RUNNING
THE COUNTRY

An Anthology of
American Politics in Action

by

A. N. CHRISTENSEN

and

E. M. KIRKPATRICK

HENRY HOLT AND COMPANY
NEW YORK

PREFACE

THE United Nations won a military victory. But that victory assured neither lasting peace, nor establishment of democracy abroad, nor its preservation at home. With the world still haunted by a distressing trust in salvation through force and brutality, the ultimate goals of peace and democracy are yet to be achieved. As a first step, we must understand and critically evaluate the relation of the people to politics, to politicians, and to vital issues of our time.

The men and women who are to carry on the struggle need knowledge and understanding of the conditions under which they work. One of the most important of these is the character of the system of organized political power. They need knowledge and understanding of governmental institutions and of how and for whom these institutions work; they need to make full use of their critical powers to solve man's day-to-day problems. With this in mind the present volume has been prepared.

By making easily available to the average citizen some of the best writing about the American system of government that has been published in books, professional journals, popular periodicals, and journals of opinion, it is hoped to increase that knowledge and understanding; also to stimulate interest in, discussion about and reflection upon the many aspects of American government now vital to those seeking to win the battle of democracy.

In bringing these selections together we make no claim to have found or used all that is best among the many excellent articles available. Nor do we doubt that many readers will believe that other things should have been added or substituted for those used. We feel certain, however, that all readers will find here much that is stimulating and valuable.

Many of the selections express opinions or judgments about controversial issues, and we know that almost all readers will find themselves in disagreement with at least a few of the viewpoints advanced. Indeed, we as editors disagree vigorously with some of them and find ourselves in disagreement about others. But this does not detract from their value; it enhances it. As John Stuart Mill long ago remarked, the person who knows only his own side of the case knows little of that.

iii

We recognize also that some of the articles contain statements of fact that are now inaccurate because of events since they were written. In no case, however, do these inaccuracies detract materially from the main point of the articles in question. We have, therefore, let them stand in their original form, though we have made corrections in brackets in instances where that seemed necessary.

We have tried to give order, coherence, and continuity to the collection as a whole by grouping the selections into chapters and by providing brief introductions to the chapters and individual selections where that treatment seemed useful. In addition, so that the reader may know something about all the authors represented, we have included brief biographical notes at the end of the volume.

We offer the book, then, in the hope that the material included will help others—as it has helped us—to understand and evaluate our times and our government.

A. N. C.

E. M. K.

April 1946

CONTENTS

CONTENTS

Chapter I

CRITICAL THINKING, POLITICS, AND THE POLITICIAN

No. 1

[WITH one country after another falling beneath the gigantic boot of fascism, with a distressing trust in salvation through brutality reigning from Moscow to the Mediterranean, with American democracy facing the greatest challenge of its history, it is more important than ever before that we have a critical examination of the relations of the people to politics and the politician. As one writer has said "It Is Later Than You Think."

Unfortunately distrust of intellectual procedure is rampant in the world and we Americans—lay and academic alike—while having the virtue of the power of sustained practical activity, have the vice of reluctance to test the quality of that activity by reference to principle. We have an aversion to theory. In political science emphasis has been upon constitutional law and the organization of the governmental machinery. There has been more concern with description than with evaluation, more learning than thinking. Histories of political theory have been written, but very little political theory. This is due, in part, to belief in crude empiricism, to the belief, first, "that if you collect all of the relevant facts and classify them they will speak for themselves and, secondly, that preconceived theories or ideas about the facts are not only unnecessary but positively dangerous."

As a result we Americans have been inclined to take fundamentals for granted. We have tended to walk in a path neither made nor discovered but accepted. We have been blinded by the illusion of objectivity and have worn the blinkers of empiricism in order that we might trot all the more rapidly along the beaten road undisturbed about our destination. We have acted as if we had made our deal with fate.

But this is not the practical pathway for a people who are at the crossroads of their destiny. The practical thing is to consider where we are and whither we are going. Decisions must be made even if a nation refuses to decide. It *is* later than we think. The time has come when we must use our minds to evaluate as well as describe our institutions. Social scientists, and political scientists in particular, must put aside their blinkers and go beyond

1

the philosophy of the moment. Students, both in and out of school, must be encouraged to formulate utopias, clarify problems of right and justice, and organize a social and political philosophy adequate to meet the turmoil and strife through which the world is passing.

The purpose of instruction in politics is to socialize the individual—to teach him to see himself as part of a vast socio-political complex which is the world to-day, to end his isolation, to so stimulate his imagination that he will come to see society as one vast inter-related whole, in which the problems of geographically or socially remote persons are in some fashion connected with his own. Facts about political institutions and their operation are essential to this end, but facts in themselves are valueless unless fitted into a completed mosaic embracing not only what *is* but what *ought to be*. Surely if the collective life of the human race is to become increasingly a matter of conscious human control, the attempt to formulate goals, to set up ideals and values, is, however difficult, a task which politics cannot shirk without dishonor to itself.

The following passage by Professor Rosen discusses the task of the social sciences, of which political science is one, and should be given full consideration by those who seek to convert the promise of American life from a promise into an actuality.]

THE TASK OF THE SOCIAL SCIENCES [1]

by S. McKee Rosen

IN 1929, there was appointed from among leading educators in the United States a Commission on the Social Studies in the Schools. After five years of investigation accompanied by the publication of particular studies from time to time, the final conclusions of the Commission appeared in June, 1934. Charged with making recommendations concerning education in the social sciences, the Commission reported: "The emerging age is particularly an age of transition. It is marked by numerous and severe tensions arising out of the conflict between the actual trend toward integrated economy and society, on the one side, and the traditional practices, dispositions, ideas, and institutional arrangements inherited from the passing age of individualism, on the other. . . . The Commission deems possible and desirable the attainment and spread of accurate knowledge and informed opinion among the masses of the American people both concerning the realities, tensions, and problems of the emerging era and concerning the ideals, traditions, and experience of other ages and other peoples in order that all choices may be made with reason, with understanding, and with due re-

[1] S. M. Rosen, *Political Process* (New York: Harper and Brothers, Publishers, 1935), pp. 3-13. Reprinted by permission of the publishers.

gard to their moral and cultural, as well as their narrowly economic, implications."

In somewhat similar vein, the Report of the President's Research Committee on Social Trends (1933), viewing the need for social thinking, warns us that: "Nothing short of the combined intelligence of the nation can cope with the predicaments here mentioned." However, "the Committee does not wish to exaggerate the role of intelligence in social direction, or to underestimate the important parts played by tradition, habit, unintelligence, inertia, indifference, emotions, or the raw will to power in various forms." Nevertheless, "the progressive confusion created in men's minds by the bewildering sweep of events revealed in our recent social trends must find its counterpart in the progressive clarification of men's thinking and feeling, in their reorientation to the meaning of the new trends."

Two outstanding committees of scholars and scientists have thus spoken of the need for social intelligence. Yet a keen observer of the contemporary scene has described the abandonment of democratic institutions and the flight to faith in dictatorships as a "failure of nerve"—a flight from responsibility, accompanied by a fatigue of the individual will and a blunting of the individual intelligence. Men seem to have regressed from the adulthood of decision-making to an infantile dependence upon one-man rule. Eternal vigilance appears as too high a price to pay for liberty when new and easy gospels abound. And yet who are the critics that they should decry the lack of reason and intelligence in such a confused world filled with uncertainty and insecurity?

Nevertheless, if anything is clear, it is the fact that critical times are just the ones in which people must remain sane and sensible. When the ship of state is making heavy weather, both the captain and the crew must be on the alert. No man is dispensable in the crisis, and each must pull his weight if the storm is to be weathered. Both the plea for the development of social intelligence and the warning of its apparent decline are challenges which the student and the scholar may not neglect. The present return to infantilism may be not the result of the decay of individual integrity, as Dr. Kallen believes, but rather a genuine perplexity at the complexity of social and economic affairs. Why this emphasis upon "research in the social sciences," and upon "objectivity in social solutions"? What is this "race between real education and chaos"—these "social conflicts and tensions" of our transitional order? What, broadly, are we faced with—what, boldly, is the problem with which the social sciences must cope?

Diagnosis may well begin, perhaps, with the reminder that until recent years our main interest has been in man's mastery over nature—his physical universe. The nineteenth century in American history, which in many respects ended in 1929, was characterized by the triumph of science and technology. In the last one hundred years, the advances in the physical sciences, in physics and chemistry, have been outstanding. Scholarship, research, money, effort, attention—all of these were focused upon the physical sciences and the results which we realize so thoroughly today in technology. This was the building era; and from straggling villages, hundreds of cities arose, to be closely interlaced by the development of vast facilities of transportation and communication. One hundred years ago Chicago consisted of a few hundred frame dwellings and a few thousand ardent souls. In the northwest and the southwest the Indians had not yet been subdued. Men were to cut down the forests, literally, so as to build their cities. The conquest of the frontier; the binding together of the country with networks of rails, roads, and wires; the application of technology to all branches of industry, the results of which we see in radios, motor cars, airplanes, and a thousand other mechanical adjustments so deeply effective of American life—this was the work of the generations which followed the pioneers.

The machine does not exist in a vacuum. While it yields social results it also raises numerous social problems and complications. Invention gave us the radio, but the radio raises a whole host of questions in economics, politics, and social policy. Regulation, censorship, control of advertising, the use in education—these are but a few of the many questions raised by the applications and implications of one single technological invention. This is but one example of the numerous technological advances which have altered profoundly in the last fifty years our whole material culture, raising problems of social adjustment which we have been negligent in meeting, and bringing ever more complications and complexities into our midst. In similar fashion, the spread of education, communication, and the increase of mobility have brought new demands and created new horizons.

But while the physical sciences and technology so deeply effective in the making of our material culture received major attention, by comparison, the social sciences, whose problems arise from the relations among men, were neglected. Too busy with the job of building and acquisition, men found little time in which to ask: *What kind of a social order is arising in our midst?* The lure of more worlds to conquer combined with a Victorian faith in the automatic and endless increase of wealth, precluded careful inquiry into the frictions and tensions which were slowly but surely developing in the American scene. Thus the social sciences—politics, economics, sociology—those disciplines which have for their province the problems which arise wherever individuals live and labor together, but reflect the temper and spirit of growing America.

In short, on the one hand, the machine has transformed rapidly our whole material culture, affecting and raising numerous political, economic, and social problems. On the other hand, the social sciences and thinking generally have not kept pace, leaving largely untouched and unsolved the whole adjustment necessary between machine development and social and economic institutions and arrangements.

Is it to be wondered, then, that keen observers may describe our condition in the twentieth century as one of quasi-chaos; that having raised the question of "whither mankind?" they are led to foretell the decline of western civilization due to its complications with attendant frictions and tensions? Is there not the distinct possibility that our civilization has become too complicated, so complex that it cannot be kept moving in orderly fashion? While recognizing that the process of social change, as a rule, is much slower than a participating generation realizes, it is to be noted that the Committee on Social Trends reported that "it would be highly negligent to gloss over the stark and bitter realities of the social situation, and to ignore the imminent perils in further advance of our heavy technical machinery over crumbling roads and shaking bridges."

An analogy, for the moment, in the international situation may lend some clarity to discourse. The various sovereign states, each with its own highly nationalistic aspirations, observing the old rules of "dog eat dog" in its relations with its neighbors and competitors, may be compared to a series of machines. While those machines are running at an increasingly rapid rate in an international order which has become closely interrelated and interdependent, there has been little provision made for integration, for gearing together these machines. Thus, this lack of gearing together tends to result, inevitably, in collision or war.

In the same way, in the internal affairs of our country we are witnessing increasing friction which may lead us into social and economic class warfare. For in a community whose main trends have been away from an individualistic and frontier way of life and toward integration and interdependence, we are still thinking in terms of a social economy of the past, an economic individualism which has proved highly detrimental to the development of vast masses of our people and threatens, perhaps, the survival of American society itself. The Report of the Commission on Social Studies warns us: "If education continues to emphasize the philosophy of individualism in economy, it will increase the accompanying social tensions. If it organizes a program in terms of a philosophy which harmonizes with the facts of a closely integrated society, it will ease the strains of the transition taking place in actuality. The making of choices cannot be evaded, for inaction in education is a form of action."

"Go West, young man, and grow up with the country." This was the advice to youth given by Horace Greeley in the editorial pages of the New York *Tribune* ninety years ago. The following generations witnessed the conquest of a continent by a nation turned to individual profit and acquisition. A wide, open country with plenty of land and abounding in natural resources gave ample opportunity to the man of energy and enterprise to make good. Nor is it to be wondered at that the old principles of individualism and free competition formed adequate explanations of economic and social success. The log cabin rearing presidents, the world of hard knocks producing industrial and financial titans—these were the symbols which adorned the credo of business enterprise in America. That every boy could become president of his company was a belief which encountered little doubt well into the twentieth century. These were the predominant pictures in people's heads, pictures which still linger on though their correspondence to real life has long since ceased to exist.

For the frontier disappeared, for all intents and purposes with the cessation of free land in 1890. The growing concentration in large industrial centers of a wage-earning class dependent upon and attached to machines, together with the development of an integrated and corporate economy, has made a myth of the individual moving freely, bargaining effectively, and receiving a just reward for his talent and ingenuity. Yet when the old deities are unkind, it is the habit of the tribe to redouble its appeal to ancient gods. Thus, at present, people still cling to the ideas of an individualistic order, believing that the old gods will be propitious and that automatically all will be arranged if we but leave individuals alone. They shout "competition," and expect manna to fall from the heavens; and they give their support to the panegyrics of a great newspaper: "The Gibraltar of American Civilization is the right of every man to make as much money as he can." The philosophy of a pre-machine age, in short, has us by the throats.

It is easy, no doubt, to underestimate the vast energies released by, as well as the great achievements of, the age of individualism which seems at present to be coming to a close. Finding its inception in the sixteenth century and gaining support from the faith of Martin Luther that nothing and no one can stand between man's conscience and the Creator, the rise of individualism marked the downfall of a society held in servility by a medievil church and feudal hierarchy. From the plea for religious liberty there was not a far step to the demand for release from political and economic restrictions. In the name of individual rights, the seventeenth and eighteenth centuries assumed the task of clearing away feudal and church encumbrances, fighting the new political despotisms which had arisen to displace those which were decaying. This new creed not only rationalized the coming to power of business enterprise, but to the eighteenth century of craftsmen, small business men, and farmers, it stood as a creed of enlightenment and humanity. The *Wealth of Nations* of Adam Smith summarized well the new dispensation:

> All systems of preference or of restraint being thus completely taken away, the obvious and simple system of natural liberty establishes itself of its own accord. Every man, as long as he does not violate the laws of justice, is left perfectly free to pursue his own interest his own way, and to bring both his industry and capital into competition with those of any other men, or order of men.

For the medieval conception of a world based on divine guidance and governed by the theological sanctions of heaven and hell, there was substituted a natural order governed automatically by natural laws in which man's reason led him inevitably to follow his own enlightened self-interest, and in which the sum total of all private interests was the public good.

Nor is it at all difficult to understand how such a creed was found eminently fitting to the westward march of American democracy, a democracy of frontiersmen unfettered by the divisions of class and caste of older cultures. Frontier traditions, enhanced by the eighteenth-century faith in reason and the Protestant ethic of thrift and hard work, made adequate foundations for a philosophy of economic individualism. The small independent worker, merchant, or farmer, by using his intelligence, working hard, and saving, could and did attain very often power and prestige among his fellow men. The accumulation of material wealth did betoken a state of grace in the new scheme of things.

The United States, like most other countries, has had a glorious past. To weigh and balance its achievements ought not to preclude a recognition of the fact that the past is over, never to return. Moreover, the new economic and social contours are becoming sufficiently clear for us to realize, at any rate, that it is a new road which we are traveling. The numerous instances indicating the shift from the America of the small independent farmer and enterpriser to what John Dewey has so aptly designated as "United States, Incorporated," have been too well elaborated by economists to need detailed repetition here. In 1870, 52.8 per cent of all gainfully occupied persons, sixteen years of age and over, were to be found in agriculture; the total percentage engaged in mining, manufacturing, trade, commerce, and clerical services was 34.3. In 1930, agriculture had dropped to 21.3 per cent, while the total for the latter had risen to 59.5 per cent.

Of the 8.8 million wage earners employed in manufacturing industries in 1929, 6.2 millions, over 70 per cent, were engaged in factories with one hundred or more employees. The degree of concentration becomes even more impressive when we consider such corporations as the American Telephone and Telegraph Company with its 324,343 employees, the United States Steel Corporation with 211,055, General Motors with 172,938, the Standard Oil Companies with approximately 192,000, and Armour and Company with 60,000. Messrs. Berle and Means, in their comprehensive study, *The Modern Corporation and Private Property,* have estimated that at least 78 per cent of American business wealth is corporate wealth, and that two hundred of our largest non-banking corporations (42 railroads, 52 utilities, and 106 industrials) controlled, in 1930, 38 per cent of all business wealth.

The corporate rule which has been established in almost every aspect of economic life, and which in the latest decades seems more than likely to become dominant in merchandising and banking, presents a new framework to which older motives and standards appear unrelated. Such an organization of economic activity in bringing an increasingly large number of workers, both by brain and by brawn, under single management has transformed the old independent worker into a wage or salaried laborer receiving orders from his boss. The property owner who invests in a modern corporation, on the other hand, has so far surrendered his control that from an independent owner he has become a mere recipient of the wages of capital. When there is added the fact that as a result of this concentration approximately two thousand individuals are in a position to control and direct half of our whole industry, the outlines of the picture become even sharper.

While such bold contours of economic change throw little light upon the more detailed changes in the lives of individuals, they do furnish a clue to the more widespread movement toward combination and association which has affected every aspect of the American scene. It is by and through associations tightly or loosely organized that the individual's choices, opportunities, and actions are largely determined. The United States has moved steadily away from its pioneer individualism to a society closely interdependent and interrelated and, in short, corporate and consolidated.

Nevertheless, the old patterns persist; and our schools, churches, and the press—the guardians of education and public opinion—still continue to stress primarily a cultural tradition as a means of induction into life, a tradition which thoroughly confuses the individual facing the real questions of today. For the problems of crowded cities and shops, the solutions appropriate to an age of agriculture and small commerce are prescribed. Clear recognition of the lag between traditional heritage and present needs, a first step to clear thinking in the social sciences, remains largely undefined and unstressed.

This, then, is the task of the social sciences. Their first function, obviously, is the acquisition of accurate information and insight into the problems of man and society and the transmission of such information and insight to the individuals composing society. But the social scientist cannot remain passive "until the evidence is all in." Even if it were at all possible, the exigencies of the times cannot await the development of complete and scientific data in the social studies before action takes place. Despite the fact that the scientific method in the social studies is applicable to a mere fragment of human experience, a "narrow land of rational certainty, relative, conditional, experimental," and despite the fact that processes and forces clearly discernible are yet unmeasurable, the social scientist cannot remain unconcerned and aloof, quietly contemplating the universe. Unless he is to limit himself to the barren transmission of established social habits and traditions, he must explore the trends and potentialities of the evolving situation. He needs to recognize the limitations of his own discipline; but he should realize also that "there are times when silence is not neutrality, but assent."

The responsibility of aiding to equip the rising generation to cooperate effectively in an increasingly interdependent society cannot be met by a conspiracy of silence. Either the social studies must aid in crystallizing, guiding, and making clear the meaning, purpose, and potentialities of the actual trends which are already bringing the future; or they may continue to emphasize, as they have in the past, the motives, desires, and aspirations of an individualistic and competitive order. To follow the latter would mean to intensify the tension and frictions of the transition through which the country is at present struggling. If, on the other hand, the social studies turn their efforts to the development of a point of view, an approach, expressive of and meaningful in a closely integrated society, they may fulfill their task of aiding the rising generation to face its problems with intelligence and knowledge rather than with fear and ignorance.

No. 2

[IF we are to fulfill our obligation to examine critically the role of people, politics, and the politician in American life we must begin with a re-examination of the role of the politician, who in the final analysis, is the practitioner of political science. It is safe to affirm, with Mr. Davenport, that the number of persons in this country who would regard this as important is not large for Americans have traditionally held the politician in low esteem. The labelling of an individual as a "politician" is with but few exceptions an act of opprobrium. This is partly due to the lag in the social sciences discussed in the preceding selection, and it is also based on the almost universally accepted belief that politicians are, as a general rule, incompetent and probably not uncorruptible. A few dead political leaders may be canonized and admitted to the ranks of statesmen but even they were labelled "politicians" by their contemporaries and their now respected policies were regarded as cheap political gestures. An editorial writer in 1793 believed that Washington should "retire immediately; let no flatterer persuade you to rest one hour longer at the helm of state. You are utterly incapable to steer the political ship into the harbor of safety." The now respected Jefferson was described, in his time, as "a man without religion, a statesman without principle, and a patriot regardless of his country's welfare and entirely devoted to raise himself and his partisans upon the nation's ruin." One of the leading papers of the nation portrayed Lincoln as "an uneducated man, a vulgar village politician, without any experience worth mentioning in the practical duties of statesmanship."

This tendency to damn "politicians" is therefore an old American custom. The descendants of the writers just quoted are probably now busily at work keeping it alive. The results are, of course, unfortunate. One of the reasons why we in the United States have long neglected reconstructing our political machinery is this easy explanation that the trouble is explained only by the presence of "politicians." For the poor performance of badly organized legislatures we blame legislators, if the administration of public policy is badly done we find some administrator to blame, when the courts fall behind in their dockets undoubtedly a judge is at fault. Basic faults in our governmental machinery have long been perceived by a few who were not too enmeshed in the crude empiricism of American political thinking. But their attempts to point out and correct these faults have been thwarted by the popular disposition to blame only the "politician."

A democratic society cannot long endure if little attention is given to the defects in its institutions and if we unthinkingly feel we can exorcise the evil spirits who plague our political practices by frequently chanting the word "politician." A full appreciation of the process of American government can be obtained only by a knowledge of the intricate structure of American government and the highly complex interrelationships that characterize this structure. And it is on the "politicians" we place the heavy burden of making it work. A fuller realization of the magnitude of his task will lead not only to a greater appreciation of his real contribution to American life and culture but also to a keener insight into the basic processes of American government.]

THE MAGNITUDE OF THE TASK OF THE POLITICIAN [1]

by Frederick M. Davenport

IT is a safe venture to affirm that the number of persons in the country, who would regard as important a discussion of the task of the politician, is not large. A much more popular and intelligible topic would be the task of ridding ourselves of the politician. Very few lift hand or pen or voice in his defense. In recent times Wallas, Lippmann and Frankfurter have given more than fugitive evidence of an appreciative understanding of him, but it has been left for F. S. Oliver, in the opening chapter of his work upon the endless adventure of governing men, a chapter in praise of politicians beginning with Walpole, to present in terms of whimsical, yet profound social, insight the service and function of the politician under any government, particularly a democracy.

It is true about politicians in general that there is much that is unlovely. The public has in mind the unintelligent, brawling, municipal wardheeler, who preys upon the widespread helplessness of large elements in the population, whose economic underpinning is graft and corruption, who fattens upon the incompetence and failure of the underprivileged. The public has in mind the machine boss who is mentally pictured as seeking and gaining power for his own upbuilding, and as pursuing at all times his own selfish interest. The public thinks of the legislator as one who is likely to lack courage, to prove the proverbial opportunist, the temporizer, the arrant compromiser. The public thinks of a political organization as built upon the lowest instincts which human beings possess, and of the politician as the man who must, in order to win, fall in with the method and the technique associated with the management and mastery of the baser qualities of mankind.

The public knows the evil in politicians, and very little about the good in them. The press attends to that. Virtue is rarely worth a headline.

Formerly the banker, the financier and the captain of industry were merciless critics of the politician. This criticism has not been so severe recently, since glass houses became more common habitations. The wholesale condemnation of the public men known as politicians, whether in high place or low, has become shallow and menacing. It has helped to undermine the

[1] F. M. Davenport, "The Magnitude of the Task of the Politician," *Harvard Business Review* (July, 1933), Vol. XI, No. 4, pp. 468-477. Reprinted by permission of the author and the *Harvard Business Review*.

prestige of the public service and to weaken the leadership of the country. It is not without reason that we take stock afresh of the real function of the able and useful type of politician and his place in the governmental order.

As a matter of fact, the politician is the person who actually brings things to pass within the fabric of government. Nothing much would happen in that field without him. He is the expert in the political behavior of the electorate. He understands human nature. He charts human prejudices and prepossessions and emotions. He knows his social psychology. The political thinker, the advisory counselor, may furnish the idea. The politician knows whether the idea is practical and can be maneuvered through the channels and past the reefs of public sentiment and into safe harbor in the Law and the Constitution. He is the navigator of the Ship of State. No one can take his place in a storm. What Lincoln did in the years 1861-1865 was to bring into safe harbor the idea of Webster that the Union must be preserved. When Lincoln entered the presidency, his position on slavery was Webster's position: it must not extend into any new territory. Lincoln navigated Webster's ideas through to success and broadened them into the policy that all men everywhere under the American flag should be free. Lincoln was the master of his country's fate and the captain of her soul, because he was the master politician of her history.

The most successful presidents have been the best politicians in a high sense—but politicians. The American people do not appreciate administrative capacity in the presidency to anything like the degree that they appreciate a sense of human contact with the President: that he is par excellence, their voice, their spokesman, their friend.

Contrary to the usual belief, a great part of the success of the American Revolution and of the new government of 1789 was due to the amazing political instinct of George Washington. If you wish a picture of the politician who became our first President, hear this description of him in Philadelphia—as a member of the Continental Congress, accompanied by loyal Virginians ready to join with the other colonies in a martial adventure which might lead to infamy or renown. His latest biographer writes:

> When Colonel Washington strode through the streets of Philadelphia, his imposing ways, his tall form in his handsome uniform . . . attracted a great deal of notice. He went here and there everywhere in the city, buying provisions, arms and munitions for his Virginians. He did not talk, but quietly purchased and paid. He made a profound impression. He was seen everywhere. In the morning and afternoon in Congress, in the evening at the tavern with the merchants, or dining in society . . . with the ostentatious banker Morris or with the well-known lawyer Dickinson, with Mayor Fisher,

with the leading Quakers. . . . He was untiring. One Sunday morning he appeared at a Quaker meeting. In the afternoon he attended the service in the Church of England. On the Sunday following he went to hear a morning sermon in the Presbyterian Church, and attended benediction at the Catholic Church after lunch. He frequented the taverns where the New England delegates were lodged, as well as those where the delegates from Carolina were dined, and going everywhere, wherever he went he gave the same telling impression of force, resolution and calm.

There was your political genius. In the living room at Mt. Vernon and in the House of Burgesses he met and learned to influence his own aristocratic class, and after his campaign around Boston and his association with the free and independent Yankees, who went off home whenever it struck their fancy and came back when they were ready, he learned to understand and to manage the peculiarly free and easy traits of that inchoate and loosely organized body of human beings, later to be known as the American people. Washington and the Declaration of Independence were at the moment the only genuinely fusing forces in the population.

Theodore Roosevelt was a great public leader because he was a great political craftsman. His genius, as I observed it when he was President, lay in his capacity to listen to a half dozen differing views upon a problem which he himself did not yet understand; and when the experts were through, he then knew which one of the various ideas was practical and would pass muster with the informed sentiment of the country. He took the Government of the United States out of a rut for the first time in a generation, and the country liked it.

The able and useful type of politician is the man who persuades people to behave like rational human beings when they are in danger of milling around like muddle-headed cattle, something that now and then happens in the best-regulated democracies. He understands the management of the gregarious instinct in mankind. He has a peculiar sensitivity to the mental, and particularly to the emotional, processes of the popular mind. He knows how to mellow and mollify, if anybody can, the pressure groups, such as the newspapers, the financiers, the labor leaders, the veterans, the farmers. His is the task in a modern democracy of moulding these disparate and often hostile interests into something like mutual understanding. It is his business to refine and combine the two kinds of energies which are ever fighting for the mastery in a democracy—the ignorance, the folly, the envy, the passion, the prejudice and the self-interest on the one hand, and the virtue, the kindliness and the idealism of the masses of the people on the other.

The mind of the able politician is a social laboratory. There he tests social experiments by his intuitive reactions. There are no laboratories for the social sciences in the sense that there are for the natural sciences. There is past experience, but that is no demonstration of future experience, because too many social variables are constantly appearing. The changes going on all the time within the consciousness of a mighty, turbulent democracy such as we now have in America, the shifting of effective motives, the transitoriness of sentiment, the social forces on the march which are dimly forming and cannot be resisted, these the true type of politician detects and respects, even when he seeks to alter their course or clarify their objectives, or perhaps attempts to thwart them altogether.

It is in this field that the politician completely overtops the academic thinker upon public affairs. It is his awareness of new premises and of invincible psychological realities which leads him sharply to check up on the policies of the university expert, the advisory counselor or the member of a brain trust. For example, it was upon the rock of the inner feeling and bitter economic necessity of distraught mankind that the successive agreements about reparations and war debts came to wreck. It was the sense of injustice in the breasts of German youth, faced with the black cloud of 62 years of economic despair, which produced Hitler instead of payments on account. Expertly well-wrought-out plans they were, but they paid little attention to the processes of human nature in vast populations. In the midst of many intricate devices proposed in Washington to create a rise in the price level, we are obliged to remember that if schemes are framed without the divination of political genius, they are sure to fail. Whether it is the economic rule of supply and demand or the subtler psychological behavior of human nature in an emergency, if the rule or the trend is violated, there always remains the law of gravitation to bring the schemes to earth.

So far as it is necessary for us to go on employing the method of trial and error in the social process, and that is still likely to be for a good while, the politician will continue to be a useful individual. He will even change his mind, and that is painful business, as every academic person knows. In a changing world there is much to be said for such a practical mental trait. So far as we can bring ourselves to provide in advance against our catastrophes and miseries, we shall find the predictive capacity of the true politician to be of inestimable advantage in determining what method of defense and adjustment will work, and what will not. In helping to bring the right thing to pass, there is nobody who can gauge so well the probable political behavior of masses of men.

Even in what we regard as the submerged areas of municipal politics, which have their foundations in graft and the spoils system, the politician and his organization perform indispensable services. In ordinary times as well as in critical times, the political machine in New York City or Boston or Philadelphia is busily finding employment for those who are out of work, is feeding the hungry without ostentation, is maintaining the morale of the plain citizen in difficulty whose actual government seems to be far away from him. There is an intimate friendliness about the neighborhood political clubhouse which, alas, government cannot match. It is true that warm shoes against the winter slush and happy picnics for the district are no fair shield for governmental incompetence and political exploitation and corruption. But it is also true that there are real human traits in these political organizations which are deep and true; and that is the reason, I take it, that the shifting masses of our metropolitan populations in the long run respond more naturally to the humanness of the machine than to the mechanical shortsightedness and cold efficiencies of reform governments. As a bulwark against proletarian revolution in certain large cities of the United States, I put the politician and his organization at the head of the list. At least where he is in the flower of his control, men will never riot because they are hungry.

There is another point. The large municipalities of the country have built up a complicated system of government. There are certain functions within their borders exercised by the Federal Government, certain by the states, certain by the counties, certain by the boroughs perhaps, certain by the municipal entities themselves. In the city of Chicago there are scores of independent local governments operating within the limits of the city. There are boards of estimate and aldermen and sinking funds and taxes and assessments, and many more. In order to get effective government there must be a correlation in action, in planning, in progress. The parts must fit together and work reasonably smoothly, if the man on the street is to get anything out of it. For example, the plain citizen is interested in good health. He wants the Federal Government to quarantine the plague cases in the port. He expects the municipality to inspect the milk. He depends upon the state to deal with river pollution. But it is the invisible politician, and he only, who establishes unity and coherence of protection for the common man.

The government of the state and nation has become a vast, technical tangle of activities, necessarily administered by bureaucratic competence or incompetence, as the case may be. But the contact of bureaucracy with the desires and ambitions, the hopes and the needs of the average man, no one supplies but the politician. That is practically one-half the task of the conscientious member of Congress. The human relation of a genuine representative with hundreds of his constituents is as intimate as that of the doctor, the lawyer, the priest or the minister. The taxpayers, the veterans, the immigration derelicts, the citizens with business troubles, job-hunters and information seekers, not to mention the postmasters—the political representative in Congress has these groups always with him, sleeping or waking.

The Congress of the United States, made up largely of politicians, is sometimes a very foolish body, but it is a true cross section of the American people. Its very faults and blunderings are the faults and blunderings of the American people. Its aspirations and ideals, its yearnings for a better economic and social order, are the yearnings, the aspirations and the ideals of the American people. It has given evidence of futility in the presence of pressure groups and crises, but the way out in the long run in America, let us hope, is not through dictatorships within or without the Constitution. Pouring difficult and dangerous problems into the lap of the President of the United States, in the hope that the zeal and toil of his advisory experts will prevent his being overwhelmed, is not an inspiring sight. It is not the way of hope or courage or intelligence in the long run. The way out is through more and better politically and socially minded leaders in Congress, recruited especially from the young men and women to whom the country has given the higher training at great cost, looking appealingly to them to support this country with their intelligence and character in the hour of her need. Instead of contemptuously sniffing at politicians and denouncing those who occupy positions of authority and power, we should look to them to give a fair portion of their energy, their time and their integrity to the development of political talent and genius in the rough and tumble reality of citizenship. The American people, their humorists, their editors, their critics, ought to teach the young men and women of the present generation that, next to enlisting in war in a great emergency, there is nothing more difficult or more important than enlisting and fighting in the public service.

In my opinion there is no more alarming symptom in the American democracy than the tendency on every hand to point the finger of scorn at the Congress of the United States. There is nothing which has had more certain effect in enfeebling that body, burdened as it is with complexity of problem and gravity of decision. If the sentiment of millions at home is hostile to the army, the army must collapse. If the sentiment of the people at home is hostile to their public servants, consciously or unconsciously their public servants cannot do their best. If the American people expected more from the Congress of the United States, they would receive more.

America never stood in greater need of exponents of social wisdom. Such persons, I suppose, are university experts, and others. Also the country never stood in greater need of leaders with practical judgment and skill to put wisdom into action. Such persons in a democracy are and always will be politicians. And it is no easy job. In modern governments we have entered upon the path of attempting the deliberate direction of human affairs by conscious intelligence. There is no other way; certainly not for America, in spite of the contention of Burke and Disraeli that the reason of men is inadequate for any great political or social achievement. The study of Recent Social Trends by a Federal commission indicates clearly enough that the only hope is in a new leadership of social wisdom. In that report we find abundant evidence, if it were needed, that "the capitalist economic system is collapsing under pressure and that problems of great variety and complexity are upon us—the poverty of the marginal farmer; the insecurity of wage earners; the perplexity of consumers; the plight of the railways; the speculative instability of the banking system; the failure of the flow of credit and purchasing power to synchronize with the flow of production; the weakness and dishonesty of the corporate structure; the chaos of international relations, communication among peoples proceeding more speedily than the reorganization of goodwill; great strain and tension resulting from changes in phases of national and world economy at different rates of speed." Furthermore, there is no likelihood that the issues will grow less complicated with time. There is no evidence that the problems can be solved or even analyzed without technical knowledge of the highest order.

Government is called upon to ease the tension, to lessen the strain, to mend the broken circuits, to stimulate social invention so that it may keep pace with mechanical invention. Private initiative and intelligence have failed. The quality of instruments of government is imperfect. Above all there still remains in the American population a dangerous amount of heterogeneity, unintelligence, inertia, indifference. Inventive social ideas are not enough. They are valueless except when combined with knowledge of the principles and practice of political navigation. None can pilot the Ship of State in such mounting seas except those possessed of the highest type of political talent and genius. But the attitude of public opinion is hostile to the normal functioning of such individuals, highly unfavorable to the breeding or training of the kind of leaders we need most. The traditional ill-repute of the politician is so firmly fixed in the popular mind that it is difficult to secure the enlistment of the most intelligent and the ablest.

Democracy is in trouble. Other forms of government like fascism or bolshevism look like temporary expedients, useful though they may be in their place and time. The only way out appears to be through a better government by better politicians, supported by a better quality of trained intelligence. And let me now speak up for the expert. It is very evident that I put the politician ahead of him. The place of the expert, as somebody has said, is "on tap and not on top." The university expert who has not associated much with politicians is a dangerous person in public affairs, but he learns a great deal from association with politicians. He learns that it is one thing to spawn ideas and another thing to keep them alive and potent. He learns that the field of theory may be on a different planet from the field of reality. He learns that it is one thing to invent a political policy and another thing to make Congress or the country believe in it or vote for it. The expert learns from the politician that he must keep his premises up to date. The consent of the governed is no more an infallible political principle than the theory that all men everywhere follow the line of their own self-interest is an infallible economic principle. The politician must deal constantly with social variables. Sometimes the expert learns that, too.

When he is able to find his way around in public affairs, it is true that the university expert is able to furnish a rich background of fertile and alternative suggestions to the politician. For example, the politician could never interpret and discuss the gold and credit and price-level problem without the expert at his ear. The politician would be quite out of his depth in the midst of the agenda of the world economic conference without the self-same life preserver buoying him up. So it boils down to the point that good experts can make good ammunition, but it is the politician who shoots it and knows when. The politician takes dough from the expert, but if it ever becomes well-baked bread, it will be in the politician's oven.

Business leaders are constantly being importuned to be more active in the political field. It is important that they should be, but they have equally to remember with the academic expert that business acumen and political skill are quite different characteristics. Business men in political affairs may fail because they may not possess, or even succeed in developing, this particular political skill. They may have neither the indirect technique nor the camaraderie of the politician. Unless they, too, have come along the path of a reasonable amount of everyday political experience, they are pretty certain to get into hot water unless escorted about by a lieutenant who does understand political human nature.

Having thus prepared the way, I hasten to say that day-by-day government at Washington would be paralyzed without the expert. There are ten thousand civil-service positions scattered throughout the departments of the Federal Government which are nearly all filled by college and university men and women—medical experts, legal experts, engineering experts, chemists, physicists, biologists, economists. Of course the range and quality of the civil service of the United States does not approach that of England. For example, after the British political revolution of 1924, when the Labor party came into power, I am informed that the shift in personnel was less than a hundred persons in the British Government. When it becomes strategically safe in Washington to distribute the patronage following the political revolution of 1932, it will be a miracle of grace if there are not tens of thousands of changes entirely outside the limited range of the civil service. Unfortunately that is likely to be true in this country, no matter which party happens to profit by a political revolution.

The houses of Congress gingerly employ the expert. Of course Congress has an excellent staff of legislative draftsmen. But at the most important point of testimony-taking before committees, there is a curious futility. The committee advertises a hearing upon an important measure and opens it wide to all who come. Those who have especial interest on one side or the other appear and overwhelm the committee with statistical tables and reams of alleged information and *ex parte* material. The university expert is heard if he is interested enough to appear, and occasionally he is sent for, but he is usually under the suspicion of some member of the committee as having been planted for a purpose. Far better results would be obtained, I think, if the committees of Congress themselves habitually called in trained university experts, from various fields, whenever needed, and paid them from contingent appropriations. These experts might well meet in advance of the hearings, in executive session with the committees, to aid in marking the bounds of useful inquiry. There is now a vast waste of time and energy in excursions far afield. It would be good practice, I think, if these experts called by the committee were to sit throughout the hearings and listen to the testimony, master it, help to evaluate it, and interpret it finally in executive session with the committee. Such a use of experts would be more helpful to Congress than the system which now prevails.

There is a feeling in this country that advisory commissions appointed by executive or legislature are likely to be unproductive. If there were a better tradition, like the tradition which supports the British Royal Commission, the plan would be less objectionable. When the Government of England asks the King to appoint a Royal Commission, it is practically the delegation of the matter to arbitration—the relation at least borders upon the arbitrative—and the Government is bound to take favorable notice of the report. This tradition about it is generally accepted in English political thought. Of course it is not so in this country because we have no fixed nonpolitical authority like a king. Without some such tradition, the expert member of a commission in this country often finds himself in an unpleasant dilemma. Before he knows it he is in danger of becoming a tame expert, chained to the person of the executive who appointed the commission or to the majority-party organization in the legislature. The self-respecting individual finds himself unable to accept this relationship and is driven either to run the commission or write his own report. A commission of this kind must be free from political pressure or its purpose fails.

It requires some refinement of method to fit the university expert into the structure of American Government, but, nevertheless, his service is indispensable. In a world increasingly dominated by economic and techno-logical methods and forces, there is no getting on without his trained intelli-gence. The passions and imaginations of men still startle us in political crises with bursts of instinctive power, but they are far less sure-footed than they were in simpler times with simpler issues.

If the question were asked whether popular government on the whole has grown stronger and more effective in the last 25 years in the United States, I do not think it could be answered whole-heartedly in the affirma-tive. A good deal of democratization of society is clear enough. Dress and fashion are for all, or nearly all. They no longer establish a line of demarcation between economic classes. Public education is for all, although we are by no means sure that public education is what it ought to be. The motor car, the moving picture, the radio are for all. But of democracy as a way of government, not so much that is favorable can be said.

Twenty-five years ago we entered upon a crusade to break the politician and the party machine. They had developed forms of autocracy and rela-tions with corporate wealth which were obnoxious to the American people. We established the direct primary, not as a far-sighted student of govern-ment like ex-Governor Hughes of New York would have had us do it, with organized leadership at the heart of it, but in a heedless and irresponsible form. We were through with politicians and bosses and machine managers who had led us astray and left us in the wilderness. We sought to strip political parties and political organizations of their power. We idealized the common man in the direct primary. We assumed that he would do right under all conditions, that he would show himself unselfish, unpreju-diced, unbiased. It is difficult to conceive that the popular primary will ever be taken away from the common man. No power of that sort, once granted is ever withdrawn. Sometimes the common man has made good use of it. But having learned the trick of popular organization, he has more or less left the direct primary to shift for itself or to be run by the politician behind the scenes, and has gone off to form blocs and willful minorities and pressure groups to confound representative popular govern-ment and to land it in a political morass.

The American people have been startled at the ineffectiveness of their Congress in recent emergencies. The houses of Congress themselves have recognized their own helplessness and have delivered their authority to the executive to exercise for them. There are, I think, two outstanding causes of the present weakness of congressional government in Washington. The first, of course, is the presence of widely heterogeneous elements in the population itself, as well as diverse sectional backgrounds and interests. Representatives in Congress are dependent for their political lives upon the diverse and heterogeneous temperaments and sentiments of their own districts. Out of such extreme divergence of viewpoint upon many questions, it is hard to get a national program even in time of dangerous stress and strain.

The other cause of the present weakness of Congress is the influence of pressure groups which are no longer secret lobbies of the old order, but open organizations of men and women out to punish any Representative who opposes the particular special interest of their own enthusiasm and desire. The number of these open associations, which are bent on ending the career of members of Congress whom they cannot control on some one issue, is large and increasing. The most independent and far-sighted Representatives from the standpoint of the nation are most exposed to the ravages of these pressure groups.

I do not believe that the effective corrective of this growing menace to American nationality and liberty is to be found in the movement, which is now going on apace, to organize pressure groups on the other side of these issues to do battle with their adversaries for the voting bodies and souls of their elected Representatives. The transfer of the field of political conflict to this extra-legal area of voluntary associations pitted against each other, will not, it seems to me, help the Government or the country, but will make confusion worse confounded.

We must come back to the business of strengthening and improving the genus politician. He is the man who knows how in a democracy. Only there must be more of him, possessed of higher intellectual and moral quality than at present. He can make democracy work and nobody else can. In order to widen the field of selection of the politician, there must be many thousands of recruits from the younger citizenship who, as a part of their regular and ordinary lives, begin the practice of politics at the grass roots.

Many persons have learned to be politicians by seeking office. That is a good method of finding out whether a man or woman has political intuition, but it is economically a hazardous way unless the individual can afford it. Politicians are of little use to the country unless they are willing occasionally to lose elections for their own convictions. But there must be at least a willingness to set aside a reasonable portion of one's time to learn to practice the political process, to gain, as Oliver says:

an understanding sympathy with one's fellow creatures, to mix and fight and fraternize with all sorts and conditions of men, to have the good fortune to meet people face to face whose opinions you abhor, and be buffeted by them, and give as good as you get, and know how to take it.

It is in this rough and tumble that politicians are made. When they are made and have the right quality, they can do swiftly for the country more than the clash of pressure groups can ever accomplish. They can establish personal loyalties which will mellow and melt even racial heterogeneity into national unity. For what is politics but courage and common sense and the capacity to understand people, to harmonize and compromise, and yet have strength of character enough to stick to what you believe is right for the community and the country?

You may win very little appreciation and you are sure to win almost no gratitude, but there is nothing comparable with it as a field of potent endeavor for one's country and mankind. The chief reason, next to softness of fiber, that far larger numbers of the young men and women of the country do not employ their energies in this field, and that the best brains of the country are not enlisted in its political defense, is the almost universal and shameless denunciation of public servants in America, which has made it impossible for the right tradition to grow.

Once more, a supporting comment from Oliver:

> Politics is the most hazardous of all professions. There is not another in which a man can hope to do so much good to his fellow creatures, neither is there any in which by a mere loss of nerve he may do such widespread harm, nor is there another in which he may so easily lose his own soul, nor is there another in which a positive and strict veracity is so difficult. But danger is the inseparable companion of honor. With all the temptations and degradations that beset it, politics is still the noblest career that any man can choose.

Chapter II

THE RULES AND HOW THEY WERE MADE

[AMERICANS have a curious reverence and respect for the Constitution. We say curious because the reverence and respect does not result from any clear and accurate knowledge of either the nature of our Constitution or the history of its formation. Instead it grows out of the belief that the Constitution sanctions those policies with which they agree and prohibits those that seem dangerous or oppressive. It is a common belief of Americans that any action contrary to the conception they have of their own interest is unconstitutional.

This results, as we have said, partly from a lack of information and understanding of the real nature of a constitution and partly from the lack of a critical appraisal of the origin of our own Constitution. It is important, therefore, that those who wish to understand our governmental system understand that the Constitution is something more than a written document and at the same time recognize that it was the product of the conservative reaction that followed the revolution. While it is true that our own constitutional history has been one of gradual democratization of our institutions, a true picture of the origin of our Constitution is impossible unless one recognizes that the chief concern of the framers was to guard against the development of popular sovereignty in the sense of unlimited majority control.]

No. 3

CONSTITUTIONS [1]

by Howard Lee McBain

IN the most generous sense of the term every country is and has been historically, except in time of revolution or other serious upheaval, governed under something that may be called a constitution. But governments vary greatly in pattern and principle, and their constitutions vary even more greatly in such matters as form and content, source and tangibility, stability and permanence. It is in consequence difficult to define a constitution save

[1] McBain, H. L., "Constitutions," *Encyclopedia of the Social Sciences* (New York: The Macmillan Co., 1930), Vol. 4, pp. 259-262. Reprinted by permission of the publisher.

in terms of rather precisionless and therefore rather useless generality. This difficulty has not daunted publicists and other commentators. Scores of definitions might easily be assembled. Some of these define with reasonable accuracy a particular constitution or group of constitutions. But few if any of them suffice to include all that may properly be regarded as constitution and to exclude all else. Yet constitutions are not generically unreal because they elude the grasp of words. Perhaps as safe and close a definition as any is that they are the fundamental laws and practises in accordance with which governments commonly operate. But manifestly the use of the word fundamental introduces a wide margin of indefiniteness in respect of which opinions will differ.

It has long been customary to distinguish between written and unwritten constitutions, and the constitutions of the United States and of Great Britain have usually been cited as the examples par excellence of these respective types. This aspect of the subject, although a matter of schoolboy erudition, no doubt requires some mention in any general consideration of constitutions. The written constitution is usually a single document, amended or unamended from time to time as the case may be. But no constitution in the form in which it functions is wholly written; for most of these documents are relatively brief and require supplementation in important particulars. In addition to this, time invariably weaves about them political customs that become durably fixed. Occasionally such customs very nearly belie the written words of the instrument. Well-known instances in point are the customs connected with the machinery of electing an American president and the custom of holding him politically responsible as the leader of national legislation despite his designation of chief executive and despite the doctrine and constitutional rule of the separation of powers.

Even so, in the case of most written constitutions a comparatively large number of the fundamental principles or arrangements upon which the government of the country is organized for operation are found in the words of the constitution itself. It is certain that from a study of the written constitution of the United States or the French Republic or the German Reich a person wholly ignorant of the politics of the particular country could form at least a blurred mental picture of its political and governmental outlines. For a picture of such outlines under an unwritten constitution he would be compelled to rely upon commentators and explanators.

The relative merits of written and unwritten constitutions have often been debated. But much of this debate appears to proceed from the specious assumption that a people can ordinarily elect to be governed under the one or the other type of instrument. It is easy to choose to be governed under a written instrument, but probably no people ever deliberately chose the unwritten type. Unwritten constitutions have invariably been evolved from absolute monarchies or autocracies. Indeed, this would seem to be an almost indispensable condition, for unwritten constitutions rest upon customs and time is a requisite ingredient of custom. Meanwhile, however, the power of government must be exercised by someone or some group. It must, so to say, be seized. Now while the seizure and direct exercise of power by an absolute monarch or relatively small group are not only conceivable but have not infrequently happened, it is very nearly inconceivable that a large group—all of the adult males, for example—could seize power and proceed to govern without committing to writing anything concerning the organization of the government. For in any sizable country government by the many involves of necessity the application of some kind of representation. And although more or less spontaneous and irregular conventions or congresses of delegates are not unknown to history, nevertheless the representative idea, if it is to continue any length of time, invites if it does not actually compel, written arrangements. While therefore an unwritten constitution may develop around a going monarchy or close aristocracy and may in the course of time become broadly democratized, it is difficult to see how a democracy, lacking these agencies, could carry on the necessary processes of government during the period that would be required for the gradual building up of customs.

In the case of federal governments, which have in most instances been dictated by expediency if not necessity, the imperativeness of a written instrument is even more obvious. The essence of federalism is that governmental powers are divided between a central or national government and certain definitive local units of government and that this division may not be altered by the independent action of either the one or the other. Such a division even when committed to writing usually involves a considerable number of legal and practical difficulties. That it should come into being in any true form by the evolvement of mere use and wont would be almost unimaginable.

"Flexible" and "rigid" are also terms that are sometimes applied to unwritten and written constitutions. At least Lord Bryce, who coined this classification, used these terms interchangeably. But surely this is to confound substance with legalistic appearance. An unwritten constitution may or may not be flexible; a written constitution may or may not be rigid. In legal theory the British Parliament may at a stroke alter the British constitution in any respect that it chooses or the prime minister may destroy the convention of cabinet government by the simple expedient of not calling the cabinet together. But such things do not happen. In the realism of history the British constitution is not flexible. It changes very slowly.

Apart from the several extensions of the suffrage, the subordination of the House of Lords in 1911 and the altered imperial status of the self-governing dominions since the World War it has flexed very little in the course of a century. Indeed, despite the potentialities for change that exist under unwritten constitutions it is probably true to say that they tend toward rigidity rather than flexibility. Nor is this surprising, for they rest largely upon customs and customs commonly wax and wane but slowly.

On the other hand, written constitutions may prove to be very malleable instruments. Mussolini has had no difficulty whatever in warping to his wishes the written constitution of Italy. In Russia under the Soviet regime, although there is a written constitution, it is completely subordinated to the Communist party. The Politbureau of this party, unmentioned in the constitution, is nevertheless the most powerful governmental agency in the country. It is a law unto itself above and beyond the constitution. It may be argued, however, that such instances are exceptional and probably ephemeral. But instances may be cited of other written constitutions which in practise have lent themselves readily to change. The constitutions of many of the American states are in this category. Some of them are amended with great frequency. The constitution of Austria has been amended in numerous important and unimportant particulars since it went into effect in 1920.

The flexibility or rigidity of a constitution can best be tested pragmatically. If it is often altered it is certainly flexible. If it is rarely or never altered it probably should be classed as rigid. But the curious fact is that in many if not most instances the difficulty or facility of the amending process appears to have little to do with the matter of flexibility or rigidity. The French constitutional laws may be amended almost as readily and as quickly as ordinary statutes. But the fact is that they have been seldom changed and that no amendment was adopted from 1884 to 1926. This is certainly not referable to the perfection of the French system of government. The constitution of the old German Empire which lasted from 1871 to 1918 was not difficult to amend but was infrequently amended. An amendment to the Constitution of the United States may be proposed by a two-thirds vote of the houses of Congress and must be ratified by the state legislatures or conventions in three-fourths of the states. History discloses that the difficulty of this process lies in the requirement of a two-thirds vote of the houses, for amendments are very rarely proposed to the states by Congress. Since the adoption of the three Civil War amendments [seven] amendments have been so proposed, and only one of these has failed of ratification. But the constitutions of a number of the American states also require that amendments be proposed by a two-thirds vote of the two legislative houses and in some of these experience has demonstrated that this requirement presents no obstacle whatever to frequent amendment. The test of rigidity in a constitution is therefore not necessarily to be found in the difficulty of its amending process. It is quite possible that amendments to the American constitution would not be frequently proposed even though an ordinary majority of the houses were empowered to propose them. It is also quite impossible to say how serious the obstacle of ratification by three-fourths of the states might prove to be if Congress proposed amendments more frequently.

Since the launching of the American nation under written constitutions both for the several states of the union and for the national government the practise of committing the fundamentals of governmental organization to writing has become increasingly common. These instruments, however, have sprung from a variety of sources. A few of them have been drafted and promulgated by more or less regular legislative bodies. Such, for example, were the American Articles of Confederation of 1781 and the Austrian Constitution and Austro-Hungarian Ausgleich of 1867. During the nineteenth century a number of constitutions were granted by kings and princes —the so-called octroyed constitutions—but these instruments, whatever their legal appearance of voluntary concession or gift, were usually wrested from more or less absolute monarchs by popular demand. Such were the French constitutions of 1814 and 1830, the constitutions of the several German states proclaimed prior to 1850 and the Sardinian constitutions of 1848 which by successive proclamations became the constitution of a united Italy in 1861. The vast majority of constitutions, however, have been formed and adopted by special constituent assemblies convoked for the express purpose of making a constitution, although as might be conjectured the popular basis of these conventions has varied widely. Practically all of the American constitutions have originated in such conventions, and among those in Europe of similar source may be mentioned the constitution of Belgium, 1831, of Switzerland, 1848, of Denmark, 1849 and 1866, and of France, 1875. The constitution of the North German Confederation of 1867, which substantially became the constitution of the German Empire in 1871, was drafted by the Prussian autocracy and was accepted by the governments of the other German states; but between these important steps in the process it was also ratified by a popularly elected assembly. All of the European constitutions that were adopted after the World War were drafted by specially convened assemblies. Of similar origin are the constitutions of the British self-governing colonies, for although these are in ultimate law acts of the British Parliament they have in fact emanated from dominion conventions.

The practise of drafting constitutions by constituent assemblies was to some extent a logical outgrowth of the development of the democratic idea. Power to govern was regarded as proceeding from the people acting through a relatively wide electorate. A constitution embodying fundamentals came to be conceived as a superior kind of law. But in a country of size the people's power could be exercised only by representation. An ordinary legislature was scarcely an appropriate representative body for the enactment of an extraordinary law such as a constitution. Hence a special representative assembly was called into being. While this trend of thought—not to mention the more abstract theory of social contract—must have exerted considerable influence, the role of political expediency and practical necessity must not be disregarded. For not a few constitutions were liquidations of revolutionary movements that resulted in the shattering or undermining of existing institutions. In such emergencies if the principle of democracy was to find expression an ad hoc constituent assembly for the setting up of new or the remodeling of old institutions was certainly a rational, indeed almost an indispensable, mode of procedure. It is worth noting, however, that except in the diminutive state of Switzerland the democratic principle has nowhere prevailed to the point of submitting national constitutions to acceptance or rejection by direct popular vote.

The degree to which written constitutions are regarded as superior laws varies from country to country. It finds most complete acceptance in those countries in which the courts exercise the power of refusing to give effect to laws which they hold to be in violation of the constitution. The superiority of the constitution is thus vindicated in a practical way. By this process legal theory as well as popular sentiment is distilled into reality by the more or less frequent assertion and specific application of the principle of constitutional superiority. The exercise of such a veto by the courts arose in the United States, where it has played an important institutional role not only in molding the popular conception of the sacrosanctity of the "supreme law of the land" but also in influencing the course of economic, social, and political trends and events. Despite the long period of time during which judicial supremacy has flourished in the United States and despite the numerous constitutions that have been drafted and effectuated since it first took root in American soil, it has not been widely transplanted. It was servilely copied in a number of Latin American countries but the instability of their governments has deprived it of a suitable stage for adequate performance. It operates in Australia much as it does in the United States; and to a vaguely limited extent it was incorporated into the post-war constitutions of Austria and Czechoslovakia.

Elsewhere the supremacy of a constitution over statutory law and executive order depends for its effectiveness largely upon the degree of deference which the government of the moment accords it. Naturally this varies with country, time and circumstance, and it affects and is affected by the prevailing popular attitude. But generally speaking, at least in countries of reasonably stable politics, the prescriptions of a written constitution are not often ruthlessly ignored by those who hold the reins of government. For the most part constitutions are in a very real sense supreme laws.

No. 4

THE AMERICAN GOVERNMENT OF THE REVOLUTIONARY PERIOD [1]

by J. Allen Smith

THE American colonists inherited the common law and the political institutions of the mother country. The British form of government with its King, Lords and Commons and its checks upon the people, they accepted as a matter of course. In their political thinking they were not consciously more democratic than their kinsmen across the Atlantic. Many of them, it is true, had left England to escape what they regarded as tyranny and oppression. But to the *form* of the English government as such they had no objection. The evils which they experienced were attributed solely to the selfish spirit in which the government was administered.

The conditions, however, were more favorable for the development of a democratic spirit here than in the mother country. The immigrants to America represented the more active, enterprising and dissatisfied elements of the English people. Moreover, there was no hereditary aristocratic class in the colonies and less inequality in the distribution of wealth. This approach to industrial and social equality prepared the mind for the ideas of political equality which needed only the stimulus of a favorable opportunity to ensure their speedy development.

This opportunity came with the outbreak of the American Revolution which at the outset was merely an organized and armed protest against what the colonies regarded as an arbitrary and unconstitutional exercise of the taxing power. As there was no widespread or general dissatisfaction with the *form* of the English government, there is scarcely room for doubt that if England had shown a more prudent and conciliatory spirit toward the colonies, the American Revolution would have been averted. No sooner,

[1] J. A. Smith, *The Spirit of American Government* (New York: The Macmillan Co., 1907), Ch. 2. Reprinted by permission of the publisher.

however, had the controversy with the mother country reached the acute revolutionary stage, than the forces which had been silently and unconsciously working toward democracy, found an opportunity for political expression. The spirit of resistance to what was regarded as unconstitutional taxation rapidly assumed the form of avowed opposition to the English Constitution itself. The people were ready for a larger measure of political democracy than the English Constitution of the eighteenth century permitted. To this new and popular view of government the Declaration of Independence gave expression. It contained an emphatic, formal and solemn disavowal of the political theory embodied in the English Constitution; affirmed that "all men are created equal"; that governments derive "their just powers from the consent of the governed"; and declared the right of the people to alter or to abolish the form of the government "and to institute new government, laying its foundation on such principles and organizing its powers in such form, as to them shall seem most likely to effect their safety and happiness." This was a complete and sweeping repudiation of the English political system, which recognized the right of monarchy and aristocracy to thwart the will of the people.

To what extent the Declaration of Independence voiced the general sentiment of the colonies is largely a matter of conjecture. It is probable, however, that its specification of grievances and its vigorous arraignment of the colonial policy of the English government appealed to many who had little sympathy with its express and implied advocacy of democracy. It is doubtless true that many were carried along with the Revolutionary movement who by temperament and education were strongly attached to English political traditions. It is safe to conclude that a large proportion of those who desired to see American independence established did not believe in thorough-going political democracy.

Besides those who desired independence without being in sympathy with the political views expressed in the Declaration of Independence, there were many others who were opposed to the whole Revolutionary movement. The numerical strength of the Tories can not be accurately estimated; but it is certain that a large proportion, probably not less than one-third of the total population of the colonies, did not approve the war.

"In the first place, there was, prior to 1776, the official class; that is, the men holding various positions in the civil and military and naval services of the government, their immediate families, and their social connections. All such persons may be described as inclining to the Loyalist view in consequence of official bias.

"Next were certain colonial politicians who, it may be admitted, took a rather selfish and unprincipled view of the whole dispute, and who, counting on the probable, if not inevitable, success of the British arms in such a conflict, adopted the Loyalist side, not for conscience' sake, but for profit's sake, and in the expectation of being rewarded for their fidelity by offices and titles, and especially by the confiscated estates of the rebels after the rebels themselves should have been defeated, and their leaders hanged or sent into exile.

"As composing still another class of Tories, may be mentioned probably a vast majority of those who stood for the commercial interests, for the capital and tangible property of the country, and who, with the instincts natural to persons who have something considerable to lose, disapproved of all measures for pushing the dispute to the point of disorder, riot and civil war.

"Still another class of Loyalists was made up of people of professional training and occupation—clergymen, physicians, lawyers, teachers—a clear majority of whom seem to have been set against the ultimate measures of the Revolution.

"Finally, and in general, it may be said that a majority of those who, of whatever occupation, of whatever grade of culture or of wealth, would now be described as conservative people, were Loyalists during the American Revolution."

These classes prior to the Revolution had largely shaped and molded public opinion; but their opposition to the movement which they were powerless to prevent, destroyed their influence, for the time being, in American politics. The place which they had hitherto held in public esteem was filled by a new class of leaders more in sympathy with the newly born spirit of liberalism. This gave to the Revolutionary movement a distinctly democratic character.

This drift toward democracy is seen in the changes made in the state constitutions after the outbreak of the Revolution. At the close of the colonial period, nearly all the state governments were modeled after the government of Great Britain. Each colony had its legislative body elected by the qualified voters and corresponding in a general way to the House of Commons. In all the colonies except Pennsylvania and Georgia there was also an upper legislative house or council whose consent was necessary before laws could be enacted. The members composing this branch of the legislature were appointed by the governor except in Massachusetts where they were elected by the lower branch of the legislature, subject to a negative by the royal governor, and in Rhode Island and Connecticut where they were chosen by the electorate.

The governor was elected by the voters only in Rhode Island and Connecticut; and in all the other colonies he was appointed by the proprietaries or the Crown, and, though independent of the people, exercised many important powers. He was commander-in-chief of the armed forces of the colony; appointed the judges and all other civil and military officers; appointed and could suspend the council, which was usually the upper branch of the legislature; he could convene and dissolve the legislature and had besides an unqualified veto on all laws; he also had an unrestricted pardoning power.

The possession of these far-reaching powers gave to the irresponsible executive branch of the colonial government a position of commanding importance. This was not the case, however, in Connecticut and Rhode Island. Although the governor in these two colonies was responsible to the voters, inasmuch as he was elected by them, still he had no veto, and the appointing power was in the hands of the legislature.

The tidal-wave of democracy, which swept over the colonies during the Revolution, largely effaced the monarchical and aristocratic features of the colonial governments. Connecticut and Rhode Island, which already had democratic constitutions, were the only states which did not modify their form of government during this period. All the rest adopted new constitutions which show in a marked degree the influence of the democratic movement. In these new constitutions we see a strong tendency to subordinate the executive branch of the government and confer all important powers on the legislature. In the four New England states and in New York the governor was elected by the qualified voters; in all the rest he was chosen by the legislature. In ten states during this period his term was one year; in South Carolina it was two and in New York and Delaware it was three years. In addition to this the six Southern states restricted his re-election. Besides, there was in every state an executive or privy council which the governor was required to consult on all important matters. This was usually appointed by the legislature and constituted an important check on the governor.

The power to veto legislation was abolished in all but two states. In Massachusetts the governor, and in New York the Council of Revision composed of the governor and the chancellor and judges of the Supreme Court, had a qualified veto power. But a two-thirds majority in both houses of the legislature could override the veto of the governor in Massachusetts, or that of the Council of Revision in New York. The pardoning power of the governor was quite generally restricted. In five states he was allowed to exercise it only with the advice or consent of the council. In three states, where the advice or consent of a council was not required, he could, subject to certain restrictions, grant pardons except where "the law shall otherwise direct." The constitution of Georgia in express terms deprived the governor of all right to exercise this power.

The appointing power of the governor was also taken away or restricted. In four of the eleven states adopting new constitutions during this period he was allowed to exercise it jointly with the council. In six states it was given to the legislature, or to the legislature and council. The power of the governor to dissolve the legislature or either branch of it was everywhere abolished.

The supremacy of the legislature under these early state constitutions is seen also in the manner of the appointment, the tenure and the powers of the judiciary. In nine states the judges were elected by the state legislature, either with or without the consent of a council. In Maryland, Massachusetts, New Hampshire, and Pennsylvania they were appointed by the governor with the consent of the council. But this really amounted to indirect legislative appointment in Maryland, since both the governor and council in that state were elected annually by the legislature. The legislature also had a voice in the appointment of judges in Pennsylvania, New Hampshire and Massachusetts, since it elected the executive in the first and the council in the others. In nine states, then, the judges were elected directly by the legislature; in one indirectly by the legislature; in the other three the legislature participated in their election through an executive or a council of its own choosing.

In every state the judges could be impeached by the lower branch of the legislature and expelled from office on conviction by the senate or other tribunal, as the constitution prescribed. Moreover, in six states they could be removed according to the English custom by the executive on an address from both branches of the legislature. The term of office of the judges in eight states was during good behavior. In New Jersey and Pennsylvania they were appointed for seven years, and in Rhode Island, Connecticut, and Georgia they were chosen annually.

The legislature under these early state constitutions was hampered neither by the executive nor by the courts. It had all law-making power in its own hands. In no state could the courts thwart its purpose by declaring its acts null and void. Unchecked by either executive or judicial veto its supremacy was undisputed.

From the foregoing synopsis of the state constitutions of this period it is evident that their framers rejected entirely the English theory of checks and balances. The principle of separation of powers as expounded by Montesquieu and Blackstone, found little favor with those who controlled American politics at this time. Instead of trying to construct a state government composed of coordinate branches, each acting as a check upon the others, their aim was to make the legislature supreme. In this respect the early state constitutions anticipated much of the later development of the English government itself.

The checks and balances, and separation of powers, which characterized the government of England and her American colonies in the eighteenth century, resulted from the composite character of the English Constitution —its mixture of monarchy, aristocracy, and democracy. It is not surprising, then, that with the temporary ascendancy of the democratic spirit, the system of checks should have been largely discarded.

This democratic tendency is seen also in our first federal constitution, the Articles of Confederation, which was framed under the impulse of the Revolutionary movement. This document is interesting as an expression of the political philosophy of the Revolution, but like the state constitutions of that period, it has had few friendly critics among later political writers. Much emphasis has been put upon its defects, which were many, while but little attention has been given to the political theory which it imperfectly embodied. That it failed to provide a satisfactory general government may be admitted; but this result must not be accepted as conclusive proof that the principles underlying it were altogether false.

The chief feature of the Articles of Confederation was the entire absence of checks and balances. All the powers conferred upon the general government were vested in a single legislative body called the Continental Congress, which was unchecked by a distinct executive or judiciary. In this respect it bore a striking resemblance to the English government of to-day with its omnipotent House of Commons. But, unlike the English government of to-day, its powers were few and narrowly limited. Its failure was due, perhaps, not to the fact that the powers granted to the confederation were vested exclusively in a single legislative body, but to the fact that the powers thus granted were not sufficient for maintaining a strong and effective central government.

The reason for the weakness of the general government under the Articles of Confederation is obvious to the student of American history. It was only gradually, and as necessity compelled cooperation between the colonies, that the sentiment in favor of political union developed. And though some tendencies in this direction are seen more than a century before the American Revolution, the progress toward a permanent union was slow and only the pressure of political necessity finally brought it about.

As early as 1643 Massachusetts, Plymouth, Connecticut and New Haven formed a "perpetual confederation" under the name of the "United Colonies of New England." The motive for this union was mainly offence and defence against the Indian tribes and the Dutch, though provision was also made for the extradition of servants and fugitives from justice. The management of the common interest of these colonies was vested in a board of eight commissioners—two from each colony—and, in transacting the business of the confederacy, the consent of six of the eight commissioners was required. Any matter which could not be thus disposed of was to be referred to the four colonial legislatures. The general government thus provided for could not intermeddle "with the government of any of the jurisdictions." No provision was made for amending the "Articles of Confederation," and only by the unanimous consent of these colonies could any other colony be admitted to the confederacy. This union lasted for over forty years.

Again in 1754 the pressure of impending war with the French and Indians brought together at Albany a convention of delegates from seven colonies north of the Potomac. A plan of union drafted by Benjamin Franklin was recommended by this convention, but it was not regarded with favor either by the colonies or by the English government. The former regarded it as going too far in the direction of subordinating the separate colonies to a central colonial authority, while for the latter it was too democratic.

The union of all the colonies under the Articles of Confederation was finally brought about through the pressure of military necessity during the Revolution. Nor is it surprising, in view of the history of the American colonies, that they reluctantly yielded up any powers to a central authority. We must bear in mind that the Revolution was in a measure a democratic movement, and that democracy was then found only in local government. The general governments of all countries were at that time monarchical or aristocratic. Tyranny in the eighteenth century was associated in the minds of the people with an undue extension or abuse of the powers exercised by the undemocratic central government. It is not surprising, then, that the Revolutionary federal constitution, the Articles of Confederation, should have failed to provide a general government sufficiently strong to satisfy the needs of the country after the return of peace.

It must not be inferred, however, that the political changes which immediately followed the outbreak of the Revolution were in the nature of sweeping democratic reforms. Much that was thoroughly undemocratic remained intact. The property qualifications for the suffrage were not disturbed by the Revolutionary movement and were finally abolished only after the lapse of nearly half a century. The cruel and barbarous system of imprisonment for debt which the colonies had inherited from England, and which often made the lot of the unfortunate debtor worse than that of the chattel slave, continued in several of the states until long after the Revolution. Marked as was the democratic tendency during the first few years of our independence, it nevertheless left untouched much that the progress of democracy has since abolished.

No. 5

WRITING THE NATIONAL CONSTITUTION [1]

by J. Mark Jacobson

WE cannot hope to understand the political theory underlying the framing of the Constitution without an analysis of the conditions existing between the battle of Yorktown and the calling of the Philadelphia convention. No movement in world history is a better illustration of social and economic determinism; no accomplishment, a more complete rebound of the pendulum.

During the Revolution democratic political ideas had run rampant. The social contract theory, especially that of Paine, had glorified the "people." And under the leadership of such men as Samuel Adams in Massachusetts and Patrick Henry in Virginia, political control had passed from the aristocratic merchants and plantation owners to the petty traders and small farmers. In the struggle to determine who should rule at home, the conservative elements had lost ground. Revolutionary thought had looked upon government as a necessary evil. Government consequently became weak and decentralized. State governments had powerless executives and omnipotent legislatures. The central government under the Articles of Confederation was almost non-existent. Congress could act only through the states; it possessed no authority over individuals. It could raise no taxes; it could only request requisitions from the states. The Articles endowed Congress with authority over foreign affairs, but granted it no power to enforce treaties. The Continental Congress had carried the Revolution to a successful conclusion, but before long some states refused to send delegates or to pay their quotas. Congress remained only an ineffective symbol of a loose union.

As a consequence of this political disorganization, and as an aftermath of the war, economic chaos set in. Colonial independence from Great Britain meant withdrawal from the British mercantile system. The American

[1] J. M. Jacobson, *The Development of American Political Thought: a Documentary History* (New York: D. Appleton-Century Co., 1932), pp. 164-179. Reprinted by permission of the publisher.

merchants found the ports of England and the West Indies closed against them; and the impotent central government could not negotiate favorable trade agreements with other European powers. The loss of foreign trade threatened to wipe out those merchants who had cast their lot with the Revolutionists. Interstate trade became even more chaotic; jealousies developed among the states; each desired to keep money from going beyond its boundaries. Like modern nations, they endeavored to build up their own business prosperity at the expense of their neighbors. Thus New York taxed the produce of Connecticut farmers and destroyed their only profitable market. The seaport states financed their governments through imposts on European goods passing through their harbors, but destined for consumption in neighboring states. Madison thus picturesquely depicted the unhappy plight of those states not having seaports: "New Jersey placed between Phil^a and N. York, was likened to a cask tapped at both ends; and N. Carolina between Virg^a & S. Carolina to a patient bleeding at both Arms." The existence of different currencies in each of the thirteen states likewise hampered interstate trade. A Rhode Island merchant could not trade in Massachusetts without first exchanging his money into the currency of Massachusetts. The financial mechanism of present-day foreign trade did not then exist; even if the value of money had remained stable, the necessity of exchange would have discouraged trading. The continuous fluctuation of the depreciated state currencies, however, made commerce so hazardous as to be almost impossible. Furthermore, the attitude of the state courts toward non-resident creditors frequently prevented the collection of debts contracted in interstate trade. Truly, Madison wrote: "Most of our political evils may be traced to our commercial ones."

Chaotic finances likewise characterized the post-Revolutionary period. In an effort to finance the Revolution, the Continental Congress and each of the states had floated large bond issues and had printed much paper money. Both the securities and the money, unsupported save by the hope of victory and of possible payment, depreciated rapidly in value. In Virginia by 1781 the Continental notes "fell to 1000 for 1," wrote Jefferson, "and then expired, as it had done in other States, without a single groan." Jefferson records that he sold some land before the issuance of paper currency, but that he "did not receive the money till it was not worth Oak leaves."

The depreciation of money resulted in an interesting and important class struggle. The creditor groups suffered greatly. The merchants who sold on credit received upon payment a greatly decreased purchasing power; meanwhile, they had to pay their European creditors in gold or silver. The debtor groups, on the other hand, benefited from this situation. In the spring the farmer bought seed and provisions for repayment at harvest season; also, his farm usually had a heavy, long-term mortgage. With the declining value of money and the corresponding increase in farm prices, the farmer could repay his debts with fewer bushels of wheat or corn. Paper money thus proved valuable to him. It supplied the frontier communities for the first time with a sufficient medium of exchange. Consequently, the debtor groups opposed a stabilization in currency and favored further operation of the money presses.

The debtor-creditor conflict, which, as we have noted, began in the pre-Revolutionary days, now took an acute form. Constant agitation in favor of fiat money, lax bankruptcy acts, and installment laws punctuated politics. In some states, as Rhode Island, the agrarians dominated the legislature and enacted debtor laws. In Massachusetts the attempt of the courts to enforce debts and foreclose on mortgages led to a violent reaction on the part of the agrarian debtors. Led by Shays, the farmers of western Massachusetts rose in revolt. By armed opposition, they shut the courts—those pernicious institutions of aristocracy—and prevented the legal collection of debts. The militia, financed by the private subscriptions of Boston merchants, put down the rebellion. But the memory of Shays's attack struck terror into the conservative hearts of the commercial and financial class. This incident, more than any other, brought about the Constitutional Convention of 1787.

The depreciation of public securities and paper currency led to another important phenomenon. Just as after the World War heavy speculation occurred in the depreciated German mark and Russian ruble, so during and after the Revolution speculation took place in bonds, money, and land certificates. The moneyed men gambled on the possibility of repayment. But as long as the central government could not raise revenues, it could not redeem its issues. As long as agrarian debtors controlled the state legislatures, the value of their securities declined. And until the central government was sufficiently strong to build roads to the West and to afford protection against Indian attacks, settlers would move there in but small numbers, and the value of land certificates would not rise. The immediate outlook for the speculators was thus dark and uncertain.

These political and economic factors characterized the post-Revolutionary period and produced the American Constitution. The principal purposes to be served by the new government, according to *The Federalist*, were:

> The common defence of the members; the preservation of the public peace, as well against internal convulsions as external attacks; the regulation of commerce with other nations, and between the states; the superintendence of our intercourse political and commercial, with foreign countries.

Edmund Randolph, in the opening address of the Constitutional Convention, expressed a similar view of the needs of the existing situation. Commercial chaos, depreciated currency, Shays's rebellion, loomed large in his mind.

> The character of such a governme(nt) ought to secure 1. against foreign invasion: 2. against dissentions between members of the Union, or seditions in particular states: 3. to p(ro)cure to the several States various blessings, of which an isolated situation was i(n)capable: 4. to be able to defend itself against incroachment: & 5. to be paramount to the state constitutions.

In speaking of the defects of the Confederation, Randolph professed:

> A high respect for its authors, and considered them as having done all that patriots could do, in the then infancy of the science of constitutions, & of confederacies,—when the inefficiency of requisitions was unknown— no commercial discord had arisen among any states—no rebellion had appeared as in Massts.—foreign debts had not become urgent—the havoc of paper money had not been foreseen—treaties had not been violated—and perhaps nothing better could be obtained from the jealousy of the states with regard to their sovereignty.

The existing political and economic conditions injured the large property groups. The merchants and manufacturers suffered through the loss of foreign trade and the chaotic obstacles against interstate commerce. The creditor class, in general, lost through the constant decline in the value of money. Speculators in securities, currency, and land desired a rise in values. A swing of the pendulum in that direction was impossible under the political situation of a weak central government and agrarian and popular control in the state legislatures. At this time, too, the large plantation owners of the South feared slave uprisings and preferred a strong central government for defense. And finally, possible repetition of Shays's rebellion of agrarian debtors frightened the conservative lovers of law, order, and security.

It was the representatives of these economic and social groups that convened in Philadelphia in May, 1787. They framed the American Constitution. Not one member represented, in his immediate personal economic interests, the small farming or mechanic classes. The agrarian legislature of Rhode Island refused to send delegates to such a capitalistic gathering. Patrick Henry, the populist leader of Virginia and a delegate from that state, "smellt a rat" and refused to attend. A majority of the delegates were lawyers by profession, and most of them came from towns, on or near the coast, where property was largely concentrated. Forty of the fifty-five members were public security holders. With the exception of New York and possibly Delaware, each state had one or more prominent representatives who held large amounts of securities. At least fourteen members held lands for speculation, and twenty-four had property in the form of money loaned at interest. Eleven delegates were interested in mercantile, manufacturing, and shipping lines. And fifteen were slave-owners. Beard, in his *Economic Interpretation of the Constitution,* has declared that:

> The overwhelming majority of members, at least five-sixths, were immediately, directly, and personally interested in the outcome of their labor at Philadelphia, and were to a greater or less extent economic beneficiaries from the adoption of the Constitution.

Beveridge, in his monumental study of Federalism, *The Life of John Marshall,* writes:

> Too much emphasis cannot be put upon the fact that the mercantile and financial interests were the weightiest of all the influences for the Constitution; the debtor and agricultural interests the strongest groups against it. It deserves repetition, for a proper understanding of the craft and force practiced by both sides in the battle over ratification, that those who owed debts were generally against the Constitution and practically all to whom debts were due were for the new Government.

The experience and the economic needs of the conservative propertied group that met at Philadelphia fashioned their attitudes. The delegates distrusted popular democracy and state legislatures, frequently agrarian in composition. Their main desire was for stability. Beveridge thus cogently depicts their mental state:

> Since the victory at Yorktown a serious alteration had taken place in the views of many who had fought hardest for Independence and popular government. These men were as strong as ever for the building of a separate and distinct National entity; but they no longer believed in the wisdom or virtue of democracy without extensive restrictions. They had come to think that, at the very best, the crude ore of popular judgment could be made to enrich sound counsels only when passed through many screens that would rid it of the crudities of passion, whimsicality, interest, ignorance, and dishonesty, which, they believed, inhered in it. Such men esteemed less and less a people's government and valued more and more a good government. And the idea grew that this meant a government the principal purpose of which was to enforce order, facilitate business, and safeguard property.

American historians have long written the story of the Constitutional Convention as an epic of conflict and compromise. They have devoted much attention to the struggle between the large and small states, with the resulting equal representation in the Senate. Attention, too, has been paid to the battle between the commercial North and the agricultural South, and to the compromises over the slave trade and the counting of slaves in connection with representation. But an examination of the realities of the proceedings at Philadelphia reveals, amidst the discord, a fundamental harmony. In the essential objectives of the Convention, virtual unanimity existed. The delegates differed only in the means of achieving their common ends. Not the conflicts and compromises, but the uniform distrust of democracy and the universal desire for stability, stand out in clear perspective.

The secret sessions of the Convention permitted the members utter freedom of expression. No speeches to the gallery, no orations for popular consumption, marked the meetings. With brutal frankness, the delegates passed judgment on the demerits of government by the people. Randolph of Virginia struck the keynote in the opening speech of the Convention:

> Our chief danger arises from the democratic parts of our constitutions. It is a maxim which I hold incontrovertible, that the powers of government exercised by the people swallow up the other branches. None of the constitutions have provided sufficient checks against the democracy. The feeble Senate of Virginia is a phantom. Maryland has a more powerful senate, but the late distractions in that State, have discovered that it is not powerful enough. The check established in the constitution of New York and Massachusetts is yet a stronger barrier against democracy, but they all seem insufficient.

Alexander Hamilton, a leader at the Convention and later the moving spirit in Washington's administration, "acknowledged himself not to think favorably of Republican Government." He addressed his remarks to "those who did think favorably of it, in order to prevail on them to tone their Government as high as possible." An economic determinism characterized Hamilton's speeches. In every community where industry is encouraged, he maintained, there will be a division into the few and the many, into creditors and debtors; hence separate interests will arise. If you give all the power to the many, they will oppress the few.

> To the want of this check we owe our paper money—instalment laws &c. To the proper adjustment of it the British owe the excellence of their Constitution. Their house of Lords is a most noble institution. Having nothing to hope for by a change, and a sufficient interest by means of their property, in being faithful to the National interest, they form a permanent barrier agst. every pernicious innovation, whether attempted on the part of the

Crown or of the Commons. No temporary Senate will have firmness en'o' to answer the purpose.

Inequality of property would, he felt, exist as long as liberty lasted, and would unavoidably result from that very liberty itself. This inequality of property constituted the great and fundamental distinction in society.

> All communities divide themselves into the few and the many. The first are the rich and well born, the other the mass of the people. The voice of the people has been said to be the voice of God; and however generally this maxim has been quoted and believed, it is not true in fact. The people are turbulent and changing; they seldom judge or determine right. Give therefore to the first class a distinct, permanent share in the government. They will check the unsteadiness of the second, and as they cannot receive any advantage by a change, they will ever maintain good government. Can a democratic assembly who annually revolve in the mass of the people, be supposed steadily to pursue the public good? Nothing but a permanent body can check the imprudence of democracy.

What is the remedy? "We ought to go as far in order to attain stability and permanency, as republican principles will admit." Hamilton was willing to grant life tenures to the senators and the President. At the very least, the Constitution should, he said, provide a seven-year term for the Senate in order that the upper chamber might have "a permanent will, a weighty interest, which would answer essential purposes." Thus did Hamilton express his distrust of democracy and his desire for stability.

James Madison played a leading role at the Convention; his influence was such that historians have labeled him "the Father of the Constitution." While he later became a follower of Jefferson, at this time he was an ardent nationalist and conservative. Madison frequently rose to demonstrate the necessity of checks upon the propertyless classes. In a speech on the suffrage, he felt that the freeholders of the country would be the the safest depositories of "Republican liberty." In future times, he feared, a great majority of the people would be not only without land, but without any sort of property. These would either combine under the influence of their common situation, in which case the rights of property and the public liberty would not be secure, or they would become the tools of opulence and ambition. In discussing the Senate, Madison's anti-democratic attitude again found expression. He argued that a limited number of enlightened citizens was a necessary defense against the impetuous counsel, fickleness, and passion of a numerous popular assembly. Like Hamilton, he held that in all civilized countries the people fall into different classes having a real or supposed difference of interests. Creditors and debtors, farmers, merchants and manufacturers, rich and poor—these classes divide society. In time a growth of population would of necessity increase the proportion of those who labor under all the hardships of life. While no agrarian attempt at a more equal distribution of property had as yet been made in this country, symptoms of a leveling spirit had, he claimed, appeared sufficiently in certain quarters to give warning of the future danger.

The government we mean to erect is intended to last for ages. The landed interest, at present, is prevalent; but in process of time, when we approximate to the states and kingdoms of Europe; when the number of landholders shall be comparatively small, through the various means of trade and manufactures, will not the landed interests be overbalanced in future elections, and unless wisely provided against, what will become of your government? In England, at this day, if elections were open to all classes of people, the property of the landed proprietors would be insecure. An agrarian law would soon take place. If these observations be just, our government ought to secure the permanent interests of the country against innovation. Landholders ought to have a share in the government, to support these invaluable interests and to balance and check the other. They ought to be so constituted as to protect the minority of the opulent against the majority. The senate, therefore, ought to be this body; and to answer these purposes, they ought to have permanency and stability. Various have been the propositions; but my opinion is, the longer they continue in office, the better will those views be answered.

A few other statements will indicate the existing distrust of democracy and the prevalent desire for stability. Elbridge Gerry was a leading Massachusetts merchant; a decade later he turned against the Federalists, and even in 1788 he found the Constitution drawn up by the Convention too aristocratic for his support. Yet, even Gerry admitted that heretofore he had been too republican; he had, he said, been taught by experience the danger of the leveling spirit. "The evils we experience flow from the excess of democracy. The people do not want virtue; they are the dupes of pretended patriots."

Governeur Morris of Pennsylvania held that there was as much reason to intrust the suffrage to children as to the ignorant and the dependent.

Give the votes to the people who have no property, and they will sell them to the rich who will be able to buy them.

The time is not distant when this Country will abound with mechanics and manufacturers who will receive their bread from their employers. Will such men be the secure & faithful Guardians of liberty? Will they be the impregnable barrier agst. aristocracy?

Roger Sherman of Connecticut was one of the few delegates who had risen from poverty through his own efforts; but with his rise in the economic scale, he had left behind all sympathy for the masses. The people, he held, should have as little as may be to do about the government. "They want information and are constantly liable to be misled."

John Dickinson of Delaware had written learned dissertations against British taxation of the colonies; at the Convention, however, he argued for vesting the rights of suffrage in the freeholders of the country. He considered them the best guardians of liberty, and felt that to restrict the suffrage to them was a necessary defense against "the dangerous influence of those multitudes without property & without principle, with which our country like all others, will in time abound."

Thus spoke the framers of the Constitution. Distrust of democracy, acquired through a decade of proletariat-agrarian-debtor control in local politics, dominated their thinking. A desire for stability, developed through commercial and fiscal chaos, directed their construction of the new governmental system. Benjamin Franklin, an aged delegate at the Convention, cynically remarked:

> Few men in public affairs act from a mere view of the good of their country, whatever they may pretend; and though their activity may bring real good to their country, they do not act from a spirit of benevolence.

The American Constitution is the resultant of two important factors: the economic and political situation after the Revolution, and the attitude which this situation inspired in the delegates at Philadelphia. The framers of the Constitution were not visionary idealists; they were practical men of affairs. They opposed popular democracy and desired upper class control in government. Naturally, they wrote their economic and social views into the document.

The Revolutionary theorists had glorified the "people"; the Convention delegates considered the masses, "turbulent and changing." The early state constitutions had trusted the legislature as the safest agent of the sovereign people; the Constitution of 1787 placed checks on the fickleness and passion of popular assemblies. Just as the Revolutionary state constitutions had accepted the thesis of the separation of powers, so likewise did the framers at Philadelphia; but in their equilibrium of departments, the scales weighed heavily against the legislature.

The Constitution minimized the role of the legislature and endeavored to prevent that organ from coming under popular domination. The Convention encountered considerable difficulty in framing the suffrage restrictions to operate in electing members of the House of Representatives. Finally, they adopted the provision that: "The Electors in each State shall have the Qualifications requisite for Electors of the most numerous Branch of the State Legislature." On its face, this section appears extremely liberal. But we must remember that almost every state had at this time property qualifications for voting. The turbulent masses were to play no role in the new regime.

Even after such restriction, the framers still distrusted the legislature. They adopted a bicameral system so that the permanency of the Senate might check the impetuous counsels of the lower chamber. Furthermore, to the independent executive they gave a strong veto; and no elected council shared the power with the executive, as was the case in several of the states. Congress could override a presidential veto only by a two-thirds vote of each house; and at the end of a congressional session the legislature could not check the President at all. Finally, the framers subjected Congress to judicial control. Critics of the Supreme Court frequently accuse Marshall of usurping the power of judicial review in the case of *Marbury* v. *Madison*. A careful analysis, however, of the debates at Philadelphia, of the proceedings of the state ratifying conventions, and of the Federalist Papers, shows that the framers of the Constitution intended that the Supreme Court should act as a check upon Congress. Suffrage restrictions, bicameralism, executive veto, judicial review—all were brought into play to guard against the dangers of populist or debtor legislation.

The Constitution-makers not only feared democracy, but also desired stability. Above all, the new government must render their property and social system secure. Consequently, they constructed a government of balances devised to prevent the majority from ever dominating "the minority of the opulent." They erected four separate units of government: a House of Representatives, a Senate, a President, and a Supreme Court. For each they provided a distinct method of selection. The qualified voters of each state were to elect the representatives; both branches of the legislature were to choose a state's senators. A specially constructed and entirely independent electoral college was to select the chief magistrate. The framers wanted no popular participation. Each state, through either its legislature or its electorate, was to choose a body of men; these colleges, each meeting in its own state, were to be uninstructed; they were to deliberate, to nominate, and to elect the President and Vice-President. Should this scheme fail, then the choice was to fall to the House of Representatives—the House, however, elected two years previously. And finally, the President was to appoint the justices of the Supreme Court, subject to senatorial confirmation. Similarly the framers established a different time-schedule of election for each unit. To the House of Representatives they gave a two-year term. The Senate was to stay in office for six years, one-third retiring biennially. The President's tenure was made four years; and the Supreme Court justices were to hold office during good behavior.

This scheme of balances, with its different methods and time-schedules of election, rendered the new government virtually safe from the dangers of popular, agrarian domination. In order for the debtor class to bring about issues of fiat paper money, they must now so dominate the state electorates as to win the House of Representatives, the state legislatures for a period of years as to win the Senate, and the electoral colleges as to win the presidency. Should the agrarians or the propertyless townspeople, by any chance, break through this carefully arranged system of different methods and times of election, the Supreme Court would still stand intact as the bulwark of property. The life tenure of the judges would render them independent and fearless in their opposition to the legislature. Later events actually demonstrated the foresight of the framers in this important matter. In 1800 the Jeffersonian Republicans captured the national government; but the judiciary, entrenched with staunch, conservative Federalists, acted as an effective check. Marshall and his associates, as we shall see, safeguarded the propertied classes.

A popular majority, during a period of temporary control, might, however, contrive to subvert this carefully arranged scheme. Against even this exigency the framers provided. They established a difficult method of constitutional amendment. A constitutional revolution must secure the sanction of two-thirds of the House of Representatives, two-thirds of the state-controlled Senate, and both legislative branches, or special conventions, in three-fourths of the states. The framers built well. Thus far only nineteen amendments [now twenty-one] have run this difficult gauntlet. Of these, the first ten, or the Bill of Rights, became law immediately as part of the bargain of ratification. The thirteenth, fourteenth, and fifteenth amendments were the aftermath of civil war. . . . two amendments passed Congress during the upheaval of the World War. Thus, only four [now six] constitutional changes have occurred during periods of normal political functioning. Truly, said Madison, "The government we mean to erect is intended to last for ages."

The powers granted to the federal government reflect the economic and political needs of the framers. The old Confederation acted only through the states; the new government could act directly upon the individual. The federal government was to have its own tax collectors, its own attorneys, its own marshals, its own criminal courts, its own army. The Constitution empowered Congress to lay and collect its own "Taxes, Duties, Imposts, and Excises"; no longer need it beg requisitions from the states. Direct taxes, however, Congress must apportion according to population—a provision included with a view to reconciling the rural interests. The taxing power and the immediate control over individuals formed the basis for all the other powers granted to the federal government.

Congress was given authority "to regulate Commerce with foreign Nations, and among the several States, and with the Indian Tribes." No longer was a labyrinth of state regulations to render trade chaotic. National commerce demanded national uniformity. The power "to coin Money, regulate Value thereof . . . and fix the Standard of Weights and Measures" likewise eliminated the previous obstacles to profitable interstate commerce. Thus did the mercantile and manufacturing groups at the Convention guard their interests.

Speculators, too, found protection. The Constitution provided: "All Debts contracted and Engagements entered into, before the Adoption of this Constitution, shall be as valid against the United States under this Constitution, as under the Confederation." This section guaranteed the repayment of the securities issued by the Continental Congress. To Congress the framers gave power "To dispose of and make all needful Rules and Regulations respecting the Territory or other Property belonging to the United States." Congress could admit new states into the Union and could establish post roads. By the exercise of these powers, the western lands would be opened, migration encouraged, and land certificates increased in value.

Still further, the framers provided for national peace and domestic security. Congress could raise and support an army, provide and maintain a navy, call forth the militia "to execute the Laws of the Union, suppress Insurrections and repel Invasions." These military provisions would enable the federal government to defend itself against foreign and domestic foes. The navy would defend our commerce, and the President might threaten its use to secure favorable trade treaties. The army and militia would put down class uprisings and slave revolts. The framers had not forgotten Shays's Rebellion. Shortly afterwards, the propertied Federalists were to use military force against a second agrarian revolt—the Whiskey Rebellion of the Pennsylvania corn growers.

In establishing the federal judiciary, the delegates at Philadelphia wrote into the Constitution safeguards for their commercial interests. Under the Articles of Confederation, New York merchants, for example, had experienced considerable difficulty in collecting debts in Connecticut; the state courts, often popularly controlled, had discriminated against non-resident creditors. To the new federal courts the framers granted jurisdiction in controversies between citizens of different states. Collection of interstate debts now rested in impartial courts. The federal judiciary also heard cases between a state and citizens of another state. Holders of state securities and land grants could now sue for the collection of their claims. All such grants of power to the federal government tended to eliminate those political and economic ills that had plagued the propertied classes. The new regime could maintain domestic peace and security, develop commerce and industry, and repay public security holders in full.

The framers, however, did not stop here. The populist state legislatures had attacked their property. This danger, too, they must eliminate. Article I, section 10, of the Constitution placed rigid restrictions on the states. No state hereafter should coin money, emit bills of credit, make anything but gold and silver legal tender in payment of debts, pass any *ex post facto* acts or laws impairing the obligation of contracts, or, without the consent of Congress, lay any taxes on imports or exports, or collect tonnage duties. Thus the Constitution-makers ruled out paper money, installment acts, lenient bankruptcy laws, repudiation of securities, and interstate tariff barriers. Thus they prevented any direct attack upon property. It is instructive to note that the Convention adopted these prohibitions with virtually no debate.

The framers of the Constitution distrusted popular democracy and desired stability. They built with their eyes well trained on their economic and political experiences. The structure of the new government eliminated popular rule and emphasized stability. The powers granted to the central government permitted it to eradicate the economic evils that oppressed the propertied groups. And the restrictions upon the states prevented future agrarian attacks.

The framers of this economic and social document naturally faced a serious problem in its ratification. In the first place, the state legislatures had authorized their delegates merely to amend the Articles of Confederation; the Convention, however, had drawn up a new document. In the second place, the Articles of Confederation had provided for amendment only by the unanimous consent of all thirteen state legislatures; and Rhode Island had refused to send delegates. And finally, the agrarians and urban wage-earners controlled some of the state legislatures; they would surely resent the restrictions on their authority. The Convention took the bull by the horns and engineered a peaceful revolution. It provided for ratification by nine states only and by special conventions. To the election of these conventions, the framers could more successfully devote their efforts.

Almost everywhere the people distrusted the new Constitution. They feared lest the new government would overawe the state sovereignties; they suspected that the new regime, being byond their reach, would prove subversive of their liberties. Four groups, in the main, were in opposition:

the small farmers, the town mechanics, the petty traders, and the politicians at the state capitals. The latter feared the decline of their importance and influence through the enlargement of the political pond; and they frequently became the leaders in expressing the more genuine popular fear of federal centralization. Amos Singletary, a rural member of the Massachusetts convention, typified the populist distrust of the new Constitution.

> These lawyers, and men of learning, and monied men, that talk so finely and gloss over matters so smoothly, to make us, poor illiterate people, swallow down the pill, expect to get into Congress themselves; they expect to be the managers of this constitution, and get all the power and all the money into their own hands, and then they will swallow up all us little folks, like the great *Leviathan,* Mr. President; yes, just as the whale swallowed up *Jonah.*

The speeches of Patrick Henry and George Mason at the Virginia convention likewise voice the popular fear of the political and economic domination of the propertied groups. Only through the superior ability of the Federalist leaders and the promise of numerous amendments—but ten of which later prevailed—could the supporters of the Constitution secure its ratification. The Bill of Rights thus resulted from the populist fears of the new oligarchic centralization. Rhode Island and North Carolina did not join their sister states until after the new government began operation.

No. 6

ADOPTING THE NATIONAL CONSTITUTION [1]

by Charles A. and Mary R. Beard

FULLY aware that their plan would be bitter medicine to a large part of the public, the delegates were puzzled about the best method of getting their instrument ratified. The lawful constitution, the Articles of Confederation, and the call under which the convention had been elected decreed that their project should be laid before the existing Congress for approval, transmitted to the states for ratification, and go into effect only after receiving unanimous consent. Now, the state legislatures, the Fathers knew by bitter experience, had been the chief assailants of public credit and private rights; they had repeatedly refused to indorse restraints on their own powers and their unanimous consent was hardly to be expected.

Having regard for realities rather than theories, the Fathers departed

[1] C. A. and Mary Beard, *The Rise of American Civilization* (New York: The Macmillan Co., 1934), Vol. I, pp. 328-335. Reprinted by permission of the publisher.

from the letter of the existing law in the interest of higher considerations. They did, indeed, provide that the new Constitution should be sent to the old Congress as a matter of form but they advised the Congress merely to pass the instrument along to the states with a recommendation that special conventions be called to decide the issue of ratification. Many citizens of the right sort, they reasoned, who would not take the trouble to serve in a local legislature, would be willing to participate in a ratifying convention; if once the barrier of the populistic state legislatures could be forced, they saw hope of victory.

Still the specter of unanimous ratification remained. After much debate on the point, the convention laid that ghost by an audacious proposal, namely, that the Constitution should go into effect, as between the states concerned, as soon as two-thirds had given their consent. This program, the learned commentator, John W. Burgess, makes plain, was a project for a revolution, a break with the prevailing legal order, a coup d'état, an appeal over the heads of established agencies to the voters, or at least to that part of the electorate prepared to overthrow the Articles of Confederation.

On September 17, after nearly four months of arduous debate, the convention brought its labors to a close. The Constitution was finished and the scheme for ratification formulated. Aggrieved by the decisions of their colleagues, some members had gone home in anger and some who stayed on refused to sign the document, denouncing it openly and opposing its adoption by the people. On the other hand, thirty-nine of the fifty-five members who had attended one or more sessions put their names on the parchment and sent it forth with their benediction, even though they differed widely among themselves in the degree of their enthusiasm for the common handiwork.

Hamilton thought the new government would not be powerful enough and entertained grave doubts about its success. While admitting that they were merely "making experiments in politics," and while expressing his disapproval of many provisions in the document, Franklin declared his faith in divine guidance in the matter. Standing then within the shadow of death, he wrote of the convention's achievement: "I can hardly conceive a transaction of such momentous importance to the welfare of millions now existing and to exist in the posterity of a great nation should be suffered to pass without being in some degree influenced, guided, and governed by that omnipotent, omnipresent, and beneficent Ruler, in whom all inferior spirits live and move and have their being."

With his customary practical view of things, Washington doubtless voiced the general sentiment of his fellow signers when he said: "The Constitution that is submitted is not free from imperfections. But there are as few radical defects in it as could well be expected, considering the heterogeneous mass of which the Convention was composed and the diversity of interests that are to be attended to. As a Constitutional door is opened for future amendments and alterations, I think it would be wise in the people to accept what is offered to them."

On receiving at Paris reports of the proceedings at Philadelphia, Jefferson was at first much troubled. He thought that the proposed House of Representatives would be incompetent to great tasks, that the President, aided by the army, might become a dictator, and that the convention should have been content to add a few sections to the Articles of Confederation, "the good, old and venerable fabric which should have been preserved even as a religious relique." Later, however, he changed his mind and on considering the possibilities of amendment came to the conclusion that the Fathers had done about as well as human circumstances permitted. In the end he came to view the whole operation as a noble triumph for humanity. "The example," he said, "of changing a constitution by assembling the wise men of the state, instead of assembling armies, will be worth as much to the world as the former examples we have given them."

Acting on the recommendations of the convention, the Congress submitted the Constitution to the states for their approval or rejection and in turn the local legislatures called upon the voters to choose conventions to pass upon the new project of government. In a trice the country was divided into hostile camps as all the engines of propaganda and political maneuvering were brought into play either to carry or to defeat the plan for a new government. With a bitterness that recalled the factional dispute in the revolutionary party a few years before, both sides resorted to strenuous tactics.

When, for example, certain opponents of the Constitution in the Pennsylvania legislature sought to win time for deliberation by leaving their seats and breaking the quorum, a federalist mob invaded their lodgings, dragged them through the streets, and pushed them back into the assembly room. Applauded by the victors, the vote was then taken and the election of delegates to the state ratifying convention was fixed at a date only five weeks ahead, reducing to the minimum the period allowed for taking "the solemn judgment of the people." Doubtless some gentlemen of the old school entertained regrets that the new law had been ushered in with disorder but the emergency was great.

Again when the New Hampshire convention met and a majority opposed to the Constitution was discovered, the assembly adjourned to prevent an adverse vote and give the friends of the new instrument a chance to work on the objectors. In one case haste, in the other delay, favored ratification.

As the winter of 1787-88 advanced into spring, the conflict was waged at close quarters, with steady gains among the supporters of the new form of government. Promptly and with little tumult, four states, Delaware, Connecticut, New Jersey, and Georgia—among the smallest and least powerful members of the confederation—ratified the Constitution. With similar promptness Pennsylvania added its approval following the events narrated above. Equally emphatic, Maryland and South Carolina, having given the voters ample time for deliberation, decided with a generous gesture in favor of ratification. In Virginia, where the popular verdict was doubtful, the weight of great names, such as Washington, Marshall, Randolph, and Wythe, finally carried the day. In New Hampshire, New York, and Massachusetts, where the election returned avowed majorities opposed to the Constitution, a great deal of clever engineering induced several delegates to depart from their apparent instructions and cast their ballots for ratification. But to the very end, two states, North Carolina and Rhode Island, refused to give their consent, allowing the new government to be erected without their aid and remaining isolated until the pressure of powerful economic forces brought them under the roof.

Intense as it was, the excitement that marked the struggle did not bring out an avalanche of voters to express their opinions at the polls. From the fragmentary figures that are available, it appears that no more than one-fourth of the adult white males in the country voted one way or the other in the elections at which delegates to the state ratifying conventions were chosen. According to a cautious reckoning, probably one-sixth of them—namely, one hundred thousand—favored the ratification of the new form of government. In any case, it is employing a juristic concept, not summarizing statistical returns, to say that "the whole people put restraints on themselves by adopting the Constitution."

Broadly speaking, the division of the voters over the document ran along economic lines. The merchants, manufacturers, private creditors, and holders of public securities loomed large among the advocates of the new system, while the opposition came chiefly from the small farmers behind the seaboard, especially from the men who, in earlier years, had demanded paper money and other apparatus for easing the strain of their debts. In favor of the Constitution, wrote General Knox to Washington from Massachusetts on January 12, 1788, was "the commercial part of the state to which are added all the men of considerable property, the clergy, the lawyers—including all the judges of all the courts, and all the officers of the late army, and also the neighborhood of all great towns. . . . This party are for vigorous government, perhaps many of them would have been still more pleased with the new Constitution had it been more analogous to the British constitution." In the opposition, General Knox massed the "Insurgents or their favorers, the great majority of whom are for the annihilation of debts public and private."

During the battle over ratification, advocates on both sides produced a large and, in the main, illuminating literature on the science of human government, a literature reminiscent of the grand style of the Revolution. Though time has sunk most of it into oblivion, especially the arguments of the defeated party, the noblest pieces of defense, namely the letters to the press written by Hamilton, Madison, and Jay in support of the Constitution, were rescued from the dust and given immortality under the name of *The Federalist*.

In the tenth number of this great series, Madison, who has been justly called the "father of the Constitution" and certainly may be regarded as a spokesman of the men who signed it, made a cogent appeal for ratification on practical grounds: "The first object of government" is the protection of "the diversity in the faculties of men; from which the rights of property originate." After enumerating the chief classes of property holders which spring up inevitably under such protection in modern society, Madison proceeded to show that "the regulation of these various and interfering interests forms the principal task of modern legislation and involves the spirit of party and faction in the ordinary operations of the government."

Then Madison explained how political strife involved economic concerns at every turn: "The most common and durable source of factions has been the various and unequal distribution of property. Those who hold and those who are without property have ever formed distinct interests in society. Those who are creditors and those who are debtors fall under a like discrimination. A landed interest, a manufacturing interest, a mercantile interest, a moneyed interest, with many lesser interests, grow up of necessity in civilized nations and divide them into different classes actuated by different sentiments and views. . . . From the protection of different and unequal faculties of acquiring property, the possession of different degrees and kinds of property immediately results; and from the influence of these on the sentiments and views of the respective proprietors, ensues a division of society into different interests and parties."

Of necessity, according to Madison's logic, legislatures reflect these interests. "What," he asks, "are the different classes of legislators but advocates and parties to the causes which they determine?" For this there is no help. "The causes of factions cannot be removed," and "we know from experience that neither moral nor religious motives can be relied upon as an adequate control." Since that is true, there arises a grave danger, namely, the danger that certain groups, particularly the propertyless masses, may fuse into an overbearing majority and sacrifice to its will the interests of the minority. Given this peril, it followed that a fundamental problem before the Philadelphia convention had been to "secure the public good and private rights against the danger of such a faction and at the same time to preserve the spirit and form of popular government." And the solution offered was in the check and balance system which refined and enlarged public views "by passing them through the medium of a chosen body of citizens." This, in the language of a leading Father, was the spirit of the new Constitution—the substance of a powerful appeal to all practical men of affairs.

By argument, by negotiation, and by the weight of personality the friends of the proposed revolution triumphed in the end. On June 21, 1788, the ninth state, New Hampshire, ratified the Constitution and the new system could then go into effect as between the parties that had sealed the contract. Within a few weeks, Virginia and New York, aware that the die had already been cast, gave their reluctant consent. With victory thus doubly assured, the Federalists could ignore the smoldering anger of the opposition that had proposed many amendments and could laugh at the solemn resolve of New York calling for another national assembly to modify the Constitution. Leaving North Carolina and Rhode Island still outside the fold unconvinced of its advantages, the old Congress made ready to disband by calling elections for the choice of men to constitute the personnel of the new government.

No. 7

THE STATE CONSTITUTIONS AFTER 1787 [1]

by J. Allen Smith

THE effects of the conservative reaction were not confined to the general government. The movement to limit the power of the popular majority was felt in the domain of state as well as national politics. Even before the Constitutional Convention assembled the political reaction was modifying some of the state constitutions. This is seen especially in the tendency to enlarge the powers of the judiciary which was the only branch

---

[1] J. A. Smith, *The Spirit of American Government* (New York: The Macmillan Co., 1907), Ch. 9. Reprinted by permission of the publisher.

of the state government in which life tenure survived. This tendency received powerful encouragement and support in the adoption of the Federal Constitution which secured to the judiciary of the general government an absolute veto on both federal and state legislation. For as the state courts were not slow in following the precedent set by the Federal courts, what had been before the adoption of the Constitution a mere tendency soon became the practice in all the states. This in reality accomplished a revolution in the actual working of the state governments without any corresponding change in their outward form. It effected a redistribution of political powers which greatly diminished the influence of the popularly elected and more responsible branches of the state governments and gave a controlling influence to that branch over which the people had least control.

Not only was the state judiciary allowed to assume the veto power, but their independence of public opinion was more effectually safeguarded by depriving a mere majority of the legislature of the power to remove them. The provision of the Federal Constitution requiring a two-thirds majority in the legislative body for removal by impeachment or otherwise was quite generally copied. Without some such safeguard the party in control of the legislature could prevent the exercise of the judicial veto by removing from office any judges who dared to oppose its policy.

New York and South Carolina were the only states adopting constitutions during the Revolutionary period, which included provisions limiting the power of the majority to impeach public officials. The New York constitution of 1777 required a two-thirds majority in the lower house, and the South Carolina constitution of 1778 a two-thirds majority in both houses. Pennsylvania copied the impeachment provisions of the Federal Constitution in her constitution of 1790; Delaware went even farther, and in her constitution of 1792, required a two-thirds majority in both houses; Georgia followed the example of the Federal Constitution in 1798; Virginia, in 1830; North Carolina, in 1835; Vermont, in 1836; New Jersey, in 1844; and Maryland, in 1851.

With the progress of this movement to restore the system of checks in the state constitutions the governor regained his independence of the legislature and also many of the rights and prerogatives of which the Revolution had deprived him. He was made coordinate with the legislature, set over against it and generally clothed with the qualified veto power, which made him for all practical purposes the third house of that body. Georgia increased the governor's term of office to two years and gave him the qualified veto power in 1798. Pennsylvania made his term of office three years and gave him the veto power in 1790. New Hampshire conferred the veto power on him in 1792 and New York in 1821.

This tendency to make the public official less directly dependent upon the people or their immediate representatives is clearly seen in other important changes made in the state constitutions during this period. Popular control over the legislature was diminished by lengthening the terms of the members of both houses and by providing that the upper house should be elected for a longer term than the lower. Georgia established an upper house in 1789 and made the term of office of its members three years. In 1790 Pennsylvania also added a senate whose members were to be elected for four years, and South Carolina increased the term of its senators from one to four years. Delaware extended the term from one to two years for members of the lower house and from three to four years for members of the upper house and made the legislative sessions biennial instead of annual in 1831. North Carolina increased the term of members of both houses from one to two years and adopted biennial sessions in 1835. Maryland in 1837 extended the term of senators from five to six years, and in 1846 established biennial sessions of the legislature. The responsibility of the legislature was still further diminished by the gradual adoption of the plan of partial renewal of the senate, which was incorporated in the Revolutionary constitutions of Delaware, New York and Virginia and later copied in the Federal Constitution. This ensured the conservative and steadying influence exerted by a body of hold-over members in the upper house.

With the exception of five states in which the members of one branch of the legislature were elected for terms varying from two to five years, the Revolutionary state constitutions provided for the annual election of the entire legislature. This plan made both houses conform to the latest expression of public opinion by the majority of the qualified voters at the polls. And since neither the executive nor the courts possessed the veto power, the system ensured prompt compliance on the part of the law-making body with the demands of the people as expressed in the results of the legislative election.

The influence of public opinion on the state governments was greatly weakened by the constitutional changes above mentioned. The lower branch of the legislature, inasmuch as all its members were simultaneously elected, might be regarded as representative of recent, if not present, public opinion, though effective popular control of that body was made more difficult by lengthening the term of office, since this diminished the frequency with which the voters could express in an authoritative manner their disapproval of the official record of its members. Under the plan adopted present public opinion as formulated in the results of the last election was not recognized as entitled to control the state senate.

These changes in the state constitutions by which the executive and judicial branches of the government acquired the veto power amounted in practice to the creation of a four-chambered legislature. By thus increasing the number of bodies which it was necessary for the people to control in order to secure the legislation which they desired, their power to influence the policy of the state government was thereby diminished. And when we reflect that not only was legislative authority more widely distributed, but each branch of the state government exercising it was also made less directly dependent on the qualified voters, we can see that these constitutional provisions were in the nature of checks on the numerical majority.

A consideration of the changes made in the method of amending the state constitutions leads to the same conclusion. During the Revolutionary period, as we have seen, the tendency was strongly toward making the fundamental law the expression of the will of the numerical majority. Difficulties in the way of change were reduced to a minimum. But under the influence of the poltiical reaction which followed, and which produced the Constitution of the United States, the state governments were so organized as to make it more difficult for the majority to exercise the amending power. Georgia in 1789 changed the method of amending the state constitution by requiring a two-thirds majority in a constitutional convention, and made another change in 1798 by which a two-thirds majority in each house of the legislature and a three-fourths majority in each house of the succeeding legislature was required for the adoption of an amendment to the constitution. South Carolina in 1790 adopted a provision guarding against mere majority amendment by making the approval of a two-thirds majority in both branches of two successive legislatures necessary for any changes in the constitution. Connecticut in 1818 restricted the power of amending by requiring a majority in the house of representatives, a two-thirds majority in both houses of the next legislature, and final approval by a majority of the electors. New York in 1821 adopted a plan which required that an amendment should receive a majority in each branch of the legislature, a two-thirds majority in each branch of the succeeding legislature, and be approved by a majority of the voters. North Carolina in 1835 made a three-fifths majority in each house of the legislature and a two-thirds majority of each house of the following legislature necessary for changes in the constitution.

The judicial veto served the purpose of preventing majority amendment under the guise of ordinary legislation, while a safeguard against constitutional changes favored by a mere majority was thus provided in the extraordinary majority required in both houses of the legislature to propose or adopt amendments. This, as has been shown in the case of the Federal Constitution, is a formidable check on the majority. In view of this restriction upon the proposing of amendments the provision for ratification by a popular majority, which owing to the progress of the later democratic movement has now been generally adopted, is no real concession to the principle of majority rule.

Assuming that a two-thirds majority in the legislature is required to propose an amendment, and that the principle of representation is so applied that each party is represented in the legislature in proportion to its popular vote, it would scarcely ever be possible for any party to propose an amendment to the state constitution, since it cannot be expected under any ordinary conditions to control two-thirds of the popular vote. But inasmuch as the successful party often secures under our system much more than its proportional share of representation in the legislature, it is by no means unusual for a party to have a two-thirds majority in both houses of a state legislature. This would appear to give the numerical majority under such conditions the power to propose and adopt amendments. Such would be the case if the party were really responsible to those who supported it at the polls. But this would assume the existence of a purely state party, organized with reference to state issues only, and carrying the election as the advocate of a definite state policy. Moreover, it would presuppose all those means, political and constitutional, by which the majority in the legislature would be accountable to the popular majority in the state. This is rendered impossible, however, as has been shown, by our system of government.

The above-mentioned changes in the constitutions of the older states may be attributed in large measure to the reaction against democracy which brought about the adoption of the Federal Constitution. They may be regarded as an expression of that distrust and fear of democracy which filled the minds of those who framed and set up our Federal government. It is not contended, however, that they are now so regarded by the masses of the people. The work of deifying the Federal Constitution was soon accomplished. And when the people had come to venerate it as the most perfect embodiment of the doctrine of popular sovereignty that the intelligence of man could devise, it was but natural that they should acquiesce in the proposal to make the state governments conform more closely to the general plan of that instrument. In view of the wide-spread sentiment which amounted to a blind and unthinking worship of the Constitution, it is not surprising that the political institutions of the general government should have been largely copied by the states. The only surprising thing in this connection is the fact that they did not follow the Federal model more closely, since every feature of it was the object of the most extravagant eulogy. Here we see, however, an inconsistency between profession and practice. The people who tolerated no criticism of the Federal Constitution showed nevertheless a distrust of some of its more conservative features. Much as the indirect election of President and United States senators was favored by the framers of our Federal Constitution, there has been no tendency to apply that principle in the selection of the corresponding state officials.

In all the states framing new constitutions during the Revolutionary period, except Massachusetts, New Hampshire, and New York, the governor was elected by the legislature. Pennsylvania abandoned indirect election and adopted election by the qualified voters in 1790; Delaware, in 1792; Georgia, in 1824; North Carolina, in 1835; Maryland, in 1837; New Jersey, in 1844; Virginia, in 1850; and South Carolina, in 1865. South Carolina and Maryland are the only states which have ever had indirect election of the upper house. Both adopted it in 1776, the constitution of South Carolina providing that the members of the lower house should elect the members of the upper house, and the constitution of Maryland requiring that members of the upper house should be chosen by an electoral college. This was abandoned for direct election in South Carolina in 1778 and in Maryland in 1837.

The conservative reaction was soon followed by a new movement toward democracy. This no doubt largely explains the failure of the people to reproduce in their state constitutions all those features which they professed to admire in the Federal Constitution. Not only did they not copy all the new features of that document, but they even discarded some of the then existing provisions of the state constitution which had been copied in the Federal Constitution. The principle of indirect election which was everywhere recognized in the choice of the state judiciary during the Revolutionary period was gradually abandoned for the more democratic method of direct popular choice which has now become the rule. The life tenure of judges which formerly existed in most of the states has almost entirely disappeared. In all but four states the judges are now chosen for terms varying from two to twenty-one years—the average length of the term being eight or ten years. The combination of direct popular choice with a fixed term of office has had the effect of making the state judiciary much more amenable to public opinion than the corresponding branch of the Federal government. By reason of the relatively long term for which the judges of the state supreme court are elected, however, and the plan of gradual renewal which prevents present public opinion from ever gaining the ascendency in that body, it is still the least responsible and most conservative branch of the state government.

We see, then, two motives exerting an influence in the remolding of the state constitutions, one being the desire to copy the Federal Constitution and the other the belief that the state government should reflect the will of the people. That the attainment of one of these ends would inevitably defeat the other was not generally recognized. The conviction which had become thoroughly rooted in the popular mind that the system of checks and balances was the highest expression of democratic organization ensured the embodiment of the general features of that system in the constitutions of the various states. The constitutional changes having this end in view largely destroyed the responsibility of the state governments to the people and thus prevented the very thing they were designed to accomplish. But however much this system was in reality opposed to the principle of direct popular control, it was adopted by the people with the idea of making the government more readily reflect their will. They were not conscious of any inconsistency in holding tenaciously to the doctrine of checks and balances and at the same time seeking to give the people more control over the state governments. The latter purpose is clearly seen in the constitutional changes relating to the tenure and manner of election of the judiciary and in the adoption of universal suffrage. Summing up the effects of these changes in the state constitutions, we may say that the suffrage was placed upon a democratic basis, the state judiciary was organized on a less irresponsible plan and the appearance of political responsibility secured by applying the principle of direct election to every branch of the state government. The longer term of office established for the legislative and executive branches of the state government, however, together with the increase in the authority of the judiciary and the adoption of the system of checks and balances has upon the whole had the effect of making the state government less responsive to the electorate.

As seen in preceding chapters, the framers of the Federal Constitution made use of the scheme of checks and balances for the purpose of limiting the power of the people. There is little evidence that they favored diffusion of authority except in so far as that authority rested upon a popular basis. Hence they carried the plan much farther in curtailing the power of the House of Representatives than a logical application of the doctrine would have justified, while at the same time giving more authority and power of independent action to the other branches of the general government than was consistent with their avowed, if not real, purpose.

They gave to the executive and judicial branches of the general government power to control the administration of Federal laws. The enforcement of all laws and regulations of the general government, in so far as the President and Senate might desire to enforce them, was guaranteed through the power to appoint and remove those who were entrusted with their execution, while the right of appeal from a state to the Federal courts precluded the possibility of enforcing a state law deemed to exceed the proper limits of state authority.

In the state governments on the other hand we find a high degree of administrative decentralization. The governor, unlike the President, was not given any adequate power to control those entrusted with the execution of state laws. A multitude of directly elected local officials are the agents of the state for this purpose. And since they reflect the sentiment of the various local interests to which they owe their election, it may and often does happen that a law to which those interests are opposed is rendered practically inoperative through the efforts of those local officials who are sworn to enforce it. The practical working of this system often gives to a local community an administrative veto on such general laws of the state as may be opposed to local sentiment. By this means the general executive authority of the state is weakened and its responsibility correspondingly diminished.

In still another respect the policy of dividing authority and parcelling it out between separate and distinct organs of government has been carried much farther in the state than in the Federal Constitution. Unlike the Federal government in which executive power is centralized in the President, the state constitutions have created a number of separate officials, boards and commissions, some directly elected and some appointed, independent of each other and irresponsible except in so far as a fixed term of office implies responsibility. This means that instead of one executive the state has many. Only one of them—the governor—has, it is true, a veto on the enactment of laws; but this, as we have seen, is really a legislative and not an executive power. Each of these has what may be termed an administrative veto; that is, the power to negative the laws which they are expected to administer by simply not enforcing them. The impossibility of securing an honest and faithful administration of the laws where the responsibility for their enforcement is divided between a number of separate and practically independent officials, is clearly shown in the experience of the various states. The evils of this system are illustrated in the state laws enacted for the purpose of controlling the railway business. Provision is usually made for their enforcement through a railway commission either directly elected or appointed by the governor. That direct election by the people for a fixed term, thereby securing independence during that term, fails to guarantee the enforcement of such laws is strikingly shown in the experience of California, where this body has been continually under the domination of the railway interests. [This was an appraisal of the situation in 1907.]

Under a system which thus minutely subdivides and distributes the administrative function, any effective control over the execution of state laws is made impossible. The governor, who is nominally the head of the executive agencies of the state, is not in reality responsible, since he has no adequate power to compel the enforcement of laws directly entrusted to other independent state officials. Any interest or combination of interests that may wish to prevent the enforcement of certain laws may be able to accomplish their end by merely controlling the one official or board whose duty it is to enforce the law in question. Their task would be a much more difficult one, if it were necessary to control for that purpose the entire executive arm of the state. The opportunity for the corrupt use of money and influence is thus vastly increased, since the people, though they might watch and judge fairly well the conduct of one state executive, can not exercise any effective censorship over a large number of such officials.

This irresponsibility which arises out of a wide diffusion of power is not confined to the executive branch of the state government. The legislature in the course of our political development has taken on the same elaborate committee organization which characterizes, as we have seen, our Federal Congress. The same sinister influences working through similar agencies oppose needed legislation. But although the good bills are frequently killed or mutilated in the secrecy of the committee room, the skilful use of money or other corrupt influence often secures the enactment of laws opposed to the interests of the people. Moreover, the practice known as log-rolling by which the representatives of various local interests combine and force through measures which secure to each of certain localities some advantage at the expense of the state at large are so common as to excite no surprise.

The relation existing between the executive and legislative branches under our system is another source of irresponsibility, since it does not follow simply because a law has been placed upon the statute books of a state that it can be enforced. An act may be passed in response to a strong public sentiment, it may be constitutional and the executive may be willing and may even desire to enforce it, and yet be unable to do so. The legislature may, and frequently does, enact laws under the pressure of public opinion while at the same time quietly exercising what is, in effect, a veto on their execution. In the case of much important legislation it can accomplish this by merely not appropriating the funds which are required for their enforcement. The laws against adulteration are a good illustration. An official known perhaps as a dairy and food commissioner may be provided for, whose duty it is to enforce these laws. The nature of the work entrusted to him requires that he should have a corps of assistants, inspectors who are to keep a watchful eye on the goods likely to be adulterated and collect samples of such goods from the various places in the state where they are exposed for sale, and chemists who are to analyze the samples thus procured and determine whether manufacturers and dealers are complying with the law. Unless an adequate sum is appropriated for this purpose, and for prosecuting those who are violating the law, such laws can not be enforced.

In our state governments the subdivision of authority has been carried so far that no effective control over the enactment or enforcement of state laws is possible. Under the influence of the doctrine of checks and balances the policy of widely distributing political authority has inured to the benefit of those private interests which are ever seeking to control the government for their own ends, since it has supplied the conditions under which the people find it difficult to fix the blame for official misconduct. Indeed it may be said that wherever power should be concentrated to ensure responsibility, it has been almost invariably distributed.

Chapter III

CHANGING THE RULES FOR A CHANGING SOCIETY

[As J. Allen Smith long ago pointed out, all democratic constitutions are flexible and easy to amend. This follows from the fact that in a truly democratic government the people are in control, and a constitution must be a means of securing supremacy of the public will and not a means of thwarting it. Such a constitution must not be a check upon the people themselves. It must be an instrument for securing popular control over the agents and representatives of the people without which popular government is only a name. A government is democratic in the proportion that it responds to the people's will, and since one way of defeating the popular will is to make it difficult to change the fundamental rules, it follows that any constitution that is truly democratic must yield to changes in public opinion.

Now, if we examine American history we shall see that the society for which our original constitutions were framed has changed fundamentally since the late eighteenth century. With changes in society there have naturally been changes in the political needs and desires of the people, and the politician has accordingly sought to adapt the framework of government to the new conditions. It should surprise no one, therefore, that American constitutions have been materially altered in the last century and a half. It does surprise a great many people, however, to learn that these changes are primarily not changes in the written document. Indeed the document drafted in 1787 has been changed less than fifteen times since 1800. It is important therefore to examine our constitutional history in order to determine how such changes have come about and whether the informal and formal means of adapting our fundamental rules to changing conditions are such as to make our constitution one that is truly democratic.]

No. 8

OUR UNWRITTEN CONSTITUTION [1]

by William Bennett Munro

THE written Constitution of the United States is a document that occupies five pages of print in the World Almanac and can be read in half an hour. But alongside it, and based upon it, there has developed during the past hundred and forty years an unwritten constitution of vastly greater dimensions. It fills the statutes-at-large, the law reports, the printed laws of the individual commonwealths, and constitutional treatises to the extent of a million pages or more. This unwritten constitution is made up of federal and state enactments, judicial decisions, usages, doctrines, precedents, official opinions, and points of view which have profoundly altered the implications of the original instrument. It has made the government of the United States a different affair from that which the framers of the written Constitution intended it to be.

So great has this divergence become at the present day that no one can now obtain even a silhouette of the American political system if he confines his study to the nation's fundamental law as it left the hands of its architects in 1787. Its words and phrases have been "twisted and tortured" during their journey down these fourteen decades, as Lord Bryce once said, until they now imply things widely remote from what they were originally thought to mean. Governmental powers of vast import have been nurtured from these few pages until we can now speak of the written Constitution as merely the taproot from which the tree of American nationalism has grown. Its branches increase their spread year after year. In a word the national government has become far more powerful in relation to the states than it was at the beginning—more democratic, more efficient, more far-reaching in its influence both at home and abroad.

The makers of the American Constitution neither began nor finished their work in the summer of 1787. Their ancestors began it at Runnymede and continued it at Westminster. Their descendants have kept bravely at the work ever since the Great Convention adjourned. It is often said that the last framer of the Constitution passed off the scene with Madison's death in 1836; but Marshall and Jackson were giving new significance to the supreme law of the land when Madison died. Nor were they the last of

[1] W. B. Munro, *The Makers of the Unwritten Constitution* (New York: The Macmillan Co., 1930), pp. 1-22. Reprinted by permission of the publisher.

the line. In the wider sense of the term the makers of the American Constitution form a great and still growing company. The list will not be closed until the end of time.

What has been said in the foregoing paragraphs is commonplace, or ought to be. Every textbook of American government adverts to the great discrepancy between what the government of the United States was intended to be and what it has become. This, moreover, in spite of checks and balances, limitations and prohibitions, and all the other artifices for preserving equilibrium that eighteenth-century minds could suggest. Such a phenomenon all the more deserves comment because it has not come to pass by reason of the nineteen [twenty-one] amendments. Among these additions to the original document only one enlarges the powers of Congress. All the rest impose restraints or change methods. The growth of the national government in strength and prestige has not been achieved by broadening the original foundation upon which it rests. Were there no other channels of federal expansion than that which the process of formal amendment has provided, the national government would now be relatively weaker than it was when it started. It has gained virtually the whole of its political and economic hegemony of to-day from statutes, from judicial decisions, and from usages. Together these make up the unwritten constitution, a structure which is the work of many hands, a rambling edifice to which successive generations of statesmen and jurists have each added wings and gables and pillars until only a semblance of the original architecture remains.

In this development of an unwritten constitution the United States has not been unique among countries which possess free government. All political systems are continually in process of change; like living organisms they must adapt themselves to an altered environment or die. You cannot encase a living organism in a marble urn and keep it alive. No more can one century be held in bondage to another. The written word, as a basis of popular government, must have the power to expand and contract. This adaptation will be by frank and formal change if the methods of constitutional amendment are easy (as they are in England and Italy); but it will follow other channels when the routine of amendment is roundabout and difficult as in the United States. The instinct of self-preservation in a government will impel it to find such channels, or to make them if need be.

Strange as it may sound to-day, the statesmen of 1787 intended to make the process of constitutional amendment an easy one. That is why they provided four alternative ways of putting an amendment through. They made it possible to initiate amendments in Congress, or without action by Congress. They provided for ratification by the state legislatures or without action by these legislatures if the occasion required. Hamilton devoted

almost an entire Federalist letter to proving the proposition that the amending process could not be made any easier without serious danger of constitutional instability.

Of course it was not anticipated that only one of the alternative methods
would ever be used. There was a feeling that the ratification of amendments by conventions in the states would often prove easier than ratification
by state legislatures. The situation in 1787 warranted that impression. If
the acceptance of the original Constitution had been left to the state legislatures, rather than to conventions called for the purpose, it would almost
certainly have been rejected by some of them. Nevertheless, after the Constitution had been ratified by these state conventions, the first series of
proposed amendments were initiated by Congress and sent to the state
legislatures as the quickest way of getting them into effect. This set a
precedent which has ever since been followed. But with this important
difference: that it required action on the part of only eleven state legislatures to add these first ten amendments, whereas it now requires affirmative
action on the part of thirty-six. [Since this was written the twenty-first
amendment was ratified by the convention method.]

The framers of the original Constitution anticipated, moreover, that from
time to time a national convention would be called for the purpose of
undertaking a general revision. If Thomas Jefferson could have had his
way he would have made such revision mandatory at least once a generation. Nothing, in fact, was farther from the expectations of Jefferson,
Madison, Franklin and the rest than that this roll of parchment would
remain unrevised to help govern their children's grandchildren, or that more
amendments would be added during the first ten years of its operation than
in the succeeding hundred and thirty. We are sometimes cautioned nowadays against a too-receptive attitude toward constitutional amendments;
but it would be difficult to find, at any subsequent stage in American history, a group of men more benevolently inclined toward amendments than
were the Fathers themselves.

In any case formal amendment has been only one of the agencies of
constitutional flexibility, and by no means the most important one. More
has been accomplished by statutory elaboration. The statesmen of 1787
did not desire or deem themselves competent to perform a task of encyclo-
pedic proportions. In eighty-one days they put together and agreed upon
only eighty-nine sentences; their four hundred hours of debate and deliberation eventuated in a document of only four thousand words. It was not
that they were lacking in vocabulary, but simply that they felt insistent
upon leaving the details of government as a hostage to the good sense of
those whom the people would elect as their representatives under the new

order.   So they bequeathed an abundant legacy of problems to the state legislatures and the new Congress.   To take a conspicuous example, they did not stipulate how the presidential electors should be chosen but merely dictated that "each state shall appoint, in such manner as the legislature shall direct, a number of electors equal to the whole number of senators and representatives to which the state may be entitled in Congress."

Again, they provided that members of the House of Representatives should be elected by the voters—but by what voters?   The decision of that question they also devolved upon the state legislatures.   To Congress they committed an even more formidable mass of routine to be worked out.   The whole structure of the federal judiciary they left to be created by law.   On the matter of administrative departments they said next to nothing.   How many departments?   Their functions?   Their relation to Congress?   On these and a score of other important matters of governmental practice the statutes have had to supply the omissions.

Some of the statutes which Congress has enacted during the past hundred years are, therefore, to all intents a part of the Constitution—for example, the Act of 1887 which supplements the Twelfth Amendment by fixing in detail the method of counting electoral votes and determining the way in which electoral controversies shall be settled.   Another illustration is the Statute of 1886 which fixes the presidential succession in case both the President and the Vice-President are unavailable.   In the French Republic these enactments would be called "organic laws," that is, laws which are theoretically open to amendment or repeal by exactly the same process as ordinary laws, but which supply certain important cogs in the mechanism of government and hence are virtually permanent and no more likely to be changed than is the Constitution itself.

Alexander Hamilton was the first to demonstrate how the words of the original Constitution could be given an expansive quality by legislation. His great fiscal statutes were the first of a series that has kept lengthening year by year.   Congress has pressed its economic powers to the limit and at times has overstepped the bounds, as in the child labor laws.   If the opponents of the Constitution could have foreseen the way in which Hamilton would wring economic domination out of its words by the process of statutory elabration they would have redoubled their opposition.   Lawyers use the terms statutory and constitutional in antithesis; but if by a constitution we mean "all the fundamental rules which directly or indirectly affect the distribution and exercise of sovereign power," then there is no practical difference between some provisions of the American Constitution and some of our organic statutes.

The statutory provision for a Secretary of State is not less firmly anchored than is the constitutional provision for a Speaker of the House. The secret ballot, which rests on legislative enactment, would be harder to displace than freedom from unreasonable searches, even though the latter rests on a constitutional guarantee. The National Defence Act circumvents an implication of the Constitution and makes it possible for the President to call forth the militia of the states for service outside the United States (which clearly was not intended), by the artifice of "federalizing" these militia organizations overnight. Hence it is sometimes said, and with reason, that for governmental principles one may look in the Constitution, but that for governmental practice one must look in the statutes.

At any rate most of the things that the student of actual government desires to know are in the statutes, not in the four thousand words of the Constitution. Even the process of lawmaking itself has had to be built up without guidance from those who laid the foundations. The Constitution declares, for example, that the House of Representatives shall choose its own Speaker, but it does not say what his powers shall be. These are fixed by the rules of the House. It requires the assent of both House and Senate for the enactment of laws, but says nothing about how a disagreement between the two chambers shall be settled. The whole system of conference committees is based upon rules made by the two legislative bodies themselves. The Constitution does not even require that bills be given three readings, or referred to committees, or placed on the calendar. It says not a word about budgets, deficiency appropriations, filibustering, time-limits, lobbying, leave to print, riders, suspension of rules, and the countless other incidentals of the lawmaking industry which attract so much interest nowadays.

Judicial and administrative decisions form the second cornerstone of the unwritten constitution. It is one of the fictions of juristic philosophy that the courts do not alter constitutions. They only interpret them. But Justice Oliver Wendell Holmes blurted the truth when he declared that courts "do and must legislate," despite their professions to the contrary. Likewise administrators do and must make laws—notwithstanding Montesquieu, Madison, John Adams and their devotion to the theory of separation of powers. It must inevitably be so, for to give a rule a new interpretation is to give it a new meaning, and to give it a new meaning is to alter it.

The course of actual alteration has now proceeded so far that the student who desires to know the actual powers of Congress will get a very inadequate, and often a misleading idea of their scope and ramifications if he merely runs through the eighteen formal powers granted to Congress by the Constitution itself. Hundreds of judicial decisions have widened these original powers beyond recognition, yet never in a single instance has any

American court asserted its power to make actual changes in the phraseology of the Constitution or the laws. It is merely that the stretching of a phrase in one decision provides the basis for a further elongation in the next; the lines of alteration are pricked out gently by one adjudication after another until a great divergence appears between the finish and the start.

Let one or two illustrations suffice: The framers of the Constitution gave Congress power "to regulate commerce with foreign countries and among the several states," intending thereby to enable the nation to set up a tariff of its own while preventing the states from setting up tariffs against one another. Then, in 1824, the Supreme Court ruled that "commerce" included not only the merchandise but the carriers of commerce; thereby inaugurating a long series of decisions in which it has held that commerce also includes the transportation of passengers by land and water, the sending of messages by wire, and the transmission of electric power; but that the term is not flexible enough to include life insurance, or the making of commercial contracts, or the protection of migratory birds. Hence it is that a word which was put into the Constitution by men who knew only sailing vessels and stage coaches has been broadened to include steamships, railroads, trolleys and motor busses, telegraph and telephone lines, radio broadcasting and traffic by airplane.

Or, to give another example of this verbal expansiveness: The Constitution provides that Congress shall have power "to support armies." To the eighteenth-century mind these words meant feeding, clothing and paying armed men in the field. But during America's participation in the World War they proved flexible enough to authorize the fixing of meatless and wheatless days for the whole civilian population, the stoppage of building operations, the cessation of industry on certain days of the week, and the taking over of the railroads. A vast amount of federal authority lies embedded in these three words!

The framers of the Constitution realized, of course, that differences of opinion would arise as to what the words and phrases of the Constitution expressed or implied, and they took for granted that the courts would resolve such difficulties just as they had been doing under the state constitutions. But they could not have foreseen the stupendous amount of interpreting that would be necessitated by the growth of the country, nor could they have envisaged the subtle way in which this interpreting process would redound to the advantage of the federal government. Most of the strength with which Hamilton unavailingly sought to endow Congress in 1787 has been imparted by Marshall and his successors. The stone which the builders rejected has become the chief stone of the corner.

And it is not the courts alone that interpret the words of the Constitution.

Administrative officers, from the President down, are almost daily confronted with the necessity of taking certain actions in virtue of what they deem to be their legal or constitutional powers. Such actions, although they may be challenged and subjected to judicial review, are for the most part allowed to pass without protest on the part of anyone and thus form precedents for the future. It is true, of course, that no administrative ruling, however long acquiesced in, is immune from reversal at the hands of the judiciary. Nevertheless when important private rights have been established under some such ruling, the courts are reluctant to disturb it. Executive orders and administrative regulations have been increasing at a rapid rate during the last twenty-five years. To-day they may be counted among the important agencies of constitutional development. Incidentally it ought to be explained that where there are any serious doubts as to the constitutionality or legality of an administrative regulation, the usual practice is to seek the opinion of the Attorney-General. The opinions of this officer are not given until after careful study has been made by his subordinates.

"Time and habit," said Washington, "are necessary to fix the true character of governments." Usage is merely habit long-continued and writ large. Governments, like men, adopt ways of doing things and in time these ways become traditional. In other words they become stereotyped in the national thought. To change a tradition involves re-educating a whole people, which is a long and difficult task. The written Constitution, for example, permits both the President and the Vice-President to be chosen from the same state. But that has never happened and probably never will. The usage is that they shall be chosen not only from different states but from different sections of the country, and any departure from this practice would be resented. So strongly is this usage entrenched that it would be easier to ignore a specific constitutional requirement (e.g., that a senator must be thirty years of age) than to place two Rhode Islanders, let us say, in the nation's chief executive posts at the same time.

Governmental usages are sometimes more constraining than the laws, and much has been written about the way in which the original Constitution of the United States has been modified by the influence of "time and habit." In general, however, too much emphasis has usually been placed upon usages which are, after all, of secondary importance. The example of an American constitutional usage most commonly cited is the one that now controls the method of choosing the President. Textbooks rarely fail to explain how the framers of the written Constitution desired the people to have no direct share in the choice of the chief executive and how usage has nevertheless given them a share which is both direct and complete. But such discussions regard the forms too much and the facts too little. It is true, no doubt, that some members of the Philadelphia Convention distrusted the competence of the electorate and were averse to the choice of the President by the people; but it was not out of deference to them that the plan of indirect election was finally adopted. Far more influential than any distrust of the populace was the argument that indirect election would give candidates from the smaller states a chance. Their merits could be much more easily made known to small groups of electors than to the people of the whole nation.

Moreover, it should be borne in mind that the men who framed the Constitution had scant expectation that the President would regularly be chosen by the presidential electors. On the contrary they assumed that these electors would in each case be likely to vote for someone from their own states and hence that no one would get a majority of all the electors, save in very exceptional circumstances. Mason of Virginia predicted on the floor of the Convention that not once in twenty elections would any candidate get a majority of all the electoral votes. This meant that under normal conditions the electors would merely nominate, and the House of Representatives would make the final choice from among the five highest nominees. In making this final choice, however, the House was to vote by states, each state having one vote irrespective of its size. That is where the small states scored in the Convention of 1787.

But their victory turned out to be a hollow one. Usage presently determined that nominations should be made by political parties, that the presidential electors should be pledged in advance, and that Mason's prediction should be almost exactly reversed. Since 1788 there have been thirty-five presidential elections and on only two of these occasions has the House made the decision. The last occasion was over a century ago, before the two-party system had become definitely established.

Many other usages have caused departures from the intent of the Fathers, and some of these usages will quickly come to the mind of anyone who is familiar with the practice of American government. The President's cabinet embodies one of them. Governor's councils were well known in 1787, but no provision was made for a President's council. Apparently it was the intention that the Senate to a limited extent should serve as one, and Washington tried to utilize it in that way, but his experience did not warrant a continuance of the attempt. So the heads of departments began to meet —occasionally at first and then regularly. The term "cabinet" was not applied to them collectively until the early years of the nineteenth century.

The usage which restricts a President to two consecutive terms has received new emphasis in recent years. Lord Bryce was hardly justified in his statement, a few years ago, that this tradition seems to have "lost nearly all its influence." The likelihood that it will ever be upset seems smaller to-day than at any previous time. [This passage was written in 1930.] So with the popular insistence on resident congressmen. In the written Constitution there is no requirement that a member of the House of Representatives shall live in the district from which he is elected. It was not definitely intended that there should be congressional districts. But as a practical matter the requirement is hardly less constraining than if it were a specific constitutional one; and unfortunately so, for it needlessly limits the range of popular choice and accentuates the spirit of localism in national politics. A dozen other examples of the influence of usage might be given; but this is not the place for them.

If the men who set up the political framework of 1787 were to rise from their narrow cells, after their long sleep of more than a century, what departures from their original conception would be the most astonishing to them? Without question they would be profoundly impressed by the far-reaching influence upon the nation's economic life which the federal government has been able to wrest from the first three paragraphs of Article I, Section 8. It would dawn upon them that what they intended to be a political instrument has become the basis for a vast endowment of economic authority and influence.

It is true, of course, that these paragraphs of the Constitution grew out of the economic necessities of the day. The whole document, indeed, was not so much a declaration of faith as of fears, for it was put together in an atmosphere of restlessness, at a time when business conditions in the thirteen states were about as bad as they could be. Independence had been gained by the war, but not prosperity. The war had burdened both the states and the Confederation with debt; the country had been deluged with paper money; prices were excessively high; trade was not reviving; and there were no agencies of credit able to cope with the situation. In their bewilderment the people of the various states were clamoring for the establishment of tariffs, each against the others, and seeking to better their own economic situation at the expense of the rest. There was a Congress of the Confederation, sitting at Philadelphia whenever it could muster a quorum; but it was without power to tax, without capacity to borrow, and without authority to enact the only measures that would secure economic prosperity.

The Philadelphia Convention of 1787 was called together for the purpose of dealing with this emergency. Its leaders had, as their primary motive, the desire to endow the central government with three powers which it did not possess, namely, the power to tax, the power to borrow (with means of repayment), and the power to regulate commerce. All else was incidental and subsidiary. Had it not been for the economic crisis it is difficult to believe that the states would have responded to the call for a convention.

Nevertheless, the framers of the Constitution did not venture to give the new federal government a single jot or tittle of economic authority beyond the limits of actual necessity. They gave Congress the power to tax, but circumscribed this taxing power with three severe restrictions. Federal taxes, they provided, must be uniform; must not be levied on exports; and if direct, must be apportioned among the states according to their respective populations. So with the commerce power. Trade with foreign nations and among the several states might be regulated by Congress, but no preferences among ports would be tolerated and the whole field of trade within each state was left to local self-determination.

The Constitution, accordingly, is eloquent in its economic omissions. There is no mention of banks or banking. It was assumed that the power to charter and to regulate banks would devolve upon the states along with all the other non-delegated powers. So with the issue of paper money. Congress was given exclusive control of the coinage, but no express authority to issue bills of credit. All this points to a full recognition of the jealousy with which the states regarded their own economic independence. Any attempt to set up a central government which obviously could exert a dominating influence over the financial and commercial affairs of the nation would have roused the states to a rejection of all that the convention proposed.

So the makers of the Constitution proceeded cautiously. They gave the new federal government, in express terms, that small modicum of economic authority that seemed to be imperative at the moment, leaving the rest to the individual commonwealths. Nothing could have been further from their minds than that even this small endowment of authority would enable the federal government in due course to control the prime interests of agriculture, manufacture, trade, communication, banking and credit throughout the length and breadth of the land. Certainly there is no such implication in the original document, especially when one joins with it the explicit declaration of the Tenth Amendment.

The government of the United States, at its inception, was a weak government. It was weaker than the leaders of the convention desired. The powers assigned to it were not those which they thought the federal government ought to have, but merely those which they hoped the states would consent to give. There were those who doubted that these powers were enough to produce any substantial amelioration in the existing economic confusion. Hence the first few years of the Constitution were its critical years. If Washington's first administration had failed to utilize every ounce of its power to improve the economic situation the revival of material prosperity would have been delayed and there would have been a general disillusionment. As it was the new government rode into the confidence of the people on a wave of economic prosperity which it helped in large measure to create. It found men who had the discernment to see that a union could not be strong unless its people were prosperous, and that national unity could be best promoted by a common interest in national economic legislation.

During the past hundred and forty years many minds have helped in the making of the unwritten constitution by drafting and enacting organic statutes, by framing administrative and judicial opinions, by setting precedents, and by developing habit into usage. Their number runs into the thousands. But among them there are four great historical figures whose work may be singled out as of conspicuous and enduring importance. These are Alexander Hamilton, John Marshall, Andrew Jackson, and Woodrow Wilson. They, not less than Washington, Madison, Franklin, and Morris, are entitled to be known as Fathers of the Constitution in the broader sense of the term. Hamilton took hold of the economic provisions, gave them reality, and made them function. He seized the right psychological moment to start Congress on its way to supremacy in the economic life of the nation. A dozen years later it would have been too late. Marshall, during his long term as Chief Justice, reinforced Hamilton's work by widening the implied powers of the national government and making the Supreme Court their guardian. To Andrew Jackson we are indebted for having infused into the American political system a large part of the democracy which the framers of the original document did not intend it to possess. Finally, Woodrow Wilson demonstrated the latent powers of the chief executive and set presidential leadership upon a new plane.

No. 9

AMENDING THE FEDERAL CONSTITUTION [1]

by Howard Lee McBain

WITHIN the calendar year 1933 two amendments were added to the Constitution of the United States. One of these abolished "lame duck" Congresses by changing the dates of the convening of Congress and of the inauguration of the President; the second repealed national Prohibi-

[1] H. L. McBain, "Amending the Federal Constitution," *The American Mercury* (February, 1934), Vol. 31, pp. 204-210. Reprinted by permission of *The American Mercury* and Mrs. Agnes Bartlett McBain.

tion. The event of amending the Constitution—never a common experience—is not without special significance at this time. For since March 4, 1933 our politico-economic structure has been undergoing swift, novel, and radical changes. Already the old Constitution finds itself groaning with the strain of stretching its terms to meet the new order. It may well be that at no distant date other amendments may have to be proposed to square the letter of the Constitution with already existing or coming events. It seems worthwhile, therefore, to take a new look at an old subject—the process by which the Constitution may be formally amended.

For a long time the difficulty of the amending process has been the subject of criticism. As everyone knows, an amendment must be proposed by a two-thirds vote of the members of each house of Congress—not two-thirds of the total membership, but of the members present at the time the vote is taken. Thereafter the proposal must be ratified by the legislatures or by conventions in three-fourths of the States as one or the other mode of ratification may be determined by Congress. This sounds formidable. It is. But what most people do not appear to know is that if history be taken as our guide, its formidableness consists in the two-thirds vote of the houses of Congress rather than in the extraordinary majority of the States that is required for ratification.

Literally hundreds of amendments have been introduced into one or the other or both houses of Congress. A few of them have run the gauntlet of one house but not of the other. Only twenty-six in all have run the gauntlet of both, and twelve of these were proposed at one time by the first Congress that assembled after the Constitution went into effect. Since 1789, therefore, a period of 145 years, only fourteen proposed amendments have passed the two houses of Congress, and three of these were of Civil War origin. It is thus evident that the big hurdle for amendments is the two-thirds vote. The difficulty that inheres in the ratifying process does not appear to have had any inhibiting effect upon Congress. Indeed, the contrary is probably true, since on doubtful proposals Congress would more readily pass the buck to the States, knowing how easily any proposal can be defeated by the action or inaction of a few of them.

I wonder, for example, how many members of the last Congress, in spite of the apparent mandate of the election of November, 1932, voted to support the Prohibition repeal amendment with the covert thought and hope that it would have difficult sledding in at least the minimum thirteen States that could have prevented its ratification. Certainly few people thought in early 1933 that it would sweep the States as it did.

To emphasize the obstacle of the two-thirds vote is not, of course, to minimize the obstacle of ratification in three-fourths of the States. It is impossible to say how large this latter obstacle would have proved had Congress been more prolific with proposals. Yet the fate which proposed amendments have met at the hands of the States is not without interest. Of the twenty-six amendments proposed by Congress only five have failed of ratification. Two of these were among the original twelve amendments submitted in 1789. Both were inconsequential, one relating to the apportionment of representatives and the other to the compensation of members of Congress.

Likewise inconsequential was a proposed amendment of 1810 relating to titles of nobility. The fourth amendment which failed of ratification was one which on the very threshold of the Civil War sought to prohibit the abolition of slavery. The war killed its consideration. The fifth and last instance of failure to ratify was the child labor amendment proposed in 1924. It thus appears that only two amendments of any importance were ever defeated by the states, and one of these was a futile attempt to stem the tide of abolition at the peak of its flow.

Moreover, the States have usually acted with rapidity, especially when it is considered that few State legislatures meet annually and that they do not convene at any uniform time. The first ten amendments were under consideration by the States for less than two years. The eleventh, relating to suits against the States, required nearly four years for its adoption. The twelfth, dealing with the matter of electing the President and Vice-President, was ratified in nine months. The thirteenth, abolishing slavery, in ten months. The fourteenth, designed to protect the Negroes, in two years. The fifteenth, giving Negroes the right to vote, in one year. The sixteenth, authorizing income taxes, in three and a half years. The seventeenth, providing popular election of United States Senators, in one year. The famous eighteenth, in thirteen months. The nineteenth, providing woman suffrage, in fourteen months. The twentieth, abolishing "lame duck" Congresses, in one year. The twenty-first, repealing the eighteenth, holds the record of ratification in eight months, despite the fact that the procedure calling for ratification by State conventions required action not only by State legislatures but also by the voters and lastly by the elected conventions.

Another point of interest in this connection is that no proposed amendment has ever been positively turned down by one-fourth or more of the States. On the contrary, the necessary three-fourths have simply failed to ratify. Defeat has come by inaction rather than action. Theoretically, the five unratified amendments are still before the States for their approval. Indeed, it may happen that revived interest in the subject of child labor may yet result in the ratification of that amendment, though this appears unlikely.

The rapidity with which most proposed amendments have been ratified by the States, thus indicating wide approval, is in itself perhaps a commentary on the reluctance of Congress to submit amendments. Consider the facts in respect of those which have been ratified in the last twenty years. The Federal income tax amendment proposed in 1909 had been actively agitated ever since the Supreme Court in 1895 had put the stamp of invalidity upon that form of taxation by Congress. For fourteen years Congress failed to propose the necessary amendment. Popular election of United States Senators had been urged for a generation or more and two-thirds of the House of Representatives had more than once approved a proposal to that end before the Senate finally yielded to public pressure in 1912. Indeed, a national constitutional convention was threatened if the Senate continued its obstinacy.

While the prohibition amendment and the woman suffrage amendment were not many years actually on the table before they were swept into the Constitution, it must be remembered that both propositions were unquestionably accelerated by the World War, and that support for them had been gathering strength by the steadily increasing roster of States that had adopted them as State policies. The evil of the "lame duck" Congress, curable only by process of amendment, had been the subject of popular complaint and demand for reform over a very long period of time. The repeal of national Prohibition, though it had advocates for a decade or more, was agitated as a serious possibility for a shorter period of time than was any other amendment of the modern era. Probably never before in our history was there such a swift change of popular sentiment on a contentious public issue. The very Congress that proposed it would not have dreamed of proposing it a year earlier than it did.

Before 1913 commentators had for a long time been saying that the Constitution of the United States was for practical purposes unamendable. History seemed to bear them out. In that year, however, the ratification of the income tax amendment broke the spell of inertia and proved the falseness of their criticism. Advocates of other amendments were heartened, and, as we have seen, five such were added in the next score of years. It seems clear nevertheless that, except in the event of some wide and sudden wave of public opinion, as in the case of sentiment for Prohibition repeal, it requires years of agitation and effort and apparently large popular demand to squeeze a proposal for amendment through the halls of Congress. This was true even of the child labor amendment, which to date has been defeated by the inaction of a sufficient number of States, perhaps proving thereby that public support was not as strong and general as many had supposed.

Should the amending process be made easier? The question might be and has in fact often been phrased thus: Should the amending process be democratized? The answer depends upon a larger number of considerations than are commonly advanced.

It is child's play to cite extreme figures of possibilities in denunciation of the present process. One-third plus one of the Senators can block any proposal to amend the Constitution. This would be thirty-three out of the ninety-six Senators, provided every Senator were present and voted. If these thirty-three chanced to be from the most sparsely settled States, they might represent only about 7% of the population of the Union. That is a ridiculously low representative percentage in which to vest such powers of obstruction.

But the fact is that Senators do not combine to vote on constitutional amendments in accordance with the census reports from their respective States. I suppose one might conceive of a proposed amendment in which the weight of the small States would be marshaled in opposition, but it would be highly exceptional in character. Despite the fact that the smaller States are much over-weighted in the United States Senate, some of the most conservative and reactionary of our Senators have come out of them. This goes to prove, if proof were necessary, that relative population figures are not a definitive factor in votes on constitutional amendments. In the election and the viewpoint of Senators sectional interests unquestionably play a part, but the comparative population of the several States has little relation to this except that most of the smaller States are predominately agricultural, Delaware and Rhode Island being conspicuous exceptions. In the votes of Senators numbers of dollars are sometimes more controlling than numbers of heads—by which I do not mean to imply bribery or corruption but merely an economic bent.

In the requirement of a two-thirds vote in the House of Representatives little complaint can be made of population inequalities since State quotas in the House are based on population. But the fact is that a two-thirds vote is difficult to get on any important matter in any non-homogeneous assembly. And certainly our houses of Congress, whatever the appearances and fictions of our two-party system, are sufficiently heterogeneous in character.

The answer to the question whether the two-thirds requirement should be reduced, say, to an ordinary majority appears to depend upon one's opinion as to how quickly responsive the Constitution should be to popular views of the moment. I can think of a lot of foolish amendments that have been introduced into Congress which luckily never got through.

In considering any proposal to ease the amending process it may be well to recall an historical fact or two. For example, from the era of Jacksonian democracy the doctrine impregnated our political philosophy for many years that a government was democratic in proportion to the number of officials that were chosen by popular vote. This doctrine, as applied, drove our State and local governments not only into administrative chaos but also into the almost unbreakable grip of machine politics. While it held sway amendment after amendment was introduced in one or the other house of Congress providing for the popular election of members of the President's Cabinet, of United States judges, and of a variety of Federal local officers, such as postmasters, district attorneys, customs officers, etc. Fortunately, the Federal government was saved this catastrophe and probably was saved by reason of the difficulty of the two-thirds vote. The appointive system has undoubted evils, but popular election would have been unthinkably worse. Ultimately the States and cities were impelled to retrace their steps in this matter.

Or to go back no further than 1912, Colonel Roosevelt apparently would at that time, if he could, have put through an amendment for the recall of judicial decisions, than which nothing could have been sillier, though no doubt the agitation on this whole subject of the recall of judicial decisions and of judges was wholesome in directing the attention of a good many judges to the seriousness of their public trust, and to the fact that the changing spirit of the times would not brook a too rigid Bourbonism on their part.

While I can recall these and other examples of foolish proposals that were forestalled, I cannot, on the other hand, think of any amendment which, having enlisted genuine and widespread interest and support, and having sustained that interest and support over a number of years, has been finally stifled by Congress. It is all a question of time. As matters now stand, a proposal for amendment cannot ordinarily be got through Congress unless a lot of people have done a lot of hard work in its behalf through a long number of years. If the requirements for proposals were reduced from a two-thirds to an ordinary majority this work would probably be lessened and the time shortened. For example, the Eighteenth Amendment was voted favorably by a majority of the House of Representatives as early as 1914; it mustered two-thirds only in 1918, in the midst of our participation in the war.

There are two points, however, that ought to be noted in connection with the consideration of any proposal to change in this respect the method by which the Constitution may be amended. In a country as large and diversified as is the United States the formation of positive public opinion on a national scale is difficult. The result is the formation of high-powered propaganda groups which in actual membership represent a small minority of the people. In our politics we are accustomed to the pressure of such groups. Their activities are widely denounced, especially, of course, by those who are opposed to their particular policies.

The Anti-Saloon League is probably the best example in recent history. The Women's Suffrage organization, of a wholly different character, was another. The wets have repeatedly declared that the Anti-Saloon League represented a minority of the people, even at the high point of its influence. Whether this was true or not it would be impossible to prove. Certainly there were large numbers of persons who adhered to belief in national Prohibition, whatever their relation to the League. The point is, however, that to reduce the majority required for the proposal of a constitutional amendment would manifestly increase the power of these fighting organizations. That should be recognized.

The second point to be observed is one that very few people appear to know. It is that the difficulty of the amending process seems often to have little to do with the number of amendments that actually triumph under it. This could be illustrated by reference to the actual practice of amendment under certain European constitutions. But we need go no further for illustration than our own States. A majority of the State constitutions require a two-thirds or three-fifths vote of the two houses of the legislature for the submission of an amendment to a vote of the people. Louisiana and Utah are two of these States. Contrast the results. The constitution of the former has been amended considerably over a hundred times in the twenty years of its existence. The constitution of the latter has been amended less than twenty times in the nearly forty years of its existence. The constitutions of about one-fourth of the States require that proposals before submission to the people shall be passed by two successive legislatures. New York and Iowa are in this group. The constitution of the former has been amended thirty-odd times in nearly forty years of its existence; that of the latter fewer than a score of times in a period of seventy-five years.

Though these figures are by no means conclusive, they at least illustrate that there are factors of importance other than the difficulty of amendment that determine the frequency of amendment. If we look only at the mathematics of the process, a two-thirds majority ought to be as easy to secure in Washington as in Baton Rouge. But it has not been. Nor would it be certain that the requirement of a simple majority in Congress would result in a marked increase in the number of amendments proposed.

Votes are often cast in Congress, as elsewhere, in the light of results that are known or closely guessed in advance of roll calls. The affirmative vote of a member under a two-thirds requirement might easily, in certain circumstances, become a negative vote under a bare majority requirement.

Let us look now at the requirement of ratification by the States. In spite of the fact that the States have failed to ratify only five of the twenty-six amendments that have been submitted to them by Congress, here again it is easy to cite extreme possibilities. One-fourth plus one of the States, that is, thirteen, can by mere inaction defeat any proposed amendment. If these thirteen States be those having the smallest populations, this means that fewer than 5% of the people of the country can defeat any proposed amendment. That seems absurdly small. Its possibility was greatly and naturally feared by those who promoted the repeal of the Eighteenth Amendment. But the point may again be made that it would have to be a very exceptional amendment that would unite in opposition only the smallest States in the Union.

Even so, in the last analysis both the proposal and the ratification of amendments is based upon an equality of the States, for each State has two Senators and each State has one ratifying vote. Considering the vast inequalities among the States in the matter of population as well as differences in economic and social interests, this extraordinary ratifying majority is certainly open to grave criticism. Ratification by a majority of the States containing a majority of the people would seem to be sufficient. But one has to attack the existing plan largely on grounds of theory, for the reason that there has been so little actual opposition in practice. The three-fourths vote has usually not been difficult to obtain, because proposals have seldom come out of Congress until the country as a whole has been thoroughly worked up to receive them.

In one most important respect democratization of the ratifying process has at length been achieved. The Prohibition repeal amendment was submitted not to State legislatures but to conventions elected in the several States for the sole and specific purpose of passing upon the proposal. This in effect amounted to a referendum to the people of the several States, though not, of course, a referendum to the people of the country as a unit. The vote was still by States. The referendum resulted from the fact that these conventions in the nature of things could not be deliberative assemblies. They could be nothing more than rubber stamps of the voters' will.

There was nothing to debate. National Prohibition had been discussed so freely and furiously throughout its short and inglorious existence that practically every numskull in the land was either for or against it. In most of the States the entire convention was elected on a Statewide ticket, there being a set of wet candidates and a set of dry candidates. The voters could scarcely have had the proposition put before them in a more direct "yes or no" fashion.

While this plan of submission to State conventions was before Congress a host of objections were raised: The State legislatures might not make provision for the call of conventions. The Governors might not call special sessions for this purpose. The plan would be expensive. It would delay the whole procedure. As usual, also, the legalists found grave difficulties: There were no precedents except the State conventions that ratified the original Constitution back in 1787-88. Did the Constitution authorize or require that Congress prescribe the time, place, manner, and all the other paraphernalia of procedure by which these conventions should be brought into being? or were all these matters left by the Constitution to the determination of the State legislatures?

Such were some of the bogies that raised their heads. They were definitely answered by swift-falling facts. Congress left all these matters to the State legislatures. Governors called State legislatures in special session where that was necessary. State legislatures provided for the call of conventions. Except for a very few matters, including the nomination of candidates, the ordinary election machinery of the State was employed. The voters voted and the conventions rubber-stamped. Precedents were established and a good many questions were answered, for the most part most sensibly.

It may well be that the drys will attempt to upset the amendment by raising technical points in regard to ratification in this or that State. Of this the wets cannot complain. Certainly they raised every conceivable and a number of inconceivable points against the Eighteenth Amendment. But if they attempt this the drys are as doomed to failure as were the wets. There is not a chance in the world that the Twenty-first Amendment will be upset by the Supreme Court because of the manner of its adoption.

More important than that, it is scarcely to be believed that, having once tried this method of ratification with undreamed of success, Congress will ever again resort to the method of proposing that an amendment be ratified by submission to State legislatures. The evils of that method, whatever the virtues of its practical simplicity, have so often been pointed out that they no longer call for comment. I think we may now regard that method as one of the dead letters of the Constitution. In highly significant degree, therefore, the amending process has been democratized.

There remains only the possible abolition of the two-thirds vote in the Senate and the House and the even more desirable provision that ratification shall require a vote of a majority of the people of the country as a whole as well as a majority in a majority of the States. The latter requirement would probably be advisable not only as a sop to State equality but also because of the preponderant concentration of population in certain of the large industrial states. Such a change can be brought about only by amending the amending article itself, which has often been proposed. If it is ever accomplished, the useless conventions should doubtless be dispensed with and the respective powers of Congress and the State legislatures over the conduct of such referenda should be clarified in the newly phrased article.

No. 10

SOCIAL REFORM AND THE CONSTITUTION [1]

by Marshall E. Dimock

THE amending of the federal Constitution was clearly intended to be a difficult procedure. The British and French constitutions can be amended by a majority vote in the two houses of their national legislatures. In the United States, however, adoption of an amendment by both houses of Congress, followed by ratification by three-fourths of the states represents a conservative limitation upon majority rule. On the other hand, it has been demonstrated that when there is a strong demand for a constitutional amendment, the actual time necessary for adoption need not be very long. This is illustrated in the cases of the Eleventh and Twenty-first amendments. On the other hand, the Eighteenth and Nineteenth amendments required the strenuous efforts of their proponents for over a generation before success was achieved. But it is not the ease or difficulty with which individual proposals can be added to the basic law that constitutes the acid test of institutional fitness. The real question is whether the constitutional adjustments necessitated by changed social conditions are made effective without undue delay. It is to be expected that there will be a certain amount of social lag. The difficulty of amendment makes the lag period longer than would otherwise be the case.

In 150 years, eleven amendments have been added to the federal Constitution. The Bill of Rights is really a part of the original document because Jefferson secured agreement to its provisions before the Constitution was finally ratified, and the adoption of the first ten amendments was taken care of by the First Congress. Between 1789 and the Civil War, there were only two additions; from 1860 to 1900, three amendments were

---

[1] M. E. Dimock, *Modern Politics and Administration* (New York: American Book Co., 1937), Ch. VII, pp. 206-212. Reprinted by permission of the publisher.

adopted; and six have been ratified since the turn of the century. Of these six, four have been added in the last twenty years. The average rate of constitutional amendment has been one in fifteen years; in the last generation, it has been one in five years. This may suggest that the need for constitutional change has become increasingly apparent.

The eleven amendments which have been adopted since the Bill of Rights may be conveniently classified under four headings: machinery, powers, rights and privileges of citizenship, and governmental immunities. There is only one amendment which falls into the last-mentioned category: the Eleventh provided that no state shall be sued without its consent. This amendment was adopted a short time after the case of Chisholm *v.* Georgia, which excited fear in the several states that the federal courts might be used by citizens to invade sovereign immunities. The Twelfth Amendment changed the procedure in electing the President and, hence, represented an alteration in machinery. The Thirteenth, Fourteenth, and Fifteenth amendments added to the rights and privileges of citizens. The Sixteenth dealt with the income tax and was an addition to federal power. The Seventeenth provided for the direct election of Senators, a change in governmental machinery. The Eighteenth Amendment, establishing national prohibition, constituted an accretion of power. The Nineteenth gave the franchise to women, extending to a large bloc of the population the privileges of citizenship. The Twentieth did away with the "lame-duck" session of Congress—a mechanical alteration. The Twenty-first nullified the prohibition amendment, and, hence, was a change in governmental powers.

Three amendments, the Twelfth, Seventeenth, and Twentieth, have dealt with governmental machinery. A like number, the Sixteenth, Eighteenth, and Twenty-first, have been concerned with powers. Four amendments, the Thirteenth, Fourteenth, Fifteenth, and Nineteenth, have added to the rights and privileges of citizenship. One, the Eleventh, has created a governmental immunity. Since the Eighteenth and Twenty-first amendments canceled each other, there have been only nine amendments added to the permanent constitutional edifice in 150 years of American history.

A sound rule of constitutional government is that the basic charter should contain only matters of prime importance, namely, principles of government and protections to citizen rights. The federal Constitution comes close to satisfying this standard. A perfect record is spoiled by the Eighteenth and Twenty-first amendments, which represent restrictive legislation. They are concerned with people's personal habits and, therefore, fall into the same category as do laws affecting eating and recreation. Compared to most state constitutions, however, the federal charter is superior indeed. State constitutions are almost invariably too long, too detailed, and contain much that belongs in the statute books rather than in the basic law.

No one of the federal amendments is a fundamental principle of constitutional government. This is not to belittle their importance. The amendments which have been added to protect human liberties are the most important ones. The others are chiefly concerned with mechanical changes which have little, if any, bearing upon governmental principle. Basic matters are exemplified by the separation of powers, federalism, cabinet responsibility, and judicial review of legislation. No amendment of this type has yet been adopted.

One possible way of adding to federal authority would be to adopt an amendment to Congress's enumerated powers giving the national authority jurisdiction of a broad character. Such an amendment has already been discussed and written about. It would not be necessary to alter by specific reference the division of authority between the states and the national government; for example, Congress might have power "to pass all laws necessary for the social security of the individual and the economic stability of the country." A clause as sweeping as this would make the federal government virtually unlimited; however, it is an example of how fundamental change might be brought about with a minimum of textual addition or modification. Similarly, a clause might be drafted which would secure the essentials of responsible party government. However, this would be more difficult to do without modifying existing provisions.

A more far-reaching and continuous method of constitutional reform would be to adopt an amendment stipulating that a constitutional convention should be called at stated intervals, say every twenty years. Such a procedure would be particularly beneficial to state governments. The calling of the convention should be made mandatory. The delegates might adjourn after having concluded that minor, if any, changes were required. Even so, this would be a good investment of public money. Proposed reforms should be submitted in advance of the convention, giving the people a chance to think about the issues and providing the delegates with an opportunity to sound out public sentiment. Naturally, all delegates should be elected by popular vote. There should be a requirement that any changes proposed by the constitutional convention would require approval of the people at the polls. Legislatures should not be permitted to exercise this power, because some proposed changes might deal with the organization and relationships of the popular assembly. Such a system would encourage the careful and periodic consideration of basic governmental questions, would be an educational force of considerable importance, would do away with the complaints of those who say that constitutions are rigid and belong to the "horse-and-buggy" age, and yet would be surrounded with sufficient checks to give reasonable assurance that ill-considered or precipitate alterations would not be rushed through.

At various times since Theodore Roosevelt's presidency, there have been proposals to limit the powers of the Supreme Court. For that matter, dissatisfaction with the judiciary's influence goes back to the early years of the nineteenth century. The number of justices on the Supreme Court bench has been added to in an effort to produce a majority favorable to the administration's program. This is theoretically possible at any time, and is a powerful reserved weapon; moreover, the President has the power of filling vacancies, an important means of controlling the judiciary. Executives see to it that judges are elevated who share their economic and social views. In more than one way, Mr. Dooley was right when he observed, "The Supreme Court follows the election returns."

There is no question that the Supreme Court is responsive to strong popular approval or disapproval; moreover, the tribunal is influenced considerably by current thinking and trends in the social, economic, and political fields. Most of the justices are assiduous readers. The influence of the average age of Supreme Court members is usually made too much of; Hughes, Brandeis, Cardozo, and Stone, for example, are certainly young in their outlooks and mental vitality.

What is to be done if the judiciary refuses to assume further responsibility for expanding the Constitution to meet new conditions? How can five-to-four decisions be justified? Will a democratic people long permit so few men to pass finally on the most vital social questions affecting the future of the country?

The objection to decisions by a bare majority might be met by requiring at least two-thirds agreement among the membership of the court. If there were nine members, as at present, this provision would mean that six justices must be in agreement before an act could be declared unconstitutional. Certainly, most people readily agree that five-to-four decisions are unsatisfactory; moreover, a number of the most important cases have been decided on this slender margin. When one of these cases goes against the general public's interests, there cannot help but be disappointment and resentment openly expressed. A change to the two-thirds rule would assure a judicial veto when there was no question about unconstitutionality, and yet prevent some reversals which merely reflect the majority's doubt and differences due to their views on economics and government. It would take away much of the policy power from the courts and restore it to the legislature and the voters.

Another possible limitation would be to authorize Congress to re-enact any law declared unconstitutional whenever a two-thirds vote could be secured in both houses of Congress. So large a majority would be reasonably sure proof that the measure was really needed and demanded. "Whose government is it," people ask, "the people's or the courts'?" Chief Justice Hughes, as Governor of New York, once said, "We are under a Constitution, but the Constitution is what the judges say it is." Repassage of a law by a two-thirds vote would restore the government to to-day's electorate. The Supreme Court would still have a great deal of preventive power. This proposal, however, is objectionable on the ground that laws repassed after a judicial decision could not help but hurt the prestige of the judiciary. It is of the nature of courts to be final. If either the legislative or executive branch were able to change its decisions, courts would lose one of their essential characteristics. Any reform dealing with judicial review should aim to increase the objectivity and prestige of the judiciary, not expose it to possible disparagement.

Several foreign jurists have expressed the wish that judicial review might be limited to procedural matters and to the protection of individual liberties, and still not be concerned with social legislation involving highly controversial matters. Is a limitation of cases which courts will review a possible method of constitutional reform? The compromise is an attractive one, if it could only be made to work; but due process of law is the stumbling block. Even though Congress and the state legislatures were to amend the judicial statutes in such a way as greatly to restrict the review powers of the highest courts, the tribunals could still bring up cases and examine into their conformity with the due-process clauses. That is, of course, unless these provisions were to be removed by constitutional amendment. Still another possibility is that judges might limit their own review powers, but this seems quite improbable.

The most drastic reform would be to amend the Constitution in such a way that all power of judicial review over congressional legislation would be prohibited. This suggestion sounds radical to us Americans; but, after all, it is nothing more nor less than the rule which exists in most countries outside the United States. It would mean the acceptance of the principle of legislative supremacy. The people's elected representatives would be able to shape social destinies by expanding or altering the Constitution as the necessity and desire therefor arose. We would then be much nearer to popular self-government and democratic control than we are now. Do the people want it? Are we capable of it?

Irrespective of whether the judicial power is curbed or which of several alternatives is adopted, it is important that the improvement of public confidence in the objectivity of judges be made a prominent consideration.

A distinguished French professor, Edouard Lambert, has pointed out that judicial review of legislation results in the Supreme Court's being drawn into the center of the political arena, where passions run high and powerful groups are resentful, no matter which way the decision goes. This is inevitable, he says, so long as courts are called upon to be social umpires and expanders of the fundamental law. Judges can be objective only when they are relieved of the responsibility of shaping social and economic policy. If they permit themselves to make policy, they cannot expect the respect and deference due to men who hold the scales of justice.

An ideal constitutional system is one in which there is a full and immediate response to the people's will, yet one in which government operates through established legal principles. Can this compromise be effected more satisfactorily than it is at present?

Chapter IV

THE SEPARATION OF POWERS

[IT is one of the dogmas of the American people that our governmental system does and should embody the theory of the separation of powers. They have accepted this dogma without critical thinking, and have given little attention to the real reasons for its adoption or the actual development of its operation. Perhaps the majority is of the opinion that the incorporation of this theory into our basic rules of politics was simply the result of a desire to avoid the tyranny of whatever politicians might be in control of either the executive or legislative branches of the government. Few perceived that, like the Constitution itself, the theory of the separation of powers was the product of the conservative reaction that followed the Revolution. Fearing control of government by the masses, the chief concern of the framers of the Constitution was to make the government stable and unresponsive to the popular will. They believed in a limited government, it is true, but it was popular rather than governmental aggression that they feared.

The theory of the separation of powers, however, was never as completely adhered to as many would like to believe. Its fundamental implications were, at the outset, violated by giving to each of the departments some controls over the other two; in other words the system of checks and balances was interlaced with the doctrines of the separation of powers. Furthermore, changes in our fundamental rules occasioned by basic changes in our society, have materially altered the application of even that part of the theory that was formally expressed in written constitutions. The emergence of the executive as a policy determining officer, and the enormous legislative powers exercised by the courts in the process of judicial review, amply illustrate these changes. With reference to the executive and the legislative departments, many have advocated further formal changes in their basic relationships in order to bring the two into closer harmony. While these proposals seemingly have much merit in them, they would involve very basic changes in our fundamental rules, changes which should be clearly and fully perceived before the step is taken.

The relationship of the judiciary to the legislative and executive branches of government is, of course, a part of the whole problem of the separation of powers. This relationship is, in the American system, however, so closely bound up with the problem of judicial review that a full discussion is reserved for a separate chapter. Those who wish to consider the problem at this point may refer to Chapter XXII.]

No. 11

THE SEPARATION OF POWERS IN AMERICAN GOVERNMENT [1]

by W. F. Willoughby

NO idea is more firmly held by the mass of the American people than that the most fundamental principle upon which their government is based is that of a separation of powers. It is in this separation of powers which they believe to exist that they find the greatest guarantee of their political liberties and safeguard against a despotic use of power by public officials. To this characteristic, on the other hand, is attributed many, if not most, of the evils which our system of government presents in actual operation; and in doing away with this separation of powers is believed to lie the only effective remedy against such evils. . . .

The fact of the matter is that our government represents one in which neither the theory of the union of powers nor that of a separation of powers has been consistently carried out. In framing our constitution, its authors proceeded upon the theory that all of the powers of government were divisible into the three great branches of legislative, judicial, and executive, and that separate provision should be made for each. They failed utterly to recognize, or to make any direct provision for, the exercise of administrative powers. In consequence of this failure, our entire constitutional history has been marked by a struggle between the legislative and the executive branches as to the relative parts that they should play in the exercise of this power. This is a matter to which we will give special attention in another place.

Disregarding this point for the present, we find that the framers of the constitution, in acting upon this theory that the powers of government fall into the three classes of legislative, judicial, and executive, proceeded to provide for three organs, a Congress, a Judiciary, and a President, which should constitute the three branches, or departments, of government corresponding to these three powers. Having made provision for these separate organs, they, however, refused to vest in them the exclusive exercise of the powers to which they correspond. On the contrary, they so defined the powers of each and so distributed the exercise of the three powers among them that

[1] W. F. Willoughby, *The Government of Modern States* (New York: D. Appleton-Century Co., 1936), pp. 241-249, 256-257. Reprinted by permission of the publisher.

no one can act independently in its own field. In almost all vital matters, the concurrence of one or more of the other two organs is required. A rapid survey of some of the more important provisions of our constitution bearing upon the exercise of the three powers will show to how great an extent this is true.

Though the first section of the constitution provides that "all legislative powers herein granted shall be vested in a Congress of the United States which shall consist of a Senate and a House of Representatives," active participation in the exercise of this power is in fact conferred upon the executive branch by the requirement that no bill shall become a law until it is referred to the President for his approval and by the power that is granted to the latter to veto such bills as do not meet with his approval. It is true that such veto may be overridden if a two-thirds majority vote for such action can be secured in both houses. This, however, does not negate the fact that the executive is given an active participation in the exercise of the legislative power and that this participation, in the great majority of cases, determines whether a given measure shall, or shall not, become a law. In this connection it is important to note that this veto power of the President, though negative in form, can be and is used to influence legislation in a positive way. This is done by the President letting it be known that if certain provisions are omitted from, or allowed to continue in, a measure it will receive his veto. In considering measures, Congress has constantly to bear in mind this contingency of a presidential veto. Through the possession of this power, the President thus exercises a very positive influence in determining the character of the laws that are drafted by Congress and sent to him for his approval.

This power to veto bills represents, moreover, but one of the ways in which the President participates actively in the exercise of the legislative power. The provision of the constitution that the President "shall from time to time give to the Congress information of the state of the Union and recommend to their consideration such measures as he shall judge necessary and expedient" has been interpreted as conferring upon the President, not only the authority, but the obligation, to propose legislation. In the early days of the Republic, it was believed that the President had exhausted his authority under this grant when he had brought to the attention of Congress action which in his opinion should be taken: responsibility for taking action upon these recommendations was deemed to rest wholly with Congress. Within recent years, however, a radical change of attitude towards this function has taken place. The people now look to the President, not only to formulate a definite legislative program, but to exert all his influence and power to secure favorable action upon it. A few years ago, Congress would have resented as an infringement of its function any attempt on the part of a President to embody his proposals in the form of definite drafts of bills. Now the President boldly puts his proposals in this form, declares them to be administration measures, and takes the position that support of them is a test of party fealty.

The President, moreover, does not stop with this formulation of a legislative program. He thereafter exerts himself to the utmost to secure favorable action upon his proposals. He is in constant consultation with the leaders of his party in Congress. By personal interviews and other means, he seeks to overcome the opposition of members not favorably disposed. If need be, he uses the great powers which he possesses to bring pressure to bear upon individual members to support his measures. Patronage can be liberally bestowed or wholly withdrawn, special action desired by members can be supported or opposed. In extreme cases, the fight can be carried into a member's district and his renomination or re-election to office can be supported or antagonized according to the position taken by him in relation to administration measures. The extent to which such a use of power by a President to coerce a member of Congress in the exercise of his function as a legislator is legitimate raises an important question which will be considered elsewhere. Here it is desired only to bring out the extent to which the President both has and uses the power to influence legislation and thus to make of himself one of the distinct organs through which the legislative function is performed. There can be little doubt that this increased participation on the part of the President in the field of legislation meets with popular approval.

The same demand that the chief executive shall formulate and seek to secure action upon a legislative program is equally evident in the administration of the affairs of the individual states. The assumption of this important function in relation to legislation by the chief executive, both of the federal government and of the constituent states, thus bids fair to harden into one of the firmly established conventions of our constitutional system. In virtue of this convention and the existence of the veto power by the President, it is thus not going too far to say that the President now constitutes an organ of legislation scarcely second in power and importance to Congress itself.

The chief executive is not the only organ, however, with which Congress has to share the legislative function. It has now become firmly established that upon the courts falls the function of determining whether the several branches of government in the exercise of their powers have kept within the limitations imposed upon them by the constitution through which they were established and their powers defined. Attention has already been called to the fact that one of the serious consequences of the attempt to define by constitutional enactment the extent of governmental powers and the manner in which these powers shall be distributed territorially and functionally is the establishment of a system under which many questions are bound to arise regarding the exact meaning and intent of these provisions and their application to particular concrete cases. This renders it imperative that authority shall be vested in some organ to pass upon these questions. In the United States, this power has been assumed by the courts as a part of their general duty to interpret the law of the land. The result is that all laws must finally pass the test of judicial approval if any question regarding their constitutionality is raised.

It might seem that this power possessed by the courts to construe laws is distinctly a judicial power and in no way partakes of the nature of the exercise of legislative power. Strictly speaking, this is so. Two facts, however, have made the exercise of this power by the courts one profoundly affecting the exercise of the legislative power. The first is the fact that, in practice the provisions of the federal and State constitutions determining the powers of government and the manner of their exercise have proved of such a character that it is almost impossible for Congress or a State legislature to depart in any way from the beaten path without giving rise to the question of the legality of their action. The result is that almost every attempt made by them to break new ground for the purpose of solving social problems has been questioned in the courts, and the latter have therefore the final say as to whether they should prevail. The second is that, in passing upon these questions, the courts have taken the position that it is a part of their function to determine the facts to which the laws are intended to apply as well as to interpret the language of the laws themselves. For example, the legislature, when it passes a law fixing the maximum number of hours of labor in a given industry, does so in the belief that the conditions are such as to bring such action within the police power of the State and thus to meet any objection that may be raised that it represents an improper infringement of the constitutional provision that no person shall be deprived of life, liberty, or property without due process of law. The courts, in passing upon laws of this character, have, however, assumed the power of questioning the soundness of this belief. If, in their opinion, such laws are not required for the proper protection of the individuals that may be affected by them, or the general public, they have not hesitated to declare such laws null and void, as not representing a proper exercise of the police powers and consequently as being instruments violating the constitutional provision just cited. The issue between the legislature and the courts is here one purely of fact and expediency. The propriety of the courts taking this position regarding their power is seriously questioned. This, however, is a matter into which we cannot here enter. We are concerned now merely with the fact that in our governmental system, as it actually works at the present time, the courts play a very large role in determining the character of legislation that the country shall have.

To sum up, it will thus be seen that our governmental system, instead of being one of the definite separation and segregation of powers, is, as far as the exercise of the legislative power is concerned, so decidedly the reverse that all three departments of government, the legislative, the executive and the judicial, participate in the exercise of this power. Authority and responsibility, instead of being concentrated in a single organ, are distributed among a number.

If we turn from the legislative to the executive power, we find here too a failure to vest the exercise of this power wholly in one organ. It is true that the constitution provides that "the executive power shall be vested in a President of the United States." Subsequent provisions, however, provide for the participation by Congress in the exercise of the power. The more important of these provisions are those which provide that the President shall have power to make treaties with foreign powers only by and with the advice and consent of the Senate and upon the concurrence of two-thirds of the Senators present, that Senatorial approval shall be had of the appointment of important officers, and that Congress and not the President shall be the authority to declare war and to provide for the calling forth of the militia.

Notwithstanding these provisions the principle of vesting the executive power in the hands of a single organ prevails to a far greater extent than it does in the case of the legislative power. The President, moreover, has been able effectively to protect himself from encroachment upon the exercise of his executive powers. The only possible exception exists in respect to the exercise of the treaty-making power. Here it is believed by many that the Senate has pushed its power to greater lengths than was originally contemplated. In this the author does not concur. It is significant that the provision granting the power to the Senate does not provide simply that treaties before becoming effective shall be approved by the Senate, but stipulates that they shall be made by and with the advice and consent of the Senate. Clearly this anticipated that the Senate should be consulted throughout the work of negotiating treaties. If anything, the practice on the part of Presidents of negotiating treaties without seeking the advice of the Senate and only bringing the treaties as negotiated before that body for approval or rejection represents an encroachment on the authority of the Senate as defined by the constitution.

Of the several powers, the judicial power is the one which has been most definitely concentrated in a single organ. The exercise of this power is vested solely in the judiciary. Neither the legislative nor the executive can be said to exercise this power in any way unless, possibly, the impeachment power of Congress be deemed to be judicial in character. Notwithstanding the dependence of the judiciary upon Congress and the President as regards the determination of its organization, procedure, and personnel, the judicial power itself is not distributed among two or more organs as is the case in respect to the executive, legislative, and administrative power, but is vested exclusively in one organ, the judiciary. In exercising its functions, the latter, moreover, enjoys a practical immunity from pressure of every sort from the other departments of government. This is due partly to the provision of the constitution that the judges shall hold office during good behavior and their compensation shall not be reduced during their terms of office, but chiefly to the tradition now firmly established that judges should exercise their judgment in an entirely independent manner. This tradition prevents the other departments from attempting to influence the judges and causes the judges to repel any such attempt should it be made. That in practice the United States has had a remarkably independent judiciary is beyond question. . . .

If now we seek to sum up and characterize in general terms the system of government of the United States from the standpoint of the manner in which this problem of distribution of powers functionally has been met, it will be seen that the system established, instead of being one of separation of powers, as is popularly supposed, is one which, while not embracing the principle of union of powers, in fact provides for a joint exercise of powers from both the organic and personal standpoints. It is true that special organs have been created for the exercise of legislative, executive, and judicial powers, and that general provisions have been incorporated in the constitution that the legislative, the executive, and the judicial powers respectively shall be vested in these organs. Actually, however, as we have seen, no one of these organs is independent and supreme within its own field. Especially is this true in respect to the two branches which are most directly concerned with the actual conduct of the internal affairs of government—the legislative and the executive.

This system under which each branch in its operations is more or less subject to the control of one or both of the other two branches is one which has been aptly designated as a system of checks and balances. The explanation of the adoption of a system of this character lies in the apprehension that existed at the time of the adoption of the constitution of the danger which was believed was inherent in any governmental system of the abuse of power by those in authority. One has but to read the discussions of the period to see how the framers of our constitution were dominated by the fear that either the popular branch of the government, the legislative, or the executive would so exercise its powers as to establish in effect a popular or autocratic tyranny. All governments, they believed, had to steer a difficult course between the Scylla of executive tyranny on the one hand and the Charybdis of democracy, or mob rule, as it was designated, on the other. Safety, they believed, could only be secured by making it possible for one branch of the government to check the other at all vital points. Due to this belief, the framers of our constitution were more interested in the negative than in the positive aspects of government, or at least gave undue prominence to the former. They were more concerned about preventing abuses and forestalling possible dangers than about establishing an efficient governmental organization.

No. 12

CABINET MEMBERS ON THE FLOOR OF CONGRESS [1]

by William C. Redfield

A FEW years ago my attention was called to a speech which had just been made in the House of Representatives about the Light House Service, then part of the department under my care. The address of the honorable member contained few, if any, accurate statements. It fairly bristled with errors. No personal or political motive existed for the attack. It was clear the member had been grossly deceived. In time it developed that an employee, who was disappointed at failing to receive a promotion which he did not deserve, had made charges against the Service to the Congressman which the latter had accepted at par without inquiry, and which he made the basis of his address in a mistaken but sincere effort to remove faults which proved to be wholly imaginary. The incident has importance only as showing how easy it was—and is—to waste the time of the National Legislature on matters remote from fact. No one was present who knew even a part of the truth. No committee had such service details within its ken. There was nothing to prevent the member from imposing the statements of a mendacious employee upon the Congress and

[1] W. C. Redfield, "Cabinet Members on the Floor of Congress," World's Work (May, 1920), Vol. 40, pp. 69-71. Reprinted by permission of Humphrey Redfield.

the country as truth. Nor was there—nor is there—provided any effective means of reply. A service when so attacked has no direct power of self-defence. When the facts were later made clear to the orator he said in all simplicity (as did another in a similar case) that if he had known more of the facts he would not have made the speech. No attempt at correction was ever made.

This story teaches also how simple and how safe it is to make addresses on almost any governmental subject when no one is present who understands the matter, especially when speeches are made under a constitutional provision that no member can be called to account for what he may say on the floor of either House. It also teaches, *per contra,* how direct a limit would be put on Congressional eloquence by the mere presence of men who thoroughly knew the subject under discussion. There would be far less said in both Houses of Congress about the executive departments if someone representing them were present and free to ask and answer questions and ready at all times to substitute facts for fancies. This confusion of facts and lack of reliable information concerning the executive departments takes place constantly and inevitably, for Congress has no direct and simple means of learning the facts, and without its fault and, of course, without its knowledge "spins on blindly in the dark" so far as detailed accurate understanding of the work of executive services is concerned.

There are sound and necessary reasons why this is so under our present system. One reason is that the task of learning the executive work of the country is too large to be accomplished in the time available. Another is that Senators and Representatives have too much else to do. A third is that the task itself is underestimated and the existing knowledge of it is overestimated. No one thinks it necessary to give the matter the time and effort it requires.

How long would it take one unfamiliar with the details of railway operation to learn enough of the Pennsylvania system to be able to make rules for the conduct of every branch of the work of that great organization? How much more difficult such a task would be, and how much more time would it require if the student were a busy man, able to give to the study only such limited time as could be spared from other exacting duties? Yet large as the Pennsylvania system is it is not as large, or as varied, or complex as is the Post Office Department alone. Yet men essay to discuss the Post Office Department (in the absence, be it observed, of those in personal touch with the facts) who would not think of glibly discussing details of railway management if they had to do so in the presence of an operating officer. On the other hand, there is much to be said on behalf of the Senator and Representative. He has to attend to the duties arising from the calls from his state or his district, and these are constant and absorbing. The mail arising from this source is at times a cause of exacting labor. The presence in Washington of constituents with their families who expect "their member" to show them around is not conducive to close study of government processes meanwhile. Again, the Congressman is probably on two committees of which one at least is active, and these take always some of his time and sometimes all of his time. If this committee work happens to cover in detail the operations of a government service, and if the other demands upon the member permit his regular attendance at the committee sessions, he will in time absorb knowledge of that phase of government activity. By the same token he will not become informed of other sides of the administrative work of the country. It should, however, be noted that many, if not most committees, do not directly relate to details of organization or operation, and some hardly touch them at all—for example, committees on pensions, foreign affairs, etc. When our Senator or Congressman has release from duties incident to his representative character and from those arising from committee obligations, he has his legislative duties to perform.

The wonder is not that so little is clearly known in Congress of executive details, but rather that so much is known. In the course of time and debate a good deal of general information—and misinformation—is picked up, and so long as no one is present in either House who really does know, almost anything that is said passes for truth. Somehow the public seems to assume that mere physical presence in Washington is itself informing as to what there goes on, as if one absorbed it from the air. There is "atmosphere" in Washington, indeed, but not that arising from knowledge. Nowhere are there better (or worse) examples of the truth that "a little knowledge is a dangerous thing."

From the conditions described arises another which is in its results most mischievous. Members of both houses often hear the government departments discussed in debates with more vigor than veracity. With individual exceptions they do not know how accurate the statements are. No one is present who knows the truth at first hand, the orator is often uncontradicted, and what he says is accepted. The member furthermore visits some of the departments at times concerning appointments or promotions, etc., and in this way learns, or believes he learns, something about those particular offices and their work. Nevertheless, it remains true that misunderstandings are common, which are amazing and which would be amusing but for their serious effects upon the country's work. In the recent discussions respecting the continued existence and the proper placing of the commercial attachés, even those members having the matter in their charge showed such lack of knowledge of the subject as would have disqualified them for advisers either in similar work in the department concerned or in any industrial enterprise.

The one most serious practical weakness in the daily operation of our government is the gap between the legislature and the executive. This works harm and wastes money every day. Congress is without accurate knowledge in any general way of the details of the work for which it provides the means. It thinks it knows and constantly asserts its knowledge in sweeping statements which to those who are informed carry evidence of their inaccuracy. It must in fairness be said that there are in both houses men who know some services very well, and some of the older members have broad comprehension of the general scope of government operations. It is, however, not uncommon for these very men, because they have clear and inquiring minds, to express interest and surprise at finding, as they constantly do, some useful function of whose existence they were not aware. In the course of six and a half years spent in the Department of Commerce, I repeatedly invited both Senators and Representatives to visit the service and see for themselves what the work was. Those who accepted these invitations invariably expressed themselves as surprised and informed by what they saw. Ordinarily the invitations were declined on the true ground that time did not permit. On one occasion after an appropriation for a lithographic press had been repeatedly refused, the Chairman of the Appropriation Committee was asked to visit the service and see for himself what the need was, and it was pointed out that this would not require his going more than a few hundred feet from his office. He declined saying that he did not care to make such a visit for "it was too expensive."

Anything that will provide team-work that does not now and cannot now exist between Congress and the departments should be welcomed. . . . The world has found a way, and in one or another form it has generally adopted it. No constitutional change is either required or suggested. It is not a subject for experimentation, but a matter of common experience in other lands. Bring the spender face to face with the provider. Let the responsible men on the administrative side front directly the responsible legislators. Let there be the give and take of open debate between them. Give Congress in its daily sessions the opportunity for getting facts it now sadly lacks by personal question and answer between those who seek knowledge and those who have it. Now they are poles apart, and each functions with excessive friction. As this is written, there comes to me a statement of a senator so far from true as respects a matter in his care as to be amazing alike in its sincerity and its error. The public service concerned could not convince him of his mistake, and private parties knowing the truth were asked to aid in making it clear. If that senator had to run the gauntlet on the Senate floor of debate with an administrative officer who was accurately informed, his conclusions would be at once more accurate and less hasty.

It is not necessary to accomplish the desired purpose that we swing to the extreme of a responsible ministry. That is not proposed or implied. It is enough to bring men face to face with one another who seek and who know the truth. Congress thinks, if the words of some of its spokesmen are to be accepted, that the representatives of the public departments would be on the defensive. Those who hold this idea would at times have a rude awakening. There have been occasions when certain measures were pending when the simple question from one who knew: "Mr. Chairman, why was so and so omitted?" would "start something," as the phrase goes, which would not down until the suppression was brought to light and its purpose made clear. We are organized to-day so as to conceal truth. This is not deliberate but it actually works that way. The public business is in a large and true sense not "public." It is discussed with a considerable and at times a controlling amount of sincere ignorance.

It is argued often against the plan proposed that the Secretaries have too much to do to make their presence in legislative halls possible without harm to the work for which they are responsible. This, of course, ignores the fact that such nations as Great Britain, France, and Italy manage it somehow and get along rather well. Nor is it pertinent to reply, as is commonly done, that they have a responsible ministry which under our institutions is hardly possible. If we will give the second in command in each department, the Assistant Secretary or one or more of them, more or less permanent administrative authority, then the department head would be freed of the mass of executive details that now presses upon him. Furthermore, the Secretary might be permitted to send as his deputy such chief of service as might be most directly in touch with the matter in hand. Permanent undersecretaries would be a most desirable addition to our executive staffs. They are not indeed unknown to us. Mr. Adee of the State Department is an example. Chiefs of great services change with less frequency than is supposed. If we have but the will to get together, it will not be difficult to work out details, and in the writer's belief one month's trial would fix the reform permanently in our system. It would clarify and simplify the work of our government; would enormously add to the efficiency of Congress, and relieve it from much labor and unnecessary debate and expense; would keep the executive in touch with the thought of Congress which is something greatly to be desired, and we should soon wonder how we ever got along without so simple and commonsense an arrangement.

No. 13

AN ANALYSIS OF THE PROPOSALS TO ALLOW CABINET MEMBERS ON THE FLOOR OF CONGRESS [1]

by Harold J. Laski

AS long ago as February, 1864, Mr. Pendleton, a congressman from Ohio, sought to secure that "heads of executive departments may occupy seats on the floor of the House of Representatives"; and his proposal was strongly supported by James A. Garfield, then also a congressman from Ohio, in a remarkable speech. The committee to which the resolution was referred then introduced a bill containing two proposals: (1) cabinet officers were to have the right, in their own discretion, to attend debates when matters concerning their departments were under discussion; and (2) their attendance was to be made compulsory on certain days for the purpose of answering questions. An ardent discussion took place upon the bill, but it was not voted on. Fifteen years later, Pendleton, then a member of the Senate, raised the question a second time. The committee to which his resolution was referred produced a long and valuable report; but, as in 1864, no vote was taken upon the proposed measure. In 1886, Mr. J. D. Long, later a secretary of the navy, introduced a measure which permitted members of the cabinet to attend and speak, at their own pleasure, in the House of Representatives; but, on this occasion, the bill was not reported out of committee. The proposal then slumbered for twenty-five years. It was revived by President Taft who supported the idea of cabinet representation in Congress with considerable vigor; but his proposal came to nothing. It was renewed in 1921 and 1924; in neither case did it arouse any serious public interest or discussion.

The case for the Pendleton proposal has been well stated by President Taft. "Without any change in the Constitution," he wrote, "Congress might well provide that heads of departments, members of the president's cabinet, should be given access to the floor of each house to introduce measures, to advocate their passage, to answer questions, and to enter into the debate as if they were members, without, of course, the right to vote. . . . This would impose on the president greater difficulty in selecting his cabinet, and would lead him to prefer men of legislative experience

[1] H. J. Laski, *The American Presidency* (New York: Harper and Brothers, 1940), pp. 96-110. Reprinted by permission of the publisher.

who have shown their power to take care of themselves in legislative debate. It would stimulate the head of each department by the fear of public and direct inquiry into a more thorough familiarity with the actual operations of his department and into a closer supervision of its business. On the other hand, it would give the president what he ought to have, some direct initiative in legislation, and an opportunity, through the presence of his competent representatives in Congress, to keep each house advised of the facts in the actual operation of the government. The time lost in Congress over useless discussion of issues that might be disposed of by a single statement from the head of a department, no one can appreciate unless he has filled such a place."

The case is obviously a powerful one; and it has had the support of men so experienced as Mr. Justice Story, Senator Ingalls, and James G. Blaine. The case is the stronger with the immense growth, in recent years, of the congressional appetite for information from and investigation of the departments, much of which, if it is to be really effective, demands their friendly collaboration. There can be little doubt that it would greatly enhance the significance of congressional debate; and, thereby, it would give to it a character of responsibility and a popular significance which, compared to those of the House of Commons, are in considerable degree lacking. There is, too, much to be said for breaking down the antagonism between Congress and the departments; at present it is not untrue to say that many of the amendments each house makes to bills derive less from a knowledge of their value than from a desire to emphasize its power. I have myself heard Mr. Theodore Roosevelt insist that this method was not only likely to produce a wiser selection of cabinet officers; it was also, in his judgment, the best way to deal with the inherent difficulties of tariff legislation and of the "pork-barrel" bills which still remain a blot of no mean dimensions on the record of the legislature.

The argument, however, has not yet penetrated deeply into the popular consciousness. It is notable that in neither of his remarkable books on the American system did Woodrow Wilson think it worth while discussing, though he paid great attention to the relation between the executive and the legislature; while Lord Bryce, who knew Senator Pendleton personally, relegates it to a footnote in his *American Commonwealth*. The reason, I think, is clear. The change is not a superficial one. Its ramifications are, in fact, so wide that they might easily change the whole balance of power in the American system. They might change it, not merely as between the executive and the legislature, but within the elements of the executive itself. The failure to give the plan the consideration it deserves is not, I think, due to inertia, but rather, as Professor Cushman rightly suggests, to "the vaguely uneasy feeling that the plan would unwisely upset the traditional and established relationship between the executive and legislative departments with consequences that cannot be accurately foreseen and appraised."

Close analysis makes this at once apparent. If the cabinet is to sit in Congress, the president must choose its members from those who are likely to be influential with it. This at once narrows his choice. It makes him think of the men who already have some standing in its eyes, and some direct knowledge of its complicated procedure. But this means putting a premium on the experienced members of either house as cabinet material. It means, further, that the more successful they are upon the floor of Congress, the more independent they are likely to be vis-à-vis the president. They will develop a status of their own as they become known as the men who are able to make Congress take their views about the bills they promote. They are likely, in fact, to become rivals of the president himself for influence with Congress. The problem, in this situation, of maintaining cabinet unity would necessarily become a difficult matter. Congress might easily tend to weaken the administration by playing off the cabinet, or some part of it, against the president and some other part. The loyalty of the cabinet officer would be divided. Is he, for example, to support the president on a scheme like the Court plan, and thereby to weaken his standing with Congress; or is he discreetly to make known his dislike for the plan in the hope that he may thereby win approval for some bill in which he is interested?

The president's problem of changing his cabinet would, moreover, be immensely intensified. Is he to keep an officer about whose full loyalty he is dubious, but whose influence on Congress is clearly great? Can he prevent such an officer's so nearly rivaling his own authority as to make his own position exceptionally difficult? Would not the position of a president like Lincoln, whose hold on his own colleagues was small when he assumed power, became virtually untenable if Congress were in a position to play them off against him? Is there not, indeed, the danger of a powerful cabal of cabinet officers' becoming the effective mediator between the president and Congress with a vital shift, as a consequence, in the present delicate balance of power? Would it not, further, be likely that a tendency would rapidly develop for any cabinet officer who became outstandingly influential with Congress to become the rival of the president himself, and, where the latter was weak, in actual fact his master?

More than even this is, I think, involved. There would develop the tendency for the president to choose his cabinet from Congress in order to maximize his influence with it, and thus to transfer the leadership of his party there to a room, so to say, of which he only had the key. There would be a tendency for cabinet officers to use their relation with Congress as a platform from which to reach the presidency, with all the difficulties of colleagueship of this position, and more, that Polk emphasized. It is difficult, moreover, not to feel that, in these circumstances, the advice of the cabinet member upon questions of patronage would be given under conditions altogether different from and inferior to those upon which they now depend. The danger of trading posts for measures is already profound enough in the American system; it is difficult not to feel that it would be greatly intensified if a cabinet officer were independent of the president in his power to influence Congress. The coherence that is now given to administrative action by the supremacy of the president might easily be jeopardized by this aspect alone.

The Pendleton scheme suggested that cabinet members should have access to debates upon the floor of the House. But in fact, the main business of Congress is performed in secret committees to which the public has no access. No cabinet officer could adequately look after his measures unless he penetrated the committee rooms also. But were he to do so, the control over him of the president would be still further diminished; and the relation between him and Congress would rival in closeness that with the executive of which the president is the head. This seems scarcely desirable in a system where there is no collective cabinet responsibility, and where the unity of the executive structure is supplied by presidential control. In these circumstances, no cabinet member can be transformed into an automaton who merely reflects the presidential will. For first, in such transformation as this innovation portends, he would have been chosen just precisely because he is not an automaton; and second, to the degree that he seeks to act like one, he defeats the whole object of the innovation.

There are two further difficulties in the scheme, moreover, to which adequate attention has hardly been given in discussion of it. It raises most delicate and complicated questions of the relation between the cabinet officer, as a quasi-member of Congress, and the senator or congressman who is in charge of the bill in which he is interested. By whom is the concession to be made to a proposed amendment? How will chairmanships be arranged so as to secure a proper harmony in congressional proceedings between the cabinet officer and the chairman of his committee? On a bill, for example, like that of President Roosevelt's Court plan, the position of the attorney-general would be well-nigh intolerable unless he were at one with the chairman of the Judiciary Committee. The fact is that, on the present system, where the chairmen of the important committees of both houses form a kind of quasi-executive within the two branches of the legislature, the position of cabinet officers would be impossible at every point where they disagreed with that quasi-executive. Either they would be tempted into a position of continuous inferiority for the sake of agreement, in which difficult questions of loyalty to the president would be involved; or they would differ openly with the official chairmen of the legislative committees, in which case, they would greatly add, by that difference, to the burden the president had to carry.

Nor is this all. The Pendleton scheme seems to assume that each cabinet officer is to sit in Congress merely in relation to his own department. But the categories of government are far from being as simple as this view would make them appear. The range of modern legislation makes the secretary of the treasury as ubiquitously relevant as the chancellor of the exchequer in relation to most government proposals. The interrelations of modern problems of defense make half the issues which arise matters of coordination to which the secretary of the treasury, the secretary of war, and the secretary of navy are all relevant. On foreign affairs, every vital matter is at least a joint operation between the president and the secretary of state; the latter could hardly offer an opinion in Congress save as he affirmed that outlook for which he had prior approval from the president; and in matters of supreme importance it is the president only whose attitude it is vital for Congress to know. There, as the Wilson administration makes clear, he supersedes the secretary of state far more emphatically than, in an analogous situation, the prime minister of England supersedes (he rather supplements) the foreign secretary. Similar difficulties arise as between the Departments of Commerce and Labor; and the Department of Justice, especially in the context of prosecutions such as those under the Sherman Act, has a vital relation to many other departments. It is, in fact, difficult to see how any cabinet officer except the postmaster-general could be confined within any rigidly defined domain. In the result, most cabinet officers would—whatever the system started as—be bound to develop roving commissions of general relevance not very different from the part that a cabinet minister plays in the British House of Commons.

It must, moreover, be remembered that in the American system the initiative in legislation does not lie, as with Great Britain, for effective purposes in the government only. No doubt a special pre-eminence attaches to bills which have, so to say, the imprimatur of the president. But the source of a good deal of important legislative action lies in the hands of individual senators and congressmen; in this respect it is only necessary to remember how much has been done, often despite the administration, by men like the late Senator La Follette and by Senator Norris. It would be far from easy to adjust the delicate relations which would arise from this dual relationship, not least if the president were in a minority in Congress. And if members of the cabinet were admitted only to the floor of both houses, they would, for the most part, miss the chance of participation in the pivotal consideration of bills; while, if they were permitted their full share in the committee processes, the duality of leadership would create almost insoluble problems.

The Pendleton scheme, in short, does not meet the real problems created by the presidential system. The facts of American life have concentrated literally enormous power in the hands of the president; and it is no doubt true that the exercise of this power produces, above all in a second term, grave congressional doubts of the wisdom of its extent. At some time in the tenure of a president with a majority, the accusation of autocracy is almost bound to arise. But the real outcome of the Pendleton scheme, or any variant upon it, would be, I think, to transfer the essential features of presidential leadership to the cabinet. Its operations in Congress would be bound, sooner or later, to become the axis upon which the authority of the administration turned. I believe, indeed, that properly to perform its function in Congress the cabinet would be bound to try and discover the terms upon which it could become a unity; a unity, be it noted, not only against the Congress, but against the president also. The latter would be compelled to spend a good deal of his energy in maintaining his authority against colleagues who would have developed an interest and prestige at least parallel to his own, and, conceivably, different from it. None of them could fail to be aware that outstanding success in the handling of Congress was the highroad to the kind of reputation out of which a presidential nomination could be secured. Some of them, at least, would be bound to play for that nomination; and the problem, in those circumstances, of maintaining presidential supremacy would be at every point delicate and complicated.

The real result, in a word, of the adoption of such a scheme as Senator Pendleton proposed would be very rapidly to transform the president into a person more akin to the president of the French Republic than to that of the United States. He could not avoid the certainty that his colleagues who became pivotal in Congress would soon become indispensable to him. He could hardly avoid the concentration of public attention upon their activities in Congress rather than upon his relations with it. He would have to watch those activities with a jealous eye lest they impinge upon the sphere of influence that is at present his own. The man among them who became the congressional leader of the cabinet would soon become a figure akin in character and influence to the prime minister; the president would be dependent upon him for every legislative move in the fulfilment of his program. Indeed, I think it not unlikely that the president would become rather the adviser than the master of the man to whom Congress looked for the formulation and defense of the presidential program; he would be moved to second place. He would find it difficult to resist the pressure of a cabinet officer who was influential with Congress; he might well jeopardize his own position if he asked for his resignation. A hostile Congress might even play off the cabinet, or some section of it, against him.

On any showing, this is to say, the Pendleton scheme would wholly alter the balance of forces history has evolved in the American system of government. I do not say that it would necessarily alter them for the worse; any such estimate depends upon a comparison between the presidential and parliamentary systems that is here out of place. All I am concerned to argue is that latent in the scheme is a revolution in the historical conception of the presidency. As it now operates, the nation looks to the president for executive leadership, and, in the long run, circumstances make it difficult for that leadership to be found elsewhere. Such a scheme as Pendleton's inherently threatens that authority. While it separates him from his cabinet, on the one hand, it builds a bridge between the cabinet and Congress, on the other; and the president cannot walk across that bridge. It gives the cabinet an interest against him, not only with the legislature, but also with the party. A generation which has seen the vice-president of the United States use his influence in Congress to intrigue against the president should have no difficulty in seeing what his position might become if his influence were joined to that of any considerable part of the cabinet. At present, at any rate, when the president and Congress are at odds, the former's power of direct appeal to the nation makes the issue between them a clear one upon which public opinion can make up its mind. A cabinet that moved toward independence of him would make such a clarity of choice a difficult matter. It would, almost necessarily, divert a good deal of attention away from the case the president has to make. It would offer the possibility of great rewards to those about him who were prepared to risk the penalties of disloyalty to him. Anyone who reflects upon the position that might have arisen if Stanton had been able to utilize Congress as a platform against Andrew Johnson can see the potentialities that are latent in this change.

It may be, as I have said, that it should be attempted; for it may well be that the burden which the present situation imposes upon the president is greater than any statesman, above all in a democratic community, should be asked to bear. But the change should not be attempted without a full knowledge that it will profoundly alter the historic contours of the presidential system. It may not, in the first instance, transform it on the lines of the parliamentary system; it is bound, I have argued, in the long run to move it toward those lines. It cannot do so, on all experience, without two results. It must first depreciate the position of the man who cannot directly influence the congressional process; those, to use my earlier metaphor, are bound to be nearer to it who cross the bridge than those who stay on the other side. And if men are sought who can influence Congress, men are bound to be sought by whom Congress is prepared to be influenced. That does not only mean the device of a different kind of cabinet officer from those of the past. It means also, in the long run, men who realize that the way to influence a legislative assembly is to be responsive to its will; and that is the first step toward responsibility to its wishes. Fundamentally, this is to alter the whole balance of the American Constitution. It is to make it desirable to build a cabinet which can sway Congress. That makes the main lever of executive authority resident in the cabinet rather than in the president. While this may be a better scheme than the present one, its possible merits cannot conceal the fact that it is a constitutional revolution of the first magnitude. It is to dig into the foundations of the state; and that, as Edmund Burke insisted, is always a dangerous adventure.

Chapter V

THE GEOGRAPHICAL DISTRIBUTION OF GOVERNMENTAL POWER

[As we have already seen, the fundamental rules under which any government is organized are embodied in its constitution. This constitution, written or unwritten, rigid or flexible, is the primary authority for the distribution and allocation of governmental power. Every nation is constantly faced with certain basic questions in this respect. Should one central government exercise all of the power to govern or should it be divided between a central government and major political subdivisions? If the latter, how should power be distributed within these subdivisions? These questions must be met by those who frame the rules. The British in the eighteenth century failed to meet them and the result was the American Revolution. Those who fought and won that war likewise failed to answer them and the result was the political failure of the Articles of Confederation. One of the major concerns of the Constitutional Convention was with these questions.

In the United States we chose to adopt what is known as a federal system of government, that is a system of government in which there is a constitutional division of powers between a central government and major political subdivisions or states. The reasons for our choice were many and varied. They are found in the economic, religious, and racial differences extant in America of the late eighteenth century, and also in the antipathy of those who wrote the rules towards any strong and centralized government.

All federal systems show much the same strength and weakness, and in all similar problems emerge. Society is never static, and a division of powers which is adequate for one generation may be totally inadequate for the next. One sees in all federal systems a constant readjustment in the original division of powers, and in almost every instance this readjustment has resulted in a flow of power from the major political subdivisions to the central government. Centralization is not a phenomenon peculiar only to our federal system.

Within our major political subdivisions, the American states, the problems are basically the same. On what principle should power be divided between them and the local units of government, the cities, villages, counties, townships, etc.? Our choice in this field has been that of a unitary system of government; that is, we have constitutionally vested with the states complete power over all local units. Cities and counties are creatures of the state, their powers

110

are given to and not reserved for them, and they may be abolished by the unilateral action of the state. However, our tradition has departed from a strict application of this unitary principle. We have extended considerable power to local units in the past but to-day one sees a trend towards centralization.

A third question also is daily becoming more important, namely that which concerns the relationship of the central or national government to the local units in the states. Here, too, new relations of a centralizing character have developed. Cities, counties, towns, and other local units are turning to or being turned to Washington rather than to their respective state capitals.

Critical understanding and evaluation of these vertical relationships are essential to a real grasp of the role and operation of government in the United States. Every student of American government must not only visualize the situation as it is to-day, but he also should make every effort to know whither we are bound, and, more important, where our destination ought to be.]

No. 14

THE OBSOLESCENCE OF FEDERALISM [1]

by Harold J. Laski

NO one can travel the length and breadth of the United States without the conviction of its inexpugnable variety. East and West, South and North, its regions are real and different, and each has problems real and different too. The temptation is profound to insist that here, if ever, is the classic place for a federal experiment. Union without unity—except in the Soviet Union and China, has variety ever so fully invited the implications of the famous definition? Geography, climate, culture, all of them seem to have joined their forces to insist that, wherever centralization is appropriate, here, at least, it has no meaning. Tradition demands its absence; history has prohibited its coming. The large unit, as in Lamennais' phrase, would result in apoplexy at the center and anemia at the extremities. Imposed solutions from a distant Washington, blind, as it must be blind, to the subtle minutiae of local realities, cannot solve the ultimate problems that are in dispute. A creative America must be a federal America. The wider the powers exercised from Washington, the more ineffective will be the capacity for creative administration. Regional wisdom is the clue to the American future. The power to govern must go where that regional wisdom resides. So restrained, men learn by the exercise of responsibility

[1] H. J. Laski, "The Obsolescence Of Federalism," *The New Republic* (May 3, 1939), Vol. 98, pp. 367-369. Reprinted by permission of *The New Republic*.

the art of progress. They convince themselves by experiment from below. To fasten a uniformity that is not in nature upon an America destined to variety is to destroy the prospect of an ultimate salvation.

This kind of argument is familiar in a hundred forms. I believe that, more than any other philosophic pattern, it is responsible for the malaise of American democracy. My plea here is for the recognition that the federal form of state is unsuitable to the stage of economic and social development that America has reached. I infer from this postulate two conclusions: first, that the present division of powers, however liberal be the Supreme Court in its technique of interpretation, is inadequate to the needs America confronts; and, second, that any revision of those powers is one which must place in Washington, and Washington only, the power to amend that revision as circumstances change. I infer, in a word, that the epoch of federalism is over, and that only a centralized system can effectively confront the problems of a new time.

To continue with the old pattern, in the age of giant capitalism, is to strike into impotence that volume of governmental power which is necessary to deal with the issues giant capitalism has raised. Federalism, I suggest, is the appropriate governmental technique for an expanding capitalism, in which the price of local habit—which means, also, local delay—admits of compensation in the total outcome. But a contracting capitalism cannot afford the luxury of federalism. It is insufficiently positive in character; it does not provide for sufficient rapidity of action; it inhibits the emergence of necessary standards of uniformity; it relies upon compacts and compromises which take insufficient account of the urgent category of time; it leaves the backward areas a restraint, at once parasitic and poisonous, on those which seek to move forward; not least, its psychological results, especially in an age of crisis, are depressing to a democracy that needs the drama of positive achievement to retain its faith.

Before I turn to the case for this view, it is worth while to dwell for a moment upon the lessons of non-American experience. It is not, I think, accident that the heavy weather encountered by the federal system in the United States has been experienced also by the three major experiments elsewhere—by Germany, by Canada and by Australia. In the first, significantly, both federalism and democracy have gone. In the others the need for constitutional revision, the sense that the historic division of powers hampers the need for social and economic reconstruction at every turn, is one of the major themes of debate. Commissions seek to discover desirable terms of effective revision in both of them. Their literature speaks of "breakdown" and "collapse." In each, also, the federal government lacks, by its bondage to a past shaped in the faith of unlimited expansion, the power effectively to cope with its outstanding problems. In each, too, the older political parties are geared psychologically to that past; and their inability to escape from the framework in which it has imprisoned them, leads to the emergence of new political orientations which threaten alike their unity and their democratic foundation. Proportionately, I suspect, their problems are less susceptible of direct solution than those of the United States. But it is, I think, an expression, not of local circumstance, but of world-historical causes, which has made federalism everywhere in the world to-day a handicap and not a help to governmental progress.

Giant capitalism has, in effect, concentrated the control of economic power in a small proportion of the American people. It has built a growing contrast between the distribution of that economic power and the capacity of the political democracy effectively to control the results of its exercise. It has transcended the political boundaries of the units in the American federation so as to make them largely ineffective as areas of independent government. Whether we take the conditions of labor, the level of taxation, the standards of education, public health, or the supply of amenities like housing and recreation, it has become clear that the true source of decision is no longer at the circumference, but at the center, of the state. For forty-eight separate units to seek to compete with the integrated power of giant capitalism is to invite defeat in every element of social life where approximate uniformity of condition is the test of the good life.

The poor state is parasitic on the body politic. It offers privileges to giant capitalism to obtain its taxable capacity, offers escape from the impositions of rich states, in order to wrest from the wealthy some poor meed of compensation for its backwardness. It dare not risk offending the great industrial empires—cotton, coal, iron and steel, tobacco—lest it lose the benefits of their patronage. Their vested interests thus begin to define the limits within which the units of the federation may venture to move. And since the division of powers limits, in its turn, the authority of the federal government to intervene—the latter being a government of limited powers—it follows that the great industrial empires can, in fact, prevent the legislation necessary to implement the purposes of a democratic society. The situation may, briefly, be summarized by saying that the Constitution inhibits the federal government from exercising the authority inherent in the idea of a democracy; while the risk to a state government of attack upon the conditions exacted by those industrial empires for their patronage is too great to permit the states to jeopardize what they have by issuing challenge. Whether, therefore, it be the hours of labor, the standards of health and housing, the effective organization of the trade unions, at every point the formal powers of the states are rarely commensurate with the actual authority they may venture to exercise. And it is the common citizen of the United States who pays the price of that margin between formal and effective power.

Political systems live by the results they can obtain for the great mass of their citizens. A democracy is not likely to survive on formal grounds merely; it will survive as it is able to convince its citizens that it adequately protects their powers to satisfy the expectations they deem their experience to warrant. In the present phase of American capitalist democracy, the central government largely lacks the power to implement the ends it is essential it should serve if its democratic context is to be maintained. It cannot obtain adequate standards of government in many of the major fields it seeks to enter. It is hamstrung, partly by the division of powers from which it derives its authority; partly because the Constitution has not enabled it to develop the instrumentalities essential to the purposes it must seek to fulfill. Its effort to obtain the proper recognition of collective bargaining may be stricken into impotence by a state law against picketing. Its effort to produce proper control of public utilities may be rendered vain by local franchises granted in a period when the recognition of the need for uniformity in this field had not dawned upon the public consciousness. So, also, with conservation; with the provision of adequate educational opportunity; with the effective prohibition (a commonplace of any well-ordered state) of child labor; with the coördination of relief for unemployment; with public works, especially in the utilization of the possible sources of electric power; with public-health legislation, not least in the field of maternity and child hygiene; with a proper policy of public roads—witness the breakdown of federal-state cooperation in Arkansas in 1923, in Kansas in 1926 and Maine in 1929; with a proper policy in housing. I take examples only. The central point of my argument is the simple one that in every major field of social regulation, the authority of which the federal government can dispose is utterly inadequate to the issues it is expected to solve.

I do not think this argument is invalidated by the rise of cooperation between the federal government and the states, or between groups of states. That use has been carefully investigated in detail by Professor Jane Clark in an admirable and exhaustive monograph ("The Rise of a New Federalism," 1938). When all is made that can be made of the pattern she there reveals, I think it is true to say that, compared to the dimension of the problem, it amounts to very little. And set in the background of the urgent problems of time, it is, I think, clear from her account that in no fundamental matters will the pressure of political interests (behind which can be seen at every turn the hand of giant capitalism) permit the necessary uniformities to be attained by consent within the next fifty years. Not even the resiliency of American democracy can afford to wait so long. Professor Clark demonstrates admirably the inescapable interest of the federal government in a hundred subjects at every turn of which it encounters the power of the states; but she also demonstrates that the problems of dual occupancy of the same ground hinders at every turn the creative solution of the problems involved unless we conceive of those solutions in terms of geological time.

I am not arguing that the administration of government services ought to be centralized in Washington. It is true, as Professor Clark says, that "there is a line beyond which centralized administration cannot go without falling because of its own weight." My argument is the very different one: that (a) there are certain objects of administrative control now left to the states for which they are no longer suitable units of regulation. Economic centralization makes necessary at least minimum standards of uniform performance in these objects, e.g., health, education, unemployment relief; and in others, e.g., labor conditions, railroad rates, electric power, complete federal control without interference by the states; and (b) that the proper objects of federal supervision cannot any longer be dependent upon state consent. Where this dependency exists, state consent will be, in its turn, largely controlled by giant capitalism. That is why Delaware is merely a pseudonym of the du Ponts, and Montana little more than a symbol of the Anaconda Copper Corporation. That is why the people of the state of Washington, who ought long ago to have been permitted to have the advantage of the municipal electric-power plant of Seattle, still suffer from the division of its potential benefits through the survival of the Puget Sound Light and Power Company.

Nor would the problem be met if, instead of the states, America were divided, as writers like Professor Howard Odum suggest, into regions more correspondent with the economic realities of the situation. If America were to consist of seven or nine regions, instead of forty-eight states, that would still leave unsolved the main issues if they operated upon the basis of the present division of powers, and if their consent were necessary to any fundamental change in that division. Once again, it must be emphasized that the unity which giant capitalism postulates in the economic sphere postulates a corresponding unity in the conference of political powers upon the federal government. There is no other way, up to a required minimum, in which the questions of taxation, labor relations and conditions, conservation, public utilities (in the widest sense), to take examples only, can be met.

At this point, of course, the relation of a federal system to the power of judicial review becomes fundamental. No one now believes Marshall's famous assertion that "courts are the mere instruments of the law, and can will nothing"; it has been obvious, above all since the Civil War, that the Supreme Court is the effective master of federal legislation. And it is clear, further, that this mastery is exercised in the main not on obejctive tests of constitutionality (which do not exist), but upon the accident of a temporary majority's view of what it is "reasonable" for the federal government to undertake. The Court has become a non-elective third chamber of the government which may, as in the income-tax cases, defeat for many years purposes of which its members do not happen to approve. In an epoch of rapid change, it is a grave danger to any society that the will of a federal legislature should be subject to judicial control, and more especially when, as Marshall said, the amending process is "cumbrous and unwieldy." In a phase of liberal construction the difficulties of judicial review are obscured from the public. But the years before the controversy over the President's Court plan should be a sufficient reminder of the immense dangers lurking within it.

The view here urged, of course, looks toward a fundamental reconstruction of traditional American institutions. It is not impressed by the view, associated with the great name of Mr. Justice Brandeis, that the "curse of bigness" will descend upon any serious departure from the historic contours of federalism. The small unit of government is impotent against the big unit of giant capitalism. It may be that the very power of giant capitalism is no longer of itself compatible with the maintenance of a democratic political structure in society; there is much evidence to support this view. What, at least, is certain is this: that a government the powers of which are not commensurate with its problems will not be able to cope with them. Either, therefore, it must obtain those powers, or it must yield to a form of state more able to satisfy the demands that it encounters. That is the supreme issue before the United States today; and the more closely it is scrutinized the more obviously does its resolution seem to be bound up with the obsolescence of the federal system.

For that system presents the spectacle of forty-nine governments seeking to deal with issues for many of which they are inappropriate as instrumentalities whether in the area they cover or in the authority they may invoke. They are checked and balanced upon a theory of the state completely outmoded in the traditional ends upon which its postulates are based. Giant industry requires a positive state; federalism, in its American form, is geared to vital negations which contradict the implications of positivism. Giant industry requires uniformities in the field of its major influence; American federalism is the inherent foe, both in time and space,

of those necessary uniformities. Giant industry, not least, requires the
opposition of a unified public will to counteract its tendency to undemocratic procedure through the abuse of power; a federal system of the
American kind dissipates the unity of public opinion in those fields where
it is most urgently required. And, above all, it is urgent to note that giant
industry, in an age of economic contraction, is able to exploit the diversities
of a federal scheme, through the delays they permit in the attainment of
uniformity, to reactionary ends. Thereby, they discredit the democratic
process at a time when it is least able to afford that discredit. For, thereby,
the confidence of the citizen body in its power to work out democratic solutions of its problems is gravely undermined.

Men who are deprived of faith by inability to attain results they greatly
desire do not long remain content with the institutions under which they
live. The price of democracy is the power to satisfy living demands. American federalism, in its traditional form, cannot keep pace with the tempo of
the life giant capitalism has evolved. To judge it in terms of its historic
success is to misconceive the criteria by which it becomes valid for the
present and the future. No political system has the privilege of immortality; and there is no moment so fitting for the consideration of its re-
making as that which permits of reconstruction with the prospect of a new
era of creative achievement.

No. 15

EFFECT OF THE DEPRESSION ON STATE-LOCAL RELATIONS [1]

by Howard P. Jones

THE depression has had its effects upon the relations between states
and local units as it has upon almost every other activity and relationship of local government. These relationships, however, have been peculiarly subject to adjustments forced by the strain of local financial difficulties because of the legal dependency of cities and other local units upon
state government as well as because of the state's greater revenue-raising
capacity.

But a discussion of trends is apt to be highly theoretical unless it has its
foundation in recorded happenings. A brief summary of some of the out-

[1] H. P. Jones, "Effect of the Depression on State-Local Relations," *National Municipal
Review* (August, 1936), Vol. 25, pp. 465-470. Reprinted by permission of the *National
Municipal Review*.

standing events in the field of state and local government during the depression may prove worth while.

Since the beginning of 1930, these events have taken place:

27 states have adopted sales taxes. (6, however, have dropped them in this period, leaving 21 with sales taxes now.)

22 states have adopted income taxes or increased income tax rates. (The state of Washington, where both personal and corporate income taxes were held unconstitutional, is not included.)

20 states have adopted or increased gasoline taxes.

The following miscellaneous taxes were adopted or increased:

Chain store.. 23 states
Liquor .... 31 states
Non-alcoholic beverages................................. 31 states
Cigarettes and tobacco.................................. 17 states
Public amusement.. 16 states

37 states have increased state aid to local units of government.

7 states have adopted over-all limits on real property taxes.

8 states have adopted homestead exemption laws.

14 states have adopted county home rule laws or laws granting counties an opportunity to revise their structure in the interests of greater efficiency.

7 states have transferred important functions from local units to the state.

94 cities have adopted the city manager plan.

7 counties have adopted the county manager plan.

Approximately 3200 counties, municipalities, and special districts are now in default on their obligations. Only two-thirds of these, it should be said, are in default on general obligation bonds, the remainder being in default on special assessment district obligations.

1 state has defaulted on its bonds but satisfactory arrangements for payment have been reached with its creditors.

Through 1935, 14 states had issued bonds for unemployment relief.

Many cities, it is impossible to say how many, have issued bonds for unemployment relief or deficiency bonds for current expenditures.

4 states have abolished property taxes as state revenue. (In addition South Dakota eliminated the state general tax levy for 1934 and California eliminated it for 1933-1934.)

21 states adopted laws increasing financial supervision over local units of government since 1930.

The picture is at first glance a peculiarly confusing one. Side by side with laws providing for a greater measure of home rule stand laws providing for a greater degree of administrative supervision over cities. Side by side with laws increasing state taxes stand laws decreasing the general property tax for state purposes. Side by side with measures for additional state aid to local units of government during a period of financial stress stand laws restricting the amount of taxes these local units may levy upon real property.

Such apparent inconsistencies become understandable, however, upon closer scrutiny. Home rule, applying as it does primarily to the structure of local government and important matters of local policy, is not necessarily inconsistent with a greater measure of state administrative supervision. Increase in state taxation from sources other than real estate developed not only from a desire to relieve real estate so far as possible but from the impossibility of real estate in a period of declining values supporting the additional burdens heaped upon state and local government. For the same reason, property tax limitation laws were established (in my opinion in a misguided effort) to relieve real estate—replacement revenues coming from state aid, in turn obtained from sales taxes, income taxes, or other sources of revenue available to the state but not to the local units.

Phrased another way, we see in these happenings the breakdown of local finance due to the depression, the state's coming to the rescue through the establishment of additional taxes from sources other than real estate and the distribution of some of these revenues to the localities, the tendency to restrict further the power of local units to levy real estate taxes, the increase in state supervision over local finance and the effort to achieve greater efficiency in local administration by the improvement of municipal organization.

It should be apparent that the subject of "state-city" or "state-local" relations is so vast that volumes have been written about one corner of the problem in a single state. What we perhaps should be primarily concerned with here, then, is what might be termed the *flow of power*. In what direction is power flowing these days—from the center to the extremities or from the extremities to the center? Is there a tendency for local government to become stronger and more vigorous as the state government becomes less so, or is the state government becoming stronger at the expense of the local units? Or, another possibility, are they both following similar trends, that is, both expanding in certain directions or contracting?

The local units, are, of course, the legal creatures of the state. It is hardly necessary to recall that the constitution of the United States does not mention local units of government, although such existed when the constitution was adopted, and that all powers not specifically delegated to the federal government are reserved to the states or to the people. Legislative abuse of this power, however, led to the municipal home rule movement which in sixteen states freed cities and villages to carry on their functions of local self-government as a result of amendments to state constitutions limiting the power of legislatures in the regulation of municipal affairs.

Such amendments took various forms, the most satisfactory simply forbidding the legislature to pass special laws on any subject, and granting municipalities simultaneously the necessary power to draft their own charters. It is at this point that we run into one of the chief legal distinctions between cities and villages and other units of local government. In most states, although not in all, this restriction on legislative power applied to cities and villages but not to other local units of government and special legislation applying to these other units remains to this day a serious abuse in many states.

These home rule laws in some instances permitted the legislature to pass special legislation to meet emergencies.

Thus section 2 of article XII of the constitution of the state of New York provides that: "The legislature shall not pass any law relating to the property, affairs, or government of cities, which shall be special or local either in its terms or in its effect, but shall act in relation to the property, affairs, or government of any city only by general laws which shall in terms and in effect apply alike to all cities except on message from the governor declaring that an emergency exists and the concurrent action of two-thirds of the members of each house of the legislature."

As a result of the depression there has been definite incursion by the state upon this home rule power. The emergency message has become a formal gesture on the part of the governor as a result of precedent established by former Governor Alfred E. Smith after passage of the home rule law in 1924. As a result a large number of special laws have become fastened upon the municipalities covering all sorts of subject matter which should be dealt with by local rather than state law. For example, at this last session of the New York legislature an emergency message from the governor accompanied a law requiring dog licenses in one municipality. Of the 944 laws passed by the 1936 session of the New York legislature, sixty were special acts applying to New York City, covering subjects usually within the realm of local action under the home rule law. An emergency message and a two-thirds vote of the legislature were required to pass a law regarding the licensing of plumbers and one concerning birth reports.

Not only is this serious from the standpoint of the violation of the principle of home rule involved in the passage of such special legislation—it is perhaps even more serious because of the uncertain status of such laws. Can they be repealed by local law? Probably not, and if not, then presumably they must be repealed in the same manner they were enacted—by special law under authority of an emergency message from the governor and a two-thirds vote.

While this may be true only in New York State, it is an example of the kind of paring away of the power of local self-government against which it is necessary to be constantly on guard if municipal home rule is to remain anything more than an agreeable fiction.

Of greater general significance, however, is the incursion on the power of local self-government from the financial side that has developed in practically every state that has had home rule.

It is almost axiomatic that financial control follows financial assistance. The tendency of state legislatures to pass laws providing for a greater degree of supervision over local finances is apparent. Most of these laws, exerting more stringent control over the incurring of indebtedness and providing for more adequate budget and accounting procedures, have been constructive. Some of them, however, such as those establishing rigid limits on property taxation, can hardly be so regarded. Under the guise of restricting taxation, they constitute serious incursion on home rule and a definite flow of power toward the state.

Since the state of Missouri in 1876 made its pioneer effort in the direction of municipal autonomy, "home rule" has been a slogan and a philosophy of local self-government that has exerted tremendous influence upon the development of our cities in the last half century and bids fair to do the same with respect to county government of the future. Reformers of the generation just past fought, bled, and died for municipal home rule which meant in general the right of a municipality to run its own affairs without interference from the state legislature. Then came the depression. The rush of municipalities to the state and federal government for financial assistance was like a herd of cattle plunging toward a water hole in a drought. The assistance was granted but not without its price. It is difficult for a suppliant to remain quite independent. Little did most advocates of municipal home rule realize that the work of two generations was to be undermined from the financial side. Picture a city, operating under a home rule charter, but hemmed in by stringent limitation on the amount of taxes it may levy which forces it to become dependent upon the state government. What reality is there to local self-government if taxpayers are unable to determine what services they want and are willing to pay for?

Perhaps equally important, what stimulus is there to economy in local government? There are inevitably two questions that must be answered whenever state aid to local government is mentioned. First, where is the state obtaining or to obtain the money and how is this money to be distributed? The popular sources of state aid at present are income tax, gasoline tax, and state-wide sales tax. Practically every state which has adopted over-all tax limitation, for example, has had to go to the sales tax. The small home owner, to whom tax limitation is so frequently presented as a panacea, is most naive to think he will incur a net saving in his tax bill as a result of tapping some other sources of revenue through the state government. The sales tax, for example, would undoubtedly cost the average home owner more than the amount he would save through his real estate taxes, and in addition he has lost one of the most important pressures for economy in local government—the scrutiny of local budgets by the real estate taxpayers who must support the services rendered their property.

As for the method of distributing state aid to the localities, this presents a knotty problem that has yet to be solved on any satisfactory basis. It must not be forgotten that the original conception of state aid was a grant to be matched by the municipality for the purpose of stimulating local expenditure in certain functions in an effort to raise local standards. We have not yet generally developed brakes for state aid. Under tax limitation, for example, is a given city to draft its own budget and then receive from the state the difference between the amount of its local revenues and the aggregate amount of its budget? The question answers itself. It is impossible to have a satisfactory system of state aid without some measure of distribution. The ideal measure would be directly related to local needs and requirements. But where are we to find such a measure? Failing this, would our units of local government willingly submit this determination to a state agency? It would be tantamount to letting the state determine the aggregate amount of the local budget. If not, we are exactly where we started. So long as the requirements and desires of communities differ, just so long is it necessary for them to have the power to tax themselves to obtain the services they demand. This is important for two reasons: first, they are thus able to get what they want by paying for it: second, their demands are controlled by their capacity to pay.

Whether we like it or not, the predominant trend today in state-local relations is toward the greater dependency of local units upon the state. Startling illustrations of the trend are: (1) the establishment by New Jersey of state receiverships for insolvent municipalities; (2) direct supervision over the affairs of three cities in Massachusetts by state-appointed finance commissions; (3) the establishment of the North Carolina Local Government Commission with broad powers of control over local debt and other matters of local finance. Accompanying it, interestingly enough, is also a movement for county home rule. While this latter trend is important because it leads in the direction of improved structure of county government, it is questionable whether counties, since they are primarily administrative agencies of the state, will ever achieve any substantial degree of autonomy. The exceptions to this will probably be suburban counties.

In all this, however, we should not lose sight of the fact that while local units are the legal creatures of the state the simplicity of this conception is apt to lead us into half truths. The modern city is the most dramatic and most complex of all the present-day social and economic phenomena. Realistically the city is an entity whose existence cannot be challenged. While legally it may be the creature of the state, realistically, the state to-day is much more the creature of its cities. Remove the cities of New York State, for instance, from its taxing jurisdiction and the financial effect upon the state government would be well nigh disastrous. But the cities for the most part would go their way relatively unconcerned, and the taxpayers within their boundaries would no doubt be somewhat better off. New York City, for instance, in various forms of taxation, contributes probably $160,-170,000 to the state government. It raises from property taxes approximately $471,296,000 for its own purposes and receives about $89,240,000 back from the state in the form of state aid. Its net loss, therefore, to the state, is approximately $72,930,000. Albany County contributes about $4,-288,000 to the state and receives from the state in the form of state aid $2,540,000. Its loss to the state is therefore approximately $1,748,000. Erie County, the majority of whose population live in Buffalo, contributes approximately $3,527,000 more to the state than it receives back in the form of state aid. Monroe County, the site of Rochester, contributes $3,-000,000 more than it receives.

This is the realistic side: the wealthier areas, comprising largely the urban and suburban territories, are actually contributing far more to state government than the local units of government operating in those areas are receiving in the form of state aid. Part of this money goes to support the state government but part of it also goes to support local units of government in other sections of the state in the form of state aid. It is impossible with available statistics and standards of measurement to estimate the net benefit accruing to the wealthier areas as a result of this process. The benefits are as much intangible as they are tangible. No criticism of this policy is involved here. The only purpose of these figures is to show that, after all, the dependency of the city upon the state is legal rather than economic in origin. Our review of depression legislation established rather clearly the fact that local units of government were becoming more dependent upon the state for their revenues. It is important to understand the nature of this dependency and to realize that it flows in the first instance from the legal status of the city or other local unit as a creature of the state and second from the fact that, because it operates over a wider area and has broader powers, the state is a better collection agency.

There is another important trend in state-local relations that must be considered here. What of the transfer of functions from local units to state government? Is this trend to be considered favorable or unfavorable? The question is more likely to be answered with prejudice than with facts. The facts apparently are these: (1) the smaller local units generally have not been operating efficiently; (2) their areas have been too small to administer and to finance adequately the services demanded; (3) the resistance to consolidation and reorganization in the interest of greater efficiency has prevented the correction of this situation. Taxpayers have been in no mood to trifle. The farmers of North Carolina in insisting that the state take over certain county functions may have been selling their home rule but they were keeping their farms. The same tendency is noticeable in many other states, particularly Virginia; but those who believe in a vigorous system of local self-government will regret this trend and believe it can be headed off by adequate legislation permitting transfer of functions as between local units, the abandonment of unnecessary local units, and the consolidation of others, together with opportunity for local adoption of improved forms of government and better methods of administration.

There is not the slightest question that local government in the United States is showing rapid improvement these days. Better personnel, improved methods, modernized structures are evident on all sides, particularly in our cities. The same may be said of state governments generally. But the increasing financial dependency of cities upon state government is in the direction of weakness rather than strength. We need not regret the transfer of functions from ineffective rural units to state government—in that way may lie efficiency; but our city governments, which have contributed so much to the experimental process of government and administration, can only lose vigor in an artificial dependency upon the state. This is not to say that state aid to cities should be abandoned as a fiscal policy but rather to urge the necessity for invention of devices which, while supplying cities with the funds they require, will enable the taxpayer, directly or indirectly, to exert a healthy control over expenditures.

In brief, we must recognize that local government serves common needs and that civilized progress demands continuance of the opportunity to serve future needs yet unseen. It is essential that citizens have adequate ways to control expenditure but it is equally important not to establish artificial limits that prevent the achievement of socially desirable objectives. The healthy city is not one that waits hat in hand at the state capitol for alms.

The way probably lies in the direction of state specification of high administrative standards and state supervision of local units to make sure that these standards are upheld, in reorganization and consolidation of local governments to give us units capable of administering services efficiently, together with a degree of local autonomy insuring the responsibility of local officials to those who foot the bills.

No. 16

THE FEDERAL GOVERNMENT RECOGNIZES THE CITIES [1]

by Charles E. Merriam

FOR the first time, it has been recognized that cities have a place in the sun. It might also be said that the United States Government has discovered the urban communities. This union is not a league of states but government of the people; and now it appears that cities are people too.

The position of cities has been made clearer by two events of recent days. One of these is the reorganization of our national industrial life under the "New Deal," and the other the repeal of the eighteenth amendment.

These two situations have made the place of American cities plainer than ever before in our history.

In the repeal of the eighteenth amendment we have lifted from the city a burden greater than it could bear, and have made possible the elimination of the gangs of bootleggers and gangsters who have lorded it over many of our metropolitan areas.

The way is now open in cities for the emergence of new types of municipal leadership advancing to higher levels of municipal achievement.

Neither the underworld as seen in Al Capone nor the upper world of rotten finance as seen in the exiled utility king Insull, will be as powerful in the affairs of cities in the next generation as they have been in the past.

It was the combination of these forces that made the way of city government difficult, for the interests of the mass of the citizens were sacrificed to the greed of a few, who piled up vast fortunes through their control of city government.

In the reorganization of our industrial life, we have found the state incompetent and almost useless, and we have found out the importance of the city as a unit.

The state has not been able to deal effectively with the banking situation.

[1] C. E. Merriam, "The Federal Government Recognizes The Cities," *National Municipal Review* (February, 1934), Vol. 23, pp. 107-109. Reprinted by permission of the *National Municipal Review*.

The state has not been able to deal effectively with the unemployment situation. The state has not been able to deal effectively in many cases with the educational needs of the time. The truth is that in this emergency period it has become clear that the national unit is the only one which can deal effectively with problems which are in their very nature nation-wide. Local questions can be dealt with locally, but national questions must be dealt with nationally; or not at all. This is not a problem in constitutional theory, but a decree of the practical situation in which we find ourselves.

In these recent days, the relations between cities and the United States have become increasingly close. This is plain in the administration of unemployment adjustment and relief; this is seen in the loans made by Public Works Administration to municipalities without the intervention of the state.

City representatives have been heard before congressional committees and their proposals seriously considered by the solons in Washington.

When the first plans were made for unemployment adjustment, the cities were not consulted; but now they are in intimate touch with what is happening.

In many instances the state is a fifth wheel as far as city government is concerned. The state will neither grant autonomy to the cities, nor will it assume the burden of administrative supervision over them. The state will neither rule, nor permit any one else to rule over metropolitan regions.

It cannot be too often reiterated that the chief problem of cities is that of authority to act promptly and effectively in the peculiar metropolitan situations which are constantly arising. Too great deliberation and delay, too much small trading for petty or personal favors, too much raising of the war cry against urban domination, too great consideration for the special and vested interests in cities which often trust their case with someone well outside the city—these are the conditions that render it hard for a city to advance in the directions indicated by urban needs. A housing problem, a park or recreation problem, a question of the city's relations to public utilities, a reorganization of courts or judicial procedure in an urban area, any of these raises a flood of objections from those unfamiliar with the stress and pressure of urban conditions. This may cause disastrous delay, mangling of enabling legislation, crippling of the plans proposed in one form or another. Out of all this comes the ghastly frustration of the community's effort toward the goal of public welfare.

It can hardly be supposed that Chicago could be held indefinitely in check, if with half the population of the state it was actually determined to make its influence felt in the state capitol. The prospect of a long period of such political maneuver is not pleasant to contemplate, however, either from the point of view of the city or of the state.

Nor can it be forgotten that many other municipalities in Illinois are in almost as unfavorable a position as Chicago. They also lack authority to deal with their local questions and suffer from the delay and uncertainty of legislative action; and they are likely to make common cause with the larger city in an effort to obtain what they regard as proper recognition by the state. The powerful Illinois Municipal League under strong leadership has long taken a definite position in regard to the importance of home rule powers, and there is every reason to believe that it will become more vigorous in the future.

If the state is able to provide a framework in which such a metropolitan community may live and move and have its being, appropriate arrangements should be promptly and energetically made. If this is either inherently or practically impossible, then advance may well be made toward some other plan. The present situation can be continued only with great waste of funds, great loss of efficiency, and grave danger of the collapse of one of the most important units of government in our great democratic experiment.

This is not primarily the fault of the states, for they were never designed to supervise large cities, and in recent years modern trends have rendered the states as useless for city purposes as for national.

There is reason to believe that it would be easier for cities to set up relations with the United States government than with the state in many instances.

Education, health, engineering and public works, police and judicial systems, parks and recreations, public welfare services, the interests of business and of labor, would be fitted in with the federal pattern of things far more readily and far more intimately than is now the case while the wearisome, ineffective, expensive, and confusing intermediation of state and county and other minor administrative agencies would have disappeared. It goes without saying that there is no magic in such a formula, but it might form the basis of forward-looking experimentation in simpler and sounder methods of local government and local-national relations.

In considering this whole problem, it is important to take a forward look at the actual trends of American government. We may anticipate fundamental governmental changes in the near future in the direction of (1) the interpenetration of industry and government, and (2) the interpenetration of modern scientific techniques of behavior control and government.

The relationship in such fields will be closer between the city and the nation than between city and county or between city and state. Urban industrial problems are more likely to be understood and appreciated, with less suspicion and more sympathy, by the national government than by the states.

The federal government is more modernized in point of view than is the state government. Most of the states are not interested in local civil service, to say nothing of more advanced public administration. The impulse to state civil service came from the city and the pressure has continued to come from the same point. The federal government is deeply concerned with housing and city planning, with child welfare, with the problems of commerce and labor. And indeed in almost any direction in which we turn we find a more modern and progressive attitude in the national administration than in the state. This is a matter of deep importance for those who look forward to the advancement of social and industrial living in the city.

But would cities be left too dependent on a centralized federal government under such a plan? It seems unlikely. Already there are thirty-five members of the Senate from cities in the ninety-six metropolitan regions, and one hundred and seventy-one in the House. There is a large and increasing municipal bloc in Congress.

The American Municipal Association, a league of state leagues of municipalities with headquarters in Chicago, is already actively working in the field of municipal cooperation. Urban communities are organized under the International City Managers' Association, and the United States Conference of Mayors is a growing power. Thus there is little ground for anticipating that municipal affairs will be inadequately protected under a federal-city arrangement.

In the next decade or so the difficulty may be not that of the suppression of the cities but that of adequate administrative control over their services. They are likely to dominate states, singly or in cooperation, and to form a bloc in Congress of formidable proportions and with powerful political backing in great states of the size of New York, Illinois, and Pennsylvania. Their force in national nominating conventions alone will be such as to enable them to have the ear of the party, of its presidential candidates, indeed, of the President himself. It is not urbanism that is in danger of being left behind politically in the new organization of national forces.

The way is opening out for the city of the future. But it is too easy to conclude that the urban community will find the road to the millennium over home rule or state rule or federal supervision or any reorganization of its governmental and legal relations alone.

Important changes of this sort must and will be made. But they will not be enough.

The city of the next generation will find itself woven more and more closely into the web of our social and economic development. The elimination of waste and graft and spoils is a means—an important and indispensable means, it is true—to an end; and that end is a richer and fuller life for the people who make up the community. The ideal city government will not be a bootleggers' government; nor will it be a bankers' government. The ideal government will be directed toward broad social purposes in the light of modern and emerging ways of life. The city may well concern itself with housing, with recreation, with leisure time, with education, with human welfare broadly conceived.

Cities like nations are not built upon selfish economic interests alone. They rise upon the ruins of lives devoted to the greater cause. They are built by a great community of effort nobly directed toward a common end, by the silent daily offerings of many unknown men and women whose efforts will never be rewarded except in the triumph of the city's cause.

If the nation reaches out a friendly hand to the city, it must find a willingness to go along on the roads that lead away from privilege and exploitation and up to higher levels and finer ways of life. The city too must be willing to say that there are greater goods than gold; that human welfare is greater than human wealth; or better yet, that real wealth is the priceless possession of human welfare.

Chapter VI

INTERGOVERNMENTAL PROBLEMS—CAN WE SOLVE THEM?

[WE have already seen that every political society is faced with the problem of distributing governmental power between a central government and some kind or kinds of political subdivisions. Once the distribution is made, other and equally vital problems arise. It becomes necessary, for example, to work out a way of life governing the relationships between the units of government that have been created. In a federal system, such as that in the United States, this is especially difficult because there is a constitutional division of power giving the major political subdivisions, or states, power to act independently of one another and independently of the central government in a number of fields.

As long as the United States was an agrarian nation with a poorly developed system of transportation and communication, the states could be relied upon to handle a great many of the social and economic problems independently. But this situation no longer obtains. It is now obvious that our social, political, and economic life is a vast, complex, and interrelated whole. There are few questions that are purely state or local in character. This means that we must submit to a greater degree of centralization or work out new means of interstate cooperation or both. Actually, trends in both of these directions are already observable.

The existing competition between states in matters of taxation and trade, the inertia of some states, and the latent fear of every state as to what her sister states may or may not do, offers little cause for undue optimism, however, as to the possibility of cooperation. Yet, at the same time, there are encouraging signs. Brought face to face with the problem, the states are seeking and finding new ways of living together harmoniously. It is our task as Americans to try to understand what is happening and make some evaluation of the means by which our government is meeting the problems that confront it in this field.

Intergovernmental problems, however, are not confined to relations between the states. Within the states we have a large number of local units of government—cities, towns, counties, school districts and the like. Problems involving the relationships of these units with one another are, if not as spectacular, equally as important as interstate relations. Many of these units were unwisely established and badly planned. Much duplication of effort and considerable waste of public money attend their labors. Their existence makes the governmental machine more complicated and the task of the politician, who must keep the machine operating smoothly, more difficult. Yet it is also true that they perform in many, if not most cases, functions that are essential and vital to our society. The problems they raise, therefore, cannot be solved either by abuse of the politician or by the simple formula of consolidation and elimination. We must carefully examine the things they do and how they do them. We must devise means of coordinating their work, and, as with so many other things, the road to improvement must be paved with knowledge and understanding.]

No. 17

SHOVE THY NEIGHBOR [1]

by John T. Flynn

The Constitution says they can't, but the Supreme Court said the Constitution didn't mean it. So we're a union of 48 individual countries all jealously taxing one another's products.

BACK in 1933 all the politician-economists were telling us that the trouble with America was that she had lost her frontier. Maybe she has. But she has gained forty-eight new frontiers. Now every state has a frontier and most states are working overtime building trade barriers around themselves.

It is harder for an American to get into some American states with an automobile than to get into Mexico or Canada. Particularly if he is a traveling salesman. Many of the states have now classified traveling salesmen with the Japanese beetles. In fact, the same officials at the borders of many states watch for autos carrying in Japanese beetles and traveling salesmen. They are afraid the beetles will eat up the crops and that the drummers will take some business away from the home-town merchants.

In other words, the states have gone in for protection—protection of home industries. And they have been busily inventing various kinds of devices and taxes to keep the hated merchandise of their sister states from crossing their frontiers. We began by calling on Americans to "Buy American!" We've gotten around to a new slogan—"Buy Wisconsin!" "Buy Oklahoma!" And we're even going a little further. The towns and villages are looking for ways to thwart the competition of neighboring towns. "Buy Prairie City!" "Buy Squirrel Corners!" We began by demanding that Americans buy only from American industries. We end by demanding that they buy

[1] John T. Flynn, "Shove Thy Neighbor," *Collier's Magazine* (April 30, 1938), Vol. 101:2, pp. 14, 22, 48, 49. Reprinted by permission of *Collier's Magazine* and the author.

from their neighborhood grocer. We may wind up with a customhouse on every main road leading into every state, border patrols and, of course, an army of smugglers and bootleggers.

You may think this a bit fantastic. The Constitution says the states cannot impose duties and imposts on products from other states. Of course, the Constitution says that. The Constitution says the colored folks can vote in the South. The Constitution says a lot of things. That doesn't prevent the state of Kansas, just the same, from having sixty-six ports of entry surrounding the state—sixty-six customhouses, more than the federal government has around two oceans and a Class A gulf. And it doesn't prevent about seventeen other states from splitting themselves off into as many little economic republics surrounded by border patrols to keep out the beetles, the salesmen, the trucks, the gasoline, the liquor, the cigarettes and various other kinds of merchandise that have been made the subject of those states' customs regulations against "foreigners." And besides, we can change the Constitution if necessary.

This thing began to get serious about 1933. Kansas is an oil state. Also Kansas, like other states, learned how to raise money by putting a high tax on gasoline. Then the state found that a lot of gasoline from outside the state was flowing in—bad gasoline and, what is worse, gasoline free of the tax. Bootleg gasoline.

This was a perfectly natural abuse to guard against. So the state set up a group of border police at what it called "ports of entry"—little spots on the great highways leading into the state. The idea turned out to be a good one. First, it gave work to a number of folks, as they like to call them in Kansas—about 175. And you mustn't sneer at the importance of this. Over in Nebraska a lawmaker rose in his seat when a similar bill was being voted on and said: "I vote aye on this bill because it will give employment to 120 men." Kansas thus employed 175.

Next it could be used not merely to keep bootleg gasoline out of the state, but it could be used to make difficult the entry of all sorts of things that compete with the Kansans. Then, besides, the railroads discovered that they had been handed a neat little weapon with which to swat their most hated enemy—the automobile. The truck that wants to go through Kansas has to pay a "ton-mile" tax to do so. Of course, the truck uses the Kansas roads. But Kansas has a good, stiff gasoline tax that is supposed to pay for the roads—and it does pay for them and some more besides. But when the truck passes the port of entry—well, here is what happens, in the words of a gentleman truck driver who went through Kansas:

I had never heard of such a thing as a port of entry. So as I was approaching the state line I saw a big sign which read: "All trucks entering

Kansas must register at the Port of Entry. Penalty $100 fine." A man in uniform stepped out into the road and put up his hand. He asked me where I was going. I told him. So he said I had to pay a tax of 1½ cents per ton-mile. My truck was five tons and it was 420 miles to my destination. So I had to fork out $31.50 to get that truck into Kansas for two days. Besides that, of course, I had to pay a heavy gasoline tax on every gallon I bought going and coming. I figured I paid $31.50 in ton-mile taxes and $16 in gasoline taxes or $47.50 to the state in the two days I was there. Which is not so good.

The transcontinental traveler who sets out for the Pacific Coast in a car must brave these custom and inspection guards as he enters and leaves Kansas, Colorado, Utah and California and, if he chooses the Southern route, New Mexico and Arizona.

All sorts of uses are made of these ports of entry. At some of them the trucks, and in some cases private cars, are stopped and compelled to pay a gasoline tax on the gasoline in the tank. The motorist has, of course, already paid a tax on the gasoline in the state in which he bought it. He must now pay another one at the port of entry.

In other states, like Oklahoma, the car is stopped at the state border if it has an out-of-state license and the driver must declare his cargo of cigarettes, beer or gasoline. Having done so, he is then taxed on them and this tax must be paid at the state capital. At other ports of entry the vehicle, whether truck or car used for business purposes, is stopped and forced to register. If it is an out-of-state truck it must take out a regular state license, paying an application fee of $25 and one twelfth of the usual yearly plate fee. In most places there is a special lookout for the traveling salesman.

The traveling salesman is the symbol of the monster Trade. He is coming into the state with his samples to get some of the people's money. He's going to take business away from the "native" merchant to make a profit for the "foreigner." Therefore these taxes add to his costs and his burdens.

In states with large gasoline taxes, of course, the port of entry is used to force motorists to buy their gasoline in the state. It is obvious that as the motorist approaches such a state line he will fill up with cheaper gas before he goes in. But of course if he has to pay a tax on the gas anyhow, he will do the opposite. He will be careful not to have any more gas in his tank than is necessary as he approaches the state line. There are about seventeen states with these port-of-entry laws, though there are not that many actually in effect because some of them are designed merely as retaliatory and have not yet been used. But the trend is toward increasing that number of states, the number of ports of entry and the number of uses to which they are put, and of course toward multiplying and intensifying the inconveniences and discouragements to interstate traffic and business by means of the automobile.

Back of these laws are the gasoline sellers, the local merchants in many states, the wholesalers and producers in certain states, and in nearly all of them the common carriers and the railroads. The railroads, of course, keep busy with every kind of obstacle they can put in the way of their greatest rival.

Thus, for instance, in Kansas, the railroads own the large common-carrier trucks, and there the common-carrier trucks have warred on every other kind of motor vehicle in support of the port-of-entry system. In Rhode Island the four railroads entering the state made the fight before the legislature for the port-of-entry law.

The whole movement is serious in that it marks one of the most dangerous drifts in business that have appeared in this country in years. It is the most advanced expression of the struggle of industrial and merchant groups to hold on to their markets for the home boys.

Of course it is entirely possible that certain special individuals may be, temporarily at least, aided by these devices. But the whole movement is based upon a complete ignoring of the fact that every town and village is not a little market to itself but part of the great market that in most cases embraces the country.

For instance, in Iowa you do not travel very far beyond one of the ports of entry that are supposed to help the local businessman before you come to a great cereal factory that makes its product out of Iowa corn and spends its entire pay roll on Iowa labor, but sells almost all of its product outside the state. It may be all right for Iowa to set up barriers to prevent the people of other states from selling things in Iowa and "taking good Iowa money" out of the state, but Iowa would be in a very sad condition if it were prevented from selling its products in other states and bringing good New York and good Illinois and good Alabama money into Iowa. Every state in the Union shelters hosts of industries and plants and farms that find their markets all over the country; while, in turn, all of the forty-eight states send their products into that one. It is this vast, untrammeled, free market that has been one of the explanations of the amazing growth of this country, while Europe has been one series of hampering, restricting, tax-eating and trade-killing frontiers.

But it's happened here before. In fact, we started this country off that way. Of course we didn't keep it up very long or there probably wouldn't be any country here now. In fact one of the driving forces for the adoption of the present Constitution was to save us from this.

In those simple days, apparently every town, every state, was afraid of the monster Trade. They built walls around themselves. They hemmed themselves in with restrictions. They had taxes and ports of entry to keep their sister states from slipping in with a bill of goods and running off with some of their precious money.

In those days Massachusetts began it, right after the Revolution. She put a tariff on British ships and goods. Then New Hampshire and Rhode Island joined her. But this hurt Connecticut, which resented Massachusetts' action because it kept out all British goods, which Connecticut needed. So Connecticut put a retaliatory tariff on Massachusetts and threw her ports wide open to Britain. Pennsylvania made discriminatory regulations against Delaware.

In those days New York got her fuel from Connecticut rather than from Pennsylvania. It was wood, not coal. She got a large amount of her vegetables, her butter, her cream, eggs, cheese and poultry from New Jersey. The New York dealers began to growl about the thousands of dollars that were carried away each year by the greedy Yankees and the hated Jerseyites. So she did what Kansas and Iowa and New Mexico and Oklahoma and many other states are now doing. She set up ports of entry. She laid a tax on every boat that sailed across the river bringing merchandise from New Jersey. She refused to let firewood come in from Connecticut until it paid a duty.

Then the war was on. New Jersey realized that New York had built a lighthouse on Sandy Hook, which belonged to New Jersey, so she imposed a tax of $1,800 a year on the lighthouse. In Connecticut the merchants decided to boycott New York, so they made an agreement not to ship anything to New York, under heavy penalties.

Where all this would have ended no one can say except probably in the establishment of thirteen small, isolated little republics whose history and fate cannot be guessed.

To put an end to this—and of course some other abuses—the Constitution was adopted. And it is a fact that while there was bitter controversy on many if not most of the subjects, the ending of this sort of thing was one upon which there was no disagreement in the convention. And, therefore, in the Constitution appears Article 1, Section 10, which provides that "no state shall lay any impost or duties on imports or exports, except what may be absolutely necessary for executing its inspection laws, and the net produce of all duties and imposts, laid by any state on imports or exports, shall be for the use of the Treasury of the United States, and all such laws shall be subject to the revision and control of the Congress." And the next paragraph provides that no state without the consent of Congress shall lay any duty on tonnage. How they manage to get around these provisions must be left to the constitutional lawyer.

Of course the isolationist states do not stop at the port-of-entry laws. California is a great wine state. She wants her citizens to drink wine—if they drink at all. Beer competes with wine. And if her citizens drink beer she wants them to drink California beer. So California imposes a special tax on beers made outside California and brought into the state.

Wisconsin is a great dairy state. She makes butter, as California makes wine. She wants no makers of vegetable fat sending in rivals of butter made from peanut oil and cottonseed oil and other such noxious growths. So she has pressed down a special tax on oleomargarine. The United States government already does that. But it's not enough for Wisconsin, which adds another tax for good measure to keep oleomargarine out of the state.

As a matter of fact, nearly all the butter sold in commerce in this country is made in six or seven states. The federal tax on oleomargarine is roundly denounced by the producers of vegetable fats in other states as a tax imposed by the Federal government to keep the products of one set of states from going into another set of states.

But, alas! There is one human weakness that the tax collector cannot suppress. It is a man's eternal yearning to escape taxes. A man will walk miles to avoid paying taxes. And it happens that in every state and most cities there is a large piece of the local geography that the state or town does not control. New York City can lay a two-per-cent sales tax on its citizens, but it cannot prevent them from stepping a few rods or miles up or down the road or across the river and doing their buying in Nassau or Westchester or dear old Jersey—the tax fugitive's paradise. And they do —by the millions. And these sales taxes have led various states into some strange vagaries of taxation against the neighbors who get some of the dollars of their citizens.

Out in Washington state they adopted a two-per-cent sales tax in 1935. Of course all of the merchants and dealers who do business outside the state and on its rim thus enjoy an advantage. For Washingtonians could go to various points beyond the state's borders and buy without paying the tax. To offset this, Washington adopted a curious new kind of tax called the "use tax." Washington cannot, of course, force you, when you are in an Oregon store buying merchandise, to pay a sales tax to the state of Washington. But if you bring the article into the state of Washington you will have to pay a two-per-cent "use tax" on it—that is, you will have to pay the tax for the privilege of using that article in Washington.

That smells powerfully like an impost or duty. But the great Supreme Court in Washington says "No." And it does so by means of one of those powerful explosions of reasoning for which it is famous. When Uncle Sam was building the Grand Coulee Dam, the contractors bought a lot of machinery, material and supplies in other states and proceeded to bring them into Washington. But the Washington tax collector or customhouse pounced on the purchases and proceeded to load them down with "use taxes." The contractors resisted, took the matter to court and ultimately it got up to the Supreme Court.

The contractor said this was a tax upon the operation of interstate commerce. The Supreme Court said it wasn't. When goods start from Pennsylvania and travel to Washington they are in commerce while they are moving. When they get to Washington commerce is over. And this was a tax not on the goods while they were moving to Washington but on the use of the goods after they got there. Which gives you an idea of how far the court can stretch these articles against interstate custom duties if they ever settle down in earnest to the job.

Since Washington got away with that, at least eight other states have gone in for "use taxes"—California, Colorado, Ohio, Oklahoma, Iowa, Kansas, Utah and Wyoming. There are twenty-four states with sales taxes ranging from two to three per cent. At least a third of these have turned to the "use tax" and in good time, doubtless, most of them will. For nothing in this world can come into style so fast as a new tax in this country. If you can't think up a new mousetrap all you have to do is think up a new tax and the legislators of the states and the aldermen of the cities will beat out a new express highway to your door.

And now a new idea makes its appearance. At a glance, at least, it seems to be as full of explosives as a Japanese war plane. At the moment, Congress is locked in a struggle over the issue of minimum wages and maximum hours. Primarily this is a drive for the protection of workers in the lower wage brackets against exploitation. But beneath the stormy surface waters of this fight another struggle is in progress. Down in Washington they sometimes call it the "Second War between the States." The wage scale in the North is of course higher than in the South. And this presents at once a grave problem, for it is contended that what is a just minimum-wage level in the North would not be feasible or just in the South. Therefore Southern senators and congressmen and great groups of Southern businessmen are bitterly opposed to the movement.

But still deeper lies the effort of particular industries in the North, principally the textile industries of New England, to recover some of their lost ground. They have lost factories to the South because, they insist, the Southern states have given the factories tax differentials and because wages are lower in the South. New England has been slowly correcting its tax troubles, but finds itself helpless against the lower wage scales in Georgia, South and North Carolina and other competing states. New England, therefore, has thrown itself back of the minimum-wage bill with all its energy in the hope that the Southern textile mills may be forced to the same wage scale as those in the North. This is an issue of extreme delicacy, which I merely outline here without undertaking to discuss or decide it. And, as I write, it has in it the threat of a split of the Democratic party.

All this is merely a preface to enable the reader to understand another movement that is taking shape. It grows out of this minimum-wage battle. The advocates of this new idea say that each state is best placed to decide what wage standards should eixst in that state. Wages, they assert, must be proportioned to the standards of living and to the price structure of each community. If fifteen dollars a week will buy as much in South Carolina as twenty dollars in Massachusetts, why should the South Carolina mills be compelled to pay the Massachusetts wages? Therefore, they contend, each state should be permitted to settle this matter for itself.

But, of course, they are instantly confronted with the objection that this is a grave injustice to those states that are willing progressively to improve the condition of the workers. Always there have been states that have adopted more stringent factory laws, compensation insurance, protective laws for women and children workers, wage minimums. And always there have been states near by that have opened their arms to the factories and employers who were willing to flee from the first state to escape its more civilized labor regulations. Therefore, as soon as a state seeks to improve the condition of its workers by progressive laws it loses factories through emigration. Therefore, the standards of the lowest wage states and lowest standard states tend to pull down the standards of all.

It is right here that this new and dangerous idea creeps in. Here it is. The proposal is that when a state adopts a wage standard for its factories, then it shall be permitted to prevent the products of factories in other states with lower wage standards from coming in. South Carolina would not be permitted to ship into Massachusetts. Alabama would not be permitted to ship into Michigan. In turn Michigan might be prohibited from shipping into Massachusetts. In other words, around each state a great wall would be built to keep out the products of industries that pay lower wages than the walled-in state. This, of course, is the protective-tariff principle applied to the states. And it would mean, if adopted, the creation of forty-eight independent states, each nestling behind a wall of embargoes and trade restrictions and tariff taxes.

Could it be done constitutionally? That, of course, is a question for the great court in Washington. The Constitution prohibits states from imposing import and export duties. But perhaps there is nothing to prohibit the federal government, which has power over Congress, from passing a law prohibiting shipment of low-wage goods into high-wage states. The federal Congress has forbidden the shipment of liquors into prohibition states. In any event, the proposal is filled with alarming potentialities.

But it is definitely in line with the wave of sectional trade restrictions that are sweeping the country. Even the cities and towns have joined in the movement. They use, of course, an old device, but they are using it now extensively. This is found in the town ordinance, which requires canvassers and peddlers to have special licenses and which puts various kinds of obstacles in the way of new department stores, new chain stores entering the town.

The young man with the portmanteau filled with samples going from door to door, rousing the housekeeper from her evening nap and calling her from her morning duties, is oftener than not the representative of a "foreign" merchant. The ordinances designed to render him invalid are, of course, often based on the alleged necessity of protecting the housewife. But in fact it is always sponsored by the local merchants who wish to keep out "foreign" competition.

The fight against the chains is also partly spurred on by this battle against the foreigners. Advocates of anti chain-store taxes point out that the wicked chain store owned by some commercial monster in Wall Street takes the money of the people of Valley City and drains it all into Wall Street. And some of the chain-store laws are specially designed to keep out "foreign" chains. For instance, in various states the law imposes a progressive tax on chain stores—ten dollars per year on each store up to the first ten and then increasing on each additional store until it rises to as much as $550 a store. But in at least one state such taxes are assessed whether the stores are all in the state or not. For instance, if the chain-store owner has eleven stores in the state and 490 stores out of the state, he will have to pay ten dollars tax on each of the first ten and $550 on the eleventh. A chain store that has all its stores in the state would be in a different position. If it owned eleven stores, it would have to pay ten dollars each on the first ten and about eleven dollars on the eleventh. The tax is an obvious effort to keep "foreign" chain stores out of the state.

The big question is—where will all this end? The utter blindness of communities to their real interests where these powerful sectional and community emotions are aroused is startling. For instance, some years ago I was in Alabama for *Collier's* looking into business conditions. In one small town I found in progress an amazingly bitter drive against chain stores. In fact, there were threats against the mayor for his apparent indifference to the fight. The mayor told me that he was deeply concerned about it because, he explained, this town is absolutely dependent on the chain store for its existence. "We have several textile mills here," he told me, "which sell their entire output to several large chain-store systems in the North. And while it is true that the few chain stores we have here take some of our money, it is also true that in literally hundreds and hundreds of cities and towns in the country the stores of the chains our factories sell to are taking the money from the people of those towns and piping it down here to us."

The understanding of this supremely important fact is none too common. In Iowa, in 1933, I was in a small village. There a farm association secretary told me that that town was, as to all essentials, completely self-sustaining. We could put a wall around ourselves and we would have, as he put it, "eatin' and sleepin' and wearin'" to get along on. That was probably true. But it wouldn't have much. Because, as that town was organized, its one source of money revenue was corn and hogs and, save for a trivial amount, all the produce of the farmers, on whom that town depended, was, and still is, sold outside—probably in far-distant states. That town and its farms have got to tap the pockets of people in every state of the Union. In turn it must submit to a little tapping itself.

The development of this country has been built on several forces. But certainly one of them has been its vast, free market. If we are now to turn back the clock 150 years and are to break the country up into forty-eight small markets, and even hundreds of smaller markets, the end of our progress is in sight.

No. 18

A MORE PERFECT UNION [1]

by Alan Hartman

THE Governors' Conference at Oklahoma City in September 1938 broke a precedent when it issued a statement condemning trade barriers. Then the governors boldly faced the long range job of setting their own houses in order. To prevent federal whittling down of state authority, and to preserve the flexibility of the federal-state relationship, they had to restore the balance between the national economy and the economic life of the states as units in the federal system. Governor James H. Allred of Texas appointed the first state commission to study the problem: "We must

[1] Alan Hartman, "A More Perfect Union," *Survey Graphic* (August, 1940), Vol. 29, No. 8, pp. 431, 446. Reprinted by permission of *Survey Graphic*.

not only recognize that the free and unhampered American market has accounted largely for our greatness," he said in *State Government,* magazine of state affairs, December 1938, "but we must be constantly on guard lest that market be destroyed by the insidious growth of laws which chip away at the foundations of this structure."

Four months after the Governors' Conference, the General Assembly of the Council of State Governments at Washington condemned trade barriers and instructed its secretariat to move in on the problem and call a national conference for April. The Council's flying-wedge tactics drove clean through the problem in four months, and the mopping-up operations after the conference bespoke something new in democratic teamplay. Frank Bane, executive director of the Council, synchronized the diverse talents of economists, newsreel men, politicians, radio commentators, public relations experts, business executives, and college professors in a publicity campaign which made the nation thoroughly trade barrier conscious.

The Council of State Governments is a joint governmental agency—a medium through which interstate and federal-state problems are resolved and a forum for the consideration of the increasing number of problems which overlap state boundaries. Mr. Bane and his staff coordinate the activities of the forty-four official state Commissions on Interstate Cooperation, which are the component parts of the Council of State Governments. The Council also is the permanent secretariat of the Governors' Conference, the National Association of Secretaries of State, and the National Association of Attorney Generals. They do not arbitrate or umpire like a court of appeals, though being a channel of negotiation between the several states and the federal government often leads to the same results. Mr. Bane and his staff are fundamentally responsible for placing facts where they will do the most good. Facts came thick and fast when Mr. Bane got to work with his special advisory committee, of which Governor Stark of Missouri was chairman, and which included key representatives of business, government and education. Six nation-wide commissions were set up to report on specific phases of the trade barrier problem at the national conference.

In February and March, at the Council's Chicago office, the trade barrier problem was removed from the realm of academic discussion and made the subject of realistic news stories. These news stories, combining background information with pertinent facts about trade barriers in special localities, were published throughout the country. The Bureau of Agricultural Economics, with the collaboration of the National Association of Commissioners, Secretaries, and Directors of Agriculture, provided the backlog of information in a special report to the Secretary of Agriculture, "Barriers to Internal Trade in Farm Products." The WPA Marketing Laws Survey prepared comparative charts of state statutes illustrating trade barriers. State governors discussed trade barrier problems in their press conferences. News magazines, and syndicates, economic writers and cartoonists took up the theme.

When the national conference met at the Stevens Hotel in Chicago on April 5, 1940, the lobby was lined with enlarged photostats of the Marketing Law Survey. State governors discussed trade barrier problems for newsreels and radio against a background of illustrative maps of the United States. The publicity director kept open a central office for interpretation of problems to newsmen and commentators as these developed on the floor of the conference—modern publicity techniques adapted to the advancement of the social sciences. Not the least interested group in attendance, though not official, were representatives of scores of business interests and lobbyists whose future was at stake. For overall effectiveness, the Council of State Governments' campaign against trade barriers before, during, and subsequent to the Chicago meeting, ranks with the drive which the U. S. Public Health Service launched against venereal diseases in 1936. It put to an end the casual acceptance of a national evil.

After the Conference, the Council of State Governments declared open season on trade barrier laws projected in 1940 legislative sessions. State legislators found themselves hemmed in by an aroused public opinion and Commissions on Interstate Cooperation were ready to pounce the minute a law which smacked of trade barrierism reared its head. In fact, trade barrier had become so malodorous a term that many governors stated publicly that any trade barrier laws passed by their legislatures would be vetoed immediately.

Cooperation committees, on the alert at 1940 legislative sessions, saw to the repeal of Oklahoma's port-of-entry system and downed a bid for a similar system in Texas. The strong opposition of the New York Joint Legislative Committee on Interstate Cooperation killed seven bills this year, notably one requiring that all materials for public buildings not mined or quarried in New York must be processed within the state. In Ohio, a bill to limit the purchase of coal for state institutions to that mined in Ohio went down. Public purchase preference bills were defeated in Connecticut, Texas and Kansas. New Hampshire rejected a bill discriminating against out-of-state salesmen.

Oregon, Vermont and Iowa defeated margarine taxes. The agriculture departments of the western states are cooperating in an effort to eliminate discriminatory quarantines.

Now that the states are organized to hold up their end, they welcome benevolent intervention by the federal government in the trade barrier problem, particularly in the vexed question of freight rate differentials and conflicting tax systems where comprehensive solutions call for vertical action by federal, state and local governments.

While officials of the Council of State Governments believe congressional action to be helpful in establishing basic standards, they are anxious to avoid broad national legislation to cover problems where state-by-state adjustments are satisfactory. Likewise, they warn against the rigidity of court action in trade barrier cases. "The whole history of interpretations of the commerce clause," reports the New York Regional Committee of the Council, "is a demonstration of the fact that this clause cannot be interpreted in terms of absolutes." Trade barrier questions, being questions of degree, are not solved by Yes or No answers; nor does judicial action allow for constant adjustments necessary for the maintenance of state-federal balance.

When Mr. Bane appeared before the TNEC hearing on trade barrier problems in March, he pointed out that recent Supreme Court decisions revolved around this statement: "Spasmodic and unrelated instances of litigation cannot afford an adequate basis for the creation of integrated national rules which alone can afford that full protection for interstate commerce intended by the Constitution." And the Court suggests that Congress should proceed, "on the basis of full exploration of the many aspects of a complicated problem, to devise a national policy fair alike to the states and our union."

Mr. Bane linked the Court's mandate to his own conclusion that it is no longer possible to draw sharp lines between the three levels of government, federal, state and local. He recommended the establishment of a continuing committee on federal-state relations, composed of representatives of both Houses and the administrative branches of the government. This committee would work with the Council of State Governments, surveying the entire situation, with a view to offering the next Congress a comprehensive plan looking toward cooperation and participation by all levels of government for a practical solution of the problem of interstate trade barriers. The committee might explore other major questions of federal-state relationships—problems arising from conflicting and overlapping tax laws, grants in aid, and their effects on education, and problems of personnel in federal, state and local government.

The Council of State Governments' campaign, publicizing collective responsibility for the trade barrier problem, was built around painstaking legal research, the vision of historians, and the liveliest advertising mediums. Such progressive use of publicity techniques must have been something of a shock to publicity-minded state officials, whose heated, interstate rivalry

in advertising scenic grandeurs and flavorful qualities of their fruits and
vegetables has developed into a minor interstate trade skirmish. The anti-
trade barrier campaign demonstrates that you can advertise your way out
of, as well as into, bad neighborly relations. And in the process, the states
have begotten a new efficiency of action.

No. 19

INTERSTATE COOPERATION [1]

by Charles J. Calrow

IT is probably entirely pardonable for a Virginian to take his text from
the writings of that master planner, Thomas Jefferson. Jefferson states
in his autobiography: "but it is not by the consolidation, or concentration
of powers, but by their distribution, that good government is effected.
Were not this great country already divided into states, that division must
be made, that each might do for itself what concerns itself directly, and
what it can so much better do than a distant authority. Every state again
is divided into counties, each to take care of what lies within its local
bounds; each county again into townships or wards, to manage minuter
details; and every ward into farms, to be governed each by its individual
proprietor. . . . It is by this partition of cares, descending in gradation
from general to particular, that the mass of human affairs may be best
managed for the good and prosperity of all." The language of this statement is, in the light of to-day, highly significant.

In this statement Jefferson justified the division of the country into certain administrative areas on the grounds of necessity, realizing that even
for the country, as it stood in his day, partition into administrative units
was needed, if the public business was to be expeditiously conducted.

The language which Jefferson employed, in addition to saying that each
of these administrative units might do for themselves that which a distant
authority could not do so well, implies the passage of laws by these administrative units distinct from either amplification or extension of laws passed
by a higher authority.

Jefferson's theories concerning government really involve two series of
gradations, one downward, the gradation from "general to particular" in
which the application of authority became more intensive as the area involved decreased, and one upward, with respect to the area over which

[1] Charles J. Calrow, "Interstate Cooperation," *National Municipal Review* (August, 1936),
Vol. 25, No. 8, pp. 445-451, 464. Reprinted by permission of the *National Municipal
Review*.

the authority should extend, the powers granted growing less as the so-called higher levels of government were reached.

But the form of government which we actually have fits neither of the Jeffersonian theories. We have neither the gradations downward from "general to particular" nor the gradations upward with the partition of cares proceeding from particular to general as the area increases.

Theoretically, the authority still flows from the people, but not through the lower levels of government controlling the minor geographical divisions to the higher, but directly from the people to the state, and from the people direct to the nation. In this last case it is, in certain particulars, restrained by the limitations erected by the same creators of authority acting in their capacities as citizens of the states. The tenth amendment to the federal constitution defines these limitations.

While Jefferson wrote in terms of geographical-political areas with their compartmentalization of authoritative control, the government which he administered was far from meeting his specification.

Under the present system there is really no series of planes of government. Such gradations as exist flow from "general to particular" both ways from the state, on one hand to the federal government, and on the other hand to the state's political subdivisions.

It is because the system of governmental levels described as desirable by Mr. Jefferson does not exist that, when problems which transcend state lines demand solution, the necessity for interstate cooperation appears. Interstate problems are all around us. Changing conditions in agriculture, industry, trade, transportation, and communication have transformed problems which were once localized into problems which refuse to be bounded by lines created by the King's Charter, Orders in Council, or determined by transit and compass. Many social, economic and physical problems arising in a single state cannot be solved by that state alone without a sacrifice of interests. Particularly is this true of those problems in which social and economic interests are simultaneously involved.

Of course, one method of handling such interstate situations is by the amendment of the federal constitution and the further delegation of particular authority to this unit of our governments. This is a form of interstate cooperation whereby three-fourths of the states may establish particular policies but of general application controlling in all states. Where this form is applicable it has many advantages, not the least of which is the designation of an authority with power to enforce and courts to adjudicate the disputes which may arise. Another advantage of this type of cooperation lies in the peculiar duality of relationship which the citizen of this country has, making him directly amenable to the laws of the United States as well as to laws of the state.

This method of cooperation has, however, certain limitations of desirability when the problems are not nation-wide but regional with reference to the area involved or particular with reference to type. For such cases interstate cooperation seems desirable.

We have recently had considerable discussion of the question of regions, and some of the supporters of the "region" concept have gone so far as to suggest the creation of regions having administrative and legislative power interposed as another level of government between the states and the federal government—a multiplication of governments. From a recognition of the fact that many of the social, economic, and physical problems are regional in character and not limited by state lines, and from the studies of this fact, it has been but a ready jump to the assumption that a regional governmental organization was a happy method of obtaining solutions of such group problems. But is it? How will such a region be delimited—by geography or function, by river basin, coal-bearing area, or maybe by particular type of agricultural production? If regions are delimited according to one of these characteristics, how will an area having a number of these types of characteristics be assigned? There is possibly some confusion of thought on this subject. Let us take Virginia as a case in point.

The economic, social, and physical problems of Virginia are shared with other states in many ways and many directions and in varying volumes. In the realm of agricultural economics Virginia shares with North Carolina, South Carolina, Georgia, Tennessee, and Kentucky the problems arising from the processes of tobacco production and tobacco marketing. With respect to mineral resources Virginia shares with Pennsylvania, Ohio, West Virginia, Kentucky, Tennessee, and Alabama, and to a certain extent with Indiana, Illinois, Iowa, Missouri, Kansas, and Oklahoma, in those problems arising in connection with the production and marketing of coal. In the realm of those resources taken from the sea Virginia shares with North Carolina, South Carolina, Maryland, Delaware, and New England the problems of distributing and marketing the products of commercial fisheries and in competitive markets meets the industries of the states on the Gulf. In the industrial world Virginia shares in production of rayon with the following states: Massachusetts, New York, Pennsylvania, Ohio, Tennessee, and eleven other states, and with New England, North Carolina, South Carolina, Georgia and Alabama in the cotton textile industry. It also shares its rivers with Maryland, North Carolina, Tennessee, and West Virginia.

The very plain fact is that in the case of Virginia the lines of certain regional area problems refuse to coincide with those of certain other regional area problems and for the problems of this state the region which would encompass them all would be so extensive that it would cease to be a convenient unit. Nor is this all, for in the territory included in such a region there would necessarily be other states which would have interlocking interest with still other areas outside of the region embracing the Virginia problems and thus a need for further regional extension.

The point may be taken further. Any division of the country into regions with limits fixed with relation to one set of problems would arbitrarily divide the areas of other problems and these last questions could only be handled by interregional cooperation or by some superior governing unit, so that all which would be accomplished by the new order of things would be a multiplication of problems both intra- and inter-regional.

A further point to be considered in connection with this regional doctrine is the question as to whether the regional authority is to be state-like with general sovereignty or to have only delegated powers like the federal government. If the former, then there is conflict of sovereigns and if the latter, nothing has been accomplished which could not have been done under the present constitutional forms.

The setting up of the regional organizations as additional levels of government between the states and the federal government is of course unthinkable under our present system but, if possible, it should not be done for the reason that it would tend to weaken the federal union.

It is believed that the regional government scheme as a method of interstate cooperation may be dismissed from further consideration and attention given to those methods which do not involve the creation of new governments.

As has been pointed out, the scheme of government outlined by Jefferson in the passage first quoted is far from being parallel with that under which we are operating. Our governmental system being what it is, our interstate problems, except in a relatively few cases, must be handled by the states severally as sovereign bodies or jointly through inter-state compacts approved by Congress, or by the federal government.

Interstate cooperation of this classification may be sub-classified under five heads:

(1) Under the first heading there may be placed that type of interstate cooperation which results in the establishment of uniform laws, uniform regulations, or uniform methods of administration. This cooperative effort toward standardization may spring from state action alone or as in the case of certain technical activities, cooperatively with federal departmental agencies.

As participation in such cooperative effort is entirely within the powers of the states and may be taken without action by the Congress, it has possibilities of expansion or limitation which permit its adaptation to any local conditions, social or economic, which may demand special consideration, thus meeting Jefferson's specification. With this plan of interstate cooperation there is, however, a possibility that some of the states, most in need of the beneficial results which may flow from its operation, may refuse to participate and thus destroy or at least weaken the cooperative plans, or else a state having once entered the cooperative plan may, for various reasons, withdraw and thus endanger the whole cooperative scheme. Lack of permanency, failure to attain or maintain sufficient coverage and, possibly, the lack of uniformity in enforcement are the weak points of this plan.

(2) In a second grouping are those state relations which are reciprocal in nature and are also without the necessity for federal approval. Many state acts of this type are on the statute books. Usually they take the form of a grant of privilege or license by the legislature of one state to the citizens or officers of other states in return for similar grants of privileges or authority for its own citizens or officers by the said other states. Reciprocity in recognition of professional registrations is an example.

An act of the Virginia General Assembly of 1936 providing for reciprocal agreement with consenting states as to the laws of "close pursuit" is another example of provision for this type of interstate cooperation.

Under plans for interstate cooperation of this type there are set up penalties for non-conformity; namely, the non-grant to non-conforming states of the rights and privileges given those entering into and holding to the agreement. This gives this cooperative effort an element of strength not possessed by the efforts grouped under the first heading.

(3) A third grouping of interstate cooperative activities is that under a plan for the conduct of a joint enterprise of a physical nature, as for example, the construction of a bridge over a boundary river. In this case a simple contractual relation exists between the states and neither functions as a governing unit. In this case while two states may by agreement regulate the use of the utility, the collective action proceeds no further. The relationship between the states is simply that of partners in a joint enterprise. This is not an exercise of sovereignty. Either party to the enterprise may sue upon the contract and such suits come within the jurisdiction of the federal Supreme Court, not because of the nature of the activity but because of the nature of the litigants.

A modification of this type of interstate cooperation is the joint agreement for the construction of certain kinds of public improvements such as roads with common points at the state line permitting the flow of interstate traffic. In this case each state would construct that portion of the road lying on its side of the state line and thus, despite joint agreements, the relation of any state to the enterprise is not that of a partner, and there is no controlling enforceable contract between the states. There is no authority to which appeal may be taken in case of failure to carry out the provisions of such an agreement.

(4) A fourth type of interstate cooperation is one in which the states may by treaty and with the approval of the Congress, engage in a joint enterprise administered by a governing body separate and distinct from the administrative departments of the cooperating states. The administrative authority may be of commission or corporation form and have, in so far as the particular enterprise is concerned, certain regulation-making authority. In this case the state acts creating the commission are, to a certain but minor extent, a degree of surrender of sovereignty by delegation of authority, as no state engaging in such an enterprise would possess the right to require the commission or corporation to commit acts in conflict with the rules laid down for its guidance in the approved treaty or compact.

This delegation of authority has, however, certain advantages, as the controlling unit thus set up acquires none of the general attributes of sovereignty and an aggrieved state has recourse through the courts without directly involving another sovereign in the proceedings. Needless to say, such a corporation or commission can have no power to enforce regulations except where it receives this authority by delegation from the states creating it; neither can its authority be extended or curtailed except with the approval of all of the parties to the original compact. In some ways, limited it is true, such a corporation or commission acquires, in relation to the contracting states, some of the same status as has the federal government.

It may be said in passing that the approval by Congress does not under the present constitutional limitations give to the federal government any administrative authority, and even though the approvals of compacts are required the so-called "upper level" of government acquires thereby no rights over the states.

(5) Still another class of interstate cooperative action is one of the Congress-approved compact type, in which each state reserves to itself the administration of the terms of the compact within its own borders. Here no authority or corporation is created. This form is generally applicable where the police powers of the states are to be employed and it is not suitable for enterprises in which the joint construction and operation of public works or public facilities are attempted.

An example of this type of cooperative effort is the Virginia tobacco control act, chapter 183 of the acts of the General Assembly of 1936, which in the draft of the proposed compact provides among other things that the states which are parties to the compact do jointly and severally agree "to cooperate with each other in formulating such regulations as will assure the uniform and effective enforcement of each of the aforesaid state statutes" and further "not to depart from or fail to enforce, to the best of its ability, any regulations concerning the enforcement of the state statutes, without the consent of a majority of the members of the tobacco commissions of each of the several states which is a party to this agreement."

It will be noted that while elsewhere within its stipulations the act provides for the enforcement of the regulations within each state and penalties for noncompliance therewith, nowhere does it provide penalties for the failure of the tobacco commission of any state to see that its own regulations are enforced; neither is there any recognition of a common authority before whom an appeal for such enforcement could be carried.

The failure of a superior state authority such as the governor, the legislature, or the courts to displace a recalcitrant commission would raise petty questions of conflict between interstate policies and constitutional law.

There may be other forms of interstate cooperation, but the list just given covers all the major types. Such others as may have developed will probably be found to be modifications of some one of these five.

Some of these interstate cooperation types are particularly applicable to certain joint enterprises having to do with things rather than with persons, and this is an important point. The problems arising from cooperative action by states as proprietaries are quite different from those which appear when joint action is taken concerning matters which call into play the police powers.

The time element is also another point which needs attention even in those cooperative plans involving only things. Certain affairs may be settled once and for all and the legislative acts providing for or ratifying the cooperative plan may well and fully provide for objectives complete within themselves and requiring no continuing administration. Where the project is one of a continuing nature the necessity for administration arises and with it troublesome questions. In all cases where the police power is invoked consideration of the time element is most important.

Despite the difficulties attendant upon interstate cooperation, the need for such action is so well recognized that every effort should be made to find a way to make cooperative effort effective. The number of matters in which joint action by two or more states would redound to the "good and prosperity of all" has vastly increased.

In summing up the weaknesses of various recognized forms of interstate cooperation it will be found that the chief of these is the failure to provide for uniform authoritative administration where the project is of a continuing nature or where it invokes the police powers of the cooperating states. The major problem, therefore, is one of providing for administration, and it must be admitted that none of the existing or suggested forms of interstate cooperation seem to provide this necessary element without some degree of conflict with "states' rights."

Even where the federal constitution has already provided for uniformity of enforcement, as it does under the provisions of section 2 of article 4, we have states refusing to recognize the extradition requisitions drawn by the executives of other states.

If it were not for the weakness due to lack of uniformity of enforcement, the uniform law plan (type 1) would, where police power alone is involved, be the easiest way out of the dilemma and, if the difficulties which arise from the tendency to delay and confuse the problem by bargaining for advantage could be overcome, the compact-commission form of cooperation (type 4) would probably settle the administration question for cooperative plans involving only things.

The reciprocity plan of cooperation (type 2) applies to only a few kinds of problems, and in the case of those problems involving economic as well as social questions it has an exceedingly limited application. This plan, however, may well be extended to cover those cases in which it would be useful. The administrative program here is not complicated and the question of states' rights does not arise.

The simple cooperative plan (type 3) has such limited application and only to specific physical problems that it needs no further consideration than already given it.

When we reach a discussion of the compact plan, which involves the use of the police power or seeks to control persons as well as things, we then enter a field in which the question of states' rights immediately comes to the front.

As has been stated, the present compact plan does not involve the federal government in the administration of the plan. It has, however, been suggested that this be changed and a three-point compact plan may solve the problem of regional controls. Under this changed plan the federal government or one of its agencies would supply the administrative authority for the cooperative region.

The plan involves first the adoption of suitable amendments to the federal constitution and next a limited delegation of authority to the federal government by interested states, and in this respect it departs from the present method of delegating authority to the federal government by constitutional provision chiefly by limiting the application of the authority thus granted to the subscribing states and omitting its application in the non-subscribing sovereignties. The delegation of authority, it is suggested, may also depart from the general constitutional form by limiting the scope of those laws needed to be passed by the federal legislature.

This form of provision for administration of interstate cooperative effort will be recognized as a modification of the compact plan heretofore described as type 4, the chief modification being that a federal agency would be substituted for the commission or corporation form of control.

The plan may also be considered as one in which the federal government places at the disposal of the states involved in the cooperative plan the facilities of the federal government for its administration. One example of such a plan, although not exactly parallel in form, was the municipal bankruptcy act. This particular act placed the facilities of the federal courts at the disposal of the municipalities of those states which by suitable legislation ratified the act. This act has been declared unconstitutional on the ground that it would lead to an invasion of states' rights, a view not shared by the minority of the United States Supreme Court.

Those upholding states' rights will object to this form of cooperative administration on the ground that it substitutes administration by federal bureau or department for that by state agency, and is thus a surrender of sovereignty, and so it would be. It is generally true that partners in a joint enterprise must waive the exercise of certain individual rights if they are to profit from the partnership.

It may also be said that the suggested plan tends to build up a federal bureaucracy at the expense of the states, and this may be true or not, depending on the nature of the enacted laws. It might be possible to so limit these laws by the acts of the delegating or ratifying states as to substantially give them the status of state-made laws.

Another plan proposed is one in which federal acts to accomplish specific purposes in limited areas are made applicable only to the areas of those states which, by suitable legislation, should permit the laws to be effective. In this case the ratification by two or more states would be a form of interstate cooperation, an interstate agreement to pass to the federal government the burden of taking care of specific problems. This transfer of burdens from the states to the federal government has been done in the case of specific purposes for the whole national area, as for example, in the case of the maintenance and government of the army, the navy, and the postal service. An extension of this system but with application only to those areas or states accepting it would be an innovation.

There is, however, one form of interstate cooperation which may be carried out without conflict with states' rights and this is cooperative plan-

ing by the states. In this case, as there are no administrative problems
involved, there are none of the embarrassments arising from conflicts with
state sovereignty. As the boundaries of the problem regions change, various combinations of states may join in the study of different specific problems and thus problems which transcend state lines may be completely
covered. From such planning there should be developed such convincing
evidence of need for state action that the several states interested in particular problems may be induced to enact suitable uniform legislation for
remedying the troubles uncovered. Where uniformly capable administration
is provided this is the least involved and may prove the most practicable
method of providing for interstate cooperation.

The general purposes of the federal and state constitutions are to insure
domestic tranquillity, promote the general welfare, and protect the liberties
of the people. If to accomplish these purposes the people, in whom all
powers are vested and from whom all powers are derived, find that in their
capacities as citizens of problem regions having specific problems they are
stopped from having these problems efficiently solved by reason of their
own acts as citizens of the nation or as citizens of a state, then the people
will in the end find a way out of this "no man's land" of government. Let
us hope that this may be done without an increase in government.

No. 20

A PLAGUE OF SPECIAL DISTRICTS [1]

by Kirk H. Porter

A COMPLAINT frequently heard about local government is that there
are altogether too many separate jurisdictions and too many local officers who have power to impose taxes for this, that, or the other purpose. In addition to the county, city, and township jurisdiction, the taxpayer is likely to find himself living within many other minor jurisdictions
and subject to their taxes. There are school districts, park districts, drainage districts, forestation districts, road districts, mosquito abatement dis-
tricts, sanitation districts, etc., etc. Each district has its own set of officials
and its own precious tax rate, so that taxpayers come to feel that they are
smothered with government, and lost in a maze of expensive complexities.
Unfortunately, our American way of dealing with governmental abuses is

[1] Kirk H. Porter, "A Plague of Special Districts," *National Municipal Review* (November, 1933), Vol. 22, No. 11, pp. 544-547, 574. Reprinted by permission of the *National
Municipal Review*.

to do nothing at all until the abuse has become well nigh intolerable an
then to rise up in wrath and go at the trouble with radical remedies tha
promise dramatic changes but oftentimes no genuine correction of the rea
evil. Thus reformers want to sweep away all these special districts witl
bold gestures, to consolidate counties, to abolish popular elections, to se
up county managers, or to establish full state control over local governmen
and administration.

However, there is a reason for the special district; even though like man·
other useful institutions it has been grossly perverted, not only by corrup·
tionists, but also by well-meaning people who have seen in it an agency o·
genuine democracy, and a safeguard against overweening power.

The special district was early designed to serve a purpose that existin,
governmental areas did not seem well adapted to serve. Thus, for instance
perhaps it becomes desirable to carry on a drainage project in a farm lan·
area. But, it appears, the swampy lands involved, the streams that must b
straightened or dealt with in some way, extend partially into the jurisdiction
of two or three counties, to say nothing of a lot of townships. In a word
the physical, topographical, engineering problem does not conform to th·
rigid governmental areas.

One solution would be to turn the problem over to the state. But ou·
devotion to old concepts of local self-government has stood in the way o
this. Another method would be to get the governing authorities in th
various jurisdictions to cooperate in the enterprise. But, when it comes t·
letting lucrative contracts, to employing workers, and most of all to levyin,
the taxes to finance the undertaking, the good spirit of cooperation all to·
frequently evaporates; bickering, sharp practice, bitter rivalries and selfisl
interest creep in, and either the project is abandoned altogether, or else i·
goes forward accompanied with unwise compromises and much extravagance

An obvious solution is the special district. Let the area of operation b·
marked out and surveyed. Let there be local referenda upon the broa·
question of going forward with the undertaking. If the popular vote b·
favorable let a special board of trustees be set up. Allow them to levy a
certain rate upon all property within their district, and let them carr·
through the project, largely independently of all other local authorities
For good or for ill this type of special district has been resorted to for man·
years, and it does indeed seem to have served a good purpose, thoug·
many people to-day think such problems ought to be handled by the stat·
directly.

But obviously, the justification for this particular type of special distric
exists only when the undertaking must needs reach into two or more existin,
jurisdictions,—that is, when it must cross county lines, or city boundaries

But there are not many legitimate cases of this sort. Drainage projects are perhaps the clearest. The forest preserve, or large park project may present the same problem. But it is interesting to observe that for the most part, to-day, state departments are assuming full control of these undertakings. This is much to be preferred, and the practice would seem to make unnecessary for the most part any further application of the special district idea as applied in the past years.

Another type of special district appears when it is desired to get a given undertaking "out of politics." This reflects deep distrust of the "regular" governmental authorities, and a wish to get the project into the hands of a "better class" of people who presumably will have a keener interest in the work to be done, a minimum of ulterior motive, and a considerable spirit of noble self-sacrifice.

The school district is the classic example of this type. Specially selected school trustees, or directors, are elected. Their powers are prescribed in the law, they may levy a prescribed rate, and thus conduct school affairs independently of the "regular" governmental authorities. Not everywhere is this high degree of independence permitted, however. Sometimes mayors, or city councils, or county supervisors select the school authorities; but they usually are free in the matter of actual administration.

Here again, the *reason* for having a special district is clear enough. And there is something in it. And it is interesting to observe that criticism of the special school district system today is directed largely to the point that there are altogether too many districts, and not that the special district idea should be abandoned. Arguments against preserving the vast multitude of tiny school districts that spatter the land would seem to be overwhelming. And many educators would be only too thankful to see the county accepted as the unit of school administration. But there is by no means a unanimity of opinion as to the wisdom of abandoning the "special" district idea and turning school administration over to the "regular" authorities, i.e., county supervisors or commissioners, or city councils. Many a reform advocate would throw up his hands in horror at that, and would plead instead for completely centralized state control.

Now the reason that lies behind the special school district has been invoked again and again to set up special districts for other purposes. Thus, well-meaning people have wanted to get public libraries out of the hands of the "regular" city officials. City parks and playgrounds, it has been thought, ought to be taken "out of politics." One of the latest manifestations of this urge for exclusiveness and purity is seen in the practice of taking county hospitals "out of politics" and of setting up separate boards with their special tax rates to carry on this service independently of the so-called politicians.

Thus has come into being a considerable number of what may be called "disguised" special districts. This type of district is disguised because it is literally coterminous with an existing area—a city or a county. In this way a city virtually becomes a special district for library administration and a special district for city park administration, and the county virtually becomes a special district for hospital administration. And each of these disguised special districts has its independent authorities,—its trustees, directors or commissioners, and its inevitable special, precious, tax rate. Furthermore it should be pointed out that often it has been the very "best" people in the community that have insisted upon this exclusiveness. These well meaning people are deeply interested in the particular service—*for the time being, anyway*—and want to keep it "out of politics."

In addition to all this, the time-honored system of fixing special tax rates for specific purposes aggravates the situation, even though it does not bring into existence either the genuine or the disguised special district. And again it is often the deeply interested, well-meaning people who are responsible for it. In the case of the special rate they wish to coerce the regular authorities—the county governing board or the city council,—or to circumvent them, or to prevent them from curtailing a given service. Right there begins the procession of special rates for special purposes. A certain rate is made mandatory, and the funds must be spent for a certain purpose—highway patrol, for instance. Then a certain rate is fixed and *must* be applied for poor relief. Presently this is split and two special rates appear—one for institutional relief, one for out-door relief.

Then there must be the fixed mandatory rate for maintaining a cemetery another for the care of old soldiers, one for the care of orphans, etc., until the list of special rates includes perhaps a score or more. To be sure, most of these rates are maximum rates. But the constant pressure that is brought by those who are particularly interested in each of these activities, make it next to impossible for the governing bodies to keep these rates below the maximum. And it should be observed that the basic idea back of the special rate is to deprive the governing body of much discretion with respect to a particular service. Thus, suppose the council of a small city either cannot or will not maintain a municipal band. Music lovers want a band. The statutes afford an opportunity. A referendum is held—that glorious instrument of direct democracy! The people vote: Shall a special rate be applied to maintain a municipal band? A handful of people vote, and most of them vote "yes," and lo! there is a band! And another rigid tax rate is fixed upon the city.

Sometimes local governing authorities, county board members and city councilmen, are quietly active at the state house seeking themselves to have those special rates applied. To have them in the statutes relieves the officials of much responsibility. They can take refuge in the fixed rate, and honestly declare that it is beyond their power to economize with respect to the services thus bolstered.

The result of all this is an astonishing complex of overlapping jurisdiction: —the "regular" areas, i.e., counties, cities, towns, and townships, the legitimate special districts, a number of wholly unnecessary special districts, several disguised special districts, and overlaying the whole, a strangling net of special rates that makes it impossible for local governing bodies to budget their resources wisely, even when they have the best of intentions.

Reform is not easy. Mere sweeping away of the special districts will not solve the problem. In fact, the good that would come of this is often very much exaggerated. The citizen is told that he lives under so many separate jurisdictions, each with power to tax; and is led to believe that if the jurisdictions were not so numerous the costs would disappear. But this is in part a vain hope. If a government service is to be maintained it makes but little difference whether one body or another imposes the tax rate. If a county hospital is to be maintained it makes relatively little difference whether the necessary taxes for the purpose be levied by a board of county supervisors, or by a board of county hospital trustees. If a city park is to be supported, or a library maintained, or a mosquito abatement project carried through, or a municipal band subsidized, or a county poor farm supported, it makes little difference who applies the rate. A dozen given rates applied by one board would be about as heavy as a dozen similar rates applied by a dozen different boards.

"But," one is quick to say, "we would get rid of all these useless officials, we would cut down personnel and the salary burden." A little could be saved this way, perhaps, but not a great deal. Libraries, hospitals, parks, drainage projects, etc., cannot be conducted without people to give time and attention to them. In brief, we should not get the idea that by abolishing districts we abolish the basic costs of the services involved. This seems to be a great delusion of those who advocate county consolidation. They seem to forget that there would be just as many miles of highway to keep up, just as many bridges to build, just as many poor people to feed and clothe, just as many criminals to prosecute, just as many children to educate, just as many land transfers to record, etc., etc.; and after all, these are the basic costs of local government.

However, the prime evil of the special district is that it grossly decentralizes administration. It tends to exalt each little service. It tends to make those who are in charge lose their sense of proportion. It relieves the principal local authorities of the power and responsibility they ought to have. It helps to let large sums of money dribble through the fingers of woefully incompetent people who often give but scant attention to the problems with which they are supposed to deal. And it makes very much easier the nefarious work of grafting politicians and crooked contractors, every one of whom is in favor of local self-government to the last degree, and more and stupider special boards and commissions.

These complexities of local government make intelligent budgeting almost impossible. A very homely illustration will make this clear. Imagine a householder trying to budget his household expenses for a year. And imagine that the amount to be spent for most of the important items were rigidly fixed. His budgeting becomes a farce! If the sums that he must spend for clothing, for food, for recreation, etc., are all fixed, there is no point to budgeting. Furthermore the decentralization in the actual conduct of services through independent agencies makes for much trouble, lack of ccoperation and duplication of effort;—not to mention the evils of the long ballot.

On the whole, county governing boards and city councils stand to acquire greatly increased power as a result of doing away with special districts— genuine or disguised;—and certainly they would gain greatly in power by abolition of many special rates. But increased power means increased opportunities for doing the things that need to be done—chiefly an opportunity for budgeting wisely. Any attempt to effect economies through a structure of many jurisdictions, and within the ambit of a complicated net of fixed rates is almost sure to fail. City and county officers must be released from their strait-jackets and given a chance to assume real power and responsibility. If we are afraid to give them such power because of the evil they might do, we are indeed afraid to put modern democracy to the test.

Chapter VII

CIVIL LIBERTIES—AN ESSENTIAL OF DEMOCRATIC GOVERNMENT

[THERE are, in the world to-day, two great classes of government: democratic or popular government and autocratic or authoritarian. This classification is based upon an analysis of the amount of protection given individual rights and liberties.

The autocratic or authoritarian system is one in which government is not responsible to the people, in which there is a concentration of the lawmaking and executive powers in the hands of one group, in which there are no independent parliaments, in which there is no guarantee of individual rights or equality before the law, and in which arbitrary judgments on the part of the rulers are substituted for rational consideration of cases according to the rule of law.

This system of government has become widespread in the modern world and includes among its adherents the Fascists and the Communists. The proponents of this system ridicule democracy, recognize no individual liberties, monopolize the press and the schools as agencies of propaganda, ruthlessly suppress free speech and assembly.

The democratic system, on the other hand, is one in which the government rests upon the consent of the governed, is responsible to the community, and governs in accordance with the rule of law. The rights of citizens are guaranteed by independent judges acting in accord with the general law laid down by representatives of the people. The individual is an end, not the state or government; the government is the tool by which the good life is constructed. This system is one which has been rapidly disappearing in the world, but to which we, to a great extent may lay claim in the United States. It is essential, in order that we may preserve it, however, that we maintain our freedom of speech, press and assembly and that we defend our system of free schools. To understand the true value of the essential freedoms, without which a true democracy is impossible, is to take the first step toward its defense.]

159

No. 21

INDIVIDUAL LIBERTY AND GOVERNMENTAL AUTHORITY [1]

by J. Allen Smith

AMERICAN writers on political science, especially those with a conservative bias, take it for granted that the chief merit of our particular form of government is that it guarantees individual liberty through an effective limitation of political power. The rights of individuals, being expressly enumerated in our federal and state constitutions, are supposed to be thus placed "entirely beyond the power of the government to curtail." This viewpoint, which is quite generally presented in American textbooks on political science, is merely an expression of the prevalent anthropomorphic conception of the Constitution of the United States as the guardian and protector of the rights of the people.

That the notion of the Constitution as self-enforcing was not accepted by the people in the early decades of American history, the emphasis on the right of revolution abundantly proves. Gradually, however, under the influence of skillful conservative propaganda, the fiction gained acceptance that the government was powerless to disregard rights enumerated in the fundamental law. The Constitution, having come to be regarded as an expression of the popular will, was relied upon to prevent the government from interfering with the liberty of the individual.

The growth of the new conception of sovereignty as unlimited political power, as well as the deification of the Constitution as the palladium of democracy, tended to modify the popular conception of constitutional law in its relation to individual liberty. The original idea of the Constitution, as a check on the power of the people no less than on that of the government itself, was difficult to reconcile with the new doctrine of popular sovereignty, which ascribed to the people untrammeled authority. The rights of individuals, as they were understood at the time of the American Revolution and in the period immediately following, constituted a recognized check on all political power, even that of the people themselves. This original conception of individual liberty has, however, been supplanted by the professedly more democratic one implied in the artificial distinction

[1] J. Allen Smith, *The Growth and Decadence of Constitutional Government* (New York: Henry Holt and Company, 1930). Chapter XIV. Reprinted by permission of the publisher.

between state and government. The chief significance of the attempt on the part of recent American writers to make this distinction is to be found in the need for some means of harmonizing a check and balance constitution with the notion of popular sovereignty. According to the supporters of this distinction, the people politically organized constitute the state, make and amend the Constitution, through it control the government, and are the final repository of unlimited power. Governmental authority is represented as being subject to the restraints imposed by a check and balance plan of organization, while the state, somewhat vaguely conceived as the people, is supposed to be subject to no limitation whatsoever. Although individual liberty is represented as effectually safeguarded against governmental encroachment, the individual, we are told, "has no rights which the state is bound to recognize."

To create belief in a human power that can legally override all restraints imposed for the protection of individuals is to supplant the basic idea in the theory of individual liberty by one which serves as a foundation for governmental absolutism.

It is interesting to note that the conception of the ultimate unlimited power of the people had a distinctly conservative origin; that its object was not to establish popular supremacy, but to ensure the subordination of the popular will to governmental authority. Superficially viewed, this interpretation of our political system seems to concede to the people, acting as the state, a degree of political power which would satisfy even the advocates of the most extreme form of democracy. But only in appearance is it a concession to the demand for an extension of the power of the people. Under the pretense of subordinating governmental authority, it in fact makes that authority supreme. By reason of the fact that the government controls the interpretation and enforcement of the fundamental law, it has the power in no small degree to remove, evade, or ignore the restraints by which its authority is supposed to be limited. The people having no part in the interpretation of constitutional law, except through the public officials who exercise this power, are as a matter of course bound by the Constitution as thus interpreted. Instead of controlling the Constitution, they are controlled by it as interpreted and enforced by governmental agencies.

No one can understand clearly the status of individual liberty in this country without bearing in mind the place occupied by the judiciary under our constitutional system. The effectiveness of our constitutional guaranties of individual liberty was greatly impaired when the government, and especially the branch of it farthest removed from popular influence, the Supreme Court, acquired the recognized right to interpret them.

The attempt to promulgate the idea that back of the government and the Constitution are the people organized as an omnipotent state, subject to no legal or constitutional restraints, tends to destroy the philosophic foundation on which the conception of individual liberty rests. Although the rights of individuals are supposedly protected against the government, they are represented as at all times subject to abridgment or abolition by this so-called state. And when we realize that this supposed political entity, in so far as it has any real existence, is only another name for purely governmental agencies, we can see that the natural effect of this fiction is to clothe the government itself with that unlimited power imputed to the mythical state.

That liberty for the individual is desirable would be readily conceded by the great majority of the people in all enlightened countries. Their practice, however, seems to be but slightly influenced by what they profess to believe. They may accept individual liberty as a purely abstract principle, and yet, in applying it, they may defeat its purpose, by giving it a narrow and illiberal interpretation. Everyone believes in individual liberty for those whose economic interests and whose opinions on social, political, and religious questions are identical with his own. What is meant by individual liberty, however, is not the right to conform, which no one questions, but the right to act as one's own judgment dictates where his opinion is opposed to that generally held. There is no need for the advocacy of freedom for individual conduct that conforms to generally accepted standards. Liberty for the individual means nothing if it does not imply the right to pursue a course of conduct and to hold and advocate views which do not have the approval of the majority and which may even be strongly condemned by that majority.

Individual liberty is inseparably connected with the theory of progress. Individuals must be free to advance new ideas and try new methods if a higher type of civilization is to be attained. The only possible guaranty of progress is the freedom of individuals and groups to criticize any belief or doctrine—religious, social, political, or economic—and to advocate any change in institutional arrangements which to them may seem desirable. Our beliefs at any given time are at best only partially true. We approach the truth only by a slow, laborious process in which competition between opposing views gradually eliminates error.

That which is established needs no special protection against that which is merely proposed. The old and generally accepted is always difficult to discredit and supplant with the new. The very fact that it has the stamp of social approval gives it a prestige which the advocates of change can not easily overcome. In actual practice the burden of proof is always, and of course ought to be, on those who attack the old. The almost universal tendency to be skeptical concerning the merit of any new idea or proposed innovation is a sufficient guaranty that there is not likely to be any undue haste in discarding the old for the untried.

The chief danger is not that false ideas and doctrines will supplant established truth, but that established error will seek to protect itself against the truth by suppressing all dissenters. That this is not a purely imaginary danger is easily understood when we reflect that, while the general mental inertia of the people disinclines them to accept new ideas, there are almost always important vested interests whose material prosperity largely depends upon the retention of the old. Every important idea or belief that has been long accepted has the support of influential classes whose interest in protecting it against attack has a more selfish basis than a purely disinterested desire for the truth.

Liberty for the individual is necessary if we are to realize the Christian ideal of personal responsibility or the democratic ideal of self-government. Men can not be morally accountable for their conduct or politically self-governing unless they possess the degree of freedom from external control which individual liberty connotes. The theory of individual liberty recognizes that there is a field of human conduct within which the coercive power of the state or of the organized church should not be allowed to intrude except for the purpose of guaranteeing this freedom by punishing those who abuse it.

It would be wholly incorrect to say that majority rule necessarily implies individual liberty. Both are the outgrowth of the struggle against irresponsible power. But the conception of individual rights as a check on governmental authority is not closely related to the growth of modern democracy, except in so far as the former was one of the influences which paved the way for the latter by limiting the power of king and aristocracy. Since the majority have come to regard themselves as the final source of political power, their attitude toward the theory of individual liberty has profoundly changed. It was to the advantage of the majority in the eighteenth century to defend the rights of individuals against the state. Having accepted the idea of popular sovereignty, however, they now regard individual liberty as a check on their own power.

We may concede that democracy is more desirable than any other form of government, and yet realize that individual liberty is not necessarily secure where the majority are in control. The rights of individuals are supposed, it is true, to be most respected in a society organized as a political democracy. As a matter of fact, however, the majority may be fully as intolerant of dissenting opinion as kings and aristocracies have always been.

Indeed, there is some justification for the conservative view that in a democracy personal liberty is more likely to be abridged than under a government in which the people have less influence. The reason for this is obvious. A government which is supposed to represent the majority, and has its support, is more confident of ability to override all opposition than one which does not recognize the right of the majority to rule and which must avoid the danger of arousing too much popular opposition. Since democracy is less exposed to the danger of effective popular resistance, it may with impunity invade the sphere of individual liberty. A strong government—one that has no fear of effective opposition on the part of the people—is almost certain to disregard the rights of individuals whenever the recognition of such rights would seriously hamper it in carrying out its policies. But where the state rests upon a basis generally recognized as undemocratic, those who exercise authority are constantly reminded of the need for a cautious moderate policy—one which will in so far as possible conciliate all important elements in the population and thus safeguard the country against the danger of revolution. Respect on the part of the government for the rights of individuals is due in much larger measure to this balance of opposing interests within the state than it is to formal constitutional guaranties. De Tocqueville in his *Democracy in America,* published in 1835, recognizes this fact when he refers to the tyranny of the majority in the United States.

I know no country (he tells us) in which there is so little true independence of mind and freedom of discussion as in America. In any constitutional state in Europe every sort of religious and political theory may be advocated and propagated abroad; for there is no country in Europe so subdued by any single authority, as not to contain citizens who are ready to protect the man who raises his voice in the cause of truth, from the consequences of his hardihood. If he is unfortunate enough to live under an absolute government, the people is upon his side; if he inhabits a free country, he may find a shelter behind the authority of the throne, if he require one. The aristocratic part of society supports him in some countries, and the democracy in others. But in a nation where democratic institutions exist, organized like those of the United States, there is but one sole authority, one single element of strength and of success, with nothing beyond it.

The old conflict between liberty and authority does not end with the emergence of democracy; it merely enters a new phase in which we must look to public opinion for the protection of individual rights. Political democracy is in no sense a substitute for individual liberty, which means the right of individual self-determination. Without individual liberty, political democracy is not likely to contribute much to the world's progress. If popular government is to free the world, it must exercise such self-restraint as may be required to keep it from encroaching on the rights of individuals. This, however, can not be ensured by formally proclaiming these rights in a written constitution. Such self-imposed checks are wholly ineffective, unless they are supported by a public opinion so clearly defined and so active that no government could afford to antagonize it.

Individual liberty in the United States to-day not only lacks the support of an active, intelligent public opinion, but often encounters a degree of popular hostility which renders constitutional guaranties wholly ineffective. The rights most likely to be abridged or denied by the government, or by the irresponsible and misguided groups who are constantly interfering with the constitutional rights of others by resort to mob violence, are those most fundamental—the ones our American constitutions have sought to preserve by express guaranties of freedom of speech, press, and assembly.

Although the hostility to free discussion in present-day society is, of course, not entirely due to any one single cause, it may be regarded as mainly economic. Wherever there is a conflict of interests we may expect to see some opposition to the recognition of this fundamental right. Let any class feel that it is enjoying advantages or privileges, of which society, if fully informed, would disapprove, and it will inevitably regard with disfavor any attempt to bring them to the attention of the public. No doubt, so far as the masses are concerned, the hostility to free discussion is largely due to a blind instinctive fear that it will undermine opinions and beliefs which they associate with the well-being of society and not to any consciously selfish interest. This is not true, however, of the opposition to freedom of speech and discussion which comes from the more intelligent classes, who take a leading part in every attack on this right.

The formal acceptance of the democratic idea by the modern world has emphasized the importance of public opinion. To-day it is conceived to be highly desirable, if not necessary, to have the support of public opinion for any economic arrangement which we wish to preserve. Quite naturally, then, every important economic group seeks to control public opinion where its material interests are involved. And since opinion is largely determined by what one is permitted to see, to hear, and to read, it can be controlled only through some form of censorship and propaganda, such as was formerly exercised by church and state—as the history of religious and political persecution clearly shows.

Propaganda, in the sense of an organized effort either to popularize or to discredit some idea, viewpoint, institutional arrangement, or economic system, has a sinister significance when through a monopolistic control of news sources it is accompanied by the suppression of all competing propaganda. The power to establish a monopoly of this sort is one that society could not safely entrust to any agency, public or private. Monopoly in such a field is infinitely more dangerous than monopolistic control of industry. There can be nothing worthy of the name of intellectual freedom without free competition between ideas.

The control of opinion by purely private interests, which modern capitalism has made possible, has come to supply an effective substitute for the old form of avowed class control. From the point of view of the capitalist class, this new form of control has some distinct advantages over the old system. It is indirect and not obvious to those who lack political and social intelligence, and, therefore, not recognized by many as class control. Concealed, as it is, under the outward form of political democracy, it is less exposed to the danger of popular attack than was the old avowed and generally recognized class rule. Moreover, it gives to capitalists the benefits of actual control without requiring them to assume any of the responsibility which should accompany it.

The efficacy of capitalistic control of opinion depends upon the extent to which organized wealth owns or controls the various agencies through which public opinion is formed. Ownership of the press, news associations, theaters, moving pictures, and broadcasting stations, as well as some measure of direct control over public school education, is prerequisite to an effective scheme of propaganda. Complete monopoly of these is perhaps not attainable, though a capitalistic control, sufficiently extensive to afford some of the advantages of monopoly, has actually been brought about.

The influence which the capitalist class may exert directly through ownership is, however, much less of a menace than the indirect pressure it may bring to bear upon those supposedly independent. The economic and financial power of this class may be used quite effectively to control those who are outside of its organization and legally independent. There are many kinds of discrimination possible against those who refuse to recognize its unjust and illegal authority. An independent paper will soon discover that one penalty for independence is the loss of all advertising controlled by this class; and this loss is usually sufficient to mean the difference between success and failure. Had any newspaper in any conservative American community during the last few years frankly defended the constitutional right of free speech, it could hardly have failed to lose its most profitable advertisements. Of course, it might have defended freedom of speech, press, and assembly as a purely abstract principle with suitable qualification, without incurring the active hostility of business—provided that it condoned the frequent interferences with the exercise of this right by mobs and by equally irresponsible public officials. But this purely formal acceptance of the principle of free speech is not to be confused with the defense of it as a practical policy. No one can be regarded as a real supporter of this fundamental right, who is not ready to condemn the violations of it that are so frequent in present-day society.

No. 22

FREEDOM TO END FREEDOM [1]

by Archibald MacLeish

IN an age of political paradox the greatest of political paradoxes is provided not by the reactionaries who invented the technique but by the liberals who detest it. Hitler frees provinces by conquering them. Chamberlain keeps peace by losing wars. Franco saves Spain for the Italians. But it is the liberals who declare that the only way to preserve the gentle heifer of liberalism from the Fascists is to shoot her through the head.

They don't put it that way but it comes to the same thing. What certain liberals now propose is that the threat of totalitarianism to free institutions should be met by limiting freedom of expression in democratic states to those who believe in freedom of expression and denying it to those who do not. Specifically, what they propose is that the privilege of freedom of expression in democratic states should be denied to the Fascists and their congeners, the Communists.

The argument runs something like this: The Fascists and their congeners, the Communists, who, incidentally, are their congeners not by choice but because the Fascists have imitated Communist techniques while ignoring Communist purposes, do not themselves believe in free speech. Therefore, they have no right to exercise free speech. Therefore, the state is entitled to refuse free speech to them. For if they are granted freedom of speech they will use that freedom to capture political power. And if they capture political power they will deprive others of freedom of speech. And if they deprive others of freedom of speech, liberalism and democracy are dead. From which it follows that a liberal and democratic state, if it wishes to be realistic and hardheaded rather than foolish and visionary, will deprive both Fascists and Communists of freedom of speech forthwith.

It is a persuasive argument. No one doubts that Communists and Fascists, when in a position to do so, forbid the expression of views other

---

[1] Archibald MacLeish, "Freedom to End Freedom," *Survey Graphic* (February, 1939), Vol. 28, pp. 117-119. Reprinted by permission of the *Survey Graphic*.

than their own, and no one imagines that American Fascists or American Communists would be more tolerant than any other variety. It requires an exceptionally catholic imagination, perhaps, to imagine a Communist dictatorship in the United States, but it is easy to imagine what a Fascist America would be like. Sinclair Lewis was able to see it in his mind's eye with the most prosaic literalness. A Fascist America would not be tolerant. Indeed, Americans being what they are, there is every chance that an American dictatorship would be even more repressive, obscurantist and bloody than anything Germany, Italy or Russia has produced. It is one thing to dictate to people who have never governed themselves, or whose experiences in self-government have been brief and footling—people as congenitally subservient and orderly and obedient and patient as the subjects of the old European autocracies. It is quite another thing to attempt to dictate to people whose notion of government is a postoffice building, a revenue agent and the Marine Band over the radio on the Fourth of July.

The nervous liberals are certainly right, therefore, in asserting that American Fascists or Communists, if they came to power, would suppress the publication of all opinion other than their own. They have done so abroad and they would do so here. Newspapers in Germany, Italy and Russia are so obviously house organs for the regime that no one in or out of the dictatorships reads them for anything but the light they may or may not shed on the regime's spoken or unspoken intentions. The same thing is true of other forms of communication. The Nazi burning of the books is the characteristic expression of the Fascist attitude toward art; and even the Russians, who can hardly be dropped into the same category, have provided unforgettable examples of artistic intolerance. An American dictator who discouraged all American music not based on Swanee River or Alexander's Ragtime Band or Boola-Boola would merely be emulating the Russian dictator who violently attacked the distinguished composer Dmitry Shostakovich in the official newspapers for "leftist stress of ugliness," for destroying harmony, and melody and for sympathy with the bourgeois heroine of his opera *Lady Macbeth of Minsk* while granting a flattering interview to Dzerzhinsky, the composer of an insipid patriotic opera based on Cossack folk-tunes and entitled *Quiet Flows the Don*.

It follows that the liberals who would deprive Communists and Fascists of the right of free speech are thoroughly justified in asserting that the Communists and the Fascists would have no just cause to complain. People who lay claim to a right only in order to destroy it may fairly be charged with hypocrisy. And hypocrisy, despite the efforts of the British Tories to give it international standing and diplomatic repute, is still one of the less attractive human characteristics.

But the argument of the nervous liberals does not end with proof that the Fascist and Communist concern for civil liberties is pure hypocrisy. It moves on to draw deductions as to the proper policy of the democratic state. And it is precisely there, in that transition from the moral standing of the parties to the proper policy of the state, that the persuasiveness of their argument leaves them. It is precisely in the argument that *because* the advocates of dictatorship have no right to claim freedom of expression, therefore freedom of expression should be denied them, that the fundamental liberal paradox appears.

For this transition is what the lawyers call a complete non sequitur. Its end has nothing to do with its beginning. And the reason its end has nothing to do with its beginning is that its beginning and its end are joined by an assumption that should not be made. That assumption is the assumption that the right of freedom of expression in a liberal democracy is nothing more than a privilege granted by the state to the citizen for the citizen's private profit and satisfaction. Only on that assumption is it possible to argue that because a group of citizens do not deserve, or have ceased to deserve, or have not the right to demand, freedom of expression, therefore the state can and should refuse them freedom of expression.

Historically it may be true that the right of free speech, and the rest of the rights guaranteed by such instruments as the American Bill of Rights, were wrung from autocratic monarchs as grants of privilege. But nothing could be further from the truth than the supposition that these rights are still mere privileges in a modern liberal democracy. In American constitutional theory the right of freedom of expression was thought of as a "natural right" and the only effect of the first amendment was to forbid Congress to abridge it. The implication is very clear that the right antedated the constitution. To-day, when "natural rights" are no longer in favor it is still true that freedom of expression antedates the constitution. And for a very good reason. A liberal democracy, such as the American democracy is supposed to be, would be unthinkable without that right and without the other personal liberties commonly grouped with it. So far is it from being true that the right is a privilege granted by the state, that the opposite is the case. *The right is one of the basic conditions precedent to the existence of the state in the form in which the state exists.* It may be—it is at least arguable—that the liberties of the Bill of Rights could exist in some other state than a liberal democracy. But it is certain that a liberal democracy could not exist without the liberties of the Bill of Rights. Popular government without them would be worse than a farce. It would be an impossibility. Unless the people of a self-governing society can assemble freely and speak their minds freely and criticize their government freely, self-government cannot exist.

It is therefore highly misleading to talk about these liberties as though they were privileges granted by the state and had the attributes of privileges. A privilege granted by the state to the citizens for their private profit could of course be withdrawn without injury to any but the citizens deprived. It could be withdrawn in whole or in part. More importantly, it could be withdrawn from one group while still permitted to another. But a right which is one of the foundations of the kind of society on which the state must depend for its own existence cannot be withdrawn in this way. And above all it may not be withdrawn from one section of that society while left in the enjoyment of another section of that society. For one of the characteristics—one of the observed, habitual, realistic characteristics—of such rights as this is that they must exist generally within clearly formulated and universally applicable limits if they are to exist at all. Nothing is more certain than the fact that the restriction of the right of freedom of expression to those holding certain beliefs, and its denial to those holding other beliefs, would sooner or later destroy the right for those holding any belief. The very essence of the right is that it should be effective against majorities and that it should protect the most unpopular opinions. To set up one political exception is to set up all political exceptions. And so even though the exception is phrased in terms of the right itself. It is as dangerous to deny the right of free speech to those who do not believe in free speech as to deny that right to those who do not believe in war or Herbert Hoover or fundamentalist Baptist biology.

The one certain and fixed point in the entire discussion is this: that freedom of expression is guaranteed to the citizens of a liberal democracy not for the pleasure of the citizens but for the health of the state. It makes no considerable difference whether those who enjoy the right of freedom of expression wish to enjoy it or whether they do not. It does not even matter that they would gladly destroy the right if they could. What does matter is that the right should exist and that it should exist in form of right, equally available to all. For unless it exists, and unless it exists in such terms, the kind of state which is built upon its existence can no longer be maintained.

As a practical matter, therefore, the proposal of the nervous liberals comes down to this: that the liberal democracies should protect themselves against dictatorship by an act of mayhem which might very easily become an act of suicide. They should protect themselves against the loss of the priceless right of free inquiry and free expression by themselves infecting that right with death. They should protect themselves against the burning of the books by starting a fire to which books will almost certainly be fed.

This fact should be borne in mind when the supporters of this proposal talk about the extremity of the Fascist danger and urge the voters to be "realistic." The dangers of fascism do most certainly exist. The Fascists, as we are continually told, need win only one election to win all elections whereas the democrats must win every election to win any other. But though these dangers exist they are less fatal than the danger proposed by way of remedy. For once the right of free expression has been mutilated from within, the eventual death of liberalism is inevitable, whereas so long as the danger outside in the street remains outside, it may perhaps be avoided. The fact that Hitler was able to use the fifteen-year-old Weimar constitution to destroy the Weimar constitution does not mean that an American Coughlin or Long or whatever could use the one-hundred-and-fifty-year-old American constitution in the same way. America is not Germany. The Americans are not the Germans. And being warned by history we are not altogether unarmed.

It is that circumstance which the nervous liberals leave out of account. They do not consider that the classic American doctrine of freedom of speech recognizes a somewhat blurred but nevertheless legible causative relation between speech and action, and permits the state to defend itself from treason not after treasonable speech has turned into action, but before. They do not consider, further, that the existence of a constitutionally guaranteed right of freedom of expression strengthens rather than weakens the hands of the state in dealing with other practices dangerous to free institutions. The constitutional guarantees of personal liberty and republican government in the United States do not mean that private armies and private uniforms and all the rest of the chicanery employed by the Nazis could not be suppressed in this country. On the contrary they mean they could be, and with the full power of the government.

The truth of the matter is that the necessary weapons for the defense of liberal democracy against the advocates of dictatorship in the United States already exist, without mutilating the one or imitating the other. The present police power exercised under present court decisions should enable a people devoted to democracy to protect their democracy; and the present control of radio, movies and the press should enable the defenders of the existing order to talk at least as loud as those who would replace the existing order with something else. The only doubtful element is not the armament for defense but the will for defense. And it is here that the weakness, not to say the mischievousness, of the proposal to deny freedom of expression to the Communists and Fascists becomes most obvious.

The will to defend democracy demands a belief in democracy. And belief in democracy demands that democracy should be a way of life with future and unachieved objectives such as men can continue to desire.

If the democracy to be defended is merely the status quo which the great corporations and the reactionary newspapers call democracy when they shout for its defense, then the belief will be cool and the will feeble.

If, however, the democracy to be defended is a future democracy, a true democracy which will admit the failures of this democracy and set them straight—if the democracy to be defended is a free man's way of dealing with a free man's evils in order to create a free man's world, then the will to defend and protect that democracy will be strong enough to sweep over any challenge. But that kind of will and that kind of belief are not achieved by refusing to permit democracy to be attacked. To refuse to permit democracy to face attack is to turn democracy into the status quo and freeze it in a form in which only a small minority can believe.

Democratic belief in democracy, and the popular will to defend it, are achieved only by permitting democracy to face any attack, however slanderous, however murderous, answering the proposals of the attackers with such proposals as a democracy can make. Those who believe in democracy because they believe in the people will have no fear of the outcome. Those who believe in democracy for another reason may very well fear but their fears will be irrelevant.

No. 23

THE BILL OF RIGHTS TO-DAY [1]

by Ralph M. Blagden

THE historic struggle to preserve individual liberties—the touchstone of democracy—is taking place to-day on a new and in some respects a more deceptive level.

The cruder devices of strikebreakers, soapboxes, arbitrary injunctions against labor, and criminal syndicalism laws have been curbed and in their places there is propaganda—subtle, concealed, playing on the emotions and fears of the people. If, for instance, sober citizens can be induced to believe there is a Communist menace, they may be persuaded to organize "law and order" societies and vigilante groups to do the work formerly done by strikebreakers in suppressing labor's rights.

Put most simply, one of the gravest dangers is that the public may be decoyed by fear of the radical fringe of Bunds and Communists to adopt

[1] Ralph M. Blagden, "The Bill of Rights in 1939," *The Christian Science Monitor* (April 1, 1939), pp. 6, 12. Reprinted by permission of *The Christian Science Monitor*.

repressive measures that would actually restrict the rights of the more liberal elements and impede essential social reforms.

The average citizen is sorely perplexed, however, over the issue of civil liberties to-day. Within the last few months he has heard what, perhaps, he never expected to hear in the United States—a prominent priest whipping up hatred and prejudice against the Jews. He has seen what he may never have expected to see—uniformed Storm Troopers in New York City's Madison Square Garden.

All about him the common, middle-class member of society hears reports of the Knights of the White Camellia, the Crusader White Shirts, the Silver Shirts, the German-American Bund and others. He hears their attacks on American institutions, their ridicule of American leaders, their praise of dictators. He has even heard his President's name publicly perverted to the accompaniment of the raucous laughter of Bund members.

This average citizen begins to wonder if it is wise to accord these enemies of democracy the right to speak, write and assemble as they please. He wonders if, in these tense and disturbed days, men should be permitted to contemn the nation that shelters them. He wonders if it is not criminal negligence to shelter the would-be destroyers of democracy—to permit men to urge revolution and violence when society appears like an unlighted bonfire of isms awaiting the match.

Concern of this kind is already manifesting itself in a rash of bills. Typical of these measures is the extreme proposal advocated in Pennsylvania, which, among other things, would make it a misdemeanor to "abet in any manner in inciting, counseling, promoting or advocating hatred, violence or hostility against any group in this state." In other states there are proposals to make groups and voluntary associations subject to the laws of libel.

Laws dealing with "criminal syndicalism," "criminal anarchy" and sedition are in force today in 34 states. They represent in large part national hysteria that followed the World War over the prospect of violence and industrial sabotage from Communists and members of the IWW. To-day there is a resurgence of public alarm. This time it is directed against the agitator of religious and racial prejudices as well as against the Communist.

The American citizen to-day, however, has available an important mass of material to moderate any temptation he may possess to rush ahead toward repressive laws. If he reads the record, he may learn that restrictive laws have not been used against actual advocacy of violence as they were intended so much as they have been used against labor and liberal elements.

Thus the American Civil Liberties Union could say after years of exhaustive observation:

In all our experience of the last 17 years in handling free speech cases all over the country, we do not know of a specific incitement to violence by any radical.

In New Jersey a bill was recently passed to protect Jews from anti-Semitic attacks. The only case that arose concerned a member of Jehovah's Witnesses, who was charged with distributing anti-Catholic literature.

The history of these repressive laws reveals that they have been a net with which to catch strikers, labor organizers and Socialists, more, perhaps, than instruments with which to protect society against the really dangerous radical. The United States Supreme Court's general rule that the right of free speech should be curtailed only when there exists a genuine threat of "clear and present danger" has not been generally followed. Indeed evidence is readily obtainable that will show that these laws have not always been administered in accordance with immutable and immaculate precepts of justice but frequently in response to the climate of local opinion, the prejudices of the era or of the judge and the dictates of class bias or interest.

Experience with these laws, therefore, furnishes a warning to the perplexed citizen to-day. It suggests that Justice Holmes may have understood the safest means of procedure when he wrote in the Abrams case:

> But when men have realized that time has upset many fighting faiths, they may come to believe that the ultimate good desired is better reached by free trade in ideas—that the best test of truth is the power of the thought to get itself accepted in the competition of the market—

The Bill of Rights is beset by daily invasions—a Negro is denied his right to serve on a jury; a permit is denied a legitimate organization to assemble in a public hall on some trumped-up pretext; a pamphlet is barred from the public on the grounds that a city ordinance against littering the streets is violated; motion pictures are censored. Endlessly varied are the assaults on civil liberties.

Running through this protracted struggle, however, one basic conflict of rights accounts for more invasions of the Bill of Rights than, perhaps, any other. It is the right of property and the right of labor to economic independence. The core of that struggle has often resided at the point where labor costs have threatened profits. Property, having been better organized and more powerful, has possessed a decided advantage, at least, until very recently. What labor deemed to be its right to organize had been successfully fought by resort to the Common Law against conspiracies. Free speaking on the picket line has been constantly limited by injunctions and martial law. Public halls have been and are still being mysteriously closed to the union organizer.

But the last five years have witnessed a tangible balancing of labor's power in this central struggle. Martial law is not so prevalent; the Norris-La Guardia Act has curbed the issuance of injunctions against labor. No criminal syndicalism laws have been passed in any state during the last three or four years—several have been repealed.

Most important of all, perhaps, is the Wagner Labor Act. This measure has tended to collectivize labor as business has long been collectivized. Labor and capital to-day confront each other as highly organized groups. The struggle, wherein it still continues, is being fought on a different plane and with new tools. Thus the threat to civil liberties may now appear in different forms.

For clarity's sake and at the risk of oversimplification we might identify the chief threats to civil liberties to-day as:

1. Propaganda—the clever and organized effort of some reactionary elements to stigmatize all liberal and reform efforts as Red.

2. Middle-class "law and order" and vigilante movements which reflect both propaganda and the excesses of labor itself.

3. Intensification of the class struggle, in which labor sees the threat of Fascism and capital sees the threat of confiscation of property in accordance with the Communist formula.

If it is true, as the facts seem to indicate, that civil liberties are trampled, mainly in the clash of economic interests, then the solution is obviously one of economics, not one of repressive legislation. The essential economic adjustments to mitigate this clash of contending rights certainly represent a matter for the educator and idea-man. If this line of reasoning is right, then the commanding, overweening need of the moment is to keep open the media of communication—the radio, the press, and the schools.

For this reason it is important to leave the educator untrammelled by "gag" laws and petty repressions, which many states have adopted. For this reason bills that would restrict the spread of ideas on the radio, because of fear of racial and religious agitation, are dangerous. If the United States is in for a battle of propaganda, its safety lies in keeping its educative and communicative lines free to carry information and counter-propaganda. If the public in a panic is tricked into restricting these media, it may discover it has clamped its hand across the mouth of truth itself.

In the meantime as we have indicated there is heartening evidence of an increased and a better balanced vigilance in the protection of civil liberties. The La Follette Committee with its disclosures of strikebreaking, abuses by company guards and "law and order" groups is indicative of growing respect for the Bill of Rights, particularly those of the more humble citizens.

The new Civil Liberties Unit in the Criminal Division of the Department of Justice is another indication of growing watchfulness over civil liberties. Youthful but seasoned Henry Schweinhaut is in charge of this new agency, which reflects mounting pleas for federal action against local repressions.

Daily the petitions for federal aid pour into the Department of Justice. It may be a protest from New Orleans that labor organizers are being interfered with—or one from New York City that WPA workers are being finger-printed—or one from Tennessee that the Ku Klux Klan is riding again —or one from the Imperial Valley in California that the Associated Farmers are harassing union men—or one from Kansas City that there is evidence of election frauds. Five hundred such protests in one month mean that the new unit needs more lawyers and faster legal highways to centers of repression.

The Department of Justice may enter local jurisdictions only when a federal statute has been violated or when there exists some other legal basis for federal intervention. Mr. Schweinhaut was in Harlan County last summer helping prosecute a historic case. In this instance the Federal Government had been obliged to join a new statute, the Wagner Labor Law, and an old section of the criminal code, in order to proceed against some 30 coal companies on a charge of conspiracy to deprive labor of its rights. Section 51 of the code is a museum piece, drafted during the Reconstruction Period to protect Negroes in their newly acquired rights. The new unit is thus impeded by old tools and would profit by a Supreme Court decision that would give the Government a clearer, more direct, avenue by which to intervene in cases of local violations of the Bill of Rights.

The philosophy of civil liberties holds that the individual possesses certain inalienable rights beyond the arbitrary and capricious interference of the state or of private individuals or groups. The United States Constitution is an imperfect guarantee of these rights, since it expressly limits only the national Congress from interference with the civil liberties of the individual. Interferences from the 48 states, colonial governments, and from other persons and groups is not yet unequivocally outlawed by the Constitution. While state constitutions and the courts have supplied the individual with substantial protection, the American citizen to-day possesses no absolute and clear guarantee of his civil "liberty" as freedom of speech.

It would be a fairly simple matter, however, to amend the Constitution so that the individual was protected against the suppressive acts of the 48 states. The Fourteenth Amendment provides that no state shall deprive any person of life, liberty, and property without due process of law. The United States Supreme Court has already interpreted "liberty" to mean free speech. If the Fourteenth Amendment were now amplified by reading in the definition of "liberty" as freedom of speech, of the press and of assembly, the civil liberties of the individual would finally not be secured against state interferences. There would still remain the suppressions practiced upon the individual by other persons or private groups, but these may be curbed in some measure by federal laws against strikebreakers, industrial espionage and company police, as well as by the Wagner Labor Law and the Norris-La Guardia Anti-Injunction law.

These circumstances indicate in some degree the legal and constitutional hiatuses that have vexed and narrowed the channels of federal action. But the new unit in the Department of Justice is determined to examine every plea to see if anywhere there exists the basis for federal intervention. Thus there is a new instrument and a new disposition to rally the Federal Government behind the Bill of Rights.

While the Federal Government has stepped in to help balance the status of civil liberties as between labor and capital, there is, of course, potential danger in this very extension of central government. There is consequently need for vigilance lest Government in redressing the balance may prove careless of the rights of property and contract.

While there is probably far more danger in repressive laws than there is in free speech, free press and free assembly, there are steps that society may sensibly take as means of protecting itself against subversive elements. Federal legislation forbidding private military forces and private military training is feasible since it follows the general rule which limits all civil liberties when used for violence or preparation for violence. Carefully qualified laws requiring that sources of propaganda be revealed are also tenable. Beyond such laws, society runs the risk of establishing precedents that can be employed to stifle discussion and therefore democratic change and progress. In every nation where democracy has collapsed, repressive laws have been the forerunner.

Laws against incitement to violence are not perhaps in themselves repressive, but their application has generally proved to be. Thus there is need for legislatures to repeal or redraft these laws, guarding against their abuse. There is an accompanying need for courts to enforce these laws only against a proved incitement to violence or against utterance that constitutes a "clear and present danger."

The final destiny of human liberties is probably in the hands of the social and economic groups themselves. So long as labor permits itself to make unreasonable and violent demands upon the property group, it will provide an excuse for the invasion of the workers' rights. So long as the property classes are greedy for excessive profits and resist labor's need for economic independence, just so long will labor be provoked to invade the rights of property.

There is also need for sincerity and tolerance in the application of the Bill of Rights. To-day each group is swift to wrap itself in this document and cry that its own rights are assailed, while often failing to defend similar rights claimed by other groups. Thus the Communists insist upon their rights to speak, write, and assemble freely. Yet when the German-American Bund assembled in Madison Square Garden to exercise such rights, the Communists behaved so threateningly that 1,400 New York policemen were needed to guard the Bund. The American Liberty League marshalled wealth and influence to defend property rights but neglected to defend the rights of humbler men. Labor unions defend their rights to picket and organize, but in assailing the professional strikebreaker, are less quick to assail the "goon" and the thug in the racketeering union. Businessmen have shuddered over the "bureaucratic tyrannies" of the Minton and Black committees but have weathered quite placidly the threats to labor's rights in arbitrary injunctions and martial law.

When men concede the other man's right, vigilance will no longer be the exacting price of liberty. Meanwhile nothing would go further to diminish infractions of the Bill of Rights than for the class struggle to be mitigated by a series of compromises that would assure each group that it may safely permit the other to talk, write, and assemble to its heart's content.

No. 24

HOW FREE IS OUR PRESS? [1]

by William Allen White

TO-DAY it is not considered at all significant that publishing a newspaper is a business, a legitimate business, which in certain of its higher realms may be reasonably called big business. But I came into the newspaper business fifty years ago and more, when journalism was passing out of its status as a trade and becoming a profession. As a profession it lasted for a generation or two. And in that period what once ideally might have been called a noble calling was transformed into a fairly safe 6 per cent investment.

Before the Civil War, back to Benjamin Franklin's time, an editor was generally an emeritus printer. The rules and traditions of his trade guided him, and the mechanical end of his day's work often interested the editor quite as much as his editorial policies. Which was natural enough. For

---

[1] William Allen White, "How Free is Our Press?" *The Nation* (June 18, 1938), Vol. 146, pp. 693-695. Reprinted by permission of *The Nation*.

often his editorial policy was a nice compromise between blackmail and begging. In my day, that is to say, beginning with the middle 1880's, the newspaper business began to merge into what was called in highfaluting terms "journalism." We reporters and editors fifty years ago scorned the term. But it prevailed over us. Journalism became a profession, not exactly one of the learned professions but a profession of sorts. It was still recruited, even at the turn of the century, largely from the composing-room of the printing office. Horace Greeley's festive phrase for college graduates—"other longhorn critters"—still echoed in the American newspaper offices in McKinley's day. Fifty years ago a fast-talking printer could borrow money from his friends or from a political banker and could establish a newspaper in a town for a sum that might be roughly estimated as a dollar for each five of the town's population. The country editor in a town of anywhere from a thousand to fifty thousand made about as much money as the local lawyer or doctor or grocer, not so much as the banker or the merchant prince of the drygoods store, and rather more but not much more than the preacher. The editor of McKinley's time belonged to the ruling class and took off his hat only to the town banker or maybe the men who owned the street cars and the waterworks. But he was a free man, this American editor of the last quarter of the old century. And being a free man, barring the tentacles of his mortgage, he ran a free press, restricted only by his courage, his honesty, and his intelligence. No outside influence restrained his powers.

With the turn of the century something new appeared in the country newspaper business. It was the linotype, the mechanical typesetter, and along with it came the rotary press, both expensive contraptions and both made necessary by expanding business which came to the editor's door. Common schools were increasing his subscription lists, and merchants found that by advertising they could create wants where no wants normally existed. So under the impulse of more subscribers and bigger and better advertisers, slowly in the first two decades of this century the costs of producing a newspaper began to rise. No longer could a man go to a county seat with $1,500 in cash and a good line of talk and buy or start a newspaper. When the armistice of the World War was signed, the business formula of the mechanical requirements of a country newspaper changed, and it required something like $10 for each head of population to buy the machinery, the typesetting machines, the press, and the stereotyping equipment, and to provide the working capital necessary to go into competition with the established newspaper in an American rural community, say a town of from one thousand to one hundred thousand population.

Obviously the young man whose father had breezed into town with a good line of talk and had persuaded the country banker to put up from $1,500 to $2,000 to start a newspaper could not get into the newspaper business himself as a proprietor in the machine age. And the old itinerant printer of Horace Greeley's day, who, according to the colloquialism of that ancient time, could start a newspaper with a shirttail full of type and a cheese press, had gone to join the troubadours, the mound builders, and the gay dancers in the Dionysian revels.

The trade which had become a profession turned into a business, and there it is to-day. And now an editor in a little country town all of whose inhabitants could be herded into a good-sized skyscraper comes before you as a small business man with a pay roll of $1,200 a week. When I bought the *Emporia Gazette* the pay roll was $45 a week, and twenty years before that the pay roll of the country newspaper in my town was less than $25 a week. Behold a miracle of the machine age.

In the next ten years the press may change again—certainly in its material aspect. Rotary presses, linotypes, stereotyping machinery may join the crossbow, the neckyoke, and the portcullis upon the ashheap of forgotten gadgets. But the merchandising of the news for a long while to come will be affected as it is now with a strong property interest. It will require machinery to assemble the news. It will require capital to distribute the news. And capital to-day or to-morrow always has a lively sense of its own advantage. Capital is instinctively, for all the noble intentions of us capitalists, class conscious. It is that class consciousness which is discrediting the press of the world to-day, particularly the press of the English-speaking democracies. Any newspaper in any American town represents a considerable lot of capital for the size of the town. The owners of newspaper investments, whether they be bankers, stockholders of a corporation, or individuals, feel a rather keen sense of financial responsibility, and they pass their anxiety along to newspaper operatives whether these operatives be superintendents known as managing editors, foremen known as city editors, or mere wage-earners known as editorial writers, copy-desk men, reporters, or what not. The sense of property goes thrilling down the line. It produces a slant and a bias that in time becomes—unconsciously and probably in all honesty—a prejudice against any man or any thing or any cause that seriously affects the right, title, or interest of all other capital, however invested. It is not the advertising department that controls the news. Newspapermen may lean over backward in their upright attitude toward the obviously unfair demands of advertisers and the moronic prejudices of subscribers, and still may be poor miserable sinners when they discuss problems affecting the stability of institutions that are founded entirely upon the economic status quo.

We editors realize that we have lost caste with the American people. We are on the bad books of public esteem, not heavily in the red but teetering back and forth between the right and the wrong side of the ledger. Labor as a class distrusts us. It wouldn't distrust us entirely without reason. The labor press sneers at us—that is to say, those class-conscious newspapers that are circulated entirely in what is known as labor circles. But one discounts frankly labeled class papers. It is a shame that the public also has to discount certain areas of the plug-hat section of the newspaper gallery, which is supposed to be impartial, high-minded, absolutely dependable. One should quickly qualify this statement. It is not true of *all* papers or of any paper at all times. Moreover, in the last three years great improvement has been made by the metropolitan press as a whole. Trained reporters who know the implications of labor's struggle are now used by certain great newspapers to get at the exact truth, but reporters trained to handle labor struggles are few, and the struggles are many. And much room remains for improvement in the handling of labor news by the American press.

The deficiencies of American journals in treating the news of what we might as well frankly if regretfully call the class struggle in this country are found largely in unconscious political attitudes. It is so easy to "policy" the news. Indeed, it is so hard not to policy the news when the news is affected with a vital bread-and-butter interest to the capitalist who controls a newspaper, great or small. And strangely and sadly enough, capital is so fluid that a threat to the safety of any investment seems to be a threat to all investments. Therefore newspapers which represent sizable investments are tempted to shy off and shiver when in Congress, in the legislature, or in the City Hall a man or a group threatens an investment in any kind of patent medicine, in any kind of holding company, in any kind of misbranded food, in any kind of railroad security, in any kind of banking affiliate, good or bad. It is no longer the advertiser who puts on the pressure. It is not even the boss back of the pay roll who begins to quake. It is the whole middle and upper structure of society. Sooner or later the truth about any social abuse is gladly received by the middle class and by those who own and control newspaper investments. But off the bat, the newspapers representing the innate conservatism of property interests which crystallize middle-class psychology are sometimes unfair in their treatment of men or movements that threaten to disturb property in any form.

Which is only another way of saying that every new day produces its own peculiar threats to liberty. A decade or so ago it seemed likely that the direct pressure of large advertisers, as for instance department stores, might affect the press with a bias. Probably that danger is decreasing. The newspaper publisher stands the economic equal of his largest advertiser, and to-day the average publisher is wise enough to know that in the newspaper business it pays to be honest. But to-day we are faced with a new menace to the freedom of the press, a menace in this country vastly more acute than the menace from government. And this menace may come through the pressure not of one group of advertisers but of a wide sector of newspaper advertisers. Newspaper advertising is now placed partly, if not largely, through nation-wide newspaper advertising agencies. Some of these agencies have lately become advisers of great industrial corporations, which also advertise. These advertising agencies undertake to protect their clients from what the clients and agents may regard as real dangers from inimical social, political, or industrial influences. As advisers the advertising agencies may exercise unbelievably powerful pressure upon newspapers. There is grave danger that in the coming decade, as social, industrial, and economic problems become more and more acute, this capacity for organized control of newspaper opinion by the political advisers of national advertisers may constitute a major threat to a free press.

And while we are on the subject of a free press this black mark must be put down against editorial judgment in general: it rises in the circulation department—a low subconscious lust to acquire circulation and hold it in the moron latitudes of the population. It affects all editors more or less. I am guilty of this sin for all my noble protestations. And because I am guilty I realize that the circulation department of a newspaper is as dangerous as the advertising department in menacing the ultimate freedom of the press. It is not that we play up sex crime like Bernarr Macfadden or amplify the details of murder. Our sin lies deeper than that: we do not use the same talents to expand and elaborate good news that we almost instinctively use in writing and displaying human weaknesses and depravity. For instance, I had to find the news of the Scandinavian Neutrality Pact on the seventh page of my favorite newspaper, which is commonly accounted a decent newspaper. As far as I know, it was not in the press report that came to the Missouri valley. If it came here, the *Gazette's* telegraph editor, who is trained to look after such things and play them up, missed it. Yet the news that Sweden, Norway, Iceland, Denmark, and Finland had signed a declaration pledging their forces to a common neutrality policy in the event of war between other states was worth more than any rape in the country that day, worth more than the story of any lovelorn lady who shot her man to death, worth more than the news of capers cut by any Hollywood star or Long Island socialite. It is because we overlook opportunities like this that the people have a keen and accurate sense that much of editorial anxiety about the freedom of the press rises out of editorial greed.

The problem of the American newspaper to-day is to open its channels of cordial reception to new social ideals and to insure fair treatment for any reform or any reformer who is obviously honest, reasonably intelligent, and backed by any considerable minority of the public. How can this be done? How can the newspapers become open-minded? I don't know. They might try to hire as doorkeepers in the house of the Lord, at copy desks and in editorial chairs, men who are free to make decisions about newspaper copy, guided by their own instincts, following their own hunches, and not controlled by an itch to move to the next higher desk by pleasing his High Potency who sits in the mahogany-paneled room in front of the front of the front office. If owners would encourage a little chronic arthritis of the knee in the lower realms of reporting and copyreading we might come out from the clouds of suspicion that envelop our noble profession at the moment. But I suppose in the end newspapers cannot be free, absolutely free in the highest and best sense, until the whole social and economic structure of American life is open to the free interplay of democratic processes.

Chapter VIII

THE ALIEN—A POTENTIAL CITIZEN

[THE population of every country is made up of citizens and aliens. The United States is no exception, and the problem of the alien, as a result of recent events in Europe, is being brought home to us in a way we have never before experienced. Through most of our history we have been a young and growing nation with an expanding economy. As a result we have, until recent years, sought to encourage immigration. Our expanding industrial machine has been in need of cheap labor. In more recent years, however, as we have found this need declining, and as European events have made us aware of the dangers of international espionage, we have seen the alien in a different light. We have restricted immigration and have begun a process of discriminating against the alien in a way no one would have prophesied only a generation ago.

While no one holds that we may not act to protect ourselves against the enemies of democracy, it is essential that we examine the position of alien and citizen in a sensible and thoughtful way. Most of our aliens—and we have fewer than five million—are loyal to this country and believe firmly in the democratic way of life.

While it may be argued that they should have become citizens, we have done very little to encourage them and we have been negligent in not making the process of acquiring citizenship more meaningful. We should, therefore, devote careful consideration to the alien problem. We must not make those who are loyal to our way of life embittered, we must encourage these people to become active citizens and participate in making our democratic institutions more effective. We must make the process of acquiring citizenship more meaningful. We must, in short, handle the alien problem in accordance with our democratic way of life. And there is no better way to begin than by examining the problem in a deliberate and thoughtful manner.]

No. 25

THE ALIEN MYTH [1]

by Lucille B. Milner and David Dempsey

THE tragic events in Europe and the disclosure of fifth-column activities in those countries which have gone down before the German machine have made Americans more keenly aware than ever of the dangers of international espionage. Europe has been honeycombed with agents of the Third Reich and, though the United States is three thousand miles away, fifth columnists are at work in this country also. It is nonsense to hold that Democracy may not act to protect itself against these enemies of Democracy. In the light of the experience abroad, no government, unless it is moribund, will let itself be overthrown by Nazi subverters within its borders. Yet in defending itself Democracy must not give up those democratic institutions which alone assure its survival.

There is no mistaking the fact that the United States has learned from the events in Europe. We are feverishly preparing to protect ourselves from within as well as from without. Our defense program is moving at almost panic speed. Industry has cleared its decks for aggressive action, and we are attempting to readjust our economy to a world of Nazi economic control. The Government has strengthened its forces and extended its work to guard against espionage and sabotage.

The problem for us is how to protect Democracy from internal attacks through the framework of democratic processes. Hysteria, vigilante groups, and self-appointed spy-hunters have no place in national defense. Widespread alien discrimination, outlawing minority political parties, hysterical and often unconstitutional anti-alien edicts of governors and mayors, compulsory oaths of allegiance and flag salute will not ferret out spies. On the contrary, such action will confuse the innocent with the guilty and hamper the work of government agencies. We have adequate machinery, both legal and administrative, for dealing with spies and saboteurs. If the Department of Justice really means business its recently organized Neutrality Unit, created for the express purpose of enforcing federal laws against espionage and sabotage, can keep the operations of foreign agents in this country well under control, without broadside attacks against whole classes of the population.

[1] Lucille B. Milner and David Dempsey, "The Alien Myth," *Harper's Magazine* (September, 1940), Vol. 181, pp. 374-379. Reprinted by permission of *Harper's Magazine* and the authors.

It has been taken for granted that the first step against the enemies of
Democracy must be directed to the non-citizen. He is generally looked
upon as the "termite" in our structure. Every home with a foreign-born
head is believed to be the nucleus of a fifth column, and a hue and cry
has been raised against the alien which is mounting to proportions unheard
of since the First World War. In reality, our widespread preoccupation
with the "alien menace" is diverting America's attention, particularly of
her lawmakers, from the genuine fifth-column possibilities of native groups
—the Christian Front, Silver Shirts, Ku Klux Klan, and the German-American Bund—all of which have taken precautions against discrimination by
closing their ranks to aliens.

The alien has long been deemed guilty of many of our shortcomings.
Constituting slightly more than two per cent of the population, he has been
the victim of an attack by those who would deport him, register him, finger-
print him, impound him, and discriminate against him economically. He
has, in fact, become our economic scapegoat. Fantastic as it appears as a
solution to what ails America, it has nevertheless been advocated for many
years, in Congress and out, that there would be plenty of work for good
Americans if all aliens could be deported. He has been held responsible
for a disproportionate share of our unemployment, crime, and radicalism.
In addition, he has been accused of threatening the American standard of
living, lowering the cultural level of the country, and menacing the American way of life.

To meet this "problem" patriots, professional and legislative, have called
for stringent curbs on alien activities. More than seventy bills discriminating in some way against the alien have been introduced in both houses
of the 76th Congress (1939-40). Many of these are dangerous not only
to the civil rights of minorities but to the rights of all Americans, and if
passed would be nothing short of a travesty on the "equal rights" clause
of the Constitution. One of these measures has already become law. In
order to catch the small group of undesirable aliens, it requires *all* aliens,
no matter how good their record or how long their residence in this country, to be fingerprinted and to register and report to the authorities at regular periods. Certain classes of non-citizens subject to deportation but without a country to accept them would, under the provisions of another bill,
be interned indefinitely in concentration camps. For the first time in American history we should imprison men without trial.

If, up to the present time, the efforts of Congress have been somewhat
less successful than has been hoped for by the alien-hater, he is undoubtedly
heartened by his less spectacular accomplishments along the lines of economic discrimination. Both the Federal and State governments have used

their powers to keep the alien from getting an even break with his brother citizen. Public and private jobs, relief and the benefits of social legislation, are more and more being closed to the non-citizen. Aliens are barred from employment on WPA, even though they have taken out their first papers but have not yet completed the five-year process of becoming citizens. The number of aliens dropped by the government in 1939 when this provision went into effect was 30,000, out of the 3,000,000 persons then on WPA. A California study indicated that 70 per cent of the membership of the families headed by aliens are American citizens. With the cutting out of 120,000 aliens employed on certain non-relief government projects, 160,000 American citizens, dependent upon the employment of the alien head of the family, were denied benefits.

The present old-age pension system of most States denies benefits to aliens. Blind pensions are denied to aliens in most States, although the disability may have occurred in the course of their occupation in this country. Much of this legislation, which demonstrates our change in policy, was a product of the fear set up by the depression, although in this period immigration was practically at a standstill.

The refugee influx has accelerated this trend toward the regulation of alien activities. This is particularly true of the professions but by no means confined to them. Despite the fact that no more than 2,500 refugee physicians have entered this country since July 1, 1934, twenty-eight States require full citizenship as a prerequisite to the practice of medicine and twenty-six categorically refuse to examine graduates of foreign medical schools. The attitude behind much of this legislation is expressed in the language of one bill which set forth, in justification of its purpose, that "an alien physician is incapable of fulfilling social and spiritual obligations toward the community." As further defense it is stated that the profession is over-crowded. The ratio of physicians to the population, however, is declining. In 1886 there was one doctor to every 662 inhabitants; in 1934 the ratio had dropped to one for every 784 persons. It is difficult to see where citizenship and medical competency bear any relationship.

The situation is no better for the other professions. Eleven States require full citizenship for optometrists and seven others require graduation from an American school. Dentists must be citizens in order to practice in seven States and in ten others they must have graduated from an American school. South Dakota and Wyoming demand that an engineer be a citizen and seven States require first papers. Eighteen States make citizenship a requirement for the licensing of an accountant and fifteen States impose the same legislation on pharmacy. The list is constantly growing, and the scope is widening to include less professional types of employ-ment.

Bus drivers, veterinarians, undertakers, peddlers, auctioneers, pool room operators, barbers, and liquor dealers must be citizens in various States, under protection of court decisions. Untested legislation applies to real estate brokers, salesmen, employment agents, private detectives, bankers, insurance agents, pawnbrokers, plumbers, and mine foremen. A Seattle, Washington, ordinance was upheld providing that only citizens could col-lect garbage. In many States aliens are not allowed to own land. In Pennsylvania an alien may not kill game. In Oregon he may not engage in commercial fishing. Seven States directly prohibit aliens from obtaining hunting and fishing licenses and five prohibit them from carrying firearms. In short, the alien is systematically being excluded not only from the pro-fessions but from a wide variety of ordinary businesses.

What the States are doing now by law, private business has to a great extent been doing all along. As far back as 1928-29, with unemployment at a minimum, industry denied work to aliens in three out of every five cases and labor unions refused to accept aliens in four out of every five memberships. Since then this ratio has grown. It is estimated to-day that eight to nine out of every ten jobs are closed to aliens in this country. Musicians, electricians, carpenters, and bricklayers are among those who require citizenship for membership in their unions. The American Federa-tion of Labor has in many cases pursued this policy further by having un-written agreements with employers not to employ aliens.

The roots of this anti-alien attitude go back to the period of hysteria and red-baiting after the World War. At that time the alien symbolized the radical. Thanks to our patriotic societies he has never lost this stigma. The old association of aliens as radicals has persisted; the new association of aliens as criminals, persons uninterested in their community welfare, and pre-emptors of jobs in a nation of jobless, has fortified the anti-alien feel-ing.

The situation to-day is in many ways comparable to that which existed immediately following the First World War. The alien, being a conspicuous and on the whole defenseless minority, became an object of hate. The forces of fear and repression set in motion in 1917 have been revived, more systematically and in the last analysis more dangerously. Alien-baiting is no longer a franchise of irresponsible public officials or of the swivel-chair patriot or night rider. The halls of Congress, business—big and little— public opinion, labor unions all have "cracked down" on the alien. He has become the common carrier of the economic, social, and cultural ailments of the country—the "typhoid Mary" of modern America.

A survey of the restrictions placed on the non-citizen in the United States leads one to question whether some basis exists for the belief that the alien threatens the security of our institutions and economy. The fact is that in periods of "security" we have bothered hardly at all about the alien; only in periods of crisis and uncertainty such as war and depression have we looked about for a scapegoat and made the aliens a class apart.

To look upon the alien as pariahs, moral untouchables, and criminals intent on destroying and subverting our government is to make fiction out of whole cloth. It is a product not of fact but of prejudice created by the increased tension of a contracting economy and a war-maddened world. That the alien immigrant played a great part in the building of our country is denied by no one; that he is now intent on tearing it down is assumed by all too many, most of whom should know better. There is not one documented piece of evidence to show that he is guilty as a class of the things of which he is being accused. On the contrary, on almost all these charges—crime, civic responsibility, standard of living, literacy, self-support —he has a better record than his native and naturalized brother American.

In the one hundred years preceding the First World War we invited thirty-seven million immigrants to this country. Indeed they were urged, exhorted, and all but dragooned into coming by labor agencies during the great years of expansion. We needed them. We were willing to allow them their political and religious freedom in return for their manpower. We taught them to read and write English, to adapt themselves to American customs. We gave them the protection of our laws and the right to engage in almost any business and we levied taxes against them. At one time we even allowed them to vote.

Under our Constitution the alien was entitled to those rights which appertain to all men. A clause in the Fourteenth Amendment established the alien inhabitant in the eyes of the law as an equal of the native and naturalized citizen: ". . . nor shall any state deprive any person of life, liberty, or property without due process of law, nor deny to any person within its jurisdiction the equal protection of the laws." *Any person,* the courts pointed out, meant just what is said—the foreigner as well as the native.

Increased interest in the acquisition of citizenship, and the high death rate that is inevitable in a population group that is old are factors testifying that the "problem" has been taking care of itself. According to the 1930 census there were 6,234,613 foreign-born persons in the United States who were not naturalized. By July, 1938, this number had dropped to 3,838,928 and of this total at least 700,000 had taken out their first papers. During the nine fiscal years between July 1, 1930, and July 1, 1939, the excess of immigrants over emigrants was only 19,398. During the same period an actuarial calculation of the number of deaths which must have occurred among the unnaturalized amounts to 901,334. Furthermore, an estimated 237,100 alien children derived citizenship from the naturalization of their parents.

What are the facts in regard to the number of aliens illegally in this country? Are there, as some claim, anywhere from 3,500,000 to 10,000,000? The Commissioner of Immigration, whose business it is to know, describes these figures as "fantastic exaggerations." The best available estimates, he reports, are that the number of aliens who have entered illegally and are now subject to deportation is less than 100,000. The total number who either entered illegally or who cannot after the lapse of years prove their legal entry is less than 400,000.

Are aliens, by and large, "radicals"? Under our laws an alien who is proved a member of the Communist Party at the time of his arrest is subject to deportation. Between 1907 and 1939 the Commissioner General of Immigration reported, exactly 1,230 aliens were deported as "anarchists and kindred classes." During this same period 14,079,272 aliens immigrated to this country. At one time—1910—we had 18,000,000 unnaturalized foreigners living in the United States. The number has never fallen below three and a half million. Yet an average of only 40 aliens a year have been proved dangerous enough, from the standpoint of political opinion, to deport.

Are aliens criminals and racketeers? The Wickersham report on "Crime and the Foreign Born" in 1931 concluded that in crimes for personal gain the native white rate rises conspicuously higher than that of the foreign-born. The records of the Department of Justice lead to the same conclusions. FBI figures for years past reveal that criminality among aliens is decidedly lower than among native-born whites. The most recent figures, those for 1939, indicate that while 607 citizens out of every 100,000 have been arrested and fingerprinted, only 203 non-citizens had undergone the same experience. In 1938 the ratio for the citizen was 571 and 209 for the alien. Whereas, in a year's time crime among the native-born had gone up by 36 points, it had dropped among aliens by 6 points. For only one offense did the alien top the native-born in 1938, namely, "buying, receiving, or possessing stolen property," and then only by one-tenth of one per cent. *In 1939 the criminality of aliens was lower than the citizens in all offenses including robbery, murder, sex offenses, and fraud.*

FBI statistics show further that the high crime rates are chiefly in the South where foreign-born and their children constitute a very small proportion of the population. Tennessee, Georgia, and North Carolina rank among those States having the highest rates for such crimes as murder and manslaughter, robbery and aggravated assault. Foreign stock in these States constitute less than 2 per cent of the population.

Does the alien lower the American standard of living? This is perhaps the oldest and most consistent anti-alien argument. The facts point to the opposite conclusion. Where the immigrant has settled in the largest numbers the standard of living, as measured by *per capita* income, is highest. The ten States with the highest proportion of foreign-born in their population have more than twice the per capita annual income of the ten States with the lowest proportion of foreign-born. One may reasonably argue of course that the States with high per capita incomes have prospered for reasons quite unrelated to the presence in them of the foreign-born; nevertheless the fact that the presence of the foreign-born has not materially altered their status is significant.

Similar conclusions are reached in regard to the popularly held idea that aliens and immigrant stock tend to hold down the cultural level of the community. Measured by illiteracy, the ten high-immigration States have almost three times as high a level as the ten low-immigration States, the percentage of illiteracy in the former being 3.5 as compared with 9.2 in the latter. Likewise with other indices of cultural interest—the newspaper and the radio. Each of our ten high-immigration States shows a net paid daily circulation of more than 250 per 1,000 population, while each of the ten low-immigration States shows a net paid daily circulation of less than 250 per 1,000, and all but two of these States range below 150 per 1,000. Although radio ownership may not be a test of high cultural achievement, it nevertheless implies a certain interest in music, entertainment, and contemporary affairs. In the States where the foreign-born are most thickly settled an average of 52.4 radios per 100 families is reported. Where the foreigner is least in evidence this average is 12.6.

Many of the anti-alien laws have been passed on the theory that the alien does not have as great an interest in the welfare of his community as the citizen. But if home ownership be taken as a criterion of responsibility and community interest the result is equally challenging: 51.8 per cent of the foreign-born owned their homes in 1937, as against 48.9 per cent for the native American.

Is the alien a burden on the relief rolls? Despite the fact that the alien has contributed his share to public relief funds through payment of taxes, the alien is discriminated against in public relief and employment. State and Federal laws bar him from scores of professions and occupations; he cannot get on WPA, yet the ratio of aliens on relief is less proportionately than that of citizens. Nearly half the alien population is over fifty years of age, but less than 3 per cent of all cases receiving relief in 1938 were non-citizens. Thus in matters of crime, housing, literacy, civic responsibility, self-support, and cultural standing, the record of the alien is not only defensible but enviable.

What, under the circumstances, can the alien do? The answer to this, by the average man, is that he should become naturalized. And this, precisely, is what he is doing—in greater numbers than the present naturalization service is prepared to handle. If anything, the present rate of alien naturalization is unhealthy. Coerced or forced naturalization has never been a policy of the government. The spirit of American citizenship rather than the form is what is desired. The alien who is dragooned into citizenship by legal and economic discrimination and now by the war threat can hardly be expected to cherish his newly acquired status as the prize that we have taught him to believe it is.

Yet this is what is happening. More aliens were naturalized in the year ending June 30, 1939, than in any other year for which statistics are available, with the exception of 1919 and the three years 1927-29. For every immigrant alien admitted in this country in 1939, 2⅛ aliens already here became citizens. Applications for first papers were taken out by an additional 294,203. The number would undoubtedly have been larger if the naturalization service had been equipped to handle applications more expeditiously. Few persons are aware of the obstacles to citizenship. Expense is one of them. Many aliens, like many citizens, have a marginal standard of living. The cost of acquiring citizenship, including government fees, expense of witnesses, and fares averages from $20 to $40 and may reach $100.

A large proportion, 43.7 per cent, of the non-citizens are more than fifty years old and have spent most of their lives here. Many entering before the days of the literacy test, too busy in the interim to become educated, still cannot pass the test for citizenship. Another large group consists of minors who cannot become citizens until they are twenty-one years of age. Hundreds more are excluded from citizenship because of race. Pacifists who refuse to take the oath of arms are barred. (Recently a seventy-two-year-old woman was denied citizenship because she refused to swear to bear arms.) Exclusion for reasons of political opinion is being extended. When proposals are made to simplify the naturalization process by reducing fees, eliminating red tape, and discrimination on the grounds of race, nationality, and political or pacifist opinion, Congress has brushed them aside as not worthy of consideration.

In hundreds of thousands of cases it is not the fault of the alien that he is not a citizen. In some districts citizenship papers are denied him because he is on relief; in others he is denied relief and so cannot pay for

citizenship papers. There is no apparent limit to this legal and social discrimination. Such prejudice and discrimination would seem to make a solution impossible; the alien must ever remain an alien. He is caught between two fires. The more his rights are denied, the more his protest is
silenced; the more his protest is silenced, the more are his rights denied.

No. 26

GOOD BUSINESS [1]

by Dorothy Canfield

ONE morning last month I made the rounds of a number of refugee
committees in New York City. I had wanted to see for myself who
these émigrés were of whom I had heard so much. In each waiting room
where they were sitting in dignified suspense I discovered the same thing.
These men and women look so exactly like any of us anywhere, so like the
people I had just left in the lobby of my hotel that it was with astonishment I noticed the signs on the walls were in a foreign language. Immeasurably different from the Europeans who used to wait on Ellis Island
benches for the end of immigration formalities, shawls and skull caps on
their heads, big bundles of household goods tied up in bedding by their
sides.

A hard-headed and successful business man of my acquaintance was
asked in my hearing the other day what he thought about letting in refugees
now dashing themselves against the almost closed doors of our immigration
rules. I winced, thinking I knew what, as a "practical man," he would
answer. For he is a very practical man; one of those who "do not believe
in charity." But I was wrong. This was what as a practical man—and
with some heat at what he evidently considered the utter foolishness of the
question—he did answer:

Let them in! Of course! Why should we be such fools as to miss taking
advantage of this tremendous stroke of luck.

They have in their brains exactly the skill in industrial organization which
this country needs to develop its resources into prosperity for all. Far from
taking away from us any part of our national wealth, they will by their
trained intelligence and practiced experience greatly increase the sum total
of what is to be shared by all.

Europe has expensively trained them in fine schools, given them years

[1] Dorothy Canfield, "Good Business," *Survey Graphic* (February, 1939), Vol. 28, pp.
122-125, 166. Reprinted by permission of *Survey Graphic*.

of irreplaceably valuable practical experience, has at no expense to us brought them to a high degree of productive ability of exactly the kind we need. If we show the most ordinary good sense, we can reap a rich harvest which Europe has sown and cultivated for us.

In all the fields of human activity outside buying and selling and manufacturing, everybody (yes, even that great dumb shortsighted "everybody" who proverbially cannot see beyond his own nose) has been vividly aware of the obvious truth of this plain saying. Even he who runs at top speed as he reads can hardly pick up a daily tabloid without seeing yet another news item about a contribution of golden value made to science, medicine, education, the arts, human learning, by one of our new citizens, or citizens-to-be. Once in so often a chronicler tries to draw up a list of the great personalities in music, art, literature, research, medicine, whom the tornado of dictatorship has blown from their comely and useful life in Europe into the United States, and to set down the most brilliant of their services to the common good on this side of the Atlantic. But the list is always incomplete because almost every day brings a new name, a new unique contribution: one day it is Thomas Mann, the next day the doctor with a device which will make it infinitely more possible for all our doctors from now on to save their patients from the long slow deadly torture of cancer of the stomach; one day we hear that the adored Toscanini is to be one of us; the day after we learn of the presence in our midst of the group of famous German savants of the International Institute of Social Research, formerly of Frankfurt, who are now carrying on at Columbia University their searching, thorough attempts to integrate all that we know of the social sciences into an understanding of human society, an understanding which may save the human future. We are fairly swamped under the pouring-out of artistic and intellectual riches from this huge Horn of Plenty. We blink, we rub our eyes, we say feebly: "Aren't you talking about that fine University in Exile, made up of distinguished scholars? It doesn't seem possible that there is yet *another* group of brilliant European savants carrying on here!" We think of Chancellor Bruening, statesman and sage, and Professor Salvemini, fine flowering of European learning, at Harvard; and Borgese, brilliant, poetic, creative, at the University of Chicago. Reflecting that we just happen to know personally of them, and that there is hardly an institution of learning in our country which is not profiting by the backwash from the dirty doings in Europe, we really hold our heads in astonishment

Yes, this much we know of the treasure the émigrés are bringing us. Because its splendor is so great it cannot be hidden, this much is read in his country newspaper by the farmer or the small-town citizen or the city reader of the tabloids, whose father, perhaps in the Ku Klux Klan, was told to hate Catholics, Jews and Negroes; whose grandfather in the APA was told to hate Roman Catholics in general; whose great-grandfathers, in the 1840's, were incited to hate Irish Catholics in particular. The noble light of the great names in the arts and in the professions of these new citizens of our country shines out in radiance even into the far and dark corners of our big sprawling country. Such great names "are news" in the newspaper sense and so get continuous and favorable publicity.

But there are other dark corners that need lighting up, and by no means only in remote corners of the country. In our own cherished brains, yours and mine, superior people though we think ourselves, there are corners dark in ignorance, dusty with idiotic prejudice. And what we need to light them is practical good sense of which that business man gave his questioner a dose. We can see—yes, who cannot—what a doctor gives to our future, who brings a new saving help in a terrible disease of the stomach. We can see that in feeding and lodging and clothing such a man we are getting back from him infinitely—in the literal meaning of the word "infinitely" —more than we give. But we are still capable of saying and thinking, thick-witted and ignorant of the most obvious mechanisms of the society of our time: "But there aren't jobs enough to go 'round, now. If we let in these new people, they'll take the work away from good Americans. We better save our jobs for our own folks." You've heard that said in the last week, you know you have. Maybe you said it yourself. Even if you didn't, it's pretty certain that you did not leap, between laughter and exasperation, to refute the really idiotic economic fallacy so simple-mindedly stated. You did not say as you might have:

Carry that conception of economic life out to its logical conclusion, and it would be stated this way, wouldn't it? One man alone on this continent would be in fine shape because he would have everything there was for himself. But let one other man arrive and he would take away from the first man half of everything he had. Who is fool enough not to see the obvious fact that two men together could make themselves immeasurably more comfortable, richer and more secure than one man?

But rather than analogies and figures of speech what is needed to cure the shortsightedness of people who talk about the refugees "taking away jobs from our own people" is factual information about the kind of people the great majority of the refugees are, and what—already—they are doing for our industrialized country. That kind of information is not news, in the newspaper sense, and so does not get country-wide publicity. Indeed

it gets no publicity at all, except an occasional news item in a local newspaper, to the effect that:

> The old Hart and Warren building is to be reopened as a box factory
> under the management of Mr. Rudolph G. Busch, formerly of Germany.
> About sixty men will find employment in the business. It is hoped this
> number will soon be greater.

A transposition of course. The name is not Busch and the factory is not
going to make boxes—the terror of the German secret police is so great
among these new citizens of ours that they dread to have any news of
their doings get back to Germany, because it may mean more suffering and
torture for the old mother or the helpless grandfather still there.

But under a name which is not his, and with a business other than his
real one, it is safe to set down the chain of events which took Mr. Busch
from his large factory in an industrial suburb of Berlin to set the wheels
in motion in the little factory in the small town in northern Indiana. It is
so typical of a host of such stories that it can stand for all of their kind.
He and his wife and their children and two of the four grandparents were
pillars of the local Protestant Church in the Berlin suburb. Two of the
grandparents—Mr. Busch's father and mother—both now dead, had Jewish
blood. At almost the speed with which one scene in a movie dissolves into
another, to an accompaniment of horrifying indignities and brutalities, their
home, their business, their money, all their possessions were taken from
them. Mrs. Busch had a widowed sister living in Indiana, and this alone, enabled them to fight their way through all the thicket of red-tape difficulties
of getting papers to come to the United States. They landed, determined
whatever else happened not to be a burden to the Indiana sister. They had
the clothes on their backs and in their suitcases, and a very few dollars in
a lean purse. Everything else had been snatched away, even her grand-
mother's lace collar which Mrs. Busch had put into her handbag to take
along as sole link with their family past, even the gold medal given Mr.
Busch for his invention of an important manufacturing device.

No, not everything else. They brought some things of which not the
most rigorous and humiliating stripping and searching at the frontiers
could deprive them: the excellently thorough, specialized and experienced
knowledge in Mr. Busch's head of how to manufacture boxes (it wasn't
boxes, remember, but something else as commonly needed), the beautiful
skill in music at the end of Mrs. Busch's fingers, and the vigor, vitality
and courage of their personalities. Of these priceless treasures, fine fruit
of the civilization of the older Germany, the new Germany made a free gift
to America.

America was slow to appreciate this gift. Landed in New York the Busches lived through some dreary months of a kind of Hades of poverty, a fumbling search for work, snatching at whatever employment the hard-pressed refugee committees could find for them. Mrs. Busch got a job as scrubwoman, plunging her pianist's fingers deep into pails of soapsuds; the oldest daughter, a fourteen-year-old girl, got her food and lodging in return for taking care of a professor's little children. Mr. Busch got work on the night shift of a printing establishment. The sister, writing anxiously from Indiana, "Are you all right? Do let me know how you are getting on," chanced to mention among other general news in a letter the disused factory, the unemployed workers sadly kicking their heels in idleness, the wheels of the small town running down, running down.

Mr. Busch knows how to make boxes out of an inexpensive material by a process not yet brought to this country. One more spasm of collective effort on the part of the refugee committee, its financial advisers, Mr. Busch, the sister, the chamber of commerce of the Indiana town—and the little news item appears in a local newspaper. What it does not say is that the carefully trained Busch children, attending the local public schools, set an example of mannerliness, musical skill and earnest, impassioned eagerness to learn which makes them invaluable pacemakers, stimulating and stirring, such as that little inland school has never had. It does not set down that the Busches became pillars of the local Presbyterian Church. Nor does it mention—because it does not guess it—the way in which Mrs. Busch's accomplished piano-playing begins to raise the level of musical appreciation all around her.

This is what happens when things go well, when the wheel of chance runs smoothly, for alas! so far pure luck, not intelligent purpose still rules in this field, vital to the development and prosperity of our country though it is. By such good luck as this, many an émigré already, in the incredibly few years since the beginning of dictatorship in Europe, by highly trained specialized skill and knowledge of advanced processes of manufacturing and business, has opened up new possibilities in the use of our vast national resources which have given employment to twenty, thirty, fifty Americans for every refugee.

The best thing that can happen—and it does—is to have a refugee fit into a need in our American life so special that we are not aware of it. Such is the story of a brilliant young physician who, on Hitler's coming to power, left Berlin and went to Yugoslavia to practise, learning to speak, read and write the Croatian language, an extraordinary feat. When his successful new career was broken by the appearance of anti-Semitism around him, he set out resolutely for America, and is now learning English. But, here is the point, his purpose is to settle in some settlement of Croatian workingmen, and work among them, ignoring the poor material returns which are all he can expect in such practice. Is there anything but pure gain for everybody in our country, in such a life?

Here is another story, illustrating the scattering of the seeds of culture which always goes on with such a dispersal of superior and highly trained people: an Austrian musician and his wife (an actress), arriving with no money and no prospects, went out to a town in the Middlewest for a visit, which was to be short, with a relative. The husband, finding musical leadership needed, began to help with a high school band, with a church choir, organized a town chorus with those of the citizens who loved to sing but had been playing bridge because the road to cardplaying was open through organizations already existing, but not to choral singing. His wife, acting on a kindred professional instinct, encountered a group of amateurs beginning to rehearse for a play, coached them with such success that they formed a drama club, gave a pageant with her help, got the children together for a singing comedy, gave a mystery play. The cultural life of the region widened before their very eyes. When the time came for the departure of the exiles, the town just could not spare them. And there they are now, in a home of their own, displacing no one, adding greatly to the color and warmth and pleasure of the life of their new community.

Here are three brothers, men of character and experience, arriving in New York, with a suitcase apiece. By great good fortune, part of their capital had been invested in England; hence was available here. In less than a year they kindled the fires in three dark, empty factories in small towns, starting up the manufacture of—well, call it clothes-pins—to the accompaniment of new opportunities for employment of the towns' wage earners disheartened by long idleness.

From time to time a refugee appears who has, safe inside his head, an expert knowledge of certain secrets used in the fine German dyeing establishments, as yet unknown here. Let your imagination play cheerfully for a moment over the possibilities implied in such cases for the expansion and development of commercial chemistry in this country, so vital to our standing in the world markets.

Naturally one of the great difficulties of the situation is that most of the refugees land in one city. Much of the work of the refugee agencies, toiling night and day in bare offices to cope with this flood so full of fruitful possibilities for our culture, our business, our education, is to open the doors of opportunity in smaller cities, more like the old home towns where the newcomers lived in Europe. This is one of the most vital needs for the émigrés, and for us, and it is one in which nearly every one of us outside of New York can be of use. The figures show that resettlements of this kind in smaller inland cities have a remarkable success. Of those thus sent out of New York half have been able to continue in the situation where they were first placed; almost half have, managing themselves, moved to new work where they are permanently established.

Here is where our personal, individual help can count most. And the best of our traditions prepare us for such usefulness, for although we have a black and bad American tradition of KKK and APA intolerance, we have to offset it a fine tradition, uniquely American, of pride in our Huguenot, Pilgrim, Quaker refugee ancestors and a later tradition of appreciation of what the highly civilized German refugees of 1848 did for our young country.

It is a platitude of our period to say that in the United States the pioneer phase is over, that the doors of the frontier are closed, once for all. Our forefathers went out, axe on shoulder, to the undertaking they euphemistically called "conquering" the continent. It is now "conquered" and needs civilizing, and finer, keener, more accurate tools than axes are needed for that great work. It is exactly at this moment, at this turn in our road, that Europe pours out on our shores not agricultural workers used to hand labor, not illiterate ditch-diggers to become public charges because here great machines dig the ditches, but precisely the skilled, educated, specially trained experienced workers we need to help us advance in the path open to us. Book designers from the finest printing establishments abroad whose work has always been better than American, workers in fur bringing heretofore secret processes which revolutionize that industry and give employment to hundreds of Americans, manufacturers of—but I am forgetting the horrified plea for silence and anonymity which goes up from these terrorized victims as they look back at those of their family circle still threatened by the boots of the Storm Troopers.

It is unthinkable that a people with our practical good sense, to say nothing of the warm hearts we Americans are proud to claim, should continue to let blind chance rule in a movement of such importance to our nation, should leave the enormous task—for it is enormous, we must understand that—of directing these newcomers into the right places and occupations in the hands of a few hastily organized, understaffed, underfinanced (indeed scarcely financed at all), desperately toiling emergency relief committees in a few of our cities. We have shown over and over an ability which has astonished the world for rapidly coordinating our forces when confronted with flood, earthquakes, fire, hurricane, war. It is not to be believed that when the emergency pours out on our land seeds of priceless value to our nation we will not bestir ourselves to plant them in soil where they will grow.

For they will not grow in brambles or on stony wastes or in deserts. The heartbreaking cases, all too many of them, of émigrés who have not had good luck but bad, show us the insanely tragic waste that will follow neglect to take advantage of our opportunity. These refugees are human, and being highly organized, they are sensitive. They have been through, most of them, frightfully harrowing experiences—like people suddenly set upon by a band of scalping Apaches and barely escaped with their lives. If to that shock is added too hard an ordeal in the new country at the beginning of their lives here, too much poverty, hardship, hopelessness and utterly unsuitable work, why their mainsprings will snap—whose would not? —and they will become useless flotsam and driftwood. And, entirely apart from natural decently human feeling—the loss is ours. Toscanini forced to earn his living by washing dishes in a hash-house would be no more (probably less) useful than any moron, and really *would* "keep an American out of a job." Toscanini at his right work gives employment to hundreds of Americans, and floods our country with new beauty.

To ensure saving at least a decent proportion of émigrés to health and usefulness to America, what is needed is that every one of us should consider himself a volunteer member of an emergency relief committee, governing this committee of one by some such elementary rules as these:

1. No case of exploitation of the distress of the émigrés allowed when I can prevent it. For since we are all human and since shortsighted greed is, alas, a very human trait, we must look out for the temptation, mean and ignoble as it is, to get more than we pay for by taking advantage of defenselessness. The relief committees always have plenty of letters from people who would be glad to get high grade domestic servants and office employes for much less pay than is current around them. To permit this kind of thing would really, of course, do exactly the harm to our American working people which is denounced—often by the very men and women attempting thus to profit by human misery.

2. Let's take special precautions against Ku Klux Klan barbarism, plainly one of the evil traditions of our country which has so many fine traditions. Knowing beforehand that America has a bad record of ignorant and brutal treatment of people of other races and creeds, I will strengthen the guards set against this danger. And this does not mean only that I will denounce the excesses of illiterate mobs at a distance; it means that I will recognize for what it is, the Ku Klux Klanism in my own nature, and will try to repress it as I try to repress other dark and savage inheritance. I will understand that such chance phrases of contempt as "That's the Jew of it!" imply that any bad qualities of a certain individual are not his but his race's; and that means that the next man of the race encountered by any of those who hear my slur will have less of that opportunity to be judged for himself.

3. Patience and the long view. The process of adjustment will be complex and every phase of every case will by no means be a success. In sowing a great field some seeds, always, will not germinate, grow and bear.

Great-grandson of persecuted refugee ancestors as I am, I will keep towards these new refugees, the warm-hearted, hopeful, generous attitude which I would have had America show to my great-grandparents. Only in an atmosphere of hope and friendliness can human beings thrive.

We are—most of us—descendants of persecuted European minorities, and very proud of the courage and endurance they showed in escaping to this country, and the resourcefulness they employed in helping to build it up. We know—most of us—how to read and we have read, since it is one of the most familiar episodes in even eighth grade history books, about the great transfusion of rich new blood into European veins when the Turks took Constantinople and, stripping their possessions from them, drove out a flood of well-educated refugees and émigrés. We know that their presence took Europe in a generation farther into learning and civilization than it had gone in centuries before.

But we don't need even that elementary knowledge of the lessons taught by the past. We can consider that "history is the bunk" and still in the light of practical, everyday good sense, which comes from ordinary experience with human life, perceive that the shrewd practical man of business is right when he exhorts us—to use the rustic Yankee phrase—that the time to help yourselves to cookies is when the cookie plate is being passed.

No. 27

THE MAKING OF AMERICANS [1]

by Louis Adamic

MY friend Bigelow, well known in the eastern city where he lives, and an American of pre-Revolutionary stock, had just served as a witness at the naturalization of his friend, Dr. Kraus, a refugee scientist from Germany. "I've never seen anything so sloppy!" Bigelow exploded. "It was like getting a liquor permit or a driver's license. No dignity. No suggestion that the citizenship which these immigrants sought had any cultural or spiritual value. I was ashamed before Dr. Kraus and within myself as an American.

"Though the courtroom was already crowded with aliens and their witnesses, attendants kept herding more in—*herding* is the word—arranging them in alphabetical order. To the bored-looking judge it was obviously

[1] Louis Adamic, "The Making of Americans," *Current History* (March, 1939), Vol. 50, No. 1, pp. 17-19. Reprinted by permission of *Current History and Forum*.

something to get over with by lunch time. The oath of allegiance was administered by an unshaven man in a sort of rat-tat-tat manner, in a language which might have been English.

"Dr. Kraus came up. Rat-tat-tat, and we were shunted to the rear, just in time to hear a bewildered ex-alien inquire, 'When do I become a citizen?' —and the response, 'Whatsamerra wichya? You just became one!' Finally, looking at his clasped hands, the judge made a speech in a low, spiritless voice—the same speech he had delivered scores of times before, a string of hollow phrases. And so to lunch, the United States having acquired a bunch of new citizens.

"Think of it!" Bigelow went on. "To most of these people the attainment of American citizenship was a fine and glorious dream that took years to reach fulfilment. And to have that dream come to its final realization in this banal, dismal, ill-tempered display of bad manners, squalor and boredom! What I want to know is: Was this typical of naturalization in the country generally? If so, who is to blame—government officialdom, the courts, or you and I?"

Bigelow's experience, while not typical, is unfortunately not unique. The blame cannot be put on the Immigration and Naturalization Service, nor on the Secretary of Labor and the President, nor too severely on the courts. Naturalization is a long-neglected problem, worthy of scrutiny at a time when American citizenship is more and more precious to growing numbers of people. Despite reduced immigration, more than 150,000 aliens are being naturalized annually, and close to a million have declared their intention to seek citizenship.

The Constitution gives Congress power to "establish a uniform rule of naturalization." The basic act under which aliens now are naturalized says that "the Immigration and Naturalization Service, under the direction and control of the Secretary of Labor, shall have charge of all matters concerning the naturalization of aliens." Reading on, however, we find that the act does not mean that at all.

Final naturalization procedure is by law made the "exclusive jurisdiction" of the federal courts and those state courts of record which want to assume that jurisdiction. The Secretary of Labor has no control over these courts. The judges are free to make the naturalization ceremony dignified and inspiring or hum-drum and sloppy. This legal set-up splits responsibility and is to blame for much of the haphazardness.[1]

There are now slightly more than 200 federal courts which naturalize approximately two-thirds of the applicants for citizenship, and about 1,800 State courts which naturalize the other third. After witnessing naturaliza-

---

[1] The Immigration and Naturalization Service was transferred to the Department of Justice in 1940.

tion proceedings or ceremonies lately in several courts, and comparing notes with people in various parts of the country who share my interest, I can say that of these 2,000 courts a few score are nearly everything one can desire with respect to making naturalization dignified. About a thousand, including some of the federal courts which turn out the highest number of new citizens, are so-so—at best marked by a cold business-like efficiency. The rest swing somewhere between "pretty bad" and "awful."

In most cases, the judges who permit careless naturalization procedure in their courts are not to be blamed too harshly. Many judges are over-burdened with their regular duties. To nearly all of them naturalization is a side line which comes up in the midst of a crowded calendar. Some naturalize thousands yearly, and it is understandable if they look upon the nervous and nondescript aliens before them as though they were un-important units in some mass-production process calling for brusque effi-ciency rather than gracious and patriotic ceremony.

When the alien decides to become a citizen he must show that he is in the country legally. Thus even before he can file his "declaration of inten-tion" and get his "first papers" he must seek from the Naturalization Service a certificate of arrival that is issued only after careful checking of the rec-ords. His declaration of intention then is recorded in court by the clerk, largely on the say-so of the Naturalization Service.

Not less than two nor more than seven years later, the applicant can apply to the Naturalization Service for second papers. Some time after he files this petition, he and his two witnesses appear before a naturalization examiner who questions all three as to his fitness to be an American citizen. If the applicant passes this examination and is to be naturalized in a fed-eral court, he is passed on to the so-called "designated examiner"—desig-nated, under the law, by the judge whose time and energy do not permit him to examine carefully all applicants in person.

This examiner recommends to the court whether the applicant ought to be made a citizen. Most federal judges rely upon the examiners entirely, and on the day of naturalization the judges serve merely as a front for what has been decided weeks before. An alien recommended by a "desig-nated examiner" becomes a citizen in ninety-nine cases out of a hundred. Actually, therefore, examiners are often more important in the making of new American citizens than are the judges. There are now about 150 of them distributed through the twenty-two naturalization districts. The great majority are excellent, well-trained men who take their jobs seriously and conduct the examinations of applicants in a conscientious, efficient man-ner.

The Naturalization Service as a whole is in better shape than it ever was. But it has no control over the judges nor over the manner in which naturalization proceedings or ceremonies are conducted in courts. The extent to which an individual examiner can influence the judge depends on both of them and on all manner of circumstances in the local courthouse and the community. Examiners are urged by the central office in Washington to cooperate with the courts toward making naturalization ceremonies as dignified and beautiful as they ought to be.

The naturalization ceremony need not be wretchedly squalid, despite inadequacies of the present system. In some places it is conducted with dignity and beauty. A few years ago, for instance, Judge Robert A. Inch of the federal court in Brooklyn undertook to inaugurate more inspiring ceremonies. In this he had the active support of his colleagues—Judges Grover M. Moskovitz, Marcus B. Campbell, and Clarence S. Galston—who take turns with him in conducting naturalization ceremonies.

Their idea was not to kill but kindle more warmly the well-nigh religious light in the eyes of many aliens as they approach naturalization. Their courtroom was large and pleasant, without unnecessary noise and the would-be citizens were considered important persons in the drama. The climax came when they were grouped by nationalities and asked to renounce allegiance to their old countries and to swear loyalty to the United States. This done, the several groups converged into one group, all Americans now, in front of the judge, who then delivered a brief address in which he went into the meanings of American citizenship, congratulated both the country and the new citizens on the step they had just taken. It was a pleasure to watch their faces.

In Cleveland I visited the federal court where Judge Paul Jones conducts the naturalization ceremony with fitting dignity. A strikingly handsome man in his lower fifties, a former football star over six feet tall, his very presence creates an atmosphere of dignity and respect. He knows the naturalization laws as well as the examiner; and in contested or dubious cases he is solicitous of the applicant's rights and devotes time and patience to a hearing of his cause. In contrast to the cold, challenging attitude that in many a court makes the applicant feel almost like a lawbreaker, Judge Jones shows kindly and democratic interest.

Cleveland is fortunate, too, in having its Citizens' Bureau, partly supported by community funds. The Bureau holds excellent courses in citizenship in a score of neighborhoods, and an annual Fourth of July picnic to give the new citizens public recognition. Last year, 5,000 attended the picnic. Mayor Burton and other prominent citizens spoke. The next day, as usual, the Cleveland *Press* issued a special edition including the rosters of the new citizens since the previous picnic and of the recent graduates of the Citizens' Bureau courses who were now available for naturalization.

A noteworthy naturalization ceremony was held last year in South Bend, Indiana, under the chairmanship of Judge Dan Pyle. The previous month, 350 aliens had been examined and sworn in; now a great, well-publicized occasion was made of giving them their final citizenship papers. One of the city's large auditoriums was jammed. The band from nearby Culver Military Academy played. Many foreign-born wore their native costumes, with representatives of each national group carrying a flag of his old country. The judge made a brief speech, outlining the progress of naturalization in St. Joseph County, of which South Bend is the seat. District Director Fred J. Schlotfeldt, of the Immigration and Naturalization Service, who had had a hand in arranging the affair, was present.

The new citizens received their documents, whereupon Colonel Ralph H. Mowbray, educator and leading citizen thereabouts, delivered an address, the keynote of which was: "We need you. You can help us. The more you feel a pride in what you have been and what you can be, the more you can contribute to your adopted country, and the more you can help make America the best country for all of us." In conclusion, while the band played a few bars of each national anthem, the foreign flags were taken to the platform and exchanged for American flags; "The Star-Spangled Banner" was played, and the new citizens filed out amid the cheers of the community.

Elsewhere I find organizations which feel about naturalization in courts as does Judge Pyle, and try to do something about it. Here and there the American Legion, or one of the service clubs, or the local school system or public library, sponsors a dinner or reception for new citizens. In the spring of 1937, a civic group in Omaha, Nebraska, which included the local naturalization examiner, sponsored an impressive Reception for New Americans. On the printed program appeared the names of the newly naturalized. Some towns form similar committees, usually headed by the mayor, which issue to the ex-aliens embossed documents welcoming them to citizenship.

All of which helps a little. Certainly all of it is well-intentioned. But all of it, also, is sporadic and haphazard.

The core of the trouble unquestionably is the split of the naturalization function between the Naturalization Service and the courts. Most persons with whom I have talked in recent months, who are deeply interested in naturalization problems but are neither judges nor Naturalization Service officials, favor taking naturalization out of the courts, which now have "exclusive jurisdiction," and placing it entirely in the hands of the Naturalization Service. The most ardent advocate of this idea is Harold Fields, of the National League for American Citizenship. His plan would facilitate the uniformity in procedure that is called for by the Constitution. It would center responsibility. It would relieve the crowded courts of an extra chore and permit them to function better in their regular duties.

Mr. Fields would create the Constitution-required uniformity, which would lead to desirable results. Now there is no uniformity, not only in court ceremonies but in the interpretation of the law by judges and in the purpose of the questions which applicants are asked. Quoting Mr. Fields: "A case involving rape was held by one judge not to have come within the province of immoral conduct"—which is a bar to naturalization under the law—"even though the crime took place within the five-year period for naturalization; in another state immoral character was construed to cover a single traffic violation." The thousands of judges never meet to gain unanimity in, or compare notes on, naturalization matters. Some are poorly grounded in naturalization law, yet they frequently overrule the examiners who are experts in it.

Under the present set-up of two departments, neither subordinate to the other, there is no sense or center of responsibility for decisions. This leads to confusion. Responsibility could well be centered in the Naturalization Service with its assumption of full administrative authority in naturalization. There would be unanimity; definition of "moral conduct" and other such vital phrases would be agreed upon.

Arguments against this idea exist, though they seem to me to be weak. It is said, for example, that the courts now annul the bureaucratic character or tendencies of the naturalization examiners, tendencies common to all permanent government administrative employees and bureaus. If naturalization is taken out of the courts, it is said, it will become a bureaucratic business, shot through with petty abuses and unnecessary strictness toward the would-be citizens. Also, the very idea that mere clerks should have the power to create citizens!

Personally, I suggest that Congress might well consider the creation of well-paid naturalization judgeships—a corps of specially qualified men who are interested in, and expert in, naturalization and have some idea as to the value and significance of American citizenship. They would, perhaps, be nominally attached to the Naturalization Service, but under no rigid administrative control of the Commissioner or the Secretary of Labor. Yet they would consistently cooperate with the rest of the Service toward bringing about uniformity and unanimity. Restricting themselves to judiciary or formal functions in naturalization, these judges would travel from place to place conducting the final naturalization ceremonies with impressive formality.

But there is no reason why we should tolerate the present appalling condition while a new system is being perfected. There are many organizations in this country which profess to be interested in a higher type of citizenship. Let them welcome the new citizens with a gracious and colorful ceremony that would make the bestowal of citizenship seem impressively significant. A citizen is either an asset to his country or a liability—there is no compromise status.

Most new citizens want desperately to be assets. It would be such a little thing, but it would help so much, if we could send them forth with their final papers with a feeling that they are important to us, instead of in the mood of bewildered disillusionment in which so many of them go forth now.

Chapter IX

THE PEOPLE AND THE SUFFRAGE

[MODERN government consists, for all practical purposes, of a relatively small number of persons who formulate and execute policies which affect the lives of all who live within the territory it governs. It is the essence of its character that these persons are legally bound by the policies it lays down. In a democratic government, however, those who formulate policies are chosen by and held responsible to the whole citizen body, and those who execute the policies must, in one way or another, share the same responsibility. In the United States this is, in part obtained, through the popular election of the chief executives as well as the legislative bodies in both the nation and the states.

It is important, however, to recognize the full implications of the necessity, in a democratic system, of providing direct channels by which the will of the ordinary man may have some influence on those who exercise political power. Most important of these is the right to the franchise. Every adult citizen must have the right to participate in the choice of those persons who undertake the task of making the rules under which he is to live. A democratic government has no alternative to universal adult suffrage. There are no practical tests for the exclusion of citizens from participation in the process of choosing those who are to rule. Neither sex nor property, race nor creed, economic nor social position, ought to prevent the citizen from participating in the choice of his rulers. Whenever the body of voters is limited, those persons excluded do not receive their share of the benefits of government. A franchise based upon property limits the interests of the state to the owners of property. Educational qualifications are, in effect, partial substitutes for property holding qualifications and, in addition, there seems to be no technique for correlating educational qualifications with political fitness. Exclusion on the basis of sex means inadequate protection of women where their interests conflict with those of men. To deprive those on the relief rolls of the right to vote is to stigmatize economic misfortune as a crime.

If it is argued that such an extension of the suffrage will result in unwise choices and mistaken policies, it must be answered that democracy is a process of trial and error. If it is argued that the common man does not have the knowledge to make a reasoned choice, the answer is that the state must make that knowledge accessible to him. If it is argued that the common man can not know enough about the intricate problems with which government must deal to make wise decisions in the realm of public policy, it must be answered that widespread participation is not to give to all men the power to govern, but to give them an opportunity to prevent misgovernment. For, in the end, it must be realized that whenever a group of voters is excluded from participation in the franchise that group is also usually excluded from the welfare realized by the exercise of the power to govern.

Realizing the significance of the franchise, many have gone ahead to hold that those who fail to use it should be compelled to do so. A policy of this kind is built upon a failure to comprehend that there "can be no substitute for an alert civic interest on the part of those who vote." In addition, those who have argued the case for compulsory voting fail to realize the extent to which such argument diverts attention from the real problems of democratizing our governmental system. To make government responsible we need to direct our attention to governmental organization. The federal distribution of power, the principle of separation of powers, checks and balances, and judicial review call for our serious consideration. We need to examine the possibilities for friction and deadlock which cause the voter to become lost; we need to shorten the ballot and to simplify governmental organization. The reduction of the number of elective officers to those concerned directly with policy determination would not only relieve the voter of a great burden but also would enable him to see the effect of his decisions more directly. We do not need to compel men to vote. What we need is to make the system one in which the voter feels that his vote really counts for something. To divert attention from these important considerations by advocating compulsory voting is to divert attention from the essentials of our democratic system.

The following articles by Professors Smith and Eagleton discuss the problems of the suffrage and of voting and non-voting in detail. They both show a keen insight into the operations of a democratic system of government.]

No. 28

THE STRUGGLE FOR A DEMOCRATIC SUFFRAGE [1]

by J. Allen Smith

PROMINENCE was given in the public documents of the American Revolution to the social contract theory, the doctrine of natural rights, the idea of equality, and other conceptions more or less closely identified with the belief in political democracy. This tended to give to the Revolution the appearance of a genuinely popular movement, and thus aided

[1] J. Allen Smith, *The Growth And Decadence of Constitutional Government* (New York: Henry Holt and Company, 1930), Ch. 3. Reprinted by permission of the publisher.

materially in developing and crystallizing public opinion in support of the war for independence.

To proclaim that "all men are created equal" and that they are "endowed by their Creator with certain unalienable rights" which governments "deriving their just powers from the consent of the governed" are instituted to protect, may not be a positive and unequivocal statement of belief in the justice and desirability of a widely extended suffrage; but inferentially, at any rate, it constituted a solemn indictment of the then existing restrictions on the right to vote.

This Revolutionary enthusiasm for the rights of man, which found expression in the official pronouncements of representative bodies, did not commit the political leaders of that time, by any direct and specific statement, to the policy of democratizing the suffrage. It was no doubt clearly seen, however, that the doctrine of natural rights, which served the practical end of justifying the Revolution, could also be used effectively by those who wished to abolish property qualifications for voting and officeholding. That this was recognized is evidenced by certain qualifying statements, obviously designed to safeguard property qualifications against an attack based on the theory that suffrage is a natural right. Thus the Virginia Bill of Rights, adopted June 12, 1776, after declaring "that all men are by nature equally free and independent" and "that all power is vested in, and consequently derived from, the people," adds the saving clause "that all men, having sufficient evidence of permanent common interest with, and attachment to, the community, have the right of suffrage." Provisions identical in substance were incorporated in the Bills of Rights in Pennsylvania, Maryland, New Hampshire, and Vermont. The effort to reconcile the theory of natural rights with a restricted suffrage probably had little effect on the outcome of the suffrage controversy. Nevertheless, it was half a century after this outburst of Revolutionary enthusiasm for democracy in the abstract, before the movement to democratize the suffrage was well under way.

Neither at the beginning of the Revolution, nor later when the Constitution was framed and adopted, was the extension of the suffrage included in the list of proposed reforms. According to the viewpoint of the official and ruling class, government existed primarily for the protection of property and property rights. This was well expressed by John Adams at the beginning of the American Revolution:

> The same reasoning which will induce you to admit all men who have no property, to vote, with those who have, . . . will prove that you ought to admit women and children; for, generally speaking, women and children have as good judgments, and as independent minds, as those men who are wholly

destitute of property; these last being to all intents and purposes as much dependent upon others, who will please to feed, clothe, and employ them, as women are upon their husbands, or children upon their parents. . . . Depend upon it, Sir, it is dangerous to open so fruitful a source of controversy and altercation as would be opened by attempting to alter the qualifications of voters; . . . women will demand a vote; . . . and every man who has not a farthing, will demand an equal voice with any other. . . . It tends to confound and destroy all distinctions, and prostrate all ranks to one common level.

Forty-one years later, in a letter to James Madison, he said:

The questions concerning universal suffrage and those concerning the necessary limitations of the power of suffrage, are among the most difficult. It is hard to say that every man has not an equal right; but, admit this equal right and equal power, and immediate revolution would ensue. In all the nations of Europe, the number of persons, who have not a penny, is double those who have a groat; admit all these to an equality of power, and you would soon see how the groats would be divided. . . . There is in these United States a majority of persons, who have no property, over those who have any.

Adams expressed the ruling class conviction of the time, that government is, and ought to be, founded on property, and that only those who have sufficient property to ensure their support of the established order can with safety be allowed to vote. In the earlier statement of his reasons for opposing manhood suffrage, he based his objection on the ground that the propertyless laboring man is dependent on his employer, and consequently is not a free moral agent in casting his vote. On this assumption, the enfranchisement of the laboring class would not in reality place political power in their hands, but would merely increase the number of votes controlled by their employers, and thus have the effect of making government more oligarchical in character than it was before property qualifications were abolished. This argument was frequently used by the opponents of manhood suffrage, and was designed, no doubt, to influence the attitude of that large class of small landowning agricultural voters, who would not regard with favor any measure which would be likely to result in a substantial increase in the political influence of the wealthy employing class of the large cities. This particular reason for opposing the extension of the suffrage seems to have been a favorite argument of those who accepted the notion, then more or less prevalent among the ruling class, that political rights should be the exclusive privilege of landowners. Indeed, the idea that government should be controlled by landowners survived in many of the original states until well into the nineteenth century. After the Revolution there were ten states in which there was a freehold qualification for voters, though in five of these there was an alternative personal property qualification. The control of the state government by the landholding interests was still further safeguarded by means of substantial property qualifications for public office. The viewpoint of the ruling class at the time the Constitution of the United States was framed is reflected in the act of Congress providing for the government of the Northwest Territory. Under the provisions of this act, the governor was required to have a freehold estate of one thousand acres in the territory; the secretary of the territory and the territorial judges, estates of at least five hundred acres each. A freehold of two hundred acres was necessary for membership in the general assembly, and no one could vote who did not own fifty acres of land in the district.

By 1821 the suffrage question was receiving serious attention in the state of New York. In the constitutional convention of that year, the committee on the elective franchise reported in favor of giving the suffrage to every adult male citizen who contributed toward the support of the government by payment of taxes on real or personal property, by service in the state militia, or by work on the highways, provided he had resided within the state for a period of six months. This proposal was debated at length, being strenuously opposed by the conservative members of the body. In the course of the debate various amendments were offered, the object of which was to defeat the proposed extension or to nullify its effects. Two of the most active opponents of a liberal suffrage policy were Chief Justice Spencer and Chancellor Kent of the supreme court. Both believed that the proposal to extend the suffrage was revolutionary, and that it would destroy the security which property owners had up to that time enjoyed and in the end bring chaos and ruin upon the nation. Chief Justice Spencer thought the time not far distant when the agricultural interest would be in a minority. "And what," he asked, "is there to protect the landed interests of the state, the cultivators of the soil, if the wide and broad proposition on your table be adopted?" He predicted "that the landed interests of the state will be at the mercy of the other combined interests; and thus all the public burthens may be thrown on the landed property of the state." "Is it desirable," he asked, "that we should remove the safeguards of property, and destroy the incentive to acquire it, by rendering it insecure?" After attributing to the beneficence and liberality of property "all the embellishments and the comforts and blessings of life," he warned the members of the convention to take care, "whilst we nominally give the right of voting to a particular description of our citizens, that we do not in reality give it to their employers." On another occasion in the convention, he said: "Let me ask to whom this right will be extended? It will principally be . . . to those who work in your factories, and are employed by wealthy individuals, in the capacity of laborers. Now, I hold . . . that it will be one of the most aristocratic acts that was ever witnessed in this community— under the pretence of giving the right to them, we in fact give it to those who employ, clothe, and feed them."

Chancellor Kent expressed the fear "that our posterity will have reason to deplore in sackcloth and ashes, the delusion of the day." He contended that the landed interest of the state should retain the exclusive control of the senate, as a guaranty of protection to the owners of the soil. In reply to those who like Chancellor Kent desired special protection for property, David Buel, Jr., said:

> One ground of the argument of gentlemen who support the amendment (to retain the freehold qualifications for senatorial voters) is, that the extension of the right of suffrage will give an undue influence to the rich over the persons who depend upon them for employment; but if the rich control the votes of the poor, the result cannot be unfavourable to the security of property. . . .
>
> I contend, that by the true principle of our government, property, as such, is not the basis of representation. Our community is an association of persons —of human beings—not a partnership founded on property. . . . Property is only one of the incidental rights of the person who possesses it; . . . it must be made secure; but it does not follow, that it must therefore be represented specifically in any branch of the government. It ought, indeed, to have an influence—and it ever will have, when properly enjoyed. So ought talents to have an influence . . . but you surely would not set up men of talents as a separate order, and give them exclusive privileges.
>
> The truth is, that both wealth and talents will ever have a great influence; and without the aid of exclusive privileges, you will always find the influence of both wealth and talents predominant in our halls of legislation.

The effort to make men instead of property the basis of the state government was only partially successful. Several important changes were made in the plan submitted by the committee on the elective franchise which were designed to make the qualifications of voters less objectionable to the property holder. The residence requirement recommended by the committee, of six months in the state, was raised to one year, and a local residence requirement of six months in the town or county was added. The suffrage was given to adult male citizens who had paid taxes on real or personal property, or performed military service in the state militia within the year preceding the election. Adult male citizens who had not paid taxes on real or personal property, or had not served in the state militia, but who had been assessed and had performed labor on highways were allowed to vote, subject to a state residence requirement of three years and a local residence requirement of one year. No colored man was allowed to vote unless he had been for three years a citizen of the state, and owned, and had paid taxes on, a freehold estate of the value of $250.00.

The representatives of the landholding interest in the convention were unsuccessful in their effort to deprive non-freehold voters of a voice in the selection of the members of the upper house; but they did succeed in limiting the influence of this class of voters by retaining the freehold qualification for membership in that house.

The varying and conflicting opinions concerning the suffrage which were expressed in the New York constitutional convention of 1821, may be regarded as fairly indicative of ruling class sentiment at that time. There was an increasing number who favored the view that government was an institution established and maintained for the benefit of all citizens, and that to guarantee an equitable diffusion of the benefits derived therefrom it was necessary to abolish the special constitutional protection given to property owners through property qualifications for voting and for holding public office. But only a small minority of the members of the convention it seems, favored the abolition of all property qualifications. Martin Van Buren, afterwards President of the United States, declared that he did not believe that there were twenty members who, were "the bare naked question of universal suffrage put to them, would vote in its favor."

Broadly speaking, there are but two theories of the suffrage; one may be called the aristocratic and the other the democratic. The aristocratic theory, which found expression in our state constitutions during the first half century of our history as a nation, held that voting was a privilege to be conferred upon such of the adult citizens as were fit to exercise it. The advocates of this theory made use of it for the purpose of justifying the then existing restrictions on the right to vote. They did not really believe in the doctrine of equality or the theory of natural rights, nor did they accept Aristotle's definition of a citizen as one who shares in governing and being governed. A citizen, as such, was at the most, they thought, only a potential voter. Mere citizenship did not confer upon the individual nor entitle him to claim, any active civic rights. The right to vote and to be elected to office did not belong to him as a citizen, but accrued to him incidentally as the owner of property. In order to justify this contention it was necessary to make the assumption that participation in the political life of the state was but a privilege, which those in control might confer or withhold. The conservative believed then, as he does now, that men their civic activities are very largely guided by what they consider to be their material interests. This stands out conspicuously in all the debates and other literature in opposition to the extension of the suffrage.

It has almost always been assumed, as a self-evident proposition, by the advocates of a restricted suffrage, that the poor, if granted the privilege of voting, would use the power thus given them to bring about a redistribution of wealth. It does not seem to have occurred to them that, if this contention has any merit, it could also be claimed with as much reason that under a property holding suffrage the material interests of property owners will be advanced at the expense of the classes who have little or no property. We are all too prone to assume that our particular interest is the best and most trustworthy indication of what is for the public good. It is, therefore, not difficult for any class to believe that its interests are representative of the general interests, and that legislation advantageous to it is also beneficial to the state as a whole. Without imputing, then, any consciously selfish motive to those in control, we may accept as true Professor Dicey's statement, "that from the inspection of the laws of a country it is often possible to conjecture, and this without much hesitation, what is the class which holds, or has held, predominant power at a given time."

The ruling class believed in the right of the politically fit to control the state. The test of fitness, however, was not personal worth, character, or intelligence. These qualities might make one respected and trusted as a man; but they furnished no assurance that political power, if placed in his hands, would be wisely and conservatively used. James Monroe in 1831, after he had been for eight years President of the United States, wrote:

> The danger is, if the right of suffrage is extended to the whole population, without any qualification, as to property, that as the difference of interest begins to operate, as it will soon do, that the mass of poor, which will be by far the most numerous, will elect persons who will be instruments in the hands of leaders who will overthrow the government. . . .

To the political liberal, citizenship implied the right to participate in the civic life of the community. To deny the individual the ballot was to deprive him of that which constituted the essence of citizenship in a democracy.

Those who believed in democracy repudiated the idea that government should be controlled by the property holding class. Citizenship, they maintained, implied the right to vote, which was a personal right of the citizen and not contingent on the ownership of a specified amount of property. Like any other right of the individual, it was subject to reasonable regulation for the common good. It was, however, a right, and not, as the conservative claimed, a mere privilege. It could and should be withheld from such as were clearly not fit to exercise it. But in determining the question of fitness, the state should not be guided by any external test such as the ownership of property. The grounds upon which exclusion from the suffrage could be justified were personal and such as clearly made one incapable of a wise use of political power. Thus naturally followed the exclusion of criminals, paupers, minors, and even women, who in the early days of democracy were classed with the politically unfit.

With the growth of democracy, the old or aristocratic view of the suffrage has been largely, though not entirely, abandoned. The idea that government exists primarily for the protection of property still survives in the thinking of the well-to-do classes; and, while property qualifications have in large measure disappeared, the influence of those who favor suffrage restrictions has been more or less effective. Even without property qualifications many adult male citizens are practically disfranchised. The chief substitute for the old property holding or taxpaying qualifications for voters is the more stringent requirement concerning residence. This is illustrated in the New York Constitution of 1821, which abolished the freehold qualification for the suffrage. The extent and character of the increase made in the residence requirement at that time clearly indicate an intention to make it serve the purpose of minimizing the effect of the non-property holding vote. While a residence requirement of one year in the state was added to the local residence requirement of six months for such voters as paid taxes or performed military service in the state militia, for all other voters, a residence of three years in the state and one in the locality was required, together with a highway tax to be paid in labor or its equivalent. For colored voters, a freehold qualification was retained.

No doubt the chief purpose of these more stringent residence requirements was to limit the wage earning vote, as may be most clearly seen in the case of the southern states. North Carolina, in the Constitution of 1876, increased the period of residence for voters from one to two years in the state, and from thirty days to six months in the county, and added a supplementary residence qualification of four months in the precinct or election district. Virginia, before 1850, required a residence of one year in the county, city, town, or borough. The Constitution of 1850, which removed property qualifications for voters, retained the local residence requirement of one year and added a state residence requirement of two years. After the Civil War this was reduced to one year in the state and three months in the locality. The movement to restrict the Negro vote, which culminated in the Constitution of 1902, restored the residence requirement of two years in the state and one in the locality. This increase in the residence requirement is an essential part of the suffrage restrictions contained in the more recently adopted constitutions of the southern states.

The Rhode Island Constitution of 1842 distinguished between two classes of voters, those who paid taxes on a freehold of a specified value and for whom a residence of one year in the state was prescribed, and those who paid taxes to the amount of at least one dollar on an estate. For the latter class of voters, a residence of two years in the state was required. When the property qualification for the suffrage was removed in 1888, the two years residence requirement was extended to all voters.

The effect as well as the evident purpose of these residence requirements is to diminish the influence of those who would have been excluded under the old property holding qualifications for voting. It is the tenant farmer and the wage earner who are most likely to be disfranchised by these restrictions. Even moderate residence requirements, under present-day conditions, disfranchise many members of the wage earning class.

Educational qualifications for voters may also be regarded as a partial substitute for property holding and taxpaying restrictions. They are, for the most part, a recent development, having little practical importance outside of the southern states, where they are utilized to limit the influence of the Negro vote. Until the adoption of the Fourteenth Amendment after the Civil War, the states could disfranchise the Negro, or, as in the New York Constitution of 1821, provide special and more restrictive qualifications for colored voters. The suffrage provisions in the recently adopted constitutions of the southern states, with the exception of the residence qualifications, which exclude many of the poorer class whether white or black, may be regarded as an attempt to accomplish by indirection a disfranchisement that is racial in purpose and effect. The restrictions upon the right to vote, such as the property owning, taxpaying, and literacy tests found in these constitutions, when viewed in connection with other provisions which have the effect of exempting white voters from their operation, are as clearly designed to limit the colored vote as were the direct and express provisions of this sort in some of the earlier state constitutions.

What the framers of the later constitutions did was to revive the old property holding and taxpaying qualifications, supplemented by an alternative educational test, and to make them apply in practice exclusively to colored voters. These provisions are an expression of the conviction that the political supremacy of the white voters must be maintained. The Fourteenth Amendment made it impossible for the southern states to retain the form of manhood suffrage without incurring the danger of political control at the hands of those elected by the colored vote. The expedients resorted to for the purpose of guarding against this possibility would probably have been adopted in any northern state confronted by similar conditions.

In many states where the right to vote for elective officials is not limited by property or taxpaying restrictions, these restrictions, nevertheless, apply to the more important matter of a vote on a proposal to incur public indebtedness for some specific purpose. In this way, the control over policies is kept very largely in the hands of the property owning class, though less obviously than was the case under the early state constitutions. The difference between total disfranchisement of non-property holders and the limitation of their influence by means of constitutional provisions of this sort, is only one of degree. Under the latter system we really have two classes of voters: those who, as property owners and taxpayers, have the unrestricted right of suffrage; and those who neither own property nor pay direct taxes and whose influence as voters is rigidly limited by constitutional provisions. Restrictions of this kind may be regarded as a compromise forced upon the advocates of manhood suffrage by those who were seeking to perpetuate the influence of property.

The demand for manhood suffrage as a political right paved the way for the woman suffrage movement. The mere fact that men had monopolized political power could not be accepted as a sufficient reason for denying women the right to vote. In an age when time-honored institutions and practices were being examined and criticized in the light of reason, it was inevitable that, with the extension of the suffrage to men, a further extension of the right to women should be demanded. Indeed, even under the theory which supported the system of property qualifications, there could be no logical defense of the practice which withheld from property owning taxpaying women the right to vote. But the question of woman suffrage did not secure any recognition until the agitation for manhood suffrage had succeeded in breaking down the more obvious and direct barriers erected in the earlier state constitutions against popular control.

The rather close connection between the general movement for the extension of the suffrage to men and the woman suffrage is indicated by the fact that the first woman suffrage convention in the United States was called in 1848. The movement, however, made but little progress until after the Civil War. In 1869 women were granted the suffrage in the territory of Wyoming. The question of equal political rights for women was beginning to receive serious consideration in the early seventies. The Prohibition platform of 1872 demanded equal rights for women, and the Greenback platform of 1884 favored a woman suffrage amendment to the Constitution of the United States. Generally speaking, the woman suffrage movement has had the support of the more radical minor parties for the last fifty years

In 1912 the Progressive party proclaimed its belief that "no people can justly claim to be a true democracy which denies people rights on account of sex," and in 1916 both the Democratic and the Republican parties included in their national platforms declarations favoring the extension of the suffrage to women by the states. Fifteen states had enfranchised women when the woman suffrage amendment to the Federal Constitution was adopted in 1920. Moreover, progress toward woman suffrage had been made in many other states by granting women the right to vote in school elections or on other local questions.

Women are citizens, and citizenship, to be real and effective, must confer the right to vote. One can hardly appeal to democracy in defense of manhood suffrage, without seeing that a further extension of the suffrage to women could be justified on the same grounds. From the viewpoint of democracy, suffrage is an essential right of the normal adult citizen, necessary in order that he may be guaranteed adequate protection under the laws of the state. Governmental policies are the resultant of the various interests which find expression in the votes of the people. A disfranchised class is deprived of the only means by which its interests can be adequately protected. A class thus divested of political rights is invariably discriminated against. We need not assume that this discrimination is in any sense conscious or intentional. It may be due to the more or less obvious fact that no group or class of persons having group or class interests peculiar to themselves are, or can be, adequately represented unless they have a voice in the making of the laws by which they are governed. The history of legislation shows that women as a class are no exception to this rule. Man-made laws, even in the most democratic communities, have failed to give women adequate protection where their interests conflict with those of men. The growth of democracy has brought about a much closer approximation to equality in the civil rights of men and women; but equal protection of women, where their interests as a class conflict with those of men, can be guaranteed only by an intelligent exercise of political rights by women themselves. "Men, as well as women," says John Stuart Mill, "do not need political rights in order that they may govern, but in order that they may not be misgoverned."

The democratic theory of the suffrage, which would grant the right to vote to every normal adult citizen, is regarded by those who oppose democracy as an unjustifiable attempt to establish an artificial political equality. Men, they say, are not equal in physical strength, intelligence, or moral character. Why should not this natural inequality be recognized in the organization of the state, by such restrictions on the suffrage as will keep political power in the hands of the fit? Those who emphasize inequality

as an argument against democracy, however, always include themselve
among the fit. The democrat might reply to them in the language of tha
advocate of monarchy, Thomas Hobbes, who after affirming that men are
all things considered, substantially equal, says: "From this equality o
ability, ariseth equality of hope in the attaining of our ends." His argu
ment is to the effect that whether men are equal or unequal, no man i
willing to admit his own inferiority, nor will he be satisfied under institu
tions and laws which discriminate against him. Since every man think
himself the equal of other men, it is necessary for the peace and safety o
the state to treat all men as equals.

The conservative not only assumes the existence of marked inequality
but believes that such inequality is highly desirable. According to his sys
tem of political philosophy, only those whom nature has designated as th
fit should be endowed with political rights. He fails, however, to recogniz
the important fact that any class or groups of classes that may happen t
be in control of the state will always seek to justify their political privilege
and to retain the material advantages derived therefrom. Moreover, th
inequality that now exists is, as Hobbes says, very largely the product o
unjust laws. Democracy could not, it is true, remove inequalities fo
which nature is responsible, but it is unalterably opposed to any polic
which would make inequality more pronounced. A widely extended su
frage is necessary to safeguard society against an artificial, state-created in
equality. One may be a firm believer in political democracy, withou
believing that men are equal in ability or worth. The conservative wh
conceives of democracy as a plan to establish and maintain an artificia
equality is setting up a man of straw.

A democratic state with a widely extended suffrage is designed as
means of establishing and maintaining equality of political opportunity
It seeks to give to each man, not equal influence, but equal opportunity t
exert such influence upon the state and its policies as is implied in the rigl
to vote. The fact that each man may have one vote, and only one, doc
not make men politically equal, nor is it intended to do so. Qualities c
mind and character which command confidence and respect will alway
give to their possessor an influence over the votes of others. True leader
men of superior intelligence and worth, who have faith in democracy an
are recognized as representing its aims and aspirations, may have fa
greater influence in a democratic society than would be possible under
restricted suffrage. In giving each individual the right to vote, a democrati
system of government merely abolishes the political privileges which hav
made it possible in the past for the favored classes to control the stat

without due regard to the wishes or interests of the disfranchised elements in the population. With the extension of the suffrage, this power has, to some extent at least, disappeared. Classes formerly disregarded, since they had no means of registering an effective protest, must now be placated in order to secure their political support. The extension of the suffrage abolished the form, if not the substance, of the political monopoly of the ruling class. It left the members of this class, however, in possession of whatever influence was due to their wealth, intelligence, or social prestige.

Closely connected with the influence of the dominant class was the method of voting. To enfranchise the wage earning population without at the same time ensuring a secret ballot was to give, in large measure, the form without the substance of political power. This fact the wealthier classes were quick to recognize. Long before the suffrage was extended, indeed, conservatives appreciated the advantages of the *viva voce* form of voting. Their point of view is well expressed by Montesquieu:

> The people's suffrages ought doubtless to be public; and this should be considered as a fundamental law of democracy. The lower class ought to be directed by those of higher rank, and restrained within bounds by the gravity of eminent personages. Hence, by rendering the suffrages secret in the Roman republic, all was lost.

The wealthy class clearly saw that its political influence might be endangered if secret voting should be established. A system of secret voting would deprive the rich of the opportunity to use economic pressure for the purpose of controlling the votes of those dependent upon them. Landlords would have less influence over tenants; creditors, over debtors; and employers, over employees. Dependent voters, who under a system of public voting could be counted on to be amenable to advice and influence, would no longer be subject to these wholesome restraints. Even under a system which limited the suffrage to property owners and taxpayers, the well-to-do regarded the political influence of the rank and file of voters with more or less apprehension, which was reflected in the high property qualifications for the important offices under the early American state constitutions.

In any political election [says John Stuart Mill], even by universal suffrage (and still more obviously in the case of a restricted suffrage), the voter is under an absolute moral obligation to consider the interest of the public, not his private advantage, and give his vote, to the best of his judgment, exactly as he would be bound to do if he were the sole voter, and the election depended upon him alone. This being admitted, it is at least a *prima facie* consequence that the duty of voting, like any other public duty, should be performed under the eye and criticism of the public. . . . Undoubtedly neither this nor any other maxim of political morality is absolutely inviolable. . . .

It may, unquestionably, be the fact that if we attempt, by publicity, to make the voter responsible to the public for his vote, he will practically be made responsible for it to some powerful individual, whose interest is more opposed to the general interest of the community than that of the voter himself would be if, by the shield of secrecy, he were released from responsibility altogether.

As a rule, secrecy in voting has accompanied or followed, and not preceded the extension of the suffrage. It was opposed by the same classes that defended property qualifications and for the same reason—the desire to keep political control in the hands of the well-to-do. A widely extended suffrage without the secret ballot, was, after all, less of an evil than it had seemed. The proposal, however, to make voting secret was clearly a plan designed to make it possible for members of the dependent classes to cast independent votes. A long period of agitation and discussion was required before the secret ballot in an effective form was finally and generally established. It was not until a full half century after the suffrage was extended in the American states that laws adequately safeguarding the secrecy of the ballot were generally adopted.

Even now, the fight for secrecy has not been entirely won. Under the election laws of some states, voters in primary elections must declare their party affiliations and receive a ballot on which are printed only the names of those from whom their party candidates are to be selected. This type of primary election prevents some voters, perhaps many, who would vote with a radical minor party, from voting with their party in the primary. The penalty for taking part in the selection of candidates for whom they expect to vote in the final election may keep many voters from the polls, or perhaps make it seem expedient to vote in the primary with a party which they do not intend to support. Among those who vote the Socialist ticket, for example, are many who would be made to feel the effectiveness of such discrimination as is often made use of to discourage radical voting by those economically dependent.

The opponents of the secret ballot professed to be the defenders of a high type of political morality. Those who are fit to vote, they contended, do not need nor desire secrecy; inasmuch as voters exercise a power conferred on them by the state, the public have the right to know how it is used; only harm would be the result of the secret ballot; fraud and deception would be encouraged.

It is difficult, for one reviewing this controversy from the standpoint of the present time, to credit the opponents of the secret ballot with a high order of political intelligence and not impute to them a certain amount of insincerity. Fraud in elections was often perpetrated under the old system of public voting. The fact that this method of voting encouraged fraud and intimidation was one of the most telling arguments for the secret ballot. Political corruption has not entirely disappeared with the introduction of secret voting; but the direct purchase of votes is no longer good business, since those who supply the funds for this purpose can have no assurance that the votes paid for will be delivered.

In England at the beginning of the World War, there was much dissatisfaction with the antiquated suffrage laws which permitted plural voting and excluded women from parliamentary elections. The plural voting system gave an undue share of political influence to the landowning class, since a landowner could vote in all districts in which he owned sufficient property to qualify him for the exercise of this right. This feature of the English suffrage laws made it possible for a minority of conservative voters to cast a majority of the votes and to control a majority of the members elected to the House of Commons. Naturally enough, the efforts of the Liberal party to abolish plural voting encountered determined opposition in the House of Lords.

The adoption of needed suffrage reforms was made possible by the abolition in 1911 of the veto power of the House of Lords. A comprehensive bill, systematizing and simplifying the qualifications of voters, was introduced in the House of Commons May 15, 1917. The enactment of this law increased the number of voters by extending the suffrage to about six million women. No woman can vote, however, until she has reached the age of thirty years, a discrimination against women which would seem to indicate that the members of the House were reluctantly recognizing the principle of woman suffrage. [This was changed in 1928; the same age qualification now applies to both sexes.] Plural suffrage was not entirely abolished, but no one may now have more than two votes.

Belgium has had a system of plural voting since 1893. To every male citizen who has attained the age of twenty-five years, is given one vote. An additional vote is conferred upon those who are heads of families and pay as householders a tax of not less than five francs, or who own land or securities of a specified value. Two additional votes are given to such as are presumed to have high educational qualifications. These include graduates of higher schools, members of the professional classes, and such as have held public office. Those who had more than one vote in 1908-9 were 40 per cent of the total number of voters and were entitled to cast 62 per cent of all the votes.

Prussia, until the reforms instituted as a result of the World War, had a system of voting which distributed political power in the state according to the amount of taxes paid. The very wealthy class, which was numerically but an insignificant minority of the population, had one-third of the representation. The larger taxpayers among the remaining population constituted another political class having one-third of the total representation. The third class, which included an overwhelming majority of the people and which with manhood suffrage would have elected practically all officials, was allowed to choose but one-third of the representatives. In this way, the public interest in state and local government was effectively subordinated to the interest of the wealthy classes.

Various devices were resorted to for the purpose of restricting still further the influence of the third class of voters. They voted less frequently than the other two classes; property qualifications were required for a certain proportion of their representatives; and the absence of the secret ballot made it possible for the small minority included in the first two classes to augment their own political predominance through economic pressure.

On account of the size of Prussia and its peculiar relation to the German Empire, the spirit and character of the Prussian state government largely determined that of the Empire. Imperial elections, at which were chosen the members of the lower house of the Parliament of the Empire, were conducted on the basis of manhood suffrage and the secret ballot. This afforded some opportunity, it is true, for the expression of national public opinion. But on account of the subordinate place of this body in the general scheme of government for the Empire, it lacked the positive power which would have made it an adequate organ of public opinion. Moreover, the Reichstag was not a body which really represented the public opinion of the Empire inasmuch as the conservative rural districts were grossly over-represented.

The German system of government as it existed until 1919, in so far as it was elective, may be described as avowedly plutocratic. It would be difficult to contrive a scheme of voting that would more effectively ensure the political supremacy of the wealthy class. But although there was no adequate popular check on the power of this class, the hereditary element was a restraining influence. Moreover, the very fact that the ascendancy of wealth in the elective part of the government was legalized and generally recognized had a moderating effect. A wealthy class thus clothed with political authority, and recognized by the public as morally accountable for the use made of its privilege, is less of a menace than it would be if its control were less directly and obviously exercised and if in consequence it were less influenced by a sense of responsibility.

The suffrage may mean much or little. Its significance depends partly on the form of government and partly on the intelligence of the citizens. It may give to the people the appearance without much of the substance of political power. Where the state is of the check and balance type, the voters have less influence than under a governmental system in which the directly elected branch is supreme. Democracy, even in the negative sense of the term, would allow the people to exercise, either directly or through representatives chosen by them, a veto on all acts and policies of the government.

A government may, however, be thoroughly democratic in form without being democratic in its practical operation. According to the democratic theory of the state, public opinion should be a controlling influence. But the state as we think it ought to be is an altogether different thing from the state as it actually is. We have not yet reached the stage in political development where the people generally have sufficient civic intelligence to enable them to play the important and responsible part which is assigned to them in the theory of democracy. The extension of the suffrage to the masses does not mean effective popular control, even where the entire structure of the state has been democratized, unless the people have acquired an active and intelligent interest in the political and economic problems with which the government has to deal.

The idea that public opinion should be a determining political force is in fact a very recent development. Even in the Declaration of Independence, which formulated the most advanced political thought of the time, there is little to indicate that the people were expected to have more than a passive part in public affairs. Democracy in the active sense of the term is, even in this twentieth century, scarcely more than an ideal.

The growth of popular government by transforming subjects into citizens is supposed to have changed fundamentally their relation to the state. But this transition from subject to citizen, from passive submission to active participation, calls for a more radical change in the political outlook of the average individual than it is possible to bring about in a comparatively short period of time. Many of those upon whom the modern democratic movement has attempted to confer political power have not been able to adapt themselves readily and promptly to changes in political institutions which require them to abandon the ideas and habits that have become more or less fixed through centuries of experience. Consequently, a new system of government is always more like the old one in its actual operation and in its spirit and results than the differences in form would indicate.

The mere fact that a man votes does not prove that he is a good or useful citizen; his duty to the state is discharged only by voting wisely and with due regard to the larger social interests, to which his interests as an individual may at times be somewhat opposed. This ideal is impossible of realization, however, no matter what the form of government may be, unless the people have political convictions that are the result of civic intelligence. An unintelligent vote will always be a menace to popular government in that it tends to perpetuate, under the forms of democracy, all the evils which prevailed under the old political system of class rule with its restricted suffrage and its subordination of the general interests of society to the interests of the ruling few. The vote of the unintelligent citizen is likely to be counted against, rather than for, democracy.

Unless one can vote intelligently, it is his duty to leave the determination of public policies to such as measure up to the standard of civic intelligence which democracy has a right to expect of its citizens. It is not the number of votes cast but their quality that determines the success of democratic government. If a man lacks sufficient interest in public questions to vote when important matters are up for actual determination, it is obvious that he does not feel keenly enough his responsibility for the outcome to make his participation desirable from the viewpoint of the public interest. The citizen who understands what citizenship means in a democracy, who knows the extent to which individual success and well-being depend upon wise laws well administered, will no more think of ignoring his civic obligations than of neglecting his private business. No artificial devices are needed to ensure a full vote on the part of such as are fittest to share in democratic government.

There are some who believe that voting should be made compulsory. But this is, to say the least, a debatable question, whether we believe in a restricted or a widely extended suffrage. If we favor restricting the right to vote, our object is the exclusion of the unfit. But while no standard of fitness that could be adopted would exclude all of the unfit, they largely disfranchise themselves where voting is not compulsory. The view that suffrage is a right which may justly be claimed by every normal adult citizen furnishes as little justification for the policy of compulsion as does the theory that voting is a privilege. Compulsion is not needed for those who have an active interest in the outcome of the election, nor is the welfare of the state likely to be advanced by the votes of those whose chief motive in appearing at the polls is the desire to escape a legally imposed penalty.

Compulsory voting is not a recent innovation, nor should it be regarded as essentially democratic either in origin or purpose. It existed in some of the American colonies before the Revolution, along with a greatly restricted suffrage. Virginia had compulsory voting throughout the colonial period; Maryland had it in the beginning and revived it in 1715; Delaware also had compulsory voting. The constitution of Georgia (1777) imposed a penalty of not more than five pounds for failure to vote without reasonable excuse. Under the Belgian Constitution of 1893, compulsory voting is combined with a form of plural suffrage, while in some of the Swiss cantons it exists in connection with manhood suffrage.

Compulsory voting is an attempt to transform, through the imposition of penalties, the passive element of the citizenry into an active element. A policy of this sort fails to recognize the fact that there is no satisfactory substitute for an alert civic interest on the part of those who vote. It would be far better for the state if those who are not keenly alive to their civic responsibilities would stay away from the polls, than that they should vote under any form of compulsion. Indeed, democracy has far more to fear from, than to gain by, a vote cast for the purpose of securing some immediate personal advantage or avoiding some personal penalty. A vote cast under any form of compulsion, whether that compulsion comes from the state itself or from some powerful private interest, is a vote not for, but against, democracy. A free ballot is the foundation of free government, and means the right to vote without being influenced by any form of coercion, either political or economic. The chief danger to democracy lies not so much in its large non-voting citizenry as in the large proportion of actual voters who do not have sufficient information concerning the questions presented to enable them to vote wisely, or who, through pressure of some private or partisan interest, cast votes which do not represent their independent political choice. How to safeguard the ballot so as to ensure intelligent and independent voting is a problem for which democracy must find a solution.

It is no doubt highly desirable that all normal adult citizens should have the right to vote. Democracy in the true sense of the term can not exist where any considerable part of the population is outside the pale of political rights. Equality of opportunity is a principle which must be recognized in the organization of the state, or democracy will exist only in name. The right to vote and, through the vote, to share in determining the policy of the state is the indispensable guaranty of equality of economic opportunity, which it is the duty of every free government to establish and maintain.

The right to vote, properly viewed, is an opportunity extended by the state to the citizen, and he should be free to take advantage of it or ignore it. Sound public policy points not in the direction of compelling citizens to vote, but rather in the direction of making the exercise of this right purely voluntary by removing every influence which now militates against free choice. We can readily see that a man who must be paid to go to the polls is not likely to advance the welfare of the community when he votes; nor is that man actuated by a much higher motive, whose main interest in politics depends upon some concession, favor, or office at the hands of the party to which he is giving his support.

We should discourage by legislation when possible, and by every other practicable means, all efforts to influence the outcome of elections by bringing to bear upon the individual voter either the threat of individual punishment or the promise of individual reward. To allow intimidation or coercion, direct or indirect, or the promise of some personal favor or advantage, to be a factor in determining whether or not votes are cast and how they are cast, is to place such votes at the disposal of those interests against which it behooves democracy to be on its guard.

We should not be oblivious of the fact that the right to vote is of value to citizens only to the extent that it gives them the power to control the government. If the constitutional system be such as to tie the hands of the majority, as is the case in this country, the natural and inevitable result is, by limiting the influence of the vote, to discourage political activity on the part of citizens. An election must be the means of determining legislation, or intelligent citizens are likely to feel that suffrage is the empty form of a political right without its substance. A system of government which makes it possible for a small minority to prevent the enactment and enforcement of laws which a large majority may have endorsed at the polls naturally operates to discourage political interest and activity on the part of citizens.

No. 29

A DEFENSE OF THE NON-VOTER [1]

by Clyde Eagleton

MANY attacks are being directed nowadays against the American voter—a most reprehensible person, if one believes these critics, whose negligence is plunging democracy to ruin. At Albany a bill has been introduced imposing a fine upon all non-voters. The revered Elihu Root, the Vice-President of the United States, and others have emphasized the citizen's duty at the polls. And Mr. James Beck has gone so far as to compare the non-voter to the traitorous Man Without a Country, who damned his own fatherland.

Certainly statistics are sufficiently impressive to cause some reflection. It has been pointed out that in the last fifty years the percentage of the American electorate actually voting has diminished from 80 to 50; and it

---

[1] Clyde Eagleton, "A Defense of the Non-Voter," *The South Atlantic Quarterly* (October, 1928), Vol. XXVII, No. 4, pp. 341-354. Reprinted by permission of *The South Atlantic Quarterly*.

fell to 38 in the elections of 1922. At the same time, in England today [1928], the voting percentage is 80, in Germany, 89, and in France around 70. We rank, in this percentage, along with the illiterate Caribbean states. And when to this statement is added the significant claim of the ward boss, that he can count upon 85% of those who do vote to cast their votes as the party organization directs, it is a fair conclusion that the American voter is displaying but little of that intelligent judgment to be exercised at the polling-place upon which democracy is said to be founded. This, of course, is contrary to present democratic principles, as taught in citizenship courses and expounded from the Chautauqua platform. Unless each citizen thinks out for himself all the problems of government, and contributes his voice to the majority which instructs the legislators as to the best solution of these problems, the democratic system of which he is the foundation, cannot function properly. If he performs this duty conscientiously, all will go well with the Ship of State; if he fails, it is sure to founder.

But is this, after all, true? or rather, is it possible? Would it serve any good purpose to compel the citizen to vote? It would be confusion worse confounded. It is an utterly hopeless waste of time for the average citizen to attempt to form an individual judgment upon the various questions which confront him; and if, by superhuman efforts, he does succeed in giving answers to them all, his vote, under the present system, is of little or no avail in determining what the action of the government will be upon those issues. If his opinion counts at all, it will probably be because he has expressed it in some manner other than voting.

Why, then, should he vote?

It must be recalled that life, and therefore government, is not nearly so simple a matter as it was in the days when our forefathers, freed from a monarchical form of government, made their proud way to the voting places, there to lay the foundations for the greatest democracy in history. The needs of government were few, so that the Supreme Court could run for several years with no cases upon its docket, and newspapers could print the oratorical efforts upon the floor of Congress and feel confident that they had reported the full legislative activity of the nation. But now the Supreme Court is several years behind in its efforts to hold the various parts of the governmental machinery within their constitutional boundaries, and to give constitutional protection to the individual; while the newspapers, despairing of discovering, much less of reporting, the obscure and multifold activities of Congress, content themselves with the conjectures of expert writers as to what is actually happening, or perhaps supply for our occasional delectation an especially luscious bit of governmental scandal. And in the meantime, department after department and bureau after bureau has been created, to care for interests the most of which the makers of the Constitution never heard of; and statutes pour from the legislative mills in such unceasing flood that it becomes no more than a vain hope for the citizen to know the laws under which he lives. He can only flounder about helplessly, wondering whether the Board of Estimate or the Transit Commission should be blamed for the subway *impasse,* or whether the exclusion of certain aliens as undesirable really represents the will of the people. And even more despairingly, he wonders what he could do about it if he did know!

It all results inevitably from the complexity and the interdependence of a social and economic system developed within the last century—that is to say, since the Constitution was made. The citizen who favored the ratification of the Constitution had no idea of the burden which was ultimately imposed upon his great-grandchildren. His life was simple, and government played but a small part in it. If he needed milk for his baby, he had not to concern himself with the establishment of an Interstate Commerce Commission, which would insure its safe delivery, nor with a national or state or local health bureau which would guarantee it to be Grade A when delivered. He could go out into his back yard and extract it for himself, or run over to his neighbor and purchase a pail-full. If he attempted such courses to-day, he might be subject to a penalty for maintaining a cow upon his premises, or his neighbor might be arrested for selling milk without a license. And he has about as little chance of supplying himself with other needed articles. The very glass of water which he draws from his faucet represents, perhaps, hundreds of millions of dollars, a governmental bureau, and a large technical staff for maintenance. He must to-day depend upon persons not only in his immediate vicinity, but throughout the nation and the world, to supply him with his everyday needs; and to protect him, the government has been forced to intervene more and more, to create vast organizations, to employ specialists to solve the problems therein arising, and to engage in international agreements and enterprises.

It has been said that the discovery of the germ revolutionized the science of government; and if this statement bears the distinguishing features of hyperbole, it is nevertheless true that the discovery of how one's own health might be affected by the personal hygiene of one's neighbor constituted a powerful wedge through whose use the government has been able to force its way into the domain of personal liberty, and has come to regulate the most intimate details of one's private life. Social measures of a thousand kinds have followed, until now one can not build a house or a factory, or carry on any sort of an undertaking, or even cross the street, without coming into contact with some department of governmental activities. Not even the inalienable right of the American citizen to expectorate where he pleases has been left to him! The average citizen does not pause to think of the source of any of the articles which he uses daily, much less of the governmental agencies which have made their use possible; yet he is expected to vote upon the intricate problems arising out of this complexity of life. It is a fascinating study, this great Juggernaut of modern civilization; but our question here is, Where does it leave the voter?

In the first place, there is far too great a number of, and an ever-increasing difficulty in mastering, the matters upon which the citizen must inform himself, if he is to perform the duties of his office with conscientious intelligence. The mere number of problems upon which he is supposed to reach a decision is appalling. In national affairs he can vote only for President, Vice-President and Congressmen; but in order to do this intelligently, under the American theory of representation, he must study questions involving almost every conceivable subject of human endeavor. For the Congressman, under this theory, is no more than a messenger-boy. He must vote, upon each bill as it comes up, as his constituency directs—which, of course, implies an ability upon the part of his constituency to direct him, and machinery for the expression of their desires. But in each term of Congress something like twenty-five thousand bills are introduced. It is worse in state government. In the last legislative year [1927], thirteen thousand statutes were actually passed and inscribed upon the books of the states; and this does not take into account those which were proposed—over three thousand in New York alone. Upon each of these the voter is—in theory, at least!—presumed to have instructed his legislators. Certainly he should have voted directly upon constitutional (state) amendments; and the increasing distrust of legislatures has led to hypertrophied constitutions full of details which the citizens dare not trust to their representatives. The constitution of Oklahoma contains over fifty thousand words, a fair-sized book, whereas the national Constitution requires only eighteen pages. So weary have voters become of this load that states have adopted special devices to compel their attention to constitutional amendments; but when one state forbade the proposal of new amendments until a certain percentage of votes should have been cast upon pending amendments, it was some fifty years before any change in the constitution of that state could be had!

Aside from the mere overwhelming number of matters upon which the voter must decide, the problems have themselves become so technical that only a trained specialist is competent, in each case, to render a fair decision. The average citizen must know economics, and decide what is the best fate for Muscle Shoals [now a part of the TVA], and whether a protective tariff on cotton is desirable; he must be acquainted with high finance, and instruct his representative upon the income tax; he must estimate the possibility of maintaining a five-cent subway fare, and calculate the roads upon which county bonds may most profitably be expended; he must understand the intricacies of international relationships, and determine whether to spend the national money upon submarines or warships or aeroplanes, or upon a World Court and a League of Nations. He should be able to pass judgment upon such abstractions as the doctrine of sovereignty, theories of socialism as against individualism, or federalism against states' rights; upon the more concrete questions of immigration, labor, farm relief, and an interminable list of others, upon any one of which a political scientist would habitually spend a lifetime of study. Yet to the illiterate Italian laborer of the East, or to the irresponsible Negro of the South, is entrusted the determination of problems which call for the best of technical training. What can they know—what, for that matter, does the average intelligent voter know?—of cycles of prosperity, or the causes of panics? Nothing, one may be sure; but if times are prosperous they vote confidently for the return of the current administration; and if money is scarce, they vote as confidently for the opposite party!

The burden of the voter is more directly in evidence in the number of persons for whom he must vote. Ballots sometimes contain several hundred names, in addition to constitutional amendments. It is manifestly impossible for the voter to become acquainted with more than a very few of those for whom he votes. And how, for that matter, is he to know who is properly equipped to become an efficient State Superintendent of Education, or a good County Judge? The greatest absurdity in American government to-day is the popular conviction that capable and responsible officials are to be obtained only through the elective process. There is no Republican or Democratic criterion for passing upon the qualifications of a tax collector; and yet most officials are chosen upon a party basis. A voter would probably consider himself incompetent to pass upon the qualifications of an electrical engineer for any ordinary purpose; yet Steinmetz, the electrical wizard, was defeated for the office of State Engineer in New York because of his Socialist tendencies! It is as absurd to think of the voter as capable of judging whether a man has the technical training necessary for a Supreme Court Judge, or to handle the records in a County Clerk's office.

If it be argued that the people have an innate ability to judge of the honesty and character of a candidate, it still remains to be discovered how they are to become sufficiently acquainted with the personal characteristics of the hundreds of persons whose names appear upon the ballots. What opportunity have they for reaching a fair and unbiased opinion, either upon candidates or upon issues? Without taking into account that we have not in this country learned to administer government upon a basis of efficiency apart from sentiment and passion and prejudice, it would be difficult for the most cool and detached intellect to make a fair judgment upon the basis of the information put before the voter. Certainly the material supplied by his party, or by propagandist institutions concerned with the questions, will not be unbiased; and he can hope for little better from his newspapers. If they do not frankly represent a party, they at least have their own well-fixed viewpoints. The paraphernalia or research is manifestly useless to the voter.

The question can not be resolved by deciding to vote exclusively for men or exclusively for measures: there are too many of either, and they are too far distant from the voter. It is quite impossible in most elections for the conscientious voter to go home from the polls, after having surveyed the long list of names before him, with his conscience clear in the belief that he has voted intelligently for every office. He is forced either to vote the straight party ticket, or else to leave many names unmarked. And if this be true, of what possible value could it be to compel him to vote, or even to place the names before him? He is expected to vote for a candidate not only upon the basis of acquaintance with his personal worth, but also on the expectation that when elected the candidate will represent his views. What possible views can he have as to how the books in the County Treasurer's office should be kept? Just how he is to instruct his representative upon problems which arise after election day, is not clear; but it is sufficiently clear that the average voter is not prepared to give instructions as to the best means of raising the national revenue, or of solving the coal-mining problem, or of supplying adequate transportation facilities in New York City. Perhaps it is his duty, as a patriotic citizen, to puzzle all such things out carefully; but if you tell him so, he will reply that he has a living to make. It is well enough to say that the success of democracy depends upon an educated electorate; but what is asked of the modern voter, absorbed as he is in the intricate struggle for existence— which must come first—is a physical and a mental impossibility.

But grant that the citizen is able to reach an intelligent decision, through some inconceivable educative process, and succeeds in conveying his will to his agent through his vote or in some other manner—of what use is it for him to do so in our present system? Democracy, if it means anything at all, means the control of government by the people; and yet there is no means provided in the American machinery of government by which the people can express their wishes upon any one given national issue. The

British have, even if they rarely use it, the opportunity of a general election upon a dissolution to ascertain exactly what the people wish on the point under debate; and other states use the referendum, or other devices. But we have no such opportunity—nothing except the national elections, in which issues are so jumbled together that it is impossible to say what the vote means when applied to any one question. Consider, for example, the famous election of 1920. Anti-Wilson, anti-Lodge, anti-League, anti-prohibition, anti-woman suffrage, and a thousand other negative impulses were thrown together into an utterly inextricable tangle. To say that a Presidential election means a popular majority upon any one issue, is mechanically impossible. Not even a constitutional (national) amendment is submitted to the people, but to state legislatures whose members are elected upon quite irrelevant pledges.

Nor is there adequate machinery through which the citizen may instruct his representative after he has taken up his office. The latter is at a loss, for he may not be able to discover until the next election day, and then too late, what his constituency desired. It is not sufficient to do as one Senator admitted doing—to pile up letters and telegrams for one side in one pile, and for the other side in another pile, and then vote for the tallest heap. Only those who have a special interest at heart, or propagandist organizations formed to overcome the inertia of the average voter, will make such an effort. The great majority of the people may be opposed, and awake to express their opposition too late.

And even if the President (or other official) should be able to detect a clear mandate for a certain policy, there can be no assurance, with our present intricate distribution of governmental powers, that the policy indicated could be put into effect, granted the best of intention upon his part. In one of the most recent textbooks upon American Government, Maxey remarks:

> The fact of the matter is that the American system is one of the most intricate and complex on earth; and it therefore requires a great deal more information and a great deal more mental effort to understand our system of government than almost any other. Compared to the intricate and highly involved scheme which we have in this country, the governments of such countries as Great Britain, France and Italy are simplicity exemplified.

The federal distribution of powers, and the principles of separation of powers, checks and balances, and judicial interpretation, provide ample opportunity for friction and deadlock; and in the process the voter loses track. The result is that if the will of the voter, initiated as a bill in Congress, successfully passes through the labyrinth of committees, bicameral action, and archaic rules of Senatorial procedure, and does not come out a monstrous malformation of amendments and reservations, it may still be killed by the President's veto, or by the decision of the Supreme Court. Even if the voter does not succeed in putting into Congress a majority of opposite party to the President, with a resultant deadlock, there can be no certainty that the two will work together. Mr. Bliven has pointed out that with an overwhelming majority in favor of Mr. Coolidge, the chief measures which he advocated have nevertheless been defeated. If the party, imposing a collective responsibility, is to be the answer to our problem, it must surely devise more effective machinery for harmonious action than this; and even more surely it must be brought under responsive control.

Why should one vote? The only reward for an honest attempt to vote intelligently is a vista of increasing trouble in the future, as the range of government widens; and there can be no assurance, as we are now organized, that the vote will be effective in the actual operation of the government.

This does not necessarily mean that democracy, as a theory of government, is a failure, as is so frequently being said to-day; but merely that the methods of American democracy are inadequate to meet modern conditions. The fact must be recognized that many people do not vote; and the fact may as well be recognized also that there is ample justification for their failure to vote. Even those who do vote are unable to do so intelligently; and this is true of the best educated as well as the most illiterate. Pure democracy was long ago admitted to be impossible with the huge populations of our day; but representative democracy will prove equally as unworkable so long as it is taken to mean that voters must form and express opinions for the guidance of their representatives upon all matters now thrust upon them. The very existence of the principle of representation implies a devolution of authority from the people to their representatives. Our problem is in large part the degree of devolution which the people should admit.

The answer is not to be found in coercive voting, nor in educating the people. The burden would be too great, under present conditions. We live in an age of increasing social and economic interdependence, in which the problems of government are more and more technical in character. They cannot be settled by the expressed whims of the people; they must be adjusted according to the laws of nature, interpreted and applied by experts. Many years ago Carlyle wrote:

Your ship cannot double Cape Horn by its excellent plans of voting. The ship may vote this and that, above decks and below, in the most harmonious exquisitely constitutional manner: the ship, to get around Cape Horn, will find a set of conditions already voted for, and fixed with adamantine rigor by the ancient Elemental Powers, who are entirely careless how you vote. If you can, by voting or without voting, ascertain those conditions, and valiantly conform to them, you will get round the Cape; if you cannot, the ruffian Winds will blow you ever back again.

So long as technical problems are left to be solved by the voter, he must, if he is bound by any sense of patriotic duty, stagger along under an ever-growing political burden, overwhelmed as he may be by his economic situation. We struggle to equip the voter with the requisite education for the performance of these duties; but as fast as we do, so fast is he loaded with new burdens. It is a hopeless race, a veritable Tantalus-task, in which the voter must always drag behind with lolling tongue.

What, one may ask, is the purpose of the elective process? Why should a person desire to vote? Apparently, there are two objects in view: to choose men for office in whom you have confidence, and who will, you believe, represent your own views in office; and to hold them responsible by failing to elect them again, if they have not proven satisfactory in office. Both rest upon the conviction that the people are capable of choosing capable men for office, and of holding them responsible for properly supporting the views of the voter. This conviction, under present day circumstances, is a fallacy. The number of men and of issues has increased to such a degree that the voter can no longer keep track of them; and the organization of the government has become so complex that it is impossible to allocate responsibility. The President blames it on Congress; the Senate blames the House; the Congressmen pass responsibility to the Committee, and the Committee to the sub-committee. The elective process, as now employed, has become unworkable. Nevertheless, it can not be discarded, if the people are to retain control.

The first need of the people is a shorter ballot; and this means, of course, far more than a reduced printing bill. It signifies a revised theory of representation on the part of the American people, who at present distrust their representatives and are convinced that the voter must himself oversee all the activities of the government. But this is no longer possible; and it is clear now that he must delegate some of his powers. Nine-tenths of the offices for which he now votes could be profitably removed from his control. By far the greater number of these are petty administrative or judicial offices upon which he is not competent to make a decision, and which could be more efficiently filled by appointment upon merit, through civil service machinery or in other non-partisan manner. If he fears this as risky, he may be reminded of the half million and more now appointed, rather than elected, in the Federal Government, which is conceded to be more efficient than any other part of the American system. At any rate, the process of appointment could scarcely be more disappointing in its results than the present process of election; and the voter at least would be relieved.

We have not yet learned to distinguish between politics and administration. Legislative and constitutional action should be concerned only with the formulation of general principles of public policy in accordance with the will of the people, leaving methods to be worked out by trained men, independent of party machinations; and this is the more needed to-day when governmental action has become so specialized in nature that only experts can handle a great part of it. As it is now, legislatures and constitutions are so overburdened with useless trivialities and complexities of procedure that important measures are passed by for lack of time. It is within the competence of the voter, for example, to determine whether as a matter of policy a five-cent subway fare should be maintained, even if from the city treasury; but he is not capable of knowing whether the subways may be properly operated for a nickel fare, or of knowing what is the best method of organizing and laying out the transportation routes. The election of judges, who should be experts rather than demagogues, and the tying of their hands by legislative rules for judicial procedure, has made our judicial administration a laughing stock.

The reduction of the number of elective offices to those of a policy-determining nature—say, the legislative body and the chief executive in each governmental unit—would not only relieve the voter of a great many decisions which he is incompetent to make, but would educate him, and would lead automatically to further improvements in government. One of the chief defects in the American governmental system is its inability to attract the highest type of man into its service. At present, the tenure in office is too uncertain, dependent not upon merit but upon a demagogic ability to please a necessarily ignorant and uninterested constituency. A capable man can not therefore afford to choose government service as a career. If elective positions were made fewer, their attraction and prestige would be greater in various ways. Officials hitherto dependent only upon the will of the people would now be made responsible to the fewer elected officials. The result would be not only increased power for the latter, but less friction, a more centralized and efficient administration, and a better opportunity for them to work out their plans. Abler men would therefore be attracted to these offices, not only for the above reasons, but also because the electorate, having fewer offices to study, could take a greater and more intelligent interest in them.

This means, of course, the concentration of greater power in the hands of fewer men, and raises the question of securing responsibility. It is a question that needs to be raised, for it reveals the defect in our system which is in greatest need of correction. Responsibility, the most essential element in democratic government, is at present impossible to locate. It is scattered out between the States and the Nation, between the President, the Courts and Congress; it is hidden away in caucuses and committee rooms and floor leaders; it can be traced down to political parties and ward bosses and lobbyists. And if the responsible person could be found, there would be no means of dealing with him, except through the failing system of perennial elections, or the awkward and practically useless weapon of impeachment. Except in appointive offices, nothing can be done to remedy mere inefficiency in office, or to prevent discretionary action contrary to public will. The American people have recognized this, and have attempted to correct it by a wider extension of the direct control exercised by the electorate; but in so doing they have overburdened themselves. To-day, much greater efficiency and more responsibility is to be found in appointive than in elective offices. Instead of many offices separately responsible to the people, who would need to be Argus-eyed to watch over them all, it would be much simpler to have, as is done by the Federal Government, only two or three elected officials, with all administrative officials below answerable to them.

. No business corporation—and the American Government should be regarded as one of the greatest upon earth—could live if organized in such haphazard fashion. The mighty motive power of public opinion which is supposed to run the government is dissipated to the four winds. But the prodigality of frontier days, when abundant resources were available and energy could be wasted, is no longer possible. Business organization points the way; and government becomes more and more a matter of business. The tendency everywhere is toward the concentration of power with corresponding responsibility. It is inevitable in government, as the cries of administrative tyranny occasionally to be heard in our country testify. To concentrate political power in the hands of a few elected officials will concentrate the attention of the people upon these offices, and will interest them in the problem of securing responsibility. Advances in the science of government are most successfully made by slow evolution. *Solvitur ambulando*. Radical reorganization of the governmental system is impossible in the present state of public opinion, and in all probability would be dangerous. A few simple changes to relieve the present intolerable situation of the voter would be the best guarantee of advance in the proper direction.

Why prod the voter? If he were compelled to vote, the problem would not be solved—it would merely be intensified. What we need is to put his power to work in the machinery of government, instead of dissipating it uselessly, as we now do, in trivial and unimportant tasks.

Chapter X

PUBLIC OPINION, PROPAGANDA, AND DEMOCRACY

[THE opinions people entertain, the beliefs they hold, the ideals they cherish have, in a democratic society, a real influence upon public policy. As a consequence those who wish to influence that policy seek to mold the opinions, beliefs, and ideals of people. This means, in turn, that those who wish to maintain and improve the democratic way of life must seek to provide real freedom in the opinion industries—the schools, the press, and the radio, to improve the ability of the common man to analyze and evaluate propaganda devices, and finally to devise some valid way of differentiating the opinions of the majority from those opinions that special interests would have us believe the majority holds. Mr. Lerner, the Institute for Propaganda Analysis, and Mr. Gallup discuss certain aspects of these problems in the following articles.]

No. 30

FREEDOM IN THE OPINION INDUSTRIES [1]

by Max Lerner

LIKE other Americans I get letters from Europe that have always the same note: Europe is doomed; can a free society survive in America? It is now fashionable to answer Yes. The new note in speeches, books, and editorials is either "the coming victory of democracy" note or the "America is different" note. A native democratic élan is excellent, but, aside from the fact that every exhorter uses democracy in a different sense, it has thus far been left largely in the realm of exhortation. The New Deal program has bogged down not only because of its own lack of plan and cohesion, not only because of the bitter opposition of its enemies, but also because of the sabotage of those who should have been its friends—the very liberals

[1] Max Lerner, *Ideas are Weapons* (New York: The Viking Press, 1939), pp. 13-19. Reprinted by permission of the publisher. This material also appeared in *The Nation* (Nov. 4, 1939), Vol. 149, pp. 495-497.

who have been whipping themselves to new heights of fervor in defense of the democratic principle.

If we are honest with ourselves we will not blink the fact that we are entering one of the blackest crisis periods in our history. The outlook is bearish from any humanist angle. Already budgets are being cut, taxes eased for big enterprise, labor-protective legislation repealed, new labor-smashing laws introduced, strikes met with repression, educational expenditures whittled away, alien-baiting and red-baiting measures passed—and all while we engage in top-flight oratory about making democracy work. I have been reading a recent history of criminal-syndicalism legislation after the World War, and the story is a grim one. But nothing in the palmiest days of Palmer, Lusk, and the Centralia hysteria can equal the new tidal wave of reaction that is descending upon us. From Boston to San Francisco, from the Mexican border to Madison, there are ungentle preparations being made by corporate capitalism to take over just as soon as the New Deal has relaxed its grip.

I do not say this to register myself on the Jeremiah rolls. I say it because the fact that the once advancing democratic armies in America are now in full retreat is a fact that needs explaining. The current explanations run in terms either of "the swing of the pendulum" or of "the tyranny of words." But pendular theories are only a polite way of saying: "I don't know, but I won't admit it." And before words can have the power to become tyrants, the minds of people must be prepared for the tyranny through demoralization. My own belief is that the turning-point in that demoralization came with the 1937 "recession." The reactionary press campaign, which had reached a fierce intensity during the 1936 elections without showing any marked effect on them, was now resumed with a much greater probability of success. The masses had voted for Mr. Roosevelt not for any sophisticated reasons but because he had reached them by the propaganda of the deed—the actual accomplishments of the New Deal. They had caught the contagion of his assurance and felt that, whatever happened, he would be master of the occasion. But such a sense of confidence could not survive a new and drastic depression. The Roosevelt image lost much of its magic, and it became easy for the Coughlins and Gerald Winrods and Fritz Kuhns and their fellow-travelers to marshal their forces effectively on the battleground of opinion.

We are in the midst of a sharp struggle over opinion, and there is a sharper one still to come. Everyone feels a swing of the country's mood to the right—a swing well engineered and maneuvered. The pattern itself is clear: anti-Semitic (Coughlin, Kuhn, and eight-hundred-odd fascist organizations), anti-labor and vigilantist (Ford, Girdler, Associated Farmers), red-baiting (Dies, the Catholic hierarchy), anti-alien (the xenophobes in Congress and out), anti-democratic (all of them). What is not so clear is how far the swing will go before it is checked, and what is likely to check it. One answer is that a direct grappling with the problems of unemployment and shrinking capital investment will check it. And it is a good answer—if it can be translated into reality.

In short, we are in what may be ironically called a new Golden Age of propaganda. The last Golden Age came with the discovery and spread of advertising technique, the revelations in the army intelligence tests of the low level of popular thinking, and the underscoring the World War gave to the irrational character of all political thinking. The new Golden Age, using all that, has added to it the control—either by a state monopoly or by a class monopoly—of the channels and sources of opinion, and their systematic exploitation for state or class ends. As Harold Lasswell says, "A new skill group has come into existence in modern civilization . . . skill in propaganda has become one of the most effective roads to power in modern states." And that propaganda skill is at the service of those who are ruthless enough to use it and can pay for it.

As there is a new Golden Age of propaganda, so also there is a new Unholy Alliance in the winning and maintaining of power. There was once a phrase that passed current among historians—"the barons of the bags and the barons of the crags." There are groups in every culture to-day corresponding to these—and the Unholy Alliance is between them. The barons of the bags are the holders of economic power, acting through their government and dependent upon it. The barons of the crags are the newspaper publishers and editors, the masters of the radio, the propagandists, the back-stage manipulators of opinion—those who occupy the strategic passes to the castles of the mind and exact their heavy toll.

The vast new fact that is emerging out of the struggle for majority rule is that our fates are currently being determined by two sorts of minority strategy. A few men within the political governing group make decisions that condition the destiny of peoples. Nothing is clearer than that Chamberlain's whole appeasement policy was dictated by the fear that the defeat of Hitler and the collapse of fascist prestige would mean a genuine democratic victory throughout Europe. And the important thing is that he was able so to play on the fear of war of the English people that they accepted this appeasement policy; and then, when Hitler's territorial ambitions turned west rather than east, Chamberlain was able to play upon the English instinct for survival and modify his appeasement policy even to the extent of introducing conscription and finally going to war. Moreover, nothing could be clearer than that Czechoslovakia would have chosen to fight rather than be absorbed if a few men in the governing group had not preferred German domination to the acceptance of Soviet aid. One of them expressed it: "I would rather be invaded by Hitler than helped by Stalin"; and the important thing is that he was able to make his own personal preference override the exactly opposite preference of millions.

What happened yesterday in Spain and Czechoslovakia, what is happening to-day in England and France, may happen to-morrow in America. The Roosevelt government has weakened the hold of the Big Money group and has even succeeded in undermining the blind faith we once had in the barons of opinion, but it has not succeeded in controlling or displacing either group. They are still in control in the two strategic centers of American life. Their great weakness used to lie in their pathetic reliance upon money in the old sense—money to be used in buying power; and Chamberlain's government in England, with its cowardly betrayal of Spain to Franco and its bewildered hope that it could then buy Franco off by loans, is the classic illustration of this. But that is an old-fashioned and vestigial capitalist view. The new groups are to-day learning the subtler uses of money. They understand not only that money must be used very delicately and indirectly —behind the rhetoric of majority rule and the screen of a free press—to buy power, but also that power must be captured and retained in order to protect money. I should be greatly surprised if the economic groups behind the Chamberlain government ever allowed their kind of Cabinet—whether under Chamberlain or Halifax or Churchill or some essentially reactionary coalition—to be replaced by a genuinely democratic government, short of civil war. I should be equally surprised about France. Nor do I think a civil war will be necessary. In a time of confusion, when the big battalions of the majority are distracted and demoralized, the compact and ruthless storm troopers of opinion march in and take possession.

That is beginning to happen to-day in America. If the liberals do not know it yet they are blind. If they fail to act they are committing suicide.

How have they acted thus far to insure the survival of a free society? Whatever the contribution of the politicians and administrators, the contribution of the intellectuals seems to have been the fetishism of the principle. Many of them recognize the extent of fascist propaganda and the preparation of fascist terrorism in America to-day. Some of them even recognize the extent to which the formation of opinion in America to-day is a class monopoly, and the hopelessness of taking active measures for greater economic effectiveness and social well-being while that is true. Nevertheless, they persist in asserting that though the heavens may fall and the democratic state be destroyed, they will do nothing to qualify the principle of laissez faire in the opinion industries.

Of course, they do not see it quite that way. To them the realm of opinion-formation is not an industry but the sacred and untouchable province of the individual. They do not see that since Jefferson's day two things have happened that have wholly changed the conditions of freedom —first, the unremitting thrust of economic empire until it has subdued the political and the social unit of the corporate sway; second, the replacement of the free small newspaper by the mastodons of the press and radio, and the perfection of propaganda techniques to swell the power of those who control opinion.

The newspaper industry is one of the outstanding examples of the crowding out of the relatively free small enterprise by big capital. One reason why William Allen White is so tragic as well as so exciting a figure in modern journalism is that, as the editor and publisher of the Emporia (Kansas) *Gazette,* he stands for a world that was but that is no longer— stands for it with complete integrity but with a final ineffectiveness. The huge independent newspaper, such as the New York *Times,* which could not be replaced or effectively met in competition except by an enormous capital investment; the newspaper chains, like those of Hearst, Scripps-Howard, Gannett, Paul Block; the powerful press associations, such as the Associated Press or the United Press; the special-feature syndicates; the new and powerful pictorial weeklies; the advertising agencies—these have left the William Allen Whites in splendid isolation, attractive but none the less museum pieces. The temper of this group may be judged by the fact that for seven years now it has been consistently anti-New Deal while a majority of the people have been consistently pro-New Deal. It may be judged even better by reading the speeches and resolutions at the last convention of the American Newspaper Publishers' Association—one that had every index of a convention of the right-wing Republicans after the dissenters among them had been expelled and only a rump was left. The fact is that these gentlemen express the interests and the sentiments of big enterprise not only because of advertisers' pressures, but basically because they are themselves big enterprise. We cheer when a J. David Stern attempts to break this solid phalanx as he did for a time with the New York *Post;* but the reason Stern failed was that no single individual alone can break the phalanx, so long as the rest remain solid. And while a Stern was trying to do that in New York, hundreds of cities and towns had only a single newspaper or several owned by the same company—with no competition of ideas in either case.

Given these conditions, it is idle to talk any longer of "freedom" of press and opinion as though it were synonymous with the absence of governmental intervention of any sort. The fact is that here, as in other industries dominated by big corporate enterprise, laissez faire has come to mean not the freedom of all but the tyranny of the few.

No. 31

A "TVA" FOR THE OPINION INDUSTRIES [1]

by Max Lerner

LIBERALISM fights for its dogmas inch by inch before it yields them. The doctrine of the final triumph of the idea—that the truth, even though unaided, must prevail—died a hard death, if indeed it may be said to have died at all. But even more tenacious is the linked notion that there exists anything like a competitive system for ideas. To say that because I can get up and spout on a soap-box in Union Square or write in *The Nation* or start a newspaper in competition with Mr. Hearst or Mr. Howard I have freedom of opinion comparable to theirs is fantastic. I speak with the voice of one, Mr. Howard with the voice of millions. It is not because he is a better man than I, or because his ideas are truer or sounder, or because they represent more authentically the humanist tradition. It is because he has a major control in the opinion industry and I have not. My freedom to start a newspaper in competition with him is as real as my freedom to enter the field against the United States Steel Corporation. The fact in each instance is that it is hollow to talk of "freedom," whether economic freedom or freedom of opinion, except where there is equality or at least a framework of governmental control to reduce inequality.

Freedom is not laissez faire. We have come by this time to recognize that in the area of our economic life, but in the area of opinion we still cling to the belief that it is. It has taken us decades of social blundering to understand that economic freedom in the sense of the unregulated decisions of an irresponsible capitalism is no longer possible. We had better face the fact that the opinion industries are as much "affected with a public interest" as any others. A nation that has decided on a program of democratic control of the rest of its industrial area endangers the entire structure of control by allowing the corporate interests to shape public opinion at will. It is very well for liberals to speak of making a weapon of liberalism; but to make a fetish of the principle is far different from wielding the weapon.

[1] Max Lerner, *Ideas are Weapons* (New York: The Viking Press, 1939), pp. 19-24. Reprinted by permission of the publisher. This material also appeared in *The Nation* (Nov. 11, 1939), Vol. 149, pp. 522-524.

But all ideas have their uses. There has been much discussion among liberals of the problem of means and ends. We tend to forget that here, as elsewhere, absolutes are arid, and that ends and means are interrelated. Freedom is an end with respect to economic security; a culture that does not give scope to diversity of opinion is an unfree culture no matter how economically secure it may be, and the whole economic life of that culture is truncated. But freedom is also a means with respect to economic security, majority rule, cultural creativeness. To have an abstract freedom of opinion in a culture that is so organized that freedom—or, better, laissez faire —of opinion plays into the hands of economic scarcity and economic tyranny is but sand in our mouths—not nourishing but a matter for gritting of teeth. And that is actually the case with us. Freedom of opinion is precious in itself, yet it is also self-defeating if it is not used to insure the free building up of majority opinion, the orderly replacement of one majority by another, the refashioning of economic institutions to achieve the maximum security for all. Freedom has little meaning except in the context of equality, just as economic equality has only a stunted meaning except in a free society.

We must organize our freedom of opinion in such a way as to make it usable and not academic. But how do it? It is not an easy task, and it has its risks. The first step is to face the problem and face it in a tough-minded way. The question of means can then be tackled. My own preference is to extend the principles of the TVA "yardstick" and the SEC "truth in securities" into the opinion industries.

We must avoid a government-operated radio as in Great Britain, and we must avoid a government-monopolized press as in Germany, Italy, Russia. I propose the TVA principle in our radio system: in addition to, and side by side with, the great private broadcasting chains, let us have two major airways reserved for the government and run for it not by its bureaucrats but by the guild of radio artists. That it can be done has been demonstrated with brilliant success by the Federal Theater, which has prodded the creative forces of the theater from their slumber. Why should not a similar Federal Radio chain, run non-commercially and without advertising, serve to set a standard for the other chains to live up to, and serve to broadcast the merciless truth about our social conditions when the other chains fear to? The radio is inherently a better mechanism to use the competition of ideas than is the press. To begin with, the air already belongs to the nation and there can be no question raised legitimately of confiscation. The radio chains have their present position on sufferance. It would be only a step forward to use two of these strategic airways directly for public purposes and turn them over to the technicians, just as the actual teaching in our school and university system is in the hands of technicians.

With respect to the movies, the TVA principle would have to be different: it would have to be a private TVA. But why should not socially conscious money enter the movie industry, and set up great producing units that would put out the sort of film toward which Hollywood is only now beginning to make some feeble gestures? And why should not an RFC that finances all sorts of schemes be used to finance culturally productive enterprise of this sort? This would involve tackling the problem of distribution outlets as well; and there is much to be said for a framework of governmental controls over these outlets. It would involve also using the new film consumer organizations to give utterance to protests against the cowardly and the shoddy and to shape the supply in relation to the demand.

As for the press, the only solution is the long and hard road of creating competition by the deliberate and large-scale process of creating new competitors. There is no inherent economic law toward gigantism among newspapers. We could do with a good many more newspapers, even though it meant that none of them could be leviathans. Here, too, in every locality where there is no competition of ideas in the press, socially conscious money must enter to create competition—and it would be a legitimate function of the government to subsidize individuals and cooperatives that want to start such newspapers, much as we subsidize new housing. In the end, in the hands of good working newspaper men and women, they would pay for themselves financially and more than pay for themselves in cultural enrichment. Alexander Meiklejohn has suggested that our press be socialized like our universities. We could do much worse and we are doing much worse. But there is another possibility: to use the government power and the whole liberal tradition to bring about competition of ideas in a press that remains free from government control; which is, in the best sense, to socialize the press.

Given the reorganized opinion industries, one can turn to the problem of the control of outright propaganda with some hope of success. The problems of the internal organization of the opinion industries are problems of power; the propaganda problem is one of truth. The first involves the adequate representation of diverse points of view, equality of bargaining power in opinion, the accessibility of adequate information for the common man; the second involves a ban on flagrantly distorted information, intended deliberately as a poison for the public mind. The first involves the break-up of the opinion monopolies and the creation of a positive framework for competition in ideas; the second involves the regulation of cut throat competition and fraudulent practices in opinion. Of these the first is most important in the long run if we are ever to have a genuine market for ideas; but the second is more urgent in the short run as a matter of sheer democratic survival.

In meeting the propaganda danger, something like the SEC pattern would be the most effective procedure. We have a Truth in Securities Act to make sure that there is no rigging of the stock market, no false prospectuses, no unethical practices in the marketing of stocks and bonds. Are our securities more precious to us than our security, our stocks more delicate plants than our ideas, our investors more in need of protection than our common people? We have a Wheeler-Lea act against false advertising of drugs and cosmetics; are we to have nothing to protect us against the infinitely more dangerous advertising of anti-labor, anti-democratic, anti-Semitic lies?

I know that liberals will immediately say: Why could not a Truth in Opinion Act be used against the left as well as the right? The answer is that it is already in use against the left. Anti-alien and anti-radical measures are already being passed in Congress and in virtually every state legislature. Have any of the corporate heads or any of their legal aids protested against them? The Dies committee is already smearing the left with its so-called investigations; has it done anything substantial to investigate corporate fascism and regional fascism in America? We know perfectly well that before the legislation was enacted to control business, labor was already hemmed in by a de facto regulation. There was always a danger that the regulatory structure imposed upon business would be turned against labor as well; and, indeed, the Supreme Court tried its best to do so. Yet the total effect has been on the whole to carry through the original legislative intentions. The liberals and the left need not fear the creation of precedents that may be used against them. When a time of crisis comes, it will not be past precedents that count; new precedents, as Hitler has shown in Germany, can easily be created in the interests of ruthless power. What must be feared is not precedents but the sort of social breakdown that will make all precedents, good and bad, equally irrelevant.

To avoid this social breakdown we must move in the direction of a clear economic program, calling for democratic control of industry, and at the same time in the direction of regulation of anti-social propaganda. Individuals of the highest caliber would be required to man a board such as I have suggested. There come to my mind men like Lloyd Garrison, Alexander Meiklejohn, Alvin Johnson, William Allen White—men wise and tolerant in the way of words but so tenacious of the ethics of the thinking craft that they could recognize the spurious and dishonest. The task of such a board would be to require complete information about the provenience and financing of political statements, to see that all inflammatory radio statements are backed up by a bill of particulars, to allow for the answering of controversial material—and, if necessary, to ban material that is poisonous and spurious. The decisions of this board would be, of course, reviewable by the courts under the rule of law. With any sort of good direction the task of the board would become that of monitor rather than censor; and as one of the consequences the press and radio would in the long run set up their own code of ethics. Such a law would be hard to write. Yet surely it would be no more difficult than the drafting of the SEC.

This would not proceed on the principle that there need be no tolerance for the intolerant. I think that is an unnecessarily dangerous principle. To pick the intolerant would be a subjective matter; to hound them, an all-too-easy absolutism. What we want to create for all is a set of rules within which tolerance and intolerance shall operate.

What chance has such a program of becoming a reality? In the immediate future, very little. The confusion between laissez faire and genuine freedom in the opinion industries is unlikely to be dissipated easily, and as long as it remains in the popular mind any attempt, however prayerful and innocuous, to restore competition in ideas will lead to anguished howls from the monopolists—and the howls will be echoed through the entire country. Nevertheless, we must continue our attempts to clarify our thinking in this area. One of the crucial reasons for the failure of progressive movements in the past has been their unwillingness or inability to operate in this area, with the result that the mass mind has been turned against them and they have been doomed to a melancholy soliloquy.

American history is the story of the attempts of the minority will to suppress the democratic consciousness. It is the story, therefore, of successive upsurges of democratic strength, each of which has threatened to break the minority power. In 1932 there was such an upsurge. There will be another. When it comes, the progressives must understand that unless they can restore freedom in the opinion industries, they are again doomed to a brief flurry of excitement and reformism and then to a frustrated soliloquy.

No. 32

PROPAGANDA ANALYSIS AND HOW TO DETECT PROPAGANDA [1]

by The Institute for Propaganda Analysis

*T*HERE is to-day especial need for propaganda analysis. America is beset by a confusion of conflicting propagandas, a Babel of voices, warnings, charges, counter-charges, assertions, and contradictions assailing us continually through press, radio, and newsreel. These propagandas are disseminated by political parties, labor unions, business organizations, farm organizations, patriotic societies, churches, schools, and other agencies; also by word of mouth by millions of individuals.

If American citizens are to have clear understanding of conditions and what to do about them, they must be able to recognize propaganda, to analyze, and to appraise it.

But what is propaganda?

As generally understood, *propaganda is expression of opinion or action by individuals or groups deliberately designed to influence opinions or actions of other individuals or groups with reference to predetermined ends.*

Thus propaganda differs from scientific analysis. The propagandist is trying to "put something across," good or bad, whereas the scientist is trying to discover truth and fact. Often the propagandist does not want careful scrutiny and criticism; he wants to bring about a specific action. Because the action may be socially beneficial or socially harmful to millions of people, it is necessary to focus upon the propagandist and his activities the searchlight of scientific scrutiny. Socially desirable propaganda will not suffer from such examination, but the opposite type will be detected and revealed for what it is.

Propaganda which concerns us most is that which alters public opinion on matters of large social consequence often to the detriment of the majority of the people. Such propaganda, for example, is involved in issues such as these: Henry Ford and Tom Girdler should or should not recognize the CIO; Hitler and Mussolini and many dignitaries of the Catholic Church are right or wrong in siding against the Spanish loyalists; Japan

---

[1] The Institute for Propaganda Analysis, "Propaganda Analysis" (October, 1937), Vol. 1, No. 1, pp. 1-2; and "How to Detect Propaganda" (November, 1937), Vol. 1, No. 2, pp. 1-4. Reprinted by permission of *The Institute for Propaganda Analysis,* 40 East 49th Street, New York City.

is right or wrong in attacking China; Congress is right or wrong in rejecting President Roosevelt's Supreme Court plan; the President is to blame or not to blame for not knowing that Supreme Court Justice Black once was or was not a member of the Ku Klux Klan; "exposure" of Justice Black represents or does not represent the interests of persons opposed to the New Deal program of social legislation.

Many opinions or propagandas are highly charged with emotion, prejudice, bitterness. People make a virtue of defending their own opinions or propagandas. Many would deal with opinions or propagandas they don't like by suppressing them, by violence, if need be. But suppression of unpopular opinions or propagandas is contrary to democratic conceptions of government. A heresy or an unpopular propaganda or opinion may be bad, or good. One way to find out is by analysis and classification according to types and interests.

    •   •   •   •   •   •   •

We are fooled by propaganda chiefly because we don't recognize it when we see it. It may be fun to be fooled but, as the cigarette ads used to say, it is more fun to know. We can more easily recognize propaganda when we see it if we are familiar with the seven common propaganda devices. These are:

1. The Name Calling Device
2. The Glittering Generalities Device
3. The Transfer Device
4. The Testimonial Device
5. The Plain Folks Device
6. The Card Stacking Device
7. The Band Wagon Device

Why are we fooled by these devices? Because they appeal to our emotions rather than to our reason. They make us believe and do something we would not believe or do if we thought about it calmly, dispassionately. In examining these devices, note that they work most effectively at those times when we are too lazy to think for ourselves; also, they tie into emotions which sway us to be "for" or "against" nations, races, religions, ideals, economic and political policies and practices, and so on through automobiles, cigarettes, radios, toothpastes, presidents, and wars. With our emotions stirred, it may be fun to be fooled by these propaganda devices, but it is more fun and infinitely more to our own interests to know how they work.

Lincoln must have had in mind citizens who could balance their emotions with intelligence when he made his remark: ". . . but you can't fool all of the people all of the time."

NAME CALLING

"Name Calling" is a device to make us form a judgment without examining the evidence on which it should be based. Here the propagandist appeals to our hate and fear. He does this by giving "bad names" to those individuals, groups, nations, races, policies, practices, beliefs, and ideals which he would have us condemn and reject. For centuries the name "heretic" was bad. Thousands were oppressed, tortured, or put to death as heretics. Anybody who dissented from popular or group belief or practice was in danger of being called a heretic. In the light of to-day's knowledge, some heresies were bad and some were good. Many of the pioneers of modern science were called heretics; witness the cases of Copernicus, Galileo, Bruno. (See *A History of the Warfare of Science with Theology*, Andrew Dickson White, D. Appleton & Co.) To-day's bad names include: Fascist, demagogue, dictator, Red, financial oligarchy, Communist, muckraker, alien, outside agitator, economic royalist, Utopian, rabble-rouser, trouble-maker, Tory, Constitution wrecker.

"Al" Smith called Roosevelt a Communist by implication when he said in his Liberty League speech, "There can be only one capital, Washington or Moscow." When "Al" Smith was running for the presidency many called him a tool of the Pope, saying in effect, "We must choose between Washington and Rome." That implied that Mr. Smith, if elected President, would take his orders from the Pope. Recently, Mr. Justice Hugo Black has been associated with a bad name, Ku Klux Klan. In these cases some propagandists have tried to make us form judgments without examining essential evidence and implications. "Al Smith is a Catholic. He must never be President." "Roosevelt is a Red. Defeat his program." "Hugo Black is or was a Klansman. Take him out of the Supreme Court."

Use of "bad names" without presentation of their essential meaning, without all their pertinent implications, comprises perhaps the most common of all propaganda devices. Those who want to *maintain* the status quo apply bad names to those who would change it. For example, the Hearst press applies bad names to Communists and Socialists. Those who want to *change* the status quo apply bad names to those who would maintain it. For example, the *Daily Worker* and the *American Guardian* apply bad names to conservative Republicans and Democrats.

GLITTERING GENERALITIES

"Glittering Generalities" is a device by which the propagandist identifies his program with virtue by use of "virtue words." Here he appeals to our emotions of love, generosity, and brotherhood. He uses words like truth, freedom, honor, liberty, social justice, public service, the right to work, loyalty, progress, democracy, the American way, Constitution defender. These words suggest shining ideals. All persons of good will believe in these ideals. Hence the propagandist, by identifying his individual group, nation, race, policy, practice, or belief with such ideals, seeks to win us to his cause. As Name Calling is a device to make us form a judgment to *reject and condemn,* without examining the evidence, Glittering Generalities is a device to make us *accept and approve,* without examining the evidence.

For example, use of the phrases, "the right to work" and "social justice" may be a device to make us accept programs for meeting the labor-capital problem which, if we examined them critically, we would not accept at all.

In the Name Calling and Glittering Generalities devices, words are used to stir up our emotions and to befog our thinking. In one device "bad words" are used to make us mad; in the other "good words" are used to make us glad. (See "The Tyranny of Words," by Stuart Chase, in *Harper's Magazine* for November, 1937.)

The propagandist is most effective in use of these devices when his words make us create devils to fight or gods to adore. By his use of the "bad words," we personify as a "devil" some nation, race group, individual, policy, practice, or ideal; we are made fighting mad to destroy it. By use of "good words," we personify as a god-like idol some nation, race, group, etc. Words which are "bad" to some are "good" to others, or may be made so. Thus, to some the New Deal is "a prophecy of social salvation" while to others it is "an omen of social disaster."

From consideration of names, "bad" and "good," we pass to institutions and symbols, also "bad" and "good." We see these in the next device.

TRANSFER

"Transfer" is a device by which the propagandist carries over the authority, sanction, and prestige of something we respect and revere to something he would have us accept. For example, most of us respect and revere our church and our nation. If the propagandist succeeds in getting church or nation to approve a campaign in behalf of some program, he thereby transfers its authority, sanction, and prestige to that program. Thus we may accept something which otherwise we might reject.

In the Transfer device symbols are constantly used. The cross represents the Christian Church. The flag represents the nation. Cartoons like Uncle Sam represent a consensus of public opinion. Those symbols stir emotions. At their very sight, with the speed of light, is aroused the whole complex of feelings we have with respect to church or nation. A cartoonist by having Uncle Sam disapprove a budget for unemployment relief would have us feel that the whole United States disapproves relief costs. By drawing an Uncle Sam who approves the same budget, the cartoonist would have us feel that the American people approve it. Thus, the Transfer device is used both for and against causes and ideas.

TESTIMONIAL

The "Testimonial" is a device to make us accept anything from a patent medicine or a cigarette to a program of national policy. In this device the propagandist makes use of testimonials. "When I feel tired, I smoke a Camel and get the grandest 'lift.'" "We believe the John Lewis plan of labor organization is splendid; CIO should be supported." This device works in reverse also; counter-testimonials may be employed. Seldom are these used against commercial products like patent medicines and cigarettes, but they are constantly employed in social, economic, and political issues. "We believe that the John Lewis plan of labor organization is bad; CIO should not be supported."

PLAIN FOLKS

"Plain Folks" is a device used by politicians, labor leaders, business men, and even by ministers and educators to win our confidence by appearing to be people like ourselves—"just plain folks among the neighbors." In election years especially do candidates show their devotion to little children and the common, homey things of life. They have front porch campaigns. For the newspaper men they raid the kitchen cupboard, finding there some of the good wife's apple pie. They go to country picnics; they attend service at the old frame church; they pitch hay and go fishing; they show their belief in home and mother. In short, they would win our votes by showing that they're just as common as the rest of us—"just plain folks"—and, therefore, wise and good. Business men often are "plain folks" with the factory hands. Even distillers use the device. "It's our family's whiskey, neighbor; and, neighbor, it's your price."

CARD STACKING

"Card Stacking" is a device in which the propagandist employs all the arts of deception to win our support for himself, his group, nation, race, policy, practice, belief or ideal. He stacks the cards against the truth. He uses under-emphasis and over-emphasis to dodge issues and evade facts. He resorts to lies, censorship, and distortion. He omits facts. He offers false testimony. He creates a smoke-screen of clamor by raising a new issue when he wants an embarrassing matter forgotten. He draws a red herring across the trail to confuse and divert those in quest of facts he does not want revealed. He makes the unreal appear real and the real appear unreal. He lets half-truth masquerade as truth. By the Card Stacking device, a mediocre candidate, through the "build-up," is made to appear an intellectual titan; an ordinary prize fighter a probable world champion; a worthless patent medicine a beneficent cure. By means of this device propagandists would convince us that a ruthless war of aggression is a crusade for righteousness. Some member nations of the Non-Intervention Committee send their troops to intervene in Spain. Card Stacking employs sham, hypocrisy, effrontery.

THE BAND WAGON

The "Band Wagon" is a device to make us follow the crowd, to accept the propagandist's program en masse. Here his theme is: "Everybody's doing it." His techniques range from those of medicine show to dramatic spectacle. He hires a hall, fills a great stadium, marches a million men in parade. He employs symbols, colors, music, movement, all the dramatic arts. He appeals to the desire, common to most of us, to "follow the crowd." Because he wants us to "follow the crowd" in masses, he directs his appeal to groups held together by common ties of nationality, religion, race, environment, sex, vocation. Thus propagandist campaigning for or against a program will appeal to us as Catholics, Protestants, or Jews; as members of the Nordic race or as Negroes; as farmers or as school teachers; as housewives or as miners. All the artifices of flattery are used to harness the fears and hatreds, prejudices, and biases, convictions and ideals common to the group; thus emotion is made to push and pull the group on to the Band Wagon. In newspaper articles and in the spoken word this device is also found. "Don't throw your vote away. Vote for our candidate. He's sure to win." Nearly every candidate wins in every election—before the votes are in.

PROPAGANDA AND EMOTION

Observe that in all these devices our emotion is the stuff with which propagandists work. Without it they are helpless; with it, harnessing it to their purposes, they can make us glow with pride or burn with hatred, they can make us zealots in behalf of the program they espouse. As we said in our first letter, propaganda as generally understood is expression of opinion or action by individuals or groups with reference to pre-determined ends. Without the appeal to our emotion—to our fears and to our courage, to our selfishness and unselfishness, to our loves and to our hates—propagandists would influence few opinions and few actions.

To say this is not to condemn emotion, an essential part of life, or to assert that all pre-determined ends of propagandists are "bad." What we mean is that the intelligent citizen does not want propagandists to utilize his emotions, even to the attainment of "good" ends, without knowing what is going on. He does not want to be "used" in the attainment of ends he may later consider "bad." He does not want to be gullible. He does not want to be fooled. He does not want to be duped, even in a "good" cause. He wants to know the facts and among these is included the fact of the utilization of his emotions.

For better understanding of the relationship between propaganda and emotion see Chapter 1 of *Folkways* by William Graham Sumner (Ginn and Company). This shows why most of us tend to feel, believe, and act in traditional patterns. See also *Mind in the Making* by James Harvey Robinson (Harper Bros.). This reveals the nature of the mind and suggests how to analyze propaganda appealing to traditional thought patterns.

Keeping in mind the seven common propaganda devices, turn to to-day's newspapers and almost immediately you can spot examples of them all. At election time or during any campaign, Plain Folks and Band Wagon are common. Card Stacking is hardest to detect because it is adroitly executed or because we lack the information necessary to nail the lie. A little practice with the daily newspapers in detecting these propaganda devices soon enables us to detect them elsewhere—in radio, news-reel, books, magazines, and in expression of labor unions, business groups, churches, schools, political parties.

No. 33

POLLING PUBLIC OPINION [1]

by George Gallup

ON a street corner in Boston a stock broker stops to answer the questions of a young man with a sheaf of ballots and a lead pencil:

"Whom would you like to see elected President in November?" the young man asks.

"Well, my first choice would be Wendell Willkie," says the stock br
"but I doubt whether the politicians would take to him. Put me
Willkie, but say I'm still not quite decided. What's your ne

"If Canada is actually invaded by any European pow
the United States should use its Army and Navy to

[1] George Gallup, "Polling Public Opinion," *Current Hist.*
pp. 23-26, 57. Reprinted by permission of *Current History*

"Yes, that's one case where I'd be willing to see this country go into action. But I'm against our looking for trouble overseas."

The scene shifts to a backwoods road in Arkansas. The man who is asking the questions wears a cap, and the man who answers wears the faded overalls of a back-country farmer. But the questions are the same. Both the stock broker and the farmer agree that the United States should come to the aid of Canada if the Dominion should be invaded. The Arkansas farmer wants a third term for President Roosevelt. Both men are chance cogs in a continuous process of sampling American public opinion. Both were selected on the initiative of the field investigator, but only after careful and detailed instructions from his home office. Multiplied hundreds of times, the interviews give a week-by-week picture of what Americans are thinking about the Presidency, about the war in Europe and the dozens of other issues in American national life.

What do the new surveys of public opinion contribute? How are they conducted? What are the limits of their usefulness?

The year 1940 is a Presidential election year, and more people will be asking these questions about this new kind of research than ever before. Many of the questions imply a criticism. The questioners recall the epic failure of *The Literary Digest* "straw vote" in 1936, and they wonder whether the new surveys of public sentiment are not "some kind of a stunt" which will go the way of *The Digest* in coming election tests. Most of the criticisms, however, indicate a misunderstanding of the nature of the new science of public opinion measurement.

The problem which the new surveys seek to solve—finding out what a nation of more than 80,000,000 adults thinks—is not new. Congressmen, legislators and Presidents have applied their ingenuity to the problem since 1789. Their chief reliance has been letters from constituents, editorials in the press and in party organs and "keeping the ear to the ground" in general. A kind of "straw vote" was conducted by *The Raleigh* (N. C.) *Star* more than a hundred years ago on the Presidential chances of Andrew Jackson.

What the new surveys of public opinion have done is to apply scientific methods to the old problem of finding out what the people of this free-thinking, free-speaking democracy wish to do with their society.

In the 1936 election, while most American readers were following the widely publicized reports of *The Literary Digest* "straw vote," which sent out more than 10,000,000 straw ballots, the new *polls* were undergoing their ¬st big test. Using only a small fraction of the gigantic sendout employed The Digest, the American Institute of Public Opinion, the Crossley poll The Fortune Survey all forecast a Roosevelt victory while *The Digest* predicted a landslide for Landon. While some of the new surveys weren't quite as accurate as their sponsors hoped, the experiences of the 1936 election did point the way to invaluable refinements in method and approach. Most important of all, the election validated the principle of the scientifically selected cross-section over the mass-balloting methods used by earlier polls and straw votes.

As the new surveys of public opinion venture into another Presidential year, their distinguishing mark is the use of this cross-section principle. Briefly it means that interviews must be obtained from each of the important and heterogeneous opinion groups in the United States *in exact proportion to the size of that group in American life or in proportion to its numbers on election day.* In the great majority of cases six main "controls" have been found to suffice: The sample must contain the proper proportion of (1) voters from each state, (2) men and women, (3) farm voters, voters in towns of 2,500 or less, and voters in towns and cities of more than 2,500, (4) voters of all age groups, including those who will come of age by election day, (5) voters of above-average and below-average incomes, as well as persons on relief, and (6) Democrats, Republicans and persons of other political affiliations.

In the state of Iowa, for instance, approximately 12 per cent of the total population are receiving relief or old-age assistance or are on WPA projects. Hence, in a typical Institute survey, 12 per cent of the interviews would have to come from persons in these various "relief" categories, and so on for the other income levels. Approximately 39 per cent live on farms, while 61 per cent live in cities and small towns, and interviews must be assigned so as to reflect this residential division accurately. In the last Presidential election Iowa cast 56 per cent of its major party vote for Roosevelt, 44 for Landon. Hence 56 per cent of the major party interviews in Iowa must be with Roosevelt voters, 44 per cent with Landon voters, and appropriate numbers for the lesser parties, and, of course, for persons who have just come of voting age. Approximately 10 per cent of the state's population are between the ages of 20 and 24, and so the proper number of interviews must come from this group and from other age groups.

And finally, since Iowa counts for about 2½ per cent of the nation's voting population, 2½ per cent of the interviews in a national survey must come from that state.

Essentially there is nothing new in the principle of cross-section sampling. The county bacteriologist who takes specimens of the water in a neighborhood stream at different points, to determine its purity, is making use of the principle. So is the ore-tester who calculates the richness of a lode of iron ore by thrusting a scoop into the ore at different points. What is new is the application of cross-section sampling to the much more difficult business of sampling public opinion. Surprisingly enough this major principle has been completely overlooked in nearly all previous surveys of the public.

"Public opinion," wrote Michel de Montaigne, the eminent sixteenth century philosopher, "is a powerful, bold and *unmeasurable* party." (Italic ours.)

Even fifty years ago, the famous student of the American form of government, James Bryce, thought that the problem of ascertaining true public opinion was almost insurmountable. But Bryce foresaw a day when some new machinery for registering the public will at frequent intervals, between elections, might be set up.

While many students of public opinion are chiefly interested in the new public opinion measurement as a political instrument and as an answer to Bryce's problem, the questions most commonly asked of those who conduct the news surveys are questions of detail. By far the commonest of all is the query: *"Why haven't I been interviewed?"* The question comes from men and women, in honest perplexity, who sit down and write to the American Institute of Public Opinion about it, and it comes from persons who would like to see the polls discredited for some reason of their own. One of those who has raised the question in good faith is General Hugh S. Johnson, who has asked various audiences whether anyone present has ever been interviewed. In a recent column the General reported that in an audience of 1600 "little businessmen" only one hand was raised.

Results such as General Johnson's cause the American Institute no surprise. Indeed, we should have been disturbed if several hands had been raised. In modern polls of public opinion the *number* of persons interviewed is almost the least important factor. Far more important in assuring accuracy is the representativeness of the cross-section. Indeed, it is even possible that a perfectly satisfactory nation-wide poll could be conducted with only 500 or 1000 interviews *provided they were properly selected*. It is safe to say, certainly, that no poll in the history of the United States ever went wrong because too few persons were reached.

If these statements seem strange, it is because most Americans still cling to the notion that the accuracy of *The Literary Digest* prior to 1936 was the result of its millions of ballots. But while millions of ballots are justifiable from a publicity standpoint, experience and statistical theory both indicate that a point is speedily reached in nearly every survey, *usually within a few thousand interviews*, where the addition of further interviews does not materially alter the total vote.

Consider, for example, the Institute's study of opinion on the NRA. In 1936 a survey of 30,000 ballots was conducted on the question: "Would you like to see the NRA revived?" The first 500 cases showed a "no" vote of 54.9 per cent. The complete sample of 30,000 cases returned a "no" vote of 55.5 per cent. In other words, the addition of 29,500 cases to the first 500 cases in this instance made a difference of only six-tenths of one per cent in the national findings. Here are the figures:

Number of Cases	Per Cent Voting Against Reviving the NRA
First 500 Ballots	54.9
First 1,000 Ballots	53.9
First 5,000 Ballots	55.4
First 10,000 Ballots	55.4
All 30,000 Ballots	55.5

In its studies on national issues the Institute generally uses from 3,000 to 60,000 interviews, depending on the statistical problems involved. In a country with an eligible voting population of more than 60,000,000 voters, this means that when the minimum number of persons are interviewed in a weekly survey an individual's chance of being polled is about one in 20,000. The odds against his being polled even in a year's time are overwhelming.

"How accurate are the new polls of public opinion?" is a second common question that grows naturally out of the first. As compared with the 1936 record of *The Literary Digest*, certainly, the record so far is good. In the poll conducted for *Fortune* magazine, Elmo Roper's cross-section sampling came within 1 per cent of President Roosevelt's election percentage. The Institute, which sampled on a state-by-state basis, indicated the dimensions of Roosevelt's landslide and placed 42 of the 48 states correctly for Roosevelt and Landon. In the 1938 Congressional elections, in the "purge" primaries of 1938 and in numerous other state and local elections, the Institute has had an average error of less than 2 per cent.

But while the new surveys of public opinion should generally prove to be within 3 or 4 percentage points of the public's true division on national questions, it is well to remember that the polls have important limitations. Their accuracy is usually the rough accuracy of the yardstick rather than the precise distinctions of the scientist's micrometer. It is easily conceivable that a national election will be decided sometime—in 1940 or afterwards—by a very close margin. The sampling method cannot be refined to the point of forecasting the close ones with absolute accuracy. The "normal expectancy of error" in samples of different sizes has been worked out, as a matter of fact, by Professor Theodore Brown of Harvard. Professor Brown's tables of probability show that with a cross-section of 900 cases the chances are 997 in a thousand that the range of error will not exceed 5 per cent—even where opinion is divided 50-50. With a much larger sample, say of 2,500 cases, the normal error will be within 3 per cent.

The Institute does not believe it can be right 100 per cent of the time. Indeed, by the same token that we expect to be right 95 times out of a hundred, we expect to be wrong five times in a hundred. The Institute's goal in a national forecast is to keep its error within 4 percentage points and to be on the right side at least nine times out of ten. Surveys on issues, of course, are a relatively simple problem in accuracy as compared with election surveys, since the latter actually involve at least four separate forecasts: (1) the division of sentiment between the candidates, (2) the proportion of voters who will go to the polls, (3) the effectiveness of political machines in getting out their share of the vote, and (4) the extent of such external factors as political corruption, if any, and the effect of the weather on turnout. A serious miscalculation in any one of these phases may be enough to cause an entire survey to go awry.

One of the bogeys which is sometimes raised regarding research in public opinion is the fear that they may create a "bandwagon" rush to what appears to be the popular side. Politicians especially have paid so much attention to attempting to create "bandwagon" movements themselves that not a few of them look with suspicion on polls for this reason. Congressman Pierce of Oregon has introduced a bill in every recent Congress since 1932 calling for an investigation of polls on two main grounds:

1. That they tend to destroy the democratic process by discouraging people from going to the polls; that "winning" voters would feel that their votes were unnecessary, and that "losing" voters would remain away from the ballot box on the theory their votes would not help.

2. That polls handicap the losing side because, in Congressman Pierce's opinion, a substantial number of voters are fickle and can be swung onto the "bandwagon" of the winning side.

How much substance is there to such observations? And how much shadow? Is there a real "bandwagon" influence, or is the "bandwagon" theory merely one of the delusions which has survived the days of "ear-to-the-ground" political methods? Do polls cause the voters to stay away from the ballot box on election day?

In the first place, polls have no monopoly on the forecasting of elections. Forecasts by newspaper correspondents, party leaders and candidates have been an accustomed part of every political campaign in the United States for generations. In the Presidential election four years ago, the most accurate state-by-state forecast was not made by a poll but by Democratic Party Chairman Jim Farley. If in 1940 the polls are to be scrutinized on the grounds that they may discourage voting, or cause a "bandwagon" effect, undoubtedly some attention should also be paid to the pronouncements of genial Jim. How many Republicans will turn around and vote for the Democratic candidate this November if Mr. Farley says that the Democrats will carry every state but Maine and Vermont?

Fortunately there is considerable evidence to answer both points made by Congressman Pierce. In the first place, a careful examination of the record gives no clue that polls decrease voting participation. On the contrary, since 1933, the period when election polls have risen to national prominence, the popular vote has shown a steady proportionate *increase*.

It would be just as plausible to argue that, by stimulating political discussion and adding to the interest and liveliness of a compaign, the polls have actually helped to increase voting participation. A look at the record shows that in 1936, the peak-year of poll interest, more than 45,600,000 Americans cast their votes, an increase of 6,000,000 over 1932 and the highest proportion of voting participation in the history of the nation.

Secondly, an investigation of dozens of state and local elections in the past three years shows that—as far as the rank-and-file of voters are concerned—the bandwagon theory has little existence in fact. The bandwagon theory assumes, of course, that when Candidate A has once been shown in the lead there will be a substantial shift of voters to his side; that his majority in succeeding polls will be increasingly large, and that he will poll a still larger majority on election day.

It is hard to say how the theory can be accommodated to the hard facts of the 1936 election, in which *The Literary Digest* consistently, week after week, and over a gigantic newspaper and radio network, forecast the election of Alf M. Landon. Here was a straw vote that had never been wrong, that commanded a far larger audience than the new polls of public opinion commanded at that time. And yet more than 27,000,000 voters cast their votes for the predicted *Digest* "loser," while less than 17,000,000 voted for *The Digest* "winner." If the "bandwagon" moved at all in 1936, it apparently moved in reverse.

An even clearer laboratory case is the instance of the 1938 Democratic primary in Kentucky. Here Senator Alben W. Barkley, the Presidential favorite, was running the race of his life against Governor "Happy" Chandler for the senatorial nomination. The Institute entered the state and conducted a series of polls between April and the August election day. The first survey showed Senator Barkley far in the lead with 67 per cent of the Democratic vote. The results were widely circulated in Kentucky. According to the "bandwagon" theory, Mr. Barkley's margin should have increased in subsequent Institute tests. But what occurred? Instead of increasing, Mr. Barkley's popular support shrunk as Governor Chandler carried his aggressive campaign to the "one-gallus" citizens along Kentucky's unmapped back roads. With further hectic campaigning by both candidates the Barkley vote dropped to 61 per cent, then to 59 per cent. On election day, a few days after the Institute completed its series of studies, the Barkley vote was 57 per cent. *The Institute has conducted more than fifty surveys of elections and spaced issues, where the movement of votes to candidates in successive surveys was charted, and continuous studies on this point are being made at the present time, yet little or no evidence of the existence of a bandwagon vote has ever been detected.*

Two final points are frequently made (1) by those who assume that the measurement of public opinion is desirable, but who point to possible weaknesses and defects in present methods, and (2) by those who view such research as a revolutionary attempt to substitute "pure" democracy for America's carefully cherished system of representative democracy.

The first of these two types of criticism is distinctly valuable; it comes chiefly from students of politics and sociology and from the Institute's own staff of specialists. This type of analysis centers on the problem of question-wording (including the view that "you can get any answer you want by wording the question appropriately"), the problems of the cross-section, and the character and value of the opinions obtained. Here, in the field of methodology, there will be constant material for self-examination and self-improvement by the polling organizations. It is the real field in which constructive criticism has not yet gone far enough.

As Professor Studenski has pointed out in a recent article, polls can be misleading when they are poorly conducted. But a badly worded questionnaire is self-exposing. It does not require an expert to know that a question worded: "Should President Roosevelt stop oppressing business?" (suggested by one reader of the polls) is stacked with bias. To eliminate both bias and unintelligibility, the Institute participates in constant testing and retesting of the questions which it selects for study. Questions are phrased in a tentative fashion and put into the hands of special investigators for actual street and home interviewing. Included among those interviewed are persons drawn from all walks of life, including sharp-eared professional people and students.

Finally, to discover valid differences which may be caused by variations in wording, the Institute uses a "split-ballot" technique in numerous instances. In these experiments, two similar wordings are used on separate questionnaires. One form of the question is put to half of the voters in the cross-section, the other to the remaining half. The tabulation soon reveals the difference, if any, which is caused by the wordings. If the difference is greater than the expected variation due to the size of the cross-section, then new and neutral phrasings must be found.

In a recent compilation of more than 200 such instances of the "split-ballot" technique the Institute found a greater-than-expected difference in only a small fraction of the cases, although many of the wordings were substantially altered in the twin forms. Experience seems to show that *where there is no material alteration in the thought expressed, there will be no material difference in the result, no matter what wording is used.* In fact, on many of the most deeply-held opinions in America to-day—such as the popularity of President Roosevelt or the question of American participation in the European war—a very stable opinion can be elicited by merely mentioning the subject, without phrasing a formal question at all.

Another sphere in which constructive criticism and research are being employed is in the direction of "intensity" measurements. Here, the object is to determine which views, as expressed to the interviewer, are deeply held and which only shallowly. Numerous checks, both subjective and objective, are being employed. A voter is asked his opinion, for example, on the Wagner Labor Act, and is then asked: "How convinced are you of that—completely convinced or only partly convinced?" The replies to the second question provide a means of singling out the undecided individual or the person with little interest in the issue. It may well be, however, that the most effective way of measuring the intensity of a "public opinion" will continue to be the study of majority and minority *trends* over spaced intervals. A proposition that gains the support of an increasing number of voters, whether intensely approved by all of them or not, is a proposition which must be reckoned with in the legislatures and forums of American life.

Only a word need be said about the final criticism of the surveys—the charge that they constitute a threat to America's cherished representative democracy. Often this charge indicates more about the critics than it does about the polls themselves, for American political theory has long been divided between those who would place more power in the hands of the people, and those who are fearful of the people and would limit that power sharply. Through the history of the last 160 years the lines have formed, with Alexander Hamilton on one side arguing that "your public, sir, is a beast," and Thomas Jefferson on the other, arguing that the majority of the plain people are less likely to misgovern themselves, in the long run, than any smaller and more exclusive group of the elite.

Interestingly enough, most of the observations on the wisdom of the majority have been based on speculations, or on the actions of small groups of people, such, on the one hand, as New England town meeting groups or, on the other, the red-handed mobs which took control of the French Revolution and who left such an impression upon Edmund Burke, De Tocqueville and others.

Are these fears of the common people justified, or are they merely hobgoblins? In the last five years the researches of the American Institute have begun to chart some of the coastlines of the largely unexplored American mind, probing into just what the majority of the American people do hold to; whether they are responsible or irresponsible; blindly radical, blindly conservative or somewhere in between; and whether their judgments may or may not make sense when viewed in perspective.

A final answer to some of these questions can only be given by history, but I am personally convinced that the average American is more competent to judge what his best interests are than ever before. In part this is the result of the revolutionary impact of mass education, of moving pictures, of daily newspapers and of the million-tongued radio. As individuals, these people may not be brilliant or intellectual or particularly well-read, but they possess a collective quality of good sense which is manifested time and again.

The important point is, however, that under a system of representative democracy like our own, public opinion may only be useful in determining the fundamental human *ends* of public policy, not the important ways and means by which these ends may be obtained. The people cannot be expected to express judgments on complicated technical or administrative policies. As society becomes more complex there is a greater and greater need for experts. Nor is it in the province of the people to initiate legislation. The need for the Congressman, the intelligent representative, remains as great as ever. What has been provided by the polls is a means of ventilating the gigantic structure of modern government with fresh draughts of what the usually silent and inarticulate people are thinking.

Chapter XI

THE POLITICAL PARTY

No. 34

[WE have already seen that a democratic government is one in which the mass of adult citizens have the opportunity to choose and to hold responsible those charged with the formulation of public policy. This necessitates some instrument of choice and the political parties are that instrument. The political parties are the foundation upon which the life of the democratic state is built. The parties arrange the issues and present the candidates upon which the people are to vote. This enables the mass of men to make a decision as to whether the party in office is acting in accordance with their interest.

Admittedly the parties do not function perfectly in the performance of these functions. Yet, when every criticism of the party system has been made, the service which it renders to the democratic state is tremendous. It is, if nothing else, the greatest obstacle in the path of dictatorship. It enables the electorate to choose between alternatives; to change its rulers.]

THE DUTY OF AN OPPOSITION PARTY [1]

by Harold J. Laski

GOVERNMENT by discussion is effective only when the institutions exist which enable its results to compel action. That is why the party system at its best is the foundation upon which a representative democracy is built. For when the issues between parties are real the clash of opinion is bound to illuminate. The need to convince involves intellectual exploration. Men seek to make a case for their policy not only to persuade themselves, but to transfer the support of others to their side. Where the administration of the State is built upon a coherent philosophy it is only by its critical analysis that its truth can be rationally weighed. This is the real case for democratic government. No dictatorship can

[1] Harold J. Laski, "A Word to the Republicans," *Harper's Magazine* (October, 1935), Vol. 171, pp. 513-523. Reprinted by permission of *Harper's Magazine*.

afford to put its ultimate principles to the test of analysis, for its basic assumption is that they are beyond discussion. It is bound, therefore, by the logic of its nature to regard all criticism of essentials as treasonable by definition since it is, inherently, an invitation to its destruction. A Russian citizen may attack the record of a motor factory's output; he cannot with confidence attack the basis of Marxian socialism. A German citizen may maintain the view that Europe cannot afford a new war; but he cannot safely insist that the persecution of Jews is a barbaric adventure or that General Goering's behavior over the Reichstag fire trial makes him clearly unfit to hold office in any civilized country. No Italian citizen may hope to argue in public that the corporative state is merely a mask behind which capitalism protects itself from the claims of economic democracy, though he has, of course, a wide freedom in the niceties of archaeological discovery or the radical emendation of a classical text. A dictatorship, by its nature, hears only the opinion it wants to hear, by the convenient, and relatively simple, method of suppressing any alternative which may prove in experience to be uncomfortable.

Yet it is the main lesson of the human adventure that alternative opinion cannot, in the long run, be suppressed in this way. There is, given a long enough time, a stark objectivity about fact which prevents its interpretation from remaining in a condition of permanent subservience to any dictatorship. Had it been otherwise, Christianity would not have survived the Pagan persecutions; had it been otherwise also, militant Christianity would not have retreated before the persistent claims of free thought. Every great novelty in history which has expressed some wide and deep experience among men has been able, in the long run, to triumph over the most urgent effort at its destruction. Truth, doubtless, is slow and painful in its search for acceptance; but its rejection has always, in the long run, been fatal to those who have refused to see its significance.

An adequately organized democracy is at least a safeguard against this inherent weakness of dictatorship; but it is upon the sovereign condition that it is in fact adequately organized. To be so it must not merely provide the opportunity for discussion; it must provide the institutions through which hostility to the will of government may have the means to effect a transfer of political power. Whatever reasons, that is to say, there are for the existence of government in a democratic society, these are also reasons for the existence of an opposition. The grounds for this view are simple enough. Men live differently; they move, by different paths, to the achievement of opposed desires. Either a government must prohibit desires alien from its own or it must admit their right to be. But in social life, to be is to seek to grow; and the purpose of growth in all matters of social constitution is translation into the ultimate fabric of the society. The idea seeks inevitably to impose itself by reason of the experience it embodies. Men who seek to infer the meaning of their experience are driven by an inescapable impulse to win for their insight the status of a universal.

Discussion in a democracy is the highroad along which they must move. But it is the price of social complexity that private insights must achieve organic form if they are to attract attention. In political life this seems to involve adoption by a party as the means which makes an insight originally private a matter of public consequence. For what a party does in the life history of a community is to act as the broker of ideas. From the mass of claims which present themselves as valid it selects those which, in its judgment and, as a general rule, from the intellectual standpoint it broadly represents, are most likely to win the favor of the multitude. It seeks to make them acceptable by all the arts that human ingenuity can invent. It uses them as its instruments in its efforts to persuade men that its title to supreme power is greater than that of its rivals.

The technic, of course, is slow; and it has a pathology of its own which not even its most enthusiastic advocates can reasonably deny. The high-sounding phrases of a party platform always conceal some body of economic interests it is seeking to preserve or promote. No party has ever been magnanimous enough to put its essential confidence in the rational value of its claims. No party has ever resisted the temptation to exaggerate its objectivity. No party has ever been able to avoid the danger of faction. It evokes a loyalty to which impartial truth and justice are easily made subservient. It tends quite inevitably to feel—though less seldom to think —that the principles in which it puts its trust, the interests it seeks to protect, are part of the unchanging order of the universe.

These are grave faults; and yet, when the last word has been said against it, the party system is the only way known to us by which, over long periods of time, changes in social constitution may be made peaceably. The conditions indeed for its success are not easily attained. The parties must dispose of philosophies which differ seriously from each other; but they must not differ so seriously that one party would prefer to see conflict rather than accept its opponent's access to power. Government by party is built upon the assumption that the issues raised are susceptible of illumination by public debate, and that the matters discussed will secure an alert attention from those who are to be affected by the result. On experience, moreover, it is tolerably certain that the success of party government depends in large degree upon its simple bifurcation. There must be a party which favors slow adaptation; there must be a rival which seeks a more drastic rate of change. Both must accept aims which have sufficient in common to enable them to be tolerant of each other. If the divergences are too wide for tolerance, as with those between the Fascists and the Socialists in Italy, or between the Communists and their rivals in Russia, party government is a useless adventure.

Nor is it likely to be creative where there is a multiplicity of parties. For the experience of Western democracy has been the clear one that such multiplicity prevents clarity of purpose from emerging into policy. A group-system, like that of France, or of Germany and Italy before their Fascist revolutions, has the wholly evil result of substituting the politics of maneuver for the politics of ideas. The consequence is always an evasion of substantial issues, a chaos of irresolute compromises, which destroys coherence in decision and firmness in administration. For the group-system means coalition government; and this has always meant on all substantial questions of principle that the government searches not for a policy which represents an organized outlook, but a strategy which maximizes its chances of survival. Each group within the coalition has to think at least as much of its individual future as of the corporate whole to which it belongs; with the result that its loyalty is rarely so permanently engaged as to permit it the luxury of reflection upon foundations. Its mind is too constantly absorbed in the tactics of combination for a long-term view to be possible. And this psychological habit has the natural consequence of taking the mind of the public away from the issues about which its thoughts should be engaged. Its attention is directed to the petty drama of personal differences in an atmosphere without relation to major principles.

The conditions, therefore, under which representative democracy may function effectively are tolerably clear. The electorate must have the great ends of life in common; those fundamentals upon which men are prepared to die rather than give way are not the fit subject-matter of rational debate. But having those great ends in common, the differences upon which debate is possible must be set for them in fairly clear alternatives. They must be able to choose the general direction and progress of the march. They must know that their rejection of one route involves the choice of the other. They must associate men with principles, and recognize that their unwillingness to be governed by one set of persons involves the acceptance of a different set of principles in the business of administration. Where all this is well understood representative democracy has the chance of major historic achievement; but in the absence of such understanding the overthrow of the representative system is only a matter of time.

This may be put in another way. So long as the differences which divide men on matters of social constitution are differences of degree, and not of kind, they may be resolved by the peaceful compromise of intellectual discussion. In this circumstance, representative democracy is the only form of government with the prospect of serious stability, for it is the only one which effectively attempts the weighing of experience. But the success of representative democracy depends, in its turn, upon its association with a two-party system each partner to which is measurably differentiated from the other on philosophic grounds without being so differentiated as to deny the claim of its rival to win power when the electorate so decide. In these conditions, clearly, government and opposition are the warp and woof of representative democracy; neither can function adequately without the other. The idea of opposition with the same title to respect as the government, on the ground that it may itself at any moment become the government, is the essential feature by which democratic systems are distinguished from dictatorships.

What is the function of an opposition in such a society? It was said by Disraeli in a classic aphorism that the function of an opposition is to oppose; and there is a sense in which, as an expression of the historic consequence of the party-system, the remark is an exhaustive definition. Certainly no organized body of men will be likely to view their exclusion from power with equanimity; and they are bound, in the nature of things, to use their opportunity of conflict to expose the blunders of their rivals. But it has been rare for any party to obtain a new lease of office merely because it attacked the government. No purely negative criticism has ever won the suffrages of an electorate. The function of an opposition is criticism of the party in power in terms of an alternative program. It has to show the democracy that its accession to office would result in positive achievements, from the performance of which its rivals are debarred no less by their philosophic outlook than their blunders in administration.

The post-war years in British politics provide many illustrations of this truth. The Labor Party won the election of 1929 because, in the main, the voters were persuaded that the Baldwin government did not understand the problem of peace and that the Labor Party did understand it. There were, of course, contributory causes, not the least of which was the conviction of the main body of the working class electorate that the handling of the General Strike by the Tory Cabinet showed its inability to understand those industrial problems which a predominantly Trade Union party might be expected to grasp. The landslide to conservatism in 1931 was born, in part, of disillusion with the feeble record of the MacDonald Cabinet and, not less, of the more positive conviction that only a party pledged to a capitalist solution could see the country safely through the crisis of that year; while the association of Mr. MacDonald with the new administration reinforced that view by suggesting that Labor itself was far from anxious to apply the ultimate principles which it declared to be the only real remedy for British ills.

The history of Great Britain since 1931 strengthens this conclusion. The opposition has consistently opposed; and the record of the government has for most observers been enough to justify passionate hostility. But the bye-elections do not reveal anything more than a widespread disillusion with the momentary enthusiasm of 1931. They suggest that the electorate is gravely dissatisfied with the government without having reached a positive conviction that the opposition knows in a definite and coherent way what alternative policy it would pursue. This is a reasonable attitude on the part of the electorate. For while the Labor Party has since 1931 been able to reveal, especially in international affairs, blunders of high magnitude on the part of the "National" Government, it still reveals itself as uncertain how rapidly it would travel if returned to office to its Socialist goal, or how decisively it would deal with the vital obstacles likely to be encountered on the road. Merely by being an opposition, that is, it has performed a vital negative function; but it has not yet displayed either the integrity or the coherence which enables it positively to assume the status of an alternative administration in the next immediate years.

The American position, perhaps because it is more complicated, is also more fascinating. From the accession of President Harding to the defeat of Mr. Hoover there were no essential differences between American parties. The electorate was asked to choose between persons rather than issues; and the criticism of the government by its opponents never suggested a coherent philosophic alternative. It was not until the depression of 1929 revealed a relationship between Republicanism and the vested interests which had to be broken, if the small man was to have a chance of effective response to his experience, that Mr. Roosevelt was enabled not merely to attack the record of his predecessor but also to indicate an intelligible alternative. His election was, under the conditions of economic disaster, a foregone conclusion. . . .

Both British and American experience point, therefore, to a principle of representative government of which it is vital to seize hold. No criticism is ever likely to be seriously effective in government unless it is accompanied by two qualities. It must be a criticism conceived in terms of a general outlook which represents a wide electoral experience, and it must be a criticism which has behind it in the legislative assembly a driving force powerful enough to compel the government to take account of its import.

Each of these qualities merits some amplification. It is obvious that no government is ever good enough to deserve immunity from attack. Such an atmosphere engenders complacency about its own performance. But it is obvious also that any government can afford to neglect an attack which does not express a considered and alternative outlook which the people can grasp sympathetically. . . .

Nor is it less important that criticism should have effective force in the legislative assembly. A discussion that is always followed by an overwhelming government majority rarely makes a profound effect on the public mind. It is discounted beforehand by the government; it is a process through which its measures have to pass rather than a dissection which may injure its prestige. It has little effect on the public for two reasons. The knowledge, in the first place, that whatever the argument the government is safe, already destroys most effective interest in the discussion. People do not watch a boxing match of which the result is known beforehand. Interest is created by suspense, the unexpected, the dramatic; and the absence of these prevents the mergence of the audience which makes discussion significant. The public, further, needs to recognize in the argument of the opposition a policy which is clearly driving toward the recovery of power. No opposition can create a receptive atmosphere unless it is winning an increasing hold of public opinion. If its strength, whether in a House of Commons or a House of Representatives, is too small to be effective in making an impact upon the government's view, it will be treated with indifference because it is not expected to do anything. An opposition can never afford to be treated with indifference; for when a party has lost its power of attacking significantly, as with the Liberal Party in Great Britain, it rapidly ceases to have meaning for the electorate. In politics, as in life, nothing succeeds like success.

This does not indeed mean that a government can assume a sovereign indifference to the attacks that it encounters. It is always tempted to this attitude, for there is a subtle poison in supreme power which only the greatest men are able to resist. The Lloyd George government of 1918 and the MacDonald coalition of 1931 are both examples of the error inherent in this attitude. Each developed, out of its very assurance of authority, a forgetfulness of its temporary character; so that both lost fairly early an adequate psychological relation to their constituents, with results that were quickly fatal. Both had brought Great Britain through a crisis, and both assumed that the duration of electoral stability is a function of gratitude for past favors. There is no political error more grievous, for it fails to take account of the vital fact that all mass judgments have short-time significance. They are built much more upon the pungent impact of immediate experience than upon a long view which envisages some distant end. That is why Karl Marx, who saw more clearly than most people the significance of public opinion in a revolution, emphasized the urgency for the revolutionists of taking the offensive, and of being able to report even small successes every day. For the initiative goes with success; and they who possess the initiative in matters of public moment are already on the highroad to the possession of power.

Effective opposition, this is to say, is the one certain method of keeping a government mindful of its declared objectives. How vital an adventure this is becomes clear from historic experience. All governments confront the temptation to make their survival the real end of their effort; and the main technic of survival is to avoid a positive policy. It is, moreover, a technic that works sufficiently well in periods of prosperity; even acute observers during the great American boom were persuaded to mistake Mr. Coolidge's negativism for intelligence. So Guizot sought the *juste milieu* in the reign of Louis Philippe; and confounding pursuit of principle with balance of interests, he produced that state of public indifference of which, as Lamartine said, the climax is always a grievance which wears a revolutionary air. Governments which do nothing in order to minimize opposition destroy interest in themselves in the same way as governments which seek to do everything in order to maximize support. The business of their rivals is always to compel them to face the alternatives inherent in the nature of their effort. . . .

The failure to develop a coherent opposition means that the conduct of the debate fails to illuminate the public. Because principles are not discussed, men are driven to acerbity in detail, or to those marginalia about persons which reduce political conflict to the status of a society-gossip column in a provincial newspaper. A great emergency ought to elevate the public mind; but it can only do so when the opposition takes its criticism to a high level. . . .

All this may be put in another way. If a society is to continue as a democracy based on universal suffrage, its existence depends upon the volume and intensity of interest its political processes can arouse. A successful administration may effect this for a period, if its ends and methods arouse, as in a war, a sympathy that is practically universal. But a division of sympathy produces inertia and fatigue unless the level at which the opposition is conducted arouses new interest in the struggle. The opposition, in a word, must provide a focal point round which the forces of discontent can reasonably group themselves. Thereby it is making possible that shift in the basis of policy which is the necessary end at which representative democracy aims. There is no other way in which popular preference can rationally express itself; and, if that way is not provided, representative democracy is not likely to survive for any long period of time.

That this is the case is obvious from experience, most notably, of Russia before the revolution of 1917, but also in a lesser degree of France before 1870 and Germany in the past hundred years. In each case, the opposition to the government lacked the means whereby its will could secure translation into the event by a direct institutional process; and when the government had to be changed, the only way of effecting this result was by its direct destruction. Any political system, in other words, that is non-representative in character must end in revolution if it fails, simply because by being non-representative it has failed to provide a peaceful mechanism for the transition to an alternative system. A dictatorship cannot simply transform itself into a representative system; the law of its being is its hostility to its critics, so that these at some point must rise against it if they are to have access to power.

But in a representative system there are similar dangers when the opposition is functioning inadequately. If it cannot make itself seem a necessary alternative the assumptions of the system do not work. This does not matter seriously in epochs where prosperity is pervasive because in such circumstances the reaction of governmental policy upon the national life is not profound. But in epochs like our own, where governmental policy is fundamental in its reaction, the failure of the opposition has momentous consequences. By failing to make its alternative seem rational, it either fails to win power, in which case long exclusion from office makes it in terms of governmental failure more and more extreme; or, alternatively, it secures office in a wave of disgust at its rival's failure but has no clear policy to implement or no positive opinion in its support. Representative democracy cannot support such a temper. Party differences must be real in an era of crisis or there will be, first, a continued failure on the part of governments to solve its problems, then indifference to the system of the regime, and, finally, its overthrow by men who argue persuasively that it is the regime itself that is at fault. Only an effective opposition, that is to say, can prevent a representative system from degenerating into dictatorship.

This is clear from post-war British history. None of its governments in the past fifteen years has had the courage to deal drastically with its economic problems; even the two Socialist governments have followed traditional paths in this regard. The result has been a growth of skepticism in Great Britain about the validity of parliamentary institutions which is already significant and might easily assume serious proportions. The issue now raised by the relationship of the major parties is a momentous one. It has become clear that to follow the traditional path is incompatible with the maintenance of Great Britain's pre-war position; but it is also clear that to desert it, as a considerable part of the Labor Party now proposes to desert it, may well impose a strain upon the parliamentary system it is unable to bear. Each of the Labor governments, even though in a minority, had a chance by the introduction of great measures, to shift the general axes of policy to which parties have to conform; each lacked the courage to embark on the adventure. Each, therefore, left the horizons of policy unaltered when it went out of office and, accordingly, confronted the situation, in opposition, of urging remedies as a policy which, when a government, it had lacked the courage to undertake. This timidity not only produced disillusion among its own supporters; it encouraged its opponents to believe, not unnaturally that, whatever its professions, the Labor Party did not mean what it said. This, in its turn, has engendered in its rivals a confidence in the security of their privileges the disappointment of which may make it difficult to maintain parliamentarism; while if the next Labor Government acts in the traditional way of its predecessors, it is certain that masses of its own supporters will cease to have faith in representative institutions.

An opposition, this is to say, must have a faith and a policy which makes it possible to express that faith in terms of legislation. It must have a faith upon which it is prepared to act as a government; and it inflicts injury that is often grave and sometimes irreparable when it fails to apply the measures in which it declares itself to believe. For the life of representative democracy depends upon its ability to retain the good-will of its constituents; and this, in its turn, depends upon the ability of those constituents to find among the political parties one which, as a government, will be able to govern with success. The survival of governments is never a function, in the long run, of their intentions; their survival depends upon their ability to increase material well-being. For it is the natural logic of universal suffrage that the electorate should use its political power to secure an increase in its material well-being, above all, in a society which, like our own, is so grimly divisible into rich and poor. If such an increase cannot be obtained under the governments which representative democracy creates, it is sooner or later certain that the drift of opinion will be away from that system; and when opinion is sufficiently impatient a Hitler or a Mussolini will emerge to seize his opportunity. Ancient Athens and the medieval cities, the England of the Commonwealth and the France of the revolutions, Russia in 1917 and Germany in the post-war period do not in essence teach us a different lesson.

If representative government is to survive, it must be successful; if it is to be successful, its citizens must have the choice between parties which, while they have the great ends of life in common, yet so differ in character that they can proffer the prospect of great alternative experiments the profundity of which elicits public interest, and so creates a moral allegiance to the system which makes them possible. On such a hypothesis, the urgency of the task an opposition must perform hardly requires a detailed emphasis. The purpose of its criticism, the objective of its attack, is to prove the elasticity of the regime, its power and width of creative experiment, its title to preserve faith in its possibilities among those who live by its results. There is no more final proof that a social system is nearing its end than its failure to provide opposition of this kind. For when there is such a failure the regime is incapable of experiment; it has then lost the power of adaptation, and, in political history, the loss of such adaptability has always been the premonition of death.

One final word may be said. It is the underlying assumption of this argument that representative government is possible only where the members of the society are agreed upon the fundamentals of political life. It is worth noting that in an unequal society like that of Great Britain or America this agreement cannot be long maintained in a period of economic crisis. Grave social disparities are never easily defensible in terms of reason when despair drives men to extremes; for it is the inevitable habit of despair to examine the traditional foundations upon which they rest and proclaim their inadequacy. We have obviously entered upon one of those epochs of historical transformation in which our institutions are likely to be tested as at no time since the French Revolution. It is quite uncertain whether they are strong enough to stand that test. Their survival is going to depend upon the rapidity with which they can adjust themselves to the need of profound experiment.

Unless this experiment can be conducted in a temper of creative criticism, fatal errors are certain to be made; and such criticism there will not be unless there is a strong opposition to make it. Habit without philosophy never yet surmounted an historical crisis; and unless we can provide our system with a philosophy while there is yet time we shall lose our grounds for hope. But hope is the condition of peace; and the breakdown of the opposition in a period such as ours is equivalent to the certainty of social disruption. If that disruption comes, Western civilization is not unlikely to enter upon a new and uglier Dark Age.

No. 35

[ASIDE from the examination and analysis of the character and value of the political party and the party system in its broadest sense, it is important to examine the detailed character of the organization of political parties. The following selection discusses one of the most important features of American party organization, namely, the local political club. Written by a man who has been engaged in practical politics for many years, and who was both governor of New York and a candidate for the presidency of the United States, it offers a first hand view of this important aspect of American party life.]

THE POLITICAL PARTY AND THE LOCAL POLITICAL CLUB [1]

by Alfred E. Smith

THE first thing to consider in a discussion of "the citizen and his government" is the smallest and most basic unit of political organization under our party system—that is, the local political club. Naturally, and because of geographic rather than any other influence, local political clubs find their greatest development in the cities and in the areas of cities where the population is most concentrated. The fact that country or suburban dwellers maintain a more natural sort of neighborliness than the city man who lives in an apartment or tenement house probably has something to do with this. Farmers or suburbanites usually know their next-door neighbors and a good many others within a short distance of their homes well enough to mingle with them socially and secure companionship or, if need be, assistance.

In the cities, however, the great variance in the backgrounds and living habits of the millions of citizens, as well as the very closeness with which they are packed into the houses in which they live, has resulted in an almost complete lack of the quality of neighborliness. Most city people do not even know the names of those living in the same house with them, much less have much social contact with their close neighbors.

Therefore the local political clubs, which in the last analysis exchange social contacts and political and economic services for votes, offer a natural and much used gathering-place for the citizens, young and old, of the cities and particularly of the neighborhood in which each club may be located.

When young Johnny Brown reaches the age to possess a night-key of his own he is going to be attracted to the local political club. In spite of the fact that the city in which he lives may offer a thousand and one different attractions, amusements, and educational opportunities, the local political club is going to seem a natural center of interest and excitement for everyone in the neighborhood. In it Johnny will see the people of his own district, sharing his own economic and social interests, given an oppor-

[1] Alfred E. Smith, *The Citizen and His Government* (New York: Harper and Brothers 1935), pp. 3-19. Reprinted by permission of the publishers.

tunity to enjoy contact with their friends and neighbors which they could not otherwise enjoy; and in it he will especially realize that he and his family may obtain the highly prized "favors" and services of the political leader and his assistants.

At some stage in Johnny Brown's career he has probably attended a picnic under the club's auspices in the summer. In the fall, especially in the exciting pre-election weeks, he has seen great activity and much to interest him around the clubhouse. Bands play and parades carrying the traditional red fire, political signs, and orators set out to stump the neighborhood for votes. Many other social and political events of great glamour to a young fellow center around the club.

Johnny may have an older brother or father who is a member, and if he is an alert young man who watches what is going on about him he will inevitably look forward to the day when he will be able to join the club and himself take part in the political meetings. When Johnny comes of age there will be no trouble about becoming a member of his local political club. There is nothing exclusive about it. The most necessary qualification for membership is simply the ability and legal qualification to vote. Johnny's name will almost automatically be added to the rolls of eligible voters and placed in its proper alphabetical order. This may be done at the suggestion of one of his relatives; or perhaps one of his pals who is active in the club and anxious to receive the credit for bringing in a new member may see to it that he is properly enrolled.

From this point on Johnny's prominence in local affairs and city, state, or nationwide politics will be entirely dependent upon himself: first upon his natural ability for politics and for developing friendships and a following; and second upon his desire to make politics a career or on the other hand to use the club simply as a social meeting-place.

Johnny Brown will unquestionably be anxious to become acquainted with the district leader himself. This leader will be a man of whom he has heard much, a man who takes the position of a sort of neighborhood idol, interested in all affairs, personal and political, large or small, of the people in his neighborhood; a man able to accomplish things in a very definite manner and a man looked up to by a large number of people in the neighborhood who depend upon the political organization for assistance in a thousand and one different matters.

Johnny soon finds that the district leader is a busy man, probably to some extent a fairly mysterious individual—most of his club members believe there is some occult political power through which the leader moves to perform his wonderful acts and favors for his people. But yesterday or to-day, the district leader's primary responsibility is to deliver as many solid and definitely countable votes as possible for his party from the neighborhood around his clubhouse. Upon his ability to deliver at every election and to repeat unfailingly his delivery of a definite and preferably growing party strength, depends his survival as a leader, because a man who cannot keep his people in line cannot qualify as a leader in any sense of the word, political or social, and will not last long as a political power.

Contrary to the belief of Johnny Brown and a great many others unschooled in the political system, the district leader's job is not entirely confined to securing employment for those in the district who may be in need of it. On the other hand, we do find that a great many people in the district turn to the leader for every sort of assistance and advice, particularly on many matters that have nothing to do with government. It is through these services that the district leader gains the loyal following which enables him to deliver votes that make him a power to be reckoned with and considered in the larger party organization.

Therefore, the district leaders set up in their clubhouses a sort of modern organized counterpart of the old trade guilds or other community centers where the people of earlier days were able to find advice, counsel and assistance. The difference is that the trade guilds of the middle ages were simply social organizations designed to set up a system whereby families might share prosperity and assist one another. The man who had steady work and a good income for a long period might be able through a common organization to help another member of the same craft who was destitute and had not been able to make enough money to keep his family in food and clothing. There was no necessity in those past centuries for a political organization. Such activities were either forbidden or seriously discouraged because the ruling powers wanted no interference with their own government and did not wish the people to have any organized voice.

To-day under our democratic system, it is very necessary that the people have these local political units where they may gather and where the political thoughts and aims of individuals may be consolidated into an organized powerful voice of the group or the political party. Just as the score or more of neighborhood clubs in a big city combine their views and their sentiments to make the sentiment and power of the Democratic or Republican party of the city as a whole, individuals within the district clubhouse and its leader express the wishes, thoughts, and aspirations of all the voters of the neighborhood.

The clubhouse provides almost everything that a poor man may need and which he cannot find elsewhere. No loyal member within the district will ever be forgotten in the apportionment of assistance. A destitute family in one tenement house may be noticed and sought out by a captain in the next house who is responsible for the votes of the families in his immediate block or street. The clubhouse will be notified and coal, food, cash, or medical aid obtained through the district leader or his assistants. This applies whether or not that family includes actual members of the club.

Every clubhouse of any prominence has a lawyer or local judge present most of the time, and citizens of the district, irrespective of their membership in the club, can come to these people for free legal advice. Small business men come to the leader with their business troubles. I have myself seen the secretary of a local organization making out a statement of loss because of fire for a storekeeper unable to read or write English.

The local clubhouse can make no distinction between citizens or aliens. If the alien does not vote this year, he may become a citizen and have a vote next year, and certainly if he is helped while an alien and learns to depend upon the district organization for assistance in earning a living and becoming an American, the club can count on his support when he receives his citizenship papers.

The district leader is a slave to his voters from morning until midnight and for three hundred and sixty-five days in the year. No exertion is too great, no favor too insignificant, to obtain his attention, and in return he asks only loyalty and a measure of help at election time from his people.

District leaders are not paid for their political or community services. They draw no salaries from their clubhouses or local organizations, and to the best of my memory I cannot recall a clubhouse which made a profit or which was even able to meet its expenses. Therefore most district leaders are unable to devote all of their time to clubhouse activities and must engage in other businesses to support themselves and their families. Between the two functions of earning a living and retaining political leadership by service to the party and its people, the leader finds more than enough to occupy the working hours of each day.

A considerable part of the district leader's time has to be spent in attending to the many personal affairs of his neighbors and club members. It is a necessary part of his efforts to cement and foster the warm feeling and personal friendship of the people in his neighborhood which are essential in his political work. Therefore the district leader attends funerals, wakes, marriages, and christenings. He makes himself a leading figure at any neighborhood dance or social function. In some districts the summer picnics and winter balls given by the district club under the personal auspices of the leader are notable affairs that are awaited the year round by the people of the neighborhood, both young and old.

One organization holds a yearly party in Central Park at which several thousand mothers and children get a day in the open, free milk and ice cream, sandwiches and athletics, and at which a money prize is awarded for the most beautiful children, the most freckled boy and girl, and so on.

Another neighborhood organization holds a great yearly dance at the Hotel Astor in New York, where the grand march is always led by the leader, and at which the attendance includes many of the notables and officials of the city and state.

In a great many cases the interest of the leader and his organization in the personal affairs of a family means a great deal more than just participating in their social affairs. There is the concrete and specific matter of supplying the means to live. Families in distress because of death, sickness, or unemployment are aided in thousands of instances by the local club, and it is through such activities that our young friend Johnny Brown learns to count on the district leader and his clubhouse for warmth and friendly spirit in any trouble he may come up against in the conduct of his daily life, or that of his family.

Of course, one of the great features of the club is that if functions all year round. The leader or his representative is available at any time, Sundays and holidays included, and this means much in meeting the inevitable emergencies that will arise in the lives of the several thousand families concentrated in a crowded city district. A friend or relative may get in some sort of trouble in the middle of the night. Perhaps he is arrested and the family does not know where to turn for bail money. The district leader, if he knows the family and has faith in their honesty, will find a bond and obtain the prisoner's freedom until the case comes up and the district club can provide a lawyer to help defend him against the charge.

It is easy to see why the district leader becomes a sort of neighborhood idol, a real figure of pure sympathy and help in human form, and why he is able to command political loyalty in return for the manifold acts he is able to perform for his people.

Along about this point I can hear our friend Johnny Brown asking how the district leader gets to be in such a position, how he becomes leader, and why he retains the job.

It must be borne in mind that while political parties have their form of organization, selection of officers, time of meetings, and such provided by law, the district club itself has no official standing in the governmental set-up. The organization of the Democratic and Republican parties as well as the minor parties, the manner in which their meetings are to be held and their officers elected, are all specified in state laws. The district club is only a unit of a larger party, and its operations and the manner in which it elects its officers, collects its dues, and conducts its activities are governed entirely by tradition and by the wishes of the club members and their leader.

The district leader, as such, holds no political office, has no power of an official nature, but most of them are appointed to public position, and therein lies their aid to clubhouse activities.

The district leader is usually someone who has been active and well liked in the social and business and political life of his neighborhood long before his actual participation in official party activities.

The district club is made up of two classes of membership—first, those who belong by actual and official registration to the political party represented by the local club; and second, those who, while not actually enrolled on the lists of the party, support the policy of the party and generally may be expected to adhere to its ticket on election day.

Since the district leader's position and the manner of attaining it are not defined by law, it is up to these club members to select from their ranks a person in whom they are all willing to repose confidence and whom they wish to elevate to the post of leader. The method of doing this has become so basic a part of the modern political picture that everyone should thoroughly understand it. The state law provides that in each county there shall be a County Committee made up of as many members as the rules and regulations of the party provide. This rule is usually based on a ratio of one representative in the County Committee for a given number of votes cast for the particular party at the preceding general election. That would mean that in a strong democratic district in New York City there would probably be two hundred or two hundred and fifty members of the County Committee. In another county of the state the ratio of one representative for only twenty-five party votes may be adopted, and in still another the ratio may be one for each fifty votes. Therefore the size of the membership of the various county committees throughout the state varies with the wishes of the local organization.

The Democratic County Committee of New York County (Manhattan Island) is composed of more than six thousand people, and the membership is kept at a large figure intentionally in order to bring as many of the voters as possible into prominence in party affairs. The County Committee is made up of delegations from the Assembly Districts, with each individual delegate representing a few voters in his immediate neighborhood in the selection of candidates and in the guidance of party policies.

The district leader is always a member of the County Committee and meets with this committee, at a time specified by law after the members are selected by the voters at the primary election, to elect a chairman and other officers. These officers are charged by law with the conduct of the party's affairs.

Obviously the great number of members from each district makes the

County Committee as a whole too large to transact all its business directly. Therefore the members of the County Committee in each district meet and select a representative to sit on a central committee known as the Executive Committee, which conducts the party affairs. The members of this Executive Committee are the district leaders, and their continuance as members of the Executive Committee is only an official symbol or notice of the fact that they are continuing as leaders of their own local political organizations.

The law, of course, does not provide for the existence of an Executive Committee. It is a voluntary body representing the wishes of the larger committee, and the men selected to sit in the Executive Committee have in turn control over the election of a county leader, who becomes the most publicly known of his party in the larger city organization. Obviously the Executive Committee, unofficial as it is, is a more powerful body than the County Committee, although the County Committee enjoys a legal standing which is denied to the Executive Committee.

In the event that any considerable number of the party members of a political district become dissatisfied with their leader and wish to oust him and place someone else in his position, it is necessary for them to contest at the next primary election his candidacy for membership in the County Committee. If the incumbent leader is unable to marshal enough votes in his own district to keep his place on the County Committee, he is considered to have lost control of his district and is replaced by a new delegate to the Executive Committee from his district. Thus we see that the present political system in New York City is a mixture of legal and traditional practice, with only a part of the party organization specified and supported by law and the rest of the system created and continued under rules of usage rather than those of law.

The social activities of political organizations of the lower East Side were more important in the time of my boyhood than they are to-day. Any boy or girl of my generation will remember most vividly from his New York childhood the political chowder parties, ox-roasts, picnics, and banquets sponsored by the local political clubs. Every man, woman, or child of the district, irrespective of party affiliations, was invited to attend, and there would be a great junket up the river to some resort or beach point on Long Island.

It must not be thought that all political activity either in the old days or to-day is restricted to the Democratic party. The Republicans, as well have their noted leaders, their district clubhouses, their parties and parades and although they seldom win an election in New York City they keep up the local organization.

All in all, district leaders of old New York, and those of to-day as well have done perhaps more than any other individuals to promote the welfare of their communities and to give opportunity for political and personal advancement to deserving young people.

If it had not been for Tom Foley, leader of the Second Assembly District, in which I was born and raised, and for the genuine care he took in fostering my career and giving me an opportunity to get ahead in public affairs, I should certainly never have been able to travel the long road of politics which I have seen in my lifetime. I think that most men in public office, or men who have gained prominence partly or wholly through politics, will bear me out when I say that without the help of their old-time district leaders they would never have been given the chance to show their mettle and to place their feet upon the first rung of the ladder of success. Tom Foley did no more for me than many another leader has done for other young men of his district. He gave me my chance at election to the Assembly because he thought I was capable and well enough known in the district to get the winning vote.

Leadership in a district is really a matter of the survival of the fittest. No leader gets or keeps his position without a genuine understanding of and sympathy with his own people—the people that make up his district and who are members of his club. Successful leaders spring from the rank and file, practically all of whom are struggling for power—practically every one of the rank and file hopes to become a leader himself. Leadership in a political organization, as in every other field of human endeavor, must be reached by hard work, brains, and a thorough ability to deal with people. There is no other way in which the ambition to become a leader can be achieved or a position of leadership retained.

My remarks about the district leaders would be incomplete if I did not record the fact that some of them, in the past, have been unfaithful to their trust and have used the power of their leadership to benefit themselves in a manner with which nobody could concur, but the answer to that is they only hold their positions by and with the consent of the majority of the members of the County Committee which they represent.

All that I have written upon this subject has reference to the past. I am firmly of the opinion that the younger generation now coming into power, because of numerical strength, are not going to be so easily led by the old-time political methods that I have herein described. I feel very strongly that consideration will in the future be given for service to the whole city by the political party rather than the ability of the district leader to hold his forces by personal favor. Shifting of population, change in conditions, make it difficult to operate under the old-time methods, and I feel that our younger people growing up will look to party achievement in the

city as a whole rather than to the favor, friendship, or whatever you may
desire to call it of the local political leader. Both of the major political
parties lose their power when the great masses of the people became dissatisfied with their administration, and in that event I do not believe that the
power or the influence of the district leader can avert political disaster. No
matter how highly organized a political party may be, the people, when
given a definite issue, decide elections without any consideration of political
leadership. As far as patronage is concerned, it means nothing when there
is an issue that appeals strongly to the people themselves. That fact has
been demonstrated times without number in elections within the last twenty
years. In other words, the younger people want the leadership of thought,
the thought that means the betterment of the whole city.

No. 36

[THE preceding selection by Alfred E. Smith gives a good indication of the
character and importance of the local political clubs. The following selection
presenting the views of a typical district leader in New York City, throws further
light upon the character of the activities of local political leaders and their
influence upon elections.]

TO HOLD YOUR DISTRICT—STUDY HUMAN NATURE AND ACT ACCORDIN' [1]

by W. L. Riordon

"THERE'S only one way to hold a district; you must study human
nature and act accordin'. You can't study human nature in books.
Books is a hindrance more than anything else. If you have been to college, so much the worse for you. You'll have to unlearn all you learned
before you can get right down to human nature, and unlearnin' takes a lot
of time. Some men can never forget what they learned at college. Such
men may get to be district leaders by a fluke, but they never last.

"To learn real human nature you have to go among the people, see them
and be seen. I know every man, woman, and child in the Fifteenth District
except them that's been born this summer—and I know some of them, too.
I know what they like and what they don't like, what they are strong a
and what they are weak in, and I reach them by approachin' at the right side

---

[1] W. L. Riordon, *Plunkitt of Tammany Hall* (New York: McClure, Phillips and Co
1905), pp. 46-53. Reprinted by permission of Doubleday, Doran and Company.

"For instance, here's how I gather in the young men. I hear of a young feller that's proud of his voice, thinks that he can sing fine. I ask him to come around to Washington Hall and join our Glee Club. He comes and sings, and he's a follower of Plunkitt for life. Another young feller gains a reputation as a base-ball player in a vacant lot. I bring him into our base-ball club. That fixes him. You'll find him workin' for my ticket at the polls next election day. Then there's the feller that likes rowin' on the river, the young feller that makes a name as a waltzer on his block, the young feller that's handy with his dukes—I rope them all in by givin' them opportunities to show themselves off. I don't trouble them with political arguments. I just study human nature and act accordin'.

"But you may say this game won't work with the high-toned fellers, the fellers that go through college and then join the Citizens' Union. Of course it wouldn't work. I have a special treatment for them. I ain't like the patent medicine man that gives the same medicine for all diseases. The Citizens' Union kind of a young man! I love him! He's the daintiest morsel of the lot, and he don't often escape me.

"Before telling you how I catch him, let me mention that before the election last year, the Citizens' Union said they had four hundred or five hundred enrolled voters in my district. They had a lovely headquarters, too, beautiful roll-top desks and the cutest rugs in the world. If I was accused of havin' contributed to fix up the nest for them, I wouldn't deny it under oath. What do I mean by that? Never mind. You can guess from the sequel, if you're sharp.

"Well, election day came. The Citizens' Union's candidate for Senator, who ran against me, just polled five votes in the district, while I polled something more than 14,000 votes. What became of the 400 or 500 Citizens' Union enrolled voters in my district? Some people guessed that many of them were good Plunkitt men all along and worked with the Cits just to bring them into the Plunkitt camp by election day. You can guess that way, too, if you want to. I never contradict stories about me, especially in hot weather. I just call your attention to the fact that on last election day 395 Citizens' Union enrolled voters in my district were missin' and unaccounted for.

"I tell you frankly, though, how I have captured some of the Citizens' Union's young men. I have a plan that never fails. I watch the City Record to see when there's civil service examinations for good things. Then I take my young Cit in hand, tell him all about the good thing and get him worked up till he goes and takes an examination. I don't bother about him any more. It's a cinch that he comes back to me in a few days and asks to join Tammany Hall. Come over to Washington Hall some night and I'll show you a list of names on our rolls marked 'C.S.' which means, 'bucked up against civil service.'

"As to the older voters, I reach them, too. No, I don't send campaign literature. That's rot. People can get all the political stuff they want to read—and a good deal more, too—in the papers. Who reads speeches, nowadays, anyhow? It's bad enough to listen to them. You ain't goin' to gain any votes by stuffin' the letter boxes with campaign documents. Like as not you'll lose votes, for there's nothin' a man hates more than to hear the letter-carrier ring his bell and go to the letter-box expectin' to find a letter he was lookin' for, and find only a lot of printed politics. I met a man this very mornin' who told me he voted the Democratic State ticket last year just because the Republicans kept crammin' his letter-box with campaign documents.

"What tells in holdin' your grip on your district is to go right down among the poor families and help them in the different ways they need help. I've got a regular system for this. If there's a fire in Ninth, Tenth, or Eleventh Avenue, for example, any hour of the day or night, I'm usually there with some of my election district captains as soon as the fire-engines. If a family is burned out I don't ask whether they are Republicans or Democrats, and I don't refer them to the Charity Organization Society, which would investigate their case in a month or two and decide they were worthy of help about the time they are dead from starvation. I just get quarters for them, buy clothes for them if their clothes are burned up, and fix them up till they get things runnin' again. It's philanthropy, but it's politics too—mighty good politics. Who can tell how many votes one of these fires bring me? The poor are the most grateful people in the world, and, let me tell you, they have more friends in their neighborhoods than the rich have in theirs.

"If there's a family in my district in want I know it before the charitable societies do, and me and my men are first on the ground. I have a special corps to look up such cases. The consequence is that the poor look up to George W. Plunkitt as a father, come to him in trouble—and don't forget him on election day.

"Another thing, I can always get a job for a deservin' man. I make it a point to keep on the track of jobs, and it seldom happens that I don't have a few up my sleeve ready for use. I know every big employer in the district, and in the whole city, for that matter, and they ain't in the habit of sayin' no to me when I ask them for a job.

"And the children—the little roses of the district! Do I forget them? Oh, no! They know me, every one of them, and they know that a sight o. Uncle George and candy means the same thing. Some of them are the

best kind of vote-getters. I'll tell you a case. Last year a little Eleventh
Avenue rosebud whose father is a Republican, caught hold of his whiskers
on election day and said she wouldn't let go till he'd promise to vote for me.
And she didn't."

No. 37

[UNFORTUNATELY, not all of the methods employed by the professional politician in obtaining and holding power are harmless. The local political leader
may, by all sorts of corrupt devices, become a political boss with his hand on
the throttle of the political machine. He may, by secret and corrupt means, by
terror and threats, by trickery and violence seize almost complete power in his
own hands. The many studies on bossism in our cities testify to the fact that
all of these devices have been and are being used to maintain corrupt local
machines. In the following article Mr. Coghlan gives us an intimate picture of
a contemporary American city boss, and of the techniques of his rise to power.
Since this article was written the "hero" was convicted of violating the federal
income tax laws and sentenced to a term in the federal penitentiary. The removal of Mr. Pendergast from the scene coupled with judicial investigations of
corruption in elections has apparently broken the hold of the machine.]

BOSS PENDERGAST [1]

by Ralph Coghlan

TO get to the great man, we climb a long flight of stairs in a rather
dingy two-story brick building at 1908 Main Street, Kansas City,
Missouri. One name for it is the Jackson County Democratic Club, but
it is better known as the headquarters of the King of Missouri Democracy.
The steps are worn. They have borne the weight of United States senators,
governors, mayors, councilmen, bankers, beggars, and gangsters—yes, and
the lame, the halt, and the blind.

At the top, we are in a large room. It has the stark atmosphere of a
lodge hall. Men are sitting around puffing cigars, chatting, reading. They
are the King's courtiers. Are they an unprepossessing lot? Never mind.
On the walls as we gaze around we see photographs of Woodrow Wilson
and of James A. Reed and we see something else we are more interested in.
It is a painting of Thomas Joseph Pendergast, the man we came to see.
Let's look at it a minute.

It is a face and figure that remind us of something—of a creature of the

[1] Ralph Coghlan, "Boss Pendergast," *The Forum* (February, 1937), Vol. 97, pp. 67-72.
Reprinted by permission of *Current History and Forum*.

artistic imagination of Homer Davenport, of Rollin Kirby, of Daniel Fitz-patrick—the American boss type. Massive head; thinning, sand-colored hair; a wrestler's corded neck set firmly on a huge torso. The face is strong, the kind of face which is molded in a jungle background where primeval emotions are stamped and there is no time for nuances. The eyes are arresting—"an eye like Mars to threaten and command"—gray, and piercing.

We think, as we gaze at this portrait of the man, of Kansas City, boss-ridden, rotten with corruption. We know that, in this, his own private barony, there have been placed on the registration rolls 268,000 names of a total population of 415,000—64.5 per cent. According to U. S. census estimates, only 60 per cent of the people are over 21. If that holds true of Kansas City, it means that more than the total adult population—including aliens, the sick, the insane, the imprisoned, the indifferent—are on the rolls. In the First Ward, where Pendergast got his start, the registration figure was 21,073, though federal census figures show a total population of only 19,923. In the Second Ward 23,469 voters were registered, though census figures show a total population of but 18,478.

And most of these names are voted.

In the August, 1936, primary, Lawrence McDaniel, well-known St. Louis lawyer, was running for the State supreme court against Judge Ernest S. Gantt, a Pendergast machine candidate. McDaniel carried a substantial majority of the 114 counties in Missouri and the City of St. Louis, and, not counting Kansas City, he had a comfortable lead. Here's what became of him there. In the First Ward Gantt got 18,919 votes to eighteen for McDaniel—a ratio of 1,045 to one. In the Second Ward Gantt got 19,201 votes to thirteen for McDaniel, a ratio of 1,469 to one.

In the last presidential election a vote of 41,805 was cast by the 38,401 babies, children, and adults of these two wards!

In the August primary, the Pendergast candidate for the gubernatorial nomination beat his opponent, a highly respected and widely known citizen, by the ratio of 29 to one.

We know that in the last Kansas City mayoralty election, when a group of independent citizens attempted to defeat the machine candidate, corruption and brutal force decided the issue. As Jesse W. Barrett, Republican candidate for governor in the recent election, told a Kansas City audience:

> We all remember the pictures of the hospital wards filled with men who were broken and bruised by the gangsters who assaulted them at the polls. You remember that flood of fraudulent votes. You were baptized in blood, but the contest was won by the machine. The score was four murders, two hundred assaults, and one hundred thousand felonies.

We know that the Pendergast machine enjoys all the political patronage in Kansas City and Jackson County, but that is only a small part of the machine's perquisites. It controls State and city contracts. It sells the construction materials which go into public buildings. It can, if it wishes, exercise a virtual monopoly of Kansas City's liquor business and its soft-drink business. The jackals of the machine enjoy the slot-machine, dice, roulette, and prostitution rackets—and a Parisian who recently visited Kansas City described it as the wickedest city he had ever seen. There is hardly a phase of Kansas City's life untouched by this monstrous outfit.

Do the citizens complain? Well, many of the outstanding ones do business with the machine or by its favor. They are mum if, indeed, they are not the machine's apologists. Others cry out, and are intimidated. Their assessments are raised. Their buildings are found defective.

The wife of the pastor of the Broadway Baptist Church believed the youth of the city corrupted by the gambling joints. She carried her complaint to the city manager—a Pendergast devotee, of course. He told her the place to teach morals was in the home; the government had nothing to do with it. But that was not the end. Subsequently the woman was threatened and abused until she was forced to flee from the city for her safety.

A preacher undertook to inveigh against the machine. A parishioner of his owned a chain of stores. One day this man was told his permit to do business had been revoked. He inquired the reason. "We do not like your minister," he was told. "Change your minister and you will get your permit back." Other members of the congregation had their assessments increased. Some were trebled. "Change your minister," these persons were told when they complained.

We know that the man we are about to see lifts men to high office with the utmost arrogance and the utmost contempt for all but the form of democratic processes. "I will make you mayor," "I will make you governor," "I will get you a seat in the Senate of the United States," he says.

In the fall of 1932, the Democratic candidate for governor died. There was a meeting of the Democratic State Committee. It was informed that the deceased candidate should be succeeded, by order of the boss, by an obscure Platte County circuit judge, Guy B. Park. The committee affixed the rubber stamp.

In 1934, there was to be an election for the United States Senate. There was also to be an election for Collector of Jackson County. To this latter post, a county judge (an administrative, not a judicial, post), Harry Truman, passionately aspired. It was a job paying a large sum of money, and Truman could use the money. The boss was sorry. He could not endorse

Truman for the collectorship but he would put him in the United States Senate. He did. In doing so, he defeated one of the finest public servants Missouri has produced—Congressman John J. Cochran, chosen in a poll of Washington correspondents some time ago as one of the five or six most useful members of Congress. (Fortunately for the public, Cochran got a place on the ticket, and was re-elected to the lower house.) In the senatorial primary, believe it or not, the county judge who wanted to be a collector polled 120,180 votes in Kansas City; and a brilliant and tremendously popular veteran, Mr. Cochran, got 1,221 votes.

Such is the power of the man we are about to see.

We move through the large room into an antechamber. It is choked with a line of people, some of the three or four hundred who will call on the boss this morning. It is a cross-section of all types, from the neatly groomed aspirant to the boss's favor to the disheveled importunate. It winds its way into the small office of Captain Elijah Matheus. Cap is an old-time steamboat pilot. He is of huge proportions. They call him the boss's secretary.

As we stand here, we notice that the boss's callers are quickly disposed of. The door to his private sanctum closes and opens, a caller leaves, a heavy voice from within says, "Who's next?"

Most of the boss's callers say: "Will you?" "May I?" "Please give me—." The answer is "Yes," or, "No." Long-winded palaver is distasteful to the boss. Talk is for editors, lawyers, and other persons far removed from the arena of immediate action.

We want to ask the boss some questions. We want his philosophy of life. We are not wanted here. Let us then be as quick about it as possible. Let us even spare his time completely by constructing a synthetic interview of what he has said brusquely to other interviewers from time to time.

But, if we pretend we have arrived in the inner sanctum, we find the man in the oil painting sitting before us on the edge of a swivel chair. He is dressed sedately. His hat is on. He seems to be about to spring. It is not the tautness of strained nerves, merely the barely repressed energy of a person whose physical movements are of tigerish speed.

Before we permit his piercing gaze to fix our own, we note quickly that the room is elaborately unpretentious. It is tiny, twelve by twelve. It has a green rug, a roll-top desk, a couple of chairs, and a brass cuspidor. We get a fleeting glimpse of a framed cartoon. It is a cartoon, printed in the *Kansas City Star* many years ago, showing the late Jim Pendergast, brother of Tom, holding the First Ward vote of Kansas City in a box.

An irony in that cartoon. The man who now impatiently demands our business holds the vote of the entire State of Missouri in a box.

"What can I do for you, gentlemen?"

"Mr. Pendergast," we begin, "you are a great power in this State. You were recently called in the *New York Times,* in an article written by its Washington correspondent, Arthur Krock, the most powerful boss in America and one of the most interesting citizens of America."

"Well!"

"We want to know something about you, about your philosophy, if not of life, of politics. You are a realist, are you not?"

"What do you mean?"

"You take a practical view of things?"

"That's me."

"Why did you go into politics?"

"I went into politics because it appealed to me and it looked like a good business. My brother, Jim, was in politics, and I started helping him. We got along because we made friends and because we gave the people good men. How could we get along in Kansas City for fifty years without giving the people good men?"

"Mr. Pendergast, we notice a long line of people waiting to see you. Do you see so many people every day?"

"I function year in and year out. I don't wait until three weeks before the election. I'm working all the time. I'm kind to people because I like to be. I never give an argument when a man comes in for a dollar and wants help. Maybe he's having an argument with his wife he wants settled —you'd be surprised how many men come in to get things like that fixed up. Maybe he wants a job. I always go out of my way to help."

"So you believe it is the function of the head of a political organization to help people?"

"What's the government for if it isn't to help people? They're interested only in local conditions, not about the tariff or the war debts. They want consideration for their troubles in their own house, across the street, or around the corner. Something like paving, a water main, police protection, consideration for a complaint about taxes. They vote for the fellow who gives it to them. We never ask about their politics. We know pretty well how they'll vote after we help them."

"What are the methods by which you rose to power?"

"I've never bulldozed anybody and never let anybody bulldoze me. Newspapers, churches, reformers, or narrow-minded fellows—they can't bulldoze me. I have never changed my mind when I knew I was right and I have never broken my word. The biggest mistake a man can make is failing to keep his word. Sometimes I've been sorry I made a promise but I've always kept it. I'm just an ordinary fellow that was able to keep his word."

"When you endorse a man for office, Mr. Pendergast—and we understand most of the officeholders in Kansas City and in the State government, besides members of the Senate and House of Representatives, are of your choosing—do you exact any promises in advance?"

"If a candidate hasn't got sense enough to see who helped him win and hasn't sense enough to recognize that man's friends, there is no use asking for favors from that candidate in advance."

"But a little bit more, Mr. Pendergast, about your methods, if you please."

"There are no alibis in politics. The delivery of the votes is what counts. And it is efficient organization in every little ward and precinct that determines national as well as local elections. National elections, national politics are just Kansas City on a big scale. It boils down to the wards and precincts. The whole thing is to have an organization that functions in every ward and precinct. That's where the votes come from. The fundamental secret is to get the vote registered—and then get it out after it's registered. That's all there is to it. All the ballyhoo and showmanship such as they have at the national conventions is all right. It's a great show. It gives folks a run for their money. It makes everybody feel good. But the man who makes the organization possible is the man who delivers the votes, and he doesn't deliver them by oratory. Politics is a business, just like anything else."

"Thank you, Mr. Pendergast. We should like to ask a question or two more. We understand that Kansas City is one of the most wide-open towns in the United States. Is that true?"

"If by calling the city wide-open, you mean gambling and poker games where the poor man obtains his recreation just as the big men do in their clubs, it is wide-open. I wouldn't put a stop to it."

"A certain former lieutenant of yours, Mr. Pendergast, a man named Johnny Lazia, an ex-convict who was machine-gunned to death in July, 1934, was in trouble with the federal income-tax authorities in 1933. The case was mysteriously hushed up for a while, but later, on demand of a federal grand juror, it was prosecuted, and Lazia was convicted. Did you, on May 12, 1933, write this letter to Postmaster General James A. Farley?

Dear Jim:

Jerome Walsh and John Lazia will be in Washington to see you about the same matter that I had Mr. Kemper talk to you about. Now, Jim, Lazia is one of my chief lieutenants and I am more sincerely interested in his welfare than anything you might be able to do for me now or in the future. He has been in trouble with the Income Tax Department for some time. I know it was simply a case of being jobbed because of his Democratic activities. I think Frank Walsh spoke to the proper authorities about this. In any event, I wish you would use your utmost endeavor to bring about a settlement of this matter. I cannot make it any stronger, except to say that my interest in him is greater than anything that might come up in the future. Thanking you for any and everything you can do, I remain sincerely,

Your Friend,

T. J. PENDERGAST.

"Yes, I wrote it. I stand by it, too. I'd do it again and I'll stand by it." Many questions about the boss are left unanswered, but let us now bow ourselves out. The boss had been indulgent enough in this synthetic interview, though on the subject of Johnny Lazia his eyes grew hard and narrow, and his voice rose in an angry roar.

It is almost noon as we leave him. He disposes quickly of the remainder of his callers and takes a light lunch, which is brought in to him. He then motors to the office of the Ready-Mixed Concrete Company. The boss owns this company. He also owns the T. J. Pendergast Liquor Company. Both are very prosperous.

It has been publicly charged that in no public building erected in Kansas City in the last ten years has there been used a single cubic yard of ready-mixed concrete except that furnished by the boss's company. One of the eyebrow-lifting uses to which it was put was to pave Brush Creek. Brush Creek is a rather harmless stream, which pursues its meandering course through Kansas City for about fifteen miles. For one reason or another it now has a concrete floor about 50 feet wide and a foot and a half thick. In many private construction projects, too, the contractors have decided to use the boss's concrete.

Let it be said of the T. J. Pendergast Liquor Company that it sells as much liquor as it cares to sell. If it wanted to, it could establish a monopoly in Kansas City, for no tavern owner could continue to do business if the forces of reprisal in the hands of the Pendergast machine were unleashed against him.

The boss is now through with politics for the day. At the office of the concrete company is a warning sign: *No politics discussed here.* He spends the afternoon at business and then he repairs to his home in a fashionable section of Kansas City. Unlike his office, the boss's home is handsome and richly furnished. No importunate callers follow the boss there. Even his key men dare not telephone or drop in. In the bosom of his family, consisting of a wife, a son, and two daughters, his privacy is inviolate.

Perhaps he will take an afternoon drive through the countryside with one of his daughters. But nine o'clock will find him in bed against a five o'clock rising to go through the grind once again at 1908 Main Street. No good fellowship. No late conferences. No carousing. No liquor. A monk in a monastery could maintain no more Spartan an existence.

One exception must be made to this. There is a race track—operated without benefit of legal sanction—at Riverside, near Kansas City, where he is to be found every afternoon when a meet is on. He loves to own horses and he loves to bet on them. This, the only personal vice of his later years, he indulges to an extreme. A New York racing paper estimated his losses in 1935 at $500,000. Nor does he confine his attendance to Riverside. He is to be found at Saratoga and at Churchill Downs, when the Kentucky Derby is run. Racing, and an occasional trip to Europe—with elaborate quarters on the newest luxury liner—are the breaks in his routine.

What are his roots?

The recorded annals of his childhood are short and simple. He was born July 22, 1872, at St. Joseph, Missouri, one of the nine children of Mr. and Mrs. Michael Pendergast. His father was a teamster employed by a St. Joseph dry-goods concern—others say he operated a small dray business of his own. In any event, it is doubtful whether the family income in Tom's youth often exceeded $50 a month.

Tom attended school at the old Christian Brothers' College, which has since been razed. Whether he ever graduated is something his surviving classmates cannot recall. At any rate, he later went to St. Mary's College in Kansas. On leaving there, he worked for a time in St. Joseph as a clerk in a railroad freight house, but was soon called to Kansas City by his brother Jim, who had found a foothold there as a saloonkeeper and politician. Tom began his Kansas City career at about the age of twenty.

As a youth, Tom was quiet and popular with his schoolmates. He was not inclined to start fights but, old friends say, he would permit no one to run over him, regardless of size or reputation. ("I've never bulldozed anybody and never let anyone bulldoze me.") He was so good a fist fighter he rarely had to prove it in St. Joseph, but it was a quality he later found to advantage in the First Ward of Kansas City. He was not a leader at school; he was below average in his studies but never failed to pass. What largely distinguished him as a youngster was his ability as a baseball player.

Around the saloon of Jim Pendergast in the mauve decade the political life of the First Ward revolved. Only the blurred memories of the old-timers remain to sketch what the Pendergast brothers were like in those days, but every student of American political history knows how the old saloonkeeper and precinct captain and ward heeler operated. Fist fights. Free lunch. A basket of coal. Menial jobs distributed here and there. Sodden figures in flophouses and tragic inmates of tenements.

A picture of Tom in the early days is now and then resurrected. John Rogers, then a young reporter, who was later to carve out a brilliant career in newspaper work and to win a Pulitzer Prize, was on his rounds in the First Ward late one night prior to an election day when he saw a strange sight. A powerfully built man, whom he afterward identified as Tom Pendergast, was walking up and down before a polling place directing the placing of chairs along the sidewalk. The man barked his orders. The chairs were lined up on both sides of the polling place, reaching to the door. Some of them were already occupied by derelicts, to whom coffee and sandwiches were passed. By the time the polls opened, these chairs were filled with adherents of Tom and his brother Jim. It was their job not only to vote but to hold the line intact to discourage Pendergast enemies from voting. When late-coming Pendergast allies arrived while voting was in progress, they were admitted to the line, while opponents were kept to the rear.

By the time he died in 1911, Jim was undisputed master of the First Ward, and control readily passed to Tom. Tom then was an alderman, in which position he served from 1908 to 1915. He had previously been a street commissioner, in the administration of Mayor, later Senator, James A. Reed, and was Marshal of Jackson County from 1902 to 1904.

To Jim's Plato, Tom played the role of Aristotle. The pupil far surpassed the teacher. Whereas Jim was content to be master of a single ward, Tom used his power there as a lever to extend his control throughout the city, then into Jackson County. By 1930, he was able to deliver 50,000 votes for Democratic candidates, and that made him a statewide power. Two years later, of his slate, only one candidate failed to win.

The Democratic landslides of 1932, 1934, and 1936 consolidated the boss's power. In 1936, his candidate for governor received a plurality of 137,791 votes in Kansas City, a plurality greater than President Roosevelt's.

It appeared for a time that, at the very pinnacle of his career, the boss was not to enjoy its fruits. He became seriously ill at the Democratic National Convention last summer, and was confined to the hospital for many months. His lieutenants were seriously worried about the succession. Tweeds, Crokers, Vares, Pendergasts are not easy to replace.

But the man on the hospital bed was not through. He recently told a public official, who came whimpering to him after being criticized in the newspapers, to resign his $5,000 job and go home. The man resigned his $5,000 job and went home. And he has "requested" the new Governor of Missouri to reappoint another official whose conduct of his office was one of the hotly debated issues of the gubernatorial campaign.

He is back at the old stand. Again the worn stairs of the Jackson County

Democratic Club sag under the weight of governors and senators and bankers and bums. Napoleon is now at Austerlitz.

But the epilogue remains to be written. Even now the forces of retribution are gathering. Though the Kansas City election and law-enforcement authorities fail to move in the public interest, the powerful arm of the federal government is now upraised. On December 14 last, Judge Albert L. Reeves instructed a federal grand jury to investigate the appalling election frauds in Kansas City. Judge Reeves said:

When a dishonest vote is introduced into the ballot box, it tends to contaminate the whole government. A fraudulent ballot is a common enemy, a canker gnawing from within. We cannot surrender our ballot box to plug-uglies and hoodlums who parade the streets with machine guns. We must not stand them any longer. I cannot sit quietly in my district and witness the open flouting of election laws.

Such was the tone of Judge Reeves's instructions. As he neared the close of his exhortation to the jury, he raised his right hand, with fist clenched, and said: "Gentlemen, reach for all, even if you find them in high authority. Move on them!"

Is the Duke of Wellington speaking?

No. 38

[IN every case the political boss must have some source of income to aid him in maintaining power. He may sell political favors, he may exact tribute from gamblers, houses of prostitution, dope peddlers, and the like; he may loot the public treasury and he may take advantage of his inside knowledge of governmental activities to profit by that information. The views of George Washington Plunkitt, a former Tammany district leader and State Senator in New York, on honest and dishonest graft give an interesting and unusual insight into some of the sources of the income of political bosses.]

HONEST AND DISHONEST GRAFT[1]

by W. L. Riordon

"EVERYBODY is talkin' these days about Tammany men growin' rich on graft, but nobody thinks of drawin' the distinction between honest graft and dishonest graft. There's all the difference in the world between the two. Yes, many of our men have grown rich in politics. I have myself.

[1] W. L. Riordon, *Plunkitt of Tammany Hall* (New York: McClure, Phillips and Co., 1905), pp. 3-10. Reprinted by permission of Doubleday, Doran and Company.

I've made a big fortune out of the game, and I'm gettin' richer every day, but I've not gone in for dishonest graft—blackmailin' gamblers, saloon-keepers, disorderly people, etc.—and neither has any of the men who have made big fortunes in politics.

"There's an honest graft, and I'm an example of how it works. I might sum up the whole thing by sayin': 'I seen my opportunities and I took 'em.'

"Just let me explain by examples. My party's in power in the city, and it's goin' to undertake a lot of public improvements. Well, I'm tipped off, say, that they're going to lay out a new park at a certain place.

"I see my opportunity and I take it. I go to that place and I buy up all the land I can in the neighborhood. Then the board of this or that makes its plan public, and there is a rush to get my land, which nobody cared particular for before.

"Ain't it perfectly honest to charge a good price and make a profit on my investment and foresight? Of course, it is. Well, that's honest graft.

"Or, supposin' it's a new bridge they're goin' to build. I get tipped off and I buy as much property as I can that has to be taken for approaches. I sell at my own price later on and drop some more money in the bank.

"Wouldn't you? It's just like lookin' ahead in Wall Street or in the coffee or cotton market. It's honest graft, and I'm lookin' for it every day in the year. I will tell you frankly that I've got a good lot of it, too.

"I'll tell you of one case. They were goin' to fix up a big park, no matter where. I got on to it, and went lookin' about for land in that neighborhood.

"I could get nothin' at a bargain but a big piece of swamp, but I took it fast enough and held on to it. What turned out was just what I counted on. They couldn't make the park complete without Plunkitt's swamp, and they had to pay a good price for it. Anything dishonest in that?

"Up in the watershed I made some money, too. I bought up several bits of land there some years ago and made a pretty good guess that they would be bought up for water purposes later by the city.

"Somehow, I always guessed about right, and shouldn't I enjoy the profit of my foresight? It was rather amusin' when the condemnation commissioners came along and found piece after piece of the land in the name of George Plunkitt of the Fifteenth Assembly District, New York City. They wondered how I knew just what to buy. The answer is—I seen my opportunity and I took it. I haven't confined myself to land; anything that pays is in my line.

"For instance, the city is repavin' a street and has several hundred thousand old granite blocks to sell. I am on hand to buy, and I know just what they are worth.

"How? Never mind that. I had a sort of monopoly of this business for a while, but once a newspaper tried to do me. It got some outside men to come over from Brooklyn and New Jersey to bid against me.

"Was I done? Not much. I went to each of the men and said: 'How many of these 250,000 stones do you want?' One said 20,000, and another wanted 15,000, and another wanted 10,000. I said: 'All right, let me bid for the lot, and I'll give each of you all you want for nothin'.'

"They agreed, of course. Then the auctioneer yelled: 'How much am I bid for these 250,000 fine pavin' stones?'

" 'Two dollars and fifty cents,' says I.

" 'Two dollars and fifty cents!' screamed the auctioneer. 'Oh, that's a joke! Give me a real bid.'

"He found the bid was real enough. My rivals stood silent. I got the lot for $2.50 and gave them their share. That's how the attempt to do Plunkitt ended, and that's how all such attempts end.

"I've told you how I got rich by honest graft. Now, let me tell you that most politicians who are accused of robbin' the city get rich the same way.

"They didn't steal a dollar from the city treasury. They just seen their opportunities and took them. That is why, when a reform administration comes in and spends a half million dollars in tryin' to find the public robberies they talked about in the campaign, they don't find them.

"The books are always all right. The money in the city treasury is all right. Everything is all right. All they can show is that the Tammany heads of departments looked after their friends, within the law, and gave them what opportunities they could to make honest graft. Now, let me tell you that's never going to hurt Tammany with the people. Every good man looks after his friends, and any man who doesn't isn't likely to be popular. If I have a good thing to hand out in private life, I give it to a friend. Why shouldn't I do the same in public life?

"Another kind of honest graft. Tammany has raised a good many salaries. There was an awful howl by the reformers, but don't you know that Tammany gains ten votes for every one it lost by salary raisin'?

"The Wall Street banker thinks it shameful to raise a department clerk's salary from $1500 to $1800 a year, but every man who draws a salary himself says: 'That's all right. I wish it was me.' And he feels very much like votin' the Tammany ticket on election day, just out of sympathy.

"Tammany was beat in 1901 because the people were deceived into believin' that it worked dishonest graft. They didn't draw a distinction between dishonest and honest graft, but they saw that some Tammany men grew rich, and supposed they had been robbin' the city treasury or levyin' blackmail on disorderly houses, or workin' in with the gamblers and law-breakers.

"As a matter of policy, if nothing else, why should the Tammany leaders go into such dirty business, when there is so much honest graft lyin' around when they are in power?   Did you ever consider that?

"Now, in conclusion, I want to say that I don't own a dishonest dollar. If my worst enemy was given the job of writin' my epitaph when I'm gone, he couldn't do more than write:

"'George W. Plunkitt.   He Seen His Opportunities, and He Took 'Em.'"

Chapter XII

NOMINATIONS AND ELECTIONS

No. 39

[ONE of the major objectives of a political party is to secure control of the personnel of government. In order to attain this goal the parties must offer candidates for elective office, candidates whom the voters may approve of or reject. The ordinary voter tends to regard the final election as the crucial point in this process and devotes comparatively little thought to the preliminary "trial-heats" in which a large number of potential candidates is reduced to one from each major political group.

We have experimented with many types of nominating procedures in the United States. Each rejection of an existing plan and advocacy of a new has been based on the desire to secure a greater democratic control over the process. Each has also been opposed on the grounds that the average voter can not make reliable judgments in the selection of candidates and that consequently it is wiser to allow a favored few to make these highly important decisions.

Few have seen as clearly as Professor Merriam the close connection between nominating systems and the democratic way of life. It is essential that all who wish to perpetuate democratic government see the full implications of the whole electoral process, nominations as well as elections. In the last analysis belief in democratic elections, unless it is supported by a similar belief in democratic nominating processes, is at best but a lip service to the cause of democracy.]

DEMOCRACY AND THE DIRECT PRIMARY [1]

by Charles E. Merriam and Louise Overacker

THE nominating system is a phase of the American party system; . . . this is in turn a phase of the larger problem of modern democracy. And democracy is a phase of the political order now existing, and this in turn of the economic and social order of the present day and the Western

[1] C. E. Merriam and Louise Overacker, *Primary Elections* (Chicago: University of Chicago Press, 1928), pp. 351-358. Reprinted by permission of the University of Chicago Press.

world. All of these are under fire and all are subject to rapid change. We do not know whether the party system may be materially modified; whether the democracy we now know is destined to survive; whether the modern political or economic order can resist the revolutionary forces that are hammering at its gates; what science will do to the whole social order in another generation.

Only the most enthusiastic and inexperienced would therefore expect that changes in the nominating system would produce a fundamental effect, whether through an indirect or a direct method.

The primary is a phase, an important phase, of our political life, and significant advances might be made in its processes, but it should not be expected that these will contribute the last word to our political problems. Too much was expected of the mongrel caucus when it was established; too much was expected of the convention when it overthrew King Caucus; too much was expected of the regulated convention; and too much was expected of the direct primary in its day. Perhaps there must always be a myth as a preliminary to progress, but the myth must not become a tradition, a memory rather than a hope. My wise colleague, Dr. Herrick, warns us to beware of making our hypothesis a religion.

The level of politics is in the long run the level of intelligent public interest in men and affairs political. Under any system the largest and most skilful group of interested and active citizens will determine public policies and will select the persons to formulate and administer them. The uninterested, or the spasmodically interested, or the ineffectual who wish well feebly will be the governed, not the governors. It was Montesquieu who said that "A slave people can have only their chains," and it is impossible to escape the conclusion that only an intelligent and interested electorate habituated to political practice can use the mechanism of democracy or the systems of nomination in use here.

There are those who foresee the decline of parties, of democracy, of politics itself, in the development of modern life. But they deceive themselves with words, for when politics is destroyed the set of relations formerly called politics emerges under some other name, whether economics or what not. Men may not be vitally interested in the mere mechanisms of government, but they were never more intensely interested than now in the patterns of human leadership, domination, cooperation; and there were never more fascinating types of political leaders in the social and political worlds than in our day. Roosevelt, Wilson, Lloyd George, Clemenceau, Stresemann, Lenin, Trotzky, Mussolini, Gandhi—these are great figures of vivid interest to mankind. In America urban and rural leaders of many colors attract the interest of millions of citizens and outshine even movie stars, boxers, base-ball heroes.

Nor was there ever a time when the functions of government were more important in the field of social relations than at the present time. Notwithstanding the furious denunciation of governmental activity and interference, it advances at a rapid rate, usually with the support in one field of those who condemn it in another. There is likely to be more government and politics before there is less, and political crises and tensions are likely to become increasingly significant. Likewise, political leaders are likely to become more important in the near future than in the past.

All systems of government require some form of general judgment on leaders and policies, and some method of indicating toleration or approval of the dominant leaders and their policies. This is necessary in times of peace as well as of war, for the sake of morale if for nothing else. Murmuring, discontent, unwillingness, scattered protest, outbreaks, resistance, rebellion, revolution—these are the classic methods of expressing these popular judgments. Democracy provides an orderly way of passing judgment upon leaders, replacing them with others, and of indicating approval or disapproval of public policies as well as of types of leaders; and further provides that practically all of the adult population shall be eligible to participate in the process. Those who are satisfied or not much dissatisfied, or lazy, or incompetent, or careless, either do not participate, or are ineffective in their participation. An election and a primary election reflect this situation. They present the issue which is basic to modern democracy, namely, Are the people interested enough and competent enough to choose leaders and determine policies? The well-known answer was, "Let them vote until their stomachs ache, but do not let them decide anything." Our political order is based upon the democratic assumption that there is material in the electorate for the formulation of sound policies of state and the choice of wise leadership, and difficulties found in this direction are on the whole less than those met with in alternative directions of dictatorship, hereditary monarchy, military or theocratic rule. We are engaged in testing this assumption.

Most of the objections raised against primaries apply to elections as well as to universal suffrage, and to the whole plan of democracy. Disbelievers in popular government are constantly asserting that many are ignorant, that many are incompetent, that many are indifferent, that many are lax, lazy, and drifting, that nothing can come from this mediocre mass of yokels and boobs, that the mass should abdicate in favor of the few and kiss the rod that condescends to rule them, thanking God that they are allowed to live and be cared for by their betters—these are common charges among those to whom modern democracy is unwelcome.

All these criticisms should be examined, and the wheat carefully sifted from the chaff, but for some time to come it is clear that the democratic experiment will continue, and the broad outlines of the basic political order will not be changed. What the outcome of the experiment may be, no one can safely predict. It seems to me that there are more signs that democracy will succeed than any of the alternatives suggested; but I do not know this and can only register my own judgment that the interests of society will be best served by the continuance of the democratic assumption and the political order based upon it.

It is quite true that there may be democracy without primaries, or without conventions for that matter. It is also possible that primary devices may develop later in the political life of a larger number of modern states. It may logically be contended that political parties should not be subject to any legal regulation of any description, but should be left to the political rebuke of the electorate. But if the objection to the primary system is to democracy itself, that should be clearly understood. And the remedies proposed need not be simply reversion to an earlier type of nomination, but should be constructive attempts to make the democratic assumption more readily workable. The short ballot, organization of conspicuous responsibility, development of technical public administration, sounder civic training, better organization of political prudence, more fundamental study of the science of politics, elimination of maladjustments in our economic and social life—all these are significant.

There is nothing sacred about our American nominating systems, direct or indirect, regulated or unregulated. They are all parts of the larger democratic experiment and should be subject to change and adaptation, as new experience or new conditions may indicate. The caucus, the convention, the regulated convention, the direct primary, the nomination by petition only, the double election, proportional and preferential voting—these are all phases of an attempt to organize the system of selecting leaders and determining policies more and more effectively, under constantly shifting conditions, rural, frontier, urban, with shifting systems of education, industry, intercommunication.

Experienced, intelligent, and disinterested men and women differ on the details of the nominating system and upon the areas within which the direct or indirect system is preferable. In so far as this represents intelligent difference of opinion and is intelligently supported, it is beneficial. It would be unfortunate, however, if this discussion were to distract interest, intelligent and persistent, from the broader problem of the reorganization of our whole electoral system, the raising of the standards of political practice, and the possibility of improvements of such types as have been discussed in previous pages of this study. The success of the democratic experiment will not be determined primarily by the direct or indirect system of nomination, but by our attitude toward the wider problems of political organization and practice which affect much more fundamentally our political future. Whether we cling to the spoils system or adopt some more scientific system of public administration; whether we retain the ballot's burden or adopt the short ballot; whether we centralize more closely authority and responsibility in cities, counties, and states; whether we develop sounder standards of leadership or fall into the hands of bosses and demagogues; whether we are able to work out a more effective system of civic training better adapted to a changing society, looking to the future as well as the past; whether we are able to adapt our representative system to modern needs and escape the gerrymanders of tradition; whether our political system reflects the deeper trends down under the surface of social and economic life and the still more revolutionary tendencies of modern science—these and many other like problems are pressing hard upon our political order, and require the united effort of those interested in the development of our political system. As these questions are attacked it is not improbable that other and better types of nomination may emerge and take their place in the political world, competing with the older for survival under new conditions.

No. 40

[SINCE 1789 the American people have been concerned with improving nominating methods. The legislative caucus was abandoned for the mongrel caucus; conventions were in part replaced by primaries. In each instance the advocate of the new plan loudly asserted his belief that *it* was the panacea that would cure all of our party and electoral ills.

Most of our nominating experimentation, however, has been built on an all too narrow base. We have been concerned only with the superficial and mechanical aspects of the problem and not with the broader questions of the relationship of the nominating (and electoral) process to the multiplicity of elective offices, and its connection with the complexity of governmental organization in the United States. Few have perceived the intimate relationship between the placid acceptance of the spoils system and the nomination of candidates for public office.

The skilled physician can not prescribe a cure until he has a complete diagnosis of the patient's condition. It is equally true that improvements in nominating methods can not be secured without a similarly complete diagnosis. The haste with which we have abandoned old systems for new, and then forsaken the new, is evidence of the need for critical thinking in this field of American government.]

NOMINATING METHODS AND RELATED PROBLEMS [1]

by Charles E. Merriam and Louise Overacker

THE problem of party nominations, it must be conceded, presents extraordinary difficulties for any system to surmount. This is especially true of the field of state and local offices, where the chief field of controversy lies. We have to deal (1) with campaigns in which there is a dearth of significant issues growing out of the local situation, and frequently a dearth of national issues; (2) with the choice of a large number of officials whose position is wholly unadapted to popular choice, as in the case of coroners, surveyors, clerks, recorders. The total number of elective offices in the United States is about 750,000; (3) with a highly developed spoils-based organization or machine on the one hand and a lack of leadership outside the machine.

This situation offers a puzzling problem, which has not yet been solved by any nominating system, and it is difficult to see how it can be solved as it stands. The Continental party system has smaller parties more compact in principle and more prolific in special types of leaders. The English party system is or has been dual in nature, but it has inherited a type of leadership on the right wing and developed a type of leadership on the other; and it has succeeded in subordinating the spoilsmen in the administrative service. In neither case is there a large number of offices to be filled by election. These conditions have greatly simplified the task of selecting party candidates, and have made it unnecessary to resort to the legal regulation of the party nominating process.

With us the number of offices is so great that the constant selection of personnel becomes almost a professional task; the task devolves upon professionals who recoup themselves through the spoils system; these professionals soon become so powerful that they dominate instead of serve the party electorate; and as a result the rank and file of the party become apathetic and indifferent, which in turn aids again the power of the machine.

[1] C. E. Merriam and Louise Overacker, *Primary Elections* (Chicago: University of Chicago Press, 1928), pp. 275-287. Reprinted by permission of the University of Chicago Press.

So we swing around a vicious circle from one disaster to another. Thus far we have not been able to extricate ourselves.

What is the next step in the improvement of nominating methods? What constructive program may be presented for the consideration of those who are not so much devoted to any existing system as to the progressive development of new and better methods? This is not a matter upon which anyone is authorized to speak dogmatically, but in the judgment of the writer the following types of change in the existing system would tend to improve its adaptability to its apparent functions. What is wanted is a system in which democratic control and popular leadership may prevail, using the framework of the party system as an agency for that purpose.

A study of primary election legislation shows that the desired results cannot be obtained until other and important political changes have been made. Unless primary laws are accompanied or followed by other developments of the political situation, comparatively little will result from the movement. No friend of direct or indirect nomination should indulge the pleasant dream that the adoption of a law providing for such a system will of itself act as a cure for all the present-day party evils. Disillusionment and discouragement are certain to follow in the wake of any campaign conducted on such a theory. It is necessary to understand that the political conditions are far too serious and far too complicated to be cured by so simple a specific.

In the first place, it is not likely that any nominating system will achieve its full results until the number of elective officers is materially reduced. When thirty or forty offices are to be filled at one primary, it is not probable that uniformly good choices will be made from the great number of candidates presented. The variety of qualifications required for the several offices, the multiplicity of candidates clamoring for recognition, the obscurity of many of these candidates, the possibility of "deals" and "slates," make satisfactory selection difficult.

The reduction of the number of elective offices is not undemocratic, as might perhaps be charged, but is, on the contrary, calculated to give the people more complete control over their own government. To provide for popular choice of a large number of officers does not increase, but, quite the contrary, diminishes their power. As was said in the *Federalist*,

> The countenance of the government may become more democratic; but the soul that animates it will be more oligarchic. The machine will be enlarged, but the fewer, and often the more secret, will be the springs by which its motions are directed.

A great array of elective public offices means control by the few rather than by the many. Amenability to popular control will be better secured by reducing the number of offices, so that the requirements of the candidates for each such position may be carefully scrutinized, and the most intelligent choice be made.

This simplification of the machinery of government may most easily be made by eliminating administrative offices from the elective list. There can be no good reason why such officers as auditor, engineer, and surveyor should be elective. An auditor must be accurate and honest, and there is no such thing as Republican auditing or Democratic auditing. Nor is there a Republican way, or a Democratic way, or a Prohibitionist way of administering the office of engineer. Certainly there can be no form of surveying that could be characterized as Socialistic or Democratic or Republican.

The true principle is that the people should choose all officers concerned primarily with the formulation of public policies. Policy-framing or legislation is a matter upon which there may be differences of opinion, and men intrusted with the work of drawing up such plans must be elected by, and be immediately responsible to, the people. Regarding the execution of policies once enacted into law, there is less room for difference of opinion. The making of the law is partisan, but the enforcement of law should be non-partisan. When the enforcement of law becomes a political issue, the times are out of joint. Laws should not be administered in a partisan way, but efficiently and justly. Administration requires technical skill, and partisanship is destructive to its best development.

If any administrative offices are to be voted upon, the number should be confined to the chief executive officers, such as the mayor and the governor. If these officers are chosen by the people and given the duty of selecting and supervising other public servants on the administrative staff, the result is certain to be a higher degree of popular control than is now generally secured. This principle has been established in the federal government from the beginning, is now being adopted in our municipal governments, and few new elective offices are being provided in state and county government. We are coming to realize that what is needed is popular control over policies, with non-partisan, skilled, and permanent administration of these policies.

Such a change may be denounced as undemocratic in spirit and tendency, but on second thought it will be seen that instead of weakening popular control over government the result will be to strengthen that control. A system that imposes upon the electorate the choice of a mass of officials strengthens the hands of partisan or private interests at the expense of the public. With a smaller number of elective officers, the results obtained under the direct primary system would be far more satisfactory than they can be under existing conditions. Public attention could be focused upon a few offices and a few candidates with better prospects than at present for the elimination of the undesirable and the survival of the fittest. Until this is brought about, the success of any nominating system must be seriously menaced.

In a discussion of nominating methods in 1909, I expressed the belief that neither the direct primary nor the convention system would work well in situations where a large number of minor administrative offices were elective. I still believe that we will not make progress in the better nomination of coroners, and surveyors, and county clerks, and state auditors under any system that the combined ingenuity of the elder and junior statesmen together may devise. The main road is the short ballot with what it involves in the way of governmental direction.

In state and county governments with which we are now concerned there is manifest a slow but strong tendency toward fundamental reorganization, somewhat resembling that which has been seen in the more progressive city governments during the last generation. More than ever vigorous and effective state and local governments are needed to offset the centralizing tendencies of the Federal government, and are desired even by the most ardent nationalists. A more modern organization of these governments would do much to clear up the difficulties surrounding the nominating system, and might change the whole character of the problem, as has happened in cities where non-partisan elections and proportional representation are now the chief centers of electoral interest. If counties were to adopt a council-manager plan, how would nominations be made? Or if, as some day may happen, a state adopts a simple form of government, such as the council-manager, or one in which executive responsibility is more strongly organized, how then will nominations be made?

The short ballot will tend to concentrate power and responsibility, and 'o focus attention upon the significant offices to be filled. If only the governor and members of the legislature, together with one or two county officials, were chosen at one time, it would be far easier for the voters to concentrate their attention upon these key officials and to exercise their powers of discrimination more effectively than at present. With the short ballot, the task of the primary will be made much lighter, while the degree of popular control will tend to be greater.

Precisely here it must be recognized that with the development of greater power in fewer officials it will be all the more necessary to exercise effective popular control over them. The larger authority conferred upon officials through the process of consolidation and through the gradually increasing authority exercised by the government over social and industrial affairs will be likely to require a balance in more direct control. This counterpart to the short ballot may be the direct primary.

But the short ballot is no more a panacea than is the direct primary, and we delude ourselves if we assume that the mechanical device of shortening the list of candidates will of itself cure all the ills the body politic is heir to. Government is no more a matter of mechanisms than it is of values and attitudes, of intelligent discrimination, of sound sense and practical judgment on the part of the community. The fundamental attitudes of the people go deeper down than either the direct or the indirect primary, important as these are. We shall be drawn aside from the main purpose and needs of our time unless we recognize the vital importance of technical administration, applying the best results of intelligence and science to common affairs, unless we recognize the fundamental need of the broadest possible social and civic training, unless we recognize the significance of the feeling of justice which the state must strive to realize in the lives of men and women.

Notable progress in the direction of simpler government has recently been made in New York State and elsewhere, but there still remain states in which no advance has been made, and even in the most progressive commonwealths there is still much to be done in the direction of the simplification of the ballot.

It is important to consider other possibilities that may arise in the course of governmental development. It may be that in the reorganization of county and state government proportional or preferential representation will play a larger role than in the past. If this proves to be the case, the methods of nominations would be materially affected, as is now seen in cities using proportional representation. Here again, of course, the question may arise as to how the primary or original selection of candidates will be made.

Another essential change is the return to the original form of the Australian ballot. The party emblem, the party circle, and the party column have nothing to do with the Australian ballot, and were engrafted on the system by American legislatures. In adopting the system, secrecy of the ballot was secured, but the party obtained the advantage of arranging party candidates in columns and permitting the voter to select a list of candidates by marking in the party circle. This mechanical arrangement places a premium upon undiscriminating voting, and often results in the election of unworthy and unfit candidates by sheer advantage of position upon the ballot. If the head of the ticket is elected, the others are likely to be carried along with the leader, regardless of their own merits. Fortunately this plan has not been applied to the conduct of preliminary elections, where voting an organization slate with one mark might have worked great damage; but the fact that this practice prevails in the regular elections throws its shadow back over the primaries. The knowledge that candidates, when nominated will be placed under the protection of the emblem or the circle makes the party, especially in districts where it is strongly in the majority, less careful in its choice of candidates than would otherwise be the case. It is only human nature to be less studious of the public wishes in a situation where a nomination is equivalent to an election and where defeat, even of the unworthy, is a remote possibility. Ballot reform is, therefore, a necessary accompaniment of primary reform. The ballot in the regular election should be made up in the same form as the ballot in the primary election, with the party designation placed after the name of the candidate.

Another constructive factor in the development of the nominating system is the further extension and enforcement of the merit system, or perhaps better stated, the establishment of sounder principles of public administration.

As long as an army of officials can be thrown into the field in support of a particular "slate," it will be difficult for the candidate not so supported to succeed. The odds are too greatly in favor of the regular army against the unorganized and undisciplined volunteers. Occasionally victory may perch on the banners of the straggling group of reformers and "antis," but habitually will rest upon the side of the well-disciplined army of office holders. The honest and intelligent application of the merit principle to administrative appointments reduces the number of workers under the control of a faction and makes the support of the "slate" far less formidable. If the group in power centers around some principle or policy it will continue to be powerful and effective in the primaries, even under the merit system; but if the chief element of cohesion was public office, it will be far less vigorous than before.

Patronage is not only the force that holds an organization together, but it is the strongest single element, and no practical politician is ever guilty of despising the power of appointing men to, and removing them from, office. There are, of course, many exceptions, but the general practice is for the appointing power to control the political activity of the appointee. When the office is obtained by merit, however, and not by favor, this sense of obligation on the part of the officer and of power on the part of the party ruler ceases. Hence the mobilization of an army for effective use in a primary campaign becomes far more difficult, and the opportunities for success on the part of the opposition correspondingly greater. To the extent that the merit system is not rigidly carried out, the effects just indicated do not follow. In any event it is not to be presumed that civil service reform is a panacea. It is merely a palliative. It will materially help, but cannot be relied upon to accomplish a complete cure for our political ills. The merit system merely abolishes the feudal tenure under which many officers now hold, and the obligations of service incident to that relationship. It will remove one handicap to an even race between candidates for nomination.

But even more important than the success of what was once called civil service reform is the recognition of the importance of public administration in the governmental system. It cannot be too strongly stated that the weakest spot in the American governmental plan as thus far developed is the lack of a permanent staff of competent public servants, adequate for the tasks of public service. With the specialization of industry and the professionalization of tasks this is rapidly coming about, but it comes more slowly than is consistent with the very rapidly growing needs of governmental service. In great fields like taxation and police, progress is very tardy, while in health and engineering we advance with greater speed. If we have a trained technical staff, the storms of political controversy may rage as they will, but the commonwealth is safe. Whatever policies are determined upon, they will be wisely and competently administered. But without such a staff, what we decide upon matters little.

A well-trained administration may also be relied upon to make many suggestions for the consideration of the legislative body, and its administrative initiative will always be of great value, even if not always accepted by the policy-determining body. The tasks of political leadership are made easier by competent administration, and the limits of danger are narrower than under other circumstances.

Raising the level of administration and leadership has its inevitable effect upon the party system and upon the nominating system of the party. The relation is not remote but immediate, and not only immediate but indispensable. It is idle to suppose that the mechanism of nominations will avail against the trend of a system in which party leadership cannot emerge without the very greatest difficulty. Forces far deeper and stronger determine the course of political events and control the political destinies of candidates for official position and popular favor and support.

Commonplace as it may seem, then, one of the basic conditions for improvement of the nominating system is the establishment of a different type of public administration upon which a different type of political leadership may rest. When all of the forty-eight states and all of the three thousand counties and all of the urban centers are under the merit system, and the federal government has reduced its "free list" of patronage, and when these systems are not merely based upon laws, but are reinforced by professional organizations on the one hand and a strong public sentiment on the other, the primary contests will take on a different color.

No. 41

[ONE of the popular indoor sports in the United States is to criticize our system of nominating candidates for the presidency. All who read this book are familiar with the "four-ring circus" analyses of the nominating conventions. The "smoke-filled room" is commonplace to everyone and the radio has brought into every home descriptions of the carefully planned "spontaneous" demonstrations which vie with one another for new decibel and time records.

The critical student must, of course, be familiar with such problems as the apportionment and selection of delegates, the control of the "organization" and the deals and trades which are associated with these conventions. On the other hand he needs proper perspective in evaluating the results of their labors. Such perspective can be obtained from Professor Laski's essay. Professor Laski, a distinguished English political scientist, weighs our conventions, balances them against the English nominating methods and finds them not wanting.]

THE CONVENTIONS AND THE PRESIDENCY [1]

by Harold J. Laski

THE founders of the Constitution were especially proud of the method they adopted for choosing the president; none of their expectations has been more decisively disappointed. The presidential candidates are now chosen at national conventions of the respective parties; and the decision is made by the electorate at large, with the reservation, as shown by the famous Hayes-Tilden case, that a plurality of votes does not necessarily carry with it the certainty of election. It is, indeed, a desirable thing that the method should be made to correspond to the facts. A constitutional amendment which simply stated that the candidate with the most votes should be deemed to have been elected would be a wise safeguard against possible difficulties in the future.

An American presidential convention is like nothing else in the civilized world; and the critics of the system—which, in its modern form, is just a hundred years old—have exhausted the language of vituperation in attack upon its character. The power of money; the persuasive power of hidden

[1] Harold J. Laski, "The Conventions and the Presidency," *Harper's Magazine* (July 1940), Vol. 181, pp. 166-171. Reprinted by permission of *Harper's Magazine*.

and corrupt influence; the undue authority of the "doubtful" State; the overt and hidden prejudices against particular types of candidates, as, for instance, members of the Roman Catholic Church; the "deals" which accompany the capture of a delegation for one candidate as against another; the mythology of the "favorite son"; the casual influence, notable in the case of Lincoln's selection, the choice of the convention city; the undue impact, as in the Democratic Convention of 1896, of a single speech by a potential nominee; the operation of the technic of the "dark horse" candidate; the exploitation of the "stalking-horse" behind whom some well-organized group has its carefully prepared selection whose name is put forward at the right moment; and, finally, the raucous, complex, and hectic atmosphere of the convention itself; its well-improvised enthusiasms; its fantastic horse-play; its immunity to thought; its wild rumors; its incredible conspiracies—all these characteristics, none of which can ever suffer exaggeration, seem to the outsider, and especially to the European outsider, about the worst possible way in which to choose a man to occupy the highest executive post in a democratic commonwealth.

The convention itself is of course predominantly an organ for registering decisions that have been made behind the scenes. Occasionally an utterance upon its floor may exercise a real influence upon its outcome. Senator Conkling did Blaine irreparable damage in 1880; and the contrast between his speech and that of Garfield, who nominated Sherman, had a good deal to do with the emergence of Garfield as the Republican candidate. So also the famous speech of Bryan in 1896 turned the balance of opinion in his favor. But in general the actual nomination is decided in part by the pre-convention campaign and in part by bargains actually concluded in and around the convention itself. The pre-convention campaign is of great importance. It was decisive, for instance, in the selection of Franklin Roosevelt in 1932; the spadework done by Mr. Farley in the two preceding years was the condition precedent to his nomination. Bargaining at the convention is of course a special art. Its importance emerges either when there are a number of outstanding candidates between whom choice is difficult—as with the Republicans in 1880 and 1920, and with the Democrats in 1924, —or when a powerful group has made up its mind to try to force a "dark horse" upon the convention.

Accident in fact plays a much smaller part in the choice of the candidate than is imagined. The public, for example, expected either Governor Lowden or General Wood to be the Republican candidate in 1920; and immense sums had been expended in promoting their interests. But the skilful proponents of Senator Harding's name had long foreseen that the acuteness of their rivalry would make neither possible, and they had long foreseen the probability of Harding's success. "At the proper time after the Republican convention meets," said Mr. Daugherty, Senator Harding's manager, "some fifteen men, bleary-eyed with loss of sleep, and perspiring profusely with the excessive heat, will sit down in seclusion round a big table. I will be with them, and will present Senator Harding's name, and before we get through, they will put him over." That is precisely what occurred.

Out of all this complexity there has emerged the doctrine of "availability." The party needs a candidate who, positively, will make the widest appeal and, negatively, will offend the least proportion of the electorate. On the whole, he ought to come from a doubtful State; a Democrat from New York is more "available" than one from the solid South because he is likely to win votes which might otherwise be uninterested. It seems still to be true that it is difficult to elect a Roman Catholic; even the solid South refused to vote for Governor Smith in 1928. He must not be anti-religious; that would offend the great vested interest of the churches. He must be sound on the tariff; he must be against wild currency adventures; he must not be too overtly internationalist in outlook. Administrative experience, like the governorship of a State, is important. It is helpful, if he is a self-made man; the "log cabin to White House" tradition is still, despite the two Roosevelts, an influential one. He ought not to possess any nostrum which can be represented as extreme. In the aftermath of a war period it is important that he should have played his part in the army; from Jackson and Taylor onward, the military hero has had an immense appeal to the electorate. It is undesirable that he should have too close an association with the big interests, especially Wall Street; Wilson, in 1912, owed his nomination to Mr. Bryan's famous pronouncement that he would not support anyone under obligation to "Morgan, Ryan, Belmont, or any other member of the privilege-seeking, favor-hunting class." He must have a sufficiently flexible mind to accept the implications of the trading necessary to build his majority. He must not be the kind of man whom it is obviously easy to ridicule in a campaign, either because he is "viewy," or for any other reason.

All of which means, as a general rule, that the outcome of a presidential convention is likely to be a compromise of some kind. But it is important to realize that it is not a compromise in which, without cause, the outstanding candidate is certain to be defeated. Henry Clay never became president because the admirable instinct of his party warned it against choosing a man whose avidity for the office was so patently excessive. Blaine never became president because even many of his admirers profoundly felt that his association, to say no more, with dubious political methods left too much to be explained away. [Clay, however, was nomi-

nated in 1831 and 1844 and Blaine in 1884.] Governor Fuller of Massachusetts could not be nominated because, as Senator Borah said, Sacco and
Vanzetti would thereby have become issues in the campaign. Senator
Lodge was for forty years an outstanding figure in the Senate. But he
could not have secured the Republican nomination simply because his own
party realized that, whatever his qualities, those years in politics were a
continuous demonstration of his unfitness for high executive office. Mr.
Hoover was undoubtedly the leading Republican in 1936; and, on the
precedent of Cleveland's nomination in 1892, was the natural recipient of
the candidature. But he was unavailable because the party leaders felt,
quite rightly, that he was too closely associated with Republican failure in
the depression to be an acceptable candidate.

It is notable, in short, that whenever an obvious contender for the nomination does not receive it there is usually a quite adequate explanation for
his failure. It is notable, further, that when a "dark horse" nominee
emerges he has been held in reserve for just such an opportunity by powerful influences which are waiting for their moment. It is possible for someone, like Franklin Pierce, who is unknown to the general public, to emerge
from the ordeal. But it is to be noticed that if he does his emergence is
always due to special circumstances, and that there is to be detected behind
him a substantial cohort who know precisely what they are doing. A "dark
horse," that is to say, is a compromise candidate in much the same way
as Mr. Bonar Law was a compromise between Mr. Austen Chamberlain
and Mr. Walter Long in 1911, or Sir Henry Campbell-Bannerman as Liberal
leader after 1895. Much the same situation obtains in the complicated
intrigues of French politics. It is difficult for the outsider to follow the
tortuous internal events which make now Mr. Herriot, now M. Chautemps,
and now M. Daladier the leader of the Socialist Radicals. Immediacy on
the basis of "availability" there also explains the result that is reached. It
is as natural for Henry Clay or James G. Blaine to have missed the presidency as it was for Mr. Churchill or Sir Austen Chamberlain to have missed
the premiership in their country.

The real difference of course lies in the prior experience of those who
are chosen as nominees. Other things being equal, a prime minister in
Great Britain or France will have served a long apprenticeship in the legislative assembly before obtaining the supreme office. He will be a figure
in the House. He will be known to the party. He will probably have had
considerable administrative experience in a lesser office. He will be pretty
intimately known to those whom he is to lead. In the United States none
of this is necessarily true. Since the Civil War a distinguished career in
Congress has rarely been a passport to the nomination. Attainment of

cabinet office has had no direct relevance to a candidature in any except two cases; and, of these, Mr. Hoover's name was made rather by his war record than by his experience in the Department of Commerce. A State governorship has counted for much. But it is pretty true to say that most of the chosen candidates have been names in the nation rather than in Washington. They have not known with any intimacy those with whom they would, as president, be expected to work.

The position is in curious contrast with the pre-Civil War period. The first four presidents of the United States almost nominated themselves; and among their successors there was hardly a candidate for the nomination who was not a person of considerable political consequence. One feature, indeed, is constant. No presidential candidate in the whole record has been a business man. [This article was written before the 1940 conventions.] The vocation, clearly, is a full-time one; and the qualities which make for business success make also against the possibility of nomination. It is true that in his engineering period Mr. Hoover was mainly a company organizer. But after his return to America all his energies were devoted to politics. Business men have played a not inconsiderable part in the conventions as king-makers; but it is a curious fact that in a civilization perhaps more dominated by business men than by any other they have had to surrender the hope of being king. The lawyer, the soldier, the rentier, and politician —these are the types from whom the candidates have been chosen. The business man may hope for cabinet office. He is likely to be important in negativing ambitions the realization of which would not be regarded with favor by the big interests. But, on the record, he must be the power behind the throne; he cannot hope to occupy it.

The reason, I think, is simple. The small man cannot hope to afford the risks of a political career. The great one, a Rockefeller, a Vanderbilt, even an Owen D. Young, would not be an "available" candidate simply because he would arouse the suspicion that the party which nominated him was in bondage to the money-power. The influence of the business outlook upon the parties must, therefore, be indirect. It is real enough, as the election of McKinley makes clear. But it must always seek to veil itself in a decent obscurity if it is not to prove a source of violent opposition from the interests of labor and the small farmer. Franklin Roosevelt gained great strength from both these sources by the fact that the Liberty League an organization dominated by the great business interests, was opposed to his re-election.

The big problem that is raised by the American method of nominating presidential candidates is whether it puts a premium, as Lord Bryce argued against the opportunity of first-rate men to receive consideration. I do no think his case is proved by making a list of first-rate men, Calhoun and Webster, for example, who missed nomination. The answer to that argument is, first, that many first-rate men have become president by reason of the system; and second, that the reasons which stopped others would have been powerful reasons against their elevation in any representative democracy. It is, I think, at least doubtful whether the elevation of a Roman Catholic to the premiership would be regarded favorably in Great Britain. A great business man, both in England and France, will operate mainly behind the political scene rather than in front of it; of our three business men who have become prime ministers one was, in fact, a rentier, and the others had long retired from active participation therein. Few people could easily explain the nuances that account for the failure of one man to reach the top, and the success of another. And in estimating the meaning of "availability" we must remember always that there is a real sense in which the more strong the candidate, supposing that he represents a special point of view, the more strong also are likely to be his enemies. Not infrequently an easy nomination—so long as the renomination of an existing president is not involved—merely means, as it meant with Horace Greeley in 1872, with Judge Parker in 1904, with Governor Landon in 1936, that rival candidates do not consider there is much prospect for their party's success, and they are not anxious to be associated with a dismal failure at the polls, with a view of a later nomination.

Granted, this is to say, the greatness of the prize and the necessity of popular election, it is difficult to see what other method than the nominating convention is available; more, it is true to say that, on balance, it has worked well rather than badly. The criticisms that are brought against it are rather, in their real substance, criticisms of the place of the presidency in the American constitutional scheme than of the method whereby the president is chosen. It is regrettable that an inexperienced man may come to reside in the White House; the answer is that few of those who have reached it have been inexperienced men. If it be said that men like Harding and Coolidge were unfit for the great post they secured, the answer is that the first had considerable experience both in the Ohio legislature and in the Senate, while the second had been a successful Massachusetts politician, twice occupying the governorship. If we take the presidents of the twentieth century, there is not one who had not been prepared for presidential office by a long experience of politics; and, with the possible exception of the Democratic candidate in 1904, that is true also of their defeated rivals. What is lacking in their training is mostly the art of handling Congress; and the rules of that art are only partly dependent upon the character of the president for the time.

It must be remembered that in making the choice there are two funda-mental considerations in the background of which the meaning of "avail-ability" must be set. The first is that the party choosing a candidate wants, if it can, to win; and second, it knows that if it does win, and its nominee becomes president, there is great likelihood of its having to adopt him a second time, since not to do so is to condemn an Administration for which it has to bear responsibility. While, therefore, it is quite true that a party convention provides an opportunity for the art of such a wire-puller as Mr. Daugherty, it is also true that the managers of a great party are anxious to avoid, if they can, the consequences of success in that type of manipu-lation. One has only to read the account of an experience of conventions like that of Senator Hoar of Massachusetts to see that a scrupulous and honorable man will approach the task of selection with all the seriousness that its consequences require.

All in all, I doubt whether the methods of the system are very different from those of other countries. They are perhaps more open and crude than in Great Britain. There is no generosity in the fight for power. There is a passionate determination on the part of organized interests to get the "safe" man who can be relied upon to live up to the commitments exacted from him. There is the fierce conflict of rival ambitions. There is the organization of every sort of cabal to win a victory for its man. Press and radio and platform are vigorously manipulated to this end. Immense prom-ises are made, pretty ugly deals are effected. Yet I suggest that anyone who knows the life of a political party from within Great Britain will not feel inclined to cast a stone at the American system. It fits well enough the medium in which it has to work. It achieves the results that the needs of the people require.

For there is at least one test of the system that is, I think, decisive. There have been five considerable crises in American history. There was the need to start the new republic adequately in 1789; it gave the American people its natural leader in George Washington. The crisis of 1800 brought Jefferson to the presidency; that of 1861 brought Abraham Lincoln. The War of 1914 found Woodrow Wilson in office; the great depression resulted in the election of Franklin Roosevelt. So far, it is clear, the hour has brought forth the man. It is of course true, as Bagehot said, that "success in a lottery is no argument for lotteries." I agree that no nation can afford a succession of what Theodore Roosevelt termed "Buchanan Presidents"— men whose handling of the issues is uncertain and feeble. But the answer is that the nation has never had that succession; an epoch of Hardings and Coolidges produces, by the scale of the problems to which it gives rise, its own regeneration. The weak president, as I have argued, comes from the fact that a strong predecessor has set the ship of state on an even keel. He is chosen because after a diet of strong occasions a nation, like an individual, turns naturally to the chance of a quiet time. "Normalcy" is always certain to be popular after crises.

The issue is whether, when crisis comes, the system can discover the man to handle it. On the evidence, this has so far been very remarkably the case. To urge that it is chance is, I think, a superficial view. It is the outcome of the national recognition that energy and direction are required, and the man chosen is the party response to that recognition. The more deeply we penetrate the working of the system the more clearly does it emerge that the result is inherent in its nature.

No. 42

[As soon as the candidates are nominated, the details of the compaign must be mapped out. This task not only involves decisions on broad issues but also careful attention to every last detail of the appeal for votes. The voters are familiar with but a part of the magnitude of this work. To many of them a campaign involves little more than the choice of the issues which are to be emphasized and the subsequent delivery of speeches and distribution of campaign literature in which these issues are discussed. In general the public has little information relating to the *minutiae* of an electoral campaign.

In the following selection Alfred E. Smith discusses these small but highly important details. As he points out, the failure of a candidate to visit a given state in his campaign tour may result in the loss of that state whereas an appearance in another area may be a complete waste of the time and energy of the candidate. If a presidential nominee fails to see a prominent local party leader, or if he has even a brief chat with the wrong leader, he may lose the whole-hearted support of a local organization and thus jeopardize his chances of carrying that locality and perhaps the state. It is indeed true in politics that "for the want of a nail" the campaign may be lost. Few persons in American public life are better qualified to write on this subject than Mr. Smith. As a state legislator, governor of New York, and presidential candidate he has had a long and intimate contact with every phase of local, state, and national politics and campaigning.]

BACKSTAGE IN A NATIONAL CAMPAIGN [1]

by Alfred E. Smith

FROM the instant of his nomination the candidate is plunged into a frenzy of time-wasting, harassing work, publicity operations, speech-preparing and other activities—all mingled with the brief opportunity given him to seriously plan and consider his campaign. Naturally, every voter in the country is interested to the extent that they want the newspapers, radio, and moving pictures to describe to them every minute of the daily habits of the candidate and his family. As a result the candidate is immediately surrounded by an army of newspaper reporters. Two daily press conferences must be planned and held, one for the morning and one for the evening representatives. Time must be devoted to picture-taking, meeting delegates, hand-shaking, talking for the talking pictures, making radio speeches, and signing autographs for well-meaning but bothersome voters. Questions of all kinds from the press and the public, covering every conceivable subject interesting to various localities but about which the candidate may actually know little or nothing, must be received, answered, or parried by members of a staff who know that it is important that no local leader or voter be offended or get the impression that the candidate is not giving his personal attention to that section of the country. Thousands of letters pile up daily. Every one must be answered and it takes a vast organization of skilled workers to sort, read, digest the contents of, and answer a presidential candidate's correspondence, particularly since it is through this correspondence that he must learn to a great extent the individual opinions and wishes of the voters whose favor he is seeking.

There is no real rest for a candidate. If he desires a few days off for himself and goes to some country spot which he had previously found lonesome and restful, he will find camera men, movie men, newspaper reporters, and the radio broadcasters his constant companions. There is no use trying to avoid it or to rebuff these representatives. They are doing their job and are under the orders of their editors or other bosses, who in turn are simply carrying out the desires of their millions of readers to know every detail of a candidate's life while he is before the public in a pre-election campaign.

But during this period the swirl of activity that immediately surrounds the candidate himself is only part of a large organization that is being arranged and set up in the various sections of the country to carry on the

[1] Alfred E. Smith, *The Citizen and his Government* (New York: Harper and Brothers, 1935), pp. 119-139. Reprinted by permission of the publisher.

vote-getting campaign. Each local political committee has definitely fixed its mind upon the fact that its particular community will respond vigorously on election day to the plea of the candidate.

To organize these committees through a central office, supply them with money, campaign literature, and enthusiasm, is a tremendous job which must be handled by a central organization which in recent years has almost always been set up in New York or Washington. A vast labyrinth of campaign departments must be set up to cater to the wishes and needs of every conceivable class or race of voters. There must be departments to deal with various races of people, departments to handle fraternal organizations, to handle war veterans, the farmers, the labor-union members, the first voters, the colleges, and many others.

Each of these activities must be placed in the hands of some one skilled and familiar with the work, and the whole thing headed by responsible executives who will represent the candidate and who can be trusted not to place him in any embarrassing situation.

It is a job in itself for the people at campaign headquarters just to see and handle the thousands of people who wander in for one reason or another, and in doing this to avoid offending anyone, thus saving the important executives from the necessity of wasting their time seeing the various types who seem drawn to a campaign headquarters as flies are to sugar.

There is a widespread impression that political parties have practically unlimited funds to spend on campaign activities, and although nothing could be more erroneous, especially in recent years when money-raising has been one of the most difficult parts of a political campaign, there are still thousands of people who think that all they have to do is go to campaign headquarters, convince some one that they can get votes, and be handed a check.

All the world's "unemployables" are among the thousands who come around looking for some sort of hand-out. People who never seem to exist at all except during campaign time reappear. They fill the reception-rooms and take up endless time of the personnel managers, volunteer assistants, chairmen of committees, and bureau heads. They claim to know how to do everything from typing to publicity and public speaking. They offer to sell valuable secrets which will demolish the opposition, or to make an investigation of the opposing candidate that will bring out such damaging facts about his character and record as to make further campaigning unnecessary.

There are always hundreds who offer to deliver vast blocks of votes, practically without further effort, if they are paid a suitable sum which may range anywhere from ten to ten thousand dollars. This sort of thing is not peculiar to any one party. They appear in every campaign headquarters.

For a person interested in personalities or humanity in general a few hours spent in a national campaign headquarters is a lesson in the handling of human beings. Here are the dignified, courtly gentlemen with their big black "senatorial" hats and heavy Southern accents, wearing thick gold watchchains, laden with fraternal emblems, each one announcing his ability to deliver the vote of an entire Southern state, if not the whole of the South and Southwest. Sometimes these gentlemen are so impressive that campaign managers hesitate to offer them compensation, but these fears are usually dispelled by a request for a little recompense for the effort and expense involved.

Then there are the Western people, attired in a sort of citified cowboy fashion and guaranteeing to deliver their cattle-raising sections of the country. The agricultural experts are likewise on hand, as well as the inevitable labor-union official who is willing to accept a well-paid position to organize the labor vote.

Most of these people have nothing genuine to deliver. The most one can say for them is that they imagine they have, but I do not hesitate to state that there are many conscious fakers among them. Nevertheless, they come to campaign headquarters with every kind of claim and sometimes succeed in getting themselves on the payroll. If they are successful in this, they often look upon a campaign job simply as an opportunity to loaf. Few expect to work hard and they all expect salaries that will enable them to live for a few months in the sunshine of campaign prosperity, after which they can retire somewhere for another four years, perhaps being able to make a few dollars in local campaigns between times.

As a way to waste money, nothing exceeds the employment of this type of people. Even the important political leaders, the members of the National Committees, local or state officials, and others who come to campaign headquarters or are in touch with the guiding minds of the campaign are troublesome to deal with, consuming a great deal of time uselessly, and must be taken with a grain or two of salt.

Every political leader has the notion that he will be unable to carry his locality alone. Notwithstanding that their candidate may speak nightly on the radio, supply them with vast quantities of literature or even money they insist that real results can be accomplished only if the people of the locality can see the candidate, have him smile at them, ride through their city and wave his hand in friendly greeting while engaging in personal conversation with the local leaders. This brings to the presidential candidate the same problem faced by a candidate for Governor who finds that there are just not enough days in the campaign period for him to be transported to every locality where he is informed that his presence is indispensable and it will be realized that when this is applied to the nation as a whole the problem is an impossible one.

The question of what states and cities the presidential candidate should really visit, and what subject he should discuss when he arrives there, is one of the most troublesome and trying parts of the campaign, both for the candidate himself and for his managers. It takes people with real political acumen and a genuine knowledge of the needs and interest of the voters in various parts of the country to decide on these points. But some one must spend a lot of time listening to the claims and arguments of all these local leaders. In the end there must be a considerable amount of heartlessness in making these decisions. Old friends and stanch supporters must be firmly and definitely turned down, and the candidate's itinerary carefully planned so as to enable him, with a minimum of time and effort expended, to cover the really necessary ground and to show himself and talk in the places where the real campaign-planners feel that there will be a genuine chance of changing votes.

Of course, the radio has made this situation a little easier. If a candidate cannot appear in a particular town he can at least arrange through the speakers' bureau and the radio department for a near-by broadcasting station to be hooked on to the network carrying his speeches, so that this locality may hear his voice.

But even this is not a complete solution. There are still some places at which a candidate must actually show himself, where perhaps there may be such doubt as to his personality or his convictions that he and his advisers may honestly feel that the only way to gain votes and change sentiment in his favor is to circulate in person, shake hands with the proper people, and show himself in a large hall to as many of the citizens as possible.

But when the campaign is all over and the candidate sits back in his easy chair and looks back over his experiences, he will usually find that ninety per cent of the political committees who urged him to appear in their towns or states, and whose requests were granted, were really more eager for local glory and the benefit they might gain for their individual organizations, than they were for the ultimate success of the party in the entire nation. I cannot say that this is done deliberately, but nevertheless it is often the case.

It is practically impossible, during the heat of the actual national campaign, for a candidate to find time enough really to think out the speeches he is about to make. Particularly is this true of a candidate who cannot or does not wish to rely upon some other person who is willing to spend his time preparing the material for his speeches, but who desires to take a personal and individual responsibility for everything that he says. When you get right down to it, a candidate on tour does not have a single moment to think out the things that represent his own thoughts unless he is prepared to satisfy himself and try to keep going with only a couple of hours' sleep every night.

An amusing anecdote illustrating this is told of Bryan's first campaign for President. A newspaper man asked former Governor Hill of New York what he thought about Bryan. Mr. Hill said, "Well, I guess he is all right." When the newspaper man replied, "Why, he makes sixteen speeches a day," Mr. Hill inquired, pointedly, "Yes. But when does he think?"

The trouble with campaign trips, while they accomplish something worth while in the way of exhibiting the candidate to the people, is that the trip is more of a general reception than a business proposition aimed at intelligently discussing the issues of the campaign before the people. Countless thousands of people who have no real interest or reason for meeting the candidate are anxious to shake his hand and gain the glory of a personal introduction.

About the most trying and tiring part of the whole 1928 campaign trip was the necessity of spending most of every day shaking hands with people whose only desire was to meet the candidate and who could not by any stretch of the imagination be supposed to be capable of materially helping the cause of my election. Nevertheless, it is impossible to offend any one of the thousands of local leaders, politicians, and just plain friends and admirers who make these requests, even if their fulfillment means occupying almost all of the candidate's time. Well-meaning railroad men conspired to help aggravate this situation. Even if the local political committees had not arranged receptions, the train could be sure of a waiting crowd at every water-tank or other stop along the line because the railroad men wired ahead word of the campaign train's arrival.

Of course, every village, town, and hamlet wants a speech from the traveling candidate, and none of them takes into consideration the fact that the candidate may have nothing left to say after days or even weeks of active campaigning, and that he must save the discussion of important matters for the nightly radio speeches broadcast to the entire country.

All in all, I found it next to impossible to get enough sleep or even to keep up with the necessary campaign work of my 1928 trip through the country.

But, nevertheless, the tour goes on. The better organized a candidate makes his personal staff, the easier things will be for him. Good publicity men, secretaries, research assistants, and others can assume a considerable part of the vast burden of campaign work, but no one can take over the job of personal meetings and greetings, hand-shakes, autographs, impromptu speeches and receptions to local political people who will be gravely offended if they have no opportunity to meet the candidate personally.

Another job the candidate has to assume for himself is meeting the press in daily conferences. The candidate must depend upon the press to be helpful to him in carrying his utterances widespread to the people, and he must hope for the press to be friendly enough to support him editorially, as well as to carry his speeches and activities in the news columns. That is necessary, but it takes a great deal of the candidate's time and energy to attend one, or usually two, daily press conferences, answer or parry the questions of anywhere from ten to one hundred eager and intelligent reporters, among whom there are sure to be many who represent hostile newspapers. In addition to these conferences there is the continual necessity of meeting feature writers, artists, photographers, and pen sketchers, who have been assigned by their editors to use their artistic talents in writing about the more personal life of the candidate and his family, or to picture him in the various activities of a campaign.

The campaigner for the Presidency had better be ready to accept with good grace every conceivable type and kind of gift. The well-meaning Democrats of the United States loaded the baggage-cars of my 1928 campaign train with every sort of present from pipes, tobacco, clothing, and underwear, to animals, such as large dogs and even a live donkey meant to represent the Democratic emblem.

Of course, one genuinely useful function of the campaign tour is the opportunity it gives a candidate to hear and sense at first hand the sentiment of the parts of the country through which he passes and the feeling of the voters toward his candidacy. One of the most difficult, and at the same time useful, political attributes is a genuine sense of perspective in such matters. It is extremely hard for a candidate to look with proper abstraction upon the noisy, cheering, and vast signs of approbation he may see around him every time his train stops, and yet to penetrate through the noise and the flattery and cheering and music and see dispassionately what impression he is really making on the voters and how the country feels toward him. It must be remembered that the crowd that usually turns out to see a candidate upon his arrival in town, or to listen to and cheer his speech, is usually largely composed of people who intended to vote for him anyhow, whose very attendance was prompted or encouraged by the local organization of his party, and who would scarcely be expected to do anything but show the highest approval of the candidate's every word, no matter what the sentiment of the voters as a whole or of the majority of them may be in that town or state.

It is worth remembering that in the 1928 campaign, when my tour through the South and West attracted the largest and most enthusiastic crowds that had ever greeted a Democratic candidate in those parts of the country, I nevertheless learned a different story when the votes were counted on election day. It takes a trained and experienced political sense to know what really lies behind the cheers of the crowd.

None the less, a candidate who has the ability to sense what is really going on and see back of the noisy receptions will gain much by his tour, for he will learn from day to day and week to week what issues can really swing votes in any given part of the country, and can thus decide what he really means to do or say about such issues.

Of course, if the local leaders would be willing to meet some intelligent member of the candidate's staff and explain their needs and desires to him and enable the staff member to digest and pass on the information in more readily usable form to the candidate, a great saving in time and effort would be effected on the part of the candidate himself. But the wise men and party wiseacres are not thus easily satisfied; each of them has an entirely different system for the candidate to follow if he is to finally enter the White House, and each of them has an insatiable desire to tell his story in person, shake the candidate's hand, and receive his personal thanks for the information, whether or not it is useful.

Therefore, even when he stops for a day or two to visit some locality and address a meeting, the candidate finds little rest and no solitude. If he dines in a public dining-room, the back-slapping and handshaking will not only prevent the consumption of any food, but will undoubtedly delay the candidate to such an extent that he will be late for the public meeting. If he attempts to dine in his own room, he is equally unlikely to get any dinner because of poor service in the unusually jammed hotel, and the persistent attentions of callers anxious to see him for one reason or another.

After the meeting there is still little rest for the harassed candidate. More and more people of the locality insist on a personal hand-shake and an opportunity to express approval of the speech or to make suggestions for the next one. But out of it all the keen-minded candidate can gain political information of vast value to the conduct of his campaign; information which must, however, be combined with the news which reaches him from the nerve center at national headquarters, where the personal communications, letters, and visits from political leaders and plain voters in every part of the country are continually being digested and prepared by a competent staff into information easily translated into oratory or statements calculated to win votes.

But the activities immediately surrounding the candidate are only a small part of the whole campaign organization. At national headquarters hundreds, even thousands, of people are laboring to gather in a harvest of votes in various specialized fields. The publicity bureau must grind out a continual grist of statements, not only by the candidate, but by the party chairman, local leaders, members of Congress, and every person prominent in the public eye whose support is worthy of publicity.

Scores of specialized bureaus which I have mentioned previously must continue their specialized appeals to special racial, fraternal, or other groups of voters. The speakers' bureau must function in a business-like and efficient manner to supply the necessary personal oratory or material for speeches to every locality that feels it needs that sort of support.

The life blood of political campaigning is money. One cannot conceive the vast number of demands made upon the party treasurer during national campaigns. Every party worker and every voter from one end of the country to the other feels that the party treasury is fair game. Letters, telephone calls, and personal requests for places on the payroll or just plain hand-outs of money pour into the national headquarters by the thousands. Naturally these tremendous demands for funds place upon the party treasurer and his organization one of the most important duties of the entire campaign organization.

Of course, one of the most difficult parts of a money-raising campaign in recent years has been the necessity for a swift, almost instantaneous, organization of all the vast facilities necessary for money-raising on a national scale, and the necessity for creating such an organization practically out of a clear sky within a very few weeks. This was the case right up to the 1932 campaign. Previous to that date it was customary for the party committees to lapse into almost complete inactivity for the period between the presidential election and the date on which it was necessary to make plans for the next presidential nominating convention.

But between 1928 and 1932 all this was changed. Mainly due to the activity of John J. Raskob, as party chairman, and his willingness to supply funds for the cause and to help raise them from other sources, the Democratic party entered on a program of real minority activity, even though the Republicans were in power. An aggressive, efficiently organized office was opened in Washington under the able direction of Jouett Shouse, and the policies and activities of the Republican administration and Republican Congress systematically exposed for the inspection of the people of the country. Naturally, such activity on behalf of one of the great parties caused the opposition to enter into an equally aggressive program—a change in political tradition that I feel has meant a great deal for the betterment of our party system.

But to return to the question of money-raising. The first decision to be made by the campaign managers is how much money will be needed and where it is to come from. Where no plans have been made in advance, the situation is just that much more difficult, but where the National Committee has been in active operation for years ahead of the presidential campaign, it is not too difficult a job to organize an appeal to the public for funds. Practically every form of money-raising activity has been tried at one time or another by the various parties. Newspaper advertising on a national scale in 1928 did not bring enough return to pay for the advertising expenditure; but on the other hand, appeals over the radio for financial support brought immediate and startling results. On one occasion $5,000 expended for radio time brought in contributions of $85,000, and in the whole 1928 campaign over $1,500,000 was raised by radio appeals directly from the party leaders to the people.

Personal solicitation, letter-writing by men prominent in party circles or in industry, women's committees, hundreds of other forms of activity, are used to raise money. The cost of the national campaign in 1928 was approximately $6,000,000 for the Democratic party, and $8,000,000 for the Republican party. But in 1932 the stress of economic conditions brought the capacity for money-raising, and necessarily the capacity for spending, down to $1,638,177.58 and $1,916,640.93, respectively.

Of course, the business management of a campaign must be vitally concerned with the expenditure of this money. What is it used for and why? Campaign managers must become hard boiled and dispassionate in their considerations of the thousands of proposals that are made for the expenditure of campaign money. There is no sum on earth that could be raised during campaign time sufficient to cover the expense of every one of the proposals that reaches a national headquarters.

But there are certain necessary and definite things that must be done. The candidate's tour costs a lot of money, the purchase of radio time a great deal more. (In the 1928 campaign $600,000 was paid to the radio companies.) The printing of literature, posters, campaign manuals, and other such material is another large item; the rental of vast office space, furniture, and salaries of clerical help another big item of expense.

The vice-presidential candidate must be helped in his campaign. The expenses of his tour about the country are met by the National Committee, even though his activities may attain only a small place in the national party picture. High-priced services of experts in publicity, research, economics, and other lines must be retained to insure the accuracy of the party's utterances and claims.

According to party tradition, divisional headquarters must be opened in three or four sections of the country, each duplicating in its small way the larger activities of the national headquarters and each spending a considerable sum which must be supplied from the central party pocketbook. If I had my way future campaigns would eliminate these divisional headquarters, as well as a great many of the expenses connected with them, particularly those in the way of supplying them with vast quantities of literature, buttons, and other campaign paraphernalia which cannot in the long run really make votes, but only serve to add to a general atmosphere of ballyhoo, and which in some cases are not even distributed by lazy or uninterested local leaders.

Most important of all, and perhaps the only really vital expense of all the campaign, is the sending into the various states of money to be expended during the last few days of the campaign at the discretion of the leaders, to get out the vote and see that it is recorded in the right way. Under this heading also come efforts in various cities in which the party must contend with a corrupt opposing machine and where it is necessary to hire a large number of watchers in order to insure the honesty of the vote and its counting.

The man who rules the party treasury must be equipped with an iron hand and a clear head if he is not to be fooled by the cupidity of local leaders who flock to the national headquarters and insist that the lack of additional funds stands between them and the loss of their locality to the party. Only a well-grounded political experience and ability to resist oratory and all sort of cajolery will prevent the party treasurer from being almost literally robbed of hundreds of thousands of dollars by leaders who claim, almost with tears in their eyes, that for the lack of anywhere from a thousand to one hundred thousand dollars, as the case may be, the candidate and his party may lose out in their home town or state.

The treasurer must know where to draw the line. Each state is entitled to something, some more than others, and the sum cannot be determined only by the size and population of the area affected, but by its past political complexion and the treasurer's personal knowledge of the party's vote-getting possibilities, as well.

It is inevitable that some of the funds will be wasted, for, unfortunately, the chief interest of some local leaders is simply to line their own pockets at the expense of the national campaign; but most of them are loyal and honest and use the campaign funds to the best possible account to bring out the votes.

Adding all these items up, one quickly reaches the vast total of money collected for national campaigns, and in most years even more. This deficit must be met by money raised on the part of the National Committee from banks or individuals willing to advance some money. Of course, it is traditional that the winning party has little difficulty in wiping out this deficit. Collections are comparatively easily made from those among the wealthy and well-to-do who always want to be on the band wagon of the winner, no matter what. The losing party must often go through a painful period of years gradually collecting a few dollars here and a few dollars there before the deficit is cut down to such a point that the party will not be hampered in its activities during the next election.

No. 43

[IN the preceding article Mr. Smith raised some questions concerning the raising and spending of party campaign funds. Such problems have long been before the American people, and have frequently been the subject of legislative action. Generally this legislation has dealt with such matters as the amount of money that may be spent in any given campaign, the sources of campaign contributions, and the legal and illegal objects of expenditure.

The problem of party finance however has a much deeper significance than legislation of this kind indicates; it has a vital relationship to democratic government. In such a government we assume that all parties may place their policies and candidates before the voter and thus may have an equal opportunity to claim his attention and support. The huge costs of campaigning, however, deny to all but a few parties this equality of opportunity. A campaign is, of necessity, a costly enterprise. In an American presidential election over sixty million potential voters must be reached by the radio, the press, and the motion picture. These channels of publicity are expensive and, whatever the issues of an election may be, it is clear that only the two major parties can raise the necessary millions of dollars. This means that third parties, regardless of the merits of their policies or the abilities of their candidates, can never compete on a basis of equality with their richer rivals. Furthermore, the existence of huge war chests may lead to reckless and questionable expenditures, and thus may affect not only the outcome of an election but also the whole operation of the democratic process.

In the following essay, Professor Charles A. Beard discusses the significance of the whole problem of campaign finance and outlines the federal legislation in this field. Since this article was written, new federal legislation has been passed which places a limit upon the sum which may be expended in a presidential election and limits the size of campaign contributions. The problems of enforcement that are noted in this essay, however, remain much the same as they were when Professor Beard wrote "Money in Federal Politics."]

MONEY IN FEDERAL POLITICS [1]

by Charles A. Beard

PERIODICALLY the country is shocked by investigations revealing the expenditures of huge sums of money by candidates for Congress; these shocks have been intermittent since the close of the Civil War. A great deal of heat has been generated, escaping usually in talk, and Congress has skirted around the edges of the subject in several statutes. Generally speaking, "nothing has been done about it"; yet there are signs of change. Not long ago the Senate in the Vare case added a new qualification for membership in that body: a citizen presenting his election credentials to the Senate must show that he has not spent too much money in an irregular fashion in winning his seat. A short time before this significant incident, Senator Bronson Cutting forcibly raised the whole question of political expenditures in a searching speech in the Senate and introduced a program of legislation designed to cope with some of the worst evils in the present practices. Judging by his pertinacity, we may assume that Mr. Cutting will not let the matter rest and that Congress, in its next session, will have to face the issue of money in federal politics.

Under the prevailing system of popular elections, thousands and even millions of voters must be reached through various agencies, such as the press, meetings, the post, telegraph, radio and party workers. Huge expenditures are necessary even for legitimate purposes, to say nothing of bribery direct and indirect. To win party nominations for offices in large jurisdictions, individual aspirants and their supporters must ordinarily make considerable outlays of money, and to win elections, party organizations and candidates must do likewise, if they have any formidable competitors. Here the American theory of democratic equality absolutely breaks down in fact. Although it is not true that the longest purse always wins, it is certainly true that without a purse of some kind to aid him, no citizen can expect to win the office of President or a seat in Congress.

Ordinarily money for such expenditures comes from four prime sources —disinterested persons of wealth, office holders, office seekers and citizens with economic undertakings which may be benefited by action or inaction on the part of the government. Attempts to raise large sums through petty contributions by the masses are not usually crowned with success. Inevitably this brings about a concentration of immense power in the hands

[1] Charles A. Beard, "Money in Federal Politics," *The New Republic* (July 30, 1930), Vol. 63, pp. 305-307. Reprinted by permission of *The New Republic*.

of a relatively small number of people. And recent investigations, not to say scandals, have revealed a widespread use of money by individuals and groups in primaries and elections—money derived from sources economically interested and sometimes expended in a fraudulent manner. In 1928 and 1929, two men were excluded from the United States Senate on the ground that their campaign expenditures were highly irregular, if not tainted with corruption. In recognition of such facts, the most advanced states have enacted elaborate campaign-practices laws and Congress has tardily but gingerly dealt with the subject.

Federal legislation in this field is of four types:

First of all, Congress has imposed certain limits on the collecting and giving of money in connection with elections. According to the terms of a law originally passed in 1883, no Senator, Representative or federal officer may solicit or receive any contribution, subscription or assessment from any officer, clerk or other employee drawing a salary from the federal treasury. Thus, an effort was made to dry up one of the prime sources of political funds. Cut off from this assistance, political leaders came to rely more and more on the contributions of great financial and industrial corporations. To counter this movement, Congress has made it unlawful for any national bank or any corporation whatever to make any money contribution in connection with elections at which presidential and vice-presidential electors, Senators or Representatives are chosen; furthermore, candidates, political committees and all other persons are forbidden to receive any contributions from these sources.

While attempting to combat the collection of political funds from three interested groups in society—office holders, national banks and business corporations—Congress has placed limits on the amount which candidates for Congress may spend in elections. In no case can they exceed the sum set by state legislation in this relation. In the absence of a state law fixing a smaller figure, a candidate for the Senate may spend $10,000 and a candidate for the House of Representatives, $2,500. However, if the size of the constituency permits it, this amount may be increased to a figure obtained by multiplying by three cents the total number of votes cast at the last general election for all candidates for the position in question—that is, for Senator, or Representative. Even then, no matter how large the vote, no candidate for the Senate may spend more than $25,000 and no candidate for the House more than $5,000.

But highly significant exceptions must be recorded. In summing up all his expenditures under the federal limit, a candidate may omit outlays for his necessary personal, traveling and subsistence expenses. He may likewise leave out of the reckoning money spent for stationery and postage, for distributing circulars and for telephone and telegraph service. Also excepted from the accounting are all assessments, fees and charges levied on him under the laws of the state in which he resides.

Meager as are the provisions of federal law on political contributions and candidates' expenditures, they are still more meager with respect to the purpose of outlays—the uses which may be made of money and other objects of value in elections. It is unlawful for any candidate for Congress to offer directly or indirectly any public or private employment in exchange for support, or to promise his influence to secure such employment on this condition. It is likewise unlawful to offer to make, or to cause to be made, any expenditures to any person with a view to inducing him to vote for or against any candidate or to withhold his vote. The acceptance as well as the offering of money for these purposes is also prohibited. In some measure, no doubt, the comparatively slight federal limitations on the uses of money are due to the fullness of state laws dealing with bribery and other corrupt practices in elections.

A further restraint on the collection and use of money is supposed to be afforded by a federal law providing for the publicity of campaign funds. Every candidate for Senator or Representative must file with the secretary of the Senate or the clerk of the House, as the case may be, both before and after election, a statement showing in detail contributions received in support of his candidacy and itemized expenditures made by him or by any person with his knowledge and consent. And, curiously enough, he must add a statement of pledges or promises made by himself, or with his consent, relative to offering public or private employment in exchange for support.

Besides requiring candidates for Congress to file reports of their outlays, the law prescribes publicity for political committees. Within the scope of the law is every committee, association and organization which accepts contributions or makes expenditures for the purpose of influencing or attempting to influence the election of candidates or presidential or vice-presidential electors in two or more states. The law does not stop here. It also applies to every other committee, association or organization engaged in influencing elections, whether it operates in more than one state or not, if it is a branch of a subsidiary of a national committee, association or organization—excluding duly organized state and local committees of political parties. All political committees covered by this legislation must file periodically fully itemized statements containing receipts and expenditures. The list of outlays must show in great detail the purposes as well as the dates and amounts of the expenditures.

After the federal legislation respecting the use of money in elections was consolidated and amended in 1925, some of the most extraordinary scandals in the long history of campaign funds occurred. Coupled with independent criticism from the outside, the discussion of these scandals in Congress has raised anew the question of providing a complete national code regulating and restricting the use of money in politics. In this relation numerous deficiencies of the existing laws have been pointed out and remedial bills proposed.

Perhaps the greatest gap in federal legislation is the total exclusion of primaries from the scope of control. The publicity act of 1911 covered both primaries and elections, but the Supreme Court in the Newberry case in 1921 held that the power of Congress to regulate the manner of holding elections did not extend to senatorial conventions and primaries. Subsequently Congress, in consolidating the corrupt-practices acts, expressly provided that the term "election" does not include a primary election or convention of a political party. Yet it is doubtful whether this exception is required by the Constitution. In the Newberry case mentioned above, only four of the nine judges of the Supreme Court agreed that Congress had no power over primaries. Another judge joined them in holding invalid a part of the law enacted previous to the adoption of popular election of Senators, but reserved judgment as to whether the authority of Congress in this respect had not been increased by the subsequent change in the Constitution. Thus, in fact, the power of Congress over primaries and political conventions is clouded with uncertainty.

And yet in a large number of cases it is the primary, not the election, that counts in the choice of Senators and Representatives. Wherever one political party continuously dominates a state, as, for example, the Democrats in Alabama or the Republicans in Pennsylvania, the real fight is over the nomination; the election is secure. It has been estimated that in a majority of the congressional districts the chief contest is the primary. It was in the primaries in Pennsylvania and Illinois that a part of the enormous expenditure was incurred which led to the exclusion of two men from the Senate on grounds of corruption or misuse of money. To clear the way for federal control over primaries, an amendment to the Constitution has been proposed, vesting in Congress supervision over nominations as well as elections.

A second criticism of the present corrupt-practices legislation bears upon the clause which exempts from the limits fixed on expenditures money spent by candidates for stationery, postage, printing, personal uses and publicity in general (except for newspapers and billboards). Under this rule a candidate may spend as much as he pleases for effective campaigning—letters, telegrams and circulars, for instance. Thus, outlays for most of the purposes which may be called "legitimate" are in fact not at all restricted in amount, and the man or woman with a long purse is given a decided advantage.

Besides leaving the candidate absolutely free to spend as much as he likes for such publicity purposes, the law allows his friends and supporters to spend all they please on his behalf without accounting for it. It is in this connection that some of the worst abuses have arisen. Frequently it is not the candidate but some powerful economic interest behind him that makes huge outlays in primaries and elections. As long as the candidate is not held personally responsible for all expenditures in support of his candidacy in primaries and elections, and the amount not strictly limited, wealth has a decided advantage in every contest.

Through another hole in the corrupt-practices law money may creep. Political committees may have large deficits in their funds at the end of the campaign and raise the money to meet these deficits long after the period for making public their accounts of the election has expired. As Senator Cutting once remarked: "A contribution made to a preëlection fund would have been in the nature of a gamble, but a contribution made to a deficit, and particularly to a deficit of the party which had been successful in the election, was simply putting . . . money over the counter and getting a return for his investment. That is a danger which is not dealt with under our present statutes at all." This practice was illustrated in connection with the campaign of 1920, when a big deficit in the Republican fund was covered by Mr. Harry Sinclair, who was later charged with fraudulently obtaining oil leases from the politicians who benefited from his campaign contributions. Mr. Sinclair stated at the time that he did not know whether he was a Republican or a Democrat, but at all events he staked his money on the winning horse.

In addition to its structural defects, the corrupt-practices law is weak on the side of enforcement. The provisions for publicity are not effective. Statements of campaign receipts and expenditures are carelessly filed in irregular form, they are not published, and after a period of two years they may be destroyed. Most of them merely accumulate dust. Eager newspaper reporters may dig out certain figures that will make news or a sensation, but as a rule candidates and committees can be fairly sure that little will be heard or known of their "public" statements. While the national committees of the great political parties report in detail, other political committees and many candidates for Congress are, to say the least, extremely careless in making their returns. It is doubtful whether the news of their publicity statements often reaches their respective districts. In this relation the law has no teeth.

Furthermore, no agency is responsible for enforcing its terms. A defeated candidate may attack his opponent in the federal courts for some infraction, but there is no permanent machinery to investigate charges of irregularity. Committees on elections in both houses of Congress and special committees for inquiring into campaign expenditures do go into specific cases as they arise, or make hurried searches when scandal breaks out, but they are almost always partisan in character and concerned primarily with immediate issues. It is not the business of any non-political federal officer or agency to maintain constant scrutiny over the operations of the election laws.

From these criticisms it follows that any thoroughgoing revision of the corrupt-practices acts should include primaries and conventions as well as elections within the scope of the law. It should fix limits to all expenditures, define the purposes for which they may be made, place full responsibility for expenditures on candidates and committees and abolish exemptions in accounting for campaign outlays. If publicity is to be more than a farce, then provisions must be made for giving effect to it in a form that will reach the voters. Deficits present a knotty problem, but committees that incur them can be made accountable and conditions may be prescribed for meeting unpaid bills. With reference to the issue of enforcement, Senator Cutting has proposed the creation of an election commission to audit reports, investigate credentials, deal with contested cases, serve as a factfinding body, and report results of its inquiries to Congress for final determination.

If the defects in the present laws are cured by new legislation, the problem of money in politics will not be entirely solved. Indeed, there are Senators who hold that it cannot be solved until the use of private money in primaries and elections is forbidden entirely. But this involves heroic action. Especially does it throw upon the federal government the burden of providing machinery by which all aspirants and candidates may present their claims to constituents on an even plane at public expense. It will take more thought than has yet been expended on the subject to evolve a scheme that will place the long head on a parity with the long purse. Perhaps it can and may be done. But no matter what restraints the law may put on the use of money in politics, it cannot by that process separate politics and economics.

Chapter XIII

THE JOB OF THE LEGISLATOR

No. 44

[EVERY individual and every association of individuals are constantly faced with the problem of making decisions about matters they feel to be important. The individual must ultimately make these decisions himself and most associations can make them at a meeting of their entire membership. But there are a great many associations, of which the state is one, that have so many members and extend over such a wide territory that it is impossible for the members to meet together. Under such circumstances it becomes necessary to establish some kind of a representative body to act for the association as a whole. In the state this body is known as the legislature.

We have already seen that where the state is democratic in character, its legislature or legislatures are elected by the great body of adult citizens and are held responsible to them. This immediately raises important questions. From what kind of groups are representatives to be chosen? How are they to be chosen? What is their function, once they are chosen? Should they be organized into one or two bodies? These and many other questions must be answered.

Professor Beard, in the following selection, points out some very significant things about the popular attitude towards, the basis of representation in, and the kinds of influence playing upon the modern legislature. The problems raised by this article are the kind to which everyone who is seeking to improve the democratic way of life must give attention.]

WHOM DOES CONGRESS REPRESENT? [1]

by Charles A. Beard

FOR more than a year newspaper headlines have been snapping with electric alarms over lobbies in Washington. The most moral nation on earth is in confusion respecting its morals. Senator Bingham places the Secretary to the President of the Connecticut Manufacturers' Association on the pay roll of the Senate and introduces him, as an "expert" on tariff schedules, into the sanctuary of the Republican finance committee in charge of the tariff bill. In this action the Senator sees no impropriety. "Nothing was done," he says, "contrary to good morals or senatorial ethics." Senator Bingham is a scholar and a gentleman. He is the son of a clergyman; he was brought up in a moral atmosphere, educated at Yale and Harvard where morals are strong, and seasoned in the moral climate of New Haven. If he is not a good one hundred per cent American, then the species is extinct. Those who know him best bear witness to the rectitude of his intentions in public and private life. At most they would be merely willing to admit, with one of his Connecticut constituents, that "the Senator has been a leetle bit careless."

And yet the Senate of the United States, after full debate and by a considerable majority, censures Senator Bingham, declaring that his action is contrary to good morals and senatorial ethics, and tends to damage the honor and reputation of that august body. Great as is the authority behind it, this resolution does not dispose of the issue. When does the innocent and accurate representation of economic interest in the Senate become immoral? As Wendell Phillips once remarked, a majority settles nothing; one man on God's side may be right and prevail. Hence the incident merely illustrates the confusion that exists in the mind of the most moral of all nations.

Now Senator Norris, who led in censuring Senator Bingham, is undoubtedly a gentleman also and a hundred per cent American—from an agricultural state. He was born in Ohio, educated in American institutions of learning, and early imbued with the doctrines of Abraham Lincoln. He is one of the most useful members of the Senate, acknowledged by foes as well as friends to be beyond reproach in public and private life. Over the long years of his service hovers not a single cloud of suspicion. The fierce

[1] Charles A. Beard, "Whom Does Congress Represent?" *Harper's Magazine* (January, 1930), Vol. 160, pp. 144-152. Reprinted by permission of the author and *Harper's Magazine*.

glare of scrutiny to which powerful opponents have subjected his character has revealed no flaws in it. He was not educated at Yale and has never written any books, but the authenticity of his Americanism cannot be questioned. This is the good citizen who finds that other good citizen, Mr. Bingham, guilty of conduct contrary to morals and senatorial ethics, and sets the whole country at work talking about its conscience.

The moral chance medley thus created was further addled by the frank declarations of Mr. J. R. Grundy, President of the Pennsylvania Manufacturers' Association, before the Senate subcommittee investigating lobbies. Manufacturers, he said, had raised a large sum of money to help elect Mr. Coolidge and a larger sum to help elect Mr. Hoover; the Republican party pledged itself to high protection; the people approved that party; and manufacturers were entitled to the benefits contemplated when they made their contributions of cash.

If necessary to gain his ends, Mr. Grundy would lay his hands upon the sacred muniment handed down by the Fathers—the Constitution of the United States. He openly said that it was a misfortune that the Fathers had given each state two Senators. He insisted that the states in which industries have been largely developed and the tariff is best understood should control in the making of tariff schedules. "The backward states," as he called them—Arkansas, Georgia, Mississippi, North Dakota, South Dakota, Montana, and Idaho—"shouldn't be allowed to throw the monkey wrench into the machinery twenty-four hours a day." He remarked that if "the volume of voice" of these states in the Senate were reduced to the proportion of their tax contributions to the support of the Government, some of them would have to use an amplifier to be heard at all. Mr. Grundy saw no "impropriety" in Mr. Bingham's action which the Senate censured. In short, he was businesslike. And many good people, especially Democratic editors, were shocked to hear that the manufacturers wanted political power graded somewhat according to the size of their economic stake in the country. To philosopers of this direction, Mr. Grundy seemed positively immoral.

Why this confusion in morals, this opposition of good men, tried and true? What is the Congress of the United States anyway? Whom and what does it represent? What principles or forces should control the action of the statesmen who compose it?

These questions cannot be answered by mere reference to yesterday's tabloid newspaper, nor to Senator Sugarbeet's last Fourth of July oration, nor to Senator Pigiron's eulogium at the tomb of his colleague, Senator Citrusfruit. A quest for the answer runs deep into the history, theory, and practice of representative government; and those who cannot bear the thought of such a dusty search must forego the pleasure of illuminating the daily headline grist.

Representative government originated in Europe in the Middle Ages, in the necessity of kings. They had to collect money to pay for their wars and support their courts. When their private purses ran short, they invited the various classes of potential taxpayers to send delegates to some central place to speak (*parler*) with the king about the amount and manner of their coming taxation. In calling on his subjects for financial aid, he invited only the possessors of goods to take part in elections and representative assemblies. There was no use asking anybody to vote or serve as a delegate who had no property out of which to contribute to the royal chest.

If Mr. Bingham and Mr. Norris were sitting in King Edward III's parliament instead of the Congress of the United States, they would frankly represent and speak for the commercial and agricultural interests respectively. For all parliaments, in their origins, were mirrors of the estates of the realm—clergy (as proprietors of lands and goods), baronage, landed gentry, burgesses, and sometimes free peasants. Broadly speaking, land and commerce was each given "a volume of voice." People who had no land or were not engaged in business simply were not heard at all. A member of the English House of Commons from London in the days of Elizabeth and Essex was an agent of the merchants of the metropolis, openly and without sense of sin. In his speeches he did not feel bound to refer every few sentences to "the majesty of the people."

When the representative system was transplanted to these shores the old English practice of associating representation with property came with it. To be sure, there were no estates in Colonial America—clergy, barons, and burgesses—in the legal sense, but there were men with different degrees and kinds of property, to use James Madison's accurate phrase. These people alone could vote and sit in colonial assemblies in the great year of grace, 1776.

And the principle was continued in the first American state constitutions. For example, Massachusetts distributed representation in her senate among the towns on the basis of tax contributions, and gave the vote only to men who held land or personal property worth so much a year. Against fundamental changes in this perfect order John Adams and Daniel Webster, one looking to the past and the other to the future, lifted their voices high in the Massachusetts constitutional convention of 1820. Even the Better America League, as well as Mr. Norris, would have to admit that the Fathers connected representation with taxation.

But just at the very moment when the Fathers were setting up their first state governments on the foundation of property, on the age-long assumption that only the possessors of goods should have a "volume of voice" in representation, a new doctrine was spreading throughout western Europe. Though ancient in its origins, this new gospel was strikingly presented by the French radical, Rousseau, in his flaming diatribe, *The Social Contract*. In brief it may be outlined as follows: Human society began in an original contract made between free and equal men, and the true and moral source of all political authority is the general will of such men. In the formulation of this will all individuals (men) share alike.

With logical vengeance, Rousseau carried this theory to mathematical finality: if there are ten thousand active citizens in any society, then each citizen has one ten-thousandth part of the political power. But what if they cannot all agree? Rousseau anticipates this possibility: the general will is expressed by the majority—in some cases, by an extraordinary majority of three-fourths. What of the minority outvoted? Rousseau has an answer. "When," he says, "the opinion contrary to mine prevails, it only shows that I was mistaken, and that what I supposed to be the general will was not general."

In this scheme of politics there is no property, there are no classes, groups, or estates. All heads are, for political purposes, equal and alike; each individual has the same amount of power; the voter is an abstract man, a disembodied spirit; he is not engaged in agriculture, or in running a factory, or in speculating on the stock market. And this order is based on "natural rights," on the dignity, worth, and value of the human being as such.

A revolutionary doctrine opposed to the "divine right" of kings, Rousseau's creed served well the French people in the lurid days when they were levelling the ancient monarchy to earth.

Searching in old English writings, Thomas Jefferson found a similar doctrine and elaborated it with fundamental distinctions of his own. As Professor Chinard points out in his recent book on Jefferson, the Virginia philosopher may not have known Rousseau's theory. At all events, in the Declaration of Independence he starts with the fundamental proposition that "all men are created equal, that they are endowed with certain unalienable Rights, that among these are Life, Liberty, and the pursuit of Happiness. That to secure these rights, Governments are instituted among men, deriving their just powers from the consent of the governed."

It is to be noted that Jefferson did not include "property" among the inalienable rights. Nor was this omission due to inadvertence. Years later when Lafayette laid before Jefferson his "Declaration of the Rights of Man," containing among them "the right to property," the Sage of Monticello suggested the elimination of property from the list. This did not mean that he was opposed to private property, but that it was not to be included in the program of natural rights strictly considered. Here is the root of that Jeffersonian philosophy which "exalts the man above the dollar," which assigns people with little property "a volume of voice" louder than that of their money (even though cash may talk in subterranean places).

In the long contests of parties and states, surging up in wars and revolutions, the doctrine of "free-and-equal men," associated with the names of Rousseau and Jefferson, triumphed throughout the Western world as the accepted talking-point of politics. And indeed it was not all window-dressing. It became a force in itself: ideas as well as facts influence the conduct of human beings. It softened the sharp edge of propertied classes by imposing upon them moral obligations running counter to pure self-interest. It inspired whole movements and great programs of humane legislation, assisted of course by agitations and revolutionary threats on the part of propertyless persons.

In spite of the contempt poured upon it by the spiritual heirs of Alexander Hamilton, it has become so enshrined in American traditions that it is safe to keep copies of the Declaration of Independence in public school buildings and to read it to immature school children—except in times of war and rebellion when the exigencies of public safety makes it inexpedient. Whatever he may think, no candidate for Congress would now dare to say openly in any part of the Union that those who own the property of the country ought by rights to govern it. Of course, Mr. Grundy may bluntly assert, in effect, that the manufacturing capitalists ought to make the tariff schedules, but doubtless the Senator and Representatives from his state look upon his statement as a *faux pas*, if nothing worse.

As a matter of fact, the general structure of the American government is apparently reared on the "free-and-equal principle." Members of the House of Representatives are apportioned among the states on the basis of their respective population—free-and-equal heads—not on the basis of the amount of property owned or taxes paid. They are elected by the head-counting process. In the House all heads are equal on roll call. If two Senators are assigned to each state, irrespective of their populations, this is a historic concession to political entities, not to any rights of property. The arithmeticians of politics have pointed out that during the fiscal year ended in June, 1929, the state of New York contributed to the Federal Government in income and miscellaneous taxes more than twenty-eight times the amount contributed by eight of Mr. Grundy's "backward states" combined: Arizona, Arkansas, Idaho, Georgia, Mississippi, Montana, North Dakota, and South

Dakota. In short, according to outward signs, the Congress of the United States is based on free-and-equal heads and free-and-equal states.

Did the Fathers who framed the Constitution and set up this Congress really believe in Jefferson's free-and-equal doctrine? The answer is emphatic: most of them certainly did not, least of all James Madison, who succeeded Jefferson in the presidency. Did classes, groups, estates, property owners, and economic interests disappear when government was turned over to free-and-equal heads, irrespective of their goods? The census returns give a negative reply. In the ample days of Andrew Jackson, when white manhood suffrage practically triumphed over property, there were still in the country planters, freeholders, manufacturers, bankers, mechanics, factory operatives, farm hands, and many other orders and estates. No doubt, the owners of goods were at first somewhat afraid lest "horny-handed sons of toil" despoil them of their possessions by political processes, but their alarms were groundless and they managed to hold to what they had. The only great expropriation that has taken place in America since that day is the confiscation and emancipation of the planters' property in slaves (about four billion dollars), and that high act had the sanction of Northern manufacturers and farmers—all property owners. No, the shift in political creed meant no fundamental changes in the distribution of wealth and the structure of economic society.

And to some extent this outcome was due to the fact that the framers of the Constitution did not believe in Jefferson's free-and-equal creed but concerned themselves extensively with projects for preventing its strict and logical operation in politics. In other words, the creed proclaimed for popular uses did not correspond to the realities of life and politics as seen by the Fathers. Eleven years after the Declaration of Independence, James Madison, in a number of the *Federalist* pleading with the voters to ratify the pending Constitution of the United States, pointed out the perils of majority rule—government by headcounting. More than that, he showed that the principal business of legislation was the regulation of various and interfering economic interests and that the various and interfering economic interests affected by it (favorably or adversely) would have the making of such legislation.

Let Madison speak for himself: "A landed interest, a manufacturing interest, a mercantile interest, a moneyed interest, with many lesser interests, grow up of necessity in civilized nations and divide them into different classes, actuated by different sentiments and views." Here, says Madison, is the prime source of political parties and factions. Of course, no sacred Republican or holy Democrat would admit it to-day, but such was the view of an influential framer of the Constitution.

And Madison goes on remorselessly to add: "And what are the different classes of legislators but advocates and parties to the causes which they determine? Is a law proposed concerning private debts? It is a question to which the creditors are parties on one side and the debtors on the other. . . . Shall domestic manufactures be encouraged, and in what degree, by restrictions on foreign manufactures? are questions which would be differently decided by the landed and the manufacturing classes, and probably by neither with a sole regard to justice and the public good." Mr. Grundy was anticipated.

Leading members of the Constitutional Convention of 1787 foresaw that a conflict of economic interest, especially between commerce and agriculture, would always run through the politics of the Federal Government whatever obeisance was made to "free people" or "backward states" as such. Moreover, they believed that in the long run head-counting on the principle of equality would not create equality in political power and "volume of voice," no matter how firmly established in legal declaration.

On this ground, Gouverneur Morris advocated giving one branch of Congress, the Senate, directly and frankly to the concentrated wealth of the country. He was convinced that if no distinction was made between the Senate and the House, if both branches were elected by general suffrage, the rich would control both of them. It is true that he feared the masses, perhaps as much as Hamilton, but he feared also the classes.

To obviate danger from this source, he proposed to give the masses their own legislative chamber and the classes theirs; he thought that, by recognizing economic facts in our constitutional system, moral confusion would be cleared up and public business would be conducted on the philosophy of "as is."

"The rich," he said, "will strive to establish their dominion and enslave the rest. They always did. They always will. The proper security against them is to form them into a separate interest. The two forces will then control each other. Let the rich mix with the poor and in a commercial country they will establish an Oligarchy. Take away commerce and the democracy will triumph. Thus it has been all the world over. So it will be among us." Under Morris's scheme, Mr. Grundy and Mr. Eyanson's chief (not Mr. Eyanson, the hired man, or Mr. Bingham, the scholar) would be in the Senate. They would not have to resort to lobbying, propaganda and back-stairs methods to gain their ends. They would not be subjected to charges of violating the "ethics" of the Senate. But the Morris project failed in the Constitutional Convention.

So did all other schemes for frankly bringing economic interests to focus in various branches of the Federal Government. A proposition to apportion representation on the basis of wealth was defeated; it would have put agriculture in the saddle in 1787 and, besides, it ran counter to the vested interests of politicians in the small states, bent on equality. At one time the convention carried a motion instructing a committee to fix property qualifications for members of Congress. Only one delegate spoke against it on principle. Benjamin Franklin, who was familiar with Pennsylvania politics, said that "some of the greatest rogues he was ever acquainted with were the richest rogues." The convention adopted also a resolution favoring a property qualification for the presidency; Pinckney of South Carolina (state of Tillman and Blease) thought that this was highly desirable. Gouverneur Morris wanted a property qualification put on voters. A careful student, S. H. Miller, who has examined all the evidence on these points, correctly concludes that the lack of property qualifications for office in the Constitution is not owing to any opposition of the Convention to such qualifications *per se*.

The absence of such property qualifications is certainly not due to any belief in Jefferson's free-and-equal doctrine. It is due rather to the fact that the members of the Convention could not agree on the nature and amount of the qualifications. Naturally a landed qualification was suggested, but for obvious reasons it was rejected. Although it was satisfactory to the landed gentry of the South, it did not suit the financial, commercial, and manufacturing gentry of the North. If it was high, the latter would be excluded; if it was low it would let in the populistic farmers who had already made so much trouble in the state legislatures with paper-money schemes and other devices for "relieving agriculture." One of the chief reasons for calling the convention and framing the Constitution was to promote commerce and industry and to protect personal property against the "depredations" of Jefferson's noble freeholders. On the other hand a personal-property qualification, high enough to please merchant princes like Robert Morris and Nathaniel Gorham would shut out the Southern planters. Again, an alternative of land or personal property, high enough to afford safeguards to large interests, would doubtless bring about the rejection of the whole Constitution by the trouble-making farmers who had to pass upon the question of ratification.

None of the Fathers appears to have called the agrarians of his day "sons of wild jackasses" or "sons of the wild jackass," after the fashion of Doctor Moses, the cultivated graduate of Dartmouth (Webster's institution), but they entertained sentiments akin to those of the New Hampshire Senator. Unable to agree upon any satisfactory scheme for keeping such "creatures" out of the Federal Government, they trusted to checks and balances to prevent damage, and left land and commerce to battle as best they could under a constitutional system that, in the nature of the circumstances, had to recognize free-and-equal heads and free-and-equal states rather than proud and-efficient dollars.

To check, balance, and refine the views and sentiments of groups and classes—that was the great object to which the framers of the Constitution directed their attention. They assumed that these diverse interests would endure, and they sought "to secure the public good and private rights" against the assaults and ambitions of mere numerical majorities representing one or more major interests in society. They foresaw the Hannas and Grundys, the Bryans and La Follettes of the modern age. They did not expect the government to be conducted by disembodied spirits without reference to the practical interests of their constituencies. And in their writings and speeches they tried to instruct the American public in the true nature of political substance.

But they failed. Their Constitution endures, a monument to their amazing wisdom, and the Government of the United States operates very much as they expected it would. But few people read their writings or pay any attention to the sound political science which they formulated. American citizens act like Alexander Hamilton and talk like Thomas Jefferson, and that largely accounts for their confusion in morals. Instead of studying and carrying forward the principles of the Fathers, they grope around in an atmosphere of verbiage that has little or no relation to the motivating forces of politics.

There is no use in talking about removing economic interests from politics. It cannot be done, at least in any civilized or half-civilized society. Even if capitalists and farmers could be abolished by confiscating their property in the name of the state, economic interests would remain—farms, factories, railways, mines, banks, government officials, technicians, and various groups of workers powerfully organized. Questions of hours, wages, and working conditions would still perplex and would have to be decided with reference to the parties in the case. Even the most obtuse Bolshevik has learned this from the battle of Trotsky against the bureaucrats, if from no other source. Misunderstandings, hatreds, and perils arise from the refusal to recognize what the Fathers well knew, namely, that the chief business of government is the regulation of various and interfering economic interests—regulation to which the interested persons are themselves parties.

Suppose that we should eliminate from the Congress of the United States all members who hold land, or stocks, or bonds, or other property affected by laws enacted by that body, who and how many would be left? Jefferson once suggested some such removal with respect to certain measures before Congress. In the early days of the Republic, when many Senators and

Representatives were enriching themselves by voting laws raising the prices of the government bonds which they held, Jefferson declared that "decency and honesty" required that such members should have refrained from voting. And yet he himself proposed to fill Congress with men representing primarily the agricultural interest, who, it may be presumed, would have voted laws in favor of, rather than against, their economic advantage. Were not slaveholders pushing a fugitive-slave bill about as much "interested" in the enterprise as stockholders in factories engaged in pushing a protective tariff bill? The matter is not so simple as some of our chimney-corner moralists would have us believe.

Doubtless the investigating Senators from agricultural states would admit that in promoting the interests of farmers they are fixing their minds on economic things quite as much as Mr. Grundy in advancing the interests of manufacturers. Perhaps farmers did not give as much to Mr. Hoover's campaign fund. It may be that they have no lobby in Washington as powerful as Mr. Grundy's Association. Yet, though a minority in the country, they have a "volume of voice." Certainly statesmen from their regions, like all other statesmen, have their ears to the ground; if they did not, they would soon cease to be statesmen—at least gainfully employed. According to one of Ex-President Coolidge's favorite stories, the late Joseph G. Cannon vowed that William McKinley kept his ear so close to the earth that it was always full of grasshoppers. The yarn may be apocryphal; if not that, it is ancient in technology. Statesmen now have microphones so finely tuned that they can hear in Washington the hops of grasshoppers in Iowa.

And what about the relation of lobbies to this process of hearing, seeing, and feeling? Suppose a summary removal of all the oil, railway, shipping, steel, farm, and other economic agencies engaged in "building fires" behind Senators and Representatives, giving "information" to them, stirring up "public sentiment," advancing their interests "in the name of public welfare." Suppose that only disembodied righteousness were left—the people who want to do good—the anti-cigarette committee, the Sunday observance association, and the like. Could we be sure that only good would result? By no means. It is notorious that some of the worst oppression and most disastrous mistakes in history must be ascribed to the honest good. Although some cynic has suggested that the heretic burners of the Middle Ages often had their eyes on the lands and chattels of the condemned, the point cannot be pressed; the operators of the Spanish Inquisition were holy men, fairly devoid of economic interest, and hell-bent on doing good. On the other hand the mercantile capitalist, while looking out primarily for himself, has been one of the humanizing forces of the modern age, incidentally working for freedom of intercourse and toleration. Those who try to do good frequently do harm, and those who pursue their own interest intelligently frequently do good. Such is the economy of Providence!

If so, what then is the upshot? Certainly we can never clear up our confusion by prosecuting amid great uproar fellow-citizens who occasionally allow cupidity to get the better of discretion, by censuring the blunt for doing openly what the sophisticated do artfully, or by cheering and weeping when "shocking" revelations break into the headlines. Some of our perplexity would be eliminated, of course, if we adopted Mr. Grundy's proposition to abolish the equality of states in the Senate and distribute representation in that chamber according to free-and-equal heads. In this case, the industrial states would have no effective opposition and Congress would be run to suit the manufacturers; Mr. Bingham would be praised for his perspicacity, not censured for violating senatorial ethics. In this case also agriculture would be at the mercy of machine capitalism and would swiftly sink to the position it occupies in Great Britain—with similar fateful consequences. An ever larger proportion of the sons and daughters of farmers would be herded in the dreary tenements of industrial cities—transformed into tenders of engines or unemployed proletarians. And the economy of those who remained on the land would be "controlled" as Mr. Grundy suggested. That would be a way of carrying a class fight unintelligently to a disastrous finish. That would be one way of dissipating our moral miasma.

There is, however, another and better way. If the above analysis is sound, our confusion in morals is due to the intellectual climate we have created for ourselves. Our political theory and our Sunday loquacity do not conform to the pattern of our week-day economic conduct. Our teachers of ethics give too much attention to Aristotle and Kant and too little to the reports of congressional investigating committees. Our psychologists, deep in a world of dreams and instincts, refuse to recognize the place of economics in behavior. Our biographers are busy making heroes big or little rather than intelligible. Above all, our political science, as taught, sung and praised, leaves economics out of the picture, and our economics, as taught, sung, and praised, neglects politics. Both are fictitious, misleading and demoralizing to our youth, for they spread false notions of the world in which life must be lived.

The solution of our problem, therefore, lies in a return to the Fathers, a restoration of political thinking to the economic foundation from which it has been removed, but with wide-open regard for the potentialities of the engineering age which they did not foresee. Science and machinery have made crude class fights archaic; contestants by their folly annually waste more than the marginal amount at stake in their disputes. Hence a mere balance of powers is not enough. The necessary rediscovery of the Fathers means a new Science of Political Economy that transcends the everlasting battle of capitalism and agriculture for advantage—a science that has its points of reference or bench marks, not in the bald interests of cotton spinners or wheat raisers, but in the very center of Planned National Economy. If the American mind can emerge from the smoke of "moral turpitude," it will be equal to the task of creating this Science. Emergence, therefore, is the beginning of achievement.

No. 45

[IF the legislature is adequately to perform its function of determining public policy and controlling the administration it must have facts with which to work. In fact-finding the legislature has found the investigating committee its most effective weapon. The Pujo, Teapot Dome, Nye, Black, La Follette, Dies, TVA and Temporary National Economic Committee investigations offer examples of what may be done through this peculiarly American instrumentality of government. The following article by Professor Rogers offers an interesting discussion of this phase of legislative activity.]

THE INQUIRING CONGRESSMAN [1]

by Lindsay Rogers

TWENTY-FIVE years ago the late Professor A. V. Dicey, whose name is still honored by students of political institutions, lamented the fact that "political inventiveness has in general fallen far short of the originality displayed in other fields than politics by the citizens of progressive or civilized states." The United States, however, can boast of at least two political inventions—that is, of two devices which have no counterparts in foreign governmental systems.

One is the Presidential press conference which, invented by Woodrow Wilson, was so adapted and improved by President Roosevelt that it produces news which in importance ofttimes rivals the news that results from congressional deliberations or even from the relations of executive and legislature. The second invention is the congressional committee of investigation. This, to be sure, is nothing new. It has roots in sixteenth-century England; the colonial legislatures set up committees to inquire into various matters, and the Congress at its second session asserted its prerogative of

[1] Lindsay Rogers, "The Inquiring Congressman," *Survey Graphic* (January, 1939), Vol. 28, pp. 5-8. Reprinted by permission of *Survey Graphic*.

investigation. Since the war, however, congressional investigations have increased in number and importance. Nowhere else do investigations by committees of the legislature constitute a major and customary instrumentality of the government. . . .

Given our form of government—the separation of the executive and legislature—congressional committees of inquiry are absolutely necessary. The fact that, under a cabinet form of government, ministers must defend themselves in the legislature results in parliamentary knowledge of and control over administrative policy that are far greater than congressional knowledge or control can be. As Woodrow Wilson wrote a half century ago: "Congress stands almost helplessly outside of the departments" with the result that "hostile or designing officials can always hold it at arm's length by dexterous evasions and concealments." The only whip that Congress has is investigation. That whip must be used by committees. But Mr. Wilson went on to say that "even the special, irksome, ungracious investigations, which it (Congress) from time to time institutes in its spasmodic endeavors to dispel or confirm suspicions of malfeasance or of wanton corruption, do not afford it more than a glimpse of the inside of a small province of the federal administration." During the last two years of his Presidency, when the Democrats had lost control of Congress, Mr. Wilson had to submit to inquiries into many "small provinces" of his administration. Fifty-one congressional investigations were in progress at the same time.

Manifestly a party which controls one or both branches of Congress wishes to use the power of investigation to hamper and discredit an executive from the opposing party. But Congress declines to be incurious when the same party controls both the legislature and the executive. It is thus that the inquisitorial power of the Senate becomes more frequent and more formidable than that of the House of Representatives.

There party control is more rigid than it is in the Senate. Representatives live in the shadow cast by the always imminent congressional elections. Hence the majority party in the House is reluctant to probe for possibly embarrassing disclosures. The result is that when the same party is in control in Congress and in the White House, investigations are frequently asked for in the House and refused, but are allowed by the Senate. That the Senate and not the more popular branch of Congress should be more important as the grand inquisitor is somewhat ironical. But in the Senate bondage to leaders is far less prevalent than in the House; because there are few limitations on debate, the need for investigations can be clearly set forth; and if the party steam roller is brought out, the minority may have an effective defense in a filibuster that can endanger the majority's legislative time table.

Thus, in the period which followed the conclusion of the war, with the exception of the Graham Committee that scrutinized military expenditures at a cost of half a million dollars), Senate committees conducted practically every important investigation. They inquired into charges of corruption in the Veterans' Bureau, the oil land leases, the Bureau of Internal Revenue and its tax refunds, Mr. Daugherty's conduct of the Department of Justice, the failure to prosecute the aluminum trust, and the internal workings of the Tariff Commission. Through its committees, the House investigated matters that were much less spectacular: the administration of the Stock Yards Control Act, the operations of the Army Air Service and the Shipping Board. It was during the Harding administration that the Senate became the grand inquest of the nation and that congressional investigations were recognized as being a regular and highly important part of the governmental machine.

When they probe into important issues and when they seem to be endeavoring to besmirch executive officers, senatorial investigations may encounter bitter opposition and severe criticism. Complaints are made that committees throw out their dragnets blindly and pry into irrelevant and innocent matters; that a wrong construction may be put on honest actions; that the course that investigations follow is determined by the idiosyncrasies of individual Senators; that those Senators are more concerned with securing headlines in the newspapers than they are in uncovering abuses.

Occasionally, what a committee and its investigators do seems designed to escape any taint of legality. Thus the committee headed by Mr. Justice (then Senator) Black, which was inquiring into "all lobbying activities and all efforts to influence, encourage, promote or retard legislation, directly or indirectly, in connection with the so-called holding company bill." The committee wanted to see all the telegrams that had been sent to Washington by opponents of the legislation. Unable to procure them from the companies, the committee persuaded the Federal Communications Commission to obtain the messages for it. In granting such a power to the commission under the Communications Act of 1934, Congress was of course doing nothing more than enabling the commission to obtain the information that might be necessary for the efficient performance of its duties and for the formulation of new legislation. It did not intend that the commission would be the assistant of a Senate committee. Nevertheless, agents of the commission examined thousands of telegrams and handed many on to the Black Committee.

The United States court of appeals for the District of Columbia declared that such "a dragnet seizure of private telegraph messages . . . whether made by persons professing to act under color of authority from the govern-

ment or by persons acting as individuals is a trespass which a court of
equity has power to enjoin." The trespass was complete, however. The
telegrams had been handed over to the Senate committee and the court
refused to enjoin the committee from disclosing the contents of the messages.
"The universal rule, so far as we know it, is that the legislative discretion
in discharge of its constiuttional functions, whether rightfully or wrongfully
exercised, is not a subject of judicial interference." The court suggested,
however, that Congress was as "much the guardian of the liberties and welfare of the people as the courts" and indulged in the hope that "attention
being called to the unlawful nature of the search, the Senate will not use
its proceeds in disregard" of the rights of the individuals whose telegrams
were in its possession.

Here the appeal to the court for relief was too late. Other Senate committees may act in such a fashion that appeals to the courts will be successful. Witnesses who refuse to testify can be punished for contumacy if the
Senate committee has stayed within its terms of reference.

Nevertheless, the protection that may be afforded by the U. S. courts is
more theoretical than real. Senate investigations are public, and hostile
and irresponsible cross-examiners can do considerable harm to individuals
who must appear without the protection of counsel who can insist on an
observance of the rules of evidence. The remedy, however, is not to hamper
the investigations. As Professor Frankfurter once said: "The safeguards
against abuse and folly are to be looked for in the forces of responsibility
which are operating from within Congress and are generated from without."
If the alternatives are no inquiry at all or an inquiry that is abused, then
the choice must be for the latter. If it is not, then there is no method by
which Congress may perform its duties of seeing to it that the administration of law, which Lord Morley called the "keystone of all civilized government" is neither corrupt nor incompetent. As legislation becomes more and
more complex, and those who execute it become more and more numerous
the keystone is a capstone and a foundation as well.

Under a parliamentary system of government, as I have said, the presence
of the executive in the legislature permits something of a day to day supervision of administration. Occasionally, however, there are matters that
have to be inquired into by some special inquisitorial process. Thus, the
Marconi scandal in Great Britain in 1912—cabinet ministers were accused
of speculating in the shares of a company which had relations with the
government—was investigated by a select committee of the House of Com
mons. When there was a leakage of budget information from the cabinet
in 1936 and some who had thereby become forewarned insured themselves
against an increase of taxes, the government set up a special tribunal to

conduct the investigation. There followed the resignation of the indiscreet minister, Jimmy Thomas.

Last spring, when it was suggested that a member of the House of Commons might be liable to prosecution under the Official Secrets Act because of military information that was contained in a question that he asked in the House of Commons, the procedure was to set up a Select Committee on the Official Secrets Act. It proceeded with a minimum of publicity and investigated with "no strangers present." The reports of such committees are intended to ascertain whether there has been wrongdoing and who is responsible—not to secure publicity for their members. Occasionally the committees may divide on partisan lines, but the inquiries are not partisan. Since headlines are not sought for, there are few abuses such as those which have not been altogether unknown in the procedure of congressional committees.

During Mr. Roosevelt's first administration the inquisitorial branch of the governmental machine was used for a new purpose. One of my colleagues, M. Nelson McGeary, has made a detailed examination of congressional inquiries from 1933 on. He points out that "for the first time since investigations were well publicized, a strong party majority, Presidentially led, was committed to a program of social change."

To an extent this was true of the first two years of the Wilson administration, and he used a congressional investigation into the tariff lobby to facilitate the passage of the Underwood Tariff revision. But it is true to say that, at the request of Mr. Roosevelt, congressional leaders demonstrated in a large way "that investigations may serve as valuable aids to an administration." Governor Landon did not like this. He objected to congressional committees "out to get the critics" as distinguished from committees that were "out to get the crooks." This was more epigrammatic than profound. If an administration has a legislative program why is it not legitimate for it to use congressional inquiries as an aid in driving that program to the statute book?

During Mr. Roosevelt's first administration there were fifty-one inquiries which could be thought of as intended to aid the administration. Some of them were of minor importance and got little publicity. But the investigations into lobbying by public utilities had a good deal of attention paid to them. After committees had turned up details about amounts of money spent on the lobbying activities of public utility agents, the House of Representatives reversed itself on the so-called "death sentence clause" of the Holding Companies Act. Similarly, the inquiry into stock exchange practices was a potent influence in smoothing the way for the Securities Act of 1933 and the Securities Exchange Act of 1934.

The banking investigation had begun before the advent of the Roosevelt administration—in the days when there were so many cruel jokes about bankers. At the time, the investigation furthered the political career of Justice Ferdinand Pecora and will always be remembered because of the midget that climbed into J. P. Morgan's lap. This was showmanship of an order which the Dies Committee has not been able to equal. In comparison, its methods have been humdrum but public expectancy has been great. Thus there seemed no inherent probability in the rumor that one of the witnesses on "un-American" activities was to be Sally Rand.

Some investigations are difficult to classify. That was the case, for example, with the Senate committee—the so-called Nye Committee—which inquired into the manufacture and sale of arms and other munitions of war. Its record was extremely voluminous. It proposed a good deal of legislation. It went into the question of the responsibility for the entrance of the United States into the war. It heard testimony on whether President Wilson had known of the secret treaties between the allies. One witness secured large headlines for the committee here and abroad by charging that, as Prince of Wales, the then King of England—Edward VII—had been a salesman for British munition firms. Extremely useful work that the committee did was discounted in the public mind by the extravagant claims made as to the importance of disclosures and as to the existence of a munitions ring which brought on wars.

Mr. McGeary classifies some inquiries as for the purpose of exercising " 'social leverage' through publicity." He instances inquiries into real estate, bond holders' reorganizations and the La Follette investigation into strikebreaking and industrial espionage. Some investigating committees which are charged with highly important terms of reference show disappointing results. That, for example, was the case with the Wheeler Committee investigating railway financing. It had the opportunity of producing a thoroughgoing scheme for a new federal policy toward the railroads. It did little. What will be the result of the TVA investigation remains to be seen. That committee has a two-fold task: of reporting on responsibility for the long continued battle within the TVA board; and of making policy recommendations.

Some congressional investigations have been conducted without a fanfare of trumpets and with few clicks of cameras. Thus the National Monetary Commission, which consisted of an equal number of Representatives and Senators, initiated the studies and engaged in the deliberations which in the end led to the Federal Reserve System. Such formulation of legislation is in Great Britain considered primarily a function of the executive. The cabinet takes responsibility for the creation of a royal commission, a committee, or a conference out of whose deliberations legislative proposals are expected to come. While these agencies are at work there is no desire to stir up public opinion. In fact the theory underlying them is that it is better to take the issue out of current political discussion for the time being, to inquire into it, and then to lay non-party proposals before the government and the public. The government will then decide on the extent to which it will endeavor to have the proposals put on the statute book. With something of this thought in mind, Mr. Hoover appointed the Wickersham Committee on Prohibition, but thereafter he made the fatal mistake of being interested in the nature of its report.

The Temporary National Economic Committee which is now investigating monopolies seems to me of a different character. It includes representatives of the legislature and of the executive in equal numbers. It has half a million dollars to spend—far too much to be spent prudently in any reasonably short period. It may produce something that is worthwhile, but if this happens, tributes will be paid to personnel rather than to the nature of the device. Bagehot once said that the men of Massachusetts could have worked any constitution. Perhaps the men on the O'Mahoney Committee will be able to work an inquiry under the joint control of Congress and the executive. The start has been good. The publicizing has been designed to take the nation to school. But it will probably not be long before devils are produced for excoriation by a shocked public. In the end Congress will be given drafts of bills. Before that happens we shall probably learn something about the difficulties inherent in an inquiry which is based on responsibility that is divided and which will be influenced by allegiances that are not identical. Congressional inquisitions and inquiries are American political inventions that are of great importance but we have not yet learned how to use them to the best advantage.

No. 46

[ALTHOUGH most of us look upon the American legislature as performing purely legislative functions, a closer examination would reveal that it performs constituent, judicial, electoral, and executive functions as well. American legislatures—state and national—have an important part in changing American constitutions, have the power of impeachment, take part in the election of certain public officers, and play an important role in the making of appointments. One of the least understood of these functions is that of Senatorial participation in the appointing power.

In the national government, the President has the power, with the advice and consent of the Senate, to make a great many appointments. The normal process is for the President to nominate an individual to the Senate and, if the Senate consents, the appointment is made. Actually, of course, the President in making such nominations must seek advice from many quarters. There has grown up, however, a tradition that the members of the Senate will not consent to an appointment that is objected to by a Senator from the state in which the appointment is made if the Senator is a member of the President's own party. This tradition is known as "Senatorial Courtesy."

An example of the operation of Senatorial courtesy is to be found in the Senate's rejection of President Roosevelt's nomination of Floyd H. Roberts as Federal District Court Judge in Virginia. The following opinions by President Roosevelt and Senator Glass, occasioned by the above case, throw some light on the full meaning and character of this constitutional tradition.]

THE SENATE AND THE APPOINTING POWER— SENATORIAL COURTESY[1]

(President Roosevelt's letter to Floyd H. Roberts, whose nomination as a Federal Judge was rejected by the Senate, precipitating a controversy over the appointive powers of Senate and President, follows in full text:)

My dear Judge Roberts:

I feel that in justice to you and your family I should write to you in regard to the refusal of the Senate to confirm your appointment as United States District Judge for the Western District of Virginia.

First of all, I tender you my thanks for the honorable, efficient, and in every way praiseworthy service that you have rendered to the people of the United States in general and to the people of the Western District of Virginia in particular.

Second, I wish it known that not one single person who has opposed your confirmation has lifted his voice in any shape, manner or form against your personal integrity and ability.

In order that you may know the full history of what has occurred, I take this opportunity to summarize the story.

On March 17, 1938, I received a letter from Senator Glass enclosing a clipping from a local Virginia paper. This newspaper article, quoting an editorial in another local Virginia paper, made the assumption that it would henceforth be necessary to receive the backing of Governor Price of Virginia before any Virginian could hope for a Federal appointment.

---

[1] The letter from President Franklin D. Roosevelt to Floyd H. Roberts and the statement by Senator Carter Glass are reprinted from the *United States News* (Feb. 13, 1939), an independent magazine on national affairs issued weekly at Washington, D. C.

Senator Glass in his letter asked if Federal appointments, for which Senate approval was necessary, would be subjected to the effective veto of the Governor of Virginia.

To this I replied on March 18, explaining to the Senator the difference between the appointive power, which is in the President, and the power of confirmation, which is in the Senate. I pointed out to the Senator that time-hallowed courtesy permits Senators and others to make recommendations for nomination, and, at the same time, that every President has sought information from any other source deemed advisable.

On March 19 Senator Glass wrote me again, covering his construction of Article II of the Constitution, and asking me again as to the accuracy of the newspaper statement. He winds up by saying "the inference is, of course, that you approve the offensive publication which was the basis of my inquiry."

I replied to this letter from the Senator on March 21 in a personal and friendly vein. I stated that I was glad that we seemed to agree in our construction of the Constitution. I told him that I was not in the habit of confirming or denying any newspaper article or editorial. Obviously if I were to begin that sort of thing, I would have no spare time to attend to my executive duties.

I told the Senator to go ahead as before and make recommendations; that I would give such recommendations every consideration; but that I would, of course, reserve the right to get opinions from any other person I might select. I ended by asking the Senator to forget the newspaper article and wished him a good vacation and expressed the hope that he would come to see me on his return.

Subsequent to this date, I received a number of recommendations for the position of United States District Judge for the Western District of Virginia —among them recommendations in behalf of two gentlemen from Senator Glass. I am not certain whether these recommendations were at that time concurred in by the Junior Senator from Virginia, but this is possible. Other recommendations were received from citizens of Virginia to a total number, as I remember it, of five or six.

The Attorney General was asked by me to report on these recommendations, paying attention as usual to the qualifications of each person suggested. I might add that your name was on this list but that at no time, to my knowledge, did you seek this office of Judge.

The Attorney General and I held several conferences with the result that we concluded that you were best fitted to fill the Judgeship.

As a result, I wrote on July 6 to both of the Virginia Senators stating that I had concluded to appoint you, that a number of gentlemen had been suggested for the place, but that I believed you to be the best fitted.

The following day, July 7, I received a telegram from Senator Glass stating that he and his colleague would feel obliged to object to your appointment as being personally objectionable to them, and that a letter would follow. A few days later I received a letter from the Senator stating that he could not conceive any fair reason why one of his candidates had not been appointed.

It is worth noting that neither Senator on July 7 or subsequently raised any question as to your integrity or ability, and the only objection was that you were personally objectionable.

In regard to the original newspaper article suggesting that Governor Price had been given the veto over Federal appointments, this and similar stories are, of course, not worth answering or bothering about, for the very simple reason that no person—no Governor, no Senator, no member of the Administration—has at any time had, or ever will have, any right of veto over Presidential nominations. Every person with common sense knows this.

Your appointment followed, you took the oath of office, and have been serving with great credit as District Judge since then.

Your name was sent by me to the Senate in January, 1939, together with many other recess appointments.

We come now to the last chapter. Your nomination was referred to the Judiciary Committee of the Senate and by the Chairman of that Committee to a subcommittee of three. It appears from the record that both Senators from Virginia registered their objection with the subcommittee, saying "this nomination is utterly and personally offensive to the Virginia Senators whose suggestions were invited by the Department of Justice only to be ignored."

The subcommittee reported back the nomination to the full Committee without recommendation, stating the raising of the matter of Senatorial courtesy and saying that this matter had not been a direct issue since 1913.

At a special meeting of the full Committee on the Judiciary and before the Committee went into executive session, attention was invited to the presence of the Governor of Virginia, to the presence of two former Governors of Virginia, and to the presence of the nominee and his counsel.

After lengthy discussion the Committee went into executive session, reopening the doors an hour later.

The record shows that at this time the Committee heard the Governor of Virginia in favor of the nominee and also former Governor E. Lee Trinkle and former Governor Westmoreland Davis; also, George M. Warren, Esq., counsel for nominee.

Thereupon the Committee, instead of hearing other witnesses in behalf of the nominee, many of whom were present, moved that a list of these further witnesses be incorporated in the record without hearing them. The Committee also agreed to receive certain letters and editorials in behalf of the nominee, and, finally, a record of designations you have received from former Governors of Virginia to sit in other judicial districts, this list including many designations of you made by former Governor Harry F. Byrd.

That was followed by your own testimony.

The privilege of making the closing and sole arguments against you was accorded to the two Senators from Virginia.

Senator Glass stated that neither he nor his colleague had formally or definitely made any statement affecting your capabilities.

He proceeded to review the newspaper reports of last March, stated that he had not communicated with the Governor to ascertain whether or not the latter had authorized the publication, and spoke of his letter to me. He went on to state that the President had not answered his question up to this date, except by sending the nomination to the Senate.

You will recognize from what I have written you that as far back as last March, in reply to Senator Glass' letters, I told him categorically that I never answered any questions relating to the credibility or otherwise of newspaper articles or editorials, and I asked him to forget the newspaper article altogether. Therefore, the statement of Senator Glass to the Committee does not square with the facts.

Continuing, the Senior Senator from Virginia referred to other newspaper articles which spoke of "rebukes" to the Senators. It is almost needless for me to suggest that neither you nor I pay any attention to such excuses.

Finally, Senator Glass stated "as a matter of fact, the President of the United States did give to the Governor of Virginia the veto power over nominations made by the two Virginia United States Senators."

I am sorry, in view of my long personal friendship for the Senior Senator, that he has made any such statement, and I can only excuse it on the ground of anger or forgetfulness.

At the end of his speech Senator Glass says "Mr. Cummings never had the slightest idea of giving consideration to the recommendations of the two Virginia Senators because the Governor of Virginia had been promised the right of veto on nominations that they made." Neither of these statements is true.

Senator Glass was followed by Senator Byrd, who stated that your nomination was personally offensive to both Senators, in fact, "personally obnoxious."

At the very close of the Judiciary Committee hearing Governor Price stated "Senator Glass has made a charge against me. He is entirely mistaken about it." The Governor further stated that he was not involved in the newspaper story.

The Committee thereupon abruptly closed the matter and went into executive session, with the result, as you know, that your nomination was reported adversely to the Senate.

This brief history repeats several episodes in the history of the United States, which have occurred from time to time during the past one hundred and fifty years. In other cases nominations by former Presidents of men of outstanding ability and character have been denied confirmation by the Senate, not on the plea that they were unfitted for office but on the sole ground that they were personally obnoxious to the Senator or Senators from the State from which they came.

During this whole period Presidents have recognized that the constitutional procedure is for a President to receive advice, i.e., recommendations, from Senators.

Presidents have also properly received advice, i.e., recommendations, from such other sources as they saw fit.

Thereupon Presidents have decided on nominations in accordance with their best judgment—and in most cases basing their judgment on the character and ability of the nominee. In many cases, of course, the recommendations of Senators have been followed, but in many other cases they have not been followed by Presidents in making the nominations.

Thereupon, under the Constitution, the Senate as a whole—not the Senators from one State—has the duty of either confirming or rejecting the nomination.

If is, of course, clear that it was the intention of the Constitution of the United States to vest in the Senate as a whole the duty of rejecting or confirming solely on the ground of the fitness of the nominee.

Had it been otherwise, had the Constitution intended to give the right of veto to a Senator or two Senators from the State of the nominee, it would have said so. Or to put it another way, it would have vested the nominating power in the Senators from the State in which the vacancy existed.

On somewhat rare occasions the Senate, relying on an unwritten rule of Senatorial courtesy, which exists in no place in the Constitution, has rejected nominees on the ground of their being personally obnoxious to their Senators, thus vesting in individual Senators what amounts in effect to the power of nomination.

In the particular case of which you are the unfortunate and innocent victim, the Senators from Virginia have in effect said to the President—

"We have nominated to you two candidates acceptable to us; you are hereby directed to nominate one of our two candidates, and if you do not we will reject the nomination of anybody else selected by you, however fit he may be."

Perhaps, my dear Judge Roberts, the rejection of your nomination will have a good effect on the citizenship and the thinking of the whole nation in that it will tend to create a greater interest in the Constitution of our country, a greater interest in its preservation in accordance with the intention of the gentlemen who wrote it.

I am sorry, indeed, that you have been the victim. Against you not one syllable has been uttered in derogation of your character or ability in the legal profession or your record on the Bench.

Very sincerely yours,

FRANKLIN D. ROOSEVELT.

Honorable Floyd H. Roberts,
Bristol, Va.

(A statement by Senator Carter Glass (Dem.), of Virginia, on President Roosevelt's letter to Floyd H. Roberts, whose appointment as a judge was rejected by the Senate, follows in full text:)

The only reason I think the President's extraordinary letter to his rejected nominee for judge of the Western District of Virginia deserves the slightest notice is the fact that some of the covert implications should be brushed away.

The Senate itself is amply able to attend to his attack upon the time-honored custom of respecting the reasonable objections of its members to executive nominations intended to be offensive to them; but I think it pertinent to summarize the relative facts in order that the public may determine the exact truth of the matter at issue.

On last March 16, under a two-column picture of Governor Price and Hon. James A. Farley, characterized as "chief patronage dispenser in the Federal Government," thus obviously to accentuate the significance of the subjoined announcement, there appeared in heavy headlines in *The Richmond Times-Dispatch,* an article captioned "Price Backing Seen Necessary for Federal Job."

The body of the article, being largely quoted from an editorial of the chief proponent of Judge Roberts, printed at his home, stated that: "Henceforth the indorsement of Governor Price will be necessary before any ambitious Virginian may hope to land an important Federal job."

Stating that the editor of the paper quoted from had "conferred with the President in Washington the preceding Monday," the paper stated without reservation that "President Roosevelt himself has made this decision, which means the Governor is to have the veto power on all appointments of any consequence in Virginia."

As incredible as this publication seemed, it did not shock the Virginia Senators, because they had previously learned that Governor Price, eagerly accepting the delegated function of Federal patronage dispenser in Virginia, had theretofore communicated with certain Federal officials recommended by the two Senators for reappointment on their assured record as "among the most outstanding officials of their class in the United States."

To their credit it must be said that not one of these officials had sought the Governor's proffered indorsement and none had been willing to join in the effort to discredit the Virginia Senators.

After waiting a day for Governor Price to contradict this extraordinary statement published right under his nose, I addressed the President a note on March 17, drawing his attention to the obnoxious publication. In this note I ventured to say: "I desire to ask if recommendations made by me as a Senator of Virginia for important Federal appointments, requiring the advice and consent of the United States Senate, are to be subject to the effective veto of the Governor of Virginia?"

It seemed to me then, as it does now, that this was a perfectly reasonable and simple question which might be answered directly and, of course, without evasion of any kind. It was not answered then, directly or otherwise. Instead, the President wrote me a page essay on the requirements of the Constitution as to Federal appointments, whereupon I ventured to reply that I had a fairly intimate knowledge of the fundamental law and nowhere discovered anything in it requiring Federal appointments to be made by and with the advice and consent of a State Governor.

Failing to get anything of a pointed nature, beyond this lecture on the Constitution, it seemed to me then, and in my mind is now confirmed, that the President approved the offensive publication which was the basis of my inquiry. This I stated in another note.

The answer of the President to this note, which he now thinks was "in a personal and friendly vein," still failed utterly to deny or affirm whether recommendations by the Virginia Senators were to be subject to the veto of the Governor of the State. True, I was told to go ahead in the usual way; but the President added that he would reserve the right to consult "Nancy Astor, the Duchess of Windsor, the WPA, a Virginia moonshiner, Governor Price or Charlie McCarthy." I cheerfully absolve Charlie McCarthy from giving the advice designed to discredit the Virginia Senators, and the record shows that none of the persons named was consulted except Price.

The President, indulging in this trivial evasion and having disdained a frank answer to my simple question as to whether he proposed to subject the recommendations of the Virginia Senators to the veto power alleged to have been delegated to Governor Price, my colleague and I hesitated to make any suggestions at all. We did not do so until specifically asked by the Department of Justice to send in a nomination at once, as it was desired to submit the name to the Senate for confirmation before adjournment.

We desired to present the name of former Governor George C. Peery, but I was told by the President he would not appoint a man over sixty years of age. By the Attorney General I was urgently advised to name a man between forty and fifty years of age, with prospect of long service. Incidentally, this only piece of advice by the Department of Justice was totally disregarded in the nomination made by the President.

The Senators prevailed on Judge A. C. Buchanan, forty-eight years old, of the Virginia Circuit Court, to permit the use of his name, and also on Frank Tavenner, forty-three years old, an assistant United States District Attorney, saying that either would be acceptable to the Virginia Senators. Can any human being conjecture why any one or the other of these men was not appointed, except that the Governor of Virginia, in conjunction with the only hostile Congressman of the six whose districts are embraced in the Western Judicial District, were promised the appointment regardless of the Senators and with the ill-disguised purpose to discredit them?

Tavenner is one of the brightest young lawyers in the Western Judicial District, of fine antecedents and himself a splendid character, with useful experience in Federal court practice. He was indorsed by every Bar Association in the second largest Congressional district of the State.

Judge A. C. Buchanan is a notable character on the bench and Supreme Court records attest that he is incomparably superior in legal knowledge to the nominee rejected by the Senate. Time and time again, as I pointed out to the Senate Judiciary Committee, the State Supreme Court had adopted Buchanan's opinions textually in important cases as its own.

Some years ago, when it was thought desirable to revise the State's judicial procedure, Buchanan was by the Supreme Court put on the judicial council to do this work. There is no man in Virginia, on or off the bench, who stands higher in reputation for probity and learning.

Although petitions for the President's nominee were circulated through the Congressional district before the ink was dry on the bill creating this judgeship, scores of lawyers indorsed Buchanan when he was reluctantly induced by the Virginia Senators to permit the use of his name. Every lawyer of his circuit indorsed him and lawyers in every county of his Congressional district. George Peery, Governor until last January; the presidents of outstanding colleges and universities, judges on the bench, members of the General Assembly as well as many men of character and great worth, approved the recommendations of the two Senators.

What objection was there to his appointment except that he had been recommended by the two Virginia Senators, charged by the Constitution with advising and consenting to such Federal appointments?

Did the President ever open his lips or communicate directly or indirectly with either of the Virginia Senators concerning their recommendations for the judgeship? He did not. Did his Department of Justice discuss with them in any wise the relative fitness of the six applicants for the position? It did not.

Was not Judge Roberts promptly brought to Washington for a conference? I am reliably told he was. Was any one of the other six persons mentioned for the judgeship brought to Washington or communicated with in any respect? Not one of them, I am told. Governor Price's own testimony, of official record, shows an admission that he was called over long-distance phone by the Department of Justice and asked his opinion of Roberts. Was he asked his opinion of Buchanan or Tavenner, or any other one of the six persons mentioned for the judgeship? He was not.

Was Governor Peery, four years ago, asked about the qualifications of Judge Pollard for the Eastern District of Virginia? He was not, nor, in my belief, was any other Governor since the foundation of the State invited to project himself into a scheme to "purge" the two United States Senators from a State by practically vetoing their recommendations for executive appointment.

Before the Judiciary Committee, I ventured the opinion that the Attorney General "never had the slightest idea of giving consideration to the recommendations of the two Virginia Senators because the Governor of Virginia had been promised the right to veto on nominations that they made."

The President says neither of these statements is true; but, with as much deference as the occasion requires, I believe the record demonstrates that both statements are true. If the Attorney General had any such intention, he never made the slightest effort to carry it into effect, not even the common courtesy of communicating with either United States Senator on the subject.

If the President did not delegate the veto power on Senatorial nominations to the Governor of Virginia, why did not the latter deny the offensive assertion published in all Virginia papers and by nearly all of them condemned, and why should the President of the United States have declined to answer a simple question propounded to him by a United States Senator for whom he had repeatedly professed friendship?

Governor Price, as may be seen from the stenographic report of the proceedings before the Senate Judiciary Committee, virtually, if inadvertently, admitted he had been given the privilege of vetoing Senatorial nominations when he said: "It was an empty honor. All the patronage had been distributed."

What was an "empty honor"? Why, of course, the delegated power to veto Senatorial recommendations. And why was not the privilege immediately exercised?

Governor Price says because the Federal patronage had already been distributed; but he failed to say he immediately projected himself into the matter of Federal appointments by trying to make the officials renominated by the Senators understand that his indorsement was essential. And his chief newspaper advocates boasted that the names of these four officials were held up by the Justice Department until Price gave his approval. This is a record of that point which I confidently submit to the public for its own intelligent conclusion.

The President in his unprecedented letter to his rejected nominee expresses the opinion that "every person of common sense knows" that "no Governor, no Senator has at any time had or ever will have the right of veto over Presidential nominations."

This is as inaccurate as many other statements and inferences made by the President are. Ninety-six Senators have the right of veto over Presidential nominations in specified cases, and on last Monday seventy-two of them against nine to the contrary exercised their right of veto on the President's nominee for judge of the Western District of Virginia, and I am assured that others would have done likewise had they been present at the vote.

But, of course, persons of common sense or uncommon sense will readily understand that the Virginia Senators were not primarily discussing veto by the Governor of "Presidential nominations." We were discussing the delegated power of the President's political vice-regent in Virginia to veto Senatorial nominations, exercised so conclusively in the case of Judge Buchanan and Frank Tavenner.

The most extraordinary statement in the President's lament to his rejected nominee is contained in the forty-fifth of his forty-six paragraphs. He states that the Senators from Virginia have in effect said to the President: "We have nominated to you two candidates acceptable to us; you are hereby directed to nominate one of our two candidates; if you do not we will reject the nomination of anybody else selected by you, however fit he may be."

Of course, everybody knows that this implication has not the shadow of fact to support it. The Virginia Senators neither said nor intimated anything of the kind and in making such a statement the President must have been actuated by a vastly greater measure of anger than he was pleased to ascribe to me.

As the record shows, his Department of Justice asked the two Virginia Senators for a recommendation. For years this courtesy has prevailed, and a reading of the debates shows that the writers of the Constitution intended it to be perpetual. Complying with the request, the Virginia Senators named two men against whose eminent capabilities and character no man has dared utter a word.

The President not only ignored the recommendations of these men, but did not extend to the two Virginia Senators the common courtesy of discussing with them the appointment of a Federal judge in their State.

We were prepared to accept any capable man who was not deliberately intended to be offensive to us, by himself completely ignoring us and willingly making himself the beneficiary of an attempt to dishonor us in our State and among our colleagues. The Virginia Senators are still perfectly willing to accept any capable nominee of the President who is not willing to concede to the Governor of Virginia or a bitterly hostile Congressman the right to veto suggestions by the Senators of men of the highest character and capability.

This is no fight for patronage. I do not care a tinker's dam for patronage. I do not recall that I ever met Judge Buchanan. I do not know, nor have I ever inquired, whether or not he approved my course in the Senate. I inferred his appointment would not get either Senator a vote he would not receive anyhow, because I know Buchanan has too much character and too great a sense of propriety to be a judicial "sniper" or to permit politics of any description to enter his court.

I was looking for a judge, not for a job. I was not seeking a man under my political patronage, nor one under the patronage of any politician.

Buchanan would have been an ornament to the Federal bench, as he has been to that of the State, and it is to be deplored from every point of view that he should have been rejected by the appointive power merely through a desire to "purge" the junior Senator next year and the senior Senator of Virginia later should I live longer than the intriguers hope.

Chapter XIV

LEGISLATIVE ORGANIZATION AND PROCEDURE

No. 47

[ALTHOUGH the advantages of a legislature in which responsibility is centered in a single house are, for the most part, undoubted, the American states with but one exception follow the bicameral principle. The original reasons for the establishment of bicameral legislative bodies in the United States are relatively easy to discover. Our federal Congress followed the two-house plan for several reasons. The framers of the Constitution had the model of the British Parliament before them, and they were faced with the problem of reconciling the views of those who believed the new Congress should represent states with the beliefs of others who felt that it should represent groups of persons. Furthermore their lack of confidence in the full democratic process led them to erect a second chamber which could check the feared excesses of the more representative house.

These same factors were influential in the original adoption of the bicameral system for state legislatures. The early state constitution makers had both the British Parliament and the new Federal Congress to imitate. They too had to reconcile opposing views of representation. They also had a desire to check the more popularly elected house by a second chamber, chosen by a more restricted electorate. To-day, although most of the reasons for the adoption of the bicameral system have disappeared in our states, the structure still stands. Cities in the United States, having sensed this change in basic conditions, have reorganized, with but few exceptions, their legislative bodies in accordance with the unicameral principle.

Students of American government must understand not only the bases upon which the bicameral-unicameral argument rests but also the full theoretical implications of both systems. The following selection by a distinguished American political scientist offers an exceptionally penetrating insight into these theoretical factors.]

A COMPARISON OF THE BICAMERAL AND UNICAMERAL SYSTEMS [1]

by W. F. Willoughby

ALTHOUGH, as has been shown, the general adoption by states of the bicameral legislative system has been due to historical accident, to the necessity believed to exist for meeting certain special conditions, or to a mere copying of existing institutions, rather than to a reasoned belief in its superiority as an instrument of legislation, there is nevertheless a strong body of opinion that this system has certain intrinsic merits which, apart from all other considerations, justify its employment.

As a preliminary to a consideration of the extent to which this opinion has a sound basis of fact, it is desirable first to point out what are the undoubted advantages of the unicameral system. Briefly to recapitulate them, they are: it is simple; it entails less expense in its operation; it permits of expeditious action; it furnishes the means for a direct, authoritative representation of the electorate; and that, under it, responsibility for action is definitely located. To these may be added the fact that it represents the system generally adopted in making provision for the exercise of other governmental powers, and that it is the one invariably employed by private corporations in making provision for the exercise of general direction and rule-making powers. In marked contrast with this, the bicameral system is one which is complicated and entails additional expense. It leads to delay in action. Two separate bodies have to be brought into accord before any action can be taken. In many cases this means that proposed action will be defeated, while, in almost all cases, the result is a compromise. And, finally, it has the serious disadvantage that, under it, responsibility is divided.

As regards these relative advantages and disadvantages of the two systems there can be, and is, no question. What then are the advantages claimed for the bicameral system that would lead to its being preferred to the unicameral system. Generally speaking, they are that such a system compels delay and deliberation; it makes it impossible for a legislature to be swept from its feet by a sudden wave of unreasoning emotion; it ensures that opportunity will always be given for a sober second thought; it ensures that measures, before their adoption, will undergo a careful revision; and

---

[1] W. F. Willoughby, *Principles of Legislative Organization and Administration* (Washington, D. C.: The Brookings Institution, 1934), pp. 222-234. Reprinted by permission of The Brookings Institution.

that it furnishes a means of preventing the legislature from being dominated by a single city or metropolitan area embracing a majority or a
large proportion of the population of the state.

All of these are, undoubtedly, desirable ends. It remains, however, to
be considered whether the bicameral system, as it obtains in modern states,
and particularly in the United States, is so devised as effectively to achieve
these ends; whether adequate means for securing them are not already provided by other features of the political machinery; whether these ends are
not more than offset by the disadvantages that have been pointed out, and
which are inherent in the system; whether these ends are, in fact, achieved
by the system in practical operation; and whether, even if they are, the
system does not give rise to other difficulties in the operation of the political system which more than counterbalance the advantages that the system
is supposed to afford.

As regards the first of these functions, it has already been pointed out
that, whatever may have been true in the past, the bicameral system as it
now exists, in both the national government and those of the states, no
longer is so constituted as to give separate representation to different interests; nor is it any longer the desire of the American people that special
provision should be made in this way for the representation and protection
of property rights. Such protection, it is believed, and properly so, is
afforded by the numerous safeguards set up in our constitutional documents
such as those which prohibit the taking of property without due compensation, the requirement of due process, the prohibition of bills of attainder
and the like, and the provision for an independent judiciary.

Turning now to a consideration of the second important function that a
second chamber is supposed to perform, namely, that of acting as a brake
or curb upon democracy, there can be no doubt but that it does act in this
way, since anything that makes more difficult the carrying out of the popular will cannot but have this effect. It is more than a question, however,
whether in so doing, it renders a valuable service. When our government
was first established popular government as applied to any large body of
people was in the nature of an experiment and it was but reasonable that
serious apprehensions should exist as to how it might operate in practice
if adequate safeguards against an abuse of powers were not provided. This
system, however, has not justified itself upon that ground. If our political
system is open to criticism from this standpoint, it is to be found in the
difficulty that exists in giving expression to the popular will rather than in
making it possible for such will to find too free expression. In considering
this matter it is important to realize that a profound transformation has
taken place with respect to the demands made upon governments. The old

belief that that government is best which governs least has long passed away. The requirements of the present time are, not so much the prevention of unwise action, as the securing of wise action. The harm that may be done by unwise action is more than outweighed by the damage that may result from failure, or delay in, taking action that is urgently needed. One of the most significant political developments of recent times is the disrepute into which the parliamentary system in European countries has fallen and the constant criticism that is made of our own legislative bodies. This disrepute is due in no small degree to the dilatoriness with which legislative bodies respond to popular demands.

It is important to note that, in our own system at least, the second chamber does not constitute the only means available for the prevention of undesirable action. There exists, in the first place, the great safeguard against an abuse of powers resulting from the numerous constitutional limitations upon the powers of our legislative bodies, limitations which exist to a like extent in no other political system. Secondly, and of still greater importance, is that characteristic feature of our legislative system which requires that all acts of legislation, before becoming effective, must be submitted to the executive for his approval. As regards the importance of this method of preventing unwise legislation, in comparison with that provided by the provision that the acts of one chamber must be ratified by another, Mr. Colvin, who made an exceptionally careful study of the working of the bicameral system in the State of New York, has the following to say:

> A comparison of the bills checked by the executive with those checked by the second house shows that the quality of the check exercised by the governor was far superior. Many of the bills defeated in the second house, especially those defeated by the assembly, suggested a hit-or-miss method of dealing with the bills and that there was little discrimination between those which passed and those which were left, other than that they were subject chiefly to the discrimination measured by the political influence behind them. On the other hand, the check of the governor showed a careful choice and a comprehensive grasp of the needs of the State, and a wise elimination of the undesirable and unnecessary, hasty, or ill-considered bills. . . . There seems to have come to be a dependence upon the governor to act as an efficient check rather than upon the second house.

That these two features greatly weaken, if they do not entirely do away with the need for a second chamber as a brake upon legislative action can hardly be questioned.

As regards the argument that a second chamber furnishes the means for securing a careful revision of legislative proposals as first formulated careful examination of the system, as it actually exists and operates, shows that the advantage thus claimed is more theoretical than actual. In the first place, it must be evident that, if a second chamber is really to perform this function, it should be specially constituted with this end in view. Preferably, its members should be selected in some manner other than that obtaining for the selection of the members of the lower house, the emphasis being laid on securing members of high technical qualifications rather than the giving expression to the representative principle, to the end, not merely of securing greater competence in the exercise of the revising function, but of putting such members in a position where their action will be determined by the technical merits of the propositions coming before them rather than by purely political, party considerations. No such special qualifications, however, are provided for in the United States. The members of both houses are selected in practically the same manner; they have the same representative character; they are equally dominated by political considerations, and there is no assurance that members of the upper house will be more technically qualified or be actuated by higher motives than those of the lower chambers.

Secondly, it should be noted that this need for one chamber to exercise a revising function with respect to the acts of the other is not so great as at first thought might appear. As has elsewhere been pointed out, the tendency is more and more for all important general legislative proposals to originate with the administration where they receive careful consideration both as regards their substantive character and their technical formulation. In the federal government at least, it is, moreover, the general practice to have all bills affecting governmental action in any way referred to the proper administrative authority for its consideration and recommendation. As a result of these two practices, all bills of real general importance already undergo the examination and scrutiny of two independent agencies.

Finally, it should be observed that the system of having the acts of one chamber reviewed by another has the serious defect of tending to induce lack of care on the part of the chamber first acting, and to lead it to pass bills that it would not pass if it knew that its action would be final. Often a chamber will shirk the duty of making needed changes in a pending bill on the ground that it is not necessary to do so since such changes can be made in the other house. In other cases, the responsibility for the defeat of an undesirable measure is shifted to the other chamber.

There remains for consideration the final argument brought forward in favor of the bicameral system that, through it, means are provided for meeting the special problem of preventing the legislature from being dominated by a single large city or metropolitan area containing a majority or a large proportion of the state's population. Undoubtedly, provision for a second chamber can be made to serve this purpose, but the complicating of the legislative structure and the legislative process in this way would seem to be an excessive price to pay for achieving this end, especially in view of the fact that it can be equally well attained by so apportioning representation in a single chamber among the political subdivisions of the state as to prevent any one city or metropolitan area from having a majority or an undue proportion of the total representation provided for. That action in this way is quite possible is demonstrated by the fact, as is later pointed out in our special discussion of the problem of apportionment, that, in practically all states having a city or metropolitan area embracing a majority or a large part of the population of the state, the principle of apportioning representatives in the lower house according to population is departed from, and such areas are given a smaller representation than they would have were strict adherence had to this basis of representation.

Before leaving this subject of the relative merits and demerits of the two systems, a further feature of the bicameral system which, in practice, has produced results far from satisfactory, should be commented upon. An essential feature of the bicameral system is that means shall be provided by which differences arising between the two houses with respect to legislation may be adjusted. In the United States, as is elsewhere pointed out in our consideration of the problem of the organization and procedure of legislative bodies, this means is provided by the setting up of what are known as conference committees; that is, committees composed of representatives of the two houses to which bills as passed by them are referred for the purpose of recasting in a form which will meet the approval of both houses. An essential feature of this system is that the measures as so redrafted must be either accepted or rejected by the two houses substantially without modification. This not only means that the character of much of the important legislation enacted is determined by these committees, but that other conditions of a highly undesirable character are set up. The defective working of this system is pointed out in a forcible way in the following quotation from a contribution to the *New York Times* of January 28, 1923, by one who has had exceptional opportunities to observe them. Writing under the title of "One Branch Legislature for States Would Improve Results," Senator George W. Norris, of Nebraska, says:

> In every legislature composed of two branches . . . the only thing that emerges from the conference is the final agreement. The individual legislator must then vote upon a conference report without any opportunity of expressing by his vote his opposition to anything that the bill in this form contains.

The citizen is deprived entirely of an opportunity to pass a just and fair judgment upon the result. In conference provisions are often put in and other provisions taken out, where an entirely different result would be obtained if the action took place in the open, where a record vote could be had upon all provisions of the bill. . . . Experience has shown that it is within the privacy of the conference committee room that jokers get into legislation, and that provisions of law demanded even by a majority of both branches of the legislature are sometimes not included in the finished product. . . . It very often happens that the most important features of legislation are put into the bills while they are being thus considered. Members of conference committees are often compelled to surrender on important items where no surrender would be even demanded if consideration of the legislation were in the open where a public record could be had of the proceedings. When the bill emerges from conference it is not then subject to amendment. It must be accepted or rejected as a whole. The conference is held in secret. There is no record vote on any proposition decided at the conference. . . .

A one-branch legislature would obviate all these difficulties. There would be no way for any member of the legislature to conceal his opposition upon any legislative proposition that comes before the body. The citizen would be able to absolutely and without difficulty place responsibility where it properly belonged for every act of the legislature. It would thus be easy to punish those whose records are unsatisfactory and to reward those whose services are meritorious.

There remains yet another objection of a practical character that can be raised against the bicameral system. The bicameral system came into existence before the development of political parties in the modern sense. This is true of the United States as well as of England where it took its rise. With the rise of the party system, an entirely new element was injected into the problem of legislation. Opinion is now fairly unanimous that this system gives its best results where what is known as party government obtains, that is, where responsibility for action can be definitely placed upon the party commanding the majority support of the people. Even in a state having the responsible type of government, the effective operation of such a system is seriously interfered with where the legislature consists of two houses, one of which is not directly representative of, and responsible to, the electorate. In England, this difficulty was only in part met by the development of the principle that majority support in the lower house alone should determine the continuance in power of a ministry representing the majority party, since, under that system, it was still possible for the upper house to prevent such majority party from having its way. It was finally overcome only by the passage of the Parliament Act of 1911, which, in effect, abolished the bicameral system, though it retained the upper house as an organ for the exercise of what is in effect a qualified veto power. In France, where no such modification of the bicameral principle has been effected, the complications introduced into the working of party government are constantly in evidence.

It is when one turns to the United States, however, that the extent to which the effective working of the system of party government is interfered with by the existence of two co-ordinate branches of the legislature is most apparent. As is well known, under our system of government, the contingency that the two houses of the legislature may be of different political complexion is not always present but is in fact of frequent occurrence. When this is the case, it is impossible for the principle of party government to find proper expression, and when party differences and animosities are acute it may result in a practical deadlock so far as the enactment of legislation of general importance is concerned. At best, it means that the whole process of legislation is slowed down and that much of the legislation that is enacted will be of a compromise character thoroughly satisfactory to no one. That such a condition constitutes a serious defect in our political system can scarcely be doubted. That it exists is wholly due to the existence of the bicameral system, and its correction is only to be found in the abolition of that system or its modification in such a way as will destroy the position of the upper house as co-ordinate with the lower house.

The foregoing critical study of the bicameral system has, it is believed, established, not only the disadvantages inherent in that system, but the further fact that the particular objects sought by its adoption, are either not achieved, or are amply provided for by other features of our political system. This being so, the conclusion inevitably follows that the system is one that should only be adopted where very special conditions exist rendering it employment desirable. No such conditions exist in the case of our states. Few things, in the opinion of the writer, would contribute more to the improvement of the whole system of state administration than the abolition of this system and the substitution in its place of a single chamber with a comparatively restricted membership. By such action the structure of government would be materially simplified, responsibility for action would be more definitely located, the establishment of effective cooperative relations between the legislature and executive would be rendered easier, and the whole process of legislation would be facilitated and made more responsive to public opinion. Added advantages would be a reduction in the cost of government and an increased probability of securing as legislators those persons who are best fitted to perform the duties of that office. One of the gravest criticisms of our state legislatures, as they now exist, is the mediocre character of their memberships. Their failure to attract to themselves persons who, as the result of their personal attainments or experience in other walks of life, are specially qualified to participate in the conduct of public affairs, is undoubtedly due in part to the difficulties that such persons would encounter in making their influence felt under conditions now existing where responsibility for action is so widely diffused. With a single chamber of comparatively small size, the post of legislator would become one of greatly enhanced power and prestige, and, as such, could not fail to make a greater appeal to men of ability, and a knowledge of this changed condition on the part of the electorate could not but tend to make it exercise greater discrimination in selecting its representatives.

In thus arguing for the abolition by the states of their bicameral systems, the writer voices the conclusions that have been reached by those students of political science who have given special attention to the problems of state government. Thus the distinguished group of scholars which cooperated under the auspices of the National Municipal League in the drafting of a model state constitution, made the unicameral chamber the central feature of their recommendations regarding the set-up of the legislative branch. Both on account of the weight of the authority carried by them, and because they summarize in an exceptionally forcible way the considerations previously presented, the comments of the committee upon this feature of their recommendations are here reproduced:

The committee believes that a single body, chosen by proportional representation and not too large in number, will be at once more representative and efficient than the present two-chamber system. The old arguments for two houses claim that they are more representative and more deliberative than a single body can be. But state senators are now chosen in the same manner as state assemblies. The senatorial district may be larger but the qualifications and weight of individual voters are the same in both districts. They represent the same people in the same way as the lower house does. As long as European nations accepted an aristocracy of higher degree than the multitude there was a reason for an upper chamber. But the many now no longer concede special privileges to the few; and the upper house, although perhaps retained in law, has abroad been rendered almost impotent in fact. The state senators likewise are not now regarded as rational checks upon legislation. Doubtless they increase the effort necessary to pass legislation just as a rough road impedes the passage of an automobile, but mere obstruction is not a virtue. Intelligent obstruction may be, but the upper house rarely renders such obstruction because it is merely a pocket edition of the lower house.

A division of power between the two houses leads to a division of responsibility, to political trades, to "passing the buck." Measures often pass one house with the understanding that they will be killed in the other and from such transactions the people get a false impression as to the checking influence of the bicameral system. As former Governor Hodge of Kansas said: "About the only purpose I have ever been able to see for the two-house system is that it enables a legislator to fool his constituents by getting a measure demanded or promised them through his branch of the legislature and then using every effort to have it killed in the other branch."

A distinct advantage of the single-chamber system is the encouragement that it affords to the development of public, responsible leadership within the legislature, and to closer cooperation between the governor and the legislature. We are all familiar with the situation which arises when the two houses are of different political complexions, or when the governor and a branch of the legislature are at odds. And yet the governor by reason of his grip on the administration and his knowledge of the working of law is naturally the one person whose work the legislature should be able to enquire into with the greatest ease. The governor should be closer to the legislature, both as a leader and as a servant, but this can only come about if there is real centralization of authority within a well organized and smoothly running body. The voters can keep track of such a legislature. We mistrust our present legislatures because they so easily slip out of our grasp.

In view of these manifest advantages of the unicameral over the bicameral legislature, it is rather remarkable that proposals looking to the changing from the latter to the former have made so little headway in the various conventions in recent years for the revision of the constitutions of the states. The only explanation of this is to be found in the inherent conservativeness of the American people in political matters. There is great reluctance to depart from any long established practice. Should one state however, make the break and go over to the new system of a single chamber it might easily result that others would speedily follow the example. [Since this was written one state, Nebraska, has established a unicameral legislature.] It is not so long ago that the bicameral system was the prevailing one in providing for the exercise of the ordinance-making, fund-raising, and fund-granting power of our municipalities. With the movement once started for the substitution of the unicameral system, the change over to this system took place with great rapidity until at the present time the bicameral system is found in few of these governments.

No. 48

[IF the stockholders of a railroad company believed that the members of the board of directors were unqualified to hold that office or incapable of making wise decisions, they probably would not attempt to solve their problems by ordering the board to meet only once a year for a half-hour session. More likely they would inquire into the factors that gave them unqualified men, or into the reasons why these men could not act with competence. But in dealing with their state legislatures, the American people have done exactly what the railroad stockholders would not do. Believing that legislatures make mistakes and that legislators are not too well qualified to do their work, the American people have severely restricted the frequency and length of state legislative sessions.

This problem is primarily a problem of the states, as Congress now meets in annual sessions beginning January 3 each year—and each session may run until the following January 3—and city councils in our larger cities meet weekly or bi-weekly. Only the states adhere to the belief that we can get along without fairly frequent and extended sessions of the policy-determining branch of government. The problems raised and difficulties encountered because of this belief are the subject of the following article.]

PROBLEMS PECULIAR TO THE SHORT-SESSION LEGISLATURE [1]

by William E. Treadway

WHETHER the legislative session limited by organic law in frequency and duration should be abrogated in favor of one unlimited in times of convening and of indeterminate length, is a question wholly apart from this discussion. The short-session legislature, where it exists, is so firmly embedded in tradition and so generally accepted that to propose its abandonment at this time would be to precipitate a highly controversial debate. It will be assumed, therefore, that the constitutional limitations upon the legislative department of government in a number of states will continue. An effort will be made to point out some of the problems existing under such limitations, and to suggest their remedies where possible.

[1] William E. Treadway, "Problems Peculiar to the Short-Session Legislature," *The Annals* of the American Academy of Political and Social Science (January, 1938), Vol. 195, pp. 110-115. Reprinted by permission of the author and *The Annals* of the American Academy of Political and Social Science. Footnotes in the original article are omitted here.

Indiana is fairly typical of the states having short-session legislatures and for reasons of familiarity and convenience will be drawn upon for occasional illustrations. Prior to the constitutional convention of 1850 the Indiana Legislature had met annually, and the frequency of its meeting seems to have been one of the outstanding questions upon which delegates to the convention were elected. A proposal to limit the General Assembly to triennial instead of biennial sessions mustered a now surprising vote of 43 for the resolution to 83 negative votes. Only 5 of the 129 delegates voting upon the adoption of this section of the constitution favored a retention of annual sessions.

The successful argument advanced at the time was that the laws of the state had been continually fluctuating.

> The changes made were of such frequent occurrence that the people did not know what the laws were; and, of course, they could not be obeyed by men who did not know when they had violated them. That was impossible. And a further evil resulting from this continual change was, that they were not administered a sufficient length of time for the people to ascertain whether their effect was good or evil.

Section 9 of Article IV of the Constitution of Indiana as adopted in 1851 provides:

> The sessions of the General Assembly shall be held biennially at the capital of the state, commencing on the Thursday next after the first Monday of January. . . . But if, in the opinion of the governor, the public welfare shall require it, he may, at any time by proclamation, call a special session.

An amendment offered at the convention seeking to limit the matters to be considered at such special session to subjects specified by the governor in his proclamation was defeated.

Section 29 of the same Article limits the duration of regular sessions to a maximum of sixty-one days, and of special sessions to a maximum of forty days. There is no limitation upon the number or the frequency of special sessions, other than that their convening is only upon the call of the executive, and under such a constitutional arrangement it is conceivable that the legislature might remain in continuous session should a governor see fit to issue his proclamation prior to the constitutional adjournment. The experience of years, however, has demonstrated as strong a reluctance on the part of the executive to prolong the assembly as was shown in the convention. Hence, certain problems have arisen inherent in the short session.

A lack of continuity from session to session is one of the major problems. A heavy turnover in membership is noted at each assembly. New members constituted 62 per cent of the Indiana House of Representatives in 1935, and 43 per cent in 1937.

This enormous turnover is accounted for probably more by voluntary withdrawals than by primary and general election defeats. The short-session legislature is the one department of government to which no one can afford to devote himself exclusively and continuously. All members must, of necessity, have superior outside interests upon which to depend for a livelihood and to which they must direct their energy and thought during the time between sessions. The irritating interruption from the normal pursuits of professional and business men and the physical strain accompanying the short sesion are the reasons most frequently given for voluntary retirement. While a rapid turnover in the legislature may appear in keeping with democratic theory, in practice it will be seen that this phenomenon operates for inefficiency.

This disruption is most damaging within standing committees. The life of the committee is limited to that of the session. Experienced chairmen and committee members, if available, could give invaluable counsel upon numerous questions that recur at each succeeding session. Not infrequently, during a session an industrious committee may gather a wealth of information upon a subject of great public concern, only to have its knowledge dissipated for all practical purposes by a substantial if not complete change in personnel of the committee at the ensuing session.

This situation might be materially improved if such important committees as those upon the subjects of taxes and finance, judiciary, public safety, and interstate and Federal cooperation were empowered to meet from time to time, as their business requires, during the interim between sessions, and to maintain a continuous secretariat.

A single legislative council composed of representative members of the more important committees of the House and the Senate and supplemented by certain lay members having special knowledge of problems of government, is another possibility.

The experience in Indiana with special study commissions appointed at the close of one session with a mandate to report its findings at the beginning of the next has been disappointing. Selections to such committees have been made more upon the basis of geographical or political distribution than upon the personal fitness or the special interest of the appointees. The result has been a disorganized and unscientific attack upon the problems assigned. Such a commission appointed in 1935 spent considerable time in touring eastern states in a superficial "study" of tax laws. No analysis of comparative legislation was made, and as a result the commission was unable to make an intelligent report of its findings. Conversely, a similar delegation from an eastern legislature visited Indianapolis during the same year, and while it did actually publish a report, its findings disclosed that Indiana was operating successfully with the income from a 2 per cent sales tax, whereas Indiana has never had a sales tax. Except in a few isolated instances, it has been fairly well demonstrated that little value may be expected from such special commissions.

Possibly the greatest single problem presented by the short-session legislature is that of an economical and efficient use of the time allotted to lawmaking. Much of the physical and mental exhaustion which has been so inseparably associated with the closing days of the session could be alleviated and the chaos of adjournment avoided by a more orderly conduct of the assembly's affairs from the beginning.

As much as several days' time may be consumed at the start of a session in the matter of reorganization. The election of officers and the appointment of employees and committees cannot precede the opening of the session, constitutionally. However, with the more-and-more accepted theory of party responsibility, it is possible for the members-elect of the party naming the largest membership in a legislature to meet in advance of the constitutional day of opening and to complete the organization of each house in caucus, subject to a formal ratification on the first day, thus being prepared for normal functioning from the hour of convening.

With the typical legislature meeting a few weeks after an election, the membership of the house and of that part of the senate up for election cannot be known long in advance of the session to the members themselves or to others. While in theory the legislators arrive freshly instructed from the electorate, in reality there has been little opportunity for a mature consideration of desirable legislation in advance. Comparatively few members bring with them any bills prepared beforehand. Soon the congestion of the short session makes heavy demands upon the time of all. And while many legislators avail themselves of the facilities of legislative drafting bureaus during a session, the fact remains that a very considerable number of bills are prepared by outside interests, both public and private, and are introduced, in fact, by request. Thus many legislators suddenly find themselves the "authors" of measures which they had not the slightest idea of sponsoring, prior to the session. This accounts for the inability of so many to give an intelligent and satisfactory explanation of their bills on the floor.

A lack of time for the proper consideration of bills in committees is deplorable. A number of committees, by reason of the subjects with which they are concerned, are idle much of the time, and designations of membership thereon serve principally as handy vehicles in making committee assignments go the rounds. Other groups may be known, notoriously, as "graveyard" committees, to which measures are consigned with a tacit understanding that they are not to be reported upon. For the most part, the other committees are greatly overworked. It is not uncommon for some committees to have as many as fifty bills on hand for consideration.

A lack of some systematic arrangement for committee hearings is a cause of endless confusion. Rules ordinarily prohibit the meeting of committees during sessions. Announcements of meetings frequently are made just prior to a daily adjournment, and are often for an immediate convening of the committee without other notice to parties interested in bills to be considered. Some fairly important committees seldom, if ever, actually meet, the chairmen "explaining" such bills as are desired "out" to a majority of their committee members and filing their reports. Committee amendments are not frequent, and minority reports are rare except upon bills of highly controversial subjects. The pressure exerted upon committee chairmen to release or to hold bills during the short session might be compared to the display of conflicting interests in a football game with a limited time to go. A "pocketing" disposition of a bill by a chairman is made relatively easy by the excuse of lack of time for consideration. Motions to discharge one committee from further consideration of a bill, with a request that the bill be recommitted to another, are seldom heard.

Under the ordinary situation, only one typewritten copy of a bill is available for the study of an entire committee. To "save time" the bill is usually "explained" by its proponent. Unless the subject matter is such as to draw the attention of an adversely affected party, there is seldom anyone present to make any explanatory remarks in opposition.

A sufficient amount of time of a session should be definitely allocated for work in committees. Certainly every member of a committee should be furnished a copy of all bills under consideration. Without an opportunity for an actual study of bills in committee an intelligent report is impossible, and legislators in the short session must of physical necessity rely to a large extent upon committee reports in determining their votes.

In Indiana, a bill ordinarily is printed before being placed on second reading, and at no other time. As a result, by the time it is eligible for a vote upon final passage, the bill may contain far-reaching amendments that are not apparent on the members' printed copies. Upon third reading, the bill, as amended, is explained meagerly on the floor by its sponsor, who, under pressure of time if not also from a want of facts, may often preface his brief remarks by saying, "This bill merely provides for . . ." It would seem obvious that all amended bills should be reprinted as amended or that a rule should be adopted requiring all amendments not so printed to be read in full before such bill is placed upon its final passage. No member is in a position to cast an intelligent vote upon a measure which he has had no opportunity to read or to hear read in its final form, and such a change in rules would conserve the time of the conscientious and energetic member who makes an effort to inform himself upon amendments during the short session.

Bills are not actually read in full upon any one of the three "readings" required by the constitution. It would be physically impossible for most members to read and digest every bill up for consideration, as long as the volume of legislative business keeps its present stride. No limit is placed upon the number of bills that may be considered for final passage in one day. It is not unusual, toward the close of a session, for thirty or forty bills to be passed in a few hours. In fact, a member may often consider himself lucky to have thumbed through the sheaf of bills upon his desk and to have found his copy of the one under final consideration by the time the polling clerk calls his name.

During a day on which the legislative mill is geared to high speed, a great many bills may be passed "on faith." Confusion is generally apparent, with even veteran members striving with some difficulty to keep abreast of the day's rapid developments. Time and again during rapidly succeeding roll calls are heard the questions: "What are we voting on now?" "Is this bill all right?" "How should I vote on this bill?" At times the situation would furnish a most interesting laboratory study for the mob psychologist. Rumors may be the means of passing or killing some measures even after a roll call has been commenced. Anonymous whispers such as: "This is a bad bill," "This is a dangerous bill," or "This bill will bankrupt the taxpayer," have been known to kill many meritorious bills through a stampede of a sufficient number of uninformed, uninterested, or exhausted members; while a last-minute whisper of some word of popular appeal, similarly, has made possible the enactment of some questionable legislation.

This extremely chaotic condition would be greatly improved if an impartial, printed synopsis of every bill introduced were made available to all members as an additional service of the legislative bureau. Such a synopsis should be sufficiently concise to be readable, but at the same time sufficiently informative to convey the full import of the bill. This service could be rendered daily by a cumulative looseleaf system. A daily calendar might also be made available, showing the current status of every bill introduced, the committee action if any, and the legislative day upon which the bill will be open for amendment on second reading or for final passage on third reading.

Mutual "back-scratching" seems to be almost inevitable in the short session. But little business ordinarily is transacted during the first few weeks. The tendency is for bills to accumulate in committees and in the various channels of enactment. Short-session legislators are all conscious of the disastrous consequences of delay upon bills of their introduction. Usually by mid-session a wave of resentment on the part of all those having bills unacted upon has reached such proportions as to offer a potential threat of retaliation. The jam is then broken by a series of bargains and concessions, express or implied, and the race against time moves into the home stretch. This situation can best be remedied by a forceful demand from the chair for a prompt and routine expedition of business from the very beginning.

An attempt has been made in Indiana to ease the pressure of the closing days of the session by a rule requiring unanimous consent for the introduction of bills after the expiration of the first forty-five days. In operation, this rule has failed to accomplish its purpose. The member desiring to present a bill during the period covered by the rule merely asks consent of the house to introduce the measure, and no one ever voices objection.

Approximately one-third of the time of a lower house in each session is consumed in roll calls. The roll of the Indiana House of Representatives was called 518 times during the session of 1935. The usually estimated time for taking and verifying a roll call is twelve minutes, and the average legislative day is five and one-half hours in duration. Thus it will be seen that of the total of sixty-one days allotted by the constitution as a biennial season for lawmaking, which incidentally includes Sundays and two holidays, about nineteen legislative days were required for calling the roll.

Roll calls are not to be discouraged. They are much more satisfactory than a mere voice or division vote, and a roll call upon every step of the progress of important measures would tend to make of the legislature a more responsible body. Members frequently hesitate to demand a roll-call vote on a question of consequence, solely because of the time required in calling the roll.

In several states the roll-call problem seems to have been solved satisfactorily by the installation of mechanical voting devices. By means of electrical switches upon members' desks they are enabled to cast their votes simultaneously and with a minimum of confusion. The vote is displayed immediately upon an indicator in full view of the members, and at the same time is permanently recorded by means of a photostatic impression or by perforation upon a specially designed ballot. The complaint of frequent errors in the hasty recording of oral votes by clerks is overcome by mechanical precision. In Wisconsin and Virginia, with lower houses identical in size to that of Indiana, a complete roll call is now taken and recorded within one minute by mechanized voting. Thus science now makes available the use of several additional legislative days for committee study and for a more intelligent consideration of proposed legislation. The adoption of such a device should expedite business to a point where the frenzy of the last days could be avoided and perhaps even an earlier adjournment could be made possible.

An effort has been made herein to paint an authentic picture of the short session with some of its more apparent problems. A pessimistic note has not been intended. The short-session legislature is a time-honored institution in state government and is likely to continue in substantially its present constitutional form for some time. However, a frank consideration of its shortcomings as they exist will convince the observer that a correction of the two major problems, that of a lack of continuity between sessions and that of an economical and efficient use of the limited time within sessions, should be expected to result in fewer and better laws.

No. 49

[THE apportionment of representatives to a legislative body has always been a difficult and perplexing legal and political problem. Not only is there the initial difficulty of fairly determining the number of representatives each group or unit is to have but also there is the political problem of securing legislative assent to a new apportionment scheme which, by definition, will alter the status quo and will favor some political or economic group at the expense of another

Students of American government are familiar with this problem as it exists with reference to the national Congress; the now well-known act of 1929 attempted to obtain a rational and fairly permanent solution to the difficulties raised by the question of reapportionment. The problems of apportionment in state legislatures, however, are not as familiar to students of American government, yet they have a double significance. First, the fair or unfair solution of these problems bears directly upon the representative character of the state legislature insofar as the state itself is concerned. Second, the solution of state apportionment problems affects the national Congress. Once Congress determines the number of representatives that each state is to have, it is the task of the state legislature to apply that apportionment to the state by a redistricting measure. If that legislature itself over-represents one group it is more than likely that this one-sided emphasis will be reflected in any act realigning Congressional districts.

The following article by Professor David O. Walter is concerned with the underlying factors in state legislative reapportionment. The urban-rural conflict which he discusses not only exists in all of our states but also affects the whole course of policy making by state legislatures.]

REAPPORTIONMENT AND URBAN REPRESENTATION [1]

by David O. Walter

ONE of the traditional features of the American state constitutions is a provision for periodical rearrangements of legislative districts in order to maintain equality of representation in spite of a changing population. The theory of representation embodied in these provisions was expressed by Judge Willis in *Stiglitz* v. *Schardien,* as follows:

> Equality of representation in the law-making tax-levying bodies is a fundamental requisite of a free government, and no unbiased, fair, or just man has any right to claim a greater share of the voting power of the people than is granted to every other man similarly situated. It is vain for the people to hope for reforms of abuses or righteous results in legislation if the legislative bodies are not fairly representative of the spirit, purpose, and will of all the people, without discrimination.

To carry out this theory, there are inserted in the constitutions various limitations on the legislature to prevent gerrymandering or inequalities. Except for New Hampshire, where representation in the upper house is based on the amount of direct taxes paid in the senatorial districts, representation in the senates is usually on the basis of population, subject to various limitations. In twenty-one states the constitutions specifically provide for a straight population basis; eleven others modify this, slightly, by excluding aliens or untaxed Indians or by a progressive ratio; three others use legal voters and two use adult males as the basis. In most of the consti-

[1] David O. Walter, "Reapportionment and Urban Representation," *The Annals* of the American Academy of Political and Social Science (January, 1938), Vol. 195, pp. 11-20. Reprinted by permission of the author and *The Annals* of the American Academy of Political and Social Science. Several tables included in the original article have not been reprinted here. The footnotes also are omitted.

tutions there are provisions to prevent gerrymandering: twenty-seven provide for contiguous territory in districts; nine specify compactness; eighteen particularly require equality, and in others equality is implied from other provisions; six provide that no county shall be divided, and fourteen that no county shall be divided except to form two or more districts wholly within the county; eight others have prohibitions against dividing other areas of government.

In regard to the lower house, eighteen states provide a strict population basis for representation; nine limit this by a progressive ratio; eight others make some unimportant exclusions; two base representation on adult males, two on legal voters, and one on votes cast for governor. As in the case of the senate, population is implied as the basis where there are no contrary provisions. There are similar protections against gerrymandering.

The courts have consistently enforced such limitations. In no state has the court denied that it has the power to review on the ground of failure to observe the constitutional limitations, such legislative action or the districtings by county boards. In twenty-two states the courts have exercised the power, or specifically stated that they have the power, to review such acts on the question of equality. There have been twenty-five cases in which the courts have so acted: in eight of these the acts were upheld; in seventeen they were invalidated. Since the general principles were laid down in cases decided between 1890 and 1900 there have been no changes in doctrine, but a few cases every decade call for the application of those principles.

In general, the courts distinguish between two types of constitutional limitations: mandatory and discretionary. In the first class are such provisions as that no county shall be divided, that two or more counties in a district shall be contiguous, and that the number of legislators shall not exceed the constitutional maximum. In the latter class, in which the courts concede considerable leeway to the apportioning agency, are the requirements of equality (usually, "as nearly as may be") and of compactness (usually, "so far as practicable"). The principle in deciding these cases is simple—the act must be so arbitrary as to be unreasonable before the courts will invalidate it. As in other fields of constitutional jurisprudence, such a test leaves room for dissent. There are variations, not only as between courts of various states but also within one state at different times, as to the range of discretion permitted to the redistricting agency.

One weakness of judicial control is that the court cannot assure an entirely equitable apportionment, but must leave the initiative to the legislative body. Hence when the districting of Suffolk County came up to the

Massachusetts court for the third time within a year, it was permitted to stand, with the unenthusiastic comment:

> With some hesitation we are brought to the conclusion that the inequalities of voting power between the several districts . . . are not quite so great and the means for avoiding them not quite so clear as to leave fair-minded men in no reasonable doubt that there is a grave and unnecessary inequality between the different districts.

More serious limitations on the theory of equality are to be found in the constitutions themselves, especially in the guarantees of representation by counties, applying to both houses. In twenty states the composition of the senate favors the less populous areas: in Arizona, Delaware, and Mississippi the apportionment is set out specifically in the constitution; in four others, the constitution says there shall be one senator from each county; to protect the rural areas, four provide for at least one senator per county; to restrict the more densely populated areas, seven provide that there shall be not more than one per county. In addition, California, New York, Pennsylvania, and Rhode Island have other definite restrictions.

Even more in the case of the lower houses, equality is subordinated to other constitutional provisions, so that in twenty-seven states the less populous areas are favored. The most common feature, found in nineteen states, is the guarantee of at least one representative per county. In eight other states, Texas just having been added to the list in 1936, other types of restriction on the populous areas are found, notably through the New England traditional representation of towns.

In spite of the notorious examples of Illinois and New York, it is not generally realized that a more frequent cause of inequalities than any constitutional restrictions is the inaction of the legislature, the customary agency for reapportionment. Although most of the constitutions provide for an apportionment and districting at least after every Federal census and sometimes after a state census, these provisions are frequently ignored. The state census may not be taken, or if taken, it and the Federal census may be disregarded. Most of the states have apportioned one or both houses since the 1930 census, although, as in the case of the California Senate, this may be merely repetition of the existing arrangement, rather than a reorganization. But eleven states have failed to reapportion since then, eight others have failed to act since the 1920 census, and there are six cases where the apportionment is from thirty-five to forty-five years old, because of failure of the legislature to act.

There are inequalities in senate districts in twenty-six states due primarily to legislative inaction, in contrast to only fifteen states where the constitutional provisions are primarily responsible for the inequalities. Similarly as to representative districts: in twenty-two states noticeable inequalities are due mainly to legislative action or inaction, and in only fourteen states are they due mainly to constitutional limitations.

Where the duty of reapportionment is vested in the legislative body itself, there is no way of compelling action. Under the doctrine of the separation of powers the courts cannot interfere to force the legislature to perform a legislative duty, even if that performance is required by the constitution. In a series of cases brought by John B. Fergus and John W. Keogh during the last ten years directly on this point, the Illinois and Federal courts have consistently refused to reach the same result indirectly, whether by restraining payment of salaries of the legislators, by declaring invalid laws passed by a legislature which had not been reapportioned, by quo warranto proceedings against the senators and representatives, or in any other way.

It is obvious that inequality among legislative districts is the rule rather than the exception, but the question arises as to what effect this has beyond mere lack of consistency in adhering to the principle of equal representation. In Pennsylvania, the senator from the Third District (Philadelphia) represents 95,843 people, and the one from the Fourth District (Philadelphia) represents 411,636. In New York, the senators from Manhattan represent on an average 207,479 people; those from Queens, 534,565. This is a matter of immediate concern to the politicians in these districts, but is of relatively remote concern to the public at large. It is seldom that a legislative proposal of public importance will affect one ward of a city favorably and another unfavorably; both legislators will vote alike on matters affecting the city voters. What is important is the under-representation of aggregates —of a group of correlated interests. The most significant general line of demarcation between interests in American state politics has been the cleavage between country and city. Whatever the future of class politics may be, it is certain to be modified by this older political division.

The result of the combination of constitutional provisions and legislative failure to reapportion is a general over-representation of the less populous areas, the rural districts, as compared with the urban districts. Although in twenty-one states the urban population is now in a majority, in only eleven of them can that majority control the legislature. It happens that in the ten others the rural dominance is due primarily to constitutional restrictions rather than to obsolete apportionments; but that is not true of the general over-representation of rural areas.

This over-representation is reflected in an under-representation of some of the metropolitan cities, due in some cases to constitutional restrictions and in others to legislative action. In the state senates, the constitutions discriminate noticeably against Atlanta, Baltimore, Los Angeles, New York, Portland, Providence, San Francisco, and Wilmington. To these, legislative apportionments add Chicago, Detroit, Minneapolis, St. Louis, and Kansas City. In the lower houses, constitutional provisions again discriminate against some of the same cities: Atlanta, Baltimore, Cleveland, Detroit, Portland, Providence, St. Louis, and Wilmington; and legislative action adds to these Chicago, Milwaukee, Minneapolis, and New York. Boston, New Orleans, and Seattle are notable for their absence from these lists. The ninety-six metropolitan districts listed in the 1930 census are located in thirty-six states, in which they have on an average only three-fourths of their proper representation in each house of the legislature.

The rotten boroughs of Connecticut, Rhode Island, and Vermont have long been familiar to students, as have the recent struggles in California, Illinois, Michigan, Missouri, New York, Ohio, and Washington. Examples of urban and metropolitan under-representation could be given in detail, but the table [Tables included in the original article have not been reprinted here.] will give an indication of how repeatedly this situation occurs.

There are some considerations regarding farmers as legislators worth mentioning in regard to this particular problem of apportionment and representation. One indirect effect of rural over-representation in the legislatures is a corresponding rural over-representation within the party organizations. In many states representation on state committees is based on legislative districts, as is apportionment of delegates to state conventions. Where the party division in the state parallels the urban-rural population split, the result is to give a rural tinge even to the party which is based primarily on city voters. In the so-called "one-party states," as in the solid South, the effects are even more noticeable. It is an axiom that in those states the party nomination is equivalent to election; it is not always emphasized that control of party nominations is in the hands of delegates from the rural, sparsely populated sections of those states. In Alabama, Georgia, and Louisiana there are conflicts within the party between rural and urban areas as bitter as those fought out along party lines in other states. And this same factor may help to explain why discrimination in apportionment continues.

Similarly, the rural areas are over-represented in the process of constitutional amendment. This in turn tends to prevent any change in the status quo as regards apportionment. In Delaware, where the process of amendment is in the hands of the legislature, it is idle to hope that that same legislature, dominated by rural representatives, will change its own composition so as to give Wilmington more representation. Even in other states, where the legislature does not have such close control over the amending process, delegates to constitutional conventions are usually elected on the basis of legislative districts. The New York constitutional convention to be held in 1938 seems likely to show how this leads to inertia if not active opposition to prevent any change in the existing arrangements. Further, a more important result of rural over-representation in the amending process is the weight given to the rural viewpoint as regards any reforms in the state government, especially those designed to remove limitations on governmental power or to increase the effectiveness of administrative or legislative leadership. Incidentally, rural interests again have dominance when the legislature acts to ratify amendments to the Federal Constitution.

Elihu Root, in the New York constitutional convention in 1894, claimed that rural over-representation was necessary in order to overcome the greater cooperation among urban representatives. That city delegates work together better than country delegates is by no means proved, and the experience of New York and Ohio at least seems to show the contrary. Further, rural constituencies seem to be more stable than urban ones, so that there is a slower turnover of rural representatives, with the result that leadership through seniority shows a trend toward the rural representatives apart from other considerations.

Not only is rural over-representation in the legislature reflected in over-representation in the party organizations and in constitutional conventions; it is also mirrored in the "invisible government"—the lobbies. As far as the legitimate activities of the lobbies are concerned, their function is to represent the specific interests of their constituents to the legislator and to create or clarify the public opinion of the voters on particular issues. Besides the force of argument and reason which the lobbyists bring to bear on the legislator, they have the pressure of votes, and a legislator is not unlikely to consider the influence pressure groups may have on his chances for reëlection. But in recognizing this, it is important to note that a legislator need fear or heed only the interest groups of his own district.

With due allowance for the value of organization, it remains true that the influence of the pressure group depends in the last analysis on the question of whom the legislator represents; for the strength of such a group depends not only on its numbers and effective organization, but also on the number of legislators on whom it can bring pressure to bear. And it is on this point that the fact of rural over-representation has significance. If the number of legislators subject to its influence is larger than a strictly proportionate representation would indicate, the result from the point of view of the pressure group is as beneficial as if its own membership were increased. The 25 per cent under-representation of the metropolitan areas in the state legislatures to that extent diminishes the influence of industrial and labor organizations, whereas it magnifies to the same extent the influence of farm organizations and others representing the rural viewpoint.

The urban-rural, conflict is rather one between the metropolitan cities and the rural areas than between all those places classed as urban in the Federal census, and the rural areas. Many villages classed as urban with 2,500 or more inhabitants are rural in feeling. Even the larger towns and small cities, especially those in dominantly rural states, are dependent on the prosperity of the rural regions of which they are the trade centers, and in turn reflect the interests and desires of those regions. On the other hand, the small manufacturing cities of Connecticut, New York, and Pennsylvania are not rural in outlook, although they may line up in those states, as in Ohio and Rhode Island, against the metropolitan centers.

The bitter cleavage between those centers and the rural areas, with the other urban population aligning with one side or the other in different states, is unlikely to diminish. The census returns show a steady drift toward the large cities, which in 1930 had 44.6 per cent of the total population, and a continuation of this trend will stimulate the urban-rural antagonism. Further, this antagonism can fairly be considered an industrial-agrarian conflict; for despite the large number of individual factories in small cities and towns, the bulk of American industry is concentrated in some two hundred metropolitan counties, with no evidence of any considerable prospect of deconcentration. We may expect, then, that the urban-rural or industrial-agrarian conflict will continue along the lines already laid down.

The rural areas are generally conservative, and at a time when urban problems are primarily industrial, the presence of a large group of legislators uninformed as to those problems and antagonistic to legislative attempts to deal with them is deplorable. One result is that in some of the eastern states the urban-rural conflict tends to shade off into a class conflict and into a party conflict. In Rhode Island, even more than in Connecticut and New York, the industrialists, though themselves resident in Providence, use the votes of the small towns to help to suppress labor and progressive legislation wanted by the majority of the population of the State. In other states a lack of interest in industrial problems on the part of the farmers is no guarantee of disinterest. Traditionally in national politics the rural areas have been the home of third-party movements, but there is an implicit recognition of the difference between agrarian radicalism and industrial radicalism. One of the frequent arguments the spokesmen of rural interests use to justify over-representation is that the cities stand for "radicalism." And as in so many other respects, here the institutional framework of government is the bulwark of the traditionalists. The urban-rural, industrial-agrarian, labor-capital, and Democratic-Republican divisions seem to overlap so that those who are interested in maintaining the status quo in economic affairs have the most to lose in any change from the status quo in political affairs.

This increases the difficulties of making any change in regard to apportionment. And not only are the legislators subject to pressure from the groups that would be adversely affected by any rearrangement, but the individual legislators themselves can have little enthusiasm for it. Even in the case of the Federal House of Representatives, one decade passed without a reapportionment although the task of allotting representation to the states could have been and later was made almost mechanical; and many states have failed even yet to redistrict for representatives, even though the state legislators have little direct interest in the districting. It would be interesting to speculate as to what would have happened if Congress had had the task of drawing up Congressional districts as well as apportioning representatives to the states. Yet that is just what takes place in the state legislatures.

In view of that and of the constitutional provisions inserted to protect the rural areas, it is almost surprising that there are as many as seven or eight states with equality of representation in both houses. Of these, Arizona and Wyoming are overwhelmingly rural and Massachusetts is overwhelmingly urban, so an urban-rural conflict can hardly arise in those states. Nebraska is exceptional with its unicameral legislature. Colorado and Washington owe their fair apportionments to the determined use of the initiative and referendum by the urban voters. Utah, which is about half urban, is an unusually homogeneous state politically. In Ohio, which is just within the limits of equality, the districts are fixed by the constitution and the apportionment is performed by administrative officials.

The experience of these states gives one or two hints as to possible changes in the method of apportionment. As pointed out above, the fact that the legislature is the apportioning agency and fails to act is a more frequent reason for inequalities than any constitutional restrictions. As long as it remains so, the only remedy is the ancient one of "tears and

prayers." So far these have not proved effective, and various other expedients have been tried or proposed.

One of the most successful methods is the use of the initiative and referendum to pass such statutes, in which the example of Colorado and Washington is encouraging. Another method is to have an apportionment and
districting by the governor and other specified administrative officials in
case the legislature fails to act within a certain time. Missouri formerly
had such a "miniature legislature," and California provided for one ten
years ago. That this method is gaining in popularity is shown by the
adoption by South Dakota last year of a somewhat similar constitutional
amendment. A third protection against legislative inaction, used in Florida,
is that the governor shall call a special session of the legislature for apportionment if the regular one following the census fails to act. Long since
repealed is the provision in the Louisiana Constitution of 1845 that after a
census was taken no law should be passed until a reapportionment was made.
In Ohio the governor, the auditor, and the secretary of state—in Maryland
the governor—apportion senators and representatives after each census, but
have no power to alter the districts.

Of particular interest is Amendment 23 submitted to the voters of Arkansas in 1936 through the process of popular initiative, and approved at the
November election; it takes away from the legislature all power over reapportionment and redistricting. An Apportionment Board, composed of
the governor, the secretary of state, and the attorney-general, has the duty
of apportioning representatives to counties and senators to senatorial districts immediately following each Federal census. The board may from time
to time divide the State into senatorial districts. According to Section 5,
any citizen and taxpayer may sue in the Supreme Court of Arkansas to
compel, by mandamus or otherwise, the board to perform its duties or to
revise any arbitrary action in disregard of the requirements of equality.

Since the main weakness in the present method of apportionment is the
failure of the legislature to act rather than inequalities among the districts
when laid out, the provision for action by administrative officials in case
the legislature refuses to carry out the constitutional mandate seems the
most satisfactory solution. One additional safeguard, as in Arkansas, might
be inserted in any such constitutional amendment that such officials should
be specifically subject to mandamus by the courts in this respect; otherwise it might be argued that when acting as such a "miniature legislature" they are no more subject to judicial control than the legislature
itself.

In some states, a change to the Ohio method would be desirable; that is, to have the electoral districts laid out in the constitution with apportionment of members to those districts by administrative officials according to ratios fixed in the constitution. In order for this to achieve approximate equality, one of two things would be necessary: either to have a large number of members in proportion to the number of districts, so that the smaller ones might have one or two members and the larger ones seven or eight; or, as in Ohio, a provision that districts might have members during some session of the decennial period and not others, in order that fractions of the electoral ratio might be taken into consideration. This of course would result in fluctuations in the size of the legislature.

Where neither of these situations is feasible, there is little to be gained from dividing up the tasks of arranging districts and apportioning members. In the case of the lower house of Congress, such a division of labor is natural; but in the states, where the creation of a single-member district is at the same time an apportionment, it is impossible to separate the two functions. There the task of redistribution involves an amount of discretion which should be vested primarily in the legislature.

To make any of these changes would of course require a constitutional amendment, and this would require in most cases the acquiescence of the rural areas.

Further, important as is a modification of the present technique of redistribution, that alone would not solve the problem of rural over-representation. It is commonly argued that the purpose of the bicameral system is to allow representation on two different bases, these to-day being considered "area" and "population," the senate presumably representing the former and the lower house the latter. Incidentally, in fourteen states the senate represents population better than the lower house, in twenty-two states there is no difference, and in twelve states the lower house represents population more nearly than the senate.

But more important than the question as to which house is the popular one is the fact that in two-thirds of the states the rural areas are over-represented in both houses—not merely in one house. This is frequently due to apportionments which have not been changed to keep pace with shifts in population, but in twelve states it is due either primarily or exclusively to various constitutional restrictions. The most common of these is the practice of representation by counties. In California, county representation for the State Senate was defended as analogous to the Federal Senate, where states are represented as such. Even though such an analogy between counties, which are often merely administrative areas, and the sovereign states may not be convincing, there is a definite feeling in the states that the rural areas should control one branch of the legislature in order to protect their interests. That does not justify the urban under-representation in both houses in thirty-two states, but it is a factor which must be taken into account in considering the present possibilities of constitutional change.

For that reason, the most that can be hoped for in any modification of the basis of representation appears to be that one house represent population exactly, while the other continues to represent primarily the rural areas. This would maintain the representations of different interests in a bicameral system; but it would also tend to emphasize the defects of such a system—deadlocks, friction, evasion of responsibility, lack of leadership.

Unfortunately, the other proposed methods of securing a more nearly adequate representation of cities are confronted by various obstacles. Proposals for functional or occupational representation are unlikely to gain a sympathetic hearing among the voters, and it is more likely that direct representation of economic interests will take place in a more restricted sphere, distinctly subordinate to the political institutions. Secession of metropolitan cities from the rest of the state has been suggested for New York, Chicago, and Los Angeles, but it is doubtful if any state legislature would permit the loss of so much taxable wealth.

The problem of representation in states with one or two large metropolitan areas is also an obstacle in the way of the movement for one-house legislatures. Would this legislature be controlled by the cities or by the rural areas? That question alone is enough to block any such reform in Illinois or New York. Current proposals for a one-house legislature in Ohio provide that representation shall be so divided that no metropolitan area or group of areas can obtain a majority in the legislature.

In states where the urban-rural division has not reached such an acute stage as in the East and the Middle West, the disadvantages of possibly permanent under-representation of cities in a one-house legislature are considerably less than the advantages to be gained from abandoning the bicameral principle. In the others, however, in preference to a gerrymandered single chamber, advocates of a more efficient and responsible legislature should seriously weigh the desirability of other improvements in legislative organization and procedure in order to minimize the defects of a reformed bicameralism in which the urban voters may be assured of adequate representation in at least one branch of the legislature.

No. 50

[EVERY American government textbook has a long section devoted to the facts and details concerning the organization and procedure of the Congress of the United States. It is, of course, highly essential for the student of American government to master this material. Unless he knows how Congress is organized, the functions and the roles of the speaker and the committee system, and the actual procedure that is followed in the introduction, consideration, and passage of bills, he cannot critically evaluate its performance.

It is also important for him to understand how these details fit into the everyday work of Congress, to translate them, so to speak, into more popularly understood terms. Mr. Jay Franklin, the well-known political journalist, illustrates how Congress puts into operation all of the machinery with which the student has become familiar.]

CONGRESS PASSES A BILL [1]

by Jay Franklin

CONGRESS is the people of the United States, reduced in numbers for convenience. It is democracy in action, showing forth its weaknesses, but also its strength. Congress is unwieldy and often verbose. Yet, though few American voters realize it, the process through which 531 harried and diverse individuals make the nation's laws is a triumph of organization.

Laws originate from four sources. The Bill of Rights guarantees to all citizens the right of petition, and how they do use it! Thirteen citizens of Hutchinson, Kans., want a law to tax chain stores. The Apostle Thomas Holy Name Society wants a committee to investigate spies. Tens of thousands of such proposals pour in; few get beyond the waste-basket and those which are introduced are invariably marked, "By Request," meaning that the legislator washes his hands of them. Only when there is strong pressure back home, as for the Townsend Plan, will he act as sponsor.

Much legislation originates with the Administration. The President by message suggests measures he thinks necessary. Recently such messages have often been accompanied by complete drafts of legislation, ready-made for Congressional action. But the most prolific source of legislation is the Senators and Representatives themselves. Some members deluge the bill

[1] Jay Franklin, "Congress Passes a Bill," *Current History* (March, 1940), Vol. 51, pp. 19-20, 59. This article also was printed in *The Reader's Digest* (March, 1940), Vol. 36, pp. 67-72 and is reprinted by permission of *Current History and Forum* and *The Reader's Digest*.

clerks. The late Senator Royal S. Copeland of New York introduced as many as 300 bills in a single Congress. Veterans like him become authorities on certain subjects (his was commerce) so that they are asked to frame and introduce any legislation in their field. Congress is predisposed to pass measures thus sponsored.

Final source of bills is the government departments. Their estimates of the money they need, filtered through the Budget Director, the President and the proper committees, become appropriation bills. By Constitutional provision, all revenue bills, and by custom all appropriation bills, originate in the House.

Let us follow a bill through the gauntlet it must run if ever it is to become law. We can begin by estimating its chances mathematically. At the last regular session, 17,906 measures were introduced; 720 reached the statute books.

In the Senate, the bill may be introduced during "morning hour," actually the first two hours, of any legislative day. The Senator rises, is recognized by the chair, and offers his bill. The President of the Senate (the Vice President of the United States) assigns it to the proper committee. It is numbered, noted in the journal and sent to the printer.

There is a catch in this. The "morning hour" is observed not every day, but every legislative day. Precisely to save the time used up in the prayer, the introduction of new bills, and other routine, the Senate frequently recesses overnight, instead of adjourning. Thus in 1922 and again in 1938 one legislative day spread over 105 calendar days.

In the House, a Member just drops his typewritten bill into a small black box on the right of the Speaker's desk. Lewis Deschler, House Parliamentarian, collects the bills from this "hopper" and designates the committees to which they go. This is one of his lesser chores. Principal duty of the Parliamentarian in each chamber is to keep the chair straight on the complicated status at any moment of a tangle of motions, amendments and so on, and to cite upon the instant the precedents covering any parliamentary situation. He advises Members as well; Deschler answers at least 500 questions a day. Parliamentarians acquire their unique lore by long service on the Congressional staffs. Deschler started in 1925 as the "Messenger to the Speaker's Table," who holds the stopwatch on House speeches,—which, in contrast to Senate rules, always have a time limit.

Bills fall into two great classes, public and private. Private bills deal with specified individuals—to reimburse Ezra Jones for the damage a CCC truck did to his fence, or—these by the thousands—to increase the pension of the Widow Scraggs, or to "correct" the spotted military record of Bill Smith so that he will become eligible for a pension. Of these last two types, few get by. The War Department has become tough about them. So is the President.

Unknown to fame is the House "Objectors' Committee" of three Democrats and three Republicans. Theirs is the drudgery of scrutinizing every private bill. Unless wholly satisfied, they object, which usually kills it. Despite this double check by the standing committees and the informal committee, three bills of every seven passed last session were private.

The Senate maintains 33, the House 47 permanent or standing committees, each a little legislative body in itself. The chief error into which the public falls in judging Congress from the visitors' gallery or by reading newspapers, is not to understand that the real work of Congress is done by these standing committees.

They are filled by the majority party leaders in House and Senate, acting as a "committee on committees." The leaders apportion memberships roughly in ratio to party strength, not through compulsion, but because they prudently look ahead to the inevitable day when they will not be on top and will expect a square deal themselves. Committee members move up toward chairmanship in order of seniority as vacancies occur. Vacancies are filled from among applicants in order of their length of continuous service in Congress.

Each committee has a number of clerks, of whom the chief clerk, at least, is generally a fixture because his guidance is invaluable to the chairman. Chief clerk of an important committee typically spends 20 years at the job, knows all there is to know about affairs of the Navy, let's say, and draws $5,000.

To the proper committee is referred each bill, as we have seen. Large committees, and some have 40 members, split into sub-committees to consider specific bills. The chairman naming a sub-committee frequently will load it with friends or foes of a bill according to how he feels about the measure. He likewise will be careful to name a majority of his own party.

If a bill is of any importance, the subcommittee will call hearings so that all persons interested may come and express their views. Special invitations will go to outstanding authorities on the subject—leading bankers, maybe, or prominent duck hunters.

As many as a dozen such hearings go on at the same time in the Capitol, the Senate and House Office Buildings. This is where your Congressman was when you visited the gallery and saw the floor half empty. True, no committee may sit while the Congress is in session, except by special permission. But it is routine for the important committees to get this permission, and the members come trooping through the underground corridors and onto the floor only when bells have warned them that a roll call vote is about to be taken.

Committee hearings may last a few hours, or many weeks. The Appropriations Committee in the last Congress worked eight hours a day for five months. It is a grind. You will see the office buildings blazing with light night after night and long ranks of Congressmen's cars parked outside.

Small hearings are likely to be held somewhere in the Capitol. Committeemen and the witness sit at one long green table. The atmosphere is friendly, informal, and thick with smoke. Big hearings are more ponderous, held in magnificent marble rooms, with committeemen on a raised dais so that the witness has to look up awkwardly. Crowds sometimes attend, particularly if some notable is to take the stand.

When the committee decides it has heard all the testimony it needs, it goes into closed session to deliberate what recommendations it will make. It is likely to redraft the bill in the light of the information it has gathered. Whereupon it will call in the Legislative Counsel.

The Legislative Counsel expresses no opinion on policy; he is an expert at writing laws. He will undertake to see that a bill conflicts with no existing law, that it will stand up in court, that its intent is clear, and that in so far as possible it facilitates the work of whoever must administer it.

Such counsel first appeared as volunteer assistants to two Congressional committees, sent by Columbia University Law School. The two attorneys made such a hit that both the House and the Senate formally created the office. Middleton Beaman was one of the men; he still is Legislative Counsel to the House.

The new bill drawn, or the old bill amended, the majority report framed —again with assistance of Counsel because courts in construing a law sometimes look back to the legislative proceedings—and perhaps a dissenting minority report written, the matter goes before the whole committee. It accepts, rejects or amends the work of the subcommittee and reports to the Senate or House. Or maybe decides not to report the measure at all. In fact, that is what happens to nine out of ten bills—they go to committee and are never heard from again. When a Congress goes out of office, they all die automatically.

Now the bill goes on the calendar, a list of bills ready for action. Broadly speaking, bills earliest reported stand best chance of passage, being at the top. But there are exceptions. In the Senate anyone may move to take up any bill regardless of its place on the list. The majority leaders take advantage of this rule and form a "steering committee" to decide which pet measure shall be pushed ahead.

Any Senator has the right to propose amendments to any bill under consideration and, unless it is a general appropriation bill, the amendment need not bear the remotest relation to the bill's subject matter. Of these "riders," a famous one is the Thomas amendment to an agricultural bill authorizing the President to print up to three billion dollars in greenbacks. The House, by contrast, enforces strictly the "rule of germaneness."

Each and every Senator talks as long as he pleases on any bill unless, as rarely, a cloture rule is applied. Unlimited debate is a Senator's most jealously guarded prerogative; a Senator will fight tooth and nail for some bill, yet refuse to vote to limit opponents' debate on it. Once a Senator has the floor, he need not yield it, and may continue to talk until he drops from exhaustion. And if he can outtalk the clock, a session may expire without taking action on the measure to which he is opposed. Huey Long staged the last notable one-man filibuster, but a group of Senators, yielding the floor only to one another, ran a disguised filibuster against repeal of the arms embargo.

Since the final vote on a measure is usually determined in advance, by party politics, by conference behind the scenes, and very largely by confidence of Congress in the wisdom of its own committees, spectators in the galleries wonder what purpose is served by the long hours of debate on the floor. They see a Senator rolling out rhetoric to an almost empty and completely inattentive chamber and they know his speech will rarely change a single colleague's vote. But Congressional debate, besides helping the members impress their constituents, has a democratic value. It educates the voters on national issues and it often builds up a weight of public opinion which does in time alter votes on the floor.

In the House, with its 435 members, unlimited debate like the Senate's would be utterly impractical. Hence the limit of one hour for any one speaker on one subject.

House leaders have their devices, too, for pushing pet measures ahead. The Rules Committee can suspend the regular rules in order to consider a measure out of its turn.

Most mystifying of all Congressional devices is the House resolving itself into a "Committee of the Whole House on the State of the Union," to consider a major bill. The Speaker's chair is taken by some veteran member well versed in parliamentary procedure. A different set of rules now prevails. The "Committee" specifies a time limit for general debate and then a clerk reads the bill, paragraph by paragraph, for amendments. These may be offered ad infinitum, except that no member may offer two amendments to the same section. Members may not speak more than five minutes on each amendment. Voting on amendments is by "voice" as in the Senate, or, if 20 members demand it, the Chairman appoints two Congressmen to act as tellers. Members favoring the amendment then pass down the aisle and are counted. Next, members opposed parade and are counted. Thus votes are anonymous. Sometimes this anonymity is pierced to the great embarrassment of certain members; reporters in the press gallery have pooled their efforts and made an almost perfect record of teller votes—a remarkable feat, to spot several hundred men by name in the time it takes them to walk down an aisle.

When all amendments have been considered, the "Committee" again becomes the House. Some opponent moves to "recommit" the bill—send it back to committee, in effect killing it for the session. The House passes on this motion. If the motion is rejected, roll call on passage of the bill follows.

A bill passed by one chamber is "messaged" to the other. A Senate clerk, for instance, comes to the House. Obtaining recognition from the Speaker, he announces that the Senate has passed a measure in which the concurrence of the House is requested. All this is most ceremonious, the clerk bowing stiffly before and after his announcement.

No measure can become law until both Senate and House have passed identical bills. When their versions vary, as often, each chamber appoints three or five conferees to try to adjust differences. They cannot introduce new matter, must try to compromise within the limits set by the difference between the two bills. When a compromise has been reached, the conferees send their report to their respective Houses. Conference reports cannot be amended and they cannot be debated; they must be passed or defeated as is.

The bill is now ready to be enrolled as an Act of Congress, i.e., printed on parchment. Signed by the Speaker and the Vice President, it goes to the President, who has ten days, not counting Sundays, in which to act upon it. He may sign it, whereupon it is law; or he may veto it, sending it back with a message explaining his action. To override the President's veto, Congress must repass the bill by a two-thirds vote of both Houses. If the President fails to act within the ten-day limit, the bill automatically becomes law. If, however, Congress should end its session during this ten-day period, the measure automatically dies. This is the "pocket veto," a device adopted by all Presidents from Washington to Roosevelt. It saves the work of writing veto messages in the busy closing days of a session, and it enables a President to kill a distasteful bill without making a public statement that might embarrass him.

Once the bill has become law, it must then stand its chance with the lawyers and the Federal courts—and that is another story. Congress, at least, has done its hard, thankless and necessary job.

Chapter XV

ADVISING THE LEGISLATOR

No. 51

[LOBBYING is closely connected with the character of representation provided for in our basic laws, and also with the nature and operation of our political parties. A member of a legislative body represents a large and heterogeneous group of individuals, each of whom has his own particular demands to make on government. Given this fact, it is not strange that our party system is one in which job politics figures more prominently than policy politics; that the resident of any legislative or congressional district tends to feel that neither his representative nor the party to which he belongs fully represents his views on any particular piece of legislation. Professor Sabine in his penetrating essay, "What Is the Matter with Representative Government?" points out how this feeling of inadequacy has caused an ever growing number of Americans to rely more and more on the lobby to represent them and their views.]

WHAT IS THE MATTER WITH REPRESENTATIVE GOVERNMENT? [1]

by George H. Sabine

HARDLY more than a century ago, the hopes of liberals were centered in the creation of representative legislatures. Popular assemblies were established where none existed, and everywhere the assembly was made representative of a larger part of the population. In the end the suffrage was extended in many countries to approximately the whole adult population, of both sexes and of all degrees of wealth, education, and rank. And yet, with this process now practically complete, success has brought disillusionment rather than elation. In the United States we have the last

[1] George H. Sabine, "What Is the Matter with Representative Government?", *The North American Review* (May, 1921), Vol. 213, pp. 587-597. Reprinted by permission of the author and *The North American Review*.

step still fresh in mind, the enfranchisement of women. It is safe to say
that the great majority even of those who favored it were rather listless;
certainly few believe that it solves any serious political problem or that most
legislation will be appreciably better because women have the vote. Broadening the basis of representation has ceased to seem a very important gain
in the progress of government.

The fact is that as representative assemblies have become matters of
course, we have very generally lost confidence in them as organs for making
law. It is natural that in war-time, legislatures should decline in popular
estimation, but I am not referring merely to that. The change was going
on long before the War. Americans had long been accustomed to holding
their legislatures in rather slight esteem, to thinking that the member of
Congress or of the State legislature is not a very intelligent or a very important person. In fact, one would have to go a long way back in American politics to reach a time when election to Congress was an honor eagerly
sought by men of ability and standing. The case of the State legislatures
is much worse. If anything is written large across the histories of our
states, it is popular distrust of the legislature. Our State constitutions,
with their detailed restrictions upon legislative power, are monuments to
this distrust.

The freedom of our legislatures has been limited in two chief ways. It
has been partly lost through the assumption of legislative functions directly
by the people, but still more has it been hampered by the ascendancy of
executive officers, who have had to assume more and more responsibility for
getting laws framed and passed.

It was natural for Americans to assume that the democratic way to settle
a question was to leave it to the people, and the more they distrusted their
representatives, the more they tended to think that leaving it to the people
meant letting the people vote on it. Since they did not trust the legislature
to pass the laws they wanted, they invented ways of initiating legislation.
And since they feared that the legislature would pass laws they did not
want, they reserved to themselves the right to pass upon an enactment
before it became law. More and more of our State law was written into the
State constitution, which as a rule could be amended only by a referendum.
Thus the initiative and the referendum were symptoms of the low opinion
which Americans had of their State legislatures, but they were also causes
of the further decay of those bodies, for the surest way to make a place
unacceptable to an able man is to make it a place where little or nothing
can be done.

In the case of the Federal Government, Congress lost power mainly to
executive officers. Not that it tamely surrendered, or that its legal powers

were restricted. Except in unusual circumstances, Congress has been tenacious of its Constitutional independence, and has rather enjoyed waging
guerilla warfare against a President or Cabinet officer. But in the long run,
circumstances have been too much for Congress. The power of the President, even over legislation, has steadily increased, and more and more Congress has had to accept his leadership. No theoretical independence could
free Congress from the results of the President's superior strategic position.
He could bring public opinion to bear upon them in a way they dared not
neglect. For there can be no doubt that the public by preference sides with
the President. It may grow tired at times of what orators call "one-man
government," but when some action is definitely wanted, the public rather
likes to see the President put it through. It is in fact a definite gain in
popular government to be able to hold some one person responsible for legislation, as for other results. The President, paradoxically enough, has become
the people's agent for keeping the people's representatives up to their job.
Our most successful Governors in the last twenty years have been men who
could deal with State legislatures in the same fashion.

The public esteem in which the legislature is held has thus tended to
decline in comparison with that given to other parts of the Government.
Indeed, it is not too much to say that our legislatures have come to be
distrusted, and that a very large number of persons feel that our so-called
representative bodies are the part of the Government which least represent
them in those matters which they deem of the greatest importance. It
should be noted, however, that distrust of legislatures has not meant distrust of legislation. Particular acts may be condemned, but so far as methods
are concerned, we look to legislation for the remedy of abuses almost as much
as ever we did. In fact, this faith is inevitable. Social and economic relations in an industrial society have refused to become stable and social
processes have undergone a steady and amazing acceleration. Such changes
call for corresponding changes in the legal relations of the parties interested.
Hence the law has had to change much faster in the last fifty years than ever
before in human history. And some sort of legislative machinery has to labor
at this task. Hence the appalling volume of law that our national, State, and
municipal legislatures have poured upon the world. One may believe in
particular cases that much of this law was ill-made, but he cannot escape the
fact that one way or another most of it had to be made. There is no reason
to suppose that the next fifty years will see any diminution of the need for
revising the law.

The two outstanding features of the present situation are the need of legislating and our loss of confidence in the agencies by which legislating is done.
Since there is no possibility of doing away with the need for legislation, the

only question is the possibility of more satisfactory agencies. In particular we need to get at the seat of our distrust of elected representatives. Representation, doubtless, we must have, since direct lgislation is out of the question both by reason of the size of modern States and equally by reason of the complexity of the questions involved. Along what lines may we expect our law-making institutions to move under the stress of the present discontent? But first, can we explain more clearly *why* representatives have lost touch with their constituencies and lost the confidence of those who elect them?

The general notion of representation is of course very old. For English-speaking people especially it was not at all an invention of the age of democratization. There was one element, however, in the early notion of representation which has been almost wholly lost in the course of modern political evolution. In earlier times it was a *community* which was represented. The representative was the spokesman for a unified group which might not unreasonably be expected to express itself with one voice. It was a unit in fact, in the sense that the interests of the members really were for the most part confined to the local group, and it was a unit also in the minds of the members. The community was relatively small. It was economically self-sufficing to a very large extent, and there was relatively little communication with other communities. In consequence, the interests of every person in it were almost exclusively local and were very largely bound up with the welfare of the locality. Its social and economic organization was exceedingly simple, compared with modern communities. There really were group interests and these interests really could be represented.

Moreover, the members were definitely conscious of the community as a real being. If we were to borrow a modern idea, we should say that the units of representation were corporations. The local bodies acted in all respects as if they were persons. A county was in no sense merely the indefinite number of persons who happened to live in a given area. In fact, though the word county (*comitatus*) does refer to a geographical district, it means equally the county court, or local representative body, which chooses members to sit in Parliament. The county has duties, rights, guilt, judgment, will, and organs for performing or expressing these. The looseness of the individual from the locality in which he lives, which is natural to our way of thinking, is essentially a modern idea. The correlated notion of the locality as merely a square mile of land inhabited by some indefinite number of persons is equally modern. In the past the local group was a community. Sometimes it was a guild with a definite unity of economic interest, but in any case the members were united by ties which seemed to them entirely tangible and the group thus formed was in their eyes a permanent, living, acting entity. Representation always involved the idea of such a unified group which spoke through its sworn mouthpiece.

The evolution of modern social and economic conditions, and the accompanying growth of modern government, have conspired, one might almost say, to crush the life out of the smaller units and localities which were once its living elements. It was inevitable under the circumstances that government should become more and more highly centralized, and that localities should be subjected more and more to centralized control. In the nature of the case the small local group could not preserve its individuality and self-sufficiency. More and more politics became a relation between two sharply contrasted extremes. On the one hand is the very powerful national state which knows no limit to its legal competence, which claims the power, —and sometimes exercises it,—of regulating all phases of the citizen's life, from his religion to his industry and from his education to his hygiene. On the other hand there is the citizen himself whose local attachments and communal bonds often have singularly little to do with his political activities and relationships. No doubt he still belongs to a community of some sort, but the community has largely ceased to be local and is not at all a political entity; on the other hand, the local political districts in which he votes have never become communities in any real sense of the word.

Thus we come to our present notion of representation, which is purely geographical and numerical. The constituency has become merely the indefinite number of heterogeneous individuals who happen to live inside an arbitrary line. If a State has sixteen members in Congress, a Congressional district is merely an area containing one-sixteenth of the population of the State. By no stretch of the imagination can the Congressional district be called a community: it need have no common interests; its people are held together by no conscious social bonds; and they may in fact be heterogeneous to any extent. The other units of local government are no different. Our cities are divided mechanically into wards; our States are divided mechanically into counties; and the States themselves, if they ever had any real unity, have ceased to have it. By this I mean that there is little or nothing in the social and economic relations between the people that correspond to the legal and political distinctions imposed upon them by the existence of the State.

Thus it is true almost universally that the local units of government have little real significance; the local governments do not stand for functionally active communities conforming to the interests and sentiments of the people. When we have wished to make really effective administrative units, such for example as the districts of the Federal Reserve Bank, we have had to neglect the legal frontiers between our local governing units. Is not this the fundamental reason why the claim to States' rights and local self-government, which has been acclaimed persistently as an ideal in American politics, has had so little practical effect? But more especially is it not at the root of our difficulty with representation? How can one man represent that which has no unity and stands for no definite purpose? Is it not easy to see why men feel that a representative who is shared among a heterogeneous mass is no representative at all? In the nature of the case he cannot stand for that which vitally interests anyone, for if he does, he becomes antagonistic to someone else who has an equal claim upon him. Thus he is smoothed down to the level of the man who is everybody's friend —the very symbol of futility. In a word, our political representation has lost touch with the social and economic relations which make up most of the life of the community.

The fact is that while political representation has adhered rigidly to the locality in the mere geographical sense, the general tendency of social and political development has been to make human communities independent of locality to a degree that would have been utterly inconceivable a century ago. Stripped of their traditional associations in the local community, men have set themselves to the making of new ties and new associations which are for the most part not local. Wide and easy communication make it practically certain that human associations will never again depend so much upon locality as they have in the past. What is essential to an association is not that the members should be in the same place, but that they should be convinced of a common interest in uniting, a common purpose to be attained, a common cause to be served. If this interest is a permanent one and if it is one which can obtain the adherence of large numbers of men, great and enduring associations can result which awaken a high degree of loyalty in their members. There is one such association which has played a great part in human life and which is by no means modern, viz., the Church, but the last generation has seen an amazing proliferation of associations of this sort. We have, for example, all the manifold associations with an economic basis,—the chambers of commerce, the employers' associations, the federations of labor, the cooperative consumers' leagues, the farmers' marketing and purchasing associations. It is extraordinary how easily and rapidly men ally themselves in these ways when the conditions are right to make them aware of a community of interest. Moreover, by no means are all these modern associations economic in origin. The lawyers' bar associations, the physicians' medical associations, and the engineering associations appeal in part no doubt to an economic motive, but certainly to many other motives besides. The many associations of scholars are for the most part not economic at all. In general, any permanent basis of common interest that can be furthered by cooperation offers the ground for an association of this sort.

The great number of these non-local associations that are based on common interests, and the rapidity with which they grow in size and power, make a striking phenomenon of present-day society. They have increased as the local community has declined, and for the same reason: under modern conditions it is simply impossible that interests should be confined within the bounds of local groups. Modern men in increasing numbers are but loosely attached to local groups and on the other hand have more and more interests in common with other men who are widely scattered. The interests which unite them with other persons of the same occupation outside their locality may easily be more vital than those which unite them with their neighbors, and the associations which result may command a correspondingly larger share of their attention and loyalty. In short, they feel that this association, or its agents, is a more adequate representative of their real interests than the political representative whom they must share with all sorts and conditions of men because of the merely external identity of residence.

Though non-local associations based upon common interests have become a serious social phenomenon, it should be noted that they have not as yet attained the standing of a political phenomenon, at least in the United States. By this I mean that they are wholly outside the law, though of course not contrary to it. They are private associations and nothing more. Government does not recognize them or make any use of them, except under unusual circumstances. Indeed, it has sometimes tried to hinder them, especially in the case of labor organizations, though with no great success when many persons were convinced of their utility. I do not say that they have played no part in government. They have, for in many cases an important part of their purpose is to influence legislation. They try to supply indirectly the representation which their members do not feel that they get from their political representatives, but such activity is extra-legal; it is no part of the organized agencies by which our laws are made.

This extra-legal influence upon law-making, though it doubtless always existed in some degree, has grown to be one of the paradoxes of representative government. We solemnly elect our representatives and send them to the State or National capital to make our laws. But when we want something, or believe that something needs doing, we show little confidence that our representative will know about it or give his help if he knows. We forthwith begin to devise ways of convincing him that we want it and of putting pressure upon him to help us get it. What we actually rely on is the extra-legal, voluntary association which we feel can really be trusted to look after our interests. The merchant or manufacturer looks to his chamber of commerce or his employers' association to secure the legislation he needs or to prevent the legislation he fears. Even the citizen who wants nothing more from the legislature than an adequate provision for the public schools, finds that he must work through associations organized to bring political pressure to bear upon State officials. We are in the position of the man who kept a dog but had to do his own barking.

Thus every legislative assembly is attended by a great pulling and hauling of interests, but this in itself is not what makes the paradox. The purpose of law is to harmonize and adjust conflicting interests in behalf of the whole community. It is right and proper, therefore, that all interests should be represented and heard. The paradox lies in the fact that the real representatives are not the responsible legislators, that the most decisive part of the session is likely to take place in the lobby, and that the duly elected "representative" constantly tends to become a puppet whose strings are pulled by someone in the background. And the public generally expects that results will be got by pressure or persuasion, by methods which it vaguely hopes will be legitimate but which it knows often are not so. Thus our laws are passed under conditions which are merely another chapter in the old story of bad government: power without responsibility and responsibility without power. The real representative who commands the support of an organized and interested part of the voters is a private person who need only keep on the right side of the corrupt practices act, while the man who is elected ostensibly to make law is politically responsible to an unorganized constituency which has no unified purpose to be represented. Is it strange that men with real ability and serious purposes should be loath to undertake such a job?

In the meantime, organization for the cooperative furthering of common interests grows steadily and rapidly. It is idle to blind ourselves to the fact that there are great possibilities of danger in this. A powerful association to promote a particular interest becomes a public menace when it uses its power in an irresponsible or purely selfish manner. But of course it is equally idle to suppose that we can influence such associations by treating them as if they were somehow abnormal. The danger lies not so much in the fact that they are powerful, as in the fact that they are irresponsible. Both labor unions and employers' associations as we know them have been organized mainly to wage war on their enemies and to win advantages for the interests they represent, whatever other interests may suffer in the process. So long as they remain of this sort they are seeds of disorder; it is just this which no statesmanlike solution of the problem can tolerate. Conflict of interests we shall always have and these conflicts will call for continual readjustment. But the adjustment must itself be an obligation upon the organizations which exist to maintain the interests. They must be made responsible for the adjustment of conflicts and for a due regard to other interests.

When an organization reaches a certain degree of power, it is really a pretense to go on treating it as if it were merely a private and more or less casual association. Already there exist associations both of labor and of capital able to exercise a power of life or death over the industries upon which the community has to live. Though nominally voluntary, they exert a control over their members which is sometimes more binding than law itself. In fact, they have at their command much of the psychological apparatus that goes to the making of law. In a word, they are institutions, or at least they are clearly on the road to becoming institutions, though they lack recognition. In one way or another, government must take account of these vast organizations; it must utilize them as responsible agencies in the public control over the vital organs of the community.

The problem of representative government is to get back to a representation of vital interests by responsible representatives. It is not my purpose to discuss the plans by which it has been proposed to bring this about. Proportional representation would at least permit men to group themselves as their interests might dictate. The representation of industrial interests permitted by the German Constitution [of 1919] is a recognition of the problem, if not a solution. Perhaps in the end we shall be driven to the much more radical expedient of organizing our basic industries as self-governing units having more or less of legal competence and subject more or less to some kind of outside regulation. Such plans for the future contain necessarily a large element of speculation. But it is not speculation to say that representative government as it now exists is far from being an unequivocal success or that it has grievously disappointed the hopes which liberals built upon it. It is not speculation to hazard the forecast that representation will never again be made effective upon a merely local or geographical basis. The modern community has outgrown the limits of locality, which, from the beginning of man's experience down to the end of the eighteenth century, were natural to all communities. When essential human interests and the associations built upon them have ceased to be local, it is idle to suppose that locality can continue to serve as a sufficient basis for political representation. We cannot go on forever with a twentieth century society and an eighteenth century system of government.

No. 52

[FOR many years, but in the last two decades especially, the lobbyist has been the object of editorial attack and political controversy. In this period he has also been the subject of a considerable amount of legislative regulation. The evils for which the lobbyist is supposedly responsible are now so well known that even the term "lobbyist" has a sinister connotation. That much of evil has been committed by well-financed pressure groups cannot be denied. On the other hand, few realize that this same lobby has contributed a great deal towards the political education of America.

Mr. Henry A. Bellows, the author of the following article, was at one time a member of the Federal Radio Commission. Following this work he was engaged as the legislative counsel for the radio industry of the United States. In this latter capacity he not only frequently appeared before Congressional committees but he also gained much first hand information on the contributions of the lobby to American politics. His article "In Defense of Lobbying" is based on his close association with the federal government as an administrator and as a member of the "third house."]

IN DEFENSE OF LOBBYING [1]

by Henry A. Bellows

NO other trade in America to-day is subject to such widespread vilification as that of the lobbyist. The departed gangster is at least
deemed worthy of a flamboyant funeral, and uproarious crowds cheer the
acquittal of a confessed beer runner, but for the lobbyist nothing is audible
but scorn and contumely. Ordinarily a Congressional investigation is a ready
road to popularity; the man who has been quizzed by a Senatorial committee emerges a hero. But the pilloried lobbyist has no such consolation.
Before his testimony is fairly out of his mouth, he is on the front pages
of the newspapers, a hapless target for national reviling. Whenever any
form of financial interests conceives that it has a right to present its views
on pending legislation, and to try to convince Senators and Congressmen
that they ought to give fair consideration to those views, then the hue and
cry begins.

There is a natural reason for this. The financial interests have, or are
supposed to have, lots of money, and some of them have been found none

[1] Henry A. Bellows, "In Defense of Lobbying," *Harper's Magazine* (December, 1935),
Vol. 172, pp. 96-107. Reprinted by permission of Mrs. Philip W. Pillsbury and *Harper's
Magazine*.

too scrupulous in its employment, particularly in connection with State and municipal affairs. There have been ugly revelations in connection with expenditures for propaganda. A well-filled "war-chest" inevitably evokes the horrid specter of bribery, and even though in recent times there have been no proved Congressional instances of such corruption, the public is prone to believe that where there is so much smoke there must be some fire. Above all, a single egregious blunder, such as the fraudulent York telegrams (although no lobbyist deserving of the title would be stupid enough to countenance such practices) casts its black shadow over every effort to affect by whatever means the legislative process.

The very term "lobbying" is in itself suggestive of sinister methods. It paints a grim picture of a furtive individual lurking in the byways of the Capitol, buttonholing a Senator here, a Congressman there, whispering secrets into quivering ears, a stealthy, malevolent perverter of truth. And in recent years this hideous figment of the imagination has grown to gigantic proportions. Not content with his pernicious activities beneath the dome of the Capitol, the lobbyist must needs reach out into every city and hamlet, and there stir up tornadoes of propaganda that writhe their way back to Washington in the form of myriads of letters and telegrams.

All very horrible, no doubt, but far from the whole story. Go to any committee hearing on an important bill. Who is that man in the witness chair, answering innumerable questions, generally of a technical nature, and, as he finally withdraws, receiving the cordial thanks of the committee chairman? He, strange to say, is a lobbyist. He is paid to represent a group or an industry for the express purpose of affecting the course of legislation. It is quite possible that he will ultimately urge those whose interests he represents to communicate with their Senators and Congressmen regarding the pending bill. The members of the committee know all this, and yet it is clear that they look upon him, not as Public Enemy Number One, but as a serviceable and trustworthy ally.

The plain fact is that lobbying, properly conducted, is not only a perfectly legitimate exercise of a Constitutional right, but a direct benefit both to Congress and to the country at large. Most important bills involve the consideration of complex problems, which can be solved only on the basis of long practical experience and careful research. The lobbyist places at the disposal of Congress the collective experience of those whom he represents. That in so doing he is unbiased he would be the last to claim. Of course he is biased, but so are all the other witnesses, including, be it noted, such representatives of the government itself as may testify. The whole business of Federal law-making is, in this respect, remarkably like the functioning of the courts. An attorney is not expected to be nonpartisan, and the judge does not condemn him because he brings out the strongest points in favor of his client. Rather, the ends of justice are considered as best served when both sides are fully and ably represented, when all the evidence is clearly set forth, and when judge and jury have the benefit of whatever technical guidance the issues in the case may require.

The analysis and discussion of a proposed law, if it is to amount to anything more than superficial guesswork, normally requires weeks or months of intensive preparation. It cannot be done adequately by untrained persons, or even by experts who can devote to it only their spare time. Many a capable executive makes a lamentable witness before a Congressional committee because he neither speaks nor understands the special language of legislation; many an eloquent lawyer falls down when searching questions reveal his limited familiarity with practical details. The experienced lobbyist, on the other hand, intimately acquainted with his subject through long association with the people he represents, and fully cognizant of the special complexities of legislative procedure, including the peculiarly difficult technic of phraseology, frequently can and does render invaluable assistance in the shaping of proposed laws.

Proof of this is spread all over the pages of the published records of legislative hearings. Obviously there is nothing secretive or surreptitious about a type of lobbying that is thus publicly recorded, and yet lobbying within the ordinary definition of the term it certainly is. It is an effort to affect the course of pending legislation; it is openly conducted in the interests of some particular group, and not infrequently it costs a good deal of money. And yet the records show both its value to the public and the almost invariable cordiality with which it is welcomed by committee members.

During the past eight years I have appeared many times on behalf of one industry before committees of both Houses. I have yet to experience anything other than the utmost consideration, and I have never left the witness stand without the friendly thanks of the chairman, and frequently of other members of the committee. Even when the questioning was incisive, as it frequently was, the purpose remained perfectly clear: the committee collectively was trying to elicit whatever information might help it in drafting a satisfactory bill. I never pretended to be anything but what I was—the legislative representative of a single industry; but whenever legislation affecting that industry was under consideration, I always found that Senators and Congressmen were eager to understand its point of view and the reasons therefor. If, in the end, I did not always succeed in convincing them, it was never for lack of ample opportunity. I am quite sure that this summary of personal experience can be duplicated by almost everyone who has practiced this form of lobbying.

It will, of course, be argued that this is not the type of lobbying to which anyone seriously objects, that it is a far cry to the activities which warn Senators and Congressmen of dire consequences at the polls if they do not vote in such and such a way, that shake down avalanches of telegrams and letters on their defenseless heads, and, going one step farther, in the ominous vocabulary of practical politics "put pressure" on them.

After all, however, our entire system of government is based on the principle of representation, and each legislator must consider all questions of national scope as they may affect both the general welfare and that of the locality which has empowered him to represent it. A keen and constant interest in what people think "back home" is by no means, as is so often inferred, exclusively indicative of vote-counting spinelessness. It is distinctly and properly a part of the job, inherent in the provisions of the Constitution itself. The lobbyist in Washington, from the very nature of his residence and work, is commonly without immediate State affiliations; he must study pending legislation from the national rather than from the local point of view. Is he, therefore, to assume that Senators and Congressmen will disregard their direct accountability to those whose special interests they are required to safeguard?

The people "back home," however, normally have very limited access to detailed information about legislation. It is seldom that an issue is so sharply defined that the question is simply one of voting for or against a bill in its entirety. Even those whose interests are directly involved are, as a rule, far from clear in their own minds as to the precise things that they do or do not want. And yet, with complete propriety, every Senator and Congressman is eager to know what his constituents, and particularly the better-informed among them, really think about the matters on which his vote will be recorded.

At this point the lobby inevitably broadens its scope. Consider any extended group which may be directly affected, either favorably or the reverse, by some pending item of legislation. Its lobbyist has painstakingly analyzed the bill; he knows, as well as anyone can know, what effect it is likely to have on those whom he represents. He understands what amendments will increase the benefits or mitigate the hardships. From all over the country he receives urgent calls for information and advice, in order that the members of his group—and it does not matter whether they are producers or consumers, employers or labor, lenders or borrowers—may more intelligently transmit their own views to their Senators and Congressmen.

And so the lobbyist perforce launches a service of information. If he knows his business, his reports attempt no concealment of their frankly partisan nature. They do not try to hide their origin by masquerading as impartial news. They are careful never knowingly to misstate facts, and clearly distinguish between established facts and the inferences drawn therefrom. Above all, the wise lobbyist sees to it that his reports never contain a single line that cannot invite the widest publicity, and that is not actually, in substance at least, a matter of record. Provided such legislative service is honest within the requirements just set forth, it may be intensely partisan.

"Propaganda!" shout the hot-heads. Of course it is propaganda, and why not? How long since it has become a crime to disseminate legislative information? Is the political education of the American people to be left entirely to public agencies with an itch for self-perpetuation? The lobbyist's report is no whit more selfishly motivated than many a departmental press release or franked Congressional speech. Admit that it is not the whole truth; its openly proclaimed source is a virtual guarantee of that. Nobody is capable of telling the whole truth about any important legislative matter; otherwise there would be no debates in Congress. The legislative news service sent out by lobbyists, provided always it makes no concealment of its origin, is a definite and wholly legitimate contribution to public education, and to brand it as in any way improper is rank injustice.

Such information is sent out for the manifest and admitted purpose of influencing public opinion "back home." What are the recipients to do with it? File it, read or unread, in the wastebasket? By all means, if it does not coincide with their views. But if it provides satisfactory answers to the questions they have been asking themselves, and if they feel that they are in any way personally concerned in the matter, then it is not only their right, but actually their duty, to see that their chosen representatives are made acquainted with their opinions.

Occasionally some Congressional sleuth makes the amazing discovery that since many of the communications he receives are similar or identical in wording, they must have had a common origin. Certainly they had. How many good citizens and conscientious voters know enough about the details of any significant piece of pending legislation to frame a really helpful letter or telegram regarding it? Even the relatively well-informed and actively interested are commonly inarticulate when it comes to giving specific recommendations for action. And yet, as the numerous insertions in the Congressional Record demonstrate, Senators and Congressmen are keenly interested in such communications from their constituents as evince genuine understanding and provide logical reasons for the opinions set forth. It is, therefore, quite understandable that the lobbyist is constantly being asked to suggest the most effective wording for such letters and telegrams.

This, of course, leads into the dark side of the picture—the obvious opportunity for fraud. The evidence in the matter of the York telegrams is conclusive, and there have been other instances in which there has undoubtedly been a greater or less degree of falsification. Any mass appeal for signatures, even if it is conducted with the utmost scrupulousness—which it generally is not—always involves some element of deception, as anyone who has ever dealt with widely circulated petitions well knows. The things that otherwise sane men and women will sign, and the uses to which they will lend their names, mostly from an easy-going inability to say "No," are unbelievable. And when the request is coupled with an offer to pay for the telegram—a wholly vicious and indefensible practice—the result is an appalling distortion of the truth. Moreover, it is impossible to undertake any task of this kind without entrusting the actual work to canvassers whose ethics may be on a level even below that of their intellects.

The answer—as the York telegrams proved—is that such tactics almost always defeat themselves, and that no lobbyist of experience, let alone integrity, sanctions them. Fraud in such matters is peculiarly easy to detect, and irretrievably damning when exposed. Most Congressmen, and their secretaries, know their home districts pretty well, and in any batch of unauthorized messages there are bound to be a few that instantly disclose their fraudulent character. A message from even a defunct Legionnaire has caused embarrassment. The lobbyist who indignantly and truthfully denies ever having had anything to do with such methods proclaims not only his honesty but still more his common sense.

Furthermore, there are relatively few legislative proposals regarding which mass communications are effective. In practice the thing generally works just the other way round. When a Senator or Congressman finds his desk littered with telegrams from people who, in the nature of the case, cannot possibly have a considered opinion, he is instantly and naturally suspicious, and his tendency is to swing sharply in the opposite direction. No one who has noted the customary fate of petitions to Congress, fortified as some of them are with thousands and hundreds of thousands of signatures (on one occasion I was confronted by documents aggregating well over two million names, most of which I believe to have been authentically signed) retains much faith in the general efficacy of mass communications, except, indeed, in those rare cases wherein the issue immediately and obviously affects vast numbers of people, and where advice can be simplified down to a flat "Yes" or "No." It is safe to say that ninety per cent, and more, of this kind of activity is engineered, not by the much-abused Washington lobbyists, but by people on the outside whose zeal atrophies their brains, and also occasionally their ethical sense. This is not because the lobbyist is purer than his fellows, but because he knows Washington and they don't.

Any form of legislative propaganda, however, undeniably opens the way for the sort of thing that has brought lobbying into such evil repute. Money can be and has been viciously used, and direct financial pressure of all sorts exerted, to color the views and actions of those who have influence either at home or with their Congressional friends. It may be impossible to buy a Senator or a Congressman, but it is sometimes quite feasible to purchase those to whom Senators and Congressmen must listen—the local political bosses who control the machinery of nomination and election. The most honest legislator who values his job—and the majority of them do—has his vulnerable spot, and if he owes his office to the support of crooks, money will talk to them and they to him. Many of the most outrageous political scandals have been of this type, with the elected representatives of the people, and still more, the appointed incumbents of high offices, mere pawns in the unscrupulous hands of local politicians who cynically offered themselves for sale to the highest bidder.

When, recently, Mr. H. C. Hopson testified that Associated Gas & Electric had attempted to influence editorial opinion by placing or withholding advertising, he gave an excellent illustration of anti-social methods of propaganda. It may be hard sometimes for a corporation to see why it should go on spending its money to support a publication which attacks it; but any use of financial pressure for the purpose of controlling editorial expression is clearly an outrage against public decency. This sort of thing, be it observed, is not lobbying or the work of lobbyists. It is something much more far-reaching and infinitely more pernicious than lobbying at its very worst—the secret use of money to buy public opinion. It is closely akin to the methods formerly charged against certain of the power interests, whereby the very children in the grade schools were supposed to learn from their teachers the iniquities of government ownership.

The seamy side of all attempts to influence legislation is, in truth, the ugly background of our entire politico-economic system of conventions, nominations, and elections, of the whole complex relationship between wealth and public service. With most of this the legislative lobbyist has little or nothing to do. In the scandals of the Ohio ring in its palmy days, for instance, lobbying was a relatively unprofitable side-issue; there was far more to be made out of the administrative branches of government. Any State or community which permits its elections to be dominated by bosses or gangs will inevitably face corruption, and that corruption will show itself in attempts to influence legislation as in everything else in which there is a possible shake-down. But it is utterly unjust to blame lobbying for such a condition.

To what extent, and through what channels, it may be legitimate to spend money—in the long run the people's money—for the purpose of affecting public opinion is wholly problematic. It costs money, for instance, to be elected to Congress. The laws provide, not that a candidate shall spend only a specified sum, but that he shall fully and truly account for whatever he does spend—and also tell where he got it. A like rule would help to eliminate many of the evils in the employment of money for purposes of propaganda, and, incidentally, would relieve the lobbyist of much of the opprobrium now thrust upon him because of acts for which he is seldom responsible.

In all this matter of seeking to influence public opinion, whether legitimately or otherwise, there is nothing of the traditional activity to which lobbying owes its repulsive name. The man who appears at public hearings, generally by express invitation, as the representative of some particular group, who assists, again commonly by invitation, in the drafting of legislation or of amendments thereto, and who sends out legislative information for the guidance of his clients or for distribution to the public, has so far done nothing which would require him ever to ask whether the Capitol has any architectural features denotable as lobbies. But the lobbyist is likewise accused of conversing privately with individual Senators and Congressmen. Well, why shouldn't he? Usually he calls on them, like any other visitor, in their offices, but there are times when he does have to earn his title by seeking them in the fusty purlieus of the Senate and House chambers. It is no indictable crime—though it may well prove an error of judgment—to talk with a Congressman even amid the blended aromas of the House restaurant, or to confer with a Senator on that scenic railway that careens underground between the north wing of the Capitol and the Senate Office Building.

This—this holding converse with legislators individually—is lobbying in all its pristine nakedness. It is excoriated as if it were a consorting of habitual criminals. And yet its hideous immorality is singularly hard to discover. Practically everyone who goes to see a Senator or Congressman "wants something"—a job, an introduction, a departmental favor, a card to the galleries. Why should it be perfectly proper to talk to him about anything else, but indecent to confer with him about his most important duties.

The lobbyist, indeed, is often at a peculiar disadvantage in this respect; he has a far harder time in capturing ten minutes with any legislator who doesn't want to see him than the camel had in squeezing through the Needle's Eye. He lacks the "Open Sesame" of the voter from the home district, and if he is, or is guessed by the secretary to be, in the least unwelcome, he will cultivate the patience of Job in the outer office while the magic doors fly open to those who, on election day, may remember. And if he seeks his prey in the Capitol itself, though from the gallery his own eyes may have told him that the gentleman is safely in his seat reading the comic page of the morning paper, the attendant who condescends to bear his card into the sacred precincts of the Senate or House chamber returns with the curt advice, "Isn't there."

Most lobbyists waste very little time in seeking to make possibly undesired calls, nor is there ordinarily much occasion for it. After all, legislation is made largely in committee, not on the floor. The members of the two committees, one in each House, to which any particular bill is referred, and frequently just the members of special sub-committees of these committees, are the persons whose opinions will be guiding, and probably determining. Even in debate on the floor, the lead in almost every instance is taken by not more than half a dozen members, most of whom have already had the advantage of studying the proposal in committee. These are the people whom the lobbyist makes a point of seeing personally, and he frequently does so by express invitation.

As typical of many such conferences, I recall a hearing several years ago at which I had to testify, largely on technical matters, at a length which completely exhausted both the committee and me. Just when I thought I was through answering questions, and the chairman was about to dismiss me with evident relief, one member, who had hitherto remained absolutely silent, piped up. "I've been listening to this witness," he said, "for hours, and I've been listening to other witnesses for days, and they've all used lots of words I don't understand, and what's more I don't believe the rest of the members of this committee understand them any better than I do. Now I wish this witness would just start in now and explain what some of these words mean."

There was a bewildered pause. The request was reasonable enough, and yet to grant it meant compelling the whole committee to sit and listen to me for at least another hour. The chairman gazed at me forlornly. The other members squirmed uncomfortably in their seats. And then I caught in the chairman's eye—though he would deny this—the faintest suggestion of a wink.

"I should be delighted to do the best I can," I said, "but the committee has already been so patient and considerate that I hate to trespass further on its time"—at this point the tension began palpably to relax—"and so if the Congressman will be good enough to give me a few minutes in his office, I will try to answer any questions he may care to ask me."

Whereupon I departed with the benediction of the chair, and that afternoon I strove to answer the Congressman's questions for a solid hour. I had reckoned him as certainly among the opponents of the amendments I was advocating—so much so that in our talk I made no effort to discuss them—but when the committee reported, there, to my astonishment and delight, was my Congressman with the majority—a small one and not on party lines—recommending the adoption of the amendments in question.

The trouble with the personal conference, as distinct from most of the other phenomena of lobbying, is that since it is not a matter of record, it gives occasion for all sorts of sinister inferences. I remember once, in the Senate waiting-room, overhearing a conversation between two women, one evidently a Washingtonian, and the other a friend from afar who was being shown the sights.

"That's Senator So-and-so," said the Washington lady in the stage whisper with which one refers to marvels at the Zoo, "and that"—indicating the man with whom the Senator was in earnest conversation—"is Mr. Blank—you know—the lobbyist for the What's-its-name."

"O-o-oh," responded the visitor in awed tones. "Is he bribing him now?"

This state of mind is lamentably common. The lobbyist is supposed to go about bearing a brief-case stuffed with currency, or at the very least to do his nefarious work by the alternate application of financial threats and promises. Now, it would be absurd to claim that such things never have happened—there have been black sheep in Congress, as everywhere—but by and large there is amazingly little evidence of it. It must be remembered that every legislator who faces re-election, as most of them periodically do, lives in the most transparent of glass houses, with opponents goggle-eyed for any chance to "get the goods on him." Even for a legislator with an itching palm the risk is too great.

Of course, Senators and Congressmen are always being told that certain actions will win—or lose—untold numbers of votes, but it is hard to see what is inherently wrong in that. After all, we live in a democracy, and the only way in which a legislator can free himself from the tyranny of the ballot is by death or not choosing to run. "Pressure" of this sort is inevitable, but most of it comes, not from the lobbyist, but from the politically-minded friend from home. As for direct bribery, most of the talk about it is utter nonsense. I am told that somebody once prepared what purported to be a current market price list of Senators and Congressmen—a document which, if it ever really existed, which I doubt, would have made good reading. Washington is a hotbed of wild rumors on every subject, and anyone who has lived there awhile learns to discount them heavily. One would think, from the absurdities that periodically gain currency, that a

Congressman could not so much as dine with an old friend without thereby selling his immortal soul. Nobody with a grain of intelligence imagines that one can buy a legislative vote with a dinner. If there is ever more direct bribery than this, the secret is unbelievably well kept, and that in an environment where secrecy is almost impossible.

Back in the Hoover era, on one of Washington's hottest summer days, I encountered a certain distinguished Senator in a corridor of the Senate Office Building, and we went to lunch together. It was too hot for appetite, and our combined meal—for which, after some altercation, I paid the total sum of twenty-five cents—consisted of one order of shredded wheat and two glasses of milk. In the course of this Spartan fare, I mentioned a bill which was scheduled to come up that afternoon, and told the Senator what I thought of it, and why. Afterward, as we were walking across to the Capitol, he suddenly stopped. "What," he said solemnly, "do you suppose the Great Engineer would think if he knew there was a United States Senator who could be bought with a shredded wheat biscuit?"

It is quite true that many of the lobbyists are on friendly terms with a considerable number of Senators and Congressmen, and that this personal relationship is sometimes assisted by a certain amount of entertaining. But, here again, why not? In every other sphere a reasonable amount of luncheon- or dinner-giving is regarded as entirely fitting, and an attorney may offer a cocktail to a judge without being in contempt of court. Accepting such an invitation occasionally does not put a legislator under the slightest obligation to vote as his host wants him to. Such entertaining as is done— and for obvious reasons it is seldom lavish or costly—is partly for the purpose of establishing friendlier personal contacts, but far more because the lunch or dinner hour is often the only time when Senators or Congressmen can get away from their tasks. Even legislators have to eat, and many a conference takes place over the luncheon table. It was at just such a luncheon—given and paid for, incidentally, by a Senator who wanted me to discuss a certain legislative matter with some of his colleagues—that I last met the late Will Rogers, whom our host had run into on his way to the dining room. Mr. Rogers knew and cared nothing about the subject of the conference, but his wit gave me the best-humored audience I ever hope to have.

Not long ago I was guilty of what now appears to be a heinous crime— I gave a cigar to a Senator, and the worst of it is that I did it in public. A hearing was just getting under way, and I happened to be the first witness. As I sat down, I noticed that the Senator sitting opposite me —a warm personal friend, but notoriously likely to disagree with everything I was there to say—was fumbling in his pockets, and then making unmistakable but unavailing pantomime in the direction of one of his colleagues.

Brazenly I took a cigar from my pocket; shamelessly, in the sight of all, I handed it across the table. The official record immortalizes the sin with the one significant word "Laughter."

Admittedly, however, the personal friendliness which exists in some cases between lobbyists and members of Congress, and which it is manifestly part of the lobbyist's business to maintain, opens the way to certain grave abuses. There are, unfortunately, plenty of people in Washington who seek to trade unscrupulously on alleged present or past "influential connections." Former Senators and Congressmen, lawyers or specialists who have been associated with administrative departments of the government, publicity agents, people of all kinds who claim to be somehow "on the inside," can be found among the ranks of those who undertake to render mysterious services for their prospective clients.

The trouble, of course, lies in the abuse rather than in the use of such contacts. It is exceedingly important, and indeed essential, for anyone who has dealings with any branch of the government to be fully posted as to procedure, to know whom to see and how to see him. The person who comes on business to Washington without a competent guide and adviser is likely to waste hours and days which could easily have been saved by a little timely counsel and a few entirely proper introductions. The moment, however, any person claims to have "influence" for sale then it is time for everyone concerned to look out. This is the most flourishing of all the Washington rackets, and, like all rackets everywhere, it fattens chiefly on the gullible. Nobody knows how much money is annually wasted in fees for this sort of "service," any more than we know how much is lost in any other form of confidence game. Here, indeed, are the frayed and tattered fringes of lobbying; here are the people who have done most to bring lobbying into disrepute.

Experience of governmental methods, a wide acquaintance among Washington's official population, long and special training in the analysis and interpretation of bills, laws, and regulations, and an established reputation, all these are parts of the wholly legitimate stock-in-trade of the attorney or other representative who does work in Washington on behalf of clients elsewhere. It is likewise legitimate that these qualifications should, in some instances, command exceedingly high prices. The experienced lobbyist, whether or not he is a practicing lawyer, is a specialist, and not infrequently is paid as such. Even if he happens to have gained some of his experience in the service of the government itself, it is certainly no crime subsequently to use that experience openly for the benefit of his clients. But as for the self-advertised venders of "influence," they continue to exist only because there is apparently no end to the supply of credulous and stupid people who believe in miracles.

Many of the ablest lobbyists in Washington to-day are Republicans, whose present political influence, as former Secretary of War Hurley recently stated, is "not worth anybody's nickel." Lobbying, indeed, has always been a special prerogative of the party out of power, by reason of its much larger number of politically prominent persons who no longer have government posts. Nobody with a grain of sense supposes that a Republican ex-official collects large fees on the strength of his influence with the New Deal. Among the Democrats who are now active as lobbyists, only the least reputable—and least successful—claim to be able to exercise any "personal influence." The large majority, like their Republican colleagues, make it perfectly clear that what they have to sell is experience in a field in which long and intimate observation is peculiarly necessary.

Enough has been said to indicate that the large fees sometimes paid to Washington attorneys and others for guidance and assistance in legislative matters—in simple language, for lobbying—do not necessarily imply the slightest impropriety. A man who, in an important civil suit, pays his attorney fifty or a hundred thousand dollars is not therefore assumed to be seeking to corrupt the judge or bribe the jury. Whether the attorney's services are actually worth that much is for the client, and for him alone, to decide. In exactly the same way, there are Washington representatives who, without having or claiming a particle of "influence," and without a single word or act that will flinch beneath the spotlight of publicity, are sufficiently experienced and capable so that they are fully entitled to charge high prices for their services.

Nobody would contend that all the money used for the purpose of affecting the course of legislation is wisely or honestly spent. Some part of it is at times diverted into wrong channels, above all when it gets into the hands of irresponsible underlings far removed from Washington itself. Expenses for general propaganda, whether legitimate or not, are always open to challenge, but the mere size of some of the amounts revealed whenever there is a lobby inquiry is not of itself enough to justify such an outcry. Any adequate legislative campaign costs money, even assuming, as is generally the case, that every cent of it is spent properly. A single item, such as the preparation and printing of a brief, may easily run into many thousands of dollars, and every lobby swells the receipts of the Post Office Department. The public ultimately pays the bill, of course, just as it pays the cost of the very active and efficient lobbies maintained by the various administrative departments of the government. In both cases the essential thing is full and accurate publicity as to how the money is spent; the fact that the amount involved may be large is no indication of improper use.

But what of the poor man in all this? The corporation may be able, with its customers' money, to hire expensive lobbying counsel, but how about the consumer, the man in the street, the housewife? The answer to that is that the strongest and most effective lobbies in Washington to-day are essentially "poor men's" lobbies. The American Legion campaign for the bonus bill, compared to which the efforts of the utility holding companies have been as the crackling of thorns under a pot, was certainly no plutocrats' party. To this day people recall the efficiency of the lobby which presided over the passage of the Adamson Bill. The lobby maintained by the American Federation of Labor, which is always on the job, has no support from millionaires. As for the farmers' lobby, it has been getting bills for the relief of agriculture passed in almost every session of Congress since the World War; if the farmers have not reaped the benefits thereof, it has certainly been from no lack of lobbying pertinacity. Anyone who thinks that lobbying unduly favors the rich has only to survey the laws enacted by Congress during the past five years—the period, we are told, of the lobbies' most insidious efforts.

Furthermore, the lobbies representing "the masses" have a tremendous head start. To begin with, they have the votes. When a labor representative tells a Congressman that his support of a certain bill will infallibly cost him the labor vote in his district, that Congressman pricks up his ears. When a consumers' organization advises a Senator that every woman in his state wants a certain thing done, that Senator is going to think twice before refusing to do it. There is, too, an enormous psychological advantage in championing what appears to be the cause of the people, even though the people may be in the end the chief sufferers. And nobody need imagine that the lobbies representing the consumers, labor, and the smaller producers are inefficiently staffed. True, they seldom go out and hire expensive counsel, but they more than make up for it by keeping their people on the job permanently. The intimate knowledge that some of them have of their business makes the highest-priced attorneys look like novices.

There are abuses in lobbying, of course. There are lobbying crooks who swindle their clients with fabulous tales of the wonders they can accomplish through mysterious channels. There are blunderers with distorted moral senses who fake telegrams and advocate whispering campaigns. There are subterranean workers who intimate that every legislator has his price. Above all, there are the people whose business is to squeeze money out of every phase of politics—the bosses who control elections and therewith the men they elect. Just so in every field; there are shyster lawyers, quack doctors, absconding bankers, labor racketeers, venal office-holders. But because these elements exist, in lobbying as elsewhere, it is grossly unjust to single out for public denunciation an occupation which not only exists by legal right but which—when properly conducted, as it commonly is—is a benefit and a necessity to the American people. It is largely through the instrumentality of lobbyists that legislation is adequately studied before enactment, and it is chiefly by way of the lobbyist that detailed information regarding such legislation reaches those who are most deeply concerned with it.

There can be no serious objection to having lobbyists registered as such, with full publicity as to their relations with their clients and with the public in all matters affecting legislation—provided there is a clear realization that the badge of the lobbyist is not a Scarlet Letter of crime. When a President of the United States referred publicly to the "lobbyists who, like a swarm of locusts, infest the halls of Congress," there was more than an intimation that the people had no longer the right of petition guaranteed by the Constitution, and that our laws ought to be enacted in Star Chamber secrecy. Until that right is denied as contrary to the mechanism of dictatorship, the lobbyist has a legitimate, necessary, and honorable place in any system of government by the people.

No. 53

[THE American states for many years have sought to curb the excesses of the lobby although they have, at the same time, recognized its political value. Regulatory statutes are now in force in three-quarters of the states. These laws were occasioned mainly by periodic investigations into the sinister aspects of the lobby and by a few of the more choice political scandals which were unearthed during the course of these investigations. For the most part, these laws do not attempt to remove the basic conditions which have produced the lobby. Rather, they forbid certain kinds of legislative pressures, regulate the procedures through which the lobbyist may exert influence on the legislature, and attempt to publicize his actions in the hope that the glare of this publicity will act as a restraining influence. These laws and their general effectiveness are the subject of Professor Zeller's "Pressure Groups and Our State Legislatures."]

THE REGULATION OF LOBBYING [1]

by Belle Zeller

"LOBBYING is declared to be a crime." Since this clause was written into the Georgia Constitution in 1877, the opinion has prevailed among the states that lobbying practices and activities should be regulated. Although Massachusetts and Wisconsin had already passed laws providing for the registration of lobbyists, it was the disclosures of the New York insurance investigation in 1905 that led to the enactment of regulatory measures in many more states. This movement has continued until, to-day, thirty-six states have enacted laws regulating lobbying in some way.

It is therefore advisable to examine the more important features of these laws. Such an examination soon discloses that either no specific definition is found or at the best the definition is vague and difficult to interpret. For example, Georgia and Tennessee define lobbying as "any personal solicitation of any member of the general assembly during the session thereof . . . *not addressed solely to the judgment.*" Texas and Louisiana stress the *appeal to a legislator's reason* as the legitimate manner of influencing him. A number of states—Kansas, Kentucky, North Carolina, Rhode Island, South Carolina, South Dakota, Wisconsin—provide that the laws apply to those who promote or oppose legislation *"affecting the pecuniary interest of any individual, association or corporation as distinct from those of the whole people of the state."* In Oklahoma, a person "employed for a valuable consideration" is guilty of lobbying who *privately* attempts to influence the act or vote of any member of the legislature concerning measures before that body.

Twenty-two states provide for publicity in the form of registration of legislative agents or legislative counsel who are employed in such capacities for compensation. The required information must include the name and address of legislative agent or counsel, by whom employed, date of employment, duration of employment if it can be determined and the subject of legislation to which the employment relates. In most of these states the Secretary of State is delegated the responsibility of providing the docket for the filing of such information. For example, in Kentucky the Attorney-General has this responsibility, in Massachusetts the sergeant-at-arms, in Florida the secretary of the Senate and the clerk of the House.

[1] Belle Zeller, "Pressure Groups and Our State Legislatures," *State Government* (August, 1938), Vol. 11, pp. 144-147, 155. Reprinted by permission of the author and *State Government*.

Eight of these 22 states draw a distinction between legislative counsel and legislative agent. The compensated legislative counsel's activities center largely around his appearance before legislative committees whereas the legislative agent "for hire or reward" does any act to promote or oppose legislation except to appear before a committee of the legislature as legislative counsel. All other provisions of the laws apply to agent and counsel alike. This distinction appears to be of little significance since there is no evidence that the lobby is under any more effective control in these eight states than the other fourteen where no such distinction is drawn. Most of the laws require that the registration of legislative counsel or agent take place at a specific time—usually one week after date of employment while others simply state that *before* any service is entered upon such registration provisions must be carried out. In some states, furthermore, the legislative counsel or agent files a signed authorization from his employer, ten days after the latter has recorded his agent's name upon the legislative docket.

Sixteen of these 22 states that require registration of a legislative counsel and agent also require that a statement of all expenses paid, incurred, or promised in connection with the promotion of legislation be filed either by the employer or the counsel or agent within 30 days (in 12 states) or two months (in 4 states) after the adjournment of the legislature. In addition the Maryland statute provides that "the Governor, whenever any bill is presented for his approval, and he has reason to believe that in connection with the passage thereof by the general assembly improper expenses have been paid or incurred, may require any or all legislative counsel or legislative agent and their employers to render him forthwith a full, complete, and detailed statement duly sworn to, of all expenses paid or incurred by them, or either of them."

Some states, Nebraska and North Dakota, for example, attempt to define the scope of the activities of legislative counsel, agent, or lobbyist by stating that their service before the legislature shall be limited to "appearing before regular committees thereof, when in session, or by public addresses, newspaper publications, or by written or printed statements, arguments or briefs delivered or transmitted to each member of the legislature." By so doing, these states hope to discourage personal solicitation of legislators. Other states go one step further in requiring that written copies of these statements be placed on file before delivery to the legislature or committees thereof—in Wisconsin and South Dakota 25 copies with the Secretary of State, in Oklahoma 20 copies with the chief clerk of the house before which such person desires to appear.

A number of the state statutes grant special exemption to professional advisers who may draft bills, advise their clients and render opinions as to the construction and effect of pending legislation. A still larger number of statutes further exempt duly accredited counsels or agents of cities, counties, towns, villages, public boards and public institutions from registering under the provisions of the law. A familiar clause in the state statutes regulating lobbying is one that prohibits the employment of any person to promote or oppose legislation for compensation contingent in whole or in part upon the passage or defeat of legislative measures.

The states, of course, provide penalties for violations of the law. The penalties may differ for the same offense from state to state, or different penalties may be provided for violations of the various clauses of the law within a particular state. In most of the states, the fine may be combined with or substituted for a prison term. Where the crime committed is characterized as a felony, or a bribe is given or offered to a member of the legislature, the maximum term runs as long as five or ten years. In Florida, the penalty for false swearing is imprisonment for a term not exceeding twenty years. However, in some twelve states the maximum term of imprisonment is 30 days or six months or one year. Six states in addition to the fine and/or prison punishment, provide for the disbarment of the guilty legislative counsel or agent for a period of three years from the date of conviction.

In fourteen states the statutes regulating lobbying are brief and deal for the most part with *improper* influence on legislation. They are concerned chiefly with prohibitions placed upon the taking of bribes by, or the giving of bribes to state officials. Montana and Utah, for example, provide that "every person who obtains or seeks to obtain money or other thing of value from another person, upon a pretense, claim, or representation that he can or will improperly influence in any manner the action of any member of any legislative body in regard to any vote or legislative matter, is guilty of felony."

In Oregon, if a person having an interest in legislation does not "first duly and completely disclose to such member (of legislature) his interest therein, or that of the person he represents," he is liable upon conviction to punishment by imprisonment or fine.

This brief analysis of the provisions of the existing state lobbying laws in the United States discloses:

1. The failure to define lobbying specifically. Such a definition should cover *professional* lobbyists, and state clearly the practices that are permissible and those that are not. The existing statutes either make no attempt at definition or, as indicated above, dispose of the question in such vague and meaningless phrases as to make them difficult, if not impossible, to interpret and enforce.

2. Lack of proper enforcement provisions. It is true that several of the statutes state that "it shall be the duty of the attorney-general, upon information, to bring prosecution for the violation of the provisions" of the law.

Better results would undoubtedly be achieved even under the existing law-enforcement provisions, if the disposition and desire on the part of the public officials were present to invoke the law more frequently and to prosecute more vigorously under it. Is it not expecting too much for public officials to go out of their way to "dig up" the information upon which to support the prosecution of a violation of vague and indefinitive legislation?

Examination shows, therefore, that attorney-generals act only in flagrant cases of overt violations that have attracted wide publicity, but such occasions are rare indeed. However, some agency, perhaps a legislative committee, or the attorney-general's office, itself, should be charged with the authority to conduct periodic and frequent investigations for the purpose of determining whether or not the law has been violated. A formal report with recommendations should be submitted to the attorney-general and to the legislature at every regular session. The publicity following such a report would cause enforcement agencies to act.

It is, perhaps, of interest to note that the number of legislative appearance statements filed in the regular sessions in 1937 ranged from two in Georgia where a legislative agent prior to registering must pay $250 for every person, firm, or corporation whom he represents, to three in Idaho where personal solicitation is restricted, up to 78 in South Dakota, 107 in North Carolina, 112 in Ohio, 114 in New York, 165 in Maine, 166 in Nebraska, 248 in California. In New York during the thirty-year period, from 1908 to the end of 1937, an average of 133 legislative appearance statements were filed yearly with the Secretary of State. It is not surprising to learn that expense statements do not disclose large expenditures. They conceal more than they reveal. These may vary from reports of "received nothing and spent nothing" to expenditures totaling approximately $100,000 for a regular session of the legislature of the wealthiest state in the union.

It is recognized that it is difficult, if not impossible, to "legislate" bad lobbying practices out of existence. However, it is generally conceded that some regulatory prohibitions are needed as a check. So long as lobbying plays its indispensable role in our constitutional system, a good regulative law should be provided for each of the 48 states embodying the best features of the laws now in existence, providing for the registration of lobbyists and for the filing of expense statements, with special attention to the two cardinal weaknesses in these laws.

However, it is apparent that any attempt to solve the problem of the lobby and create a system in which the various pressure groups will exert an influence in proportion to their social usefulness, necessitates also the extension and improvement of official research agencies, a thoroughgoing reorganization of the legislative process and greater interest in affairs of state by the general public.

No. 54

[THE typical American state legislature meets for a sixty-day session every second year. The member of that legislature, in this brief period, must express a supposedly well-considered opinion on subjects ranging from abbatoirs to zoologists. He must reach decisions on bills providing for systems of social insurance, the taxation of corporations, the regulation of the medical profession, the regulation of the intricate financial operations of holding companies, and a host of other equally diversified and highly complex subjects.

Obviously no one legislator is informed on all of these items; it is indeed rare to find one who is fully informed on any one of them. He is forced to seek aid and guidance from some outside agency. Recognizing that it is undesirable for the legislator to have to rely entirely on the lobby for information, a few states have provided an expert non-partisan research agency, and a still larger number have supplied some help in the field of bill drafting. Professor Witte discusses the nature and importance of these "Technical Services for State Legislators."]

TECHNICAL SERVICES FOR STATE LEGISLATORS [1]

by Edwin E. Witte

THE major technical services for state legislators which have developed in this country are legislative reference, bill drafting, and statutory revision. Reference and research services are listed in the 1937 edition of *The Book of the States* as existing in 42 states, drafting services in 43 states, statutory revision services in 15 states; plus which there is the Interstate Reference Bureau, conducted since 1930 by the American Legislators' Association. Unfortunately, however, the existing technical services for legislators in many states appear to be almost non-functioning.

There are 19 states with functioning combined bill drafting and legisla-

[1] Edwin E. Witte, "Technical Services for State Legislators," *State Government* (February, 1938), Vol. 11, pp. 32-34. This is a shorter version of an article by the same title that appeared in *The Annals* of the American Academy of Political and Social Science (January, 1938), Vol. 195, pp. 137-143 and is reprinted here by permission of *The Annals* of the American Academy of Political and Social Science and *State Government*.

tive reference services, 4 states with substantial but separate drafting and reference services, and 4 other states which have such separate services but as to which the author is doubtful whether they are "substantial." Thirteen more states make claim to having both a drafting and a legislative reference service of a kind, but either or both are very evidently inadequate; four states have one or the other of these services; and four neither of them. Fortunately, most of the more populous states have public bill drafting and legislative reference services which are really functioning. In comparison with other activities of the state governments, however, these services are small even in California, New York, Pennsylvania, and Wisconsin, which are the states with the largest appropriations for such services. In no state is as much as $100,000 per year expended for such services.

All these three types of technical services are universally acknowledged to be very necessary to the reasonably efficient functioning of state legislatures; where established, they function without arousing serious opposition, and legislators do not hesitate to make use of them; from time to time additional services are created in states without them. But very certainly, bill drafting, legislative reference, and statutory revision services have not fulfilled the high hopes expressed by their champions when they first attracted public attention in the pre-war decade.

At that time they were hailed as a "really far-reaching reform in our legislative life." There was expectation that through such services legislation could be placed upon a scientific plane and freed from the baneful influence of the lobbyists.

It is now evident that too much was expected of the legislative reference bureaus. No matter how efficient the technical services may be, they cannot guarantee good legislation. Much more fundamental changes are required to make the state legislatures function at maximum possible efficiency.

It is also very clear that legislative reference work has suffered from administrative reorganization in many states. When a legislative reference bureau is attached to a large administrative department, it becomes more difficult to preserve the reputation for neutrality, which everyone agrees is vital in services of this kind.

Occasionally, also, legislative reference services have become involved in contests between legislatures and governors, with resulting disastrous consequences to them. Such services should serve both, but it is often difficult to do so without arousing the suspicions of one or the other, when they are in conflict.

Most of all, technical services for state legislators have suffered from too narrow a conception of their purposes and from second rate leadership. A few legislative reference executives, perhaps, attempted too much and forgo that their function was to serve the legislatures, not to boss them. Much more commonly, however, the executives of technical services have been content to conduct them in such a way that they would not arouse opposition. There is far more danger that legislative reference bureaus will do too little than that they will attempt too much. Services of this kind will, indeed, be continued if they are content to go on as they have been, but if they make their continued existence their major objective, they will fall far short of accomplishing what they should.

Many legislative reference services are merely "highly specialized libraries," as Professor Leek described them a decade ago, but they should be something very different. It was unfortunate that the bill drafting and legislative reference service which Dr. McCarthy built up in Wisconsin was called "the legislative reference library" and was attached to the free library commission. In Wisconsin this title has made no difference, and the connection with the library commission has been advantageous; but it was the Wisconsin service that first attracted attention, and other states in trying to establish a similar service made the mistake of regarding it as a specialized library.

Legislative reference work does not consist of collecting books or even the very miscellaneous fleeting literature of current legislative questions; nor does it consist merely of indexing bills and making accessible prior legislative proposals. The essence of legislative reference work is the furnishing of information in response to inquiries, primarily from legislators and secondarily from others interested in legislation. The information furnished should be accurate and as complete as possible. No less important is it that the information should be in such concise and understandable form that it can and will be used by the legislators. A library consisting mainly of materials compiled in answer to prior or anticipated inquiries will be helpful; but it is a hindrance, not a help, if it absorbs too large a part of the energies and appropriations of the service.

Likewise, bill drafting must concern itself with more than the technical details. It is not the draftsman's job to tell the legislator what sort of legislation he should introduce or support. It is for the legislator to decide all questions of policy. But it is the draftsman's responsibility to translate the decisions of the member into statutory provisions as consistent as possible with the existing body of law and the structure and functioning of the government. To do so, the draftsman must understand the member's proposal and all its implications, and it is his duty to acquaint the member with all its effects upon the existing law and government, so that the member can make intelligent decisions on alternative methods which are open to him in working out the details of his proposal.

All this means that "technical services for legislators" are fraught with many difficulties. In the last analysis, how well these services are performed depends upon the man in charge and the competency of his assistants. This is truly, as Dr. McCarthy said, "a man's work"—one that calls for all the ability that any man possesses. At one and the same time the director and his staff must have "a passion for anonymity," unusual tact, a broad knowledge, and tireless energy. But if well done, services of this kind are worth all the effort that anyone can put into them; and, while they cannot guarantee good legislation, they can be very valuable in helping legislators to do their work more efficiently.

Chapter XVI

THE EXECUTIVE IN AMERICAN GOVERNMENT

[THE executive in modern government has, in general, two functions. In the first place, the executive is concerned with a legislative program. Its business is to translate the complex pressures of public opinion into legislative recommendations. It is, secondly, an administering agency charged with the management of a large body of public employees who are applying legislation. Its business is to see that the public services apply the legislation, in letter and in spirit, as the legislative assembly intended. It is responsible, therefore, not only for the character of the legislative program but for its detailed and day-to-day application. Errors that are made are its errors; the blame is always upon its shoulders.

This being the nature of the executive in modern government, it is important to examine its detailed characteristics at the national, state, and local levels in the United States in order that we may determine whether it is properly organized to discharge its responsibilities.]

No. 55

[PROFESSOR ROGERS' article is exactly what its title implies, an examination of the American presidential system. It presents an accurate picture of the President as chief executive and makes it possible for us to assess whether the system is such that the President can effectively discharge his responsibilities as chief legislator and chief administrator.]

THE AMERICAN PRESIDENTIAL SYSTEM [1]

by Lindsay Rogers

GOVERNMENTS, like clocks, go from the motion men give them: and as governments are made by men, so by them are they ruined too. Wherefore governments depend rather upon men than men upon

[1] Lindsay Rogers, "The American Presidential System," *The Political Quarterly* (October-December, 1937), Vol. 8, pp. 517-529. Reprinted by permission of the author and the Political Quarterly.

governme,its." From what representative political institution does the
truth of William Penn's dictum receive a more convincing and more vivid
demonstration than from the American presidential system? Its history
is the history of the men who have been at its head. Some Presidents were
vigorous. Others were inert. One avoided the ruin of threatened disunion.
A century and a half after the adoption of the Constitution, the manner
of the functioning of the presidential office cannot be adequately discussed
save in terms of its occupants. The system now works differently from the
way it did under Coolidge whom the country desired to be inactive, or
under Hoover to whom the electorate administered a decisive rebuke for
vacillation and timidity.

Not of his two immediate predecessors has Franklin Roosevelt thought
when he considered his responsibilities and opportunities. He has looked
to Lincoln and Woodrow Wilson and, in a lesser degree, to Jackson, Cleveland and Theodore Roosevelt. They have been the last century's "strong"
Presidents. So far as Franklin Roosevelt is concerned, differences of opinion
exist only in respect of whether his manifestations of strength have been
expert or inexpert, wise or unwise. All of the men in the galaxy of strong
Presidents were by temperament averse to inaction, but in three cases at
least they were aided by the fact that their times clamoured for leadership.
Lincoln and Wilson led the country through two wars. Mr. Roosevelt had
to battle with a depression. Warfare on the economic terrain has proved
a more demanding, and will to historians seems a severer, test than warfare on the military terrain. When he holds an ordinary office a man is
judged by what he does, but a man at the head of affairs which call for
leadership must, as Bishop Creighton said, be judged also by what he
chooses to do. That is pre-eminently the case with American Presidents.
What they choose to do moulds the presidential system. Unlike Prime
Ministers, they have the advantage of relative freedom from the restraints
of colleagues or the command of party. They have the great disadvantage
that certain choices which they prize highly may be disapproved by the
Aristocracy of the Robe as not authorized by the Constitution.

To the draftsmen of that document there was vouchsafed no vision that
they were creating the most powerful elective office that one hundred and
fifty years later the world was to know. In method of recruitment and the
tasks imposed on it, the Presidency is now precisely the opposite of that
which the Framers contemplated and for which the written word still provides. Their scheme was for an exceptional man to be chosen by a group
of outstanding men—the Electoral College. Universal suffrage and the
growth of political parties have transformed the Electoral College into a de-

vice for recording the verdict of an electorate which is forced to choose between candidates put forward by irresponsible party nominating conventions. The race is not to the swift nor the battle to the strong, but time and chance have happened favourably to the United States in turning up at crises men of exceptional stature.

Less spectacular but hardly less complete is the change in the part that, after his election, the President is called upon to play. The Constitution provides that "The executive power shall be vested in a President of the United States" and imposes upon him the obligation of seeing that the laws are "faithfully executed." Its intention was that in law-making the President should be no more than a check or balance. Thus "all legislative powers" are vested in Congress, and the President's share in this process—according to the literary theory—is confined to summoning Congress into extraordinary session, delivering messages and vetoing proposals of law. If when this last happens, Congress is still in session, it may by a two-thirds vote of each House "override" the veto. In determining the relations between the White House and the Capitol in Washington, the laws now reach but a little way.

The President's minor rôle has become his major rôle. Nor was this development only at long last. The growth of political parties which from time to time differ on the programmes they wish to see driven to the statute book, and the clamour of interests and sections for Congressional legislation have been responsible for the change. Politics and economics have reversed the emphasis of the Constitution. The stone which the builders thought unimportant has become the cornerstone of the presidential system. The President is now chief legislator and the country judges him on the basis of his success as a legislator rather than his success as an executive.

How Franklin Roosevelt has played his more important rôle is notorious. No previous American President has been so much discussed in Europe. Great journals which have rarely paid attention to American affairs now send their most brilliant critics to see the great actor perform. It should not be thought, however, that the drama is of a new genre. Its tempo is faster, there is more action, and the climaxes are more smashing; but from Wilson to Roosevelt there have been changes of degree, not of kind, of personality but not of task. The depression called for more vigorous leadership than did the War—vigorous in that the subjects of legislation were more numerous and covered a far wider ambit. The task was greater also because in economic warfare there is no unanimity on objectives. During the World War, dissentient groups were unimportant. Under the Roosevelt Administration there have always been determined minorities who insisted that measures argued for must not be accepted because of the sacrifices they would require of individuals or groups. That, to be sure, is an obstacle that has to be surmounted in any representative government, but in the United States the separation of the President and Congress creates difficulties which can be avoided by parliamentary chief executives.

The presidential system is highly personal and Mr. Roosevelt has greatly intensified what legal structure has made inevitable. The American Cabinet is an inchoate body of clerks chosen on the basis of geography and of political followings. No more than half of the ten members of the present official family could in a Cabinet meeting furnish any ideas or criticisms worth listening to on subjects other than those immediately concerning their own departments. Moreover, great segments of public policy—interstate commerce, the control of monopolies, shipping, communications—are the province of the so-called independent boards and commissions. These are quasi-administrative, quasi-judicial bodies whose members are appointed for staggered terms and who are not easily removable by the President. As chief legislator, the President can support or oppose or supplant the proposals of these commissions but he has no power of control. Since the United States has no administrative class of civil servants, there is a lack of creativeness at this level, and the civil service is normally not the source of important new legislation. In his major rôle, therefore, the President must take much of the initiative himself and on each specific piece of legislation must determine the *ad hoc* assistance which he will require. That assistance is *ad hoc* not only on the content of the legislation but also in respect of its draftsmanship. The Senate and the House maintain legislative drafting services which are inadequately staffed, but the President has no such agency.

The most spectacular legislation which Mr. Roosevelt has proposed was the Bill to add six additional Justices to the Supreme Court of the United States. That scheme was hatched by the President in consultation with two or three intimate advisors, put in the form of a Bill, shown to the Attorney-General so that he could prepare a supporting letter (which turned out to be quite weak on its facts) and then communicated to the Cabinet a few minutes before it exploded in Congress and stirred up a bitter discussion in the country. In the ensuing debate, the President discarded the grounds on which he first urged the measure and took a more tenable position. Or, as chief legislator, the President can function in consultation with the officials immediately concerned. That has been the procedure for the preparation of much of the relief administration. Or he can appoint an

interdepartmental committee to draft a Bill. That was the course followed
when the reciprocity treaty policy was framed. Or the President may ask
that a special group—half governmental, half extra-governmental—sponsor
the studies that are necessary to serve as the base of legislation. That was
the background of the Social Security laws. Finally, the President may
emerge as an advocate of measures which have been hatched in Congress
and for which there seems to be some support. That roughly was the situation with the recent minimum wage and maximum hour legislation to take
the place of the National Industrial Recovery Act which was declared
unconstitutional by the Supreme Court.

Given such handicaps in preparing legislation, the President, manifestly,
is not happily circumstanced in dealing with Congress. He gets highly uncertain assistance from the instrument of party. The machinery of presidential nominating conventions is geared to choose "available" candidates.
It is rare that those nominated have been outstanding party leaders, and
even rarer that they have been leaders for any length of time. In 1928, for
example, Alfred E. Smith, then the Democratic candidate for the Presidency,
persuaded Mr. Roosevelt to be the Democratic party's nominee for the
governorship of New York State. Much against his will, Mr. Roosevelt
consented. He was elected and, after two years, re-elected. Albany was an
excellent vantage point from which to plan the capture of the presidential
nomination. Had Governor Smith had other preferences in 1928, or had his
importunities not been yielded to, Mr. Roosevelt could not have been the
presidential candidate in 1932. After election, however, a President, no
matter how minor a person he has been before, at once becomes the leader
of his party. If he be a man of only ordinary force, no one can challenge
his titular primacy because he has enormous powers of patronage. If he be
a man of more than ordinary force, with a programme that has support in
the country, he can translate titularity into reality.

Nevertheless, leadership is personal rather than party. The President
heads, that is to say, a national organization which is made up of sectional
organizations that have varying interests and loyalties. There is little agreement on doctrine. The paths down which the President may attempt to
lead Congress are sometimes entirely different from those promised on the
hustings. That was the case, for example, with much of the New Deal
legislation. Between the election and the inauguration the situation had
changed greatly and different panaceas seemed to be called for. Or, after
searching his secret conscience, the President may blaze a trail through a new
wilderness and ask the party to go hunting with him—e.g., the Supreme
Court proposal. In such adventures the President cannot rely on party

discipline, for there is little of that. For many years most major legislation has been pushed through Congress with the support of bi-partisan majorities, and has been opposed by bi-partisan minorities. Rarely does the President carry with him all of his party, and to carry as much as he does, he must be adept in handling patronage and artful in persuasion. Senators and Representatives follow because they wish to be known as supporters of the President. They think that such a label will advantage them when they stand for re-election. Or they oppose the President because this seems politically more expedient. Nor does a large party majority in Congress necessarily increase prospects of control. I doubt whether Mr. Roosevelt was greatly overjoyed when the last election gave him such an overwhelming number of Senators and Representatives who labelled themselves Democrats. As he looked at them when he read his message to the new Congress, he must have had something of the feeling credited to the Duke of Wellington when he was inspecting a group of new recruits for the British army. "I don't know whether they will scare the enemy, but, by God, they scare me." In the summer of 1937 Mr. Roosevelt's party majority began to scare him.

Presidential attention to drilling the recruits may be confined to Washington or it may extend throughout the country. When the latter is the case, the President concerns himself with "local situations"—with nominations and elections to state or even municipal offices. Woodrow Wilson, who attempted with considerable success to be the leader of the Democratic party in Congress and who through a party caucus (now unimportant) established more discipline than any of his successors have enjoyed, did not concern himself with local political organizations and their problems. It may be that President Roosevelt has an opposite view of his responsibilities. It may be also that by temperament he enjoys the game that the Tapers and Tadpoles play. Whatever the reason, President Roosevelt devotes a good deal of his time to the petty business of local politics, to the scufflings of the Tapers and Tadpoles. Whether from the standpoint of the presidential system the game is worth the candle is highly doubtful. It is rare that votes in Congress are thereby influenced. Moreover, in recent elections the swings of the popular vote have been so great as to suggest that an unpopular President does not measurably increase his chances of re-election by the attention which he pays to local political organizations. Indeed, he may give the country the impression that he is descending from his eminence. Perhaps his best strategy is to be as intelligent as he can be and pray that the country will be favourably impressed.

In his other rôle also, that of Chief Executive, the President must rely on

ersonal rather than on party loyalty to fill the legal lacuna which the Con-
titution permits and even desires. Throughout much of the administrative
eld, the President is unable to initiate or to prevent. The heads of de-
artments and independent establishments have authority which is theirs
) use without the necessity of securing presidential approval. Because
f the ineffectiveness of the Cabinet and because there is no centre of legal
eference like the Privy Council through which administrative legislation
ust be filtered, the President lacks machinery to turn up the information
hich he should have in order to control administrative policy. When
nformed, he can do no more than attempt persuasion, and if this fails,
emoval from office is the weapon which he must use. In that is to be
ound the sanction of administrative management under the presidential
ystem.

Hence, with the presidential system as it is now organized, the President
annot be a highly successful chief administrator. Indeed, it is amazing
aat breakdown is avoided. At the apex of the hierarchy, he is responsible
or all policy. Each of the ten secretaries who head departments and each
f the sixty or seventy heads of independent establishments have direct ac-
ess to and take advice only from him. Even within the departments there
re certain officials who on some matters deal with the President rather
aan with their nominal chiefs. Laboriously he must thread his way through
host of unrelated matters. Everything is tackled à *deux*: neutrality policy
ith Secretary Hull; Puerto Rico with Secretary Ickes or the Governor of
ae Island and the Chief of the Division of Territorial Possessions.; labour
olicy with Secretary Perkins or the heads of the various boards or a spe-
ally constituted body, as in the case of the steel strike; relief with Mr.
[opkins or governors or mayors. The President must act on a series of
x parte cases presented to him. He hears only one side. Inadequately
:affed so far as a personal secretariat is concerned, he lacks anything
emotely resembling the organization which Sir Maurice Hankey heads.
a short, the system imposes the maximum of physical burden and reduces
) a minimum the opportunities for discussion and thought before action.
he situation is far, far worse than that against which Mr. Lloyd George
evolted in 1916 when he set up his War Cabinet and made Mr. Bonar Law
ae sentinel to drive away intruders so that the members of the War Cabinet
ould have time to think.

In his uncoördinated handling of large policy and petty detail, the
merican President lives under the shadow of Congressional refusal to per-
ait any managerial freedom. With respect to personnel and the estimates,
e has hardly an iota of the authority that the British Treasury possesses.

On such matters, Congress is the dictator, and it has not yet learned th
by imposing too severe limitations on the structure and methods of a
ministrative management, it is really lessening its own authority. T
Congressional prerogative of criticizing and calling to account a man wh
has full responsibility is far more valuable than insistence on a statuto
straitjacket which may be used to furnish an alibi for delay and inefficienc
The weight of this consideration is not lessened by the President's politic
irresponsibility *vis-à-vis* Congress. His responsibility to the country wou
be less clouded if Congress could bring itself to give him a freer administr
tive hand. Congress delegates tremendous law-making authority and th
makes it difficult for the President to see that the laws are faithful
executed.

Finally, as every schoolboy knows, the American Presidency combines th
two functions of government which Walter Bagehot distinguished as cer
monial and efficient. The result is a heavy addition to the already tr
mendous physical burden of the office. But the combination has furth
unfortunate consequences. The fact that the President is the Head of th
State draws from him some of the fire to which a political leader should h
constantly subjected. Press and political opponents deal with ignorant o
mistaken presidential utterances more hesitantly, more politely and ther
fore less cogently than they would if the utterances came from a Prim
Minister facing the legislature.

These combined functions and the separation of the executive from th
legislature mean that the President must devote some attention to publi
relations—to "building himself up," to persuading the country to accept th
picture of himself which he thinks is desirable. In Great Britain, I take i
such publicizing has thus far been confined largely to the Monarchy. Ther
as Mr. Kingsley Martin's brilliant little book shows, the publicizing has ha
remarkable successes. In the United States, public relations are, to thos
who work the governmental machines, more important than they are in
country with a Cabinet system. British Ministers can be judged on the
performances in the House of Commons. Failure cannot be long conceale
Whatever may be thought of the representative character or the legislativ
efficiency of the House of Commons, or of its lack of control over the execu
tive, that body still compels Ministers to show what kinds of persons the
are. Hence there can be some measure of agreement on the characters an
abilities of men in office. Myths cannot long perdure. In the United State
those who attempt to work the presidential system do not have to prov
themselves in day-to-day dealings with the legislature. They must there
fore convince the public of their strength by resort to the press, the wireles

and the cinema. Sometimes it is difficult to demonstrate the fake of touched-up portraits. Under the presidential system, office-holders need never appear in the mental undress of parliamentary squabbling.

Since Mr. Roosevelt put forward his court proposals, some quarters have voiced fears concerning the growth of personal government in the United States. These fears seem to me chimerical—with one possible reservation and even for that Congress is responsible. Of necessity Congress had delegated to the President far-reaching law-making authority. The mathematically-minded can calculate that President Roosevelt is empowered to "make legislation" on more than seventy subjects with which his predecessors did not have to deal. But what Congress has granted, Congress can take away. Hence I see scant reason for being alarmed by the argument that the presidential system is developing into a personal dictatorship.

My reservation is in respect of the huge sums for relief and public works which have been authorized by Congress but which the President can allocate. The bulk of these moneys is distributed through state and municipal governments. Since those who head the state and municipal administrations are in part judged by their success in securing federal funds to supplement their own relief measures, the President of the United States in a sense holds the power of political life and death over a host of public officials throughout the country. That is a new and dangerous kind of political power. As a bribe or as a weapon, it can be far more important than patronage ever has been—that is, appointments to office. It can be far more insidious than Congressional "pork barrels"—that is, the appropriation acts which contain grants for post offices, river improvement, public buildings, and so on, in such profusion that representatives of the communities favoured are sufficiently numerous to make approval overwhelming. But even this spending power of the President is exercised only because Congress so wishes. Congress could set up a non-presidential—if it so desired, a non-partisan—machinery for allocating relief funds. Apparently Congress does not want to do this. The present system is wasteful and corrupting, but it is not a system which makes the head of the presidential system a dictator.

Viewing these constitutional and statutory handicaps, one naturally asks: why have they not had more serious consequences? Why does not the American presidential system work so badly as clearly to demonstrate these defects and to secure their correction? It is true that on critical occasions the United States has been fortunate in the men brought forward to work cumbersome machinery. But the success of the presidential system is not due to the factors that Bagehot had in mind when he said that the men of Massachusetts could work *any* constitution. American economics have made American politics tolerable and now—as in other countries—the great question is whether politics will be competent to provide a tolerable economic life. The size of the country, great natural resources, a small *per capita* public debt, relatively low taxation and a rising standard of living have combined to muffle the creaks and strains of the presidential system. Moreover, as in Great Britain down to the advent of the Labour party, the United States down to the advent of Mr. Roosevelt had escaped political cleavages on any matter (save slavery) that was fundamental. Even now in the United States the cleavage is not between parties. Indeed, it may conceivably force a re-alignment of parties. Publicists frequently point out that governmental insti-tutions as we have them—parliaments and executives—were set up in an age when governments dealt with problems that were largely political. Now governments must deal with a host of economic problems. Will the old institutions prove efficient instruments? By such a test the future of the American presidency will be determined. That future, however, will be shaped more by men than by laws.

No. 56

[THE tasks and the responsibilities of the executive in our state governments are not fundamentally different from those of the executive in the national government. The governors in our states, however, are, in many cases, more hampered by the organization and distribution of executive power than is the President. The following article by the late George Dern, who was at one time Governor of Utah and later Secretary of War, gives us the reflections of a successful politician and executive officer upon the operation of the executive office in the states. The main emphasis is upon the administrative rather than the legislative aspects of the executive office but is valuable for the insight it provides into the difficulties standing in the way of a governor who wishes to be an effective administrator. In addition, it raises the question as to whether the present organization of state government is such as to enable the people to hold the politicians in the executive offices responsible for the efficient admini-stration of the public business.]

GOVERNORS AND LEGISLATURES[1]

by George H. Dern

THERE is a considerable degree of misapprehension in the popular mind with respect to the proper functions of a governor. Some critics might add that occasionally there is also a considerable degree of misapprehension in the mind of a governor with respect to his own proper functions. But at any rate, it is important to have a clear conception of a governor's duties, and of his relationship to the legislature in administrative matters.

Without wasting time on non-essentials, let us dive head-first into the vital question of where governmental responsibility is situated in the American system.

It is not front page news that each state government, as well as the national government, is divided into three departments—legislative, executive and judicial. The Judicial Department is usually an orderly, well-behaved group which knows its place and keeps in it. To be sure the national legislative branch once in a while thinks the Supreme Court is poaching upon its private preserves, but as a general rule there is a satisfactory line of demarcation between the Judicial Department and the Legislative and Executive Departments, especially in the States.

This seems to leave the quarrel, if there be one, between the Legislative and Executive Departments. Do these brethren always dwell together in harmony? Do legislators work overtime praising the executive for his fairness and scrupulous regard for the rights and powers of the co-ordinate branch? Does the executive lie awake nights thinking up new ways to tell the public that the legislative branch knows its place and stays in it? Oh, we get along with each other pretty well, and the little clashes help to make life interesting. Such clashes as we have are, of course, due to the cussedness of legislators who persist in playing politics, a vice which never even enters the purer mind of the executive.

Nevertheless, there are honest differences of opinion as to the distribution of authority between the Legislative and Executive Departments. The general public is prone to hold the Governor responsible for everything that happens during his term of office, including the acts of all elective and appointive officials, if not the actions of the Legislature itself. Popular opinion thinks of him as an officer of vast power and clothed with authority

[1] George H. Dern, "Governors and Legislatures," *State Government* (August, 1931), Vol. 4, pp. 7-16. Reprinted by permission of *State Government*.

to tell everybody else what to do and what not to do. With such an impression abroad I say, "Come let us reason together."

The Governor has two functions, executive and administrative. When a Governor goes into office he ought first to get it firmly fixed in his mind that there is a vast difference between these two functions. His executive functions are inherently his own, being vested in him by the Constitution. His administrative functions, on the other hand, are all delegated to him by the Legislature, for the legislative branch is the source of all administrative authority. This distinction is of such fundamental importance that it is worthy of amplification.

A State constitution usually provides that "the Governor shall see that the laws are faithfully executed." That is his executive function, with which the Legislature has nothing to do. On its face it looks like a fine cloak of authority, but upon examination it is a flimsy garment, because the actual enforcement of the laws is in the hands of various State and local officials.

Although the Governor is denominated the chief executive, in most States he is only one of a group of constitutional executive State officers elected by the people, all independent of each other and, in their executive capacities, responsible only to the electorate, whilst in their administrative capacity they are responsible to the Legislature. The Constitution of my State, which is typical, provides that "the Executive Department shall consist of Governor, Secretary of State, State Auditor, State Treasurer, Attorney-General and Superintendent of Public Instruction." In many States the number of elective officers is much larger. Oklahoma fills 14 State offices by popular election, Mississippi 13, and Arkansas, Louisiana, Michigan, Nebraska, New Mexico and North Dakota 10 each. On the other hand, lucky Maine and New Jersey only elect one. The Governor, of course, has certain constitutional powers peculiar to his office. He is commander-in-chief of the militia; he may convene the Legislature; he may fill certain vacancies in State and district offices; and he has the appointive power. However, he has little authority or supervision over the other elective officers of the Executive Department, each of whom has his own constitutional duties. Indeed, it might almost be said that Utah, for instance, has six Governors instead of one.

Not only has he scant supervision over the other elective State officers in their executive capacity, but he is in substantially the same position with respect to them in their administrative duties and also with respect to the appointive State officials. These have their functions specifically prescribed by law, and it is their duty to obey the law, not to obey the Governor.

At the most the Governor, in his executive capacity, only has authority to see that they perform those duties faithfully.

Perhaps the Governor has come into office on a promise to enforce certain laws which are being flagrantly violated. When he gets on the job he finds that the enforcement of such laws is the duty of local officers over whom he has no control. If a complaint reaches him that the peace officers of some community are winking at law violations, about all he can do is to call the complaint to the attention of the officers who are doing the winking.

Thus he becomes disillusioned about his great executive powers, and he finds that instead of having law enforcement in his hands he is little more than a figurehead in this respect. If he is a philosophical student of our form of government he will not find fault with this arrangement. So far as the general principle is concerned he will doubtless approve the good old theory that this is a government of laws, not of men, and that law enforcement should be kept close to the people.

So much for the Governor's executive function, which, as I have attempted to show, consists of a general supervision over the law-enforcing agencies of the State government. We come now to the administrative function, which consists of actually administering the laws as enacted by the Legislature and interpreted by the Judiciary. In this field the Governor has a much wider influence. Although it is still the duty of the administrative officers to perform the duties laid upon them by the Legislature, and although the Governor is not in a position to exercise his own judgment and discretion in enforcing the laws, he will find that through his power of appointment he has a very substantial, though intangible, influence upon the manner in which many laws are enforced. In this field of administrative functions, if we except his influence upon legislation, he will find most of his own activities and most of his opportunities for useful service, provided the laws of his State invest him with the authority which he needs in order to render the services. All his administrative powers must be delegated to him by the Legislature.

Let us examine his legal powers in this field a little more closely. The National Government is the same as the State governments in that all administrative authority is derived from Congress. Because the President is the only executive officer, and since the members of his cabinet are appointed by him, there is a common belief that he is legally responsible for all their acts. That this view is erroneous was clearly explained in a Senate report during the 46th Congress, which, after enumerating the President's constitutional executive powers, used this language:

The departments and their principal officers are in no sense sharers of this power. They are the creatures of the laws of Congress exercising only such powers and performing only such duties as those laws prescribe. . . . The Secretaries were made heads of departments; they were charged by law with certain duties, and invested by law with certain powers to be used by them in the administration confided to them by the laws. They were in no sense ministers of the President, his hand, his arm, his irresponsible agent, in the execution of his will. There was no relation analogous to that of master and servant, or principal and agent. The President cannot give them dispensation in the performance of duty or relieve them of the penalty of non-performance. He cannot be impeached for their delinquency; he cannot be made to answer before any tribunal for their inefficiency or malversion in office; public opinion does not hold him to stricter responsibility for their official conduct than that of any other officer. They are the creatures of law and bound to do the bidding of the law.

The foregoing doctrine has been sustained by the Supreme Court, as witness the following extract from one of its decisions:

The executive power is vested in a President, and as far as his powers are derived from the Constitution, he is beyond the reach of any other department, except in the mode prescribed by the Constitution through the impeaching power. But it by no means follows that every officer in every branch of that department is under the exclusive direction of the President. Such a principle, we apprehend, is not, certainly cannot, be claimed by the President. There are certain political duties imposed upon many officers in the executive departments, the discharge of which is under the direction of the President. But it would be an alarming doctrine that Congress cannot impose upon any executive officer any duty they may think proper, which is not repugnant to any rights secured and protected by the Constitution, and in such cases, the duty and responsibility grow out of and are subject to the control of the law and not to the direction of the President. And this is emphatically the case where the duty enjoined is of a mere ministerial character.

The same rule, of course, applies to State governments, and hence the plan of centralized administrative control does not mean at all that the Governor will become an autocrat who will try to run every State office and activity. Personally, I have no use for dictators, whether they be of the Mussolini type or of the Lenin type. They all look alike to me, and I should be the last to advocate a scheme that would defeat or impair our representative form of government. But I do think that, in the interest of the taxpayer, our State governments should be organized in such a fashion that they may be able to approach private enterprise in efficiency.

To illustrate the statement that the legislative branch is the source of all administrative authority I need only cite one or two concrete illustrations.

Whether or not the State shall have a system of State highways is for the Legislature to decide. What roads shall be State highways is also for the Legislature to decide. Who shall construct the highways and how much money shall be expended are likewise questions for the Legislature to decide. If the Legislature prescribes a highway program, and creates a highway commission to be appointed by the Governor to carry out the program, it is the commission's duty to build the highways, not the Governor's. The Governor has nothing to do with how, when and where the roads shall be built. His duty is to appoint the commissioners, and see that they carry out the program prescribed by the Legislature. He should, however, have administrative power to see that the commission sets up an efficient organization and does not waste the State's money. He should therefore have the power of removal as well as the power of appointment.

The regulation of rates charged by public utilities is a proper function of the Legislature, but it is not feasible for the Legislature itself to perform that function in a satisfactory manner. It therefore creates a Public Utilities Commission, and authorizes the Governor to appoint its members. The Public Utilities Commission is an arm of the Legislature, not an arm of the Governor, and it would be usurpation on his part to attempt to dictate to the commission with respect to its duties. Nevertheless, even with a punctilious respect for the official powers and duties of the commission, it is entirely appropriate for him to scrutinize the organization and operation of the commission from a business or financial standpoint, with a view toward preventing waste or extravagance.

I need not multiply examples to prove that it is the function of the legislative branch to decide what activities the State shall undertake; to dictate how and by whom the activity shall be carried on; to give the necessary directions and prescribe rules of procedure; to furnish the money to carry on the activity; and to exercise control, by means of adequate accounting, audits, reports and other devices, over the persons to whom the work is entrusted. These are all the administrative functions, and constitute the means by which the Legislature confers administrative authority upon its agents.

Notwithstanding the fact that the Legislature is the source of all administrative authority, there is no reason why the Governor should not be the most important administrative officer, particularly in matters of finance. On the contrary, there is every reason why he should be. For the past 20 years or so the cry has been for greater efficiency and economy in government, both National and State. We are told that Government should adopt the methods of private enterprise where efficiency and economy have been most highly developed. The advice is good, and we ought to study the organization of private business and pattern after its good features. How does a successful corporation function?

In the first place, it has a body of stockholders, who own the business, and who are in it to make money. They elect a board of directors to run the business for them, giving it broad powers as to policies and methods. Once a year the directors report back to the stockholders. If their steward- ship is approved they are usually re-elected. If not, they are superseded by another board.

The directors, however, do not pretend to manage the business. They only determine policies and authorize projects, and they elect a general manager to carry out those policies and projects. Within the limitations imposed by the directors he has authority to conduct the business of the corporation, and he is held responsible for the results. If the Board elects other officers, such as a treasurer and a secretary, their duties are of a subordinate character, and they have no voice in the general management of the business. They have nothing to do with making profits except in so far as they are of assistance to the general manager.

How nearly analogous is the organization of most State governments to this approved type of business organization? If we consider the State as a corporation, the people are the stockholders. They own the business, but they are not in it to make money. They are in it to get certain services as cheaply as possible. They elect a board of directors, known as a Legislature, to run the business for them, giving it broad powers as to policies, direction, supervision and control. Obviously the Legislature, consisting of a large number of members, and meeting only every two years, cannot pretend to manage the business directly; hence it must delegate its authority to others. It therefore farms out its authority to sundry officers, boards and commis- sions. These should all be under the supervision of a general manager who would be responsible to the Legislature. The Legislature, however, does not elect a general manager to act as its agent. The general manager, in the few states which have one, is elected by the people and he is called the Governor. If the Governor were given full authority to supervise the finan- cial administration of the policies and projects of the Legislature, and if he were held responsible for the results, the cases would be nearly parallel, for the mere circumstance that the Governor is elected by the stockholders in- stead of by the directors does not necessarily militate against successful operation of the proposed set-up.

However, there are only a few States where the analogy is approximately complete. In my State, as I have said, we have six managers, all elected by and responsible to the people, and all independent of each other. Many States have a longer list of constitutional elective officers. Although the Governor is nominally the Chief Executive, the other officers are not subordinate to him, and if they do not like his orders they can tell him where to go. Each of these officers usually has important administrative functions added to his constitutional functions, but they are not co-ordinated under one head. They may antagonize each other and all pull in different directions. How long could a private business enterprise survive with that sort of internal discord? How long would such foolishness be tolerated by the stockholders?

It seems anomalous that in our National Constitution we should be willing to say that "the executive power shall be vested in a President of the United States of America," whilst in most of our State Governments the executive power is spread out wide and thin, and the Governor is the Chief Executive in name only. But it is far worse to spread the administrative authority all over the lot, with no centralized control over the spending of the taxpayers' money.

The Secretary of State of the United States, to whom we entrust international affairs of tremendous import, is appointed by the President, but the Secretary of State of most of the States of the Union must be elected by popular vote.

The Attorney-General of the United States, who is the lawyer for the National Government, is appointed by the President, and is therefore in harmonious relationship with the Chief Executive, but in most of the States the Attorney-General is elected by the people, so that he is not only independent of the Chief Executive, but may actually be hostile to him. Why should not the Governor select his own legal adviser, so as to be sure of having a lieutenant of whose ability he is satisfied and upon whose co-operation and loyalty he can depend?

Why should we tolerate a system under which the Governor may be pulling in one direction whilst his fellow officers are pulling in the opposite direction and frustrating his efforts? How can we enforce efficiency under such a system? I do not speak out of any personal grievance. It happens that I am receiving cordial cooperation from my fellow officers of the Executive Department, and they are my personal friends. Unfortunately, this happy condition does not always exist, and the form of organization actually is important. If the other State officers, instead of being elected by popular vote, were appointed by the Governor, they would naturally be his trusted advisers and the State would reap the advantages of the cabinet form of government.

I suppose Utah is not the only State that has worked out a fairly satisfactory form of centralized financial administration despite a multiplicity of elective State officers. The State has a budget system and the formulation of the budget is the duty of the Governor, as it should be. The Governor, the Secretary of State and the Attorney-General constitute the State Board of Examiners, who must approve all claims before payment, thereby exercising financial control. These officers also comprise the State Board of Supplies and Purchase which supervises the purchasing department and performs some of the functions of a department of finance. This triumvirate therefore exercises broad administrative powers, and we virtually have a commission form of government, instead of the Governor being the real adminstrative head of the State Government. Perhaps there is something to be said for a multiplicity of counsel. It is obvious, however, that the same system could be used with appointive officers, and also have the other advantages of the cabinet system.

There is nothing novel in this suggestion that the States should take a leaf out of the Federal Government's book, and centralize administrative authority in the Governor, because several States have already done so.

There is nothing undemocratic about it. Why should it be considered more democratic to vote for half a dozen candidates, five of whom the average voter does not know, than to vote for one whom the voter does know? For there is no conceit in the plain statement that in a State election the candidates for Governor are the ones who arouse public interest and around whom the campaign centers, whilst the rest of the candidates are usually just so many more party nominees. Democracy means that every voter uses his individual judgment and makes his own choice of candidates. In a State election not more than one voter in a thousand even knows the names of the candidates for, say, State Treasurer, and so instead of making a choice he merely registers his political party affiliation. What is there so democratic about that? What does the voter gain by it?

As Governor Alexander once said,

> A modern business institution is a true democracy, controlled and conducted by those who own its stock yet who know little about the details of the business they conduct. The American people are said to elevate the dollar above all else, including even their patriotism, yet they are content not to meddle in the details of the business in which their dollars are invested and which returns them other dollars. They never suspect that in selecting a competent manager to conduct their business they are waiving any of their rights.

This is a good place to put more business into government. Certainly one officer can be held accountable much better than can six who may all pass the buck to each other. The system of checks and balances is wholesome as between the three departments, but to let one executive officer check another leads to confusion and inefficiency.

The practice of curtailing the powers of the Governor is a relic of colonial times, when the Governor was appointed by the British Crown. The colonists had no voice in his selection and he was seldom chosen from their number. He was regarded as an outsider over whom they had no control, and who administered affairs not for the best interests of the colonists but as the agent of the mother country. There were frequent conflicts between the Governor and the Legislature, and the people invariably sided with the Legislature, especially when the arbitrary will of the Governor prevailed. The result was that the people became embittered and prejudiced against executive and one-man power.

This prejudice remained after the Revolution, and it was deemed necessary to do away with executive tyranny. The Governor was therefore generally elected by the Legislature, and shorn of all but a semblance of power, while the Legislature became supreme.

Gradually, however, the practice grew up of electing the Governor by popular vote. The people learned that when he, no less than the Legislature, was selected by and responsible to them the fear of tyranny was groundless. Furthermore their implicit confidence in the Legislature was shaken by specific cases of legislative corruption and extravagance, and it became evident that the great powers of the Legislature should be curtailed and that some of them should be transferred to another body. During the first half of the nineteenth century there came a wave of extreme democracy, which resulted in frequent elections of almost all public officials, from dog catcher to Governor and Supreme Court judges. While the Governor became independent of the Legislature his power for several decades was not appreciably increased. In fact, in some of the States his duties were so slight that it was not even deemed necessary for him to live at the seat of government.

Since the Civil War there has been a decline in public confidence in the efficiency of popular elections, and simultaneously there has been a great increase in the number of the functions undertaken by the States, which has resulted in the creation of very many new offices. When it became almost a physical impossibility to place on the ballot the names of all the officers to be chosen, many of them were made appointive by the Governor. There has come about a gradual increase in the power, prestige and influence of the Governor, until to-day there is probably more distrust of Legislatures than of Governors. Nevertheless the decentralized type of administration in the American States is still the rule rather than the exception. The object of the framers of the American Constitution was to prevent the government from becoming so strong as to jeopardize the rights and liberties of the individual citizen, and our State constitutions are still cluttered with the efforts in that direction. The inertia of governmental organization is hard to overcome.

There can be no doubt that if we want our State governments to approach the efficiency of private business, we need a more unified, concentrated and efficient type of administrative organization. All competent students of the subject are agreed on this point, and also in the conviction that it can be achieved without any sacrifice of individual liberties.

How can it interfere with individual liberties when all we are talking about is financial administration? The powers of the Legislature will not be affected at all, and the only object is to save money for the taxpayers.

It is not proposed to infringe upon the responsibility of the Legislature in determining what the State shall do and in what activities it shall engage. This does not necessarily mean that the Legislature should specify every detail. In my State, for example, the Legislature designates certain State roads, and makes certain funds available for their construction and maintenance. It is left to the State Road Commission to determine the precise location of each road, the type of construction, and the order in which the several projects shall be built. The system works admirably, and I have recommended a similar arrangement for State buildings. The Legislature, during its brief session, is poorly equipped to make adequate study of the building needs of the State institutions. I think it would be advantageous to have a State building commission make a thorough survey of the State's building needs, and report its recommendations through the Governor to the Legislature. The Legislature might well use these recommendations to aid it in authorizing a building program to meet the State's estimated needs for a period of years, and determine how much money should be spent from time to time. The building commission could then determine the order in which the buildings should be erected and the type of construction, and proceed to carry out the program. Legislative log-rolling would be eliminated, and a higher type of construction could be had at a minimum cost.

The centralized administration herein suggested does not contemplate taking away from the Legislature the function of prescribing the agencies and organizations which shall carry on the activities which it has created. Here again efficiency might be promoted if the Legislature did not attempt to be too specific in the details of internal organization of an activity. Decisions in this field made in advance of actual experience are likely to be productive of harm.

The Legislature should also be left with authority to determine the per-

onnel of the agencies which it creates, particularly the officers who are to
e responsible for the direction of the activities. That is, it should deter-
aine their number, character, compensation, powers and duties. How far
. should go in specifying the subordinate personnel is doubtful, but it can
npose a limit by the size of the appropriation. It is for the Legislature
o say that the Industrial Commission shall consist of three members, but
: is difficult for it wisely to prescribe the number of inspectors, statisticians,
eporters and other necessary employes. Centralized administrative control,
owever, contemplates that the Chief Executive shall prepare a budget of
he financial needs of the service and submit it to the Legislature. In the
ormulation of this budget a careful study of the subordinate personnel
vould be made for the information and guidance of the Legislature in
naking appropriations. A businesslike control of expenditures by the Chief
Executive is another administrative function that the Chief Executive would
erform for the Legislature.

The Legislature, as the source of all administrative authority, must obvi-
usly have power to determine means for legislative supervision and control,
nd it should exercise that right. It can do so by requiring proper records,
egular reports, accurate accounts, periodical audits, and such other means
s it may deem proper.

With all these safeguards and reservations of power in the Legislature
here can be no reason why the Chief Executive should not be invested with
he duties and powers of a general manager, and made the real business
ead of the administration, whom the Legislature will hold responsible for
arrying out its declared policies in an efficient manner. The line of ad-
ninistrative authority should run through the Governor to the Legislature,
vhich means that the purely administrative officers should be the subordi-
ates of, and subject to, the superior authority of the Governor. In his
idministrative capacity, as distinguished from his executive capacity, the
Governor will therefore be the subordinate of the Legislature, and will be
icting as the agent of the Legislature in controlling financial affairs.

I have tried to convey the idea, and I now repeat it, that there is a
undamental distinction between the responsibility of the Governor in
espect to the organization and management of the government and his
esponsibility in respect to the technical work done by the operating units.
What I mean by that is that the Governor should be held responsible for
he government being well organized and well run from the business stand-
oint, but that he should not meddle with the technical work that has been
delegated to the operating units by the Legislature. The general manager
f an industrial plant does not tell the chemist how to make his analyses,
but he does regulate the wages and hours of assistants, and he sees that

supplies are economically purchased. If the Governor finds that the opera-
ing units are not functioning efficiently from the business standpoint h
should have power to interfere, but his responsibility should be restricte
to the appointment and dismissal of officers.

I summarize by quoting from an excellent bulletin issued by the Chambe
of Commerce of the United States entitled "The Financial Administratio
of Government." This bulletin states that a proper system of financia
administration should be based on certain fundamental principles. Th
first of these is "The definite recognition of the Chief Executive as th
responsible head of the administration, and as such having general responsi
bility for directing, supervising and controlling the conduct of administra
tive affairs and particularly those having to do with finance." The secon
is, "The provision of adequate means through which the Chief Executiv
may, in fact as well as in name, meet and discharge these responsibilities.

If we accept the principle that the Governor shall be the general manage
we must also adopt the rule which is inviolable in private business that h
should have the right to hire and fire. A general manager who cannot selec
his own subordinates is a joke in the business world. Of course, this onl
refers to the responsible heads of departments, and would not interfere witl
civil service.

To give the Governor this power will generally require several importan
changes in constitutional as well as statutory provisions. In the first plac
in most of the States the chief administrative officers are elected by th
people. In the second place, the Governor can only make appointment
with the advice and consent of the Senate, and in some States he can onl
remove them with the concurrence of the Senate. The approval and con
sent of the Senate may be salutary in connection with the appointment o
judges, but when it comes to the appointment of administrative officers t
be the subordinates of the Governor it is out of place. It is absurd to hol
the Governor responsible and then tie his hands.

It seems proper for Governors to seek more power in order to make them
selves more useful to their States. But I have not suggested anything ir
this article that is not already in successful operation in several States and
advocated by competent authorities on State government.

I have not tried to cover the whole field of the Chief Executive's functions
For example, the most conspicuous service rendered by the Governor is often
in connection with his influence upon legislation. Through his powers o
recommendation and veto he has both a positive and a negative influence
upon the enactment of new laws. Moreover, if he assumes the position of
leadership which his people expect of him, he can make himself a strong
force in behalf of new policies which he considers wise and salutary. While

this function is among his chief powers, duties and responsibilities, yet it is not a part of the theme of this article. I have intentionally limited myself to the administrative side of his office, where his usefulness apparently can be increased.

No. 57

[THE form of executive organization in American counties is largely the result of the incorporation of provisions relative to it in the state constitutions. Most of these constitutions were drafted in the last century under the spell of Jacksonian democracy, and they failed to distinguish between the election of officers who would determine policy and those who would administer it. As a result there is usually a long list of elective county administrative officers provided for in the state constitution. This means that there is no single executive that can act as chief legislator or chief administrator.

This situation has led to the proposal for county executives of the elective or of the managerial type, and steps in these directions have been taken in some states. In 1927, North Carolina authorized county boards to appoint managers, and this was done by some counties with considerable success. In 1932, all counties in Virginia were given the option of adopting the manager plan or the county executive plan which provides for an elected executive. Both plans are now in use. In 1931, Montana, and in 1935, New York, established the county manager plan with some limitations.

The following article by Professor Kneier discusses the defects of the present system of executive organization in American counties and presents the manager plan as a possible remedy.]

THE COUNTY MANAGER PLAN [1]

by Charles M. Kneier

IN the organization of county government no definite plan or principles have been followed. Neither the separation of legislative, executive, and judicial powers, nor an executive responsible to a representative body has been applied with any approach to consistency. In nearly every state there is an elective county board which levies taxes and determines matters of local administrative policy; but it has very limited powers of legislation. There is also in every state a number of other officials, mostly elective, with executive, administrative, and judicial functions. These are largely inde-

[1] Charles M. Kneier, "The County Manager Plan," *Public Management* (February, 1930), Vol. 12, pp. 45-49. Reprinted by permission of the author and *Public Management*.

pendent of the county board or of any unified control; and there is no single officer who can be considered as the chief officer of the county, corresponding to the governor of a state or the mayor of a city.

In a report of a joint legislative committee on county government in Ohio in 1926, it was stated:

> In administrative organization county government presents a picture of extraordinary complexity . . . the county violates almost every principle of business and governmental organization which experience has evolved . . . the present system of county government is subject to serious criticism both from the standpoint of administrative efficiency and of popular control. As a business organization the county lacks a responsible head. . . . If democratic government . . . signifies effective popular control, the present organization of the county with its multiplicity of elective offices is fundamentally undemocratic.

A report on county government in Virginia in 1927 criticized the system in that state as follows:

> In our study of Virginia county government we were particularly impressed by the scattered, disjointed and irresponsible type of organization that exists in all the counties. . . . The present county government has no responsible head; it is without a chief administrative officer and the board of supervisors controls through appointment only a small part of the county administration.

Substantially the same statements could be made of county government as it exists throughout the United States. The criticism of county government made some years ago by Richard S. Childs still holds: "It is not a government, it is a dozen governments loosely tied together."

Various proposals have been made to remedy this situation. One suggestion is that there be elected in the county, a chief executive officer. An act of 1893 created for Cook County, Illinois, the office of county president, elected as a member of the county board, with a limited veto over the acts of the board and the power to appoint the county officers not elected by popular vote. In counties of the first class in New Jersey there is a chief executive officer. The law in that state provides for the election of a county supervisor and a board of chosen freeholders. The county supervisor is "the chief executive officer of the county, and may recommend the board of chosen freeholders to pass such measures as he may deem necessary or expedient for the welfare of the county." He must be vigilant and active in causing the laws and ordinances of the county to be executed and enforced. It is his duty to exercise a constant supervision over the conduct of all subordinate officers and to examine into all complaints made against ıny of them for violation or neglect of duty, and if he finds any officer ʒuilty of the charges brought against him, the county supervisor may sus- ɔend or remove him as the case may seem to require. The county super- ʾisor has a veto which may be overridden by a two-thirds vote.

There was formerly in Kings County, New York, a supervisor at large, vho presided over the board and exercised some executive functions. County ɛxecutives were also provided in the home rule charters which were recently ʾoted upon and defeated in Nassau and Westchester counties in New York.

The movement for an elective county executive officer has made little ɔrogress. More recently attention has been directed to the manager plan ɔf government and its extension to the county has been advocated by some ıs a partial solution of the proper organization of the county. It is held hat greater centralization of authority and responsibility is needed than is ɔrovided by the county board; and it is urged that appointment of the ɛounty executive is to be preferred to election.

There are others, however, who admit the merit of the manager plan in ɬhe field of city government but question the wisdom of its extension to ɬhe county. Emphasis is placed upon the county as an artificial unit of ʒovernment, which serves primarily as an administrative district of the ɬtate. They question whether there is a place in county government for ın "all-controlling manager."

The manager plan has suffered the same fate as the strong executive in ɬhe field of county government. The plan is found in name or in principle ɪn a few counties, in North Carolina and Virginia. General county manager ʟaws have recently been enacted in Georgia and North Carolina. County nanager charters have been proposed and defeated in San Diego and Sacra- nento counties, California, in Baltimore county, Maryland, and in Silver Bow county, Montana. While the manager plan has thus far made slow ɔrogress, at the present time there seems to be a revived interest in it as ɬhe proper solution of the unsatisfactory organization of county government.

In considering the extension of the manager plan of government to the ɛounty, there arises the question of its applicability. The argument ad- vanced for the adoption of the manager plan in city government is that the ɛity is a quasi-business corporation, a cooperative consumers' society, en- ʒaged in buying and selling services to its citizens. Since this is the case, ɪt is argued that business principles should be applied—this is secured in ɬhe manager plan. Is the county also a quasi-business corporation and do ɬhe facts warrant the extension of the manager plan of government into ɬhis field to solve the problem of unsatisfactory organization which has been ɔointed out above?

A consideration of the population of American counties and the expenditures made for governmental services is of value in a discussion of the applicability of the manager plan to the county. The average population for all counties in the United States in 1923 was about 35,000, but the few counties having a population of more than a million makes this much more than a typical figure for the country as a whole. The large counties of the West have smaller populations than the smaller and more densely populated counties of the East; and the small rural counties of the Southern states have a small population. The median county population is about 20,000 which more nearly represents the typical county in the United States.

The latest data for which complete figures for county expenditures are available is 1913, the Department of Commerce having omitted entirely the reports on county expenditures in *Wealth, Public Debt, and Taxation* for 1922. The per capita governmental cost payments for counties was reported as $4.49 in 1913. For the period 1912-22 the county tax revenues increased 142 per cent, and it may be assumed that if the figures on expenditures were available they would show approximately the same increase.

Measured by the relative distribution of local administration between the county and other minor districts, the county is of most importance in the Southern states and the Mountain and Pacific Coast states of the West. By the same tests, it is of least importance in New England, where the county is weakened by the importance of town government. In the Middle-Atlantic and North-Central states it occupies an intermediate position.

If a quantitative standard of the intensity of county administration is applied, the results are somewhat different. Judged by the per capita rate of expenditure, the county is of much the greatest importance in the western group of states. Second rank is taken by the North-Central and Middle-Atlantic states, while by this standard the Southern states fall in the third group. In three of the New England states, Massachusetts, New Hampshire, and Maine, county expenditures are of some importance; in Connecticut and Vermont, county finances are almost negligible; while in Rhode Island the county expenses are entirely included in the state budget.

The increase in the urban population is significant in a study of county functions. As more of the people within the county become subject to the control of an incorporated city or village, the functions of the county become less important, the people residing in such incorporated places depending upon this government rather than upon the county, for certain services.

By far the great majority of counties are distinctly rural in character. Perhaps a fourth of the whole number contain a city of over 10,000 population; but even in most of these the rural district predominates. There were in 1920, 12,858 incorporated places having less than 2,500 inhabitants;

his is an average of four per county. In a considerable number of counties he urban population in one or more cities will be more than the rural nhabitants; while in a limited number of cases the population of a large :ity and its suburbs will comprise the great majority or the whole of the :ounty population.

The increased use of special districts is also having its effect upon county unctions. Such districts now exist under at least eighty-nine names and orty-seven distinctive species. Many services formerly performed by :ounties have now been placed under the control of special municipal cor->orations. Thus agricultural development districts, drainage districts, good ·oads districts, highway improvement districts, library districts, park dis-:ricts, poor districts, rural improvement districts and rural community listricts are performing functions formerly entrusted to counties. This :ends to diminish the importance of the county as a unit of local government.

The increasing degree of state supervision and control has been pointed to as a significant factor in determining the future importance of the county. Thus the state has taken over the care of certain defective classes which were formerly left under the control of local authorities. This may be seen in state institutions for the care of the deaf, the dumb, the blind, the insane and the poor. State hospitals also tend to remove this function from the county. State systems of improved highways mean that this activity is being removed in part from county to state control.

Other functions which are still administered by local authorities have been placed under state supervision and control. Examples of this are education, health, law enforcement, charities, and corrections.

While the county is losing some of its functions, to the state, to cities and villages, or to special districts, newer county functions are being developed. Among these newer functions are county libraries, county hospitals, and county parks. About thirty states authorize county libraries, and county hospitals may be established in about twenty states. County parks have been established in a few states. Among the states which now empower counties to establish and maintain airports are Pennsylvania, Michigan, Indiana, North Carolina, Texas, Nebraska, Wyoming, Idaho, and California.

County aid to agricultural interests has been given in various ways, and new methods have been developed in recent years. County fairs supported from public funds were formerly held; and in more recent years farmers' institutes of a more definitely educational character have been established in several states. Giving aid to needy farmers to enable them to secure seed grain and feed is a county function in some states, as North Dakota, Minnesota, Montana, and Kansas. By 1924, county farm advisors were operating in 2,084 counties, in all of the states. About 30 per cent of the total cost of these advisors comes from the counties.

It may be seen that as the older functions are being taken over by the state and special municipal corporations, newer services are being developed by the county. That these newer functions equal in significance those that have been lost to other governmental units seems open to question.

If the functions performed and the cost of governmental services do not warrant the necessary expenditure to secure a competent county manager the question arises as to whether this does not indicate that the county is not a satisfactory unit for efficient administration and point to the need of revising county areas so as to increase their size. This would tend to reduce the cost of county government, since there is needless waste and unnecessary overhead cost where officers serve a small county. In recasting county lines an effort should be made to encourage the development of communities with common economic and social interests. County areas might be revised either by a comprehensive reorganization, state-wide in scope, or by consolidation of existing counties where local sentiment is favorable.

The tendency to place the administration of county functions in the control of some larger area indicates a recognition of the fact that the county is too small a unit for the efficient and satisfactory performance of certain services. While in most cases this has been done by the state assuming the performance of the function which was formerly under local control, in some cases the transfer has been, not to the state, but to some larger area of local administration. Provision is made in several states for the joint performance of certain functions by adjoining counties. Counties in Michigan may unite to form a district for maintaining a health department; in Michigan, Minnesota, and Texas they may erect hospitals for their joint use; Pennsylvania, Michigan, South Dakota, Kansas, and Oregon provide that they may cooperate on road-building projects; and in several states they may cooperate in maintaining joint poor farms and county libraries.

These provisions indicate a recognition of the inadequacy of many counties, as now constituted, to meet the needs for public services, and the desirability of larger areas of administration. The same considerations would seem to apply to other functions, and point to the need of larger counties. Serious study is being given to the consolidation of counties and the revision of county areas in several states; New York and Tennessee are giving more consideration to this problem at the present time than probably any other states.

The great variation of counties in the various states and sections, in size, functions, cost, and in governmental organization, makes difficult any generalizations relative to the county manager plan. It seems, however, that it offers one, if not the most satisfactory, method of improving the conditions in county government. Even though great strides have been made in the direction of state control and will unquestionably continue to be made in the future over certain county functions, it must be noted also that newer services and activities are being developed over which there is no supervision. While emphasis may be placed upon the county as an administrative district of the state, it also continues in many respects as an agent of local government. A study of its functions shows that it too, as in the case of the city, is engaged in buying and selling services to its citizens. If the county manager plan is not applicable to county government as it is at present constituted, the question arises as to whether this does not merely mean that the county is not a proper unit for efficient administration.

While some functions have been transferred to the state, to cities and villages, and to special districts, the county will unquestionably continue to perform functions, both as an administrative district of the state and as a unit of local government. Reorganization along the line proposed in New York and Tennessee may be desirable to secure efficient administration. Whether this reorganization is or is not made, the case for an appointive manager seems strong. For the greater number of counties with relatively small populations the manager could take over the functions of one or more of the existing offices, such as county auditor or county clerk, and it would not be necessary to make any addition to the list of county officers. Some improvement could be made by concentrating more fully in one of the present offices the responsibility for the business management of county affairs. But appointment seems to offer the most satisfactory method of securing a high type of executive and administrative leadership in county government.

No. 58

[THE following discussion by Professor Wager carries further some of the arguments presented by Professor Kneier in the preceding article.]

THE CASE FOR THE COUNTY MANAGER PLAN [1]

by Paul W. Wager

LAST month Professor Kneier outlined in a most illuminating way many of the arguments for and against the extension of the managerial idea to county government. The editor of this publication has asked the writer to make a further statement on the subject. Although Professor Kneier has covered the ground pretty thoroughly there are two considerations that will bear emphasis. The first is that county government must be reorganized in the interest of economy. The second is that county government must be revitalized in the interest of democracy. The case for the county manager rests on the part which he can play in both of these tasks.

Anyone who has observed the operation of county government, in the rural counties at least, must recognize a great deal of waste. Any kind of waste is to be deplored, but to waste a large fraction of the farmer's tax dollar in these depressed times is downright wicked. A few conspicuous forms of waste which are manifest in almost any rural county are: (1) Too many officials and deputies for the amount of work to be done; (2) the employment of officials who are unqualified for their work; (3) the constant "breaking in" of novices both as chiefs and clerks; (4) losses in purchasing supplies because of the lack of centralized systematic buying; (5) interest paid on temporary loans and loss of interest on temporary balances; (6) costly and dilatory methods of collecting taxes; (7) abuse and neglect of public property; (8) lack of any systematic accounting in some instances and duplication of accounts in other instances; (9) idleness or lost motion on the part of public employees because of poor planning and poor management; (10) losses resulting from delinquency or insolvency on the part of officials and taxpayers; (11) laxity and inequality in assessing and listing property; (12) unnecessary overhead because of a duplication of county institutions. Sometimes there is deliberate fraud—bribery, patronage, embezzlement—but the losses from such causes are nowhere near as great a drain on the treasury as these hidden and innocent leakages.

There is no way to measure the extent of such losses. They vary greatly from county to county and from one administration to another but one would be conservative in estimating them at from 10 to 15 per cent of the annual expenditures.

[1] Paul W. Wager, "The Case for the County Manager Plan," *Public Management* (March 1930), Vol. 12, pp. 78-79. Reprinted by permission of *Public Management*.

Can they be stopped? In the opinion of the writer they can be, but not until two conditions are met. First, there must be a unified, co-ordinated government with clear, direct lines of responsibility. The policy-determining body must have a strong executive agent or chief administrator in whom the lines of responsibility converge both from above and from below. That is the chief merit of the council-manager plan and the county is just as greatly in need of a similar organization. The manager plan is the short ballot plan. It does not guarantee good government, but it permits unity and it fixes responsibility.

The second condition which must be met before we can hope to have good government is a sustained public interest. No machinery of government is self-operative. No machine is so nicely adjusted that it cannot be manipulated. No manager is infallible, and we do not want a dictator however wise he may be. Government is for the people's business and they should rule. They will usually act wisely when they have all the facts.

The processes of government must be made visible. They must be stripped of all secrecy and mystery. It is not enough to publish financial statements; they must be interpreted. They must be made so intelligible that the average citizen can understand them. The citizen should be able to trace the expenditure of his tax dollar, and compare its distribution with that of last year, and with that of an adjoining county.

Not only must the process of government be opened up and explained, but its objectives must be stated. Too often government has had no objective, no constructive program to capture the imagination of the citizens. Government must be dramatized; it must be made interesting. The citizen should participate in the preparation of the budget and then be enabled to follow the expenditures month by month. He should share in the formation of a five- or ten-year program and then watch its development year by year. When government is made visible and purposeful the citizens will recognize it as their business and insist that the leakages be stopped. They will give it the enlightened and sustained interest essential to democracy. And they will pay their taxes as cheerfully as they meet their other obligations.

Here is where a county manager is needed. He sees the county as a unit, the county business in its wholeness. He sees the relation of one office to another and where the work of each fits into the general plan. He must be something of a seer as well as an administrator, and a teacher as well as a financial director.

We cannot hope to have efficiency in county government, or in any government, until we restore public confidence, and it will be difficult to restore public confidence until there is efficiency. Both must develop together, and both tasks are within the role of a county manager. We need a strong responsible executive in county government (1) to give the taxpayer more service for his tax payment, and (2) to serve as an instrument for a more vigorous democracy. We need him to give continuity and purpose to government as well as unity. We need managers with social vision as well as business acumen, and with deep human sympathies as well as political insight.

The elements of efficient administration are unity, co-ordination, and centralized responsibility. The elements of democracy are simplicity of organization, tangible objectives, full publicity, and direct avenues of popular control.

Chapter XVII

ADMINISTRATION—ORGANIZATION AND REORGANIZATION

THE work of government falls into two broad categories: (1) the formulation f policy and (2) the execution of policy. The first of these may be called olitics, the second, administration. As we have already seen, the chief execuive has duties and carries on activities closely related to both of these phases of overnmental activity. He has become chief legislator and has long been, in ame at least, chief administrator. Although the congress, state legislatures, or ity councils actually approve or adopt policies, create the machinery of adninistration, provide for its maintenance, prescribe its duties, and examine its esults, the chief executive and members of the administration supply informaion, make suggestions, draft legislation, and in many other ways take part in he process of formulation of policy. Thus, it should be clear that the doctrine f separation of powers is not carried out in any complete or systematic fashion a American government, and that various parts of the governmental machine do ot operate in splendid isolation from each other.

None the less, the administrative organization of government, at some risk o be sure, can be singled out for purposes of description and evaluation. Not nly can it be separated out for these purposes, but such separation, description, nd evaluation are essential for those who wish to improve the American system f government. We should not be misled by Alexander Pope's couplet:

> For forms of government let fools contest
> Whatever is best administered is best.]

No. 59

ONE of the most common charges brought against the administrative branch f government is that it constitutes a bureaucracy. Those who bring this charge o not usually define what they mean by the word "bureaucracy." They generusly imply, however, that the powers of the executive branch of government ave been expanded too rapidly at the expense of the legislative and judicial ranches and to the danger of the liberties of the people. Furthermore, they ntimate that government, at all levels, is attempting to perform too many func-

467

tions, with the result that the number of governmental employees increase
beyond all reason and that taxes become too great a burden.

Each of these three charges is a serious one. If the evidence supports th
filing of any one of them, it should be carefully considered by the America
people. Democratic self-government may be endangered by an unthinking reli
ance on executive action; liberty may be threatened by a sudden and unplanne
expansion of governmental functions. However, the accusations must be care
fully and exhaustively considered. As Professor Dickinson points out, on
neither proves the charge nor encourages careful consideration of its implication
by raising "The Perennial Cry of Bureaucracy."]

THE PERENNIAL CRY OF BUREAUCRACY [1]

by John Dickinson

NO more frequent charge is brought against some of the activities o
the federal administration than that they involve a dangerous an
unwarranted increase of bureaucracy. Behind and apart from the merel
disparaging implications of the word, this charge of bureaucracy seems mor
or less reducible in the minds of those who bring it to three specific charges
first, that there is too great an enhancement of the functions and powers o
executive agencies of government at the expense of the legislative and judi
cial agencies; second, that the government is undertaking to perform to
many functions; and, third, that for the foregoing or other reasons there i
too great an increase in the number of governmental employees, and conse
quently in the expenses of government and the resulting burden on the tax
payer.

These three charges are seldom clearly distinguished by those who fea
bureaucracy, and when thus cumulated into an undifferentiated mass im
pression, they constitute a disquieting picture, each part serving to heighte
the lurid shadows of the rest. Naturally, no part of the total impression i
more portentous than that which implies violation of supposed constitutiona
principles through the vesting in executive agencies of powers which belon
properly to legislature or judiciary.

This last charge is not new. In being urged against the so-called Ne
Deal legislation, it is simply being made to do a fresh turn of duty afte
having served steadily for fifty years against most of the important legis
lation enacted during that period. As a preliminary to examining the merit

[1] John Dickinson, "The Perennial Cry of Bureaucracy," *The Yale Review* (March, 1935)
Vol. 24, pp. 448-463. Reprinted by permission of the author and *The Yale Review*, copyrig
Yale University Press.

f the charge, it will be helpful to look at some special reasons which give
t a perennial appeal to certain elements of American opinion.

The first of these is the tendency to distrust and disparagement of the
xecutive branch of government merely as such, which results from an
versimplified and conventionalized reading of English and American gov-
rnmental history during the seventeenth century. During that period the
English executive was the Crown, a hereditary governmental organ not
hosen by any process of election, and still claiming to rule by inherent
ight rather than by delegation of authority from the people. In the Ameri-
an colonies there was the additional fact that the executive in the person
f the colonial governor represented in most colonies the alien power of
he mother country, three thousand miles away, in opposition to the will
f the local legislators. It was primarily for these reasons that the struggle
or liberty took the form of a struggle against the executive, rather than
ecause of anything inherently hostile to liberty in the nature of executive
ower. However, the result was to create in men's reading of history a
ias against the executive branch, which disclosed itself forcefully when
ur new States came to shape their constitutions during the Revolution.
"What power have you given to the governor?" a North Carolinian was
sked. "Only the power to draw his salary," was the famous reply, and it
as always remained easy to rouse those Americans who pride themselves
n some historical knowledge to a distrust of any increase whatever in the
owers or responsibilities of the executive department, even though that
epartment is, and under our constitutional system has long been, as fully
epresentative and as responsible to the electorate as is the legislature, and
ven though it has been made fully dependent on the legislature for many of
ts powers and all its funds. Identification of executive power under our
Constitution with the position of an English king like Charles the First, or
James the Second, and an attitude towards executive power, based on such
dentification, represent a misleading perversion of historical knowledge.

Just as oversimplified understanding of history constitutes one reason for
disparagement of the executive, so a second reason is supplied by an oversimplified conception of the so-called theory of the "separation of powers,"
which has become a fixed dogma in the minds of many Americans who have
had the benefit of an elementary course in political science. A number of
years ago a high school teacher was discussing with me the fact that President Harding had made a point of having the Vice President attend Cabinet
meetings, while President Coolidge after his election had given up the practice. "At first," said my friend, "I was inclined to blame President Coolidge
for the abandonment of the practice, but on reflection I saw that he was
perfectly right because the Vice President, as presiding officer of the Senate,

is closely connected with the legislative branch of the government and, therefore, his sitting with the President and Cabinet, who constitute the executive branch, would be a clear violation of the separation of powers and, consequently, unconstitutional."

The separation-of-powers doctrine apparently implies in the popular mind a government rigidly organized along the following simple lines. In the first place, the legislature, consisting of a body of elected representatives, must formulate of its own initiative, and enact in the form of laws, all state-enforceable rules and regulations governing conduct. At this point the executive steps in, in the person of the public prosecutor and the sheriff or marshal with their deputies, and undertakes to discover any infraction or supposed infraction of these laws. In the event of discovery of a supposed infraction, the individual under suspicion is brought by the executive before a court representing the third, or judicial, branch of the government, and the question of the occurrence or non-occurrence of the infraction must be exclusively for the courts to establish. Should the courts find the fact of an infraction, it is their function to pronounce the penalty prescribed by law and turn the offender back to the executive in the person of the sheriff or marshal for the execution of the sentence by way of imprisonment or forfeiture. This is the outline sketch of government which seems to lurk, consciously or unconsciously, behind the thinking of a large body of more or less informed Americans, and supplies the standard by which they are tempted to judge whether or not the legislative measures to which their attention is called are constitutional.

Of course, no government functioning exclusively along these lines could satisfy the needs of even the simplest frontier community. In the first place, they omit all provision for any public-service, as distinguished from purely regulatory, functions of government. In even the simplest and most individualistic communities such public-service functions are represented by the construction and maintenance of roads and bridges, if not of schools. Indeed, in our American communities of colonial times, they sometimes extended to maintenance of such service agencies as sawmills, grist-mills, breweries, and the like.

The discharge and oversight of public-service functions of this character find no place in the framework of government outlined above. Necessarily the agencies performing such functions are "executive" in character. Necessarily also it is impossible in the nature of things for the legislative body to lay down in the form of statutes all the rules and regulations in accordance with which such service agencies must operate. However detailed the legislative mandates might conceivably be as to the width and grading of roads, the materials and type of labor to be used, and so on, there would still inevitably arise for decision possible alternatives within the terms of the legislative mandate which the administrative agency would have to resolve. The legislature itself could not dictate these decisions unless it chose to act itself directly as the road-building agency, that is, as an executive or administrative agency actually carrying out the job.

Nor does the foregoing picture give even an adequate conception of the operation of the regulatory, or police, functions of government. Here again, the executive arm cannot act as simply a mechanical intermediary between the legislature and the courts. Since in the drafting of statutes, as in other human activities, prevision is limited, situations always emerge which raise a doubt as to whether or not they fall within the statutory language. In such cases law enforcement officials will inevitably exercise a power of statutory interpretation to determine whether or not they shall bring the matter into the courts. This is particularly true after public business increases to the point where the official must emphasize certain aspects of his work at the expense of others.

It can be laid down as a basic governmental fact that as public business increases in volume, through the mere increase in the population of the community if for no other reason, the amount of detail which can be directly handled by the legislative body itself will necessarily decrease, and correspondingly the amount of discretion which will be exercised by enforcement and other administrative officials will necessarily increase. This is a plain matter of physics and physiology, wholly apart from considerations of constitutional law or theory. Our colonial legislatures looked into and decided by statutory enactment countless matters which we should to-day regard as of a detailed administrative nature. As the colonies increased in size and became States, the legislatures had to content themselves with laying down rules for the guidance of officials, with the inevitable result that a field for administrative construction of these rules, and hence of administrative discretion, came into being.

Nor is it mere increase in the size of a community which restricts the sphere of detail open to direct action by the legislature. An even greater factor is the increase in the number and variety of human activities and interests. In a simple community the number of things which people do, and which may have to be regulated at certain points in the public interest, is relatively limited. They plough and sow and reap; grind grain into meal or flour, or brew or distil it into strong drink; breed and slaughter animals; cook, spin, weave, and sew within the home; cut timber and build houses; trade a little by way of barter or for cash; marry, bring forth children, make wills, die, and are buried. How different from this short yet almost exhaustive catalogue is the list of activities which men carry on in an advanced modern community, with its systems of credit and banking and insurance, its multiplicity of corporate organizations, its network of transportation facilities, its complicated forms of merchandising and advertising and distribution, its accounting systems and variety of intangible forms of property.

If any legislative body to-day were to undertake to give not an increased, but merely the same, measure of attention to the life of the community which legislatures gave a hundred years ago, it would find the task completely beyond its physical capacities. Unless, therefore, as the size of our communities and the complexity of our social and economic dealings increase, we are to have a progressively *decreasing* amount of governmental intervention and control, our legislatures must act in progressively less and less detail, which means that they must more and more utilize the agency of administrative officials.

One device to which American legislatures early resorted in order to increase their ability to cover the necessary field of action has been to handle their business almost exclusively through committees. The members of each committee devote practically their whole time to a special class of questions, either banking, insurance, public utilities, or the like, and, except in the case of measures of unusual public interest, the results of the labors of these specialized committees are accepted and ratified with very little question by the entire legislative body. This delegation of the functions of the entire body to a small part of the membership illustrates the same physical necessity as the further delegation to administrative officials. Even, however, after it has been carried to the utmost limits, it does not eliminate the necessity for, but still requires to be complemented by, such further administrative delegation.

Just as the inevitable increase of public business presses upon the human limitations of the legislative body, so before long it exhausts the effectiveness of the district attorney and the sheriff as the sole and exclusive agencies of law enforcement. While enforcement is limited to elementary rules of conduct, like those against murder and theft, these officials, if provided with a staff of assistants increasing in rough proportion to the population, might, no doubt, supply all the enforcement needed. When, however, with the economic progress of the community it becomes necessary to administer rules relating to sanitation and public health, transportation facilities and practices, banking, insurance, security issues, conservation of natural resources, pure food, unfair advertising, and similar matters, district attorneys and sheriffs, unless their staffs were increased to unwieldy numbers, would prove entirely inadequate enforcement agencies.

Nor in many of these fields can enforcement with justice to the individual or advantage to the public be confined to the infliction of penalties after the offense has been allowed to occur. We have learned the advantages of prevention. It is better to require that, in advance of being admitted to practice, doctors and dentists should submit to examination and be licensed than that competence should be tacitly assumed and that the protection of the public should rest wholly upon subsequent prosecution and suits by injured persons. It is more effective to require a building permit in advance than to deal with fire hazards or unsanitary structures after the erection has been completed. This system of administrative permits and licenses, which has accordingly spread in response to the need for regulation in new fields, is rooted in an old one. Even in the frontier stage of our culture we required liquor dealers to have licenses and we set up boards to grant them, and no one raised any question of a violation of the separation-of-powers doctrine.

The need for saving the time of the legislature, and the need for other enforcement devices than mere prosecution or civil suits in the courts, led as long ago as the Tudor period in England to the invention of what may be called the administrative method of law enforcement, the application of which to a new field is always met with the cry of bureaucracy. This administrative method may be described in outline as follows. When the legislature decides to provide protection for the public in some such matter as purity of food or drugs, it does not attempt the impossible task of defining specifically in the statute what particular combination of ingredients constitutes impurity in the case of each and every article of food or medicine, but indicates its purpose of requiring that the foods and medicines offered for sale shall be pure and unadulterated, and defines the broad sense in which these terms are used. The legislature then sets up a specialized agency to enforce this statute, whether by granting permits or licenses, or by receiving and passing upon complaints, or by making inspections and orders, as the statute may provide.

In the exercise of these functions the administrative agency, as its work develops, must necessarily bring the comparatively broad provisions of the statute down to specific cases by deciding, for example, whether or not the presence of certain foreign matter in a particular food, or the inclusion of a certain ingredient in a medicine, renders the food or medicine impure or adulterated. In other words, it has to interpret or construe the statute and lend it greater particularity in applying it to specific cases. This process of interpretation is precisely what the courts are continually doing every day when they apply statutes in their decisions. When the administrative body performs the same task, and announces in advance in the form of a rule or regulation that it will consider the inclusion of a particular chemical as constituting an impurity, it is said to be exercising quasi-legislative power and to be making one of those "rules having the force of law," which are so often represented in any argument against bureaucracy as an invasion of the power of the legislative branch of government.

Of course, no invasion of legislative power exists if the rule constitutes a fair and reasonable interpretation of the statute and lies within the field of construction which the legislature intended to leave to the administrative agency. Such construction, as has already been pointed out, must inevitably be performed by whatever agency enforces a law, in view of the limitations on human prevision and legislative prescience. The question is always one of degree—of whether or not the administrative delegation reasonably conforms to the legislative purpose and standard, and whether or not the expression of that standard is sufficiently clear to afford a reasonable guide to administrative action. Under our American practice, the administrative body is on both these points always subject to control by the courts at the instance of any individual alleging actual or threatened injury. Where an administrative body has made a regulation claiming to have the force of law, it is always in the last analysis for the courts to decide whether the legislature has provided a sufficiently definite standard for the administrative body to follow, and whether the administrative ruling reasonably conforms with that standard. If either of these questions is decided in the negative the administrative regulation is invalid. These safeguards, which exist in our American practice, do not exist in England, and this lack therefore renders inapplicable to our situation the arguments against delegation of legislative power which have been urged with so much force by Lord Hewart and others in England in recent years.

It must also be remembered that, apart from the protection of the courts, any interpretation of a statute laid down in an administrative regulation is subject to correction or repeal by the legislature itself. One of the purposes sought to be accomplished by the delegation of power to make administrative rules and regulations is to provide greater flexibility and adaptability of the law to changing conditions of technology and the arts than would exist if too detailed regulations were permanently frozen into the statute itself. If, however, an administrative regulation, even when sustained by the courts, is, nevertheless, thought by the legislature to be at variance with the then legislative purpose, it can be wiped out as effectively as if it had been originally written into the statute, and in all probability more promptly. There are thus two great safeguards against abuse of administrative rules and regulations—the legislature and the courts.

Administrative power exercised under such safeguards is a vastly different thing from the bureaucratic power of the Ministries of an absolute monarchy

hich John Stuart Mill had in mind in the famous passage in which he
ontrasted bureaucratic with representative government. Furthermore, it
ust be remembered that our administrative officials are as much servants
f the people as are our legislative officials. In the state governments many
f them are chosen by popular election. Even where appointed, they are
esignated by a popularly elected chief magistrate, whose policies must be
rought to the test of approval by the people at the polls. This removes
em altogether from legitimate comparison with the bureaucracies of the
oman empire or of the absolute monarchies of Continental Europe in the
ighteenth and early nineteenth centuries.

It is curious that on this point those who bring the charge of bureaucracy
gainst administrative regulation blow both hot and cold. On the one hand,
ey use arguments forged against irresponsible bureaucracies not subject
o popular control. On the other, they frequently urge against our own
dministrative agencies that they are not impartial and independent but
political" because subject to a chief executive who must justify his conduct
t the polls. If it be an argument against administrative agencies to say
at they are political, surely the same charge could be brought with at
ast as much effect against the legislative bodies whose powers these same
dministrative agencies are accused of wrongfully invading.

The final and complete answer to the argument that delegation to ad-
inistrative authorities involves an unconstitutional violation of the separa-
on-of-powers doctrine is that this argument has been repeatedly urged
pon our highest courts and in every instance rejected. It is valid only on
n oversimplified, school-book interpretation of what the separation-of-
owers doctrine means. Our courts, following Madison in "The Federalist,"
ave interpreted it in a more realistic sense, so as to render it compatible,
ather than inconsistent, with the effective functioning of government. All
hat the maxim means, says Madison, is "that where the *whole* power of
ne department is exercised by the same hands which possess the whole
ower of another department, the fundamental principles of a free consti-
ution are subverted." Where an administrative agency is authorized to
ake rules and regulations having the force of law, it does not exercise the
hole legislative power, since those rules and regulations must conform with,
nd fit within the outlines of, a statute enacted by the legislature.

It is, therefore, no argument against the constitutional validity of legis-
ation, new or old, that it delegates to an arm of the executive department
road authority to determine the details necessary to effectuate legislative
olicy. All that can be attacked are specific case-to-case instances, where
t may be alleged that the particular administrative agency in question has
verstepped the limits of the legislative grant or has acted where the legis-

lative mandate is too vague and uncertain to supply a sufficient guide. T
broad policy of delegation to the executive, whether or not we choose
disparage it by the word "bureaucracy," has been an integral part of o
governmental system since the first statutes enacted by the first Congre
under the Constitution.

Nor is there substance to the charge that the administrative system
regulation invades the proper province of the judiciary. No administrati
order can be brought home to an individual except through the instr
mentality of the courts, or under circumstances which permit court reviev
A condition of the validity of such an order is that the parties affected mu
have ample notice and full hearing either before the administrative body o
in court. No doubt, in the initial phases of the work of any new administr
tive agency, there will be certain informalities in procedure until permanei
forms can be worked out. If these informalities go so far as in the opinio
of the reviewing court to amount to a denial of a fair and full hearing, t
administrative order will be set aside.

The criticism is often made that administrative procedure is inherentl
unfair because not infrequently the same agency both presents a charg
and hears it. This claim the courts have never sustained as amounting t
a violation of the guarantee of due process or invalidating the constitutiona
ity of administrative procedure. In so far as it has any practical justific
tion, the tendency at present in the organization and reorganization o
federal administrative units is to effect so far as possible a separation withi
each unit between the personnel which initiates proceedings and that whic
passes upon them in a quasi-judicial capacity.

From all that has been said, it is apparent that the constitutional arg
ment used to support the charge of "bureaucracy" is without substance. Th
additional arguments, that government is performing too many function
and that it is increasing too greatly the number of governmental employee
are usually employed in a circular fashion. Government is said to b
undertaking too many tasks because to perform them it must increase it
personnel to the size of an enormous bureaucracy. On the other hand, it i
said that the army of government employees constitutes a dangerous bureauc
racy because they are employed in unnecessary and superfluous tasks whic
are a menace to liberty. Each argument rests on the other; separated the
lose most of their effectiveness.

It has long become apparent that no abstract formula other than th
public convenience and welfare at a given time can determine the prope
scope of governmental activities. The liberty of individuals in our Anglo
Saxon tradition means not immunity from government but liberty unde
law, and law means restraint for the common welfare. Under the increas

ngly congested and interdependent conditions of modern living, new governmental restrictions are being continually introduced, often in substitution for older forms of restriction which have become obsolete and are
abandoned. We are not permitted to operate motor vehicles on the highways without an examination to determine competency. We are not permitted to sell milk or meat without an inspection to determine its purity
and fitness for human consumption. We are not permitted to erect buildings
without a permit and inspection to determine their safety. Will anyone
claim that such restrictions are an invasion of liberty in any real sense, or
in any sense that men have fought for? Will anyone claim that we would
be better off without them?

The principal argument against many of these governmental regulations
sometimes seems to be that they must be administered through governmental officials, who, for the purpose of the argument, are thereupon oppro-
briously termed "bureaucrats." Here again the circular argument recurs.
The regulations are criticised because of the officials, and the chief ground
of criticism of the officials is that they administer the regulations. Senator
Borah warned us a short time ago of the "deadening hand of bureaucracy."
More recently another distinguished statesman has spoken of the "slow
strangulation of an engirdling bureaucracy." Are we being "strangled" and
"engirdled" by motor vehicle inspectors, or building inspectors, or medical
examining boards? Is the "dead hand of bureaucracy" upon us because
pure-food inspectors examine the meat we eat and the milk we drink? And,
if so, is not the "dead hand of bureaucracy" preferable to the death-dealing
bacilli of ptomaine or typhoid?

It may, of course, be granted that some of the regulations introduced by
the recent federal recovery legislation are different in degree, if not in kind,
from the types of regulation which have just been mentioned. No doubt,
plausible arguments could be advanced to support the charge that for one
reason or another some of these forms of regulation are not truly in the
public interest. With that question we are not here concerned. What we are
concerned with is that it is not a valid argument against a new regulation
that it must be administered by government officials who, because they have
to administer the regulation, can be impugned as an "engirdling" and
"deadening" bureaucracy. Whether or not officials constitute a "deadening"
bureaucracy depends entirely upon whether or not they perform with
promptness, efficiency, and fairness the governmental functions entrusted
to them, assuming that those functions are, on their merits, required by the
public welfare. There is no reason why governmental officials, just because
they are governmental officials, should be regarded as necessarily always
acting inefficiently and oppressively any more than the employees of a

private corporation or of any other large and important body. To believe
that they must always so act is a pure assumption inherited from the days
of irresponsible types of government when hereditary hordes of personal
servants of an absolute monarch exercised the powers of government without any obligation to satisfy public opinion, and free from the pressure
which public opinion can bring. Those conditions are gone. Under a constitution like our own, no government can remain in power if the acts of
its official subordinates displease public sentiment. To deny that government officials can act as promptly and justly as men in other stations is
not merely to accept the anarchist denial of the possibility of reasonably
good government, but is substantially to deny the effectiveness of all corporate action.

It is, of course, conceivable that the field of governmental regulation
might be extended to the point where the number of officials needed to
administer it would become so large as to constitute an intolerable burden
on the rest of the community. If that point were reached, it would no
doubt be an indication that the scope of governmental action has been unduly enlarged. That it has been reached is the impression frequently sought
to be produced by those who warn us of the dangers of bureaucracy. The
figures disprove this contention. The total number of persons employed
to-day in the combined service of the state and local as well as the federal
governments amounts to less than 3,000,000 or approximately only 2½%
of the population. This proportion would have seemed slight to our New
England ancestors with their multiplicity of fence viewers, hog reeves, hay
wards, surveyors, sealers, and other town officials. If to-day the cost of
government is high and the annual budgetary outlays large, these expenditures are not primarily for the payment of an army of officials. They are,
in great part, payments of interest on sums laid out in the construction of
roads and public buildings, and payments to contractors, material men,
laborers, and the like. In the case of the federal government approximately
30% of the ordinary budget is for interest payable to the bondholders who
advanced the funds for our expenditures in the Great War. 27% is paid
out to veterans and other recipients of war pensions. About 16% goes to the
maintenance of the army and navy and the purchase of military equipment.
The amount of the federal emergency or recovery budget which goes to the
maintenance of government officials is negligible. The large sums included
in this budget are either distributed in the form of relief to the needy unemployed or represent recoverable loans advanced to banks, railroads, home-
owners, and farmers. The payroll of officials constitutes hardly 10% of the
outlay of the federal government.

No one would deny that it is well for a democratic government to be on
its guard against bureaucracy in the sense of an inefficient, irresponsible,

and overgrown army of public employees. The weakness in the charge of bureaucracy which is so steadily dinned into our ears is, that like the cry of "wolf," it may deaden us to the danger should the danger really come. And, in the meanwhile, it serves to prevent a frank and fruitful examination of many measures on their merits by dragging a false scent across the trail.

No. 60

[THE most honest and capable administrators would have difficulty in carrying out public policy in many American governmental jurisdictions because of the out-of-date and unwieldly machinery with which they would have to work. A trucking contractor would speedily learn that a 1905 model truck is not adequate for the trucking business of to-day. His problems could not be solved by emphasizing the need of better drivers. Yet in the field of governmental business, we turn most of our attention to the drivers and are reluctant to examine the 1905 or, in some cases, the 1850 models of administrative machines with which we furnish them.

We need, therefore, not only to describe and analyze this machine, but in many cases to reconstruct or reorganize it. This need varies with the particular level of government with which we are concerned. At the national level this need has been perceived and action has been sought by every President since 1908. State government administrative reorganization has been a factor in state government and politics since 1917. The council-manager form of city government arose largely out of the crying need for reorganizing the unbelievably outmoded administrative structure of the mayor-council plan of government. A recent and highly important analysis, evaluation, and proposal for rebuilding at the national level was made by President Roosevelt's Committee on Administrative Management. The section from the report of this Committee, which is included in this chapter, presents, in brief, some of its findings and conclusions.]

ADMINISTRATIVE MANAGEMENT IN THE GOVERNMENT OF THE UNITED STATES [1]

by The President's Committee on Administrative Management

THE primary purpose of a rational reorganization of the administrative agencies of the Executive Branch of the Government is to reduce to a manageable compass the number of agencies reporting to the President. The Constitution of the United States sets up no administrative organi-

[1] The President's Committee on Administrative Management, *Administrative Management in the Government of the United States* (Washington: United States Government Printing Office, 1937), pp. 31-33.

zation for the Government. The whole matter of executive power is dealt with in a few brief phrases. First in importance is: "The executive Power shall be vested in a President of the United States of America." Reference is also made to the Army and Navy, of which the President is named "Commander in Chief," and, indirectly, to the "executive Departments"; and there is laid on the President alone the duty to "take Care that the Laws be faithfully executed." In these few words, supplemented by those defining the scope of the Legislative and the Judicial Branches, there is set forth the constitutional principle of the separation of powers, which places in the President, and in the President alone, the whole executive power of the Government of the United States.

The administrative organization of the Government to carry out "the executive Power" thus rests upon statute law, and upon departmental arrangements made under the authority of law. The history of these laws and arrangements is a reflection of our national problems and development. At the beginning, in 1789, there were but four departments: State, War, Treasury, and the Attorney General. The General Post Office was permanently established in 1794, and 4 years later, the Navy Department was created. Thus, by 1800 there were six departments, all of them directly under the President in accordance with the constitutional principle of the separation of powers.

For the next 50 years there was no change. Then came the creation of the Department of the Interior in 1849, of Agriculture in 1889, and of Commerce and Labor in 1903, from which the Department of Labor was separated in 1913.

Two new kinds of governmental agencies made their appearance in the generation after the Civil War. They were, first, executive agencies under the President but not connected with any department, such as the Civil Service Commission (1883); and, second, independent regulatory agencies, such as the Interstate Commerce Commission (1887), which were neither placed under the President nor connected with any department. Many additional agencies of these types appeared in subsequent years.

During the World War a large number of new agencies were established. These were chiefly councils, boards, commissions, administrations, and governmental corporations, and though not legally connected with the regular departments, they were definitely within the Executive Branch and under the President. In this period the innovation was the governmental corporation, which was found useful particularly in dealing with financial operations. Most of these agencies were abolished, or consolidated with the departments, in the years following the war.

During the recent depression similar need for emergency action has resulted again in the establishment of a large number of new agencies. These include administrations, boards, commissions, committees, governmental cor-. porations, and authorities. The novel elements in this period are the extended use of the corporate form and the introduction of the "authority." Most of these agencies have been placed in the Executive Branch and under the President, but in the main they have not been connected by law with the regular departments.

As a result of this long development, there are now in the Government of the United States over 100 separately organized establishments and agencies presumably reporting to the President. Among them are the 10 regular executive departments and the many boards, commissions, administrations, authorities, corporations, and agencies which are under the President but not in a department. There are also a dozen agencies which are totally independent—a new and headless "fourth branch" of the Government.

THE EXECUTIVE BRANCH TO-DAY

The Executive Branch of the Government of the United States has thus grown up without plan or design like the barns, shacks, silos, tool sheds, and garages of an old farm. To look at it now, no one would ever recognize the structure which the founding fathers erected a century and a half ago to be the Government of the United States. A careful examination of the Government shows the following facts:

1. The structure of the Government throws an impossible task upon the Chief Executive. No President can possibly give adequate supervision to the multitude of agencies which have been set up to carry on the work of the Government, nor can he coordinate their activities and policies.

2. The normal managerial agencies designed to assist the Executive in thinking, planning, and managing, which one would expect to find in any large-scale organization, are either undeveloped or lacking.

3. The constitutional principle of the separation of powers and the responsibility of the President for "the executive Power" is impaired through the multiplicity and confusion of agencies which render effective action impossible.

4. Without plan or intent, there has grown up a headless "fourth branch" of the Government, responsible to no one, and impossible of coordination with the general policies and work of the Government as determined by the people through their duly elected representatives.

5. For purposes of management, boards and commissions have turned out to be failures. Their mechanism is inevitably slow, cumbersome,

wasteful, and ineffective, and does not lend itself readily to cooperation with other agencies. Even strong men on boards find that their individual opinions are watered down in reaching board decisions. When freed from the work of management, boards are, however, extremely useful and necessary for consultation, discussion, and advice; for representation of diverse views and citizen opinion; for quasi-judicial action; and as a repository of corporate powers.

6. The conspicuously well-managed administrative units in the Government are almost without exception headed by single administrators.

7. Owing to the multiplicity of agencies and the lack of administrative management there is waste, overlapping, and duplication, which may be eliminated through coordination, consolidation, and proper managerial control.

These are the major features which stand out clearly in any examination of the structure of the Executive Branch of the Government.

There flow from these factors many obscure difficulties and problems. Among these is the time and energy which have been wasted for many years because of departmental jealousies and jurisdictional disputes among the department heads and bureau chiefs as to who should control particular activities. The people of the country have held the President responsible for failing to settle these internal quarrels, whereas in fact, because the President's authority is not commensurate with his responsibility, often he has been unable to compose the differences short of the summary dismissal of one of his Cabinet Members. The departments themselves and groups of citizens interested in particular activities often seek to settle such disputes by direct appeals to the Congress, there again only to find the same or almost the same differences represented in the jurisdictional jealousies of congressional committees.

Another difficulty is found in the nature of the regional subdivisions of the departments and agencies. At the present time there are 109 different plans of geographical subdivision of the United States in use by the various governmental agencies for their local offices. From the standpoint of the citizen this does not make good service or good sense. Government should, of course, be carried to the people through the decentralization of the Washington departments, partly to make it fit their needs, and partly to keep it from becoming distant and bureaucratic, but this decentralization need not be chaotic and conflicting, provided it is properly integrated at the center and subjected to over-all management.

The method of decentralization of necessity will vary from department to department and from activity to activity within the department. A general principle that may be laid down is that the decentralization should be geographical and that more and more of the administrative work of the Executive Branch be carried on in the field in regional units set up to cover all parts of the United States. In this way the Government will be brought nearer to the people themselves and by this regional organization the Federal Government may the better cooperate with State and local governments in the conduct of its affairs.

This geographical decentralization also will diminish the waste of time and money, to say nothing of the patience of the people, entailed by excessive centralization of administrative activities in Washington. At the same time it offers the opportunity of lessening the insensitivity of the breaucracy by bringing the persons who actually administer in detail the work of the Government into touch with the people whom they serve in their own communities.

The safeguarding of the citizen from narrow-minded and dictatorial bureaucratic interference and control is one of the primary obligations of democratic government. It can be accomplished only by so centralizing the determination of administrative policy that there is a clear line of conduct laid down for all officialdom to follow and then by so decentralizing the actual administrative operation that the Government servant remains himself one of the people in touch with the people and does not degenerate into an isolated and arrogant bureaucrat.

These difficulties and defects in the organization of the Executive Branch have been clearly recognized for a generation and have been growing steadily worse decade by decade. The structure as it now stands is inefficient; it is a poor instrument for rendering public service; and it thwarts democratic control. With such a planless organization, good management is almost impossible—a fact of great importance in the modern world in which nothing can continue without good management, not even democracy.

No. 61

[As noted in the previous section, we have long been concerned in the United States with problems of administrative reorganization. The fact that our present machinery for government is faulty may, however, cause some to support measures for reorganization without subjecting these proposals to careful examination and critical review. The following selection by Professor Hyneman is, therefore, especially valuable; it aids the critically minded student in evaluating not only the original administrative machine but the new models which some propose to substitute for it. It makes clear that we must be critical not only of what we have but also of what is proposed.]

ADMINISTRATIVE REORGANIZATION [1]

by Charles S. Hyneman

.   .   .   .

THE pattern of state administrative reorganization which came to be generally accepted was shaped by many hands. The most systematic and one of the most doctrinaire justifications of the integrated administrative structure was Mr. W. F. Willoughby's *Principles of Public Administration,* published in 1927. Mr. Willoughby wrote this book, he said, to establish the position that "in administration there are certain fundamental principles of general application, analogous to those characterizing any science, which must be observed if the end of administration, efficiency in operation, is to be secured." While many writers, before and since this work appeared, have suggested that different ills may require different remedies, almost everyone entitled to professional consideration who wrote on public administration from 1915 to 1936 accepted the "principles" which he announced; and most of them appeared as convinced of their incontestability as Mr. Willoughby himself. With virtually all students of public administration "efficiency in operation" was the end of government and integration through reorganization the only path to that goal.

As early as 1922 Mr. Francis W. Coker filed his dissent from the prevailing theory, but his essay seems not appreciably to have stayed the march to orthodoxy. In 1927, the year of Mr. Willoughby's *Principles,* Mr. W. H. Edwards published a series of articles in which he audaciously characterized the prevailing program of reorganization as the concoction of "political medicine men," and a "cure-all" which would soon "be buried in the potter's field of political panaceas." His attack, incisive and scathing, was ignored. Three years later Mr. Harvey Walker questioned whether boasted achievements were due to integration and disputed the reasoning of orthodox reorganizers so far as seemed necessary to justify a competing program of reorganization which he has had on the market ever since.

I find nothing in the literature of public administration from 1930 until 1936 that could be said to challenge the orthodox position in respect to administrative reorganization. In 1936 Mr. Leonard D. White applied a "scrubbing brush" to Mr. Willoughby's "principles" and, when he had freed them of "the layers of surface associations," found (I convert Mr. White's

---

[1] Charles S. Hyneman, "Administrative Reorganization," *The Journal of Politics* (February, 1939), Vol. 1, pp. 62-65. Reprinted by permission of the author and *The Journal of Politics.* The footnotes in the original article are not reprinted here.

clear implication into positive assertion) that they were "hopes, assertions, and opinions."

Mr. Porter's departure from the approved pattern of organization has already been noted. It remains to record the most significant challenge to orthodoxy since the blistering attack by Edwards—that currently made by representatives of the Institute of Government Research of Brookings Institution. In their report to the Byrd Committee in 1937, the Brookings group managed to challenge nearly every one of the tenets of orthodox administrative theory. Since they were concerned with national administration, their remarks constituted at best an oblique attack on the state reorganization movement. What the report to the Byrd Committee lacked in directness was supplied, however, by Mr. A. C. Millspaugh in his contribution to the *Essays in Political Science in Honor of Westel Woodbury Willoughby*. The volume contained two essays on public administration. In one Mr. W. F. Willoughby reidentified his "hopes, assertions, and opinions" as "fundamental principles" and pointed to state reorganization as their triumph in practice. In the other Mr. Millspaugh condemned the reorganization program as "theoretically unsound," suffering from "unimaginativeness, impractical theorizing, and, of course, inadequate factual support."

The "fundamental principles" which Mr. Willoughby arrived at by "rigid application of scientific methods" were found by Mr. White to be merely "hopes, assertions, and opinions," and by Mr. Millspaugh to be "theoretically unsound." What, then, is the scientific character of the state reorganization movement?

Judgments arrived at intuitively may be sound though not supported by recitation of evidence or convincing argumentation. It is nevertheless worthwhile to examine the quality of the literature which fortifies a position. That can best be done in this instance, I think, by testing the argument against a series of questions; the reasoning which supports reorganization will be convincing to one, it seems to me, only as it satisfies him on the following points.

1. *Is "efficiency" acceptable as the first objective of reorganization?* Mr. Willoughby clearly states that "efficiency in operation" is "the end of administration"; the literature makes it abundantly clear that many other writers and consultants are concerned first of all to accomplish savings in materials and effort.

There are many grounds for discontent with American state government besides its inefficiency and wastefulness. What does the administrative reorganization program, designed to achieve efficiency and economy, offer to the man whose chief concern is for certain other qualities in his government —whose chief concern is that vision, imagination, and courage predominate in the execution, adaptation, or modification of policy? "An administrative organization," says Mr. Porter, "which is designed wholly in accordance with the theory that the sole function of an administrative department is to *do* things may not be suited to the task of deciding *what* shall be done." Apparently there is a good deal of feeling in non-academic circles that organization for efficiency, by way of integration, is pretty sure to be destructive of vigorous, far-sighted development of policy.

I find nowhere in the literature dealing with state reorganization a single statement designed to put Mr. Porter's doubts at rest—nowhere a statement designed to demonstrate that a broader "social efficiency" necessarily follows upon the achievement of "efficiency in operation."

The rationalization of reorganization is addressed to the taxpayer; it makes no promise to the laboring man concerned about revision of the industrial rules and regulations nor to the investor demanding that great capitalists be forced to respect the blue sky law. If such people are led intelligently to embrace the reorganization program it is because they have themselves conceived that devices for efficiency will effectuate the policy they desire.

2. *Can work of administrative character be divorced from control of policy?* The literature supporting the reorganization movement is thick with statements that work of an administrative character should be separated from policy determination and the administrative work entrusted to officials controlled by the chief executive. If such a severance is possible, the dilemma of reconciling "efficiency in operation" with vision and courage in policy determination may be solved. In very few instances, however, does one find in the literature of reorganization either evidence or argument designed to demonstrate that such a severance is practically possible. The proposition is certainly not self-evident; indeed there is a body of experience to suggest that it cannot be accomplished. Every one of the Illinois code departments, for instance, exercises important control over persons and property; every one makes rules and regulations having the force and effect of law; every one makes adjudications in which matters vital to the livelihood of individuals are determined.

The formulation of rules and regulations and the conduct of adjudications can of course be taken from the department head and entrusted to a board. But even if this is done the department head will retain important control over policy for he will decide whether the law is to be the same for the rich as the poor; whether one interest group is to use government to enthrone its advantage at the cost of other groups. If the department head is stripped of such control over policy he becomes a mere office-manager; if such control over policy is vested in a board, then the kind of department which Mr. Porter recommends is thereby created and the departmental situation which reorganization was designed to terminate is reestablished.

3. *What evidence is there that single officers are preferable to boards for work of an administrative character?* Conceding for the moment that the chief objective of reorganization is "efficiency in operation" and that it is possible to separate work of an administrative character from policy determination, what evidence is there to establish the superiority of the single officer over the board for administrative work? The answer is—nothing that need be convincing to a skeptical mind. I find no record of an extended experience in careful observation. There is a great deal of convincing testimony that boards have proven unsatisfactory, but in no instance have I found these statements accompanied by the assertion that single officers in the same state or single officers heading like departments in other states were any more satisfactory. It is pointed out that continental European countries prefer single officers to boards; I have nowhere encountered the statement that this is the cause of some superiority of their government over ours.

It is customary to point to the business corporation as an organization that achieves efficiency through the use of single rather than plural officers. The analogy will not be of much value, however, unless the decisions made by the officer of the corporation are comparable to those entrusted to the state department. Is it not true that most of the important "administrative" decisions of the corporation go to the board of directors—the validation of major purchases, determination of pay increases, location of new plants, establishment of a basic advertising program? But these decisions are of a kind with those which confront the state department head, whether single officer or board. And what of the use of committees of officers in the business corporation? Several of the leading retail merchandizing corporations will not permit the department head to select a store site, commit the corporation to lease or purchase of real estate, or make a contract for any major alteration of store properties; such decisions go to a committee of administrative officers where to quote one department head, "they take nothing for granted; you have to satisfy them on every point." Is this not grist for Mr. Porter's mill?

The supporters of reorganization certainly have not shown their readers all facets of the corporate analogy.

Action is the imperative need in state government, says Mr. Austin Macdonald; single officers are the key to action, say all the supporters of

reorganization. When Mussolini and Hitler cry that the day for deliberation is past and the time for action is at hand they are urging a nation to
a program; they are not denying leaders the opportunity to consult with
one another. When Mr. Macdonald cries for action, he demands that
major policies be formulated before leaders can get together. His picture
of government in action is perhaps fairly accurate for the emergency ward
of a hospital; has it any validity for government where one is likely to
encounter it? Can Mr. Macdonald and other proponents of the integrated
state have misconceived that the need of firmness in enforcing compromise
is, instead, a necessity of avoiding compromise?

4. *Do we need the whole reorganization program in order to obtain central direction of administration?* All students of administration are agreed,
I believe—including Coker, Edwards, and Millspaugh—that the governor
ought to be given more supervisory power than he possesses in many of our
non-integrated state administrative systems. But in order to get a satisfactory central direction of administration, is it necessary that the governor
have power to appoint and remove department heads at will? It is Mr.
Porter's contention that if the governor had adequate financial control and
a dependable force of men to handle that and other staff functions he would
possess "the instruments through which a governor could dominate all the
administrative activities of the state if he wished to do so." My reading of
Mr. Harvey Walker and the Brookings report to the Byrd Committee indicates that Mr. Porter is not alone in his views.

Mr. Porter offers much argument but little evidence to support his point.
In this he is matched by those who demand the most thorough implementa-
tion of executive control—there is a surfeit of "reason dictates," a dearth of
"this occurrence demonstrates."

5. *What is the truth as to administrative accomplishments under reorganization?* "Where sound consolidation plans have been adopted," said the un-
repentant and unreformed Brookings Institution in 1930, "there has resulted
almost universally an improved type of public service at a decreased public
expenditure." On the other hand, Mr. Harvey Walker asserts that "it is
very difficult to point to any concrete financial advantage gained through
the adoption of a reorganization plan." Mr. Buck accredits some praiseworthy accomplishment to reorganization in practically every state that has
been reorganized. Some of the accounts appear to differ little from campaign boasts. One, at least, is a story of mid-depression reduction in the
cost of government, no effort having been made, so far as Mr. Buck en-
lightens us, to determine whether these economies were not being paralleled
in every other state in the union.

Nearly all the economies which Mr. Buck recounts are supposed to have

occurred during the administration of the governor who initiated reorganization, yet at most only two or three writers have pointed out that possibly
these men were strong executives who would have achieved the same
economies, with or without a budget, under a non-integrated system of
semi-independent departments. I have encountered only two conscientious
efforts to evaluate the accomplishments of reorganization. One frankly
admitted inability to determine what accomplishments were due to reorganization; from the other I could gather nothing which need alter any man's
prejudices on the subject.

6. *Can the governor be made responsible for the conduct of administration?* It is now more than fifteen years since Mussolini marched on Rome;
a good deal of the world's population is in the grip of dictatorship. Yet the
literature of administrative reorganization is filled with contempt for those
who warn against overarming the chief executive with power. Not until
1935 did the literature of public administration (except for the critics of
reorganization) reveal anything approaching concern to subject the chief
executive to effective popular control.

The customary reconciliation of democratic ideals with concentration of
power is presented in the following paragraph:

> If the plan here proposed is adopted, the Governor would stand out in
> the limelight of public opinion as never before. The economies of his ad-
> ministration would redound to his credit, while waste and extravagance could
> be laid at his door. He would become in reality the responsible executive of
> the State, whose duty it would be to serve the best interests of the people;
> and if he did not do this he would have to put his political aspirations forever
> behind him.

Unfortunately for the persuasiveness of the foregoing argument, the quotation is preceded by the statement that, "As a matter of fact, the voters
really look to the Governor at the present time as the responsible head of
the State administration, although they elect several other administrative
officers." If the people already believe the governor is chief of the administration, what difference does it make, so far as they are concerned, for
him actually to assume that position? What reason is there to suppose
that voters will assert a new vigilance simply because an official has assumed a power which they already thought he possessed?

Can this supposed transformation of the voter's attitude be explained
by the fact that formerly he had divided his attention between so many
candidates for state office that he was unable to scrutinize the records of
the candidates for the governorship? Evidently not, since one frequently
encounters the statement that prior to reorganization the voter gave little

or no attention to the candidates for subordinate administrative positions. What relief, in that case, does the voter obtain when the ballot is shortened? Concede that the voter did divide his attention between the candidates for the various elective offices prior to reorganization, concede that he is freed of a part of that burden so that he can give his whole attention (so far as not drawn off to national and local issues) to the candidates for the governorship, how much wiser will he be on election day? What facts or gossip concerning the candidates for governor can be expected to come his way because of the elimination of other offices from the campaign?

Perhaps there is something to the statement that the battle for the governorship, under long or short ballot, will regularly be fought out on a legislative or political issue—rarely if ever on an issue of honest, enlightened and economical conduct of administration. Perhaps the market for news and the agencies for its distribution and dramatization in many of the states are such that the public can never expect to be reliably informed on the conduct of public administration. Perhaps popular control of the executive can be achieved only when there exists a representative assembly which can match power with power—such an assembly as now exists in none of the forty-eight states.

Mr. Coker, Mr. Edwards, and Mr. Millspaugh are concerned about this. A few other students of administration are aware that the problem of popular control exists. Most of the rationalizers of state reorganization, however, appear to proceed blithely on the assumption that God looks after fools, drunkards and the liberties of the people.

It has been my intention to show, as accurately and adequately as the space at my disposal permits, to what extent the literature supporting the reorganization movement deals in demonstrable truth as distinguished from supposition born out of wish. I find my own view of the argument adequately expressed in John Locke's remarks on Filmer's *Patriarchia*.

> If he has in that chapter, or anywhere in the whole treatise, given any other proofs of "Adam's royal authority" other than by often repeating it, which, among some men, goes for argument, I desire anybody for him to show me the place and page, that I may be convinced of my mistake and acknowledge my oversight. If no such arguments are to be found, I beseech those men who have so much cried up this book to consider whether they do not give the world cause to suspect that it is not the force of reason and argument that makes them for absolute monarchy, but some other by interest, and therefore are resolved to applaud any author that writes in favour of this doctrine, whether he support it with reason or no. But I hope they do not expect that rational and indifferent men should be brought over to their opinion, because this their great doctor of it, in a discourse made on purpose,

to set up the "absolute monarchical power of Adam" in opposition to the "natural freedom" of mankind, has said so little to prove it, from whence it is rather naturally to be concluded that there is little to be said.

My complaint, up to this point, has been directed against a betrayal of the intellectual obligations of a learned profession; the evidence will also sustain an indictment of the profession on ethical grounds. Men invited to recommend a program which promises efficiency and economy for a state, as I see it, have not only mistaken supposition for fact and hypothesis for principle; they have failed to warn their clients (in the printed report at least) of the enormous risk involved in creating a powerful chief executive in a state which has no responsible legislature and in many instances no effective opposition party.

Text-book writers, while admitting that the accepted pattern of reorganization is disputed by men entitled to respect, have nonetheless proceeded, through the use of sweet and sour words, to prejudice the immature student by strictly emotional as distinguished from intellectual appeals. Senatorial confirmation of appointments is a "vicious arrangement"; efforts to transform the impeachment process into a device for establishing legislative supremacy over the executive in matters of policy are "both ridiculous and deplorable"; a "comprehensive plan" prepared by "experts" for Maryland was rejected in favor of a "makeshift scheme"—the author not mentioning that the adopted arrangement was carefully studied by responsible persons and was quite as "comprehensive" as the one rejected.

To my complaint and to this indictment it is possible, however, to enter a general demurrer. Perhaps the ideal of our profession is the faith of a priesthood rather than the skepticism of a science; if so, it is no offense to dogmatize assumptions and eschew inquiry. Perhaps a code of ethics is too dear a luxury for a profession still driving hard to establish prestige; if so, who shall condemn us if we indulge occasionally in cozenage or venture close to barratry?

No. 62

[PROFESSOR HYNEMAN has made it clear that proposals for reorganization of the administrative machine should be subjected to careful scrutiny before they are accepted. Professor Edwards, in the following discussion, presents a critical review of the actual accomplishments of the state reorganizations that have already been made.]

HAS STATE REORGANIZATION SUCCEEDED? [1]

by William H. Edwards

THE nation-wide controversy aroused by the President's plan to reorganize federal administration has revived interest in state reorganization. The federal plan is said to be based upon state reorganization principles. For that matter, state reorganizations were based upon federal principles, and were advanced as the "federal plan for states." Such mutual admiration signifies that what is good enough for the federal government is good enough for the states, and vice versa. At this turn of the federal-organization-state-reorganization-federal-reorganization wheel, information is needed concerning results in the states as a basis for evaluating the federal plan. In 1931 Charles A. Beard said: "No one has taken the trouble to examine in minute detail the achievements of the machinery which has been installed in fifteen states." The present writer has since attempted such an examination. Only a few facts and conclusions, reached by a study of what happened in the first fifteen states to be reorganized, can be cited here.

The first question to consider is: To what extent have the states actually been reorganized in accordance with the basic reorganization principle? That principle is to centralize administrative control in the governor by consolidating many agencies into a few large functional departments, each headed by one individual appointed by the governor.

Consolidation of agencies by abolishment and assignment of their functions to new code departments was not as great as has been claimed. The actual reduction ranged from thirty-seven in Illinois to three in Maryland. The average number of agencies reduced by consolidation in the fifteen states was seventeen. The average number absorbed by each code department was one and one-half. The Massachusetts consolidation, according to Mr. A. E. Buck, was so insignificant that it accomplished no reduction. Yet it leads ten other states. South Dakota, with only two reorganized departments, accomplished a greater reduction than nine other states. Thus the reductions in most states were insignificant and were not large in comparison with the number existing before reorganization, which we were informed ran into the hundreds. Now as a result of the tendency toward decentralization, there are almost as many agencies as before reorganization.

Concerning the nature of agencies abolished, many were of minor ad-

[1] William H. Edwards, "Has State Reorganization Succeeded?" *State Government* (October, 1938), Vol. 11, pp. 183-184. Reprinted by permission of the author and *State Government*. A fuller statement of the author's views may be found in the *Southwestern Social Science Quarterly*, June, 1938.

ministrative importance. Some were inactive before reorganization. Others, whose functions were important, were abolished and their functions were not given to any other agency. This was not consolidation but cessation of desirable government activities. Some proper government functions were eliminated apparently because they were performed by plural-headed agencies—the disapproved type of overhead organization.

With regard to the scope and nature of the reorganized departments, whole functional fields were left outside the code structure in nearly every state. Numerous "reorganized" departments absorbed no functions of abolished agencies, but were merely the same old departments, which were placed bodily within the code structure without alteration. Some departments are departments in name only, such as headless departments, departments composed primarily of semi-independent bodies, and departments in which divisions are in practice separate agencies. Consolidations have frequently united totally unrelated functions. Departments have also been overloaded with too many functions for one director to oversee. In short, even on paper there are fewer consolidations than claimed, and the codes as administered are more decentralized than they seem from the law, so that the administrative structure, in fact, is still a diffuse organization.

Consolidation was achieved to a greater extent by attaching semi-independent agencies to code departments than by abolishing agencies and merging their functions in integrated departments. In the fifteen states as a whole over twice as many agencies were attached as were abolished. In each of nine states the number of attached agencies exceeds the number abolished. In Maryland the proportion of attachment to abolishment is over fifteen to one. New York has 120 attached agencies. Almost all attached agencies are plural-headed and largely independent of the governor. When agencies are attached to departments which are independent of the governor, he is farther removed from control than if they had been left unattached. Departments with attached agencies are often departments in name only. Many "attached" agencies are unattached in practice. Frequently so much confusion of authority has resulted from attaching agencies to code departments that administrative functions have been seriously impaired. A device, similar to this of attaching agencies to functional departments, was adopted to give the appearance of consolidation, i.e., the creation of a "governor's office" or "executive department" to serve as a top bureau drawer. By this process five states corralled unrelated agencies which often perform operating rather than staff functions. This expedient accomplished no consolidation and no change in the relations of the governor to these agencies.

The basic reorganization principle requires code departments to be headed by individuals appointed by the governor. Otherwise the resulting structure will be worse than the former decentralized system. In only six states, however, are all code departments so headed. In six other states from one-half to less than one-sixth of their code departments are so headed. Comparing totals of all code departments in the fifteen states, plural-headed or other disapproved types are three-fourths as great in number as the governor-appointed single-headed type. Not all single-headed departments are reorganization achievements. In Minnesota all single-headed departments were such before reorganization, while all four new departments were placed under plural heads in violation of the basic principle. Divisions of headless code departments are in most instances under plural heads or elective officers. Elective officers frequently occupy positions of large influence under the codes, and the code sponsors have aided in the retention of elective officers in contradiction of the basic reorganization in principle.

The codes have not reduced the governor's burden of appointing a mass of petty subordinates. In Pennsylvania he appoints some 670 code officers. In Nebraska he must appoint every officer and employee under the code. Some reasons for this burden are: the limited scope of reorganization; consolidation by attachment rather than abolishment; the existence of large numbers of plural-headed code departments, plural-headed divisions of headless departments, plural-headed attached agencies, and many unreorganized agencies most of which are plural-headed; and the requirement that the governor appoint subordinates within reorganized and unreorganized agencies. Because the codes require him to appoint department heads and employees, and because of his opportunity to dictate the appointment of employees generally, one authority has stated that political parties support the codes to secure "a rapid allocation of spoils while retaining the fiction of efficiency and civil service."

Since reorganization, "the natural tendency toward decentralization" has reasserted itself. The selfish motives for decentralization are manifested by "ripper bills" and partisan tinkering with the administrative machine; the altruistic ones by reaction against overloaded departments and confusion of authority arising from attached agencies and by the desire of professional and reform groups to take particular services out of spoils politics. As a result, some codes have been virtually obliterated and others largely disorganized.

Reference should be made to such other reforms as the use of modern methods of budgeting, accounting, and purchasing because they are sometimes confused with the central purpose of reorganization—the concentration of power in the governor. Such reforms may be a part of many other forms of governmental organization and are not an inherent part of the one-man-control plan. Space does not permit consideration of the impact of state reorganizations upon other reforms. I submit, however, that the most useful contribution of the reorganizations is not in partially establishing the basic principle of one-man-control but in helping to install other reforms, namely, centralized purchasing and modern fiscal practices.

The major benefits expected from reorganization were "efficiency and economy." Those claiming economies gave no direct evidence that economies resulted from increasing the governor's authority. When specific claims were cited, they were generally the result of central purchasing. Indeed a major weakness of the efficiency claims is that benefits have been attributed to the one-man-control plan which should have been attributed to related reforms, such as central purchasing, fiscal improvements, or unifunctional departmentalization. Enthusiastic advocates asserted that reorganizations have saved in some states hundreds of thousands of dollars and in other states millions. More cautious advocates have repudiated such claims. Thus Charles A. Beard holds that it is impossible to show "gains in efficiency and economy," and that support should be based upon the "logic" of "lines of responsibility from bottom to apex."

Thus it seems that reorganizers have swung from exaggeration to modesty as regards evidence of efficiency and economy. But perhaps something can be said of the advantages and disadvantages accruing from reorganization. What then can and what cannot be evaluated? Specific effects can be and have been determined: the extent to which the reorganizations have helped to install other reforms, namely, modern fiscal and purchasing methods and unifunctional departmentalization; the effect of reorganizations upon civil service laws and the merit system; and the effect upon particular functional departments where the overhead organization has been changed from plural to single heads. But on the other hand, the general economy and efficiency of reorganized versus unreorganized states cannot be estimated for several reasons. One is that many reorganized states are no more reorganized than unreorganized states so far as the basic test, the preponderance of single-over plural-headed agencies, is concerned. Another reason is that accounting techniques will probably never be developed to the point where the general proposition of concentrating authority in an elective chief administrator can be evaluated in dollars and cents. Even though such an evaluation might be made, it would still be more useful to calculate this concentration in terms of representative democracy and political liberty.

In conclusion: the facts concerning reorganization, a few of which are cited here, indicate that the reorganization movement has not been able to carry through or maintain its fundamental principle of concentration of power in the governor by consolidation of many agencies into a few large

integrated departments headed by governor-appointed individuals. Consequently, it is difficult to evaluate the one-man-control plan. It is possible,
however, to make piecemeal evaluations to the extent that functional departments have been changed from plural to single heads. *If* there are any
lessons for the federal government in state reorganizations, they are: that
the limited scope of reorganizations makes general conclusions useless;
that federal reorganization will probably not carry through the basic principle; that the President will probably not be much, if any, more of a chief
administrator than now; that powerful independent agencies will probably
remain such; that, therefore, opponents of reorganization need not be unduly
alarmed because a comprehensive reorganization will probably not materialize; and that, as Dr. Beard says, it will be difficult or impossible to prove
tangible benefits from reorganization, except "logical assumptions" which
can be proved as well beforehand.

Chapter XVIII

THE GOVERNMENT AND ITS EMPLOYEES

[THERE are in the United States to-day well over four million public employees. There is almost an infinite variety in the work that they do. Some of them are legislators, some executives, some judges; but these three groups constitute only a small fraction of the total number of public employees. The overwhelming number of public workers is found in the hundreds and thousands of public offices in which the everyday work of government is done. Here every profession, trade, occupation, and skill is represented. Accountants and zoologists, janitors and pharmacists, radio operators and carpenters, teachers and actors—these, and a host of other occupational groups, are employed by us to do our public work and thus constitute our civil service.

In a broad sense the term "civil service" includes all of the civil, that is, all of the non-military and non-naval, employees of government. But the term has another and inexact meaning; many use it as a synonym for "merit system." When used in this sense it implies that the civil servant secured his position through some procedure which tested his training, aptitude, and skills, and that once he has his job he is protected from political interference. This is an incorrect usage of the term. If all of the stenographers or bacteriologists of a city public health department are chosen because of their friendship for the department head, or because of their perspicacity in backing the right mayoralty candidate, this department has a civil service in spite of the absence of a merit system.]

No. 63

[THE struggle for the attainment of a merit system for public employees has been a long and a strenuous one in the United States. The "spoils system" has shown, and continues to show, a remarkable tenacity. The reasons for its ability to withstand the movement towards a real merit system are several. Not the least of these is the current but erroneous attitudes which we, the American people, have towards our civil servants and the work which they do. The following selection discusses these fallacies in our thinking. As long as the American people retain these points of view there is little possibility of securing that energetic and thoughtful action without which we cannot hope to substitute merit for spoils.]

FALLACIES IN AMERICAN THINKING ON GOVERNMENTAL PERSONNEL [1]

UNDER the American system, our governments, federal, state, and local, constitute a cooperative enterprise through which we endeavor to maintain freedom; sustain law, order, and property; protect the individual against exploitation; conduct essential public services, such as highways, water supply, fire protection, postal service, and sanitation; guard the public welfare through the promotion of health and the care of the sick, the handicapped, the poor, and the unemployed; conserve our national resources for the benefit both of the present and of the future; furnish and encourage universal education through schools, colleges, universities, libraries, and other agencies; cooperate with private individuals and associations for economic advance through the expansion of domestic and foreign markets, the improvement of agricultural and industrial practices, the study of practical and scientific problems, the protection of patents and copyrights, and the development of standards and standard practices; provide for the creation of corporations, and regulate those which deal with the necessities of life or are by nature monopolies; protect public health, decency, and morals with controls over child labor, hours of labor, wages, foods and drugs, alcohol and narcotics, medical and other practices, housing, and the use of land; create and regulate the banking and currency system; conduct foreign relations, and maintain our national independence.

During emergencies certain of these powers and services are greatly expanded: in time of war, to mobilize men and resources and protect the nation against the enemy; in time of flood, earthquake, fire, or drought, to prevent starvation, epidemics, or further destruction and encourage quick recovery; and in time of economic collapse, to feed, clothe, and house the destitute, find work for unemployed men, restore credits, start in motion again the complicated mechanism of our economic life, and lay broad plans so that the full energies of the nation, public and private, may work to the same constructive ends.

In brief outlines, these are the responsibilities and work of the American national, state, and local governments to-day. Government is a cooperative enterprise exceedingly complicated and difficult, and supremely important to every one of us, rich or poor, employed or unemployed, wherever we

[1] Commission of Inquiry on Public Service Personnel, *Better Government Personnel* (New York and London: McGraw-Hill Book Company, 1935), pp. 13-22. Reprinted by permission of the publisher.

live. We must have government to live, to work, to advance, to enjoy the fruits of our labor.

The success or failure of that government, and the kind of service which it renders, will rest in the last analysis upon the capacity and character of the men and women who constitute it. We must therefore maintain a governmental system under which the government attracts to the public service its full share of the capacity and character of the man power of the nation. This we do not accomplish in the United States under existing conditions. The American people know it, and demand a change, though they do not clearly see the way out. The whole work of the Commission of Inquiry on Public Service Personnel has therefore been directed, first, toward finding out what are the reasons for our nation-wide failure to attract enough men and women of the finest capacity and character into state, local, and national governmental services; and, second, toward devising, on the basis of experience, a constructive program for the future which will correct this failure.

The inquiry and the program of the Commission are confined to the appointive administrative services, and do not include the elected legislators and councilmen, boards and commissions, mayors, governors, and other elected officials, nor the judiciary and military forces. These limitations have been adopted because it is apparent that the weakest link in American democracy, the point at which we fall most conspicuously behind the other self-governing peoples, is in the appointive services where the great bulk of the work of modern government is carried on. Moreover, permanent advances can be achieved in this field by united effort in a relatively short time.

The selection of appointive administrative personnel for governmental service in the United States, especially in the state and local fields, is profoundly influenced by a number of common fallacies. Though men and women of experience have repeatedly called attention in the hearings of the Commission to the falsity and absurdity of these conceptions, they nevertheless prevail in many of our public appointment policies. The evidence we have taken indicates that these wrong ideas, accepted without thought, are in large measure responsible for the failure of our national, state, and local governments to attract to the public service their due share of men and women of capacity and character.

Among these fallacies, the following may be listed:

1. The false notion that "to the victor belong the spoils." From this it is inferred that it is right and necessary for a newly elected administration to discharge incumbents regardless of their merit and appoint its own party workers regardless of *their* merit to any salaried posts which can be found, vacated, or created. This was not the doctrine of the fathers of the Con-

stitution. It is a corruption of democracy, introduced into American government between 1810 and 1824. It is of no value to government nor, in the long run, to political parties, and has been abandoned in many parts of the United States, and in most of the democracies of the world.

2. The mistaken idea that the duties of governmental employees are, as President Jackson said, "so plain and simple that men of intelligence can readily qualify themselves for their performance." Whether or not this was true in 1829, it is certainly not true to-day. On the contrary, certain of those duties are now so difficult, so complex, so technical as to require the recruitment of highly trained specialists and the training in the services of the best administrative talent which the nation produces. Moreover, experience and science demonstrate that men have different physical and mental and moral capacities, and that these differences must be recognized in their education, in their work, and in many of their other relationships, not only from the standpoint of their usefulness to society, but from that of their own happiness as well.

3. The false idea that charity begins on the public payroll. All over the United States men and women are elected or appointed to office or kept on the payroll because they need the job: someone has died, there are twelve children in the family, a leg has been lost, or some other misfortune has befallen them. The employees appointed for these eleemosynary reasons draw the pay while others do the work, or else the work is botched and neglected. The cost to the public is not only the salary involved but also the much larger social cost of poor and bungled service and of lowered morale among the other employees.

4. The erroneous assumption that "patronage is the price of democracy," that the parties which we need for self-government cannot exist without spoils. This fallacy, more than any other, is responsible for the hopeless, defeatist attitude of good citizens, deterring them from advancing to the annihilation of the spoils system. There are, it is true, large cities, certain states, and other areas where political parties and political activity are *at present* sustained by patronage. But in great sections of the United States, and in other democracies of the world, democracy exists, political life is maintained, parties thrive, without the spoliation of the appointive administrative services. The truth is, as Theodore Roosevelt once observed, that patronage is the curse of politics. It is the selling-out price of democracy, because of itself it turns the political party into a job brokerage machine, creating a mercenary army of occupation, which, under the guise of democracy, robs us of self-government.

5. The idea that "the best public servant is the worst one. . . . A thoroughly first-rate man in public service is corrosive. He eats holes in our

liberties. The better he is and the longer he stays, the greater is the danger." Though this was the printed statement of a past president of the United States Chamber of Commerce in 1928, the Commission of Inquiry on Public Service Personnel could find no support for the idea in 1934. Springing in part from the same fallacy, much vilification of public employees as "tax eaters," "payrollers," and "bureaucrats" is, however, indulged in by certain groups in certain areas. The evidence indicates that these groups either are thoughtless or else have selfish reasons for desiring bad government. Indiscriminate vilification lessens the morale of all public officials, dissuades capable persons from entering the public service, and discredits the authority of government. Such efforts to change government through personal abuse of public servants as a class, rather than through the advocacy of specific reform measures, must be recognized as thoroughly subversive. No one who goes through the country from coast to coast examining the public service, as did this Commission, can fail to be impressed by the many evidences of marked ability and loyalty in those who now serve the public. To transfer to these worthy employees the abuse earned by a few bad ones is a most unwholesome piece of demagogy.

6. The erroneous thought that "tenure is the cure of spoils." This was the central idea of early civil service reform, and is the chief objective of certain organizations of public employees. American experience shows that guaranteed tenure for public employees is, when standing alone, a dangerous thing. It tends to produce poor service and low morale, to lessen the standing and prestige of the "protected" classes, to prevent the advancement of efficient personnel, and to keep deadwood on the payroll. It is used in many jurisdictions by the politicians as a dugout for spoilsmen. The evidence presented indicates that tenure should not be established except as a part of a merit system which selects with care those who are to be given tenure, establishes a definite retirement system, and sets up the method of getting rid of deadwood. Responsible employees' organizations both in this country and abroad have not only recognized these facts but have insisted that they cannot afford to ask for the protection of incompetent personnel, as this will not only result in bad service but will undermine public confidence in all public servants.

7. The superficial thought that the way to eradicate spoils and favoritism is to begin at the bottom with clerks, stenographers, and policemen, and work up, and that the success of reform can be measured by the percentage of the total service which is placed "under civil service." All the evidence presented shows clearly that the top posts are of supreme importance, and that chief administrative officers who are spoilsmen can demoralize the rank and file and wreck the service in spite of any law.

8. The belief in "home town jobs for home town boys." Tariff wall around individual city, county, and state payrolls are a bad thing not only for the public service and the taxpayer, but also for those who desire to work for government. Residence requirements, particularly for technical skilled, and other higher posts, restrict the opportunity for selection by th employer, that is the government, and they limit the opportunities for a career on the part of the person entering the service. No such restriction have, as a rule, been imposed with regard to school teachers, nor in privat business, and they should not be imposed in connection with other appoint ive government positions. Residence qualifications are a benefit only to incompetent applicants and petty politicians.

9. The notion that "the public service is always less capable and effi cient than private enterprise." The best businesses are more efficient than the average government; while the most efficient governmental units are more efficient than the average business. At many of the hearings of the Commission the opinion was expressed that businesses and governments are apparently about on a par—what business gains through the profit motive and elasticity being apparently lost in many instances through hereditary management, labor difficulties, and outside control. It was pointed out also that in America, governments have, as a rule, undertaken no services except after private agencies have proved themselves incapable or powerless to con duct them. To achieve any measure of success under such conditions is a remarkable accomplishment for public management. Businesses and other private agencies, too, have their problems of nepotism, favoritism, sharp practice, low morality, embezzlement, insolvency, and decay, as well a the difficulties which arise from useless competition. The criticism of the public service arises by comparison not so much with the superiorities of business as with the higher standards which we expect and have a right to demand from our governments.

10. The erroneous idea that the spoils system, the eleemosynary system and the other corrosive influences can be driven out of the public servic through the prohibition of specific abuses. Time and again, the Commission has been told that laws will not cure the situation. What is clearly required is not negative laws, but the positive and militant handling of the problem of personnel with the active backing of the public and the press.

These are among the fallacies which have been more or less dominant in American thinking during recent generations, which have an important effec upon the problem of public personnel policy. The fact that the American people are now beginning to recognize the falsity of these ideas clears the way for a new constructive approach to the problem of attracting to the public service men and women of capacity and character.

No. 64

OUR first attempts at reform of the public service were directed at only two
or three objectives. It was believed by many that if we could obtain capable
persons in the civil service, through merit examination, and protect them from
political interference, the problem of public personnel would be solved. In the
half century that has elapsed since the passage of the Pendleton Act we have
learned that a sound personnel system involves much more than these two steps.
The attainment of a real merit system necessitates the adoption of sound systems
of promotion and advancement, the provision of adequate means of discipline,
suspension, and removal from the service, and the attainment of a high morale
among the civil servants. Furthermore, the relationships between the adoption
of a sound personnel policy and the functioning of democratic government must
be clearly perceived. These and other considerations are the concern of "Essentials of a Model Personnel System."]

ESSENTIALS OF A MODEL PERSONNEL
SYSTEM [1]

by Floyd W. Reeves

THERE is no such thing as a personnel system that can serve as a
model for all types and sizes of governmental jurisdiction. There are,
however, certain basic principles of personnel administration that are relatively uniform for all jurisdictions, irrespective of size or scope of operations.
Any personnel system, to be effective, must be organized and administered
in a manner consistent with these principles and with the basic objective of
personnel administration. This basic objective is to secure and retain in
the public service a quality of personnel that corresponds to the responsibilities of the service, and to achieve standards of competence that are as
high as available human resources will permit.

The first essential of an effective personnel system is that it be a part of
an effective system of government.

Laws, rules, and regulations providing that the personnel system operate
on a merit basis are essential to secure efficiency in personnel administration,
but they will not in themselves produce it. They must be enforced by a
well-established tradition of good government, a tradition of merit in per-

[1] Floyd W. Reeves, "Essentials of a Model Personnel System," *The Annals* of the
American Academy of Political and Social Science (January, 1937), Vol. 189, pp. 134-141.
Reprinted by permission of *The Annals* of the American Academy of Political and Social
Science. Footnotes in the original article are omitted here.

sonnel administration, and an enlightened public opinion. Unless they are
so enforced, they will not result in a merit system. Tradition is more important, however, than the laws, rules, and regulations. The latter constitute a
negative attack upon the problem. Building a tradition of merit in public
service requires postive, constructive action. The administration of the
personnel function in a model personnel system will be designed to increase
the prestige of the public service. Unless there is prestige attached to the
service, it is difficult to secure efficient public servants, and when they are
secured, it is difficult to retain them.

A tradition of merit in government administration recognizes such admin
istration as a profession. Public administration cannot become a profession
however, in a jurisdiction in which a large number of the major administrative officers are elected for specified terms. A short ballot is a requisite for
an effective system of government. Elected officials will include only those
engaged in major policy-forming activities. This group may include the
chief executive officer and a very few immediate assistants. It will never
include officers whose principal function is administration.

The legislative body is the major policy-determining agency in govern
ment. When this body is small, as in the case of many city councils, the
chief executive will not need to assume major responsibility in connection
with the determination of broad policies. In such cases, the chief executive
may well be a part of the professional staff, selected upon a merit basis
Such a plan now operates effectively in many cities with the city-manage
form of organization. When the legislative body is large, as in the case o
state governments, the chief executive and a few immediate assistants wil
not be members of the professional staff, since they will be called upon to
participate actively in policy formation.

The complexity of modern government requires a high degree of compe
tence, particularly at the levels at which the higher administrative officer
function. It also requires a high degree of devotion to the public service
These requirements can best be met through training for and experience in
government service. A corps of career administrators in charge of operat
ing departments and responsible to policy-forming officials is essential to
the successful functioning of the executive branch of the government. Thi
is the only means whereby the quality of personnel in public service may be
made to correspond to the large responsibilities of that service.

The effectiveness of the personnel system is affected by the soundness o
the organization of operating departments. To as large a degree as possible
each operating department will administer closely related functions. It i
seldom possible, however, to organize an operating department in a manne
such that some of its functions will not impinge upon functions performe

by other departments. The successful administration of such functions requires close inter-departmental cooperation. This, in turn, requires machinery for coordination at all major levels where these functions operate. Often this coordination can best be achieved by means of inter-departmental committees, composed of staff members of the departments affected, and reporting back to the department responsible for the administration of the function concerned.

An effective organization requires that the number of major coordinate administrative officers responsible directly to the chief executive shall not exceed a reasonable span of control. This implies the assembling of all functions of a governmental agency into a few large groups. In a state or city government, this number should probably never exceed six or seven, and might well be smaller.

Over a period of many years the activities of government have constantly expanded and become more complex. To provide for this expansion and the increased complexity of government, a heavy strain has been placed upon personnel administration. In its earlier stages of development, public personnel administration was conceived to be a function designed primarily to eliminate spoils. This idea has given way to a broader conception that places major emphasis upon developing incentives, increasing morale, and stimulating employee efficiency. The promotion of the merit system has not decreased in importance, but new methods for accomplishing this purpose, methods that do not interfere with the development of a constructive and positive personnel program, are now recognized as essential and are being employed in many jurisdictions.

Personnel functions of an administrative nature include such matters as attendance control, checking pay rolls, administering pensions, care of records, and preparing reports. Most personnel agencies also participate in one way or another in the classification of positions in the service, the determination of salaries, and the formulation of salary schedules. The negative controls on recruitment have not decreased in importance, but the technique employed to accomplish the ends sought is being constantly improved.

Personnel agencies are increasingly participating in quasi-judicial functions in connection with appeals from decisions relating to demotion, separation from the service, classification and salary status, and compensation for injuries received in line of duty.

Many of the newer and more constructive functions of personnel administration are primarily advisory in their nature. Their purpose is to stimulate desirable action on the part of employees and management. Functions of this type relate to such matters as discipline; employee-management relations; working conditions; and health, safety, welfare, and recreation.

These matters are primarily the concern of the heads of the operating units but an effective personnel service can render valuable assistance in studying such problems and suggesting means for their solution.

No exhaustive analysis of the functions mentioned above is necessary to make it clear that a continuous program of research is essential if personnel problems are to be dealt with adequately. Personnel management is not static in any of its aspects. Because this is true, no one of the personnel functions may well be excluded from the research program. This implies a personnel research agency in every jurisdiction except those that are very small. Small units may find it advisable to utilize the assistance of some outside agency in carrying on necessary research activities.

Most of the essentials of a model personnel system relate to the two major aspects of the personnel function—entrance to the service, and increasing efficiency within the service. Both of these aspects will be discussed briefly.

Effective public administration requires throughout the service men and women with adequate training for the work they are to perform and with qualities of character adequate for the positions they are to occupy. The best laws that may be devised may be virtually annulled if they are administered by an incapable or unsympathetic staff. The requirements mentioned are particularly important for those charged with the responsibility of administering the personnel function, since pressures, political and otherwise, are frequently concentrated at that point.

Within the general service, as distinguished from the major policy-determining group, the judiciary, and the military service, merit appointments will not be confined to the lower positions in a model personnel system, but will extend throughout the service. No appointments will be made for political purposes, or on the basis of personal friendship, family relationships, religious affiliations, or other non-administrative reasons. There will be no attempt to find jobs for individuals, but a constant endeavor will be made to find qualified and efficient persons to fill necessary jobs. There will be no discrimination because of the marital status of employees or applicants. Resident requirements will not be set up for technical, skilled, or higher posts, because such requirements restrict opportunity to secure the best talent for the public service, and limit the opportunity to develop a career service. For economic reasons, such requirements may be applicable for temporary positions or for unskilled labor. The conditions set forth above are necessary in order that all appointments may be made upon the basis of merit, which is a requirement of an effective personnel system.

The technique employed in the recruitment of personnel will be in accord with the democratic principle of equality of opportunity in accordance with merit. Examinations will be widely advertised and the duties and responsibilities of the positions for which the examinations are held will be adequately explained. The personnel administration will not wait passively for applicants to apply, recruitment will be active. Well-qualified persons will be sought out and urged to file applications. Cooperative arrangements for the certification of candidates will be developed with other governmental jurisdictions, with accredited professional associations, and with educational institutions.

Few personnel agencies can afford to have a permanent staff of examiners qualified to pass finally upon the qualifications of candidates for some of the more important positions requiring high technical, professional, or administrative ability. In certifying eligibles for such posts, therefore, use will be made of special boards of examiners. Such boards may well consist of a major staff member of the personnel division, a representative of the operating agency for which the candidate is to be certified, and one or more persons either from within or from without the service, qualified to pass upon the eligibility of candidates for the position.

The procedures employed in selecting personnel for entrance to the service will be in accord with the requirements for the development of career services. A career service has been defined as a "life work . . . an honorable occupation which one normally takes up in youth with the expectation of advancement, and pursues until retirement." The establishment of effective career services is essential to the development of an effective personnel program.

For each major type of service there will be an appropriate method of entrance based entirely upon qualifications to render effective service. These qualifications include not only ability to render effective service immediately after entrance, but, what is even more important, capacity for continued growth in the service. This implies that a majority of those entering each type of service will be relatively young, will enter at the lower positions within that service, and will be promoted to vacancies at higher levels entirely on the basis of merit.

It would seem inadvisable to restrict entrance to higher positions in the service exclusively to those who entered the service at the lower levels. No matter how effectively a career service system may operate, no agency is likely to secure a monopoly upon persons well qualified to fill the higher positions. It may be conceded that opportunity for promotion within the service is essential to a career service and to an effective personnel program. It may also be conceded that employees within the service, when they are equally qualified, should be given preference over candidates from without the service. An effective career service, however, does not imply filling important positions from within the service when better trained and better qualified personnel can be secured from other sources. Such action would not assist in creating a true career service, but would tend to prevent the attainment of that goal.

In personnel management, as in recruitment to the service, the techniques employed should exemplify the democratic principle of equality of opportunity in accordance with merit. Employees in a model personnel system will receive just treatment and be given reasonable security. This requires that they be placed in positions where they can render the largest service, in accordance with the total needs of the governmental units of which they are a part; that they be protected against arbitrary dismissal, demotion, or discipline; that their positions be properly classified as to duties and responsibilities; that they receive fair compensation for services rendered; that adequate provisions be made for supervision and in-service training, with opportunities for advancement or demonstrated merit; that they and their dependents be protected against the hazards of sickness, old age, and death, disability, or injury in line of duty; and that working conditions be as conducive to health, safety, and efficiency as the nature of the work and the requirements of the public interest permit.

Upon entrance to the service, every employee will be placed on probation for a definite period of time, ranging from a few months for positions of a routine nature to one or two years for important positions requiring diversified talents and involving large responsibility. During this probationary period the supervisor of the employee, in cooperation with the personnel agency, will give the employee careful supervision, assist him to become more proficient in his present work, and encourage him to take additional training when such training seems advisable. Service records will be kept, and at stated intervals throughout the probationary period, reports will be made by the supervisor to the personnel agency. At the end of this period the supervisor will be required to make a definite recommendation with reference to the future placement of the probationer in the service. He will recommend that the employee be retained in his present position, that he be transferred to some other position of equal or lower grade, that he be dismissed, or, in rare cases, that he be promoted to a position of greater responsibility. In any case, the recommendation will be definite. The employee will not be retained in his present position merely because of a lack of positive action.

Supervision and training will not cease with the end of the period of probation. Both are important throughout the entire service, and at all levels.

In-service training is of two general types—training for the position which the employee now occupies, and training for some other position in anticipation of transfer or promotion. The governmental agency, through the stimulation of its personnel division, will be encouraged to provide both types of training when such facilities are not adequately provided by the educational system or are not easily available. When agencies of public education are easily accessible to employees, such agencies will be encouraged to provide facilities for in-service training.

In filling positions that become vacant above the lower grades, it is a matter of major importance that appointing officers give proper consideration to employees already in the service. Consideration will first be given to employees in direct line within the same department and unit. Next in order will come employees available for transfer and promotion from other departments. Failing to find suitable candidates within the service, well-qualified former employees available for reinstatement will be considered before turning to existing examination registers. New open competitive examinations will be given only after failure to secure eligibles through the procedures mentioned above. Classification of positions as to duties and responsibilities is a technical function of great importance to the building of morale within the service. It is one of the major factors affecting the compensation of employees. As such, it becomes particularly important that this function be performed efficiently and fairly, in order that high morale may be achieved. As a highly technical function, classification cannot be performed effectively unless it is administered and conducted by trained experts devoting full time to such work.

Good working conditions and some degree of security are essential to high morale. The attainment of these objectives is a joint responsibility of the operating departments, the personnel agency, the chief executive of the government, and the policy-forming body responsible for the government. The central personnel agency will administer the accident compensation and retirement services. It will also cooperate with and encourage the departments to provide other services for the improvement of working conditions.

In addition to activities of the type mentioned above, an effective personnel agency will perform many functions of a broad, developmental nature. It will keep itself well informed concerning methods, policies, and procedures of personnel management throughout the service. It will encourage and support constructive personnel development, and will disseminate knowledge concerning such development to other parts of the service. It will provide machinery for the coordination of personnel policies and plans within the service. It will develop advisory relationships with personnel administrations of other governmental jurisdictions and of industries, and with students of personnel administration wherever they may be found. It will utilize every legitimate means to stimulate better personnel practices throughout the service. It will encourage officials to recognize the importance of high morale, and to become familiar with the means whereby such morale may be developed. To accomplish these ends, emphasis will be placed upon positive, constructive action rather than upon negative, restrictive measures of control.

One of the most effective ways for government to improve the development of its personnel function is through the cooperation of representative groups of employees and the supervisory staff. To secure such cooperation, recognition should be given to the right of employees to participate actively in the development of policies and plans whenever they are in a position to make a contribution. Members of the management staff and the supervised employees, together, comprise an organization for public service. To obtain the objective sought, the whole-hearted cooperation of all members of this organization is essential.

The management of personnel is and must continue to be a major function of all administrators. Some aspects of the personnel function, however, are so highly technical that general administrators are rarely found who are equipped with the technical knowledge or skill now available for personnel work. Furthermore, the burden placed upon administrators in administering the operating functions under their direction is usually so heavy that it does not permit them to devote the time and attention necessary to the successful performance of technical personnel functions. Because of this situation, specialized personnel agencies are essential at all major levels of administration.

Good personnel in charge of the administration of the personnel function is an essential of good administration. But good personnel may be rendered relatively ineffective unless it is placed in an organization framework that is structurally sound. Furthermore, good personnel is not attracted to an organization that is structurally unsound, and when secured, can seldom be retained. Therefore, the personnel administration must be given its proper position in the structural organization of the agency of which it is a part.

Personnel administration is a part of management. Functions such as selection of employees, efficiency rating, promotion, demotion, and removal from the service, are essentially management functions. Negative controls may be secured in part if these functions are performed by an independent civil service commission, but only in part. It is easy to find ways and means whereby restrictive laws, rules, or regulations may be overcome. Furthermore, such negative controls as may be necessary are more effective when operated as a part of management. Any other arrangement violates sound principles of administration, in that it robs management of initiative, and undermines responsible leadership. Consequently, negative controls can never be wholly effective if administered by a civil service commission operating as an independent agency outside of the management structure. Positive, constructive action in the performance of the personnel function almost never develops through an independent civil service commission.

The personnel agency is one of a group of service agencies established to assist operating agencies through the performance of technical functions. Other agencies of a similar type include those for fiscal control, purchasing, management of physical facilities, research, and long-range planning. Of this group, the agency for fiscal control and the personnel agency are of major importance. Their functions are closely related. At the level where the chief executive operates, these agencies constitute the major instruments through which he performs his managerial functions. Therefore it is important that the heads of these agencies be made responsible directly to the chief executive. Both functions are so important that no chief executive can afford to delegate their performance completely to others.

There is another reason, and a major one, why agencies for the performance of functions such as personnel administration and fiscal control need to be attached directly to the office of the chief executive. These agencies must be given large responsibility for the performance of their specialized functions, but these functions are performed in connection with activities for which line officers are responsible. The service agencies can never be given authority over the operating agencies commensurate with the responsibility that the service agencies have for the successful conduct of the functions with which they are charged. Therefore the service agencies need the active support of the chief executive and the prestige that will come from being attached to his office, in order that they may function in a satisfactory manner. No specialized function of major importance should be administered by a specialist primarily concerned with the administration of another specialized function. Both personnel administration and the administration of the budget are highly specialized and important functions. Therefore neither of them will be made subordinate to the other, but they will be given coordinate positions in the structural organization of the government.

Some governmental jurisdictions are so large that it is not advisable to concentrate all personnel functions in a central personnel agency. Many of these functions can be administered more effectively if placed in the operating agencies where the functions are to be performed. Some of them, such as the classification of duties and responsibilities of employees, need to be administered in part by the central agency and in part by the operating agency under the supervision and control of the central agency. In the case of functions administered directly by the central agency, such as examinations for entrance to the service, the active cooperation of the department is essential. Therefore, in each of the larger departments or other administrative units, personnel offices will be established with a relationship to the head of the department similar to that described for the head of the central personnel agency with the chief executive of the entire governmental jurisdiction.

Since in the larger jurisdictions there will be both a central personnel agency responsible to the chief executive, and departmental personnel offices responsible to the departmental heads, coordinating machinery is essential. Possibly the best way to secure such coordination is to organize the heads of the personnel offices in the departments into an advisory council, with the head of the central agency serving as chairman.

Personnel functions may be classified as quasi-judicial, administrative, and developmental. The hearing of appeals from decisions of administrative officers is quasi-judicial. Activities such as the giving of examinations or the classification of employees are administrative. Stimulating others to perform their personnel functions more effectively is developmental. The question arises as to the best type of agency through which to perform personnel functions. Should the personnel agency be headed by a board, or by an individual? There are advantages and disadvantages in both arrangements.

In the case of quasi-judicial functions there are some advantages in placing responsibility upon a board composed of three or more persons. But it is generally conceded that administrative functions can be performed best by an individual. Likewise, an individual is more effective than a board in the performance of developmental functions.

The quasi-judicial functions are important, but the administrative and developmental functions are of equal if not greater importance. The model personnel system will have a central personnel agency headed by an individual to care for administrative and developmental functions. Within this central agency it will establish a board which will be charged with responsibility for the quasi-judicial aspects of the personnel function. In this way the advantages of both forms of organization may well be secured without the disadvantages attached to either form of organization.

No. 65

[IN many communities in the United States the citizens have been perplexed by what appears to them to be a most puzzling problem. Shocked by the waste and inefficiency of a politically appointed public service, they have in scores of instances demanded and secured the adoption of the merit system. Believing the battle to be won, they thereupon have relaxed their interest and vigilance and happily awaited the coming of a well-trained and well-directed group of public servants, a corps of workers that inexplicably failed to materialize. These citizens made the mistake of assuming that the policy decision was the only battle of the war. In their concern over this battle they overlooked the equally important and decisive engagement which revolved about good administration of the personnel program.

These perplexed people can find the explanation of their predicament in the following article by Professor V. O. Key, Jr. As Professor Key points out, the ingenuity of the spoilsman has kept up with the legislative efforts of the reformer. Politicians who seek patronage as a means of building up their control over the machine have invented many techniques for evading civil service laws.]

METHODS OF EVASION OF CIVIL SERVICE LAWS [1]

by V. O. Key, Jr.

ANY systematization of the techniques of political machine formation must include an analysis of the methods of evasion and avoidance of merit system legislation. The electoral power of the "machine" depends in large measure upon the efforts of disciplined and loyal party workers who may be recruited most readily through the distribution of patronage. Almost uniformly legislators and practical politicians have opposed, at least privately, the enactment of laws providing for the recruitment of public employes upon the basis of merit. Militant reform movements compelled the enactment of such legislation and ways and means came to be devised to mitigate the requirements of the law. Without attempting an extensive survey of the present status of the merit system, examples of evasion in various jurisdictions may be brought together to indicate the more frequently recurring general types.

[1] V. O. Key, Jr., "Methods of Evasion of Civil Service Laws," *The Southwestern Social Science Quarterly* (March, 1935), Vol. 15, pp. 337-347. Reprinted by permission of the author and *The Southwestern Social Science Quarterly*.

Limiting the Scope of Merit Laws.—By framing legislation to exclude certain classes of employes from the application of merit requirements and procedures, many positions have been saved to be dispensed at the discretion of the organization. Practically every proposal in Congress for the creation of a new administrative agency is marked by a fight to exclude its employes from the provisions of the civil service regulations, and often the effort meets with success. The disastrous effects of such a step on prohibition enforcement are too well known to require comment.

Although there are some exemptions of specific administrative agencies in states and cities having merit laws, more positions are affected by the exemption of classes cutting horizontally through all the administrative departments. Heads of departments and their immediate subordinates, such as deputy commissioners, are generally open to selection upon the basis of political considerations. These jobs are extremely valuable from the patronage standpoint, for it may be said that the value of a job for this purpose increases with its altitude in the administrative hierarchy. The place which their holders occupy in the public eye serves as a constant reminder to the Italians, the Brotherhood of Locomotive Engineers, the Poles, the Catholics, the Negroes, the American Legion, or other pressure group that the administration has recognized them by placing one of their number in a post of power and honor. Furthermore, the possession of a large number of such positions greatly simplifies the matter of discipline within the organization. The leader is constantly being challenged by men who are almost his equal and the astute distribution of positions of this type among the more dangerous contenders for power helps mightily in checking insubordination.

Every important official must have his confidential assistants, personal investigators, private secretaries, or other attachés possessed of a title of relatively high prestige value. Due to the intimate relationship and the delicate matters handled by these persons, it is argued that they should be selected by their superior completely free of any requirement for competitive examination. This contention is often groundless, but after the places are created and exempted from examination requirements they may be used as rewards for deserving members of the organization.

Some positions which for other reasons are thought not to be susceptible of being filled by competitive examination are governed by pass or noncompetitive examination provisions. This type of examination gives much greater discretion to the appointing authority than the ordinary open competitive test. In effect, complete freedom may be given to the appointing officer. At the other extreme, laborers are usually exempt from the operation of the competitive procedure. There are loafers and workers, able and disabled persons, whose characteristics could be determined by a personnel officer, but the merit system was introduced with emphasis upon the academic type of examination which precluded the inclusion of this type of employe. This leaves a large number of jobs for unskilled workers which can be used with extraordinary effectiveness in building up organization support. The possible effect of all these exemptions may be seen from the fact that in 1929, of the 86,509 employes of the City of New York, 246 belonged to the unclassified service, which number included heads and deputy heads of departments; 1,024 to the exempt class; 11,694 to the non-competitive class; and 24,200 to the labor class. Over 40 per cent of the employes of the city were thus exempt from merit procedures.

TABLE I

TEMPORARY APPOINTEES OF WEST CHICAGO PARKS SYSTEM

Year	Number of Positions	Salary Paid to "Temporaries"	Percentage of Total Payroll Paid to "Temporaries"
1915	79	$ 5,021.86	0.0071
1920	234	35,132.93	3.3
1925	636	473,350.33	26.3
1928	1725	1,202,616.90	42.5
1929	1305	984,867.82	39.9
1930	1798	872,777.00	27.4
1931	2212	1,748,501.65	61.2
1932	2122	1,142,163.90	46.7

Slightly different from permanent exemptions from the merit laws is provision for the appointment of temporary employes to fill positions otherwise subject to examination. Legislation usually provides that vacancies in such positions may be filled for thirty or sixty days by temporary employes pending the holding of an examination. By filling competitive positions with temporary employes and repeatedly renewing these appointments merit laws may be practically nullified. As an example of what may be done by this method the West Parks system of Chicago may be cited. Table I shows the progressive increase in the number and proportion of temporary appointees over a period of years. About 1,900 of the 4,500 Cook County (Chicago), Illinois, jobs are subject to the merit laws. During 1928 at least 40 per cent of these positions were filled by temporary appointees. In 1923 approximately 5,000 of the 22,000 positions in the Chicago classified service were filled by temporaries. During the Cermak administration in Chicago the general trend in the number of temporaries was upward with aperiodic fluctuations nicely synchronized with the occurrence of elections. The total number of temporary employes was reliably estimated at between five and six thousand. In Cleveland in 1922 it was found that more than 2,000 of the 5,000 positions subject to examination were occupied by "thirty-day" appointees. The practice was carried to its logical conclusion in Kansas City, where at one time all positions in the city service were held by temporary appointees. In Cuyahoga County (Cleveland), Ohio, in 1929, 58 per cent of the county's 1,466 positions were either exempt, unclassified, or filled by temporaries. By renewals these positions became in effect permanent, at least for the duration of the party's power. Such appointees, however, may be removed at will, thus greatly simplifying the problem of maintaining organizational discipline.

Under certain circumstances the civil service commission usually has the authority to exempt positions from examination and this is often done, sometimes for the benefit of the organization and at other times for legitimate reasons. Without the complicity of the commission, positions in the classified service may be left unfilled by the appointing authority and the duties performed by persons appointed under some title not subject to examination. In the federal service it was found at one time that a large number of persons appointed as laborers without examination at the request of various politicians had been assigned to classified duties.

Under the civil service laws of some jurisdictions it is possible to evade the requirement of competitive examination prior to appointment by contracting for services. This exception, designed to provide for the employment of attorneys, accountants, architects, and experts of various kinds on a contractual basis, was used in New York City to furnish a berth for Dr. William H. Walker, brother of the former mayor. The Board of Education contracted for his services as a "medical consultant" to render the same service as a "medical examiner" in the competitive class. When the Court of Appeals nullified this evasion, about 250 employes hired under the contract system in New York City were affected. In Boston contracts were made for the services of laborers. The contractor made a profit in furnishing these men who could have been employed directly by the city. In Chicago it was alleged in a legal proceeding that political employes of the West Parks board were not on the personnel payroll, but were paid with vouchers for materials.

Clerical employes and other attachés of the courts on all levels of government and in practically all jurisdictions remain subject to the patronage system. Due to the insistence upon the independence of the judiciary as a coördinate branch of government, its employes are more often excluded from the operation of civil service laws than not. This action has not been unconnected with the fact that court functionaries are often in a position to render services of peculiar value to the organization, particularly in the lower courts handling minor criminal cases. Similarly, employes of legislative bodies—clerks, pages, stenographers, and the like—are in most cases selected on a patronage basis. In some instances the committees making the selections are frankly named the "patronage committee."

"Right Guys."—The early advocates of civil service reform—affectionately referred to by the "pols" as the "goo-goos"—envisaged civil service commissions as agencies independent of the administrative departments applying the merit laws stringently and without fear or favor. This conception was readily demolished by appointing "right guys," i.e., loyal organization men, to the commissions. "If the mayoralty of the city falls into the hands of the spoilsman who appoints the civil service commission, it is an easy thing to take all the starch out of the civil service requirements. The manifold ways in which this was done under the Walker administration (in New York City) revealed the abuses incident to the commission being appointed by the mayor and owing its allegiance solely to him." In Illinois during the regime of Governor Len Small the chief examiner of the civil service commission quoted one of its members as saying that "there will be just examinations enough to keep up appearances." Even when the commission is constituted of men firmly committed to the policies of the merit law and is assisted by a staff of technically proficient personnel officers, it can accomplish little without the voluntary cooperation of the chief executive and the heads of the administrative departments.

An excellent example of what can be done by appointing the "right" men to a commission occurred during Mayor "Big Bill" Thompson's first two terms in Chicago. The two Republican positions on the commission were held by three individuals at various times during his administration. Charles E. Frazier, a prominent member of the Thirty-third Ward Republican organization, was appointed, he said, with the understanding that he should "do nothing unjustified." Alex J. Johnson, vice-president of the William Hale Thompson Republican Club, replied to a query as to the relationship between his political activities and his appointment to the commission: "What of it? You don't think the Mayor would appoint an enemy, do you?" Percy B. Coffin, the third Republican holding membership on the commission during this period, served as a handy man for the mayor in various capacities, including a stint as unofficial patronage dispenser.

The appointment of loyal organization men to the commission is undoubtedly the most effective means for bringing the civil service under the control of the organization. This can be done, of course, only when there is no effective opposition to such a policy. To placate opposition to spoils practices frequently a minority of the commission consists of effective but harmless "window dressing." Or appointments of weak men without malodorous records, easily subject to manipulation, may be made for the same purpose.

Legislative Sabotage.—Control of appropriations for the work of the personnel agency may serve as a means for mitigating the severity of the enforcement of merit laws. However disposed the commission may be, without ample staff to carry on the voluminous and complex work of testing, classification, *et cetera,* it can accomplish little. By reducing the appropriations for the personnel agency the legislative body may effectively draw its fangs. The Chicago Civil Service Commission may be cited as an example.

TABLE II

STAFF AND APPROPRIATIONS FOR CHICAGO CIVIL SERVICE
COMMISSION, 1915-1922

Year	Staff	Appropriation
1915	74	$101,000
1916	63	74,520
1917	37	65,640
1918	37	61,930
1919	39	74,420
1920	31	82,070
1921	31	87,580
1922	33	104,820

When Mayor Thompson first took office in 1915 the commission had an average staff of 75 employes and an annual appropriation of about $100,000. It was recognized as one of the best personnel agencies in the country. Table II shows what happened to its staff and appropriations. Other factors contributed, but by 1923 the commission had sunk to a position of very low repute. The financial strangulation of the personnel agency has been carried to the logical conclusion in Kansas, where no appropriations are made and the state civil service law remains dormant. Short of actually cutting appropriations pressure may be brought to bear upon civil service agencies by members of the legislative body. One can not very well deny a legislator a favor one day and ask him to vote for an appropriation the next.

The Process of Selection.—In the process of examination there is opportunity for maladministration. Although safeguards are usually employed to prevent the identity of the examinee from being known to the rater, they may be evaded. Furthermore, a considerable latitude of discretion in the evaluation of papers is possible due to the type of questions often used in civil service examinations. A Cook County, Illinois, grand jury in 1922 compared the markings of papers by the civil service commission examiners and by the persons who had been brought in by the commission to prepare the questions. Although no proof of abuse of discretion was presented except by inference, the range of variation as indicated by Table III indicates the possibilities.

Numerous instances of unfair grading of examination papers are available from a study of the Cuyahoga County, Ohio, civil service commission. An examinee, who had not had the experience required to enter the examination, was asked: "When would you permit the addition of sand above the amount called for in the specifications in a batch of concrete?" The answer was: "When the weather is wet, before the engineer has been able to make a

TABLE III

COMPARISON OF RATING PAPERS BY EXAMINERS AND BY PERSONS
PREPARING CERTAIN EXAMINATION QUESTIONS

Paper	Mark by Civil Service Examiners	Mark by Person Preparing Questions
A	90	70
B	60	80
C	40	85

test." He went to the head of the eligible list. In an examination for dirt street foreman the following question was put: "Describe in detail and illustrate with a diagram a case where a drain across a street is needed." The reply was: "A drain should be placed under roadway." No drawing was furnished. Although the applicant had not had the required experience for entrance to the examination, he passed and was appointed to the service. In another examination for the same position a man who had been a barber most of his life said in his application: "I did not have any practical experience of this position, but I have a number of barber shops." He was given 70 per cent for experience. Two years' experience in dirt highway construction work was required. In an examination for sewer maintenance foreman answers totaling fourteen lines to five questions earned a mark of 98.4 per cent. A close check of 1,175 names on the eligible lists resulting from 73 examinations by the Cleveland city commission showed that 22 per cent of them had actually failed in the tests.

Members of the organization may take the examination and be appointed with or without chicanery in the ratings. Being appointed, they may do their political work "on the side," assuming, as is customary, a weak enforcement of the rules prohibiting political activity by permanent employes. In some cases positions requiring technical training and practical experience are filled by inexperienced political temporaries who acquire experience at the expense of the public and then secure permanent appointment after examination.

In case of necessity, when the examining authorities are careless, a substitute may take the examination for the applicant. Occasional instances of this have been uncovered. "James M. Curley and Thomas F. Curley were convicted," according to Foulke, "of impersonating two candidates at a civil service examination in Boston and were sentenced to two months in jail." In some cases little publicity is given to coming examinations. This may leave the organization practically free to appoint its candidates through the forms of competition.

Members of the civil service commission or its employes may be bribed to give an applicant a favorable rating. When the examinations are fairly conducted, but an atmosphere of suspicion exists, persons with "inside" information can pick up a little pin money. A municipal civil service commissioner once said that "someone would accidentally or in some improper manner" discover the results of the examination "and would go and obtain money" in return for an assurance that the examinee "would get the rating which he had already earned by his own ability." In other cases persons claiming the power to influence the selection from among the three highest in an examination have collected money from as many as possible of those likely to be appointed, keeping the amounts paid by the successful ones and repaying "those not selected, with the explanation that counter influence was too strong."

Movement of Personnel.—The control of promotion, discipline, and assignment may be employed to persuade recalcitrant members of the administrative personnel, recruited into the service by an open and aboveboard system of examinations, to serve the purposes of the organization in the same way as those appointed by an out-and-out spoils procedure. Criteria of achievement or failure of achievement in the political organization may be substituted for similar criteria within the administrative hierarchy in the management of personnel. A man may be promoted within the administrative service for gloriously carrying his precinct or he may be made to "go along" with the organization by actual or threatened disciplinary measures.

Because of the difficulty of developing an objective measure of relative merit for promotion in the administrative service, promotion is peculiarly susceptible to manipulation for political purposes. In some cases no effort is made to promote as the result of examinations. Discretion in selecting persons to be promoted is left to the head of the department or some other administrative superior. This discretion may be exercised upon the suggestion of party officials. By its power to determine the classes of employes eligible to take promotional examinations, the Chicago commission was able to favor particular individuals.

Persons entitled to promotion on the results of an examination under some laws may waive their right to someone lower down the promotional list. Pressure may be brought upon them to compel them to do so. In 1915, one Weideling, a sergeant in the Chicago police department, took the examination for police lieutenant ranking forty-fifth on the examination results. Forty-three men waived and Weideling, then becoming one of the three highest, was promoted to a lieutenancy. "It was directly charged in the press that these forty-three men were compelled to waive their rights by pressure and influence brought to bear by the head of the police department in order that Weideling's name might be reached." Control of assignments is a method often used in police departments to defeat the purpose of the merit laws among other things. Police who persist in political indifference may be sent to the "prairies" or to the "sticks." Assignment to a post far away from home is a powerful persuasive. Continual application of such measures will usually bring the most obstinate person into line.

Positions in the classified service may be abolished as an "economy" measure or on some other basis. New positions with different titles but similar duties may then be created and filled by temporary political appointees. In Chicago the license bureau which had charge of the collection of business and occupational license fees was abolished by council action. A short time later fifty clerks, selected in fact by the fifty Democratic ward committees, were stationed in police station houses to perform similar duties at a much higher cost and a reduction of license revenue. The chief function of these clerks appeared to be to sound the alarm when the police brought in persons charged with crime and to call to their rescue the ward committeemen or other party functionaries. Similarly in Columbus jobs held by classified employes were abolished and later re-created under new titles and filled by political appointees. In Troy, New York, competitive positions were abolished and new jobs exempt from examination, "executive secretaries," were created to handle the work.

It would be a grave error to say that the movement for civil service laws beginning with the passage of the Pendleton Act by Congress in 1883 has not limited to a considerable extent the patronage available to political organizations in many jurisdictions. Nevertheless, ways and means have been found to weaken in varying degrees the efficacy of the administration of these laws. The explanation is simply that the groups of citizens interested in combatting the patronage system have not been powerful enough to compel the enforcement of these rules.

No. 66

[THE best personnel legislation and the most able and honest administration of it will not, alone, assure us of a high-caliber public personnel. Several years ago Professor Harold J. Laski expressed his concern over the fact that American college men and women were not interested in careers in the public service. In a provocative essay he questioned the future of a democratic society in which the ablest minds were indifferent, or even hostile, to the idea of working for the people. Professor Leonard White has likewise been seriously disturbed over this rather anomalous situation. Few have done more than he to remedy it, and to make the public service attractive to the college-trained man or woman. As a teacher and civil service administrator in Chicago and later as a member of the United States Civil Service Commission, he has contributed significantly towards bringing the public service and the university graduate into closer contact.]

THE PUBLIC SERVICE AND THE UNIVERSITY
GRADUATE [1]

by Leonard D. White

OPPORTUNITIES for the university graduate in government work have become so numerous and varied that I cannot undertake to describe or even refer to all of them. I propose to deal only with opportunities in the national government, emphasizing especially careers in the permanent civil service.

In passing, however, I must remind you that interesting openings for university men and women are available in the states and cities. Most of these are in scientific and professional lines; engineering, public health, education and libraries, social service, forestry, and conservation presenting familiar illustrations.

New life and interest in state and local government are stirring as a result of more extensive cooperation between Washington on the one hand and state capitols and city halls on the other. Federal-state relationships between the Department of Agriculture and state agricultural experiment stations are a well-known example. Cooperative arrangements in the management of employment offices under the Wagner-Peyser Act and joint programs in the complex field of the Social Security Act illustrate a new type

[1] Leonard D. White, "The Public Service and the University Graduate," Edward Janes James Lecture at the University of Illinois, April 28, 1937. Reprinted by permission of the author and the University of Illinois.

of government opportunity which is rapidly developing midway between the national government and the states. The states deserve, and unless they are to fail in their responsibilities, will require a greater proportion of men and women trained in their state universities.

I cannot refrain, also, from passing reference to the new vocation of technical consultant on government problems. The origins of this rapidly expanding group reach back to the foundation of the New York Bureau of Municipal Research in 1906. Present opportunities for employment as consultant are found in the many bureaus of governmental research, in the state leagues of municipalities, and in associations of state and local government officials, the headquarters of many of which are in Chicago. The demand by busy and perplexed officials for the impartial advice of these consulting experts is growing by leaps and bounds. They have already become one of the important agencies for administrative improvement in national, state, and local government.

Our present interest, however, is the federal service. May we begin by clearing the ground of a few of the illusions which many people, even some university students, still cherish. For example, there is an opinion abroad that no really first-class man or woman would choose the civil service as a career. In all earnestness and with all possible emphasis I say that this opinion has no foundation in fact. Where among the engineers of his generation could be found a more distinguished member of his profession than the late Elwood Mead, for years Director of the Reclamation Service? Who in the ranks of the natural sciences is more entitled to respect and honor for his scientific accomplishments than Dr. Lyman J. Briggs, Director of the Bureau of Standards? Where in the field of personnel management can a more eminent practitioner be found than Dr. W. W. Stockberger of the Department of Agriculture, or among the statisticians one more able than E. Dana Durand, now a member of the Tariff Commission? Whose reputation in the field of transportation economics excels that of Joseph B. Eastman, for many years a member of the Interstate Commerce Commission? These are men who have made the public service their life work. He who thinks that the public service does not attract men and women of first rank or who fears that a government career would deprive him of contact with first-rate minds is simply ignorant of the quality of the public service of to-day.

Another opinion held by uninformed persons is that no really man-sized jobs exist in the civil service. This view, also, reflects a profound ignorance of the nature and scope of the tasks of modern government. One of my former students had for some time under his jurisdiction 29,000,000 acres of land for purposes of soil erosion control, and over this vast domain were moving whole armies of workers, a problem of management and direction of first magnitude. A very different and a very difficult job is the work of the conciliator in labor disputes—not a position for a man who cannot stand the heavy wear and tear of controversy. A preliminary task of the Social Security Board was to register 26,000,000 persons eligible to participate in the unemployment insurance benefits of the Act. An incidental problem faced by the Civil Works Administration on November 15, 1934, was the mailing of individual checks to 4,000,000 Civil Works Administration workers in all parts of the country.

The old agencies, too, have their large-scale problems. To give you a modest illustration, I may refer to the task of the Civil Service Commission which last year examined three-quarters of a million persons; examinations are held at over 3,500 points in all parts of the United States. It is no simple matter merely to have the right number of examination papers at the right place at the right time. This is nothing, however, compared to the task of the Comptroller General who must audit not only the transactions of the old departments and agencies, but also the millions of vouchers produced by almost any one of the new. In short, able men and women are making the public service their life work, and their job is as big as they are.

Many uninformed persons believe that civil service employees are easy-going, not to say lazy, and soon fall into an inevitable rut. On this point Mr. Eastman made the following observation at the recent semi-centennial celebration of the Interstate Commerce Commission:

> As one who has had twenty-three years' experience in the public service, nothing arouses my anger more than the idea which so many entertain who are without experience that public employees are a lazy-time-saving lot of mediocre ability, and lacking in initiative. I have never found them so. On the contrary the thing that has always impressed me has been their extraordinary readiness to put their souls into the job and often to endure overtime work without pay, when on the whole they gain so little recognition for their work.

A recent study of reported overtime showed almost 14,000,000 hours in the whole federal service in a period of six months, equivalent to about 28,000,000 hours a year. This is not the record of an easy-going organization.

Another misunderstanding is that all the good jobs go to politicians. It is true that they have too many. But there are now over 500,000 positions in the federal civil service; thousands of these involve high responsibility and are regularly filled by promotion from below. Professor Macmahon of Columbia University demonstrated ten years ago that most bureau chiefs are career men. The situation in the civil service agencies has not changed for the worse since his study.

In an organization as huge as the federal civil service one may fear to get lost and eventually become only a very small cog on a very small wheel of a very intricate machine. The civil service is a huge organization, but like a great university, it falls into separate units, each of which has its own *esprit de corps,* and within each of which one may build up pleasant and effective working relationships. The University of Illinois with its thousands of students may very well seem to the freshman who comes to its campus for the first time a forbidding and complex organization. He quickly learns, however, that the university is a group of schools and departments, and that within each, individual professors and their students come into close and friendly contact.

During the last few years university and college graduates have entered the civil service in larger numbers than ever before. Cynics say that this is a temporary trend, due to the depression. Lack of employment elsewhere has certainly played a part in the new interest of graduates in the public service, but this is too shallow to serve as a complete explanation. The crisis in our economic and governmental system and a realization of the vital importance of government in working out our economic salvation have challenged the imagination of college men and women. They have discerned a major task and are anxious to take a part in it.

The scope of civil service openings is suggested by some simple figures. On June 30, 1936, there were 498,000 positions in the federal civil service. The normal annual appointments for replacement purposes range between 40,000 and 50,000. About half of these are in the post office, where career opportunities for university men and women have not yet been developed. In the rest of the service a fair estimate of the annual number of junior professional and scientific appointments and junior clerical appointments from college registers is 3,000 to 3,500. This is a relatively steady demand and does not take into account needs caused by expansion of the service.

Appointments to these positions are made on the basis of open competitive examination. The competition is strenuous, and under present conditions a college or university graduate in the lower half of his class has a slender chance either of passing the examinations or of securing an appointment. The beneficial effect of this situation upon the character of public service will be projected far into the future.

We may now pass directly to a brief survey of the principal examinations which provide the normal avenue of entrance to a civil service appointment. These examinations fall into two major groups. On the one hand there are examinations in the professional and scientific field, including economics and the social sciences. On the other hand, there are examinations leading into the clerical, administrative, and fiscal service, to which the United States Civil Service Commission has made some notable additions in recent years.

The professional and scientific branch of the federal service has grown rapidly in recent years. A study published by the Census Bureau in 1896 revealed about 3,600 professional and scientific positions, two per cent of the total employment. In 1930 the number of professional and scientific positions had increased to over 35,000 and amounted to about six per cent of the total service. At present we may estimate at least 40,000, not including over 10,000 more in the noncivil-service agencies. We will consider engineering, agricultural and biological sciences, medicine, law, economics and social science.

Engineering.—The federal service requires engineers in practically every specialized field. Among the agencies to which engineers are supplied by the United States Civil Service Commission are the Engineer Department at large, the Navy, the Bureau of Public Roads, the Reclamation Service, the Soil Conservation Service, the Bureau of Mines, the Geological Survey, the Forest Service, and the Procurement Division.

Many such engineers are concerned primarily with research. Thus engineers in the Bureau of Standards, aeronautical engineers at Langley Field, highway engineers in the Bureau of Public Roads, Bureau of Agricultural Engineering, Forest Products Laboratory at Madison, Wisconsin, Naval Research Laboratory, are deeply concerned with research problems.

For the engineering field the United States Civil Service Commission usually holds once a year a comprehensive examination for junior engineers, as well as specialized examinations for higher grades. In September, 1935, an examination was announced for junior engineer in the following optional subjects: Aeronautical, agricultural, ceramics, chemical, civil, electrical, mechanical, mining, petroleum, and structural steel and concrete. The options vary somewhat from year to year. This examination is the normal avenue of entrance to the engineering field. The prerequisites are graduation from a college or university of recognized standing, requiring the completion of a full four-year course, and a maximum age limit of thirty-five. Original appointments are at $2,000 a year, the standard rate for all junior professional appointments.

The United States Civil Service Commission also holds from time to time a student engineer examination for seasonal employment during the summer. For illustration, I refer to the student engineer examination announced in June, 1936, with optional subjects in chemical engineering, civil and highway engineering, electrical and mechanical engineering. The Bureau of Public Roads and the Engineer Department at large use this examination as a testing ground for students who are completing their junior year, giving them a summer appointment, at the end of which they return for the final year of their engineering work. After taking their engineering degree, they may then qualify as junior engineers upon passing a noncompetitive examination.

In addition to these junior examinations the commission holds from time to time examinations for higher and more specialized engineering positions with salaries running up to $5,600 and occasionally $6,500 per annum.

Agricultural and Biological Sciences.—The second major group of scientific and professional examinations is concerned with the agricultural and biological sciences, leading to appointment principally in the Department of Agriculture, one of the great research scientific institutions of the country. This department includes the Forest Service and the Soil Conservation Service, as well as the former Resettlement Administration. The 1935 announcement included junior entomologist, forest pathologist, plant physiologist, plant quarantine inspector, and pomologist. The 1936 announcement carried ten options, including among others junior agronomist, biologist, soil technologist, and zoologist. While the specialties will vary somewhat from year to year, the basic biological sciences are regularly represented.

Here it is appropriate to refer to the examination for junior forester and junior range examiner. These examinations are required once a year, and the demand for qualified men is brisk. The prerequisite for the junior forester examination is a full four-year course leading to a bachelor's degree from a forestry school of recognized standing, or from the forestry department of a college or university, or a master's degree in forestry in addition to a bachelor's degree in some field other than forestry. Senior graduate students are regularly admitted in this as in many professional examinations. A similar examination is that for park ranger, National Park Service, except that the educational prerequisites are much less severe.

Medicine.—Practically the entire medical service maintained by the national government is under civil service regulations. Three great branches are the United States Public Health Service, the Veterans' Administration, and the Indian Service. Examinations for medical officer are held from time to time for appointments in these well-known medical services. The medical staff of the famous St. Elizabeth's Hospital, Washington, D. C., is also maintained through examinations offered by the United States Civil Service Commission.

Law.—The only professional and scientific field which is not generally recruited by the Commission is law. Most appointments to the junior attorney positions are outside the civil service system. Several important exceptions, however, exist, to wit, attorney positions in the Interstate Com-

merce Commission, the Veterans' Administration, the Federal Communications Commission, and the Employees' Compensation Commission. Examinations for law positions are held from time to time. By way of illustration,
I refer to an examination announced in 1934 for the Federal Communications
Commission, carrying appointments ranging from $2,000 to $5,600 per
annum.

Appointments to attorney positions in other departments and agencies
are usually made directly by the General Counsel. In many instances the
General Counsel writes to the deans of the law schools for recommendations.
Many excellent appointments are made in this way, although I believe that
equally satisfactory results could be secured for the junior attorney positions
by means of a properly constructed competitive examination.

Economics.—May we turn from these older professions to the somewhat
more modern group, the economists and the statisticians. In 1896 it appears that the Government employed only 87 statisticians. Apparently the
only economist was one "economic ornithologist" in the Department of
Agriculture. From these slender beginnings the demand for economists and
statisticians has expanded until we now find an estimated 1,600. They are
found principally in the field of agricultural economics, social economics,
and business economics. The agencies in which the greatest expansion has
occurred are Agriculture, Labor, Farm Credit Administration, and the Social
Security Board.

One or two illustrations of the type of work in the higher realms of government economics may be of interest. The Executive Secretary and Director of Research of the Central Statistical Board, a position paying $8,000
per annum, has these duties:

1. Directing all investigations undertaken by the Board.

2. Making plans and formulating policies for the work of the staff.

3. Acting as chief contact officer of the Board in negotiating with the
technical, professional and working staffs of other organizations.

4. Preparing final reports upon all work undertaken.

5. Keeping accurately informed of current developments in the statistical services.

This work is "original and almost entirely supervisory, requiring the highest
order of initiative, judgment, and independent thinking."

The work of chief economist of the Mineral Production and Economics
Division of the Bureau of Mines ranges over a broad field. He conducts
primary economic and statistical research on problems of the mining industry, as well as difficult analytical studies concerning the relationship of

various mineral groups to each other. Illustrative cases include the study of potential supplies of monetary metals in relation to the price level; development of techniques for forecasting demand for copper, lead, zinc, coal, and other minerals; capacity of the mining industry to absorb labor at various levels of economic recovery; relation of reclaimed metal supplies to future rates of reserve depletion. Conference with other economic and statistical units is frequent. The position is paid on a scale from $4,600 to $5,400.

What examinations lead to such exalted positions? A number of specialized examinations in economics are likely to be announced in any year, as, for example, junior agricultural economist, junior financial economist, and junior social economist. In 1936, the Commission announced a general examination for economist, including positions ranging from $2,600 to $5,600 a year. This examination was intended to cover all fields within the broad subject of economics except home economics and social economics. The results were satisfactory, and a general examination in the field of economics is likely to be repeated from time to time.

In the closely related field of statistics the Commission holds a series of general and specialized examinations. The principal entrance gate is the test for assistant statistical clerk. Specialized examinations in the higher grades are held from time to time, carrying salaries from $2,600 a year to $5,600 a year. At the top of the statistical hierarchy we find the examination for assistant commissioner of labor statistics at $6,500 per annum.

Social Science.—New programs of government work have created a new demand for social scientists. The United States Civil Service Commission is experimenting to find the best way of securing highly qualified personnel trained in one or more of the social sciences.

The most recent experiment in the social science field is the examination for social science analyst. This examination is of such general interest to college seniors and graduates that it is desirable to examine it for a moment. The initiative for the examination came from the Research Division of the Social Security Board. Interest, however, quickly spread to other agencies, including the Central Statistical Board. The examination is held with three optional subjects: economics, sociology and social research, and political science.

The prerequisite for the junior social science analyst is successful completion of a full four-year course leading to a bachelor's degree in one of the social sciences, senior students being admitted subject to proof of receiving a diploma at a later date. The assistant grade, commencing at $2,600 a year, requires in addition two years of postgraduate study, or two years of full-time experience in teaching a social science, or two years professional or research experience in the optional subject, or any time equivalent of these. The requirements for the higher grades, which rise to $5,600 a year, vary with the grade. We hope that this examination may become a convenient means of recruiting economists, political scientists, and sociologists.

Recent discussion of careers in government has been directed toward the increasing number of administrative supervisory positions. Administration as such, however, is not yet a frequent subject of examination by the United States Civil Service Commission.

The Commission is experimenting in this field in response to the increasing demand for qualified administrative personnel. For instance, in 1936 for the first time in its history, the Commission held an examination for personnel officer, and secured a small register of well-qualified applicants. This type of examination will doubtless be repeated from time to time, inasmuch as the demand for personnel officers in the federal service is increasing steadily.

Another illustration is the recent examination for administrative officer for the Social Security Board, covering positions ranging from $3,200 a year to $5,600 a year. Such examinations point to the gradual recognition of administrative service as a special type of work. At the present time, however, it is premature for college or university students to prepare specifically for this type of work in government.

One other examination of special interest to the liberal arts student whose asset is a broad education remains. This is the test for junior civil service examiner. This examination was developed in 1934 with the hope that it might serve as a convenient means of permitting the nonspecialized liberal arts college graduate to enter the federal service. The results have far exceeded our expectations. In the 1934 competition over 7,000 college graduates took part, of whom the severe general intelligence test eliminated about one-half. During the last two years the Commission has placed over 1,200 men and women from this register in a wide variety of positions and in nearly twenty different departments and agencies. The examination was given again in the summer of 1936, attracting 21,000 competitors, of whom 6,400 passed the examination and are now available for certification to the departments. This register is popular with the appointing officers, and it seems reasonable to suppose that it will provide the principal means by which the nonspecialized liberal arts college and university student may enter the federal service in substantial numbers.

These are the principal but by no means the only examinations of interest to college and university graduates. All announcements are posted in the first-class and second-class post offices, all college grade announcements are sent to every college and university, and individual notice for specified examinations can be arranged upon request.

One important question remains. What is the probable financial return to college men and women in the federal civil service? The entrance rate of pay for scientific and professional positions is $2,000 a year. The highest rate under present pay scales is from $8,000 to $9,000 a year. In the clerical, administrative, and fiscal service, a common entrance rate is $1,620 a year, rising to the same maximum, $8,000 to $9,000 a year. The rate of progress from the bottom rung of the ladder to the top depends on the same circumstances as elsewhere, and no general statement can be made. Unusually competent men and women, however, move up rapidly—certainly as rapidly in my judgment as in the field of college and university teaching. In the government service, as in private employment, there is an insatiable demand for exceptionally qualified employees.

Choice of a life work is governed in each individual case by a complex set of imponderables. Not everyone should try to enter the public service. Those who wish to amass a fortune should stay in the world of private enterprise. Those who prefer to work alone, free from supervision and direction and the requirements of teamwork, should stay out of public offices. Those whose working habits are impulsive, who are driven to work feverishly for two or three days and nights and who then expect to loaf for a week, will find adjustment to the more settled ways of government offices rather difficult.

Is it, then, worth while to prepare for the civil service? May I repeat the answer to this question which I gave in a recent article in *Scribner's Magazine*.

For the individual who seeks a spectacular career, who desires to wield public influence publicly, or who wants to make money, I would say, no. But there are young men and women who want to work with one of the principal agencies for the progressive improvement of our national life, who are content with private sources of personal satisfaction, who command patience, and who can be satisfied, if successful, with an eventual income of six or seven thousand dollars a year. For them the public service has much to offer, and they are choosing it for their life work. They are marching forward confidently to take over administrative responsibilities which older hands are relinquishing year by year. The public service will not suffer when they come of age.

Chapter XIX

THE COURTS AND THE LAW

No. 67

[IT requires very little reflection upon the circumstances of our everyday lives for us to see the necessity of some kind of rules if people are going to live together peacefully. The following article by Professor Radin illustrates this point in describing the origin, necessity, and nature of law.]

THE HAPPY ISLAND [1]

by Max Radin

THE Island Mas-a-tierra, some centuries ago, was a wholly deserted member of the group called Juan Fernandez, about four hundred miles off the coast of Chile. There, in the month of September, 1704, a Scottish sailor named Alexander Selkirk was marooned and there he lived quite alone for five years, till he was rescued and taken back to his home. His adventures gave Defoe the idea of *Robinson Crusoe* and became the subject of a great many poems, essays, and sermons. Perhaps the most famous poem about him is the one by the English poet, William Cowper, of which the first stanza runs:

> I am monarch of all I survey—
> My right there is none to dispute;
> From the centre all round to the sea,
> I am lord of the fowl and the brute.

If Alexander Selkirk had been given to thinking hard and carefully about his surroundings, he would have realized that his condition was even stranger than he supposed. Instead of everything on the island belonging to him

[1] Max Radin, *The Law and Mr. Smith* (Indianapolis: Bobbs-Merrill and Co., 1938) Ch. 1, pp. 1-5. Reprinted by permission of the publisher.

the truth was that nothing belonged to him. He had no rights, because there was no one against whom he could claim them. He had no privileges, because there was no one who disputed them. Whatever he did, he had no duties and no liabilities. So far from being a monarch or lord, he no more ruled or owned the place he occupied or the things he used, than the sea-gull owns the portion of the ocean over which it flies. Whether he moved or stood still, ate or walked or slept, hunted or planted, he was completely lawless.

Now, mark how different all this would be if he had found another human being there or if another human being had joined him. Perhaps we shall understand it if we recall the delightful ballad by W. S. Gilbert, entitled "Etiquette," which tells the story of the *Ballyshannon*, which foundered, drowning all the passengers but two, Gray and Somers:

> These passengers, by reason of their clinging to a mast,
> Upon a desert island were eventually cast.
> They hunted for their meals, as Alexander Selkirk used,
> But they couldn't chat together—they had not been introduced.
>
> And somehow thus they settled it without a word of mouth
> That Gray should take the northern half while Somers took the south.

These two perfect Englishmen managed their living together on the island in their own way, but the most important thing was that there had to be some way. The moment two persons are in the same place, where they might conceivably run into each other or where the one might want what the other had, they must in some fashion decide how to avoid conflicts. If they do not, the only possible result will be that the stronger will kill the weaker or make him his slave.

When there are only two, the way to avoid conflicts is simple. One way is to act like our two Englishmen, each keep to his own side and never so much as nod to the man on the other side. There are other ways, of course, but they are all pretty easy to understand and pretty easy to follow.

But when, instead of two, there get to be a great many people on our island, the ways that have to be arranged so that people do not run into each other, interfere with each other, take things away from each other, hurt and abuse each other, are much more complicated. We cannot simply let Somers take the southern side and Gray take the north, because there are only four points of the compass and there are, let us say, many thousands of persons. We must, therefore, manage it so that everybody can go somewhere, live somewhere, get something to eat and something to wear, assuming that there is enough to go round in all these matters, as there generally is.

We could manage it easily enough, with or without "word of mouth," if we could divide the island up into exactly equal parts, each one of which was in every respect as good as the other, and if we could then divide the commodities in the island, the things that could be used and enjoyed, into exactly equal portions. Then, if everyone would remain perfectly satisfied with his share and never want any other or any more, our way of living together on our island would be simple enough. The rules of our society would be easy to understand and there would be no difficulty about keeping the rules, because no one would have any reason for breaking them.

Obviously, what we have assumed is impossible. In the first place, no region can be divided into exactly equal parts; and, if it could be so divided, these parts would not have the same qualities. For many purposes, one could not possibly be as good as another. The same is probably true for the commodities on the island. Secondly, it is impossible to suppose that all the islanders would be satisfied or remain satisfied. The strong, the good, the industrious, the competent, would feel that they ought to have more things or better things than the weak, the bad, the lazy, the incompetent; and the greedy, the avaricious, the selfish, would certainly wish to have more, whether they ought to have them or not.

We might be willing to admit that those in the first group ought to have more than the others and we might even assist them in getting it, but we should certainly not do so in the case of the second group. On the contrary, we should do everything we could to prevent them from getting what they wanted. The simple rules of living together would, consequently, have to be modified. We should have to find some way of discovering who the good, the strong, the competent, the industrious, are. We should then have to keep in restraint the greedy, the selfish, the avaricious. The rules would no longer enforce themselves, because there are now many people who might want to break them, and we should have to do more than establish rules; we should have to get some sort of force to compel those who wish to break the rules to keep them.

Our Happy Island has already got to be a pretty complicated place, but real life is far more complicated. After all, our island is imaginary. No country we know ever began with even a pretense that all its inhabitants had an equal share of the good things in the country. Every country has rules about living together, established long ago, and the first thing we note about these rules is that they have nothing to do with either the deserving or the undeserving classes of the community.

There is one further thing which we must try to understand. Let us go back to our Happy Island for a moment. We have discovered that we need rules. Gray must know that Somers will not be found on the northern side—that is, on Gray's side—and he must know that this arrangement is lasting. Or else he must know that Somers will not be there on Monday, Wednesday, and Friday. In any case, the rule means that the situation is to be repeated; it is something that happens many times in the same form. If Gray could never know whether Somers would be there or not, life under the circumstances would, we are told, be intolerable to him.

So also when there are thousands of persons instead of two involved. If anything might happen any day, there would be no rule, and living together would be really impossible. John Smith, peering out from his refuge, might see Thomas Brown and Brown might rush on him to kill him, or he might leave him alone. Smith might exchange goods with Brown and Brown might take his goods back again or leave them. Smith could never be sure about his safety or his property. Life would be one constant terror-ridden anxiety. Rabbits might live that way, but certainly not men.

And it is almost as bad when there are rules but we do not know them. Suppose Smith comes to a wholly foreign and previously unknown country —let us call it Laputa. He sees from a hiding-place people acting in a way that seems entirely without rule or method. Sometimes one Laputan attacks another and sometimes he leaves him alone. If Smith knew Laputan, he would have understood that the Laputans always attacked each other unless one of the two made a certain gesture, and that if he wished to go about peaceably he had only to make that gesture.

In other words, there are two things necessary. There must be rules, and there must be some way of finding out what they are. In most countries, in our own country particularly, most people have somewhere to go, some place to live in, and some means of getting the commodities necessary for living. How much they can get, and the number and variety of things they can do, depend upon rules which number over a million and which are sometimes extremely hard to understand.

Of these rules, some, for reasons we shall try to discover, are called legal rules, and the sum of all of them is called THE LAW, a phrase which we often write in capitals, but which is not half so awe-inspiring as it sounds.

No. 68

WE have already seen that government has two main functions: (1) the formulation of the rules under which the community is to live and (2) the enforcement of those rules. We have seen, also, that these two functions are carried out by a variety of governmental agencies and that there is no clear-cut division and separation of powers relative to them.

It should be no surprise to us, therefore, to learn that the functions of the judicial branch are not confined wholly to the execution or enforcement of public policy, but that they include the actual determination of what the policy shall be in many cases. In other words, while it is the job of the court to investigate and determine facts and apply the law to the facts thus determined, there are many cases in which there is doubt as to what the law is and its applicability to the case at hand. Laws are, of necessity, general in character. They are, in many cases, worded so that their exact meaning is in doubt. Conditions arise which present issues not considered when laws were framed. Laws often conflict, and there is doubt as to which is applicable; in some cases there seems to be no clear-cut law at all. As a result, courts have the important task of determining what the law is, what scope and meaning it is to have, what law shall prevail when there is conflict, and what the law shall be when there is no rule available to fit the case at bar.

These functions are of great importance in any country, but in the United States they are particularly important because we have a system of jurisprudence known as the "common law." This means that the rules governing the relations of individuals have not been reduced to statutory form to a very considerable extent and that the law has come into existence as a result of a long line of judicial decisions in particular cases. This in turn produces certain results. The law built up in these decisions comes to be looked upon as composed of a body of "deathless truths" to which those who interpret it can turn for a solution of their problems. It comes to have a meaning and significance, especially for lawyers and judges, of more importance than any other kind of law. Both statutes and constitutions come to be interpreted in the light of it; it becomes, in a sense, the high priest and oracle of our legal system. It becomes "THE LAW"; and an understanding of this fact is a valuable aid in the evaluation of our whole judicial system.]

"THE LAW" [1]

by Fred Rodell

THE Law is the killy-loo bird of the sciences. The killy-loo, of course, was the bird that insisted on flying backward because it didn't care where it was going but was mightily interested in where it had been. And certainly The Law, when it moves at all, does so by flapping clumsily and uncertainly along, with its eye unswervingly glued on what lies behind. In medicine, in mathematics, in sociology, in psychology—in every other one of the physical and social sciences—the accepted aim is to look ahead and then move ahead to new truths, new techniques, new usefulness. Only The Law, inexorably devoted to all its most ancient principles and prece-

[1] Fred Rodell, *Woe Unto You, Lawyers!* (New York: Reynal and Hitchcock, 1939) pp. 23-38. Reprinted by permission of the publisher.

dents, makes a vice of innovation and a virtue of hoariness. Only The Law resists and resents the notion that it should ever change its antiquated ways to meet the challenge of a changing world.

It is well-nigh impossible to understand how The Law works without fully appreciating the truth of this fact:—The Law never admits to itself that there can be anything actually new under the sun. Minor variations of old facts, old machines, old relationships, yes; but never anything different enough to bother The Law into treating it otherwise than as an old friend in a new suit of clothes. When corporations first came on the legal scene, The Law regarded them as individual persons, in disguise, and so, for most legal purposes, a corporation is still considered, and even talked about, as a "person." A transport airplane, so far as The Law is concerned, is nothing but a newfangled variety of stagecoach. Such things as sit-down strikes, holding companies, Paris divorces, were treated with almost contemptuous familiarity by The Law when they first appeared, and the same fate undoubtedly awaits television when it grows up and begins to tangle with The Law. For all this is part of a carefully nurtured legend to the effect that The Law is so omniscient that nothing men may do can ever take it unawares, and so all-embracing that the principles which will apply to men's actions five hundred years from now are merely waiting to be applied to whatever men happen to be doing in 2439 A.D.

What The Law purports to be is a tremendous body of deathless truths so wide in scope and so infinite in their variations that they hold somewhere, and often hidden, within their vastnesses the solution of every conceivable man-made dispute or problem. Of course the truths are phrased as abstract principles, and the principles are phrased in the strange lingo of The Law. And so only the lawyers—especially those who have become judges or ordained interpreters of The Words—can ever fish the proper solution out of The Law's vastnesses. But it is the very keystone of the whole structure of legal mythology to insist that all earthly problems can and must be solved by reference to this great body of unearthly abstractions—or, in short, that they can and must be solved by the lawyers.

The chief reason why it is so hard for the ordinary man to get the lawyer's picture of The Law—as a supreme mass of changeless abstract principles—is that the ordinary man generally thinks of law as a composite of all the little laws that his various governments are forever passing and amending and, occasionally, repealing. Congress and state legislatures and city councils keep laying down rules and changing rules. Is this not clear proof that the Laws moves with the times? Briefly, it is not.

To the lawyer, there is a vast difference between The Law and the laws. The Law is something beyond and above every statute that ever has been

or could be passed. As a matter of fact, every statute, before the lawyers
allow it to mean anything—before they let it have any effect on the actions
of men—has to be fitted into The Law by "Interpretation" of what the
statute "means." And any apparently harmless little statute is likely to
mean plenty to a lawyer, just as a statute which seems to carry dynamite
in its words may mean nothing by the time the lawyers are through with it.

A few decades ago when the famous Clayton Act was passed, which was
intended to preserve competition and crack down on monopolies, a strong
labor lobby got Congress to write Section 20 into the new law. Section 20
had practically nothing to do with competition or monopolies. Section 20
was intended to restrict federal courts from granting so many injunctions
against union activities. Samuel Gompers, who was then the head man of
the unions, called Section 20 "labor's Magna Charta." But Samuel Gompers was no lawyer.

By the time the lawyers, headed by the Supreme Court, got through with
Section 20 it meant exactly nothing. Chief Justice Taft, speaking for the
lawyers, said it was *intended* to mean exactly nothing. Referring to The
Law as authority, he said that it was clear that Section 20 was no more
than a restatement of The Law as it had existed before the Clayton Act
was passed. Now, Chief Justice Taft was in no position to know, and
would have considered it irrelevant if he had known, that the Clayton Act
might not have been passed at all if it had not seemed clear to labor that
Section 20 gave strikers the right to picket without constant interference
by the federal courts. But Chief Justice Taft and his court of lawyers had
the last word. They made of labor's "Magna Charta" something strangely
resembling Germany's "scrap of paper." And all in the name of The Law.

Of course, Chief Justice Taft and his court would have found it far more
difficult to do this if other lawyers had not played a leading part in writing
the Clayton Act. Section 20 was full of those typically meaningless legal
words, like "wilfully" and "maliciously." It said, for instance, that federal
courts could not stop strikers from picketing "lawfully." "Lawfully," according to Chief Justice Taft, meant in accordance with The Law before the
Clayton Act was passed. Before the Clayton Act was passed, the lawyers
had ruled that just about all picketing was against The Law. Therefore
it still was Q. E. D. And, incidentally, the Supreme Court did almost the
same thing with the whole of the Clayton Act by picking on other meaningless legalistic words to prove that most trusts were not trusts and most
monopolies were not monopolies—according to The Law. You can change
the laws all you please, but you can't change The Law. And The Law is
what counts. It would, moreover, be a mistake to jump to the conclusion
that Chief Justice Taft and his court "interpreted" Section 20 of the Clayton

Act into complete oblivion merely because they didn't like unions or strikes or picketing. For Taft, in the course of explaining at great length why Section 20 did not really mean a thing, went out of his way to include in his opinion a rousing defense of labor unions. Of course, this defense did not do the unions any good, any more than Section 20 did the unions any good after Taft got through with it. The point is that Taft was insisting to his fellow-lawyers—the only people who ever read or understand judicial opinions—that in disappointing the unions he was merely following The Law. The choice, however distasteful, was forced upon him. For it is part of the legal legend that no lawyer—not even when he becomes a Supreme Court justice—ever does any more than explain what The Law is and how it applies. He is merely the voice through which the great gospel is made known to men.

Moreover, The Law can do strange things to man-made laws even when, as very rarely happens, such laws are not so full of "wilfullys" and "maliciouslys" and "lawfullys" that they practically invite the lawyers to write their own ticket. For example, there was the Guffey Coal Act, involving federal regulation of the coal industry. The Supreme Court first said that most of the important parts of the Act were unconstitutional. Now, saying that a law is unconstitutional is really no more than a convenient way of saying that it goes against The Law. But the whole idea of constitutionality and unconstitutionality is so mixed up with notions like patriotism and politics, as well as with the most sacred and complicated of all legal rules, that it deserves and will get full treatment a little later on. The point here is that, after saying part of the Guffey Act was unconstitutional, the judges went on to say that the good part had to be thrown out with the bad part. Not unreasonable perhaps, on the face of it. Not unreasonable until you learn that Congress, foreseeing what the Supreme Court might do with part of the Act, had taken particular pains to write very clearly into the Act that if part of it should be held unconstitutional, the rest of it should go into effect anyway. And so in order to throw out the whole Act, the Court had to reason this way:—Part of this law is unconstitutional. The rest is constitutional. Congress said the constitutional part should stand regardless of the rest. But that is not our idea of a proper way of doing things. We do not believe Congress would want to do things in a way that does not seem proper to us, who really know The Law. Therefore, we do not believe Congress meant what it said when it said to let the constitutional part stand. Therefore, we will throw it out along with the unconstitutional part. In the name of The Law.

That reasoning is not a burlesque. It is a shortened version of part of what the Supreme Court actually said, though the Court phrased it in multisyllabic legal language, in the case of Carter against the Carter Coal Company. And the result is an example, more obvious but no more extreme than thousands upon thousands of others, of how little the laws written by our so-called lawmakers really mean until the lawyers have decided what those laws mean—or don't mean—in the light of The Law.

Thus, the common man is dead wrong when he thinks of law as a conglomeration of all the laws that are passed by legislatures and written down in books—even though it is true that practically all those little laws are phrased by lawyers in legal language. Those little laws, those statutes, are, to a lawyer, the least important and least respectable of three kinds of rules with which the lawyers deal. The other two kinds of rules are those that make up what lawyers call "the common law" and those that make up "constitutional law."

Now, the common law is actually closer to The Law with a capital L than any constitution or statute ever written. The common law is the set of rules that lawyers use to settle any dispute or problem to which no constitution or statute applies. There is, for instance, no written rule to tell the lawyers (or anybody else) whether a Nevada divorce is good in Pennsylvania. There is no written rule to tell whether a man who orders a house built with a bathroom between the kitchen and the pantry has to take the house and pay the builder if everything else is fine but the bathroom is between the living-room and the coat-closet. In both cases, the lawyer-judges write their own answers without interference from any constitution or statute. In both cases, the answers are said to be fished directly, non-stop, out of the mass of abstract principles that make up The Law.

Constitutional law is something else again. A constitution, in this country at least, is halfway between The Law and an ordinary statute. Like a statute, it is phrased by men, a few of whom are usually not lawyers, and is written down in definite if often nebulous-meaning words (though in England the Constitution isn't written down anywhere and so is indistinguishable from The Law of England). But like The Law, constitutions, except where they deal with the pure mechanics of government—as in giving each state two senators or listing the length of a governor's term of office—are made up of abstract principles which mean nothing until brought down to earth by the lawyers. If this sounds like heresy, consider, for instance the U. S. Constitution's well-known guarantee of freedom of speech. What does that guarantee mean, practically speaking? It did not stop the federal government from putting people in jail during the World War because they talked against war. It did not stop the police of Harlan County, Kentucky from beating up people who tried to make speeches in favor of unions in Harlan County. On the other hand, that constitutional guarantee does prevent the extreme restrictions of free speech which are common abroad to-day. How tell, then, which free speech is good and which is bad, under the Constitution? Only by asking the lawyer-judges. And how can they tell; how do they decide? Simply by referring to our old friend, The Law, in order to "interpret" the Constitution.

The Law is thus superior to constitutions, just as it is superior to statutes. And according to the legal legend, it is neither constitutions nor statutes which finally determine the rules under which men live. It is The Law, working unimpeded to produce the common law, working through the words of constitutions to produce constitutional law, working through the words of both statutes and constitutions to produce statutory law. All three kinds of law are merely obedient offspring of that great body of abstract principles which never changes and which nobody but a lawyer even pretends to understand.

Justice Holmes was in effect talking about The Law as a whole, when he said of its nearest and dearest offspring: "The common law is not a brooding omnipresence in the sky." But Justice Holmes, as he well knew when he said that, was dissenting not only from a decision of the Supreme Court but from the opinions of most lawyers about The Law. For practically every lawyer thinks and talks of The Law as a sort of omnipotent, omniscient presence hovering around like God over the affairs of men. Yet every lawyer purports to be able to understand and interpret a large part of that presence for the benefit of those who are not lawyers—at a price.

The strange thing is, however, that lawyers, for all their alleged insight into the great mystery, are never able to agree about the presence or its interpretation, when it comes down to applying The Law to a simple, specific factual problem. If the lawyers agreed, there would never be a law case, for every law case results of course from a legal dispute as to what The Law is. If the lawyers agreed, there would be no dissenting opinions. If the lawyers agreed, we would not have appellate courts reversing the judgments of trial courts and super-appellate courts reversing the judgments of appellate courts, and super-super-appellate courts—or supreme courts—reversing the judgments of super-appellate courts. The fact is that every lawyer claims to know all about The Law *until* it comes down to applying The Law to a specific dispute. Whereas no non-lawyer cares in the slightest degree what The Law is until it comes down to applying The Law to a specific dispute.

It is all very well for a lawyer to say, out of his knowledge of The Law, that a "mortgagor" has "legal title" to a building. That is very pretty and sounds very impressive. But if the mortgagor then wants to know if he can sell the building, and on what terms, and if he has to pay taxes on it, and if he can kick the mortgagee out if the mortgagee comes snooping around, the lawyers will begin to disagree. It is all very well, too, for a lawyer to say that The Law forbids "interference with the freedom of contract." But when fifty-seven respectable lawyers of the late Liberty League declare unanimously that employers need pay no attention to the Wagner Labor Act, because it interferes with freedom of contract, and then the Supreme Court tells them they are one hundred per cent wrong, the fifty-seven lawyers' undoubted knowledge of The Law begins to look just a trifle futile.

The Law, as a matter of fact, is all things to all lawyers. It is all things to all lawyers simply because the principles on which it is built are so vague and abstract and irrelevant that it is possible to find in those principles both a justification and a prohibition of every human action or activity under the sun.

And how does The Law, then, ever get brought down to earthly affairs? In what way does it actually succeed in building regulatory fences around men's conduct? The answer is just as simple as it is complex. The answer is that the last bunch of judges which gets a shot at the solution of any specific problem has the decisive word on The Law as it affects that problem. The solution which that last bunch of judges gives to that problem *is* The Law so far as that problem is concerned—even though every other lawyer in the world might suppose The Law was different. It might not then be irrelevant to ask just what a judge is. And it was an unusually candid judge who recently gave the best answer to that question. "A judge," he said, "is a lawyer who knew a governor."

The lawyers who knew governors—or who knew presidents—or who knew enough ward-leaders (where judges are elected)—bring The Law down to earth in all sorts of different and conflicting ways. A home-owner who beats up a trespassing hobo may be a hero in one state and a criminal in another. But no matter which he is, the legal appraisal of his actions will fit perfectly into the great and ubiquitous framework of The Law. For, no matter how differently different judges in different places may decide the same human problem, or decide it differently in the same place at different times, the great legend of The Law as steadfast and all-embracing is always adhered to. Decisions may change or differ or conflict, but The Law budges not.

And it is necessary to understand this keystone of legal reasoning—and to accept it as a fact no matter how silly it may sound—before it is possible to understand the strange processes of The Law. It is necessary to realize that The Law not only stands still but is proud and determined to stand still. If a British barrister of two hundred years ago were suddenly to come alive in an American court-room, he would feel intellectually at home.

The clothes would astonish him, the electric lights would astonish him, the architecture would astonish him. But as soon as the lawyers started talking legal talk, he would know that he was among friends. And given a couple of days with the law books, he could take the place of any lawyer present—or of the judge—and perform the whole legal mumbo-jumbo as well as they. Imagine, by contrast, a British surgeon of two hundred years ago plopped into a modern hospital operating room. He would literally understand less of what was going on than would any passer-by brought in from the street at random.

The Law, alone of all the sciences, just sits—aloof and practically motionless. Constitutions do not affect it and statutes do not change it. Lawyers talk wise about it and judges purport to "apply" it when they lay down rules for men to follow, but actually The Law—with a capital L—has no real relation to the affairs of men. It is permanent and changeless—which means that it is not of this earth. It is a mass of vague abstract principles —which means that it is a lot of words. It is a brooding omnipresence in the sky—which means that it is a big balloon, which has thus far escaped the lethal pin.

No. 69

[PROFESSOR RODELL has given us a general picture of The Law. Mr. Hibschman, in the following article, brings some of the details of that picture into focus.]

HUMPTY DUMPTY'S RULE IN LAW [1]

by Harry Hibschman

"WHEN I use a word," said Humpty Dumpty, "it means just what I choose it to mean—neither more nor less."

But Alice objected, "The question is whether you can make words mean so many different things."

And Humpty Dumpty airily replied, "The question is which is to be master, that's all."

We are not living in Wonderland, as we have reason to know every time we come to grips with actualities; and yet in this very real world what Humpty Dumpty said is true—words mean what their masters say they mean. And the masters are the courts of last resort, the Supreme Court

[1] Harry Hibschman, "Humpty Dumpty's Rule in Law," *The Atlantic Monthly* (April, 1932), Vol. 149, pp. 470-474. Reprinted by permission of the author and *The Atlantic Monthly*.

of the United States and the appellate courts of the various states. This statement a study of their decisions will speedily confirm; and it will at the same time show what a myth is that certainty of the law which laymen are assured exists.

To begin with the highest court in the land, it held many years ago that the expression "high seas" includes the Great Lakes, though the question arose in connection with the interpretation of a statute written originally by a Congressman who later became a judge, and who as a judge declared that the Great Lakes were not included. A dictionary in common use even now, in defining the words "high seas," uses the Great Lakes as an example of what the words do not cover; and to ordinary folks the dictionary definition for "high seas" as the open ocean seems still to be good.

But would it occur to you that a fence is a building? A New York court said it was. And the highest court of Massachusetts has held a tent to be a building. A railroad car is a building in Nebraska, but not in Arkansas. A corncrib is also a building in Iowa, but not in Florida—perhaps because they raise corn in the former state and not in the latter. At any rate the Florida Supreme Court argued, "We have been unable to find this word 'corncrib' in Worcester's Dictionary; and it is not necessarily a building, a ship or a vessel. . . . 'Crib' has various meanings, as the manger of a stable, a bin, a frame for a child's bed, a small habitation, and it is used in the latter sense by Shakespeare. Nowhere else do we find it used in the sense of a building." That was in the year of the Lord 1882, and as a consequence of the court's conclusions a defendant who had been convicted of burglary went free.

On the other hand, a Texas court, in order to sustain a conviction of burglary, held that an office in one corner of a hardware store, made of pickets about four feet high, three inches apart, with a plank on top used as a shelf, was a building, though it is clear that it was nothing more or less than a corner fenced off within a building. By the same reasoning the part of a court-room railed off from the public is a building.

A jackass is a horse. The Tennessee Supreme Court settled that many years ago. And, according to the Illinois Supreme Court, asses are cattle. So are goats under a ruling of the North Carolina Supreme Court. The latter court cited in support of its conclusions the well-known case of Laban and Jacob.

Snakes are "implements, instruments, and tools of trade," at least when Uncle Sam is collecting his revenues. For the same purpose a new metal called "bouchan," used in watches, is a jewel. In Georgia a minor who has a separate estate is an orphan. In Pennsylvania a bicycle is an animal and in the Federal courts it is also a business vehicle.

Chinamen in California were formerly held to be Indians, which disqualified them as witnesses against white folks and made it possible for good white men to rob and assault them with impunity. A Chinese merchant sent to the penitentiary is no longer a merchant, but a laborer, so that the exclusion acts may be applied to him. For the same purpose a gambler is a laborer. According to a very recent decision, however, an air pilot is not a laborer.

In New York, under the sanitary code, candies are vegetables; and in Georgia a watermelon is both a fruit and a vegetable. Pipes, tobacco, cigars, and newspapers are not "articles of comfort" for a poor husband, but mere luxuries. So says the Alabama Supreme Court, which might be expected to have a deeper sympathy for the downtrodden male. In Massachusetts a college education is not a necessary under present-day conditions, according to a decision rendered last year.

In Michigan a dentist is a mechanic. In Mississippi he is not a mechanic. And in North Carolina he is not a physician, within a statute allowing the sale of liquor on the certificate of a physician. Otherwise, says the court, "toothache would be more welcome and more prevalent than snake bite."

A gelding is not a horse. At least both the Montana and the Kansas Supreme Courts have held that, where an indictment charges a defendant with having stolen a gelding, his conviction cannot be sustained if the evidence merely shows that he stole a horse. And a charge of stealing a hog cannot be supported by testimony of the stealing of a dead hog. In other words, a dead hog is not a hog. We have the word of the Supreme Court of Virginia for that.

A question that often arises in connection with certain crimes is the meaning of the term "daylight," or "daytime." This is also an important matter in connection with the service of search warrants. In such a case decided in 1923, it was held by a Federal court that a search warrant providing for a search in daytime only was no justification for a search made at 5.15 P.M. on December 22. In another case decided in 1927, however, it was decided that thirty-eight minutes after sunset was "daytime" in Georgia. The test applied was the so-called burglary test, which is whether there is sufficient light from the sun to recognize a man's features. Judge Sibley said in that case: "Daytime does not in law or by common understanding begin at sunrise, and end at sunset, but includes dawn at one end and twilight at the other."

But in 1929, in a case involving a search under a daytime warrant, Judge Norton, another Federal district judge, reached a conclusion directly contrary to that of Judge Sibley. Judge Norton said:

"Daytime" in this statute is used in its ordinary meaning at the present time. . . . What seems to me to be the correct rule is stated in Murray's Dictionary, where "day" is defined as "in ordinary usage including the lighter part of morning and evening twilight, but, when strictly used, limited to the time when the sun is above the horizon." This rule has great practical advantages. . . . Sunrise and sunset will make a much better working rule than the vague and shadowy boundaries adopted for humanitarian reasons in defining burglary.

So there you are. Which is right? I confess that I do not know.

Is an airplane a "self-propelled vehicle"? A Federal district court held it was and convicted a defendant of the crime of having transported a "self-propelled vehicle," which had been stolen, from one state to another, where the facts showed that he had flown a stolen plane across the state line. But the United States Supreme Court held only a few months ago that the district judge was mistaken—that an airplane is not "a self-propelled vehicle."

In Missouri a pistol so defective that it could not be discharged even if it were loaded is a firearm. In New York it is not.

Nowhere is it more evident that the prejudices and predilections of the courts determine the meaning of words than in the decisions interpreting Sunday laws, particularly with reference to baseball. Thus, the Supreme Court of Kansas has held that baseball is not a game under a statute forbidding "games of any kind." The Missouri Supreme Court has laid down a similar rule, saying that baseball is a sport. But the Nebraska Supreme Court has held baseball to be a game within a statute forbidding "sporting" on Sunday. The New Mexico Supreme Court, on the contrary, has held that baseball is neither a sport nor labor. But it is labor in Virginia, at least when played by professional players, though no admission is charged. In Tennessee it is not the exercise of "any common avocation of life"; and in Oklahoma it is a public sport and banned if played by professionals, but a private sport and not within the statute when played by amateurs.

Turning away from the criminal law for a moment, let us take a look at the exemption laws and the laws of estates. How would you define the words "household effects"? In Vermont it was held some years ago that they did not include a piano. In Michigan there has been a similar holding; but in Missouri, Oklahoma, and Texas the term "household effects" has been held to include a piano. In New York it has recently been held that "household effects" included two automobiles, a riding horse, and a speedboat; and an earlier New York decision was to the effect that wines in a well-stocked cellar were "household goods." It may be interesting in this connection to note that the Iowa Supreme Court held in 1929 that a radio had "no likeness or kindred relationship with a musical instrument."

Another word that has puzzled the courts from time to time and led to conflicting rulings is the word "accident." According to a Pennsylvania court, the bite of a dog is an accident. So is being shot by an assailant or robber; and so was the shooting of a husband by his wife, when, following a quarrel, the husband approached the house, swearing and carrying an axe, and the wife took a pistol and killed him. The latter holding was made to enable the wife to recover on an insurance policy containing a provision that there could be no recovery by the beneficiary if the insured met his death at her hands other than by accident. Suicide in a fit of delirium or insanity is an accident; but electrocution following a conviction of murder is not an accident according to a decision of the United States Circuit Court of Appeals handed down last June. However, death by lynching is an accident in the opinion of the Kentucky Supreme Court, whatever it may appear to the victim.

"Colored person" in Virginia means one having one-fourth or more of Negro blood. In North Carolina, on the other hand, it means a person having Negro blood of any degree. In Oklahoma it is held to mean Negro so clearly that a white person charged with being colored can maintain an action for libel. But in Mississippi it has been held that the term "colored races" includes all races except white. The Court of Appeals of the District of Columbia, on the other hand, held in 1910 that "colored" referred only to persons of the Negro race, and that, regardless of the slight amount of Negro blood that might be in their veins,—the determining factors being "physical touches, whether of shade, hair, or physiognomy,"—they were "colored" if there was the least admixture of Negro blood.

The word "collision" is another that has demanded a great deal of attention on the part of the courts, and their conclusions as to its application have been varied and conflicting as usual. The Michigan Supreme Court, for instance, held in 1920 that "an object coming from above" might be considered as constituting a collision, the object in that case being the shovel of a steam shovel that fell upon a loading motor truck. The Texas Court of Civil Appeals, on the contrary, decided in a somewhat similar case that an object falling from above could not be considered as constituting a collision, the object being the upper floor of a garage that gave way and crushed a car standing on the floor below.

In New Jersey a recovery on an insurance policy on the ground of a collision was allowed where the car went through the guard rail of a bridge and was damaged by falling to the ground below. Where a car was backed into an open elevator shaft and fell to the floor below it was held to be a collision by the Pennsylvania Superior Court. But in Wisconsin it has been held that where a car ran off the road, and down an embankment into a river, the facts did not justify recovery as for a collision. In Missouri, on the other hand, recovery as for a collision was allowed under almost identical circumstances. Where, in order to avoid striking an approaching car, a driver turned out and his car left the road, fell down an embankment, struck a rock, and turned over, it was held in New York that the injury to his car was due to a "collision," the court saying, "In simple words it is a striking together of two objects. The road is an object, likewise the earth. Whether vertical or horizontal makes no difference." But the Washington Supreme Court held in 1924 that it was not a collision where a car skidded off the road and rolled and bounded down a mountain side, striking stumps and trees as it went. Again, on the contrary, the Alabama Supreme Court held that same year that where a car was left standing on a hill and started by the force of gravity, going over a cliff and hitting the ground a number of feet below, damages were recoverable as for a collision.

There is one other troublesome word that needs to be noted—namely, the word "drunkenness." The Nebraska Supreme Court held that a man might be under the influence of liquor without being drunk, and gave as the test the one of whether or not he had lost control of his bodily and mental faculties. But the Iowa Supreme Court in a case involving the removal of a mayor on the ground of intoxication, after saying that intoxication and drunkenness meant the same, held, "It means not necessarily that he is so drunk as to be unable to walk straight or show outward signs to a casual observer, but is satisfied if he is sufficiently under the influence of liquor so that he is not entirely himself."

A Texas court more wisely said, "A person may be intoxicated and not drunk. One drink will not ordinarily make a man drunk. Defendant had the appearance of a man who was drinking some but able to attend to his business." But the same court had said previously with even a greater exhibition of wisdom, "It is extremely difficult to draw the line on a 'drunk.' There are various stages, such as quarter drunk, half drunk and dead drunk. There are the stages of being vivacious, foxy, tipsy, and on a 'high lonesome,' and it is as difficult to determine when a young lady gets to be an old maid as it is to tell when a man has taken enough alcoholic stimulant to pass the line between 'jolly sober' and 'gentlemanly drunk.'"

And now, approaching the end, let us see what "end" means according to an august appellate tribunal. Said the Virginia Supreme Court: "It imports what will be when the Apocalyptic Angel, with one foot on the sea and the other upon the Earth, shall lift his hand to Heaven and swear, by Him that liveth forever and ever, that there shall be 'Time no longer.'"

It is well, however, to note that at least in one instance a high court was stumped by a problem of definition. It was the Supreme Court of Georgia, which in 1925 admitted and explained:

> From the days of Socrates and Xantippe, men and women have known what is meant by nagging, although philology cannot define or legal chemistry resolve it into its elements. Humor and threats are idle. Soft words but increase its velocity and harsh ones its violence. Darkness has for it no terrors, and the long hours of the night draw no drapery of the couch around it. It takes the sparkle out of the wine of life and turns at night into ashes the fruits of the labor of the day. In the words of Solomon, "it is better to dwell in the corner of the housetop than with a brawling woman in the wide house."

And further deponent sayeth not.

No. 70

[THE nature of the rules applied in particular cases, as we have seen, is determined to a considerable extent by the judges who find the rules by peering into the crystal ball of The Law. Unfortunately the rules that are to be seen there are often archaic, but tradition coupled with a reactionary judicial psychology makes reform difficult. This situation is made clear in the following article by Mr. Hibschman.]

LEGAL COBWEBS [1]

by Harry Hibschman

JAMES HARRIS, a gentleman of color, was indicted in the State of Delaware in 1841 for having stolen "a pair of boots." But at the trial it appeared that, in the excitement of acquiring new footwear in violation of the law, he had seized and asported, not two boots that were mates, but two that were both for the right foot. He was convicted as charged in the indictment; but on appeal the high and honorable Superior Court reversed his conviction on the ground that a charge of stealing a pair of boots could not be sustained by proof of the stealing of two boots that were not mates. "The object of certainty in an indictment," said the court, speaking didactically, "is to inform the defendant plainly and precisely of what offense he is charged. This certainty must be not merely to a common intent but to

---

[1] Harry Hibschman, "Legal Cobwebs," *The American Mercury* (December, 1931), Vol. 24, pp. 455-460. Reprinted by permission of the author and *The American Mercury*.

a certain intent in general, which requires that things shall be called by their right names." (3 Harrington 559.)

To be sure, that was ninety years ago. But the rule applied in the Harris case has not yet been sent to limbo. In fact it still works. For, in law, rules and precedents are like musty bottles in old wine cellars—they are esteemed for their age. In 1881, for instance, the Kansas Supreme Court decided with all due judicial solemnity that evidence of the stealing of a gelding would not sustain a charge of stealing a horse. (State v. Buckles, 26 Kan. 237.) In 1912, the Alabama Supreme Court held that a charge of a violation of a statute making it a felony to steal "a cow or an animal of the cow kind" could not be sustained by evidence of the stealing of a steer. (Marsh v. State, 57 So. 387.) And in 1917 it was decided in Missouri that a conviction under an indictment charging a man with stealing hogs would have to be reversed where the evidence showed that the hogs were dead when taken. The august appellate tribunal that handed down this illuminating decision went across the seas for its main precedents and cited three English cases as authority, two of them decided in 1823 and the other in 1829. It reached the conclusion that "the carcass of a hog, by whatever name called, is not a hog." (State v. Hedrick, 199 S. W. 192.)

A very recent example of a reversal of a conviction because of "variance," as the courts call the vice condemned in the cases already cited, is the Texas case of Prock v. State (23 S. W. (2nd) 728), decided last year. Here the complaint on which the defendant was arrested and bound over for trial described him as a "male person," and the information filed against him and on which he was tried described him as an "adult male." It was held that this difference required the reversal of his conviction of aggravated assault on a female, though where the harm to him lay is beyond the imagination of an ordinary man.

Another Texas case was reversed in 1910 on the ground that the indictment in which the defendant was accused of burglary described the burglarized premises as being occupied at the time of the crime by six Japanese mentioned by name, while the evidence was to the effect that there were only five. (Grantham v. State, 129 S. W. 839.) In 1917 the Illinois Supreme Court reversed a conviction for embezzlement because of a mistake in the name of one partner out of more than thirty named in the indictment as the injured parties. (People v. Dettmering, 116 N. E. 205.) And in 1919 it similarly upset a conviction in a liquor case because in one count out of forty-nine, under all of which the defendant was found guilty, his name was spelled Holdburg instead of Goldburg. (People v. Goldburg, 123 N. E. 530.)

Judges whose morning prayer is, "Keep my feet in the paths of Coke and Blackstone, for precedents' sake!" may, of course, find complete satisfaction for their souls in such decisions. But if one dares to be captious and ask what difference it can make to a defendant—what rights of his are jeopardized—if two unmated boots are described as a pair, a gelding as a horse, a steer as of "the cow kind," or a dead hog as a hog, or if he is proved to have burglarized the premises of only five Japanese instead of six, or embezzled from thirty men properly named and one misnamed, or has the first letter of his last name given wrongly in one count out of forty-nine, one is moved to repeat with the Oklahoma Criminal Court of Appeals that a technicality is "a microbe which, having gotten into the law, gives justice the blind staggers" (Ryan v. State, 129 Pac. 685.), and to exclaim with the Wisconsin Supreme Court that "there is little wonder that laymen are sometimes heard to remark that justice is one thing and law is another!" (Gist v. Johnson-Carey Company, 158 Wis. 204.)

With many American appellate tribunals the point of view, regardless of the breakdown of the judicial machinery and the increase of serious crime, is still that expressed long ago by the Supreme Court of Massachusetts in the case that is said to have driven William Cullen Bryant from law to literature as his life's work. "In a matter of technical law," said the court, "the rule is of more consequence than the reason for it." (Bloss v. Tobey, 19 Mass. 320.)

American courts have been especially fearsome of permitting one jot or tittle to be taken from, or changed in, indictments. This attitude is due to the supposedly sacred character of the Grand Jury as an institution and of the indictment as its solemnly begotten child.

Thus, it has been held within the last five years that a Federal court is absolutely without power to amend an indictment—even to strike out by stipulation of the defendant's counsel the words "and feloniously" as surplusage. (Stewart v. U. S., 12 Fed. (2nd) 524.) The leading Federal case on the subject was decided by the Supreme Court in 1886, when it was held that, if a change is made in the indictment, "the power of the court to try the prisoner is as much arrested as if the indictment had been dismissed or a nolle prosequi had been entered." (In ex parte Bain, 121 U. S. 1.)

Applying this rule, our appellate courts, both State and Federal, have handed down decisions that seem the height of folly if justice is really the end sought by the judicial process and if individuals are expected to retain a modicum of respect for the law and for the tribunals established to administer and interpret it.

Among the most notorious are the "the" and the "did" cases. Of the former the best known is a Missouri case, decided in 1908, in which a verdict of guilty was set aside because the indictment read "against the peace and dignity of State of Missouri" instead of "the peace and dignity of *the* State." (State *v.* Campbell, 109 S. W. 706.) But there had been a similar holding in Texas as far back as 1883. (Thompson *v.* State, 15 Tex. App. 39.) The leading "did" case was decided in Mississippi in 1895, when a conviction was reversed because the word was omitted from the indictment. Then in 1907 this original case was followed as a precedent in a murder case. In the murder case the fact that the word had been omitted in the indictment before the words "kill and murder" was discovered in the lower court at the time of the trial, and its insertion was permitted by the trial judge. In spite of this amendment, the defendant's conviction was reversed and the case ordered dismissed. (Cook *v.* State, 17 So. 228; and Hall *v.* State, 44 So. 810.)

The "the" cases have been overruled in Missouri, and there have been no recent "did" cases; but that does not mean that the technical approach to the consideration of indictments has been rejected, not by any means. That reversals still continue in many jurisdictions as of old will be evident from a few cases out of many decided during the year 1930.

In South Carolina, for instance, it was held that, where an indictment for murder charged that death occurred in the same county as the assault but the evidence showed that death occurred in another county, though the assault causing death occurred in the county in which the trial was being held and, therefore, the defendant was properly brought to trial there, still it was error to permit the indictment to be amended at the trial to show that death occurred in the other county. (State *v.* Platt, 151 S. E. 206.) In Louisiana an indictment charged the defendant with forging a certain order for $6 on a corporation and, on motion of the State's attorney, the indictment was amended to give the value of the forged order as $4 instead of $6. This was held to be reversible error. (State *v.* Sylistan, 125 So. 859.)

In Illinois a conviction was set aside because the indictment charged an attempt to open a showcase with intent to steal its contents but failed to allege that the attempt was unsuccessful. (People *v.* Donaldson, 173 N. E. 357.) In Texas an indictment was held fatally defective because it alleged that the defendant deserted his complaining wife "unlawfully and willingly" instead of "unlawfully and wilfully." (Carter *v.* State, 27 S. W. (2nd) 821.)

And in a New Jersey case, where an indictment for larceny was amended by striking from it the name of the party found by the grand jury to be the owner of certain alcohol alleged to have been taken and by substituting the name of another as owner, the appellate court held that the trial judge was without authority to permit such change, saying: "There can be no conception of the crime of larceny without ownership of the property alleged to have been stolen being in someone. It is therefore quite clear that the allegation of ownership in an indictment is a matter of substance and not of form." (State *v.* Cohen, 147 Atl. 325.)

But there are a number of late cases in which it is held that such amendments as those just mentioned are permissible. The substitution of a different name for that given in the indictment in connection with the ownership of the property taken, for instance, was upheld in Iowa in 1922 and in Mississippi in 1929. (State *v.* Luce, 191 N. W. 64; and Wood *v.* State, 124 So. 353.)

The difference of opinion in these cases lies largely in varying conceptions by the courts of what is a change in substance and what merely a change in form. That is the rock on which they split, one stream of decisions flowing in the most ancient channels and the other breaking through the banks of hoary precedent and cutting new passageways through the legalistic débris of the centuries.

The strange thing about American adherence to outworn doctrines and practices is that we claim to have inherited them from England. And yet England and her dominions have long since cast most of them overboard as so much rubbish. The judge who sits in an English criminal court may wear an ancient garb, but the procedure he follows has been modernized until an American hardly recognizes its semblance to what we are supposed to have derived from the same source. Since 1851 such defects in the indictment as have been discussed above have been of no importance whatever in English jurisprudence. The insertion of words like "the," "did," and "against the peace and dignity," or amendments to show true ownership or description of property or identification of persons are permitted as a matter of course.

The fundamental difference between present-day English criminal jurisprudence and American criminal jurisprudence may be graphically illustrated by quoting the indictment in the famous Sacco-Vanzetti case and comparing it with a similar indictment in Canada. The Sacco-Vanzetti indictment read as follows:

COMMONWEALTH OF MASSACHUSETTS

Norfolk, ss.

At the Superior Court, begun and holden within and for the County of Norfolk, on the first Monday of September in the year of our Lord one thousand nine and twenty, the Jurors for the Commonwealth of Massachusetts on their oath present That Nicola Sacco of Stoughton in the County of Norfolk and Bartholomeo Vanzetti of Plymouth in the County of Plymouth on the fifteenth day of April in the year of our Lord one thousand nine hundred and twenty at Braintree in the County of Norfolk did assault and beat Alexander Berardelli with intent to murder him by shooting him in the body with a loaded pistol and by such assault, beating and shooting did murder Alexander Berardelli against the peace of said Commonwealth and contrary to the form of the statute in such case made and provided.

In Canada that indictment would have read:

In the Supreme Court of Ontario

The Jurors for our Lord the King present, that Nicola Sacco and Bartholomeo Vanzetti murdered Alexander Berardelli at Ontario on April 15, 1920.

Compare this last, too, with an indictment returned by a grand jury in the District of Columbia in 1891. It charged that the defendant

did cast, throw, and push the said Agnes Watson into a certain canal then situate, wherein there then was a great quantity of water, by means of which casting, throwing, and pushing of the said Agnes Watson in the canal by the aforesaid Frederick Barber, in the manner and form aforesaid, she, the said Agnes Watson, in the canal aforesaid, with the water aforesaid, was then and there mortally choked, suffocated, and drowned.

This indictment was held defective on the ground that it did not allege that Agnes Watson died by reason of "the defendant's homicidal act." (U. S. *v.* Barber, 20 Dist. of Col. 79.)

If England and Canada have been able to modernize and simplify indictments and other elements of their criminal jurisprudence, why can't we? Do our inflexible constitutions stand in the way? Are we helpless in the face of the rising tide of criminality?

The answer is that what our co-heirs of the English common law and English jurisprudence have done, we can do. And we have already made a beginning in some states. California is, despite the Mooney case, perhaps the most striking example; and her accomplishments are worth noting as proof that we are not altogether helpless.

California's record of reversals in criminal cases, while not among the highest, was formerly, unlike her climate, nothing to brag about. In the period extending from 1900 to 1909, for instance, 22.5% of all criminal cases appealed were reversed. True, the record for Illinois for the same period was 37.3%; but that of New York and Massachusetts was under 15% each.

The old attitude of the California courts is evidenced by a case decided in 1880. It involved an indictment charging "entry into a stable to commit *larcey*." This was held not to describe any offense because of the simple omission of the letter *n*, notwithstanding the fact that there was a provision in the Penal Code, reading: "No indictment shall be deemed insufficient, nor shall the trial, judgment, or other proceedings thereon be affected by reason of any defect or imperfection in matters of form which shall not tend to the prejudice of the defendant." (People *v.* St. Clair, 55 Cal. 524; 56 Cal. 406.)

All of which goes to show that judges, like horses, may be led to the trough but can't be made to drink by mere legislative enactment. Judicial reform by statute can be, and repeatedly has been, thwarted and prevented by the wrong kind of men on the bench. One thing the layman groping for something better in the field of law needs to realize is that in the end, regardless of what the law-makers may say, it is the judges who determine what the law is and how, if at all, it shall operate.

But in 1911 the following section was added to the California constitution:

No judgment shall be set aside or new trial granted in any criminal case on the ground of misdirection of the jury or the improper admission or rejection of evidence, or for error as to any matter of pleading or procedure unless, after an examination of the entire cause including the evidence, the court shall be of an opinion that the error complained of has resulted in a miscarriage of justice. (*Constitution, Art.* VI, *Sec.* 4½.)

The first case involving this provision to reach the Supreme Court of the State seems to have been approached somewhat doubtfully and apprehensively. The court did, however, go so far as to say that "Section 4½ of Article VI must be given at least the effect of abrogating the old rule that prejudice is presumed from any error of law." (People *v.* O'Bryan, 130 Pac. 1042.)

That was in 1913. But by 1924 the Court had become bolder, and now it laid down this rule: "It is now incumbent upon the complaining party to make an affirmative showing that prejudice followed from the error relied upon." (People *v.* Mahach, 224 Pac. 130.)

The result of the recognition and application of this new constitutional provision is manifest from the fact that, while from 1910 to 1912, over 23% of the appeals in criminal cases were reversed, the percentage from 1916 to 1918 was only 12 and from 1918 to 1920 only 11.

Then in 1927 the Penal Code was amended so as to permit a short form of indictment or information and so as to make many other radical changes. The former crimes of larceny, embezzlement, false pretenses, and kindred offenses, for instance, were amalgamated into one crime, theft. And many of the old, technical rules were wholly abrogated. All these provisions have been sustained by the higher courts, and the spirit in which they were adopted was completely recognized in People *v.* Campbell, 265 Pac. 364, where the Supreme Court said:

Much of the time of courts has been consumed in the consideration of technical objections to pleadings in criminal cases; yet it is probable that few judges are able to recall a single case in which a defendant was actually in the slightest doubt as to the crime with which he was charged. Modern legislation is endeavoring to cut the Gordian knot by which the trial of criminal cases has so long been fettered, and the courts ought not to thwart that laudable effort by an adherence to mere technical precedents which regard form rather than substance.

The short form referred to has also been adopted in Maryland, Massachusetts, Alabama, Iowa, New York and other states and has the endorsement of the American Law Institute. So we are making some progress, and there is some reason for hope. But before we can travel very far, the comparatively few enlightened jurists and members of the bar who are striving for a better judicial system must be supported and reinforced by an awakened, insistent and clamorous laity. Tradition, the self-interest of certain groups, indifference, conservatism, and a reactionary judicial psychology constitute almost insuperable barriers to even the degree of reform attained in England. And a sane system, truly modernized and humanized, must carry us far beyond it.

No. 71

[THE particular role and function of the courts in any governmental system are determined not only by the nature of the system of jurisprudence and the kind of rules enforced but also by the procedure that is followed in enforcement. If results are to be satisfactory, the procedure must be such that the work is done with economy and dispatch while at the same time the rights of the interested parties are protected. Our system is more defective in these respects than in almost any others. The following article by Mr. Fred B. Morrill well illustrates this fact.]

FARMER JONES GOES TO LAW [1]

by Fred B. Morrill

FARMER JONES was troubled. He had never experienced any legal entanglements, and up to the time the S. C. & Z. R. R. began to lay its new line through his farm he had never even had occasion to consult a lawyer.

[1] Morrill, Fred B., "Farmer Jones Goes to Law," *The American Mercury* (February, 1931), Vol. 22, pp. 219-222. Reprinted by permission of the author and *The American Mercury*.

His experience in courts of justice was limited to serving a couple of times as a juror, and he firmly believed that under our judicial system justice was bound to prevail. But it was not until the railroad had cut down part of his orchard and commenced to make a deep and unsightly cut through his most fertile field, and one of his barns and a part of his wheat crop had been destroyed by fire through the negligence of the construction gang, that he consulted a lawyer about beginning proceedings to enforce his rights.

His lawyer advised him that he could enjoin the railroad from further interfering with his property, and thus compel it to pay for the property taken, and for any damages he might sustain by reason of the taking, or institute condemnation proceedings to determine the amount he was entitled to receive, and which the company would have to pay. The first seemed the course to pursue until he was advised that, on bringing such an action, he would be required to execute a bond to indemnify the company for any loss it might sustain, if by chance his suit should fail.

Not being able to furnish such a bond he was precluded from bringing an injunction suit, and so decided to bring an action to recover the damage he had sustained. His lawyer seemed to think that it would be necessary to commence two actions: one for the loss occasioned by the fire, and another for the damage to his farm, and for the property taken by the railroad. But Mr. Jones could not see any reason why he should be put to the expense and trouble of two suits, so he instructed his lawyer to proceed with the first.

As the company was entitled to be fully advised—in a legal way—of the grounds upon which he expected to recover, he was required to file his complaint in court, setting forth, under oath, the facts he expected to prove, and to serve the same upon the company. In order to prevent him from obtaining judgment against it for the amount of his claim the company could either demur to his complaint or answer under oath, denying, either in whole or in part, the allegations therein set forth. Its attorney adopted the first procedure, demurring on the ground that the complaint did not state a cause of action—which under the law amounts to an admission that all of the material allegations therein set forth are true—and on the further ground that several causes of action had been improperly united.

This made an issue of law to be decided by the court, and in due course of time the demurrer was argued and the contention of the attorney for the railroad sustained. The court held that those engaged in the construction work were independent contractors and that therefore the railroad company was not liable for their negligent acts. Thereupon the action was dismissed, and a judgment for costs entered against the plaintiff. Instead of having a judgment against the railroad company, Mr. Jones was surprised to find that it had a judgment against him, which he must either pay or take an appeal to the Supreme Court of the State.

Believing he was in the right, he decided to take the appeal, and within the time allowed his attorney served and filed his notice of appeal and appeal bond. The printed record and briefs of the attorneys were also served and filed, and after several months the case was placed on the docket for argument. On the date set for the hearing, the issues of law involved were argued by the attorneys and the case taken under advisement by the court.

Although court costs, appeal bonds, printing bills and attorney's fees made the appeal more expensive than he had anticipated, Mr. Jones's faith in the American judiciary system was still strong, and so he looked confidently for a favorable decision and an end to his troubles, which by this time were continually on his mind and the principal subject of discussion in his family circle and of much concern to the entire neighborhood.

Month followed month without any news from the Supreme Court. But at last, when nearly a year had elapsed, the long-looked-for decision came. To Farmer Jones it was like a thunderbolt out of a clear sky. For the Supreme Court decided that the railroad's demurrer was well taken, and thus there was another judgment for costs against him. Over two years had elapsed since the action was commenced. Its net result to date was two victories for the railroad company, and two judgments in its favor.

In most cases the decision of the Supreme Court of a State is final, but Jones was advised by his attorney that a Federal question was involved, in his case, and that in consequence it could be taken to the Supreme Court of the United States. Although that proceeding involved the giving of more bonds, the payment of more court costs and attorney's fees, and the printing of additional records and briefs, he decided that he must go on to the end of his legal journey.

At last the date for presenting the case was set and he sent his attorney to Washington to make his oral argument before the court. And after a few more months of anxiety he was advised by his attorney that the case had been decided in his favor. The highest court in the land had reversed the State Supreme Court and the trial court, holding that his complaint stated a cause of action entitling him to a trial of the case upon its merits.

Nearly four years had now elapsed and he was at the point from which he started. His opponent had not even been required to answer his complaint, and thereby state the grounds upon which it relied as a defense to his claim. By a demurrer that did not cover a sheet of paper, and with very little cost outside of attorney's fees, the defendant, during all these years, had been able to prevent a jury trial.

But now, after the highest court in the land had decided in his favor, and stated in language that could not be misunderstood that the allegations of his complaint set forth a cause of action, Mr. Jones felt confident that his legal difficulties were nearly over. During the following year the record was remitted to the trial court; the answer was filed, denying under oath all of the allegations of his complaint, and the case was brought on for trial before a jury. The first two days were occupied in impaneling the jury and hearing the opening statements made by the attorneys; after which the testimony of himself and his witnesses was submitted—testimony he was sure could not be controverted by the defense.

Then followed a proceeding that he could not comprehend. The jury was excluded from the court-room and the attorney for the railroad company made a motion for a non-suit, a motion that was followed by arguments of counsel and the reading of many decisions to the court. Toward the end Mr. Jones felt that he could no longer bear the suspense and left the court-room. When he returned the attorneys were gathering up their papers and law-books and he was advised that the motion had been granted—that his case had been dismissed without a verdict of the jury and that a judgment for costs would be entered against him.

As a layman he had always understood that in a case of this kind trial by jury was guaranteed under the Constitution, and the ending of his suit without a jury passing upon the facts gave him a shock he would not soon recover from. He was now forced to either take an appeal or pay the judgment.

His only hope of recovering from the railroad company lay in an appeal and he was obliged to continue on. This involved more bonds, costs, attorney's fees, delays and anxieties. However, after weary months of waiting the Supreme Court decided that the trial court had erred in granting the non-suit, and the case was remanded for another trial. Again a jury was impaneled and after a trial lasting ten days a verdict was rendered in Jones's favor for the full amount of his claim.

He was now jubilant. At last he had a judgment against the railroad company, and he could see no reason why it should not be paid. But when he called upon his attorney to ascertain how soon the company could be made to settle he was informed that its attorney had moved for a new trial upon errors of law occurring at the trial, and on the ground that the damages assessed by the jury were excessive; and had also made a motion for judgment *non obstante veredicto*. After another delay these motions were disposed of, but not entirely to Jones's satisfaction. The court denied the motion for a new trial, and the motion for judgment *non obstante veredicto*, but decided that the verdict was excessive, and reduced it by $1000. No action being taken by either party, judgment was entered accordingly.

Either party could now take an appeal. Jones firmly believed that he was entitled to the full amount of the verdict, but in order to close the litigation he was willing to accept the amount called for by the judgment and instructed his attorney to take such action as might be necessary to enforce payment. As soon, however, as an execution was issued, the company perfected an appeal to the Supreme Court of the State, claiming that the trial court erred in its instructions to the jury, and by giving a *supersedeas* bond the execution of the judgment was stayed.

Jones now saw before him another long delay and more expense. There was the usual printing of records and briefs, followed by oral arguments before the court. But at last the decision was rendered, and to his great joy the judgment of the trial court was sustained. He now had in his favor a decision of the Supreme Court of the United States, a verdict of a jury, and a judgment thereon sustained by the Supreme Court of the State. The end of his lawsuit seemed to be in sight. His attorney advised him that the Federal question involved had been finally disposed of by the Supreme Court of the United States, so that the railroad company was precluded from having the last decision reviewed by that tribunal, and as soon as the remittitur—whatever that might be—was filed in the lower court the judgment would have to be paid.

Unluckily, the joy of Farmer Jones was of short duration. He did not know that, though the court had decided the case in his favor and written an elaborate and lengthy opinion on the law governing the issues involved, and cited numerous decisions of other courts, the company still had an opportunity to cause delay. It could, and did, file a petition for a rehearing *en banc*.

And the petition was granted. The granting of this petition required more printed briefs and another oral argument at the next term of the Supreme Court, and another delay before that tribunal rendered its decision. And while Jones felt confident that it would be a final decision in his favor the waiting from day to day became almost unbearable.

At last the long-looked-for decision was rendered. Alas! it did not end the legal journey of Farmer Jones. In this decision the court found that in rendering its former opinion it had overlooked a legal point, now more forcibly brought to its attention by the attorney for the railroad company upon the reargument, and, revoking its former opinion, it remanded the case for another trial.

Jones was now ready to give up all hope. He had been in the courts for seven years and nothing had been accomplished. Seven years of trouble,

expense and disappointment and he was again at the place from which he
started. Trials, verdicts and decisions were of no avail. They only served
to make him more expense and anxiety. He felt that he was bound hand
and foot, his body, arms and legs entwined in the meshes of a legal entangle-
ment from which there was no escape.

But he was wrong, for notwithstanding more dilatory moves made on
behalf of the company, in due course of time, after a long, hard-fought trial,
another verdict of a jury for the full amount was rendered in his favor.
Again there were the usual motions for a new trial and for judgment notwithstanding the verdict, and also a motion to have the verdict set aside
upon the ground of misconduct of the jury in arriving at a verdict, and
after they were disposed of in his favor, another appeal was taken. But
this time the railroad company was not successful; its petition for a rehearing was denied, and the case was remanded to the trial court and a
final judgment entered.

The attorney for the company had now exhausted every legal quibble
known to the law. There had been numerous decisions and two verdicts in
the trial court, six decisions by the State Supreme Court, and one by the
Supreme Court of the United States, and at last, after more than ten years
of litigation, Jones heard the jingle of the dollars due him from the railroad
company.

Ten years of litigation and that long line of decisions and verdicts, and
all the while the railroad company had legally admitted by its first pleading
that every material allegation set forth in his complaint was true!

And during all those years the railroad had been operating its line through
his farm; notwithstanding that Article V, amendatory of the Constitution
of the United States, provides that: "No person shall . . . be deprived of
life, liberty, or property without due process of law; nor shall private property be taken for public use without just compensation."

Chapter XX

THE COURTS AND PUBLIC POLICY

[In addition to participation in the formulation and execution of public policy as discussed in the preceding chapter, the courts in the United States have the power to invalidate acts of the legislature on the ground that they are contrary to the constitution. This is known as the power of judicial review and, in the form in which it is now exercised, amounts to actual participation in the legislative or policy-determining work of government. The claim is made that much of the social and economic legislation invalidated by the courts throughout our history has not been held void because it was in clear and unmistakable conflict with the constitution but because it was in clear and unmistakable conflict with the economic and social views of a majority of the court. Thus the court exercises what is essentially a legislative veto and, in essence, does the legislature's job over again.

In order to understand the role of the judiciary in American government, it is essential to appreciate the nature of the power of judicial review and the way in which it has been exercised by American courts. The following articles will give to anyone who will reflect upon the material they present a better understanding of the processes of American Government.]

No. 72

THE ROLE OF THE SUPREME COURT IN A DEMOCRATIC NATION [1]

by Robert E. Cushman

BACK in 1801 Jefferson wrote to a friend: "The Federalists have retired into the judiciary as a stronghold—and from that battery all the works of republicanism are to be beaten down and erased." Some people to-day believe that in a democracy no court should have power to invalidate

[1] Robert E. Cushman, "The Role of the Supreme Court in a Democratic Nation," Edmund Janes James Lecture at the University of Illinois, March 9, 1938. Reprinted by permission of the author and the University of Illinois.

laws passed by the representatives of the people. Many others believe that we need a Supreme Court with power to declare laws unconstitutional; but they also feel that in the use of that authority the Court has dangerously assumed powers which belong to the legislature, powers which in a democratic government ought not to be exercised by a court of law. This is the problem which I wish to explore. What is the rôle of the Supreme Court in our constitutional democracy?

I should like to divide my discussion into three parts. I should like *first* to show the nature and growth of the Supreme Court's power to invalidate laws. *Second,* I wish to show that the Court in reviewing legislation determines not merely the constitutionality of law but the wisdom and desirability of legislative policy. *Third,* I shall explain how I think the Supreme Court can best be restored to its proper rôle in a democratic government.

I. *The nature and growth of the Supreme Court's power over legislation.* Let us turn to the first of these three topics,—the nature and growth of the Supreme Court's power over legislation. I do not enter here upon any analysis of the theory of judicial review. I do not wish to make any comment upon the old, old dispute as to whether the framers of the Constitution intended to have the Supreme Court invalidate acts of Congress. We may accept judicial review as a going concern without worrying about its lineage. I should like, however, to trace the stages in the development of the power of the Supreme Court to declare laws unconstitutional, from the rather modest beginning in John Marshall's famous decision in the case of Marbury *v.* Madison, to the broad and drastic power which the Court now enjoys. This will make more clear the actual working relations between the Supreme Court and the Congress. There are at least four stages in this evolution of the Court's power, and these I wish to discuss.

First, let us examine briefly the case in which the Supreme Court first declared an act of Congress unconstitutional. This was the case of Marbury *v.* Madison, well known to every college student. President John Adams, about to retire from office, had appointed some sixty loyal Federalists to judicial positions created two weeks earlier by the Judiciary Act of 1801. The commissions of all these appointees had been signed and sealed, but John Marshall, Adams's easy-going Secretary of State, had not gotten around to deliver them when at midnight on March 3rd Thomas Jefferson, the newly-elected President, took office. Jefferson regarded these so-called "midnight" appointments to be an outrageous assault upon the principles of democratic government and common decency and ordered his Secretary of State, James Madison, not to deliver the commissions still left in the office. One of these had been destined to make James Marbury a justice of the peace in the District of Columbia, and Marbury, not wishing to be done out of his job, brought an action in the Supreme Court of the United States to compel Madison to give him his commission. He brought his suit under a section of the Judiciary Act of 1789 which authorized the Supreme Court to issue writs of mandamus and prohibition in the exercise of its original jurisdiction. After much delay the case reached the Supreme Court in 1803 and Marshall, as Chief Justice of the United States, was confronted with the fruits of his own negligence. The Court's decision and Marshall's opinion announcing it made history. Marshall began by scolding the Administration for not delivering Marbury's commission to which he was clearly entitled. This was just the kind of case in which it would be proper to mandamus Madison to deliver the commission. Unfortunately, however, this could not be done because the section of the Judiciary Act purporting to give the Supreme Court the power to issue a mandamus in the exercise of its original jurisdiction was unconstitutional. The Constitution clearly states the limits of the original jurisdiction of the Supreme Court and those limits Congress may not change. It could not, therefore, authorize the issuance of mandamus in original actions. The law purporting to give this new jurisdiction conflicts with the Constitution, and the Supreme Court, sworn to uphold the Constitution, must refuse to enforce the invalid statute. Thus was the doctrine of judicial review announced by the Supreme Court.

Now there are two facts about Marbury v. Madison which should be carefully noted. In the first place, the act of Congress held void was an act in which Congress had, in the Court's opinion, unconstitutionally tampered with the Court's own jurisdiction. It had tried to give to the Court powers which could not validly be given and the Court had protected itself against this legislative assault on its own integrity. Jefferson himself could not logically quarrel with the basic theory of the Court's action. He believed that each of the three departments of the Government must interpret the Constitution in so far as it bears upon its own powers and status, and may properly follow its own interpretation. No department is bound by the constitutional interpretation of any other department. In Marbury v. Madison the Court is simply saying to the Congress, "You must keep your hands off from us. You cannot enlarge our jurisdiction beyond constitutional limits." While some of Marshall's language is more generous, the case of Marbury v. Madison, viewed on its facts, does not establish the power of the Court to reach over its own fence and pass upon the validity of Congressional or Presidential acts which in no way affect the prerogatives or jurisdiction of the Court itself. Marshall nowhere asserts the superiority of the Court over Congress or the Executive, nor does he lay claim on the Court's behalf to any general power of supervision over the other two departments. In the second place, no other act of Congress was invalidated until the Dred Scott case in 1857. If the Supreme Court, under the doctrine of Marbury v. Madison, was supposed to enjoy the broad power to supervise the constitutional correctness with which Congress and the President exercised their own powers, it is rather surprising that during the fifty years following no attempt was made to seek the Court's decision as to the constitutionality of the Bank of the United States, a protective tariff, the acquisition of Louisiana, the annexation of Texas, and numerous other legislative or executive acts which aroused bitter constitutional dispute.

The second stage in the development of the power of judicial review was reached in the Dred Scott case decided in 1857. We cannot go into the fascinating story of this great case. It is enough for our purposes to know that the Court held that a Negro slave could not become a citizen of the United States, and that the Missouri Compromise Act of 1820, which forbade slavery in the federal territories north of 36° 30″, was unconstitutional. In thus forbidding slavery in the territories Congress had exercised a power not granted to it in the Constitution, a power which could not validly be implied from the delegated power to govern the territories. This represents an important enlargement of the scope of judicial review over the doctrine of Marbury v. Madison. Marshall's early decision had held that the Court could refuse to enforce laws purporting to change its own jurisdiction when the Court believed those laws to be invalid. In the Dred Scott case Taney and his colleagues go much further. They hold that the judgment of Congress as to the scope of one of its own legislative powers, this time a power in no way concerning the Court, is wrong and that the act so passed is unconstitutional. The Court, in other words, takes on the task of determining whether Congress has exercised powers which the Constitution has not delegated to it. Congress must stay in its own constitutional backyard and the Supreme Court, not Congress, is to determine whether it has done so.

The third stage in the growth of judicial guardianship over legislation came in the late eighties with the emergence of the Court's modern doctrine of due process of law. Here the Court added to its power of deciding whether Congress exercised undelegated power the much more far-reaching power of deciding whether Congress has exercised delegated power in an improper manner. Due process of law is a test, not of the existence of legislative power, but of the method of its exercise. The story back of this can be sketched only in the briefest way. The guarantee of due process of law traces its ancestory back to Magna Charta. After many permutations we find it set forth in the Fifth Amendment of the Federal Bill of Rights. There we read, "no person shall be deprived of life, liberty, or property without due process of law." Similar clauses are found in most state constitutions, and in 1868 the Fourteenth Amendment included an identical due process clause which applies to the states. The early history of due process of law was not spectacular. For a hundred years due process was held to be a limitation upon governmental procedure and not upon the substance or content of legislative policy. It required notice and hearing and a fair trial, but it did not forbid the legislature to regulate a social or economic problem. After the Fourteenth Amendment was adopted the Supreme Court, in its first case construing it, held that the due process clause had no relevance to, and could not, therefore, forbid an arbitrary state police regulation setting up a slaughterhouse monopoly in New Orleans. Due process seemed destined to remain the "forgotten clause" of the Constitution. But vast economic changes were taking place. The states began to deal with social and economic problems through more drastic exercises of their police powers, while the regulatory powers of Congress, especially under the commerce clause, were pushed far beyond previous limits. All this legislative activity was a sharp challenge to our American pioneer philosophy of *laissez faire*. Vested interests felt keenly the need of a constitutional weapon with which to combat the onward march of the new social control, and after a period of some wavering and uncertainty the Supreme Court, abandoning the precedents of a hundred years, converted the due process clauses of the Fifth and Fourteenth Amendments into judicial yardsticks by which to measure the validity of the substance and content of social legislation. Under the new rule a state or federal law was void as a denial of due process of law if in the opinion of the Court it impinged in an "arbitrary" manner upon the liberty or property rights of the individual. This step, taken without ostentation, constituted the greatest expansion of the Court's power to review legislation which has thus far occurred. Let me give a single illustration of the way in which the new doctrine enlarged judicial power. In 1898 Congress passed the Erdman Act regulating interstate railroads. One section of that act, aimed at the promotion of collective bargaining, forbade any interstate railroad to discharge one of its men because he belonged to a labor union. The Supreme Court held the act void on two grounds. It held first that this provision was not a regulation of interstate commerce because the relations between the railroad and its men had nothing to do with interstate commerce and did not, therefore, fall within the delegated power of Congress to regulate that commerce. It held, secondly, that, even if Congress had exercised its commerce power in passing the act, it had exercised it in so arbitrary and unreasonable a manner as to deprive the railroads of their liberty and property without due process of law. Congress had tried to exercise a power it did not have, but even if it had had the power, it had exercised it in an unconstitutional manner.

There is a fourth step in the development I am tracing. By it the Court has added to its scrutiny of the constitutional propriety of the *method* by which a granted power has been exercised by Congress, the further job of judging the constitutional propriety of the *purpose* for which the power has been used. This new technique was first employed in invalidating the first federal child labor act in 1918 in the case of Hammer *v.* Dagenhart. This act had forbidden the shipment in interstate commerce of the products of mines and factories in which children were employed in violation of standards set up in the act. In a five-to-four decision this was held void on two grounds. First, child labor is not closely enough connected with interstate commerce to make the statute a bona fide exercise of the delegated power to regulate commerce. Secondly, even if the statute were a bona fide exercise of the commerce power, it was an exercise of the commerce power for an unconstitutional *purpose,* namely, the regulation of child labor, a matter lying within the powers reserved to the states by the Tenth Amendment. Three New Deal measures of importance were invalidated on this same ground, that they constituted exercises of valid federal powers for invalid purposes. These acts were the Agricultural Adjustment Act, the Municipal Bankruptcy Act, and the Guffey Coal Act. In invalidating the AAA in the Butler case Mr. Justice Roberts did not hold the processing taxes and the paying of crop reduction benefits void on the ground that Congress was not exercising its delegated power to spend money. He held it void because the tax was levied in order to raise money to be spent for financing a scheme for the regulation of agriculture, an object which lies outside the delegated powers of Congress. The power was there, the method was regular, but the purpose was wrong. The Court has thus extended its supervision to the *motives* which have led Congress to exercise its delegated powers. "Thus," as Mr. Justice Cardozo put it, "the process of psychoanalysis has spread to unaccustomed fields."

To summarize this whole growth of judicial power, we find the Court at the outset protecting itself and its jurisdiction from unconstitutional interference by Congress. It next assumed the power to keep Congress from exercising powers not delegated to it by the Constitution. By a third step, the Court took over the authority to see that Congress and the States do not exercise their admitted powers by methods which seem to the Court to be arbitrary. Finally, the Court has undertaken to scrutinize legislative motives and to invalidate exercises of valid powers, by valid methods, but for wrongful purposes. Thus the judicial camel has got himself pretty completely into the legislative tent.

II. *The legislative and policy-determining character of the Supreme Court's power to declare laws void.* This brings me to the second major part of my discussion—the substitution, through the Court's power of judicial review, of judicial for legislative judgments on major questions of legislative policy. Has this come about in any large measure? If so, how has it come about, and with what practical results? My own view is that the Supreme Court now exercises wide power over the actual content of legislative policy. A very large proportion of the social and economic legislation invalidated in recent years has been held void not because it conflicted clearly and unmistakably with the clauses of the Constitution, but because a majority of the members of the Supreme Court believed the legislation to be economically unsound and objectionable. The Court exercises what I believe to be essentially a legislative veto. It is doing the legislature's job over again.

I am well aware that this charge would be sternly denied by the Supreme Court. As Professor Thomas Reed Powell has neatly put it, the Court has a very keen appreciation of "the rôle of rigmarole" in the judicial process. Proceeding on the theory "let not thy left hand know what thy right hand doeth," the Court continues to insist that the invalidating of a statute is an almost mechanical judicial process in which there is no room for personal opinion as to the social or economic merits of the legislation involved. In the very process of holding the Agricultural Adjustment Act void on grounds so strained and loosely reasoned as to reach almost a new low in judicial technique, Mr. Justice Roberts takes time out to restate the old orthodox incantation:

> When an act of Congress is appropriately challenged in the Courts as not conforming to the constitutional mandate, the judicial branch of the Government has only one duty—to lay the article of the Constitution which is invoked beside the statute which is challenged—and to decide whether the latter squares with the former. All the Court does, or can do, is to announce its considered judgment upon the question.

All of which sounds as though the justices, with the aid of compasses and slide rules, should reach a perfectly accurate result with which there can be no disagreement.

Now, certain clauses of the Constitution can be interpreted by the Supreme Court in this coldly mechanical manner. If Congress should fix federal income tax rates at a higher level in Illinois than in New York there could not be the slightest doubt that such an act violates the requirement of geographical uniformity in accordance with which the Constitution states that such taxes must be levied. It would be impossible for Congress to regulate criminal procedure in the federal courts in such a way as to violate the provisions of the federal Bill of Rights guaranteeing trial by ury, or protection against compulsory self-incrimination. It may be readily agreed that in such cases the Court could put the statute and the constitutional provision side by side and see at a glance that they do not jibe. Cases of this kind are exceedingly rare. They are rare because legislatures are not likely to indulge in self-advertised violations of the Constitution.

But these are not the cases in which the validity of social and economic legislation is involved or in which broad questions of legislative policy are at issue. If we examine the cases in which important legislative measures have been held by the Supreme Court to be valid or to be invalid over the last twenty years, we shall see that the constitutional provisions which these laws are supposed to violate do not have any clear, certain, and established meaning. What, for instance, are the major constitutional issues on which the validity of the principal New Deal measures turned? They are three in number. *First,* has Congress exercised some power not delegated to it? Or, concretely, can you reasonably hang the National Industrial Recovery Act on the constitutional "peg" of the commerce power, which Congress thought it was exercising when it passed the statute? *Second,* has Congress, or have the states, exercised some power in a manner so arbitrary or unreasonable as to amount to a deprivation of liberty or property without due process of law? *Third,* has Congress exercised some delegated power, such as the commerce power or the taxing power, for a purpose believed by the Court to be unconstitutional? There are no sharp, clear lines here between the constitutional and the unconstitutional, no categories of black and white, and in settling these issues the Court has come to exercise a type of judgment and discretion which is essentially legislative in character. Let us examine more closely just how the judicial process actually works in dealing with problems of this sort.

Let us turn first to the Minimum Wage Cases. In 1923 the Supreme Court by a five-to-three decision held that the due process clauses of the Constitution guarantee the right to pay women and children starvation wages. The Court clung to this shocking doctrine until last year when it held by a five-to-four vote that its previous decision was wrong and that minimum wage laws for women and minors do not deny due process of law. Now what actually happened here? A minimum wage law is an exercise of what we call the police power. The police power is that vital power of the American states to legislate for the public welfare. More specifically it is the power of the state to restrict individual freedom of action, or the free use of private property, in order to protect the health, morals, good order, convenience, or general welfare. A parking regulation, a quarantine of contagious disease, or an act forbidding gambling is each an exercise of the police power. Each exercise of the police power contains two elements. It restricts individual liberty and it protects or promotes some public social interest. The Court's task when it applies the test of due process of law to a legislative exercise of the police power is to weigh these two conflicting interests one against the other. If, in the opinion of the Court, the restriction upon individual liberty outweighs the social advantage claimed for the act, then it denies due process of law. Thus a majority of the Court prior to March, 1937 believed that minimum wage laws imposed upon employers and employees a burdensome restriction of their right to make free contracts with each other about wages, and that this restriction was not offset or compensated for by any equivalent social gain. The valued right of women and minors to work for next to nothing was at stake, and there was no substantial advantage to the community in having them paid a living wage. Then suddenly light came to one of the members of the Court and this balance between social advantage and restricted bargaining power was reversed. There were now five justices who believed that starvation wages for women and children were a sufficient social menace to warrant a legislative restriction on the free bargaining power of employers and employees, and as a result minimum wage laws suddenly became constitutional.

Now in reaching these important decisions the words of the Constitution have played no real part. The Constitution does not mention minimum wages and it does not explain what it means by due process of law. The Court therefore must decide whether or not a minimum wage law is valid without any direct help from the Constitution itself. The question is in essence not a legal question at all. It is a question of individual judgment and opinion and the answer which the individual judge makes to it will depend upon his social and economic philosophy, which, in turn, will depend upon his early environment and education and his business or professional associations. This is what Mr. Justice Stone was driving at when he said "It is difficult to imagine any grounds, other than our own personal economic predilections," for holding a minimum wage law void. And when the Supreme Court invalidates important legislation on the basis of its "own economic predilections" it is doing the work of a legislature and not of a court; it is determining questions of legislative policy and not questions of law. Minimum wage laws were unconstitutional for fourteen years not because the Constitution forbids them but because a majority of the Court believed them unsound and objectionable.

Let us examine next the Schechter case in which the Supreme Court held void the National Industrial Recovery Act. We may pass by that part of the Court's decision holding that the NIRA invalidly delegated legislative power to the President, because the statute could easily have been amended to avoid that constitutional defect. The crucial issue in the case was

whether Congress in the exercise of its delegated power to regulate interstate commerce could validly authorize the application of a code of fair
competition to a Brooklyn wholesale poultry market and punish violations
of that code. The Court, in a unanimous decision, held that it could not.
The Government urged that the transactions in the Schechters' poultry
market, and other similar establishments covered by the code, vitally affected the stream of interstate commerce in poultry in the metropolitan
area. Congress therefore could properly take measures to protect that interstate commerce against the harmful effects of bad labor conditions and unfair
competitive practices prevailing in the local markets. In a substantial number of cases the Court had permitted federal power to penetrate into local
affairs in order to protect interstate commerce from the effects of local evils
or local discrimination. The Supreme Court did not repudiate these earlier
decisions. It did not even deny that conditions prevailing in the Schechters'
poultry market had an influence upon the interstate commerce which Congress might lawfully regulate. It merely held that that influence was "indirect" and not "direct" and therefore the code could not be sustained under
the commerce power. Here is an important act of Congress stricken down
by the Court because it falls on the wrong side of the line by which the Court
separates those transactions and interests which are "directly" connected
with interstate commerce from those which are only "indirectly" connected
with it. It is perfectly clear that in making such a decision and in drawing
such a line the Court translates into a rule of constitutional law its own
opinions as to how far the policy of federal centralization under the commerce power should be permitted to go, again a question of policy, a question
of expediency, thinly disguised as a question of law.

There is a third type of decision in which the Court even more clearly
assumes the rôle of the lawmaker. These are the cases in which the Court
invalidates acts of Congress because delegated powers have been used for
what the Court regards as wrongful purposes. Some of the best illustrations
have arisen under the federal taxing power. In 1902, Congress, under pressure from the powerful lobby representing the dairy interests of the country,
drove colored oleomargarine out of the market by levying on it a prohibitive
tax of ten cents per pound. Two years later in the McCray case the
Supreme Court upheld the statute against the charge that it was an abuse
of the federal taxing power since its purpose was not revenue but destruction.
The Court refused to inquire into or worry about the motives which had
led Congress to pass the act. Such motives cannot properly be made the
subject of judicial scrutiny. The oleomargarine tax is "on its face" a
revenue measure. It is, in short, "objectively" constitutional, and whether
it is "subjectively" unconstitutional, whether Congress had an ulterior and

unconstitutional purpose in levying it, is none of the Court's business. A year ago this doctrine was reaffirmed in a case in which Congress had im posed a special license tax of $200 per year upon those engaged in sellin, machine-guns, sawed-off shotguns or rifles, and silencers. "On its face," says Mr. Justice Stone, "it is a taxing measure" and "inquiry into the hidden motives which may move Congress to exercise a power constitution ally conferred upon it is beyond the competency of the Court." The good faith of Congress is evidenced by the fact that twenty-seven people paid the tax in 1934 and twenty-two in 1935, so it must have been a revenue measure In 1919, however, Congress imposed a tax of ten per cent upon the net in come of those employing children in violation of the standards set up in th act. It had also passed the Future Trading Act by which a tax of twent, cents a bushel was laid upon all grain sold on future contracts upon grai exchanges which were not registered with the Secretary of Agriculture an subject to his regulations. The Supreme Court held both of these statute unconstitutional. The taxes levied were not really taxes at all. They wer penalties imposed on those who indulge in practices which Congress object to but may not directly forbid. Speaking of the child labor tax Chief Justic Taft declared, "Its prohibitory and regulatory effect and purpose are pal pable. All others can see and understand this. How can we properly shu our minds to it?" How indeed, except by just following the sound an wholesome doctrine of the oleomargarine tax case that the motives leadin, Congress to exercise a delegated power are not a proper subject for judicia examination. But this the Court was not willing to do. Last year the cour applied the rule of the Child Labor Tax Case to a federal statute imposin, an annual license tax of $1000 upon anyone engaging in the business o selling liquor in violation of the laws of a state. This, again, is a fisca penalty and not a tax and encroaches, therefore, upon state power.

Now the Court in these tax cases has very deftly managed to eat its cak and keep it too. It invalidated the child labor tax without overruling it decision in the oleomargarine tax case. It has, therefore, both rules t play with and can select with a good deal of freedom which prohibitory o regulatory federal taxes it is going to hold valid and which it is going t hold void. Looking at them realistically there is no essential differenc in the nature of these taxes or the privileges or interests upon which the fall. Congress taxes the privilege of making colored oleomargarine, th privilege of employing children, the privilege of selling the kinds of weapon with which gangster crimes are usually committed, or the privilege of oper ating as a bootlegger within a state. Congress could not directly forbi anyone to exercise any of these privileges on which it has laid its tax. I every case the tax is for a non-fiscal purpose and everybody knows i

When the Court approves of the regulatory policy involved in the tax it turns a blind eye to the obvious effect of the tax and applies the test of "objective constitutionality." But with equal ease it can invalidate a similar regulatory tax, by taking into account "what everybody knows" and applying the test of "subjective constitutionality." In deciding which formula to use the Court is able to give effect to its own views as to the expediency of the legislative policy involved, it is able to exercise a policy-determining power.

I have no patience with the pious verbal expressions and legal epigrams by which certain judges and lawyers seek to camouflage or to conceal the essentially legislative power which the Court exercises in the handling of these three groups of cases and many others. In applying these vague and general clauses of the Constitution to concrete cases the Court has the opportunity, and it embraces the opportunity, of giving effect to its hunches, its predilections, and its prejudices. In interpreting due process of law it may read into the Constitution either a progressive social philosophy or a Mid-Victorian theory of "rugged individualism." In setting the limits to the commerce power it may swing the balance toward an aggressive federal centralization or toward an equally vigorous protection of state rights. In my judgment the legislative power which the Supreme Court now wields in the exercise of its power of judicial review of legislation is far greater than can be soundly adjusted to the principles of democratic government. Our constitutional system rests on the principle that the legislative power of the United States is vested in the Congress. It is not vested in the Supreme Court. It seems to me one of the vicious paradoxes of our national democracy that so many vital questions of national policy are determined in the last analysis by the "personal economic predilections" of Supreme Court justices.

III. *Can the Supreme Court be divested of its undemocratic assumption of legislative power?* This brings me to my final and very practical topic—Can the Supreme Court be divested of its undemocratic assumption of legislative power? How can we establish a sounder and more democratic balance between the legislative and judicial powers under the American Constitution? I have two answers to this question, but before explaining them, may I mention some proposals which I do not favor? I do not believe that the Supreme Court should be deprived of its power to declare acts of Congress unconstitutional. I do not attach much importance to the suggestions that Congress should so alter the appellate jurisdiction of the Supreme Court as to reduce substantially the number of chances the Court would have to pass on the validity of laws. I have never been enthusiastic about the proposal to require seven or more of the nine members of the Supreme Court to concur in declaring a statute void. Such a rule does not go to the root of the problem and I doubt if it would accomplish any very important results. I am not in favor of giving Congress the power to override decisions of the Supreme Court declaring acts of Congress void, although I should be glad indeed to see rather similar results attained by making our clumsy process of federal constitutional amendment simpler and more democratic. I merely state my views on these points as I do not have time to explain my reasons for holding them.

The first of my proposals is a very simple and wholly unspectacular one. It does not upset anything and it would, I believe, increase rather than weaken the Court's prestige. It is the simple proposal that the Court shall of its own volition abandon the job of legislating and confine itself to the task of judging; that in reviewing legislation it shall accord what Mr. Justice Washington over a hundred years ago called "a decent respect due to the legislative body by which any law is passed." This is, of course, exactly what the Supreme Court officially claims that it does, and no one would endorse my suggestion more heartily, in all probability, than those justices who have been among the most ruthless in overriding legislation on the basis of "personal economic predilections."

But what I have in mind is not a matter of words. It is a thing of the spirit, a positive and aggressive determination on the part of the Court to encroach just as little as possible upon legislative discretion, a complete unwillingness to invalidate a statute if any reasonable ground can be discovered upon which it may be sustained. This was the life-long judicial philosophy of Mr. Justice Holmes. Justices Brandeis, Cardozo, and Stone now uphold this doctrine of judicial tolerance. It claims the adherence of Chief Justice Hughes not infrequently and of Mr. Justice Roberts once in a while. This attitude is peculiarly necessary in applying the nebulous test of due process of law to social and economic legislation. Whether such legislation is "arbitrary" or not, is, after all, a matter of opinion and the legislature is entitled to its opinion even if that opinion be mistaken or foolish. "There is nothing that I more deprecate," said Mr. Justice Holmes, "than the use of the Fourteenth Amendment beyond the absolute compulsion of its words to prevent the making of social experiments that an important part of the community desires, in the insulated chambers afforded by the several states, even though the experiments may seem futile or even noxious to me and to those whose judgment I most respect." There is certain irony in the fact that Holmes came to be universally regarded as a great liberal. Every advocate of social and economic reform regarded him as an ally. And so he was—but not always in the sense in which they thought him to be. There is reason to believe that Holmes had little use for a large amount of the social and economic reform which he voted to hold constitutional. In his own social philosophy he was a fairly conservative man. But he believed firmly in two things—first, as he neatly put it, "I am not God"; second, an American legislature possesses what Lowell called in the Bigelow Papers "the right to be a cussed fool," and that right must be respected and protected by the Supreme Court. Holmes's liberalism was the liberalism of tolerance, often a disgusted tolerance, a tolerance grounded on respect for the integrity of the legislature's own job no matter how stupidly that job was done. That attitude on the part of the Court is vitally necessary at the present time. Its attainment and the development of a tradition which would make it permanent would do more to restore the Supreme Court to its proper place in the American Constitutional system than any of the drastic proposals which I mentioned and discarded a moment ago.

Is there any hope of securing such an attitude upon the part of the Court towards legislation? I believe there is even if results of this somewhat intangible sort may not be achieved all at once. There are two ways in which progress may be made. One is by the slow process of education. This means education within the legal profession so that lawyers who attain seats on the Bench will have a sound and wise understanding of the nature of the judge's job with respect to legislation. It means education on a broader base so that there may be an increasingly well-informed public opinion to insist upon the appointment to the Bench of men who have this attitude. We are beginning to profit from the results of this educational movement which has been going on for twenty years or more. A second way in which progress may be made is by focusing attention and public pressure upon the Presidential appointment of judges of the right kind and upon their confirmation by the Senate. I cannot develop this in detail. Our existing system of choosing Supreme Court justices does not give us as good results as it should. We get a few distinguished men, a good many able men, and now and again somebody definitely below par. The country is entitled to have on the Bench judicial statesmen. The traditions surrounding Supreme Court appointments must be so shaped as to secure them. It must be made good politics for the President to name such men and for the Senate to confirm them. The making of these vitally important appointments should never be casually inadvertent. It might be wise if the rules of the Senate should forbid the confirmation of major judicial appointments in less than thirty days so that full and open hearings may be had upon the qualifications of the men named by the President. Progress along these lines may be slow and erratic, but I believe that public opinion in this country is coming to see the importance of securing the right kind of Supreme Court justices and that we shall build up the kind of traditions which will insure their appointment.

I have a second proposal to make. This we may fall back on if we fail to persuade the Supreme Court to abdicate voluntarily its legislative and policy-determining functions and to adopt the wise tolerance toward legislative discretion which Mr. Justice Holmes preached and practiced. This proposal is that we adopt clarifying amendments to the Constitution which will sharpen the meaning of its clauses, make clear the scope of its delegations of power, and the impact of its limitations. The Court in construing the commerce clause or the due process clause is engaged in making broad decisions of policy which do not properly belong to a judicial body. We could relieve it of that power by clarifying those clauses so that their meaning and application is no longer a matter of honest dispute. If we wish to make sure that the power of Congress under the commerce clause includes the regulation of laboring conditions under which goods are made for the interstate market, then let us say so with definiteness and precision. If we are tired of having the due process of law clause used by conservative judges to throttle needed social legislation, let us make clear what we wish the due process limitation to mean, or discard it altogether. I believe that the Court itself would welcome such a change. I believe we should all be better satisfied if, without impairing the integrity or the traditions of our judicial system, we left to the Court the task of applying constitutional clauses which have reasonably definite meaning, instead of attacking it for giving what we feel is the wrong meaning to clauses so vague as to have no clear and concrete meaning of their own. Our whole judicial system would gain in efficiency, and in public confidence, under such a change.

I have traced the stages through which the Supreme Court has gradually acquired the vast and far-reaching power over legislation which it now exercises. I have undertaken to show that this power has enabled the Court to dominate wide ranges of legislative policy in the light of the opinions and prejudices of the justices, and I have suggested that this exercise of essentially legislative power by a court of law conflicts with the democratic principle upon which we have built our governmental system. I have no patience with the attitude of constitutional ancestor-worship which rejects as sacrilege any change in the Constitution or in the Supreme Court's power of judicial review, but I have no desire to see the power of judicial review pulled up by the roots or mutilated. Let the Supreme Court clean its own house. Let it replace an arrogantly ruthless attitude toward the exercise by Congress of its legislative discretion, by the tolerant aloofness which bespeaks the judge and not the lawmaker. Let the President and the Senate place on the Supreme Court men who appraise correctly the relation between the Court and Congress. If the Supreme Court cannot or will not do this let us, instead of changing the Court or changing its power of judicial review, change the concrete nature of the job which we give it to do. Let us withdraw from the reach of its interpretation those vast uncharted ranges of discretion which come from vague and general clauses of the Constitution. Let us sharpen and clarify the sections in the construction of which the Court now finds it possible to impose its policy judgments upon the country. By following this course we shall preserve and strengthen the best features of the American system of judicial review of legislation. We shall get rid of its weaknesses and its dangers. The Supreme Court of the United States will become not an obstacle but an aid to the smooth and efficient working of democratic government in a great nation.

No. 73

THE DIVINE RIGHT OF JUDGES [1]

by Max Lerner

A LONG view of the power of the Supreme Court is difficult to achieve in the midst of immediate issues and angry passions. But it would start with the fact that what the court is doing now, in smashing the best legislative efforts of the community, is no novelty, just as the attacks on the court are no novelty. It would try to get at the nature, the psychological roots, and the economic consequences of the power of judicial review —presumably America's most beautiful and original gift to the art of government.

Judicial review is a political device by which the court passes on the constitutional validity of legislative and executive acts. It enables the judges to apportion powers between the states and the national government, and between the legislative, executive, and judicial branches. This is a power nowhere to be found expressly granted in the Constitution itself. But it has by this time written itself into the Constitution by court interpretation, and although only a custom it has become as commonly accepted as if it were clearly granted in the document.

There are two opposing theories as to how the power grew up. One is the usurpation theory. It goes back to Jefferson and is repeated afresh in every period of constitutional crisis. It holds that judicial review is sheer usurpation and that the Supreme Court has deliberately filched powers belonging to other departments. This point of view is generally highlighted with charges of tyranny that transport us back into the pages of Plutarch.

[1] Max Lerner, "The Divine Right of Judges," *The Nation* (January 29, 1936), Vol. 142, pp. 121-123. Reprinted by permission of *The Nation*.

The other is the Federalist view that the judicial power flows inherently from the nature of our federal system, and that without it our government would be unworkable and our democracy unthinkable.

I shall confess I cannot subscribe to either of these theories, although they both offer fragments of the final answer. It is true that there have been some men on our court with a will to power. And it is true, on the other side, that given our federal-state governmental system, if both the states and the nation try to ride the same horse someone must finally decide who shall ride in front. But a clearer answer than either would be that the court's power is a natural outcome of the necessity for maintaining capitalist dominance under democratic forms; that judicial review has proved to be a very convenient channel through which the driving forces of American economic life have found expression and achieved victory. Such a view could be documented by reference to the history of the judicial power since Marshall first established it in 1803 by his decision in Marbury *vs.* Madison. The high points in the story would be Marshall's use of the judicial power to give enlarged scope to the expansion of business enterprise, the development of the doctrine of due process of law after the Civil War, and the reading of a laissez faire social philosophy into the Constitution in the decades around the turn of the century.

To-day the court is reenacting the role it has always played whenever a resurgence of popular feeling has threatened to sweep away some of the established power of business enterprise. Nor has there been in all this any consistency of judicial doctrine or political theory. When the people have gained control of the state legislatures, as happened in Marshall's day and in the decades of agrarian revolt, the court has denied power to the states and concentrated it in the federal government. But when, as is true now, the people have captured the federal offices, then the court denies power to the federal government and reserves it where it must be ineffective in the task of business regulation—with the state governments. The Republicans now find themselves amazingly the devoted adherents of states' rights, and the Democrats (shades of the Jeffersonian tradition!) are earnestly seeking to increase the national power.

There are several rather striking misconceptions to-day about the court's power and function. One is that judges decide as they do because they can do no other—that they follow an inflexible path of constitutional doctrine. Only a little less far from the truth is the second and opposite misconception—that the judges are untrammelled in the expression of their own social attitudes and that they can play ducks and drakes with judicial precedent. What are actually the limits within which the Supreme Court has to work? It can decide only specific cases and not abstract questions

—the case of the Schechter brothers, for example, and how they sell their chickens—and out of those specific judgments the body of constitutional law grows up. Once a case is settled, however, a rule of law is established for future decisions, and every judge must abide by it (*stare decisis*) regardless of his previous views. The court works, moreover, within a difficult technical tradition, under a limited jurisdiction, and with severe procedural regulations. Finally, its role with respect to legislation is negative and passive. It can initiate nothing of itself. But after you have said all that, the fact remains that the judge retains a great latitude of decision. On the same set of facts in the Hoosac case, after hearing the same arguments and reading the same briefs, with the same body of precedent to draw on, possessed of the same degree of integrity and patriotism, Mr. Justice Roberts comes to one constitutional conclusion and Mr. Justice Stone to exactly the opposite one. What can explain this? Only the hypothesis that the judge works within limits and with material flexible enough to allow for personal choice. The *determining* factor becomes not some rigorous rule but the judge's own social philosophy. This in turn is shaped by his class roots, his education, his experience, and the elements in the contemporary climate of opinion to which he is responsive.

There is another misconception. We tend to believe that the court shows its power only when it declares an act of Congress unconstitutional. Actually the court has exercised this judicial veto only on some sixty occasions, many of them of slight moment. The judicial veto represents the outer limits of the court's power. It shows how far that power can go. But usually the court influences the shaping of an act even before it is passed, for the knowledge that the act will have to run the gauntlet of judicial review is a sovereign acid for eating away features that the court will predictably disallow. Once the act is passed it may be whittled into ineffectiveness (as happened with the antitrust legislation) without any actual declaration of unconstitutionality, or the agency set up (like the Federal Trade Commission) may be crippled by court interpretation without being destroyed outright. Thus the court's power is broader and more continuous than the exercise of its veto. Even when it upholds legislation it is directing our economic life. The entire landscape of life as it is lived to-day by the common man is ultimately at the mercy of the court's action or sufferance.

The essence of the court's position in our system is that it takes problems that are primarily economic and clashes of interest that are economic, and translates them into terms of legal doctrine. It thus becomes the bottleneck of economic policy. I believe that is the one overwhelming fact that we must face to-day. As long as economic issues are fought out frankly as such, their solution lies with the people and with their representatives in the legislature. But when economic issues are translated into legalistic terms, when the question of the fate of the farmers and workers and housewives and working children becomes a matter of hosts of none-too-angelic lawyers dancing on the needle of due process of law, then the big electoral battalions are left helpless. If we face it clearly, looking beyond the tangle of our traditional usages, the question of what we shall do with our farms and our factories is not ultimately a question for lawyers or judges to settle. It is a question of economic and social policy. To allow our economic policy to be shaped by the judges is wrong whichever way you look at it. If they decide, as is often claimed, on purely legal grounds, then those are the *wrong grounds* on which to decide questions of economic policy. If they decide, as is sometimes admitted, on economic and social grounds, then they are the *wrong people* to be intrusted with decisions on these grounds, for they are judicial and not economic technicians.

In passing thus on economic policy the Supreme Court has throughout our history functioned as the last bulwark of the possessing classes. It has always been a final line of defense for them, a sort of Hindenburg line that would stand fast when all else crumbled. Beaten at the polls, in danger of having the economic institutions of a plutocracy leveled by the political forces of a democracy, the defeated group has always turned to the court for shelter and has found it in the safe haven of constitutional law. Jefferson discovered this fact when he and his party of small farmers and mechanics turned the Federalist propertied interests out of Congress and the Presidency in 1800, only to find them dug in again behind the earthworks of the court. Jackson discovered it in the 1830's, Lincoln in the 1850's, the agrarian leaders in the eighties and nineties, the Progressives such as La Follette and Theodore Roosevelt as the century ended. And now Mr. Roosevelt is discovering it afresh. It seems to be the fate of American reformers to conduct their education in public.

Each of these men sought to attack the court. In no case has the court's power been successfully limited. What accounts for this extraordinary toughness and viability of the court? The defenders of the court answer that its survival indicates the hollowness of the attacks on it. What is involved is evidently a medieval ordeal by fire, proving innocence. But the successive crises of the judicial power can no more be exorcised by this sort of mumbo-jumbo than can the crises of the economic system. Each attack on the judicial power in America has not been merely an unaccountable bit of behavior of the democratic mass. It has been the expression, in constitutional terms, of the inability of our state to adjust its own power-relations and resolve its own contradictions. And for that reason each successive crisis of the judicial power has taken its color, its substance, its tension from the contemporary stage of the struggle of economic groups and classes.

This is happening to-day too. And to-day, as in the past, the court will survive the attack on it, not because of any inherent rightness in the judicial power, but because the larger number of our people still have a sense of the sanctity of the court. What used to be the divine right of kings has now been replaced by the divine right of judges.

There are several elements in this pattern of divine right as it exists in the popular mind. One is the fact that we have been encouraged for over a century to make a fetish of the Constitution. Every people needs some form of anchorage, some link with the invariant. The Rock of Ages is as essential to political as it is to religious life. In fact, the habits of mind begotten by an authoritarian Bible carry over to an authoritarian Constitution; and a country like ours, in which our early tradition had prohibited a state church, ends by getting a state church after all. To be sure, not all who make a fetish of the Constitution believe in it. There are many newspaper and political groups which appeal to the sanctity of the Constitution with their eyes fixed on the immensities and their hands reaching out for their own special interests. And yet with the larger number of our people the belief that the Constitution is sacred beyond change is a genuine belief, and must be reckoned with.

The second psychological element in the tradition of the divine right of judges is the belief that the Supreme Court is the special guardian of the Constitution—and a better guardian than Congress or the President. Part of John Marshall's genius lay in his skill in pushing into the background the power that the court was gaining over economic policy, and thrusting into the foreground its role of guardianship. This the later judges have encouraged by their continued utterances, and it has become the official theory of the court's power. The judges have thus been associated in our minds with the function of protection rather than with the struggle for power.

The third element has been the tradition of judicial neutrality. We have somehow placed the judges above the battle. Despite every proof to the contrary the common man attributes to them the objectivity and infallibility that are ultimately attributes only of godhead. The tradition persists that they belong to no economic group or class; that they are not touched by economic interests; that their decisions proceed through some inspired way of arriving at the truth; that they sit in their robes like haughty gods, unaffected by the prejudices that move common men.

How long a myth built of such baseless fabric can continue is another matter. It is undoubtedly weakening and may be expected in the end to crumble. Meanwhile, however, its force and its hold on the popular mind are enough to daunt Mr. Roosevelt and keep him from making an open attack on the court's power. In the end it will not be the Roosevelts who will restore to the popular will the power of deciding on economic issues. The Supreme Court may be expected to be its own bitterest enemy. Even the myth of the divine right of judges will not survive many more decisions like Mr. Justice Roberts's masterly essay in obfuscation in the Hoosac case.

No. 74

THE INCIDENCE OF JUDICIAL CONTROL OVER CONGRESS [1]

by Henry W. Edgerton

JUSTICE HOLMES said: "I do not think the United States would come to an end if we lost our power to declare an Act of Congress void. I do think the Union would be imperilled if we could not make that declaration as to the laws of the several States." It may be necessary to national survival that some national tribunal have authority to decide that acts of state legislatures are inconsistent with the Federal Constitution. Judicial supremacy over national legislation rests on no such necessity. Whether to preserve, restrict, or abolish the power of courts to hold acts of Congress void is a pure question of policy, the answer to which should depend on the character of the results which the present system has produced and is, therefore, likely to produce. How and when the system originated, what were the attitudes of the founding fathers toward it, whether it is in some sense a usurpation are questions with which scholars have dealt. There has been much discussion of the relation in which particular constitutional decisions stand to other decisions and to the original Constitution and its amendments. Little serious attention has been paid to the practical question of the incidence of the courts' control over Congress, i.e., its effect or tendency,

[1] Henry W. Edgerton, "The Incidence of Judicial Control over Congress," *The Cornell Law Quarterly* (April, 1937), Vol. 22, pp. 299-301, 246-248. Reprinted by permission of the author and *The Cornell Law Quarterly*. As the analysis of specific cases and the footnotes are omitted from this material as reprinted here, everyone is urged to read the article in full as it appeared in *The Cornell Law Quarterly;* Reorganization of the Federal Judiciary: Hearings before the Committee on the Judiciary, United States Senate, 75th Congress, 1st Session, on S. 1392, A Bill to Reorganize the Judicial Branch of the Government (1937), pp. 1881-1912; or *Selected Essays on Constitutional Law,* published under the Auspices of the Association of American Law Schools (1938), Book 1, pp. 793-844.

as between different social groups and interests. On that point there has been much summary assertion but little proof.

A full treatment of this subject would deal with all reported cases in which any court has held an act of Congress void; the number and character of the acts which Congress has been deterred from enacting, or encouraged to enact, by the prospect of judicial review; the uncertainty which often exists between the passage of a law and the Supreme Court's disposition of it; the question whether the relative abstinence from political effort of American as compared to European intellectuals is due to the knowledge that desired legislation, even if its passage is secured, may not become "law." With most of this the present article will not deal. It will consider only the cases in which the Supreme Court has held an act, or part of an act, of Congress unconstitutional. Decisions of the same sort by other courts which were reversed or not passed on by the Supreme Court are too many to be treated in an article; moreover, they have been relatively local in their effects. The difficulty of dealing objectively at present with the Supreme Court's disposition of "New Deal" legislation, and the inherent uncertainty regarding the effects of much of it, seem sufficient reasons for not considering statutes passed after March 4, 1933. This article aims to consider briefly all the cases in which earlier acts of Congress have been annulled by the Supreme Court.

Congress does not contravene the black-and-white clauses of the Constitution, like that which allots two Senators to each State. The conflicts between Congress and the Court have related to the indefinite clauses, like those which deal with interstate commerce, due process, and executive power. It is familiar that the relation of a law to these broad clauses is not a matter of fact but a matter of opinion. Congress in all the cases to be considered, and members of the Court in many, differed in opinion from the majority of the Court. This paper is not concerned with the question whether the congressional or the judicial opinion seems, in general or in a given case, the more reasonable. In other words, it is not concerned with the soundness or propriety, from a technical point of view, of the decisions. It does not discuss the commerce clause or any other clause of the Constitution. Neither is it concerned with the backgrounds, beliefs, and desires that led Congress to pass the laws, or the Court to annul them. There is no question, in my mind, of the high motives of the Court. I am concerned only with the practical effects and tendencies of the nullifying decisions. What interests, individual or social, do they protect; and, conversely, whose ox is gored? Has judicial supremacy been, on the whole, neutral in its incidence; or has it tended to protect the interests of a relatively poor and unprivileged majority on the one hand, or of a relatively well-to-do minority on the other?

It is always difficult, and usually impossible, to determine how different things would be if they were not as they are. The effects of the decisions cannot be fully known. The possibilities in that direction cannot be exhausted in one article, or by one man. A vast amount of contemporary material would need to be studied. Treatises would have to be written, from a special angle, on all the topics with which the various decisions deal, including, for example, taxation and trial by jury. This paper is offered as an introduction to a neglected subject. It deals, for the most part, with direction rather than distance. If the tendencies of the decisions fit into a pattern, conclusions not too tentative can be drawn regarding their collective incidence.

[The detailed analysis of the acts of Congress held unconstitutional by the Supreme Court is omitted here. Everyone interested in the subject, however, is urged to read the examination of these cases in the original article.]

CONCLUSION

To repeat, with motives, and with the relative reasonableness of conflicting congressional and judicial views on vague standards like interstate commerce and due process, this paper is not concerned. It is concerned only with the practical effects and tendencies of judicial supremacy. The discussion might be expanded by considering acts of Congress which the Supreme Court has upheld against attack. But apart from the period of uncertainty which precedes the decision, judicial supremacy produces, in connection with a statute which is upheld, no effect whatever, since the statute would necessarily be upheld if there were no such thing as judicial supremacy. Some of the cases in which the Supreme Court has annulled state legislation have had more effect than many in which it has annulled acts of Congress. But cases involving state legislation, besides being too many to be treated in an article, are foreign to the subject of this one. The supremacy of courts over state legislatures and the supremacy of courts over Congress stand on different ground. If the one sort of control is a practical necessity, it does not follow that the other is; and if the one sort has protected certain interests it does not follow that the other has protected like inerests. In the control of state legislation there have been deviations, including certain free speech cases, from the pattern of the federal cases. What should be done about the one sort of control and what should be done about the other are different questions.

Exhaustive investigation would reveal more than this brief inquiry about the effects of many of the decisions. It might modify the views expressed here regarding some of them. It is unlikely that it would seriously qualify the conclusions which follow.

Of the pre-New Deal cases in which the Supreme Court annulled acts of Congress, one group protected mistreatment of colored people; another group protected businesses or business methods hurtful to the majority; another, comprising employers' liability, workmen's compensation, minimum wage, child labor, and union membership cases, protected owners of business at the direct expense of labor; another protected owners of business against taxation; another protected the recipients of substantial incomes, gifts, and inheritances against taxation; and other cases protected the interests of property owners in other ways. Not many cases of any importance fall outside these categories. A few decisions were approximately neutral in their incidence as between different social groups. Rich and poor were given theoretically equal assurance that for various offenses they must be indicted before they are tried, and must be tried by a jury of twelve. But few persons ever find themselves in a position to be affected by such decisions, and any benefit which they may confer is uncertain, slight, and probably less equal in practice than in theory. Moreover, the statutes which those decisions annulled were limited to Chinese, to Alaska, or to the District of Columbia, and there is no reason to assume that their principle would have been extended, as the principle of the minimum wage would obviously have been extended, if its local application had been upheld. There is not a case in the entire series which protected the "civil liberties" of freedom of speech, press, and assembly; on the contrary, over the protest of Holmes and Brandeis, the Espionage Act was not merely upheld but extended by the Court. There is not one which protected the right to vote; on the contrary, congressional attempts to protect the voting rights of Negroes were defeated by the Court. There is not one which protected the vital interests of the working majority of the population in organizing or in wages; on the contrary, congressional efforts to protect those interests were frustrated by the Court.

So much is objective, more or less. Subjectively, according to one's social philosophy, it may follow that judicial supremacy over Congress is good, bad, or indifferent. The cult of "the Constitution," which contemplates chiefly this power of the courts, illustrates the connection between conventional standards and the interests of dominant groups. In one who identifies the country with the well-to-do minority of its population, enthusiasm for judicial control over Congress is as logical as enthusiasm can be. It is hard to see why, apart from convention, one who does not make that identification should share that enthusiasm. When a legal scholar says,

"I am for continuance of the Supreme Court's power of review. I think that it has proved its worth. . . . I think that over the long haul the Court has done a superb job," I wonder what cases seem to him so valuable as to outweigh the *Dred Scott* case, which helped to entrench slavery; the *Civil Rights* and related cases, which protected the oppression of Negroes; the employers' liability and workmen's compensation cases, which denied relief to injured workmen; the child labor and minimum wage cases, which protected the hiring of women and children at starvation wages; the income tax cases, which prevented the shifting of tax burdens from the poor to the rich; and the many minor instances in which the Court's review has done harm to common men.

No. 75

THE FATE OF THE SUPREME COURT [1]

by Max Lerner

IN the halcyon days before the Schechter decision Professor Corwin of Princeton had the courage to write a book under the title *The Twilight of the Supreme Court*. He said that the court was on its way to a dignified but ineffectual old age, and that its sun was setting. The book was a good book and a learned book. It was well reasoned, and its conclusion should have been a sound one. But scarcely was the ink dry on its pages when the court handed down the first of its series of hostile decisions on the Roosevelt legislation. Instead of subsiding into twilight, it shone forth with the blaze of noonday strength.

The moral is, I suppose, that it is always bad policy to compose a man's obituary before he is for certain dead. Yet Professor Corwin was less wrong than would appear. During the next decade or more the power of the Supreme Court will undoubtedly be challenged as never before. But if there is a decline in the court's power it will not come about by any gentle slipping into euthanasia. It will come about only after a stiff fight. There are any nummber of evidences that the fight has already begun. The court is now entering its iron age.

For one thing we are witnessing the first signs of a crack-up in what I called in my first article the sense of the divine right of judges. While Americans are still strongly imbued with it, they are no longer in a complete innocence about such matters. They are beginning to learn that judicial decisions are not babies brought by constitutional storks but are

---

[1] Max Lerner, "The Fate of the Supreme Court," *The Nation* (March 25, 1936). Vol. 142, pp. 379-381. Reprinted by permission of *The Nation*.

born out of the travail of economic circumstance. The poll held after the Hoosac decision by the American Institute of Public Opinion showed that some 53 per cent of those polled were in favor of requiring more than a Supreme Court majority to invalidate an act of Congress. That is in itself almost a revolution in American opinion. And the crack-up in opinion will grow every year as economic collapse makes legislation on a national scale more necessary.

But the court will have ample support in the struggle that lies ahead. It will have of course the driving force of the vested interests with all their control over the molding of public opinion. But it will have even more powerfully the strongest support that any tribunal or institution can have— namely, fear. I do not mean fear of the court, fear of the judicial power, the fear that one has of the whiplash of tyrants. I mean fear of not having the court. I mean the terrible fear of change and the unknown, which is to so many people more powerful than the felt needs and pressures of to-day. It is fear and not will that underlies a good part of our politics— the creeping fear of people who do not want to make decisions, and prefer to surrender their decisions to others. This sort of womb-retreat is no unknown thing to political psychology. It is a phenomenon familiar enough in fascism. We are just beginning now in America really to explore and understand the length and breadth and depth of the middle-class mentality in our politics. For that mentality the court's ancient sureness seems something not to be abandoned, lest we confront an uncharted future. If this is only a social myth it has thus far been a necessary one. It will have to do until we build a new set of necessary myths that are emotionally rooted not in fear but in the collective will, and economically rooted not in the class power of the dominant group but in an expanding economy for all. When that has happened, the struggle over the judicial power will be over, and the Supreme Court's iron age will be at an end.

Proposals for dealing with the court have been thick as blackberries. They have come from professional and amateur constitutionalists of every kind. They fall into three general groups: the remedial proposals, those looking toward a Congressional curb on the court's power, and those looking toward a constitutional amendment.

The first group, the remedial, implies the existence and desirability of the court's power. They are more concerned with lopping off the excrescences of that power than with challenging it. Perhaps the simplest proposal is that of a eugenics program for the court. Just as the vitality of the race is held by some to depend on selective breeding and thus getting the right babies, so the proper functioning of the judicial power is held to depend on getting the right judges. And that of course goes back to getting the right Presidents, who will appoint the right judges, who will in turn render the right decisions. This view, of course, sees judicial decisions as almost entirely a matter of the personnel of the court. Everything depends on the individual judge. In this sense, such a view is too optimistic. Individual judges are themselves products: their minds and their direction have been shaped by the dominant institutional forces of our life. Another difficulty is that getting the right President does not seem to insure getting the right judge. Examine the present composition of the court and you will find that Justice Brandeis, leader of the liberals, and Justice McReynolds, the most inveterate tory of them all, were appointees of President Wilson. Justices Roberts and Cardozo, confronting each other in opposite judicial trenches, were appointees of President Hoover.

More drastic than the pious hope that better justices will be appointed is the movement for advisory opinions. At present a law is enacted, administrative machinery is set up to enforce it, taxes are levied, government and business expenditures are made on the strength of it, men are set to work—only to have the court, in passing finally on a specific case, declare the whole thing unconstitutional. The proposal for advisory opinions would have Congress get from the judges their opinion on the constitutionality of a projected law before it had come into force and economic interests had become entangled with it. The great merit of this proposal is that it would do away with our present uncertainties. And one of the refreshing things about it is that, like the child in the Hans Christian Andersen tale, it innocently announces the nakedness of the king. It recognizes frankly that the court is a third legislative chamber, and insists that since this is so we ought to know the fate of our legislation as quickly as possible.

But for that very reason the proposal runs counter to the entire tradition of the court. That tradition is the tough, concrete tradition of Anglo-Saxon case law, in which the individual case has to bear the freightage of weighty issues. An issue of constitutional law does not arise until a specific case has arisen that involves it. Until then the heavens may fall, but the court knows no generalizations and will give no advice. Its wisdom is a pragmatic one. There is a good deal to be said in support of this approach. The true meaning of a law is not to be found in the bare statute. The statute must take root, like a tree, in the soil of actual circumstance, it must bear a leafage of functioning and consequence before it can be seen as a reality. "How do we know what we think," the judges may ask, "until we see how things work out?"

The proposal from the liberal members of the court is the exact opposite of advisory opinions—namely, judicial self-limitation. This tries to carry the implications of case law all the way. It denies that the court has anything to do with legislation directly, and insists that the judges must restrict themselves to the narrowest issues in the cases that arise. Judicial self-limitation of this sort was an integral part of Justice Holmes's entire philosophy of judicial tolerance. It is part also of Justice Brandeis's philosophy that a case cannot be torn out of its context—and that context includes the impulsions to the legislation, its consequences, and the entire economic and procedural history of the case itself. Judicial self-limitation has always been given some lip-service by the court, as in the rule that the judges will consider no "moot" cases, nor any cases raising only "political questions" (blessedly vague phrase). The deliberately adopted strategy of Justices Brandeis, Stone, and Cardozo at present is to push this form of judicial hara-kiri much farther. It has found its best expression in Justice Stone's dissent in the Hoosac case, Justice Cardozo's dissent in the Mayflower Farms case, and Justice Brandeis's concurring opinion in the TVA case. These opinions not only made the general plea of judicial restraint (in Justice Stone's words, "The only check upon our own exercise of power is our own sense of self-restraint") but pointed out the two directions in which it is to be exercised: always passing on as few issues as the court can get away with, and always giving the legislature the benefit of any reasonable doubt.

It may well be asked how dependable such a method is in solving the problem of the court's power. It involves not only the selection of extraordinary judges who will be willing to limit their own power. It involves the shaping of a new method, a new mood and temper, a new conception of the scope of the court's power. And to achieve changes in the midst of the present social tensions is a heroic task. The court has never operated in a social vacuum. It has always been an integral part of the social struggles of every period in our history. It has taken its temper from the prevailing ideology of an aggressive individualist capitalism. It has been part of the fiber of a culture dominated by business enterprise. It is terribly hard to expect the court to generate a new humility now. The whole idea of judicial humility is strikingly like the plight of the gigantic Serrovius in Shaw's "Androcles and the Lion," whose powerful frame shakes with all the passions of a healthy beast, yet whose Christian principles bid him stay his hand whenever it is raised to strike. How can a court cultivate this sort of humility when issues are at stake throughout our national life that touch the justices as much as they touch anyone else? . . .

I have mentioned the remedial proposals at some length partly because it is unlikely that we shall get anything more than that in the immediate future, partly because they go to the heart of the problem of the judicial power. But the most discussed proposals are the group that seek directly to curb the court's power. These are the proposals that rouse Liberty Leaguers to the highest pitch of fury. But they are not new. Although they have never been advanced in such profusion until this year, they have cropped up periodically when the court was under attack.

The simplest way to curb the court would seem to be to "pack" it. Congress has undisputed power to determine the size of the court. In Jackson's Administration the number of judges was increased from seven to nine in order to counterbalance the influence of the Marshall tradition. Under Lincoln, during the Civil War, the court was conveniently increased to ten, to make it safe for the war powers of the President. There seems to be ample proof that Grant packed the court in order to get a favorable decision on the Legal Tender cases. This is a technique that Mr. Roosevelt might have used if an unfavorable NRA decision had come down earlier than it did, while the country was still under the spell of the New Deal; and especially if the court had been closely divided on the issue. . . . Eventually of course an Administration with enough temerity may do what the liberals did in England to the House of Lords—threaten the creation of so many new justices that under the threat the court would yield up some of its power.

The most frequent suggestion for a judicial curb is to regulate not the numbers on the court but the manner of their voting. It would provide that a majority of the justices were not enough to invalidate an act of Congress. Some number such as seven or eight or more than two-thirds of the court is usually suggested. The obvious answer is of course that, granted the existence of the judicial power, this would leave the decision on constitutionality in the hands of one or two justices. The answer to that answer is that just such an event is intended: that since you can usually count on one or two justices who will vote on the side of Congress, this leaves the decision on economic issues where it belongs—with Congress and the President. Another device, intended to have somewhat the same effect, would be to provide that unfavorable court decisions could be overruled by a two-thirds vote of Congress. Still another would be to abolish entirely, by Congressional action, the court's right to invalidate acts of Congress; or to take certain types of cases or certain issues of legislation out of the jurisdiction of the court.

About all of these the same three questions arise. Are they constitutional? Would they be effective? Could they be accomplished? A strong case could be made out, on the basis of precedent, that Congress has the power to set the conditions under which the Supreme Court shall function, and that such a power would include the regulation of its numbers, voting, jurisdiction. The supreme irony of the whole situation is of course that whether Congress has such a power would have to be finally decided by the court itself.

And it is very unlikely that, given the present temper of the court and the present tension of the country, the court would be willing to sign its own death warrant. If it did, some such proposal would seem an eminently desirable one.

One proposal for dealing with the court's power that has the amazing distinction of being favored by both sides is the amending process. The liberals and radicals want it because it seems to them a fundamental attack on the whole problem. The conservatives don't object to it because they don't really think an amendment has any chance of being adopted. The idea is therefore one calculated to assuage them in their present constitutional agony, and postpone a reckoning to the dateless future.

The questions that have been most often raised as to what form a constitutional amendment would take seem to me comparatively unimportant. We are not lacking in the political inventiveness and legislative draftsmanship adequate to solve the problem. More serious is the question whether the court will not interpret away any amendment, no matter how skilfully and shrewdly drawn, just as it has interpreted away many a statute in the past. But most serious of all are the issues of power. An amendment giving Congress the right to legislate on all issues affecting agriculture, industry, labor, and finance on a national scale would be so direct a path to the control of business enterprise by the state that it would meet the massed force of opposition from business enterprise. What lengths that opposition would go to it is now difficult to say. But it is clear that such an amendment could be carried through only as part of a larger movement not only to curb the court's power but to establish a controlled economy. Such a movement involves a greater degree of organization of the productive groups in our society than has yet been achieved, and a new political alignment. Into it the best democratic energies of the country will be poured. The court and the country are both entering on an iron age. The struggles of that age will determine whether the promise of American life can be made constitutional.

Chapter XXI

SOME ASPECTS OF JUDICIAL ORGANIZATION

No. 76

[PROFESSOR RADIN, in the first selection in this chapter, carries on the discussion of the role and function of the courts. In addition, he points out what a court is, how and from what group the judges are chosen, and gives us a brief and general description of the hierarchical arrangement of American courts, federal and state.]

WHO SAYS IT IS THE LAW? [1]

by Max Radin

IF an observer with a telescopic eye powerful enough to see things some two hundred and fifty thousand miles away as clearly as though they were right at hand, were to seat himself in the moon and turn that eye of his on our Earth, he would see, moving about chiefly on the land, some eighteen hundred millions of beings who would puzzle him greatly. He would see them walk or run, or refrain from any action whatever. He would see them put things together and pull them apart, work side by side in some cases and in others violently attack each other, and he would certainly make little sense of what they were doing if he tried to keep all the eighteen hundred millions in view at the same time. He might note that they all ate and breathed and slept, but otherwise he would find it hard to discover anything that they all did, or even anything that nearly all did.

But if he gave up trying to keep track of the entire eighteen hundred millions and directed his gaze at some smaller part of the world—the United States, for example—he would discover, if he watched carefully, that there were a great many things after all that nearly everybody in that region did,

---

[1] Max Radin, *The Law and Mr. Smith* (Indianapolis: Bobbs-Merrill and Co., 1938), Ch. 2, pp. 6-13. Reprinted by permission of the publisher.

and he would further note that the same people were likely to repeat certain of their actions over and over again. And if our observer with the monstrous eye were a reflective kind of person, who liked to arrange his knowledge and put it in order, he would soon be busy with these repetitions, classifying them and working out some scheme to explain them to himself.

Now let us leave the moon and get back to Earth, particularly to our part of the Earth, the United States. Nothing can be more obvious or significant than the similarity among the actions of most of us. Men, for example, all dress in almost exactly the same style and use in their clothes only black, brown, gray, or blue colors, almost never red, green, yellow, or purple. Women's clothes vary more but still in a general way follow a common, if new, style every year. Almost everybody eats set meals at about the same time. In the city, men leave their homes after breakfast and go to a different place where they do nearly the same kind of work every day and return about 6 P.M. to eat their dinner. When letters are written, they begin and close with set phrases which are very like each other. People in speaking to each other use the same language; that is, they use the same words for the same ideas and utter them in a fixed order which they would not think of changing. People walking or riding on the street keep to the right, and so avoid colliding with each other. A great many men raise their hats when they see women whom they know. When they are told to stop or keep in a certain direction by a uniformed policeman, they obey his orders. If they want anything displayed in a shop window, they know they will have to pay money for it and they usually do.

These are only a small selection of the number of acts that all or most men in any one country do. Many of these things they do without thinking about them, and some of them they do consciously but still without objection on their part and without any reluctance. Some of them they do because they see other people doing them and have fallen into the way of imitating them. Some of them they have been told to do by parents, employers, foremen, teachers, friends, policemen, or even casual strangers who seem to know. If they do these acts unconsciously they are apt to call them habits; if they do them consciously they may think of them as *rules;* that is, as things which for some reason they feel they ought to do, or ought to do in a particular way.

Their reasons for thinking they ought to do them vary a good deal. Sometimes they think so because everybody else does them, sometimes because they are the easiest way of getting a certain purpose fulfilled, or because someone they respect told them to do them, or else because they are satisfied that some Higher Power would like them done. And among all these rules, there are some of a peculiar sort which are called *rules of law.*

What is peculiar about them? A great many persons have said wise and rather mysterious things on the subject and have phrased the difference in words that are a little hard to follow, but to the Ordinary Person the difference does not seem a particularly mysterious matter. If you asked this Ordinary Person why he raises his hat to a lady of his acquaintance, he would probably reply in a lofty tone that all gentlemen do, and he would not be impressed if you proved to him that in many parts of the world gentlemen do not, and that in western Europe they have been doing so for only some three or four hundred years. He would retort that what gentlemen do here and now is a good enough rule for him.

If, on the contrary, the Ordinary Person were asked why he does not snatch a desirable tie from a haberdasher's shop and make off with it, there can be no doubt that the first reason which would occur to him would be that he might be arrested and imprisoned for acting in that way. It is not the only reason, surely, but it is a good one and, I think we may say, it is the one most likely to be given. We might take another example. If the Ordinary Person were asked to put on green silk knickerbockers and go to work daily in them, he would surely decline, and his reason, if he condescended to give one, would be that he did not wish to make himself ridiculous. Again, if he wished to buy a house, he would not be satisfied with an oral promise on the part of the seller, but would insist on having one in writing. And in this case the reason would be, not that an oral promise is ridiculous or unmannerly, but that without a written promise he would be unable to prove in court his right to the house, if it should come to that.

We could follow this through. There are a great many rules of all sorts— rules of morals, of fashion, of manners, of religion, of convenience, of common sense, and any of them may be rules of law as well. But we think of them as rules of law only when and if they call up in our mind a court or else a policeman, a sheriff, or other officials who have some connection with a court. That is not quite the whole story, but it is much the greater part of it, and it answers well enough to what in most people's minds is the test of whether a rule is a legal rule or not. It is not a legal rule to refrain from wearing green silk knickerbockers in our daily routine of business, because a court will not care whether we do or not. But we had better not come to work in no clothes at all, because a court is very likely indeed to care about that.

What is this court which we have to keep in mind so much? Why should our plans have so frequently to depend on what this court will do or will say? And how do we know what it will do or say? For I hope it has been noted that we have been using the future tense. In describing whether a thing is *now*, at the present time, a rule of law, we are indulging in prophecy.

We are imagining a future situation in which the rule will be considered by a court, and we are forecasting the result of that consideration. If the court will enforce it, when in the future it has occasion to, it is a rule of law *now*. We cannot get this too early in our minds or keep it there too firmly.

It is therefore highly important to know what a court is. And though it may sound childish to start out by saying what a court is not, it is on the whole well to remember that a court is not a building or an institution, but a man or else a very small group of men, practically never more than nine. The court is the judge or judges, and the judge—there is usually but one—is the court. Everything else is secondary. And this judge is a human being and a citizen, extremely like the rest of us in character, feelings, manners, and habits. He is in no sense inspired; he possesses no mysterious powers which the rest of us do not have, and, to do him justice, he does not pretend to have such inspiration or such powers—at least the vast majority of courts do not. For that reason, sensible courts would be very glad if people stopped speaking of them in figures of speech or in grand and high-sounding phrases. They are not Priests of Justice, or Bulwarks of the State, or the Foundations of Society, or Lighthouses, or Rocks, or Anchors, or any of the other things that eloquent and well-meaning people have called them, but merely fellow citizens who have been elected by the people or appointed by Presidents and Governors to do a certain particular job. They are almost always selected from among lawyers, a class of people of whom we shall have to say a great deal later, but whom we shall describe for the present as men who for a number of years have educated themselves intensively by study and practice, so that judges—that is to say, courts—can be selected from them.

Our courts, then, are men who have had a particular kind of education and who spend most of their lives in close association with lawyers; that is to say, with men who have had the same kind of education. Not only are they subject to error, but they may properly assert—in spite of popular notions to the contrary—that they are readier to admit their mistakes than other professional groups and have created more ways of correcting themselves than have other professions. And surely it does no possible good, and may do a great deal of harm, if these particular public officials are separated from all others and considered to be sacred or holy or somehow entitled to a particular kind of reverence, over and above the respect which they may claim by reason of their abilities, education, and character.

Having settled in our minds what courts are not and in a very general way what they are, let us look at them more closely. These men about whose words or actions we must prophesy, if we wish to know what the law is, are not very numerous. They number about one in thirty thousand of the population, or, if we include justices of the peace or police judges, about one in twelve thousand. In most of the United States, they have been elected by the people; in a very few of them they have been appointed by the Governor with the consent of the State Senate. There are, besides, Federal Courts, which have been appointed by the President of the United States with the consent of the United States Senate.

Evidently we cannot, in a book like this, learn all the details of the organization of all the courts. Nor if we could learn them, would it do us much good to remember them, because changes so frequently occur in details. But we might get some notion of how these things are managed, because we shall have to refer to certain special courts again and again.

First of all—in order to get them out of the way—there are the United States Courts. Certain things are reserved for them; things we had better omit for the present. They are not many, although, as we shall see, they are important enough. If we wish to know what the law is on one of these matters, we must put the following question: "What would Judge Blank of the Federal District Court decide about it, since we live in his District?" We should have to ask that, knowing that if he does not say what we think he should say, we could "appeal," i.e., take the matter to a higher court, consisting of three judges higher in rank than Judge Blank, called Judges of the Circuit Court, who sit often in a distant city. The law, instead of being as Judge Blank will say, will turn out to be as the Circuit Court will say. There, we shall have to stop in most cases. In a very few cases— highly important ones—we may get a chance to correct even the Circuit Court. We may get permission to go to the United States Supreme Court at Washington, where nine judges will make up their minds whether Judge Blank was right after all. That often takes a great deal of time; we sometimes do not discover until many years after an event has happened what the law *was,* according to which it should or should not have taken place.

Except for this small number of important things which are reserved for the Federal Courts, everything else, large or small, may come before the State Courts. If we live in Chicago and wish to know the law of the state of Illinois on a particular question, we ask ourselves what Judge Bracton of the Superior Court will say about it, since we have reason to think the matter will come before him. If the arrangement in the city is such that we cannot be at all sure it will be Judge Bracton, but know merely that it will be some one of the forty or fifty Superior (or Circuit) Judges in the city, we must try to imagine what any one of them would say. That will be harder, but if they are all sensible persons and we are sensible ourselves, it will not be impossible.

And just as in the case of the Federal Courts, we shall have a chance of "appealing," first to the District Appellate Court, in which three judges sit, and finally to the State Supreme Court of seven; and we can usually do so without asking anyone's permission. In this way, just as in the case of the Federal Courts, it will sometimes take many years before we can find out whether we were right or wrong when we said, about a particular thing that happened, that it was or was not in accordance with a rule of law.

Not only does it take time but it takes money to find out. Judges, being public officials, are paid salaries. They do their work in buildings that often cost a great deal of money to build and a great deal of money every year to keep in order. In every case there are many records which must be kept, and it costs much money to make these records and take care of them. Now, most of this money is taken from the public treasury, but some of it—a very small amount—comes from the fees which people must pay to get a case decided by the court. They must pay a small fee when they start, a larger one while the case is in progress, and further fees when they appeal. All these fees together do not amount to very much but they may run in a simple case to as high a sum as $150, which for extremely poor people is a large sum of money.

This, then, is the way our courts are organized, and it is not a very complicated matter. It used to be far more complicated and may soon become so again. For, while we have described two systems of courts running more or less parallel, we have not described them all. For small matters, where small sums are involved or slight injuries done, we do not go to a Superior Court at all, although we sometimes may if we want to, but we usually find ourselves before a justice of the peace or a police judge. He does not have to be a lawyer but he usually is. We generally do not spend much time in conjecturing what he will say about a rule of law, because if there is doubt about it we are pretty sure to appeal to the Superior Court. None the less—although once more we must wait till later to discuss the question—this court of small matters has a great power and can do a great deal of good and a great deal of mischief.

We are not yet through with courts. If the question is whether under a legal rule an injured workman is entitled to compensation and how much, that will not go before the ordinary court at all, but before a Compensation Commission which is really a court under another name. Similarly in some states, questions of workmen's wages, rates for gas and electricity or railroad rates—all these things will go before special commissions, not before the regular courts. That makes things fairly complicated; and, as it is likely that there will be more commissions rather than fewer, what with Federal

Courts, State Courts and Commissions, it will be something of a problem to know just which court we are to have in mind when we try to foretell what the law is. Evidently we shall need guidance.

Where this guidance comes from is the subject of a later chapter. For the present, let us ask ourselves a more important question. These judges have as their sole task that of stating whether an act was or was not in accordance with a rule of law. How do they know?

No. 77

[THE organization and jurisdiction of the federal constitutional courts are familiar to all who are interested in the study of American Government. Not so well known, either with reference to their organization or to their highly specialized jobs, are the legislative courts. The Court of Claims is one of the oldest of this latter type but, as Miss Stern points out, it is so unknown that many Congressmen and lawyers are unaware of its existence and work.]

THE UNKNOWN COURT [1]

by Edith M. Stern

"THE sovereign cannot be sued" is an axiom of law, a corollary of the ancient doctrine that "the king can do no wrong." Every school child knows that the United States repudiated kings and their infallibility in 1776, but comparatively few citizens know that the United States, alone among all the sovereign states of the world, may be sued by right and without special permission. The special court which keeps hard at work on such cases alone attracts so little notice that long ago it was dubbed The Unknown Court.

Its shabby red brick and brown-stone home, a block from the White House, is never pointed out to sightseers. Yet it disposes of claims running into hundreds of millions of dollars annually. Its decisions have established vital principles of law, and there is no appeal from its findings of fact. Only the Supreme Court can reverse it on points of law.

In this U. S. Court of Claims an inventor can sue the Government for infringement of a patent that the very same government has granted. Even the humblest citizen may seek justice from the "sovereign." Duke Stubbs, for instance. Duke and his wife had been on relief for some time. But he

---

[1] Edith M. Stern, "The Unknown Court," *Current History* (November, 1938), Vol. 49, No. 3, pp. 35-36. Reprinted by permission of *Current History and Forum*.

won a judgment of $50,000 from the Court a few months ago because the government had ruined his silver fox farm in Alaska.

Duke Stubbs' suit against Uncle Sam followed extension by the Government of the boundaries of McKinley National Park. Forest rangers, tramping across his premises, made breeding impossible; foxes are such temperamental animals that even a change in the wearing apparel of their attendants is said to keep them from mating or make the vixens miscarry. Mr. Stubbs and his wife had sunk everything they had into their venture, and just when it was beginning to pay handsomely it had to be abandoned. Responsibility for compensation, the Court decided, lay with the Government.

Duke Stubbs was fortunate in getting the right lawyer. He might easily have failed to hear of the Court of Claims. Even the dean of a midwestern law school told a building contractor that his only recourse was to write to the Treasury when he complained that his costs had been increased because the Government had held the plans submitted for approval an unreasonably long time. A congressman not long ago told a constituent that the Court had no power to award damages. One of the leading lawyers of New York didn't know where to seek justice for a client who had a claim against Uncle Sam.

But though the Court is a stranger to most people and even to some lawyers, enough cases are brought before it to keep judges and clerks busy the year round. Many of the suits seek indemnities far out of proportion to actual damages, for Uncle Sam is not only vulnerable but rich. When army bombers miss their target and set fire to a farmer's crops, he may be tempted to place a value of $10,000 upon the destroyed hay and wheat, or more than what his entire farm may be worth. So that in addition to being a boon to the humble citizen who has an honest grievance against the Government, the Court is a careful guardian of the public funds, saving the taxpayers from paying millions of dollars to satisfy unjust claims.

Recently, an Illinois landowner claimed $1,000,000 because his lands were flooded by a new federal spillway. The Court decided that his lands had been flooded often before the spillway was built, and that he was therefore not entitled to recover. The verdict ended at the same time 80 similar lawsuits, involving tracts of fifty to thousands of acres, and sums of $10,000 to $60,000,000.

That decision, involving millions of Government money, got not a line in the Washington newspapers the day it was handed down, though the papers gave plenty of space to police court items. But the Court is accustomed to being ignored, and it goes on quietly doing its work without expecting public recognition.

The Government's interests before the Court of Claims are represented by the Department of Justice. Skilled attorneys of the Department resist unjust claims to the limit—and with remarkable success. Last year they defended action in 1600 cases and succeeded in limiting recoveries to one-half of one per cent of the amounts sued for—the finest record they have made to date.

Claims against the Government are nothing new, but in the early days of the Republic they could be settled only upon passage of special legislation by Congress. This meant confusion, caprice, corruption. There was the notorious Fisher case that Mark Twain immortalized, in which it is said that the heirs of a farmer whose crops were destroyed by troops during the War of 1812 milked the Government of $67,000. The widow, during her lifetime, would have been content with $600.

To relieve this situation, the Court of Claims was established in 1855. Originally it merely reported its recommendations to Congress. Lincoln, in his first annual message, 1861, urged an enlargement of the Court's powers. "It is as much the duty of Government," he said, "to render prompt justice against itself in favor of citizens as it is to administer the same between private individuals." Since 1866 the Court has been empowered to render judgment. Now its findings of fact are final; they cannot be reversed by appeal to any higher tribunal. And only the Supreme Court can reverse it on the law.

The three judges who sat first soon found themselves overburdened with the handling of intricate cases "involving enormous amounts in a country of 25,000,000 people." The Court was expanded to five judges in 1863, and in 1925 seven commissioners were added to assist in sifting evidence.

The claims that come before it are of many kinds. The Government is not an abstraction, but an aggregate of federal employes who, like other human beings, make mistakes. A navy vessel collided with a fishing boat, and the owner sued. During the war, when the Government was running the railroads, a spark from an engine started a great forest fire in Minnesota. A Government dredge, deepening a harbor on the Atlantic coast, ran over a man's oyster bed and destroyed the breeding mollusks. An army post had been using coal for fuel; the heating system was changed to oil, and the coal company whose contract was cancelled sued for damages.

Formalities and technicalities are few in the Court of Claims. Suit is started by a petition, to which the Government replies. Then follows a unique procedure for taking testimony. Instead of witnesses coming to court, the Court—in the person of a commissioner—goes to the witnesses. Both sides may select the places most convenient or economical for the examination of witnesses.

A contractor, for instance, claimed that the Government should have informed him that the "borrow pit" (place from which earth is removed), used in the construction of a levee near New Orleans, was over what was once a cypress swamp. A dozen engineers were prepared to testify, for the Government, that the possibility of buried stumps is characteristic of the lower Mississippi and that the contractor should have calculated the chances of running into them. Oldest inhabitants averred that the existence of this particular swamp was not a matter of common knowledge, and that there was no reason why the Government should have known about the obstacle. To move such a crowd to Washington would have been costly for the Government, so a commissioner and the attorneys on both sides trekked to Louisiana.

The process of fact-finding often goes on for years when the matters involved are immense and complex. When inventors have claimed, for example, that the War Department infringed upon their patents for a tin helmet, an airplane propeller, or a potato-peeling machine, the Court had to determine the validity of the patent, the actuality of the infringement, and the extent of the damages. In patent and contract cases 5000 pages of printed records are not uncommon; 10,000 not unheard of.

Indian claims—98 of them are pending—involve staggering sums and intricate details. The Sioux entered suit 17 years ago and to-day their claim, with interest at six per cent since 1876, amounts to over $900,000,000. During the course of westward migration the Government appropriated their lands, and promised that it would use any money from the sale of such land for the benefit of the tribe. That it has failed in its trust is the subject matter of a petition that runs 4835 printed pages—eight bound volumes —and during the course of the suit, not yet decided, 162,899 claim settlements, 600,000 vouchers and 1900 appropriations have been examined.

Once the evidence is complete the Court considers the findings of fact and then the five judges assemble to hear the argument. Often the argument takes no more than an hour. Since there is no jury, there is little oratory. Later the Court renders judgment. And though a claimant may at times feel that a verdict is mistaken, at least he knows that its side of the story has had thorough consideration by judges appointed for life, free of political influence—judges who never since the beginning have been touched by the slightest breath of scandal or corruption.

Only a small part of the cases affected by the Court's decisions are ever tried. Sometimes by agreement a suit for a small amount is instituted as a test case for a whole class of similar claims. At the moment 1400 soldiers are claiming $75 to $300 allowances for re-enlistment in the U. S. Army. Soldiers who leave the army, and then re-enlist, are given a gratuity for every year of previous enlistment. During the economy legislation following the depression, these allowances were not paid. Only one of these claims will be tried. If the claimant wins, all other soldiers with similar claims will get their money. If he loses, none of them will. Similarly, after the war, 4500 officers banded together to finance, and win, a test claim for $150 for dress uniforms.

It is a demonstration of democracy-in-action when a corporation claims and recovers $16,000,000 in taxes and a clerk in the Department of Agriculture claims and recovers $1.50 for lunch money.

True, the Court does not cover personal-injury cases. If you are run over by an army truck, you have no legal right to sue the Government. All you can do is entrust your claim to your senator or representative. If he has the time, the inclination, and the influence, he may get Congress to pass a private act for your benefit, which can take the form either of a direct appropriation or special permission to sue.

But even with its limitations the Court of Claims is something for Americans to regard with pride. It is a living negation of the dangerous doctrine that the state can do no wrong. And it is an evidence of high national morality that, in a world of increasing arbitrary dictatorships, to sue the United States rests upon a right and not a prayer.

No. 78

[IT is difficult to classify the courts which are found in our state governments. Their number, type, and jurisdiction, and the manner in which their judges are selected vary widely from state to state, even though they follow, in general, the pyramid arrangement which Professor Radin outlined. One state court which is almost universal in the United States is the justice of the peace. Overlooked because of the petty nature of the cases which he hears and decides, the justice of the peace is nevertheless an important judicial officer. His work and how he performs it are the subject of the following article; it is based on a series of investigations into the functioning of "justice" courts.]

J. P.[1]

RECENT studies of the justices of the peace indicate that the people's courts are frequently neither popular nor judicial. Investigators in as widely separated states as New York and California, Michigan and Mississippi, conclude that the present system of rural justice is uneconomical and inefficient, and that it should undergo drastic reorganization.

[1] J. P., *State Government* (March, 1934), Vol. 7, pp. 69-71. Reprinted by permission of *State Government*.

One of the most striking points brought out by these studies is the large surplus of justices. For example, Professor Sunderland found that, out of the 290 justices who had been elected in six Michigan counties, only 21 ever did any judicial business—the other 90 per cent never tried a case. The New York Commission on the Administration of Justice, in its report this year, states that "out of a total of some 3,600 justices of peace, only 1,500 perform judicial functions of any kind." In the metropolitan region of Chicago, Dr. Albert Lepawsky reported that one-tenth of the justices never hear a case, and that about one-half of them try the great bulk of the cases. This situation is not due solely to the fact that these three states are among the half dozen in which the justices perform some slight administrative duties in addition to their judicial functions. Dr. Douglass found that two of the 26 justices in Hamilton County, Ohio, handled two-thirds of the garnishment and attachment suits, while three justices heard 91 per cent of the speeding cases.

The reports also indicate that, in some of the states at least, there is justification for the old saying the "J. P." stands for "judgment for the plaintiff." The report of Dr. Sikes on the justice courts in Mississippi, for example, contains the statement that only two per cent of the civil cases in those courts were decided in the defendant's favor. In criminal cases the defendants were almost equally unsuccessful.

In Ohio, however, the defendants seem to have a somewhat better chance of a favorable decision. A study of 5,820 civil cases and 1,239 criminal cases revealed that defendants were successful in four per cent of the former and that they were discharged in 21 per cent of the criminal prosecutions. However, half of the discharges, it should be noted, were for want of prosecution.

Among the 926 civil cases brought before the justices in the six Michigan counties which Professor Sunderland studied, only seven—or less than one per cent—resulted in judgments for the defendant. In contrast, the defendant succeeded in more than a third of the cases brought before the circuit or superior courts of these same counties. A study of criminal cases confirmed the findings of the civil cases—the defendants were adjudged guilty 95 per cent of the time.

A much greater problem than this monotony of judgments for the plaintiff is the distortion of justice directly traceable to the fee system. Dr. Sikes, for instance, contends that the administration of justice should not be on a competitive basis; that the judges who receive fees for each case decided can scarcely be expected to remain strictly impartial in their decisions. Many states have remedied the evils of the fee system, but some still retain this method of remuneration in spite of a denunciation of it by a Chief Justice of the United States Supreme Court.

Unfortunately, however, the mere removal of the fee system is apparently not a complete solution for all of these problems. A recent survey of the justices of Los Angeles county—where these officers are paid an annual salary—shows that even there many of them are inactive. There were 46 justice courts which heard no cases during the year 1931-1932, and the number of cases heard by individual justices ranged from seven per year to 3,000 per year. Per capita expenditures for these courts ranged from 26 cents to 61 dollars.

Several of the investigators criticized the records—or rather, the lack of records—covering the work done in the justice courts. For example, Professor Sunderland pointed out that some justices kept no records at all, and that the few records which *were* kept were inaccurate, inadequate, unsystematic, and lacking in uniformity. Such records are, of course, worthless for supervisory purposes. Those whose official duty it is to superintend and inspect the work of the justice courts are blocked at the outset by inadequate reports.

Private "supervision" of an efficient and effective character, however, may —as Dr. Lepawsky states—step in to take the place of nonexistent public control. He found that, in the metropolitan region of Chicago, agencies like the larger department stores, mail order houses, and motor clubs have taken active interest in these inferior courts in order to insure favorable decisions for their cases.

Qualifications for the office of justice of the peace are not specified by most of the states. In fact, only one state requires that such officers have even modest pretensions to learning: in Louisiana a justice must be able to read and write the English language. Under such circumstances, one would not expect to find many lawyers among these minor officials, and the studies by Dr. Douglass in Ohio and Professor Manning in Kentucky reveal that the percentage is not, indeed, very large. One-third of the justices of peace in Hamilton County, Ohio, are members of the bar, but less than one per cent of the Kentucky justices are lawyers.

A composite picture drawn from all of these studies shows the typical rural magistrate as a man of between forty and sixty years, with only a common school education, who has never held any other political office. The judicial duties are, of course, assumed in addition to the regular "private business" of the justice which, in three-fourths of the cases, is farming. Although the office frequently possesses a certain popular appeal, the typical justice serves only one or two terms.

The facts presented in these studies are by no means new developments, nor were they previously unknown. *State Government* cannot refrain from quoting a few lines from the interesting volume by Bruce Smith, entitled *Rural Crime Control,* in which he recalls the colorful Roy Bean, who

> . . . was born one day near Toyah
> Where he learned to be a lawyer
> And a teacher and a banker and the mayor,
> He was cook and old shoe-mender,
> Sometimes preacher and bar-tender,
> And it cost two bits to have him cut your hair.

Mr Justice Bean was the sole peace officer in the 35,000 square miles, more or less, lying west of the Pecos River in Texas. A photograph, dating so recently as 1900, shows him holding court, in shirt sleeves and a five-gallon hat, on the "veranda" of his establishment in Langtry. Three signs adorn his one-story shack. One, over the door, reads "Justice Roy Bean, Notary Public." A second, placed just below, but in much larger capitals, declares for "Law West of the Pecos." A third and comparatively modest shingle bears the legend "Beer Saloon." While it may seriously be doubted whether the same combination of callings would produce satisfactory results in more settled communities, it seems to be agreed among those most likely to know that "Cold Beer" and "Law" labored together amicably in establishing order throughout the vast territory "West of the Pecos."

Quite as significant as the general dissatisfaction which is expressed with these rural justice shops are the suggestions for their improvement. Professor Sunderland recommends: "a county court, properly organized and housed, having a trained judge, a competent clerk, office equipment sufficient for the keeping of proper records, and sitting at such times and places as the needs of the community should indicate," to replace the obsolete justice courts.

But a mere consolidation may be only a first step. Bruce Smith concludes:

The lessons of English experience with local courts will in large measure be lost if we do not make some provision for a justice's clerk. In many instances this will prove to be the only effective means for bringing administrative competence and some degree of procedural expertness into the conduct of daily routine of rural justices' courts. Moreover, if such course be followed, it will prove possible to attract to the rural bench men of local standing and ripe wisdom who are now unwilling to serve because of the burden imposed by petty detail. If the personal qualifications of justices were improved there would need be less concern about their professional training, and other problems surrounding the justice of the peace would have a fair prospect of early solution.

No. 79

[FOR more than a generation American jurists, lawyers, and scholars have been subjecting our judicial machine to a careful and critical examination. These inquiries have followed several channels and from each have come suggestions for change and proposals for reconstruction. As was the case in the field of public administration, these proposals must themselves be subjected to examination, and Professor Haines does this in the following article.]

THE GENERAL STRUCTURE OF COURT ORGANIZATION [1]

by Charles Grove Haines

THE present system of court organization presents certain characteristics which are the natural outgrowth of the common law background of American law.

In the first place, a hierarchy of courts was established with relatively little in the way of cooperation or mutual adjustment among the courts, whether of different or of the same grade. Each court or group of courts had, as a rule, an independent status incased in the provisions of the constitution and statutes providing for its organization and jurisdiction. Higher courts, of course, reviewed the decisions and judgments of lower courts in accordance with well-defined statutory requirements and common law procedure; but administratively, each court was a separate entity and was seldom subject to direction or control by any superior body.

In the second place, as judicial business increased or new types of controversies arose, new courts were established or additional judges were authorized. The change from a pioneer, rural type of life where a few judges acted as community arbiters, to an urban industrial economy with a multiplication of cases to be settled, resulted merely in more courts and more judges. These judges continued to apply what Mr. Justice Cardozo termed "a system of case law, with powers of innovation cabined and confined."

Though a detailed analysis of state judicial machinery is impractical and would serve no useful purpose in this connection, it is well to recognize that much greater diversity prevails in the state judicial establishments and their practices than is generally recognized. Little progress will be made

[1] Charles Grove Haines, "The General Structure of Court Organization," *The Annals* of the American Academy of Political and Social Science (May, 1933), Vol. 167, pp. 1-11. Reprinted by permission of *The Annals* of the American Academy of Political and Social Science. Footnotes in the original article are omitted here.

in the scientific study of the administration of justice until broad generalizations regarding state administration are replaced by observations and conclusions resulting from thorough and independent investigations in many states. Some investigations of this type, such as those of the Johns Hopkins Institute of Law, are under way and promise interesting revelations regarding the operation of courts.

Realizing that details vary in the systems of courts established in the states, certain common features usually belong to the structure of court organization as formulated in constitutions and statutes. Thus, there are as a rule four grades of courts: first, local peace magistrates and inferior courts for petty causes; second, county and municipal courts with a limited jurisdiction in civil and criminal matters and a variety of duties administrative in nature, such as the disposal of probate matters, and in certain communities a separate tribunal for the trial of equity cases; third, superior, district, or circuit courts of general jurisdiction at law and equity, with authority to try more serious offenses and to review the decisions of inferior magistrates; fourth, a supreme court of review.

A marked increase in the causes to be disposed of, both in the trial courts and in the appellate tribunals, resulted in only two significant changes during the latter part of the nineteenth century—the establishment of more trial courts or provisions for additional judges, and, to relieve the strain on appellate courts, the authorization of intermediate appellate tribunals. As a rule the constitution prescribed the system of courts for the state, defined in a general way their jurisdiction, and surrounded court procedure with some specific limitations. It was this general type of court organization which was challenged when, at the beginning of the present century, the administration of justice in the states was subjected to serious criticisms on the ground of inefficiency.

In a report of a special committee of the American Bar Association "to suggest remedies and formulate proposed laws to prevent delay and unnecessary cost in litigation," two principles were proposed as involving the central issues in the reform of court organization and procedure in the United States. These principles were as follows:

I. The whole judicial power of each state (at least for civil causes) should be vested in one great court, of which all tribunals should be branches, departments, or divisions. The business, as well as the judicial administration of this court, should be thoroughly organized, so as to prevent not merely waste of judicial power, but all needless clerical work, duplication of papers and records, and the like, thus obviating expense to litigants and cost to the public.

II. Whenever in the future practice acts or codes of procedure are drawn up or revised, the statute should deal only with the general features of procedure, and prescribe the general lines to be followed, leaving details to be fixed by rules of court, which the courts may change from time to time, as actual experience of their application and operation dictates.

These suggestions for reform in the field of court organization were made for the committee by its chairman, Dean Roscoe Pound, who summed up the situation in relation to court organization in the comment that

with respect to anachronisms in the machinery of justice generally, I submit that relief is to be sought in a modern, unified, flexible, judicial organization in which judicial power is conserved, the administrative activities of the tribunals are systematized, and provision is made for expert and responsble supervision.

The English Judicature Act of 1873 and the administrative arrangements which developed therefrom served as a model for the proposed reforms.

The changes suggested, which were intended to bring about a unification of the existing scattered and more or less independent state and local judicial tribunals, were expected to involve large powers of general direction, supervision, and control over the work of the courts, including authority to establish divisions, control assignment of judges, formulate rules of procedure, and supervise the types of records and reports, and to insure a more definite standardization of practices in the administration of justice.

Dean Pound's proposals for reorganization of judicial machinery, which soon received the support of bar associations, of the American Judicature Society, and of numerous other organizations, took concrete form in the establishment of special municipal courts.

The first city to secure a partial unification of its court system was Chicago. The court established in that city, and placed under the direction of Chief Justice Olson, involved the following features: first, a single court in place of numerous justices of peace and police magistrates; second, the chief justice as an administrative head acting as a general manager; third, the chief justice and associate justices constituting an administrative council for the general supervision of rules and regulations and of the administrative activities of the court; fourth, rules of procedure to be formulated by the court, with their preparation largely in the hands of the administrative council; fifth, provision for specialization and accordingly for the establishment of separate branches (among the branches established were the following: domestic relations, traffic, morals, boys, and small claims courts); sixth, a psychopathic laboratory, in charge of an expert who was expected to act as consultant and adviser to the justices. For a number of years this court performed its functions so successfully that it was deemed a model for similar courts to be established in other metropolitan centers.

Among the cities which followed Chicago in the effort to unify the judiciary was Detroit, where a single court was established for the handling of criminal cases. A number of reforms were instituted, such as the establishment of special divisions, the elimination of unnecessary steps in trial procedure, and improvements in the keeping of records. The first years of this court resulted in noteworthy improvements in the administration of criminal justice in Detroit.

Only a few cities have adopted the plan of a unified court system, but the principles of consolidation, specialization, and flexibility in administration have been accepted and applied in varying degrees in a number of cities. The scope and significance of the application of these principles are exemplified in the Philadelphia Municipal Court. This, according to a recent appraisal, is

a court with jurisdiction to hear initially the smallest case, yet manned by judges learned in the law, as compared with the magistrates' courts, with their lay judges, before whom it was practically compulsory to bring small claims prior to the establishment of the municipal court; a court "of record" in which trial of civil cases without a jury is encouraged and before which a number of minor criminal offenses not requiring jury trial are regularly tried; a court in which thousands of juvenile offenders are handled with a view to their welfare and in disregard of the requirements of the criminal law; a court which begins desertion and nonsupport proceedings with a letter asking for a conference rather than by an arrest plus imprisonment or bail; a court which helps the unmarried mother to get not only the father's support, but prenatal care and medical and hospital service at the birth as well; a court which has ordered the dispensing of thousands of dollars of public money to widows, that they might keep their children with them; a court which adjusts many of its cases without formal court proceedings; a court with investigators to supply the judges with information which might not be forthcoming from the parties themselves; a court with physicians and psychiatrists to diagnose the ills of its wards and recommend treatment; a court specializing in sex offenses, in which the presence or absence of venereal disease is a fact of great weight; a court which hears its juvenile and domestic relations cases without the preliminary hearing before a magistrate that once was necessary; a court which uses probation and parole extensively, and has many probation officers to aid in the rehabilitation of individuals and families; a court which has experimented with a "poor man's court" and has established a "conciliation, small claims, and legal aid division," a labor bureau to find employment for its wards, and a statistical department to interpret the court's work to the court and to the public.

These steps toward unification for a metropolitan community were followed by attempts to unify and centralize the entire judicial system of a state. Constitutional conventions in New York, Illinois, and Missouri incorporated in draft constitutions all or part of the program for unification. New York adopted only part of the unification plan. Illinois proposed to unify the courts of Cook County and granted the rule-making power to the Supreme Court. The draft constitution of Missouri included the essential features of the model unification plan as proposed by the American Judicature Society. The entire judicial system of the state was to be under a single administrative direction. With the rule-making power in the courts and a judicial council established, the process of central control and supervision was to be rendered effective. But these draft constitutions were rejected by the voters, in state-wide political contests waged only in small part around the changes in the judicial systems.

The model state constitution prepared by a committee of the National Municipal League also includes a plan for consolidation. Under this plan a general court of justice is to be established, comprised of three departments to be known as the supreme court, the district court, and the county court. The supreme court is authorized to sit in two or more divisions and to make rules for the distribution of cases between divisions and for the hearing of certain cases by the full court. The district court is to have original jurisdiction in certain cases, and such appellate jurisdiction as shall be conferred upon it by the judicial council or by law. County courts are granted original jurisdiction to try all cases heretofore considered within the jurisdiction of county courts and those cases which formerly were tried by justices of the peace or local magistrates.

Provision is also made in the model constitution for a judicial council consisting of the chief justice, the presiding justices of the supreme court, and two county court judges to be assigned each year by the chief justice. The chief duties of the council are to make rules and regulations respecting the business of the courts and to assist in the division of business and the assignment of judges in the various tribunals. All of the judges of these courts are to be appointed by the governor, subject to approval, in certain instances, by a majority of the legislature. This plan provides for a unification and centralization of the judiciary which has appeared on the whole too revolutionary to be adopted by any state.

In the general discussions over these and similar plans for structural reorganization of the courts, there is rather general agreement upon certain fundamentals; namely, that there should be:

First, a General Court of Judicature for the state.
Second, three main divisions of the court:

I. A supreme court, with two divisions, criminal and civil, and other divisions if necessary.

II. District courts—intermediate courts of appeal—with original jurisdiction in a limited number of cases.

III. County courts—with original jurisdiction over civil and criminal cases and appellate jurisdiction over cases from local magistrates; with special supervision and control over local magistrates or justices of peace (certain plans do not make any provision for local magistrates); with authority to establish divisions for probate, juvenile cases, and so forth.

Third, establishment of a judicial council

(a) To make rules of practice and procedure.

(b) To control the business of the courts, supervise judicial statistics, assign judges, and generally exercise administrative supervision.

The grant of the rule-making power, which is a significant feature of all plans according to Mr. Justice Roberts, should be so broad in its scope

that the question of forms of action, the question of the initiation of an action, the question of pleadings, the question of proofs, the question of trial procedure, the question of appellate procedure and the whole genus of procedural things, from the start to the end of a litigation, ought to be in the hands of those who know best about it and who, from time to time, can make rules to meet situations as they arise in the actual practice of law.

The extent to which the courts of a state can be unified is one on which opinions differ widely. Though few would defend the existing arrangements in most of the states, it is doubtful whether so thorough a centralization as designed in the above plans would be practicable. In the first place, it must be recognized that conditions in the states vary to such an extent that generalizations on the matter of unification should be made with due caution. The problems of states like Connecticut and Rhode Island are scarcely analogous to those in Texas, Montana, and California; so that general principles of centralization cannot be applied without doing violence to local conditions and requirements. The abolition of local magistrates or justices of peace may be desirable where a county covers no more acreage than a great many farms in the states of the West. But when a county has a population of a million or more inhabitants and comprises a territory almost equivalent to a small state, a single county court scarcely meets the situation. Nor does the proposal to have the county court sit in different parts of the county meet every condition.

Some direct control and supervision over the entire court system, such as is being developed through the judicial councils, is undoubtedly desirable and can be applied to advantage in most of the states. On the other hand, if the results of centralization in other fields can be taken as indicative of what is to be anticipated from this movement, it is doubtful whether the authority to appoint judges for the entire judicial system should be placed in the hands of the governor without more definite restrictions and limitations than the model constitution or other plans for judicial reform provide.

Neither the system of appointment of judges nor that of election has worked satisfactorily. If appointments are to be made by the governor, it is believed that an eligible list should be prepared by committees of judges and lawyers who can form estimates of the professional qualifications of those recommended. Or, if the state judicial system is placed under the direction of a minister of justice or chief judicial superintendent, judges may be appointed by this officer with the advice and consultation of the judicial council. But there are good grounds to question too great a concentration of power as to the appointment and control of judges in all the cities and local communities of a state. After all, much is to be gained by placing special responsibilities in the administration of justice upon local communities, provided a flexible plan of judicial organization and administration is adopted and limited central control and supervision are established.

Certain guiding formulas in court organization and administration which may be adapted to a variety of conditions are: first, centralization and general administrative control in the making of rules of procedure, in the distribution of cases among the various courts, and in the assignment of judges; second, specialization in court trials and administration for the handling of those cases where peculiar technique and intimate understanding of conditions are imperative; third, flexibility in the establishment of separate departments or divisions and in the provisions which are made for the handling of various types of cases. These formulas can be carried out with a limited amount of central supervision and control, and with the placing of greater responsibilities on local communities for the conduct of judicial administration.

It is doubtful whether general approval can be given to the proposal that the centralization of courts under a strong chief justice is desirable, though certain gains are likely to follow from unification. Centralization may readily be carried too far, so that the special interests and circumstances involved in such fields as juvenile offenses and probate matters may be forced into mechanical and undesirable channels. Administrative unification has distinct advantages in preparing uniform and flexible rules of procedure for all courts, in developing an effective system of reports and of the use of reliable judicial statistics, and in adjusting the personnel of the bench in order to expedite the disposition of cases; but it cannot be deemed as a corrective of some of the most serious ills which now affect our administration of justice.

There is a point in the process of centralizing administrative responsibilities where an increase in duties results in a diminution of efficiency. This has been rightly termed "the inherent vice of centralized authority." Professor Laski says:

It is so baffled by the very vastness of its business as necessarily to be narrow and despotic and overformal in character. It tends to substitute for a real effort to grapple with special problems an attempt to apply wide generalizations that are in fact irrelevant. It involves the decay of local energy, taking real power from its hands. It puts real responsibility in a situation where, from its very flavor of generality, an unreal responsibility is postulated. It prevents the saving grace of experiment.

Another difficulty with unification of the courts lies in the fact that a mere change in organization cannot be effective unless it involves also an improvement in the personnel of the judiciary. After a number of years in operation, Professor Moley remarks that the municipal court of Chicago is

still as inefficient and confused and political as most unreformed courts in other cities. . . . The majority of the judges now sitting are fitted neither by experience, education, nor, what is more important, sufficient professional standards to discharge with credit the great responsibilities and powers which they possess under the law. The court is full of incompetence, of political influences, of lamentable laxness in meeting an unprecedented tide of crime. In the hands of such a staff the court, technically well organized and full of possibilities for good, yields a sorry product.

In Detroit a deterioration of the personnel of the court had similar, though not as serious, results. Other cities with less effective organization and a better personnel on the bench have secured more effective results than either Chicago or Detroit. It not infrequently happens that the results secured by a court depend more on the ability, the courage, and the independence of the judges than upon the particular form of court organization.

With proposals for improvement in the administration of justice, as with reforms in other divisions of government, there has been an overemphasis on the mechanics of court organization, and too much has been expected from mere changes in the organization and administrative arrangements of the system of courts. In the advocacy of both the commission form of city government and the commission-manager type of organization, claims have been made assuring improvement in city administration which have not been satisfactorily or permanently fulfilled unless other important factors were favorable to the new administration. So enthusiastic proponents of reorganization of the administrative services of the states, coupled with an executive budget, predicted a transformation in the control of the public business which has not been realized, except in a few conspicuous instances where forceful personalities secured remarkable improvements in the state public services, or other fortunate combinations of circumstances gave to administrative centralization a success only partially to be attributed to structural reform.

Though there may well be no diminution of effort to eliminate weaknesses in organization, whether in the legislative, the executive, or the judicial branch of the government, little is gained by giving attention to faults of organization unless other factors vital to successful administration are given equal scrutiny.

A consideration of the structure of the courts in the American states involves also certain questions which require brief observations, namely: whether there are too many courts, and hence a reorganization should mean the abolition of some of those now functioning; whether civil and criminal cases should be considered by separate tribunals; whether misdemeanors and felonies should be merged in the trial process and be dealt with by the same court; and whether greater flexibility can be secured both in the trial of cases and in the administrative arrangements among the several courts.

It is difficult to give an answer to the question whether there are too many courts under existing arrangements. As cases are now dealt with in our judicial tribunals, there certainly are not enough courts; but apparently the increase in judicial business is so great that the mere multiplication of courts is creating a situation which from many standpoints is both impracticable and intolerable. In Los Angeles County the number of superior court judges has been doubled in a five-year period, with approximately fifty judges trying cases, and considerably behind in the docket. At the same rate of increase, it is difficult to imagine the situation in the next fifty years.

Instead of an increase in the number of courts functioning as they are at the present time, it would undoubtedly be advisable to reduce the number of trial courts and judges. Other and more effective methods must be devised, however, to take care of the increasing number of controversies which come to the courts for trial, if the judicial system is to be saved from functional paralysis.

On the other hand, if the reduction of the number of courts would mean the concentration of judicial business in a few centers and the removal of the trial of minor and petty offenses a considerable distance from the litigants, with increasing delays and expense, the expedient of a reduction of courts would indeed be questionable.

There are serious doubts whether the proposals to eliminate the justices of peace or petty magistrates is a step in the right direction, provided measures may be adopted to secure more competent justices in the minor courts and improvements may be inaugurated in the procedure followed.

In both England and France, important and effective use is made of the justices of the peace in the disposition of minor causes. The main function of the French justice is to bring parties to an informal conference and to adjust disputes by methods of conciliation and to pass on minor infractions of the laws and ordinances. Those selected for this position must have a degree of license in law and two years' practice or experience in a law office, and must pass a professional examination.

Though the English justices of peace as a rule are not professionally trained, they develop a successful technique as a result of experience, and, with the aid of competent clerks, render a type of justice which is generally deemed satisfactory. Even in graver offenses a trial may be had in "petty sessions," a court of summary jurisdiction composed of at least two justices usually residents of the immediate neighborhood.

In both countries, an inexpensive and informal justice is kept close to the people, rather than removed to distant courts with a high degree of formality and expense.

Ultimately the issue as to the number of courts is tied up with the introduction of more effective methods in the handling of minor cases, in the sifting of evidence by informal examination, by affidavits, and by the discovery of documents, and the determination of issues involved, in advance of trial, so that only controverted points need to be proved in court. In civil cases, much more extensive use of arbitration and conciliation may well be made before the controversy reaches the stage of trial. The problem of the determination of the number of courts must also be adjusted in accordance with the marked differences in the size of the states, the necessary distances to be traversed, and the complexity of conditions which arise over an extensive territory such as is comprised in many of the states.

As in the answer to other questions, the separation of civil from criminal jurisdiction can scarcely be dealt with in general terms. The practice prevails in the United States and in foreign countries for the same court to try both civil and criminal cases. The Municipal Court of Chicago, deemed a model for court organization, combined the trial of both civil and criminal causes. On the other hand, the Detroit plan separated the trial of civil from criminal business.

The main argument for the combination of civil and criminal trials is that the arrangement provides a more effective use of the personnel of the bench. It is a question, however, whether better results may not be secured by greater specialization, whether under a unified court arrangement or in separate courts. So many fields of trial work to-day require a special knowledge and technique that it seems unwise to expect judges to be familiar with the details and the technique necessary for the trial of all kinds of civil and criminal causes. Better results would undoubtedly be secured so far as the dispatch of business is concerned if the judges were given definite assignments either to the civil or the criminal division of the court and thus put into a position where they could acquire specialized knowledge and skill. Though there are advantages in having judges broaden their interest and activities by the trial of different types of cases, most of the advantages thus secured can be gained by the separation of the civil from the criminal business, with an occasional exchange of judges in divisions or branches involving similar facts and circumstances.

Unfortunately, too much dependence has been placed upon the necessity of structural changes in court organization to secure an informal and flexible type of justice. Without any specially planned or advertised reorganization, a chief justice was placed at the head of the Common Pleas Court of Cuyahoga County, Cleveland, and by this simple device one of the most efficient and successful trial courts in the country has been functioning for a number of years.

Whether the trials of misdemeanors and felonies may appropriately be merged under a single tribunal also depends to a considerable degree upon local conditions and interests. The general attitude of neglect and indifference toward justices of peace and minor courts, it is often claimed, can be changed by putting all courts on a basis of equal importance. Why tolerate inferior courts? is the query often raised. The term "inferior" attaches to the courts the stigma of unimportance, and hence neglect and contempt on the part of the public. Should not all courts be potentially equal in importance? And as these are the final courts for the majority of the people, should they not be placed on a par with the higher courts? Thus, it is contended, the stigma attached to courts of inferior jurisdiction may be removed and the disposal of petty misdemeanors may be placed on the same plane as the trial of serious felonies. Since able judges will not accept positions on existing inferior courts, the trial of petty offenses is to be combined with the hearing of charges of graver importance.

Much as it may seem commendable to make this kind of a combination, in practice, results come therefrom which are not so favorable as are usually predicted. Where the trials of felonies and of misdemeanors have been combined, it frequently happens that men of force and character will not accept positions on the courts. They are unwilling to devote their time to the hearings in petty conflicts. The doctrine that all courts are potentially equal in importance, though a well-sounding phrase, does not seem to work out well in practice.

It is frequently not realized that much greater flexibility, both in the methods of trial now in use and in the administrative adjustments among courts, could be secured without drastic changes in the legal arrangements now prevailing regarding court organization. Some of the most important and effective changes in law enforcement can be accomplished by the adoption of simple, reasonable, and effective administrative devices with a minimum of permissive legislation. Effective as the administration of criminal justice is in England, it is carried on through a set of courts which have not been seriously changed for generations. Such devices as have been evolved in England and Continental European countries for securing and sifting the evidence prior to the trial of a case could be adopted to great advantage in this country.

Without any marked changes in the structure of courts, it would be possible to accomplish the result which was thus described by Lord Bowen as applicable to the administration of justice in England. In every cause, whatever its character, said Lord Bowen,

> every possible relief can be given with or without pleadings, with or without a formal trial, with or without discovery of documents and interrogatories, as the nature of the case prescribes—upon oral evidence or affidavits, as is most convenient. Every amendment can be made at all times and all stages in any record, pleading or proceeding, that is requisite for the purpose of deciding the real matter in controversy.

Could not the English plan of summons for direction before a master, by which the vast scheme of discovery is largely administered, be utilized without waiting for the adoption of an elaborate scheme of court organization?

Three significant factors account in large part for the efficiency which prevails in the administration of justice in England and in France. They are: first, the central position and the authority of the judge; second, the lack of technical rules of evidence and the relative informality of procedure which prevails in the actual trial and consideration of cases; third, the subordinate position of the lawyer, who is deemed primarily an agent and assistant of the court, aiding the judge in securing accurate data regarding the case and the selection and determination of the vital issues involved. Most of these advantages could be gained in the actual administration of justice in the United States with relatively few important changes in court organization. In practice, individual judges assume the functions comparable to those of a French or an English judge, with results that are considered satisfactory to all parties concerned.

Principles which require special consideration in any plan to revise existing judicial machinery may be briefly summarized as follows:

First. Flexible constitutional provisions for court organization. The Federal plan vesting judicial power in a Supreme Court and such inferior courts as Congress may establish, which has been followed in a few states, is preferable to the usual clauses of the state constitutions covering the details of court organization and jurisdiction. Progress in remolding judicial machinery is always slow, and is greatly retarded by the difficulties involved in the adoption of frequent constitutional amendments.

Second. Establishment through constitutions and statutes of a certain degree of unification of the court system involving a limited supervision over all inferior tribunals by the Supreme Court and a judicial council authorized to prepare and issue rules of procedure, to assign judges for special duties in accordance with the pressure of causes to be determined and the special capabilities of the judges, and to develop uniformity in records and statistical information.

Third. Expeditious procedure in the preparation of affidavits and in the discovery of documents, with greater use of masters and judicial assistants, to dispose of issues before the stage of trial is reached, as is done in a large percentage of cases in England.

Fourth. Flexible administrative arrangements, to permit specialization where required, to provide for conciliation and arbitration as well as other devices to secure informal and inexpensive proceedings in the adjustment of small claims, and to facilitate the settlement of controversies by summary judgments, declarations of right, or any other device which serves to secure the ends of justice.

The adoption of the above principles will require not a few structural changes in court organization, but they can be applied by degrees, without a radical reconstruction of present judicial machinery. A considerable part of such a program will necessarily have to become a part of American law and practice if we are to accept Elihu Root's challenge to put our judicial house in order.

Chapter XXII

THE EXPANDING WORK OF GOVERNMENT

[IN the preceding chapters we have examined the structure and operation of the governmental machine; it is now time to examine the nature of the load it pulls. Government is not an end in itself; it is an instrument for the accomplishment of certain common purposes of the community. Its character is determined not only by its organization but also by what it does, and to-day it is doing more than ever before.

Whether the organization of government is democratic or autocratic, whether rule is by majority or by dictator, a world-wide trend is observable. The role of government is constantly expanding. The load it is pulling is getting bigger and bigger. The reasons for this are many, but among the most important is the rapid transformation of our society from a rural agricultural to an urbanized industrial one. If we were still living under eighteenth-century conditions, we would have little need for many of the things now being done by government. Slum clearance is essentially a problem of an industrial and urbanized community; the protection of the rights of labor is not of primary importance in an agrarian nation; the question of old age insecurity is primarily a problem of urban industrial workers. If each of us lived on our own farm, the simple activity of securing a pure water supply would be a concern of each family. When millions of us live in small areas, it becomes a concern of the whole group and government takes over the task.

Advances in science and technology have forced the government to assume many jobs never before considered as properly within its sphere. When evidence was obtained that yellow fever was carried by mosquitoes, control of these insects became an essential function of government. When we became aware that impure milk was an important factor in the spread of such diseases as typhoid fever and tuberculosis, we insisted that government regulate the production and sale of milk. One only needs to examine the relationships of the radio, the automobile, the railroad to the community to see still further tasks for which government has had to assume responsibility.

In other words, we no longer believe that that government is best which governs least. More and more we are inclined to look upon government as a huge service agency and to judge that government best that serves best.]

No. 80

THE CHANGING ECONOMIC FUNCTIONS OF GOVERNMENT [1]

by Ernest L. Bogart

MAN is a social animal and, since the beginning of recorded human history, has always shown a capacity for organizing systems of control over divergent interests and for adjusting common relationships. Such were the institutions of monogamy and the family, religious organizations, and shifting social groups. As life became more settled and civilization advanced, political organization developed with definite legal systems to enforce and direct the increasingly complex institutional life. But government could develop only within the framework of accepted social mores and customs, and could not, if it would maintain itself, contravene prevailing standards of right human relationships. Government is society organized for certain desirable purposes, but these purposes have varied from time to time.

An examination of the theories of the functions of government shows that these have run the gamut from the philosophical anarchism of Bakunin to the leveling communism of Babeuf. Anarchism is the negation of government, which, it insists, rests upon coercion. Their motto, "every man is free to do what he will provided that he does not infringe the equal right of every other man," assumes a society of high-minded, cooperative, and rational human beings, but scarcely fits the conditions of modern complex industrialism. Scarcely less applicable is the "administrative nihilism" of Herbert Spencer, who severely limited the functions of government to the protection of life and liberty and the enforcement of contracts. Adam Smith's theory of laissez faire slightly widened the permissible functions of government, for he admitted education, some public works, and even, under special circumstances, a protective tariff. John Stuart Mill, although a stalwart defender of laissez faire, is said to have opened the door to socialism when he admitted that the delimitation of the proper functions of government could not be brought within the ring-fence of a definition. "There may be occasions," he wrote, "when it is necessary for the government to undertake almost anything."

[1] Ernest L. Bogart, "The Changing Economic Functions of Government," *The Annals* of the American Academy of political and Social Science (November, 1939), Vol. 206, pp. 1-5. Reprinted by permission of *The Annals* of the American Academy of Political and Social Science.

It remained for the German historical school, however, to change this negative philosophy and to assign to government a positive role in improving economic and social conditions. Instead of the "police state" they substituted the concept of a "welfare state," which had the positive mission of controlling and directing economic forces so as to promote social well-being. From this school it was a short step to the "socialist of the chair," who stood midway between individualism and socialism. The socialists advocated the extension of the functions of government to the point of taking over all means of production, and the communists took the last step by making government supreme over every step in the industrial process, from production to distribution and consumption.

The list of theories, revealing as it is of the attitude of scholars to this problem, does not throw adequate light upon the historical changes in practice which have taken place. Three fairly well-marked stages may be noted since the beginning of our present capitalistic industrial system. At the beginning of the industrial revolution, all the governments of Europe administered systems of extensive and minute control of industry, commerce, and other forms of activity. The reaction from his oppressive mercantilistic policy gave birth to the theory of individualism and free enterprise, which reached its height about the end of the third quarter of the nineteenth century. Nowhere, however, except perhaps in the United States, did this theory find full expression, for, from the beginning, restraints were everywhere imposed upon competition. The factory acts in England were a notable instance of state interference in private industry when unsatisfactory conditions developed. The prevailing theory held, however, that such interference was admissible only under exceptional circumstances, and that the general rule should be laissez faire. That government was best which governed least.

The principle of individualism never took such deep root on the continent of Europe as it did in England and the United States, and government never abdicated the industrial sphere so completely. In certain fields, as transportation, forestry, and municipal public works, the government shared with private capital the task of development, and in others it exercised powers of control. But even in the two countries where liberalism and individualism progressed farthest, the last quarter of the nineteenth century saw a change in the direction of increased governmental interference. Legislation in England was tinged with social objectives and, under the influence of Fabian socialism and other liberal forces, undertook broadening programs of human betterment. Even in the United States, with the disappearance of the frontier and the narrowing of the opportunities for the common man, legislation was enacted and administrative commissions were established to correct abuses and exercise control. There was an enlargement everywhere of governmental powers and an extension of governmental activities. The prevailing theory remained, however, one of individualism, and departures from it were made pragmatically to meet particular conditions, rather than as the result of a reasoned and farsighted policy as to the proper functions of government.

Since the World War a significant change has taken place. The school of thought which believed in political democracy and economic liberalism— that is, a representative government determined by the will of the electorate, and an economic system based on free initiative and independent enterprise —has been subjected to many assaults, both theoretical and practical. The influence of socialism has been widespread and has inclined people to regard the expansion of governmental functions with indifference if not actual approval. The industrial countries of Western Europe have been moving away from both democracy and individualism and towards systems of state planning and collective control—that is, the assumption by government of greatly expanded functions. This has taken different forms in different countries, such as Sovietism in Russia, Fascism in Italy, and National Socialism in Germany; but fundamentally, each of these is a system of government-controlled and managed economy. Even in Great Britain and the United States, many observers claim that a similar movement is under way; in support of this contention they cite the adoption of a protective tariff and the extension of government control over railroads, coal mining, industrial combinations, housing, and other lines in Great Britain, and the varied activities of the New Deal in the United States.

There were many reasons for the assumption of new functions and the enlargement of old ones by governments, but only the most outstanding need be mentioned.

In the first place, technical improvements had broadened the markets, brought about keener international competition in those markets, and led to larger undertakings and groupings. In no field had technological changes been more revolutionary than in the leading heavy industry, iron and steel. These had tended to reduce the differential advantages enjoyed by the citizens of one country or another in the manufacture of particular products, and had brought them all into the world markets under conditions of intense competition. The textile industries—the most important producers of consumers' goods—presented another outstanding example of keen international competition, owing to the rapid rise of the cotton industry in the Far East, especially in Japan, and to the growing efforts of other countries to supply their own needs. As a result of the strong pressure exerted by these forces, a great increase in industrial combinations was taking place and industries were consolidating in larger and more effective groupings, national in scope. The independent individual or small company became an anachronism. The great combinations were government-aided by loans, by discriminating railroad rates, by import quotas and protective duties, and by foreign exchange manipulation, and were at the same time made to serve state policy by strict methods of control and even by partial ownership.

The World War had shown the possibility of government participation in industry on a new scale for the purpose of achieving definite ends. The war brought about compulsory organization under government control in every country, rationing raw materials, labor, transportation, and credit with a view to their most effective utilization in winning the war. A free economic system is impossible during a war, and the more in fear of war a nation is, the more will it expand powers of government at the expense of the rights of individuals. Modern warfare, which involves the utilization of all the material and human resources of a nation, inevitably means the most extreme extension of the functions of government into every domain of activity—economic, political, social, intellectual, and even religious. After the World War, in spite of the removal of controls at the insistence of industry, a larger measure of govermental authority remained than had ever existed before.

Finally, the war bred a feeling of insecurity, which led each of the twenty-six states into which Europe was now divided, into a policy of exaggerated nationalism. In no sphere was this more rampant than in the economic. Barriers were set up against the free movement of goods, of capital, and of labor. Higher tariffs, import quotas, and currency juggling kept out competing goods. Each little state set up its own textile mills, its locomotive works, its factories of various sorts. Economic self-sufficiency was thought to be essential to the achievement of political nationalism, and autarchy became the goal of countries sadly deficient in national resources and capital.

Upon the basis thus laid it became possible for new authoritarian groups to seize the power of the state and to expand this to a point just short of socialism, establishing systems of organization which are a negation of political democracy and of freedom of initiative and enterprise. The political liberalism of the nineteenth century, which allowed small scope for government functions, and the concomitant philosophy of laissez faire with its freedom from political control, both yielded to the new forces of nationalism and authoritarianism, which stretched the powers of the state to the extreme limit. Democratic forms of organization and control were thought to be too clumsy, slow, and uncertain to fit the needs of these new states, and the internationalism of free enterprise was equally inconsistent with their economic aims. In some countries these liberal institutions have been practically destroyed, and even in those countries where the form has been preserved they have been greatly modified.

Although war and threats of war have served in recent years to enlarge the functions and powers of government, the tendency in this direction had been proceeding steadily for the previous half-century. When Professor Henry C. Adams, in a report to the American Economic Association on *The Relation of Modern Municipalities to Quasi-Public Works,* defended the right of the government to control private business, he was regarded as a somewhat dangerous radical. Since that time, however, the Federal and state governments in this country have not only set up many regulating commissions, but have also greatly expanded government enterprises and have entered many fields previously occupied exclusively by private industry. Although over one-third of the railroad mileage of the world is publicly owned, the governments of the United States have left this field to private enterprise, except for a short line in Alaska; but the Federal Government owns a barge line on the Mississippi River, and at one time owned and operated a considerable merchant marine. It has entered the express, banking, and public utility fields directly, and indirectly a great many others. State and local governments operate practically all sewage disposal systems, most of the water plants, and many other municipal utilities, such as lighting and electricity.

So gradually has the extension of government participation in these varied activities proceeded that it has not met serious opposition. Down to the period of the World War, most of this extension occurred in municipal ownership. Since that event, the Federal Government in the United States and the central governments in other countries have greatly expanded their functions. It is a world-wide trend, in which we on the whole have lagged behind. Regulation rather than ownership has been employed in this country, although the net has steadily been tightened about private enterprise.

A historical survey of the changes that have taken place in both our philosophy and our practice supports certain tentative conclusions. In the first place, we must realize that economic and political institutions are not immutable. As they now exist, they are the product of a long historical evolution under changing environmental conditions, and are themselves subject to further change. The institutions of political liberalism, of private property, of freedom of economic enterprise, of freedom of choice of occupation, and of freedom of mobility of persons are all comparatively new, and rest solely upon broad principles of expediency. If they are now

undergoing processes of further change or modification, we need not therefore conclude that the basis of our traditional economic and political world
is threatened.

In the next place, there is need for adaptation to changing social environment in the case of political and economic institutions, just as there is in
the biological world. Certain institutions of great value in a certain stage
of social evolution, as was feudalism or the Canonist doctrine of usury,
become outgrown and serve then only to hinder progress. It is often difficult if not impossible to determine, in the midst of a period of change and
resulting conflicts between the forces of radicalism and conservatism, to
just what extent the status quo should be preserved; but certainly all who
urge change or reform are not therefore destroyers of society.

And finally, we must realize that the aim of organized society is the promotion of the common welfare. Government is a most important and
powerful agency in achieving this result, and has positive and beneficent
contributions to make. The pendulum has swung far from an unrestrained
regime of laissez faire in the direction of increasing powers of control and
operation. To conclude, however, that it will reach equilibrium only when
complete socialism has been attained is to misread the lesson of history.
Equilibrium is the result of the movement of opposing forces. Human institutions resist change, and usually yield only because of inherent weakness.
If political democracy and economic liberalism are to survive, it will be
because they can prove their capacity to meet the problems of to-day.
Government must be admitted as a partner if it is not to be master.

No. 81

DRUGGÈD INDIVIDUALISM [1]

by Ernest Boyd

IN a country where so much has been achieved through large-scale production and standardization it is natural that there should be an almost
nostalgic insistence upon the virtues of individualism. As the period grows
more remote when the conditions of American life brought individual effort
and enterprise to the fore, there is an increasing tendency to substitute the
legend for reality, to employ the language of another age for the expression
of ideals no longer attainable. Individualism that once was rugged is now
druggèd, drugged with the heady vapors of a terminology that becomes

[1] Ernest Boyd, "Druggèd Individualism," *The American Mercury* (November, 1934),
Vol. 33, pp. 308-314. Reprinted by permission of the author and *The American Mercury*.

more and more meaningless as the circumstances which inspired it change. The process of emerging from this hypnosis, like that of shaking off the effects of any drug, is unpleasant, and it is not rendered any less so by the fact that one is immediately brought face to face with the realities from which one wanted to escape.

The mark of the druggèd individualist is his inability to comprehend the rôle of the state in modern civilization; he lives on in the dream that this is a pioneering era whose needs can best be fulfilled by leaving as much as is humanly possible to private enterprise. When a nation occupies a territory so vast as the United States, this collective sense of the state as the embodiment of the national will is often merely embryonic. It is not easy to feel patriotic about half a hemisphere in the same degree as one can feel patriotic about a limited, homogeneous area, such as nature and history have allotted to all other Western democracies. Local loyalties, therefore, are more real than national loyalties, since men are naturally devoted to the soil in which they have their roots. The New Englander's roots are not in the South, nor are the Southerner's in the West. The Federal tie is abstract rather than concrete, as is evidenced by setting the capital of the United States in a District artificially created for the purpose. There is no doubt as to the power of the Federal government to command and receive the loyalty of every American citizen in times of national crisis. But the emotional quality of that loyalty must necessarily differ from that of smaller nations in similar circumstances.

The fact that America has so rapidly and recently advanced from the status of a small pioneering country to that of the most influential of the first-class powers helps to preserve the illusions of the druggèd individualist, since it seems only yesterday that all the slogans and catchwords which beguile him were true. Every modern industrial country has undergone profound changes in the last hundred years, but elsewhere the evolution of the idea of the state, the building up of the social organism has been gradual, so that the older nations have been more prepared to accept that relationship towards the state which is nowadays essential. Only in America is government service regarded as an inferior occupation, as tantamount to a confession of failure, or of lack of ambition, at least. Where other peoples are proud to serve their country by accepting government employment, America shows her deep-seated indifference to the state by rendering such employment both socially and financially unattractive. Why it should be ignominious for the best brains in the country to be drawn into the Civil Service, that is, into the service of the state, only the druggèd individualist can tell. Let us listen to one.

A short while ago, Mr. Mark Sullivan was reported as bemoaning the fact that the young men coming out of college who consult him as to their careers are losing hope of "attaining success by individual enterprise," owing to the "regimentation" of business under the New Deal. The deplorable prospect of giving their talents in the service of the state, instead of going into business and making money, provokes in Mr. Sullivan these reflections:

> The youths who have come to me for advice this year have been puzzled and troubled in spirit. I should say that hardly one young man in ten, so long as he remains young, really likes the notion of a government career. Instinctively he feels that it is a little stifling, that it has the depressing quality of routine and regimentation, that its main recommendation is permanence and security. By instinct the larger number of normal young men prefer the competition that goes with careers in private business, the greater element of adventure and the chance, not possible in government careers, of really striking material success and reward.

Mr. Sullivan then proceeded to enlarge upon the subject by pointing out that "as surely as human beings are divided physically between blondes and brunettes" so surely are they divided between individualists by nature and collectivists by nature. This division he calmly defined as "those who instinctively prize independence and those who instinctively prefer supervision." And his conclusion was that America's choice between the individualist and the collectivist way of life will be determined by whichever of these two temperaments dominates. Holding up Lindbergh as the perfect type of triumphant individualism, he declared that there are "some millions of Lindberghs. There are a score in every village, hundreds in every town, thousands in every city," men who "were diligent in work and ambitious in spirit, who by character and personality impressed themselves on older men, who were thereby able to borrow money and get credit, and who came to the top of their respective lines in their respective communities."

All the fallacies of druggèd individualism are beautifully displayed in these quotations. There is, first of all, the gratuitous insinuation that young men should have no desire to serve the state, that the Civil Service is a sort of asylum for the disabled and incompetent and aged, with its corollary that profit-making is the first and highest ideal of youth. Then comes the misleading suggestion that anyone has ever proposed that everybody is equipped for government service, and that the natural differences of human temperament should be obliterated in one vast routine bureaucracy. Very adroitly the sense of collective duty is branded as a preference for "supervision," while the slow, onerous, and frequently subservient stages of a business career are glowingly described as "independence." The professions which are not primarily chosen for gain seem to be ignored, unless one is to assume that every activity outside a government department is "business,"—a very sweeping assumption. In conclusion, of course, comes the inevitable "success story" of the village lad who made good, Lindbergh being a veritable godsend for the purposes of argument in these times of universal depression, with the American figures of unemployment in the neighborhood of 10,000,000.

In citing such exploits as that of Lindbergh the druggèd individualist implies, without daring to say so explicitly, that an individual of this type would be completely discouraged if in the service of the government. Yet, one seems to have heard of aviators who have flown the Atlantic and undertaken other comparable flights while members of the army, navy or air forces of their respective countries. Even under the dictatorship of Mussolini, Balbo and his armada managed to accomplish a remarkable task without having to borrow money from skeptical business men to finance the undertaking. Balbo's initiative was not stifled by bureaucracy, nor has he since been used as a cat's-paw by airline promoters. If, as Mr. Sullivan says, Lindbergh's spirit of rugged enterprise so deeply impressed those who advanced him the money for his flight, it is curious that he arrived in Paris so disarmingly unconscious of this backing that he was astonished at not being called upon to identify himself by means of letters of introduction. He clearly left America in ignorance of the proud confidence he is now alleged to have inspired.

Whenever the profit-making motive lands our rugged individualists in disaster, then they are only too eager for government assistance, just as they are at all times ready to use the knowledge and information which the work of various government departments places at their disposal for the further exploitation of the public whose taxes pay for these departments. When the slogan is raised: "Keep the government out of business"—this invariably means, either that an attempt is being made to protect consumers, or that, as a result of pioneering and foresighted government expenditure, new sources of money-making have been opened up, as in the case of Boulder Dam. Why, one naturally wonders, is this precious spirit of individual, private initiative never in evidence when any project is afoot which promises benefits to the community as a whole, but only a very moderate profit in actual cash? Can it be that this boasted individualism without which, we are told, this country will go to the dogs, is essentially none other than plain commercial greed?

This suspicion is confirmed by the history of business as contrasted with governmental enterprise. While it is conceded that many great fortunes have been made and are maintained by methods based upon something more than "diligence in work" and "ambition in spirit," as these terms are commonly understood, it is always the practice to dwell with vast pride on the success story in all its variants. The effect of success of this kind on character is never discussed, nor the question as to whether the victor in the struggle is a finer human being, a more civilized asset to the community as a result of his gratifying bank balance. Yet, it may well be that a country too thoroughly imbued with crude mercantilist philosophy, a nation of bagmen, cannot survive in a world which is growing increasingly collectivized. Whatever illusions on this score may haunt the dreams of our druggèd individualists, every great industrial nation in the world, except America, is only too well aware that the present is not a simple pioneer period in history, nor one whose problems can be met in terms of eighteenth century radicalism.

Yet, whenever anybody condescends to disentangle druggèd individualism from the mere profiteering motive and to expound the philosophical background of this point of view, nothing emerges save this confusion of eighteenth century ideology and pioneering conditions. Thus Representative James M. Beck at the Calvin Coolidge anniversary exercises:

> The Constitution is the greatest charter of individualism in the annals of the world, and under it our government, once one of the smallest nations in the world, became the master state of the world.
>
> Certainly we built up in little more than a century, a civilization greater in diffused comfort, in equal conditions and general happiness than any other nation. We shared this mighty spirit of individual initiative with our English forebears, and it is humiliating to recall that to-day the people of England have retained to a greater extent the spirit of individual initiative, and as a consequence are farther advanced on the way to recovery from a world depression than we, who have in the last twelve months substituted a stupendous and unprecedented Federal bureaucracy for the initiative of the individual.

Here is the frank admission that America has far transcended the rôle foreseen by the Founding Fathers and long since passed beyond the stage of a small pioneering country. Yet, the only remedy proposed is that the government should ignore both these vital facts and revert to methods which have been proved so injurious that the only further demonstration can be to prove them ruinous. A "stupendous Federal bureaucracy" may be "unprecedented," but that does not prove that it is not desirable. The growth of America is also stupendous and unprecedented, so why should not stupendous and unprecedented methods be singularly appropriate? Mr. Beck, it will be noted, ignores the possibility that a bureaucracy, that is, the servants of the state, can have any other function than to be obstructive.

If it is incompetent, if it is obstructive, if it is dishonest—why not improve it, why not devote the time wasted on advocating impotent "individualism" to building up the prestige of the public service, to making it more worthy and representative of the community?

Nevertheless, Mr. Beck extols the individual initiative of England, from which he derives the American variety. Yet, bureaucracy in Britain has functioned for generations on the very scale that the druggèd individualists denounce. There the best brains of the universities and public schools are drawn upon by the state for the army, navy and Civil Service. No young Englishman would understand Mr. Mark Sullivan's theory that government employment is the refuge of spineless creatures who are afraid of responsibility. Bureaucrats most efficiently administer services which do not even exist in this country, as they administer others which are a source of profit to the nation as a whole, whereas here those same services benefit chiefly and extravagantly those rugged individualists who happen to be large stockholders. The result of that British individual initiative which Mr. Beck so rightly admires is that the government can call upon as highly competent, as well equipped, and as experienced a group of experts in their various fields as has ever been produced even by the most generous money rewards offered by American business.

The advantage of attracting first-rate men into the service of the state is obvious both in foreign and domestic affairs, but druggèd individualists are still convinced that money-making is the only worthy objective of man, even when making a bare living is becoming more and more hazardous. The result is that, when men of genuine ability accept Federal appointments, they very soon succumb to the persistent, all-pervasive, anti-government propaganda, and are lured into private business by monetary and other considerations. They are richer for the exchange, Uncle Sam the poorer, so much so that, in emergencies, the government has to borrow qualified men from business, whereas other nations maintain their services, civil, military, and naval, in such a fashion that a man would feel as disgraced in abandoning them for trade as any soldier or sailor would feel disgraced if he started huckstering and bargaining for better terms, before going into battle.

"The individualist," said Mr. Beck, in the address from which I have quoted, "is a citizen who first creates and then controls his government. The collectivist is a subject who surrenders his own judgment to the arbitrary dictates of a governmental bureaucracy." The exact opposite of this is the case. A collectivist first creates and then controls his own government, thereby controlling his own bureaucracy. An individualist of the druggèd variety surrenders his own judgment to the arbitrary slogans and politicians, thereby losing control of his own government. Mistrust of the state, bordering on an almost total misconception of its functions in the modern world, is illustrated by this striking distortion of the meaning of "collectivist," which by definition involves an active belief in the use of government for collective purposes, i.e., for the benefit of all. This is described as "surrender," just as the service of the state is called a desire for "supervision," and the endless kowtowings, concessions, and servilities of the business world are fondly referred to as "independence."

One would imagine that, at least since the crash of 1929, the precise limitations of our anti-bureaucratic exemplars of private enterprise and individual initiative had become such a matter of universal knowledge, and often contempt, that it would be impossible to argue seriously that such leaders are reliable guides in national affairs. The most incompetent bureaucrats in history have never been shown up to worse advantage, while few of similar rank, standing, and responsibility have been convicted of such ruthless indifference to the public welfare, on the one hand, and of such childish helplessness and ignorance, on the other, in precisely those matters in which public confidence had vested them with complete and untrammelled authority. Yet, we find Representative Beck declaring that, "if men at times make mistakes, and all do, their mistakes are not as great or so harmful as those of the typical bureaucrat. . . . If the individual makes a mistake, it is his own error and he suffers accordingly, but if the bureaucracy makes a mistake, the individual suffers for something for which he is not responsible."

Here, again, we note the familiar technique of the druggèd individualist in argument. There are two false assumptions. The first is that, when a government official blunders, he does not pay the consequences. The second is that, when the industrial and financial masterminds misled the country with bad advice and wholly fallacious prognostications, when they continued, after the crash, to misinterpret or misrepresent the facts, they alone paid the penalty, that their mistakes were less harmful and of less importance than those of a government department. Yet, statistics based on Dun's *Review,* on October 17, 1931, quoted the amount of liabilities in failures as $332,425,638, $473,043,174, and $531,776,004, for the years 1929, 1930, and 1931, respectively. In December, 1929, the rugged individualism of the National City Bank found expression in the statement that "there are no great failures nor are there likely to be." In the spring of 1931 the equally rugged individualism of Andrew W. Mellon assured the Congress of the International Chamber of Commerce that reductions in wages would be avoided "at all costs."

A couple of months later he reduced the wages of all employés of the

Aluminum Company of America by 10%. In fact, during those years of acute crisis, the stream of childish platitudes and evasive untruths was so promptly and regularly contradicted by the facts that Senator Simeon D. Fess had to confess indignantly that "every time an Administration official gives out an optimistic statement about business conditions, the market immediately drops." This, the druggèd individualist declared, was all because of a concerted effort to discredit President Hoover.

No bureaucracy could have been more helpless or more costly to the country than these exponents of private enterprise and initiative proved themselves and were proven to be. The only difference is that, however competent or incompetent, the bureaucrat is not out for personal gain; by the very nature of his position he has renounced money-making to devote his abilities to the public service. Whatever the anti-brain trusters may say about "professors," the latter do not, as a rule, so conduct themselves as to merit such criticism as that recently published by the Senate Banking Committee: "Many of the abuses have resulted from the incompetence, negligence, irresponsibility or cupidity of individuals in the profession." Cupidity is a powerful factor in the career of the rugged individualist. It is automatically eliminated from a first-class Civil Service. It is incredible that politicians and publicists can still continue to argue as if the choice lay between a wasteful, extravagant, ineffectual bureaucracy and the shrewd, foresighted and self-sacrificing men of affairs. As the Senate Banking Committee's report pointed out:

> Despite the grave responsibility which his fiduciary position imposed upon him, the investment banker took no steps to curb the speculative fervor which swept over the investors in his field from 1926 to 1929. On the contrary, he was content to float new issues as long as the investing public was willing and able to absorb them, regardless of the inevitable consequences.
>
> The colossal loss sustained by the public on bond issues sponsored by the investment bankers manifests that those bankers were either incompetent or derelict in the performance of their duties.

Rugged individualists all! No wonder, when times are good, that they want the government to keep its hands off business.

One might continue indefinitely citing cases to prove that government servants are not necessarily incompetent and unenterprising, and that private enterprise and initiative are not always to the advantage of the community. A vast number of services of all kinds are collectivized, more in some countries than in others, and they are as efficiently conducted as those in the hands of private ownership. The point is that, whether efficiently or inefficiently managed, their aim is not profits but the public welfare. Inefficiency and even downright dishonesty in business can exist as well as honesty and fair play. In neither case does the community benefit as it would under public ownership. In this country the legend persists from pioneering times, and is carefully cultivated for obviously interested reasons, that public ownership is always and everywhere bad, and that the faintest approach to government control should be resisted as an attack on the liberty of the people.

The result is that there is less public ownership in America than in the other great Western democracies. In fact, nothing that can conceivably show a profit has been left to the government, State or Federal, although many services could be more economically performed by one or another of these agencies. For historical and geographical reasons, the American sense of the state is more embryonic than that of other nations, and expresses itself differently. The question, therefore, arises as to whether, in the crisis through which civilization is passing to-day, America can afford to indulge in the daydreams of druggèd individualism, that is individualism based upon outworn phrases and having no relation to the realities of contemporary industrial and economic conditions. Collectivism has made the army and the navy of the United States. Why should the spirit that inspires it be anathema? It also, by the way, built the Panama Canal, after the scandalous and ignominious failure of private, profiteering enterprise.

Chapter XXIII

RAISING THE MONEY FOR GOVERNMENT

[As noted in the preceding chapter, the field of governmental activity is rapidly expanding both in scope and intensity. The remaining chapters of this book are devoted to a consideration of old and new governmental functions. Our concern here, however, is with the relationship of these functions to the problems of public finance. If the people demand schools and highways, policemen and health officers, regulation of business and protection of the consumer, and if these demands on government continue to increase, it is clear that the government must, by some means, raise more money to-morrow than it is securing to-day. If revenues fail to meet proposed expenditures, any of several consequences may follow. It may result in an increase of taxes, either by increasing the rate of taxation or broadening its base. A second possibility is to curtail or reduce the activities of government. A third is to borrow. No magic formula can be found, in spite of the desires of candidates for public office, which will enable government to continue its services and not at the same time force it to continue its programs for the raising of sufficient revenue. The question of taxes is consequently directly related to public policy on governmental activities. The complaint over high taxes cannot be divorced from it.

If we can decide on what we wish government to do for us, and how much this will cost, we have by no means solved our tax problems. Taxation, although the major, is not the sole source of public revenues. Government derives income, for example, from borrowing and from the earnings of its enterprises. Taxation is, however, the most important item on the revenue side of the governmental ledger. If we know how much we wish to spend, and what portion of this sum must come from taxes, we must then determine what kinds of taxes should be levied and which should be avoided. Furthermore we must decide which level of government shall use, exclusively or in conjunction with other units, the various kinds of taxation. Our federal system of government and the number and complex structure of local government units make this latter problem a particularly difficult one in the United States.

There is finally the problem of evaluating the tax structure we now have with reference to the possible demands that may be made on it in the future. If reconstruction or reform is needed, the issue must be faced directly and now. The essays in this chapter throw light on all of these questions of tax policy.]

No. 82

A TAX POLICY FOR THE UNITED STATES [1]

by Harold M. Groves

FOR the last ten years powerful interests in this country have been quietly working for a sales tax. Their position is summarized as follows by one of the Hearst papers: "When the Democratic party has the sincerity to be democratic, when it has the patriotism to be American, it will substitute excise taxation and sales taxation for undemocratic, un-American, discriminatory, income taxation with its crooked evasion and equally crooked enforcement." The American Bankers' Association Journal in a leading article not long ago sang the praises of the sales tax as follows: "The sales tax is the most effective, the most just and the most equitable of all taxes. Its adoption is only a question of time."

It will be recalled that the manufacturers' sales tax was presented to Congress in the spring of 1932 as the logical measure for removing the huge federal deficit. And it will be remembered that it brought forth such an avalanche of opposition both in and outside of Congress that the House voted it down by 263 to 161. Following this defeat, it was thought by many that the decisive battle concerning this issue had been fought.

Now it looks as if this country might have a sales tax after all, adopted not by the federal Congress, but by the legislatures of the various states. . . . Fifteen such laws were enacted during the depression and thirteen were passed during 1933 alone. [More than half of the states now have a sales tax.] Already Congress is being urged to relieve the states of a difficult administrative burden by enacting a federal sales-tax law with a return of 50 per cent of the revenue to the states. The spread of the sales tax in this country has been compared with that of the gasoline tax, which came into general use within a period of two or three years and into universal use within a decade.

Why are the states accepting an instrument of taxation that Congress dropped like a red-hot coal? The answer is to be found in their experience during the depression. The property tax, which has always been the mainstay of the states, has lost its elasticity. As soon as the depression began, property owners entered a vigorous protest against the high fixed charge which the property tax exacted from them even when their property was

---

[1] Harold M. Groves, "A Tax Policy for the United States," *The New Republic* (February 7, 1934), Vol. 77, pp. 357-359. Reprinted by permission of *The New Republic*.

unproductive. The states yielded to the taxpayers' demands, first, by decreasing assessments without changing tax rates, then by decreasing rates, and finally by recklessly imposing statutory and constitutional maximum rates beyond which municipalities could not levy on property.

The states as well as the federal government have had extraordinary expenditures to meet during this depression. Much of the time the states and their subdivisions have carried the full burden of relief. And even now the federal relief administration requires, as a condition of federal assistance, evidence of local effort to meet the cost of relief. Some states have interpreted this as a federal mandate to enact a sales tax.

The states could not greatly reduce their normal expenses without defaulting or seriously sacrificing standards in some extremely essential public services. Many states and their subdivisions have heavy fixed charges in the form of interest on debt, and over a thousand municipal units are, or have been, in default. Yet most of the primary functions of government, including education and highways, are their direct responsibility. The federal government, for example, has contributed practically nothing toward the support of education. The states and their municipalities normally spend about two-thirds of the citizen's tax dollar. . . .

Very few untapped sources of revenue were available to the states. Of these the most important were the state income tax and the general sales tax. The state income tax met with strong objection in the claim that "you can't tax net income when there isn't any." It was asserted to be quite impossible, within the limits prescribed by administrative feasibility, interstate competition and the resistance of the taxpayers, to raise worth-while sums from a net-income tax in some of the agricultural states like South Dakota. While only partially valid, these assertions carried great weight. Moreover, the federal government was already in this field and the net-income tax encountered constitutional barriers in many states. Under these circumstances it is little wonder that new ground has been gained by the sales tax.

It is plain enough that the state sales tax does not escape the cogent objections that were offered in Congress against a national sales tax. In fact a state sales tax is more objectionable, since it is far more difficult to administer and creates more problems in interstate competition between industries. The fact that 60 per cent of the purchases of goods and services are made by consumers receiving less than $2,000 a year is as important in the one field as it is in the other. Moreover, a large share of state and local revenue is already raised by a definitely regressive tax that is paid directly or indirectly by the humblest citizen. No one escapes the general property tax, for it is reflected in rent. The tax is regressive in actual practice both because local assessors quite universally favor large property owners, intentionally or otherwise, and because a large part of the tax is shifted and—like the sales tax—is paid by the consumer. To use the sales tax as a supplement is to add a second regressive tax and a further burden to those who are already staggering under the load of the property tax. Surely there is some better alternative to closed schools and half-paid public employees.

Three lines of action that will make a state sales tax unnecessary can be urged. The first is to use the federal income and estate taxes to help support education. Unrestricted interstate travel, migration and trade are steadily creating a closer knit and more interdependent country. A national minimum standard of educational opportunity has become of universal interest. The people of Massachusetts are no longer unconcerned if 25 per cent of the children of Arkansas are allowed to grow up in ignorance. The educational system, now financed almost exclusively by local districts through taxes upon property, should be a first charge upon the ability to pay of the entire nation.

It is true that federal aid involves difficult problems of distribution, supervision and federal finance. These problems will require the best efforts of experts and statesmen. But they are not insuperable. And it must be remembered that the alternatives may be the sales tax or closed schools or both.

The second plank in the program is to continue the fight for state income taxes. Only about half [now three-fourths] of the states have a net-income tax, and among those which do not are the rich and populous states of Michigan, Illinois, Ohio, Pennsylvania, New Jersey and Indiana.

There is much room for improvement in existing state laws. They are quite as leaky as the federal, but no more difficult to mend. Many impose rates that are little more than a gesture. The recent New Mexico law imposes a top rate of 4 per cent, and applies this rate only to income above $100,000. In addition, the law offers the taxpayer generous property-tax offsets. New Mexico apparently has taken no chances of driving wealth from the state by this law; nor can it have taken very seriously its resolution to substitute income taxes for other sources of revenue.

Further development of state income taxes is often resisted on the ground that the federal government has preëmpted the field. Or it is said that since the federal government has many advantages in the administration and collection of the net-income tax, it should be given a monopoly. The case for this proposition would be much stronger if the federal government were to assume some responsibility in financing education, as recommended in our first plank. Until the federal government adopts such a policy, the states have only the grim alternatives to the net-income tax stated above—

excessive taxes on property, the sales tax, starving necessary public services or default. The net-income tax is clearly better than any of these. Moreover, unless the states are to be entirely deprived of their financial independence, which seems neither likely nor desirable, taxes based on ability to pay—which means income and inheritance taxes—will continue to have a legitimate place in their tax systems.

It will be said, of course, that a state income tax will amount to confiscation if added to the federal tax, which now runs up to a maximum rate of [75] per cent. But the argument is misleading. The federal rates are not so high as they seem, for nobody pays the maximum rate on his full income. The [75]-per cent rate is actually applied only to that portion of a taxpayer's income which exceeds [five] million dollars. Moreover, the federal government permits a deduction of state taxes as an expense before calculating its tax. This means that the federal government collects only on that portion of net income not taken by the states. Many of the states permit a deduction of the federal tax and some of them permit a deduction of their own taxes as well. This procedure in itself is an assurance that overlapping taxes are not likely to become confiscatory.

Those who fear the cumulative effect of federal and state income taxes should indorse the suggestion frequently made that the federal government give the taxpayer a credit against his federal tax for any income taxes that he pays the states. Such a credit would go much further than the federal deduction already allowed, which is merely against the taxpayer's income, whereas the proposed credit would directly decrease the taxpayer's federal taxes. There is precedent for the proposed credit in the federal estate tax, which allows the taxpayer to pay 80 per cent of his federal tax with a state inheritance tax receipt. In addition to putting a check upon double taxation, a federal credit would tend to eliminate territorial competition in the taxation field. States that seek to attract industry and wealth on the ground that they levy no net-income taxes would lose the advantage of the federal credit for their taxpayers. Now that the federal government is spending large sums for relief in all states, it might reasonably collect an extra surtax in those states which refuse to tax on the ability-to-pay basis. The suggested federal tax credit is a sound device for doing exactly that.

The third plank in the no-state-sales-tax program is to relieve the property taxpayer by modifying the property tax rather than by reducing assessments, rates and revenues. One of the principal objections to the general property tax is that it is not based upon the net property of the taxpayer, but upon his gross assets. Thus if Farmer X buys a farm worth $10,000, pays $2,000 down and gives his note and mortgage for the remainder, he will be taxed from the outset on $10,000 worth of property. On the other hand, the mortgagee, who has an $8,000 claim against the farm and is probably better able to pay taxes than Farmer X, will, as a rule, pay no property taxes upon his claim.

We have heard much during this depression about the necessity of helping the debtor in various ways, through moratoria on foreclosures, refinancing farm and home loans and so forth. The property tax as conducted in the American states is a device by which a large part of the communities' taxes are loaded upon the debtor class and escaped by the creditors. Tax relief for the debtor is both timely and fundamentally sound at the present time.

If the states wish to make the property tax more in accord with ability to pay, they can do so by making it apply to the "net worth" of the taxpayer—including all assets both tangible and intangible. A property tax so conceived would be a personal tax. It would not apply to corporations. Debts would be deductible and credits (stocks, bonds and mortgages) would be included among assets. The rate might be moderately graduated where state constitutions would permit, and appropriate exemptions provided to protect small savings. It would be unnecessary to substitute such a "net worth tax" for the property tax all at once. Instead, the new type of tax could be inaugurated as a supplement to the present tax.

The objection which will be offered against such a tax is that it is impossible to administer. The net-income tax encountered the same objection many years ago. The administrative difficulty was largely overcome by centralized administration and civil-service administrators. The "net worth tax" might escape its administrative difficulties by using the same formula. The estate tax is based upon the net value of all the property of the deceased at the time of death. This tax, too, involves difficult problems of evaluation and detection of property. But, nevertheless, it is now very well administered.

Professor Seligman once said that "the sales tax constitutes the last resort of countries which find themselves in such fiscal difficulties that they must subordinate all other principles of taxation to that of adequacy." The most fortunate and best endowed country in the world ought not to accept a tax measure with so little to recommend it. Rather it should seize one or all of the much better alternatives outlined above.

No. 83

LOCAL FINANCE [1]

by Philip H. Cornick

EACH of the forty-eight States seems to have at least two systems of local finance in operation; many States have more than two. In some of the older States there is what is entitled the general tax law, cited in practically all compendiums on the subject, although it is no longer general except in name. It is operative in all of its provisions only in rural areas if at all. Elsewhere throughout those States local finance is governed by special acts applicable to individual cities, to classes of cities or villages, or to urban communities as a whole.

Paralleling the general and special tax laws there are other acts controlling the financial operations of local governments in general or by more or less arbitrary classes—budget acts, bond acts, acts stipulating what expenditures may be made and what expenditures must be made. Under the systems in vogue in the several States—systems which frequently suffer from lack of internal coordination—the 160,000 overlapping units of government are spending ordinarily out of current revenues about one and a half times as much as the State and federal governments combined. To indicate the scale of local expenditures from borrowings, it is only necessary to say that before the federal government embarked on its program of depression borrowing, the local governments had debts outstanding which approximately equalled those of the federal and State governments in conjunction.

The entire fabric of local expenditures, furthermore, has in the course of years been welded in many States into a rigid structure by such devices as minimum tax lexies for certain functions, maximum levies for others; maximum aggregate levies for all purposes (sometimes for single units of government, sometimes for all overlapping units within a given area); fixed pay scales for certain types of civil servants, and progressive pay scales for other types of civil servants.

To finance these expenditures, the laws provided, first, a loosely hung revenue system and, second, a loosely controlled system of borrowing, in both of which the valuations of property played an important part. Taxes on the capital value of property as indicated by market prices provided

[1] Philip H. Cornick, "Local Finance," *The Nation* (November 21, 1934), Vol. 139, pp. 586-588. This article was reprinted with some changes in Paul Studenski and others, *Taxation and Public Policy* (New York: Richard R. Smith, 1936), Ch. 5, and is reprinted here by permission of Richard R. Smith and *The Nation*.

two-thirds or more of the current revenues. Ratios based on those capital values provided the legal limitations on the aggregate local debts which could be incurred. As property values increased, the limitations on revenues and on debts increased hand in hand; as they declined, those limitations declined similarly. Unfortunately, the debts already incurred could not be reduced at the same rate. Therein lies one of the major causes of the present financial stringency of local governments.

The items included in the property tax base vary widely from State to State and sometimes even from locality to locality within the same State. In at least one city in Pennsylvania the list of taxable properties includes only the full value of land and, in effect, one-half the value of buildings. In the rest of that State, as well as in New York, the list is restricted to lands and buildings, both taxable on full value. In other States the list includes such items of tangible personalty as the assessors can find; in still others, even stocks, bonds, mortgages, and other intangibles are also taxable on full value, in law if not in practice.

Judged by purely pragmatic tests, these diverse systems served their purpose reasonably well from about 1897 to 1929, while property values were generally advancing. In 1907, in 1913, and again in 1921 there were disquieting symptoms. To-day thousands of local governments are in default on their bonded debt. Others have avoided default in that field only at the expense of not meeting current pay rolls. In many areas some essential local services have been eliminated and others drastically curtailed. While levies have tended to mount, revenue receipts have declined markedly. On the basis of these facts, each of them indisputable, a large and noisy segment of the general public is busily voicing the conclusion that the existing system of local finance has broken down and must be made over on a new pattern.

On the other hand, there are facts which would warrant conclusions diametrically opposed to this. For example, while it is true that a distressingly large number of cities have been forced to default on bond payments or pay rolls and to cut down on essential services, it is equally true that for every local unit in this group there are scores which have met every obligation as it fell due, and which have succeeded in retrenching in the costs of services without serious curtailment in the quality or quantity of the services rendered. In other words, while the existing systems of local finance in this country have nowhere escaped the effects of the world-wide financial stringency, they are in a state of collapse only in certain local areas.

It is significant, furthermore, that the local governments which are in direst distress are not distributed at random throughout the nation. Instead, they preponderate in certain fairly well-defined types of community and tend to concentrate in certain regions. Resort cities built on no firmer foundation than that of catering to the needs, whims, and weaknesses of tourists; satellite cities in the suburban fringes of metropolitan areas; farming counties which built rural highway systems on specifications suited to streets in congested cities; rural school districts which erected buildings of a type devised to meet the needs of densely populated urban areas; mushroom oil cities in the West; and here and there a great city prostrated by the almost complete paralysis of its overexpanded industries—these and other local governments of equally abnormal types have contributed defaults out of all proportion to their total number. Many of them were merely real-estate promotions. All of them suffered from temporarily inflated land prices out of all proportion to past, present, or probable future incomes.

Even in areas, however, where the local governments have succeeded in discharging faithfully and economically every obligation to citizens and creditors alike, the burden of taxation is painful, and the chorus of protest grows. Under competent leadership this protest might be used as a means to a much-needed simplification of the structure of local governments, to the reallocation of functions among federal, State, and local governments, and to the erection of an integrated tax system for federal, State, and local purposes. But leadership is absent. The checks and balances, the blurred lines of authority and responsibility within units of local government, and the conflicts of authority among overlapping units—all imposed from without—have made a career in municipal government singularly unattractive to able and high-minded citizens. In some of the State governments the situation is worse. When one party or faction at election after election places its candidate in the governor's chair, and the opposing party or faction just as consistently dominates both houses of the legislature, party responsibility becomes a memory, and party leadership a farce. To put the other side in a hole becomes the aim of political strategists.

Having looked vainly for leadership in that quarter, the people are turning to obscure, inexperienced, and often ignorant leaders. In State after State loosely drawn constitutional amendments providing for a rigid limitation of property taxes have been proposed by such men and adopted by overwhelming majorities. In Michigan and West Virginia local government in the larger cities would have been paralyzed if the courts had not found ways out of the dilemma created by such enactments. In Ohio a similar crisis impends. In other States comparable amendments are on the ballots. In California, before this is printed, the voters will have made their decision on a constitutional amendment designed to wipe out every existing tax and to substitute therefor a general tax on sales and transactions. In spite of its new-fangled name, the "syncrotax," this proposed substitute belongs in the category of taxes so aptly described by Edwin Cannan when he said that they were "well concealed from their ultimate payers by being administered in small doses wrapped up in prices."

In other sections relief for real estate has long been sought, not by tax limitation, but by the imposition of taxes on occupations in the guise of business licenses. The area within which they are being resorted to is steadily expanding. Almost half a century ago, in a book which has been out of print for so long that it has been forgotten even by its authors, Richard T. Ely and John Finley made a harsh but just appraisal of these taxes.

> The license system may be fairly called medieval in its character. . . . It pushes the comparatively weaker elements and the industrially unfortunate down. . . . Licenses like many of ours remind me of taxation in the time of feudalism, when only those were taxed who were too weak to resist.

But while these misguided efforts at tax reform are in progress, the old property tax is showing sturdy qualities which even its few friends had not suspected. In cities of 30,000 and over, municipal revenue receipts as a whole declined from 1929 to 1932 (the last year for which comprehensive figures are available) 16 per cent. It is interesting, therefore, not to say amusing, to observe that the receipts from taxes on property declined only 11 per cent, and those from all other sources together 24 per cent. As the receipts from these other sources declined—including the receipts from municipal shares in State-administered taxes on sales and incomes—the levy on property had perforce to be increased. Fixed charges and the costs of providing local services essential to the public health, welfare, and safety cannot lightly be evaded. The conclusion is therefore inescapable that if the heterogeneous group of tax reformers which has stood for "broadening the tax base" had had its way, and if our municipalities during the period of prosperity had erected their revenue structure more largely on those other bases, they might well have faced a decline in revenue more serious than that which actually confronted them.

The reason for this state of affairs is not far to seek. The tax on property is an assessed tax. The valuation, at least, of real estate can be established by public officials on the basis of objective indices, and the rate of the tax is computed to meet revenue requirements. The taxpayer has the right to administrative review and of appeal to the courts, but when he has exhausted these remedies, the levy becomes effective. Taxes on sales and on incomes, on the other hand, are self-assessed taxes. The rates are established beforehand and are then applied by the taxpayer himself to the value of the base which he certifies in his return. While the public officials have a right of audit and review, the objective indices available for this purpose, in the overwhelming majority of instances, cover a very narrow range. The tax base, therefore, may fluctuate widely, not only because of a decline in honesty. Honesty in all but a few exceptional individuals is probably too fragile a quality to survive the strains imposed by self-assessed taxes during a depression.

But the property tax has another quality which adds to its toughness. Once the tax has been levied, it remains a lien until paid. Under the first impact of the depression the collections of current taxes declined drastically, but a correspondingly large volume of receivables accumulated on the books. Some of these are wholly uncollectable, chiefly those outstanding on vacant lots for which there is no demand whatsoever either in the present or within a predictable future. The remainder will become cash receipts sooner or later. In one city which was on the verge of financial collapse less than a year ago the combined cash receipts in current and delinquent taxes this year have already reached a sum in excess of the current levy. Conditions in that city are probably not wholly unparalleled elsewhere, as the statistics should prove when they become available. Should cases of this nature be indicative, it is not too much to say that the most urgent need of American local finance in the immediate future is a cessation of attempts to cripple, by hampering limitations, the operations of the only important element in the existing tax system which has been sturdy enough to come back in the face of the depression.

For the more distant future other remedies are indicated. As one looks back over the checkered history of American local finance, three great crises stand out. These came in the periods following 1837, 1873, and 1929. Each had been preceded by almost insane booms in land prices, accompanied by lavish expenditures of public funds on improvements designed to serve the lands lying at the centers of most intense speculation. The last two of these booms, furthermore, were accentuated by the dislocations in the normal economy of the nation by the great wars which immediately preceded them, and by the methods used in financing them. Who shall say that these conjunctions came about by chance—that these wars and land booms were not the primary causes of the subsequent crises in local credit? The greatest obstacles in the way of stable systems of municipal finance would seem to be wars and speculation in land. How the first evil may be minimized will no doubt be adequately treated in an article later in this series. The elimination of the second lies within the scope of local finance itself. An adequate tax on land values will do it. Henry George outlined the method in his analysis of what happened after the collapse of 1873.

No. 84

COORDINATION OF AMERICAN FINANCE [1]

by Clarence Heer

RESPONSIBILITY for the raising and spending of taxes in the United States is divided among no fewer than 180,000 independent and semi-independent political units. Yet however badly we may need to coordinate federal, State, and local finance in certain particular respects, the present predilection for coordination as an abstract principle represents a distinct danger. There is of course no more virtue in coordination per se than there is in decentralization per se. Coordinating devices are merely means for obtaining certain ends. Their value can be judged only in terms of the objectives they are designed to achieve. One recent proposal for obtaining a greater degree of coordination between federal and State finance, for instance, would have the effect of firmly fastening the sales tax on us as a permanent part of our revenue system.

It is beginning to dawn on us that governments, through their taxing and spending programs, exercise, willy-nilly, a profound influence upon the course of private business. We are beginning to see that fiscal policies may be deliberately framed with a view to promoting economic stability. But a tax policy for recovery, or for any other purpose, cannot be made effective in the United States as long as tax-raising and tax-spending functions are distributed among 180,000 political units which are grandly left to shift for themselves. Only the federal government has made any attempt in the last two fiscal years to adapt its fiscal program to the requirements of recovery. During that time it has expended some three billion dollars on emergency public works and unemployment relief. Very properly it has financed these expenditures by means of credit rather than increased taxation.

Unfortunately, the recovery efforts of the federal government have been largely nullified by efforts in an opposite direction on the part of States and localities. During the seven years ending in 1930 the net long-term borrowings of State and local governments, after allowance is made for re-

[1] Clarence Heer, "Coordination of American Finance," *The Nation* (December 19, 1934), Vol. 139, pp. 705-707. This article was reprinted with some changes in Paul Studenski and others, *Taxation and Public Policy* (New York: Richard R. Smith, 1936), Ch. 8, and is reprinted here by permission of Richard R. Smith and *The Nation*.

funding and retirements, averaged very close to a billion dollars per annum. These borrowings were spent for the most part on permanent capital improvements, became income to someone, and helped swell the stream of current purchasing power. In 1932, according to the *Commercial and Financial Chronicle,* the net long-term borrowings of States and municipalities for purposes other than refunding dropped to about two hundred million dollars. In 1933 net borrowings disappeared altogether, the volume of bonds retired exceeding the volume of new issues. This is, of course, only part of the story of deflation as practiced by State and local governments during the current depression. State and local budgets have been everywhere cruelly slashed. Educational expenditures were reduced by half a billion dollars between 1930 and 1934. School expenditures per child enrolled declined from a national average of $90 in 1930 to $67 in 1934.

Had State and local governments adapted their fiscal policies to the requirements of recovery, they would have refrained as far as possible from levying new taxes or increasing the rates of old ones. To the extent that new taxes were unavoidable, they would have selected such taxes as were likely to trench on savings rather than on necessary consumption. Actually, as we all know, the outstanding fiscal invention of the depression period was the sales tax. It is a fact worth pondering that more money was raised through State sales taxes during the fiscal year just closed than was raised through State income taxes.

The States and their subdivisions carry the responsibility of financing a major share of the normal costs of government. But only the federal government possesses the credit resources and is capable of adequately exploiting the types of taxes needed to execute a fiscal program for recovery. It is clear, then, that there must be a considerable degree of financial cooperation between federal, State, and local governments if a fiscal program for recovery is to succeed.

Economic stability will of course be only one of the objectives toward which the fiscal policy of the new social state will be directed. Since the importance of other objectives is more generally recognized, they may be passed over rather hurriedly. It goes without saying that the new social state will seek to distribute the burden of taxation in an equitable manner. It will endeavor to distribute the services and benefits of government in accordance with social needs. In the case of functions, such as education and health, which are of vital interest to the nation as a whole, it will assure to all of its citizens, in whatever part of the country they may reside, a national minimum of services. It will budget the total tax funds of the country among various functions with due regard to the relative social importance of each function. Finally, it will seek to secure as much economy and efficiency in tax administration as is compatible with its other aims.

It is easy to understand why we cannot hope to come within reaching distance of any of the objectives mentioned under our present scheme of intergovernmental fiscal relations. Under this scheme the functions of government are parceled out among a multitude of more or less independent jurisdictions. The range of taxes which the various jurisdictions are in a position to administer effectively is largely conditioned by their territorial extent. Altogether apart from legal restrctions, the only form of taxation from which local governments are likely to secure much revenue is the general property tax, or more correctly the tax on real estate. The situs of real estate is fixed. In an extremely mobile world most other subjects of taxation are too active and elusive to be caught in the small tax nets which municipalities, counties, and districts are able to spread.

State governments, because of their wider areas, have a broader range of taxes at their disposal, but even they are subject to handicaps which the federal government escapes. Lack of uniformity in the taxing systems of the various States stimulates tax avoidance and evasion. The avenue of escape opened up by the interstate commerce clause makes certain forms of State taxation inequitable. Interstate tax competition makes it difficult for any State to depart too widely from the pattern of taxation set by its neighbors. No single State, for instance, could proceed very far with a program of steeply progressive income and inheritance taxes. There are too many other States in which less democratic ideas on taxation prevail.

Modern economic life is closely integrated. Wealth and income are to an increasing extent the result of processes to which all sections of the country contribute. But the legal bases of taxing jurisdiction are not founded on any ultimate inquiry into economic origins. They depend on such criteria as the location of physical property, the domicile of owners and income recipients, and the presumed situs of business operations. Since these criteria tend to be concentrated in a few urban areas, there are wide variations in the capacity of both localities and States to support public services. Notwithstanding these differences in ability, certain functions which are affected, to a degree at least, with a national interest are now supported almost entirely on a State and local basis. This makes for gross regional inequalities in respect of services which ought to be subject to nation-wide standards. Another serious shortcoming of our present fiscal order is that it militates against a rational budgeting of the total tax funds of the country. The relative amount of support accorded any particular function is now determined to no small extent, not by the relative importance of the function itself, but by the relative efficiency as a tax-raising unit of the level of government to which the function has been assigned.

Little need be said about the administrative wastes and duplications which are inevitable under a regime of fiscal separatism. The dual administration of the same types of taxes by both the federal government and the States is naturally a source of annoyance and expense to the taxpayer. When States attempt to administer types of taxes which they are not capable of administering as effectively as is the federal government, taxable assets are wastefully dissipated. When federal, State, and local governments vie with one another in the competitive exploitation of the same tax sources, the result may be a net loss to the country at large. The current situation in the matter of liquor taxation supplies an excellent case in point.

It is clear that some form of coordination of federal, State, and local finance is needed, but what kind of coordination shall it be? One proposal is that the device of federal credit for State taxes, which has been used for a number of years in the field of inheritance taxation, be extended to other taxes, specifically income taxes on individuals and corporations. The one virtue of the federal crediting device is that it effectually eliminates intergovernmental tax competition. Its extension to the field of income taxation would force all States to levy income taxes at rates high enough to absorb the federal credit. The crediting device, however, would contribute very little toward the attainment of the major objectives set up for the new social state. Its chief beneficiaries would be the wealthy industrial and commercial States. It would not solve the problem of regional inequalities in taxable capacity, nor would it do away with duplicate tax administration.

Other proposals contemplate the exclusive collection of certain taxes by the federal government and a sharing of their proceeds with the States. From the standpoint of efficiency it is certainly desirable to give the federal government a monopoly of all taxes in respect of which it enjoys a marked administrative advantage. The difficulty comes in agreeing upon a formula for distributing the proceeds of such taxes among the States. State-shared federal taxes raise other questions, too, which cannot be pushed aside. As long as the States and localities remain solely responsible for supplying certain vital governmental services, can they afford to jeopardize those services by accepting a fixed percentage share of specified federal taxes in return for a partial surrender of their present taxing powers? Is it wise to divorce the raising of taxes from control over their expenditure? Ought the proceeds of national taxes to be expended for any functions or services which are not invested with some degree of national interest?

If one answers any or all of these questions in the negative, another plan of coordination which retains the advantages of centralized tax administration is still open. According to this plan the federal government would be given exclusive jurisdiction over income, inheritance, liquor, tobacco, and all other taxes which it is in a position to administer more effectively than the States. In return for this addition to its taxing power, and to compensate the States for their loss, the federal government would assume financial responsibility for the maintenance of minimum national standards in respect of such State and local functions as education, health, and welfare, which are of more than purely local concern. Administration of the functions in question would remain with the States and localities, but the federal government would see to it that its standards were enforced. This is, of course, merely an application of the familiar subsidy principle and is no novelty in federal and State finance. It would appear to come closer to achieving the objectives set up for the new social state than any other plan currently suggested.

But genuine fiscal coordination will not be achieved through piecemeal expedients directed at one or more specific abuses which happen to afflict us at the present moment. In a highly dynamic age intergovernmental arrangements such as tax credits, nationally administered State-shared taxes, or federal subsidies will have to be constantly readjusted to meet changing conditions. We cannot expect to navigate the tortuous financial channels of the future by setting our ship on a predetermined course with the tiller firmly lashed. What we need above everything else is intelligent pilots, and at present such pilots are lacking.

This lack may easily be remedied through the creation of a federal-State commission on fiscal coordination. A central coordinating agency of this kind would not in any sense constitute a super-government. Its duties would be purely planning and advisory. It would perform much the same function for the country at large as federal, State, and municipal budget-making bodies now perform for their respective governments. The commission would, first of all, schedule the financial requirements for all essential governmental activities and services, whether federal, State, or local, with regard to their relative importance for the country as a whole. It would then formulate a master plan of federal, State, and local taxation which would raise the needed revenue in an equitable and rational manner. On the basis of its financial plan the commission would submit recommendations for specific legislation to the Congress and to the legislatures of the several States. For the purpose of coordinating the credit operations of the various levels of government, it would, when necessary, act as a go-between in arranging for advances of federal credit to the States and localities.

A coordinating body of the type proposed might be set up on the initiative of the President and Congress. To emphasize its intergovernmental character, however, it might be expedient to establish it through reciprocal federal-State legislation, or even on the basis of an interstate compact to which the federal government became a party by virtue of the terms of the initial consenting act. Whatever the procedure used, the establishment of a central commission on intergovernmental fiscal relations represents a necessary first step toward coordinating federal, State, and local finances.

No. 85

A TAX PROGRAM FOR THE FUTURE [1]

by Paul Studenski

．　　　．　　　．　　　．　　　．　　　．

IT should be understood at the outset that no reduction in the emergency expenditures of the federal government can be considered until there is ample evidence of the capacity of private industry to employ more workers, and when that evidence is available, the reduction should be carried out gradually, according to a prepared plan. Nor has the time arrived when federal borrowing should be completely stopped. But the time has come when this borrowing should be diminished. Taxation should be used from now on with much more determination. The fact that the downward movement of business activity has been arrested, and that in some fields of business even a slight improvement has taken place, amply justifies the imposition of heavier taxes. These taxes will not interfere with an improvement in business conditions; on the contrary, a failure to impose them will interfere with it.

There must be no inflation of the currency through the issuance of non-convertible, non-interest-bearing Treasury notes to cover budgetary deficits or to defray any wildly conceived new expenditures, such as those proposed under the Townsend plan. Apparently there is little danger of such inflation as long as the present Administration continues in control of Congressional legislation. The Treasury has been able to obtain all the funds required, over and above those furnished by taxation, by means of legitimate credit operations at low rates of interest; and unless some unexpected political or economic developments of a disturbing nature should occur, the Treasury will be able to obtain in the same way the five or six billion dollars

[1] Paul Studenski, "A Tax Program for the Future," *The Nation* (March 6, 1935), Vol. 140, pp. 274-276. This article was reprinted with some changes in Paul Studenski and others, *Taxation and Public Policy* (New York: Richard R. Smith, 1936), Ch. 12, and is reprinted here by permission of Richard R. Smith and *The Nation*.

more that it may need during the next two or three years. There is of course a possibility of inflation occurring in the future as a result of an overexpansion of private credit on top of the existing great expansion of public credit at a time of a rapid and somewhat speculative recovery of business.

The evil consequences of currency inflation need not be considered here. There is a general agreement among most groups that it should be avoided at all costs. Of all devices to prevent inflation taxation is the most effective, and should be resorted to at once. A tax program capable of yielding additional revenue of at least half a billion dollars per annum under present business conditions, and more if conditions improve, should be developed and enacted at once. The essential elements of such a program should be an increase of from one to ten points in the rates of inheritance and personal-income taxes and a broadening of these taxes at the base. The required supplemental revenue cannot be obtained by additional impositions on the wealthy classes alone. There must be additional impositions also on people of medium and small means, but these should, as far as practicable, take the form of direct taxes so that they may be adjusted in accordance with ability to pay, and the payments should be undisguised. The level of exemption from the inheritance tax should be lowered to $25,000, and life insurance should be treated in the same way as estates. Personal exemption from the income tax should be lowered for married persons from [$2,000] plus $400 for each child to $1,500 plus $250 for each child.

The tax program should also include moderate increases in the corporation-income tax and in the tax on cigarettes and other tobacco products, and the addition of a gross-receipts tax levied at a fraction of 1 per cent on all business except that done by extremely small concerns. The gross-receipts tax, which is collectable on the current gross income and payable monthly, would reflect any improvement in business conditions as it occurred and would therefore be especially valuable during a recovery. If levied at a low rate it would in large measure be absorbed by business.

At the first sign of inflation the government should be ready to impose taxes of a deflationary character. It should be ready to impose a capital levy and possibly a sales tax of the character suggested by Professor Colm, the rate of which would increase progressively and automatically with the rise of the price level. A capital levy of a substantial nature would cause an immediate shortage of funds in the money markets, it would force some property-owners to liquidate a part of their holdings in order to obtain cash with which to pay the tax, and it would in this and other ways exercise a restraining influence on prices. A sales tax of the nature indicated would discourage sellers from raising prices and buyers from buying and would thus deflate prices. Odious as is the sales tax as a mere device for raising revenue, it would become a serviceable tax if used in this way to prevent inflation. Plans for these two taxes should be worked out immediately and powers conferred on the Administration to impose them as soon as the price level begins to rise more rapidly than a predetermined rate per month.

The federal government should enact a tax on interest from mortgages. The tax might be so levied as to exempt interest rates up to 4 per cent and then be so steeply graduated that by the time it is applied to a 6 per cent rate, nine-tenths of the excess would be taken by the government. Such a tax would either yield substantial revenue or else impel mortgagees voluntarily to readjust interest rates downward and thus ease the burden of the mortgagor. It would cause interest rates generally to decline and stimulate capital to engage in new enterprises offering possibilities of profit.

The present high rates of taxation should be continued after the emergency has passed, and even raised to still higher levels. In the course of seven or eight years of relative prosperity, we should liquidate the entire increase in the public debt of the past few years, while at the same time supporting adequately the newly organized social services. . . .

Some of the recent expansion of government expenditures should no longer be considered as of an emergency nature but be treated as permanent in character and even carried farther as business conditions improve. This holds true particularly of proposals for the planned development of the country's natural resources and the development of cheaper electric power, for the inauguration of federal and state expenditures for old-age pensions and annuities, unemployment insurance, and social security generally, for the construction of new housing facilities for the low-income groups of our population, and, finally, for the extension by the federal authority of aid to states and local governments for purposes of education. Expenditures in the field of education (including higher education), public health, public recreation, and utility services should be increased as soon as economic conditions permit. The national, state, and local budget systems should be improved and the budgets themselves planned, executed, and accounted for more efficiently than they are to-day. In addition to annual budgets governments should develop and maintain programs of capital outlays and financings covering periods of from five to ten years. Before we can expect effective government participation in the coordination of the various features of our broader national economy, we must have better planning and control in the traditional spheres of government activity.

As a part of a permanent program the tax system of the country should be brought into closer accord with the principles of ability to pay and of the use of public finance for social control. Taxes on personal incomes should be made more universal in their application and more steeply graduated. Sales taxes should be remodeled so that they would become elastic business taxes usable for social control; and the rate of the corporation-income taxes should be increased. The present so-called emergency rates of inheritance taxation should be continued and even carried to a point of taking for the use of the state any excess fortune above a fixed sum, say $5,000,000. Only by limiting the fortunes that may be transferred to beneficiaries shall we be able to preserve democracy and relative equality of opportunity in this country. The rates of the taxes on personal and corporate incomes, excess profits, capital stock, and undistributed surplus of corporations should be adjusted so that within certain limits they would automatically fluctuate with the rise and fall in business activity and in the volume of investments. This can be accomplished, as recently suggested by G. T. Altman in the *Tax Magazine*, by relating the rates to an index of business activity and capital accumulation. The Treasury could announce annually by reference to these indices the rate to be applied to the taxes of the year. The surpluses resulting from rising rates might be used for debt retirement, the expansion of social services, and the accumulation of reserves. Deficits caused by dropping rates could be covered from reserves or new borrowings. Public finance might thus serve to stabilize our national economy. . . .

The country's tax system should be considered as a unit and not as a conglomeration of a number of unrelated systems—federal, state, and local. The federal credits for inheritance taxes paid to states should be applied to the existing rates, instead of merely to the lower 1926 rates, but the credit should be fixed on a regressive scale, so that the federal government should receive 80 per cent of the amounts levied in the case of the large estates and a diminishing share, dropping to 20 per cent, in the case of smaller estates. Such an arrangement would end litigations over the question of whether large estates should be taxed in one state or another; and it would also introduce greater stability in state revenue. The crediting device regressively adjusted might advantageously be extended to the personal income tax. The states should cease taxing corporations on a basis of net income and alcoholic beverages on a volume basis, and should content themselves with a share of the proceeds of a federal corporation-income tax and a federal liquor and beer tax.

The coordination of federal, state, and local finance should be concerned, however, not only with taxation. It should also embrace the current budgets, capital-outlay programs, and credit operations of the various authorities, and be accompanied with a coordination of their administrative activities as well. Some of the functions of government would need to be reallocated as between these several layers of authorities. Before any such coordination can take place, a series of comprehensive studies of the underlying problems must be made by staffs of experts. It is to be hoped that the study of coordination of tax systems which is about to be made by the Treasury will be productive of a sound plan and will be followed by studies of the other fields of federal, state, and local finance and administration. Such studies should be conducted under the direction of a specially created commission on federal, state, and local relationships, which should be transformed eventually into a permanent body. Its establishment should be followed by the organization of twelve permanent regional commissions of the same order. The task of the national and the regional commissions would be to develop intergovernmental unity and cooperation on a national and regional scale so that the government might emerge from its present state of chaos.

A substantial reorganization of local finance and administration should be undertaken. The administration of the property tax should be improved as regards assessment and like matters; the existing limitations on the rate of the property tax should be removed, and the local revenue system broadened through larger distributions to localities of shares of state-collected taxes. A more effective supervision by the state over the budgetary practices and credit operations of the smaller spending units should be established. Those local units which are incapable of an effective independent operation should be consolidated, and the entire structure of our county government modernized. The states should give cities wider powers to own and operate utilities.

An amendment to the federal constitution that would permit the federal, state, and local governments to tax the income from federal, state, and municipal bonds on the same basis as income from any other securities should be adopted; and after its adoption bonds should be issued without the tax-exemption feature. [Court decisions in 1938-1939 indicate that such an amendment may not be necessary.] The munitions industry should be nationalized and a plan of steeply graduated war taxes developed that would make the accumulation of large fortunes in consequence of war contracts impossible.

Instead of merely conforming with the changes occurring in the social order, taxation should induce them. Of all the peaceful means of bringing about a new social state, taxation is the most potent one. It should be used not merely as an expedient to raise revenue, but as a positive force for social reconstruction.

Chapter XXIV

PUBLIC SPENDING, DEBTS, AND BUDGETING

[THE government, as most of us are aware, can supply the community with certain services more efficiently and economically than each individual in the community could supply them for himself. These services must, of course, be paid for. In order to pay for them the government must raise money. Most of this money is raised by taxation, but governments, like individuals, sometimes have to borrow. They borrow whenever it seems impossible or undesirable to obtain sufficient funds for current expenses from current sources of revenue.

Throughout most of our history governmental income has managed to keep step with increased expenditures. In fact prior to 1929 the national government had done little borrowing for peacetime purposes. More recently, however, expenditures have gone up so rapidly that they could not be met out of current revenues. The government has had to fight the depression, relieve the unemployed, and build up the defenses of the nation. As a result each new year has found the nation with a larger public debt. By the end of Franklin Roosevelt's second administration it had reached an all-time high of over forty-five billion dollars.

A great many see in this situation an omen of disaster. It is said that the government is headed toward bankruptcy, that the debt will have to be paid by our children, that we are on the road to inflation, that the government credit will eventually be exhausted. In this chapter Mr. Coyle examines the debt and the prophecies of calamity in a somewhat different light than we usually find them examined.

It is not only the increased spending and increasing debt of the national government that have been subjected to criticism, however. The state and local units of government also have been faced with increased expenditures and ever-larger debts. Here, too, many see evil days ahead. The result is often a panicky slashing of expenditures with little or no real examination of the situation. This is unfortunate because we do not want to save the pocketbooks of this generation at the expense of the education, health, and welfare of the next. Instead, as Professors Merriam and Buck suggest, let us abolish the spoils system, eliminate graft, reorganize our governmental machinery and create an adequate system of public budgeting.

In any event, the problems of public spending and the public debt call for serious analysis by those who seek to understand and improve the American way of life.]

No. 86

BUT IS THERE A FEDERAL DEFICIT? [1]

by David Cushman Coyle

IN Washington, under the crystal chandeliers of the big Senate hearing room, two men were talking across the table. One of them was Senator Byrnes, the Chairman of the Committee on Unemployment and Relief, the other was Mr. Winthrop W. Aldrich, Chairman of the Board of the Chase National Bank. According to the record, the Senator and the banker had happened to meet that morning, and the banker had consented to come to the afternoon hearing and give his advice informally on the problems facing the Committee.

Under the circumstances neither senator nor banker could be expected to weigh each word of the informal questions and answers nor to take responsibility for all the divergent trains of thought that their words might set in motion. On the other hand, it is proper to sit in with the official reporter and the newspaper representatives and listen to the public conversation of these two men, and then to speculate on the consequences that might flow from such ideas as they expressed.

Senator Byrnes: Do you consider the conservation of soil and forests a good investment?

Mr. Aldrich: Definitely yes, sir.

Senator Byrnes: If the United States were a business corporation dealing with you, you would consider an expenditure for conserving assets of that kind as a sound use of funds, would you?

Mr. Aldrich: Yes.

. . . .

Senator Byrnes: If the Government spends money for purposes of that character you would consider it in a different class from expenditures that were not conserving assets?

Mr. Aldrich: Yes, I would.

. . . . .

Senator Byrnes: Would you think that a public work of undoubted value would have to be self-liquidating in order to make it a sound investment,

[1] David Cushman Coyle, "But Is There a Federal Deficit?", *Harper's Magazine* (April, 1938), Vol. 176, pp. 449-457. Reprinted by permission of the author and *Harper's Magazine.*

or would you consider it in some instances just as the construction of the home office of a corporation might be; it might bring no dividends but it would be essential? It would be an investment of the corporation.

Mr. Aldrich: I think, undoubtedly, there are a great many public works that are necessary that are not self-liquidating.

Senator Byrnes: And they would, undoubtedly, be of value, such things as a school building or a bridge?

Mr. Aldrich: Undoubtedly.

Senator Byrnes: You would not think it was an unwise policy on the part of a corporation to issue bonds to construct a home office building or a thing of that kind?

Mr. Aldrich: No, sir.

In these few minutes of quiet talk history may have been made, but if it was there was no excitement about it at the time. Perhaps the newspaper men had heard the same ideas before. The ideas expressed are not new though they have had little public discussion in this country. Back in 1932 Senator Byrnes introduced a bill directing the Government to adopt the usual business practice of separating capital investments from the operating budget. The business form of budget is used in Australia, and the country's credit is good. But the United States was not ready for such a change in 1932. The New Deal budget was set up to show ordinary and emergency accounts, a distinction that failed to impress the critics of the Administration. More recently, however, from half a dozen different sources in Congress and outside have come criticisms of the lack of information about our public investments.

If the Federal Government is regarded as a business corporation, according to the principles that Senator Byrnes and Mr. Aldrich were discussing, the striking conclusion is that no one knows whether the budget is balanced or not.

Anyone can see with half an eye that the nation's budget of production and consumption is not balanced. We consume more than we produce, despite the surplus in a few lines such as cotton and corn. We make up the difference by liquidating our natural resources. We know that the nation is living by destroying its capital, though we do not yet know the exact amount of our deficit.

With the Federal budget the case is different. The good old days when the Government cured every depression by giving away the public domain to all comers have passed forever. To-day the Government is building up its property, not tearing it down. Anyone can see that the Government is investing money each year in new capital assets. It is also borrowing money. But no one knows whether it is piling up a book surplus or falling behind.

If we are going to try to find a sensible answer to public financial questions it seems evident that a good way to begin would be to strike a balance and see how we stand.

The essential peculiarity of the Federal budget is that it does not show a clear distinction between investment and spending.

A corporation may have an income of two million dollars and expenses of one and a half million. Its budget is not only balanced: there is half a million profit; the stockholders are well satisfied that the company is in the black. But suppose that during the year the company has issued five million dollars' worth of bonds and has built a new plant worth five million dollars. Its debt has increased. Is it, therefore, in the red? On the contrary, the stockholders note with satisfaction that the company is bigger and presumably richer than ever.

But note what happens when the Federal Government plants trees on its own land. Senator Byrnes and Mr. Aldrich are not alone in considering this to be a sound investment. In 1936 the Government planted 215 million trees in the national forests, at a cost of $1,828,000. To pay for this work, the Government has issued bonds and has increased the national debt. It reported this expenditure as an expense, added with the rest to give us an unbalanced budget. The fact that the Government added nearly two million dollars' worth of young trees to its assets is left out of account.

The Government gives a list of assets in its budget report, but in its general treatment of the budget it lumps the investments with other expenses and tries to balance the whole sum by the revenue of each year.

Any corporation that will not make any capital investments except out of its current income is not only being extremely conservative but is also imposing on itself limitations that may easily become disastrous. A common example is the manufacturer who sees his competitors putting in a new process by which their costs will become less than his own. If he refuses to follow suit because he fears to go in debt he may have to pay for his conservatism by losing his business.

Governments, while they are less likely to be run out of business than some industries, are equally subject to losses if they cannot keep up to date. For example, there are some 15,000 one-room, one-teacher schools in this country, with less than eight pupils per school. The Little Red Schoolhouse is a romantic theme of song and story, but in brutal fact it costs about $200 per year per pupil to run one of these romantic institutions. A consolidated school with 40 or more pupils can be operated at a cost of $50 or less per year per head, provided the roads are good enough for economical bus transportation.

The rural school districts with their high-cost schools are heavily burdened with expense, overstraining the taxpayers and leaving no surplus for repairs or textbooks. A building program is usually beyond the capacity of the local budgets; for a new school building requires a capital investment of about $400 per pupil, and many of the local governments are already over their ears in debt. But if only half of these 15,000 smallest schools are favorably situated for consolidation there is a good opportunity to invest some $12,000,000. About 30,000 children could be put into modern grade schools for this sum, making an annual saving of $4,500,000, or 37 per cent. The Office of Education estimates that all together about 1,000,000 children could be moved into larger schools at a total saving of about 50 million dollars a year. Incidentally, their schooling would be improved, not to speak of sanitation. But these latter points are intangibles, which a bank would set down at a value of one dollar.

Everyone agrees that what the country needs, in addition to kind words from the White House, is more investment in capital goods. Is there any reason why the government, while patting the backs of worried business men, should not do a little investing in its own business? Yes, there is a reason. When the government makes an investment everyone calls it spending. I am one of those who have called it spending and who have said that spending was what this country needed. The fact is still there, but the name was wrong. It is time to adopt a more accurate vocabulary. When the Federal Government borrows a billion dollars and buys a billion dollars' worth of valuable assets it is no more unbalancing its budget than is a corporation that borrows a million dollars and uses the money to buy a million dollars' worth of property. The bookkeeping methods of the Treasury should make this fact clear. Then we could begin to see what we are about.

Corporations do not always invest their capital wisely and neither do governments. That is another reason for wanting the bookkeeping to represent the facts as accurately as possible. Even with the best of bookkeeping we shall need to understand clearly what sort of a business our government is, and what kinds of investment it can properly credit to its capital account.

The chief job of government is not that of a manufacturer but is more nearly that of a broker or business agent. Through government we buy various goods and services at wholesale, usually at a distinct saving compared with the price of similar products bought at retail. The reason we use government to supply us with roads, schools, police protection, postal service, and national defense is simply that we cannot get these benefits so cheaply in any other way, if at all. As our agent, the government builds or buys physical plant, durable goods, and property of all sorts; like any merchant, it has both inventory and plant which expand as the business grows.

Like any merchant, the Government has intangible assets, which are by no means to be neglected. The chief of these intangibles is the taxpaying ability of the citizens or the ability of the government to collect revenues. This asset is comparable to the going value of a business concern. A progressive corporation will spend millions of dollars on an advertising campaign to increase its future income and, therefore, its going value. The Metropolitan Life Insurance Company spends large sums to promote health and cut down the death rate of its policy-holders. On the same principle, the Government spends money, for example, to conserve the soil, from which future taxes will come.

Mr. Aldrich told Senator Byrnes that he considered soil conservation a sound investment, but it is difficult to find a way of crediting to the Federal budget the values created by the improvement of privately owned farm land. The land will not even pay Federal taxes. But someone will pay Federal taxes, if the land is fertile and productive, who would not be able to pay if the land should become desolate and the market town a deserted ruin. Soil conservation with the help of Federal money is a true investment in future Federal revenue, but it is not one that can be easily measured. Probably the best procedure is to list it at only one dollar, but to list it as an asset, so as to keep the fact from being overlooked that, though not measured, it is still a real investment.

In its capacity as buying agent and as managing agent for various public properties, the Government is required to collect the costs from the people for whom it is acting. These costs are collected in two ways: by fees and charges on the one hand, and by taxes on the other. There is no absolute difference between these two kinds of public revenue. There is a wide borderline where the choice between toll services paid by the consumer and "free" services paid by the taxpayer is entirely a matter of convenience.

In the bookkeeping, however, a toll bridge is different from a free bridge in the fact that tolls are thought to be more certain than general tax revenues. The toll bridge is said to be "self-liquidating" because the people pay for it directly as they use it. In the same way, municipal bonds bought by the PWA for the Federal Government are held as self-liquidating investments because they are paid by local consumers or taxpayers without calling on Congress to levy taxes.

This distinction between "self-liquidating" property, on which the costs can be collected by direct fees or assessments, and ordinary property to be paid for out of general taxes, must be recognized in Federal bookkeeping if the balance sheet is to be easily accepted as valid by the public.

The degree to which new public assets can be fully credited against expenditures will necessarily depend, therefore, on how clearly they can be proved to have a definite capital value. At the head of the list will come self-liquidating paper, such as municipal bonds and private notes and mortgages in proportion to their probable repayment. Next comes self-liquidating property owned by the Federal Government, such as certain national forest areas, with proper allowances for increase and decrease in value. Third is necessary physical plant for the efficient carrying on of public business, such as a post office which actually saves in rental costs, also with proper allowance for depreciation. Last is the long list of intangibles, including soil conservation, aids to navigation, education, public health, and scientific research, all of undoubted value but not clearly measurable in dollars.

Business men who, in their own affairs, insist on efficient machinery and adequate maintenance will naturally insist on the same principle in public affairs when the bookkeeping is done in a way to show the true conditions. Business men are most insistent that the Federal budget should be balanced; but no one is clear as to whether, in the common business meaning of the words, the budget is balanced or not.

There is, accordingly, a certain inconsistency in the thought that lies back of the advice pouring into Washington. This inconsistency of standards cannot be suddenly rectified by a magazine article, or even by a pronouncement from the White House. But a beginning could be made if the Government would distinguish between its capital budget and its expense budget. If a bookkeeping system, set up and checked by a well-recognized firm of public accountants, should show the Federal government to be in the black, a large part of the fear that now oppresses the American people would disappear.

When we come to realize that much of our expenditure can properly be charged to capital account, we may easily go so far, so that no sensible business men would not admit the soundness of the bookkeeping. First steps should, therefore, be cautious, and a highly conservative attitude should be adopted.

First let it be admitted that if a profitable opening for public capital exists, and the money to invest is not available from revenue, it is a good economy to seize the opportunity even with the use of borrowed money. This is the practice of well-managed private business, and it should be possible to apply the principle to public business.

. . . The Government should select a number of public works that are clearly recognizable as new assets, and transfer them to capital accounts, so as to release a part of the current revenue for investment in intangible but useful operations.

The capital list might include loans for local public works, such Federal buildings as are shown to produce a money saving in operating costs, the self-liquidating fraction of multiple-purpose projects such as the TVA, and a conservative percentage of the cost of forestation work on public land. Housing loans, and rehabilitation loans to farmers, and any other private business paper acquired by the Government in course of helping business revival, may properly be listed as assets in the proportion in which experience shows such loans to be usually repaid. Against the addition to assets there should of course be a write-off for depreciation and obsolescence.

Note that WPA projects, where the completed property becomes an asset of a State or municipality, are not included here as Federal investments. Neither are subsidies to soil conservation on private land, to education, or to public health. All these operations are investments more or less, but they cannot be listed as having any definite asset value to the Federal Government without arousing uncertainty and distrust. They should, therefore, be financed out of current revenue, without forgetting, however, that they add largely to the wealth of the American people in general.

The Government need not take credit for all public investments, tangible and intangible, because the true surplus of revenues over current non-investment expenses is so large that the Treasury can afford to be thoroughly conservative. No exact figures are available because of the traditional method of bookkeeping. It would take an official order and considerable expense to make over the accounts so as to show the investment or expense status of each item of expenditure. But in the 1938 budget there are two items called Investments and Acquisitions of Property that are probably more or less the same items that a corporation would put in its capital account. These items total $1,630,000,000. Another item that may shed some light on the amount of investments is one called "recovery and relief expenditures up to Oct. 31, 1936." This shows a total of 17 billion dollars, of which nearly 7 billions is "repayable."

In the absence of detailed analysis, it seems reasonable to suppose that the Federal budget each year includes a billion dollars that would be admitted as additions to assets if the United States were a business corporation dealing with a conservative bank. If that is correct, the budget is almost "in the black," in the common meaning of the words as they are used in private business. If the budget is nearly balanced—and a small increase of taxation will produce a surplus—there is no need for letting budgetary troubles stand in the way of efficient operation of the public services. In private business the only excuse for poor equipment and wasteful economics is absolute inability to get money enough to afford more profitable methods. With proper bookkeeping it should become evident that the Government can afford to do a good job. True economy calls for appropriations that will do away with some of the present loss and inefficiency.

To quote Alexander Hamilton: "How is it possible that a government half supplied and always necessitous, can fulfill the purposes of its institution, can provide for the security, advance the prosperity, or support the reputation of the commonwealth? . . . How can its administration be anything else than a succession of expedients temporizing, impotent, and disgraceful? How will it be able to avoid a frequent sacrifice of its engagements to immediate necessity? How can it undertake or execute any liberal or enlarged plans for the public good?" (Federalist, Dec. 28, 1787.)

For example, it is inefficient to require that WPA workers should be chosen from the relief rolls. They should be drawn from the rolls of the U. S. Employment Service, without requiring proof of pauperization. This reform would take more money, but the real returns would be higher.

It is inefficient to pay prevailing wages on WPA for part-time work, causing the workers to look for other part-time jobs, in which they accept low wages and demoralize the market. Full-time work might cost a little more, but the benefits would offset the extra cost.

It is inefficient to require heavy contributions from local "sponsors" for WPA projects. The effect is to skimp other local services, increasing the need for relief and disorganizing the local governments. A more generous policy would pay dividends in the long run.

It is inefficient to relieve the Federal budget at the expense of municipal budgets, because local taxes are chiefly on real estate, and a rise in local taxes will injure property values. Federal taxes can be placed on personal incomes without injuring business or property values.

It is inefficient to cut the allowance for overhead on any kind of public relief, because experience has amply shown that crowded relief offices result in chiseling, mistakes, and waste of many kinds. It is no accident that the City of Washington, for example, where relief overhead is kept to a minimum, stands near the wrong end of the list in tuberculosis, juvenile delinquency, and crime. The fact that a dollar saved on relief administration wastes a dollar or more in crime is well established by the studies that are on record.

It is inefficient to cut the CCC, when the work that it can do still needs to be done. Much of the work of the CCC is of a kind that cannot be admitted to the Federal list of investments because it serves to improve local or private property. But it is sound investment in land, trees, and boys nevertheless, and to cut the CCC is to waste resources for the sake of a false economy.

It is inefficient to economize on the service of public health, for it is cheaper to spend ten dollars to keep one workman from getting syphilis, than to have him become unemployable and infectious.

Why do we now practice all these kinds of inefficiency and many more besides? Because the Federal budget seems to be unbalanced. The Federal budget is probably not unbalanced. The chances are that it is really piling up a surplus. No private business with good credit facilities and good management would operate in such a slipshod manner. By being over-conservative and straining for the ideal of paying for all our investments out of current revenue we fall just enough short of the ideal to throw us into a state of penny-wisdom and pound-foolishness.

This point should be made clear. An intangible investment such as public health is just as sound an investment as the Bonneville Dam, and maybe a good deal sounder. I am not suggesting that in order to ease the budget we should confine our Federal operations to self-liquidating construction projects. I am suggesting that by removing from the budget all capital items that a bank would admit as assets in examining a private corporation we can make room for the intangible investment items and can put them on an efficient basis. In any case there is bound to be a large proportion of sound investment concealed in the current expense account of the Government.

There are several collateral points that have to be considered, though they cannot take much space in a magazine article.

One point is the relation of capital debt to inflation. In the universal demand for an expansion of private investment the danger of inflation is not considered, but a proposal to borrow a few billions more for public investment will immediately be met by cries of fear lest we start a runaway inflation. The relation between borrowing and inflation is the same in private as in public capital expansion. It is quite simple.

If the capital is borrowed from banks that deal in check-account money, money is created by the borrowing; it is inflation.

If the capital is borrowed from people, insurance companies, savings banks, or others who cannot create credit, the money is not created; it is not an inflation. The exceptions to these two rules are not important for the present discussion.

The financing of the Government deficit during the depression was chiefly through banks; it was in the main inflationary. That was good at the time because there was a scarcity of money. At present there is no scarcity of money. New borrowings, private or public, ought to be largely from sources that do not create new money.

With suitable co-ordination between Treasury and Federal Reserve, the Government can borrow and invest money as any private business can do, with little or no inflation.

There is another principle that applies to Federal debts as distinguished from municipal or corporate debts. The Federal taxing power covers practically all those to whom the Federal Government owes money. To a considerable extent the taxpayers and the creditors are the same people. In so far as the bonds are distributed in the same proportion as the tax load they are book items of no weight. All that has happened is that the taxpayers have invested in assets held for their account by the government, and have accepted bonds on which they will pay the interest to themselves. The difference between this way of financing and paying for the assets directly by taxation is not as great as it seems to be. Federal debts are, therefore, partly self-cancelling, and are accordingly on a sounder basis than any conventional business bookkeeping would show. The chief reason for not paying the bonds is that the creditors do not want them paid.

The principle that the French call *"fonds perdus,"* or the asset without debt, represents an ideal like the New England conscience that yields its best fruits when cultivated with moderation. Whenever the Government can buy a valuable property for cash out of its surplus revenues that investment is peculiarly sound from the political point of view. The funds are "lost," or written off. No interest has to be paid on them. Any profit resulting from the investment appears to be pure gravy. The principle is not one of economics but of human nature. If we invest for future profits and make no written promises about paying them, we soon forget the cost; when the results come in we get a pleasant surprise. Any democratic government does well to lay up pleasant surprises for the voters instead of unpleasant ones like 1929.

But though it is undoubtedly good politics to make only such investments as can be paid for out of current revenue, it is bad politics and bad economics to fail to make necessary investments and thus lay up trouble for the future. The principle of cutting our capital outlay to fit our cash surplus can be carried to an unprofitable extreme. To lie awake worrying because some of our investment was made with borrowed money is hardly necessary. It is like a New England housekeeper who has reached a stage where her much needed sleep is disturbed by fears that dust may have settled on the mantel when she opened the door to let the cat out.

Like any well-established corporation, this nation is a going concern, with good credit and access to capital. Whenever there is a good opening for new capital in its business the company will lose if it fails to take advantage of the opening. Such opportunities come up in Washington almost every day—as for example the suggestion of the president of the Pittsburgh Coal Company last January that the Government buy coal reserves. The Government could hold these coal lands off the market, to relieve the pressure of royalty payments that forces the opening of new mines and leads by a short and obvious chain of cause and effect to heavy public relief burdens. Everyone agrees that it would be profitable, but "we haven't the money." Why not? If we could make the investment out of surplus income, so much the better. But if we have to borrow the money at three and one-half per cent to make a saving of several times as much, that is not a national disaster. The national disaster is more likely to follow if we are too cautious to protect ourselves against future expense.

Although there are certain political advantages in building up public assets without public debt, there is another side to the matter that every banker or trustee will recognize. Banks, insurance companies, foundations, and universities must have a supply of gilt-edged bonds to serve as the foundation of their investment portfolios. U. S. Government bonds are the standard for this purpose.

Consider the operations of the Home Owners' Loan Corporation, a Federal concern which has taken over a great mass of unsound home mortgages. Many of these loans were a year or more behind with their interest and taxes. They were no comfort to the banks and insurance companies that held them. But when the Federal Government threw them all into one pool, using money borrowed on its own credit at a low rate of interest, this mass of sour loans turned into a sound investment in which the HOLC will have little if any loss, and perhaps a modest profit. Meanwhile the private institutions, in place of these highly questionable mortgages, were supplied with gilt-edged Federal debt. They growled about New Deal extravagance, but they over-subscribed the Treasury issues five to ten times.

It should be made clear that one of the duties of the national Government is to buy and sweeten certain kinds of business paper, turning it into national debt that is almost or entirely self-supporting, and that is available for institutions to carry in their vaults as an investment backlog. It should also be made clear to frightened taxpayers that debt of this kind will not be paid out of taxes. In fact it will probably become a revolving fund and never be paid at all. Taxpayers who tremble at the burden that is going to crush their children and grandchildren are mainly the victims of inaccurate Treasury bookkeeping. War debts may have to be paid out of taxes, because the assets for which the money was spent have been thrown, pointed end frontward, at the enemy. But self-supporting Federal debts are no mortgage on the revenue system. On the contrary, they are the standard ballast that business concerns use to prevent being upset by sudden squalls.

Suppose you are the owner of a chemical plant, located on a river above a growing city. You have received a court order to cease polluting the river water. Your engineer offers you two plans. The first plan is to put in a purification plant at a cost of $100,000, from which you will get no return except the privilege of continuing in business. The second plan is to remodel your plant to use a new process that salvages the waste chemicals and does not pollute the stream. The second plan will cost $200,000 but will add $150,000 to the productive value of your business. Which is the cheaper—to spend $100,000 net or to invest $200,000 at a net loss of only $50,000? Other things being equal, almost any business man would choose the second plan.

Now suppose you are the responsible head of a government, with a mandate from the sovereign people. The people will continue the mandate of democratic government only on one of two conditions. First is that you give them one billion dollars of straight relief, for which you get no return except the temporary foiling of the villain who lurks in the shadows. The alternative is that you put two billion dollars into public works, with not over half a billion wasted. Which is the cheaper?

Believe it or not, many people still feel that a billion down a rat hole is cheaper than two billions invested. They are not to blame for feeling this way. It is the Government's fault. The Government ought to learn how to do its bookkeeping so that this optical illusion would not be fostered by an unbusinesslike accounting system.

Our Federal Government is the agent of the American people, appointed by the people to buy, manage, and distribute various goods and services that for one reason or another cannot be profitably or efficiently handled by private business. In relation to the public debt, the government business can be divided into three categories. First is the list of profitable assets which the government buys for public use and which it holds and manages in the public interest. Any such asset can properly be bought with borrowed money, to be repaid out of the profits of the property itself. There is no need to pay for such acquisitions by means of taxes unless the people wish to pay in that way so as to save interest. In fact, if too much of this public debt should be paid off, banks and insurance companies would be hard put to it to find sound investment for their money.

Second is the list of profitable investments such as schools and public health, which the government buys and distributes to the smaller governments or to the public.

The third category is made up of current public services, such as national defense and the deficit portion of the postal service, which are more properly classed as running expenses of our national life.

The second and third classes of expenses should be paid for out of tax revenues, not necessarily in the same year that they occur, but within a reasonable time. If they are so paid, the budget will be balanced.

Once the people understand this distinction, they can be shown that the Federal finances are in a sound condition and that a bold policy of building up the material and human resources of the nation is not beyond our means. Let us hope that this understanding may come soon, for the lack of it is the chief cause of our present confusion, our widespread fear of the future, and our costly delay in putting men to work.

No. 87

A DIFFERENT PRESCRIPTION [1]

by Charles E. Merriam

THE genuine reductions in American governmental costs will not be made by alarmists in a panic, but by careful examination of the underlying difficulties. I confess to a very genuine alarm at the activities of some well-intentioned citizens who are carrying on a crusade against high costs—sincerely but, as it seems to me, destructively. In the old days out in the country when a fire broke out, there was sometimes as much damage done by the amateur fireman as by the flames themselves.

I venture to offer to citizens and taxpayers, concerned as they should be about a sound fiscal policy, the following suggestions, which are widely different from those commonly presented, but which in my judgment and experience are likely to prove more useful in the long run.

1. *Abolish the spoils system* now found in 3,600 counties, 38 states, and hundreds of cities; and enforce and develop the merit system where already found. The spoils system is the beginning of evil in governmental expenditures, and out of this come graft, corruption, and incompetence. Unless the spoils system can be abolished, not only will taxes mount higher and higher, and public services lag, but the industrial future of the nation will be seriously jeopardized by incompetent dealing with the vital economic affairs of the republic.

2. *Encourage the organization and training of responsible governing offi-*

---

[1] Charles E. Merriam, "A Different Prescription," *State Government* (June, 1932), Vol. 5, page 1. Reprinted by permission of the author and *State Government*.

cials. There are some 800 organizations of officials in the United States, some of which are very active although a few do little more than hold an annual banquet. The development of these responsible governing groups is full of promise for the future of American government.

3. *Reorganize the government units and departments* in such manner as to prevent the great wastes of overlapping and duplication. There are now in the United States more than 200,000 independent governing and taxing bodies. No one seems to know within a good many thousand just how many there are, but everyone knows there are too many, and that they are very expensive.

From another point of view, I venture to offer the following suggestions as to how governmental burdens may be lightened.

1. *Stop boycotting the governmental service.* There is throughout the United States a widespread and vociferous propaganda against government. This is not only the attitude of certain radicals, but of certain conservatives. This boycott of government and public life makes difficult the recruitment of the personnel necessary for government. It makes government inviting for spoilsmen, grafters, and racketeers and drives away many of those who might best serve the state. It produces higher costs and lower achievement levels. Unless we lift the boycott on government, there can be no substantial economy.

2. *Do not be misled by propagandists who say "economy" when they mean "immunity" from public regulation.* They wish to save money in order to conserve their own special privileges. We might save money by abolishing the Interstate Commerce Commission or the Federal Trade Commission, or by getting rid of the Public Utilities Commission of the state. But we might save a nickel and lose a dollar.

3. *Cultivate the forward look in government.* Unless our attitude toward government can become more flexible, there will be no permanent and substantial reduction in the expenditures of government. There may be panicky and foolish slashing of budgets, but there will not be that sound and prudent advance toward better use of the public money.

I have not been officially notified, as was Noah, of the coming flood, nor do I share the pessimism of Spengler in his gloomy prediction of the decline of western civilization. But unless I misread the signs of the times, our political and economic theory and practice must soon move up to a higher level and adjust themselves to the new conditions inexorably imposed on us by modern industrial and scientific development.

No. 88

PUBLIC BUDGETING [1]

by A. E. Buck

REGARDLESS of its political environment, a system of public finance may be said to depend for its continuity and effectiveness upon the extent to which it utilizes the process of planning and control, now commonly termed public budgeting. If a government does not obtain year after year, or within a reasonable period, enough taxes and other revenues to cover its total expenditures, it will eventually accumulate a deficit which will lead to the necessity of debt repudiation, the cessation of essential activities, and finally a state of insolvency and complete impotence.

Although many Americans regard budgeting as a recent development in government, such is not the case. Nearly two centuries ago the budget was fairly well established as an essential part of the British parliamentary system. It was initiated in France more than a hundred years ago. Then it was gradually adopted by other European countries, by Japan, and by the British dominions. But as late as the beginning of the present century the United States was still without an established budgetary practice. Only within the last twenty-five years have we made some progress, although merely a beginning, in budgetary development, first in the cities, then in the States, and finally in the federal government. The National Budget and Accounting Act was not passed until 1921.

As applied in the various countries of the world, the budget may be said to have three essential elements: (1) a financial plan, (2) a procedure for formulating, authorizing, executing, and controlling this plan, and (3) some governmental agency responsible for each successive step in this procedure. When viewed as a plan, the budget sets forth the monetary requirements of a government for a definite future period—usually a year—and in doing so exhibits a balanced relation between anticipated income and estimated outgo. As a procedure, the budget involves certain definite steps: first, in preparing estimates and framing the financial plan; second, in voting or adopting the plan; third, in carrying out the plan as authorized; and, fourth, in auditing and reviewing the resulting fiscal operation. The governmental

---

[1] A. E. Buck, "Public Budgeting," The Nation (October 24, 1934), Vol. 139, pp. 472-474. This article was reprinted with some changes in Paul Studenski and others, Taxation and Public Policy (New York: Richard R. Smith, 1936), Ch. 2, and is reprinted here by permission of Richard R. Smith and The Nation.

agency responsible for each of these steps is determined more or less by the pattern of government under which the budget operates. In the United States, for example, the executive should be responsible for the first and third steps, while the legislature should be responsible for the second and fourth. The executive, by virtue of his authority over the administration, is in the key position not only to prepare the financial plan but also to carry it out. The legislature, according to its historic right, holds the purse-strings in our government. It accomplishes this through authorizing the financial plan presented to it by the executive, and through establishing accountability on the part of the executive for carrying out this plan. The latter feature, involving an audit and review of financial operations, is as yet far from being properly developed.

The most essential feature of the budget, as a financial plan, is equilibrium, that is, a balanced relation between revenue and expenditure. Under existing economic conditions, unbalanced budgets are among the most baffling problems that governmental authorities have to face. Ordinarily these authorities have attempted to balance their budgets by increasing tax rates, by decreasing expenditures, or by a combination of the two methods. And when they have failed by such methods, as has often happened, they have resorted to borrowing. The policy of contraction—enforced economies in expenditures—has apparently produced balanced budgets in a few instances. One of the most successful attempts to apply this policy is embodied in the so-called Premiers' Plan of Australia, which was carefully worked out on the basis of "equality of sacrifice" and adopted in 1931. It has been employed in the balancing of the Commonwealth and state budgets, and thus far has shown remarkable results.

Opposed to the policy of contraction in balancing the budget is the expansionist theory. The latter proposes the use of public credit to increase expenditures for capital improvements and to aid in the planned extension of private production. It is claimed that the effect of applying this theory, once its full force is felt in a country, is to increase revenues and to decrease unemployment relief. Thus the budget is eventually balanced; furthermore, the causes of budgetary disequilibrium are largely removed. The authorities of several governments have seemingly accepted this theory, at least in part, and have provided funds for a program of capital improvements and national development. The United States government has embarked upon such a program under the New Deal. It has not, however, gone whole-heartedly in this direction, but has attempted to carry out at the same time a policy of contraction with respect to the ordinary services of administration. While it is too early to indicate the economic effects of this approach to the problem of budgetary balancing, hopeful signs are not lacking.

A second essential feature of the budget is comprehensiveness, signifying that the budget includes all the financial requirements of the government, that no receipts or expenditures are omitted. The idea of budgetary comprehensiveness has not been particularly stressed in the United States, and has not as yet been widely realized. Not all the receipts and expenditures of the national government are shown in the budget, although this document is perhaps as comprehensive as any of the State or municipal budgets. In many State and municipal governments, the stock method of producing a balanced budget is to omit the requirements for certain governmental agencies and funds. Public-works requirements are frequently excluded from the general budgets of States and municipalities on the pretext that the necessary planning for such works cannot be done at the time the budgetary estimates are prepared. These budgets are therefore little more than programs for current expenditures. Both current and capital expenditures should be shown in the budget, with the means of financing in each case clearly set forth. Capital expenditures may be effectively supported by long-term programs of development. These programs may be prepared for a period of five years without great difficulty and with a fair degree of accuracy, assuming that economic conditions are fairly stable. The experience of some American and British municipalities, as well as that of Soviet Russia, has demonstrated that five-year plans are feasible.

Budgetary unity is seriously affected by splitting the budget into two parts, ordinary and extraordinary. It is then possible to balance the ordinary budget by transferring to the extraordinary budget certain expenditure requirements which should be met from current revenues. The latter budget is balanced, if at all, by the use of public credit. In general, the tendency is for the two budgets to become separated, legislative attention being directed less and less to the extraordinary budget, which remains chronically out of balance. According to European experience, the extraordinary budget has shown serious weaknesses and has sometimes led to grave abuses, especially in France. Nevertheless, the United States government, on July 1, 1933, embarked upon a scheme for a so-called "double budget," which resembles in certain respects an ordinary and an extraordinary budget. This scheme anticipated that the ordinary expenditures would be met by the receipts from current revenues, while the extraordinary expenditures, to which were assigned all outlays arising from emergency legislation, would be met by moneys obtained from the sale of bonds.

As yet there is no established practice in the United States with respect to gross and net budgets. In an effort to produce comprehensive budgets, the present trend, if any, seems to be in the direction of gross budgeting. The requirements of undertakings, services, and funds, previously omitted, are now being brought into the budgets of the national, State, and municipal governments. However, at this time the budget of the national government is neither gross nor net, at least in so far as public undertakings are concerned. The requirements of the Panama Canal, for example, are included in the budget in gross amounts, while those of the Post Office Department appear simply as net deficits. Practically the same thing is true of the State and municipal budgets, the requirements of public undertakings appearing either in gross amounts or not at all. In many cases one would not know from an examination of these budgets that such undertakings even existed, except when it became necessary, owing to poor or incompetent management, to replenish wasted capital assets or to meet current operating deficits. Such practice is not net budgeting in the real sense of that term; moreover, it encourages loose financial administration on the part of the governmental authorities. Net budgeting can, however, be made quite effective, especially in relation to public undertakings. It simply requires an annexed or subsidiary budget for each of these undertakings, which is keyed into the general budget by carrying forward the net surplus or deficit.

While the technique of public budgeting is not of special interest to the layman, there are certain major handicaps to budgetary practices in the United States which should be touched upon. First, we have an inflexible scheme of federal organization which tends to separate national and State finances. There can be little doubt that this rigid federal structure hampers budgeting in the interest of all sections of the country, a handicap that unitary forms of government do not experience. The national government of the United States has practically nothing to say about the budgets of the forty-eight States and their local subdivisions, or the extent to which their governments may incur debts. Through improper handling of its finances, each State may create an embarrassing situation for the nation as a whole. No central machinery exists, such as some other federal governments have already found necessary, for coordinating in a degree the budgetary needs and required loans of the federal and State governments. A comprehensive plan for the coordination of federal and State finances should be worked out, which would require the application of budgetary methods on a uniform basis, the integration of federal and State revenue systems, the regulation of expenditures in keeping with the nature and importance of governmental tasks, and the supervision of indebtedness in all State and local units.

Secondly, the unwarranted separation of powers, especially between the legislative and the executive branches, is a stumbling-block to budgetary development in the United States. An intimate relationship between the two branches is necessary to perfect the working of the budget system. Under ordinary circumstances party control affords practically the only unifying force between the legislature and the executive; and even so, the habit of separation has become so strongly fixed that it often persists although both are controlled by the same political party or faction. Only under the pressure of major emergencies, when the legislature temporarily defers to the leadership of the executive, do the two branches actually work together. Efforts should be made in the national and State governments to bring the legislature and the executive into intimate contact and place greater responsibility upon the executive for the budgetary program. Certain devices to this end have been suggested: to give the executive the right to introduce financial and other measures in the legislature; to allow the executive the privileges of the floor to explain and defend his proposals; to permit the executive, in the case of a deadlock, to dissolve one or both houses of the legislature and to carry the issue to the electorate.

In spite of the handicaps just mentioned, it is possible to improve very greatly the budgetary methods of the United States. The executive's powers in the preparation of the budget for legislative consideration may be extended without in any way doing violence to the legislature's prerogatives under the American system of government. Furthermore, instead of restricting the executive's authority in carrying out the budget by detailed appropriations and numerous legal limitations of one kind or another, it is suggested that appropriations should be made in lump-sum amounts rather than in segregated items; that the administrative officers should not be permitted to spend these appropriations without the approval of the executive's central finance office; and that this approval should be obtained on the basis of monthly or quarterly programs of work prepared by such officers. It is also suggested that during the fiscal year comparison between revenue and expenditure, actual and prospective, should be made at frequent intervals, and that the executive should take steps to bring them into line with each other whenever the budgetary balance appears to be threatened.

It would be to the advantage of each State legislature in the United States to consolidate the committees having charge of budgetary matters into one joint committee which would consider all phases of the budget for both houses. It would be helpful, too, for the Governor, or his chief finance officer, to sit with this committee while it is discussing the budget. In Congress it would seem advisable to consolidate the committees of the two houses now dealing with budgetary matters so that one committee in each house would examine both the income and the expenditure sides of the budget, or even to go a step farther and establish a Joint Committee on the Budget. The use of committee-of-the-whole procedure has been suggested as a remedy for some of the abuses growing out of the standing-committee system of American legislative bodies. With the executive present on the legislative floor, such procedure would make it possible to stage a genuine discussion of the budget—a discussion that would arouse public interest in the problem from coast to coast.

Suitable financial machinery and methods, not to mention adequate personnel, are indispensable to the executive in carrying out the budget. These instrumentalities are either lacking or are defective in one way or another in many of our units of government. In the national government, for example, the Treasury Department needs some adjustments in its organizational machinery. Provision should be made for the exercise of real budgetary control through this department by transferring from the General Accounting Office its accounting functions, leaving with that office only the post-auditing and investigational functions. The central accounting system of the government should undoubtedly be maintained under the Treasury Department; the executive would thus have control over the sources of accounting information necessary to the realization of the budget. The Bureau of the Budget should be made, actually as well as legally, a part of the Treasury Department, thus obviating the present anomalous situation in which the President has two chief financial officers, the Secretary of the Treasury and the Director of the Budget.

Finally, the enforcement of accountability on the part of the executive for carrying out the budget is an important role of the legislature, now practically neglected in the United States. In the national and in nearly all the State governments the methods employed to enforce accountability at the present time are largely makeshifts—audits improperly performed and without legislative review. As a remedy for this situation in the national government it is suggested that the existing General Accounting Office should be reorganized into a General Auditing Office, headed by an Auditor General responsible to Congress. This office should be concerned mainly with post-auditing the accounts kept by the Treasury Department and by the various operating departments. Annually it should submit a report to Congress embodying its findings on all post-audits, its criticisms of faulty financial procedures, and its recommendations for improvements. To consider this report, it is suggested that Congress should create a joint Committee on Public Accounts, consisting of not more than fifteen members, with the chairman and a majority of the members selected from the party or parties in opposition to that of the President. This committee would then serve as a critical body for reviewing the financial operations of the government, censuring improper practices and administrative abuses, and recommending suitable action thereon to Congress.

Chapter XXV

TREATY-MAKING AND FOREIGN POLICY

[THE day of the hermit nation is gone. Nations cannot withdraw into their shell and let the rest of the world go by. The rest of the world refuses to go by and, when it is a world of ambitious, aggressive, and warring states, national security becomes of prime importance. Without security a nation cannot develop its resources or enrich its civilization. Nor, without commerce and intercourse with other nations, can it make the most of its resources and enjoy the benefits that modern knowledge has to offer. This means that the process of conducting our foreign relations and the nature of our foreign policy are of compelling significance to every one of us. This chapter makes no pretense of offering a systematic and complete picture of these matters. It does, however, present clearly certain aspects of and certain opinions about the process of treaty-making, Latin American relations, and the relation of the United States to international organization.]

No. 89

HOW THE UNITED STATES ENTERS INTO TREATIES WITH OTHER NATIONS [1]

by William V. Whittington

THE primary classification of the procedure by which the power to make treaties has been exercised is based upon a division of our history as an independent nation into three periods.

First, that period from the date of the Declaration of Independence in 1776 to March 1, 1781, during which time there was no constitution or other fundamental law in written form.

Second, that period from March 1, 1781, to March, 1789, during which

[1] William V. Whittington, "How the United States Enters into Treaties with Other Nations," *Congressional Digest* (August-September, 1938), Vol. 17, pp. 195-197. Reprinted by permission of the *Congressional Digest*, the Washington monthly published without editorial bias or advertising, featuring the congressional controversy of the month, pro and con.

time our Government operated under the Articles of Confederation adopted by the Continental Congress.

Third, that period from March, 1789, to the present, during which time the Government has operated under the Constitution.

It must be remembered that although the Articles of Confederation were adopted in November, 1777, the required acceptance by the thirteen States was not effected and the Articles did not become effective until 1781. In the meantime, however, there were concluded and brought into force two treaties.

The Continental Congress, which was vested with the power to appoint plenipotentiaries and to ratify treaties, delegated to Benjamin Franklin and certain others authority to negotiate with the Government of France for the conclusion of a treaty of amity and commerce and a treaty of alliance. These negotiations were of great importance in the revolutionary scheme. The two treaties were signed at Paris on February 6, 1778. It was not until late afternoon of Saturday, May 2, 1778, almost three months later, that these treaties were placed before the Continental Congress. On the following Monday, May 4, the Congress considered the treaties and approved them. These treaties with France are the only examples of treaty procedure during the first of our historic periods.

During the second period, beginning with the effective date of the Articles of Confederation in March, 1781, several treaties or agreements with foreign nations were concluded and entered into force, including agreements with France, Great Britain, the Netherlands, Prussia, and Morocco. Still another agreement, a consular convention with France negotiated by Thomas Jefferson and signed at Paris, was pending.

Under the Articles of Confederation it was necessary that nine States give their sanction to a treaty before it could become effective. We have referred to the fact that the Continental Congress delegated the authority and issued instructions directly to plenipotentiaries appointed by it. The Congress, pursuant to the terms of the Articles of Confederation, had control of foreign relations. As far as the making of treaties was concerned, the Congress then performed all those functions, including ratification of treaties, which now are performed by the Chief Executive. The President of the Congress was a presiding officer, without the executive powers now vested in the President under the Constitution.

The third of our historic periods began with the date on which the Constitution of the United States entered into force. Although the Constitution provided that it should enter into force when ratified by nine states, and the ninth ratification was effected in June, 1788, it was not until the first Wednesday in March, 1789, that the Constitution was declared to be in effect.

Many hundreds of treaties and agreements concerning nearly every conceivable phase of international relations have been concluded since that time. The provisions of the Constitution altered entirely the procedure for making treaties. In the field of treaty making, the President is the sole authority for entering into negotiations and for concluding agreements with foreign countries. The one limitation upon his authority is that set forth in paragraph 2 of section 2 of Article II of the Constitution, reading:

> He shall have power, by and with the advice and consent of the Senate, to make treaties, provided two-thirds of the Senate present concur.

It is necessary that we take the time to comment briefly upon the relative functions of the President and of the Senate in regard to the making of treaties.

It is sometimes incorrectly stated that the Senate ratifies a treaty. It is true that the Constitution provides that two-thirds of the Senators present shall give their advice and consent to the making of treaties, and failure of the Senate to give such advice and consent has prevented in a few instances the ratification of treaties. Nevertheless, the approval of a treaty by the required number of Senators does not ratify a treaty and is not mandatory upon the Executive.

Perhaps the principal factor to be borne in mind with respect to the Executive authority in the making of treaties is this: At every point until an international agreement becomes effective the authority of the President is sole and exclusive, with the one exception provided in the Constitution. The President's control, therefore, may be either positive or negative. With reference to the negative control, I quote a portion of an address delivered recently by Hunter Miller, Historical Adviser and Editor of Treaties of the Department of State:

> . . . He may refuse to permit a proposed treaty to be signed on behalf of the United States; if signed he may refuse to send it to the Senate; if sent to the Senate he may withdraw it at his pleasure; if acted on favorably by the Senate he may refuse to ratify it; and he may even ratify it and refuse to exchange the ratifications. At any stage in the making of a treaty, until it is internationally complete, the President may, in the exercise of his own discretion, bring the proceedings to an end.

Before proceeding to a study of the various types of agreements and the procedure for their negotiation, we should have a definition of terms.

As to the distinction between a bilateral and multilateral treaty, I believe there is no confusion. A bilateral treaty is, in its simplest terms, an agreement or contract between two governments with respect to certain matters of mutual interest. A multilateral treaty is one that has been signed and effected as between three or more governments and dealing with matters of more or less common interest to all of them.

In using the term "treaty" we do so with the language of the Constitution in mind. That is to say, those international agreements which are submitted to the Senate of the United States for its advice and consent to the ratification thereof are deemed to be treaties in the Constitutional sense. They may be called many other things by the nations interested. For instance, they may be referred to as treaties, or as conventions, or as protocols, acts, articles, contracts, or agreements; but it is convenient and proper to refer to them collectively as treaties.

The procedure in the making of bilateral treaties may be considered in two parts, the first being that up to and including signature, and the second being that which follows signature.

Probably the first question requiring attention is this: How do the two countries get together? There are, of course, many ways in which this may be done, but perhaps the most usual method is for one or the other of the governments to communicate to the other, through diplomatic channels, its desire to negotiate an agreement covering certain matters. In such case, it is customary for the government proposing the agreement to submit to the other a complete draft or text of the proposed arrangement.

Thereafter, the actual negotiations may take place in the capital city of either of the interested nations, or at any other place, as the competent authorities may consider most expedient. Let us say that the negotiations are carried on in Washington, D. C. In such case, the ambassador or minister or other qualified plenipotentiary of the foreign country will represent his government in the negotiations, and for that purpose will consult directly with the Secretary of State or other qualified officers within the Department of State. Throughout the negotiations, the representative of the foreign country may keep in touch with his government and will pursue the negotiations in accordance with instructions from his government.

It may be that the negotiations—that is to say, the discussions and consultations with a view to reaching an agreement with respect to subject matter and terminology—will be completed within a comparatively short time. On the other hand, these negotiations may and often do require months or even years, depending upon the complexity or controversial nature of the matters to be dealt with in the proposed treaty.

Eventually, we shall assume, an agreement is reached on all points. It is probable that the text of the agreement has been prepared in the languages of both countries, carefully compared and found to be identical so far as the substance of the provisions is concerned. The treaty then may be drawn up for signature, duplicate originals thereof being prepared in what is referred to as the *alternat*—that is, with parallel columns containing the two languages side by side, the language of one of the countries being in the left-hand column of one of the originals while in the other original that language will appear in the right-hand column. We shall refer to this again.

A time and a place are fixed for the signing of the treaty. Let us say the place is an office in the Department of State. Shortly before the time fixed for signature, the qualified plenipotentiary of the foreign nation and the Secretary of State of the United States will appear, and the documents will be placed in readiness for signature. Other interested officers of both governments may be present to assist in or to observe the procedure of signing. When all is in readiness, there having been a formal presentation of full powers, the treaty will be signed, and the respective seals of the plenipotentiaries will be affixed.

The treaty having been duly signed and sealed, the plenipotentiary of the foreign nation will retain one of the duplicate originals for transmission to the foreign office of his government, and the other duplicate original will be retained in the archives of the Department of State, subject to the further procedure required in regard to senatorial approval, and ratification.

The negotiations having been completed and the treaty having been concluded (that is, signed and sealed), we are prepared to consider the method by which the treaty is brought into force. For this purpose, it is believed that it would simplify matters greatly if we follow step by step the actual procedure in effecting a comparatively recent treaty—the treaty between the United States of America and Mexico terminating article VIII of the treaty of December 30, 1853 (the Gadsden Treaty).

This treaty was signed April 13, 1937. On April 19, 1937, the Secretary of State sent to the President a letter (or report), enclosing one of the signed and sealed originals of the treaty, for submission to the Senate of the United States. On April 22, 1937, the President sent to the Senate a message, together with the letter from the Secretary of State and the treaty. On that same date, the treaty was read the first time in the Senate and was referred to the Committee on Foreign Relations, and it was ordered that the treaty, together with the President's message and the accompanying letter of the Secretary of State, be printed in confidence for the use of the Senate. Accordingly, there was printed a confidential Executive document for the use of the Senate, copies thereof being furnished to the Treaty Division of the Department of State for confidential use.

It was on June 10, 1937, almost two months after the treaty was signed, that the Committee on Foreign Relations of the Senate submitted its Executive Report, recommending that the Senate "do advise and consent to the same." As of this date, the injunction of secrecy imposed by the Senate was removed and the treaty was made public. That did not mean that the treaty was approved by the Senate, but merely that copies thereof would be available for general distribution.

On June 29, 1937, about three weeks after the Committee on Foreign Relations had submitted its favorable report, the Senate of the United States gave its advice and consent to the ratification of the treaty, without amendment or reservation. Needless to say, in some cases the Senate has given its advice and consent only with certain reservations, which it has been necessary to communicate to the other government in order to ascertain whether the latter would accept them.

At this point, the function of the Senate ends. The remaining action is for the Executive. An instrument of ratification is prepared in the Treaty Division for the Signature of the President of the United States. This instrument recites the steps that already have been taken, then usually it sets forth the text of the treaty exactly, and concludes with a statement to the effect that the treaty is thereupon confirmed and ratified. In the case of the treaty with Mexico which we are considering, this instrument was signed and sealed by the President of the United States on July 15, 1937, a little more than two weeks after the Senate had given its advice and consent.

Meanwhile, the treaty was under consideration by the Government of Mexico in accordance with its own procedure. It was not until November 9, 1937, that the instrument of ratification of that Government was signed and sealed. It sometimes happens that the foreign government will ratify a treaty before its ratification by this Government.

Under the terms of the treaty, as is now customary with bilateral treaties, the ratifications were to be exchanged at a specified place and the treaty was to go into effect when such ratifications had been exchanged. The instruments of ratification of the treaty were exchanged formally in the Department of State at Washington, December 21, 1937. The treaty thereupon entered into effect internationally, despite the fact that under our national procedure the President had yet to proclaim it.

It is the practice of the Department of State at the present time to prepare instruments of ratification in duplicate, both being signed and sealed by the President. One of these is delivered to the foreign government; the other is placed in the archives with the original signed treaty. This has not always been the case, but as we have indicated already it would not be feasible to attempt an explanation of all the variations in procedure.

There is but one other step in our national procedure, namely, the promulgation of the treaty by the President. There is prepared in the Treaty

Division, for the President's signature, a proclamation commencing with the statement that a treaty of a certain kind with a certain country has been signed at a certain place and date, and then setting forth word for word the treaty as signed, and concluding that the treaty has been made public, "to the end that the same and every article and clause thereof may be observed and fulfilled with good faith by the United States of America and the citizens thereof." The President of the United States issued his proclamation of the treaty with Mexico on December 27, 1937, less than a week following the exchange of ratifications.

Thus terminates the procedure, as far as the effectiveness of the treaty is concerned, but that is by no means the end of the work that must be done. There remains the matter of publication, of recording, of distribution, and of various other labors, which are done by the Treaty Division of the Department of State.

No. 90

THE STORM CENTER IN TREATY-MAKING [1]

by Harold H. Sprout

THE Constitution states that the President "shall have the power, by and with the advice and consent of the Senate, to make treaties, provided two-thirds of the Senators present concur." This division of power and function has provided an admirable mechanism for the protection of minority interests as well as for the expression and even promotion of antithetical conceptions of national interest and policy. It is the purpose of this paper to show how these phenomena have come to pass; to sketch briefly their effect, not only on the form and procedure of American diplomacy but also on the spirit and substance of American foreign policy; and to consider what if any revision of the treaty-making process is possible and desirable under existing conditions and circumstances.

Treaty-making under the Constitution involves four principal stages—negotiation, senatorial consent, ratification and exchange of ratifications. The Senate plays an occasional role in the first stage, a paramount role in the second, and none at all in the third and fourth. The President has, in a few instances, sought the collective advice of the Senate before entering into treaty negotiations. He has sometimes placed Senators upon commissions appointed to negotiate treaties. He has frequently consulted with individual Senators prior to or during the course of negotiations. The

[1] Harold H. Sprout, "The Storm Center in Treaty-Making," *The American Scholar* (Spring, 1938), Vol. 7, pp. 211-222. Reprinted by permission of *The American Scholar.*

trend of Senatorial opinion—in particular, forewarnings of Senatorial opposition—may indirectly affect proceedings. But the Senate as a body has
only rarely attempted to interfere with the process of negotiation. And
its incursions into this realm have not been conspicuously successful. The
Senate's great power over treaties lies rather in its veto on the completed
work of the Executive. And it is chiefly this veto which, by producing the
trends noted in the preceding paragraph, has become one of the storm
centers of the Constitution.

A draft treaty, on submission to the Senate for approval, is referred to
the Committee on Foreign Relations. This Committee has a broad discretion. It may, and sometimes does, hold public hearings at which interested
parties state their views with fair assurance of publicity in at least the
metropolitan newspapers. The Committee may then recommend unqualified
ratification; it may draft amendments, possibly changing the whole purport
of the treaty; it may propose reservations, limiting or even eliminating the
obligations of the United States; it may bring in a report recommending
rejection; or it may take no action at all.

When the Foreign Relations Committee has acted, the struggle, if there
be one, is transferred to the floor of the Senate. Here the opposition can
continue its assault by means of amendments, reservations and obstructionism in general. The Senate's rules facilitate such tactics. Although there
is now a cumbersome procedure for limiting debate a determined Senatorial
minority can still filibuster and otherwise delay final action almost indefinitely.

Consent to ratification with amendments or reservations causes further
delay and complications. A draft treaty is in a sense a contract with the
other signatory or signatories. It usually represents a compromise in which
all parties have made concessions. The effect of Senatorial alterations is
often to strike out concessions made by the United States while insisting
on all concessions of the other signatories. Such alterations may thus
defeat the whole undertaking and in addition engender resentment and
ill-will abroad. At the very least, amendments and reservations hold up
ratification while the Executive strives to secure the consent of the other
signatories. Negotiations to this end present difficulties enough when only
one other Power is involved. Such difficulties become all but insuperable when it is necessary to secure the consent of a large number of Powers,
as, for example, in the case of the Senate's qualified approval of the World
Court Protocol in 1926.

Theoretically and mathematically the two-thirds requirement enables a
comparatively small minority of Senators elected by an even smaller fraction of the country's population to defeat undertakings acceptable to an

overwhelming majority of the American people. That the two-thirds rule has had such an effect on several occasions is probably beyond dispute. But this rule is not the only or even the principal source of minority obstructionism. As already noted, the Senate's ordinary rules of procedure quite as much as the two-thirds rule offer large opportunities for obstructionism. A bare majority can incorporate amendments into a treaty or add reservations to a resolution of "advice and consent" to ratification. Such amendments or reservations may defeat the treaty's purpose even if they do not block final ratification. By skilfully utilizing the tricks and dodges of parliamentary procedure a determined minority can often delay a vote while it strives to mobilize support and can sometimes prevent the Senate from taking any action at all.

These various possibilities inherent in minority obstructionism, repeatedly stressed in criticisms of the Senate's treaty-veto, pose a fundamental question of political science: Whether and to what extent governmental institutions should protect minority interests from the consequences of majority rule. One of the principal arguments for a judicial veto on legislation—one constantly reiterated in the recent Supreme Court controversy—rests upon the assumption that it is politically expedient as well as socially desirable to safeguard minority interests from the tyranny of the majority. And this same argument has been cited in justification of the Senate's veto on treaties.

As a matter of historical fact it is interesting to note that the Senate's treaty-veto was originally conceived largely with a view to protecting minority interests. In 1786 a bare majority of the States represented in the Continental Congress (the quasi-legislative body under the Articles of Confederation) carried a resolution, against solid Southern opposition, authorizing the Confederation's Foreign Secretary in return for a general commercial treaty with Spain to relinquish the rights of Americans to ship their merchandise down the Mississippi River through the Spanish port of New Orleans. On the other hand New Englanders were fearful lest the Central and Southern States should combine in a similar fashion to relinquish American claims against Great Britain respecting the Newfoundland fishing grounds. To prevent a sacrifice of one minority interest for the benefit of another, as well as for other reasons, the members of the Constitutional Convention of 1787 deemed it necessary to impose some check on the treaty-making power. And to prevent a bare majority from overriding an important minority it was finally decided to vest the power to make treaties in the President "with the advice and consent" of two-thirds of at least a Senatorial quorum.

In practice the Senate's treaty-veto has protected minorities to an extent that the framers of the Constitution could scarcely have contemplated. Pressure by private interests held up one treaty for over 20 years. Treaties affecting the status or property rights of individuals have proved especially vulnerable. Treaties granting reciprocal tariff reductions have fared worst of all, the pressure of jeopardized minority interests having prevented affirmative action on nearly all reciprocity treaties submitted to the Senate.

Such sensitivity to the pressure of interested groups—foreseen imperfectly if at all by the framers of the Constitution—is largely a product of the residential requirement and of our system of electioneering. The Constitution specifies that a Senator must be an "inhabitant of the State for which he shall be chosen." This requirement brings to the Senate men who are keenly aware of and normally sympathetic to important group interests within their respective States. Furthermore Senatorial candidates must ordinarily rely upon these interests to provide the large sums of money necessary to finance primary and election campaigns. They must also build up voting strength among the rank and file of the electorate. Under such conditions it is only common prudence for the ambitious politician to watch closely the currents of opinion and to heed the demands of influential pressure groups within his State. Thus whenever a pending treaty imperils local interests or otherwise agitates local opinion it is certain to arouse opposition in the Senate. And by complex bargaining, one phase of which is popularly known as "log-rolling," strong opposition by even one or two Senators may suffice to prevent affirmative action on a pending treaty.

Other developments, mostly unforeseen by the founding fathers, have also complicated the treaty-making process. The Senate in 1790 had 26 members; today it has 96. As the late George W. Wickersham once remarked: "A body of ninety-six men of such diverse characteristics and opinions," while "almost hopeless as an executive force . . . is ideal for purposes of obstruction."

The rise of a bi-party system was another unforeseen development vitally affecting the treaty-making process. Political parties are pressure groups whose interests and activities affect foreign policy in various ways. Narrow partisanship has frequently characterized the Senate's action on treaties as well as on domestic legislation. And the potentialities of such partisanship are obvious when it is remembered that the President's party ordinarily controls less than two-thirds and sometimes only a minority of the seats in the Senate.

The group interest of the Senate itself has also affected treaty-making. A club atmosphere pervades the upper Chamber. To many of its members their position represents the fulfillment of a life-long ambition. A Senatorship is widely regarded as second only to the Presidency in prestige and renown. As a result the Senate collectively and Senators individually have developed a jealous concern for what they are pleased to call the Senate's prerogatives. One of the most jealously guarded of these prerogatives is the Senate's treaty-veto. And every attempt on the part of the Executive to coerce or to sidestep the Senate has stimulated the latter to assert its power, at whatever cost to the international prestige and influence of the nation as a whole.

This antagonism between Senate and Executive has received further impetus from a fundamental disagreement as to the basic aims and means of American foreign policy. American opinion has shown a marked tendency to cluster around the antithetical concepts of isolation and collective security. Those who incline toward the latter position generally feel that peace and prosperity for the United States are permanently achievable only in an orderly world and that the American people have therefore a real self-interest, not to mention a moral responsibility, in pledging their enormous power, in cooperation with other peace-loving nations, to prevent or if necessary to stop lawless aggression anywhere in the world. This view, toward which the executive branch of the Government has gravitated in recent years, stands in sharp contrast to the ancient American tradition of national security through neutrality, non-intervention and no entangling alliances. While there are various brands and degrees of isolationism those who incline toward this position generally feel that a policy of no pledges and little cooperation offers a larger assurance of peace and security—for the United States at least—than any scheme of collective action that can be operated in a world dominated by fear, suspicion, armed force, mass propaganda and mob psychology. The various brands of isolationist doctrine, always more popular in the interior than upon the seaboard, have long had vigorous champions in the Senate where the equal representation of States has resulted in over-representation of those less densely settled regions of the interior in which a narrow isolationism has traditionally had the greatest vogue.

This cleavage between the Executive and a large segment of Senatorial opinion dates from the closing years of the 19th century. In 1899 it found clear-cut expression in a Senatorial reservation to a convention for the pacific settlement of international disputes negotiated at the first Hague Conference. This formula, repeatedly used on subsequent occasions, states that "nothing contained in this convention shall be so construed as to require the United States . . . to depart from its traditional policy of not intruding upon, interfering with, or entangling itself in the political questions . . . of any foreign State; nor shall anything contained in the said convention be construed to imply a relinquishment . . . of its traditional attitude toward purely American questions."

This negative attitude toward political cooperation persisted down to the outbreak of the World War. There is abundant evidence of Senatorial antipathy to the internationalism of Secretary of State John Hay (1898-1905) and of President Theodore Roosevelt (1901-1909). And if this trend was less conspicuous thereafter it was largely because the Taft Administration (1909-1913) itself forsook the path of political cooperation with the Powers and once more sought security—for the United States—in a policy of isolation.

President Wilson's crusade for the League of Nations reopened the breach between Executive and Senate in a manner calculated to give a continuing impetus to Senatorial isolationism. Without entering into the details of Wilson's tragic struggle for the League we may simply note two developments that were vitally to affect the exercise of the Senate's treaty-veto in the post-war years. The first was the famous propaganda campaign by which the anti-League forces reawakened, stimulated and gave a new lease of life to the traditional isolationism which was still deeply rooted in American ideology. The second was the notorious packing of the Foreign Relations Committee, reorganized after the congressional elections of 1918, with irreconcilable isolationists, whose influence continued into the twenties and is undoubtedly greater to this day than it might otherwise have been.

The resurgent isolationism of the country in general and of the Senate in particular has repeatedly affected treaty-making during the post-war years. The Senate qualified its approval of the Four Power Treaty of Washington (1921) with a reservation which stated that the United States interpreted the treaty as involving "no commitment to armed force, no alliance, no obligation to join any defense." In 1926 the Senate consented to ratification of the Protocol of Adherence to the World Court with reservations which would have placed the United States in a favored position of irresponsibility enjoyed by no other member of that body. Two years later the Senatorial proceedings on the Pact of Paris revealed the isolationist forces still in the ascendency. In this instance only strong Executive pressure coupled with an official interpretation that rendered the treaty all but worthless save as a moral gesture prevented the Senate from adopting formal amendments or reservations that might well have prevented the instrument from going into effect at all. Again, in the London Naval Conference of 1930, the practical certainty of Senatorial opposition may well have been a factor in President Hoover's refusal to enter into a "consultative pact" with the European Powers in return for greater armament concessions on the part of France. And finally, in 1935, isolationist sentiment in the Senate and in the country at large as well as poor management on the part of the Administration blocked the entry of the United States into the World Court on terms almost identical with those prescribed by the Senate itself back in 1926.

This episode precipitated a lively if short-lived agitation for a constitutional amendment to deprive Senatorial minorities of their power to thwart the Executive's diplomatic undertakings. Senator James P. Pope, a strong advocate of American entry into the League of Nations, proposed an amendment reducing the two-thirds requirement to a simple majority and there was fresh discussion of an earlier proposal to abolish the two-thirds rule in favor of a simple majority approval by both branches of Congress. These and other proposals, all calculated to enlarge the President's control over foreign policy, raise several fundamental questions: First, whether the suggested constitutional amendments would really effect the reform which their sponsors desire; second, whether any constitutional amendment to this end is politically possible; third, whether it is needed; and fourth, whether any revision of the treaty-making process is really desirable.

With respect to the first question it is not clear that a mere substitution of majority rule would afford the relief which the Senate's critics desire. Such a reform would not eliminate the obstructive potentialities inherent in the discretion of the Foreign Relations Committee and in the ordinary rules of Senate procedure. Minorities could still urge amendments and reservations, bargain with their colleagues for support, filibuster and otherwise obstruct progress. A simple majority rule would admittedly place treaties in as favorable a situation as ordinary legislative proposals. But would that be sufficient? In dealing with the latter the Senate and House are framing as well as endorsing policy. In dealing with treaties, on the contrary, the legislative body is passing on a completed instrument, contractual in character, alteration as well as rejection of which may well defeat the whole undertaking. It is therefore arguable that to make the treaty-process a really effective instrument of a positive foreign policy it would be virtually necessary to abolish legislative review of treaties altogether.

Coming to the second question it is clear that any constitutional revision of the treaty-making process lies beyond the horizon of practical politics. The amending process is notoriously difficult under the most favorable conditions. But conditions here are decidedly unfavorable. And it is likely that they will remain so, so long as Senators jealously guard the prestige and prerogatives of the upper Chamber; so long as so many influential pressure groups can derive advantage from the existing treaty-veto; and so long as there remains a basic cleavage in American thought as to the national interest and destiny of the United States.

Turning to the third question it is at least arguable that no constitutional revision of the treaty-making process is really necessary. To avoid the Senate's veto, statesmen have utilized other vehicles for national policies. One of these is the informal executive agreement. The Protocol of 1901, arranging for payment of the Boxer Indemnity, was never submitted to the Senate. In 1907 President Theodore Roosevelt entered into an executive agreement with Japan for limiting emigration to the United States. An informal executive agreement, however, has certain weaknesses and limitations. It has no legal standing and imposes no more than a political or moral obligation even upon the Administration that makes it.

To meet this deficiency, statesmen have evolved another type of instrument which within a limited field offers virtually all the advantages of a formal treaty but without the necessity of Senatorial consent to ratification. Congress may authorize the President to enter into executive agreements with respect to matters falling wihin its constitutional powers. Such agreements have the force of law and are constitutional provided Congress has prescribed certain general principles to which the agreements must conform. The Trade Agreements, under the Reciprocal Trade Agreements Act, illustrate this type of procedure. Every one of these Agreements embodies tariff concessions that would never receive a simple majority endorsement in Congress to say nothing of a two-thirds vote of approval in the Senate.

The congressional joint resolution offers still a third substitute for the treaty-process. The expansionists of 1844 could not muster the two-thirds necessary to perfect a treaty for the annexation of Texas. The expansionists of 1898 found themselves in the same predicament with regard to a treaty for the annexation of Hawaii. In each instance the constitutional difficulty was sidestepped by resort to a joint resolution which required only simple majorities in each chamber and was just as much a law of the land as any treaty. This procedure has been utilized recently to effect the entry of the United States into the International Labor Organization. And it is currently advocated as a constitutional avenue for the entry of the United States into both the World Court and the League of Nations.

Considering the latitude of action possible under these three procedures one might perhaps conclude that there is no urgent reason for attempting to simplify the treaty-making power by the difficult process of constitutional amendment. Such a conclusion, which in general seems well-founded, does not, however, foreclose discussion of the final question: Whether it is even theoretically desirable to curtail or to abolish the treaty-veto of the Senate.

There can be no dogmatic answer to this question. Each person's answer will probably depend largely upon his preference as to the brand of foreign policy the United States should follow. As already noted there are many to-day who believe that national self-interest, if not moral obligation as well, demands a positive foreign policy, and that the American people should cast their lot with the great European democracies to enforce a regime of peace and collective security. Persons strongly inclined toward such a position may feel that everything possible should be done to strengthen the President's power over foreign policy and to avoid the obstructionism that so often paralyzes Senate proceedings on treaties.

On the other hand there are many who have doubts as to the advantages of a positive foreign policy; who still feel that, for the United States, a conservative policy of no commitments and little cooperation presents fewer perils in a world dominated by fear, suspicion, armed force, mass propaganda and mob psychology; and who question in any case the wisdom of large commitments so long as the nation remains hopelessly divided respecting the basic aims and methods of national policy. Persons entertaining such doubts will certaintly regard the congressional majorities necessary to authorize international commitments under joint resolution or by executive agreement as a wise restraint on the Executive's capacity to pledge the United States to act in concert with other Powers. And such persons may even view the Senate's existing treaty-veto, with all its admitted imperfections and opportunities for minority obstruction, as an anchor to windward from which we should not lightly cut ourselves adrift.

No. 91

A PEACE AUDIT OF THE AMERICAS [1]

by Josephine Schain

WHAT have our accomplishments brought us, what have been the results from the theories that have been tested? From our experience of over a century can we say with any certainty what are the essential elements that should go into the establishment of a durable peace? And what way do the signs point for the future? These are some of the questions I have posed for myself as I have reviewed the history of inter-American relations.

First we have a great idea. Simón Bolívar, a prophet with uncanny vision, challenged the new republics of this continent to join together in a union dedicated to freedom and liberty. As President of Peru he called

[1] Josephine Schain, "A Peace Audit of the Americas," *The Annals* of the American Academy of Political and Social Science (July, 1940), Vol. 210, pp. 133-138. Reprinted by permission of *The Annals* of the American Academy of Political and Social Science.

the first congress at Panama in 1826. It is interesting to note that although the United States was invited and the Senate accepted the invitation, we were so slow in getting under way that our delegates were not able to attend the conference.

During the period from 1826 to 1888, neither the public nor the government took particular interest in inter-American affairs. 'Tis true, we had proclaimed the Monroe Doctrine, but our interest in pan-America did not develop into a matter of constructive concern until later. We can claim little credit for the early work in behalf of pan-American activity. There is perhaps good reason for this. We were busy pushing our own frontiers to the Pacific coast. New land was opened up for settlement, there was gold in the hills and adventure for those with restless feet.

But the ideas of Bolívar were not allowed to die. A number of the countries found it useful to counsel together. Conferences were held, treaties of amity and commerce negotiated, and the codification of law begun. Through the persistency of some of the Latin American states a foundation was laid for the real cooperation which we are now endeavoring to evaluate. There is reason also for this persistency of the Latin American countries. Those who desired to restore the old imperialist control were a source of worry for many years after the Spanish Crown was separated from its American colonies.

Then in the early eighties our interest began to awaken. James G. Blaine cast his eyes over the inter-American export and import statistics and noted the growth of the trade between the Americas. Echoes from conflicts between several of the states to the south reached his ears, and as Secretary of State he weighed his responsibility for peace in this hemisphere. But I shall not presume to judge which motive governed his later action. As a matter of fact, in 1881 he invited the republics to a conference to be held in Washington; but this was later canceled because of a change of administration. But the great idea of Bolívar was not canceled. Congress began to take an interest. A congressional commission visited many of the Latin American countries in 1884 and returned with a recommendation that an inter-American conference be called. Finally legislation authorizing such a meeting was passed in 1888 and invitations went forth, resulting in a conference in Washington in the fall of the next year. The most important result of its sessions to be noted here was the establishment of the International Bureau of the American Republics, which later became the Pan American Union. Cooperation had now advanced to the stage of having a secretariat.

From 1889 to 1928 the United States dominated relationships in the Western Hemisphere. It not only took an interest in pan-American conferences, but through a policy of protecting the rapidly increasing investments of its citizens, a period of expanding dollar diplomacy developed. A new interpretation was given to the Monroe Doctrine, by which this country took upon itself continental police powers. It consolidated control of the Caribbean area. The "big stick" came into play. The nations to the south began to apply the term "Colossus of the North" to us. A number of these countries in Latin America were troubled by boundary disputes, by overwhelming debts, by revolutions, so that, all in all, that was far from a happy period in relationships either north or south.

But looking back upon those years, we find many items on the credit side of the balance sheet. Of these the more significant are: the growing interest in arbitration as a means of settling disputes; the proclamation by Mr. Root, the Secretary of State, of the principle that we in the United States "neither claim nor desire any rights or privileges that we do not freely concede to every American Republic"; the development of the International Bureau into the Pan American Union with increased facilities for carrying on its work; the negotiation of the Gondra "Treaty to Avoid or Prevent Conflicts" which was signed in 1923; the expansion of the idea of mediation in the acceptance by the United States of Argentina, Brazil, and Chile as mediators in a dispute with Mexico. Thus persisting through a century, the idea of pan-Americanism began to take on distinct form and substance.

Then beginning with 1928 there can be traced a steady and progressive development of cooperation among the American countries, due mainly to the change of attitude by the United States. Secretary of State Stimson withdrew the marines from Nicaragua, refused to intervene in the collection of debts, and inaugurated a change in the United States policy which refused to recognize governments resulting from revolution.

In 1933 Mr. Roosevelt, after he became President, announced that the policy of the United States in the future would be opposed to armed intervention in Latin American affairs. Mr. Hull, as Secretary of State, began to guide our policy into definite channels of cooperation on a basis of equality. The Platt Amendment which gave us the right of interference in Cuban affairs was abrogated and in general the policy of intervention was abandoned, and our influence was directed toward strengthening the inter-American efforts to work out a basis for peace in this hemisphere.

At Montevideo tariffs were discussed—a definite reversal of the United States thesis that tariffs are solely a matter of domestic concern. But more than any specific issue, the most significant thing was the marked change in the attitude toward cooperation.

Mr. Roosevelt in 1936, in an endeavor to implement the machinery for peace in this hemisphere, took the initiative and called the Inter-American Conference for the Maintenance of Peace. At this conference the agencies of peace already existing were given new scope and effectiveness. Many conflicting points of view were reconciled, and many fundamental principles basic to a durable peace were agreed upon.

At this conference collective responsibility for the security of American republics became an accepted principle. Embedded in the idea of collective responsibility were the principles: of consultation in case the peace of the republics was menaced; that such consultation could be brought about by any government, thus recognizing the equality of states; that consultation could refer not only to difficulties arising between American states but "in the event of an international war outside America which might menace the peace of the American republics, such consultation should also take place." And so the republics pledged themselves to act as a whole against aggression.

Continental solidarity was decreed at Buenos Aires and the principle accepted that "an unfriendly act toward one is an act against all." This was even more clearly and neatly stated at the meeting in Lima. The principles upon which solidarity is based read as follows:

1. The intervention of any state in the internal or external affairs of another is inadmissible.

2. All differences of an international character should be settled by peaceful means.

3. The use of force as an instrument of national or international policy is proscribed.

4. Relations between states should be governed by the precepts of international law.

5. Respect for the faithful observance of treaties constitutes the indispensable rule for the development of peaceful relations between states, and treaties can only be revised by agreement of the contracting parties.

6. Peaceful collaboration between representatives of the various states and the development of intellectual interchange among their peoples is conducive to an understanding by each of the problems of each other as well as of the problems common to all, and makes more readily possible the peaceful adjustment of international controversies.

7. Economic reconstruction contributes to national and international well-being as well as to peace among nations.

8. International cooperation is a necessary condition to the maintenance of the aforementioned principles.

Another fundamental principle of the public law of America was reiterated, namely, that the occupation or acquisition of territory or any other modification or territorial or boundary arrangement obtained through conquest by force or by non-pacific means shall not be valid or have legal effect. The pledge of non-recognition of situations arising from the foregoing conditions is an obligation which cannot be avoided either unilaterally or collectively.

After the conference of Buenos Aires and again after the conference of Lima, many questioned whether these admirable declarations were anything more than a pious hope. Then a crucial test came on September 3, 1939. The world crisis increased the tempo of the slowly emerging Latin American cooperation. The procedure outlined at these conferences was immediately followed. The foreign ministers met in Panama September 23 to October 3 to consider the defense of the American nations against involvement in the war abroad. Thus we have the first application of the procedure of consultation.

Three committees were organized: Neutrality, Maintenance of Peace, and Economic Cooperation. A General Declaration of Neutrality of the American Republics was approved, which gave notice that the rights of the American neutrals in this hemisphere must be paramount to the rights of the warring powers. An Inter-American Neutrality Committee composed of seven experts in the field of international law was created. This committee will sit for the duration of the conflict, for the purpose of advising American governments on common problems of neutrality, in the hope of preserving peace in the Western Hemisphere.

The Committee on the Maintenance of Peace established, by the "Declaration of Panama," a safety zone around the American continents. By this action the foreign ministers authorized the President of Panama to request all belligerents to keep their naval activities out of adjoining American waters. The difficulty of enforcement is obvious. What the effect of this decision will be in the future, no one can tell.

The Committee on Economic Cooperation established the Inter-American Advisory Committee on Economic Affairs, composed of an expert from each of the twenty-one republics, which has continued to function since the Panama conference.

There are those who maintain that the economic front is the only front to be considered. I would not go so far as that, though unquestionably it is one of the most important. Progress in the economic field during the last decade has been encouraging. Economic relationships between the Americas have begun to change from one of conflict to endeavors at cooperation. If temptations from the economic standpoint can be controlled and regulated, a great obstacle in the path of durable peace will have been removed.

At Montevideo, Buenos Aires, and Lima there were resolutions calling for the reduction of barriers to international trade. Then at the Panama conference the delegates leaped ahead and established the Inter-American Advisory Committee on Economic Affairs. The purpose as stated by the conference is "to study problems of an economic nature growing out of the war." One plan already projected is that of an inter-American bank, the object of which would be to facilitate bringing capital to the countries that need it, on the basis of cooperation.

Another step in economic advance which affects inter-American affairs is the renewal of the Trade Agreements Act on the part of the United States Senate. The endeavor by scientific means to find an equitable basis for the exchange of goods is indeed a step ahead. I noted in a recent copy of *Pan American News,* published by the Foreign Policy Association, that a group of United States experts has been making a survey of Colombian economy for the government of Colombia. The object is to find out whether tropical products can be produced which do not compete with United States products.

These are instances of the type of thing that can be done to remove sources of friction. Policies of aggressive expansion can be changed to cooperative development to the mutual benefit of all countries involved. As an English authority has said, "What is needed is the maximization of human well-being in its broadest sense, the advancement of social justice within and between nations."

Another item on the credit side of our ledger is the persistence of the conference method in the Americas. It is a definite proof of an underlying desire to work together. When we analyze the long list of inter-American conferences we find that war is not the only subject that they have been called upon to settle. They have focused far more on the development of peaceful relationships and on matters of importance to the everyday life of people. The list is long: conferences on agricultural problems, codification of international law, motion pictures, housing, public health, police methods, archaeology, Indian affairs, engineering problems, women's affairs, transportation and communications, intellectual exchange, copyrights, and other matters.

As this adventure in international cooperation evolves, we arrive at certain conclusions. As one reviews this century or more of effort, it is clear that substantial progress became possible only when the dominant and powerful country accepted cooperation on the basis of equality of states. There was little of permanence until the United States was willing to cooperate. With power goes responsibility. In the complicated modern world this is as true of nations as of individuals.

Another conclusion is the need for powerful and informed public opinion in every country. "War is an international affair," Mr. Root said, and added, "to prevent it there must be international opinion and international action upon that opinion, and international institutions to give effect to that opinion." It is not necessary to comment on the assertion that war is an international affair; that is a self-evident fact.

The necessity for having an informed citizenry is imperative to a durable peace. This is the crux of our problem, as witness the long years that have passed since Bolívar challenged the republics in this continent to pool their efforts in order to achieve international welfare.

We have had a few tests in recent years which demonstrate that the sentiment in favor of peaceful adjustment of disputes in this hemisphere is acquiring definite strength. At Lima the republics faced disrupting influences, but the conference took no backward step. At Panama decided advance was made, not alone in proclaiming principles but also in setting up committees to function during the war period in order to meet promptly and effectively situations that might arise.

The great problem of educating public opinion is one in which I am personally very much interested. We have a long way to travel in our own country, I know, before we can feel at all sure of a public educated to understand these problems relating to a durable peace for the Americas; as witness the Gallup poll on the Trade Agreements program. Of the persons polled, only one in ten had sufficient comprehension to be able to vote on the subject. Tremendous economic problems as an aftermath of the wars now raging will undoubtedly challenge the relations among the countries in this hemisphere and put both theory and practice to the test.

I do not mean to seem pessimistic; quite the reverse, for the period from 1930 to 1940 demonstrates the part that public opinion can play in backing up a constructive foreign policy.

A major task before the republics now is to make the principles that have been adopted work; or as Mr. Root says in the last phrase that I quoted, there must be "international institutions to give effect to that opinion." When cooperation becomes active, then the necessity for machinery becomes more pressing. There must be adequate channels for effective and full expression on the part of the differing countries. Provision must also be made for necessary change.

We must explore further the question of the means by which the principles that have been adopted may be carried out, and carried out in times of stress. I look forward to the discussions along these lines at future pan-American conferences, as I know there are several items on the agenda carried over from the conference at Lima which cover this point.

Another conclusion is that durable peace in Latin America is dependent upon a world at peace. As long as there is war in the world no area is safe, and inter-American gains might still be wiped away by conflict from without.

The reverse of this may also be true. Successful regional experience and organization may help to point the way to the solution of world problems. If the principles adopted through inter-American experiences are basic, is it not possible that they are capable of universal application? As I re-read the history of inter-American relations, I am reassured in my belief that it is possible to organize the world on a basis of order under law. We note the advance made in international cooperation on this continent since 1826. We should not be discouraged by the results of the mere twenty years of effort that have gone into the building of a world society. When we realize that nowadays distance is measured in minutes, not miles, and that the tempo of the twentieth century is double that of the nineteenth, we may be led to hope that results also will arrive more rapidly.

The world balance of power has passed to this hemisphere. It can be a tremendous force for peace if it continues to work out a cooperative policy that can stand the test. When one considers the differing backgrounds, the absence of a common cultural heritage, it is significant that a basis of co-operation among the republics has been found. If peoples as different as those of Haiti, Argentina, Brazil, Bolivia, and the United States can work out peaceful processes for settling difficulties and can cooperate on a con-structive program, then surely there is hope for a durable peace among the peoples of the world.

And what of the immediate future? For over a century we have seen the idea of pan-American cooperation weathering indifference, revolutions, and dollar diplomacy, and coming at last to a period of achievement. While acclaiming our achievements, let us look at the future realistically. Are we assured of a continuing policy of cooperation on the part of the United States? Have we built up an informed public opinion that will insist on developing the work begun, or is there danger that the "big stick" will again come into play?

We know now that in large areas of the world political and moral disin-tegration will follow the war. Has there been built up an attitude of conti-nental solidarity that can weather that time of testing? Will pan-American cooperation be able to stand against the terrific impact of the economic chaos after war? The disrupting effect of the totalitarian drives of the last half-dozen years upon the economy of many of the Latin American countries is a slight indication of what lies ahead. There is no time to be lost. Let us bend every effort toward the development and the buttressing of the fundamental principles of right international conduct, spurred on by what has been accomplished in the Americas.

No. 92

INTERNATIONAL ORGANIZATION [1]

by James T. Shotwell

IT is somewhat unreal for us to be discussing the essential bases of a lasting peace on a day in which the history of the world is perhaps being settled in a greater decision than at any previous time since Salamis. No single moment in the World War was so fateful as this moment. . . .

Let us keep that thought in mind, for I am convinced that you and I have some responsibility for what has happened. It behooves us not to blame other nations for the tragic difficulties that have come upon them, without humbly and sincerely examining our consciences as American citizens.

That is a prelude to anything I have to say on peace at this time. Yet in this hour of military decision it is evidently incumbent upon every citizen of a democratic country to consider how measures may be planned on which we can rely in the hour of crisis, so that things like this will not happen in future generations. The planning of peace in wartime is surely as legitimate as the planning of war in peacetime by the general staffs. There has been too little concrete planning by the general staffs for peace, and far too much tendency to stand back and defend and expound the prejudices of the past, which we all ordinarily make the chief motive-power of our thinking and the guide of our lives, instead of the thing we call "Reason." Yet we all recognize that it is a reasonable and decent thing, even at an hour like this, to see if we can think through plans of permanent peace among the nations.

Fortunately, there is a great deal of thinking on this subject in the world. I am struck by the almost unbelievable contrast between the preparedness for peace, or the degree of serious consideration of its problems, which we find in the world to-day compared with the situation in 1917, when a few of us met in what we called the "Inquiry" (the name adopted by the technical group which advised Colonel House and President Wilson) and tried

[1] James T. Shotwell, "International Organization," *The Annals* of the American Academy of Political and Social Science (July, 1940), Vol. 210, pp. 19-22. Reprinted by permission of *The Annals* of the American Academy of Political and Social Science.

to devise a peace conference in which American ideals might play some part in the reconstruction of the world after the World War.

At that time the problem of peace seemed abstract, unreal, metaphysical, to us all. We had no experience to guide us. We looked back to the conferences of Münster and Vienna, but there was very little there that ran parallel to the experiences and needs and problems of 1917. There was very little of anything except a few journalistic essays to guide our thinking in the world in which we were then living.

To-day there are aggregations of scholars at work on the subject in every university of any note in all the civilized world; and there are technical experts, either scholars of academic background or those who have had the practical experience of politics in operation, who are planning and working for a decent organization in which the coming generations may find some hope of escaping the menace of continuous war.

Unfortunately, in the interval since the World War, a whole series of distorting myths have given a turn to our prejudices, an accent to our supposed self-interests, which makes it all the harder for the practical, experienced thinker to make headway at the present time. The difference is something like that between the communities of the East and those of the West in the early stages of westward migration in this country, when those on the frontier could experiment with freer minds and a larger range of contact than those in the East, inhibited by vested interests.

Nevertheless, although there are difficulties of a practical character, I think we can say that we do know some of the things that are not to be done and some of the things that have to be done in the world for permanent peace. They fall in two categories: (1) the policies of nations and (2) the organization and constitution of the bodies which should carry out these policies.

With this distinction in mind, let us consider some of the elements in the field of international planning, necessary for permanent peace. Let us start not with the things we want, but with the things we have—the elements of international contact that are actually working.

The first of these is a much neglected element—diplomacy—yet it is the oldest, the largest, and in many ways the most important and most permanent thing that can be counted upon as a method of dealing between nations.

We have a good deal of very important experience in the field of diplomacy. When the World War began, there was a great reaction against what was called "secret diplomacy." It was claimed, with some justification, that war was rooted in a system of intrigue that carried nations on toward war as an ultimate instrument of policy. (I am quoting Clausewitz in his theory *On War*.) We had a feeling that we must reform diplomacy by making it public. It was a very natural thing and a necessary step, but one which none of us thoroughly understood, because in that moment of change we proposed to change almost everything—to have no private negotiations of any importance, but instead to have everything done in public conference.

This was a vast mistake. Why? Because not all the old diplomacy had led toward war; it had equally averted war. It had played its part as the normal and natural way for independent governments that stood for national, absolute sovereignty to deal with one another—the way that involved the least danger through arousing resentments. Every American knows that if the war-debt problem had not been thrown into the public arena, it could have been settled to advantage, to the betterment of the whole world, including ourselves.

So we should have retained some secret diplomacy as a part of our planning, but we should have known how to practice it. I do not mean to imply that American diplomacy has been weak; it has measured up to any other diplomacy. But we have made our natural mistakes as Americans, just as the representatives of the Hapsburgs made their natural mistakes. Our greatest blunder was the effort to register success in diplomacy, so that the newspaper headlines could justify the administration in power at any given time, by recording a triumph over the party of the other part. Now, every time that is done, the other nation or nations involved are bound to spend their very lives to get even with us in one way or another, for years to follow. In the headlines of the American newspapers, we had a wonderful success at the Conference of Habana in 1929, when our brilliant Secretary of State presented our case with reference to Nicaragua and other matters, and it seemed that at last we knew how to manage a conference. Yet Latin America spent the next ten years getting square with us!

I give you that single instance in the history of diplomacy to show what we have yet to learn. We have not learned that lesson yet, by any means. For diplomatic success, it is not enough to have the other nations convinced that our side is right; the negotiations must be so arranged that those nations can share in them and get the credit for them. We did not need to have public diplomacy to achieve decency in international relations; we needed to have decency in diplomacy. And that can be the case when men meet together quietly, just as truly as when they meet in public on the political platform, and perhaps a little more so.

The next field that we have to consider in continuing relationships is that of trade and finance. Here we have a trend toward nationalism, or autarchy, which the Germans have developed most completely in their closed economy. The object of that trend is to work solely for the interests of one nation—a policy which, when practiced, inevitably tends to pass the frontiers between peace and war in the accumulation of defense materials against the hour of danger of reprisal. That is, of course, as I said, defense, rather than war economy, and the Germans, with their acute technological information, practiced it.

"Economy" is, unfortunately, a misleading word, because it tends to make Americans think that there is something that is technical and pure, apart from politics, which is something impure and not technical. We should use the old English term, "political economy." That is what we practice—the economy of nations—and in that political economy other things than welfare have to be reckoned with. We have to reckon with the political forces and trends of the nations themselves, many of them preferring a certain measure of discomfort or even of poverty, of loss and disaster, to welfare and prosperity, if they can give a black eye to some other people against whom they cherish resentment.

Let us get down to human nature. That is what it is. We have seen it in the postwar years. Among nations, the economy of welfare is more an ideal than a practice. But, nevertheless, if we are to have peace with economic backing and a basis of economic dealing, it must be a peace that registers human welfare on the whole; and that means that we have not only economic but also social problems, which is the next point, because as a basis of permanent peace there must be a concept of justice.

There was only one grand phrase in the latter part of the Treaty of Versailles. I am not speaking of the Covenant, which had some splendid things. But in Part 13, in the Labor Section, we wrote a phrase which will stand high in history: "Permanent peace rests upon social justice." That is the point that we reach through our economic approach. There must be within the nation, in its domestic affairs, a concept and a practice of social justice, or the international relationship upon which peace depends will be a fragile thing. No nation can be accounted safe in its dealing with its neighbors which does not practice justice among its citizens at home.

The peace movement has suffered long from a failure to connect these two things. Until the years following the World War, there was a tendency in those supporting the peace movement to find a certain escape from responsibilities at home by thinking of their responsibilities in Ethiopia, for example. There was a great lack of sense of connection between the two. No nation can be sure of itself in dealing with other nations unless it is highly practiced in the administration of justice in the social life of its own citizens.

That brings me to the next point. Justice is a big word, and we have never fully understood it. We think that justice depends upon the rectitude of the individual with reference to himself and his own affairs. That is not the history of justice. The history and test of justice in the long development of jurisprudence—in the West, at least, although not in China—have been our willingness to accept the judgment of our equals, of our fellow citizens, as to whether our case is right or not. From the days of Justinian through the Roman heritage of law on the Continent, from the days of early English settlements through the English common law, this principle of allowing the truth-seeker, the jurist, to determine methods for finding right and wrong, and the application of these methods, is a fundamental thing.

What does that mean, in the long run? It means that society progresses in proportion as the conscience not of each individual but of the community as a whole progresses.

In international affairs we must learn that it is not a question of what we think is right (it may be right, but we cannot be sure); it is what a community of nations will adjudge to be the right. And that judgment can be reliable only in proportion as it schools itself through practice, and there can be no practice as long as great nations like ours refuse to adhere to institutions of international justice.

We have done irreparable damage to the justice of the world as a whole by our attitude on such matters as the World Court. Well, there is a phase that grows out of the interests of nations that clash. But we must build before they clash; we must proceed with the methods for securing that public opinion of the world to which the pacifist resorts, which he invokes, by getting that public opinion into action while it is being formed. So, instead of leaving things to courts and arbitration after the issues have become difficult, we must get adequate methods, adequate institutions for shaping the issues as they come.

And here, again, we have done almost nothing. I cannot trust myself to speak of what we did about the League of Nations. How can we ever have international peace if we do not give the international community a chance to put something in the place of war? We will never have it. As long as we allow disputes to develop so that the antagonisms and animosities which they generate cut torrent-wise across the international landscape, we are dreaming idle dreams when we talk about permanent peace.

"Oh," you say, "but we took a step in disarmament." We thought we did. We had an easy slogan for disarmament. We said the way to disarm is 5-5-3. We had a mathematical formula. Disarm in capital ships. Take out those above the ratio and sink them at sea. It was the great drama of the peace movement. But then came Japan saying, "We would like 10-10-7, or perhaps 10-10-10. The ratio of 5-5-3 is not satisfactory."

It was France that had the right idea. She said rightly that the way to disarm is to give nations that sense of security that will enable them to disarm. Disarm their fears, and then lessen their armies and navies.

Now the only practical way to do that is to erect and strengthen and fortify the institutions of international understanding—not only those of justice, but those that lead toward justice: confidence, diplomacy, and all those institutions in which the gathering storm of disagreement may be dissolved by a reasonable understanding of what the other party wants. What has been our attitude toward the Far East? One of continuance of our missionary outlook. We are going to save their souls somehow in the Far East without responsibility or risk to ourselves.

I will summarize a few points. I said at the beginning that there are two main things to keep in mind: one, the functioning and continuing policies of nations; the other, the structure in which we can embody these policies. This structural organization, the organization of peace, calls for an even larger readjustment of international institutions than the League of Nations gave us a glimpse of. I think perhaps we need to have the diplomacy and the politics practiced by themselves, or at least with due regard to their technique—to where they lead a nation; and the economy and the social and the technical, the nonpolitical, practiced without the impediment of feeling that they may lead us toward that thing known as the preservation of peace by sanctions. The sanction of the nontechnical world is in its own success or failure—not in the policing of nations. The sanction of the political world still remains where nations treasure their national sovereign power. The political and nonpolitical activities lie in different fields, but in the postwar years we tried to separate them too much. We thought we could deal with economics as if it were simply a matter of accounting; while, as pointed out above, the economic relationships of nations gear, equally with political facts, into their sense of prestige and power. We cannot entirely separate these things, but we can go a long way on the pathway toward permanent peace if at the present time, even in wartime, we plan and think and give vitality to those instruments and institutions which stand for world prosperity, world health, world understanding in the intellectual field and the common heritage in the culture of the race.

One final word: There is no permanent peace without courage. Just think that over!

Chapter XXVI

SOME PROBLEMS OF LAW ENFORCEMENT

[Wherever people have lived together, there has been need of some rules governing their relationships with one another. Society always has had to prohibit certain kinds of anti-social conduct and enforce those prohibitions. In other words, law enforcement has always been looked upon as one of the legitimate functions of government.

In the accomplishment of the task of law enforcement many agencies are at work. National, state and local governments are all playing a part in this gigantic task. The United States Department of Justice, the federal marshals, the secret service, state police, county sheriffs, chiefs of police, and courts at all levels are constantly carrying on the job of enforcing the rules that the community lays down.

Out of this welter of activity it is only natural that problems should arise. How can we prevent violations of the law and still preserve the rights of individuals? How can we modernize the law and the obsolete machinery now set up to enforce it? How can law enforcement be removed from politics? How can the lawyer criminal be dealt with? How can we get better judges? How should we reform the jury system? How can we defend the poor who are accused of crime? How can we overcome the barriers to law enforcement created by state lines? How, in other words, can we secure reliable, efficient, and just enforcement of the law? These are the questions that are discussed in the present chapter.]

No. 93

WHO'S WRONG WITH THE LAW? [1]

by Mitchell Dawson

"STRING 'em up! Burn 'em! Cut their hearts out!"
The rope tightens. The flames leap up. . . .
The Governor of California congratulates the avenging mob at San Jose: "That was a fine lesson to the whole nation. . . . I am checking San Quen-

---

[1] Mitchell Dawson, "Who's Wrong with the Law?", *The Atlantic Monthly* (May, 1934), Vol. 153, pp. 621-631. Reprinted by permission of the author and *The Atlantic Monthly*.

tin and Folsom prisons to find out what kidnappers they have. I am thinking of paroling them to those fine, patriotic citizens of San Jose, who know how to handle such situations. . . ."

"Congratulations on the stand you have taken," wires the pastor of New York's Church of the Heavenly Rest. (Later, the pastor admitted that his message was the result of being "deeply stirred," and that "it should not have been sent.")

Congratulations, pastor!

The spirit of the mob, aroused by frightful crimes, goes marching on. The Governor of Maryland impedes the course of swift, sure justice by calling out the troops. Twenty-one members of the state assembly—"almost all descendants of original Anglo-Saxon settlers"—denounce the Governor. Meanwhile the good citizens of St. Joseph, Missouri, hang and roast their man in spite of sixty-five National Guardsmen with armored tanks.

Editorial typewriters once more click out the old familiar tune: Now is the time, now is the time, now is the time for all good men . . . Something is fundamentally wrong. . . . The law has broken down. . . . Now is the time . . .

For what, gentlemen?

The cry goes up: "We need new laws, strong laws, hard laws, laws to end crime." Editors, preachers, judges, crime commissioners, and the good citizens of San Jose, point the finger of scorn at our laws. The courts are tied up by antiquated, weak, dilatory, and technical rules so that they cannot cope with the master minds of gunmen, kidnappers, bank robbers, ravishers, and street-corner bums.

In Illinois we have hard, strong penal laws. Murder and kidnapping are punishable by imprisonment or death; rape, robbery with a gun, and burglary with intent to commit a felony, by a maximum of life imprisonment; arson, by one to twenty years in the penitentiary; and other misdeeds by a sliding scale of fines and imprisonment, subject to commutation for good behavior. We have police also, and prosecutors, courts, and jails, all working overtime. Much of our procedure, it is true, dates back to mediaeval England. But in spite of that our criminal courts in Chicago, under the pressure of public opinion, are rapidly clearing their dockets.

Yet in Chicago robbery and burglary continue to flourish and people get shot as you might swat flies on the wall. From coast to coast it is the same: thousands of laws—hard laws, strong laws—thousands of police, thousands of prosecutors, thousands of courts, and hundreds of thousands of crimes.

This is the law the people built

It is built of blood and fire, of conflict, aggression, and reprisal. It was forged by the clamor of millions of ancestral voices: the voice of the tribe before the council fire howling for vengeance; the voice of the chieftain passing judgment of torture and death; the voice of fear building barriers about its belongings, its home, its lands, its wives, its maidservants and its manservants, its horses, cows, dogs, and asses, calling upon the tribe to curb the claws and fangs of rapacious neighbors; and the voice also of pity for the weak and justice for the wronged.

The law and its institutions are the fruits of centuries of collective living. Kings, princes, prelates, parliaments, presidents, governors, legislatures, and judges have all had a hand in its making, but behind them stand the people, ready at times to rise up and behead, hang, burn, and destroy in the passion of what they believe to be justice. Deep in their hearts lies a distrust of rulers and judges bred by centuries of injustice and oppression. Out of this grew the grand jury, the petit jury, the rule against self-incrimination, habeas corpus, the right to a change of venue, and other safeguards thrown about the accused.

Much of this legal machinery has, without question, become obsolete and inadequate for the handling of our increasingly complex social problems. Professors, police experts, criminologists, and lawyers have for years been suggesting improved methods for apprehending and trying criminals. Ideally, we should scrap the entire present system from police administration to the punishment or attempted reform of law violators, and build in its place a new structure in the light of more modern ideas as to ways and means of forestalling and controlling antisocial conduct. But the finest system in the world, whether devised by a practical criminologist or a social idealist, will not in itself reduce crime one iota without the spirit and will of the people behind it; and even a slight improvement is impossible as long as the nation, in the name of democracy, cherishes and applauds lawlessness and tolerates political corruption.

Our crime problem is not so much "What's wrong with the law?" as "Who's wrong, and why?"

This is the cop
Who enforces the law the people built

"Now, about this crime business," said a well-known hoodlum to Senator Copeland when he was in Chicago with the Senate subcommittee on racketeering and kidnapping, "all you need is honest cops and a little cooperation from the courts."

The average policeman must have bitterly resented the public's cynical approval of this gibe. He is in disrepute for conditions which he is powerless to change. The individual cop is no worse than the rest of us. He has a wife and children. He stands up to get shot at, and quite often is killed. His pay isn't large and sometimes it's delayed.

He may start out as a rookie with high ambitions to make a record for himself by catching crooks and cleaning up his precinct. He may dream of promotion through sheer merit, of becoming step by step a sergeant, lieutenant, captain, and chief amid the plaudits of all good citizens.

But he is soon disillusioned. He discovers that there are certain "joints" that must be left alone because they "kick in" to somebody with protection money, and that there are persons whom it is useless to arrest because they have somehow acquired "immunity" from punishment. This is lesson number one—the lesson of political corruption. It is further illuminated by the flamboyant success of certain lieutenants and captains (not all of them, by any means) who "sport" big cars and invest in stocks, bonds, or apartment buildings.

Our ambitious young cop sees evidence all around him of the profits of the "shakedown" and the "fix." He learns to keep his mouth shut for fear of being exiled to "the sticks." Yet in spite of these conditions he may still have confidence in the civil service system (established in most of our large cities for the purpose of protecting the rank and file of the police and ensuring their orderly promotion), only to realize eventually, if he is bright, that it too is dominated by the machine of the party in power.

He may even resist all temptation to take part in the corruption which surrounds him. Thousands of policemen do. But the chances are that he will succumb to another influence just as insidious and vicious—the spirit of lawlessness. Going about his business from day to day, hauling in bums, pickpockets, holdup men, housebreakers, reds, and drunks, he learns from his brothers in arms to consider his prisoners as obstinate criminal cattle to be pushed and poked and yanked around in order to make them dread forever the sight of the police. No matter how kindly he may otherwise be, he discovers that all's fair in the war on crime. He becomes familiar with the ritual of the "goldfish" room, where prisoners are threatened and beaten with rubber hose, tortured by glaring lights, kept awake for endless hours, and assailed with questions and suggestions until they confess. "You gotta give 'em the works," he is told, and, his faith in the integrity of courts, juries, and prosecutors being weakened by his own actual experience with corruption and inefficiency, he accepts this doctrine of lawlessness with enthusiasm.

To anyone who doubts the prevalent use of the third degree by the police, let me recommend the Report on Lawlessness in Law Enforcement of the National Commission on Law Observance and Enforcement appointed by President Hoover, which presents a multitude of actual instances and concludes that such lawlessness not only brutalizes the police and hardens the prisoner, but impairs the efficiency of the police by leading them to rely on force rather than wits in solving crimes. This is demonstrated by the fact that the Boston police, with little or no use of the third degree, have obtained much better results than the Chicago force with its habitual resort to torture.

Corruption and lawlessness begin at the top and work down. The enforcement of law and order in most of our cities is controlled by a politically appointed commissioner or superintendent, and through him by the bosses of the dominant party, who thereby acquire a tremendous influence over the lives, property, and happiness of the citizens. How brutally, corruptly, and inefficiently they wield it should be apparent to any reader of the day's news.

In spite of such handicaps, here and there a few zealous men, who regard police work as a profession, have succeeded in putting in practice improvements in the technique of crime detection and have tried to encourage the morale of their co-workers and win the public's respect. But they struggle like ants in a sand pit.

> *This is the culprit*
> *Who is caught by the cop . . .*

Youth, growing up in the light of the flaring beacons of lawlessness and corruption, shrugs its shoulders: "Only saps work. You can't get a job, anyway. What's your racket, kid?"

What's your racket, gentlemen, you who howl for the cutting of school taxes, the reduction of teaching staffs, the shortening of the school year, and the curtailment of every school activity except the three R's—what's *your* racket?

Organized crime, organized labor, organized business, organized politics, organized exploitation, parallel and interlock. When trouble breaks, the "big shot" escapes abroad or gets off with a Senate investigation or a light sentence for income tax evasion. The little shots—our Tonys and Joes and Ikes—take the heavy "raps" and go to Sing Sing or Joliet or find permanent surcease via the electric chair.

These are the children, boys, girls, young men, young women, in the streets, alleys, basements, "athletic" clubs, pool rooms, dance halls, barrooms, dives, on the march to detention homes, reformatories, jails. Onward, ever onward, presses the eager, adventurous throng, lured by the hope of easy, gaudy living.

Among them are many mental and emotional misfits who constitute a separate problem. Some of these crippled personalities are discovered and isolated at an early age, but many go about without restraint until they become entangled in the processes of the law. Our social agencies have made progress in the care and treatment of mental defectives, but the law and the courts have been slow to accept the recommendations of psychiatrists.

Indifference, greed, stupidity, shoddy education, and the example of corruption and lawlessness in high places—these are the culprits.

"Lycurgus left none of his laws in writing," says Plutarch, "for he resolved the whole business of legislation into the bringing up of youth."

This is the prosecutor
Who flays the culprit . . .

He begins his career usually as an assistant district attorney or as state's attorney, with little experience in trial work. He learns his courtroom tactics in conflict with seasoned criminal lawyers who delight in springing on him all the tricks and chicanery of their trade. He thinks he must fight fire with fire and dirt with dirt. If he discovers the coercion and intimidation of witnesses by defendants and their friends, he feels justified in keeping the state's witnesses incommunicado and holding over them the threat of criminal prosecution.

The prosecutor is further incited to lawlessness by the clamor of editors, ministers, crime commissioners, and business men for more and stiffer sentences. The necessity of satisfying these good people and assuaging the public appetite for melodrama drives him and his assistants to seek convictions by fair means or foul. The prosecutor joins with the police in using the third degree; in court he violates the rules of evidence, and by improper and inflammatory remarks to juries lays the ground for numerous reversals.

Through his control over the grand jury and the initiation of criminal complaints, the prosecutor wields a power superior to the police, and if he is strong and shrewd he may very well become the dominant political personage in his county. Politics, in fact, is the keynote of all his activities. He probably began as a bright boy running errands for a precinct captain, canvassing voters, or handing out sample ballots; or he may have been related to an influential politician. In either case he saw the advantages of legal training and stepped out of law school into political office of some kind, working his way up through the system to nomination for prosecutor on the party ticket.

In his campaign for election he invariably follows the well-known formula of promising to clean up vice, racketeering, gangs, and gambling, and by constant repetition he may even convince himself that he will suppress crime altogether. But the moment he assumes office he is forced to abandon all but a pretense of an honest and independent administration. In the first place, he has to accept the staff of inexperienced and frequently incompetent assistants assigned to him by the party bosses. And, secondly, the men who nominated him are after him at once to "nol pros" this case and that, to give some hoodlum a break, or to let a confessed criminal plead guilty to a lesser offense than the one he is accused of so that he will take a lighter sentence and perhaps walk out of jail on probation. At the same time the forces of bribery and corruption begin to play upon the weaker members of his staff and find ways and means of gaining their ends no matter how honest the prosecutor himself may be.

Organized gangs recognize the prosecutor's bark, but fear his bite very little. They are in far greater danger from the guns of an outraged police force than from the loud reiteration of the prosecutor that he will drive crime out of his county. Nor can anyone improve the situation very much as long as the office of prosecutor remains a political prize.

> *This is the lawyer*
> *Who fights the prosecutor . . .*

This is the lawyer, aye, and the entire bar, including your humble servant. Most of us won't sully our hands with the criminal law. It's a dirty business. You can't touch tar without getting smirched. A defendant in a criminal case expects you to get him off by hook or by crook, but mostly by crook. If you are unwilling to adopt the devious and crooked ways of crime itself, you can't be the defendant's best advocate, so you turn him down. At least that is how the argument runs.

Most criminal lawyers, therefore, belong to a race apart. Heroes in the public eye; almost but not quite pariahs among "good people." Hardy and shrewd, they know their legal tricks, their police, prosecutors, judges, and gentlemen of the jury. Above all they are realistic—champions hired to get results.

The lower-grade criminal lawyer has his hook-up with gangs and keeps his petitions for habeas corpus written up in blank ready to fill in with the necessary data, so that he can "spring" a client from the lock-up the minute the police nab him. He knows who will furnish bail. He knows who knows which judges and how to pull the strings. He asks his clients no foolish questions. If someone intimidates witnesses and bribes jurors, that's their business, not his. He may indulge in fixing cases, but you can't prove it on him. His philosophy is short and simple: "Give the customers what they pay for."

You may call this sort of unscrupulous practitioner a lawyer criminal, if you like, but he can turn the phrase neatly on other members of the bar: "How about our respectable legal friends who advised public utility magnates and others in the intricacies of floating rotten bonds? And how about eminent counsel who connive among themselves for so-called 'friendly' receiverships to keep the looting of failing corporations and the consequent fees within the magic circle of the insiders?"

The code of ethics of the lawyers is actually higher than that of the business world which supports them. It includes many niceties and is scrupulously observed by the bulk of the bar. Serious infractions of ethics usually lead to disbarment. The lawyers, on the whole, like the ministers, doctors, tradespeople, laborers, and the police, are a decent, hard-working lot. But they labor under the narrow and often antisocial necessities of advocacy.

Some lawyers, in fact, maintain a distinct cleavage between their personal conduct and their conduct on behalf of clients. They would not steal a nickel or raise a finger in violation of the letter of the law, but they will, and do, without compunction disclose to buccaneers of business ways of evading the spirit of restrictive statutes. Their concern, like that of their supposedly criminal confreres, is to give the customers what they pay for, and they will ignore every consideration of social good if it conflicts with the aims and ambitions of a powerful client. Lawyers of this sort would doubtless subscribe to the notorious view of Lord Brougham expressed during the excitement of a trial:

> An advocate, by the sacred duty which he owes his client, knows, in the discharge of that office, but one person in the world, *that client and none other*. To save that client by all expedient means—to protect that client at all hazards and costs to all others, and amongst others to himself—is the highest and most unquestioned of his duties; and he must not regard the alarm, the suffering, the torment, the destruction, which he may bring upon any other. Nay, separating even the duties of a patriot from those of an advocate, and casting *them*, if need be, to the wind, he must go on reckless of the consequences, if his fate it should unhappily be, to involve his country in confusion for his client's protection.

This low and servile conception of the duties of an advocate has been generally repudiated by the legal profession. Yet the spirit of it survives among a minority who have so identified themselves with the interests of their clients that they retain no clear conception of the public good. They are the lawyers who aided and abetted the gentlemen denounced by the President in his message at the opening of the present Congress:

I am speaking of those individuals who have evaded the spirit and purpose of our tax laws, of those high officials of banks or corporations who have grown rich at the expense of their stockholders or the public, of those reckless speculators with their own or other people's money whose operations have injured the values of the farmers' crops and the savings of the poor.

There are fortunately signs that the honest, capable, and diligent majority of the bar have been so aroused by the general outcry for a house cleaning that they may rid themselves not only of the "lawyer criminal," but also of those other malefactors who through a highly developed legal technique and political connections have assisted in looting the public in the numerous ways that democracy affords.

This is the jury
Who favor the lawyer . . .

The culprit is said to be entitled to trial before a jury of his peers. They are too often just that and no more. Therein lies the vice of our jury system as it is administered. Our twelve men may be good and true, but they are not necessarily bright.

Certain trades and professions are notably missing from the jury panel. The police, firemen, teachers, soldiers, lawyers, doctors, and ministers are exempt by law from jury service in most of our states. Bankers, high executives, politicians, and their friends are exempt in practice. Sometimes their names are drawn, but they usually manage on one ground or another to be let off. No one can really blame them. The profitless frittering away of the time and energy of veniremen by lawyers, the courts, and their attachés is notorious. A busy man is appalled at the prospect of abandoning his own affairs even for a few weeks to take part in the drab and inefficient business of the courts.

Occasionally an intelligent and conscientious citizen called for jury service will not try to get excused, and may even look forward with some zeal to participating in the administration of justice. Such a venireman, however, finds himself herded about with other victims, often in badly ventilated and uncomfortable rooms; and when he is finally called to court for examination as a prospective juror he is certain to be challenged by one side or the other if he reveals the slightest ability to form opinions of his own. In fact, unless he conceals this dangerous faculty, he may fail altogether to enjoy the doubtful pleasure of sitting as a juror in any case. If he plays dumb and is accepted and sworn in as a juror, his experience will be illuminating but not edifying. He must sit in silence and listen to constant bickering over evidence and to arguments of counsel that insult his intelligence. Of course, there are exceptions. He may be lucky enough to be picked as juror in a case defended by a brilliant and inspired advocate. But that happens only once in a lifetime.

Whether the I.Q. of the average jury is lower than that of the police, the lawyers, and the court attendants, we do not know. That it is somewhat lower seems reasonable to suppose. But it should be remembered that the jury is the great alibi for prosecutors and judges. It is invariably blamed for every "miscarriage of justice," as in the case of the acquittal of the Touhy gang of alleged kidnappers by a Minneapolis jury a few months ago.

The function of the jury is strictly limited to deciding the guilt of the defendant upon the particular evidence brought before it. It is not permitted to consider extrinsic circumstances presented in the newspapers but excluded from court. In cases of business fraud a verdict of acquittal in a supposedly air-tight case may be due to the inability of the jury to grasp intricate evidence, but in cases of murder, robbery, kidnapping, and crimes of violence generally, it is just as likely to be due to the failure of the state to prove the defendant's guilt beyond a reasonable doubt.

How far the jury system has been tampered with by the fingers of corruption we do not know. In Boston last fall twenty-five former jurors admitted accepting from twenty-five dollars to seventy-five dollars each for holding out for the acquittal of defendants. Two men were sent to jail in Jersey City a few months ago for offering to fix juries in criminal cases, and several others were indicted for jury-fixing in Passaic County last summer.

The drawing of veniremen may also be manipulated by political organizations, so that the men called for service will be of a class and character amenable to influence. The evidence of such practices in Detroit was so strong that the State of Michigan revised its jury panel system.

We have no means, however, of gauging the extent of the corruption and manipulation of juries. It is a secret locked in the hearts of innumerable individual jurors, but they certainly are not immune to the influence of the lawless forces that surround them.

This is the judge
Who instructs the jury . . .

Judge Thomas Taylor, Jr., upon retiring at the age of seventy-two from the bench of the Circuit Court of Cook County, Illinois, after nearly fifty years of the finest type of judicial service, had this to say:

We have many able men at the bar. It is a pity they will not be able to get on the bench. We do need something here. It is a calamity. I could name three hundred or four hundred of the best lawyers, fit for the bench, but no one of them will ever have the ghost of a show. Our people will not select men who are the best for them. They are plastic in the hands of the politicians.

Judges come up through the political route. The young lawyer becomes a precinct captain and a good organizer. In time he gets close to the ward committee-man.

He then tries out for the Municipal Court. After a few years here the ambitious ones aspire to the Circuit and Superior bench. Their success is at no time dependent on their ability as judges. *We get good ones only by chance.*

Judge Taylor states facts that are beyond dispute. It speaks well for the human race that we have as many fine, conscientious judges as we do. Quite often, lawyers who have shown no sign of great legal ability, or interest in public service, will demonstrate excellent judicial qualities after their elevation to the bench.

Unfortunately the work of the good judge is seldom broadcast. He labors day after day in court, in chambers, and at home, sometimes late into the night, reading and considering in the hope that by the grace of God he may arrive at just conclusions. But there is no drama for the public in the quiet researches of the human spirit. They go without acclaim. The name of the good judge seldom registers on the minds of the vast electorate, and when his term expires he is wholly at the mercy of the politicians who nominated or appointed him.

Sometimes a judge may renounce all political alliances and play directly for the support of the public, but very few judges can remain long on the bench if they utterly spurn the hands that boosted them up. This does not mean that cases are generally decided in judicial chambers before they are tried, as a large part of the public cynically believes. But it does mean that intervention through politicians is repeatedly sought by the relatives and friends of criminal defendants, and that the judges are besieged from day to day by requests from politicians, big and little, for leniency and special consideration in cases that are coming up before them.

We also have evidence in our great cities that some of the judges of the "lower" courts have tolerated or participated in the organized exploitation of accused persons, as revealed in Judge Seabury's investigation; that some judges have belonged to political organizations that were closely tied up with gangsters and racketeering; and that others have paid political debts through the appointment of receivers and their attorneys.

The aspirant for judicial office must travel the same path as the aspirant for the job of prosecutor. Very often he has been a state's attorney or district attorney, and he retains the point of view in criminal trials that he acquired in that office. He may separate his political activities from his function as a judge, but the chances are that his adjustment to the expediencies of politics will continue to have some effect upon his conduct. This is demonstrated in the common judicial practice of approving deals made between the prosecutor and attorney for the defendant, the toleration of innumerable continuances which discourage the witnesses for the state, the perversion of the ancient remedy of habeas corpus, the approval of insufficient and badly secured bail bonds, laxity in granting probation, and the distortion of many legal processes which in themselves would be adequate if properly administered.

> *This is the boss*
> *Who names the judge . . .*

He runs the show and gets things done for the electorate in a way that no one else will or can. He never turns a voter down. He formerly dispensed food, coal, and clothing to the needy through his party organization, and during the last few years he has claimed credit for getting such things for his constituents from unemployment relief agencies, although they could very well have been obtained without him. Quite recently he has tried desperately to control the distribution of jobs by the CWA as a means of keeping voters in line.

According to William B. Munro, who has studied the boss in his natural habitat, he is a necessary and almost indispensable part of our political system, not only furnishing direct contact between the citizenry and public administrative agencies, but also acting as liaison officer between the executive and legislative, yes, and the judicial branches of our government.

In return for helping his constituents, he asks only for their support at the polls. But the upkeep of his organization requires a large and constant supply of money, which he secures by indirect levies upon the entire public. He may still gather some funds through the time-honored sale of police and court protection, but his greatest revenue comes by dealing in licenses, franchises, tax rebates, public contracts, and through campaign contributions from business men, utility magnates, and job holders.

Give the boss power, and the rest of the boys may have the glory. He seldom seeks office except perhaps to grace the latter days of his life, so that he may leave to his children the tradition that their father was held in high honor and esteem.

That the boss and his lieutenants name the judges is a commonplace.

Judicial office is a political job whether filled by election or by appointment. While there is evidence that somewhat better men are obtained through the appointive system because of the focusing of responsibility, it is still apparent that a seat on the bench is considered principally as a reward for political service.

Bar association officers and committees again and again have besought party bosses to select their nominees for judicial office from a list of lawyers of unquestioned ability and reputation, but such efforts are vain. The boss knows what he is about and will never alter his purely political attitude toward the bench unless forced by the overwhelming pressure of public opinion expressed in votes.

> *These are the people*
> *Who stand for the boss*
> *Who names the judge*
> *Who instructs the jury*
> *Who favor the lawyer*
> *Who fights the prosecutor*
> *Who flays the culprit*
> *Who is caught by the cop*
> *Who enforces the law the people built*

"We, the people of the United States, in order to . . . establish justice . . ."

So said our forebears, bitter from the memory of Old World tyrannies and the cruelties of king-made judges like Jeffreys and Stubbs. The founders of our democracy stripped their judges of wigs and robes, aggrandized the jury of their peers, and sought by every possible means to protect the citizen against judicial usurpation and oppression.

And as the people spread out across the mountains and the western plains, they carried with them a relentless contempt for the pomp and dignity associated with the woolsack and the mace. Their ideal was justice—plain, swift, and sure. The outlaw—killer or horse thief—was caught and hanged without ceremony by the posse comitatus, or shot on sight by an outraged citizen. Rifle, shotgun, and six-shooter became implements of daily life, like the axe, the plough, and the scythe.

The hordes that poured in on us from the ends of the earth, with customs and traditions conflicting and diverse, eagerly embraced the ideals of democracy, which seemed to them to include not only the aversion for superimposed authority, but the right of the citizen to bear arms and to appropriate whatever property or privileges he could be the first to lay hands on. It was in this spirit that the processes of government and law

enforcement were ultimately converted both by native-born and by naturalized citizens into an organized system of plunder and political spoils. It
is against this spirit that we now begin to see signs of revolt.

The President issued a clear call for a new deal for justice in speaking
before the Federal Council of Churches in December:

> A thinking America . . . seeks a government that will be sufficiently strong
> to protect the prisoner and at the same time to crystallize a public opinion so
> clear that government of all kinds will be compelled to practise a more certain
> justice. The judicial function of the government is the protection of the
> individual and of the community through quick and certain justice. That
> function in many places has fallen into a state of disrepair. It must be a
> part of our programme to reëstablish it.

And in his address at the opening of Congress he roundly denounced
public malefactors whether operating within or without the letter of the
law:

> These violations of ethics and these violations of law call on the strong
> arm of the government for their suppression; they call also on the country
> for an aroused public opinion.

The American Bar Association at its annual meeting last summer anticipated the President's call to action by formulating a National Bar Programme for the purpose of arousing lawyers throughout the nation to a
concerted effort to solve, among other things, the problem of criminal law
enforcement. Since then the president of the association has sent out a
questionnaire to 1450 local and state bar associations asking for specific
data on the reasons for the failure of the law and courts to control and
abate crime.

The will to reform is, of course, futile without concrete plans. We must
have a programme of constructive action with the objective of divorcing
every part of the machinery of justice from the control of party politics
and of inspiring the entire nation not merely with respect for the law but
with the zeal to enforce it. Such a programme might well include:

1. A nation-wide reform of criminal procedure through the adoption by
the states of the modern code devised by the American Law Institute and
recommended by the American Bar Association, which would speed up the
work of the courts and eliminate useless technicalities. Many of its provisions could be adopted by the courts on their own initiative without legislative sanction.

2. The revamping of our police systems with a view to removing them
from the control of local politics, adopting more scientific methods of train-

ing, increasing administrative efficiency, and using every modern facility for the identification and apprehension of criminals. Consideration should also be given to Attorney-General Cummings's suggestion for the development of state constabularies, independent of county lines, working in coordination with each other and the federal authorities.

3. Federal laws for the control of the manufacture and sale of firearms and explosives, stringently limiting the right to bear arms and requiring the keeping of records which would enable the police to trace the pedigree of every dangerous weapon. Other federal laws, where practical and constitutional, to cover interstate criminal activities, not at present subject to federal prosecution.

4. A new attitude toward the problem of youthful delinquency, which goes to the root of our troubles. This would require a thorough change in educational methods in directions indicated by progressive pedagogues, the increased development of constructive habit-forming activities, the teaching of social ethics rather than merely abstract virtues, the consistent and periodical medical and psychiatric examination of all children from an early age, together with the keeping of behavior records, and the adoption throughout the nation of modern methods in the treatment of juvenile offenders. And to carry out such plans we should institute a stern and implacable offensive against the false and shortsighted educational economies which have made such disastrous headway during the depression.

5. The office of public prosecutor must be removed from politics. We should try to inspire a more clinical attitude on the part of the agencies of the state in handling offenders. Every criminal court should have a public defender and an independent staff of doctors and psychiatrists, dominated neither by the prosecutor nor by the defense, with the duty of ascertaining and reporting scientific facts to the court. The recommendations of such a body should largely determine the treatment of law violators.

6. The bar must eliminate the lawyer criminal. It is already tackling the job. The standards of conduct of defense attorneys are also likely to improve with a more scientific attitude on the part of the state.

7. The jury system need not and probably ought not to be abolished. But its function should be limited to a determination of facts. It should have no power to pass upon the moral, emotional, or mental responsibility of a defendant or his treatment and punishment. The problem of obtaining a higher grade of jurors and combating jury tampering is squarely up to the lawyers.

8. We must demand and get better judges. The problem of judicial selection is dealt with in one of the planks of the American Bar Association

platform for 1934. Its solution rests upon establishing a technique which will restrict the choice of judges to a qualified list approved by the bar.

9. As to the boss, our only immediate hope is to restrict his influence as far as possible and to use him for more constructive ends.

We have no need of Jeremiahs. The nation is already aroused, but we must find ways of directing the very real and widespread indignation against our law-enforcing agencies into effective action; and above all we must inspire the oncoming generation with an ardent spirit for justice which will burn bright and transcendent in every heart.

No. 94

BARBED-WIRE ENTANGLEMENTS[1]

by John A. Warner

" JUMPING over lines to beat a rap for crimes" seems to be the modern version of the offender's game of "hide and seek" with the forces of law and order. The lines are the invisible dividers separating state from state. The players in the game are the law-breakers versus the police. The challenger seeks immunity in the neutral corner over the boundary, and the opposition players, by statutory rules, dare not remove him from that neutral corner without the consent of the extraditing governor who constitutes the official referee. These umpires are often responsible for decisions which are difficult to reconcile. Moreover, since the rule book is cumbersome, technical, abstruse—the work of many different authors— months of deliberation are often required before a final decision can be reached. Such delay more often favors the sought-after than the seeker. A study of crime prevention teaches that swift apprehension coupled with sure punishment deters crime in no small degree, but the problem of inter-state rendition very frequently makes it impossible to act upon this knowl-edge.

The problem becomes particularly acute when the offense is one classified as a misdemeanor. In such cases, there is little inclination to spend time or funds in securing the return of the offender, although his offense may equal a felony in gravity. It is sometimes stated that crimes of misdemeanor grade are less serious than felonies and that less attention should therefore be paid to punishing them, but efficient police will not agree with that theory. So closely allied are the two classes that one sometimes wonders

[1] John A. Warner, "Barbed-Wire Entanglements," *State Government* (January, 1935), Vol. 8, pp. 285-287. Reprinted by permission of the author and *State Government*.

why the arbitrary division was made. Is a man less criminal because he succeeded in stealing only one hundred dollars' worth of property than he would have been had he been able to steal material valued at one hundred and one dollars?

The formidable barrier of state lines is seriously interfering with efficient police practice and procedure. The laborious process of requisition and extradition plus a tendency of localities to consider that the flight of criminals is "good riddance to bad rubbish," result in a condition whereby offender after offender goes unpunished for his acts against society.

State rendition laws as well as local regulations on the subject differ widely, and until some simplified and unified system is adopted, the ends of justice will continue to be defeated—in felony as well as in misdemeanor cases. A few states have amended their statutes in order to simplify the process of rendition. New York, for instance, recently prescribed that a fugitive wanted by some other state might waive his right to rendition process before a magistrate of a court of record. Whereas, of course, this is highly desirable for other states which may take advantage of New York's concession, New York itself may be balked in similar circumstances by the failure of these other states to provide a waiver clause. Until there is uniformity within all states, no general benefit may be gained by the police and prosecuting officers of the nation at large.

Many technical volumes have been written about the fugitive problem, and many court decisions on this subject—including some by the United States Supreme Court—have been handed down. It is, therefore, perhaps presumptuous for the police forces of the country to offer suggestions for the solution of the problem. It must be admitted, however, that police agencies are very often criticized for their failure to apprehend criminals, and that one outstanding reason for such failure is the intricate machinery of interstate return of offenders. While such disparity and lack of co-operation exist among the state laws, most misdemeanants and a goodly percentage of felons will continue to enjoy "out-of-state" immunity.

Another factor involved is the expense of preparing papers and of traveling to the capital of the asylum state to present these papers before reaching the place of the offender's incarceration. At times this may constitute a severe financial burden on the county, city, village, or town.

Since many so-called minor offenders committing crimes near the border lines of states seem aware of the protection offered after migration, there is a general trend toward that sort of immunity. The popularity of this form of escape has become increasingly apparent with the development of the modern system of police communication. The system exists between approximately seven hundred police departments in the states of Massachusetts, Connecticut, Rhode Island, New York, New Jersey, Pennsylvania, Delaware, and Ohio. This vast network of police teletypewriters distributes the alarms and messages from each of the states mentioned to all of the others. Supplementing this teletypewriter system, of course, are the police radio messages—many thousands of which are daily traveling the ether waves.

A study of message traffic via the teletypewriter—involving the transmission of about two hundred and fifty thousand police messages each year—indicates that the majority of the crimes are in the misdemeanor class. It also indicates that, because of the technical difficulties involved in the arrest of misdemeanants outside of the state where the crime was committed, the offender is seldom apprehended after his flight across the state lines.

When, however, with the aid of modern rapid means of communication, an asylum state does arrest a fugitive, the demanding state often fails to exercise the same vigor in securing his return as it manifested in seeking his arrest.

Both the interstate compact clause of the constitution and the so-called "Interstate Compact Act" of the 73rd Congress authorize the states to enter into agreements which would simplify interstate rendition and materially aid in the prompt return of fugitives. A study of the possibilities of such interstate compacts in the field of criminal justice might well be undertaken in the various states by legislators, crime commissions, and others interested in the subject. Undoubtedly such compacts could be broad enough to include interstate rendition on the basis of certification by the demanding state, and they might even recognize the authority of out-of-state police officials in the execution of process and apprehensions of offenders.

Another act of the 73rd Congress has made it a federal crime for felons or witnesses in criminal proceedings to flee from one state to another, but the assistance of federal authorities is necessary for the return of fugitives under this act. Strictly speaking, a criminal so apprehended is under the custody and control of the federal authority, and is subject to prosecution for the federal crime of flight. There is no definite provision for his being delivered to state authorities for prosecution under their statutes. Undoubtedly this act will be invoked in order to secure the return of criminals to a jurisdiction in which they can be tried for their original crime, but apparently the federal prosecution will always have priority.

Until the states realize the deficiencies of present rendition laws, interstate crime control will remain in an elementary stage. Simplification and uniformity of these laws are necessary if the police forces of the country are to do the work expected of them by press and public in the apprehension of law violators. At some future time uniform state legislation may be

passed which will follow the lines of federal deportation proceedings, applicable in the case of alien offenders. In other words, states should be able
to return to each other undesirable persons who have crossed state boundaries in order to escape trial and punishment for an offense committed
elsewhere.

No. 95

PUBLIC DEFENDERS IN CRIMINAL CASES [1]

by Mayer C. Goldman

IT must be generally recognized that in the administration of justice an
impartial search for the truth should be the paramount consideration.
Although many persons believe that under our present system those accused
of crime are already too carefully protected by various legal presumptions
and technicalities, the prevailing sentiment undoubtedly is that the administration of our criminal law is, in many respects, unsatisfactory and inadequate.

Mr. Chief Justice Hughes said some years ago, "The administration of
the criminal law is a disgrace to civilization." President Roosevelt stated:
"There are two kinds of justice in this country: one for the rich and one
for the poor."

There is sound basis for such criticism. A modern criminal trial is not
so much an inquiry to ascertain the truth as it is a battle of wits between
opposing forces, to obtain partisan advantage. Justice in this country is
constantly denied. The poor too frequently are the victims of their poverty.
The gangster and criminal rich too often escape merited punishment. When
two such distinguished authorities as President Roosevelt and Chief Justice
Hughes agree about our inadequate and unfair legal system, who can blame
the man in the street for saying "There ain't no justice"?

About thirty-one years ago, Harry K. Thaw, a young millionaire, went
to the roof of Madison Square Garden, approached the table where Stanford
White was sitting, and shot him dead. The case was starkly simple. Yet
to-day Harry Thaw walks the streets a free man. That same day, John Doe,
a hard-working newsboy and sole support of an ailing mother, was haled
into court on a presumably trumped-up charge. He did not have the money
to hire one of the many expensive lawyers enrolled under the Thaw banner,
or to hire any lawyer at all. His case was starkly simple, too. He went
to jail.

[1] Mayer C. Goldman, "Public Defenders in Criminal Cases," *The Annals* of the American Academy of Political and Social Science (September, 1939), Vol. 205, pp. 16-23. Reprinted by permission of *The Annals* of the American Academy of Political and Social Science.
Footnotes in the original article are omitted here.

The fundamentals of this situation have not changed. It is easier for a camel to go through the eye of a needle than it is to make a rich criminal go to prison. On the other hand, a poor man, whether he be innocent or guilty, once arrested, is already on his way to a prison cell. If he cannot afford a lawyer to defend him, he must seek charity from a legal aid society or throw himself on the mercy of the court.

The present "assigned counsel" system is farcical in its operation and tragic in its consequences. It is a mere gesture to justice. It provides no compensation whatever (in many states) to lawyers appointed by the court to defend poor persons (except in capital cases). It neither protects the accused nor satisfies the community. It is as unfair to the lawyer as it is to the accused. Even if competent and conscientious lawyers were assigned, they lack the necessary moneys to make a merited defense. Frequently they wholly fail to measure up to their job—through lack of character or ability or experience. Generally, the accused does not even know the lawyer assigned to him, does not trust him and does not want him. That is the price he pays for a defense—not because he is guilty, but because he is poor. What a travesty on justice!

Although the court has inherent power to assign the best type of lawyer, the accused often gets the worst type. The existing system is a public scandal, which has been frequently criticized by judges, sociologists, and others. It would be a simple matter, if space permitted, to point out the many striking miscarriages of criminal justice, unfair trials, wrongful convictions, excessive punishments—all due to the state's failure adequately to protect accused poor persons. The law reports and many textbooks tell the sad story only too well.

Society owes a duty to all persons, regardless of race, creed, or purse, to protect their fundamental right to a fair trial, through competent counsel. It likewise must protect itself against organized crime and desperate criminals, now entirely too well defended by disreputable lawyers, who often share the proceeds of crime. Although the duty of society is to shield the innocent and punish the guilty, it has signally failed to do either. A drastic change in criminal law is urgent. The state legislatures have been either unwilling or asleep. Neither they nor the bar associations have thus far assumed the necessary leadership in dealing with this vital social problem. An awakening of the public conscience is necessary to effect that "equality of justice" which theoretically is proclaimed under our present legal procedure.

It is as much the function of the state to shield the innocent as to convict the guilty, and the "presumption of innocence" is worthless unless it carries with it the right to the accused person to be defended by competent counsel and to have the benefit of a fair trial. If it is the function of the public to pay for the defense of indigent persons charged with capital crimes, it should be equally the function of the public to pay for the defense of such persons charged with lesser crimes.

The true solution of the poor man's problem in the criminal courts is the establishment of official public defenders, or state defense counsel, as a necessary part of the administration of criminal justice. The plan is sanctioned by historical precedent in other countries and by experience in this country.

A brief outline as to the defense of accused poor persons in foreign jurisdictions is interesting.

An official called "Pauperus Procurator" appears to have existed under the Roman Papal Government. There was such an official in Spain in the fifteenth century. In the Cortes of Madrigal (1496) and in the one of Toledo (1480),

> The judges were to ascertain every week, either by personal inspection or report, the condition of the prisons, the number of the prisoners and the nature of the offenses for which they were confined. They were required to bring them to a speedy trial and afford every facility for their defense. An attorney was provided *at public expense,* under the title of *advocate for the poor,* whose duty it was to defend the suits of such as are unable to maintain them at their own costs.

The Spanish law provides for the employment of counsel to represent indigents in both civil and criminal cases.

The criminal code of Hungary provides specifically for a public defender in certain cases.

In the Argentine Republic the defense of accused persons unable to employ counsel is intrusted to the defenders of poor and absents.

In France there exists an organization called *L'Assistance Judiciare,* through which persons without sufficient means are entitled to avail themselves of the protection of the courts. The bar in that country is unified into an order; assignments to the defense of indigent prisoners are made by the executive head of the order, from the bar in general, and accepted as obligatory.

In Belgium an indigent person has the right to choose a lawyer who gives his services gratuitously. He is called a "Pro Deo" lawyer.

The Constitution of Mexico provides for the free public defense of its citizens.

The Norwegian Act of May 22, 1902, prescribes that a lawyer must be assigned by the court for the defense of any person who is being tried for crime, the expense thereof to be borne by the state.

In England, counsel assigned to the defense of an accused person is paid by the government.

Under the Danish criminal system the court appoints in each case a prosecutor and a defender for the accused person, both of whom are selected from a competent staff.

The public defender system has worked efficiently and economically in Los Angeles, San Francisco, Oakland, Chicago, Bridgeport, New Haven, Hartford, Canal Zone, Columbus (Ohio), St. Louis, Tulsa, and other communities. Its logic and fundamental justice are no longer debatable.

All the principal theoretical objections which were at first urged against this system by lawyers and bar associations—viz.: increased expense, political control, the inability of the state to prosecute and defend at the same time, that innocent persons are rarely, if ever, convicted, and others—have been wholly discredited. Wherever this plan has been amply tested by experience, notably in Los Angeles, San Francisco, St. Louis, Oakland, and Chicago, the fact is that not only have public defenders not increased the expense to those communities, but they have materially reduced it. One notable instance will serve to illustrate the economy resulting from this office. In Chicago, very substantial savings to the tax-payers have been effected, generally speaking, as stated by Public Defender Benjamin C. Bachrach in September, 1938, as follows:

1. By holding down the number of jury trials.
2. By always being prepared and ready to proceed with trials, thereby avoiding numerous continuances.
3. By shortening trials (a) by speedily selecting juries; (b) by stipulating necessary facts to avoid continuances.
4. By advising defendants when the case is hopelessly against them to plead guilty and thereby save the time of the court.
5. By eliminating in capital cases fees provided by law for each indigent defendant.

As to the frequent objection that public defenders are subject to political influence and control, they are no more or no less politically influenced or controlled than any other public officials. It is, of course, important that they, like all other public officials, should be free from such domination—if that be possible. If our system of selecting officials is wrong, the system should be changed; but to urge that public defenders may be corrupt begs the question, since judges, prosecutors, jurors, and others may also be corrupt. They should be appointed by an appellate court to minimize political influence.

As to the so-called incongruity for the state to prosecute and defend at the same time, the comment thereon by former Attorney-General Cummings, in his 1938 annual report, is interesting. He said:

> This is a superficial point of view, for it overlooks the principle that the Government should be as anxious to shield the innocent as it is to punish the guilty. Moreover, many of those who in one breath oppose the creation of the office of public defender, in the next breath approve the system under which lawyers are in fact assigned to defend indigent prisoners. . . .

The benefits which would flow from a general adoption of the system of public defenders are both vital and numerous, viz.: (1) the rights of accused poor persons would be better protected; (2) there would be fewer unscrupulous and perjured defenses; (3) prisoners, rich or poor, would be equal before the law; (4) the truth would be more available; (5) there would be fewer pleas of guilty at the instance of indifferent and uncompensated lawyers; (6) trials would be expedited; (7) the administration of justice would be raised to a higher plane; (8) over-punishment would be prevented; (9) expense would be decreased.

It would be simple to amplify these benefits by sound argument if their logic is challenged.

The chief opposition to the public defender plan, for which the writer has fought for a quarter of a century, has come from within the legal profession. Officials of the old-line lawyers' associations have opposed the plan on the ground that its successful operation on a national scale might encourage other governmental "encroachments" on private practice. "Some among us," former President Stinchfield of the American Bar Association is quoted as saying, "say it is a step toward the socialization of the profession."

Against this timid and obviously self-centered and extremely selfish attitude of the orthodox bar groups, the newly organized National Lawyers Guild, at its first national convention in Washington, D. C., unanimously adopted the writer's resolution for the extension of the official public defender system. If the public defender plan is "socialized justice," by all means let us have more of it.

Many communities, notably Boston, Philadelphia, Pittsburgh, Houston, and Washington, are now experimenting with or considering the public defender plan in one form or another. The organized bar is finally waking up to the fact that it is its job, to a very large extent, to arouse the public to the need for more effective legal aid for the poor, in both criminal and civil cases. The trend in that direction is amply indicated by recent reports made by appropriate committees of the American Bar Association. It is interesting to note that its Standing Committee on Jurisprudence and Law Reform, in its 1939 report to the Association, recommended the adoption of the following resolution: "Resolved, that the Association approves in principle the establishment of a system of public defenders in the Federal Courts."

This resolution was adopted by the House of Delegates of the American Bar Association at its annual meeting, July 13, 1939. A similar resolution was likewise adopted by the Junior Bar Conference of the Association at the same annual meeting.

This is the first time that the subject of public defenders has been given any really favorable attention by any committee or group of the American Bar Association.

Perhaps the most significant step forward thus far taken in support of the public defender plan—with the possible exception of the actual creation of the office in various American communities—is the fact that the former Attorney-General of the United States submitted to the Judicial Conference between the Chief Justice of the United States and the nine senior United States Circuit Judges, at its 1937 and 1938 meeting, the subject of proper representation for indigent defendants in criminal cases, and that the Conference adopted a resolution in part as follows: "We approve in principle the appointment of a Public Defender where the amount of criminal business of a district court justifies the appointment. . . ."

It should also be noted that the Standing Committee on Legal Aid Work of the American Bar Association, in its 1937 annual report, gave much consideration to the public defender plan and stated therein: "We believe that every man accused of serious crime is absolutely entitled to counsel and that, if he is too poor to employ one, *society* must furnish him one." (Italics mine.)

Through the public defender plan the innocent are amply protected, while the vicious and dangerous criminals are not over-defended. In fact, the professional crook or gangster prefers private counsel, for obvious reasons. The one thing which such a criminal does *not* want is justice. Under the public defender plan the guilty get only what they are entitled to—a fair trial—and no more. Justice is the ultimate goal. All the technicalities, strategems, delays, framed defenses, and crooked alibis of the average criminal trial are eliminated through counsel having no axe to grind, but only the desire to see that justice is done.

Why should a rich or powerful defendant, or a gangster with a record—probably guilty—enjoy an advantage through the law over a poor defendant, perhaps innocent, merely because he can hire counsel of his choice and checkmate justice at every turn?

There is sound reason to urge compulsory state defense for *all* accused persons, but that is another problem. Why should one accused person be permitted to choose his lawyer while another takes the uncompensated and usually indifferent lawyer who is thrust upon him by the court? There is no constitutional right to anyone to choose his own lawyer, despite the general impression of the bar and the public to the contrary. All that the United States Constitution guarantees to *any* accused person is the right to the "assistance of counsel." That right is vindicated when the court assigns counsel to the defendant.

However, the *primary* need is for public defense for accused *poor* persons, although it is equally important that the menace of the rich or vicious criminal aided by crooked lawyers or "lawyer-criminals" should be wiped out. Eliminate the lawyer who advises the racketeer how and when to break the law, and *organized* crime will quickly disappear. We can no longer tolerate the unethical criminal lawyer, who is willing and anxious to pervert justice. Nowhere in the civilized world is crime so rampant as in this country. Nowhere are lawyers so poorly regarded by the public. English barristers are upstanding and respected by the community. Their actions are guided by a desire to do justice—not to pervert it. Lawyers must be Ministers of Justice—as they are intended to be.

For many years, legal aid societies and voluntary defender committees have been functioning throughout this country, supported by philanthropic persons and groups who are motivated by a real desire to protect the poor in our courts. Although the writer is sympathetic to the motives and aspirations of all voluntary groups and has a keen appreciation of the splendid work which they have done, he maintains that it is the duty of the *state*, rather than of private agencies, to safeguard the legal rights of accused poor persons. Justice is the concern of *all* the public.

The fine work of the private agencies will inevitably show the need for public defense and thereby overcome the handicaps of the present system. No voluntary group has the necessary money, prestige, or power to do the job efficiently. All of them have wholly failed thus far really to solve the problem. Their existence, however, proves conclusively the need for a drastic change in better protecting the indigent.

Adequate legal defense is vital to the life and liberty of the accused. It affects not only the accused and his "assigned" lawyer, but society as a whole—and the government itself. The adequate protection *by law* of the lives and liberties of accused persons is as much a logical and proper function of government as safeguarding the health or regulating the hours and conditions of labor or controlling the education of its citizens. Insuring to *all* of the people a *real* "equality before the law," through competent counsel having the financial ability and prestige to protect innocence, is of vital interest to the state and necessary to elemental justice.

1. At the 1937 session of Congress, Senator Arthur Capper of Kansas and Congressman Byron N. Scott of California introduced bills providing for the establishment of official public defenders in every Federal District Court. At the present session Senator Capper's bill was reintroduced, and Senator Henry F. Ashurst, chairman of the Senate Judiciary Committee, introduced a similar bill at the request of the Federal Department of Justice.

2. In the 1937 annual report of the Standing Committee on Legal Aid Work of the American Bar Association, there is a comprehensive discussion of "Legal Aid in Criminal Cases," with particular reference to public defenders.

3. The Committee on Public Defenders of the New York State Bar Association, of which the writer has had the honor to be Chairman for many years, succeeded several years ago in getting a resolution adopted, reciting, among other things, "That this Association approve the principle of Public Defenders"; and the Committee has for many years submitted comprehensive reports to the Association as to the progress of the public defender movement throughout the nation.

4. The National Lawyers Guild, at its organization meeting in 1937, unanimously adopted a resolution favoring the extension of official public defenders to represent indigents.

5. Former Attorney-General Cummings, in his 1938 annual report, said, among other things:

In recent years in a number of large counties and cities of the country, permanent officials have been provided to act as public defenders. In at least one commonwealth (Connecticut) this system has been adopted on a state-wide basis. Wherever it has been in operation it has proved successful both in preventing possible miscarriages of justice and in eliminating dilatory tactics and technical obstructions on the part of defense attorneys. . . . It is my opinion that the inauguration of a system of public defenders along the lines here suggested would be a distinct step toward the further improvement of the administration of justice.

6. Former Dean Charles E. Clark of Yale University Law School (recently appointed Judge of the United States Circuit Court of Appeals for the Second Circuit) recently stated: "It always amazes us in Connecticut to see the fears and worries of many of the profession about this most desirable reform which works so well in this state."

With such eloquent testimony from former Attorney-General Cummings and Judge Clark, who live in a public defender state (Connecticut), and in view of the constantly growing national interest in justice to the poor, the public defender plan must be regarded seriously.

This plan has probably made more progress throughout the country in the past twenty-five years than perhaps all the other proposed legal reforms put together, and this in spite of the opposition of the bar. Its progress is due mainly to the awakening of the public. With the coming of trial by newspaper, by radio, by newsreel, the average citizen is beginning to realize that if his rights are to be protected against a new greed for convictions there must be public defenders as well as public prosecutors. In view of these changing attitudes it seems probable that the day of the poor man's public defender in *every* criminal court is at hand.

It is no wonder that criminal lawyers are in such general public disrepute, or that there is a constantly growing popular contempt for *all* law and *all* lawyers. If unscrupulous lawyers were banished, it would be a "consummation devoutly to be wished" from the viewpoint of the public. The great body of American lawyers are thoroughly honorable and trustworthy. Unfortunately, however, on stage and screen, in newspaper and editorial comments, on byways and highways, lawyers in general are the objects of public scorn and distrust.

The leadership of the bar in matters concerning social justice has been constantly challenged. Lawyers have sat idly by while lay groups have initiated and fought for vital reforms. The legal profession must vigorously assert the power and the responsibility of intelligent leadership and direction which rightfully belongs to it. The time is ripe to throw off the shackles of an outworn legal system. It must be replaced with one adapted to present-day needs. The organized bar must meet the challenge to its leadership by championing true reforms in the law—and it seems to be finally waking up to its duty. There must be a scientific readjustment of the new sphere of social progress. Public defense is as logical as public prosecution. The assumption that the people must prosecute but may not defend is not warranted either by history or by logic, by justice or by expediency.

The public defender plan is a progressive, logical adjunct to modernized criminal law administration. Emphasis thrown on prosecution should not be to the prejudice of the defendant without money. Through public defenders, many of the scandals of private defense will be abolished. Equal justice must come *by law*—not by favor or charity or by volunteer unpaid counsel, having no definite duty or responsibility to defend. The inscription on the front portals of the new United States Supreme Court building— "Equal Justice Under Law"—is highly significant of that principle.

The medical profession is now fighting for state medical aid, treatment, and hospitalization for the poor as a necessary function of society to safeguard the health of the community. The legal profession must inevitably lead the way for true reform in the administration of justice if it hopes to survive the present antagonistic attitude of the general public.

As between the past aimless drifting and the "do-nothing" policy of the organized bar on this vital and humane legal and social problem, and the concrete and logical solution thereof through the public defender plan to insure a real Democracy of Justice, the path is clear.

No. 96

TWELVE GOOD MEN—AND "UNTRUE!"[1]

by Upton Close

FOR the first time we have an official "low-down" on the American jury. The Ruth Commission of Pennsylvania, armed by the Legislature with authority to subpoena, has put scores of ex-jurors on the stand and made them tell what really happens behind locked jury-room doors.

One result of the Commission's first year of work is that 117 individuals in Pennsylvania, ranging from professional criminals to court employees, lawyers and politicians, are under indictment by Judge Curtis Bok's special "blue ribbon" grand jury. But punishment of offenders turned up is incidental. Of first importance to everyone who must some day resort to the law, and to every American who wants justice, are the Commission's factual survey of shocking practices existing all over the United States, and its careful, common-sense recommendation of reform.

The Commission's report, going to press as this is written, and previewed only by this writer, was very nearly smothered by the bosses in Pennsylvania, who cut off funds with the hope that the findings could not be published. We shall have the report only because the fearless young director of the Commission, Chet Keyes, anticipating this strategy, wisely contracted for the printing even before the report was compiled, and put aside each month a sum now sufficient to publish the book.

It all began with a series of newspaper articles by Dave Wittals in the *Philadelphia Record,* exposing the probation racket in that city. The Legislature took notice, and Governor Earle appointed State Senator Rev. Frank W. Ruth to be chairman of a commission to investigate. That was a lucky choice. The good name of Ruth, pastor of a small-town Dutch Reformed Church, a man above reproach and beyond approach, saved the Commission from scorching when politicians turned on the heat.

[1] Upton Close, "Twelve Good Men—and 'Untrue!'" *The Christian Science Monitor* (July 20, 1938), pp. 1-2, 13. Reprinted by permission of *The Christian Science Monitor.*

The Ruth report covers a great deal of legal ground, but perhaps its most significant feature is the exposure of jury conduct. Most common of the sins of juries, says the report, is the tendency to regard lightly misconduct in office. A mayor sharing the proceeds of prostitution, a police chief collecting from illicit liquor dealers, political bosses conspiring to deprive the American citizen of his right to vote freely, seem to arouse the sporting instincts of jurors willing to have the verdict determined by the flip of a coin or pulling straws.

The Commission's post-mortems on amazing verdicts brought out the case —only slightly more ludicrous and outrageous than others—of the coin-flipping foreman at Easton.

"Let's get this over with!" he urged his fellow members as soon as the bailiff had locked them in. "It's all very confusing—none of us really knows whether to acquit or convict. Why not leave it to Lady Luck? She's always fair! I'll toss for each of you. If it's heads you're for acquittal; tails you're for conviction—O.K.?" It being a sporting proposition, all eleven agreed. The foreman outdid himself. He tossed for each of his fellow jurors, one at a time. All eleven came up heads. That decided the verdict and the jury filed into court with it. Some of the jurors had misgivings but didn't like to accuse the foreman of cheating. They didn't know then that he was a political henchman of the accused!

Jurors in one instance confessed to agreement in order to get to a lodge dance on time, in another instance to see a ball game. The ease with which one or two determined jurors can swing the remainder was evidenced by testimony after testimony. The ordinary, easily influenced juror seems to assume that his fellows who take definite stands right off know more about the case than himself.

The reasoning of the great American juror would baffle an ancient Greek Sophist or medieval logician. Certainly it did baffle several Philadelphia lawyers connected with the investigation. In one prominent case, a jury of conservative citizens received evidence, including a confession, of a fatal assault, committed by a young lady defendant. But the extraneous introduction of testimony which, in the minds of the jurors, offended the religious faith in which the defendant was reared made them decide to overlook the killing, although forgiveness was no part of their prerogative. Later, when the Commission subpoenaed the jurors in this case to find out why they had disregarded legal fact, it got such explanations as these: "There was a lot of argument—I did not know what it was all about." "I not understand English." "How do I know what happened, I wasn't there—see?" "The foreman was very stubborn."

And here is the foreman's logic: "We are not going to convict of murder!

. . . If we let her go free she will worry more about her wicked act and really suffer more than if she served a few years' imprisonment."

Is this typical of what goes on in a murder trial jury? The Commission's work shows that such warping of logic and placing of prejudice above duty are common.

Jury justice suffers, too, because courts forget the surprising ignorance of many jurors in such fundamental matters as court language and procedure. Ex-jurors in whose hands had lain the disposition of men's liberty and property admitted under oath to the Ruth Commission that they had reached verdicts without knowing who was the plaintiff and who the defendant, never having absorbed the meaning of the words from clerks, court, or lawyers.

Often, too, the juror is asked to perform unreasonable feats of memory. In one Pennsylvania case, a jury was asked to bring back verdicts against 53 defendants of varying degrees of guilt, being tried together, without so much as a written note on the evidence produced or the impressions made by the defendants at the trial. The baffled jurors couldn't remember them apart! Who could?

In states such as Kansas, jurors are provided, when they go into closet, with all trial exhibits and clerk's transcript of the testimony—material technical, rambling, contradictory and complicated, but, at least, something to refer to. In many states, however, the juror's only whack at trial exhibits is when they are waved under his confused remembrance of what witnesses, lawyers, and court said throughout the trial, which may have lasted many days.

In one case, jurors got to arguing over the phrase "undue influence," used by the judge, and found that none of them knew what it meant! Of course, they were forbidden a dictionary—all reference books are forbidden. They had not been told that they might go back and ask the judge, and, even had they known, that would have required a court session and formal re-entry and re-exit from the courtroom. A jury wants to get the thing over. And, after all, even jurors have their pride!

How much justification exists for the tradition (rather than law) that jurors may not take notes or carry memoranda into the jury room is uncertain. There is, of course, the danger that memoranda may be partial, or "loaded" from the outside. Yet a judge, or panel of judges, when serving in the function of the jury, works from copious notes. The unfortunate juror, however, is required to recall from memory the gist of 50 contradictory statements! And though he may not have notes, he may have seen newspapers, screaming sensational guesses.

The commission found that the barest start has been made in rendering simple, fundamental instruction to jurors. The judges of Northampton County, Pennsylvania, have prepared vest-pocket printed booklets for jurors. Words in common legal use have been avoided until after their meaning and effect have been stated. In some western states mimeographed instructions are provided. The Commission urges the improvement and standardization of such instructions.

Damaging to justice as ignorance may be, actual corruption is less forgivable. The Commission found it to be a custom in some counties for a defendant to look up prospective jurors directly or otherwise. Amazing industry was shown by one embezzler suspect. His first trial brought conviction, but he won retrial on a technicality. By direct visit or through intermediaries he got pretty well around to the members of two complete panels of 90 each, with disastrous expense to the State. Trial two resulted in a hung jury, trial three in acquittal—his assiduity brought results!

The Commission found the most startling and widespread jury malpractice to be service under false name. This is prevalent in large cities, and our "best citizens" are collaborators in it. A busy man or woman receives a summons to jury duty and goes to a "friend with influence" to get him out of it. The friend says: "Sure, forget it—just leave it to me!" What happens is that a henchman or favorite of the local boss turns up for jury duty, answers to the name of the impaneled citizen, and serves throughout the life of the panel for his $3 to $5 a day—meanwhile being in a perfect position to "throw" cases damaging to his political machine.

In Philadelphia and several lesser Pennsylvania cities, juror substitution has become so common as to be almost accepted practice by court officials. It has a charity angle! A Ward boss tries to have on hand a few "jury tours" for faithful unemployed voters who need to add to their relief dole.

In a sardonic case reported from Oregon the defendant's wife was on the jury—unknown to all save the defendant and his unscrupulous attorney. But when certain secrets the defendant had hidden from his spouse came out in court, the poor fellow rushed to his lawyer with the demand that he "get that woman off the jury at once!" She was in a fine position to revenge a wife's wounded pride.

The Commission received another shock when it subpoenaed jurors who had brought in a verdict of acquittal in a flagrant larceny case. Jurors testified that they followed the foreman, who blithely admitted that he had once done four years for larceny and shied away from causing such distress to a fellow being.

This case pointed up an evil existing in many states: The foreman is chosen or designated at the beginning of the trial, making him a marked man to those seeking to influence the verdict. In Kansas, for opposite instance, the jury chooses its foreman after it receives commitment of the case.

Legal qualification requirements for juries, varying in the 48 states, add up to a huge joke at the expense of society. Twenty-four states require the juror to possess "good moral character" or "one or more of the qualities of good moral character"! Thirty states, that the juror be "generally reputed to be intelligent." Eighteen states ask no positive qualities at all, but specify, more or less, against a person with a criminal record. Some say that he must be "not an idiot." Some states exempt World War veterans if honorably discharged after nine months' service. If dishonorably discharged, they can become jurors!

Men of learned professions—doctors, lawyers, and teachers—are usually exempt by statute or get off by custom. No wonder the report says: "By the time the higher type get excused, one out of three or four capable jurors remain. Our methods of selection blow away the wheat and save the chaff."

The panels from which juries are chosen are commonly made up of names drawn by lot from voters' registration lists, tax books, or even telephone directories. This proceeding is designed to insure impartiality of choice, but it offers no guarantee of the fitness to serve of any juror so drawn. In some instances politics enters into the selections, as in Berks County, Pennsylvania, where the panel is "nominated" by the big party bosses: one Republican, one Democrat. The Commission believes that a fundamental reform—procuring of good jury timber—can be brought about by pre-examination of names for fitness by a semi-judicial, semi-citizens' board. In Los Angeles, such a board has been established.

After that comes the reform of the business of challenging prospective jurors. Attorneys have a certain number of peremptory challenges—varying in the various states—whereby they can dismiss jurors without revealing any reason. Aside from this, they can ask the judge to dismiss any prospective juror whom they can cajole or bluff into admitting that he has set ideas about the case in hand. Naturally, the common result is a battle between contending attorneys, each trying to seat jurors sympathetic to his own argument. Actual fitness to serve becomes a secondary consideration.

Instead of this scandalous lawyers' game, the Commission would have the judge provided with a brief on each summoned citizen, procured by investigators who cannot know on what case he will serve. Secondly, it would have the reasonableness of all challenges ruled on by the judge. The right of peremptory challenge would be eliminated.

After an improved method of selecting juries, two final reforms are recommended. Bewildered by the inconsistency and even brutality of the law in fixing punishments, jurors frequently return arbitrary verdicts of not guilty or guilty in lesser degree than proved. If all states had the indeterminate sentence law now being tried by California, without minimum and maximum, leaving length of punishment to decision of an expert penal board according to merit, juries would bring in more honest convictions.

The last reform—which alone had wide discussion prior to the Ruth Commission's work—would authorize a "majority verdict" of ten or nine jurors. This is being tried now in a few places in civil cases. It saves many hung juries and consequent retrial costs and time. It enables the jury to get past one or two stubborn members, and makes "fixing" harder, since at least three jurors instead of one must be reached.

Americans are not purposely careless about a matter which touches us so closely as the administration of justice. But they have been at a loss to know how reforms can be made. The Ruth Commission's report gives a layman's-language picture of the abuses that exist, and the common-sense ways to correct them.

Mr. Chet Keyes and his co-workers have laid the problem out so that you in your county and state and I in mine and every voter in his can take hold of it. American justice will be just what the American public demands—and deserves.

Chapter XXVII

MONEY AND CREDIT, BANKING, AND SECURITIES

[MODERN economy is a money economy. The exchange of commodities is based upon money and credit, not barter, and power over money and credit gives a considerable amount of control over the stability of commerce and the distribution of wealth. As a result the currency question is drawn into the conflict of interests that furnishes the substance of politics. There is no way to take the question of money and credit out of the public forum and into the laboratory. Nor is this any less true of the control over banks, whether of the savings, commercial, or investment type. Whether or not they have power to issue notes or affect credit, the public will never permit them to be removed from at least a certain amount of control designed to protect the people against fraud. The question as to what kind of banking system we shall have—how much public supervision, control or ownership there shall be—can no more be removed from the public forum than can the question as to what kind of a system of money and credit we shall have.

In addition, in recent years, another question of a similar character has assumed considerable importance, namely, the amount of control government should exercise over the sale of private securities. Since 1911, and especially since 1920, this matter has been one which the people have been unwilling to leave completely in private hands and to-day the government—national and state—exercises considerable control in this field.

There are, of course, no pat answers to the questions that one can raise relative to public control of money and credit, banking, and the securities market. This chapter is designed to indicate to some extent what the problems are, what government has been doing, and what it might do.]

737

No. 97

GOVERNMENT MANAGEMENT OF CURRENCY AND CREDIT [1]

by John Parke Young

THE tendency for governments to regulate increasingly economic life has nowhere been more marked than in the field of currency and credit. Whether the phrase "managed currency" be used or not, currencies all over the world have been subjected to more and more control and management. As in other fields, controversy has waged over how far regulation should go, what can be accomplished by it, and the devices to be employed.

The earliest types of currency regulation had to do merely with physical characteristics of coins and protection against counterfeiting. When paper money was issued, if the government established rules they were intended primarily to assure redemption in specie, which was considered the end of governmental responsibility. Regulation was later extended to include bank deposits, but the duty of government as to the safety of deposits was accepted less explicitly—partly because the problem was not easy. Banks were sometimes required to keep certain cash reserves—a fraction of the money they were supposed to have on deposit. Only since the World War, in most cases only during the last decade, have governments made serious efforts to control the value and functioning of money, apart from the devices mentioned above aimed at setting rough limits to depreciation.

When we pass from an endeavor on the part of government simply to assure the general safety or validity of money, to efforts to regulate its value and to guide its functioning in our economic system, we arrive at one of the most important and most difficult of economic problems. The major role money plays in modern highly specialized society, the profound effects of price level fluctuations, and particularly the intimate relation of monetary matters to interest rates and the business cycle, make the question of special consequence. The broader aspects of the monetary problem have come to be recognized in governmental circles principally as a result of the Great Depression. Many governments are to-day endeavoring to deal with it from the standpoint of its broader implications.

Society has traveled a long distance from the simple state wherein the

---

[1] John Parke Young, "Government Management of Currency and Credit," *The Annals* of the American Academy of Political and Social Science (November, 1939), Vol. 206, pp. 100-108. Reprinted by permission of *The Annals* of the American Academy of Political and Social Science. Footnotes in the original article are omitted here.

individual was fairly self-sufficient, and has become extremely dependent upon trade—buying and selling. It has developed a complicated existence in which monetary values and price movements occupy a pre-eminent position. Wages, incomes, and values of nearly all kinds are expressed in terms of money. The vast industrial machine in which goods are produced in huge quantities by specialized processes and distributed to the four corners of the world is utterly dependent upon money, functioning according to monetary costs and prices. Our society is organized down to the smallest detail, upon a financial or monetary basis. The proper functioning of the monetary mechanism is thus a matter of no small consequence.

What is "proper functioning," and just what do we expect of the monetary system? In other words, what is the goal or objective of monetary regulation?

Here we are confronted with the facts that the problem of money and prices has theoretical aspects that tax even the best economists, and that there is a wide range of opinion on actions to be taken. It formerly was thought that the well-known quantity theory of money was a fairly simple proposition and a rather complete explanation of prices. If we expanded the volume of money, other things being equal, prices would tend to rise. What could be more obvious. "Other things being equal," however, was a catchall phrase often used to obviate further analysis.

This is not the place for a labored discussion of the theory of money, but as Keynes and others have pointed out, the problem of money involves the whole gamut of economic theory. An expansion of money tends not only to raise prices but also to lower the rate of interest, increase production, and put men to work. Short of full employment and full production, however, it may have little effect upon prices. Furthermore, whether the individual decides to spend his money or save it, to hold his assets in the form of money or in the form of real wealth, affects the whole stream of economic activity. Depending upon whether confidence is high or low, monetary expansion may or may not mean economic expansion or a rise of prices.

Thus the story goes and the debate begins. Does monetary expansion lead to maladjustments and an unstable condition? Does it upset the balance or relationship between savings and expenditures which absorb savings, such as those for plant and equipment? Does it excessively stimulate the capital goods industries, and again at times fail entirely to stimulate these industries? Do we really want a stable price level? One thing is agreed—the consequences that flow from an expansion or contraction of money affect almost every phase of economic life. But this is of little help in formulating a currency program and discovering where we are trying to go.

The implications from monetary theory regarding governmental policy are great. Should the government pursue a spending program, endeavoring thereby to expand the flow of money and income? (See the views of John Maynard Keynes, Lauchlin Currie, and others.) If we stabilize the volume of money, will economic stability follow? (See the discussions on neutral money and an equilibrium rate of interest by K. Wicksell, L. von Mises, and F. A. Hayek.) Should we constantly adjust the volume of money to the volume and condition of business, and are price movements a guide to the amount needed? (See the views of Carl Snyder, Irving Fisher, W. I. King, and others.) Is the demand and supply of gold the chief factor in price and business stability, and should we attempt to adjust the supply of gold through alterations in the gold content of money? (See James Harvey Rogers, G. F. Warren and F. A. Pearson.) Is parity with gold and foreign exchange stability a prime objective of monetary policy? (See E. W. Kemmerer and others.) Considering world economic developments of the past ten years and the difficulties of the gold standard, has gold ceased to be able to perform useful functions and should it be completely demonetized? (See Frank Graham, C. R. Whittlesey, and others.) These are a few of the questions confronting currency administrators.

While these questions remain unanswered with anything approaching unanimity, governments have proceeded with more and more management. The phrase "managed currency" has been used with various meanings and has usually referred to an irredeemable paper currency, with little or no specific backing, regulated by some governmental agency, as opposed to the semi-automatic functioning of the gold standard. Strictly speaking, however, no currency is entirely unmanaged, and the question to-day is largely one of how much management and what kind should be imposed, of the probabilities of impartial and competent management, and particularly of the effectiveness and the consequences of control devices. Looking around the world, we find that practically all currencies are now subjected to a fairly large amount of governmental regulation.

The aims which in actual practice are sought are usually rather hazily recognized, but in general are to maintain as great a degree of foreign exchange stability as possible, and at the same time to maintain as much price and domestic economic stability as possible; or to put it negatively, to avoid actions which it is felt might upset conditions. Measures toward these ends are usually taken rather clumsily and gropingly. Moreover, it must be admitted that a considerable amount of management by governments is opportunistic, or akin to blind wandering. The objectives are complicated by the needs of treasuries and the fact that most governments are operating under deficits which tend toward currency expansion.

Particularly under war conditions are currency objectives subordinated to the raising of revenue. Thus the immediate currency problem for a large part of the world is that of holding inflation in check.

The present trend toward currency management has been stimulated by the economic confusion of recent years and the necessity of taking action of some kind. It is true that much of the confusion is in itself due to unfortunate currency policies. China turned to a managed currency when her silver standard broke down. Great Britain started the ball rolling by leaving gold in 1931. Then came a period of currency chaos throughout the world unprecedented in history. It has also been a period of currency revolution, when ideas have been radically altered.

A managed currency is not the opposite of the gold standard. (Unless we define the gold standard in its completely rigid and 100-per-cent automatic sense.) The problem is not one of the gold standard versus the non-gold standard, but one of regulating the currency and credit system and the flow of money so as to yield the desired price and economic stability—in so far as this can be accomplished by currency devices.

Gold movements under the former system tended to regulate currency and economic conditions, largely by expanding or contracting bank reserves. Gold, however, has long been recognized as an imperfect regulator of such conditions. The continual inflation and deflation which took place under the gold standard sometimes became disastrous. To-day gold has little influence in currency and credit systems, and the attempt is being made to provide stability by other devices. Since the breakdown of the gold standard, few nations have shown much interest in restoring gold. Some economists would abandon gold permanently. Others feel that in spite of its shortcomings, gold has a place in currency systems.

Although surrounded by superstition and ghosts, gold can be useful in settling foreign balances and in providing exchange stability. The recent huge importation of gold into the United States, however, has not been to settle balances, but on the contrary has itself been an unbalancing item. With the world in a chaotic condition and with little interest in the gold standard, there is slight prospect of any near term arrangements wherein gold would be used extensively to clear balances between nations.

Because of the high price which the United States has established for gold and the fact that this country will absorb gold at this price without limit, the metal is now being mined in very large amounts. Most of the world's monetary gold has come to America (Gold imports for the past five years [1934-1939] have averaged $1,509,000,000. In 1938 the United States acquired $1,974,000,000 of gold, and during the first eight months of 1939 about $2,500,000,000.), and with gold production at new peaks, this country's reserves of approximately seventeen billion dollars continue to mount. If the gold standard should not be restored in the rest of the world (and such restoration appears uncertain), the United States will have had unloaded upon it most of the world's monetary gold in exchange for real values. Dug from the ground in South Africa, it is being buried in the ground in America after having been paid for with American Dollars.

While fixed exchange rates, which the gold standard helps to provide, have important advantages, the cost of maintaining such rates may under certain circumstances become excessive. Measures to maintain fixed rates in terms of gold may involve deflation, falling commodity prices, and a lack of prosperity. Currency policy, therefore, may be faced with a decision between fixed rates and domestic well-being. Thus, France prior to 1936 held the franc steady in the foreign exchange markets, but because of this suffered more acutely at home. Since 1931 Great Britain has felt that a stable pound in terms of gold would require sacrifices not compensated for by the gains, and has therefore not pegged the pound at a fixed level, although she has through her stabilization fund endeavored to provide as much foreign exchange stability as practicable. The United States and several other leading countries also have stabilization funds which endeavor to prevent fluctuations in exchange—fulfilling a function formerly performed more or less automatically by gold. (The gold standard, however, included arrangements tending toward equilibrium in the balance of payments at the fixed rates. The absence of such arrangements under a system of controlled exchange rates is likely to lead eventually to disturbance and difficulty. This was one of the difficulties in the years leading up to the currency collapse of 1931. The gold-standard mechanism during that period had been restricted or disregarded.)

It can be seen that the problem of gold is not an easy one for currency administrators. Particularly is this true in the case of the United States, with its enormous stock of gold, a high fixed price for the metal, and the rest of the world not on gold.

Regarding a practical currency program for the United States at the present time, we find two fairly well defined schools of thought. One group believe that booms and depressions can to a large extent be moderated through the use of monetary measures, and that monetary policy therefore should be directed toward flattening out the business cycle. The other group feel that the business cycle is basically a non-monetary matter, and that while at certain times monetary measures may contribute toward economic stability, under most circumstances monetary maneuvers are harmful, impeding necessary adjustments in the economic system and leading to nervousness and uncertainty in the business world. They feel (with varying emphasis) that monetary policy should concern itself primarily with such things as the quality of the assets behind currency and credit and with maintenance of parity with gold, thus contributing to confidence and order in international affairs.

The first group, on the other hand, would expand the volume of money in periods of depression and falling prices, and conversely contract the volume in periods of boom and rising prices. The reasoning is that the immediate cause of recession is a shrinkage in the demand for goods, and that this shrinkage, if left alone, feeds on itself, becoming continually worse. The shrinkage in demand is reflected in a decline in prices, in a contraction in the volume of money, and in a slowing down of the rate of turnover and the flow of income.

It is argued that the government should at such times endeavor to stabilize demand by expanding the circulating media; that such expansion of money will tend to expand spending, i.e., to revive demand; and that one of the best guides as to whether demand is stable is an index of the general price level, an index that reflects the average prices of all goods bought and sold, including securities and services. If the price level rises, it indicates that demand is outstripping supply; while if it falls, it indicates the opposite. It follows that monetary policy should ordinarily aim to maintain a relatively stable price level and that this should be accomplished by expanding or contracting the circulating media. Inflation and deflation—those great disrupters of economic life—cannot be seriously disturbing if the currency volume is controlled, expanded if deflation sets in and contracted if inflation begins. It is like steering a car—if the car starts to veer in one direction, the wheel should be turned toward the other direction; if it is turned too far it should be turned back, the aim being to keep the car constantly in the center of the road. This viewpoint, with variations, is held by a large number of outstanding economists.

The opposing view is also held by a large number of distinguished economists. The Board of Governors of the Federal Reserve System in March, 1939, issued a statement disagreeing with certain proposals, based on the reasoning of group one, to use monetary devices to stabilize business. This statement said:

> Experience has shown, however, that (1) prices cannot be controlled by changes in the amount and cost of money; (2) the Board's control of the amount of money is not complete and cannot be made complete; (3) a steady average of prices does not necessarily result in lasting prosperity; and (4) a steady level of average prices is not nearly as important to the people as a fair relationship between the prices of the commodities which they produce and those which they must buy.

Economists favoring this latter position point out that price movements are not solely the result of changes in the volume of money. Changes in the velocity of money, or the rapidity with which it turns over, are continually taking place, reflecting many forces of a nonmonetary nature which lead to a rise or fall of prices. We must go behind the velocity, they say. Furthermore, the relationships between the prices of commodities, between costs and selling prices, are exceedingly important from the standpoint of prosperity or depression.

The differences of opinion on the currency question are to a considerable extent those of emphasis, and there is basically much more agreement than might appear on the surface. Practically all are agreed that the former gold standard was far from perfect, that fluctuations of the price level were often the source of serious trouble, and that efforts to remedy this condition deserve most careful attention. There is little dispute over the fact that an intimate relationship exists between monetary and credit matters and the ups and downs of business. It is also agreed that the state of confidence exerts a powerful influence upon currency movements, upon savings and the flow of income. Probably no economist would dispute the fact that the velocity of money reflects nonmonetary forces; yet one group would deal with a disrupting change in velocity as merely a symptom of some nonmonetary movement, and to be discovered and treated as such. Another group would agree that velocity is a symptom but would remedy matters by monetary devices, that is, by compensating changes in the volume of money—not necessarily to the exclusion of other remedies.

Those who fear a large amount of currency management realize the grave conditions which can come from mismanagement and political manipulation. Those who welcome it are impressed with the grave conditions which have in actual fact resulted from lack of regulation or from uninformed actions. Events of the past ten years provide ample evidence of this. The former currency systems were unable to meet the strains of current developments, including the high-pitched international economy, however irrational it may be. As a result, whether we like it or not, positive regulation is here and will remain.

It is clear that currency devices are very powerful forces for good or evil, and that currency and credit systems have not functioned well when left to gold and so-called automatic devices. The degree to which the problem can be solved by government is still unknown. In view of the profound effects of currency disturbances, the currency question offers a challenge to the resourcefulness and ability of government. When it is remembered that prices and monetary incomes are at the heart of our economic system and that currency matters have much to do with economic and social conditions in general, perhaps with the survival of free institutions and enterprise, the currency problem is seen to be one of the major problems of to-day.

No. 98

THE NATION'S BANKS [1]

by Harry W. Laidler

ONE of the major issues before the American people to-day is how best to render the banking and credit system of the nation an instrument devoted wholly to the service of society. The banking system in the United States, like Topsy, has "just growed." At the turning of the century, as a result of various ups and downs in banking development, some 10 thousand national and state banks—10,382 to be exact—were being operated in the various states of the union. By 1921, at the beginning of the era of the New Capitalism, that number had trebled, reaching a peak of 30,812. During the booming post-war years 1921 to 1929, some 5714 banks holding total deposits of $1,625,000,000, closed their doors.

These suspensions ranged in number from 367 in the year 1922 to 976 in the prosperous year of 1926. At the end of this period, the number of banks had shrunk to about 25,000. During the succeeding 3 years of the depression, while not more than a handful of banks failed in England or in Canada, the bank mortality in this country was indeed high. In 1930, 1352 quit payments, in 1931, 2294—the greatest number up to that time in the history of the country—and in the following year, 1456, a total for this 3-year period of 5102, with deposits of over 3¼ billion dollars! Thus during the 12-year period 1921 to 1932, no less than 10,816 banks with a capitalization of $653,000,000 and deposits of $4,885,126,000 went, at least temporarily, out of business. In the same period, 1614 banks with deposits of $792,304,000 reopened.

"If the test of a sound banking system is its ability to maintain its position and usefulness through economic adversity as well as prosperity," declared the conservative National Industrial Conference Board at that time, "the American banking system failed signally in recent years." The suspensions of 1931, as it declared, "constituted one of the greatest financial catastrophes in the nation's history."

[1] Harry W. Laidler, "The Nation's Banks," *A Program for Modern America* (New York: Thomas Y. Crowell Company, 1936), Ch. 12, pp. 250-281. Reprinted by permission of the publisher.

The modern banking system had its origin in part in the desire for the safe-keeping of treasure. Citizens who had surplus gold in the old days took their treasure to goldsmiths and got the latter to put their deposits in strong safes, the tin boxes of those days, in return, at times, for a small fee. One of the prime arguments used by banks to prevent hoarding of money has been that money in the bank is safer than it is in tin boxes at home. During the post-war days it was difficult for the banker to prove that statement.

Behind the bank failures of the post-war years there were many factors. The economic depression, the worst in the last half century, and the preceding post-war agricultural depression, were responsible for many suspensions.

Many bank closings resulted from the small capital resources of individual banks. In 1929, nearly 5500 banks had a capital of less than $25,000; an equal number possessed a capital of $25,000, while over 7000 more had a capital structure of less than $100,000. During the period 1921-1929, only 12 per cent of all defaulting banks had a capitalization of more than $100,-000; 39 per cent had less than $25,000, while 49 per cent had between $25,000 and $100,000.

The reason for this greater mortality among the smaller banks of the country was not hard to seek. In many cases, particularly in rural districts, most of the loans were made to borrowers who obtained their living in the same occupation, agriculture, for instance. When agriculture flourished, the loans were sound, repayments were comparatively certain, and the bank prospered. When agriculture was in the doldrums, however, farmers and those depending upon them for their livelihood, were poor risks. They were often unable to meet their obligations when due and it did not take long before the entire capital and reserves of a bank capitalized at $10,000 or $25,000 were wiped out.

Although the smaller banks had the most difficult time during these years, the larger institutions did not escape unscathed. There were some failures among the greater banks. Perhaps the most notorious was that of the Bank of United States, with its 58 branches, its 400,000 depositors and its $200,000,000 of deposits. The suspension of this bank constituted one of the greatest single financial failures up to that time in the nation's history. If it had not been for the action of the Reconstruction Finance Corporation, many more of the great banks of the country would probably have closed their doors in the early thirties.

Failures were due during that period not only to the lack of capital resources but to the lack of uniform regulation. Most of the banks of the country were subject to the regulation of the 48 states of the union and

the laws and their enforcement in many of the states utterly failed to protect the depositors. Nor was federal regulation adequate. Nationally, "lax
and spineless comptrollers of the currency," as Professor H. Parker Willis,
formerly Secretary of the Federal Reserve Board, declared, "had suffered
the banks to get into bad and illegal condition, unchecked by any supervising activity of the reserve institutions." Of the banks suspended from
1921 to 1932 inclusive, 2030 were members of the Federal Reserve System;
8786, non-member banks.

The existence of bank affiliates was the root cause of many financial
disasters. The failure of the Bank of United States, with its hundreds of
thousands of depositors, was indicative of this evil. The officers of the
Bank of United States were officers of many of the 58 affiliates of the bank
and the existence of these affiliates made possible the juggling of millions
of dollars of the people's funds by a few officers bent on private profit.

In hundreds of instances bank officers proved incompetent or dishonest.
One-half of the banks that failed in 1929-1930 had made loans to directors
and officers, in many instances on inadequate collateral. Many of the failed
banks had spent far too much on new and elegant bank buildings. Many
of the bank directors were inactive and negligent.

In July, 1932, J. F. Sullivan, President of the California Bankers Association, thus characterized the management of the banks of the country:

> As a result of my efforts to collect some data on the subject of bank state-
> ments, I have become more firmly convinced than ever that banking, gener-
> ally speaking, is the most poorly managed business in the United States to-day.
> The sins that have been committed, the fallacious practices that have been
> allowed to continue year after year, the utter disregard shown by bankers
> generally toward sensible, intelligent methods of improving bank profits, bring
> home to me quite clearly the reason there has been such a painful lack of
> bank leadership in the country during the last two years.

In city after city the banks financed skyscrapers and mammoth hotels
and apartment houses, when the existing capacity was more than sufficient.
They placed second mortgages upon highly speculative real estate developments and poured funds like a drunken sailor into the security market. [As
Professor Warne has said:]

> Golf players, retired farmers, tradesmen, men of inherited wealth, and
> speculators sat behind polished mahogany desks and looked wise. One may
> become a lawyer or a barber only after a certain show of professional prowess.
> For banking, one apparently needed only a pleasant disposition and a suave
> method of presenting the merits of gilt edged bonds or of joining Christmas
> clubs. Bankers breathed optimism when business was good and lent to enthu-

siastic enterprisers who sought high profits. They became panicky when business was bad, called loans, and thus made a bad situation worse.

During the few years before the depression, our banks made too small a percentage of commercial loans, and loaned too much on collateral. From 1922 to 1930, their loans on securities increased from $3,909,000,000 to $8,560,000,000. Real estate loans and investments during the years 1918 to 1928 of all member banks of the Federal Reserve increased from $461,000,-000 to $3,155,000,000, an increase of 565.5 per cent.

From October, 1929, to July, 1932, the market value of all stocks on the New York Stock Exchange decreased from $89 billion to between $15 and $16 billion. This seriously affected the stability of hundreds of banks.

It is generally conceded (declared a special Senate Committee investigating stock exchange practices, in its report of June 6, 1934) that the flow of credit of the commercial banks in the form of brokers' loans, the financing of syndicate or pool operations in securities and loans on securities as collateral, accentuated the speculative excesses during the boom period. The consequent disastrous results affected not only the investing public, but these banking institutions, whose capital was substantially impaired by the collapse and shrinkage of values of securities into which banks had frozen a large part of their funds.

Many bank failures were likewise due to unsound foreign loans. The American banks invested in Germany during the boom years a sum that exceeded the amount of reparations. Within 12 years we loaned to Colombia $72,000,000, as compared with $25,000,000 of loans made in 53 years by European countries.

In 2 years we loaned to Peru two-thirds as much as the country borrowed abroad in 69 years. American investments in South America could not now be sold for 33 cents on a dollar.

Behind the bank failures was the fact that, though the banks had deposits totaling 55 billion dollars, they had a permanent gold basis of only 4 billion. Our financial institutions operated with the realization that, if a large proportion of their depositors demanded gold, these depositors could at any time compel the banks to close their doors. As the depression continued, an increasing number of depositors presented themselves at the tellers' windows and asked for their deposits. In some cases, after they counted the cash and left the banks, they redeposited their funds in other banks in the large cities, banks in which they had more confidence. From July 1932 to July 1933, the deposits in the central reserve banks of New York increased by 18.5 per cent, while in the country banks they decreased by 5.1 per cent. In some cases, depositors, after withdrawing their money, hoarded their gold. Banks began to call in their loans and to refuse to make further loans. In the 3 years, 1930, 1931, and 1932, the reported volume of total loans and investments of Federal Reserve System banks decreased by nearly 8½ billion dollars. During the same period net deposits of member banks shrank by approximately 7 billion. The calling of loans and the increased cautiousness in the financial community in extending new loans led, among other forces, to the rapid decline in the value of securities, to the closing of factories and to the tragic increase in the army of the unemployed. Runs on the banks of the country were of daily occurrence.

During 1932, to prevent further suspensions, the government stepped in and established, in February of that year, the Reconstruction Finance Corporation. During the remainder of the year this corporation was busy salvaging banks in distress. By the end of the year it had loaned $600,000,-000 to the banking institutions, $270,000,000 to railroads, pressed by banks to pay their maturing obligations, and about $150,000,000 to insurance and other institutions. Other measures were adopted to make it possible for banks to meet the demands of depositors.

These operations, however, did not stem the tide of bank failures. In January, 1933, another major hoarding period began, and great quantities of deposits were shifted from bank to bank. In February, withdrawals of gold increased in volume. Some of this gold was hoarded, some exported. Between early February and March 4, the money in circulation increased by $1,830,000,000, while $300,000,000 in gold was withdrawn from the banks. Heavy demands were made on the Federal Reserve Banks.

In the meanwhile the banking authorities in a number of states were obliged to adopt emergency measures. Louisiana declared a one-day holiday on February 4 to allow the banks to make arrangements to meet their obligations. Michigan began a 4-day holiday, later extended, on February 14. On February 25 the Governor of Maryland declared a bank holiday. On March 1, Alabama, Kentucky, Tennessee and Nevada followed suit. These were joined by 6 others on March 2 and by 7 others on March 3, the day before the inauguration of President Roosevelt. On March 4, the Governor of New York issued a proclamation declaring that day, which was Saturday, and the following Monday, to be bank holidays. Similar action was taken in Illinois, Massachusetts, New Jersey, Pennsylvania and elsewhere.

These actions in the various states by March 4 had closed or placed under restrictions practically all banks in the country. Federal banks also observed state holidays and closed on March 4. "All leading exchanges ceased operations and business in general was practically at a standstill."

On March 6 President Roosevelt issued a proclamation declaring a nation-wide bank holiday to continue through the 4 days ending Thursday, March 9, with the expectation of opening only such banks as could meet all demands upon them. Certain necessary activities were permitted to the banks. Banks were, among other things, not allowed to permit withdrawals of currency for the purpose of hoarding. The export of gold was prohibited and hoarders of gold were required to return their gold to the banks. On March 9, 1933, Congress met and gave the President large emergency powers over the banking institutions of the country. It provided, among other things, for the appointment by the Comptroller of the Currency of conservators to reorganize banks where such action was necessary in the interests of the depositor. It authorized the issuance and sale of preferred stock by national banks and the purchase of such stock by the Reconstruction Finance Corporation. It permitted Federal Reserve Banks to make loans to member banks under more liberal terms than formerly.

The President was empowered to license "sound" banks, and, from March 12 on, these "sound" banks began to reopen. Hoarded coin and gold and gold certificates began to flow back into the coffers of the financial institutions of the land. On April 12, some 4 billion dollars of deposits was still tied up in 4200 unlicensed banks and, by the end of the year, about a billion and a quarter dollars was impounded in 1900 banks.

Following the bank crisis likewise came the Banking Act of 1933, passed on June 16. Many believed that the time had come for the nationalization of the banking system, but President Roosevelt and his advisers adhered to the system of regulation. The 1933 Act, among other things, provided for the guarantee of bank deposits. To assure the safe return of such deposits, Congress temporarily guaranteed deposits of $2500 or less—thus covering over 90 per cent of the depositors of the country—and provided that a permanent system of deposit guarantee should be later developed. This act, often referred to as the Glass-Steagall Act, likewise required the divorcement of banking affiliates within a year and the separation of investment and commercial banking. It prohibited the paying of interest on demand deposits and restricted interest on time deposits. It forbade a bank to make loans to its own officers. It provided that the Federal Reserve Board could suspend a member from the use of the Federal Reserve System's credit if, after fair warning, the member bank made undue use of its credit for speculative purposes. It provided that holding companies should not vote their bank stocks except under certain specified conditions. It raised the minimum capitalization of national banks from $25,000 to $50,000. It empowered the Federal Reserve Board to warn officers of member banks whom it found engaged in unsound practices and to remove them if they persisted. And it forbade private banks of the type of J. P. Morgan and Company to conduct at one and the same time a deposit and an investment business. Either one or the other phase of its business would have to be abandoned. The act likewise created a Federal Open Market Committee consisting of 12 members, one being appointed by each Federal Reserve Bank. By this provision the bankers, rather than the Board representative of the public, were placed in charge of such operations, thus weakening the control of the government over the Committee's operations.

The act was vigorously praised and just as vigorously condemned. It permitted the extension of branch banks. But, as John T. Flynn declared, it did not strike at what was

> the greatest of all the abuses of banking—that is the control of banks by holding companies. . . . We may now expect to see the union of state branch-banking systems by means of the holding company. The bank affiliate has been made illegal. But there is nothing to prevent a holding company which owns a security corporation from also owning a banking corporation. . . . There is nothing in the law to cover a case like the Transamerica Corporation. This corporation owns a subsidiary which in turn owns the Bank of America, with 300 branches. But the Transamerica Corporation also owns the Banc-america-Blair Corporation and half a dozen other subsidiaries. The effect of this new law, therefore, will be to encourage those who want affiliates to embrace the holding-company type of banking.

To H. Parker Willis, first secretary of the Federal Reserve Board, the act was merely a stop-gap. The original Federal Reserve Act had been largely futile. The Federal Reserve Banks had been of little use to the smaller banks. At times they had been "a complete menace." They had failed, he contended, to preserve their funds for their members who were in need. They had permitted the larger banks to borrow extensively for use in stock market manipulation.

> A statistical analysis of the operations of one of the largest of the Reserve Banks during a recent year, made for the Senate Banking Committee, shows that scarcely any of its advances were for the genuine relief and aid of the ordinary member bank, and that nearly all were employed in furnishing the larger banks with cash for speculative transactions.

To this Board, possessed of enormous powers which it has left largely in abeyance or transferred to others, the Act of 1933 gave [according to Professor Willis]

> still greater and more inclusive authority which it is now asked to use sanely and constructively. The act makes this requisition at a time when the Board

has apparently reached low-water mark in prestige and probably in ability. Organized as a non-political body with membership fairly evenly divided in political preference and in no sense bitterly partisan, it is now composed 100 per cent of Democrats, recent appointees having been selected primarily on political grounds.

The act, further, assumed that it was possible to have a sound banking system in the midst of an unsound economic system. But, as Dr. Willis maintained, a nation cannot insist on indulgence in stock gambling of an extreme type, on shoddy and unsafe corporation finance, and on costly and hazardous government finance, and, at one and the same time, build up a sound banking system. "Our national banking system (declared Dr. Willis) is obsolete, our Federal Reserve System, in incapable and unsympathetic hands, our examination system hamstrung by politics and prejudice." The Banking Act of 1933 is little more than a protest against a banking world gone wrong. "It does not go to the root of the situation."

The deposit guarantee feature of the act likewise came in for much condemnation from those who maintained that state guarantees in the past had failed, and that the act would but prove an encouragement to inefficiency and make the well-managed banks pay for the inefficiency and dishonesty of their competitors. Nor did it bring about the unified banking system or the socialized system that many maintained was required by the needs of the time.

As time went on, it became increasingly apparent that the chief evils in the banking system still persisted. The country's banks were still insecure. There was no social control of the country's credit.

The first of these problems, that of the safety of deposits, had been tentatively dealt with in the Banking Bill of 1933, which set up the temporary Federal Deposit Insurance Corporation. The Banking Bill of 1935 made this corporation permanent, guaranteeing to all depositors in insured banks 100 per cent return on deposits of $5000 or less. This covered over 90 per cent of the nation's depositors. It provided that the funds for the insurance deposit corporation in addition to its capital be raised by an assessment of one-twelfth of one per cent on the average deposits of the insured banks. In case of need, it empowered the Secretary of the Treasury to come to the aid of the F.D.I.C. by purchasing a quarter of a billion dollars' worth of its obligations in addition to the sums already provided by the Reconstruction Finance Corporation and the Treasury. It further declared that no state bank with average deposits of a million dollars or more could insure its deposits with the F.D.I.C. after 1941 unless such bank became a member of the Federal Reserve System—a provision aimed at the development of a more unified banking system.

Under this set-up, the Treasury was placed, according to Harold M. Fleming, in a position of ultimate insurer, for, from the Treasury, "if for none other than political reasons, the cash would have to be forthcoming to pay the depositors in the closed banks."

As a means of protecting individual banks in case of emergency, the Act of 1935 provided that Federal Reserve Banks could make loans to member banks on "any sound asset," which means practically all assets which banks in any emergency are likely to possess. "Stated for the sake of simplicity, without certain technical qualifications, the Reserve System is practically obliged in the next serious emergency (as a result of this legislation) to 'bail out' the entire banking system."

What will be the effect of this section it is too early to judge. On the one hand it is defended on the ground that it does away with the "inelastic and restricted basis upon which accommodations have been available to member banks in the past." On the other hand it is criticized for giving the careless banker and his depositor "all too much assurance of protection from the consequences of over-extending credit." As has been before mentioned, commercial banks have tended increasingly to place a declining percentage of their deposits in short-term loans. In 1890, 61.9 per cent of all bank assets were represented by commercial loans, while, in 1935, the proportion had declined to 24.3 per cent. During the same period, bank investments of a far less liquid character increased from 13.2 per cent to 59.4 per cent of total assets. The incentives to his keeping his portfolio in a "liquid" position, that is to his keeping a substantial proportion of his assets in short-term readily marketable paper, have been, it is claimed by many, further "weakened now that comparatively 'slow' assets are to be made permanently eligible for rediscounting. . . . In the next banking emergency the entire banking system will fall back with crushing weight on the Reserve."

The second problem with which the framers of this act grappled was that of insuring additional public control over the credit structure of the country. One of the gravest indictments brought against the nation's banking system, as has been brought out elsewhere, has been that it extended far too much credit for speculative purposes in the booming days of prosperity, and far too little credit for legitimate business enterprises in the tragic days of depression. The amount of credit extended to business is a vital factor in the country's prosperity. The nation, it is true, has long had power to decide how much currency should be issued, but nine-tenths of the total supply of money in circulation consists of not currency but of demand deposits in commercial banks that circulate in the form of bank checks. Control over this larger and more important part of the money supply—bank deposit or check money—rests very largely with the banks.

Many economists have long held that the banking system can vitally affect the money supply of the country in at least three ways. It can do this first by lowering or increasing interest rates. A business man goes to his local bank to get a loan. He gives his note due, say, in three or four months. The bank lends him the face value of his note, after deducting the interest. This is called discounting the note. The local bank, however, may get its money from the Federal Reserve Bank, which rediscounts the note at a certain discount rate. The interest rate which the Federal Reserve charges the local bank is called the re-discount rate. The Federal Reserve Board at Washington had long the power to increase or decrease this re-discount rate. Whenever the rediscount rates went up, there would be a tendency to discourage borrowing and to contract credit. Whenever these rates went down, there was a tendency to encourage borrowings and expand credit. The extent of this tendency, however, in a situation where member banks possess some billions of dollars of excess reserves, is highly debatable.

Secondly, a banking system can influence the money supply by raising or lowering reserve requirements of banks which are members of the Federal Reserve System. Member banks of this system are required to maintain a reserve against their demand deposits equal on the average to 10 per cent. This reserve is deposited with the Federal Reserve Banks. "Before a bank can 'create' $10 of deposit money through lending or investing that amount, it must have available $1 of reserves in excess of its existing legal requirement." With the lowering of required reserves, the banks are in a position to extend more credit to business. With the increase in required reserves, on the other hand, the money market becomes ordinarily more stringent.

In the third place, the volume of money can be increased or decreased by the purchase or the sale of government securities, by so-called open market operations.

When a Federal Reserve Bank buys $1,000,000 of government securities it pays for them by means of a check drawn upon itself, and this check, upon being deposited with a commercial bank, gives that bank $1,000,000 of reserve money which it can make the basis of an expansion of $10,000,000 of its own credit.

Vice versa, if the Federal Reserve Bank sold government securities, it would take that much reserve money out of the market, thus tending to contract credit.

Before the Act of 1935, the reserve requirements in the banks were fixed. The Federal Reserve Board could do nothing to change these rates unless he President declared that an emergency existed. Governor Eccles and others contended that the Board should have greater power over these rates and thus over the volume of money in the country. He proposed to give the Federal Reserve Board the use of this most important instrument of control without requiring the President to declare an emergency, which might involve insurmountable political obstacles. The first draft of the bill permitted the Federal Reserve Board to change the reserve rate as it deemed it desirable. This proposal was bitterly fought on the ground that no board should be given such great power over the credit system of the country. If the Reserve Board was free to require the banks to keep not 10 per cent, but 20, 50, or 100 per cent reserves against deposits, the board could transform over night a condition of ease in the money market to a condition of acute stringency. A compromise was finally arrived at whereby the Board was able to fix the reserves within strict limits. Such reserves, however, were not to be less than those required at the time of the passage of the Act, namely 10 percent, nor more than twice that amount.

For years open-market operations had been a matter for individual determination by the Federal Reserve Banks. Later these banks organized a loosely coordinated committee consisting of representatives from each of the twelve Federal Reserve Banks to give advice regarding purchases and sales of securities. The Act of 1933 established an Open Market Committee composed of the twelve Governors of the twelve Federal Reserve Banks, with power to recommend purchases or sales, but with no power to order any such sales. The Federal Reserve Board was empowered by this act to approve or disapprove these recommendations. Power over such operations was thus thoroughly decentralized, in direct contrast to the situation in most of the countries abroad. Governor Eccles, of the Federal Reserve Bank declared during the discussion of the 1935 legislation:

> At the present time the control over this power (over open-market operations) is distributed between the committee of twelve Governors of the twelve banks, who now have the responsibility for recommending purchases or sales; the Federal Reserve Board which has authority to approve or disapprove the recommendations of the Governors, and 108 Directors of the twelve Reserve Banks, who, in turn, have the right to determine whether or not they will buy or sell in accordance with the policy that has been recommended by the Governors and approved by the Board. A more effective means of diffusing responsibility and encouraging delay could not well be devised.

Under the old system, declared Congressman Steagall, one bank had the power to nullify any policy, even though agreed upon by all the other eleven banks and approved by the Federal Reserve Board. Governor Eccles therefore urged that the power over open-market operations be entrusted to a Federal Reserve Board of eight, including the two ex-officio members, the Secretary of the Treasury and the Comptroller of the Currency. However before this Board should take any action on open-market operations as well as on discount rates, it should consult with a committee of five Governors of Federal Reserve Banks. This recommendation of Governor Eccles adopted in the House bill, was also vigorously attacked as giving great power over the business and financial fabric of the country to a "political" Board dominated by the President of the United States. As a result of a bitter attack on this provision, a compromise was effected in the House bill engineered by Congressman Steagall and the Senate bill largely formulated by the conservative Senator from Virginia, Senator Glass. In the final draft of the bill, the old Reserve Board was disbanded. A new Board of seven was created, from which the Secretary of Treasury and the Comptroller of the Currency were excluded. These seven members were to be appointed for periods of 14 years by the President, and to be known as the Board of Governors of the Federal Reserve Board. Of these seven, 2— the Chairman and the Vice-Chairman of the Board—were to be appointed by the President for a period of 4 years. The Act, moreover, created a new Open Market Committee consisting of the Federal Reserve Board of seven and five others chosen by the twelve Federal Reserve Banks from specified sections of the country.

No Federal Reserve Bank, the Act declares, shall engage or decline to engage in open-market operations except in accordance with directions and regulations adopted by the Committee. "The Committee shall consider adopt, and transmit to the several Federal Reserve Banks, regulations relating to the open-market transactions of such banks."

As a means of avoiding the interlocking directorates found in the past the Act further provided that, except under certain prescribed conditions no director, officer or employee of any bank, shall serve as director, officer or employee of any other bank.

Under the 1935 bill, the Federal Reserve Board was also given a little more control than formerly over the twelve Federal Reserve Banks. Although the Presidents of these twelve banks were to be elected as were formerly the Governors, by the directors of each of the Reserve Banks— this time for a five-year term—these selections were to be subject to the approval of the Board of Governors of the Federal Reserve Board.

The bankers in the final draft of the bill got pretty much what they wanted. They eliminated from the Board of Governors the Secretary of the Treasury and the Comptroller of the Currency, thus greatly lessening the power of whatever administration may be in power over the control of the Board's policies. They greatly limited the power of the Board in changing reserve requirements, while the bill increased the government responsibility for the deficits of the banks. The bill was in fact regarded as a distinct victory for Senator Glass, the conservative Virginia Senator, and in considerable part a defeat for Eccles and the House Committee.

Nor did the bill bring the regulation of the banking system of the country under one roof. Not until 1942 will it be necessary for state banks with deposits of more than $1,000,000 to become members of the Federal Reserve System in order to enjoy the benefits of deposit insurance. The law makes no provision for the membership of the smaller banks in the Federal Reserve set-up. These will remain for the most part state banks subject to the regulation of laws in the 48 states of the union. And yet it is among these banks that the largest number of failures have been registered.

> The multitude of small banks [maintains the New York *Times*] must be an ever-present threat to the guarantee fund. Only by a single legislative control over all the country's banks, which would enable the national government to adopt a uniform branch banking policy and uniform standards of liquidity and soundness, could the necessary reconstruction of the banking system be carried through.

During the crisis of the thirties, an increased demand has been heard for the socialization of the credit resources of the country. That socialization is seen by many as a logical and essential trend in the economic life of the nation.

Abroad a distinct development has taken place during the last few decades toward a non-profit banking system under public or cooperative administration. Cities, states and nations have long owned and operated banks in various countries abroad. In Sweden, the Swedish Riksbank is regarded as one of the soundest and best established central banks in Europe. For years this bank, administered directly under the supervision of Parliament, has served as the depository of state funds, has received time and demand deposits, has been in charge of the clearance operations of the state, has made loans and discounted bills. During the last few years, largely through its efforts, the price level of Sweden has remained remarkably stable.

For over twenty years, the government of Australia, at the other end of the world, has been successfully operating its Commonwealth Bank. This bank likewise receives deposits of the various departments of the government, and has administrative charge of the large public savings banks of Tasmania and Queensland. In 1920 it was given power to issue notes and to direct clearing house activities among the private banks. It conducts a rural credit department. Its profits, which have been considerable, have gone into a reserve fund, or helped toward the payment of the public debt. The bank has been definitely divorced from politics of the invidious sort and has aided the Commonwealth to weather the economic crisis of the thirties. In Russia, the entire banking system, as is natural, is a function of the state. Most European countries do such an extensive savings deposit business in connection with their Post Office Departments that the Postmaster Generals are the largest single bankers in their respective communities.

Throughout Europe, there are strong municipal banks of the type of the savings bank in Birmingham, England. In conservative Switzerland, public banks exist in practically every canton. They transact every phase of the banking business except that of speculative investment and the issuance of notes, and, as in the Swedish and Australian government banking systems, have been efficiently and honestly run.

Coming to America, few realize the extent to which the government has been compelled to engage in banking operations. Our Postal Savings Bank is, of course, an old story. For a number of years its deposits increased at a slow and steady gait. In January, 1930, its 6000 branches held about $165,000,000 of deposits. In 1933 these deposits amounted to about $1,200,-000,000, an increase of over 600 per cent in a three-year period, despite the absence of any governmental propaganda in behalf of its own institution. It goes without saying that no depositor in this system has lost a dollar of his saving, and there are at present some 2,000,000 depositors. Outside of our Postal Savings Banks, the government has taken an increasing interest in the financial institutions of the country. The government, as has been pointed out, selects the seven members of the Board of Governors of the Federal Reserve Banks, and three of the nine members of the Boards of the twelve Federal Reserve Banks. Through the Reconstruction Finance Corporation, for a time, one of the most powerful financial institutions in existence, we have loaned hundreds of millions of dollars to banks, and have purchased preferred stocks and capital notes aggregating over a billion dollars in some 40 per cent of the nation's banks.

From February 2, 1932, to December 31, 1935, the R.F.C. had loaned, invested or allocated the enormous sum of $10,616,833,860, including allocations of about $1,700,000,000 to other governmental agencies and for direct relief. Included in its disbursements were loans of $1,350,000,000 to banks and trust companies, $833,000,000 in purchases of preferred stock in 4134 banks and $435,000,000 in purchases of capital notes and debentures in 2847 banks; $102,000,000 in loans to insurance companies, over $1,170,000,-000 in loans for distribution to depositors in closed banks and $670,000,000 in loans to railroads. By the end of 1935, many of these loans had been repaid but the R.F.C. still owned $882,000,000 in preferred stock, capital

notes and debentures of banks and insurance companies, and still had outstanding over 1½ billion dollars in loans. Jesse H. Jones, Chairman of the
R.F.C., claimed in his annual report (January 25, 1936) that, if the policies
of the corporation continued as they had substantially been, the $115,844,000
profit for the 4 years would cover all losses, assuming the Commodity Credit
Corporation had no ultimate loss.

During 1934 and 1935 there was considerable discussion as to whether
the government, through the R.F.C., planned to dominate the banks in
which it held large blocks of stock. The first banking institution in which
the Reconstruction Finance Corporation obtained majority control was the
National Bank of Detroit, reorganized on March 24, 1933. "With the creation of this bank," the New York *Times* declared, "the United States for
the first time since Andrew Jackson's administration goes into the banking
business—half of the bank's capital of $25,000,000 being furnished by the
Reconstruction Finance Corporation."

In 1934 the Reconstruction Finance Corporation, as is well known, definitely selected the President of the great Continental Illinois National Bank
and Trust Company, in which it held majority control. Spokesmen for the
Administration, however, hastened to assure the bankers' fraternity that,
although the R.F.C. owned at that time around an eighth of American
banking capital, it was not likely to use its voting power, "except in cases
of factional dispute within banking directorates, or to bring about mergers.
Furthermore, the government does definitely intend to withdraw from this
interest at some future date."

The United States likewise boasts of a large number of mutual savings
banks. In June, 1934, there were 594 such banks operated in 18 states,
with a total of $9,720,000,000 in deposits and 13,687,000 depositors, an
increase of nearly 400,000 for the year. The average account was a little
over $700, and the average rate of interest, 3.24 per cent. The assets of
these mutual saving banks totaled around $11,000,000,000.

In 1933, there were also nearly 11,000 building and loan associations on
a cooperative basis, with a membership of 9¼ million and with total assets
of approximately 7 billion dollars.

Uncle Sam is likewise conducting extensive financial operations through
the Federal Land Banks, the Livestock Credit Corporations, the Jointstock
Land Banks, the Federal Intermediate Credit Banks and the Agricultural
Credit Corporations.

The government likewise became during the depression the principal
agency for the extension of credit to home owners. Through the R.F.C.,
the Home Owners' Loan Corporation, the Federal Housing Administration,
the Farm Credit Administration and other government agencies, it had

advanced, by December 15, 1935, nearly \$7½ billion to home owners for new construction, the refinancing of mortgages, for modernization and repair programs, etc. It had likewise allocated about \$150,000,000 for low-cost housing ventures. Its assistance to housing ventures up to that time follows:

1. Direct financial assistance in *new housing construction:*
   a. By loans through RFC .... \$ 8,000,000
   b. By loans through PWA—disbursed   29,828,000
      By loans through PWA—additional commitments   24,026,000
   c. PWA grants ....   none
                                                 \$ 61,854,000

2. Direct *refinancing* of *home owners'* mortgages which are in danger of default, including renovation and improvements in many cases:
   a. Urban loans through the Home Owners' Loan Corporation \$2,921,682,000
   b. Farm loans through the Farm Credit Administration 2,813,000,000
                                                  \$5,734,682,000

3. *Indirect refinancing* of old and new mortgages through loans to other agencies:
   a. Loans on home mortgages to Federal savings and loan associations through the Federal Home Loan Bank ...... \$ 111,655,000
   b. Reconstruction Finance Corporation loans to Federal Land Banks, mortgage loan companies and building and loan associations 1,106,000,000
                                                  \$1,217,655,000

4. Federal *insurance* of housing loans made by other agencies:
   a. "Modernization and repair notes" insured by the Federal Housing Administration .... \$ 226,000,000
   b. Home mortgages for new construction insured by the Federal Housing Administration   187,543,000
                                                  \$ 413,543,000

         Total \$7,427,734,000

In fact the depression gave rise to a number of situations which many observers claimed would lead to the permanent limitation of private banking. The banking system during the depression was called upon increasingly to buy government bonds. In an effort to liquefy their assets, they purchased many securities in behalf of the PWA, the CWA, the AAA and other institutions of the government, while, at the same time, refusing to lend money to industry. In August, 1929, the outstanding commercial loans of weekly reporting banks of the Federal Reserve System totaled \$9,390,000,000. By July 31, 1935, this had declined to \$4,360,000,000, the smallest figure since

1914, despite the fact that the excess reserves of the member banks on that date were between $2 and $3 billion, this amount increasing by December, 1935, to over $3,300,000,000. "The ultimate result of such investment habits on the part of the banks," declared Raymond Moley, "would be to liquefy them out as mere investment trusts with one kind of assets, government paper, and to bring on an irresistible call for commercial credit accommodation from other sources, presumably the government. The result would be clear long before the transformation had been completed."

In the second place, the government during the depression developed a number of financial institutions, referred to above, with the object of meeting the credit needs of various groups of people from whose support private banking had largely withdrawn. Writing in early 1934, Mr. Moley declared:

> The area of agricultural credit has been largely staked off by government. Commercial banks had already pretty largely abandoned that service, or were intending to as soon as they could. Country banks were among the first to race for liquefication through government securities. The area of industrial loans begins to be invaded by the RFC through loans to the railroads. . . . The field of city building construction begins to be invaded by the PWA through its loans for large-scale housing, although these are in neighborhoods which banks have been generally quitting for many years. . . . As the banks withdraw their lines of credit from rural and city land, battalions of governmental credit are being moved up. . . . It is estimated by George E. Anderson that all but $600,000,000 of RFC credit has been furnished to private interests which might in normal times have been taken care of by banks.

Many expected the government to leave these fields with the return to normalcy. Others anticipated a continued occupation of at least some of these fields.

The third thing which during the depression led to a limitation in the functions of the private banking system was the decrease in the type of banking asset upon which a sound banking system was supposed to be built. This decrease was noticeable even before the Wall Street collapse of 1929. In the old days, the commercial banks loaned largely to business enterprises for the purpose of helping them within a few months to complete a commercial transaction. An exporter would sell goods abroad. The money from these goods would be forthcoming within a few months. In the meanwhile the business had to incur certain definite expenses. The exporter went to his bank and secured short-term credit. When the transaction was completed, and the payment came in the normal course of business, the loan was repaid. The same thing occurred in the case of the manufacturer,

the wholesaler, the producer of raw material. During the post-war era,
with the increasing tendency of large corporations to raise their working
capital out of corporate surpluses, out of the sale of common stocks, or
through long-term security offerings, and with the development of chain
stores and large manufacturing plants with their national and international
markets, such financing was centralized increasingly in New York. This
permitted the New York banks

> to build up large corporate treasuries which were available for lending on
> call in the late days of the stock market boom, and took away from local
> banks the old-time supplies of commercial paper which provided them a liquid
> business. The Federal Reserve System was designed to rediscount these
> supplies of commercial paper, and their decline rendered the Reserve System
> largely impotent to control the use of credit through changes in the discount
> rates.

The depression likewise gave rise to a desire for a central control of
credit. The standing of private bankers in the community during those
days reached a new low.

These trends have led to the formation of numerous programs for the
reorganization of the banking system along more socially desirable lines.

One school of advanced thinkers urges the further mutualization of the
nation's banks. George Soule would have Congress instruct the Federal
Reserve Bank to buy the stock of every bank within its district which
accepts demand deposits or makes commercial loans. The value of the
stock could be estimated by assessing the market value of the bank's assets
and subtracting from them its liabilities. The owners of the national banks
could be compelled to sell by cancelling the charters of those who refused.
All state banks could be required to take out national charters.

The Federal Reserve Banks could be authorized under his plan to issue
in exchange for the stock of the solvent banks non-voting preferred stock
yielding, say, 5 per cent. Profits could be devoted to dividends on preferred stock and an amortization fund for its retirement. Any excess profits
could be devoted, first, to building up an ample surplus, and, following that,
to dividends to depositors. The result of the purchase would be 12 self-
owning commercial banking aggregates, with limited profits. Unnecessary
banks could be scrapped. The 12 Reserve Banks would, as at present,
receive most of the reserves of the local banks, rediscount commercial paper
and distribute currency.

As for the Federal Reserve Board, Soule believes that it would be desirable to substitute for it a single United States Bank, "which would centralize

the reserves of the Reserve Banks, act as a bank of issue and determine open-market policy."

This [declares Soule] would not be a "socialized" banking system. A really socialized system is impossible unless industry itself is socialized. But here is a mutualized system which could serve our present order as well as any system could be expected to serve it, and one which, if we ever create a planned society, would be capable of becoming an efficient unit of the society.

Another school urges as the next step in public control, the enlargement of the functions of the United States Postal Banks, with their 8,000 branches, their 1,500,000 depositors and their deposits of $1,200,000,000, the largest single institution of savings in the world. It has been urged that these banks permit checking accounts and deposits higher than the present limit. The deposits in the banks should be increasingly available for the purchase of government bonds. Prior to the depression, the deposits were redeposited in other banking institutions, the government obtaining 2½ per cent interest and the banks loaning this money to private or public enterprises at a good profit. During the depression, because of the low rates of interest, banks refused to take the deposits at the legal rate of 2½ per cent and the government invested large sums of money in government bonds. As a result the amount of postal funds for redeposit in banks of the Federal Reserve System decreased from $1,075,000,000 in June, 1933, to $400,000,000 in March, 1935. Many bankers fear that, when "prosperity returns" and government bond rates go up, postal savings investment in federal bonds will increase; the postal savings banks will be in a position to give higher interest on deposits and become stronger competitors. Other students of the banking system hail this trend, maintaining that there is no logical reason why the government should not utilize the funds in public savings banks in a manner most advantageous to it.

A third school would begin the enlargement of the public banking functions with the nationalization of the Federal Reserve System.

Mr. Morgenthau, Secretary of the Treasury, is quoted as saying in his testimony before the Senate Committee in the Spring of 1935:

I belong to the school which believes the government should own the stock of the Federal Reserve.

I would like to see Congress work out a plan where the government owned the stock and the trustees could be surrounded with every precaution so that they could be free from political or private influence. When it comes to the discount rate, that's a function of the government.

A similar proposal was made by Senator Frazier in 1933 (Senate Bill 806). Senator Frazier proposed that the United States organize and operate a national bank to be known as the Bank of the United States. This bank would abolish the Federal Reserve Board and transfer its powers and duties to the Board of Directors of the Bank of the United States.

The corporation, according to the bill, would start with a capital of $2,000,000,000. It would be the depository of all funds of the federal government, except gold coin, gold and silver bullion, and postal savings funds. It would be authorized to receive deposits from any bank or trust company in the United States. Such deposits would be guaranteed by the United States government.

The bank would be able to make loans to the United States government, to cities and states, to banks and trust companies, to the Federal Farm Loan Board and to other institutions. It would likewise have certain powers of stabilization.

The late Senator Cutting in 1934 introduced a similar bill, declaring that "the creation of a national bank which will eventually have a monopoly of the issuance of credit, is, to my mind, the most vital need of the country to-day."

Under the bills sponsored by Senator Frazier and the late Senator Cutting, the government would own and operate the central bank, as the Swedish government has for so many years owned and operated the Swedish Riksbank, but would leave the commercial banks of the country in private hands. It would do what it could to prevent wide fluctuations in the price level, and would lay down general rules upon which business, industry, farming and individuals had access to money and credit. To prevent manipulation by politicians or financiers, some advocates suggest that no person employed in the public service and no commercial banker be eligible for membership on the governing board of this central public bank. The central bank would thus be "a supreme banking authority, acting solely in the broad interests of the country, and subject . . . neither to private influence nor partisan politics."

H. C. Simons, Paul H. Douglas and other economists at the University of Chicago, likewise favor the nationalization of the Federal Reserve Banks on the ground that purchasing power should be created not by private bankers but by the government. The national government, Dr. Simons maintains, should take over the ownership of the Federal Reserve Banks through the purchase at par of their stocks. After this transfer, he contends, the Federal Reserve Banks should begin to buy up government bonds either from the banks or in the open market and issue in return federal reserve notes equal to the par value of the bonds.

By this means the government in effect "would be able to retire the whole government debt and to save the present interest payments of approximately one billion dollars a year."

Society has long since taken away from individuals [declares Professor Douglas] the right to profit individually by privately coining money. Why should it surrender to private individuals and corporations the similar right to levy toll upon the public by permitting them to create purchasing power in the form of credit? Should not the profits of this essentially public function accrue to society as a whole rather than to those who have placed themselves at the vantage place of industry?

As Carl Snyder has shown, production, if we take long periods of time, has increased at the rate of three per cent a year compounded. Now if the private bankers only increase the quantity of credit in the same proportion, they would gather to themselves a very large gain in wealth and power. This has most certainly been the case in the past. The volume of bank credit which has been built up from very small beginnings is now the property of the banking fraternity. By creating credit they have acquired a title to wealth and a claim upon the national income as real as if they had themselves built gigantic factories, railroads, utility plants, etc. Some idea of how much these sums amount to can be gained from the fact that if we were to take a credit total of thirty-three billion as our base, an increase of 3 per cent in this figure to match the increase in production would mean that, in the very first year, the private bankers would create one billion dollars in new credit. They would own this and would in fact increase their wealth by that much. As the total volume of credit rose, the absolute yearly additions would of course rise also. Thus, 3 per cent of 50 billion dollars would amount to 1.5 billion a year. A large part of the fruits of progress, therefore, tend to be transferred to the private bankers because their ability to create the monetary counters enables them to claim title to the goods. It is, of course, true that purchasing power is loaned out. But interest is charged for the loans and these go not only to independent business men but also frequently, as the revelations of the last ten years have shown, to persons and syndicates closely identified with or controlled by the bankers themselves.

This point of view was emphasized in 1935 by Congressman Goldsborough:

What an astounding situation it is for the government to borrow money from the banks that the banks do not have, and then, by redepositing the money, loan the same money back to the bank and pay them interest on it! The total capital surplus and undivided profits in all the banks of the United States is less than 7 billion dollars. The total amount of private loans borrowed from all banks is about 34 billion dollars or about 27 billion dollars more than the banks have to loan.

In addition to that, of those 26 billion dollars of government debt, the banks hold 13 billion dollars. You understand they have less than 7 billion dollars to loan. They have loans to private enterprise, 34 billion dollars or 27 billion dollars more than they have, and they are loaning the government 13 billion dollars on nothing in God's world but blue sky.

The treasury now has in its vaults or on deposits in private institutions amounting to 5,400,000,000 dollars, and that is doing nobody any good; and that might well be devoted to paying off government obligations.

The solution of the banking dilemma, Professor Douglas contends, lies in the development of several types of banks. There should be deposit banks. These should be institutions for safe-keeping and convenience. These banks should not be able to build up additional credits on their deposits. They should be required to keep 100 per cent reserve in cash and would in effect be "ware-houses of cash." They would obtain their income not from loans, but from charging a small sum to depositors for this safe-keeping of funds and from service charges made upon the transfer of funds by check. Under this system there would be no longer any danger of bank runs or bank failures. For behind every deposit there would be an equal amount of cash. "Deposit banking would, therefore, be absolutely safe and the age-old defect of a fractional reserve in the banking system would be removed."

As for long-term loans, they could be made by individual investors or by investment trusts. Short-term loans could be made in a similar fashion. Or deposit banks could make such loans up to the extent of their real capital and surplus. "Thus existing banks could buy bonds with these assets, present them to the Reserve Banks and obtain cash in return which would be theirs and which they could lend out. But they could not obtain credit in addition to this."

This arrangement, claims Douglas, would permit society to control the entire amount of circulating medium and would prevent the creation of commercial credit to finance investment. "Since banks could no longer create credit, all investment would have to come from savings, and while decreases in the amount of credit would still tend to cause trouble, the disturbances would be far less than those which now occur."

Moreover, if the investment trusts refused to make loans, and held their savings idle in their vaults, the government bank might come into the picture and make loans to industry. As a general rule, however, they should keep their hands off of direct loans, though they could make such loans to the government. This plan, according to Professor Douglas, would "insure the safety of deposits, give large revenues to the government, provide complete social control over monetary matters and prevent abnormal fluctuations in the capital market."

Other students of the subject would have the nation take charge not only of the country's central bank and a large part of the savings banking business, but the commercial banking business as well. They would not only convert the Federal Reserve Board into a United States Banking Corporation, as suggested in the Frazier Bill, and operate the present twelve Banks as corporations subsidiary to the central governing board, but they would empower each Federal Reserve Bank to take over directly the capital stock of all the banks within its territory, or all of the banking facilities and instrumentalities without the capital stock. "This," according to Messrs. Bauer and Gold, "would furnish immediately a countrywide system, with general control of policy lodged in the Federal Reserve Board, and with each Federal Reserve Bank responsible for the activities within its district."

After nationalization, the banks of the various districts could be consolidated and unified, eliminating the hosts of unnecessary and duplicating banking units. A policy of this sort "would furnish suitable banking provisions wherever needed, but would eliminate all unnecessary units and facilities."

> Such consolidation [Bauer and Gold maintain] would not only establish credit control in harmony with national monetary and economic policies, but would increase enormously the economy of banking operations. In communities where there are, or have been, half a dozen banks, there would be only one, but there would be the one, and it would have the entire government back of it in meeting the community needs. There would be full monopoly; no competition, duplication or overlapping. While there might possibly be loss of efficiency in personnel, there would be tremendous reduction in the number of officials and high salaries, especially in overheads connected with existing duplications and elaborateness. Each community would be assured of adequate banking means, but would be saved from the heavy costs imposed by the present system.

The banks "would be devoted exclusively to the supplying of current purchasing power according to community needs and convenience, with continued regard to the maintenance of productive and financial stability with advancing technology."

In connection with the establishment of the Bank of the United States, these authors would create a Public Improvements Corporation and a Bureau of Fiscal Control, owned likewise by the government. The board of each organization would be appointed by the President. Each member of each of the Boards would be "a person of highest standing in his profession or business," in full agreement with the purpose of the act, "and free from partisan and financial associations which may interfere with the fullest devotion to the public purpose . . . established" in the bill. "He shall not have been prominent in the affairs of any political party, nor contributed beyond nominal sums to the support of such party." Comprehensive personnel policies shall be established in the various organizations. The Board of Public Improvement shall have as its object the carrying out of comprehensive programs of public works to the end that unemployment shall be eliminated. The Board of Fiscal Control for its part "shall assemble, analyze, and make available all statistics and information needed by the related Boards and the Joint Board in carrying out the functions imposed on them. . . ."

Many are arguing that this start in banking should be but a beginning of governmental incursions into the important field of banking and credit. Banking, they declare, is so vital to the welfare of the nation, that it should not be run for private profit. A. A. Berle, Jr., declared a while ago

> that the aggregate credit of the community which is occasioned by your deposit and mine and the merchant's around the corner and every one's in a commercial bank, is the added resource of the entire community; that it belongs to the community and that managing this resource is not a matter of private property. . . . Only as it is run with an eye to public interest rather than with an eye to private profit can a banking system ultimately be safe.

Thus it is becoming increasingly evident that the present disorganized, chaotic banking system, with its quest for maximum profits for each of its thousands of separate units, is incapable adequately of serving the community. It is becoming ever more patent that the important function of creating purchasing power is a public, not a private function. A socialized banking system is the final goal of any sound banking program. As George Soule points out, socialized banking is impossible in a non-socialized industrial society. But a start toward such a system by a program of nationalized, cooperative and mutualized banking institutions can and should be made without delay.

No. 99

PROTECTING INVESTORS IN SECURITIES [1]

by Theodore W. Glocker

MANY million dollars are lost each year by investors in American securities. The Senate Committee on Currency and Banking estimated in 1933 that the loss from security investment in the United States had been twenty-five billion dollars during the previous ten years. Legislation protecting investors has been enacted in recent years by practically all states and by the Federal Government. The extent of this legislation and its effectiveness in removing the causes for losses of investors will be discussed.

Among the reasons for losses from security investment may be mentioned: (1) fraudulent practices by dishonest promoters, (2) bad faith on the part of accredited investment bankers, (3) manipulation of prices of securities by brokers and speculators, (4) betrayal of security holders by officers and directors of corporations, (5) wide fluctuation in economic conditions, and (6) ignorance and greed of investors.

The responsibility of governments to protect their citizens against fraud is generally recognized. The principle of *caveat emptor* is not applicable to investments. When buying food or clothes, the customer has a chance to learn by trial and error. In the case of investments, however, there may be error but no chance for another trial after one's money is lost.

The need for protection against purveyors of worthless securities is evident when one becomes familiar with their highly efficient methods. "Sucker lists" are carefully prepared and sold to dealers engaged in this business. School teachers, physicians, dentists, and clergymen are favorite victims. Whenever farmers in some section of the country have a good crop, impressive looking, high pressure salesmen descend on them from neighboring cities to gather part of their surplus cash. These salesmen study and take advantage of the weaknesses of prospective customers. They appeal to gambling proclivities and to the natural desire to get something for nothing. They stimulate the greed of prospects by glowing descriptions of large profits made in other enterprises, and flatter their vanity by telling them that they have been selected for solicitation because of their superior

[1] Theodore W. Glocker, "Protecting Investors in Securities," *The Annals* of the American Academy of Political and Social Science (November, 1939), Vol. 206, pp. 68-74. Reprinted by permission of *The Annals* of the American Academy of Political and Social Science.

intelligence. Hasty and ill-considered decisions to buy are encouraged by statements that only a few shares are left or that the price of the stock will rise in a few days.

The victim of these schemes has the right to sue in civil court to recover losses suffered through misrepresentation. One great difficulty is to prove intent to defraud. An oil promoter may actually own a tract of land near an oil field. He may have started drilling, and possibly there may be oil on his land. On one occasion a promoter who thought he had sold worthless securities repurchased them in a hurry at a higher price, because, overnight, his oil well became a gusher. Another difficulty is to discover the whereabouts of the swindler, who flits quickly from place to place and has probably departed for parts unknown before the victim discovers his loss.

Kansas was the first state to pass, in 1911, legislation designed to regulate the sale of fraudulent and low-grade securities, and has been followed by practically all other states. The phrase "blue-sky laws" has been applied to this type of laws to indicate that they have been enacted to regulate securities worth no more than a section of bright blue sky.

The states vary widely in their blue-sky laws. They may be roughly classified in three groups. In the first group are such states as New York, New Jersey, and Maryland, whose antifraud laws empower the attorney-general in case of fraud to enjoin the sale of the securities and to prosecute guilty persons in criminal courts. Many injunctions stopping the sale of securities have been obtained by vigilant attorney-generals. However, there have been very few criminal convictions, and many fly-by-night dishonest dealers escape to other jurisdictions. Fear of conviction may cause restitution of part of the funds taken from defrauded customers, but much of the lost money is never recovered.

In the second group are those states which have created commissions to grant licenses to dealers. An applicant for a license must submit a personal history and this is checked in suspicious cases. The main purpose of the law is to permit only honest dealers to do business. However, indirectly it provides a check on the quality of new securities, since the commission must keep in touch with the transactions of dealers, may require information, as under the Pennsylvania law, concerning each of the issues sold by the dealer, and, if it finds intent to deceive or defraud, may stop the sale. The dealer's license may also be revoked, and he is subject to fine and imprisonment.

A third group of states require, sometimes in addition to registration of dealers, approval of the sale of securities by state officials. Certain types of securities are exempt, but detailed information is required regarding other types, and approval of their sale may be withheld if there is evidence of misrepresentation, or if the sale will work a fraud upon the purchaser.

Prevention of fraud is the primary purpose of laws licensing dealers and requiring approval of the sales of securities by state commissions, and in this respect such laws are preferable to antifraud laws which attempt to punish the guilty and to reimburse the victim after loss has occurred. Nevertheless, such laws impose burdensome restrictions on legitimate dealers, whereas many dishonest ones do not apply for licenses or inform state commissions concerning securities which they are selling. However, failure of dishonest dealers to conform to the law may attract the attention of the authorities and thus lead to detection of their fraudulent activities.

There are serious defects in the administration of the blue-sky laws of the various states. First, effectiveness of their enforcement has sometimes been lowered by the poor quality of politically appointed administrative officers and by political pressure on their policies. The most serious defect of state legislation has been its limitation to intrastate transactions. Dishonest dealers may do no business in the state where they are located, but sell securities in other states by mail, telegraph, telephone, and newspaper advertisements. Some states are helping others by amending their legislation so that it covers not only sales of securities to persons within the state but also sales to persons outside the state.

The Federal law forbidding use of the mail to defraud has supplemented state legislation and has greatly strengthened government control over fraudulent transactions in securities. Federal officers have been alert to detect the use of the mail by dishonest dealers in securities, and have been able to follow their trail from state to state. "Stop orders" preventing use of the mail may be issued by the Postmaster-General, and cases may be prosecuted in criminal courts. Jurisdiction of the Federal Government has been extended by the Federal Securities Act of 1933, which makes illegal all fraudulent interstate transactions, involving use of mail, telegraph, telephone, radio, express, or other means of communication or transportation. The Securities Act was passed primarily to require accredited investment bankers to provide complete and accurate information to their customers. However, in administering the law, the Securities and Exchange Commission discovers and aids in the punishment of many cases of fraud.

Many who favor government elimination of fraudulent promoters oppose government regulation of accredited dealers. Prior to the World War there was not a great need for regulation of reputable investment bankers. Some dealers claimed that they assumed the attitude of a trustee in their relations with their customers and endeavored to map out a program of investment suitable to the latter's needs. The American Investment Bankers Association adopted ethical rules of conduct for members, and at its annual meetings responsibility of the dealer in securities for the welfare of customers was repeatedly emphasized. Members of leading, long-established firms took pride in the reputation of their organizations for conservatism and integrity.

Between 1922 and 1929 the attitude of dealers changed, and frequently little or no consideration was given to the welfare of the customer. As a rule, accredited investment bankers do not indulge in direct misstatements, but during this period unfavorable factors were often omitted in bond circulars, and figures in balance sheets and profit-and-loss statements were juggled to give a favorable impression. Sales commissions of dealers were sometimes too high for the less conservative types of securities, and stocks and bonds were sold for more than they were worth. Highly speculative securities were also sold to customers whose small capital did not permit sufficient diversification to justify the risk involved.

There were several reasons for the change in the attitude of bankers. First, their close personal relationship with customers was lost as a result of the great increase and the change in the type of persons purchasing securities. The campaigns to sell Liberty Bonds during the war popularized the idea of buying bonds, and the rich capitalists and the large financial institutions that were the chief customers during the pre-war period were submerged in a mass of ignorant and avaricious purchasers who wanted safety and 12 per cent.

A second reason was optimism. At a time when even bankers believed that a long era of prosperity lay ahead, the distinction between conservatism and speculation could not easily be maintained.

A third reason was the inexperience of commercial bankers, stock brokers, and many others who entered the business at that time. Moreover, even the old-time bankers were not well acquainted with foreign bonds and common stocks, types of securities which they began to sell in large quantities during that period.

A fourth reason was the dominance of avarice and the lowering of moral standards which takes place so often in a period of great prosperity.

Finally, a very important reason was the need for keeping busy the vast machinery for marketing securities. The large distributing houses had established branches or outlets in many communities. An efficient machine had been created capable of disposing of an issue of securities worth fifty or one hundred million dollars in a few hours after opening of the public sale. There were not enough good bonds to keep busy the small army of salesmen in the various cities, and bankers had recourse to low-grade securities in order that the machine might be kept working.

Investors have secured protection through legislation designed for other purposes. State regulation of finances of insurance companies is designed to aid policyholders, and state and Federal regulation of commercial banks is intended to protect depositors. However, stockholders benefit if such legislation strengthens the financial soundness of these institutions. As a part of the process of securing cheap rates for consumers, the Interstate Commerce Commission is given power to disapprove new issues of railway securities, and many state public utility commissions exercise similar control over the finances of local operating utilities. An unsound financial structure means, as a rule, high rates, because if a company is over-bonded or over-capitalized, its security holders may be able to prevent rates from being lowered by contending that such action would endanger payment of dividends and interest and might cause bankruptcy. The sounder financial structure of railways and utilities resulting from such regulation should make their securities safer investments.

The Federal Public Utility Holding Company Act was passed in 1935, partly to help the investor, but in large part to strengthen the power of state commissions to regulate rates. The large holding companies secured funds to purchase control over new local subsidiaries by siphoning the earnings of old ones, forcing them to make upstream loans and to pay unearned dividends and exorbitant fees for technical advice to the parent companies. Accounts were juggled to hide the extent of these transactions. The state commissions had no control over these large interstate holding companies, yet were prevented by them from lowering rates for service because of the artificial decrease in the earnings of subsidiaries. To remedy this situation the Federal Public Utility Holding Company Act gave the Securities and Exchange Commission drastic power to simplify the capitalization and regulate the finances of these holding companies, and to control relations between parent companies and their subsidiaries. The low price of utility holding company securities following 1935 has been attributed to the act. However, if administered in moderation, the law should ultimately help investors by forcing adoption of conservative financial policies and reducing the risk of bankruptcy.

States, counties, and cities should protect purchasers of their bonds from unwise financial policies of their legislative bodies and executive officers. Following periods of default and repudiation of state bonds during the last century, constitutional limitations were placed on state debt. These restrictions have sometimes been irksome, particularly during recent years, when such restrictions have prevented some states from borrowing funds to match grants of the Federal Government for unemployment relief. Nevertheless, with a few exceptions, state bonds have enjoyed a high credit rating during the past fifty years, including even the period of the recent depression, and for this situation these constitutional limitations may be partly responsible.

Supervision of borrowing policies of most local governments seems to be badly needed. The bonds of more than two thousand local governments were in default during the depression following 1929. Many statutory limitations have been imposed on local indebtedness and have been circumvented by local governments, sometimes with the connivance of state legislatures. Some states are creating state or local boards to supervise the borrowing and other financial policies of counties and cities, and such supervision should greatly improve the quality of the bonds of local governments.

In addition to the above-discussed legislation indirectly affecting certain nonfraudulent stocks and bonds, some state commissions administering blue-sky laws have attempted to check the purchase of nonfraudulent highly speculative securities on the ground that such sales would "work a fraud" to investors. However, until the passage of the Federal Securities Act in 1933, laws regulating the sale of securities were usually intended primarily to prevent fraud.

While certain provisions of the Securities Act are designed to strengthen the power of state and Federal officials to control fraud, its primary purpose is to prevent certain unfair practices in the sale of nonfraudulent stocks and bonds. Investment bankers are said frequently to omit or twist unfavorable facts in their advertisements of new securities so as to give a favorable impression. To prevent this practice, security dealers are made civilly liable to investors for misrepresentations and omissions, and the Securities and Exchange Commission withholds its approval of the sale of a new issue until satisfied that prospective customers will be given full and correct information. The Commission makes no attempt to decide concerning the soundness of securities sold to the public. Rather it seeks to secure pertinent, accurate, and complete facts which investors can use in making their own decisions.

With the exception of the stocks and bonds of local operating utilities, the Federal Act of 1933 applies to securities not regulated by other government agencies. Thus, it regulates only interstate transactions, and exempts the securities of railroads, banks, insurance companies, and domestic governments. Sales aggregating less than $100,000 are also not covered by the law.

There has been much criticism of the Federal Securities Act. Bankers claim that the provision imposing civil liability for unintentional misrepresentations and omissions is unduly harsh. However, the law cannot be considered very unjust, since it is merely transferring a loss from the investor to the banker whose carelessness caused it. The act should induce investment bankers to specialize in a single field of business, to become thoroughly familiar with that field, and to make painstaking investigations of corporations whose securities they offer to the public. With this increase in knowledge, bankers originating new issues should tend to become more conservative, and therefore security investment should become safer.

Fear of liability on the part of dealers and the high cost of securing the required information are said to have been the causes of the decline in public sale of new securities since the passage of the act. However, this decrease may be also explained by the stagnation of the capital-goods industries.

The extent to which the investing public will use the information obtained by the Securities and Exchange Commission may be questioned. Very few persons have the knowledge or the patience to analyze the mass of facts and figures contained in the registration statement. This information is digested in the prospectus used by the dealers in advertising the securities, but the law has increased the length of this prospectus, and in so doing may discourage the reading of it by investors. However, the long registration statements are studied by financial reporters, investment counselors, and other experts, and their opinion should exercise some influence on a considerable group of investors.

The Securities Act and similar government regulations tend to eliminate desirable as well as undesirable promotions. One wonders whether certain flourishing industries would exist to-day if present laws had been in effect at the time of their origin. Since a promoter does not usually possess definite information about cost of production, probable demand, and other facts concerning a new venture, he must sell its securities largely on the basis of optimistic generalizations, rosy-tinted by his hopes and desires. If, because of the Securities Act, his promises must be neutral in tone and his statements limited to cold facts and figures, the chances of selling such securities are quite slim. In the future, highly speculative enterprises may have to be financed to a considerable degree by private subscription, and new commodities and services may have to be developed largely by existing corporations. At any rate, slower progress may be the price which society must pay for conservatism and greater security.

After securities have been sold to an investor he continues to need protection, and to provide this protection, the Securities Exchange Act was passed in 1934. One purpose of the act is to vest power in the Securities and Exchange Commission to correct unfair practices on security markets. "Washed sales," "matched orders," or any other series of transactions likely to raise, lower, or stabilize prices are made illegal. No one is permitted to acquire a substantial control of the floating supply of any security so as to affect its price, and "pools" may not be organized for the purpose of manipulation. Dealers, brokers, and their employees must refrain from misleading statements and from dissemination of information intended to affect security markets. Persons injured by such price manipulations may sue for damages, and for violation of the act, brokers must be suspended from operating on stock exchanges.

A second purpose of the law is to require corporations whose securities are listed on exchanges to supply full information at frequent intervals regarding their operation and finances.

A third purpose is to check misuse of credit by operators on security exchanges. To achieve this last purpose, the Federal Reserve Board is authorized to fix the margin of cash required for loans having securities as collateral, and is given control over agencies extending such credit.

Investors should be protected from the exploitation of corporations by their officers and directors. These officials may manipulate statements of earnings and withhold important information in order to make a profit from the purchase and sale of the securities of a corporation. They may vote themselves high salaries and bonuses, sell property to the corporation at inflated values, make contracts for their company favoring other corporations in which they are interested, or fail to liquidate hopelessly unprofitable businesses through their reluctance to relinquish good salaries.

The Securities and Exchange Act attempts to control speculation by officers and directors in the shares of their own company. If the stocks and bonds of a corporation are listed on an exchange, its officials must state, monthly, the amount of its securities which they own. They cannot sell short the stock of their company, and must turn into its treasury all profits obtained by the selling of such securities within six months after their purchase.

One cause of the exploitation of corporations is the lack of control over directors by stockholders. Yet, how can twenty-five million stockholders, comprising three or four million separate individuals, exercise any real control over their respective companies? Some corporations are requesting their stockholders to vote yes or no on propositions presented in proxy statements. However, many fail to vote, and few possess sufficient detailed knowledge of the corporation to render intelligent decisions.

Another cause of these evils is ownership of an insufficient amount of the securities of a corporation by its directors. The suggestion has been made that each director of a corporation should own a minimum amount of its common stock. Some object to this regulation on the ground that it would cause many able men to refuse to serve as directors. However, such men could serve, perhaps, in an advisory capacity, and voting power could be vested in salaried directors owning a considerable number of shares of stock in the corporation. Serious consideration must be given by our business leaders to methods of correcting the weaknesses of corporate administration. Otherwise, Federal regulation of corporate affairs, with all the objectionable features of government supervision, may be inevitable.

The most efficient forms of legislation can replace only in a very small degree the exercise of good judgment by investors, and three factors make the exercise of such good judgment rather infrequent. First, successful practice of the art of investment is difficult, and many investors know as little about it as a child of six years does about original sin. Secondly, the desire to take a chance is strong in most of us. Thirdly, the avarice of investors militates against exercise of good judgment. We may laugh at the ignorance of the widow who asks for securities which are absolutely safe and yield 10 per cent. Yet, during the period of economic optimism from 1922 to 1929 we sought the same impossible combination, allowing the prospect of a high yield to blind us to the risk involved.

Education of the investor is recommended by most writers on this subject. However, educating the investor is a big job, which must be performed continuously, and at present there exists no agency whose primary function is education of the investing public. The Securities and Exchange Commission could perform a fine service by creating a department to do such educational work. The mass of information which is available in the reference rooms of the Commission for the use of financial experts could be digested and presented in diluted form to investors and an effort made to instill in the minds of the people correct points of view regarding investments.

Chapter XXVIII

GOVERNMENT AND BUSINESS ENTERPRISE

[THE transformation of American economy from one based on the Jeffersonian ideal of sturdy independent yeomen to one founded on a mass production industrial system has profoundly affected the economic activities of government. Although as yet we have formulated no general rationale of these activities, it cannot be denied that the economic relationships of government have been rapidly increasing in scope and intensity over the past seventy-five years. This trend has been little affected by changes in political administration. Both Republican and Democratic Presidents and Congresses have advocated and adopted new regulations of business activity or expanded the scope of already existing controls.

We are to-day, then, living in a society in which almost all of our economic activities come under a greater or lesser degree of control by government. To a few, the immediate need is the formulation of a logical and consistent program of action that will encompass the whole gamut of political-economic relationships. Some are of the opinion that the solution to the problem lies in well-administered and democratically controlled regulatory legislation. This is, in the main, the policy we have followed. Others are of the opinion that there is a fundamental conflict between the basic tenets of a political democracy and a privately owned economy; that political and economic power will coalesce either in a democratic or an undemocratic manner.

For the past three-quarters of a century or more our legislation has been based on the assumption that political society could control privately owned economic activity. The local and state governments early entered into the field of regulation of business, and since the latter part of the nineteenth century there has been an ever-widening sphere of federal regulation. To comprehend fully its significance and its objectives the student must be acquainted with the social, economic, and political pressures which occasioned these regulations. Government in a democratic society is and should be responsive to public pressure, and this is of course true in the field of government regulation of business. We must, furthermore, consider whether or not, in any given field of action, such pressures have evoked the proper legislative solution. Has the development of our anti-trust legislation, for example, been based on the realistic factors of our changing economy, as it must be based in order to be effective?

The problems of governmental regulation of business in the United States are more difficult to solve because of our federal system of government. Even though we can agree on basic policies to be followed, it is difficult to secure uniform action in that sphere reserved to the several states. As is illustrated by Mr. Flynn's article, if a few states are lax in their laws governing corporations all states feel the consequences, political and economic, of this laxity.]

No. 100

THE MYTH OF RUGGED AMERICAN INDIVIDUALISM [1]

by Charles A. Beard

"THE House of Bishops would be as much at sea in Minneapolis as at Atlantic City." This bit of delicious humor, all too rare in America's solemn assemblies, sparkled at a tense moment in the late conference of the Episcopalian magnates at Denver when the respective merits of the two cities as future meeting places were under debate. But the real cause of the caustic comment seems to have been a heated discussion, led by the Honorable George W. Wickersham, over a dangerous proposal to modify, not the Volstead act, but the sacred creed of rugged American individualism.

That contest had been precipitated by the report of a special commission in which occurred these highly inflammatory words:

It is becoming increasingly evident that the conception of society as made up of autonomous, independent individuals is as faulty from the point of view of economic realism as it is from the standpoint of Christian idealism. Our fundamental philosophy of rugged individualism must be modified to meet the needs of a cooperative age.

This frightful conclusion flowed from a fact statement which the commission summarized in the following language:

Side by side with such misery and idleness, there are warehouses bursting with goods which cannot be bought; elevators full of wheat while bread lines haunt our cities; carefully protected machinery lying idle, while jobless men throng our streets; money in the banks available at low rates.

These shocking passages Mr. Wickersham read to the assembled delegates with considerable indignation, and denied their truth. Then he added an

[1] Charles A. Beard, "The Myth of Rugged American Individualism," *Harper's Magazine* (December, 1931), Vol. 164, pp. 13-22. Reprinted by permission of the author and *Harper's Magazine*.

illuminating exposition all his own: "I think this is an expression of a social philosophy that is expressed by the Soviet Government of Russia. It is a negation of the whole concept of American civilization. I think it would be a sad day when the American people abandon the principles on which they have grown to greatness." Coming to specifications, he particularly attacked a point in the report, that "compulsory unemployment insurance is feasible." Realizing that Mr. Wickersham was a specialist in individualism, since he was the chief author of a collective report from which each individual signer apparently dissented, the congregated deputies at Denver voted down the proposal that the commission's statement should be taken as "representing the mind of the Church," and substituted a mere pious recommendation that it should be given "careful consideration" by members of the Church. Such, at least, is the story reported in the press.

This is only one of many straws in the wind indicating a movement to exalt rugged individualism into a national taboo beyond the reach of inquiring minds. From day to day it becomes increasingly evident that some of our economic leaders (by no means all of them) are using the phrase as an excuse for avoiding responsibility, for laying the present depression on "Government interference," and for seeking to escape from certain forms of taxation and regulation which they do not find to their interest. If a smoke screen big enough can be laid on the land, our commercial prestidigitators may work wonders—for themselves.

Still more direct evidence confirms this view. For example, in the autumn of 1930, a New York bank published, as a kind of revelation from on high, a slashing attack on "Government interference with business," written by that stanch English Whig, Macaulay, a hundred years ago; and a few weeks later one of the leading advertising firms took a whole page in the *New York Times* to blazon forth the creed anew under the captivating head: "Cheer Up! Our Best Times Are Still Ahead of Us!" And the whole gospel was summed up in these words from Macaulay: "Our rulers will best promote the improvement of the people by strictly confining themselves to their own legitimate duties—by leaving capital to find its most lucrative course, commodities their fair price, industry and intelligence their natural reward, idleness and folly their natural punishment—by maintaining peace, by defending property, by diminishing the price of law, and by observing strict economy in every department of the State. Let the Government do this—the people will assuredly do the rest." In other words, here was put forth in the name of American business, with all the pontifical assurance that characterized Macaulay's shallowest sophistry, the pure creed of historic individualism, and here was served on the Government and people of the United States a warning revelation of confident expectations.

A year later, in a release to the press, Mr. Otto Kahn discussed the subject of planning and intimated that the fortunate position of France to-day is to be ascribed to the fact that the French Government interferes less with business than does the Government of Germany or Great Britain, with the implication that the United States might profit from this experience. About the same time the Honorable Newton D. Baker made a long address at Williamstown which was evidently designed to show that nothing important could be done in the present crisis by the Federal Government, except perhaps in the way of tariff reduction by international agreement. And now comes from Chicago the announcement that a number of rugged business men are forming a national association to combat Government in business, to break up this unholy alliance. There is not a professional lunching-and-dining fellowship in America that is not now applauding to the echo such ringing cries as "Let Us Alone," "Take Government Out of Business," "Hands Off," "Unburden Capital." With an eye on such straws in the wind, President Hoover publicly states that all notions about planned economy come out of Russia, thus placing such distinguished men as Gerard Swope and Owen D. Young under the horrible Red ban. As one of the high-powered utility propagandists recently explained, the best way to discredit an opponent is to pin a Red tag on him—without reference to his deserts, of course.

Hence it is important to ask, calmly and without reference to election heats, just what all this means. In what way is the Government "in business" and how did it get there? Here we climb down out of the muggy atmosphere of controversy and face a few stubborn facts. They are entered in the indubitable records of the Government of the United States and are as evident as the hills to them that have eyes to see. Let us catalogue a few of them *seriatim* for the first time in the history of this adventure in logomachy.

1. *Government Regulation of Railways, from 1887 to the last Act of Congress.* How did the Government get into this business? The general cause was the conduct of railway corporations under the rule of rugged individualism—rebates, pools, stock watering, bankruptcy-juggling, all the traffic will bear, savage rate slashing, merciless competition, and the rest of it. If anyone wants to know the facts, let him read the history of railroading in the sixties, seventies, and early eighties, or, if time is limited, the charming illustrations presented in Charles Francis Adams' "A Chapter of Erie." And what was the immediate cause of the Government's intervention? The insistence of business men, that is, shippers, who were harassed and sometimes ruined by railway tactics, and of farmers, the most rugged of all the rugged individualists the broad land of America has pro-

duced. And the result? Let the gentle reader compare the disastrous railway bankruptcies that flowed from the panic of 1873, including bloodshed and arson, with the plight of railways now, bad as it is. Government regulation is not a utopian success, but it is doubtful whether any of our great business men would like to get the Government entirely out of this business and return to the magnificent anarchy of Jay Gould's age. . . .

2. *Waterways*. Since its foundation the Government has poured hundreds of millions into rivers, harbors, canals, and other internal improvements. It is still pouring in millions. Some of our best economists have denounced it as wasteful and have demonstrated that most of it does not pay in any sense of the word. But President Hoover, instead of leaving this work to private enterprise, insists on projecting and executing the most elaborate undertakings, in spite of the fact that some of them are unfair if not ruinous to railways. Who is back of all this? Business men and farmers who want lower freight rates. There is not a chamber of commerce on any Buck Creek in America that will not cheer until tonsils are cracked any proposal to make the said creek navigable. Dredging companies want the good work to go on, and so do the concerns that make dredging machinery. Farmers are for it also and they are, as already said, the ruggedest of rugged individuals—so rugged in fact that the vigorous efforts of the Farm Board to instill cooperative reason into them have been almost as water on a duck's back.

3. *The United States Barge Corporation.* Who got the Government into the job of running barges on some of its improved waterways? Certainly not the Socialists, but good Republicans and Democrats speaking for the gentlemen listed under 2 above.

4. *The Shipping Business*. The World War was the occasion, but not the cause of this departure. For more than half a century the politicians of America fought ship subsidies against business men engaged in the shipbuilding and allied industries. At last, under the cover of war necessities, the Government went into the shipping business, with cheers from business. Who is back of the huge expenditures for the merchant marine? Business men. Who supports huge subsidies under the guise of "lucrative mail contracts," making a deficit in postal finances to be used as proof that the Government cannot run any business? Business men clamor for these mail subsidies and receive them. Who put the Government into the business of providing cheap money for ship-building? Business men did it. Those who are curious to know how these things were done may profitably read the sworn testimony presented during the investigation of W. B. Shearer's patriotic labors on behalf of the ship-building interests, especially the exhibits showing how money was spent like water "educating" politicians.

Who wants navy officers on half pay to serve on privately owned ships? Business men. Who wants the Government to keep on operating ships on "pioneer" lines that do not pay? Business men. And when the United States Senate gets around to investigating this branch of business, it will find more entertainment than the Trade Commission has found in the utility inquest.

5. *Aviation.* The Government is "in" this business. It provides costly airway services free of charge and subsidizes air mail. Who is behind this form of Government enterprise? Gentlemen engaged in aviation and the manufacture of planes and dirigibles. Then the Government helps by buying planes for national defense. Who is opposed to air mail subsidies? A few despised "politicians."

6. *Canals.* Who zealously supported the construction of the Panama Canal? Shippers on the Pacific Coast who did not like the railway rates. Also certain important shipping interests on both coasts—all controlled by business men. Who insisted that the Government should buy the Cape Cod Canal? The business men who put their money into the enterprise and found that it did not pay. Then they rejoiced to see the burden placed on the broad back of our dear Uncle Sam.

7. *Highway Building.* Who has supported Federal highway aid—the expenditures of hundreds of millions on roads, involving the taxation of railways to pay for ruinous competition? Everybody apparently, but specifically business men engaged in the manufacture and sale of automobiles and trucks. Who proposes to cut off every cent of that outlay? Echoes do not answer.

8. *The Department of Commerce, its magnificent mansion near the Treasury Department, and its army of hustlers scouting for business at the uttermost ends of the earth.* Who is responsible for loading on the Government the job of big drummer at large for business? Why shouldn't these rugged individualists do their own drumming instead of asking the taxpayers to do it for them? Business men have been behind this enormous expansion, and Mr. Hoover, as Secretary of Commerce, outdid every predecessor in the range of his activities and the expenditure of public money. Who proposes to take the Government out of the business of hunting business for men who ought to know their own business?

9. *The Big Pork Barrel—appropriations for public buildings, navy yards, and army posts.* An interesting enterprise for the United States Chamber of Commerce would be to discover a single piece of pork in a hundred years that has not been approved by local business men as beneficiaries. When Ben Tillman shouted in the Senate that he intended to steal a hog every time a Yankee got a ham, he knew for whom the speaking was done.

10. *The Bureau of Standards.* Besides its general services, it renders valuable aid to business undertakings. Why shouldn't they do their own investigating at their own expense, instead of turning to the Government?

11. *The Federal Trade Commission.* Who runs there for rulings on "fair practices"? Weary consumers? Not often. Principally, business men who do not like to be outwitted or cheated by their competitors. If we are rugged individualists, why not let every individualist do as he pleases, without invoking Government intervention at public expense?

12. *The Anti-Trust Acts.* Business men are complaining against these laws on the ground that they cannot do any large-scale planning without incurring the risk of prosecution. The contention is sound, but who put these laws on the books and on what theory were they based? They were the product of a clamor on the part of farmers and business men against the practices of great corporations. Farmers wanted lower prices. Business men of the smaller variety objected to being undersold, beaten by clever tricks, or crushed to the wall by competitors with immense capital. And what was the philosophy behind the Sherman Act and the Clayton Act? Individualism, pure and undefiled. "The New Freedom" as President Wilson phrased it in literary language. "Break up the trusts and let each tub stand on its own bottom." That was the cry among little business men. As lawyers put it in their somber way, "the natural person's liberty should not be destroyed by artificial persons known as corporations created under the auspices of the State." Whether any particular business man is for or against the anti-trust laws depends upon his particular business and the state of its earnings.

13. *The Tariff.* On this tender subject it is scarcely possible to speak soberly. It seems safe to say, however, that if all the business men who demand this kind of "interference"—with the right of capital to find its most lucrative course, industry and intelligence their natural reward, commodities their fair price, and idleness and folly their natural punishment— were to withdraw their support for protection, cease their insistence on it, then the politicians would probably reduce the levy or go over to free trade; with what effect on business no one can correctly predict. At all events there are thousands of business men who want to keep the Government in the business of protecting their business against foreign competition. If competition is good, why not stand up and take it?

14. *The Federal Farm Board.* This collectivist institution is the product of agrarian agitation, on the part of our most stalwart individualists, the free and independent farmers; but President Hoover sponsored it and signed the bill that created it. Now what is its avowed purpose as demonstrated by the language of the statute, the publications of the Farm Board, and

the activities carried out under its auspices? It is primarily and fundamentally intended to stabilize prices and production through cooperative
methods. And what has the Board done? It has encouraged the development of cooperation as distinguished from individualism among farmers;
it has financed cooperative associations; it has denounced individualistic
farmers who insist on growing as much as they please, and has tried to get
them to increase their earnings by a common limitation of production. If
the Agricultural Marketing Act means anything, if the procedure of the
Farm Board is not a delusion, then cooperation is to be substituted for
individualism in agricultural production and marketing. If there is ever
to be a rational adjustment of supply to demand in this field, the spirit
and letter of President Hoover's measure must be realized through organized
action by millions of farmers under Federal auspices. The other alternative
is simon-pure individualism: let each farmer produce what he likes, as
much of it as he likes, and sell it at any price he can get. But under the
happy title "Grow Less—Get More," the Farm Board has given instructions to farmers: "One thing the successful manufacturers learned long ago
was that they could not make money when they produced more than they
could sell at a profit." The obvious moral is for farmers to get together
under Government leadership or hang separately.

15. *The Moratorium and Frozen Assets.* The latest form of Government
interferences with "the natural course" of economy is the suspension of
payments due the United States from foreign powers on account of lawful
debts and the proposal to give public support to "frozen assets." What was
the source of inspiration here? American investment bankers having got
themselves into a jam in their efforts to make easy money now demand
Government assistance. In 1927 one of the most distinguished German
economists told the writer of this article that the great game in his country,
as in other parts of Europe, was to borrow billions from private bankers in
the United States, so that it would ultimately be impossible to pay reparations, the debts due the Federal Government, *and* then the debts owed to
private parties. The expected result? American bankers would then force
their Government to forego its claims for the benefit of private operators
who wanted to make bankers' commissions and eight or ten per cent on
their money. Well, the game worked. American taxpayers are to be soaked
and American bankers are to collect—perhaps.

And what is a "frozen asset"? It is a gaudy name for a piece of paper
representing a transaction in which the holder expected to get a larger
return than was possible on a prudent, rock-bottom investment. A Hartford, Connecticut, municipal four is not frozen; a holder can get better
than par in the present dark hour of Wall Street's sorrows. A seven per cent

Western farm mortgage is frozen tight—and ought to be, and the holder frozen with it. So is a Bolivian seven. Why should there be Federal interference to save investors from reaping the fruits of their folly and greed? No reason, except that the latter want the Government to bring home their cake so that they can eat it. The trouble is that American capital, in finding "its most lucrative course," has fallen into a slough, and if it gets out with its gains intact the Government must bring a derrick to hoist it.

In this survey of a few leading economic activities of the Federal Government the emphasis is not critical; so far as the present argument is concerned, any or all of these functions may be justified with respect to national interest. Indeed it is difficult to find any undertaking of the Government which is not supported by some business men on the ground of national defense. In the early days of our history even those statesmen who generally espoused free trade or low tariffs were willing to concede the importance of making the nation independent in the manufacture of munitions of war. And in the latest hour, subsidies to the merchant marine, to aviation, and to waterways development are stoutly defended in the name of preparedness. Transforming a creek into a river navigable by outboard motor boats can be supported by military engineers on the theory that it gives them practice in their art. No; the emphasis here is not critical. The point is that the Federal Government does not operate in a vacuum, but under impulsion from without; and all of the measures which put the Government into business have been supported by rugged individualists—business men or farmers or both. The current tendency to describe the Government as a meddling busybody, prying around and regulating for the mere pleasure of taking the joy out of somebody's life, betrays an ignorance of the facts in the case. The Government of the United States operates continually in the midst of the most powerful assembly of lobbyists the world has ever seen—the representatives of every business interest that has risen above the level of a corner grocery; and there is not a single form of Government interference with business that does not have the approval of one or more of these interests—except perhaps the taxation of incomes for the purpose, among other things, of paying the expenses of subsidizing and regulating business.

For forty years or more there has not been a President, Republican or Democrat, who has not talked against Government interference and then supported measures adding more interference to the huge collection already accumulated. Take, for instance, President Wilson. He made his campaign in 1912 on the classical doctrine of individualism; he blew mighty blasts in the name of his new freedom against the control of the Government by corporate wealth and promised to separate business and Government, thus setting little fellows free to make money out of little business. The heir of the Jeffersonian tradition, he decried paternalism of every kind. Yet look at the statutes enacted under his benign administration: the trainmen's law virtually fixing wages on interstate railways for certain classes of employees; the shipping board law; the Farm Loan Act; Federal aid for highway construction; the Alaskan railway; the Federal Reserve Act; the Water Power Act; and all the rest of the bills passed during his régime. Only the Clayton anti-trust law can be called individualistic. No wonder Mr. E. L. Doheny exclaimed to Mr. C. W. Barron that President Wilson was a college professor gone Bolshevist! And why did Democrats who had been saying "the less government the better" operate on the theory that the more government the better? Simply because their mouths were worked by ancient memories and their actions were shaped by inexorable realities.

Then the Republicans came along in 1921 and informed the country that they were going back to normalcy, were determined to take the Government out of business. Well, did they repeal a single one of the important measures enacted during the eight years of President Wilson's rule? It would be entertaining to see the Sanhedrim of the United States Chamber of Commerce trying to make out a list of laws repealed in the name of normalcy and still more entertaining to watch that august body compiling a list of additional laws interfering with "the natural course of business" enacted since 1921. Heirs of the Hamiltonian tradition, the Republicans were not entitled to talk about separating the Government from business. Their great spiritual teacher, Daniel Webster, a pupil of Hamilton, had spoken truly when he said that one of the great reasons for framing the Constitution was the creation of a government that could regulate commerce. They came honestly by subsidies, bounties, internal improvements, tariffs, and other aids to business. What was the trouble with them in the age of normalcy? Nothing: they just wanted their kind of Government intervention in the "natural course of industry." Evidently, then, there is some confusion on this subject of individualism, and it ought to be examined dispassionately in the light of its history with a view to discovering its significance and its limitations; for there is moral danger in saying one thing and doing another—at all events too long.

Historically speaking, there are two schools of individualism: one American, associated with the name of Jefferson, and the other English, associated with the name of Cobden. The former was agrarian in interest, the latter capitalistic. Jefferson wanted America to be a land of free, upstanding farmers with just enough government to keep order among them; his creed was an agrarian creed nicely fitted to a civilization of sailing ships, ox carts, stagecoaches, wooden plows, tallow dips, and home-made bacon and sausages; and since most of the people in the United States, during the first century of their independence, were engaged in agriculture, they thought highly of Jefferson's praise of agriculture and his doctrine of anarchy plus the police constable. Cobden's individualism was adapted to capitalist England at the middle of the nineteenth century—early industrial England. At that moment his country was the workshop of the world, was mistress of the world market in manufactured commodities, and feared no competition from any foreign country. English capitalists thus needed no protective tariffs and subsidies and, therefore, wanted none. Hence they exalted free trade to the level of a Mosaic law, fixed and eternal. They wanted to employ labor on their own terms and turn working people out to starve when no profitable business was at hand; so they quite naturally believed that any Government interference with their right to do as they pleased was "bad." Their literary apologist, Macaulay, clothed their articles of faith in such magnificent rhetoric that even the tiredest business man could keep awake reading it at night.

Closely examined, what is this creed of individualism? Macaulay defines it beautifully in the passage which the New York bank and our happy advertising agency quoted so joyously. Let the Government maintain peace, defend property, reduce the cost of litigation, and observe economy in expenditure—that is all. Do American business men want peace all the time, in Nicaragua, for instance, when their undertakings are disturbed? Or in Haiti or Santo Domingo? Property must be defended, of course. But whose property? And what about the cost of litigation and economy in expenditures? If they would tell their hired men in law offices to cut the costs of law, something might happen. As for expenditures, do they really mean to abolish subsidies, bounties, and appropriations-in-aid from which they benefit? Speaking brutally, they do not. That is not the kind of economy in expenditures which they demand; they prefer to cut off a few dollars from the Children's Bureau.

Then comes Macaulay's system of private economy: let capital find its most lucrative course alone, unaided: no Government tariffs, subsidies, bounties, and special privileges. That is the first item. Do American business men who shout for individualism believe in that? Certainly not. So that much is blown out of the water. Macaulay's next item is: let commodities find their fair price. Do the gentlemen who consolidate, merge, and make price understandings want to allow prices to take their "natural course"? By no means; they are trying to effect combinations that will hold prices up to the point of the largest possible profit. Macaulay's third item is: let industry and intelligence receive their natural reward. Whose industry and intelligence and what industry and intelligence? When these questions are asked all that was clear and simple dissolves in mist.

Then there is Macaulay's last item: let idleness and folly reap their natural punishment. That was a fundamental specification in the bill of Manchesterism. Malthus made it a law for the economists: the poor are poor because they have so many babies and are improvident; nothing can be done about it, at least by any Government, even though it enforces drastic measures against the spread of information on birth control. Darwin made a natural science of it: biology sanctified the tooth and claw struggle of business by proclaiming the eternal tooth and claw struggle of the jungle. If the Government will do nothing whatever, all people will rise or sink to the level which their industry or idleness, their intelligence or folly commands. No distinction was made between those who were idle because they could find no work and those who just loved idleness for its own sake—either in slums or mansions. Those who hit bottom and starved simply deserved it. That is the good, sound, logical creed of simon-pure individualism which Herbert Spencer embedded in fifty pounds of printed matter. To him and all his devotees, even public schools and public libraries were anathema: let the poor educate themselves at their own expense; to educate them at public expense is robbery of the taxpayer—that industrious, intelligent, provident person who is entitled to keep his "natural reward."

Do any stalwart individualists believe that simple creed now? Not in England, where Liberals, professing to carry on the Cobden-Bright tradition, vote doles for unemployed working people. Why not let idleness and folly get their natural punishment? Why not, indeed? There must be a reason. Either the individualists betray their own faith, or, as some wag has suggested, they are afraid that they might find themselves hanging to a lantern if they let the idle and the foolish starve, that is, reap the natural punishment prescribed by Macaulay. Nor do American individualists propose to let nature take her course in this country. There is no danger of revolution here; as Mr. Coolidge has said, "we have had our revolution"; yet business men agree with the politicians on feeding the hungry. It is true that they seem to be trying to obscure the issues and the facts by talking about the beneficence of private charity while getting most of the dole from public treasuries; but that is a detail. Although our rugged individualists advertise Macaulay's creed, their faith in it appears to be shaky or their courage is not equal to their hopes. Then why should they try to delude themselves and the public?

There is another side to this stalwart individualism that also deserves consideration. Great things have been done in its name, no doubt, and it will always have its place in any reasoned scheme of thinking. Individual initiative and energy are absolutely indispensable to the successful conduct of any enterprise, and there is ample ground for fearing the tyranny and ineptitude of Governments. In the days of pioneering industry in England, in our pioneering days when forests were to be cut and mountain fastnesses explored, individualism was the great dynamic which drove enterprise forward. But on other pages of the doom book other entries must be made. In the minds of most people who shout for individualism vociferously, the creed, stripped of all flashy rhetoric, means getting money, simply that and nothing more. And to this creed may be laid most of the shame that has cursed our cities and most of the scandals that have smirched our Federal Government.

That prince of bosses, Croker, put the individualist creed in its bare logical form when he said that he was working for his own pocket all the time, just as "every man in New York is working for his pocket." Fall, Doheny, and Sinclair were all splendid individualists; they explained that they hoped to make money out of their transactions, even while they covered their operations with the mantle of patriotism—national defense. Tammany judges, Connolly and his iron pipe, Doyle with his split fees, and policemen growing rich on vice are all individualists of the purest brand. W. B. Shearer collecting money from ship-building concerns to make a naval scare so that they might increase their profits belongs to the same school. Britten, bringing a fleet to Montauk Point to boom real estate in which he is interested, does nothing reprehensible under the Manchester creed; his capital is finding "its most lucrative course." Wilder and Bardo, representing shipping interests, when they spend money in Washington "educating" members of Congress, are following the law of the game. They are perfect individualists. The ruinous chaos in coal and oil is to be attributed to the same Darwinian morality. Finally, Al Capone, with his private enterprise in racketeering, is a supreme individualist: he wants no Government interference with his business, not even the collection of income taxes; if he is "let alone" he will take care of himself and give some money to soup kitchens besides.

The cold truth is that the individualist creed of everybody for himself and the devil take the hindmost is principally responsible for the distress in which Western civilization finds itself—with investment racketeering at one end and labor racketeering at the other. Whatever merits the creed may have had in days of primitive agriculture and industry, it is not applicable in an age of technology, science, and rationalized economy. Once useful, it has become a danger to society. Every thoughtful business man who is engaged in management as distinguished from stock speculation knows that stabilization, planning, orderly procedure, prudence, and the adjustment of production to demand are necessary to keep the economic machine running steadily and efficiently. Some of our most distinguished citizens—Owen D. Young, Gerard Swope, Nicholas Murray Butler, and Otto Kahn, for example—have, in effect, warned the country that only by planning can industry avoid the kind of disaster from which we are now suffering; on all sides are signs of its coming—perhaps soon, perhaps late, but inevitably.

And all of them know that this means severe restraints on the anarchy celebrated in the name of individualism. The task before us, then, is not to furbish up an old slogan, but to get rid of it, to discover how much planning is necessary, by whom it can best be done, and what limitations must be imposed on the historic doctrine of Manchesterism. And to para-phrase Milton, methinks puissant America, mewing her mighty youth, will yet kindle her undazzled eyes at the full midday beam, purge and unscale her long abused sight, while timorous and flocking birds, with those that love the twilight, flutter about, amazed at what she means, and in their envious gabble would prognosticate a year of sects and schisms.

No. 101

THE CONTROL OF BIG BUSINESS [1]

by Walton H. Hamilton

OUR anti-trust laws express the common sense of another age. Toward the close of the nineteenth century a nation which had been composed of farmers and small business men was confronted by a crisis. A revolution in the ways of production which had been gaining momentum with the passing decades was no longer to be ignored. The hand trades were giving way to manufacture; the machine process was transforming the ways of production; businesses were becoming great corporations; captains of in-dustry were coming into possession of wealth and power; and the strange and wicked city was dominating the country. A society made up of almost self-sufficient farms, with its complement of local trade, was being trans-formed into an articulate, even if rather unruly, industrial system. In the whirl of change small traders who saw their enterprises crowded to the wall cried out against the iniquities of big business. The public, which distrusted size as much as it feared extortionate price, realized that untoward things

[1] Walton H. Hamilton, "The Control of Big Business," *The Nation* (May 25, 1932), Vol. 134, pp. 591-593. This article was reprinted in Henry Hazlitt (Ed.) *A Practical Program for America* (New York: Harcourt, Brace and Company, 1932), and is reprinted here by permission of the author, *The Nation*, and Harcourt, Brace and Company.

were going forward. An industrialism which had got its start by stealth came on with such a rush as to leave the people bewildered. The world was no longer as it used to be—and ought to be.

In the emergency a policy had to be formulated. In the task it seemed to occur to no one, at least among those in strategic places, to ask whether industrialism was not rather different from anything society had known before, and whether experimentation might not be used to contrive for it a suitable scheme of control. Instead, the thinkers and the statesmen of the times brought to the problem the best wisdom they could muster—and this wisdom was the product of a social experience which was passing. If the farmer found difficulty in making ends meet, or the small merchant was threatened with extinction, or the customer had his pocket picked by the extortionate dealer, or the workingman put in his long hours for a pittance, it was all because the system of free competition was not working.

At the time, the case for an enforced competition seemed to be quite reasonable. Fact may be on time, but thought usually arrives on the scene a little late. The people talked quite grandly about every man being "the architect of his fate"; and they believed quite sincerely in the creed of "each for himself and the devil take the hindmost." In that climate of opinion only individualistic notions of the province of government and the control of industry could gain currency. Moreover, a long experience with petty trade had produced its own economic policy, and the sense of the man in the street was confirmed by the wisdom in the learned books. It was perfectly clear that the competition of seller with seller and of buyer with buyer gave assurance of efficient service, high quality, and fair price. The interests of one party to a trade—seller, lender, or employer—were balanced by the interests of the other party—buyer, borrower, or employee. Nor could any trader help himself at the expense of his customer, for his desire for gain was checked by the rivalry of others for the very dollars he was trying to secure. The ups and downs in prices which came in the wake of competition attracted or repelled capital, and thus in each industry kept the capacity-to-produce adjusted to the demand for the product. In fact, free enterprise was "a great and beneficent system" which kept industries organized, eliminated the inefficient, gave survival to the fit, insured to labor good working conditions and fair wages, and protected the consumer. For all "the blessings of free competition," as the Supreme Court of the nineties called them, a single provision had to be made. Trades were to be kept open, if need be through a legally enforced competition, and an automatic, self-regulating system could be depended upon to secure for the public all the business system had to give. The thing to be done seemed obvious;

and an attempt was made to stay the development of large-scale enterprise and to make big business behave as if it were petty trade.

So it was that in the name of laissez faire the law was invoked. For some time, even if not from time immemorial, the common law had forbidden "conspiracies in restraint of trade," and a number of States had in the decades following the Civil War aimed statutes at the growing evil of monopoly. In 1890 the Sherman Act, designed to prohibit combinations in "commerce among the several States," was enacted into law. In 1914 the Clayton and the Federal Trade Commission acts were passed in an attempt to extend and to strengthen the federal anti-trust act. The great majority of the States—almost all in the South and West—passed their little Sherman acts.

The resort to law carried its own peculiar hazards. The ideas of common sense had to be translated into the language of legislation; the ends of public policy had to be vindicated through a process of litigation. Economists and statesmen might talk of an enforced competition, but the judiciary gave its attention to "conspiracies in restraint of trade." The language of the statutes caused the courts to consider modern industrial mergers in the light of precedents from a pre-industrial era. The decisions of a former age were invoked in suits to punish offenders or to "dissolve" monopolies; the litigation had to go forward, from issue to issue and from court to court, under a formal code of procedure never designed to draw a line between desirable and undesirable forms of industrial organizations. The cases were heard before benches of judges far more experienced in the discipline of the law than in business, and far better acquainted with Cooley on Blackstone than with texts on the economics of monopoly. It is hardly strange that questions of anti-social practices were subordinated to the antecedent questions of decorous procedure, and that ingenious attorneys found ways to "wear the case out" before the larger issues were raised.

It is small wonder that the resort to law has not been a conspicuous success. Our era of federal "trust-busting" covers a period of more than forty years. In this period has occurred the greatest movement in the concentration of productive wealth known to history. Yet the statisitcs of the Department of Justice present a most illuminating picture of law enforcement at work. A little more than two score criminals have been jailed, and eight have fallen afoul of the law for contempt—a matter of a little more than one person a year. A little under 1,400 persons have had to pay fines aggregating about $1,750,000—or roughly 40 offenders and $50,000 a year. A number of States have derived far more revenue from trust-busting than has the federal government. Yet the prosecution of cases has not been a profitmaking enterprise; the fines collected have fallen far short of the costs of administration. On its face this record is a glorious tribute of respect paid by men of big business to the letter, if not to the spirit, of the anti-trust acts.

This does not mean that the statutes have been without their effect upon the practices of business. They have been ineffectual in preventing corporations from acquiring the physical properties of their competitors and in staying the progress of industrial combination. They have put serious obstacles in the way of agreement among rival manufacturers to restrict output and to maintain price. The barriers have not been insuperable; captains of industry are anxious to live within the law, but they also love to have their own way, and the art of doing both is not unknown to able lawyers. If resourcefulness has often failed the emergency, the credit is not always due to the law. The ups and downs of business strain the morale of all industrial groups; and lapses into the established ways of competition are due more often to a break in discipline from within than to the vigilance of public officials. It is of interest that a number of gigantic corporations have escaped the toils of the law, and that severe penalties have often fallen upon small businesses and upon trade unions. Even where they have not been effective, the acts have been at least a petty nuisance to the interests affected.

But the roots of failure are far more fundamental than a resort to law to give effect to a public policy. The course of industrialism has come with too much of a rush to be stayed; its forces have been too turbulent to be subdued by legislative fiat and court decree; business men have been too powerful to allow their activities to be crowded into the grooves chiseled out long ago for a simpler industry. The universe of petty trade was one sort of place; the world of big business is quite another. In the small town the trader knew his customers personally; he could enlarge his business as his market expanded; his out-of-pocket expenses furnished adequate bases for his prices. As invention brought changes in technical processes, time allowed an easy accommodation. Under the prevailing system a knowledge of the future intent of customers and of the hidden plans of rivals is essential to a sound policy. The business judgments of to-day determine the capacity-to-produce of to-morrow; yet, in an impersonal market, the demand may go to a rival or pass on to another ware. In many lines of business overhead costs have become dominant; and as fixed charges are spread over a large or a small output, the market determines the unit cost of production rather than the unit cost the market. In adapting the capacity-to-produce of an industry to the demand for goods, a far neater and less wasteful adjustment is demanded than the separate judgments of business rivals can effect. They must respond just enough and not too much to market trends, and the unity in action essential to order cannot be secured by a policy of competition.

In fact, the competitive system at work presents problems unknown to the competitive system in books. The good people of the nineties were disturbed because rivals might get together and conspire to impose extortionate prices upon their customers; and that danger still exists. But quite as important is the bill of costs which competition imposes upon the producers. It makes for plant waste and surplus capacity; it fails to articulate tidy establishments into orderly industries. A capacity which cries to be used and overhead costs which click on with the clock lead as often as not to an overdone competition which drives prices relentlessly down. In its wake comes a plague of bankruptcies, irregular employment, and wages too low to support a decent standard of life. Under such conditions there is no chance to get answered, or even to have raised, the larger questions of policy which affect all who have a stake in the industry. It makes all who are concerned—executives, salaried officials, investors, laborers, and consumers—creatures of an undirected industrialism.

The cry to-day is for a revision of the statutes; and yet that revision is no easy matter. An influential group demands that trade agreements be submitted to an official body, such as the Federal Trade Commission, and that advance opinions be given upon the legality of the proposed practices. The proposal has much to recommend it; the bother is that it will probably fail in operation. The spokesman for the government is likely to be guided in his advice by what the courts have said in the past, and to hand down general and platitudinous statements which have little relation to the novel practices for which approval is sought. A business must meet changing conditions; its policies must be adapted to the course of events as they emerge; a declaration that a policy on paper is legal can hardly apply to the policy as it works out in practice. Another group demands the right to "exchange information" and promises to abstain from a regulation of output and a control of price. The bother is that if discipline can be sustained and resourceful lawyers can be retained, the practice prayed for is all that is needed to effect a rather far-reaching monopoly. A third group boldly demands the repeal of the acts and offers no constructive scheme with which to replace them. It insists upon enlarging the control of business over industry when recent events have proved the incapacity of business for the proper exercise of the control it already possesses. The anti-trust statutes are a declaration that business is affected with a public interest; the moral commitment of that declaration is much too important to be lost.

But no mere expedients can get to the heart of the problem. The demand for change comes from an industrial world; it is not to be met with the devices and procedures of a craft society. The simple idea of the uniformity of all trades, which underlies current legislation, must give way to an accommodation of public control to the varying necessities of different industries. For our businesses are not all alike; banking, railroads, power, and radio-broadcasting have already been accorded their own schemes of control. The methods of production and of marketing in various other trades—building, retailing, milk, coal, textiles, cotton-planting—have their own peculiarities with which the problem of industrial direction must come to grips. In all cases, if there is to be order, if the nuisance of bankruptcy is to be abated, if workingmen are to have regular jobs and adequate wages, there must be some central direction. The formal control, or understanding, must certainly extend to capacity, probably to output, and possibly to price. In all cases, if there is to be flexibility, there must be some local control.

This general end is to be served by no simple and uniform economic organization. We have ceased to think in terms of panaceas; and neither a return to the good old competitive system of our fathers nor the adoption of a ready-made, hand-me-down substitute will meet current need. If our industries are to become instruments of national well-being, we must employ a varied program of economic control. Three distinct types of organization seem to be promising. Industries which produce non-essentials and can win only a limited trade against the allurements of unlike wares demand little public control; their activities may well be intrusted to the capricious solicitude of the market. Industries, such as railroads and power, which are linked with all the activities of the economic order demand a large social oversight; this may be met either by an administration commission or by public ownership. Industries, such as coal and steel, which have distinctive groups of customers may be organized from within under a control in which producers and consumers alike share. Industries must be kept going and their dependents must be given adequate livings; consumers must be accorded protection against an anti-social restriction of output and a monopoly element in price. This problem is not to be solved by any "either this or that" formula; its solution demands clear vision, full knowledge, and neat adjustments.

The plain truth of the matter is that the rewriting of the anti-trust laws is the beginning, not the end, of the problem. We may indulge in tinkering and console ourselves with make-believe and pretense; but the fundamental question stands out in clear-cut relief. To-day a lack of harmony exists between the technology of industry and its organization. An economic order in which the productive processes belong to big business and the arrangements for its control to petty trade cannot abide. We cannot banish depression and summon order by invoking the ideas which the people of the 1890's borrowed from a small-town culture. We must devise a scheme adequate to the task of the direction of great industry. In a world of change a society cannot live upon a wisdom borrowed from our fathers.

No. 102

WHY CORPORATIONS LEAVE HOME [1]

by John T. Flynn

A STRANGER, dropping into the large and impressive dining room of the Du Pont Hotel in Wilmington, Delaware, might find cause for surprise in the numerous company around the tables and the metropolitan air pervading the place. These diners are manifestly not traveling salesmen. There is something about them which recalls the types to be seen lunching in Savarins near Wall Street—prosperous men, with the self-possessed bearing of those who are accustomed to deal in large affairs. The simple truth is that from forty or fifty to a hundred or more corporations, good and bad, are holding their annual stockholders' meetings, and these gentlemen, their pockets stuffed with proxies, are on the scene to vote the proxies and reëlect themselves to office in their respective corporations.

What is more, there is nothing particularly unusual about all this. It is an everyday occurrence. And if the visitor will step across the street to the Industrial Trust Building he will begin to perceive the significance of it.

This building, like all others devoted to business offices, has in its lobby, near the elevators, the inevitable black frame enclosing the names of its tenants in small white block letters. It is not a very large building, and one would expect to find a modest frame containing fifty or sixty names. Hence it is difficult to suppress surprise when one sees that the directory frame fills all the walls, on all sides, right up to the ceiling. One notices that the Standard Oil Company of New Jersey is a tenant, and that this is its principal office. That ought to take up the building all by itself, to say nothing of such huge concerns as the National Dairy Products Corporation, the Pennroad Corporation, the Pullman Company, Remington Rand, Transamerica, William Wrigley, Warner Brothers, which are also nestling somewhere under this same roof. And if one cares to do a bit of counting he

[1] John T. Flynn, "Why Corporations Leave Home," *The Atlantic Monthly* (September, 1932), Vol. 150, pp. 268-276. Reprinted by permission of the author and *The Atlantic Monthly*.

will be amazed to discover that more than 12,000 corporations have their home offices here—all of them on one floor!

For this is the corporation homeland of America. This is Delaware—"The Little Home of Big Business," as its newspapers like to speak of it. That is why the Du Pont Hotel is full of men who have foregathered from all over the country to attend stockholders' meetings. In Wilmington alone there is an average of a hundred of these meetings a day; and, since each of them involves the attendance of from two to half a dozen men, it will be seen that the city has daily as many visitors as an ordinary convention would bring. Every day is convention day in Wilmington.

The business of issuing corporation charters to companies to ply their trade in any part of the country has attained mammoth proportions in Delaware, and it is a business that is impressive and peculiar in at least one particular: it is perhaps the only one in which a whole state, in its sovereign capacity, engages, with great profit to itself and to certain classes of its citizens, and with immense mortification and embarrassment, financial and spiritual, to its sister states. Delaware, however, did not invent it, nor does she have a complete monopoly of the business. New Jersey, Maine, West Virginia, Maryland, and Arizona also have their shingles out. But Delaware is now the leader, even though it was New Jersey that began it.

Away back in the early days of the Republic, Alexander Hamilton learned how to use the "liberal" public morals of the free-and-easy State of New Jersey to organize several corporate enterprises which could never have found root in the sterile soil of New York. And, with the advent of the era of big business, the state began, about 1875, to do a good deal of trafficking in charters. By the late eighties, when the trusts were being mercilessly badgered by most of the states and were hunting for a hospitable harbor, New Jersey had already established herself as a pioneer in the benevolent work of adjusting her laws to make things comfortable for them. By this time, however, Maine and West Virginia were also in the market place. Indeed, in 1890 the Secretary of State of West Virginia arrived in New York with the great seal of the state, opened headquarters in a downtown hotel, and announced that he was ready, upon the shortest notice and at the lowest prices, to issue charters to all and sundry who wished them.

At about this same time Mr. John B. Dill, then a rising corporation lawyer, had a bright idea, and went to the Governor of New Jersey with it. He proposed that the state authorize the creation of a corporation which could act for all outside corporations in securing charters for them at the lowest rates, and which could also act for them as resident agent after incorporation. In other words, he proposed to reduce the whole matter to the basis of a highly organized business. The new corporation would be able to advertise in other states, solicit business, and bring the trade to New Jersey.

The state legislature, ever on the alert for "liberal" laws, promptly adopted the idea. Immediately several such corporations were formed. The advantages of New Jersey as a habitat for the trusts that were being persecuted by other states were widely trumpeted. The new corporations born of Mr. Dill's idea set up for business in Exchange Place in Jersey City, and very soon that small dingy street became known as West Wall Street, and some 1500 outside corporations were being regularly represented there.

It was half a dozen years later that New Jersey passed her famous holding-company law, which permitted any New Jersey corporation to buy and hold the stocks of any other corporation of that or any other state. Singularly enough, it was passed at the very moment when the Standard Oil Company was being pressed by Attorney-General Frank Monnett of Ohio to carry out the decree of the Ohio courts dissolving the original trust. John D. Rockefeller was able to find sanctuary within the broad shelter of this new statute, which became law, it is curious to note, over the signature of John W. Griggs, then Governor of New Jersey. Griggs was immediately thereafter called by Rockefeller's old schoolmate and friend, Mark Hanna, McKinley's *alter ego,* to be Attorney-General of the United States, and in this office was charged with the enforcement of the anti-trust laws. Thus did the curtain go up upon the first scene of the great comedy of American corporation law.

It was at this point that little Delaware looked with a jealous eye upon the new business which New Jersey had developed. In 1890, New Jersey derived an income of $292,000 from her corporation business. By 1896, this had risen to $707,000—and these were 1896 dollars. So the following year Delaware amended her constitution to permit incorporation under general statutes, and the legislature passed a general incorporation law in 1899. This ushered Delaware into the charter-mongering business along with Maine, West Virginia, and New Jersey.

From the first, the state did well enough for a young charter breeder, but it was not until Woodrow Wilson became Governor of New Jersey that Delaware's real opportunity arrived. Wilson put through the New Jersey legislature a series of reform measures intended to check various abuses in politics and business. Among them were his famous Seven Sisters Acts, which seriously impaired the "liberality" of New Jersey's corporation laws. This was Delaware's chance, and she rose to it. She "liberalized" her laws a little more, and the corporation traders and mongers at once

> Through the fields of Clover
> Rode right on to Dover,

and set up in business there and in Wilmington.

This, in brief, is how it has come about that in all the seas of our home trade, wherever there is a dollar for a share of stock or a banker to recommend it, corporations by the thousand can be found cruising under the black flag of Delaware's corporation laws in search of easy money.

As a business proposition, it has been an unqualified success for Delaware. The state has chartered more than 100,000 corporations. About 60,000 of them have vanished like the weird sisters into the air from whence they came, or have been conducted to their sepulchres through receiverships in the courts, to the happy chants of lawyers, appraisers, trustees, accountants, clerks, and attendants. About 42,000 of them still remain, some great and powerful, many of them all but dead, awaiting burial.

During the jolly days of the Coolidge administration, prosperity smiled upon the business. In 1927, some 5424 charters were granted, with fees to the state of $824,483. By 1929, the charters issued had risen to 7537, with fees of $3,309,698. The charter mill kept up its feverish pace to the very end of the great bull era. In September 1929, when the depression was just around the corner, nearly 600 new corporations set sail from Dover, most of them to founder before they had well begun their journey. And in spite of the depression, which, of course, has seriously interfered with the launching of new enterprises, Delaware is handing out charters even this year at the rate of about fifteen a day.

The fees for initial incorporation go into the general fund of the state, and at present this source of revenue is considerably curtailed; but there is also an annual franchise tax which each corporation must pay. The Radio Corporation pays about $4400 a year. Mr. Insull's Middle West Utilities paid about $3888 a year. Mr. Ivar Kreuger's International Match Company had to pay a tax of approximately $8000. A huge concern like General Motors pays about $39,000 a year. In 1932, the total of all these corporation franchise taxes will be about $3,500,000. The money is devoted to the support of the public schools. It has become such a lucrative business for the state that there are some who think that all real-estate taxes might be safely done away with, and that the whole machinery of the state could be supported by the taxes paid by the corporations of other states which have a mythical domicile in Delaware.

It is not the state's profits alone, however, that make the business attractive. Since there is an average of one hundred corporation meetings a day in Wilmington, as we have already observed, the hotels and merchants are greatly interested. Most of these meetings are perfunctory. The stockholders are in Wilmington to-day and gone to-morrow; but they are always succeeded by a new throng. Occasionally, however, there is a grand stockholders' fracas for control. When the Transamerica Corporation staged its big battle for control last spring, there were one hundred and fifty stockholders on the scene, and they remained for many days. One set of combatants occupied two floors in the Du Pont Hotel, and some two hundred clerks and tellers were required to count and look after the details of the fight.

Then there is the business done by the lawyers, and by more than thirty of those special corporations which handle the details of organization and represent absent corporations in the state the year round. Finally, and richest of all, are the receiverships. One may well guess that receiverships of corporations such as Delaware permits must be numerous—and they are. At the moment some of our greatest enterprises are being operated by Delaware lawyers under the guidance of Delaware courts. It is no wonder that the bar of the state plumes itself upon the almost unbelievable liberalism of Delaware's "progressive corporation laws."

There is, however, another side to it. "The suspicious," says a pamphlet advertising the state's liberalism, "harking back to the muckraking days when every corporation was guilty—of something—until proved innocent, might say that the Delaware laws must be 'wide-open' laws, attractive to 'blue sky' operators." The pamphlet assures us that "a study of corporations with Delaware charters promptly squelches any such hypothesis." It then goes on to point to some of the types of corporations which boast of Delaware's great seal. There is the Goldman-Sachs Trading Corporation, the Commonwealth and Southern Corporation, the Blue Ridge Corporation, the Continental Chicago Corporation, and the Petroleum Corporation of America. There is the Lehman Corporation, the Prince and Whitely Trading Corporation, and the Winslow Lanier International Corporation.

This boast was made, of course, in 1929. Certainly no one can say that these were "blue sky" concerns. But many intelligent students of finance are now willing to admit that the peculiar forms of capitalization employed by these concerns, and specially authorized by the Delaware law, were responsible for the loss of billions of dollars to investors—dollars which are gone as completely and effectually as if they had been invested in blue sky. The pamphleteer might have added the Insull Middle West Utilities and Kreuger's International Match Company, as well as a number of other corporations which have either failed or been seriously crippled because they suffered from the organic weakness inherent in the forms of capitalization especially favored by Delaware laws.

In the various ways I have mentioned, Delaware manages to get for herself an income of four or five million dollars every year. This, of course, is the final reason and explanation of her legal laxity. It would really pay the other states of the Union, which suffer from Delaware's delinquency, to tax themselves enough to pay the cost of running the Delaware government, absolutely free to that state, if she would just agree to go out of the business of breeding corporations.

Why do corporations leave home and go to Delaware? There need be no speculation about the phenomenon. The boosters for Delaware will tell you. Mr. Robert Pennington, who has written a book about the state's corporation laws, observes that "the liberal provisions of the law are being more constantly taken advantage of by the legal profession and corporate interests generally."

That is it—the "liberal" provisions of the law; liberal, indeed, to the point of glaring laxity. Almost anything goes in Delaware, and here are some of the things that go:

1. Directors need not be stockholders. A collection of office boys would do quite as well.

2. No officer or director need reside in the state. All that is required is a resident agent and an office with a sign out. We have already seen that some 12,000 corporations meet this simple requirement by having, all of them, the same resident agent and the same office on one floor of the Industrial Trust Building in Wilmington, with their signs displayed in its burlesque building directory. This is a part of the jolly system by which one of the most serious and important underlying facts of our business life —the management of all the vast tools of industry—is reduced to the level of *opéra bouffe.*

3. Directors' meetings may be held outside the state, but stockholders must meet there. This is an important advantage for promoters, for, as a prospectus from Wilmington puts it, "if stockholders' meetings were held in a populous place like New York, where so many stockholders would chance to live, a good many might be led to attend the meetings, if only from curiosity." They seldom show up in Wilmington. This explains the gentlemen with pockets stuffed with proxies whom one sees in the Du Pont Hotel.

4. The directors may issue new stock, and, indeed, affect the preferences on old stock, without the approval of the stockholders. They may make by-laws without the approval of stockholders. In fact, a careful study of Delaware's statutes indicates that directors can do almost anything with their corporation—which is a highly prized privilege.

5. Better than this, the right to elect all or a majority of the directors

may be limited to one class of stockholders. I am quite ready to grant that there is something to be said in favor of this provision. Our economic structure is so complex that no man holding widely diversified securities can hope to keep adequately informed about every company in which he owns an interest. There may be good reason, therefore, for providing two distinct classifications of ownership: one which carries with it the right to participate in the direction of the enterprise, and another which relieves the holder of this responsibility. I repeat that there *may* be some justification for such an arrangement, although there is always a danger in divorcing ownership from responsibility. Even at best, however, no one can doubt that this plan is subject to grave abuses.

In the old days, such amateur promoters as E. H. Harriman thought themselves quite clever when they discovered that 26 per cent of the stock of a company could control the whole, through the indifference and lack of unity of the remainder. But under Delaware law it is possible to arrive at the same result by actually investing little or nothing in the enterprise. Who is not familiar with the Class A and B stocks, Founders stock, and the like? In one of the largest holding companies, 10,000 shares of Founders stock, which cost almost nothing, controlled several million shares of cash-paid common. In another, the property was controlled with the Class B common stock, all of which was given as a bonus with the preferred shares. The promoters bought the preferred shares and got the controlling Class B stock. Then they sold the preferred shares at par and retained the common, so that they acquired the actual ownership of a $150,000,000 corporation without investing a cent.

Delaware law permits the issuance of these various classes of stock, and there is almost no limit to what can be done with this device.

6. Stock may be issued, not only for cash, but for property, services, rights, and "the product of one's brain," as an authority assures us. This may be called the waterworks department of the law. Since stocks may be issued for almost anything, the public investor is permitted to put up the cash while the promotors put in the product of their brains. If, subsequently, the investor discovers that the product of the promoters' brains is literally without value, he has no remedy, because "the judgment of the directors as to the value of the property for which the stock was issued is conclusive." Thus oceans of water may, by the magic process of "labeling," be changed into goodwill, and the goodwill may then become the basis for issuing millions of dollars' worth of stock.

7. Stock, of course, may be issued without par value. This provision becomes a deadly thing when it is further provided that the no-par stock may be issued from time to time at such terms and prices as the directors

may fix. They may issue a new batch of stock to the public at one price, to the stockholders at another, and to themselves at still another. It is within the power of the directors at any time, under this provision, to dilute the property of the stockholders, or, acting within the law, to rob them of their profits. This has actually been done on a large scale in countless instances.

8. The baleful system of issuing rights and stock purchase warrants, so generally abused before 1930, is permitted under the Delaware law. This is another method by which directors and insiders are enabled to gamble with the corporation's money without taking any risk themselves. For instance, the directors of one large holding company were given rights to purchase, at any time within three years, 100,000 shares at $20 a share— the amount at which the common stock was issued. On its face this seems fair enough, but let us examine it more closely.

Within a year after these rights were issued the stock went to about 70. At this point all that the directors needed to do was to step in, exercise their rights, put up $20 a share, and get 100,000 shares which they could immediately have sold at a profit of $50 a share. If the stock had come down, of course, they need not have exercised the rights. They gambled to win a lot without risking anything. As it happened, these chaps were reserved for a singular doom. They were too greedy. They thought the shares would go far above 70, so they waited. Then came October '29, and almost before they could say Jack Robinson those shares had tumbled to 7. But they lost nothing.

9. Less than a majority of the board may constitute a quorum; in fact, provision may be made for alternate directors. "This," one is assured in Wilmington, "is a great convenience where some members of the board of directors have varied interests which from time to time prevent their attending meetings." Thus a gentleman who sits on from forty to sixty directorates is excused from paying any but the most cursory attention to the business of the companies over whose fortunes he is supposed to watch. Instead, he may spend his time in Wall Street, speeding up one side of the business cycle on the bull's back with Coolidge and down the other side on the bear's back with Hoover.

10. In Delaware a corporation can be conjured into existence almost as fast as a magician can produce a bouquet of flowers from his hat. A fast motor car stands before the door of the leading incorporating company in Wilmington, almost like an engine in a fire house, ready for action. An idea is born in Wall Street in the morning. A telegraphic appeal goes out to Wilmington—Quick! Quick! A charter!—and the papers are drawn with lightning speed. The waiting automobile races with them to the capitol

at Dover. Only a few minutes are required in the office of the Secretary of State, then the car dashes back to Wilmington. The "incorporators" hold their first meeting and elect directors as the sun starts downward. An express train speeds the precious charter to New York, and before twilight the directors of the new Delaware corporation are holding their first meeting in their penthouse on Park Avenue.

But, you ask, how can the incorporators meet in Wilmington? Simplicity itself. The trust company which makes a business of getting out charters "will furnish the necessary incorporators, when its services are being used by attorneys, enabling the election of directors and adoption of by-laws to be taken care of at Wilmington without necessity of forwarding waivers and proxies of the incorporators to us." Thus reads the prospectus of one of the charter-mongering companies. A batch of office-boy incorporators can be delivered along with the other accommodations in much the same way that an Irish undertaker supplies mourners at a funeral.

In view of these ten specific points which I have enumerated, one need not marvel that most of our great utility holding companies, our largest railroad holding companies, and most of our great investment trusts have obtained their "letters" from the state of Delaware. It is but fair to add, however, that Maryland, Maine, Arizona, and West Virginia are also doing their share to make America safe for promoters and very insecure for investors.

There is a widely accepted notion that the corporation is just a business device—just an implement which enables business men to conduct their affairs with greater convenience. Along with this goes the notion that it is an invention of the lawyers, and that its development ought to be left to them. The truth is that the corporation is one of the most profoundly important facts in modern life. It has gone far to transform our whole economic civilization.

When two or more men unite their resources and abilities, they have an advantage over those who act singly in any business. Until the corporation was devised, the law always held men thus acting together to strict personal accountability for the acts of the partnership or association. The new form of corporate organization is quite different from mere union. In fashioning it, the government has tried its hand at outright creation. A corporation is a legal person that enjoys certain civil functions just as if it were a human being. This fictitious legal entity, endowed with the resources of a large number of men and yet acting as an individual, has enabled men to unite without compelling them to assume full responsibility for the acts of the group.

These are simple facts which must be acknowledged. The result has been to transform us completely from an individualistic people into a highly organized and collective industrial society; to take the tools of industry out of the hands of the individual entrepreneur and put them into the hands of the corporate entrepreneur. In its final form the corporation makes it possible for the men who control it to exercise a vast power. It gives them the opportunity, if they are not properly restrained, to make competition by single individuals utterly impossible, and, in certain cases, to put themselves almost beyond the reach of the law itself.

These facts are put forward, not to condemn the corporation, but rather to effect a clear statement of the problem—to point out that the development of the corporation is primarily an economic and a social problem. Here I do not speak of monopolies and trusts. I speak of corporations large and small, whether monopolistic or not. They are all charged with serious social and economic responsibilities. If this is true,—and I do not see how anyone can doubt it,—is it not strange that the economist has had almost no share in guiding corporate development in America? The economist himself has revealed an amazing indifference to the matter. Along with the social reformer, he has occasionally lifted his voice in loud protest against monopoly, and against corporations as instruments of monopoly, but aside from that he has tended to remain painfully silent.

The development of the corporation has been left, therefore, to the lawyer, and he has been moved almost solely by considerations affecting his client— some specific corporation. The early New Jersey laws and the laws still in force in Delaware were passed almost without public attention. The lawyers in the legislatures rushed them through noiselessly. As I searched through old files of New Jersey and Delaware papers in an effort to trace the history of this legislation, which has had a more important bearing upon our economic life than any other legislation ever enacted, I had difficulty in finding the meagre accounts of the laws.

Then, from time to time, changes in the statutes were made as corporation lawyers demanded them. In 1888, in New Jersey, lawyers wanted the state to permit corporations to purchase the stocks of other corporations that were necessary to their business, and the law was passed. At nearly every session this power was altered or enlarged as the corporation lawyers required. In New Jersey, Delaware, and West Virginia, the lawyers appeared each year with new proposals: to permit different kinds of stock, to increase the powers of directors, to permit proxy voting, to permit different classes of common stock, to permit multiple voting of stocks, to permit proxies for three years, to permit dividends out of capital surplus. Every suggestion was dictated by the convenience of promoters, who sought to make easier the flotation of corporate securities and the control of finances, but there was never a thought for the public interest, no consideration of the economic factors involved, no voice lifted on that phase of the question.

"Here in Delaware," one of the leaders of the bar said to me, "we have an ideal system. Our legislature would never think of passing an amendment to our corporation laws without submitting the matter to the state bar association. Proposals for change are always brought to us first. Our committee considers them, and if we approve them the legislature adopts them as a matter of course. That ensures sound laws. Don't you think it is an excellent system?"

"Well," I suggested, "has it ever occurred to anyone to call all the economists of the state into session and submit the matter to them for an opinion?"

The idea seemed to startle him because of its novelty, and, doubtless, its stupidity.

Twenty-five years ago this whole subject was being gravely considered throughout the nation. At that time almost everybody—John D. Rockefeller, John D. Archbold, Joseph Choate, Samuel C. T. Dodd, Mark Hanna, on one side, and Theodore Roosevelt, James R. Garfield, William J. Bryan, and innumerable economists on the other side—favored national incorporation. If it was important then, it is imperative now; for then we did not have in their full flower the elaborate corporation systems of Delaware and her rival states.

Some people then thought that the states ought not to surrender their power over their own business affairs. That choice no longer confronts us. The several states of the Union must now choose between incorporation laws passed by Delaware, which affect all the states vitally although the others have no voice in their enactment, and laws passed by the national Congress, in which each state will have a voice. The only protection which remains for the people in the great majority of states which do not indulge in charter-mongering lies in a Federal incorporation law.

Chapter XXIX

GOVERNMENT AND PUBLIC SERVICE ENTERPRISES

[IT has long been recognized in the United States that those public service enterprises known as public utilities present special problems of regulation and control. Because of their naturally monopolistic character, the fact that government has conferred upon them its own power of eminent domain, and by reason of the close relationship of their services to the public well-being, public utilities are now, and for years have been, subjected to close scrutiny and regulation.

The policy issues which are now before the American people do not, then, revolve about the question of whether or not to regulate the public utility. Rather they concern the most effective means of regulation, and the jurisdictions most capable of administering a regulatory program.]

No. 103

TECHNIQUES OF PUBLIC CONTROL—AN APPRAISAL OF METHODS [1]

by Robert M. Cooper

WITHIN recent years the public utility problem has assumed an increasingly significant place in the field of political as well as legal science. In certain respects the problem is universal in the sense that it it common to most systems of government. It will suffice merely to indicate that the governments of Great Britain, France, Germany, Italy, Sweden, Norway, and Switzerland, as well as the United States, have, through a variety of devices, recognized the fundamental problems created by business

[1] Robert M. Cooper, "Techniques of Public Control—An Appraisal of Methods," *The Annals* of the American Academy of Political and Social Science (January, 1939), Vol. 201, pp. 1-16. Reprinted by permission of *The Annals* of the American Academy of Political and Social Science. The views expressed in this article are to be attributed to the author alone, and not to the Department of Justice, with which he is connected.

"affected with a public interest" whose services are characterized "by public convenience and necessity."

The basis of the public utility problem, in its political aspect, is the desire to eliminate or control the enormous potential power which these enterprises possess by virtue of natural, social, or economic factors or their privileged position as compared with other, purely private businesses. Since public utility enterprise frequently assumes monopolistic form, either through natural economic circumstances or by direct governmental sanction, its operations lie beyond the reach of the automatic checks and restraints of the free competitive market. Similarly, many other economic principles, such as the law of supply and demand, are more or less inapplicable to public utility services, which are either indispensable or reasonably necessary to large portions of the public. To provide a substitute for these economic forces and competitive restraints, public authorities have been compelled to establish artificial devices for the protection of the consumer, on the one hand, from inferior services and unreasonable rates, and for the protection of the utility, on the other hand, from destructive and predatory practices.

During the past fifty years, both state and Federal governments have attempted to deal with the problem of the public utility enterprise through the increasingly familiar process of administrative regulation. Following a period of legislative hesitation, Congress has finally subjected most public utilities to a more or less constant regulation or control by means of one or more administrative agencies established for that single purpose. It may be said with little exaggeration that the rise of the "administrative commission" has been the outstanding development in the American system of government during this period. For the purposes of this discussion the general pattern of public utility regulation may be concisely stated. The general legislative policies and administrative standards are specifically set forth in the legislation creating the regulatory tribunal, whose duty it is to apply these standards and policies to concrete situations involving the operations of the utility sought to be regulated. Theoretically at least, the administration of these legislative standards provides a ready substitute for the normal checks of the competitive market and supplies a control device to offset the privileged position and potential power of such enterprises.

Following this general pattern, Congress has authorized the Interstate Commerce Commission to exercise extensive control over the rail and motor carrier industries; the Secretary of Agriculture to regulate certain activities of meat packers and the operations of stockyard companies; the Federal Communications Commission to regulate the operations and practices of the telephone, telegraph, and radio industries; the Federal Power Commission to control navigation and regulate the development of water power, as well as the interstate transmission and sale of electric energy and natural gas; the United States Maritime Commission to regulate the operations of water carriers engaged in interstate, foreign, and intercoastal commerce; and more recently, the Civil Aeronautics Authority to regulate the operations of air carriers engaged in interstate and foreign transportation.

It would be misleading to imply that these tribunals are the only Federal agencies exercising a supervisory control over public utility operations, or that such a description represents a complete survey of Federal control of such enterprises. But such a survey, if intended to be inclusive, is necessarily fraught with difficulties. One difficulty arises from the fact that in addition to the agencies just enumerated, there are various other tribunals whose authority and power extend to public utility enterprises as well as other private businesses. In addition to the Department of Justice, such agencies are the Securities and Exchange Commission, the Federal Trade Commission, the National Labor Relations Board, the National Mediation Board, and the newly appointed Wages and Hours Administrator.

Another difficulty which tends to prevent a more accurate description of public utility regulation by either the state or Federal Government is the fact that the public utility concept is no longer a definite and fixed category into which businesses may be classified with certainty. From a legal viewpoint, the public utility concept has become little more than an attempted rationalization of judicial opinion which has permitted certain types of control in one industry and condemned them in others. With a few noteworthy exceptions, the approach to the public utility problem by local governments has been similar to that of the Federal Government. The vast majority of states have established regulatory tribunals patterned after the example of the more successful Federal tribunals, with more or less extensive authority over the local operations of such industries as electric light, heat, and power companies; gas companies; street and interurban railways; motor vehicle carriers; telephone and telegraph companies; and water companies. Whatever difficulties may be encountered in measuring the precise extent of national and local public utility control, it cannot be doubted that both governments have in the main resorted to the device of administrative regulation in their attempt to meet the problem of the public utility enterprise.

In view of the extensive use of the regulatory commission in this country, it is not surprising to find a growing public sentiment that the process of administrative control is an inevitable device for solving the public utility problem. As a nation, we are rapidly developing a political attitude which accepts the regulatory commission as a permanent institution within the structural framework of our government. Unfortunately, however, this attitude frequently appears to be more the result of habit and familiarity than of rational examination. Before the stamp of inevitableness is placed exclusively upon any particular solution to such a complex problem as that of the public utility enterprise, two lines of inquiry should be carefully pursued. First, how effective is the regulatory commission and what are its outstanding defects? Second, are there any possible alternatives which would in whole or in part eliminate those defects?

In the main, the defects of administrative regulation fall into two classes —those which are minor since they may be corrected, and those which are inherent in the process of regulation. The minor deficiencies need not detain us longer than to observe that such shortcomings as the quality of personnel, the lack of sufficient appropriations, poorly drafted legislation, insufficient jurisdictional authority, lack of initiative and responsibility on the part of commissions, and improperly conducted public relations are matters of a temporary nature which may be completely eliminated by intelligent foresight and experience. Of more vital concern to those interested in the broader aspects of the public utility problem are those fundamental defects which seem to be inherent in the administrative process because of its essential characteristics and objectives. The very existence of these inherent deficiencies represents a serious compromise with the basic philosophy and purposes of the entire scheme of public utility regulation.

From beginning to end, the regulatory process operates in an atmosphere of more or less intense antagonism. In certain respects this is its outstanding defect as a permanent device for meeting the public utility problem. The idea that one group of officials may be set up to check, supervise, and control the commercial operations of another group of individuals without encouraging subterfuge, evasion, sharp practices, and animosity is inconceivable under a system of capitalistic economy. Although this antagonistic attitude is frequently driven below the surface of observation, its presence is none the less real. On the one hand, the regulatory commission is charged with the primary duty of securing efficient, widespread, economical services for the consuming public. On the other hand, the management of the public utility enterprise is forced to concern itself chiefly with securing the highest possible return to the owners of the industry. This is not to say that the regulatory commission condemns the profit motive, or that public utility management ignores the public interest in providing efficient service at low rates. It is clear, however, that the essential purposes of the two groups are socially and economically incompatible if carried to their logical conclusion.

Neither the commissions nor the public utilities have long succeeded in carrying their objectives to the stage of final accomplishment, with the result that the process of regulation has come to resemble more a half-hearted compromise than an effective instrument of control. If the profit motive continues to dominate the desires of public utility management—and there is every reason to believe that it will—antagonism and animosity are likely to grow until the entire scheme of regulation breaks down under their destructive force. While the law has definitely placed the public utility enterprise in the category of public interest for the purposes of public control, these judicially recognized prerequisites of social and economic welfare have had but little effect upon motives of public utility management.

Another more familiar defect of the regulatory process involves a consideration of the controversial subject of judicial control. Relying in part upon the Third Article of the Constitution and in part upon the due process clauses of the Fifth and Fourteenth Amendments, the judiciary has established itself as the ultimate protector of the rights and property of economic enterprise. This essentially American doctrine of judicial superiority has had an incalculable effect upon the process of administrative regulation. There are many who believe that the failure of the administrative process to function more successfully is directly due to unwarranted interference by the judiciary. Through a great variety of technical distinctions and judicial niceties, the courts have subjected the decisions of regulatory commissions to a supervision which frequently destroys the far-reaching advantages of administrative expertness and specialized knowledge presumably possessed by public officials. Judicial supervision has done much to cripple the legitimate exercise of administrative discretion which is the very essence of the regulatory device. There are few practices more disastrous to the sound functioning of the regulatory process than these frequent excursions by the judiciary into strange fields where their tools are antiquated and their knowledge only partially adequate.

Within recent years the courts have become more and more interested in the procedural elements of the regulatory process. The decisions of the Supreme Court in the cases of Jones v. Securities and Exchange Commission and Morgan v. United States are viewed with some apprehension by administrative officials. While it may be true that the techniques of certain administrative procedures are in need of improvement, any wholesale attempt on the part of the judiciary to impose its traditional methods upon the regulatory commission should be met with immediate opposition. To-day there is a serious danger that the regulatory commission may become too "judicially minded" to perform its duties in accordance with the accepted standards of sound administration. This danger increases with each attempt of the courts to impose their methods upon the regulatory agency. It should not be forgotten that the rise of the administrative tribunal was in large measure due to the complete inadaptability of traditional judicial procedure to meet the exacting demands of the regulatory process. Although the Chief Justice of the United States was considering other problems of government at the time, his observation that "our government is the most successful contrivance the world has ever known for preventing things from being done" has particular applicability to the growth of judicial supervision over administrative action.

A further inherent deficiency of the regulatory device, intimately related to that of judicial control, is the administrative process of rate making. The problem of controlling rates—and hence indirectly the income—of a commercial enterprise frequently involving hundreds of millions of dollars is a delicate task at best. But here again the courts have imposed such restrictions upon the exercise of the rate-making function that the task has become doubly burdensome. Commencing with the Smyth v. Ames doctrine, limiting regulatory control to the establishment of those rates which will yield a "fair return" upon the "fair value" of the property dedicated to the public service, the courts have developed a bewildering collection of valuation formulae which have rendered intelligent administration of the rate-making authority practically impossible. Placing its chief emphasis upon the "hypothetical" concept of reproduction cost as an essential element of present value, the Federal judiciary has grasped at first one formula and then another, with the result that the valuation problem has become the focal point of public utility litigation. The growth of valuation litigation, in addition to causing serious delays in administration, has confused the regulatory tribunal to such an extent that there has been a positive reluctance to exercise its statutory authority over rates except in the most extreme cases. For this reason, administrative rate making and control has tended to become more sporadic than continuous, more uncertain than scientific.

It makes little difference whether one considers this judicial supervision over the rate-making process as an unwarranted usurpation by the courts or an essential safeguard for the protection of the legal rights of private enterprise. The fact remains that there exists to-day a fundamental conflict between administrative rate control and judicial requirements which has proved detrimental to the sound functioning of the regulatory process.

Another inherent defect in the process of administrative regulation arises from the American doctrine of federalism. The nation-wide conduct of public utility operations has little relation to the constitutional division of powers between the Federal and state governments. Since no state can be considered as an isolated unit, socially, economically, or physically, situations are constantly developing which require the intervention of a central rather than a local control in order to secure uniformity of action. Frequently the Federal Government is without constitutional power to intervene in such matters. In other situations the constitutional power resides in the Federal Government, although the logical solution to the problem would appear to be in the direction of a varying local control.

The ultimate success of any regulatory program is subject to the unyielding principle that the area of administrative control must coincide with the area of commercial operation of the enterprise sought to be regulated. Constitutional federalism is more often than not at odds with this principle. The problem of Federal and state jurisdiction goes much deeper than the mere need for liberal interpretation of the Constitution. There can be no doubt that the Constitution contemplates a more or less well-defined division of authority between the two political entities; but the theory of dual sovereignty is seldom adaptable to the actual operations of the public utility enterprise, whose activities are dictated by economic circumstances rather than the exigencies of political federalism. A possible solution to this difficult problem appears to be in the direction of cooperation between the two governments.

Within recent years numerous experiments in Federal-state cooperation have been undertaken with rather encouraging results. A number of Congressional acts have authorized the establishment of joint boards, composed of state and Federal officers, to administer jointly the regulatory features of national laws dealing with matters of local concern. In other situations Congress has authorized state commissioners to sit with the Federal agency during hearings on matters in which the local authorities might be interested. In a few instances Congress has employed the principle of supplementary legislation, which permits each government to operate within its respective sphere of sovereignty but partially avoids the jurisdictional problem by the formulation of similar legislative objectives. Another more recent method of cooperation is the system of Federal loans and grants-in-aid to local public authorities engaged in activities which affect the general welfare of the Nation. By this device the local agency assumes the basic responsibility of administering the legislative program, and the Federal Government renders financial assistance on condition that certain national policies be made a part of the local program. Despite the increasing application of these cooperative efforts by the Federal Government to avoid the "gaps" of constitutional federalism, its practical restrictions still stand as a serious threat to the effectiveness of the regulatory device.

One of the most persistent criticisms of the regulatory process is its ultimate tendency to divide or separate managerial responsibility. The con-

tinuing success as well as the efficient operation of any commercial enterprise depends primarily upon its ability to certalize responsibility and
establish a unified management. The regulatory process is at odds with
this principle by seeking to divide the responsibilities of management between the administrative agency and the public utility official. It is a
mistake to assume that the effectiveness of the regulatory device can be
measured *solely* by the extent of interference with the legitimate functions
of management. Such administrative intervention, although necessary to
effectuate many legislative policies, may act as a barrier to the normal
accomplishments of progressive management. When considerations of
public interest compel the regulatory commission to share actively in managerial responsibility, there is a grave danger that initiative and elasticity of
operation may be subordinated to other, less consequential factors. In
many situations the rigidity and inflexibility of administrative rules, due in
part to legislative pre-definition and in part to judicial control of discretion,
tend to sap the vitality of the regulated enterprise. During the initial stages
of a regulatory program, administrative control is normally restricted to
certain obvious abuses and evils which have grown up with the industry
as a back-wash of unsound competitive practices. These regulatory activities resemble a "house cleaning" of undesirable practices, and seldom approach the realm of managerial responsibility. But as regulation increases
in intensity and drives further into the sphere of management, there is a
dangerous tendency toward a preservation of the status quo within the
industry. When administrative control supplants managerial initiative and
responsibility, regulatory standards which were intended to be merely mini-
mal in character and quality tend to become the accepted criteria of public
service. Perhaps the process of regulation may be so modified that this
tendency to divide responsibility can be eliminated, but it should be recognized that the adoption of such adjustments in the regulatory device may
involve a serious compromise with the present philosophy of public control.

One should be cautious in assuming that these deficiencies, fundamental
as they are, represent a failure of administrative regulation to solve the
public utility problem. Such an assumption would oversimplify the elements involved in an evaluation of such an extremely complex process. On
the whole, however, the Federal regulation of public utilities appears to be
more a success than a failure. In this respect the vitality of the administrative process has been demonstrated by its practical results. Federal regulation has gone far toward accomplishing its objectives, despite its shortcomings and serious handicaps. The effectiveness of local regulation is much
more difficult to measure, because of the many varying factors which accompany the administration of local policies and the lack of reliable information

as to their activities. But with respect to both Federal and local regulatory control, one may indulge in some interesting speculation as to how much more effectively the public utility problem could be met if devices not possessing such defects were utilized.

As previously suggested, the regulatory commission is a pre-eminently American method of meeting the public utility problem. Great Britain is rapidly abandoning the administrative commission for what are considered to be more efficient instruments of public control. Among European nations, the independent regulatory tribunal never achieved a position of lasting importance. In view of the more recent British experiments and the general satisfaction with other methods of public control throughout the world, an examination of these alternative devices against a background of American regulatory experience would appear to be most timely. The succeeding discussion of the operation of alternative methods is not intended to be a suggestion that they be utilized in this country in preference to any other system of control. I have no desire to advocate or seek the substitution of any of these devices for the present system of regulation. This discussion is merely a survey of the various methods which have been more or less generally employed to solve the public utility problem; but even a cursory consideration of these new techniques of social control may shed new light on the entire field of government regulation as we are accustomed to deal with the problem in America.

The rise and growth of the cooperative movement is one of the most significant developments in our social and economic history. From a functional aspect, the cooperative is not unlike many other economic organizations established to perform certain commercial or industrial services; but in other respects it is radically different. The cooperative is based upon two fundamental principles—production for use rather than profit, and substantial equality of ownership by the consumers. It is an economic organization which belongs to the people who use its services, the control of which rests equally with all the members, and the gains of which are distributed to the members in proportion to the use they make of its services.

The outstanding success of the cooperative movement abroad, particularly in Sweden, has led to its limited but relatively rapid adoption in this country. Although the American cooperative has been utilized most frequently in connection with agricultural production and distribution, its increasing use in such public utility services as electric power and light, water supply, and telephone is of more than passing significance. The nonprofit and democratic aspects of the cooperative movement tend to avoid the economic maladjustments which inevitably flow from the concentration of corporate power and the separation of ownership from control under a capitalistic economy. In one of his famous dissenting opinions, Mr. Justice Brandeis characterized the cooperative as a device "which leads directly to the freedom and equality of opportunity which the Fourteenth Amendment aims to secure," and further intimated that the rise of the movement represented an advance from "economic absolutism" of corporate domination to the ideal of an "industrial democracy."

As compared with the deficiencies of the regulatory devices, the cooperative enterprise presents some interesting contrasts. In the first place, the cooperative movement eliminates the defects which have their origin in the constant conflict between the profit motive and the ultimate objectives of administrative regulation. The cooperative is operated entirely on a public service basis—with little or no emphasis on the profit element—since consumer and owner are one and the same. The objectives of management, consumer, and owner are identical.

In the second place, the problem of judicial control as well as the cumbersome valuation-for-rate-making process is practically unknown to the cooperative enterprise, since its operations are the result of voluntary agreement between the management and the consumer. In the third place, since the public utility cooperative serves only a limited number of consumers rather than the public at large, and is thus not ordinarily subject to regulatory jurisdiction, the management of the enterprise is free to develop its own commercial policies. In this respect the cooperative is as free as private enterprise to develop the incentives and initiative of progressive management, with the assurance that such operations will not be detrimental to the public interest.

A final observation may be made with respect to the cooperative movement. From a psychological viewpoint, the cooperative acts as a stimulus to representative government by creating a sense of responsibility among the members and broadening their economic outlook. The tendency of the cooperative movement to arouse the public to their rights as well as their duties under a democratic government is a circumstance which has as yet been neither fully realized nor appreciated in this country. Its potential application to the public utility problem is only gradually being recognized.

Another method frequently utilized as a public utility control device is the program of public competition. There can be no doubt that it is an extremely effective method for creating and enforcing adequate public service standards. The theory of government competition has the virtue of going right to the heart of the public utility problem—the absence of competitive checks and restraints. In this respect it is a possible substitute for administrative regulation, just as regulation is a substitute for the forces of the competitive market. Unlike the regulatory device, government competition attacks the problem through the normal avenues of the capitalistic economy. In both instances, government provides the instruments of control, which in one case operate by means of an artificial standard of political authority, and in the other through the familiar competitive channels of commercial enterprise. Under these circumstances it is difficult to rationalize much of the contemporary argument against the use of government competition. It it quite obvious that a program of government competition could be administered with such intensity as to force rates down to the point of confiscation, or with such extravagance as to require unnecessarily high standards of service. But these arguments are hardly valid criticisms of the method per se, since they involve self-serving assumptions and may be applied with equal force to any method of social control, including the regulatory device.

Much of the resentment against competition by public authorities arises from the fact that it necessitates the entrance of government as a trader in the realm of commercial and industrial relationships. While this contention may have some merit with respect to purely private businesses, it seems strangely irrelevant when applied to the public utility enterprise, whose services are predominantly public in character. Certainly it must be conceded that government is entitled to utilize and should use the most effective method at its disposal for safeguarding and protecting the public interest. If public competition is a more effective device than regulatory control, misleading assumptions concerning the "sanctity of private enterprise" should not be permitted to halt its utilization in the public utility field. In any event, the choice between these methods of control is not aided by the characterization of public competition as "immoral," "unethical," or "unfair."

As in the case of the regulatory device, the Federal Government is presumably limited in its utilization of government competition by constitutional restrictions, although here the lines are not sharply drawn. Until rather recently, the commercial activities of the Federal Government were so clearly related to government use and consumption or so closely confined to its territorial jurisdiction, that few questions of constitutional power arose in the courts. The activities of such Federal agencies as the Emergency Fleet Corporation, the United States Sugar Equalization Board, the War Finance Corporation, the United States Housing Corporation, and the United States Spruce Corporation during the war period were hardly considered to be indicative of a permanent policy. But it should be noted that the creation of these agencies, even on a temporary basis, represented a conscious recognition of the proper role of government during periods when the economic forces of production and distribution become unbalanced.

The public utility problem to-day, as always, is no less real than the general commercial and industrial problem during the war.

The two outstanding experiments of the Federal Government with the competitive device are those operations associated with the Inland Waterways Corporation and the Tennessee Valley Authority. The first of these agencies is not so well known, and was established to regulate water carriers and operate a barge line on the Mississippi River in competition with other shipping and railroad enterprises. Although its liquidation has been recommended on several occasions, the corporation still operates as a serious competitive check on the transportation rates not only in the Mississippi Valley but throughout the entire Nation on long distance traffic.

The Tennessee Valley Authority is a more familiar Federal Agency, and a description of its functions need not detain us long here. Established for the primary purpose of erecting dams and hydroelectric plants along the navigable waters of the Tennessee Valley, its operations have been constantly extended into the electric power and distribution fields until to-day its services and rates act as an exceedingly effective competitive yardstick in the power industry throughout the entire Tennessee Valley from Little Rock to Asheville and from Cincinnati to Birmingham. Although the Supreme Court has sustained the validity of certain of these competitive activities by the TVA, the extent to which the Federal Government would be permitted to go in utilizing the competitive device on a wide scale without violating constitutional limitations remains a very much mooted question. It should be noted, however, that many of these constitutional restrictions can be avoided by the method of Federal and state cooperation, previously referred to in connection with the regulatory device. By the system of Federal loans and grants-in-aid to local authorities for the construction and operation of public utility enterprises, the government is in a position to assist in the establishment of the competitive device in areas where it cannot operate directly in the event that questions of constitutional power are raised. The Supreme Court has recently sustained the method of cooperative effort, and there is little doubt that it will be extensively used in the future.

But apart from these experiments in Federal-state cooperation, the competitive device has been most frequently utilized in the past by local governments. Local public competition in the case of electric power, gas, and water supply has proved to be an exceedingly effective method of maintaining high public service standards at low rates in many municipalities throughout the country. But since the line of demarcation between government competition and public ownership in the case of local authorities is at best uncertain, a further discussion of these matters will be reserved until later.

From an administrative standpoint, the utilization of the competitive method as a control device avoids many of the outstanding deficiencies of the regulatory process. Although the spirit of antagonism between the public authority and the private utility enterprise is probably more intense in the case of the competitive method, it does not materially alter the effectiveness of the device as it does of the regulatory process. Furthermore, the problem of judicial control is practically eliminated when the competitive method is employed, since the judiciary does not ordinarily have any power over the operations of public corporations. Due to the fact that the competitive method operates directly through the normal channels of the capitalistic economy, the administrative tendency to interfere with the independence and initiative of progressive management is completely avoided.

From an economic viewpoint, however, the competitive method presents several serious problems. The systematic utilization of public competition results in a duplication of plants and services, the additional cost of which must ultimately be borne by the consuming public. The principle of natural monopoly within limited areas is universally recognized in the case of certain utility enterprises such as the telephone industry. To permit a duplication of services in such circumstances involves an unnecessary waste and destruction of investment values which would ordinarily offset any advantages to be gained from such public control. However, the principle of natural monopoly even in those circumstances should be conditioned by the constant possibility of government competition. The threat of potential competition involves none of the disadvantages previously suggested, but its presence is frequently a decisive factor in the effort to obtain an adequate public service at reasonable cost.

Despite the fact that we live in a country where public ownership is a common spectacle, this method of social control is still considered by many to be the stepchild of socialism, communism, or fascism—depending upon the current political aversion of the writer or speaker. Social action is dictated and controlled by the practical demands of social necessity. Public ownership is one method of dealing with the public utility problem which is frank in its recognition of the true "public service" character of the functions to be performed. A recognition of the public service function entails no compromise with the ideals of democratic government and no unwarranted interference with the prerogatives of private enterprise. Although it is not the purpose of this paper to discuss the merits or demerits of the public ownership program, a brief consideration of the various factors which have caused its adoption in the public utility field may raise some interesting questions concerning its effectiveness as a control device.

The first and most significant reason for the utilization of the public ownership device is the desire to eliminate the profit motive from the management of the public service enterprise. Enough has already been said to indicate the nature of the conflict between the interests of owners and consumers, and that the desire to secure high returns on invested capital is frequently incompatible with the right of the public to obtain indispensable services at fair rates. The program of government ownership establishes a public trusteeship in which the profit motive is subordinated to the public service motive among those responsible for the management of the enterprise. In the past, private management has been conspicuous in its failure to recognize the dominant public interest in the nature of the utility enterprise and the conduct of its affairs. Then, too, private utility operators have consistently ignored the fact that government has made substantial contributions to the industry in the nature of free use of natural resources and public lands, the right of eminent domain, protection from wasteful competition, and even pecuniary gifts and bounties. The movement toward government ownership has received its chief impetus from the constant failure of private management to assume voluntarily this necessary sense of public trusteeship.

A second and equally significant reason for the extension of public ownership is the growing public dissatisfaction with existing service policies and practices of many utility enterprises. Many factors, including the persistent profit motive, have contributed to this failure to provide adequate as well as widespread utility services. Private management is frequently reluctant to extend the market for its services over wider areas unless there is little risk involved in the undertaking. The lack of a definite expansion program by many utility enterprises has virtually isolated large sections of the country from the benefits and conveniences of modern public service facilities. There are many who believe that this restrictive market policy has had a tendency to retard the economic development and advancement of the entire Nation. The failure of the electric power industry to expand its operations into rural areas was one of the chief reasons for the creation of the TVA and its subsequent program of rural electrification. In 1936 only about 11 per cent of the farms of the Nation had access to an electric power system, as compared with 90 per cent in Germany, 50 per cent in Scandinavia, 66 per cent in New Zealand, and almost 100 per cent in the Netherlands. Similarly, the rise of the cooperative telephone company in the West was symptomatic of the unwillingness of private management to expand its market into new areas. Independently of other causes which will be discussed later, it seems rather clear that the rapid growth of public ownership in Western Europe is largely explained by the fact that the people had more confidence in the ability of local government to provide efficient, adequate, and widespread service than they had in private enterprises.

The third reason for the employment of the public ownership device relates to the services performed by those enterprises which have entered an era of declining profitability. In the case of those enterprises where profits are rapidly approaching the vanishing point and new capital cannot be attracted to the industry, government is frequently forced to take over the whole industry or at least some of its weaker units. To-day there is much talk of the Federal Government's taking over the railroads because of their present precarious financial condition. Public authorities were faced with a similar situation when the turnpike superseded the canals, and even later, when the railroads destroyed the profitability of the toll-road ventures. In such situations government must first decide whether the service involved is worthy of continuation. If the service has been largely superseded by more efficient or less costly substitutes, there is no particular reason why it should be perpetuated even under a system of subsidies. On the other hand, if the service is still necessary to the economic or social well-being of the community, government should not hesitate to save the industry from complete or partial disintegration. With the exception of the railroad situation, this aspect of the public ownership program is relatively unimportant to our problem, since its utilization is generally considered to be an emergency device rather than a permanent plan of public control.

A final reason for resort to the public ownership program involves a consideration of the role of government as a pioneer in new and untried commercial fields. Frequently private enterprise is either unwilling or unable to take the initiative in supplying new services or facilities which appear to be necessary to the public interest. Under these circumstances government assumes the burden of developing and performing the service in question. The construction of highways, the provision of educational facilities, the transmission of the mails, and the development of a merchant marine are all examples of pioneering government ownership. Occasionally these enterprises are transferred to private management when they become profitable, but more often they remain under public operation and gradually assume every aspect of a traditional governmental function. It is significant to note that when government assumes the role of pioneer or risk bearer, there is seldom any objection on the part of private enterprise. Yet it must be recognized that the same fundamental principles of public control are involved whether the government operates a postal system or an electric power system; in both cases the public authority is supplying an indispensable service to the public, although for different but equally cogent reasons.

The preceding analysis of the causes and reasons for the rise of the movement toward public ownership would appear to indicate that as a method of control it avoids many of the deficiencies of the regulatory process. This is particularly true with respect to the subordination of the profit motive and the elimination of judicial supervision, especially in the direction of rate making. Public ownership avoids many of the shortcomings of administrative regulation by bridging over the constant clash of conflicting interests—between consumer and investor, between the courts and administration, between managerial initiative and administrative restrictions, and, above all others, between the public interest and industrial individualism.

But from these observations it is not meant to imply that government ownership is by any means the perfect instrument of social control. As a universal method of solving the public utility problem, it carries its own more or less serious deficiencies. As in the case of the competitive devices, future interpretations of the Fifth and Tenth Amendments to the Constitution may prevent the Federal Government from utilizing a program of public ownership as a general method of control, just as a more restricted construction of the Fourteenth Amendment may prohibit state and local governments from employing the same method. Moreover, the transition from private enterprise to public ownership may involve the creation of new problems which have their origin in the traditional shortcomings of government institutions, such as: the lack of commercial or industrial experience; disunity of management due to an excess of democratic controls; external financial supervision; questionable accounting practices; inflexibility of organization and procedure; inadequately managed public relations; and the presence of political influences. Many of these problems, if they exist at all, are remediable and may be solved by the revamping of administrative organizations under the guidance of an enlightened public opinion. Others are more deep-rooted and may involve a fundamental change in the science of government. With respect to these problems the British experiments in the public ownership of public utilities are of vital interest to those who search for new tools of social regulation.

While the Federal Government and various local authorities in this country have been reshaping and improving the regulatory device, Great Britain has blazed new trails in the inauguration of a vast program of public ownership experiments in the public utility field. At the present time government ownership in England has been applied to approximately 60 per cent of the electrical distribution; 40 per cent of the gas supply; 80 per cent of the local transport, including trams, railways, subways, and buses; 90 per cent of the water supply; and the entire radio broadcast system. The British program is built around three fundamental ideals or assumptions: first, that responsible administration is superior to regulation as a method of social control; second, that voting stockholders and speculative profits are undesirable elements in the public utility enterprise; and third, that the officials of the public utility are trustees of the public interest. Relying upon these basic principles, two somewhat different but highly effective organizations have been developed to meet these new demands—the public utility trust and the mixed undertaking.

The significant features of the public utility trust are the following: Its organization is corporate in form and monopolistic in character. The stock is held by the investing public, although they possess no voting rights by virtue of such ownership. The earnings of the trust are fixed by statute, being limited to from 3 to 5 per cent of the capitalization, its stock thus assuming the characteristics of a bond with a fixed and guaranteed interest rate. Excess earnings beyond the statutory rate are utilized to effectuate rate reductions. Sinking fund requirements are frequently established whereby the stock may be retired at periods varying from twenty to sixty years. The flotation of additional securities is subject to the approval of the Treasury.

The directors of the public utility trust are usually designated as "trustees" and are appointed by the government. The trustees are selected primarily on the basis of their ability and interest in public affairs, regardless of their political affiliations. It is expected that the trustees will represent and protect the interests of the four groups primarily concerned with the enterprise—consumer, investor, labor, and government. Selected by the trustees, the managerial function is vested in a general manager, who has wide discretion in the organization and development of commercial policies. The salaries of the trustees and the manager are established by statute and are sufficiently compensatory to attract men of considerable ability. The employees are subject to a merit system and only the more desirable features of the Civil Service law.

The interrelation between the government and the corporation is one of the most significant aspects of the public utility trust. The British practice has followed the policy of relative independence by placing the trust in a position of semi-autonomy. The Minister whose department activities are most closely related to the function of the trust is charged with an ex-officio responsibility in relation to its operations and activities. The Minister merely exercises a general power of surveillance and a reserved authority to investigate; he has no power to interfere with the managerial policy of the trust. In these respects the Minister merely acts as an advisory connecting link between the legislative body and the trustees. The outstanding examples of the British public utility trust are the London Transport Board, the Central Electricity Board, and the British Broadcasting Corporation— each of which varies only slightly from the pattern just described.

Although the mixed undertaking has points in common with the trust, such as its corporate form and monopolistic position, the two organizations are strikingly different.

The mixed undertaking is essentially a joint adventure in which government and private investors are joined to conduct a public service enterprise. The ownership, the management, and the profits are divided between the government and private interests, in proportion to the amount of capital each has contributed to the undertaking. The government owns a portion of the stock representing its investment, elects and appoints some of the executives, depending upon the proportion of the investment, and decides controversies arising between government and private directors. In these respects it is a cooperative enterprise in which public and private interests are safeguarded through a series of managerial checks. The proportion of government participation varies in those countries where the mixed undertaking is utilized; in France it is fixed by law at 40 per cent, in Germany it is usually above 50 per cent, and in Great Britain the percentage is dependent upon the type of enterprise involved. But in each instance the government reserves the right to veto any action arising out of fundamental disagreement between government and private representatives. Because of the remarkable success of the public utility trust and the comparative newness of the mixed enterprise, only a few of the latter undertakings are to be found in Great Britain at the present time.

The outstanding British examples of the mixed enterprise are the Manchester Ship Canal, the Southampton Harbor Board, and the Anglo-Persian Oil Company.

A comparison of the relative advantages of these two methods of public ownership gives rise to much uncertainty as to the problem of choice. On the one hand, the mixed undertaking permits government to participate in the operation and management of the utility enterprise with a minimum expenditure of public funds. This circumstance is becoming an increasingly important consideration, particularly where the program is to be carried out on a broad scale. The extent of participation may be varied in accordance with the needs of the enterprise and the public interest involved. As a solution to the American railroad problem, the mixed undertaking presents some interesting possibilities. Furthermore, the organization of the mixed enterprise allows the freedom and independence of managerial initiative which many governmental institutions are said to lack. However, the potential power of governmental veto with regard to matters of fundamental disagreement may serve as a serious check on developments in those directions. Finally, the mixed undertaking offers some unique advantages as an effective method of public control. The representatives of the government are familiar with the details and operations of the enterprise, since they are a part of the organization. Because of this association, government is able to obtain any information it requires, and is placed in a position where it may readily control or supervise capitalization, accounting practices, profits, and earnings, as well as service standards. The potentialities of this method of control will probably be fully appreciated only by the administrative official who has been literally bound, tied, and gagged in his attempt to obtain necessary information from private management.

On the other hand, the public utility trust possesses some significant advantages over both the mixed undertaking and the American public corporation. In the first place, the trust is semi-autonomous; government interference with managerial initiative is reduced to the bare minimum once the organization has been established. In the second place, the elimination of the profit motive effectively removes another source of trouble which could still arise in connection with the mixed enterprise. Finally, it is the only method of public ownership which makes no compromise with the fundamental postulate that the function of the public utility enterprise is predominantly public in character. The sense of public trusteeship is its outstanding characteristic.

By way of conclusion, the following observations may be made regarding the choice of control devices. In America, administrative regulation as a method of public utility control is on trial as it has never been before. Unless the antagonisms and conflicting interests can be eliminated from the regulatory process, the movement toward alternative methods, including social ownership, is certain to be given greater impetus. Private utility management, if it is so inclined, is in a crucial position to make regulation work. The denial of the profit motive as a dominant factor in the operation of the enterprise, the development of a spirit of cooperative effort and understanding between management and the administrative commission, and an enduring sense of public trusteeship—all of these represent the initial steps which must be taken to render the regulatory device an effective and desirable instrument of public control.

The principal lesson to be learned from the recent experiments in public ownership—both here and abroad—is that the effectiveness of any program of social control must depend in the last analysis upon good administration.

The public utility problem, in whatever form it is found, is primarily a question of distributing controls. The locus of ownership is merely an incidental aspect of the whole problem. Government is forced to resort to extreme measures only when its normal instruments of authority are dulled by constant impact with powerful resistance and deep-rooted hostility. When the use of sharper and more effective tools of political authority becomes necessary, new problems of administration and protection are certain to follow. The reconciliation of these new concepts of public interest with the older political ideals of freedom and individual initiative is surely one of the most urgent tasks that face democratic government to-day.

No. 104

[THE railroads have come almost completely under governmental control since the passage of the Interstate Commerce Act of 1887. The extent of this control and the difficulties in which the railroads now find themselves are more or less familiar to all. Recommended solutions of the railroad problem are legion, but more and more consideration is being given to the possibility of government ownership. Professor Daniels, in the following article, gives some of the reasons why this solution is more than a possibility.]

TOWARD NATIONALIZED RAILROADS [1]

by Winthrop M. Daniels

WHETHER the Federal Government shall take over the railroads is fast ceasing to be an academic question. It is now by no means impossible in the near future. Joseph B. Eastman, Federal Coordinator of Transportation, reported to the Senate in January, 1934, that "theoretically and logically public ownership and operation meets the known ills of the present situation better than any other remedy. . . . When an industry becomes so public in character that such intimate regulation of its affairs becomes necessary, in strict logic it would seem that it should cease to masquerade as a private industry and the government should assume complete responsibility, financial and otherwise."

It is true that the Coordinator does not at present recommend public ownership and operation "because of the impaired economic condition of the nation" and because "the immediate burden upon the public finances might be great." But his judgment as to the eventual solution is unmistak-

[1] Winthrop M. Daniels, "Toward Nationalized Railroads," *Current History* (January, 1935), Vol. 41, pp. 407-412. Reprinted by the permission of *Current History and Forum*.

ably clear, and there are some grounds for thinking that he overestimates the financial load which the government would immediately assume were it to acquire control.

For several reasons, eventual government ownership is not unlikely. In the first place, the roads as a rule have been upon a prolonged fast. They entered the period of depression fairly well able to weather a moderate recession of business, or even a major recession, if not unduly protracted. With ample cash assets, many of them continued dividend disbursements for some months after net operating income had declined or disappeared. Apparently they thought to make a calm by laughing at the storm. But the depression continued, and shows no signs of abatement.

It is frequently said that a newly launched enterprise must expect to encounter an initial "starving period" of several years before it begins its earning career. But when, after attaining maturity, it is called upon again to undergo a five-year famine, the outlook for eventual recovery is far from hopeful. In January, 1934, some 75 railroads, operating a total of 42,340 miles, about one-sixth of the total in the United States, were in receivership or subjected to court control under the Bankruptcy Act. Had the RFC not gone to the rescue with large loans the insolvent brotherhood would have inevitably grown. As a drowning man will clutch at a straw, a starving corporation will accept financial aid from an alien source even at the sacrifice of its former independence.

This dependence of the railroads upon the government is shown by the extent to which they have sought and received government aid. The PWA has advanced about $200,000,000 to roads which ventured to continue with new construction projects or to make good some part of their deferred maintenance. The RFC has lent over $400,000,000 to various carriers on the verge of bankruptcy. What is not fully realized by the roads or by the public is that every time Uncle Sam dips one hand deeper into his pockets to aid distressed railroads the further forward he reaches his other hand toward taking complete control.

The case has its parallel in the advances made by the government in the last eighteen months to needy banks. Where in return for financial assistance the government induced banks to issue and sell to the Treasury the new preferred bank stock, or to make the Treasury a preferred creditor for capital loans, the government became not a sleeping but a senior partner. Over 90 per cent of the assets of the Federal Reserve Banks and about 30 per cent of the assets of member banks consist of government securities. The Treasury has thus strengthened its stranglehold on the banks until they have become fiscal satrapies whose chief function is to absorb new government loans at dictation. Should the credit of the government fall but moderately, banks whose assets are chiefly in government bonds would see a practical disappearance of the equity of the common stockholders, and could readily be nationalized on reorganization if the Treasury asserted its preferred position.

That the borrower is servant to the lender has long been an established axiom. It applies also when the government functions in the lender's role. The situation when Federal control of the railroads was ended in March, 1920, differed markedly from the present situation. Under war emergency, the Federal Government had assumed their operation. Despite the rise in prices and costs attendant upon the war, the Railroad Administration did not deem it wise to raise rates sufficiently to recover the costs. When the roads were returned to the owning corporations it was generally conceded that until a new and higher rate structure, adjusted to the new level of prices and costs, was set up, the carriers because of their previous involuntary captivity could not pay their way. Moreover, during the government administration additions and betterments had been made with the primary objective of providing war transport, not with a view to supplying the new capital requirements which normal peacetime operation would have demanded.

The railroad loans which were therefore provided in the Transportation Act of 1920, as the outcome of previous Federal control, were intended only for the temporary assistance of the carriers, to help them emerge from a situation into which they had been plunged by previous government action. The existing loans from the RFC are of a totally different character. Instead of being a virtual reparation for embarrassments previously created by the government, they are frankly eleemosynary, with a repayment string attached. With the government in the role of Lady Bountiful, it may not be strange that the railroads sought the shelter of public credit. If it was to be the function of the government to lend to the banks, to the farmers, and to necessitous debtors generally, why not to the railroads? They but acted as did the individual who avowed: "When I saw everybody holding out his hand, I held out my hat."

Unfortunately for the railroads, by accepting government aid they expose themselves to having thrust upon their directorates a representation of the lending interest. It is difficult for them to explain why he who pays the piper shall not have a voice, at least, in calling the tune. It is not alone the "sons of the wild jackass" who ask the question and who suggest the answer. The Coordinator himself, in his first report, remarked in reference to requiring Federal incorporation to enforce railroad consolidation that "the Craven plan of public directors on the boards of such corporations should be put to the test, when and where the commission finds that it can be tried without detriment to other railroad companies not having such public directors."

It is also strongly urged that only by the intervention of public authority in the field of managerial judgment can waste and preventable expense be avoided. Thus, the Coordinator recently ordered the Louisville & Nashville to continue the interchange of through passenger-train equipment for the Dixie route with the Chicago & Eastern Illinois at Evansville, Ind., when the Louisville & Nashville had arranged to operate its equipment between Evansville and Chicago over the New York Central Lines. The Coordinator based his order on the ground that unnecessary duplication of service and unnecessary capital expense must be avoided.

Moreover, the series of reports which the Coordinator is issuing calls attention to extensive economies which might be secured by various changes in railroad operation. The Merchandise Traffic Report suggests potential annual economies of over $87,000,000. The report on the proposed pooling of box cars gives $75,000,000 a year as a "conservative estimate of the operating savings possible." No doubt when the Coordinator's staff issue their reports on the present conduct of carload freight traffic and passenger traffic, other extensive potential economies will be disclosed.

These so-called "wastes of competition," which inhere in persistent carrier rivalry, and which would be saved by a cooperative railroad policy, do not necessarily imply government ownership as the sole remedy. Either a greater degree of voluntary cooperation through a wide extension of the pooling device, or the actual consolidations of railroad properties might achieve similar economies. But if the roads are reluctant to apply pooling arrangements, and if their finances for the time being preclude consolidation, the alternative of realizing the alleged possibilities of vast economies in operation is said to lie in government compulsion or government operation.

The reason assigned by the Coordinator for not recommending government acquisition of railroad properties at the present time is the "impaired economic condition of the nation" and the heavy immediate additional burden that would be laid upon the public finances. Waiving altogether the prior question of the desirability of government-owned roads, we would suggest that the difficulties to immediate government acquisition are not as great as the Coordinator assumes.

The impaired economic condition of the nation is reflected in that of the railroad companies as a whole. The par value of their aggregate stocks in the hands of the public is about $7,150,000,000. With Pennsylvania shares, for example, selling at 45 per cent of par, New York Central at 20 per cent of par, Baltimore & Ohio at 15 per cent of par, and shares of lesser companies at prices far lower, it is conservative to estimate that the aggregate current market value of railroad equities is not one-third of their par value. Even when allowance is made for the few exceptional properties such as the Union Pacific and the Pocahontas roads, and the guaranteed stocks of certain leased lines, the aggregate market value of railroad equities cannot be more than about $2,350,000,000. It is hardly necessary to suggest that corporate control may be secured with no more than a 50 per cent interest.

A little over $1,000,000,000 would have been the cost of securing government control of the railroads of the country, had the marketing operations been possible with requisite secrecy and dispatch. Several times that sum has been spent by the Treasury on various forms of "self-liquidating" projects and public works. The so-called profit from the debasement of the gold content of the dollar would have been more than ample to finance the acquisition. Had the extreme New Dealers had the imagination and audacity which prompted Disraeli to buy the Suez Canal shares for Great Britain, or which moved Jefferson to buy Louisiana for the United States, they could have achieved government control of all railroad properties in the United States, and Congress would have fallen over itself in its haste to ratify the acquisition.

True, the roads thus acquired would have been burdened with funded debt charges of $500,000,000 a year. But this debt service charge and also annual taxes paid by the railroads are now in great part earned by the roads from their current operations; and if the economies recited by the Coordinator's reports were remotely realized, the bond interest would be taken care of by the properties themselves, with no additional burden on the public finances. In short, the prevailing market levels of railroad stocks would have afforded the government an opportunity of buying control of the entire railroad system at a minimum cost.

The final reason why government ownership seems possible in the not distant future is that holders of railroad bonds have become very much discouraged over the future of these assets and are only too ready to listen to a proposal to exchange them for government securities. Something like $3,000,000,000, or about 15 per cent of the total investments of life insurance companies, are said to be in railroad bonds. The mutual savings banks hold perhaps another $1,000,000,000 of the same securities. The Coordinator reports that numerous executives of insurance companies, banks and similar institutions, as well as large individual holders, "are beset with fears with respect to railroad investments"; that the "confidence inspired by the provisions of the Transportation Act, 1920, has gone, and disillusionment has taken its place."

"In the five years ending in 1938," says Vice President County of the

Pennsylvania, "close to $2,000,000,000 of railroad debt matures, and must be refunded, including part of the large short-term borrowings from the government for improvements and maintenance." The president of the Security Owners' Association, in the pending case asking an advance in railroad rates, testified before the Interstate Commerce Commission on behalf of the association's members, who hold in excess of 40 per cent of the par value of the total outstanding railroad funded debt, that "the confidence of investors, who have in the past provided the railroads with capital through the purchase of their bonds, has been based largely on the belief that regulation meant stabilization of return. The drastic shrinkage in market values, and the actual or threatened cutting off of return on investments, has shaken that confidence, but the belief that regulation must and does recognize its function still persists." He therefore asked on behalf of 60,000,000 life insurance policy holders and 13,000,000 depositors in mutual savings banks "immediate constructive relief." If that should not be forthcoming, he thinks "there can be little basis for the expectation that they (the railroads) will play an important part in the economic recovery of the nation."

To summarize: The likelihood of government ownership and operation of the railroads in the not distant future is due to the large existing burden of railroad indebtedness to the Federal Government; to the impending maturities of railroad debt which threaten widespread insolvencies if government loans are not further extended; to the depressed market price of railroad stocks, which would make available a controlling interest at a low figure; and to the eagerness of the largest holders of railroad bonds to surrender them in exchange for government obligations.

If one were foolish enough to essay the role of a prophet and to leave out of one's reckoning those unexpected occurrences which always bedevil the prediction of future social phenomena, the prophecy would run as follows: First, in the pending rate advance case the carriers will receive half a loaf or none at all; second, the next session of Congress will not establish effective and comprehensive regulation of the railroads' competitors, nor cease to accord virtual subsidies to motor traffic highways and to inland water routes; third, increased receiverships, in the absence of an industrial revival, will follow; and as the outcome, a substantial policy of nationalization will be inaugurated. Of course, there may be a miraculous way of escape, but unfortunately, the divinity who in the past has always been supposed to take special charge of children, drunken men and the United States of America seems to be gone on a far journey.

The probable drift toward nationalization will be speeded up, then, with the prolongation of industrial depression. But it is one thing to recognize the drift, and another to ride complacently with the current. The deadening effect of bureaucracy and the poisonous effect of politics on industry would both have to be encountered if the government owned and operated the railroads. Even the Coordinator would put control, if the railroads were nationalized, in the hands of a non-partisan political body of trustees. As he says, "the tendency in countries which have public ownership and operation is now definitely to separate the railroads from ordinary governmental activities and make them autonomous, non-political enterprises." Whether this ideal could or could not be realized, it is significant that it implies the need of supermen for the job, and evident distrust of "that crafty and insidious animal called a politician."

There is no use, however, in imagining that the imminent danger of nationalization can be avoided by the carriers through a supine policy of leaning on the government credit—while it lasts—or by invoking the special solicitude of Congress upon the widows and orphans whose income depends on railroad bonds. It is only by a rigorous self-regulation that they can escape the calamity that yawns before them. They will not be able to shame Congress into a decent respect for their rights until they have done for themselves what both prudence and principle dictate. What are some of the things that this policy involves?

First, it means eliminating from the property accounts of the railroads a quantity of alleged assets whose only title to the name is their past cost. The issue is not one of overcapitalization in the old sense of the term. Only those with "water" on the brain can be blind to the fact that the aggregate of railroad securities outstanding in the hands of the public is less than the actual investment in the properties. But there is nothing sacred, in the economic sense, in the magnitude of past cost incurred, even though it be beatified as "prudent investment." Many of these past investments are to-day one with Nineveh and Tyre.

There are thousands upon thousands of branch lines of railroad whose value to their owners, or whose necessity to the public, is wholly negative. While there have been many petitions by carriers to abandon some parts of their mileage, the corresponding duty to amortize their capital obligations is apparently neither conceded by the carriers nor emphasized by the Interstate Commerce Commission. L. F. Loree, president of the Delaware & Hudson, asserts that there are 70,000 miles of tracks that ought to be discarded. Keeping their cost in the balance sheet figure as part of the live investment in road and equipment is simply idle and misleading.

Correlative to a realistic write-down of assets is a reduction in capital liabilities, such as a lessening of the par value of stock, and eventually an amortization of the bonded indebtedness incurred for these vanished elements of value. In his supplemental report to that of the so-called Coolidge

Committee, Alfred E. Smith hit bedrock when he observed: "I am satisfied that the general public will not tolerate writing up values or increasing rates merely upon the theory that a great many railroad securities are held by savings banks, trustees and insurance companies as security for widows, orphans or other beneficiaries of trust."

In the second place, the railroads must show more disposition to effect operating economies along new lines, especially those that involve conjoint action through the use of the pooling device. Many of the paper savings that the Coordinator's staff are displaying in their reports will no doubt disappear when and if the proposed new methods are attempted. But there will probably be a considerable residuum that can and ought to be realized. In some instances demonstrable economies are obtainable by doing away with needless duplication in competing lines. Clearing house arrangements for interline settlements illustrate another possibility. Until the roads exhaust their capacity for self-help they cannot look for relief at the hands of Congress. The only possible reform that may come promptly from Congress is a statute that would forcibly expedite the reorganization of bankrupt railroads.

Even if the carriers came before Congress with an absolutely clean bill of health, it is by no means certain that they could, without tireless effort and disheartening rebuffs, obtain the legislation which they may claim as of right and not of favor. That Congress should extend regulation to the railroads' competitors by highway and waterway is abundantly clear. That subsidies should be withdrawn from these competitors is dictated by every just consideration. Eventually, when the opposition of self-interested lobbies is overcome, this result may obtain. In the meantime, the whole mechanism of transport may have been nationalized.

No. 105

[THE regulation of radio broadcasting is one of the more difficult problems with which government must deal. All will agree with John T. Flynn, the author of the following article, that the limited number of air channels makes regulation imperative, and that this regulation implies the power to determine who may broadcast, under what conditions they may broadcast, and, to some extent, the content of programs. Not all, however, will agree with the author's analysis of the relationship of the advertiser to the radio industry, but a consideration of the basic issues raised by this relationship is a prerequisite to a satisfactory determination of public policy.]

RADIO: MEDICINE SHOW [1]

by John T. Flynn

A POSITIVE, defined, recognizable policy on radio broadcasting is one of those things the national government has not yet troubled itself to form. But attention to the problem cannot be very much longer deferred. The incredibly childish approach of the broadcasters to the problem of public discussion, the vague whisperings of plans for government entry into the business of broadcasting, the scandalous rumors about the commission set up to represent the public interest, the vulgarity, banality, sheer ignorance and immaturity of the advertisers who sponsor our daily ration of culture, have so irritated the public conscience that Congress is certain to get around presently to this very serious matter.

It is impossible to consider radio without discussing the problem of freedom of speech. It is impossible to conceive of radio broadcasting without government control. The air is a series of highways over which messages may be broadcast. The number of these highways is limited—less than 100. There is therefore a sheer traffic problem to be faced. Unless these radio bands or highways are allocated everybody would attempt to use the same bands and transmission would be impossible. These highways are not like public streets which countless vehicles can use at the same time. In the air every traveler must be kept off the aerial highway while the licensed user occupies it. There is, therefore, no escape from a system of government licenses.

The privilege of granting licenses and of renewing them comprises the right to refuse them, to cancel them, to deny renewal. Therefore an arbitrary or excessively political government can employ this power as a means of controlling the contents of the broadcast. And thus arises the old ghost of invasions of freedom of speech by the political authority. Everybody will agree that under no circumstances should the government be permitted to influence or dictate the social, economic, religious, political or other intellectual content of broadcast programs, save insofar as the rights of other citizens may be involved. The slander laws and, within properly defined limits, the police power to exclude obscenity cover the government's general sphere of control, so far as content is concerned.

But freedom of speech and of the press may have other enemies than

[1] John T. Flynn, "Radio: Medicine Show," The American Scholar (Autumn, 1938), Vol. 7, pp. 430-437. Reprinted by permission of the author and The American Scholar.

the government. And this makes it necessary for us to be quite clear what we mean by freedom of speech and of the press. The man who owns a newspaper and who is free from every form of government restraint certainly enjoys freedom of speech so far as his newspaper is concerned. But we must distinguish between the individual newspaper and the press as an institution. There is a difference between freedom of the individual owners and freedom of the press as an institution. A group of men who severally own all the newspapers in a society may come together in an agreement to exclude all news and discussion of certain subjects of social concern. They do this in the exercise of their own freedom. But having done it, that society no longer enjoys a free press insofar as the censored subject is concerned. It is entirely possible, therefore, that the individual owners of the press may be free of all government restraint and yet the country be without a free press. It is this view of the matter which remains obscure in most discussions of the subject.

Every newspaper owner is subject to restraints which arise out of his own human weaknesses—fear of offending his community, fear of the hostility of its powerful leaders, fear of religious and social and political groups. These kinds of restraints can never be eliminated. They are in the order of human nature and must be accepted as inevitable. Freedom of the press and of course of the radio means freedom from such restraints as may be controlled. Against these human weaknesses there is but one safeguard—a multitude of journals and a multitude of editors who will not be subject to the same restraints. All will not be trying to please the same people. The very freedom—nay urge—of one man to print becomes a powerful corrective of the restraints upon another to omit the news. Political oppression of the press is so baleful just because it can exercise its influence over every editor, can terrorize and silence any editor who defies its interests.

The restraints upon the press which arise out of these private and social and commercial interests become a grave public problem when the powers which exercise these influences are so great and so united that their pressure may be applied to all editors and to the press as a whole.

Let us suppose that Editor Number One publishes his journal at a loss but makes up his loss through a subsidy granted by Mr. X. Editor Number Two also publishes a journal at a loss but meets his deficit by means of sums obtained for some service to Mr. Y. Editor One will feel at liberty to print what he chooses so long as he does not offend Mr. X. Editor Two will feel bound to print what pleases Mr. Y under penalty of losing Y's support. But Editor One will be hampered only by his dependence upon X and will be quite free to print what he chooses about Y. And Editor Two although restrained by Mr. Y will have no compunction about printing anything he wishes about X. But what will happen when Editor One and Editor Two are both dependent on Mr. X? If all the papers in a community are owned by Editors One and Two they constitute the press. In theory both editors are free to defy the powerful Mr. X. But in the nature of things they will not do so because the price of defiance is extinction. And therefore while these editors are legally free and voluntarily relinquish that freedom for a more highly coveted prize, namely solvency, the press is not free.

Something like this has happened to the press in this country. Few if any newspapers can publish their journals at a profit. They must employ those journals in another field than journalism—and that field is advertising, which is in no sense a part of journalism but rather a parasite upon it. It is the advertiser who makes up the editor's deficits.

It is not true, of course, that there is but one advertiser who holds in his hands the power of life and death over the editors. No one can deny, however, that the advertising interests in a community, although they have their special differences on points of religion and social principles and even of commercial policies, are generally a unit upon certain important essential principles. But even where they are not a unit there is a menace to the freedom of the press which arises out of the necessity laid upon the editor to court their favor. The publisher solicitous for the favor of Mr. X and of Mr. Y, even though these gentlemen differ upon a point, will exercise the greatest prudence in seeking to offend neither. The very number of the powerful persons who make up the patron element of the press merely multiplies the number of restraints upon the editor. Altogether it forces on him that conservative timidity which compels him to remain away from certain great areas of news and from the discussion of certain serious subjects which the commercial interests in a community as a whole and separately wish to remain untouched.

Thus it seems clear that before we can have a free press society must find means not only of protecting the individual editor from the invasions and restraints of government but of protecting the press as an institution from the editors themselves.

Thus far I have discussed this problem in terms of the press alone since that is an instrument with which we are more familiar. But the radio, like the press, is subject to the same observations. It is one of those instruments of public news and discussion which apparently cannot support itself as such and must turn to some other interest to pay its bills. Like the press it has turned to the advertiser. The advertiser is willing to pay the cost of assembling a great orchestra or of forming a troop of entertainers or supplying a dance band because he knows that millions will listen. All he asks is the privilege of interrupting the program at intervals to catch the ears of those millions of listeners. It is an old technique. The itinerant medicine man of former days carried about with him his banjo player and minstrel and clog dancer and magician to attract the crowd to his tent and to put them in a benevolent mood as a prologue to his own "high pitch" upon the wonders of his pills and lotions.

Now the radio is hopelessly committed to this form of operation. The advertiser is and doubtless for some time will remain the sponsor of the radio program. And because he pays the piper he is in a position to call the tunes. Thus the freedom of the radio as an institution of public discussion and news, not the freedom of the individual station, is threatened. The individual station is a commercial enterprise in the hands of an enterpriser who wishes to operate it as an instrument of profit derived from the commercial interests in the community. He has no wish to offend or battle or defy them. His only study is to please them to the uttermost, prove his usefulness to them and advance their interests. He has no liberty which he is deeply concerned in defending against them. But the grand result is that the institution of which he is but a part and which, as an institution, is a public and not a private function sees its freedom extinguished. Is it not clear that the freedom of the radio is destroyed if the government will not grant licenses unless it censors the programs? Is it not equally clear that that freedom is equally impaired if the advertising interests will not pay the bills unless they can impose a practical censorship?

But what then is to be done about it? There is obviously only one power with sufficient authority to do anything and that is the government, which is the trustee of the people for the adminisration of the air.

But no one will countenance a government-dominated news agency and forum. Men have not forgotten that the first struggle for freedom of speech and of the press was waged against political authority. That battle, certainly in this country, has been won. But a people vigilant for the preservation of its democratic freedoms will never cease to look with a certain suspicion upon political authorities, particularly in a world troubled as ours is to-day by so many ruling groups who assail the very existence of these rights. The radio is of necessity in the hands of the government. We cannot escape its presidency over the administration of the medium through which the radio operates. But every resistance should be offered the establishment of government-owned and -operated radio stations since these are liable to become the instruments not of the government but of the politician who operates the government. But equally we cannot tolerate unregulated private ownership of the air. And there is no regulating authority but the government. How far, therefore, may we trust the government with this function? I offer the following suggestions.

The advertising sponsor presents a twofold problem. First there is the abuse of the advertiser's privileges in the use of the air and secondly the abuse of his power to restrain free discussion over the air. On the first point the abuse arises when the advertiser is permitted to disseminate news and discussions of public questions. The advertiser wishes to advertise his product. He therefore desires to command a large audience. This is a purely practical matter of drumming up a crowd. To do this he uses the most attractive entertainment he can obtain. Having gotten his crowd he should be permitted within decent limits to advertise his product. But he should not be permitted to turn that crowd into a political, religious or economic meeting. He should not be permitted to employ the radio and the crowd to spread religious, social, economic or political propaganda. However bad the newspaper may have become it has not descended to this. It does not, as a rule, rent out its news or its editorial columns to advertisers. It does indeed succumb to the influence of commercial interests but it does not permit the editorial function to pass out of its hands. Its editorials and reports do not have to run the gauntlet of advertising agents, vice-presidents and presidents and managers of commercial corporations, as is the case in broadcasts. The handling of news and views in the newspaper is in the hands of a department separated from the advertiser. And although the advertiser's spirit broods over the editorial room the editorial room resents it, resists it as much as it can. Furthermore, thinking of its function in terms of editorial excellence and obligation, the editorial room does build up an ethical standard which stands as a barricade against the over-insistent business office.

I know too well the bad influence of the commercial spirit upon the press. I know as well as anyone how much better the press could be if it were emancipated from this influence. But I know also how infinitely worse it would be if the advertising agent and the advertiser had moved bodily into the editorial rooms. This is what has happened in the radio broadcasting station. This is what I wish to end.

I would not restrain the radio broadcaster from the dissemination of news or of discussions. But I would compel him to separate this function completely from the programs of the advertisers. To permit the advertiser to become a social and economic propagandist on the air is to give the advertising interest a disproportionate place in the great forum of public discussion. A great manufacturer can pay the immense sum required to support a great symphony orchestra on the air because he gets an advertising return for the expenditure. But having drawn together a vast audience to listen to the symphony orchestra and having subdued the mind by means of the melting music, he may then interrupt the concert for a precious five minutes while he pours into the ears of his guests his economic and political philosophies. There is no public group with sufficient financial resources to meet this kind of propaganda. The advertiser should be permitted to have his crowd and his concert and a brief period to sell his wares but no more. As a citizen with economic and social views to exploit he should have only the same right, so far as the air is concerned, as any other citizen. Although this would not free the air from the influence of the advertiser it would certainly tend to bring the distribution of the news and views of the broadcasting station under the administration of an editorial group capable of developing a far more civilized ethic with respect to the news.

I would divide the air into its three functions. In one it would be a great medicine show where advertisers, for pay, could put on entertainment and cry their wares, but the ballyhoo would be limited strictly to entertainment. In a second the air would be a great distributor of news and views which would be administered by a separate editorial board at the expense of the broadcaster. In a third I would consider the air as a great public hall which would be open to hire by persons, and by cultural and educational and other public organizations to hold meetings. And a part of this time I would compel the broadcasting station to give freely for educational and public purposes.

I would not permit any newspaper to own or operate a radio station. The newspaper is itself a dispenser of news and views. It tends to become more and more a monopoly in its community. One-paper communities, or communities dominated by a single owner, are growing in number. A multitude of journals and stations, and the inevitable competition between them, is the chief prophylactic against excessive surrender to the sponsoring advertisers in both press and radio. To permit the radio to fall under the dominion of the press as the press itself falls under the dominion of monopoly is to throw away this safeguard.

Regulations covering these points might well be made by the government without infringing the rights of anyone or without setting the government up as a menace to the liberties of the people themselves. No other agency of society can protect it from that usurpation of the instruments of communication by the great, predatory interests of the nation—which is coming to be one of the most sinister problems of the modern democratic state.

Chapter XXX

GOVERNMENT AND LABOR

[AFTER the Civil War, the United States rapidly became an industrial and urbanized nation. The West was opened up, improved technology fostered the creation of great railway systems, the invention of the automobile necessitated the development of highways, great new cities were born, monopoly organization came to be the form of capitalist production, the number of salaried and wage workers rapidly increased, and the problem of labor and labor relations became one of the major problems of the day. By the 1930's the American scene was markedly changed from the 1860's. The little man was no longer able to pull himself up by his bootstraps. Movement from class to class had grown extremely difficult, and the worker was more conscious of his position and of his rights. In 1870, 44.8 per cent of the gainfully employed were industrial and other wage workers; 4.8 per cent were salaried workers. By 1935, the percentage of gainfully employed in the first class had grown to 59.3 and in the second to 20.2. Thus over half of the gainfully employed are industrial and wage workers and almost 80 per cent are wage and salaried workers.

As a result, the solution of the problems of labor and labor relations has become a major responsibility of any government bent on serving the great mass of the people. A government fulfilling its responsibility must guarantee the right of labor to organize, help labor secure equality of bargaining power, protect labor against exploitation through the regulation of hours and wages, the employment of children, and many other things undreamed of seventy years ago.

Perhaps the most striking but least understood aspects of this picture are the industrial conflicts commonly known as strikes. Few of us know what lies behind them. Few of us know about such things as the "yellow dog" contract, the Mohawk Valley formula, primary and secondary boycotts, lockouts, and injunctions. Few of us know why we think labor organizations are good or bad. Few of us know why labor is or is not well organized. Few of us have taken time to consider what the proper role of government should be in relation to labor. Yet, it is about these things that we shall have to think if we are to solve the problems with which we are confronted.]

No. 106

WHAT'S BEHIND THE STRIKES? [1]

by Alexander H. Frey

MOST labor disputes—in fact the vast majority—have not arisen simply out of the desire of workers for more pay or shorter hours. Behind the strike has usually been a struggle for effective unionization and the resulting power of collective bargaining. The Industrial Revolution, i.e., the mechanization of the processes of production and the introduction of the factory system, brought about conditions which have terminated the ability of any but the most highly skilled workers to bargain individually with their employers on a basis of equality. In earlier times employer and employee belonged to the same community, attended the same church, participated in the same political activities, and were not very far removed in the economic scale. There was no great surplus of labor; if the terms of employment offered to a given employee by his employer were unsatisfactory more likely than not they would talk face to face and reach an accord. Or if the terms were regarded by the employee as utterly unreasonable he could do odd jobs for others, farm on his own land, and look forward to the security of at least subsistence for himself and his family for an indefinite period. And eventually either his employer would feel the need of his services sufficiently to modify his former offer or the employee would find other satisfactory work in the same community.

But with the coming of the Industrial Revolution all this was changed. Great cities developed which were the centers of the factory system. The individual worker and his employer (to-day very frequently an impersonal corporation) grew farther and farther apart socially and economically. The favorable atmosphere for personal conferences and adjustment of disputes disappeared. The individual factory worker to-day owns no land, has no tools, little or no capital, and hence has no resources with which he and his family can hope to survive an extended deadlock with his employer over terms of employment. Moreover, even if desirable jobs are available elsewhere, he cannot afford to transfer himself and his family and their few possessions to a distant city. In short, under modern industrial conditions the individual worker is powerless to bargain on an equal basis with his employer with respect to the terms of his employment. Acting alone, he

[1] Alexander H. Frey, "What's Behind the Strikes?" *Harper's Magazine* (January, 1938), Vol. 176, pp. 168-178. Reprinted by permission of the author and *Harper's Magazine*.

has no practical alternative but to accept the terms offered to him. This, in briefest outline, is the story behind the passion for unionization. To labor leaders and other students of labor problems the desirability of organizations through which workers can bargain collectively is axiomatic.

Nor is the benefit of such labor organizations confined to labor's ranks; it is important to employers and to the consuming public as well. The recent depression has emphasized the fact that ability to purchase must approximate ability to produce if periodic accumulation of disrupting surpluses of consumers' goods is to be avoided. The workers of the nation are by far the largest body of consumers. Unless they have sufficient wages —buying power—to enable them to purchase a reasonable proportion of the consumable goods which they help to produce, surpluses of goods will again arise and a new depression will be inevitable. To the maintenance of our competitive, capitalistic society the making of profits is essential. Competition being severe, there is constant pressure upon employers to reduce costs of production. Labor costs are frequently the greatest single item of expense in the production of goods. Consequently, the reduction of wages, or its corollary, increasing hours of labor, is an ever-present temptation. As already indicated, the individual employee does not have the equality of bargaining power which might enable him to counterbalance this threat. Nor can even the most generous, altruistic, and farsighted employer afford to pay wages much in excess of his competitors. If, in the interest of immediate profits, wages are reduced to a point where workers are unable to consume the products of industry, a crash is inevitable with disastrous consequences to all. But effective labor unions, operating over a wide area, can modify the development of this pernicious cycle. Herein lies the interest of employers and of the public generally as well as of employees in labor's achievement of collective bargaining.

Yet, despite this almost self-evident special interest of employees and general interest of the public in the development of effective labor organizations, the growth of union membership has been incredibly slow. In 1931 the labor unions of this country embraced only one-fifth of all wage earners, excluding agricultural laborers. The recent depression with its attendant poverty and excess of labor caused many workers to drop their union membership. Unquestionably the Wagner Act and the current activities of the CIO have stimulated an increase in the ranks of organized labor. But there would seem to be little doubt that even to-day scarcely one-quarter of the industrial workers of the country hold union memberships.

What is the explanation of this amazing paradox that laborers, whose self-interests are so dependent upon collective bargaining, have not flocked into unions—their collective bargaining agencies—almost to a man? There are four principal factors: (1) inertia on the part of the rank and file of workers, (2) deficient labor leadership, (3) the solid front of employers and effective back pressure on their part to thwart the development of unionization, and (4) the attitude of the courts when confronted with controversies arising out of labor disputes.

The first two require no extended discussion. Laborers are not exempt from the human tendency to be more concerned with the immediate present than with the speculative future. If a man has a job he has at least so much security and present income. He knows that if he joins a union his income will be decreased by the amount of the dues that he will have to pay. He knows that as a union member he may be called out on strike and thereby lose wages and perhaps even his job. He is, therefore, strongly inclined to let well enough alone and not take out the insurance for his job-future that union membership may constitute. If he subsequently loses his job or suffers a drastic reduction in pay his availability for union membership is further affected.

About the deplorable quality of labor leadership, there is not much that can be said except to recognize that it is a concomitant of the weakness of labor unions generally. So long as the efforts of employers and the attitude of the courts (along with labor's natural inertia) keep the vast majority of workers out of unions, just so long will the emergence of more intelligent, reasonable, honest labor leaders be curtailed. Heretofore the risks to labor leaders of jail sentences or other penalties have been so great that in many instances only the fanatics or the dishonest have ventured to array themselves against the opposing forces. Under the circumstances the really extraordinary fact is that many men of extremely fine character and capacity have always been found at the forefront of the labor movement.

There are serious, impartial students of labor problems who are convinced that, despite the inertia and inadequate leadership to which I have referred, labor's struggle for effective unionization would to-day be much farther advanced had employers not been so skillfully combating this movement. For many decades there has been going on a miniature civil war between capital and labor with an arsenal of weapons on each side. The employers are equipped for both attack and defense. An aggressive move on the part of employers is the lock-out, so called because it refers to an employer's act of locking his plant against employees willing to work, in an effort to get for himself more favorable labor terms. This is the counterpart of a strike. It has been held that employers may without legal penalty enter into a combination to lock out their employees.

The blacklist is another device of employers for eliminating union employees: employers furnish one another with the names of former employees known or believed to have union membership or even sympathy and the employer so notified refuses employment to the worker in question. Although this resembles a secondary boycott, it has not received judicial condemnation. Moreover, statutes which have been enacted against blacklisting have had little effect, the difficulties of proof being almost insuperable.

A prophylactic measure popular with employers for guarding against unionization of their employees has been the so-called "yellow dog" contract. This is an agreement which an employer exacts from an employee that the latter will neither join a union nor induce other employees to do so during the course of his employment. As the nickname suggests, labor particularly resents this stratagem. Such contracts are never made the basis of damage suits for breach thereof, but are intended, as Mr. Justice Maxey of the Pennsylvania Supreme Court has pointed out, merely as "an emplacement for equity's longest-range injunction gun." In other words, the purpose of a "yellow dog" contract is to enable an employer to get an injunction, not against his own employees, but against labor leaders and union officials seeking to unionize his employees, on the ground that such persons are threatening to induce a breach of contract on the part of the employees.

Once a labor dispute has started, the injunction may become the employer's main reliance. But as this is primarily a defensive measure, consideration of it will be postponed until labor's weapons in this struggle for unionization are discussed.

A number of scattered anti-union activities of employers have recently been crystallized into a cohesive technic for strike-breaking known as the "Mohawk Valley formula." This formula was distributed to the National Association of Manufacturers by James H. Rand, Jr., President of Remington Rand, Inc. It was outlined as follows by the National Labor Relations Board in its statement of a case involving that corporation, decided March 15, 1937:

First: When a strike is threatened, label the union leaders as "agitators" to discredit them with the public and their own followers. In the plant, conduct a forced balloting under the direction of foremen in an attempt to ascertain the strength of the union and to make possible misrepresentation of the strikers as a small minority imposing their will upon the majority. At the same time, disseminate propaganda, by means of press releases, advertisements, and the activities of "missionaries," such propaganda falsely stating the issues involved in the strike so that the strikers appear to be making arbitrary demands, and the real issues, such as the employer's refusal to bargain collectively, are obscured. Concurrently with these moves, by exerting economic pressure through threats to move the plant, align the influential members of the community into a cohesive group opposed to the strike.

Include in this group, usually designated a "Citizens Committee," representa-tives of the bankers, real estate owners and business men, i.e., those most sen-sitive to any threat of removal of the plant because of its effect upon property values and purchasing power flowing from payrolls.

Second: When the strike is called, raise high the banner of "law and order," thereby causing the community to mass legal and police weapons against a wholly imagined violence and to forget that those of its members who are employees have equal rights with the other members of the community.

Third: Call a "mass meeting" of the citizens to co-ordinate public sentiment against the strike and to strengthen the power of the Citizens Committee, which organization, thus supported, will both aid the employer in exerting pressure upon the local authorities and itself sponsor vigilante activities.

Fourth: Bring about the formation of a large armed police force to intimi-date the strikers and to exert a psychological effect upon the citizens. This force is built up by utilizing local police, State Police if the Governor cooper-ates, vigilantes and special deputies, the deputies being chosen if possible from other neighoborhoods, so that there will be no personal relationships to induce sympathy for the strikers. Coach the deputies and vigilantes on the law of unlawful assembly, inciting to riot, disorderly conduct, etc., so that, unhampered by any thought that the strikers may also possess some rights, they will be ready and anxious to use their newly-acquired authority to the limit.

Fifth: And perhaps most important, heighten the demoralizing effect of the above measures—all designed to convince the strikers that their cause is hope-less—by a "back to work" movement, operated by a puppet association of so-called "loyal employees" secretly organized by the employer. Have this association wage a publicity campaign in its own name and co-ordinate such campaign with the work of the "missionaries" circulating among the strikers and visiting their homes. This "back to work" movement has these results: it causes the public to believe that the strikers are in the minority and that most of the employees desire to return to work, thereby winning sympathy for the employer and an endorsement of his activities to such an extent that the public is willing to pay the huge costs, direct and indirect, resulting from the heavy forces of police. This "back to work" movement also enables the employer, when the plant is later opened, to operate it with strike-breakers if necessary and to continue to refuse to bargain collectively with the strikers. In addition, the "back to work" movement permits the employer to keep a constant check on the strength of the union through the number of applica-tions received from employees ready to break ranks and return to work, such number being kept secret from the public and other employees, so that the doubts and fears created by such secrecy will in turn induce still others to make applications.

Sixth: When a sufficient number of applications are on hand fix a date for an opening of the plant through the device of having such opening requested by the "back to work" association. Together with the Citizens Committee, prepare for such opening by making provision for a peak army of police, by roping off the areas surrounding the plant, by securing arms and ammunition, etc. The purpose of the "opening" of the plant is threefold: to see if enough employees are ready to return to work; to induce still others to return as a result of the demoralizing effect produced by the opening of the plant and the return of some of their number; and lastly, even if the movement fails to induce a sufficient number of persons to return, to persuade the public through pictures and news releases that the opening was nevertheless successful.

Seventh: Stage the "opening," theatrically throwing open the gates at the propitious moment and having the employees march into the plant grounds in a massed group protected by squads of armed police, so as to give to the opening a dramatic and exaggerated quality and thus heighten its demoralizing effect. Along with the "opening" provide a spectacle—speeches, flag raising, and praises for the employees, citizens, and local authorities, so that, their vanity touched, they will feel responsible for the continued success of the scheme and will increase their efforts to induce additional employees to return to work.

Eighth: Capitalize on the demoralization of the strikers by continuing the show of police force and the pressure of the Citizens Committee, both to insure that those employees who have returned will continue at work and to force the remaining strikers to capitulate. If necessary, turn the locality into a warlike camp through the declaration of a state of emergency tantamount to martial law and barricade it from the outside world, so that nothing may interfere with the successful conclusion of the "Formula," thereby driving home to the union leaders the futility of further efforts to hold their ranks intact.

Ninth: Close the publicity barrage, which day by day during the entire period has increased the demoralization worked by all of these measures, on the theme that the plant is in full operation and that the strikers were merely a minority attempting to interfere with the "right to work," thus inducing the public to place a moral stamp of approval upon the above measures. With this, the campaign is over—the employer has broken the strike.

To those who are unfamiliar with the extremes to which very many industrial leaders have gone in their relentless opposition to the development of labor unions the effrontery involved in actually codifying such a program of oppression, deception, violence, and corruption must seem well-nigh incredible. But that the "Mohawk Valley formula" or a definite plan closely resembling it has been utilized in combating *successfully* numerous recent strikes cannot be doubted. With Philadelphia as a reference point, one can all too readily recall the riots at the Chester plant of the Sun Shipbuilding and Dry Dock Company and at the Hershey factory of the Hershey Chocolate Company, each preceded by citizens' committees, special deputies, quasi "martial law," spurious "back to work" movements, and barrages of false propaganda eventually arousing the local citizenry to massed attacks upon the strikers. Other sections of the country can no doubt remember similar local episodes.

And the employer's most effective weapon against the development of labor unions remains to be mentioned. This consists in discharging or discriminating against individual workers for union membership or activity. The labor movement's greatest obstacle has arisen from this constant threat and the ever-present fear which it invokes. Out of the individual employee's powerlessness to combat it arises the paradox that the success of the struggle for collective bargaining is contingent upon the power to bargain collectively. When one includes in the battery of employers' guns the stimulating of so-called "company unions" (puppet employee associations dominated by the employer or his representatives) and participation in trade associations through which numbers of employers can present a united front to the demands of labor, it is amazing that the struggle to achieve organizations of employees independent of company domination has succeeded even as well as it has.

A chief reliance of workers in their campaign for unionization has been the strike. When an industry is thoroughly unionized, strikes are comparatively rare, and such strikes as may occur are called by union leaders as representatives of substantially all the workers involved in the dispute. Strikes for collective bargaining in previously unorganized areas, however, are almost necessarily begun before complete union machinery can have been set up and leaders accredited. Fear, largely generated by his employer's actions, is so great on the part of the average employee that he tends to avoid union membership. Unless stimulated by some greater fear or aroused by a dramatic appeal, he continues to ignore the safeguard for his future that would spring from the formation of a collective bargaining agency. Hence it is inevitable that whenever steps toward the establishment of a union occur the initiative is taken by a coterie of the more vigorous and fearless employees. The invalidity thus becomes apparent of the frequently voiced objection to strikes for unionization that they represent attempts on the part of a mere minority of the employees to coerce the employer into action affecting all. If, while an employer is doing all in his power to influence his individual employees to abstain from union membership, the employees must refrain from group action aimed at neutralizing the employer's efforts unless their group comprises at least a majority of the employees, collective bargaining will be an unattainable fantasy.

At one time English law forbade strikes under any circumstances. It was about four hundred years before the Industrial Revolution that the pestilence, known in England as the Black Death, swept large areas of the earth. This terrible tragedy immeasurably affected the course of the law's development with reference to the labor movement. The mortality among English workers was so heavy and the labor scarcity so great that the individual artisans and laborers who survived had a bargaining power of disturbing proportions. Consequently Parliament in 1351 enacted the Statute of Laborers which created not only a duty to work but also to work in accordance with prescribed standards. Thus there was introduced into English (and subsequently American) law the conception that the labor contract and labor relationship are subject to a different status than are other contracts and other relationships.

One of the dogmas of the common law is that if a person is caused economic injury, for example, a business loss, by the acts of others, he can either enjoin their conduct or recover money damages, unless they can prove that their purpose is lawful and that they have employed lawful means. A business man may cause tremendous economic loss to a rival, may even ruin his rival's business by deliberately selling below cost, and the courts will attach no penalty to his conduct. This is judicially regarded as only the ultimate consequence of legitimate business competition, in which the survivor was seeking merely to serve his own economic interests and not maliciously to injure his bankrupt competitor. But many courts have issued injunctions against attempts by workers or labor leaders to persuade others to strike in order to induce union recognition on an employer's part. These courts offer a wide variety of reasons for this result, but the underlying thought is that the workers are seeking to bring about a cessation of activity in the employer's business that will be economically detrimental to him, and that the employer and the employees are not business rivals, and hence this injury is not justified. In this area the courts fail to apply to the workers reasoning comparable to that used in support of injury by one business man of another, namely, that the workers are seeking merely to further their own economic interest in collective bargaining and not endeavoring maliciously to injure the employer. The explanation for these contrasting attitudes can be traced back to the Black Death, the Statute of Laborers, and the parade of statutes and decisions stemming therefrom. The culmination has been an inchoate judicial reaction that the sale of goods and the making of profits are optional with the owner, while the sale of services and the earning of wages are morally (though not now legally) mandatory, and hence that if the desire of employees to withhold services for the sake of ultimately bettering their positions conflicts with the desire of an employer to make profits by selling goods, the former should yield.

When labor in its struggle for union recognition supplements the strike with other devices this tendency of the courts to suppress interference by labor with the "free flow of business" becomes even more marked. Unless strikers can succeed in preventing their employer from filling their places with other adequate workers, they merely sacrifice their jobs and their wages without bringing economic pressure to bear on the employer. Consequently, most strikes are accompanied by some form of picketing. Picketing usually has a three-fold objective: (1) to influence public opinion in favor of the strikers, (2) to dissuade non-strikers from going to work, and (3) to provide a physical activity for the strikers which will help to maintain discipline and morale. Here again the courts have come to the aid of capital in this struggle with labor by issuing sweeping injunctions against picketing. To be sure the prevailing judicial formula is that only non-peaceful picketing will be enjoined. But as far as the second and most important objective of picketing is concerned, i.e., dissuading others from taking the strikers' places, peaceful picketing is virtually a contradiction in terms, for almost any effective action which pickets might take to keep others from replacing them might be, and indeed has been by many courts, described as non-peaceful.

If strikers or their associates beat up fellow-employees who refuse to join the strike such conduct is and always will be regarded as unlawful and subject to criminal as well as civil penalties. An express or implied *threat* of physical harm is also to be condemned and may be judicially penalized by injunction or otherwise. Unquestionably an *implied* threat may be just as real as an expressed one. But if courts go far enough in enjoining implied threats of violence virtually all picketing can be outlawed as non-peaceful. The mere presence of numerous pickets has been held to constitute such an implied threat. Dirty looks, insulting gestures, and deprecatory epithets have been relied upon by other courts in granting sweeping anti-picketing injunctions. All picketing, except possibly the simplest variety, does present an intimation of impending harm to opponents of the pickets. It may be that effective picketing inevitably involves some invasion of the rights of others. Abstractly, no violence or threat of violence by any person or group should be condoned. For this reason should all picketing be banned? In the ultimate analysis, this is a social problem, namely, is the advantage to society in removing this possibility of violence sufficient to offset society's loss resulting from destruction of one of labor's chief weapons in its struggle for collective bargaining?

Another form of pressure which workers frequently bring to bear upon their employer in the event of a struggle for union recognition is the boycott. In its simplest form a boycott is a concerted withholding of patronage, a refusal to buy the boycotted commodity. Obviously, withdrawal of the patronage of the strikers alone would have small significance. Consequently, an attempt is usually made to induce non-strikers to participate in the boycott. Such an extension of the arena of boycott is sometimes termed a "secondary" boycott. If economic pressure results, once more the injunction intervenes on the side of capital. Many courts will enjoin secondary boycotts unqualifiedly. Other courts will permit such conduct provided the persons outside the labor group have been persuaded by peaceful means to withhold their patronage. But a strict interpretation of "peaceful" can have the same practical consequences as a total prohibition of such boycotts.

Courts also distinguish between primary and secondary strikes. A secondary strike may take either of two forms: it may be a sympathetic strike in which employees who have no particular dispute with their own employer strike in order to induce him to bring pressure to bear upon another employer to agree to the demands which the latter's striking employees have made upon him; or it may be a strike by employees, who otherwise have no dispute with their employer, against having to work on goods which at an earlier stage in their processing have been produced by non-union labor. Even in jurisdictions where the legality of strikes for union recognition is conceded, courts are inclined to grant injunctions against secondary strikes at least as readily as they do against secondary boycotts.

Injunctions against strikes, injunctions against picketing, injunctions against boycotts—at every turn in its struggle for collective bargaining labor has been confronted with an injunction. Actions for damages or even fines might have been surmounted, but the injunction has devastating potentialities. It can be issued by a single judge; the defendant has no right to a jury; restraining orders and preliminary injunctions may be granted solely upon the basis of affidavits presented by the plaintiff without the defendant having been heard at all in his own behalf; violation of an injunction is contempt of court for which imprisonment may be inflicted; and most drastic of all, this punishment can be visited upon individuals not named in the injunction or even having notice of it, either by designating a class of unnamed persons as defendants, or by charging complete strangers to the proceedings with having so conducted themselves as to "obstruct the course of justice." Furthermore, the detrimental effect of injunctions issued in labor disputes is virtually the same whether the injunction was properly or improperly granted. The injunction remains in force until set aside by the issuing judge or by a higher court. Appeals are costly and slow. By the time the case has been carried to a court of last resort and there decided, a long enough interval has elapsed so that the injunction has done its work of hampering the strikers and their leaders sufficiently to cause a breakdown of the strike.

Every move of labor toward its goal of collective bargaining checkmated by injunction, every effort thwarted by the ruthless ingenuity of employers, is it any wonder that unionization has made comparatively slight progress? Yet, in the light of modern industrial developments, the need of workers for collective bargaining is increasingly clear. Moreover, the importance to the rest of the public of strengthening labor's status has gradually been dawning, and legislatures have endeavored in various ways to come to labor's aid. In 1898 Congress passed the so-called Erdman Act. This statute sought to promote unionization of interstate railroad employees by outlawing "yellow dog" contracts and forbidding employers to discriminate against union members. But in 1908 the United States Supreme Court, in the noted case of Adair *v.* United States, held the Act to be unconstitutional because repugnant to the Fifth Amendment declaring that no person shall be deprived of liberty or property without due process of law. A companion case, Coppage *v.* Kansas, arose in 1915 out of a Kansas statute also declaring "yellow dog" contracts to be unlawful. Again the United States Supreme Court thwarted the legislative effort to stimulate unionization by declaring this State statute unconstitutional as in conflict with the "due process" clause of the Fourteenth Amendment. In each of these cases Mr. Justice Holmes was among those dissenting.

Rebuffed in its effort to lessen the severity with which employers treat union workers, Congress addressed itself to another obstacle in the path of the labor movement, namely the injunction. In 1914 Congress passed Section 20 of the famous Clayton Act. Although the wording of this section leaves room for some construction (this is inevitably true of a statute covering a broad field), it might reasonably have been interpreted as manifesting a Congressional purpose to take away from the federal courts the power to issue injunctions in labor disputes except where necessary to prevent irreparable injury. But in 1921 the United States Supreme Court, in Duplex Printing Press Co. *v.* Deering, held that the benefits of this statute extended only to "those who are proximately and substantially concerned as parties to an actual dispute respecting the terms or conditions of their own employment, past, present or prospective." This decision reversed both the District Court and the Circuit Court of Appeals and evoked dissents from Justices Brandeis, Holmes and Clarke. The value to labor of the Clayton Act was largely destroyed by this narrow construction as it left union officials and other labor leaders as vulnerable to the injunction as formerly.

Not until 1932 could sufficient strength be mustered in the Senate and in the House to enable Congress to attempt to override these judicial vetoes. In that year the Norris-La Guardia Act was passed. This statute embraces the subjects dealt with by both the Erdman and the Clayton Acts. Instead of making it a crime for an employer to require an employee to enter into a "yellow dog" contract, the Act of 1932 provides that such contracts shall not be enforceable by injunction or otherwise in any federal court. The Act also denies to the federal courts the power to enjoin any person "interested" in a labor dispute from doing a number of specified acts, such as "Giving publicity to the existence of, or the facts involved in, any labor dispute, whether by advertising, speaking, patrolling, or by any other method not involving fraud or violence," and "Assembling peaceably to act or to organize to act in promotion of their interests in a labor dispute." One of the features of the Act is that it protects defendants in actions for labor injunctions from many of the grave procedural abuses to which they were theretofore subject. The United States Supreme Court has not as yet passed upon the constitutionality of the Norris-La Guardia Act in whole or in part. Its validity has, however, been upheld by the Circuit Court of Appeals (see, for example, Levering & Garrigues Co. *v.* Morrin) and the refusal of the Supreme Court to grant an appeal from the Circuit Court is at least a straw in the wind.

The most recent federal enactment on behalf of labor is the National Labor Relations Act of 1935, popularly referred to as the Wagner Act. This statute characterizes a number of acts by employers as "unfair labor practices." These "unfair labor practices" are in general the more common activities of employers in their attempts to defeat the development of labor unions. They include (a) coercing employees not to join labor organizations, (b) dominating the formation of labor organizations—this relates especially to company unions, (c) discriminating in the hiring or firing of employees against union members or against employees who have availed themselves of the rights established by this Act, and (d) refusing to bargain collectively with employees' representatives. The Act provides that representatives selected for the purpose of collective bargaining by the majority of the employees in an appropriate unit shall be the exclusive representatives of all the employees for the purpose of collective bargaining as to conditions of employment. A National Labor Relations Board of three members is set up. If a complaint is made to this Board that an employer has committed one of the unfair labor practices designated in the Act, the Board may conduct an inquiry, hear testimony, and, if the Board finds that the employer has been committing the unfair labor practice charged, it may issue a "cease and desist" order and may also direct the employer to reinstate employees with back pay where improper discharge is involved. If the employer ignores the Board's order, the Board must petition one of the federal Circuit Courts of Appeal for enforcement of the order; and if the employer desires he may petition the Circuit Court of Appeals for a review of the Board's order.

In a series of historically startling opinions delivered April 12, 1937, the United States Supreme Court completely upheld the constitutionality of the Wagner Act. This statute and the Norris-La Guardia Act are of course only applicable within the domain of the federal government, that is, where interstate commerce is concerned. But they are already being supplemented by State legislation. Twenty-five States now have strike injunction statutes patterned after the Norris-La Guardia Act. Massachusetts, New York, Pennsylvania, Utah, and Wisconsin have already adopted State counterparts of the Wagner Act, and similar legislation for the creation of State Labor Relations Boards is pending in other jurisdictions.

With the aid of such statutes, State and Federal, there should be a tremendous forward surge in the labor movement. With removal of barriers heretofore erected by employers against the establishment of independent labor unions among their employees and with a limiting of the power of the judiciary to enjoin acts in furtherance of unionization, the inertia of workers with respect to union membership will decrease, competent labor leaders will multiply, and collective bargaining will at last become a reality.

This will take time. The process will be accompanied by strife. There will still be strikes. Doubtless we have not seen the last of the "sit-down" strike, the illegality of which has not been challenged by any statute or judicial decision to my knowledge. [Since this was written the courts have refused to uphold the validity of the "sit-down" strike.] If a legitimate labor dispute develops between an employer and a group of workers sufficiently large and organized so that by the familiar processes of strike, picketing, and boycott they have a reasonable likelihood of gaining their objectives, it might be in the interests of society to avoid the physical disorder and violence and the widespread disruption of business which strenuous opposition to these orthodox labor measures often produces, by permitting *such* a group of workers to substitute occupation of a factory for the more cumbersome and wasteful methods they normally employ. On the other hand, the taking over of an entire plant by a few irresponsible and self-seeking workers should never be tolerated. But where to draw the line only patient and tolerant trial and error can determine.

Nowadays when strikes and strife occur people often ask, "Why doesn't the Labor Relations Board step in and settle the controversy?" Such a question fails to comprehend the purpose behind the creation of these Boards, State and Federal. This purpose is to prevent the major anti-union acts of employers and thus make it possible for workers to organize effective collective bargaining units as a result of which they will gain equality of bargaining power with their employers. The theory is that once this equality of bargaining power has been attained, government will thereafter keep its hands off, trusting that through the operation of economic laws labor and capital will reach agreements which will be in the best interest of society; and even before this beatitude of bargaining equality arrives the Labor Relations Boards are not to be charged with the stupendous task of regulating the relations between capital and labor through compulsory arbitration or otherwise. Much can be said in favor of the legislature establishing boards of mediation to which, if mutually desired, both an employer and his employees could appeal for aid in settling a labor dispute; but there would be great danger of limiting the effectiveness of the Labor Relations Boards if to their present functions were added those of the proposed boards of mediation.

Not infrequently one hears the complaint that the Wagner Act and kindred State statutes are one-sided in that they impose restrictions on employers without placing responsibility upon labor. Of course this legislation is partial: it was addressed to an unbalanced situation. Opponents of these measures cry that labor unions should be required to incorporate in order that they may be held legally accountable for their misdeeds as corporations are. If this plea is made in good faith it arises out of ignorance of the law; for ever since the Coronado case was decided by the United States Supreme Court in 1922 labor unions have been subject to suit by service of process upon representative officers in substantially the same manner as corporations.

It must be recognized that all this pro-labor legislation may fail of its objective: employers may in the future, as they have in the past, so manipulate legal doctrines as to defeat the legislative will and thus retain their present bargaining advantage; or it may happen that such legislative aids to labor may become so great as to create not an equality but a superiority of bargaining power on the part of labor. In this latter event far more than mere incorporation of labor unions will be necessary if our capitalistic institutions as we now know them are to be preserved.

This much, however, is certain: that the existence of collective bargaining units for all labor, independent of employer domination, and probably organized for the most part along industrial rather than craft lines, is of vital importance to the nation, and that it is fatuous to concede to labor the right of collective bargaining without also legalizing *some* effective means whereby collective bargaining may become a reality.

No. 107

THE LABOR INJUNCTION [1]

by Francis Bowes Sayre

THE adjustment and regulation of industrial conflict is one of the baffling and outstanding problems of the age. Increased production depends upon decreased human friction. Of the various forms of attempted solution none has been more discussed, praised, blamed, or bitterly resented than the labor injunction, which is a peculiarly American development. For although an English court granted an injunction in a strike case as early as 1868, it remains of negligible importance in English labor controversies.

The earliest recorded cases of labor injunctions in America date from the eighteen eighties, and their use increased with extraordinary rapidity during the ensuing ten years. Ever since the famous Debs case in 1895, when the United States Supreme Court sustained the issue of a drastic and sweeping injunction in the great Pullman strike of the preceding year, the injunction method has become in America the storm center of controversy and political discussion. What is the truth concerning the labor injunction? Is it a sound and an effective remedy in labor disputes? What are its values and what its dangers?

As an effective method for preventing conflict, actual experience has proved the futility of the injunction. If labor organizations are sufficiently powerful to dominate an industry and to control the labor skilled in that industry, they can ultimately gain their ends in spite of the most rigid of injunctions. The injunction against a strike cannot prevent individual workmen quitting employment for personal reasons. The injunction against an unfair list serves only the more widely to advertise the names of employers so listed, and to stimulate loyal union sympathizers to refrain from buying the products of such employers. The injunction against the boycott is equally powerless to compel individual union sympathizers to patronize anti-union employers or to buy non-union goods.

Naked legal processes cannot compel men as individuals to work, or to deal with, or to buy. The injunction obtained in 1919 by Attorney General Palmer to prevent a nation-wide coal strike proved ineffective in getting the miners back into the mines; they returned only after President Wilson had arranged with the union officers for arbitration of the dispute. The famous injunction obtained by the Bucks Stove and Range Company against the

[1] Francis Bowes Sayre, "The Labor Injunction," *Forum* (January, 1931), Vol. 85, pp. 56-61. Reprinted by permission of *Current History and Forum*.

American Federation of Labor in 1907, compelling the discontinuance of their name in the "We Don't Patronize" list of the *American Federationist* and restraining the defendants from "interfering in any manner with the sale of the products of the plaintiff," so stimulated union sympathizers in their struggle against the stove company that sales decreased, and within three years the company was forced not only to request the court to withdraw injunction proceedings, but to make peace with the union.

The much discussed injunction which Judge Hough issued against the United Mine Workers of America on September 10, 1927, restraining them "from interfering with, obstructing or preventing in any way . . . the carrying on of the business of the plaintiffs; from destroying or damaging . . . the plant, buildings, equipment or property at or near" the plaintiffs' mines, was followed by the dynamiting of the Bradley mine tipple and by continued property destruction for many days thereafter.

Injunctions may greatly impede and hinder organized activity, they may cause the winning or the losing of a strike, but they cannot prevent conflict. And if the trade-union organization is strong enough to dominate the industry, they will in the last analysis prove ineffective in frustrating even organized activity.

On the other hand, if a labor organization is so weak as to have no effective control over the labor engaged in the industry, employers can usually win their ends in far cheaper and more satisfactory ways than by the injunction. If the union fails to control the labor supply, it is far better business to engage fresh labor than to enjoin employees from striking; and under such conditions there is no need to enjoin boycotts since labor groups lack the power successfully to enforce them.

More effective protection against acts of violence can be secured through police protection and through criminal prosecutions. As the counsel of the National Erectors' Association testified before a Senate Committee in 1912: "It may have occurred to the Senator to inquire why we did not begin injunction suits, but an injunction against dynamite would have been far less effective than criminal action, if we had the evidence to secure it. We could not very well enjoin anyone from using dynamite until we had evidence, and the moment we had evidence, criminal action was the proper course."

The injunction can never be anything but sterile as a method for preventing industrial conflict. For the injunction rests upon compulsion; and conflict cannot possibly be prevented by force. The father with all the force at his command cannot prevent continuing conflict between his two small sons. No matter how absolute may be the power of the domestic relations court to enforce its decrees, it cannot thereby prevent conflict between an ill-mated husband and wife. In the oxidized atmosphere of repression conflict burns all the more ardently. Force methods can for a time prevent open outbreaks of violence, and are often necessary for this purpose; but actual violence means criminal activity, and the law, which provided certain constitutional safeguards in the trial of crimes, does not permit crimes to be enjoined as such.

However useful force methods may be in the prevention of open violence, there is only one effective way to prevent conflict, and that is by reaching men's minds, be it by reason or persuasion or offer of adjustment or reward. Herein lies the power of industrial arbitration, which, if it be fair, kindles men's imaginations and wins their minds. Herein lies the power of social legislation, which, if it be founded upon social justice, also wins both sides to cooperative effort. But the injunction, resting upon compulsion, by its very nature antagonizes rather than wins men's wills. It deeply irritates and provokes; it is likely to generate more violence than it suppresses. In the settlement of labor controversies it is an aggravation, and not a solution.

But the current cry of trade-unionists is, not that injunctions are futile and ineffectual, but that they are unjust and make for social danger. How far is popular criticism on this ground justified?

An injunction is merely a decree or order issued by a court forbidding specified defendants from engaging in specified conduct which would constitute a violation of law and cause irreparable injury. Thus, the owner of a patent may enjoin another from infringing upon his patent rights; one entitled to the reversion of an estate may obtain an injunction against the person in present possession in order to prevent him from wasting or impairing the property; one may enjoin the continuance of a nuisance which is injurious to his property or the closing of a road over which he has a right of way; one may enjoin another from breaking contracts of such a nature that money damages for their breach would be inadequate, such as contracts not to carry on certain trades, contracts for the conveyance of specified pieces of land, and the like. In such cases, where money damages would be inadequate, some preventive form of remedy is the only way to justice; and thus the injunction has come to be a thoroughly well-established and almost indispensable remedy in these exceptional situations.

Principles of legal justice do not change with varying parties. What makes for justice in controversies between property owners or commercial rivals will presumably make for justice in trade disputes. If an employer finds that his trade is rapidly falling off and bankruptcy is staring him in the face because of an illegal labor boycott or because of an illegal strike which he is powerless to prevent and for which the remedy of damages at law would be utterly inadequate, why should this useful remedy be denied him? Does not social justice in fact require it? Is the current criticism of the labor injunction due, after all, only to propaganda generated by trade-unions because of the very effectiveness of the injunction procedure in blocking them from conduct which is illegal and unconscionable and which therefore ought to be prevented?

To understand the problem one must bear clearly in mind that the injunction is a very exceptional kind of remedy. It clothes a single judge with the extraordinary power of prescribing what another's conduct shall be, and of punishing disobedience summarily without a jury and with all the power of government at his back. It would constitute an intolerable form of tyranny were it not for the fact that no court has the right to enjoin any conduct except that which is either illegal in and of itself or part of a larger illegal whole. Judges have no right to enjoin conduct merely because it seems to them unfair or oppressive or socially injurious; conduct is enjoinable only if it violates established law. The injunction power thus presupposes and requires as a safeguard a definite body of law clearly defining what conduct is lawful and what unlawful.

Suppose, however, that in some particular field of activity the law has not yet achieved definite formulations as to what conduct is lawful and what unlawful, so that the judge in such matters is left unguided by settled legal doctrines or established precedents, and must, whether he likes it or not, be controlled largely by his own social ideas and economic background. In such a field one can sense the social danger arising from the too frequent use of a legal remedy which clothes a single judge with arbitrary power to dictate to the defendants what their conduct shall be, which provides for the finding of facts without the safeguard of a jury, which frequently requires a vital decision to be made at the *commencement* of the suit—upon mere affidavits or at a hurried preliminary hearing—rather than, as in most judicial proceedings, at the end of a careful trial, and which often allows disobedience to be punished by the summary action of the single judge who issued the order. Use of injunctions in such an undefined sphere is particularly dangerous if the controversy involves nation-wide class-conscious groups at grips over issues of burning social importance.

Now labor law involves a peculiarly difficult field. It involves primarily the regulation of the competitive struggle between large organized groups over the price and conditions of labor; and the law has always found the regulation of competitive activity, even between individuals, a baffling problem. Since in the field of trade competition one gains ascendency by defeating one's rivals, competitive activity constantly involves conduct entered into with knowledge that it will damage a rival or even with positive intent to do such damage.

Conduct specifically intended to damage another is in general forbidden by the law and supports an action for damages; but in this field the law, in the faith that competition is worth more than it costs, justifies some forms of competitive activity but not others. One may not knock his trade rival over the head to put him out of business or physically take money out of his till; yet ordinarily one may deliberately and intentionally put him into bankruptcy by winning away his customers or underselling his goods, even though the latter method may mean to him infinitely greater damage and disaster. Just where to draw the line in the field of trade competition between what activities the law permits and what it does not is often far from clear.

If there is doubt as to what practices the law permits as between competing individuals, there is irreconcilable conflict and confusion in the law as between nation-wide organizations of employers and employees, battling and competing with each other over the price and conditions of labor. For instance, although there is no method of industrial warfare more commonly and widely resorted to than the strike, courts have not yet been able to draw the line between what strikes are legal and what illegal. A little over a century ago courts agreed in holding all strikes illegal. Judges saw in them only organized efforts to damage employers, and branded them as illegal and enjoinable on the grounds that they were activities entered into for the malicious and express purpose of damaging others.

To-day courts realize that the strike for larger wages or shorter hours is only a step in the competitive struggle over the price of labor; and just as they freely allow members of commercial organizations acting in concert to refuse to sell their products to those who will not pay their price or comply with their demands, so all courts to-day allow trade-union members acting in concert to refuse to sell their labor to employers who will not pay for labor the terms which they demand. Such conduct, although intended to do damage, is justified by trade competition.

But as to the legality of strikes to unionize a shop or an industry or to compel the discharge of non-union employees, courts are to-day hopelessly divided. Those of many states, such as Massachusetts, still brand such strikes as illegal and enjoinable, seeing in them only activities maliciously intended to damage others and resulting in an increased cost of production. Those of other states, such as New York and Illinois, have come to see that such a strike is, like the strike for higher wages, not a malevolent activity, but only a step in the competitive struggle over the price and conditions of labor, and should be legally permitted, as justified by trade competition.

The law determining the legality of strikes for other purposes is in a state of chaos; no one can say where the line of legality lies or how it is to be drawn. The granting of injunctions against such must depend very largely upon the social ideas of the individual judge.

Modern efficiency in organization methods is continually developing new forms of collective action. The term "boycott" was not invented until 1880; problems arising out of the "yellow-dog contract" are of still more recent origin. Legal formulations, which must grow out of accumulated experience, evolve slowly; courts are still groping for solutions of the more recent legal problems.

No part of the law is in a more formless or chaotic condition than the law of boycotts. Courts have been utterly unable to agree as to what constitutes a boycott, or as to what boycotts are illegal. Most hold that the "primary" boycott is legal, and the "secondary" boycott illegal; but no court has yet been able to draw a satisfactory line as to just what constitutes a primary and what a secondary boycott. Members of commercial organizations acting in concert have been permitted to refuse to buy from anyone selling to a rival group, and their conduct held not a boycott; but trade-unionists refusing to sell labor to anyone dealing with a rival group are charged with engaging in a boycott, and their conduct is enjoined. In other words, in the field of boycotts there is no established and recognized line separating what is legal from what is illegal; and to a very large extent judges are left to follow their own conceptions as to what should be permitted and what not.

The so-called "yellow-dog contract" is an agreement which some employers get each employee to sign as a condition of employment, providing that he will not join a union as long as he remains in their employ. Courts have held it illegal "maliciously" to induce another to break his contract; but no court has yet successfully defined what is meant by "maliciously." As to whether a union organizer acting openly has the right to persuade employees working under "yellow-dog contracts" to join the union is again a question upon which the law remains in the widest uncertainty; some judges have enjoined such activity and others have refused to do so.

Again, no right is more vital to the growth and very existence of labor unions than that of peacefully persuading others to join their ranks. The denial of the practical exercise of this right at critical moments of the competitive struggle strikes at the heart of trade-unionism. Yet upon the question of the legality of picketing, courts are hopelessly divided. The majority hold that picketing is entirely lawful so long as it is peaceful and does not in fact involve intimidation. A minority holds that there "can be no such thing as peaceful picketing, any more than there can be chaste vulgarity, or peaceful mobbing, or lawful lynching."

When the question came before the United States Supreme Court, the judges failed satisfactorily to settle this issue, and the actual decision only served to create fresh problems. The late Mr. Chief Justice Taft, in rendering the opinion of the Court, broadly declared that labor unions had the unquestioned right of peaceful persuasion; but by his limiting the unions to a single picket at each gate in a plant employing at the time some three hundred and fifty men, the practical exercise of the right was very seriously curtailed if not denied. Just what the law covering picketing is to-day remains in the greatest uncertainty.

Added confusion has come from the constant resort by judges in labor cases to the vague common-law doctrines of conspiracy and restraint of trade. Many trade-union activities have been enjoined as constituting conspiracies, even though no illegality could be found in the means used or in the ends pursued; but precisely what constitutes a conspiracy no court has yet been able to say. An increasing number of trade-union activities are being enjoined in the Federal courts as constituting restraint of trade under the Sherman Anti-Trust Act; but similarly, restraint of trade is something which no court has yet been able precisely to define.

As a result, when judges are asked to enjoin the collective action of labor unions on the ground of conspiracy or restraint of trade, in the absence of definite legal formulations to guide their judgments, their decisions must be largely the result of their individual social points of view. And when trade-unions are thus at times enjoined from indulging in precisely the same kind of activities as are freely allowed to competing commercial organizations, a dangerous sense of injustice at the hands of the courts is inescapably bred among a substantial portion of the population.

It is not meant to suggest that justice should be reduced to a mere process of mechanics and that judges should be stripped of all discretionary power. Decisions must and should depend to some extent upon the varying points of view of individual judges. But the play of judicial discretion should be confined within fixed limits. Above all, the injunction, which as a safeguard against abuse requires a substructure of definite, established law, should not be used as the customary and ordinary remedy in the field of labor law where there is so much uncertainty, so many ill-defined or undefined doctrines, such wide latitude for the play of social prejudice or economic bias.

This is the more important when one remembers the exceptional nature of the injunction procedure. In the ordinary legal procedure judges reach their decisions only after a patient examination of the facts in open court and after mature consideration of the law as expounded in carefully prepared arguments on both sides. But, as I pointed out, in the case of injunctions a single judge must decide whether or not to issue a temporary injunction or restraining order at the very *beginning* of the suit, sometimes at *ex parte* hearings (that is, where only one side is present) or on mere affidavits, often before the defendants have an opportunity to collect evidence or to argue their case.

Although the injunction granted may be but a temporary one and may be vacated at the conclusion of the suit or later reversed on appeal, in cases of industrial struggle this is frequently of no advantage to the defendants. For in such cases injunctions are usually sought at highly critical moments, and to tell defendants after the strike is broken or the struggle is lost that the injunction was improvidently issued or had no legal justification fails to repair the irreparable harm done them.

The reversal of a judgment for money damages carries with it its own relief; the reversal of an injunction decree frequently comes only after the complainant's purposes have already been served. The extraordinary injunction procedure seems peculiarly unsuited to achieve justice in labor controversies. Yet in this field it has been turned into the ordinary and accepted mode of legal action.

Some have proposed the complete abolition of the injunction in all labor cases. But this is too simple. Employees at times need the protection of the injunction remedy as well as employers; and in the present state of opinion, complete abolition would probably be impracticable even were it desirable. The remedy is rather to formulate and clarify by legislation or otherwise the underlying substantive law with regard to various specific forms of group competition, and at the same time to curb the abuses to which the injunction procedure has too readily lent itself.

Thus the problem of the injunction is not only a legal problem. It is a profoundly important social problem as well. Its present excessive use is not only ineffective for the purpose of preventing or reducing industrial conflict; it is tending to provoke a sense of unfair treatment at the hands of the courts on the part of substantial producing groups in the community, and thus to undermine their faith in law and their respect for the courts. Such a situation calls for constructive effort to meet the growing danger, not only by labor leaders, but by all who believe in American law and American traditions. [Since this article was written, the national government, by the Norris-La Guardia Act, and some of the states, by similar legislation, have attempted to curb the abuses surrounding the use of injunctions in labor disputes. Justice, however, cannot be reduced to a mechanical process nor can judges be stripped of all discretionary power. The problem of the labor injunction, therefore, is still important.]

No. 108

LET'S LOOK AT LABOR [1]

by William H. Davis

THE duty of labor and management in a democratic society is to perfect the democratic process within the field of production. Government's duty to workers and to management is not to interfere with the development of such processes, but to promote it.

The democratic principle is rooted in persuasion. It was Plato who first declared that the creation of an orderly world is the victory of persuasion over force. From this it follows that the enduring progress of mankind implies a continuous succession of such victories; that any resort to force means at least temporary defeat. As A. N. Whitehead has put it, "The worth of men consists in the liability to persuasion. They can persuade and be persuaded by the disclosure of alternatives, the better and the worse. . . . The recourse to force, however unavoidable, is a disclosure of the failure of civilization, either in the general society or in a remnant of individuals." The Declaration of Independence affirms this principle when it declares that "governments derive their just powers from the consent of the governed."

The duty to bring labor relations into line with this democratic principle lies at the very heart of the problem that confronts our industrial life to-day. Democratic ideas reached their fullest development in the thoughts and writings of western civilization during the revolutionary period at the end of the eighteenth and the beginning of the nineteenth century. As the industrial revolution developed during the nineteenth century it was particularly in this field of labor relations that liberty, equality and fraternity were most conspicuously absent. No one can fail to realize the importance, therefore, of practical and resolute action to make the democratic principle effective in the relations between the employers of this country and their workers. But what does this mean in practical terms?

First, the use of persuasion in labor relations calls for equality of bargaining power. Without such equality persuasion is at once driven from the field by force. In the United States there has been, within recent years, a real advance in the understanding and acceptance of that basic fact. Industrial relations commence with the individual worker and his employer. In this simplest form of bargaining the individual worker is obviously at

[1] William H. Davis, "Let's Look at Labor," *The Survey Graphic* (February, 1939), Vol. 28, pp. 106-108. Reprinted by permission of *The Survey Graphic*.

a disadvantage. The beginning of equality of bargaining power is the organization into a bargaining unit of workers in a single plant. Organization of workers for concerted action has been bitterly opposed by powerful interests in this country, even as recently as the years following the World War; but it may be said that to-day such concerted opposition is a thing of the past. Indeed, the recognition of the workers' right to self-organization, by the people of this country and by their government, has deeper roots than some people seem to think.

The right itself is one aspect of our fundamental civil liberties: freedom of assembly and freedom of speech. It was recognized as early as 1901 by the Industrial Commission appointed by President McKinley. In Theodore Roosevelt's administration it was recognized by the Anthracite Board of Conciliation in 1902. It was accepted by the War Labor Board under Mr. Taft during Wilson's administration. During the Coolidge administration it was incorporated by Congress in the Railway Labor Act of 1926. It was referred to as "not to be disputed" by Mr. Justice Hughes, speaking for the Supreme Court in 1930. During the Hoover administration it was affirmed in the Norris-La Guardia Anti-Injunction Act of 1932 and in the Interstate Railways Bankruptcy Act of March 3, 1933; and during the present administration it has been incorporated in the National Industrial Recovery Act, the Amended Railway Labor Act, and in the Wagner Act.

It is clear that this right of the workers to organize for collective action is in no way limited to a single plant or locality. It is a right that has no limit of place, purpose, or extent, until it comes into conflict with the equally fundamental rights of others or with the common welfare. The extent of union organization is, therefore, a thing that lies primarily within the choice of the workers themselves; and whatever opposition remains to the extension of organization beyond the limits of a single plant or company is no longer based upon denial of the right, but rather on arguments of expediency. It has no power to stop the wider extension of unionization.

But when the workers in an industry have spread their organization beyond the individual plants to cover a competitive area, and still further when national or federated unions are formed, the balance of bargaining power shifts from the employer to the workers. As a mere matter of self-defense, employers in turn have to combine. The history of trade union movements in this country and abroad shows that the organization of employers, initiated in each case as a defensive measure, may follow either the path of opposition to, and concerted action to break down, organization of the workers; or it may follow the path of collective dealings with the labor organizations.

Choice of the first path has led to violence and continued conflict. This is inevitable under a democratic government, which lacks the power to put down the conflict that arises when a free people are interfered with in the exercise of rights they hold "unalienable."

The second path—organization of the employers as well as of the workers for collective bargaining on an industry-wide scale—has led, on the other hand, in the democratic countries abroad and in some industries in America, to stabilized and satisfactory labor relations. This development represents the maturity of labor relations in a democracy. It is the final balance of equality of bargaining power between the parties. Any step beyond it introduces governmental regulation with a corresponding departure from the democratic principle of persuasion.

Collective bargaining on this scale is vastly different in character and results from the narrower bargaining between an individual employer and his own workers. For collective bargaining on this wider scale the organization of the workers, as of the employers, must extend beyond the individual plant or company. Either by industry-wide organization or by federation or other common action of the different unions in an industry, the organization of the workers must be at least as wide as the extent of the industry within the competitive area. In this fact lies the possibility of a practical solution of all those disputes (nearly one half of the total number of labor disputes in America) that flow out of the efforts of the workers to build up strong labor unions and the opposition of the employers to such organization efforts.

The wider scope of bargaining, with its accompanying need for a wider scope of organization, leads to an understanding and acceptance on the part of the employers of the value of strong and stable unions, capable of carrying out the agreements they make and able to maintain throughout the industry the standards agreed to by the associated employers. This enables each associated employer to know with certainty what his labor costs will be during the term of the agreement and so reduces the danger of competition from rival producers operating on a lower wage scale. Readily available evidence shows that this general extension of trade unionism has substantially eliminated inter-union disputes and has reduced to insignificance the question of the closed shop. There is also abundant evidence that collective bargaining on this scale, which because of the numbers of men and the magnitude of the interests involved carries with it a peculiarly heavy responsibility, leads to the orderly conduct of the negotiations leading up to the basic agreements or their modifications, and almost always to a peaceful outcome of these negotiations. In addition to this, agreements negotiated on this scale commonly provide for settlement of any disputes arising under them without resort to strikes or lockouts, thereby minimizing that final cause of interruption of the productive process. In short, this matured system of industrial relations is one in which the democratic principle of persuasion is fully applied and which by its clearly recorded achievements, as in Great Britain and Sweden, has demonstrated its practical value to both employers and workers.

Labor and management have a community as well as a diversity of interests, and as citizens they have interests beyond their bargaining with one another. And the bargains they make have their own effect upon the general welfare. That sound, mature industrial relations lead on to a nation-wide confederation and cooperative action on the part of both employer organizations and labor unions is clearly shown by the history of the labor movements in democracies abroad. In Great Britain, for example, the British National Confederation of Employers Organizations and the Trade Union Congress have become integral parts of the national life. They are consulted by government not only in regard to labor legislation, but in many matters affecting general economic or social conditions. The government looks to these bodies to settle by conference all problems of industrial relations that affect the general welfare; and in turn they serve as an agency for control and stabilization of industrial relations. Through them the desirability of avoiding mass conflicts that arouse hostile public opinion is impressed upon the employers' associations and labor unions, thus giving to the opinion of the community the ultimate power of control that is proper in a democracy.

What is the duty of a democratic government toward such a matured system of industrial relations? The hallmark of democracy is economy of coercion, and a democratic government should not interfere with the working of any established agency of collective bargaining unless and until the bargains concluded adversely affect the general welfare. But the government may usefully carry on activities supplementing and reinforcing the activities of employer and union organizations. Thus the government may properly provide agencies for voluntary mediation and conciliation, with, established panels of trained arbitrators who may be brought into a dispute at the joint request of the contending parties; and experience has shown that the government should have a recognized power to set up, in industrial disputes of outstanding public importance, boards of inquiry with power to investigate the issues and make findings of fact and recommendations, but without power to impose their recommendations. Compulsory arbitration has been tried over and over again in England and on the Continent, but always with unsatisfactory results. It is plain, from the evidence, that compulsory arbitration so distorts the processes of persuasion that they become practically useless.

It seems clear, therefore, that the duty of government toward such a matured system of industrial relations as has been described, is to refrain from all interference with the bargaining processes, limiting governmental activities to wholly voluntary assistance.

But the duty of a democratic government may be quite different from this, where industrial relations are in the adolescent stage in which we see them to-day in most American industries. Experience shows that trade unionism in a weak and struggling condition tends to increase the number and bitterness of industrial conflicts, and that it is in the earlier stages of organization that charges and counter-charges of provocative action, intimidation and coercion are most frequent and most troublesome. In this country, as in every democracy, intimidation or coercion by violence or threats of violence is prohibited by the general law under the police powers of the state. There is no apparent reason for any legislation specifically forbidding such activities in the field of labor relations.

It is, however, quite clear, although it is sometimes overlooked, that an employer has, with respect to his employes, a unique power of intimidation and coercion—the power to promote and demote, to hire and discharge. No doubt such authority must rest ultimately with the employer, but, like other forms of power, it is subject to abuse. It may be used by the employer to interfere with the worker's freedom to discuss wages and working conditions or to meet with his fellow workers for such discussion. This constitutes a direct attack upon the worker's basic civil rights of free speech and free assemblage, and the coercion may be as real and tyrannical as was ever true of the abuse of political powers that brought about the revolutionary establishment of these civil liberties. Even if the employer does not abuse this power, the worker's fear that he may lose his job, or that he may be discriminated against, fundamentally restricts his freedom of action. It is this situation that has led to the prohibition, in our National Labor Relations Act, of any interference by employers with the free exercise of the workers' right to organize. A parallel situation led to the passage of similar legislation in Sweden in 1936, when Swedish employers, despite the established recognition of trade unionism among industrial workers, showed a disposition to interfere with the organization of white-collar employes.

The nature of the prohibitions in the National Labor Relations Act is such that they will become a dead letter if and when employers cease to interfere with the organization of the workers; but until that occurs these special protections are justified by the fact that the employer has a special power, possessed by no one else and not covered by the ordinary police regulations, to coerce his employes.

It is clear from the very nature of the democratic principle that the entire value of collective bargaining may be defeated—it may be turned from an instrument of service into an instrument of oppression—if democratic principles and procedure are not maintained within the bargaining organizations themselves. Monopoly or monopolistic practices in associations of employers or in associations of workers is always a matter of public concern. It should be noted, however, that such practices, including what we call "labor racketeering," call for agreements behind closed doors. The wide scope of maturely developed collective bargaining affords a very real protection against them, since the greater the number of persons involved in an agreement and the wider its extent, the more difficult it is to maintain it upon, or bend it to, unlawful or unsocial practices.

This brief review omits all discussion of the economic factors involved in labor relations. They are important elements in the effect of the collective bargains made between the employers and their workers, but they have no bearing on the validity of the proposition that democratic principles should be applied in labor relations. As thus simplified, it appears that the common duty of labor, management and government in this country is to encourage the growth of organization and collective bargaining to that mature state in which, in every important industry, basic standards of wages, hours and working conditions are negotiated by national unions or groups of unions with industry-wide associations of employers.

It is easy to state broad general principles, to quote the Bill of Rights in support of them. But the test of our philosophy of government is whether it can be made to work in controversial fields. Beyond tolerance, patience, understanding, the democratic duty toward labor demands deep-rooted faith in persuasion as the only weapon democracy can use in the struggle for sound industrial relations—the only weapon it needs.

Chapter XXXI

THE PROBLEM OF SOCIAL SECURITY

[THE past decade has seen a rapid acceleration of the government's social welfare program. Although this program embodies many new lines of action they are but statutory expressions of social changes which began decades ago. The problems of social security to-day and governmental responsibility for action are quite unlike the problems and responsibilities of the last century. In the United States of the early nineteenth century the bulk of the working population consisted of small farmers and artisans. Their security was largely dependent on their own efforts and ability. Contrast this with the situation found in any American city to-day. Capable and willing workers are without jobs; most of them through no fault of their own. Unlike their grandfathers they can not provide for their various needs by farming. There are, in addition, hundreds of thousands of aged persons for whom society has little to offer in the form of jobs. A new society demands new approaches to its social problems.

Until recently we followed but one main policy in the sphere of social security legislation, namely that of giving relief when savings and jobs were lost. But even here there was a lack of critical thinking. State welfare laws in the 1920's closely resembled the poor laws of Henry VIII. The far-reaching social changes of the last one hundred years had had very little effect on our welfare policies. Relief was looked upon as a local problem although a relief crisis in Detroit affects Los Angeles, Minneapolis, New Orleans, and New York. Local control and finance meant widely varying policies, standards, and tax burdens. One effect of the depression has been to centralize controls over the giving of relief, first in the states and later in the federal government.

The federal government entered the field in 1932 by lending money to the states in order to aid them in financing their expensive relief activities. In 1933 this policy was changed to one providing for grants-in-aid and subsidies to the states. Two years later the federal government disclaimed responsibility for general direct relief and embarked on a policy of furnishing work relief for those who would work. This program, the WPA, raises such perplexing questions as what work should the WPA worker do, and how much should he be paid. Since 1935 the WPA worker has been the butt of many jokes which concern his job, and the zeal with which he performs it. Superficially these jokes may be funny; fundamentally they only illustrate how we have failed to solve these and the other pressing problems of relief and its administration.

In the latter part of the nineteenth century European countries, tiring of the expense of palliative measures, embarked on more positive programs of social insurance in order to meet the threats of industrial accident, old age, unemployment and illness. Early in this century the United States began to act along these same lines. Workmen's compensation legislation is now well established here, and in 1935 the passage of the Social Security Act initiated a comprehensive program of unemployment and old age insurance. There is little doubt that this program will be substantially changed as our experience under it accumulates. There also seems to be little doubt that the responsibility of government for providing such a program will continue.]

No. 109

WHY SOCIAL SECURITY? [1]

by Mary Ross

THE musket hung over the fireplace once stood for security in American homes. It meant game for the pot. It gave protection against unfriendly beasts and Indians. It was a first defense against hunger and danger in the new land.

Probably no families in the world ever have been as self-reliant as the Americans who wielded their muskets in the Colonies and on the frontier. They literally made their own living, for a family had little or nothing except what their members could do and make. A large family was an advantage, since then there were many hands to plant and weed and harvest, to chop wood, to carpenter, to spin and dye and weave, cook and sew. A widow with children was a matrimonial prize.

Our Thanksgiving celebrates the security of the colonists. Our turkeys are the descendants of the wild turkeys their muskets brought down; our cranberries, of the cranberries they found in the bogs. Our pumpkins, potatoes, and onions still commemorate the good harvest the Pilgrims gathered in 1623.

For 250 years and more many American families, like the first colonists, measured their security in terms of the things they could make and do for themselves. As the frontier stretched westward, covered wagons carried with them the habits and ideals that had conquered the wilderness at Jamestown and Massachusetts Bay.

Now automobiles plunge in days over the trails that a scout on horseback or a wagon could travel only in months, and airplanes cross the conti-

[1] Mary Ross, "Why Social Security?" (Washington: Social Security Board, 1940), pp. 1-28. Reprinted by permission of the Social Security Board.

nent in a single hop. The ways in which American families live have changed as swiftly as the ways in which they travel.

Within the lifetime of people still living, the frontier has all but vanished. Change is so obvious that we are likely to take it for granted. It has come so quickly that it is hard to realize what it means to us who live to-day.

The following pages outline some of the changes that have brought us to days when we reach for a pay envelope, not a musket, to get our food and protect our homes.

As late as 1890 more than a third of the Nation's homes were on farms. Country families are bigger than city families. Hence it was not until 1920 that the census found a greater number of people in the towns and cities than on farms and in villages. To-day the farms have only about a fifth of the homes and less than a quarter of the population. In hardly more than a generation we have ceased to be predominantly a nation of country people.

Boys and girls left the farms because the road of opportunity led to the city. Not so many hands were needed on the farms. Machines were taking over work that muscles once had done. Science taught more efficient ways to use the land. Up to 1870 the farms had more than half the Nation's workers, not counting children. By 1930 they had only one in five.

Farm efficiency has grown especially rapidly in recent years. Production per acre increased nearly 20 per cent between 1910 and 1930. Production per worker increased 40 per cent.

Young people from the farms went into the factories and mines. They helped build the railroads and the cities. There seemed no end to new jobs in the rapidly developing nation. From 1870 up to 1910 each census found a larger percentage of the population "gainfully occupied."

As factories turned out more goods, more people were needed to sell them and to finance the making and selling. Since 1900 literally millions of men and women have found jobs in these fields—as salespeople, stenographers, and clerks, telephone and telegraph operators, wholesale and retail dealers, bookkeepers, cashiers and accountants, insurance agents, commercial travelers, stockbrokers, and bankers.

And as invention and science multiplied the output of one field after another, more of our energy could be turned into jobs which have to do with services, rather than things. There has been a growing number of restaurant and lunchroom keepers, janitors and elevator operators, barbers and manicurists, doctors, dentists, and trained nurses; of librarians, teachers, and other public servants; actors, authors, and artists; lawyers, chemists, and technical engineers.

Some of these added jobs represent services which families formerly had done for themselves at home. Others reflect our rising standards of living —more and better education, better health, more leisure, greater comfort and convenience in daily living.

The life in all these many occupations differs in one way from that of the farms where once most Americans made their living.

To-day we do not make a living. We buy it. We make money, and that money mostly determines the kinds of houses we live in, the food we eat and the clothes we wear, the security and independence we look to in hard times, sickness, and old age.

Even in the Colonies, of course, some things were bought and sold. Paul Revere was a silversmith as well as a soldier. But the colonists used money chiefly to buy the luxuries of those days, such as Paul Revere's porringers, or fine furniture, or tea, coffee, and spices.

Many Americans lived as did a New England farmer who wrote in his diary:

"My farm gave me and my whole family a good living on the produce of it and left me, one year and another, one hundred and fifty dollars, for I never spent more than ten dollars a year, which was for salt, nails, and the like. Nothing to eat, drink, or wear was bought, as my farm produced it all."

On the farms of our grandparents where soap and candles were made and hogs butchered for the smokehouse, a family still made a considerable part of their living without using money. Even to-day, an important part of the "income" of farm families comes in the things they raise and make for themselves.

But farmers, too, now must have money. They need it for the kinds of things we no longer make at home and also for the modern tools of their trade—for machines and gas and oil to run them with, for commercial fertilizers, for radios to follow weather and market reports.

In the towns and cities, money is the means of existence from day to day.

The home of a pioneer family was a little world in itself. Members of the family were their own farm and factory workers, butchers, bakers, and barbers; policemen and firemen; often their own doctors and nurses, and sometimes their own teachers as well.

As one of these occupations after another has gone out from under a family's roof, it has become possible for us to have more goods and services than a family can produce for themselves. But most of a family's chance to have them depends on their ability to buy a living.

It is common to hear young people discussing when they can afford to marry and have children. That question would have astonished young people on the frontier.

A young man then could hardly afford *not* to marry. He needed a wife as a business partner, children as helpers. In early New England not only spinsters but bachelors were under a cloud. Bachelors, in fact, were regarded with suspicion. Usually they had to live where the court told them to. Single people had to attach themselves to a family to get a chance to work for their living.

Both the children and the old people earned their place at the family table. As we have shifted from a land economy to a money economy, the work of the young and the old no longer has the same value in helping a family to make their living.

Children need more schooling. Once they learned from their chores, while doing the family's business, many of the things they needed to know as adults. Now work at home fails to give them the background they need for jobs in business, trades, and professions. State by State, we agreed that children must go to school.

Change in the work done at home and in our knowledge and standards of child care made children almost a luxury to a family, instead of an economic asset. Families are smaller, especially in the cities. There are fewer sons and daughters to care for the old people of future years.

Old people, like children, have lost much of their economic value to a household. Most American families no longer live in houses where one can build on a room or a wing to shelter aging parents and aunts and uncles and cousins. They no longer have gardens, sewing rooms, and big kitchens where old people can help make the family's living.

Old people were not "dependent" upon their relatives when there was need in a household for work they could do. They have become dependent since their room and their board cost money, while they have little to give in return. Now they need money of their own to keep the dignity and independence they had when their share in work was the equivalent in money.

The shift of work away from homes also explains the work of girls and women to-day. Women have always worked for their living. When work left the home, they followed it into factories and offices. By 1930 the census found a quarter of all the girls and women "gainfully occupied," not including housewives working without pay for their families.

Studies of employed women have shown again and again that they, like men, get jobs in order to support themselves and their families. In other words, they, too, have shifted from making a living to making money. It is among native-born white American women that the habit of wage work has grown up so rapidly.

Married women, like single women, find it necessary to work for wages.

Between 1900 and 1930 the percentage of married women at gainful work increased six times as rapidly as that of single women of the same ages. Many married women carry the double job of housewife and wage earner. Here again, studies show that they do it because their families need their money.

Most of the work of wage-earning women represents not women's rights but women's duties.

During our lifetime it has become increasingly difficult for a family to pull together and go into business for themselves in one way or another.

For years there was good land to the westward to be had for the taking. Homesteading was an outlet for the sturdy and ambitious. In the towns, family shops and businesses were carried on with relatively small amounts of capital.

There is no more free land on which a living can be made. A farmer needs machines as well as skill and grit if he is to compete in the market. In the towns and cities, modern methods of production and merchandising have greatly increased the experience and capital needed to go into business and stay in business.

Individual enterprise, which so often meant family enterprise, now plays a minor part in earning our national income. Including the farmers, only about one in five of the gainfully occupied works for himself. As a nation, we no longer work as individuals or families, but as employees.

The safety of life has never increased as rapidly at any time on record as in the past 40 years.

Take Massachusetts, for example, where there are records over a long period. A baby born in Massachusetts in 1789 had, on the average, an expectation of a life of about 35 years. In the next century the expectation of life at birth increased about 8 years; babies born in Massachusetts in 1890 had before them a life expectation of 42.5 years for men and 44.4 for women. But between 1890 and 1930 those averages grew to more than 59 years for men and more than 62.5 for women. The gain in the 40 years following 1890 was twice as great as that of the whole century preceding.

This gain in average length of life has come almost wholly from success in saving the lives of babies, children, and young people. More of us live to reach middle age and old age. At the same time the birth rate has been declining. The result of these changes is that old pople form an increasing percentage of the population.

While life became safer, the chance to earn a living became less secure. The growth of employment in basic industries began to slow up. Machines and improved methods made it possible to increase output without increasing the number of workers needed to produce it. Then, for the first time, one important field of work after another reached its peak in employment and began to decline—began to use a smaller number of workers.

Agriculture's *share* in the total employment of the nation had been going down since 1870 but each census up through 1910 counted a larger *number* of agricultural workers. In the census of 1920 and the census of 1930 the number of workers was smaller. In 1930 there were 600,000 fewer farmers and farm workers than there had been 20 years before.

A similar change came in mining. Efficiency was growing. In 1930 two soft-coal miners could turn out as much as three had done in 1900. The peak in the census record of mine workers came in 1920. In the 10 years that followed, industrial activity was expanding, and new mine workers were needed for the gas wells and oil wells. But by 1930 the total number of miners had dropped by 100,000.

All through the prosperous years of the 1920's there were fewer workers on the pay rolls of factories and steam railroads than there had been at the start of the decade. In 1930 the average number of factory workers was 1,500,000 less than that of 1920. The average number of employees of steam railroads had dropped by 500,000.

A man no longer had the same chance to continue through his working years in the occupation he had learned as a boy. The new openings in trade and the service occupations and professions often made specialized demands which workers from the older industries found it hard to meet. It was not likely to help a jobless miner, for example, to learn that more barbers were being employed.

This shift in occupations was particularly difficult for older men. From 1890 on, an increasing percentage of the men of 65 and over has been reported as unoccupied.

With the census of 1920 a more general change appeared. In that year and in 1930 the reports showed a drop in the percentage of all men and boys of 16 and over in gainful occupations. In spite of the increasing employment of girls and women, these reports found a decline in the proportion of all Americans of 16 and over in gainful occupations.

Work has been shifting from place to place as well as from occupation to occupation. Manufacturing was declining in New England, for example, at the time when the growing automobile industry pushed it upward in the Central States. Often families must move to follow jobs or find them.

Americans always have moved in search of a living. The older migrations, however, were likely to be those of people who expected to found a new home, settle down, and grow up with the town. The quick shifts of recent years have split up families. They have weakened the old ties of kinship and neighborliness on which a family used to rely. The loss of neighborliness and the increasing size of stores and factories have weakened the personal ties between workers and their employers.

As work has become specialized, we also have developed occupations in which the demand for work shifts from season to season.

On family farms work was, and is, seasonal in the sense that each season has its particular demands. But indoors and outdoors, there is something useful to be done each month of the year. The season for wood-cutting comes when the fields are bare; for sewing, before or after pantry shelves are stocked with jellies and preserves.

But when factories began to turn out the clothing that families had made during the spring and the fall sewing, factory workers entered jobs in which they were likely to be employed for only part of the year. A cutter or a machine operator may be an expert at his own job, but he finds it is hard to earn in some other way when the factory slows down or closes.

All these changes in the kinds and places and time of work have made the demand for workers changeable and uneven. As a result, many workers —especially industrial workers—were without jobs even in boom times.

The Committee on Economic Security found that in the years 1922-29 an average of 8 per cent of our industrial workers were unemployed. In the best of those years, nearly 1,500,000, on the average, were without jobs.

When hard times came, further millions lost their chance to earn a living. By 1932 and 1933 industrial unemployment had risen to about 39 per cent. That meant two industrial workers out of five—10,000,000 or more in all.

The word "unemployment" was not used in English dictionaries before 1888. "Unemployable" came into use only a year earlier.

As far as we can look back, men and women, of course, had lost one way of earning their living and had to find others. Groups of workers, like the hand weavers, had seen their work taken away by machines. But it is only recently that we have realized that there could be a widespread situation— even in good times—in which large numbers of people who needed to work and wanted to work had no chance to do so.

It was not until machines had knit our lives closely together in industry and trade that unemployment could weigh down families throughout a community or a nation. Only recently have we realized that the requirements of work have become so specialized and exacting that at any one time some people cannot hold any paid job.

In our present money economy, unemployment has become a common hazard of family life like the epidemics which swept our cities three or four generations ago. A family's livelihood can be cut off as quickly and unexpectedly as their lives once were cut off by typhus, yellow fever, or cholera.

Unemployment is like a contagion also because it spreads. When a big factory shuts down, its whole neighborhood and city suffers. The livelihood of all who have been selling their goods and services to those wage earners is affected—storekeepers, landlords, doctors, barbers, owners of movie houses, and, in turn, the workers whom they employ and those who produce the goods they sell. When large numbers of people in one part of the country are without earnings, families on farms and in cities hundreds of miles away may find their living less secure.

Science and invention have given ordinary people ease and comfort and variety of which even rich people of earlier civilizations did not dream. A pair of silk stockings once was a present for a king or queen. But this progress has a price. It demands that we use our ingenuity to keep families independent, now that their living hinges on the judgment, skill, and good luck of many other people as well as of themselves. We have shown our ingenuity in making machines and scientific discoveries. The job now is to adapt our common life to the changes that came with our progress.

The words "social security" have become popular in the last five or ten years. Actually the right and duty of a community to protect its members is as old as the records of men. Primitive tribes have rules and customs to assure the safety of all.

Even pioneer American families, of course, relied on each other for help in trouble and emergencies. Barn-raisings and corn huskings, which have lasted down to our times, are a survival of years when a household asked the neighbors' help in an emergency, knowing it would give its help when its turn came.

But communities did not rely wholly upon the willingness of people to help each other. They did not rely wholly even on the willingness of families to support their own members. The common law of England, for example, lays down the duties husbands and wives owe to family support.

Under later circumstances we have found many of the older family laws oppressive, such as the laws which restricted the right of a woman to her earnings, or her right to hold or will property, or to make decisions about her children. Those laws, however, were intended for the protection of families under the circumstances in which they lived when the laws were made. They held a family together as an economic unit.

The great English commentator, Blackstone, wrote: ". . . even the disabilities which the wife lies under are for the most part intended for her protection and benefit. So great a favorite is the female sex of the laws of England."

In the Colonies, drawing their traditions from England, a husband was obliged by law to support his wife in the manner justified by his circumstances. He was liable for the debts she had contracted before her marriage, as well as later ones. She had a right to inherit part of his estate when he died. In these ways, law and custom, as well as affection, protected the security of persons least able to get security for themselves.

Since a living was made in families, it was through families that a community made and enforced its security measures.

Many of these measures remain with us to-day. The security of children, wives, and aged parents does not depend upon the willingness of their relatives to support them. It is written into our laws and enforced daily in our courts. It is a form of social security because we see to it as a society that relatives give this support when they can, whether they wish to or not.

As cities have grown up we have taken another series of steps for social security by banding together to pay for certain kinds of protection that no one family can provide for themselves. We have police and fire departments, for example. We make fire laws governing the kinds of buildings that people may build in safety to themselves and their neighbors. We support public-health departments. We set up traffic regulations to protect safety of life on the highways and streets.

We also have taken steps to aid helpless people who need a kind of care or an amount of protection that few families can provide for themselves. As our increasing scientific knowledge showed the need and the way, we built hospitals for the mentally sick and for people with tuberculosis. We made laws and opened clinics and special schools for crippled children.

At first these measures to help unfortunate people dealt chiefly with those who were dangerous to others, such as mental patients and people sick with communicable diseases. More recently we realized that it is public economy as well as kindness to make sure that other disabled people get care, since often they can recover enough to earn a living for themselves. It is cheaper to cure them than to care for them for years in institutions.

About forty years ago we began to realize that security in health and life must follow people out of their homes and into the factories.

Our greatest success has come in making life safe for children.

Up to about 1900 many children had gone along with their elders into the factories. In 1900 nearly a fifth of all the 10-to-16-year-old children were at work. This was a larger percentage than had been found in any previous census year.

Then State after State decided that factories were not places for children. Laws were passed to restrict child labor and to specify the conditions under which children might work, if at all. At the same time other laws made it compulsory for children to have more chance to go to school and stay in school. In 1930 less than one-twentieth of the 10-to-16-year-old children were in gainful work.

We have not yet lifted by any means all the burden of harmful labor from the shoulders of children, but most of it is gone. And in the twentieth century we have come far toward achieving what some of the colonists set themselves as a goal: the right of children to the security of an education. In 1932 President Hoover's Committee on Recent Social Trends declared that the fact that half the children of high-school age were in the high schools was "evidence of the most successful single effort which government in the United States has ever put forth."

In the past forty years many States have passed laws to promote health and safety in work for adults as well as for children—laws governing hours of work, night work, dangerous work, and the like. These are conditions which workers no longer can control for themselves as they could when they worked at home.

And in some ways we have taken steps toward assuring not only health and safety in work but also the money to which working families must look in order to buy their living.

When children were taken out of factories and put in school, it was obvious that some families suffered from the loss of the children's earnings. This was especially true in families where the father was incapacitated or dead. Widows with children were no longer a matrimoial prize.

In 1911 two States passed laws to give small money allowances to needy mothers, so that they could keep their children at home rather than put them in an institution. By 1930, 44 States and the District of Columbia had mothers'-aid laws on their books. Upward of 200,000 children were being aided.

Other laws looked to the earnings of adults.

By 1911 a majority of the States had passed laws establishing minimum wages for employees on public works.

By 1910, a tenth of the States had free public employment services. This kind of service was later established by many of the other States, and Federal interest in it dates from 1918.

In 1911 the State of Washington passed a workmen's compensation act. In the next ten years similar laws were enacted by more than forty other States. These laws required employers to insure their employees against injury. Under them the cost of industrial accidents, and to some extent the costs of sickness due to work, have become a part of the running costs of industry.

Under the old common law injured workers had a right to try to collect damages from their employers. The workmen's compensation acts established a more just and orderly way to give workers what the common law admitted as their due.

Starting in the 1920's, many States took steps to provide some security for another large group of their people—the old people who were in need and who probably would never be able to earn their own living again. Alaska had had a law since 1915 to aid old residents in the Territory who were in need. Montana, in 1923, was the first State to pass a law for this purpose, and, by 1935, 28 States, Alaska, and Hawaii had such laws.

This wave of laws to pay regular allowances to needy old people did not come by accident or imitation. It came because of the growing percentage of old people in the population and the inability of the old to work for their living. Old age was becoming an increasingly serious problem to old people and their families and their towns and counties.

Most of the allowances given to old people under State laws have been very small. Even so, they have helped many old people to stay in their own homes and to keep their self-respect when they share the homes of others. Giving allowances has been cheaper as well as more humane than caring for old people in poorhouses.

Mothers' aid and old-age allowances are not "pensions" in the sense in which we usually use that word. Widowed mothers and old people do not get assistance just because they are widowed or have reached a certain age. They also must show that they are in need.

Regular assistance was not provided for all the needy aged or all the needy mothers and children even in the States which had passed such laws. Under some of the State laws a county chose whether or not it wished to operate under the State plan. When county and State funds ran low, even eligible applicants remained on waiting lists for months or years.

Mothers' aid and old-age assistance are a modern way of meeting an old responsibility. They recognize the obligation of our government to provide basic security for these people who cannot earn it for themselves; and they offer a more just and orderly way of meeting that responsibility.

They are better methods than those which States and towns and counties long have used, such as giving baskets of food or tons of coal, or building orphanages and almshouses. They give the people they help a greater chance to choose how they will live. They provide them with what all of us now use to keep our freedom and self-respect. They give them money.

One social historian has called measures like these social inventions. They are ways we have invented to fit our social life to the changes brought by mechanical and scientific inventions.

In 1932, Wisconsin passed the first American unemployment compensation law. This was a social invention which had never before been used in the

United States. Such laws are unlike those mentioned above. Unemployment compensation does not apply to people who cannot work because they are too young or too old or too sick. Its purpose is to promote the security of the able-bodied.

Just as workmen's compensation protects wage earners from the costs of accidents at work, so unemployment compensation protects them against some of the costs of the accident of having no job at all. It is not charity or relief, but a means of preventing need for relief. Through this unemployment insurance, like other types of insurance, the loss of wages which is crushing to those who incur it in any one month or year, is made bearable by distributing the cost of unemployment over large numbers of people and over a long period of time.

For some time people had realized that the same principle—social insurance—might well be applied to the problem of old-age security. This also had become too big a risk for individuals or families or even State governments to meet single-handed.

Our expression "saving for a rainy day" recalls the times when families stored wood in the shed and food in the cellar and pantry for seasons when it was difficult or impossible to go out to fetch them. Why do they not store money in the bank now for the time of unemployment or old age when it cannot be made?

There is an answer to that question in a study made by The Brookings Institution, which analyzes the incomes and savings of families in our richest year, 1929.

In that year, the study found, families with incomes under $1,000 spent, on the average, more than they received. They drew on past savings or got outside help or went into debt. Those families with incomes of less than $1,000 represented a fifth of all the families of the nation in 1929.

Families with incomes of $1,000 to $1,500 kept even, on the average, but saved little, especially in the cities where everything had to be bought and living costs were higher. These families represented another fifth of all the families in that year.

Thus the study found that about 40 per cent of our families saved very little, as a group, in our richest year for the hard times that were coming.

Practically all the savings of that prosperous year were made by the families at the top of the money ladder.

About 10 per cent of us had family incomes over $4,600. They were found to have made 86 per cent of all the savings.

Another 10 per cent had family incomes of $3,100 to $4,600. They were found to have made 12 per cent of all the savings.

The great majority of American families—the 80 per cent who had incomes under $3,100 in 1929—were found by that study to have saved only 2 per cent of all that families saved that year.

Could the 80 per cent have saved more than they did?

The Brookings study declared that at 1929 prices a family income of $2,000 "may perhaps be regarded as sufficient to supply only basic necessities." An income of $2,500 was "a very moderate one."

Even low-income families to-day are likely to regard as necessities things which their parents may have done without, such as running water, electricity, haircuts, movies, a greater variety in clothing and diet. It costs more to be sick. Medical care is better and, hence, more expensive. An employee who loses time from his job because of sickness often loses pay and sometimes loses the job as well.

But what would be the result if all families did save as much as they could by doing without all but the barest necessities?

The families who now save little—those with low and moderate incomes—make up a large share of the markets on which our living depends. In 1929, 70 per cent of all the families were under the $2,500 mark which the Brookings study defined as "moderate." The spending of that 70 per cent is necessary to hold up the fabric of trade and industry on which the living of the nation depends.

When a large part of the population cuts down spending, that fabric sags, and workers and others feel the weight of hard times. That is what happened in the early years of the depression when fear and necessity made people stop buying.

There seems no question of the willingness of American families to save when their incomes approach a comfortable level. But the evidence of this study shows that most families, and especially the families whose risks are greatest, have little to look to when a rainy day comes. Their security lies in the steadiness of their earning and the safety of what savings they are able to make for the years when they no longer can earn.

When trade and industry gathered homes into closely built-up towns and cities, it no longer was safe for each house to have its own well. The safety of the whole town made it necessary to have a town water supply.

The safety of all of us now depends also on the general streams of earning and spending. Unless many families are buying—are paying money into a common pool by their spending—the stream of earnings is lowered, and all have less chance to earn. The well-being of country families and city families depends on the ability of other families to buy.

The security of families has followed their work out of the homes. Social security no longer is homemade.

No. 110

BUT PEOPLE MUST EAT [1]

by D. S. Howard

CHICAGO'S fighting alderman, otherwise known as economics professor
Paul Douglas of the University of Chicago, recently carried an arm-
load of groceries before an audience he was to address. The bread, milk,
cereal, prunes, and other low-cost foods were valued at approximately $1.05,
representing the amount supposedly granted relief families of four persons
for one day's food. Unfortunately, relief families had not for months been
receiving what they were supposed to get, and provision for food was only
two thirds of the established standards. To illustrate this deficiency the
alderman-professor reduced by one third the meagre groceries before him.
There remained 70 cents' worth of food. With this homemakers were expected to provide four persons with three meals each. At best only cheap
foods could be purchased, and but a minimum of those. Little could be
saved out to cover odds and ends needed in cooking, or to provide desserts,
fresh fruits, protective foods, or variety. Since purchases would of necessity
be limited strictly to penny-stretching buys, attempts to provide much of
the spice of life would be likely to leave somebody hungry. Monotony of
relief diets is almost as galling as their inadequacy.

That Chicago's food allowances fell one third below established standards
was not all, for those standards represented, not what families needed, but
only what the relief administration with depleted resources thought could
be provided. This was so much below family requirements that a well-
known Chicago social worker christened it a "skeleton budget" to make
clear its sub-minimum nature, and to distinguish it from minimum budgets
recommended by home economists. During the fall of 1939, a minimum
budget would have provided, in Chicago, $65 a month for a mother and
three young children. The skeleton standard would have given such a
family only $44. Actual relief allowances represented only two thirds of
the skeleton standard and less than half the minimum! No term to be
applied to these sub-skeleton grants has yet been coined.

Inadequacy of relief in Chicago has been so glaring that the city has been
shocked by revelations of the number of Chicagoans who have less than
enough food. The number of children found to be weakened for want of

[1] D. S. Howard, "But People Must Eat," *Atlantic Monthly* (February, 1940), Vol. 165,
pp. 193-202. Reprinted by permission of the author and the *Atlantic Monthly*.

proper food compelled one nationally famous Chicago social centre to modify its program, substituting quiet activities for games like basketball and baseball.

During the most recent of Cleveland's recurring relief crises, 16,000 were reported to have gone without relief. Under circumstances like these there is little talk of three meals a day. The problem is to find one. A Cleveland welfare official, during the relief stoppage, was quoted as saying that an expectant mother went three days with nothing to eat but apples; a mother with eight children had no food but corn meal; another woman spent her last $1.25 for a streetcar pass so that she could ride streetcars night and day to keep warm.

Low relief standards, unfortunately, are not unique to Cleveland and Chicago. They are found in every section of the country.

St. Louis's relief program, according to a newspaper dispatch, was recently termed by the health commissioner "an experiment in malnutrition." In October, families were given only $24.30 for all purposes for the entire month—approximately $6.00 per week, barely enough to feed its members, to say nothing of housing, clothing, or keeping them warm. Single persons were, on the average, given only $8.62. Whole families in Cincinnati and New Orleans in October were also granted less than $25 for all purposes for an entire month. Only three or four dollars more per family were provided in Boston and Cleveland.

Relief allowances sharply below minimum needs are more the rule than the exception in the United States. Reports received from cities as widely separated as Seattle, Denver, Minneapolis, Detroit, and Atlanta all indicate that relief allowances have, within the past twelve months, provided only a fraction—perhaps 80, perhaps 60, perhaps 40, or even but 25 or 30 per cent —of what home-economics experts regard as an irreducible minimum. As a result, many a relief recipient receives less for one day's food than is spent in some households for a dog. And although children, like monkeys in zoos, need fresh lettuce, bananas, oranges, and spinach, only the monkeys are assured these necessities. Philadelphia, the City of Brotherly Love, within the year limited relief grants, for a family of four, to approximately $12 a week, or $1.70 a day. One cannot but wonder what these might have been if Philadelphia had been merely, as some cities advertise, a friendly city. Rule-of-thumb methods used in some areas prescribe one dollar, or perhaps a dollar and a quarter, per person per week for food. These amounts, which cannot decently feed a human, are sometimes augmented by perhaps 10 or 15 per cent to cover incidentals.

Miserable as general relief standards frequently are, the whole trouble is not in the starvation level of life they impose. Almost as bad as their inadequacy is their uncertainty. Without warning, relief offices sometimes close for indeterminate periods. Or a specified percentage of relief grants may suddenly be lopped off.

Then, too, allowances granted to cover designated items (usually food and sometimes food alone) must often be used for rent, fuel, electricity, clothing, carfare, medicines, soap, or other incidentals for which no provision is made.

Although it is usually food money which is diverted to meet other pressing needs, the converse sometimes occurs. A letter received by a Chicago social worker stated the problem baldly "Miss, we have ate our budget of coal and light also rent. ples excus and help."

Worse yet, allowances wholly inadequate to meet current needs must sometimes be applied to back rent or grocery bills long overdue. This necessity not infrequently springs directly from policies which in some areas require people to exhaust all possible credit before applying for relief. The inevitable result of these practices is that when relief is granted it must sometimes be spread back over the period during which potential applicants were being forced ever deeper into the quagmire of destitution.

What standards and practices like these mean to families throughout the United States is evidenced by the average amounts actually granted relief recipients last winter. Data for winter are used here because it is then that need for food, clothing, shelter, and warmth is most acute, and the inadequacy of grants most apparent. Averages for this winter are not yet available.

In December, 1938, Christmas month (although hundreds of thousands have no reason to recall it as such), relief in 39 states for which reports were available averaged $26.15 per household. But this was only the average. At one extreme were states like New York and California, where grants for the month averaged over $30. Even these maxima, however, provide no beds of roses. This is evidenced by the fact that food allowances in New York City, where standards are among the most nearly adequate in the country, provide for a family of four an average of only 8 cents per person per meal. If food money must be diverted for other needs for which no provision is made, even this modest allowance is reduced.

At the other extreme were 10 states (Alabama, Arkansas, Florida, Georgia, Mississippi, New Mexico, North Carolina, South Carolina, Virginia, and West Virginia) in which average grants for the month fell below $10, reaching a mere $4.60 in Arkansas. In Mississippi, the average sank almost to the vanishing point, only $2.73, less than 10 cents a day. And these grants, it must be remembered, are not for individuals, but households which probably average three or four persons each. The meagre grants cited here must therefore be split at least three and perhaps four ways.

Fortunately, relief grants do not necessarily represent all that relief households have to live on in any one month. Many also have at least some other resources like those described below. Furthermore, average allowances also understate somewhat the amounts actually given to households for an entire month, since some grants included in the average are for only part of a month.

Relief (sometimes termed "general relief"), to which reference is here made, is one of the five basic types of public aid now being granted in the United States. The other four are WPA employment and three types of assistance granted needy persons under the federal Social Security program —aid to dependent children, old-age assistance, and aid to the blind. Emphasis placed upon the inadequacy of general relief must not be construed to mean that WPA wages and Social Security benefits are adequate. They are only relatively so.

When contrasted with old-age assistance, general-relief grants appear all the more insufficient. In August, 31 of 41 states reporting on a comparable basis granted more to individuals receiving old-age assistance than to relief families which probably averaged between three and four persons each. Two states, notably Arizona and Colorado, granted individual aged pensioners more than twice as much, on the average, as relief families. A number of others granted individual old-age pensioners half again as much as families given general relief. The nub of this is not that pensioners get too much but that relief families get far too little.

WPA wages, over the nation, vary from about $31 to $95 a month, averaging perhaps $50 for the country as a whole. Although this average is nearly double that for general relief, WPA wages are frequently wholly insufficient to meet families' needs. This is especially true when workers are unskilled, work in areas where lowest wages are paid, or have a number of dependents.

In a meeting of WPA workers not long ago a frail little man, nervous and tense, arose to remind his hearers of what they apparently well remembered —that he had refused repeatedly to go with delegations demanding that WPA officials increase wage rates. Apologetically, his eyes not meeting those of his hearers, he made his confession. Suddenly fire burst out of this hitherto mild man. "But now, by God," he almost yelled, electrifying his listeners, "now I'll join a delegation. By God, I had a delegation come to me, and I'm ready now to join one myself." The delegation that had come to him, he explained when the flame had subsided somewhat, consisted of his two little daughters. At the close of their evening meal they had picked up their empty tin plates and walked to their father asking for more supper, more than he felt could be provided out of his WPA wages for unskilled labor. Little wonder that these workers gather in neighborhood houses, schools, or empty stores to ask each other earnestly how they make their wages last, how they manage to find houses they can afford to rent, what they use for food.

But WPA wages are not merely too low decently to feed, house, and clothe many families. Every so often they stop completely. In this they are like general relief. Congress in its wisdom recently decreed that all workers (except veterans) continuously employed by the WPA for as long as eighteen months must be discharged for at least thirty days. Two things, however, Congress forgot. One was to appropriate funds sufficient to provide jobs enough to reëmploy these furloughed workers at the end of their enforced thirty-day layoff, if at that time they still needed work. The second was to declare a moratorium on hunger. The effect of these oversights is to sentence, not to bread and water merely, but to no visible means of support, many whose crime it was to need WPA jobs for eighteen continuous months.

Harrowing as it is to live on inadequate and intermittent relief, living without it when in need is worse. How many persons there are who need but do not receive relief is not known. That they represent several hundred thousand families is altogether likely. This very uncertainty as to their number but symbolizes the degree to which federal, state, and local governments have neglected their plight.

Who they are is clear. Some are single men and women. As a rule they are among the first to be denied relief when funds run low, a chronic condition in not a few areas. Somehow people without dependents are expected to be able to fend for themselves even though they have no jobs or resources. Some are childless couples. When there is only so much relief to be divided among so many, those with dependents are sometimes given a priority that sentences to utter resourcelessness those with none. Others are fathers, mothers, and children who have not lived long enough in one place to meet what are often stringent residence requirements. Still others are those who do not quite meet qualifications for assistance under the Social Security program—old people not quite old enough to qualify for old-age assistance, blind persons who technically can see a little too much yet not well enough to work or support themselves, young children who are a bit too old or whose fathers are incapacitated but not for a long enough period. Large numbers of those denied relief despite their being in need are able-bodied or employable persons and their families. The plight of all these is unenviable.

It is a strange paradox that wives and babies who have never lived in any other community than their present home may be denied relief because of some technicality regarding the residence of the head of the family, that children under working age are denied aid because their father is employable though without work. It is no less whimsical that, although federal-state provision is made for needy aged persons sixty-five and over, none is made for those who are only sixty-four; that although the federal and state governments cooperate to aid certain (but not all) dependent children under sixteen, there is no such cooperation to aid children attaining that ripe age. Beginning on January 1, 1940, the Federal Government can participate in assisting dependent young people under eighteen years of age provided they attend school regularly. State laws, however, must still be amended before this new policy can be effectuated.

With regard to employable persons, eight states and the District of Columbia were, within the past year, reported by the federal WPA as granting them no relief. The states were Arizona, Florida, Georgia, Mississippi, Nevada, South Carolina, Tennessee, and Texas. Another six states—Alabama, Arkansas, Kentucky, Louisiana, North Carolina, and Oklahoma—were reported as giving "practically no relief" to those who were employable. Another thirteen states—Idaho, Indiana, Maryland, Michigan, Minnesota, Missouri, Montana, Nebraska, Ohio, Oregon, South Dakota, Virginia, and Washington—were reported as having "low standards" or only "limited funds" for direct relief. Employable persons and their families in many of these states were probably aided only on a very restricted basis if at all.

Failure of a state to appear in any of these three groups does not mean that all was therefore well for employables. In New Jersey, for example, a local relief director boasted not long ago that he secured local funds for relief only by demonstrating that it would cost less to give people relief orders than to bury them. Relief designed merely to keep people out of the hands of undertakers cannot be expected to offer much to families and growing children needing more than to be kept alive.

Denial of relief to those who are really employable is bad enough. Its denial to persons of doubtful employability is worse. In one state, if a person was able-bodied he was construed to be employable, and anyone able to go to a relief office was automatically classified as able-bodied. Thus ability even to apply for relief rendered one ineligible. In another state, unless one was almost ready to qualify for old-age assistance he was regarded as employable and therefore ineligible for relief. In a third state, relief to employables might be given in emergencies. However, being foodless or evicted and on the street was not construed to be an emergency.

Why is provision for needy employable persons, and those not given assistance under the Social Security program, so inadequate? A first answer is that, for those who are employable, there are not and never have been enough WPA jobs to go round. WPA officials themselves have estimated that the federal work program has from time to time failed, by from 350,000 to 1,300,000 jobs, to provide work for all needy employable workers. This inadequacy is due in part to failure of the administration to request appropriations large enough to meet the full need; failure of Congress to appropriate even as much as requested; failure of local and state authorities to initiate and contribute toward the expense of projects; failure to create the kinds of work that can be done by those needing jobs. Most important of all, however, is the failure of the American people to demand that proper provision be made for those unable decently to maintain themselves and their children.

Since the WPA and Social Security programs do not provide for all needing aid, why do not the states and localities make proper provision for them? Some of course do. More do not.

One bar to effective action is the unsettled question whether, since the Federal Government apparently will not help to meet the whole need, the obligation is one for the states or for cities, towns, and counties. State responsibility for general relief is less widely accepted than for relief granted under the federal Social Security program. Federal law requires that states contribute toward the cost of old-age assistance, aid to the blind, and aid to dependent children. In addition, states must assure good administration of these programs in all political sub-divisions. This requirement in itself necessitates substantial contributions of state funds in order to make supervision effective. Lack of comparable provisions in regard to general relief has contributed to the present chaos. A first step obviously demanded is for the Federal Government to give to establishment of sound general-relief programs the same degree of financial support and leadership it has given to the inauguration of special programs of assistance under the Social Security Act. Only thus can a sound beginning be made at the all-important task of meeting the distress of people who are not eligible for any type of public assistance provided in cooperation with the Federal Government.

How do needy people get along when granted inadequate relief or none? Some, of course, don't. A very few don't even try. Sometimes mere anticipation of the experience is so overwhelming that people choose not to face it.

In New York City news stories have told within recent weeks of two workers who, when discharged from their WPA jobs, chose not to face what lay ahead. One of these, a woman, shot herself after one glance at the envelope known to contain her dismissal notice. The other, a man, seemingly in a daze of disappointment after discharge by the WPA, marched stolidly into the path of an onrushing subway train.

As for those who choose to "tough it out," as all but the rare exceptions do, there are other ways. What these are is by no means clear. Even social workers and public-welfare officials who are closest to the problem, when asked how people get along, reply, "We simply don't know" or "We can't imagine how they do it."

Yet only details are lacking. The broad outlines are clear enough, and first-hand observers agree that getting along without relief, or with only inadequate aid when one is in need, is a bitter, grueling experience. Those compelled to undergo it are left stunned, bewildered. A recent report by a social agency in Baltimore declared the insecurity and dependence of needy families receiving no relief to be "devastating."

Families suffering this devastation are shaken to their depths. Men become embittered over their failure to find work and to feed their families. One father, because of his inability to provide more than one bed for his entire family, was recently reported to suffer recurrent "black moods." How even the youngest are affected was evidenced by a five-year-old who looked into his father's face and said half-assuringly, half-questioningly, "But we'll soon find a job, won't we?"

Tensions and stresses among destitute families always become aggravated around Christmas time, when parents have to try to explain slip-ups in Santa's schedule. To many a family, and to several times that many children, Chirstmas is something like the twenty-ninth of February. Sometimes it comes, sometimes it doesn't.

Fortunately, people in bitter need frequently don't have to endure it for long at a stretch. Something may turn up, after a week or a month or so, to break the agonizing tension. After longer or shorter periods, families may be able to manage without difficulty. Some, however, may again fall into need when the smile vanishes from the face of fate. However infrequent, however short or intermittent, may be one's descent into dire unrelieved need, the experience leaves its mark.

One way of getting along, perhaps the first (after earnings, credit, ability to borrow, and insurance adjustments have been exploited to their fullest), is to give up cherished belongings. When sold or pawned, these may bring no more than enough for a meal or two. A wedding ring, usually the last thing of value to go, may yield food for a day, possibly enough for a week. Investigators in different sections of the country have reported finding homes of people in bitter need without one article which could be sold or pawned for ten cents. This is the Midas touch in reverse. Instead of base things turned to gold, cherished keepsakes are turned into bare crusts.

One resource almost everywhere available to needy families is federal surplus commodities. These, for hundreds of thousands, have constituted a

last thin line of defense against hunger. The commodities are those purchased by the Federal Government, not so much with a view to their appro-
priateness for feeding hungry families as to stabilizing agricultural prices.
Amounts and types of commodities available for distribution vary both from
place to place and from time to time. The range of items is so limited and
so unpredictable that they give families dependent upon them no more than
a tenuous hold on life—a *Tobacco Road* sort of existence. Commodities
granted at any one time may include, perhaps, flour, prunes, beans, grape-
fruit, and corn meal. Again they may include only onions, flour, and cracked
wheat. Butter and eggs sometimes made available are genuine delicacies.

What the government's new "stamp plan" may ultimately accomplish in
terms of augmenting relief allowances for food is not yet clear. There is,
however, the constant threat that too-low relief standards may be further
reduced as the plan develops. Should these not be lowered to offset possible
gains achievable under the plan, there still would remain an elemental difficulty. Free commodities to the value of half the amount granted in relief
for food would still not raise to a defensible level many food allowances.
Half of nothing isn't much, and half of very little isn't very much more.

Next in importance to surplus commodities are casual earnings. Driven
by necessity, needy persons sometimes work for such miserable wages that
their hourly rates are unbelievably low. Rates of ten cents or less per hour
are not unknown. Low earnings which might appear to be sufficient to
raise relief families' level of life somewhat above that afforded by relief
allowances frequently have no such effect. In the first place, it costs money
to work. Carfare, clothes, and lunches cut deeply into meagre wages. More
important is the fact that, in some jurisdictions, earnings in any amount
disqualify families for relief—this because agencies do not want to "subsidize private industry." In areas where persons having private earnings
may be given supplemental relief, allowances are usually reduced by an
amount commensurate with the earnings. Thus earnings do not raise the
low plane upon which relief families must subsist. This is particularly true
in areas having lowest relief standards.

Another way of getting along is to live off each other. The necessity of
"looking up a friend" every time he wanted to eat or needed carfare to
hunt a job was described by one man as the bitterest pill of all. One by one,
friends tired of it. Friendships waned. Gradually he was left more and
more alone, withdrew more and more into himself. Finally, as he put it,
"you feel all withered inside."

Relatives are normally expected, under our social system, to help one
another. Even here, however, there are limits which any court would
recognize. Under our relief system, however, admittedly needy people who

are denied necessary aid must sometimes be taken in or aided by almost complete strangers who for some reason are willing to share with others resources which many times are not adequate for themselves. This robbing of hungry Peters to help starving Pauls is sometimes called "invisible aid." It is frequently lauded as a manifestation of desirable social attitudes. This lauding, however, is usually done only by those not called upon to play the part of either Peter or Paul.

Another device is for someone to leave home. Or perhaps a family will split. up. Youngsters may be sent to live with grandparents, leaving the parents to face the rigors alone. Children in at least one section of New Jersey are still taken from their parents and given temporary institutional care when families are dispossessed. Among social agencies with high standards, the practice of removing a child from his family because of poverty alone has been outlawed for thirty years. Keeping a roof over a family's head, it may be pointed out in passing, is no less cardinal a principle than keeping families together.

Sometimes, instead of sending children away, the father may leave home in the hope that perhaps remaining members of the family may, in his absence, be granted relief for which they are ineligible as long as he is there.

Again a family may be broken up simply because there is no way to care for it as a whole. A family of eleven recently put into the street was thus dealt with. The father was sent to a shelter, the mother and children given institutional care. Separations of this kind may not be for long. Again, they may.

Most devices to which families resort in order to keep together and alive are legal. Sometimes, however, people in dire need do not stop when all conceivable legal means have been exhausted. Hungry men to whom relief agencies have denied food have been known to walk into restaurants and eat long-postponed meals, telling cashiers to charge them to the city.

Sheer desperation has driven men to other extreme steps. There was, for example, the case of an ex-waiter. In better times he had worked in some of the largest hotels in his city. While he was out of a job and receiving relief in that city, his little daughter fell sick. The doctor prescribed for her an extra quart of milk a day, and urged that if possible the milk be served warm. Prescription in hand, the child's father hounded and harassed relief authorities every day for seven days until the coveted "medicine" was at last authorized. Milk to that family assumed overnight a value and importance worthy of radium; gas with which to heat it couldn't have been more highly prized if it had been helium. Suddenly a new blow fell. The gas was turned off; bills had gone too long unpaid. When the gasman had left, a meter on those premises was broken. And that meter hasn't been the only one operated on. Unfortunately the ex-waiter was alone neither in what he suffered nor in what he did.

Electricity, too, has been carried into houses without benefit of meter. This involves stringing wires which at times become real fire hazards, threatening both life and property. Yet they bring light. People otherwise might have to sit in the dark. School children might otherwise have no light to study by.

However needy families get along with little or no relief, the result is likely to be the same—adults and children hungry and, on occasion, fainting from hunger; families evicted, "doubled up," living in darkness; adults too weak or improperly clothed to work; children too run-down actively to play; few properly clothed, all more or less cold—the whole constituting a mass of unrelieved misery.

In view of relief conditions, it is surprising how some federal officials can refer with ill-concealed pride to the administration's policy, adopted in 1935, of quitting this business of relief. And this despite the fact that the Federal Government has never quit, and is not now out of the business. It has only withdrawn from the one all-important field of general relief. It administers directly the work-relief program of the Work Projects Administration, pays 100 per cent of the cost, and itself administers direct relief granted farmers by the Farm Security Administration. It cooperates too with the states in continuing the business under a different name adopted when the federal Social Security program, embracing three types of relief, was established.

Needy persons not provided for through these special programs, whether because they are not eligible or because the programs are not adequate, the Federal Government passes by on the other side. This lack of federal aid and leadership has undoubtedly contributed to continuance of present chaotic, deplorable conditions. There is little room for pride in either the policy or its results.

To suggest that the Federal Government has not fully met its relief responsibilities is not to disregard the importance of possible economies in federal spending or of limiting the growth of the national debt. It is only to point out that, in the absence of federal aid and leadership in this field, people are in want or only inadequately aided. Perhaps the country's whole relief scheme needs restudy to determine whether the programs to which th Federal Government is already contributing represent the best possible use of funds available for relief. Perhaps the whole structure of local, state, and federal taxation should be reviewed to arrive at the most equitable division of responsibility consonant with the well-being of the country as a whole. Until some such steps can be taken, however, there are strong reasons for federal aid for general relief. Among these are unmet need; disparities between state and local resources on one hand and unemployment and destitution on the other; the handicap placed upon industry in one state which provides comparatively adequately for its needy as opposed to another state which levies upon its industries distinctly lower or perhaps no relief taxes.

By stressing the necessity for federal aid I do not intend to imply that relief is the best possible way of helping people eat when they lack other means. No one likes relief. Those who pay for it don't like it. Neither do those who administer it, nor those who receive it. It is not even a good second-best. Ultimately, it is hoped, some fairer way may be found to absorb into the nation's economy at least those who are able to work, thereby reducing need for relief to them. More equitable distribution of the national wealth, income, and the products of industry might also serve to reduce the need for relief. But these possibilities, though they may be for to-morrow, avail nothing to-day. In the meantime many needs remain unmet or only partially met. Relief, at least for the day, must go on.

A high federal officer in a recent radio address told workers discharged by the WPA that in the absence of jobs and relief they'd better take in their belts another notch and get ready to face a tough winter. This advice, realistic though it may have been, hardly squares with assurances that "no one in America shall be allowed to starve." Failure of the American people to aid hundreds of thousands of needy, destitute families which happen not to benefit or to benefit only inadequately from existing federal or federal-state relief programs, suggests that what is really meant is that "no one in the United States shall be allowed to starve *too long*," or, perhaps, even "no one shall be be allowed to starve *to death*." It is not the Federal Government or state and local governments which must assume ultimate responsibility for conditions as they are. That rests upon the American people. We have failed to demand a newer deal for large numbers of needy families. We have also failed properly to support proposals made by administration leaders to give greater security to those in the nation who are most disadvantaged.

But, someone may interject, there are probably millions of people in other countries living on far less than the average American relief recipient; why all the excitement? This may be attributed to at least four factors. In the first place, need is relative. It is materially affected by mores and standards of living. In the interest of public health and safety, for example, authorities in an American city might compel a relief family to vacate a house which in another country might be regarded as a quite adequate establishment. Thus, one corollary of America's relatively high standard of living is a relatively high standard of need. A second factor is the standard of life a nation can assure to even the poorest of its people. If a country is unable to provide no more than an animal-like subsistence to its most disadvantaged members, that is one thing. If a nation can do better but doesn't, that is something else.

A further consideration beyond what a nation can do is what a nation should do. If there's anything in being a good neighbor, in the Golden Rule, or in social justice, surely this has some bearing upon what a nation does for those within its borders who are in greatest need. To many Americans the failure of other nations to do more for their most disadvantaged members no more justifies this nation's failure to do all that can be done than homicide by one man gives other men a right to murder. Finally, there is the realization that needs unmet to-day may in the long future ultimately entail even greater social costs and outlays of money than an adequate relief program for the present. Relief, therefore, is looked upon as a preventive of something worse. The recent national health survey which disclosed a markedly higher incidence of sickness and more prolonged disability among those in the lowest economic groups than among those in comfortable or better circumstances again suggested that efforts to improve living conditions among needy people may, in the long run, be good social economy regardless of what other nations choose to do.

Recognition of extensive unmet responsibilities must not, however, be allowed to obscure the tremendous gains achieved in seven short years or to cloud the vastly greater degree of security now afforded millions whose very means of subsistence is vouchsafed only through the WPA and Social Security programs.

Failure to do what remains to be done reduces to a mockery our noble pretenses about establishing a minimum level below which no man, woman, or child shall be allowed to fall. It negates, in large measure, values that might otherwise accrue from broad social, educational, health, and recreational programs upon which Americans pride themselves. Can hungry children play, cold children learn, half-fed children remain well, develop properly? What of destitute and harassed parents who suffer far more from realization of what is happening to their children than from their own deprivation? Can they be good fathers and mothers? Can they rear to-day the best type of citizens for to-morrow? Difficult if not impossible as these tasks seem, miserable if not intolerable as are circumstances confronting millions of needy persons in this country, they constitute the lot of those of our fellows who are most insecure, most harried by necessity, worst fed, worst clad, and worst housed.

No. 111

THE WPA—LOAFERS OR WORKERS? [1]

by David Cushman Coyle

IS it true, as you so often hear, that people on relief acquire the habit of living at ease and thenceforth refuse to go to work? Is it true that WPA workers cling to their soft snap and refuse to take jobs in private employment? Do Americans really like to work, or would they rather loaf?

There are records in the WPA files that bear on this question, for one of the jobs of the WPA is research into the attitudes and behavior of its own workers.

It should go without saying that anyone with a little observation can find a horrible example to prove that "reliefers" are happy to relax on Uncle Sam's bosom, and no one needs to look far to find a WPA loafer or one who has to be bounced before he will go out into the cold world. For there have always been shiftless families, or shiftless men with hard-working wives, or vice versa. You remember one (at least) in your home town who had to be "helped," when you were in Sunday School, and you find them still in every community. They prove nothing about present-day relief or about the WPA.

But are there millions of them now? Have relief and the WPA turned good workers into shiftless paupers?

On the face of it and considering what has happened to some millions of helpless people, one would expect that the losses of morale would be stupendous. The astonishing thing is that so little trace of lost morale can be found in the records. Apparently the American people are tougher than anyone had a right to hope.

What sort of people are "on" the WPA?

All sorts, of course. The most striking thing about them is how very American they are.

Take this one as an example:

Bill Jones is forty-one years old, born on a Midwestern farm, one of eight children. He was a smart youngster; at fourteen he was halfway through high school. He then ran away from home because his father got drunk and knocked him unconscious.

Heading south, he picked up a few odd jobs on farms, until one day he wandered onto a race track where a jockey had just been killed. In the

[1] David Cushman Coyle, "The WPA—Loafers or Workers?" *Forum* (March, 1939), Vol. 101, pp. 170-174. Reprinted by permission of *Current History and Forum*.

emergency which developed, Bill was given a job as jockey. This lasted him six years. He worked on a commission basis and earned as much as $6,000 a year when he was eighteen.

When his employer failed in business and gave up racing, young Jones secured a job in a salt mine, where he worked until he enlisted in the World War, in 1917. He was sent to France, participated in four major battles, and was gassed; but at the time of his discharge from the army he refused disability compensation because he "objected to sponging on the government."

After a brief visit with his parents, to whom he had been reconciled, he started to look for a job. He found one as a painter for an oil company and traveled about his State painting gas stations. In his off season he traded in furs, until, in 1923, he was cleaned out by an overnight 25-per-cent drop in the fur market. He continued in the painting business and developed a keen interest in art, especially murals, read widely on the subject, and never missed an exhibition.

In 1926 he married. His wife is a good cook and has a courageous disposition, which no doubt helps to account for Mr. Jones's persistent struggle in the face of misfortune.

In 1927, he set up a sign-painting business of his own, which failed in 1933 after absorbing $500 of his veterans' adjusted compensation. After living by odd jobs for a few months, he landed in a CWA road project but quit, in the spring of 1934, to take a sign-painting job. In December of 1934 he was broke again and had to apply for relief. Before going on relief he cashed in his two insurance policies, netting himself $50. In the spring of 1935, he found another job as a sign painter, which lasted a year. On the side, he painted murals in local taverns. In 1936 he took his bonus money and again went into business for himself; but ill luck beset him. A dishonest employee cleaned him out of about $200 worth of materials. By October, 1936, he was broke again.

He applied to the WPA, and was assigned to an art job on a recreational project. He enjoyed this work so much that he hated to leave it but, as he wanted to get back on his own, he quit in April, 1937, to take a house-painting job. He earned $500 during the spring and summer but fell and broke his wrist, and was again set back by doctors' bills and inability to work. In January, 1938, he was forced back on relief.

His murals in local taverns have evoked considerable comment, and recently they came to the attention of the school authorities in his State. When last heard from, Bill Jones was negotiating for a job with the State as a traveling art teacher at $200 a month.

Bill Jones is a typical American, although probably few others could be found who had progressed from jockeying to art teaching by way of the fur trade. He is typical in his checkered career, with its ups and downs, its sudden changes of occupation, and the indication of a continuous will to live. Twice he has been on work relief and twice on direct relief but he still has his own ideas about how to get on his feet again. He represents the millions whose lives have been upset by the long depression but who are neither too sick nor too old to scramble for a toe hold. He represents millions of employable men and women, white-collar workers and laborers, skilled mechanics, scientists, experienced and inexperienced workers, who, having lost their jobs and exhausted their private resources, have needed employment on WPA projects to tide them over a desperate period.

Are these Joneses of America turning down private employment? Do they wish to remain wards of the government? Are the unemployed lazy? Is the WPA creating a labor shortage through its work-relief policy? Is Bill Jones typical or only a shining exception?

Let us look at the record.

More than five thousand cases of alleged job refusals (of both WPA and private assignments), reported since 1935, have been investigated by agents of the federal government.

Only forty-two of these refusals, or less than 1 per cent, were found to be real cases of an individual's not wanting to work.

The investigation covered large cities with diversified industries, small cities with a single industry, and farming areas of various kinds. The researchers were not content with asking the person under investigation why he failed to take the job. In all cases where the circumstances were doubtful, they investigated further to learn whether his story was true. The number of probable errors would not more than double the number of unjustifiable refusals reported.

There were even a few cases crossed off because the individuals were not "reliefers" at all. A few other individuals, it was found, were in jail or dead at the time they were reported as having failed to show a proper eagerness to take a job. These miscellaneous cases came to 14 per cent of the total of 5,055.

In 12 per cent of the cases, the job was unsuitable. The worker could not do the work or could not afford the required tools or could not get transportation to the job. Many white-collar people are not physically able to do manual labor. (And, by the way—speaking of shovel leaning—try spading a garden for an eight-hour day under the eye of a candid camera! Since the time of Frederick W. Taylor, scientific management has recognized that rest pauses add to the efficiency of labor.) Even with normal periods of shovel leaning, the pace of a manual job is too fast for the ordinary indoor man or for a laborer who has been underfed for some time.

In 17 per cent of the cases, the people under investigation were found to have moved without leaving addresses, so that the notification had reached them too late or not at all.

Temporary or permanent disability accounted for 18 per cent of the refusals. Many of those who had been ill at the time of the refusal were found to be recovered and working.

The largest number of refusals, 38 per cent, came in cases where the workers in question already had found jobs. This class includes those who refused WPA assignments because they had private jobs or who refused private jobs because they already had other private jobs.

The experience of the depression has proved that the American people still want jobs. They learned in school that in America the boy who studies and works day and night will marry the boss's daughter and become president of the company. The vast majority still believe in work.

Fortune reported, as a result of a survey in 1937, that more than two thirds of the workers on relief had at some time held one job for more than five years. In each of the eleven localities covered in the *Fortune* survey, a board of local citizens was set up to rate the WPA workers and relief recipients as to employability. Only 25 per cent were rated unemployable, the principal reasons for this being old age and poor health. Even among those who were judged unemployable by these boards, one in eight was able to find work in the prosperous period of 1937.

The stories about WPA workers or people on relief coming to jobs and walking away again are mostly based on a small percentage of cases where wages or working conditions were substandard. A few employers think a depression is a good chance to get workers for less than a subsistence wage and are happy to let the relief office make up the difference. The unskilled casual workers, on the other hand, having no chance to answer back, have perforce developed their own system of protection from such a policy. They retreat into silence, quit the job, and pass the word along the "grapevine" that So-and-So is bad medicine. Employers who have been given this silent treatment are apt to be vocal when the WPA refuses to force workers into their clutches. They originate a good many of the common stories about the WPA's creating a scarcity of labor.

There can, of course, be a scarcity of labor and a surplus at the same time, because workers are not all alike. Most of our unemployed workers are unskilled, and most of the scarcity is in the skilled trades. During the depression, the apprentice system broke down, and the usual supply of young skilled workers did not materialize. Young men and women entering the labor market remained jobless. Skilled workers who had been laid off became too old, or lost their health and skills and were no longer acceptable to industry. Many employers will not take a worker over forty years of age, and a considerable number of the skilled men on the WPA have reached their fifties.

There will continue to be a shortage of skilled labor until such time as industry can absorb young workers and train them. But such a shortage is not the fault of the WPA. The amount of training which can be done on WPA projects is limited, and the government cannot halt the passing of the years which disqualifies the older trained men.

It is generally agreed that there are from ten to twelve million unemployed in this country. The WPA has had from two to three million on its rolls. To blame the WPA for a shortage of labor is to charge that the tail is wagging the dog. What about those who are not on the WPA or on direct relief? Shortages of certain types of workers exist despite these millions who walk the streets.

The servant problem, for instance, has been acute for many years; it existed long before the advent of the WPA. Housewives who cannot or will not pay decent wages or offer attractive working conditions point to the thousands of women unemployed or working on WPA projects and charge that the fault lies with lazy workers.

The fact is that domestic service, often considered an unskilled occupation, really requires a considerable degree of skill. A servant is expected to keep a home in good order, buy food, cook, clean, and launder. She must have youth, personality, good character, and initiative.

Such a person usually either is already employed in an office or has a good chance to find a job without going into domestic service. Why should anyone who can get a better job submit to being treated as an inferior, working unlimited hours, and receiving a compensation of $3 or $5 a week?

In several cities the WPA conducts training classes for domestic servants where young women are taught the skills necessary to make them efficient household workers. But these trained workers can and do secure positions with families that offer good wages, regular hours, and pleasant working conditions. Usually, there is a waiting list of employers for the girls who complete these courses. Neither the WPA nor any other agency can solve the problem of finding first-class girls for underpaid and undesirable employment.

In some forest and farm occupations there are similar conditions of low pay and long hours, which create a scarcity of labor. Here and there, for instance, a farmer or a lumber operator is found who offers less than the going rate of wages or who has a reputation for cheating on his payroll.

Workers soon learn of such conditions and refuse to accept them. Then the would-be employers kick.

Another common reason for the shortage of workers in certain areas is the cost of travel and the workers' reluctance to move their families from one locality to another without some fair assurance of continuous employment. There may be a scarcity of farm workers in a truck-gardening area, yet in a neighboring State there may be thousands of persons on relief or employed on WPA projects. Unless the farmers can pay enough to transport the workers daily to the scene of employment or to support them while they live away from home, there is no way to get the men and the jobs together.

In the West there are thousands of migratory farm workers who travel from one crop to the next. They move in great numbers, led by stories of work to be had in one place or another. Sometimes there is an oversupply of workers in one county and a scarcity in another. Sometimes one crop is delayed, detaining the workers a week or two, while another crop comes early, placing other farmers in a tight spot for labor to harvest it.

Local WPA directors keep in close touch with the demand for workers, and whenever jobs are available they send WPA workers to apply, releasing them for private employment.

In the early stages of relief work, many workers were afraid to accept private jobs for fear they might soon be unemployed again and take months to get back on the WPA. This situation has been remedied in most localities by giving the workers assurance of re-employment after holding temporary private jobs.

It is significant that more than a million WPA workers have taken private jobs since the beginning of the program. The WPA is organized so that, with occasional local exceptions, it gears closely into private industry and serves as a reservoir of labor. It takes up some of the slack between private jobs and supplies workers, through the U. S. Employment Service, whenever they can be employed in industry or agriculture.

It is to be hoped that, by publicity and experience, employers will be led to make increasing use of the United States Employment Service, so that the WPA can place its men, rather than "dump" them, loose, into the labor market. Regardless of what cries of protest are raised, there is no apparent reason why the WPA should dump workers on the labor market in order to satisfy the demands of the few who want a surplus of labor so that they can get workers at sweatshop wages. The WPA has adopted a policy of refusing to jeopardize the wages or workers now employed by forcing its own people to accept jobs at substandard pay and under undesirable working conditions.

A half-dozen typical complaints out of the hundreds investigated by the national WPA headquarters present an interesting comparison between the charges of labor scarcity and the facts.

One letter, addressed to the President, stated that there was an acute shortage of cannery and field labor in Maryland and Delaware, caused by work relief. The writer was requested for additional information and named twenty-one canneries. Investigation proved that half of these were not operating and only one was looking for any workers; this plant wanted a few women to clean strawberries. The shortages in field labor were limited to two areas. In one, a number of spinach cutters were required for two weeks; and in the other a large number of strawberry pickers were needed for one week. Practically all the employers interviewed considered relief policies of negligible importance in accounting for labor shortages, which occur yearly because of the highly concentrated and erratic demand for workers and because earnings and employment conditions are relatively unattractive.

A Kansas farmer complained bitterly that he had driven hundreds of miles in search of farm hands but found them all on WPA projects. The unemployment census of his county showed 518 men registered as jobless and wanting work. Only 189 workers were employed on WPA projects. When interviewed, the farmer had no jobs to offer but said he might need a helper some months hence.

In New York, newspaper items reported that large numbers of Negroes were being imported for farm work on Long Island, because local workers were on the WPA. Investigation disclosed that the report concerned only one farmer, who also owned a farm in Florida and who regularly transported his help from Florida to Long Island, when the Southern season was over. A total of seventeen Negroes had been imported. To test the possibility of securing a job as a farm laborer on Long Island, a newspaper reporter applied for work—any kind—at fifteen farms, and was turned down in each case.

In Tennessee, a cotton planter complained that he could not get from fifty to seventy-five men to chop cotton, because half the Negroes approached were working for the WPA. Investigators discovered that the workers had to be transported 45 miles to the farm, leaving at 6 A.M. and returning at 8 P.M.—and that for a wage of only $1 a day. The district WPA director did not feel justified in releasing men to accept work under those conditions.

The Governor of Oregon received complaints from six employers who claimed the WPA had caused a serious labor shortage. The investigation disclosed no shortage of labor, and the complainants, when interviewed, stated that they had no jobs to offer. Previously, certain WPA projects in Oregon had been closed in response to complaints of labor shortages, but workers reported that no jobs could be found. Since then, men have been released from the projects only when real jobs were available.

In Texas, a shortage of cotton pickers, in 1937, led to many requests for the suspension of all WPA projects. It was found, however, that State and county WPA officials had already released all workers regarded as physically able to pick cotton. Actually, the labor shortage was caused by early ripening of the crop in the northern part of the State, before the migratory workers were through in the southern part.

As these reports show, the WPA has not been a large factor in the labor supply. There is a reserve of millions of unemployed, outside the WPA, to which industry can turn. Many labor shortages reported at the present time are recurring problems which first arose long before the WPA and have continued through the depression. When business is recovering, cases of local scarcity of certain kinds of labor are bound to occur from time to time.

The investigations of complaints turn up a surprisingly small number of actual cases of laziness or even of unwillingness to leave the WPA for the risks of private employment. Apparently the people who have borne the brunt of the long depression have kept their desire to work and to get back on their feet. A pretty tough race of people, these Americans, and hard to kill. They'd better be, for it takes a long time to get America straightened out.

Some shiftless people there are, as there have always been. A real loss of skill and energy through sickness and old age can be observed among the unemployed. But, in the main, the workers of America seem to be "taking it" better than anyone had reason to expect.

Chapter XXXII

EDUCATION, HOUSING, AND HEALTH—
GOVERNMENTAL RESPONSIBILITIES?

[In spite of the proud boast of many Americans that they live in a land of equal opportunity for all, it is still sound to advise those yet unborn to choose their parents and place of birth wisely. We are, regardless of fine phrases, still a nation with a great portion of our people poorly educated, badly housed, and suffering from inadequate medical care. All of us do not start with an equal chance; the status that we reach in life is not dependent solely on our own efforts. The education that we receive, the houses that we live in, and the medical and dental care that we get depend to a great extent upon the economic status of our parents and the geographical area into which we are born. Take education, for example. In 1935-36, about an equal number of pupils attended rural and urban schools. The urban schools spent about $108.00 per child, the rural schools $67.00. In addition, it should be noted that to arrive at such a high figure for rural schools, town and village schools were classed as rural. This means, for example, that in most of the 44,000 schools with from 3 to 17 pupils in 1934 the teachers were poorly paid and poorly trained, school terms were short, building facilities were inadequate, and many essential services were lacking.

The situation is made still worse by the fact that school funds are raised locally and from the property tax. There are some 127,000 school districts in the United States, most of which raise their taxes separately. This means that, if the tax base is broad, much money is available, but, if the tax base is narrow, little or no money is available. It means also that some districts can build $1,000,000 school houses with all of the latest equipment while others must use one-room shacks that cannot keep out the rain. In 1930, there were 800,000 children between the ages of 7 and 13 who were not in school at all because they lived in poor rural areas. It is obvious, therefore, that an adequate educational system is dependent upon state aid; that is, the state must raise money and distribute it—as needed—to local communities for educational purposes.

This, however, will not solve the problem. There is as great a variance between the resources of states as between school districts. In a recent year, one state had $31,000 in wealth per child; another had $4,000. This means that if there is to be equal opportunity, there must be some kind of federal aid as well as state aid; that is, the federal government must distribute funds to states, in accordance with needs, for educational purposes. But, state and federal aid are not enough. We should also have consolidation of school districts, free transportation of children in outlying areas to the schools, and many other services. Until we have made it possible for all children to be educated in accordance with ability and not in accordance with the accidents of birth, we should beware of smug satisfaction with our educational system.

If we turn to housing, the situation is little different. In a survey made in 64 cities in 1934, it was shown that only 37 per cent of the dwelling units could be considered in good condition, that over 15 per cent needed major repairs, and that 2 and 3 per cent were, by any standard, unfit for use. This gives rise to health and social problems affecting the welfare of the whole community. Slums breed crime and ill health, and are notorious for their cost to the community for fire protection. Unfortunately, the matter lies beyond individual solution.

With a high rate of unemployment, many persons are unable to provide for themselves. In the city of Minneapolis, one family in every four is on relief. These people—unemployed to a great extent through no fault of their own— cannot solve their housing problem. Our economic system has failed to achieve a well-balanced distribution of income so that all families can obtain the necessities of life. This is true with regard to medical and dental care, food, clothing, and the like as well as housing. This basic factor is not the only one causing poor housing, however. For in good times as well as bad, our economic order has not produced the kind and amount of houses needed.

The depression, however, has brought the housing problem home to a great many people, and the government has taken a hand in it. Beginning with the Federal Home Loan Bank System and the Emergency Relief and Construction Act of 1932, the government stepped into the housing field. In 1934, the National Housing act was passed and the Federal Housing Administration set up. This act was designed to create a sounder mortgage system and stimulate dwelling construction by government insurance of loans for some repairs. It also provided a permanent system of government insurance for residential mortgages made on a long term basis. Private enterprise, however, was reluctant or unable to produce low cost housing and the Housing Act of 1937 was passed setting up the United States Housing Authority. This agency was given power to make loans to local housing authorities established by the state law for the purpose of building low rent housing. In 1938, the National Housing Act was amended to provide for renewing insurance on repair loans, for insuring mortgages up to 90 per cent of the value of small owner-occupied homes, and for insuring mortgages on rental properties. The problem is not yet solved, however, and one of the major tasks of coming generations of Americans is to make a national use of our resources in the building of decent housing.

The problem of health is equally or more urgent than that of education and housing. The Committee on the Costs of Medical Care made a study from

1928 to 1931 which resulted in an estimate that the nation's sickness bill was $10,000,000,000 a year. The greatest burden of this falls, of course, on the low-income groups. The National Health Survey revealed that 57 per cent more illnesses disabling for a week or more occur among families on relief than among families with incomes of $3000 or over. The relief group had 47 per cent more acute illnesses than the highest income group and 87 per cent more chronic illnesses. In addition, the poor are sick longer. The average case of chronic illness among persons in relief families was 63 per cent longer in duration than the average case in the $3000 and over income group. It should be obvious also that the poor have less medical care. In families with incomes over $3000, 17 per cent of illnesses lasting seven days or more had no medical care; for relief families, it was 30 per cent. The cost of medical care to low-income groups is a great hardship, and they are trapped in a vicious circle. Their poverty prevents them from getting adequate medical care; their ill health reduces their earning power and standard of living. It is becoming clear that sickness is a hazard—like death and unemployment—with which the individual cannot deal. The cost must be spread over a wide group and over a long period of time.]

No. 112

THE PRESENT SITUATION IN THE SCHOOLS[1]

THE history of the United States affords no more dramatic and significant spectacle than the growth of its educational system. It is a story of the determined struggle of a free people to advance their standards through the improved education of succeeding generations. American education is a phenomenon of American democracy; and the present strengths and weaknesses of American democracy are in large part the result of the strengths and weaknesses of the educational system.

As an enterprise in mass management, public education is one of the largest of all public businesses. Its plant, its personnel, its annual expenditures all rank it among the largest governmental functions. By 1930 the total value of the property and endowments of the public schools had reached the impressive sum of $6,674,445,000. Their annual expenditures, including interest and capital outlay, were at a level of about $2,300,000,000. Drastic reduction in expenditures, followed by partial recovery, has occurred since 1930; in 1935-36 the schools were maintained with enrollments substantially above those of 1930 through the expenditure of about $2,000,-000,000.

As an enterprise in human relations, the schools deal in the human lives

[1] The Advisory Committee on Education, *The Federal Government and Education* (Washington, D. C., United States Government Printing Office, 1938), pp. 6-18.

of the future Nation. Enrollments in all public elementary and secondary schools reached a total of 26,367,098 in 1935-36. Enrollments in elementary schools reached their peak in 1930 and have since declined slightly because of the smaller number of children in the total population. In 1935-36 enrollments in public elementary schools were 20,392,561. High school enrollments continue to expand as a larger proportion of all youth enter the high schools. Youth to the number of 4,399,422 were enrolled in public high schools in 1929-30; by 1935-36 the number had increased to 5,974,537.

In the recent years of depression, the schools have been on trial. Although the influx of pupils into the high schools has continued at an undiminished rate, for several years the programs both in elementary and in secondary schools were greatly disrupted. In many areas, school terms were curtailed, entire sections of the curriculum were dropped, crowding in schools increased, fewer teachers were provided, and the salaries of those remaining were drastically reduced.

In most cases the worst injuries of the depression have now been repaired, and there is a general disposition to build anew on a sounder foundation. The tests of the depression have demonstrated, however, that the general pattern of the tax-supported school has been firmly established and will not soon be changed. In the years that lie ahead, there must be many new developments and some expansion of educational programs, but the coming decades are not likely to be marked by so great an expansion as occurred during the half century closed in 1930. Following a half century of laying of foundations between 1830 and 1880, and a second half century of rapid expansion ending in 1930, it may well be that America is now entering upon a period of evaluation—a period in which will be determined more accurately what educational policies are best suited to a modern democracy and how best they may be realized in practice.

When the work of evaluation is undertaken, it is immediately apparent that an intense localism is at once the strength and the weakness of American schools. Local interest and support have been the major factors in the development of the most democratic system of education in the world. Our folk-made schools have given us many great benefits. We also bear the burden, however, of many grave disadvantages that trace back directly to local responsibility for public education. We have in this country a considerable number of the best public schools in the world. We also have far more than our share of those of very inferior quality.

The strong public school centers in the United States are found most frequently to-day among the small and middle-sized cities. The school boards in these cities are usually free from unwise forms of political interference and tend to be made up of competent citizens, although those citizens are frequently more representative of business and the professions than of other groups in the community. Administrative control is effective and the local tax base in most such communities is adequate to support a liberal measure of educational service without reliance upon any other source of support. The leadership by school administrators is in general as good as can be found in any phase of governmental service, and in many cases reaches a very high level. The classroom teachers in those cities typically are well prepared, are seldom without experience, and are both interested in their work and desirous of improving it.

Under such conditions, schools can give effective attention to stimulating the maximum development of the children. The courses of study are adaptable and can be adjusted to changing conditions. Textbook teaching is still the rule, but some use is being made of reading materials other than textbooks. Health, welfare, and noncommercial recreational activities are provided to some extent. School and community activities are frequently blended to provide a more inspiring curriculum and to achieve other values.

The school systems in the middle-sized cities are capable of much further improvement, but their great virtue lies in the fact that improvement is going on at a rather rapid rate. They have the necessary resources and enough autonomy for leadership to function. They may well continue to provide much of the educational leadership for America. Every effort should be made to encourage them to do so.

The school situation in the great metropolitan areas is often less satisfactory. Their wealthy and autonomous suburban areas have perhaps the finest public schools in the United States, but the large cities themselves present another picture. They unquestionably have the financial resources for good educational programs, and in many cases provide educational service at a high expenditure level. They suffer, however, from the chronic handicaps of mammoth urbanism. In all cases they adapt to changing conditions only at a slow rate. They have not yet found techniques by which to instill a progressive spirit throughout the entire personnel of centralized school systems, each as large as those of many whole nations in other parts of the world. In some cases they suffer from the most flagrant applications of the spoils system and other phases of corrupt political action.

The least satisfactory schools in the United States are now to be found for the most part in rural areas. The rural schools are better than they were formerly, but under present conditions there is no prospect that the rural areas will be able through their own resources to lessen the wide gap between rural and urban levels of educational service.

In 1935-36 the average expenditure per pupil in average daily attendance in all public schools, urban and rural, was $88.30. The numbers of urban and rural children in average daily attendance were approximately equal, 11,406,380 urban and 10,892,387 rural. The average expenditure per pupil in average daily attendance in urban schools was $108.25, and in rural schools $67.40. The rural figure includes town and village schools as well as those in the open country. Expenditures in the schools of open country areas are much lower, although statistics of average expenditures in such schools are not available.

Low expenditure levels in rural areas are reflected in poorly paid and relatively untrained teachers, reliance on stereotyped forms of textbook instruction with inadequate provision of supplementary books and other instructional materials, school terms averaging a month shorter than those in cities, and a general lack of the health, welfare, guidance, and other services in addition to instruction that are needed by children in schools.

At the time of the 1930 census, about one-fourth of all children of elementary school age lived in the rural counties that a few years later were classed as serious relief problem areas. These counties even in good times are not able to supply more than a low level of educational service for one-fourth of the future citizens of the Nation. In 1930 there were 810,000 children between the ages of 7 and 13 who were not going to school at all. Most of those children were in the poorest rural areas.

The continued maintenance of large numbers of one-teacher rural schools with extremely small enrollments is responsible in many areas for both a low level of educational service and a high tax bill for the service that is provided. A study completed in 1934 recorded nearly 44,000 schools in which the attendance per school ranged from 3 to 17 pupils, and average costs per pupil ranged from $200 to $80, although the level of service provided was markedly inferior to that found in many town and village schools operating at cost levels around $40 per pupil in attendance.

In several predominantly rural States, the average compensation of all elementary school teachers is less than $600 a year. Teachers on a salary scale of this kind cannot afford to spend much on preparing themselves for their work and on keeping up with new developments. Throughout the Nation in rural schools with a single teacher, nearly a fourth of all the teachers have had no preparation beyond a high school education and seven out of eight have had no more than two years of education beyond high school. Considering the circumstances, the amount of good accomplished by these teachers is large, but the results are still inadequate.

The administration of the school system in the United States is more highly decentralized than any other public function, primarily because of the small size of most rural school districts. Data collected in 1934 show that there are approximately 127,000 separate and independent school dis-

tricts and other types of local school jurisdictions. Each of these local jurisdictions is free to decide on the type and quality of education offered, subject only to general State laws and regulations and to the limit of available
funds. Altogether there are about 424,000 school board members; in 12
States they outnumber the teachers. More efficient administration would
be possible in many areas if some rural districts were consolidated. Larger
districts could afford professionally trained superintendents who are beyond
the reach of a small rural district.

The schools generally both in rural and in urban areas are deficient in
their facilities for necessary services other than routine instruction. Training for pre-primary children has only begun to be introduced. Facilities for
physical education, for health education, and for recreation are extremely
limited in the schools attended by a majority of the children in this country.

Health and education are closely tied together in a mutual relationship.
Children who appear to be stupid are often merely suffering from some
physical defect that can be remedied by medical attention. On the other
hand, preventable diseases and defects can be greatly reduced in number
by further extension of health services and health education in the schools.

Some 2,500,000 children of school age in the United States are handicapped in some way that necessitates facilities in addition to those provided for other children. Not more than 325,000 are receiving the attention
necessary to make their education a success. A majority of the children
with defects of sight, hearing, speech, and other functions can be made
capable of supporting themselves and of living useful lives in the community if they are given a fair chance to obtain an education. To neglect
this opportunity, as is now being done in most of the cases, is to impose
an unfair burden on the children themselves and an expense on the community throughout their lives. Twenty-six States have laws concerning
special classes for some types of handicapped children, but no State is
providing funds large enough to meet the requirements. In rural areas the
available information indicates that practically nothing is being done in
the way of providing suitable education for these children.

In most of the States where there are separate schools for Negroes, the
schools for white children are below the national average, yet Negro schools
are only about half as well supported as white schools. Because of the intimate economic relations that necessarily exist between the two races, the
low level of education among Negroes is a severe burden not only on themselves but on all who must employ them or have dealings with them. Even
in Northern States, the large influx of Negroes from the South makes the
quality of their previous training a matter of vital importance to the localities where they live and work. All the statistics for length of school term,

average attendance, educational qualifications of teachers, type of school buildings, and other factors indicate that a wasteful neglect is characteristic of the treatment of Negro school children in most of the areas where they are required to attend separate schools.

In general, the outstanding impression to be gained from a survey of the schools throughout the United States is one of very uneven development. Elementary school service of some sort is now almost universally available, and the general program from the first through the sixth grade exhibits a considerable amount of uniformity. When the quality of elementary school service is considered, however, almost any measure that can be applied will reveal the widest possible variations.

The development of secondary schools has followed the development of elementary schools, but has not been carried so far. In consequence, secondary schools present a picture of even greater diversity than do elementary schools. The secondary schools, however, offer so many problems that they are given special consideration below.

The major problem of the elementary schools is one of providing financial support where it is not now adequate. Improvement is needed in many other respects, particularly in the preparation of teachers, the organization of school districts, and the supervision of instruction, but the methods of securing improvement in the elementary schools are on the whole well known.

In areas of declining elementary school enrollments, many needs can be cared for by shifting existing resources released through declining enrollments. In other areas, enrollments may and should continue to increase because many children are not now in school. The areas of poor school attendance are, in general, also the areas of lowest financial resources. They present the most acute and difficult problems of education in the United States to-day.

Education at the secondary level in this country was for a long time considered a special privilege, available only to a few on the payment of tuition fees, and designed chiefly as a preliminary preparation for certain professions. During the latter part of the nineteenth century the growing realization of the implications of democracy led to the development of the high school as a part of the common school system.

In retrospect, nothing in the evolution of American education is more striking in its sweep than the development of the secondary school. Nothing like it has ever happened before in any other country. As late as 1890 in the United States only 3.8 per cent of the number of young people 14 to 17 years of age were enrolled in public high schools; at present more than 60 per cent of the population of high school age are enrolled in public high schools. In 1937 for the first time the number of graduates from high schools in a single year passed the million mark. There are now some 25,000 public high schools in which over 230,000 teachers instruct almost 6,000,000 boys and girls, by means of a curriculum that is gradually, although inadequately, being adapted to meet the individual and social needs of American youth.

For the country as a whole, the period of phenomenal high school expansion appears to be drawing to a close. The effects of the decline in birth rate which began some years ago are already beginning to be shown in the size of the youth population; about 1940 the number of youth of high school age will begin to decrease. With 60 per cent of the number of youth in the 4-year high school age group already attending high school and with decline in the total youth population, it will no longer be possible for the high school enrollment to double each decade as it often has during the past half century.

Expansion will not stop abruptly, however; all existing trends indicate that a considerably higher percentage of those of high school age will attend high school in the future, particularly in areas where high school enrollments are still low.

School attendance beyond age 16 is not usually required by law, and many States have not accepted fully the obligation of making a high school education universally available. The limitations on existing facilities are indicated by a wide variation among States with respect to the percentage of youth of high school age who are enrolled in high schools.

There are about half as many young people of high school age as there are children of elementary school age. In 1935-36 high school enrollments in six States were in excess of 40 per cent of elementary school enrollments, while in eight States at the opposite extreme in high school enrollments, they were under 20 per cent of elementary school enrollments. These differences among States to a considerable extent reflect urban-rural differences.

Low high school enrollment figures are in many cases due to low average family incomes and to the necessity or desire upon the part of young people to go to work without finishing high school. In view of the great unemployment among youth, however, and the reluctance of many employers to hire young people who have not finished high school, many of the youth of appropriate ages who are not attending high school are out of school either because high school facilities are not available or because the available facilities are not suited to their needs.

With the radical changes in social life, brought on by the development of present industrial and economic conditions and by the rapid growth of cities, the schools have been swamped with new duties. These new duties have come along with the great increases in high school enrollments and changes in the composition of the groups of students enrolled. School administrators have often been too busy with pressing immediate tasks to think through fundamentally the necessary changes in their programs. Yet there is now no possible doubt that the school system must supply many new kinds of training, particularly in the secondary schools.

Education for citizenship, for example, can no longer be properly confined to a formal study of the structure of government, leaving the pupil innocent of all idea as to what really happens at the city hall or in Washington. Students should learn something of the economic causes of political pressure, the nature of propaganda, the democratic treatment of honest difference of opinion, and the technique of cooperation.

Most high schools offer some types of training designed specifically to prepare for employment, but programs in the vocational field are relatively undeveloped. The schools are still groping for the solution of many problems that must be solved before sound programs of occupational preparation can be provided on a substantial scale.

For adequate occupational preparation, many young people need special vocational training, but consideration should also be given to the far greater importance of general training for useful employment. Underlying each particular specialized trade or calling must be the basic skills and habits— accurate arithmetic, careful use of the language, and responsibility and conscientious work. Both elementary and secondary schools need better facilities for giving the basic training which will prepare a young person to learn a job quickly and, if the job vanishes in the course of technological change, to shift over without serious trouble to some new type of work. The useful habits and basic traits roughly included in the term "character," together with flexibility of mind and a wide range of interests, are the essential foundation for a successful working life in any occupation.

The complex opportunities and pitfalls of modern life make it practically impossible for most high school pupils to make a wise choice of future occupation on the basis of casual observation of the world around them. Yet only a few schools are providing educational and vocational guidance under trained and capable counselors. In the absence of suitable provision for guidance, much of the high school education now provided fails to meet the needs of the pupils. More attention to guidance is needed, with a more realistic definition of the requirements for ultimate employment and a better supply of data as to relative opportunities in the various fields.

The same qualities of competence, responsibility, and emotional adjustment that make for efficiency in gainful employment are equally essential for the development of successful home and family life. The operation of harmonious and secure homes in which the new generation can be given a good start is a public service of the most vital kind, affecting the stability of the social order and the whole question of the permanence of democracy. The schools can well afford to supply whatever training is possible that will help the young people of each generation to establish successful homes.

The high schools are giving some attention to education for a variety of cultural and avocational activities, but have had difficulty in establishing and maintaining well-rounded programs. Fine arts, craftsmanship, music, and similar subjects are offered in some of the schools, but are generally regarded as incidentals, to be dropped whenever there is difficulty in meeting the school budget. In view of the fact that a rapid expansion of cultural services would help to overcome technological unemployment, training along those lines is a matter of economic importance to the future prosperity of the Nation.

The expansion of high school courses to meet one new - demand after another without any fundamental reorganization of programs has brought great confusion into the offerings. The pupil, his parents, and the public frequently see no sensible or necessary meaning in the arrangement of the curriculum. There is a great need for a recodification of educational objectives and methods in the secondary schools, so that pupils, parents, teachers, and taxpayers may have a definite picture of the world of human knowledge and human attitudes into which the pupils are being introduced.

In any reorganization of secondary schools, a central place should be given to their major task of preparing all youth to the age of at least 18 for useful, self-sustaining membership in American society. This means that there must be far-reaching modifications of secondary education, new curriculums, new courses, and, possibly, new methods of instruction. These changes are essential to meet the gradual increase in the school-leaving age from its present average level of 16 years to the approaching average level of 18 years.

The high schools must also assume far greater responsibility than at present for part-time educational and related services for out-of-school youth and adults. Most of the 900,000 young people who drop out of high school each year without being graduated are in need of further educational service, and many of them would respond if suitable part-time programs were provided. Adults also have increasing needs for the services of the schools to supplement the education they received earlier in life, for vocational retraining, and for constructive leisure-time activities. In many areas the community facilities will not be complete until the high schools become true community centers for educational, recreational, and cultural aspects of community life.

In view of its terms of reference, the Committee has given only a limited amount of attention to private education. To complete the picture of elementary and secondary education in the United States, however, it should be said that in 1933-34 there were about 12,000 private elementary and secondary schools in this country. Nearly two-thirds are controlled by the Catholic Church, and about one-sixth are under other church auspices. Private schools enroll about one-tenth of the total number of elementary school pupils and about one-sixteenth of the total number of high school pupils. In general, these schools meet standards set by public authorities. Most States recognize the public service they are rendering by granting tax exemption to such of them as are nonprofit making in character.

The citizen has the right to expect that the public school will bring both to his children and to his community real opportunities for individual and social development. The following services are among those that should be universally available:

1. A well-planned program of general education for all children and youth, and also suitable preparation for particular vocations in accordance with the needs of the children and youth.

2. Instruction by carefully selected teachers who are competent and well-prepared, and who are interested in the development of community life.

3. Safe and sanitary school buildings adapted to a modern program of instruction and related services.

4. Suitable school equipment and instructional materials, including books and other reading materials adequate for the needs of the children.

5. Student aid when necessary to permit able young people to remain in school at least up to age 18.

6. Suitable opportunities for part-time and adult education.

The community facilities for educational and related services should include:

1. Adequate school and community libraries.

2. A broad community program for the protection of the physical and mental health of the children.

3. Adequate provision of educational and related services for handicapped children.

4. Well-organized and competently staffed educational and vocational guidance services for all children and youth.

The organization of the local school system should be adapted to democratic methods and needs:

1. The school district or other local administrative unit, whether urban or rural, should be large enough to permit economical organization, effective supervision of schools, and a broad base for local taxation.

2. The board of education should be broadly representative of the entire community.

3. There should be competent supervision of instruction and other services through a staff with supervisory capacity and social vision.

4. The teachers should be encouraged and given opportunity to participate actively and intelligently in the development of educational and administrative policies for the school system; they should also be encouraged to participate in community activities appropriate for public servants.

5. There should be definite cooperative arrangements for the coordination of the work of the schools with that of other community agencies concerned with the health, education, welfare, and guidance of children and youth.

6. In rural areas, the school system should be as efficiently organized and as well supported as in urban areas; so far as feasible school attendance areas should follow community lines.

7. Where separate schools are maintained for Negroes, they should be as well adapted to the needs of their pupils as are the schools for white children and youth.

This catalog of minimum standards presents no impossible demands in a country as rich as the United States, as democratic, and as convinced of the necessity for universal educational opportunity. There are many school systems, particularly in areas where financial resources are large, that meet most of these standards. There are, on the other hand, large numbers of local school systems that fail to meet them, and millions of children are enrolled in schools that fall very far short of achieving them.

No. 113

THE COSTS OF BAD HOUSING [1]

by Edith Elmer Wood

THE social and economic costs of bad housing are old subjects of discussion, but our supply of relevant factual material has increased so greatly in the last few years as to justify revaluation. Naturally, not

[1] Edith Elmer Wood, "The Costs of Bad Housing," *The Annals* of the American Academy of Political and Social Science (March, 1937), Vol. 190, pp. 145-150. Reprinted by permission of the author and *The Annals* of the American Academy of Political and Social Science. Footnotes in the original article are omitted here.

all the new material is of equal validity, and not all who quote it do so with equal care. Hasty generalizations, claiming too much, often prove boomerangs.

Social costs may be summed up in terms of sickness, injuries and deaths, delinquency and crime, decrease in industrial efficiency, lowering of the quality of citizenship, increase of family disintegration, and social unrest. This article is limited to the first-mentioned groups, where the newer material is found.

The earliest observers, a century ago, warned of the connection between bad housing and disease, especially between overcrowding and epidemic disease. Early sanitarians battled for city sewers, pure water, and collection of refuse. But in many American communities these elementary needs have never been extended to low-rent housing.

Later it was discovered that sunlight and fresh air are essential to health, from which it followed that dark and semidark rooms, or rooms without means of ventilation, are inimical to health. In such dwellings a tuberculosis patient has scant chance for recovery, and his family face greatly increased danger of infection. The prevalence of rickets among children increases sharply. Rheumatism and respiratory diseases flourish in the dampness of cellar homes or where roofs and walls are no longer water-proof.

Social phenomena are complex. Few have a single cause. Few fulfill the requirements of a controlled laboratory experiment. This is true in matters of physical health and also in matters of mental and moral health. We must be content to note that the correlation of high general death rates, sickness rates, and infant mortality rates with areas of recognized bad housing raises a presumption of causal connection, though it does not exclude the simultaneous influence of other factors such as poverty, ignorance, or race.

A careful piece of work in separating some of these factors was done by the Children's Bureau in its 1925 report, "Causal Factors in Infant Mortality," summarizing the results of a series of studies in eight American cities. Infant mortality rates were found for groups classified by race, by income, and by coefficient of room density, which is the number of persons in a home divided by the number of rooms. Where room density was less than one, the infant mortality rate was only 52 per 1,000 births, against 94 where the density was between one and two, and 135.7 for two and over. Elimination of the effects of race and income left the rate still twice as high in over-crowded as in spacious homes.

An older but much quoted example, where the housing factor is nearly isolated, is found in the before-and-after statistics of the Liverpool Health Department. Liverpool was a pioneer in municipal slum clearance and housing, and as early as 1897 adopted the policy of getting the identical families displaced by clearance into the new houses. In various projects, such rehoused families reached from 77 to 99 per cent of the total. Slum clearance being a public health measure in Great Britain, it was the health officer who recommended an area for clearance, submitting general, tuberculosis, and infant death rates in comparison with city averages to justify his recommendations. In Liverpool, at least, subsequent statistics were presented to check results. A 50 per cent cut in all these rates after a few years was not unusual. In tuberculosis, it was often more.

Among the most impeccably gathered, presented, and interpreted statistics of housing, health, and delinquency in recent years are the massive volumes on Cleveland by Howard Whipple Green. He divides the city into 14 economic areas on the basis of rentals recorded in the 1930 census. In the lowest, rents average below $15 a month; in the highest, $100 and over. In the two highest-rent areas combined, the general death rate was only 7.2 per 1,000. In the lowest two, it was 15. The average for the city was 11. These rates were standardized for age and sex. Similarly, the tuberculosis death rate per 100,000 population 25-44 years of age varied from 34 in the highest economic areas to 215 in the lowest. Separate classification of white and Negro deaths would show that part, but only part, of this enormous difference was due to race.

Similar figures could be multiplied indefinitely. The New York Health Department collects a vast amount of basic material. Some of it has been used in the spot maps and rate maps prepared by the Slum Clearance Committee in 1934 to demonstrate the general coincidence of high infant mortality, high tuberculosis case and death rates, and high venereal disease rates with areas of land overcrowding and deteriorated housing. Negro Harlem also demonstrates the racial factor. Better health conditions produced by homes built under the Tenement House Law of 1901 are reflected in the superior health records of the newer boroughs built largely since that date. Queens and the Bronx, each with population over a million, have general death rates between 7 and 8 per 1,000, while Manhattan, with 81 per cent of her residential structures built before 1900, has over 14.

Apart from its menace to health, bad housing often involves extra fire risks. The yearly death toll in the old-law tenements of New York, with their wooden stair-halls and inadequate fire escapes, is a grim illustration. Occasionally worn-out houses collapse on their inmates, as happened recently in Philadelphia. More often, tenants are injured by falling ceilings or broken stairways. Children who have no yards to play in are in daily peril on the street.

Little research has been done in tracing environmental factors in mental and nervous breakdowns and emotional instability. Addresses of mental institutional patients have been plotted occasionally and show heavy rates for slum areas, especially lodging house areas, but the study is in its infancy. Careful investigation of emotional instability in its early stages, as it develops in a hyper-excitable child who is getting insufficient rest, sleep, and fresh air, might lead to conclusions of practical value in the prevention of delinquency and crime. A crowded home in a crowded tenement is one of the noisiest, nerve-joltingest, least restful spots on the face of the earth. A young child's nervous system is far more susceptible to injury than an adult's. Case histories show the disproportionate prevalence of emotional instability among delinquents and criminals. It is hardly questionably that it constitutes an important predisposing factor. It may turn out that city tenements, in an almost mechanical way, are multiplying the number of children who suffer from this defect.

The work of Clifford Shaw in plotting Chicago's "Delinquency Areas" and calculating their delinquency rates, and his later similar studies in six other cities for "Causes and Cure of Crime," are our richest sources of information on the localization of delinquency. In Chicago, Shaw plotted some sixty thousand home addresses on maps of the city. They were in ten groups and extended over a period of thirty years. There were groups of truants, of boys brought before the juvenile court, of delinquent girls, of youths charged with crime, and of adult male offenders. What the maps showed clearly was that the homes of the individuals composing any of these groups at any time during the period were not distributed evenly over the city by area or by population, but were concentrated in certain localities of congestion and blight. In Chicago these areas were around the Loop, the stockyards, and the steel mills. Since the delinquency areas remained in the same localities during thirty years, while the racial makeup of the population changed several times, the racial predisposition theory of delinquency seemed to be pretty well refuted.

Shaw points out that while high delinquency rates and bad housing occur together, it does not necessarily follow that one is the cause of the other. Both may be the result of a *tertium quid* such as poverty. For practical purposes, he agrees that improved housing conditions in these areas would probably decrease delinquency and crime, provided whole neighborhoods were rebuilt at one time.

In this proviso Shaw is, I think, justified, for it is bad associates rather than bad bricks and mortar that incite to delinquency. But it is the lack of play space indoors and of a house yard where young children can play outdoors under their mother's eye that forces mere babies on to the street and under the influence of whatever associates they stumble on. The prolonged infancy of the human race is an advantage only if it means prolonged protection and education. Otherwise it is a handicap. A three-day-old chick is much better qualified to take care of himself than a three-year-old child. Manners and morals are acquired by imitation of associates. Three-year-olds are not discriminating. Bad behavior catches their attention more easily than good. They graduate from one ganglet to another. The damage is done before they start to school. These youngsters need new homes, but the homes must be set among new and safe playgrounds.

Within the last three years studies have been made of the excess cost of slums to the taxpayers, which have forced the tired business man to sit up and take notice. To this aspect we confine ourselves, although it must be remembered that cost to the taxpayers is only part of the economic waste involved in slums.

In the summer of 1933 a study was made in Indianapolis by the Bureau of Social Research of Indiana University, R. Clyde White, director. Eleven census tracts with deteriorated housing near the center of the city were picked as probable areas of greatest economic drain. With 10.4 per cent of the population, they absorbed 30 per cent of city hospital service during the year 1932 and furnished 24 per cent of cases treated in the venereal disease clinic and 19.1 per cent of patients at the hospital for the insane. The cost of extinguishing fires was 16.7 per cent of the total for the city. Residents of the district were responsible for 36 per cent of what the city spent to arrest, try, and imprison felons, and almost 25 per cent in the case of misdemeanants.

A small area containing only 1,500 population was selected for further study. A profit-and-loss statement was drawn up which shows the method followed. Assessed valuations for the area multiplied by the tax rate gave the theoretical income. From this was deducted the 32.55 per cent tax delinquency to show actual income. The average per capita cost of government in Indianapolis was $38.56. Within the area it was $61.85. The total cost of the area to Indianapolis taxpayers was $92,775, and its total contribution in taxes $11,312.30, leaving a deficit of $81,462.70.

Early in 1934 appeared *An Analysis of a Slum Area in Cleveland* by the Rev. R. B. Navin and others under the general supervision of Howard Whipple Green, which dug a little deeper into the subject. A deteriorated central area was chosen, containing 2.5 per cent of the population, occupying only ¾ of 1 per cent of the city area. Its population was predominantly Negro and Italian, and had decreased 27 per cent between 1920 and 1930. Income from all sources is compared with expenditures for direct service of the county and Board of Education as well as the city, but tax delinquency is not deducted. "Direct service" is the sort that can be apportioned to a locality, while general administrative expenses of the city are distributed uniformly. In 1932 the cost to Cleveland taxpayers for direct services to the area was $1,356,988, and the tax-rate income (which was not all paid) was $225,035, leaving a deficit of $1,131,953. Unofficial welfare agencies in the neighborhood spent $615,459.

Put in another way, the tax-rate income from this slum was $10.12 per capita, while the cost of operating the section was $61.22 per capita. "In other words the city of Cleveland subsidized each man, woman and child in this area to an amount of $51.10 in 1932. This seems to be a rather large subsidy for the privilege of maintaining a slum area." The private welfare societies spent $27.68 per capita in the area, making altogether "the rather stupendous amount" of $315 annually per family of four persons.

Following Indianapolis and Cleveland, a number of cities made similar studies of varying value. One stands out, however, because of its objectivity, its city-wide scope, and the new facts which it brought out. This was the 1935 report of the City Planning Board on the "Income and Cost Study of the City of Boston."

Critics of the Indianapolis and Cleveland figures had suggested that probably all residential districts paid less in taxes than they received in services, the deficit being made up by business and industry. There being no information available either in proof or in disproof, the Boston City Planning Board in 1934 undertook to test this hypothesis in six small sample areas representing business, industry, and four types of housing. It was found that the business district and the high-rent residential district gave the city a large surplus, the industrial and medium-rent districts a small one. The suburban district, with detached houses, had a small deficit, and the low-rental district a large one.

This little study aroused so much interest that it was decided to extend it to cover the whole city. A fifth residential area was added between the low-rental and suburban areas, to contain the wooden three-deckers characteristic of Boston and vicinity.

The principal correction made by the city-wide study in the results of the sample study was that the sum total of all Boston's industrial tracts showed a small deficit. There are evidently two kinds of industrial tract— the prosperous one which shows a tax surplus, and the blighted one which shows a deficit.

The method used in allocating costs results, it seems to this commentator, in an understatement of the differences between tracts. For instance, 50 per cent of the cost of maintaining the Fire Department is considered of general benefit and allotted to assessed values, while 50 per cent is allotted to service rendered by location of alarms according to average cost per alarm. In the Hospital Department, 25 per cent is considered general cost, and 75 per cent service rendered. Police Department costs are divided on a 50-50 basis. It is hard to see why all of these costs should not be charged to the areas receiving the corresponding services.

As a matter of fact, in comparing studies so differently planned, in cities of such different types as Indianapolis, Cleveland, and Boston, one is astonished not by the differences but by the similarity of essential results. Cleveland, it will be remembered, puts the per capita excess of cost over income in her selected slum area, with 22,000 population, at $51.10; Indianapolis, in a selected slum district with only 1,500 inhabitants, puts the per capita excess cost at $54.31. But Indianapolis deducted tax delinquency from income, while the two other cities did not. Making the necessary correction, her per capita becomes $50.64, which is to all intents and purposes the same as Cleveland's. And Boston reporting on all its low-rental areas, with a population of 69,000, in spite of cautious understatements, arrives at a per capita excess cost of $48.24!

The Boston study shows that 22 per cent of the gross area of the city has a net income of $18,339,714, and 78 per cent of the area shows a net cost of $18,156,419. "About 22.5 per cent of the population live in the suburban areas, which cover 45 per cent of the city's total acreage and are responsible for about 18 per cent of the deficit. About 29 per cent of the population live in the three-decker areas, which cover 11 per cent and are responsible for 41.5 per cent of the deficit. About 9 per cent of the population live in the low-rental areas which cover nearly 2 per cent of the area and are responsible for over 21 per cent of the deficit."

It is not to be concluded, of course, from these facts that all census tracts should show a balance between taxes paid and services received, or that those in the red are parasitic. Business and industry exist to create wealth to maintain homes and rear children. It is logical for taxes from the business district to pay for schools in residential districts. What is unwholesome is the excess cost of the bad housing areas due to excess illness, excess fire hazards, and excess delinquency and crime. We are indebted to the Boston study for proving that there is an average per capita deficit for non-slum residential areas which should be subtracted from the per capita deficit in a slum area to find its true excess cost as a slum. In the case of Boston the average per capita deficit for all non-slum residential areas would seem to be $10.81. Subtracting this from $48.24 leaves $37.43.

This appears to give us a fairly accurate measure of the economic cost of slum areas to the taxpayers. But we are not justified in assuming that all of it would be saved if slums were demolished and the people rehoused. Computations of excess cost of slums always and properly include the large item of relief. But families live in the slums because they are poor. They are not, to any measurable extent, made poor by living in the slums. Better health may increase earning power, and better environment stimulate ambition, but no one should expect the disappearance of slums to abolish poverty. Neither would illness, death, or delinquency be abolished.

On the other hand, European experience justifies belief that in a few years the death rates, sickness rates, and delinquency rates of a transplanted slum population would approach the city average. And what the taxpayers would save would go a long way toward paying the clearance and housing bill, which it is their duty in any case to incur in the interest of crime prevention and public health.

No. 114

THE REALITIES OF SOCIALIZED MEDICINE [1]
by H. E. Sigerist

THE National Health Conference that was held in Washington last summer was welcomed unanimously by all who have the nation's health at heart. It sounded like a bugle call, a signal for action. It meant that the period of surveys had come to an end and that, at long last, definite steps were to be taken to remedy an untenable situation. I may add that the National Health Conferencee made a profound impression abroad. I was traveling at the time through ten European countries, and wherever I went I found that the recommendations of the President's Interdepartmental Committee to Coordinate Health and Welfare Activities and the attitude of the Conference toward them were discussed eagerly. In Europe, American medicine is regarded as being extremely advanced scientifically and technically, but very backward socially. "If you are able to carry out this program," one of my public-health friends said, "you will surpass European medicine definitely. You will set an example to the whole world and will reduce death rates in a way never dreamed of. Humbly we shall send our students to America to learn from you."

After ten years of extensive surveys by private and government agencies we know what medical conditions are in the United States. No country has ever had more data available on this subject, and our present health and medical situation is unmistakably clear. We now have documentary evidence for the fact that one third of the population has no medical service, or at least not enough. We know that 40 million people live on annual

[1] H. E. Sigerist, "The Realities of Socialized Medicine," *Atlantic Monthly* (June, 1939), Vol. 163, pp. 795-804. Reprinted by permission of the author and the *Atlantic Monthly*.

family incomes of $800 or less, which just permits them an emergency standard of living and makes it impossible for them to purchase medical care; on the other hand, it is obvious that this is too large a group to be reached by charity services. We know that there is another third of the population whose family income does not exceed $1500 a year. This group is perfectly willing and able to pay for part of the medical services it needs, but finds it extremely difficult to budget the cost of illness. There are, furthermore, millions of families whose income is more than $1500 a year, but to whom medical care presents a serious problem. They are not indigent and are not entitled to free services; they are willing to pay for what they get, but, again, find it difficult to budget the cost of illness. The group that is able to purchase whatever services it needs without economic hardship is infinitely small.

Such a situation is absurd, particularly when we remember that we have available almost all the personnel and technical equipment necessary to provide complete medical services of high quality, in prevention, diagnosis, and treatment. We have more doctors per capita of the population than any other country in the world. Our medical schools were backward for a very long time, but to-day we have seventy-seven recognized schools which train highly qualified practitioners and produce an enthusiastic medical corps that is eager to serve the public and expects nothing in return but the possibility of making a decent living. We do not need a larger number of physicians—at least not in the near future. We have splendid nurses, and if all of them were permanently employed there would be no immediate need to increase their number substantially. More public-health nurses are wanted, but there are plenty of girls anxious to enter this profession and we have the facilities for training them. The hospital situation was a sore spot for a long time, but conditions have improved tremendously in the last twenty-five years. As a rule the cities are adequately supplied with hospital beds, but more hospitals are needed in rural districts. This, however, is an economic problem that can be solved without much difficulty.

We have excellent research institutions, and since the beginning of the century a generation of medical scientists has grown up that has made valuable contributions to medicine. European physicians who visited this country around 1900 had a superior smile on their lips when they watched our scientists. But conditions have changed. American leadership in medical science is universally recognized, and American publications are studied very carefully all over the world. Our philanthropic foundations are the envy of foreign countries, but let us not forget that medical research is financed to a much larger degree by public than by private agencies. The Federal Government supports some of the most important research institutions of the country. The Department of Agriculture alone is undoubtedly the largest research institute of the nation and probably one of the largest in the world. Great contributions have come from the National Institute of Health of the United States Public Health Service, and the National Cancer Institute will soon be the undisputed centre in the field. Problems of infant and maternal welfare are investigated by the Department of Labor. The states and communities also contribute substantially to the support of research. Thirty-five of the seventy-seven medical schools are tax-supported, and nobody will deny that many of them compare very favorably with some of the best privately endowed institutions. Seventy per cent of all hospital beds are in public hospitals. While private funds are shrinking steadily, more and more public funds will become available for research, and it seems to me most important that the government has recognized its obligation to support research.

In other words, we have a first-rate medical personnel and technical equipment, but at the same time large sections of the population have no, or not enough, medical care. We are told, however, that health conditions are better in this country than abroad, that in spite of unemployment they were better in 1938 than ever before in the history of the United States. This, we hear, proves that medical services are satisfactory, and that there is no reason in the world why we should bother about the present situation.

Yes, health conditions are, as a whole, better here than they are in France, Italy, Spain, Yugoslavia, or in Greece. They are not much better than in England, Germany, Switzerland, or Holland. And they are certainly not better than in the Scandinavian countries or New Zealand. If health conditions are better here than in certain foreign countries it is not because medical services are superior, but because this country was able to develop a higher standard of living. I have just studied conditions in Yugoslavia, where a public-health man of genius, A. Stampar, has organized a splendid system of social medical services. If in spite of these services, health conditions there are inferior to ours to-day, it is because the average wage of the industrial worker in Yugoslavia is forty cents a day, and the average-size farm has about ten acres of land. Health conditions have greatly improved there, but health conditions are not determined by medicine alone. Nicotinic acid cures pellagra, but a beefsteak prevents it. And if the United States was able to develop a higher standard of living, it was not because it had a system of its own. It produced food and commodities under the same system as European countries. The higher standard of living was caused by a unique combination of factors that made such a development possible.

If health conditions are better in this country, they are certainly not good enough. We still carry an enormous burden of illness, much of which could be prevented. We are far behind other countries in the incidence of venereal diseases. Over half a million people are infected every year with syphilis and over one million with gonorrhea. Annually 60,000 children are born with the handicap of congenital syphilis, and over 50,000 people die from the results of syphilis. There is no justification whatever for having such an enormous number of venereal patients among us. We have the scientific means to diagnose and cure the disease, and there is no reason why we should not eradicate it as Denmark and a number of other countries have done.

We have one of the lowest tuberculosis death rates in the world, but this low rate still means that we have about 400,000 tubercular patients under-going treatment every year, and that the disease is the second cause of death for the age group between fifteen and forty-five years of age. We have a low maternal death rate, but in spite of it 12,500 American families are deprived every year of the wife and mother, and we know that at least half of these tragedies could be prevented. Our low infant death rate means that 69,000 children die during the first month of their life, and 75,000 infants are stillborn; in other words, in any given year 144,000 young women go through the trying period of pregnancy and childbirth, and the result is a dead child or one that will die in a few days or weeks.

Every year 600,000 people are disabled by pneumonia and almost 100,000 die of it, but we have a serum and a drug that could reduce the death rate by at least one half. We have 500,000 mental patients in institutions filling one half of all hospital beds available in the country, and about one million mentally deficient persons outside of institutions. An extension of mental-hygiene services would keep many of these patients socially adjusted. One out of eight persons who reach the age of forty-five dies of cancer, and although the cancer problem is not yet solved we have methods of treatment that could reduce the death rate considerably.

Now that many acute diseases have been overcome, the chronic diseases are in the foreground and affect millions of people. Arthritis alone disables one and a half million persons every year, and even more individuals are suffering from neuralgia, neuritis, and lumbago. Diseases of the heart, the blood vessels, and the kidneys kill over half a million people every year, many of whom have been handicapped by their illness for a long period of time.

I think we cannot be ambitious enough in health matters. The fact that the United States has a higher standard of living and a superior technical equipment gives it possibilities of combating disease that no other country has, and there is no reason why we should not set an example to the world and demonstrate that many diseases can be wiped out entirely and the incidence of many others reduced considerably.

Let us not be sentimental in these matters, nor speak in humanitarian terms. Let us forget that the American citizen has a right to life, liberty, and the pursuit of happiness, which by implication should include the means of preserving and restoring health; let us not think of all the mental misery and anxiety that illness creates for the individual and his family, but let us talk plain business. This country, with its good health conditions, loses every year 10 billion dollars as a result of illness. The population spends 3.7 billion dollars for medical care. Every wage earner loses annually eight calendar or seven working days on account of illness, and the loss of earnings amounts to about half a billion dollars a year. Considering the present status of medical science, about one third of all deaths are premature, and the capital value of these preventable deaths has been estimated to be over 6 billion dollars.

I am not a business man, but I know enough economics to realize that 10 billion dollars is a heavy tax, and one which is particularly unpleasant because it could very well be reduced considerably. And who carries this enormous burden? Business and industry, which lose the services of their employees and pay high taxes for public curative services; and also the employee who is sick at home without income and spends his last savings for medical care. Every child knows that prevention is not only better than cure, but also cheaper. Would it not be better business to spend some money to prevent the incidence of illness rather than to spend many times that amount to cure it? If we agree on this principle, why, then, should we not act and organize medical services in such a way that the physicians may reach all the people, whether rich or poor, and that they may apply without restrictions whatever weapons medical science has forged for them?

The tendency to organize medical services represents by no means a new development. In the dark days of czarism, as early as 1864, Russia established a complete system of state medicine for the rural districts; since Russia is an agrarian country, this meant that the majority of the population received medical care from salaried district physicians and paid for their services through taxation. In Germany, it was under a conservative regime that Bismarck introduced a comprehensive system of social insurance, including health insurance, in 1883. He did it, not under pressure as we sometimes hear, but because, being a shrewd statesman, he recognized that a healthy working class benefits the employers as well. He found in addition that it was cheaper to make the workers pay for the services they received than to establish public or charity services. Germany's example was followed by one European country after another, by England in 1911, by France in 1928. When Alsace and Lorraine were returned to France, the two provinces had the German social-insurance system and did not dream of giving it up, so the rest of the country followed suit and adopted it.

No country that ever enjoyed the benefits of social insurance has made the slightest move to relinquish them. On the contrary, there has been a tendency to extend social insurance to include ever larger parts of the population. In the eastern European countries which had to reconstruct their public-health work after the war, medical services were organized very thoroughly. In Yugoslavia 3600 of 5000 physicians are in the service of either the government or the social-insurance organizations. Public services and health cooperatives bring medical care to the rural population, while the wage earners and salaried employees receive services from the social-insurance organizations.

The average American does not know Europe, and is convinced that there is nothing he can learn from foreign countries. There is, however, one group of European nations that he openly admires: the Scandinavian countries. He likes their democratic institutions, their high standard of living, and their high educational standard. In these countries, medicine is almost 100 per cent socialized. Public services and health insurance make the doctors available to everybody, and the health standard is remarkably high.

We often hear the naive argument that if these European systems were superior to our haphazard distribution of medical care, health conditions in Europe would of necessity be better than in America. But, as I mentioned before, the standard of living is an essential factor of health. Most European countries have not enjoyed all the natural and economic advantages of America, and if they had not organized their medical services they would not have the relatively good health conditions they actually have to-day.

We need not look to Europe alone. In New Zealand the legislature in 1938 passed one of the most comprehensive social-security acts that have ever been conceived. It aims to give every individual complete social security and provides an extensive system of pensions for all people who are handicapped economically by illness, invalidity, death of the breadwinner, and old age. It provides, further, all the means required for the protection and restoration of health. The system will in the beginning provide the free services of general practitioners, free hospital or sanatorium treatment, free mental-hospital care, free medicines, and free maternity treatment. It will, as soon as feasible, be extended to include services of specialists. The plan will be financed from three sources: (1) a social-security contribution of one shilling in the pound on the wages and other income of all persons; (2) continuance of the present registration fee of one pound per annum for males over twenty years of age; (3) subsidy from the Consolidated Fund.

The price is not too high considering the many benefits that cover almost any risk. It has been estimated that the general practitioner will make an average income of $6000 in our currency. He will receive additional compensation for midwifery, anaesthesia, traveling expenses, and so forth. Consulting specialists will be remunerated according to a fee schedule.

On the South American continent one republic, Chile, has developed in the last fourteen years one of the most progressive systems of social legislation. Social insurance is compulsory for all persons under sixty-five years of age whose annual income is less than 12,000 pesos and whose work is more physical than intellectual. This embraces the great majority of the population. Other persons whose annual income is less than 12,000 pesos can join the social-insurance system voluntarily, provided they are Chilean citizens, less than forty-five years of age, and have passed a previous health examination given by a physician of the Insurance Fund. The insurance system is financed through contributions of employer, employee, and the state. In the case of employees working under a labor contract, the employer contributes 5 per cent of the wage bill, the employee 2 per cent, and the state 1½ per cent. Insured persons who work independently and those who are insured voluntarily contribute 4½ per cent or 5½ per cent of their income according to the field in which they work, and the state contributes the same amount. The benefits consist of complete medical care, sickness, maternity, and disability benefits, and old-age pensions. Patients are hospitalized in state hospitals and sanatoria, the Insurance Fund paying the hospitals two pesos a day for each patient.

A still more progressive bill, to enforce preventive medicine, was passed in Chile in May, 1938. It requires periodic examination at least once a year, but more often if necessary, for all persons coming under the Social Insurance Act. The chief objective is the eradication of tuberculosis, syphilis, heart diseases, and occupational diseases. The examination must include a Wassermann test and an X-ray. In each case the complete clinical history and social history must be taken and a report must be made on the working conditions of the person examined. If in such an examination the doctors find that an individual is not sick but run-down, they must, as a measure to prevent disease, prescribe for him either a complete vacation or a period of half-time work, wherein the loss of wages is compensated for by the Insurance Fund. And no employee can be dismissed from his job in such a case.

These facts make it evident that the organization of medical services is not a new phenomenon, or limited to certain types of countries. It is a world-wide development. In some countries the process is finished and services are completely organized, others are half-way in the development, and in others it is just beginning; but no country can possibly escape the trend. Some people say, however, that this organization of medical services is nothing but the socialization of medicine, and the word "socialization" is a bogey—it smells of Communism. [We should not be afraid of the word, but should recognize that the socialization of services is the logical and unavoidable consequence of the industrialization of the world. If we are opposed to socialization we must also oppose industrialism and must advocate a return to the Middle Ages.]

We must realize that the structure of society has undergone tremendous changes in the last one hundred years as a result of industrialization. A hundred years ago, one out of five gainfully employed persons was a wage earner, and four owned their own means of production, while to-day four out of five are wage earners or salaried employees, and the number of independent producers has been reduced to a minimum. In a society in which four fifths of the whole gainfully employed population depend for an income on the labor market, there is of necessity a strong feeling of insecurity and as a result a pressing demand for security.

It is to satisfy this demand that social-insurance systems are introduced everywhere in order to spread unpredictable risks among as many people as possible and to pool resources. The insecurity created by illness is merely one aspect of the general insecurity resulting from our general social-economic system. [In the period of transition in which we are living to-day more and more aspects of our economic life will become socialized, and we have the choice only between two possibilities, either to socialize gradually or to let things go and wait until the pressure becomes so strong that it bursts forth in revolution.]

When we look at the development of medicine in the last hundred years we find another explanation for the present situation. Not only has the cost of medical care increased considerably with the progress of medical science, but medicine, originally a private relationship between physician and patient, is tending to become a social institution. With the progress of medical science, the scope of medicine has broadened considerably. The law could not be administered without the expert advice of the psychiatrist. The sanitation of dwelling places, the protection of society against epidemics, the protection of mother and child, the care of tubercular and mental patients, the hospitalization of the indigent, are tasks of such magnitude that they could not possibly be carried out in an unorganized, haphazard way. They require the power and scope of the state, and therefore public-health services have increased tremendously. In the United States we already have well-organized efficient state medicine in our public-health services—federal, state, and municipal; and nobody will deny that they are largely responsible for improved health conditions.

The development of industry, on the other hand, has created so many new sources of danger that provisions had to be made to protect the worker, not only in his own interest but also in the interest of the employer. Workmen's Compensation Acts are operating to-day in all but one state, and they guarantee the worker medical care and compensation for the loss of wages. These acts virtually amount to compulsory insurance against sickness caused by industrial accidents and occupational diseases. The principle has been generally accepted, even by the American Medical Association.

A great variety of voluntary insurance schemes have been applied with more or less success, and the tendency to spread the cost of medical care and to make the rich pay for the services given to the poor is expressed in charity services and in the sliding scale commonly applied by physicians. Thus we already have socialized medicine in the country, and I. S. Falk estimates that in normal years over 800 million dollars are spent for medical care through group payments under systems that are more or less socialized.

The problem we are facing to-day is, therefore, not to introduce some basically new principle, but to develop already existing services. The population still spends three billion dollars in a haphazard way, with the result that many millions of people do not have enough medical care. If this same amount of money could be spent systematically, it would carry us a long way, and comparatively few additional funds would be required to provide medical service for everybody and reduce the incidence of illness considerably.

The Technical Committee on Medical Care, which was appointed by the President, presented its report on February 14, 1938. The National Health Conference, consisting of representatives of all groups of the population, met in Washington on July 18-20, 1938, discussed the program, and endorsed it enthusiastically. On January 23, 1939, the President transmitted his annual message on health security to Congress, and on February 28, 1939, Senator Wagner introduced a bill (S. 1620) "to provide for the general welfare by enabling the several States to make more adequate provision for public health, prevention and control of disease, maternal and child health services, construction and maintenance of needed hospitals and health centres, care of the sick, disability insurance, and training of personnel." The bill is an amendment to the Social Security Act. It aims to provide funds to put the National Health Program into practice and sets minimum standards.

We no longer need discuss the health situation in abstract terms. We have a precise program before us, and the question is whether we shall accept or reject it. The initiative is up to the states. The Federal Government does not try to impose a definite scheme upon them, but is ready to subsidize any state that develops a sound health program which meets with the minimum requirements established by federal legislation. The National Health Program aims to extend existing facilities and to develop principles that have already been accepted by the people.

What are its recommendations? Public health services have developed tremendously in the last few decades and nobody can deny that they have proved their usefulness. They are primarily responsible for the reduction in the infant death rate, death rate of tuberculosis, incidence of venereal diseases, and similar achievements. An extension of such services will of necessity improve health conditions still further. This is merely a question of funds and personnel.

The state health budgets average eleven cents per capita, which is not enough. The municipal budgets run from a few cents to one dollar per capita, but very few cities can boast of the latter figure. Less than one third of the counties and still fewer cities have a full-time professional health officer. With federal subsidies the states could develop their public services, and the results would be felt very soon. Such services in no way interfere with the private practitioner. Their task lies in a totally different field, and, as they address themselves primarily to the needy population, they relieve the practitioner of a burden he could not possibly carry.

The second recommendation provides the extension of hospital facilities, particularly in the rural districts. More than 40 per cent of all counties—a population of 17 million—have no registered general hospital. Many counties have hospitals, but they are small and are neither financially nor technically prepared to admit a larger number of free patients. Many needy patients, therefore, have to be hospitalized in the large cities or they are not hospitalized at all, as happens very frequently. It has been estimated that the establishment of 360,000 new hospital beds would solve the problem, and the Federal Government is ready to give grants-in-aid to construct and improve needed hospitals and to provide special temporary grants toward defraying the operating costs in the initial period. At the same time, out-patient clinics could be developed and diagnostic centres established, particularly in the rural areas where there is a definite lack of such facilities.

Another recommendation that seems to be generally accepted concerns the compensation for the loss of wages due to illness. Once we accept the principle of unemployment insurance, there is no reason why we should not extend it to unemployment resulting, not from economic crises, but from illness. The causes may be different, but the result is the same, and the hardship on the worker just as great. The fear that such a scheme would lead to malingering is not justified. Compensation would amount to only a percentage of the wages and would be granted after a waiting period of a few days. And even if it should induce a few unbalanced individuals to malingering, it would bring tremendous benefit to the whole working population.

Two other recommendations are controversial, and indeed they touch problems which are infinitely more difficult to solve. We know that one third of the population live on an emergency standard, and it is perfectly obvious that they cannot possibly purchase medical care in the open market. It is equally obvious that medical services provided for this group can be financed only through public funds. I think everyone agrees that such services should be complete, including physician, dentist, nurse, hospital, drugs, and appliances, and that they should be of high quality. In a democracy the welfare of every individual counts, and every life is valuable. If we are unable to overcome poverty, unable to provide a job for every man and woman willing to work and to guarantee a decent standard of living to everybody, we are collectively responsible for such a condition, and the least we can do is to provide the means of protecting and restoring health to everyone who needs it.

The question is what form of services should be provided for this needy group, and this is best discussed in connection with the medical problem of the middle class. Many millions of otherwise self-supporting families—as a matter of fact, the overwhelming majority of the population—find it very difficult to budget the cost of illness, and many a budget has been wrecked by sudden illness, with very serious results. A plan that would permit families to finance the cost of treatment through periodic payments in proportion to their income would guarantee the regularity of medical services and necessarily improve health conditions. The Federal Government is willing to subsidize states that develop such a plan.

The possibilities of organizing medical care are limited. They are, to put it briefly, public services, health insurance, or a combination of both. Medical services can be made public services, financed through taxation and available to all without charge, like education or the administration of the law. This is, in my opinion, the ideal solution to which every country will come ultimately. This country, however, is not yet prepared to take such a far-reaching step. The next possibility, therefore, is health insurance, which can be voluntary or compulsory—compulsory for all or only for certain groups.

Many experiments have been made in recent years with voluntary insurance, and Cooperative Health Associations, once the initial difficulties were overcome, have given satisfaction to all persons involved. Their great advantage is that they practise group medicine, which is a superior form of medical service, the only one that permits the application of all resources of medical science. They are a solution of the problem wherever there is a large, economically homogeneous group to be served. They do not represent a general solution, however, because they do not reach all the people who need protection. Still less do the voluntary insurance schemes initiated by Medical Societies in order to compete with Group Clinics and Health Associations. They are not health-insurance but fee-insurance plans, and perpetuate the present haphazard form of medical service.

If health insurance is to be effective it must be compulsory. Compulsory for whom? For all those who need help and protection—that is, first of all, the wage earners and salaried employees up to a certain income. Most European systems include only low-income brackets. We must do more. The Capper Bill (S. 658), introduced in the Senate on January 16, 1939,— a bill that sets minimum requirements for the approval of a state system of health insurance,—provides compulsory insurance for all manual laborers and such employees whose wages do not exceed $60 per week, which is a fair limit. For some reason unknown to me, it excludes farm laborers and domestic servants, who need protection just as badly. It does not exclude them entirely, but permits them to join voluntarily, as may all such persons whose weekly income does not exceed $100. Persons who are receiving old-age or unemployment benefits or relief could be included under such a system, whereby the premium would be paid by the agency distributing the benefits.

Under any insurance scheme the benefits must be available to the insured persons and their family members, and must include complete medical service with emphasis on prevention (immunizations and periodic physical examinations), maternity benefits, and cash benefits to compensate for the loss of wages. Funds should be used for health education and research.

The fairest way to finance such a scheme is to have all those groups contribute who benefit by improved health conditions—namely, the state, the employers, and the employees, whose contributions should be in proportion to their wages. The Capper Bill foresees employees' contributions scaled from 1 to 3 per cent according to whether the weekly wages amount to $20 or less, $21 to $40, or more than $40.

The Capper Bill has had very little publicity. It has some weak points, but as a whole is a very sound and constructive project that certainly deserves to be widely discussed. It is undoubtedly a great improvement on all European schemes and demonstrates that the overwhelming majority of the population, including the needy group, can be embraced by such a combination of compulsory and voluntary insurance.

Every system of distribution of medical care requires the cooperation of the physicians. The collection of premiums and the distribution of cash benefits are administrative matters, but the medical benefits are entirely in the hands of the doctors. So far the American Medical Association and its constituent societies have violently opposed the idea of compulsory health insurance. It is not easy to understand this opposition. The A.M.A. has accepted the principle of compulsory insurance for accidents and occupational diseases. In other words, it agrees that if a worker suffers from lead poisoning, as a result of his occupation, it is unobjectionable for him to be treated under an insurance plan by a doctor who may be a salaried physician and not the doctor of his own choice. The personal relationship between physician and patient will not suffer, and the patient may be compensated for his loss of wages. If, however, his lead poisoning is due to adulterated food, the A.M.A. considers that the situation is entirely different and that insurance is undesirable. This discrimination is not very logical.

One very important reason for the physician's opposition must be that the doctor is ill-informed in these questions. He is trained as a scientist and knows very little about economics and sociology. As long as the A.M.A. had purely medical problems to solve, it did a very good job, but now it is facing a problem that is also social and economic. The *Journal* of the A.M.A. was biased in these matters from the very beginning, precluding any open discussion.

I have read dozens of articles and pamphlets written against health insurance in the last few years, and I found them full of mistakes and wrong statements. Men who are critical scientists in their own fields seem to lose every critical sense as soon as they approach a social problem.

There must be some reason for this vague fear of socialized medicine. Some doctors are afraid of mistakes and abuses that are apparent in European systems. There is no reason why we should copy these mistakes. On the contrary, we should be grateful to Europe for having done the experimental work so that we can learn from it.

Some fear political interference. Granted that this may be a menace—it is one that can be avoided. If the people have no confidence in the men whom they themselves elect to governmental positions, they can make the health-insurance system an independent corporation managed by representatives of all the groups involved: employers, employees, physicians, and government.

Others are afraid of bureaucracy. Whether there is much bureaucracy or not in such a system depends entirely on the physicians. If they are willing to serve on salaries—which can be differentiated considerably according to experience and responsibility—there will be a minimum of red tape. It will be tremendous, however, if doctors insist on being remunerated on a fee-for-service basis which requires an extensive system of checking.

But the quality of medical care will suffer under any such scheme, we are told. Is it really so very high to-day? Is it adequate in rural districts, where many doctors practise the horse-and-buggy medicine they learned in a third-grade medical school forty or fifty years ago? Quality will not be improved if insurance funds are used merely to pay the doctor's bill under the present haphazard system. It will be improved considerably, however, if funds are used to develop group medicine in health centres.

But then, we hear, the free choice of physician will be limited. The idea of unlimited free choice of physician is fine, but the fact does not exist and never has existed. The indigent patient who seeks help in a dispensary has no choice at all, but the A.M.A. has never objected to that. The patient in rural districts where only a few doctors are available has a very limited choice, and in cities the pocketbook sets definite limits to the free choice.

Some members of the medical profession are afraid of the economic consequences that health insurance may have upon them. They do not know that in every country where it has been established health insurance has always brought more money to the doctors. They pride themselves that every day they are giving one million dollars' worth of medical service free of charge. That is, they pride themselves publicly. Privately, I have heard many a doctor bitterly complain that he could not collect his bills. The Committee on the Costs of Medical Care revealed that doctors with high incomes in the cities collected as much as 80 per cent of their bills, but those with low incomes in small towns collected only 20 per cent. This is not just. There is no reason why the physician should not be remunerated for honest work. Health insurance would ensure that he would be; it would relieve him of a great burden.

By systematically obstructing experimentation, the American Medical Association has greatly harmed the reputation of the medical profession. Its indictment by the District Court of the United States for the District of Columbia has deeply impressed the public. Lawyers will have to decide whether the Sherman Act can be applied to the practice of medicine, but, whatever the outcome of the trial may be, the fact will remain that medical organizations have applied methods of coercion that are condemned when business applies them. The public, however, should know that the rank and file of the medical profession do not blindly follow their leaders. They feel greatly disturbed and do not know what policy they should follow. The Medical Society of the County of New York recently held a poll asking its members whether they would favor compulsory health insurance or not. The result was significant: two thirds of the members had no opinion and abstained from voting; only 24⅓ per cent were opposed and 9 per cent in favor of compulsory insurance. The rank and file will continue to perform their duty, and I have no doubt that they will cooperate joyfully the moment they are convinced that socialized medicine benefits the patient as well as the profession.

Health insurance is not a panacea. It is not the ideal system, but I think that, under the present social and economic conditions of the country, compulsory health insurance combined with an extension of public-health services is the best possible solution.

Medicine has had a very short history, of but 5000 years, and it has become really efficient only in the last 100 years. For 5000 years people fell sick and, once they were sick, called for a doctor. It is time that we should change this relationship and devise a system under which the doctor will call on the potential patient in the home, in the workshop, or on the farm. Such a program will not lead to regimentation, but, on the contrary, to an application of the principle of family practice never before realized.

I am confident that our medical problem will be solved in a not distant future. I believe in the common sense of the people. I know that new problems call for new leaders, and that physicians of great reputation and integrity such as Dr. Hugh Cabot and Dr. John P. Peters find an ever-increasing audience. And, most of all, I have faith in the young medical generation that is growing up under our eyes.

Chapter XXXIII

GOVERNMENT AND THE FARM PROBLEM

[IN the United States of 1850 a farm could be obtained for little expenditure of capital, and a small sum was needed to equip and operate it. Our rapidly expanding population could absorb the farmer's products, and surpluses could be readily and easily exported. Given an ever-mounting demand for farm products, farmers sought and obtained government aid in increasing their production. Land was made available at slight cost through the homestead laws; irrigation projects put fertile but arid land into use. Bureaus were established to aid the farmer by placing the results of scientific investigation at his disposal and to help him battle those pests and diseases which destroyed his crops.

The World War further emphasized the trend towards increasing production, due to the inability of Europe to grow much of its own foodstuffs. The emphasis on producing was increased when we entered the war in 1917. It was in this period that we ploughed the "dust bowl" and planted the seeds of new crops and new conservation problems. The wartime activity also created an intense activity in farm land speculation. Farms were purchased at fabulously high prices, and purchasers borrowed liberally on these new inflated values.

Since 1920 we have been confronted with a different set of circumstances. Demand for agricultural products has declined, partly because of the loss of European markets and partly because of the slowing up of our annual population increase. Farming has now become an enterprise which requires large amounts of capital; those who cannot raise this money are forced, in an ever-increasing number, to become tenants. It is now necessary to remove lands, especially those of sub-marginal productivity, from production. Some action must be taken which will solve the capital and credit problems of our farmers.

These aspects of our farm problem, and the constitutional and political difficulties that lie in the way of their solution, are the concern of the selections in this chapter.]

No. 115

AN AGRICULTURAL PROGRAM [1]

by Harry W. Laidler

AGRICULTURE in the United States is in the doldrums. In the comparatively prosperous year ending June 30, 1927, Professor Morris A. Copeland estimated that, if the farmers of the United States paid themselves for their labor an average of $540 a year, or slightly more than $10 a week, and set aside 4½ per cent interest on the market value of the equity in their farm property, they would collectively face a deficit of no less than $1,717,000,000. Only by cancelling the interest on their property and by limiting themselves to an average income of $10 to $11 a week wage, could they balance their books. Since 1927 the situation has become even more tragic.

The depression in agriculture which began shortly after the war, was, to some extent, but a reflection of the changed world situation. It is common knowledge that American farmers were faced with ever stronger competitors abroad during the first three decades of the twentieth century. One of these competitors was Canada, with its great stretches of fertile farming land in the West. In 1900, Canada grew a paltry 52 million bushels of wheat. That amount rose in 1928 to about 550 million, over 10 times as much as a generation before. To the South, Argentina increased its crop over threefold from 78 million bushels at the end of the century to 239 million in 1927-1928. The Australian figures likewise jumped during that period from 49 million to 119 million. Russia is now again invading the world market and is likely to prove a vigorous competitor in the days to come.

These increases abroad had a decidedly dampening effect on American exports. In 1897-1898, we sent out of the country 530 million bushels of the five principal cereals. Twenty-four years later, in 1913-1914, this total had declined to 108 million. The war, in the nature of the case, greatly stimulated demand and, in 1921-1922, the country was found to be exporting 533 million bushels, practically the same as a quarter of a century before. Four years later, in 1925-1926, however, exports again shrunk to 210 million bushels, and since then have fluctuated up and down.

The export market in beef also suffered severely, due largely to the rise of Argentina as a competitor for the world market. In 1900 this South

[1] Harry W. Laidler, *A Program for Modern America* (New York: Thomas Y. Crowell Company, 1936), pp. 181-195. Reprinted by permission of the publisher.

American country exported but 54 million pounds of beef. Thirty years later it sent out of the country an annual average of over 2 billion pounds. In the meanwhile, the exports of American cattle raisers became negligible. The sale abroad of pork likewise showed a marked decline.

While American agriculture, to some extent, tried to recoup by developing new specialties in the form of dairy and horticultural products, the low purchasing power of the workers abroad prevented great expansion of these commodities.

But the rise of powerful foreign competitors by no means told the whole tale. The trend among the American people toward lighter eating and drinking had a material effect in decreasing the public's demand for farm products. Americans in the late twenties ate less bread, less corn meal, and less cereal foods per person than they did prior to the war. The total per capita consumption of all cereals decreased from about 380 pounds at the beginning of the century to 330 pounds before the World War and to 250 in more recent years.

The great decrease in the number of mules and horses, looking to the farmer for a full dinner pail, likewise during these years made a big dent in demand. It was estimated that the number of horses and mules on farms shrunk in the 13-year period ending in 1931 from 26.4 million to 17.9 million heads, while the number of tractors and trucks steadily mounted. In the cities and towns during the same period the use of the horse decreased at a much greater rate. The steady substitution of machines for these beasts of burden had a decidedly disruptive effect on farm practice.

> Throughout much of the corn belt (as Dr. Edwin G. Nourse brought out), oats and hay have come over a long period of time to a very important and very firmly entrenched position in standard crop rotations. Farm equipment, the experience of the workers, and the whole farming system have grown up around this rotation plan, and as yet no fully satisfactory substitutes have been found to meet the new ratio of demands anywhere nearly as well as did the old corn, oats and meadow combinations.

So much for the question of demand for farmers' products. What about the supply side. Here we find that the number of acres under cultivation steadily increased for decades until after the World War. This development was assisted by the policy of irrigation, drainage and the clearance of timber and other lands, as well as by the building of railways and highways which made much new land accessible to markets.

More important, perhaps, than these forces was the transformation of much of our Western lands from range use to that of crop cultivation, or from extensive to intensive farming. "Millions of acres of Texas, Oklahoma and Kansas range land (declared Dr. Nourse) have, since 1920, gone into cotton and wheat, and the vineyards and orchards of California and other states have been recruited from one-time grain and hay fields at a rate which has threatened to swamp certain branches of the horticultural industry." The other side of this picture was, of course, the abandonment of many farms and the reforestation of some farm land.

Of more importance was the advancing productivity of the farmer as a result of the use of improved machinery, and utilization of electricity, and the general advance of technical knowledge among the farming population. Labor-saving machinery is not new on the farm and, from the Civil War to the World War, the improvement of farm machinery went steadily on. The high prices received for products during the World War, the dearth of farm labor, the government campaign to grow food to win the war, the pushing of agricultural production into regions requiring extensive farming —all gave a greater impetus than ever to such improvements and to the widespread adoption of tractors, trucks and stationary motors on the farm. These changes continued following the war when agriculture may be said to have entered the "power farming" stage of development. In 1918, only 80,000 tractors were used on American farms. By 1929 that number had increased to 853,000, an increase of over 1000 per cent. There had likewise been a great increase in the use of combines during the post-war years. As a result of these changes, it has been estimated that the efficiency of human labor increased approximately 30 per cent on the average for the entire United States in the decades following 1909.

These developments meant overproduction as compared with the effective demand of the community in many farm commodities. In the world-at-large, the post-war period witnessed an average production of many million bushels of wheat more than were consumed, while, in 1930, the first year of the depression, the carryover in the United States piled up to the record total of 275 million bushels.

The result was an almost steady decline of the price per bushel received by producers in 1919. On December 1 of that year, this price reached $2.15. From this high, it tobogganed down to $1.04 in December, 1929, and to less than 50 cents in October, 1931.

The decline of the price of this and other commodities was accompanied by numerous changes in agriculture during the "prosperous" twenties.

1. The ratio of prices received by the farmers to prices paid by them for needed commodities was reduced from a pre-war level of 100 to a level in August, 1930, of 72.

2. Farm-land values decreased from a peak of 170 per cent of pre-war value in 1920 to a level of 115 per cent ten years later.

3. Tens of thousands of farms were compelled to go into bankruptcy, suffer foreclosure sales or be sold for non-payment of taxes.

Farm mortgages likewise increased steadily. In 1910, they totaled $3,599,000,000 and represented only 10 per cent of the value of the farms. By 1930, this debt had increased to $9,468,000,000, constituting about 22 per cent of the farm value. The proportion of farms operated by tenants also steadily advanced from 25.6 per cent in 1880 to 35.3 per cent in 1900 to 42.4 per cent in 1930. In the West South Central states 62.3 per cent of the farms were under the control of tenants, though in New England, over nine-tenths of the farms were still occupied by the owners. In 1910, 35 per cent of American farmers were renters; by 1930, that percentage had grown to 42.5.

4. The income of the average farm remained pitiably small. From 1924 to 1929, the balance available for capital, labor and management for the average farm fluctuated between $857 and $898. In 1929 the total *weekly income* to pay for the average farmer's labor and interest on the capital invested by him, was just about $17. The average monthly wage of the farm hand was less than $36 a month.

5. Taxes ate up an increasingly large amount of the farmer's income. Tax levies in 1929 were $1.43 for each $100 of the full value of real estate as compared with only 63 cents in 1913.

6. As a result of adverse conditions, many farmers left the farm during the twenties. The net cityward movement in 1926 was 1,020,000; in 1927, 604,000; in 1928, 576,000 and in 1929, 619,000.

As the birth rate on the farms is greater than the death rate, the actual loss of the farm population was not so great as these figures may indicate. The net loss in rural population during these four years has been estimated at 1,319,000. The estimated farm population in January, 1930, was 27,-222,000 as compared with 32,077,000 in 1910. The farm population was thus a declining proportion of our total. From 1920 to 1930, it declined from slightly more than one-third of the people of the country (34.7 per cent) to about one-fourth (25.3 per cent). The number of farms in this 10-year period declined from 6,448,000 to 6,298,000.

During the early years of the depression, the agricultural situation became increasingly grave. The value of exports of the principal agricultural products declined in the fiscal year ending June 30, 1932 to 59 per cent of that of 1928-1929. The gross income from the farm declined nearly 57 per cent from 1929 to 1932, from $11,918,000,000 to $5,143,000,000, the lowest gross income in any year for which estimates were made. The gross income from cotton and wheat was about 30 per cent of that in 1929, while the total value of farm real estate decreased from about 48 billion dollars in 1930 to 30½ billion in March, 1933.

During the years 1928 to 1932 farm indebtedness, it was true, decreased by about a billion dollars to about 8½ billion, while the total of other forms of farm debt likewise decreased. Ordinarily, as the Department of Agriculture maintained, such a decline in the debt burden would be regarded as a wholesome sign. The decline from 1928 to 1932, however, was the result not of normal liquidation, "but of foreclosures, bankruptcies, and forced sales, and of the inability of local banks and other credit agencies to lend. Forced sales in 1932 constituted 37 per cent of all transfers, as compared with 27 per cent in 1928.

"Moreover, the reduced carrying charges represented that year a much larger percentage than in 1928. Interest on mortgages alone amounted to 13 per cent of the gross farm income.

"In 1932, for the country as a whole, nearly 16 per cent of all mortgaged farms were encumbered for more than 75 per cent of their value. The mortgage debt represented 25 per cent of the value of all farm land and buildings, and about 40 per cent of the value of all mortgaged farms. *It was two and a half times greater than in 1910.*" Land values, however, fell even more rapidly, with the result that, in 1932, farm taxes amounted to $1.50 per $100 of farm valuation.

Even in 1929, farmers were having a hard struggle to meet their debts. When farm prices dropped during the depression to 50 per cent below prewar, their burden became intolerable. More than a million farm families, constituting nearly five million people, were forced to accept public relief.

Practically all of the decline in agricultural income during these years was due to the lower prices paid for agricultural products. The volume of agricultural production for market or for home use in 1932 was only about 5 per cent below that of 1929, while prices received by farmers for farm products averaged 59 per cent lower in 1932 than in 1929, a drop in prices about twice as great as that witnessed in manufactured goods. The income available for the farmer's capital, labor and management shrunk from $5,574,000,000 in 1929 to $1,291,000,000 in 1932. In the latter year, this income "not only provided no return on investment but also fell short by $1,200,000,000 of rewarding the farm family for their labor even at the reduced wage rates for hired labor."

With 23 per cent of the working people living on farms, the farmers' share in the national income had dropped to less than 8 per cent.

The point was thus reached, as the Department of Agriculture declared, where it was "difficult for farmers to pay their taxes and difficult if not impossible for those in debt to meet their payments. The universal complaint is that fixed charges now swallow up all the income. Prices and markets have fallen into such stagnation that thousands of growers can get practically no returns for their crops at present."

The situation in the field of agriculture led to the sacrifice of tens of thousands of farms through mortgage foreclosure and tax delinquencies. During the five-year period March, 1926, to March, 1931, 237 farms out of every 1000 were lost to the farmers of South Dakota through foreclosure proceedings, 235 farms in Montana, 163 in Nebraska, 157 in Iowa, and 138 in Missouri. Over one-tenth of the Montana farms, in addition, were lost through tax delinquencies. In the United States generally, during the year ending March 15, 1933, approximately 15.3 farms per thousand were sold for non-payment of taxes, while 38.8 farms per 1000 were involved in transfers in settlement of debt. In many instances, farmers refused to bid on farm land. Farmers' strikes and demonstrations were frequent.

As one means of ameliorating the agricultural situation, an agricultural marketing act was passed in June, 1929, for the purpose of attempting to stabilize prices and production through cooperative methods. The legislation officially aimed:

To protect, control and stabilize the currents of interstate and foreign commerce in the marketing of agricultural commodities and their food products—

1. By minimizing speculation.

2. By preventing inefficient and wasteful methods of distribution.

3. By encouraging the organization of producers into effective associations or corporations under their own control for greater unity of effort in marketing and by promoting the establishment and financing of a farm-marketing system of producer-owned and producer-controlled cooperative associations and other agencies.

4. By aiding in preventing and controlling surpluses in any agricultural commodity, through orderly production and distribution, so as to maintain advantageous domestic markets and prevent such surpluses from causing undue and excessive fluctuations or depressions in prices for the commodity.

To put this policy into effect, Congress created a Federal Farm Board of nine members and authorized it to administer a revolving fund of $500,-000,000. The Board was empowered to make loans out of this fund to cooperatives, to stabilization associations, to clearing house associations, etc. To cooperatives, loans could be made to help in the effective marketing of products, in constructing better marketing facilities, in financing membership promotion work of the cooperatives and in advancing to cooperators a larger share of the market price of crops.

There is much dispute regarding the accomplishments of this Board in the development of cooperative societies. O. S. Moser, President of the National Cooperative Council, maintained that the Board did much to encourage farmers' cooperatives; that, in two years ending July 1, 1931, the membership of farmers' selling cooperative associations had increased 33.4 per cent, that the volume of products marketed through the cooperative system had expanded by 28.8 per cent, that some 2800 community pools of all sorts had been organized and that many scattered farmers' cooperatives had been brought into unified national sales organizations for the handling of grain, cotton, wool, livestock, pecans, beans and beets.

On the other hand, Mauritz A. Hallgren contended that this so-called encouragement of cooperatives by the Farm Board had "consisted in forcing upon the producers, or upon as many of them as will be coerced, a predetermined pattern of cooperation in the making of which the farmers have had no choice whatever." Far from encouraging the cooperative marketing movement as required by the Agricultural Marketing Act, he maintained, the Farm Board had impeded that movement, and with regard to certain commodities had "deliberately sabotaged it by delivering it into the hands of one or two small groups of professional promoters"; that it had "allowed the $500,000,000 revolving fund . . . to be used as a club to beat the grain, livestock, cotton and other producers into submitting to the dictation of these promoters"; and that these promoters had "used their position to enable them to create capital for themselves as private agents."

In its attempt to stabilize prices, the Board, through the Grain Stabilization Corporation, purchased great quantities of wheat at an average price of about 82 cents, while the Cotton Stabilization Corporation purchased millions of bales of cotton at an average of 16.38 cents a pound.

Stabilization operations of wheat carried on under the authority of the Farm Board resulted in an accumulation of 257,000,000 bushels by the Grain Stabilization Corporation by June 30, 1931. The Board then stopped further purchases, announcing that it would limit its sales on the open market to 60,000,000 bushels. Such sales, together with exports to foreign governments and a distribution of nearly 100,000,000 bushels to the Red Cross, greatly reduced the stocks on hand by the middle of 1932. The Cotton Stabilization Corporation likewise bought large quantities of cotton. By the end of 1932, the losses of these organizations, through price declines, approximated $240,000,000.

In its annual report for 1932, the Farm Board declared that its experience had demonstrated that "no measure for improving the price of farm products other than increasing the demand of consumers can be effective over a period of years unless it provides a more definite control of production than has been achieved so far."

The failure of the Farm Loan Board to meet the agricultural situation led President Roosevelt, after assuming office, to initiate the Farm Relief Act, creating the AAA, an act approved by the President May 12, 1933.

The bill set out to restore to the agricultural industry the purchasing power which it had during the years 1909 to 1914. This pre-war period has been at times referred to as the "golden age" of agriculture, on the ground that, during these years, a "normal" relation existed between agricultural prices and the prices of manufactured goods. Those acquainted with the farming situation in those years realize, however, how far farming was from an economically sound industry. The act applied not to all farm products, but only to cotton, wheat, corn, hogs, dairy products, tobacco, rice, and beet and cane sugar. It included within its scope about 3,500,000 out of the nation's 6,000,000 farms.

The Secretary of Agriculture, under the act, was empowered to make contracts with individual growers or groups of growers for the restriction of crop production. In these contracts, he was authorized to pay a rental to growers of crops in return for their keeping acreage idle, or at least free from marketable crops. The money to pay for these subsidies was to come from a tax on processors, a tax which, in the nature of the case, the processors would strive to pass on to the consumers of food in higher prices. The Secretary was likewise empowered to negotiate trade agreements between growers and distributors looking toward price stability. In the case of cotton, a plan for cotton option contracts was worked out, as a supplementary method of reducing cotton acreage. Under this plan, which had been pocket-vetoed by President Hoover, all cotton held by government agencies was to be sold to the Secretary of Agriculture, with the understanding that it be disposed of by him by March 1, 1936. The Secretary was authorized to enter into contracts under which any producer who agreed to cut his crop would receive an option to buy government-owned cotton upon terms deemed advisable by the Secretary, in combination with rental and benefit payments.

To carry out the provisions of the act, an Agricultural Adjustment Administration was set up. In June, 1933, Secretary Wallace outlined the terms of a proposal for the destruction of a part of the 1933 cotton crop, already planted, on condition of acceptance by a sufficient number of producers. Under this plan, the government expressed its willingness to give to producers who took a certain amount of cotton out of production, a cash payment of from $6 to $12 an acre, according to yield, plus a non-transferable option on government cotton at 6 cents a pound, or a cash payment, without cotton option, of from $7 to $20 an acre. Land taken out of cotton production, the Secretary declared, might be used for production of soil improvement or erosion-preventing crops or food and feed crops for home use. The administration would not accept less than 25 per cent nor more than 40 per cent of a producer's acreage for payment under this plan. The aim of the Agricultural Adjustment Administration, or the AAA, as it became popularly known, was to take out of production that year about 10,000,000 acres producing approximately one-fourth of the nation's cotton crop, in a year, be it said, when millions of the nation's unemployed were walking ragged in the streets of the great cities of the country. If such a reduction did not take place, Secretary Wallace maintained, the season with its unusually high yield would be a disastrous one for the producer.

During the few weeks following the announcement of the proposal, federal and state agents and volunteers made visits to 2,000,000 farmers, and in mid-July the Secretary announced that he had received offers from about half of the farmers to plow under more than the required number of 10,000,000 acres. About 60 per cent of those accepting decided to take option contracts for the purchase of about 2,300,000 bales. To pay for the benefits of more than $100,000,000 given the farmer for his plowed-under cotton, the Secretary levied a processing tax of 4½ cents a pound or about $21 a bale.

Wheat producers were given a subsidy on that portion of their crop during the years 1933, 1934 and 1935 estimated to go into domestic human consumption. To qualify for this benefit, the farmer was required to sign a contract to reduce his acreage in 1934 and 1935 by a percentage not to exceed 20 per cent of his average acreage for the three-year period 1930 to 1932. In addition he was supposed to sow to wheat an acreage which, on the basis of previous yields, would produce the amount of his allotment. Benefits were paid on the whole allotment, whether or not the entire crop matured. Land taken out of wheat production, as in the case of cotton land, could be used for soil-building and non-competing crops. Allotments were made to states on the basis of past yields, while the states, in turn, made them to counties on the basis of their former yields. The wheat producers themselves were given the job of organizing their own county associations and were required to pay the expenses of the directors out of the benefits received. Growers failing to make reductions forfeited all right to further payments.

In late June, a processing tax of 30 cents a bushel on wheat milling was applied. This represented approximately the difference between the average 1909-1914 wheat price of 88.4 cents a bushel and a price of about 60 cents on June 15, 1933. It was equivalent to a tax of $1.38 a barrel of flour and about a half-cent on a one-pound loaf of bread. The farmer received a benefit of 28 cents a bushel—the tax minus the two cents for administrative purposes, or $151.20 on 540 bushels. This whole crop was marketed in the regular way, so that the farmer received the market price on his entire production, in addition to the benefit payment on the amount of his allotment. Up to April, 1935, the AAA distributed about three-fourths of a billion dollars in rental and benefit payments, while a slightly larger amount had been collected through processing taxes, and $200,000,000 more on surplus-removal purchases of cattle, hogs, butter and other things. The Federal Surplus Relief Corporation had laid out some 60 to 80 million dollars in buying up other surplus farm products. During the 2 years, 1933 to 1935, as a result of these controls, of a severe drought and of a somewhat greater purchasing power among city workers, prices for agricultural products increased, bringing with them an advance in agricultural income. As the drought of 1933 was severe, and that of 1934 the worst in our agricultural history, it is difficult to say how much the cutting down in crops and the price increases were due to the adjustment programs, and how much was due to the "act of nature."

The average per unit purchasing power of farm products jumped from an index figure of 57 in February, 1933 (on the basis of 100 in July, 1929), to 82 in October, 1934, while the total income from farm products advanced by a couple of billion dollars from about 5.3 billion dollars in 1932 to about 7.3 billion dollars in 1934 and by about another billion the following year. Prices paid by the farmers for needed commodities increased during the same period, but not to the same extent as did prices of products sold by farmers. The National Bureau of Economic Research estimated that the prices received by farmers advanced from February, 1933, to October, 1934, from an index number of 37 to one of 68, while the prices paid by farmers increased during this period from 66 to 82.

The increased prices for farm products, in the nature of the case, meant higher living costs for the mass of city dwellers. They thus involved a transfer of purchasing power from the city worker to the farmer. They changed the distribution of recovery among groups of people instead of contributing to total recovery.

While the bounties given by the government increased the money income of many farmers, they caused great misery to other groups of agricultural workers, notably farm tenants and share-croppers. For, in thousands of cases, the owners of the land who received the government subsidy for taking land out of cultivation, kept the cash, failing to share it with those who were actually tilling the land.

Many thousands of tenants and share-croppers, furthermore, with the shrinkage in the amount of land under cultivation, found that their services were no longer required. Evicted from their shacks, they became outcasts in the land, face to face with starvation.

Dr. Calvin B. Hoover, after an investigation of the subject, declared:

> In a number of cases share-tenants and share-croppers were not credited with any part of the so-called option payments of the 1933 contract. In these cases the landowner obtained the tenants' share of the cotton option payments as well as his own. . . . Whether the tenant received anything at all often depended upon the charitableness of the landlord . . . cases of outright diversion by landlords of benefits properly due tenants have been charged.

Professor William R. Amberson, heading a committee of the League for Industrial Democracy and the Socialist party, testified that the committee's investigation of 500 share-cropper families in Missouri, Arkansas, Tennessee and Mississippi indicated that the acreage reduction program had forced from 15 per cent to 20 per cent of all share-cropping families into the "no-crop" class. It had likewise resulted in many plantation owners eliminating the share-cropping system in whole or in part, "forcing the former share-croppers to accept day labor instead, a lower economic status."

The committee came across instance after instance of eviction leading to intense suffering while the crop-reduction program was being carried out. Many families were forced to leave their former homes by pressure and intimidation, without the serving of eviction papers.

> Most of these people (declared the Amberson Committee in 1934) are still living in the country, some in tents, some in abandoned houses, a few in such miserable shelters as corn-cribs and cotton houses. Many of them have drifted into the cities and towns, where they are dependent upon direct federal relief. Even when working, the average share-cropper family secured hardly more than $300 a year and was living on an economic plane so low that its "buying power" was completely exhausted in obtaining the most basic necessities of life.

The 6 to 3 decision of the Supreme Court in early January, 1936, concluded a chapter on agricultural bounties to farmers the social implications of which will long be debated by students of agriculture. Following the AAA decision, Congress passed a Soil Conservation and Domestic Allotment Act. This act authorized the Secretary of Agriculture to spend not more than $500,000,000 a year to make benefit payments to farmers in the United States who carried out certain soil improvement practices. The object of the act, among other things, was to transfer 30,000,000 acres of land, formerly used to produce staple crops for export, into soil-building crops. The

Act set up a temporary plan to be in operation for 2 years, and a permanent system to be operated after January 1, 1938. Under the permanent plan, the states would develop their own production programs, subject to federal approval and formulas.

Despite the increase in agricultural income since the depths of the depression among a number of sections of the farming population, therefore, the agricultural situation is still tragic for millions of farmers and their families. In many cases, as among large numbers of tenant farmers, the farmer's lot became worse under the New Deal.

What type of agricultural program can be depended upon to yield to the farmer the abundant life?

No plan for agriculture alone will suffice to bring permanent prosperity to the farmer. Agriculture is connected by a thousand ties with the industrial life of the nation and of the world, and a sound and well-balanced agricultural economy is impossible without a sound and well-balanced general productive and distributive system at home and abroad.

No. 116

THE AMERICAN PEASANT [1]

by Wayne Gard

DESPITE the many types of forgotten men whose emergency needs were satisfied by the first Roosevelt administration, the wail of the tenant farmer reaches Washington almost as loudly as in the panicky days of early 1933. Large government checks for crop reduction have been going into the pockets of landlords, but only dribbles have reached the tenants who do the actual work of plowing and harvesting on nearly half of the nation's farms.

In no previous period in the country's history has so small a proportion of the farm land been owned by those who cultivate it. The startling increase in the per cent of farms operated by tenants, from 25.6 in 1880 to 42.1 in 1935, reveals a strong trend away from the rugged independence of the homesteader and toward an un-American system of peasantry. . . .

The American dream of the family-size farm has become so remote that action to provide security is imperative. To remedy this situation, he [Roosevelt] asked for retirement by public agencies of land unsuited for farming, credit assistance for those wishing to buy farms or in danger of

[1] Wayne Gard, "The American Peasant," *Current History* (April, 1937), Vol. 46, pp. 47-52. Reprinted by permission of *Current History and Forum*.

losing them, and cooperation with State and local bodies to improve the leasing system. The slight decline in five years from the tenancy figure of 42.4 for 1930 does not represent any real improvement in the situation. In this period, mortgage foreclosures increased farm tenancy in nearly all States outside the South. The latter region lost nearly 70,000 colored tenants, but few of these became land owners; most of them joined the ranks of wage hands or relief clients.

A certain amount of farm tenancy is reasonable and not undesirable. Unless he inherits money or land, a young farmer usually must rent for a few years before he buys a farm; but this kind of tenancy would account for only about fifteen per cent of the farms. In 1935, only the New England States, New York, Utah, and Nevada were below this figure. Even in the rich corn lands of Iowa, nearly half the farms, 49.6 per cent, were being cultivated by renters; this was more than double the proportion for 1880.

In the cotton belt, where farm tenancy has been a social cancer for decades, the figures are still higher, rising to 69.8 per cent in Mississippi. In addition to having a larger proportion of tenants than other regions, the South is saddled with an unusually vicious system of tenancy. The corn or wheat tenant usually is a cash renter; at any rate, he takes a large share of the risk and receives a corresponding share of the profit in good years. The typical cotton tenant, on the other hand, is an almost hopeless sharecropper, who is burdened by debt and disease and who, in a large proportion of instances, does not even own the mule with which he plows. Under present conditions, few cotton tenants have much chance to become farm owners.

The share-cropper system was a make-shift that grew out of conditions incurred by the Civil War and Reconstruction. Planters, left with large estates but deprived of their former help, adopted the plan of parceling out their land to former slaves and poor whites, most of whom had to be provided with tools, work animals and even food. At first, most of the sharecroppers were Negroes; but gradually these came to be outnumbered considerably by whites. The relatively helpless condition of these tenants tended to keep them in perpetual debt and to develop a paternalistic and sometimes arrogant attitude on the part of the planters.

Of course, not all cotton tenants are at the bottom of the economic scale. The South has developed a whole hierarchy of tenancy, in which the highest type of tenant is the renter who provides all equipment and work animals, takes care of the operating expenses, and pays his rent in a previously fixed amount of cash or cotton. The cash renter suffers few of the evils of tenancy, but in the South he represents only an almost negligible proportion of tenants.

Next in order is the share tenant, who also provides his equipment and work animals but may require the landlord to furnish part of the fertilizer. But he pays his rent on a share plan which usually gives the landlord a fourth to a third of the crop. At the bottom is the share-cropper, who has no capital except a little worn-out furniture. He provides only his own and his family's labor and perhaps part of the fertilizer. The landlord must supply him with tools, work animals, and seed; and usually he must advance on credit most of the food for his family. The share-cropper pays half his cotton as rent, and he is lucky when the other half is enough to take care of debits the landlord has charged against him. More than a third of all cotton tenants, and more than half the Negro tenants, are croppers.

The miserable and unsanitary homes of the share-croppers, white as well as black, have been described many times. Several years ago, a writer in the *Dallas News* asserted that "the squalid condition of the cotton raisers of the South is a disgrace to the Southern people. Their children are born under such conditions of medical treatment, food, and clothing as would make an Eskimo rejoice that he did not live in a cotton-growing country."

The typical cotton tenant's house is slapped together with boards discarded by a sawmill and never knows the feel of a paint brush. The roof leaks, even when new; and few if any of the rooms are ceiled or plastered. Window glass is a luxury enjoyed by few croppers, and there seldom are screens to keep out the flies. The tenant family of five or six persons lives in a three-room shanty. Many of the Negro croppers have only two rooms; as many as thirteen people have been found living in a single bedroom and kitchen.

The share-cropper's larder contains little beyond the traditional three M's —meat, meal, and molasses. Usually the meat is restricted to fat salt pork, called fatback or sow-belly. Sweet potatoes and dried beans often appear on the table, and sometimes there is a dish of greens. Gardens are uncommon, since landlords do not encourage them and the poorer croppers have no money with which to buy seeds. A considerable proportion of the croppers have no regular milk supply, and eggs and chickens are luxuries that some croppers do not taste in a year's time.

The cropper's diet and his living conditions encourage pellagra, rickets, anemia, malaria, typhoid, and other serious diseases, which take a heavy toll. Yet in many cases no money is available to pay for medical treatment. Arthur F. Raper's painstaking study of farm tenancy in two Georgia counties showed that nearly half the tenant families went the whole year of 1934 without the services of a physician. An earlier survey of conditions in North Carolina showed that doctors were in attendance at only 14.6 per cent of the births in families of black croppers, and at only 48 per cent in families of white croppers.

Naturally, the recent depression, with its low cotton prices, made conditions even worse in the rural slums of the South. Two years ago, Erskine Caldwell shocked readers of the *New York Post* with a series of articles in which he described conditions he found among Georgia share-croppers. Particularly explosive was his description of a two-room home occupied by three families, each consisting of a man and wife and one to four children. In one room

> a six-year-old boy licked the paper bag the meat had been brought in. His legs were scarcely any larger than a medium-sized dog's leg, and his belly was as large as that of a 130-pound woman. Suffering from rickets and anemia, his legs were unable to carry him for more than a dozen steps at a time. His face was bony and white. He was starving to death. On the floor before an open fire lay two babies, neither a year old, sucking the dry teats of a mongrel bitch.

Educational facilities provided for share-croppers' children are woefully inadequate. White children have tumbledown school houses, underpaid teachers, and short terms. At that they have six to sixty times as much tax money spent on their education as do Negro children who in many localities are equally numerous. Negro families sometimes have to build and repair their own school houses; and teaching is carried on under most primitive conditions. In Macon County, Georgia, the average teacher in rural Negro schools in 1934 received a salary of $106.93 for the year. Many Negro children are unable to attend school at all.

The share-cropper justly blames high interest rates and dishonest bookkeeping for much of his plight. Planters and merchants often mark up the prices of food and other articles sold to croppers on credit, and interest rates commonly range from 25 to more than 50 per cent. Some landlords tack on a 25 per cent manager's fee. The croppers are at the mercy of the planters and dare not question their bookkeeping. A classic story tells of one cropper who brought in five bales of cotton and was told, after some figuring, that this cotton exactly balanced his debt. Pleased at this, the cropper mentioned that he had one more bale that he hadn't brought in. "Shucks," the boss said impatiently, "why didn't you tell me about that before? Now I'll have to figure it all over to make it come out even."

The impoverished condition of the share-cropper does not mean that the planter is rolling in wealth. The whole cotton belt, except in western Texas, has a hungry look; the per capita farm income in the Southeast is only $183 a year, compared with $273 for the entire country. One recent study shows that the average Southern planter, after deducting interest on his investment, has only $855 a year for his work of farm management.

The government's crop reduction program, however, has brought large benefits to the landlords—benefits that are apparent in painted houses, new clothes, shiny automobiles, and padded bank deposits. Only a slight trickling of this improvement has reached the tenant, who has borne the brunt of the reduced acreage. The effect of the government program has been to take risks from the landlord's shoulders and throw them upon the tenant. Landowners received big checks from Washington and were enabled to obtain production credits at cheap rates. Yet many of them continued to provide supplies to tenants at 20 to 30 per cent above cash prices and refused to share their government benefits with croppers.

Complaints of tenants against the effects of the 1933 plow-up campaign led the government to insert in 1934 and 1935 acreage reduction contracts clauses intended to protect the tenants' interests. Many landlords ignored these provisions, some requiring immediate return of money paid to croppers. Thousands of share-croppers had to become wage hands or go on the dole. Tenants' complaints mailed to Washington were sent back to county agents, who in turn passed them on to the landlords against whom these accusations were made.

That a large proportion of cotton tenants are shiftless and improvident is generally conceded. Yet investigators who have studied the subject at first hand have been convinced that the tenant's laziness is a remediable result of malnutrition and disease and that when he is improvident it often is because he sees no hope of bettering his condition by trying to provide for the future. Typhoid is three times as prevalent in the cotton belt as elsewhere in the country; and both malaria and pellagra—the starvation disease —are six times as common. No one would say that any of these diseases is a spur to ambition.

The fact that many tenants are habitually in debt and seldom receive any cash tends to make them spendthrift with the little they do get occasionally. One man reported that he had been cropping for eighteen years without receiving any money. When such a farmer is paid a few dollars, it is little wonder that he may want to splurge them on fancy living, a phonograph, or even a ramshackle automobile—instead of buying the mule he may need. Even a disreputable car nourishes his starved self-respect and lends him a feeling of power and importance. It also expedites his trips to town and enables him to gain some knowledge of machinery that may come in handy if he ever gets a chance to operate a tractor. For the Negro tenant there is the additional incentive that driving a car on a public road gives him a fleeting illusion of equality with the white man.

Deprived of effectual help from the planter or from the government in Washington, the cotton cropper has been unable to make his voice felt by the ballot, even on local issues. Southern Negroes are deprived of the vote by means too well known to need listing here; one of these means, the poll tax, serves to disfranchise many of the poor whites as well. In desperation, share-croppers in eastern Arkansas and western Tennessee organized the Southern Tenant Farmers' Union; but in many neighborhoods the planters' violent reaction against the union has only added to the croppers' woes.

Armed and sometimes drunken planters have broken up meetings of the union and forced its officers to leave the county. Floggings and threats of lynching have been common; even a white woman was stripped and flogged by vigilantes. Tenants who joined the union have been forcibly evicted from houses. Often local officers have supported the law-defying planters. One former Methodist preacher who served as a volunteer organizer for the tenants' union was sentenced to six months in jail and fined $500 on an anarchy charge, and the lawyer who defended him had his practice ruined. Of course, not all Southern planters condone the violence of the Arkansas vigilantes, but they appear to be united against the union.

Despite the low opinion in which they are held by planters, most of the share-croppers are capable of greater responsibility. Those affected by the Tennessee Valley project and the Resettlement Administration have shown quick response to offers of educational and economic help. Many of the white tenants represent the country's purest strains of Anglo-Saxon blood. D. P. Trent, regional director of the Resettlement Administration for Oklahoma and Texas, has found that "there prevail among these people standards of honesty, integrity, and character which are not excelled in any other element of our population. All that is needed is a decent opportunity. Children of these families, when given an opportunity, rank with the best in intelligence, skill, and competitive achievement."

On a limited scale, the Resettlement Administration has been helping ambitious tenants to buy land and equipment on easy terms and has enabled many to acquire decent houses and gain the benefit of having a cow and a garden. Typical of resettlement clients is the Texas farmer who was on relief despite the fact that his grandfather, on returning from the Civil War, had traded his horse for 500 acres of land. The grandson was classified on relief rolls as hopeless, and his four children were so ragged that they were ashamed to go to school. Yet a small rehabilitation loan enabled him to buy a pair of mules, a set of second-hand harness, a plow, and materials with which he built a house. Thus equipped, he was able to obtain land. His first year's crop enabled him to repay a considerable part of the rehabilitation loan. To-day flowers bloom along the slab walk to his front gate, and his daughters attend school in freshly laundered dresses.

Bills introduced in Congress in January [1937] by Senator John H. Bankhead and Representative Marvin Jones would have the government undertake on a much larger scale work of the type the Resettlement Administration has been doing. This plan would establish a Farmers' Loan Corporation with an initial capital of $50,000,000, to which a like amount would be added each year for ten years. This money would be used to buy land for lease or sale to farm hands and tenants ambitious to better their condition. Those unable to make a down payment of 25 per cent would be allowed to lease land from the corporation, which would apply the rent on the purchase price in case the tenant wished to buy after his rent payments amounted to 25 per cent of the total purchase price.

Recommendations of the President's committee, which have been passed on to Congress, are in essential harmony with the Bankhead-Jones plan. It now appears likely that Congress will at least make a start toward solving the tenancy problem. The minority report of W. L. Blackstone, president of the Southern Tenant Farmers' Union, would have the government sponsor cooperative farming under Federal supervision. Mr. Wallace has opposed this plan as economically unsound and as "too much like the Russian system." [In 1937 the Bankhead-Jones Act was passed by Congress. It created a Farmers' Home Corporation with power to begin a program to reduce farm tenancy.]

In addition to making it easier for the wage hand or the share-cropper to become a cash renter or a farm owner, there is need to revise the prevailing system of leases. If leases are made for several years instead of only for one year, and if provisions are included to credit the tenant with permanent improvements he makes on the farm, he will have more incentive to practice soil conservation, raise food for his family, and repair the house in which he lives. No cropper or other tenant is likely to dig a well or build a barn or repair fences and gates if his only reward is to be moved off the place after the next harvest.

Other countries have solved tenancy problems as discouraging as that of the United States. Twelve central European and Balkan governments helped 2,000,000 tenants to become farm owners in the first ten years following the World War. The regulation of farm leases has also had more attention in some countries than it has here.

The problem of tenancy in the cotton belt may soon become complicated by the adoption of mechanized farming. Further perfection of the Rust brothers' cotton picker may lead to more farming in large units, with the help of tractors and wage hands. This mechanization might send many of the South's rural inhabitants to the cities for jobs or doles, but the process is not likely to be as rapid as some theorists predict. The present task is to improve rural education, health, and housing and to regulate farm leases —as well as to help wage hands and tenants toward farm ownership.

No. 117

THE GROWTH OF FEDERAL RESPONSIBILITY [1]

ALTHOUGH the Federal Government first began to recognize its responsibilities to agriculture a century ago, when the Congress provided a small appropriation for agricultural fact-finding purposes, our public policies did not begin to take form until 1862.

In that year the first group of major agricultural laws was enacted by the Congress. The first Homestead Act was passed; the Department of Agriculture was created to "diffuse among the people of the United States information relating to agriculture"; and the Morrill Act was passed, donating lands to the States, the proceeds from these lands to be used to support colleges of agriculture and mechanic arts. These have become known as the land-grant colleges and universities.

If teaching is to be worth while, sound information must be gathered. So, in 1887, 25 years later, Congress passed the Agricultural Experiment Stations Act. This act authorized the establishment, under the direction of the land-grant colleges and universities, of experiment stations to conduct research relating to agricultural subjects.

The experiment stations set to work gathering, assimilating, discovering, testing agricultural information. The stations published this information. Soon, however, it became evident that most farmers were lagging far behind the experiment stations. Few were using the practices recommended by the research workers. So Congress passed the Agricultural Extension Act of 1914. This act authorized the Department of Agriculture and the land-grant colleges and universities to give instruction in agriculture to persons not attending the colleges. Thus cooperative extension work was begun, with a county agricultural agent in each county working under the immediate supervision of the State college of agriculture.

Out of these activities of education and research there grew a great body of agricultural knowledge. Especially in the last several decades we have made rapid progress in the field of agricultural science. We have been successful too, through our system of extension education, in taking the

---

[1] The United States Department of Agriculture, *Planning for a Permanent Agriculture* (Washington, D. C., The United States Government Printing Office, 1939), pp. 11-18.

. results of our research from the experimental farms and laboratories to the farms of the Nation.

Another outgrowth of these activities is the close working relationship that exists between the Department and the land-grant institutions.

With the deepening of the agricultural depression in 1929 it soon became apparent that more than education and research would be required if agricultural stability were to be regained. And so, when the Congress passed the laws authorizing what have come to be called action programs, the traditional working relations that had existed between the Department and the land-grant universities for 70 years suggested immediately that the agricultural colleges be asked to assist with these programs. The colleges, through the county agents of the extension services, undertook to explain the new programs to farmers and to help farmers to set up the machinery to administer them.

The agricultural problem became a major national issue soon after 1921. That year marked the beginning of the period of acute farm trouble. The country entered into a short industrial depression, and prices fell. Although the prices of industrial goods soon recovered, the prices of farm products continued to fluctuate at the lower level. Ever since the fall of 1920, surpluses of many of the staple farm products have overhung the market, depressing prices. Why did these surpluses accumulate? Why did they not disappear in years of short crops, as they always had before?

Although most farmers are familiar with the principal answers to these questions, it may be useful to repeat them here: (1) The area of cultivated land greatly expanded during the World War and continued to expand after the armistice; (2) the automobile, truck, and tractor displaced many horses and mules; (3) the United States changed abruptly from a debtor to a creditor nation; (4) European nations increased their production of farm products; (5) foreign nations refused our farm products; (6) new producers in newer countries such as Argentina and Australia entered the world market.

Up to the beginning of the World War Europe had invested heavily in the United States. European investors helped to build railroads and factories and to develop the natural resources of a rich land. This country paid interest on these loans largely by exporting agricultural commodities. So long as we owed Europe, the channels of trade remained open. The World War reversed the flow of credit. In less than 5 years Europe owed us huge sums of money. There was but one way for Europe to pay her debts—to sell goods in international trade. This she was unable to do. Here and abroad international and national policies interfered with the interchange of goods.

Our tariffs, already high on manufactured goods, were lifted higher.

For a time we extended further credits to Europe, and Europe sent some gold to us, but this arrangement only postponed the inevitable crash. A wave of nationalism swept over the world. Countries that had passed through 4 years of war felt deeply the need to be self-sufficing. Above all, with short war rations a vivid memory, they intended to be dependent on no foreign nation for food. Europe resorted to tariffs on agricultural products, to import quotas, to subsidy programs, and to other measures to end domestic competition with food products from this country. Behind these trade barriers Europe expanded her agricultural production, just as the United States in the preceding era had expanded her manufactures behind a protective tariff.

Since colonial days our agriculture had constantly enlarged and tooled its farm plant to produce for a growing export trade. The World War only accelerated the trend. By the close of the war farmers in this country had adjusted their plant to allow for sale abroad of the products from many millions of acres. They quickly felt the gradual loss of much of their foreign market as the European nations turned from war to agriculture and erected barriers to trade. Surpluses piled high, and prices slammed down.

Prices had been abnormally high in the war years. This had caused quick, drastic shifts in the uses of land. Grazing land and forest land that had been considered until war times as unsuited to farming was brought under the plow—land that, under cultivation, could return a fair living only while prices were high and, in some localities, only while the weather favored. Grass on the Plains was turned under for wheat; more forest land was cleared; cash crops like cotton and corn replaced the grass and forage crops that formerly protected the soil from washing off the steeper slopes. Gasoline-propelled machines displaced horses and mules which had consumed the products of 35 million acres, releasing for the production of food and fiber land which had been used to produce feed. Farm machinery prices doubled. Land prices boomed. Farms sold for two or three times their former price. Lending agencies made many loans which later proved unwise. Farmers assumed obligations that could be met only if they got high prices for their products. Farm mortgage indebtedness rose from 3 billion dollars in 1910 to 9 billion dollars in 1928.

Farmers did their best to make drastic adjustments in the post-war years, but they could not make them quickly enough. Under the pinch of low incomes they were forced to overcrop their soil; they were compelled, at least temporarily, to produce more bushels of grain, more bales of cotton, more stock, to meet interest, taxes, and other inflexible production costs and to purchase nonfarm commodities at high prices, which after the war had not come down as fast or as far as farm prices. This was a losing game. Farmers lost their farms. More than 40 thousand farmers passed from owner status to tenant status each year. Millions of others cried out for Government assistance to help them bring about readjustments in farm prices. Finally, a million farm families, mostly in regions dependent on one cash crop, were lacking even the necessities of life, and they applied for relief.

The World War and other international pressures sorely aggravated our difficulties, but all of our troubles cannot be blamed on that conflict. Many of them are of domestic origin. World disturbances only hastened the arrival of problems that grew out of our heroic efforts to subdue a continent.

We know now that certain shortcomings always have been inherent in our public land policies. We have had, really, but one policy for a country of widely diverse soils, topography, and climates. We gave little consideration, at least at first, to the widely divergent adaptabilities of land. Land policies suitable for the humid East, for example, were not suited to the drier West. In many parts of the country the 160-acre homestead tracts were much too small to yield a family living. Many lands opened up to farming undoubtedly should have remained in trees and grass. Many thousands of families were permitted, and often urged, to settle on lands too poor or on farms too small to yield them an adequate living. Looking back, we find little guidance was offered settlers.

Many of the causes of land misuse in our country are rooted in attitudes developed in a period of great land plenty. Perhaps the strongest of our pioneer beliefs was the conviction that each man was entitled to unrestricted ownership of a piece of the earth. So long as we had land in abundance our principal aim was to dispose of it to settlers as quickly as possible.

To put our lands into the hands of the people was a worthy objective, but unfortunately along with the accomplishment of this objective there arose some abuses. As a Nation we came to speculate heavily in land, both in a small and in a large way. We permitted corporations to acquire large tracts of the public lands, and many millions of acres of forests were promptly devastated as one of the immediate consequences. We came to expect perpetual rises in land values and looked upon them as one of the primary compensations of farming. Much land got into the hands of non-farmer owners, and the percentage of tenant operators grew astonishingly.

To-day, partly as a result of our land policies and partly as a consequence of world-wide disturbances, we are faced with a great bundle of land problems: Eroded and worn-out farm lands; more destructive floods in areas where lands have been especially misused; overgrazed and depleted range lands; stranded communities in regions of abandoned farm lands and cut-over forests; the Dust Bowl—to name a few. And associated with these land problems are other human problems even more difficult of solution.

Lack of knowledge of good farm, range, and forestry practices undoubtedly accounts for a share of our millions of acres of wasting lands, but there are other causes which cannot be overlooked. Even were all farmers, ranchers, and lumbermen familiar with the best conservation practices and measures, many would be either unable or unwilling to put them into effect. They might not be financially able to do so. A farmer may lack sufficient land resources, as well, to do other than he is doing. Quite often private and public interests in land fail to coincide. They may in certain instances conflict violently. It is scarcely to the advantage of the tenant for a year, for example, to conserve soil resources. Few tenants will take steps to do so until they establish long-time interests in the land.

Habits of farming are hard to change. Ours were born in a day when land was abundant and cheap. When its land wore out, a family picked up and moved farther west. There is no incentive to conserve land when it is cheap and plentiful. The incentive to conserve is born of approaching scarcity. We have reached that stage with land. There are no longer new territories to open, new frontiers to cross. From now on we must live on what we have.

With so many factors beyond individual control it was natural for farmers to petition Government for assistance. Working as individuals they were unable to deal with the forces working against them. They lacked the tools with which to work. They hoped, through Government, to attack their problems cooperatively. Government, both State and Federal, responded with a series of laws. Some of these have been superseded by other legislation in the light of experience, court decisions, and changing circumstances. Together, they shape a new agricultural policy for the country.

This new agricultural policy, undoubtedly not yet mature, grew very slowly at first. It did not begin to find expression in national legislation until passage of the Agricultural Marketing Act of 1929, which created the Farm Board. The Farm Board sought to control prices by controlling marketings of the staple crops. But it was given an impossible task. Having no powers to control supplies through production limitation, it failed. Since then, other acts of Congress have been passed to aid in lifting agricultural prices. Profiting by experience with the Farm Board, Congress passed the first Agricultural Adjustment Act during the depths of the price crisis of 1933. Its principal objective was to raise farm prices and income by controlling the production of certain staple commodities through acreage limitations. An adverse court decision ended this first production-control effort. Since this decision was rendered, two major farm acts—the Soil Conservation and Domestic Allotment Act of 1936, and the act which supplemented it, the Agricultural Adjustment Act of 1938—have authorized programs designed to conserve soil resources and balance agricultural and industrial income.

It was realized meanwhile, that income improvement was only one of the adjustments needed in agriculture, even though it was inextricably related to most of them. To cope simultaneously with the other aspects of the farm problem the Resettlement Administration was created to aid in the rehabilitation of the disadvantaged in agriculture. This program, now modified, is carried on by the Farm Security Administration. To the problem of erosion control Congress responded with the act that created the Soil Conservation Service. The Bankhead-Jones Act provided for tenancy reform and for public acquisition and development of land submarginal for agriculture. The Water Facilities Act of 1937 provided for small water developments in the arid and semiarid areas where these are necessary to agricultural progress. The Flood Control Act of 1936 and subsequent amendments authorized land treatment for flood control. Other acts provided for the development of farm forestry, for crop insurance, marketing agreements, for purchase of land for public forests, for developing wildlife sanctuaries, and for other activities.

This list of public programs is only a partial one. It includes only a part of those administered by the Department of Agriculture. It does not include the programs authorized by State laws, nor does it include the programs in aid of agriculture administered by other Federal agencies. Yet it is sufficiently long to show that our traditional attitude toward farming and farm land is rapidly passing. We are undoubtedly coming to look upon farming as an industry requiring direct assistance from the Federal Government and upon farm land as national wealth entrusted to the care of an individual. Under the new concept, it is public policy to enable farmers to earn a fair share of the national income and to charge them in return with the responsibility of conserving and maintaining the land.

Chapter XXXIV

CONSERVATION, PLANNING, AND THE FUTURE

[THE United States is easily one of the leading nations of the world in abundance of natural resources. In minerals—oil, coal, copper, lead, zinc, aluminum, phosphate, and the like; in lumber, in water power, in land, we have vast resources at our command. The increased consumption and wanton waste of the last fifty years, however, has produced the growing realization that we should consider how best to conserve these resources for future generations. As the National Resources Board pointed out, "In the happy hunting stage of skimming the cream off resources, the nation has taken its abundance of mineral supplies as a matter of course. But, as we pass into the stage of maturity, it is evident that the spending habits and impetuous expansion of pioneer days must give way to a more orderly and less wasteful development. The great mineral industries of the United States have been built up through individual initiative and control. Until recently, it has been assumed that private enterprise required no guidance in developing the natural resources and needed no help from government." The Board proceeded to point out, however, that it is now "established beyond a reasonable doubt that the United States is deficient in many minerals necessary for industry, both in respect to its present and future requirements; that for others, the supply is limited to a decade or a few decades; that, aside from building materials, only a few of the minerals, such as coal and iron, exist in quantities sufficient to supply the nation for long periods of 100 years or more, and even those are more limited in regard to the higher grade preserves. Present over-development of some minerals has tended to obscure the central and dominant fact that, in relation to what we hope will be the life of the nation, our mineral supplies are too limited to excuse the wasteful exploitation that now prevails." The Board maintained, for example, that a billion cubic feet of natural gas was being blown into the air daily and pointed out that this was enough to supply the United Kingdom twice over and was forty times as much as all the Scandinavian countries use together. Similar wastes in the field of mineral resources, land, water, and forests are also in evidence.

The growing evidence of the wasteful use of resources led, at the beginning of this century, to a realization of the need for conservation and planning.

964

Since 1900 there has been a steady development in both of these fields and it is important to recognize that conservation and planning are here and that their further development is inevitable. One should keep in mind that planning constitutes an added power in the hands of government, and that it gives the politician an added responsibility. The power can be used for bad as well as good purposes, and it can be developed efficiently or inefficiently. One thing is certain. We shall not plan well if we continue to pretend, as many wish us to do, that planning does not exist. The modern state has become a positive state; it has become a social service state. If it is to remain a democratic state the people must be eternally vigilant against those forces that, in the end, would deny the promise of a democratic and abundant life.]

No. 118

CONSERVATION OF NATURAL RESOURCES [1]

by Robert H. Randall

WEALTH of natural resources is a dominant factor in the American economy. We are a prosperous country primarily because we are a richly endowed country. If we continue to dissipate this natural heritage, if we fail to conserve our land, our forests, our oil and coal and minerals, we shall lose our sources of raw materials and of energy, and shall be hard pressed to maintain or improve our standard of living.

Conservation of natural resources does not mean, however, that these resources should be preserved for the use of future generations at the expense of the present. It simply means that we cannot be so profligate with our capital as we have been in the past—that a balance must be struck between present and future needs. To strike such a balance calls for careful planning in the use and the development of our resources.

To the Colonial settler and to the pioneer, pushing the frontier of the United States ever westward, land and forest, fish and game, and mineral deposits were so abundant as to seem inexhaustible. They were to be had for the taking, and they were recklessly and wastefully exploited. Little if any thought was given to the future. However, as the frontier receded and the land came to be more densely populated, it became apparent that inexhaustibility was a myth—that our resources were being rapidly depleted. The idea of conservation came to be accepted first in the older, eastern

[1] Robert H. Randall, "Conservation of Natural Resources," *The Annals* of the American Academy of Political and Social Science (November, 1939), Vol. 206, pp. 142-146. Reprinted by permission of *The Annals* of the American Academy of Political and Social Science.

sections of the country, where the results of wasteful exploitation had long been apparent, and then moved slowly westward, advancing with settlement. But it was not until the close of the nineteenth century, with the disappearance of the frontier and the passing of the era of free and good public lands, that the threatened exhaustion of our natural resources became sufficiently apparent to arouse any nationwide interest in their conservation and managed use.

Although the earliest attempts to protect such natural resources as forests and wild life date back to the Colonial period, little progress in conservation was made from that time until after the middle of the last century. In the 1860's, however, certain states undertook to control stream pollution and to protect fish; in the 1870's steps were taken for the protection of game; in the 1880's for the preservation of forests; and in the 1890's for the prevention of oil and gas waste.

These state activities in the field of resource management gradually developed from mere legislative declarations of policy to administrative control over specific resources. The degree of control exercised has varied with the resource; for example, much greater progress has been made in forest than in land management. It has also varied with the state. The methods used, either singly or in combination, have ranged from the acquisition of land by the state and the withdrawal and reservation of public lands, the purchase of consent from private owners by direct payment, services, or tax adjustments, and regulations under the police power, to education and the application of scientific techniques, as in fish and game restoration, and reforestation. Legal justification for this expansion of governmental activity has been found in the police power of the state, buttressed by the legal theories of sovereign ownership and the prevention of waste.

The early state agencies concerned with the management of natural resources were numerous and operated quite independently of one another. Little or no recognition was given to the fact that the use and development of one resource might affect other resources. There was no concept of co-ordinated resource management or of comprehensive planning for the use and development of all resources, on which such management, to be successful, must be based.

During the same period, the Federal Government also began to manifest an interest in conservation. In 1871 the office of Commissioner of Fish and Fisheries was established to prevent the decline of fisheries. Somewhat later a Federal forest agency was set up, and in 1891 the first national forest reservation was created. It was not until the first decade of the present century, however, that conservation became a national issue.

Though the conservation movement of 1908, which produced the National

Conservation Commission, the Governors' Conference, and the Joint Conservation Conference, succumbed in the face of the political controversy it had aroused, and though only four of the state conservation commissions established at that time have survived to the present day, three major accomplishments must be accredited to this movement: It brought about popular recognition of the need, in the public interest, for governmental control over the use and development of our natural resources; it emphasized the interrelationship of these resources and the need for co-ordinated resource management based on comprehensive planning; and it established a precedent for state conservation agencies and for interstate and Federal-state cooperation in this field.

In the postwar period, numerous state conservation agencies were set up as part of state administrative reorganization plans or were established separately to integrate the various state activities in relation to natural resources. However, even in those states having consolidated conservation agencies, this consolidation was seldom all-inclusive, and other agencies still exist with functions in the resources field. Moreover, the state conservation commissions were primarily concerned with resource management, and only incidentally with planning. Prior to 1933, only three states —New York, New Jersey, and Wisconsin—had specifically recognized planning as an important function of state government and had made provision for it. The stage, however, had been set, and with the establishment of the National Planning Board in 1933, the states hastened to take advantage of the Federal aid offered, under the emergency relief grants, for the setting up of state planning agencies.

Though the constitutional division of powers between the states and the Federal Government has placed the burden of resource management on the states, the Federal Government has endeavored to ease this burden by making grants to the states, by providing them with the services and advice of such agencies as the Forest Service, the Biological Survey, the Bureau of Fisheries, the Bureau of Mines, and the Geological Survey, and by undertaking conservation work in those areas over which the Federal Government itself has jurisdiction. Prior to 1933, however, there was little more opportunity for co-ordinated resource management based on comprehensive planning on the national level than there was within the states.

With the depression came the realization of the imperative need, in order to mitigate such crises in the future, for integrating the many state and Federal functions pertaining to resource management into a co-ordinated and comprehensive program for the wise conservation and use of the Nation's resources. It was seen that such a program, to be successful, must be nationwide in scope, since conditions in one section of the country were bound to affect other sections, and that it would call for effective cooperation among the different Federal agencies and between the Federal Government and the states.

> To advise and assist the Administrator . . . through the preparation, development, and maintenance of comprehensive plans . . . through surveys and research . . . and through the analysis of projects for co-ordination and correlation of effort among the agencies of the Federal, State, and local Governments,

the Public Works Administrator, in December 1933, set up the first National Planning Board. This was succeeded by the National Resources Committee, established by Executive Order in June 1935,

> to prepare and present to the President a program and plan of procedure dealing with the physical, social, governmental, and economic aspects of public policies for the development and use of land, water, and other national resources and such related subjects as may from time to time be referred to the Board by the President.

The National Resources Planning Board took over the function of the Resources Committee on July 1, 1939.

The National Planning Board, through the services of its consultants and with Civil Works Administration funds allocated for local planning projects, encouraged the states to set up state planning boards to undertake planning at the state level and to cooperate with the national planning agency. Since 1933 forty-seven states have set up planning agencies, of which forty-two were in existence as of May 1, 1939, and about four hundred county planning commissions and a number of regional planning commissions and special interstate committees have been established.

These local, state, regional, and national planning agencies have undertaken to formulate programs for the best use and development of our resources. This planning, by the very nature of the problems to be solved, must be largely a cooperative enterprise, since the solution calls for concurrent action at all levels of government. State and national programs cannot be considered as distinct and separate entities, nor can the exercise of the planning function be confined solely to the planning agencies.

The National Resources Planning Board and its predecessors, therefore, have continually endeavored to stimulate planning in the states and by the Federal agencies concerned with resource management, and to correlate this programming both as among Federal agencies and as between the states and the Federal Government. To this end special committees have been organized, made up of representatives from interested Federal agencies and state planning agencies and of outside technicians, to study and make recommendations relative to the conservation and use of our land, water, mineral, and energy resources. These technical committees have worked in cooperation with state and local governments. The solution of regional problems on a regional basis has been facilitated by the establishment of permanent regional commissions, such as those in New England and the Pacific Northwest, and of special regional committees, such as that in the Northern Lakes States, to further interstate and Federal-state cooperation in attacking these problems.

The state planning boards have undertaken the collection of those basic data on state resources which are essential to the formulation of any sound program for resource use, whether state, regional, or national in scope. These boards offer an opportunity for the co-ordination of the plans of other state agencies in the resources field and provide the necessary machinery for comprehensive planning of resource management at the state level. Their existence has greatly facilitated the preparation and carrying out of regional plans; and since state activities coincide at many points with Federal jurisdictions and services, the state planning boards and the National Resources Planning Board together, through their respective co-ordinating functions in relation to other state and Federal agencies, are in a position to foster the cooperation of these agencies and to assist in the correlation of their long-range programs.

Together, the various planning agencies established since 1933 constitute a means whereby the objective, advanced in 1908, of co-ordinated resource management based on comprehensive planning may be realized. They are, therefore, to some extent an outgrowth of the earlier conservatiion movement. However, in response to new conditions, the concept of conservation which was held at the beginning of this century has had to be expanded.

According to the laissez faire philosophy of the nineteenth century, the automatic working of the self-regulatory features of the competitive system might be depended upon to keep individual initiative within the bounds of reason and to maintain an equilibrium within the economic structure. Governmental interference in the business of the banker or the industrialist, in the relations between employer and employee, or on behalf of the underprivileged was thought to be warranted only in cases of extreme maladjustment, too patent and too productive of human suffering and social unrest to be tolerated.

The obvious dissipation of our forests and pollution of our streams forced the gradual abandonment of this attitude as it affected the utilization of natural resources. The need to conserve our human resources is only now being made equally apparent by widespread unemployment, limited opportunities for individual enterprise, and the obviously inadequate standard of living of a great body of the population. Therefore, there is to-day a strong tendency to include human resources when we speak of conservation, and the work of the National Resources Planning Board, the regional planning agencies, and to some extent that of the state planning boards, has not been confined to natural resources but has been extended to human resources as well.

Since the purpose of conservation of natural resources and of careful planning for their use is to obtain the greatest general benefit from them and to protect the public interest in them, it is obvious that no useful plan for their development can be made without taking into full account its social and economic aspects and consequences. Only by relating natural resources to the economic and social life which they support, in planning for their utilization, can the general standard of living be improved and the interests of future generations be protected. Planning for human resources in conjunction with physical resources is, therefore, an integral part of comprehensive planning and a natural development, rather than an innovation, in the evolution of the concept of conservation.

Planning as a governmental function has been necessitated by the facts that the machinery of contemporary society is too complicated to be self-regulatory, and that the consequences of its breakdown are too grave and far-reaching to be chanced. Planning agencies are no more than a concrete recognition of the great variety of conflicting and diverse interests which go to make up the modern state. They have become essential to permit representative government to function effectively in reconciling these interests in the public welfare. The National Resources Planning Board and the local, state, and regional planning agencies are instruments for the formulation and correlation of plans to govern the management of our various resources, both physical and human, as conditions and public opinion warrant this long-range programming. They can neither force the adoption of these plans nor supervise their execution. Their function is to advise the executive and legislative branches of government and to co-ordinate the administrative activities of the different divisions and levels of government.

No. 119

THE ROLE OF GOVERNMENT IN ECONOMIC PLANNING [1]

by Raymond T. Bye

IN the early stages of capitalism, industry was carried on by many small, competing enterprises, whose proprietors were free to formulate their own policies with very little interference from the state. Such a system of industry can be described as unplanned, because it was extremely decentralized, depending for its guidance not on the will of any controlling body, but on the ups and downs of prices, which, through their effects on profits, were supposed to keep production in rough balance with consumers' demand. It was a process of trial and error, comparable in some respects to life in the jungle, where many different plants and animals struggle for existence with no other guiding principle than the law of survival. Like the jungle, it was both wasteful and cruel. The waste appeared in the inefficiency of small business units, in errors of individual judgment leading to business failures, in competitive duplication of facilities, in unemployment and periodic depressions. The cruelty was evidenced by ruthless competitive practices, by intolerable factory conditions, by starvation wages, child labor, and poverty.

In an effort to correct these weaknesses, two developments ensued. In the first place, small individual proprietors were replaced by corporations, and these in turn by supercorporations, which subjected portions of industry to a considerable measure of central guidance. Competition was in some cases eliminated, in others tempered by mutual understandings and trade association rules. Similarly, the wage earners banded together into trade unions. In the second place, government stepped in to prevent abuses. Workers were protected by factory legislation, public utilities were regulated, trusts were restrained, banks were partly centralized, and so on. This evolution has continued, so that the character of the industrial system has been greatly changed.

The deeper meaning of all this is that the various processes of industry are gradually being brought under centralized control. Just as the jungle has been replaced by man's cultivated fields, so the chaos of thousands of

[1] Raymond T. Bye, "The Role of Government in Economic Planning," *The Annals* of the American Academy of Political and Social Science (November, 1939), Vol. 206, pp. 126-132. Reprinted by permission of *The Annals* of the American Academy of Political and Social Science.

competing enterprises is being replaced by organization. Little by little, industry is being *planned,* instead of being left to the automatic guidance of natural economic forces. The planning is being done partly by the large corporations and trade associations which dominate their respective branches of production, and partly by the state, through such agencies as the Federal Reserve System, the Interstate Commerce Commission, the Securities and Exchange Commission, the National Labor Relations Board, and many others, Federal, state and local.

However, such measures of planning as the above are separate and disconnected; they are not integrated into a unified whole. The result is that the processes of industry are not yet well articulated. Indeed, the plans effective in one part may work at cross-purposes to those in another. For example, anthracite and bituminous coal, natural and manufactured gas, petroleum, and electricity are all sources of fuel for the production of heat and power. Efficient utilization of our natural resources would require that these several industries be fitted together in such a way as to avoid waste and to conserve as much as possible for the future; yet they are notoriously disorganized. The anthracite industry is paralyzed, the bituminous industry chaotic and continually in the throes of labor disputes, the petroleum industry a confusion of exploitation, instability, and profligate waste, while the gas and electric industries, although better integrated and publicly regulated, have been characterized by financial mismanagement and exorbitant costs. These are typical of the results which naturally follow from a system of independent free enterprise.

The controls introduced into the situation by government are little better. Laws affecting industry are enacted under the pressure of special interests instead of being framed with regard to the smooth functioning of the whole economy. Such laws are often in direct opposition to each other. Witness the efforts of our Federal Government to persuade foreign governments to pay their debts to it, while at the same time protective tariffs are established to prevent the importation of goods by which alone these debts might be paid. Because private business does not fully employ all our labor, we embark upon programs of public works intended to fill up the gap, while at the same time we enact measures designed to raise the wages of workers and thereby discourage an increase in private employment.

If industry is ever to function smoothly and consistently, a greater measure of unity in its processes must be achieved. No other way to accomplish this seems possible than through planning of a more general sort than that which now prevails. Some kind of central guidance is needed.

Some business leaders, conscious of this need, have advocated that each industry develop its own program of planning, with only enough participation by government to give the plans its blessing and to prevent any flagrant abuses. Something of this sort was attempted by the National Recovery Administration, and similar schemes have been favored by prominent business leaders, such as Gerard Swope, and by the United States Chamber of Commerce.

Although many of the people who have advanced these proposals are men of high motives, such planning would almost inevitably degenerate into exploitation of the public. If each industry is allowed to plan for itself, there will be a strong temptation for it to suppress competition within its own ranks and to limit the output of its product, to the end that high prices, with resulting high profits, may be secured. This was what happened under the NRA, and it is what might be expected under any similar program.

Even at its best, independent planning by separate industries could not achieve balance in the economy as a whole. Railways must be co-ordinated with other kinds of transportation, and transportation facilities as a whole co-ordinated with the industries which employ their services. Fuel and raw materials industries must be co-ordinated with the manufacturing groups which use their products, and manufacturing industries in turn must be co-ordinated with the wholesale and retail establishments through which they find their outlets. In the end, the output of all the industries must be co-ordinated with the needs of consumers. Planning of this broad type can be done only by the Federal Government, for it alone is competent to deal with so vast a problem on a national scale. It alone is sufficiently catholic in its interests to represent all of the people, and sufficiently wide in its jurisdiction to control the various industries that must be included.

Under a dictatorial form of government, planning can readily become ruthless regimentation. This has been the case in Soviet Russia, where general economic planning is most fully developed, and in Germany and Italy. But the extreme suppression of the individual which is characteristic of these systems is largely political in character and is rooted in the traditions of the people. Russia has never known anything but autocracy, which was exericsed long before the advent of the Communists; the Germans have always been used to a good deal of regimentation; and the traditions of democracy have not been so fully developed in Italy as among English-speaking peoples. Moreover, planning in these countries came about by revolution, not by evolution. If developed in a more orderly manner and kept within the framework of democratic institutions, it ought to be possible to achieve unity and co-ordination in our economic life without the sacrifice of essential liberties.

To accomplish this, the program of planning would have to meet two basic requirements. In the first place, it should retain the essential features of the existing price system. This means that demand and supply should be the guide for production to follow. The planning authorities should not decree what things were to be produced and what should be the output of the various industries and enterprises on the basis of arbitrary decisions or intuitive guesses, but should seek to achieve that balance in industry which would naturally result if production were nicely adjusted to demand. The difficulty with the present system of unplanned industry is that this adjustment is not well attained. The planning authorities could presumably replace the erroneous guesses of the thousands of enterprisers who now follow their individual judgments, by informed decisions based on adequate information. Thus they would enable business men to proceed with a program which would offer less risk and more assurance of a market for their outputs at prices which would cover their costs than they can possibly have at the present time.

Because planning of this sort would follow the natural tendencies of the present economic system, and thereby help business men toward correct policies instead of hindering them, it seems likely that it could enlist their willing cooperation. They would not have to be forced to conform to the plans if the plans proved by experience to reduce losses and to provide wise guidance. Similarly, the plans would help investors to place their savings in profitable rather than losing ventures, and they would help employees to find lucrative positions where their innate capacities could be more sure of a market and where employment would be more steady than is now the case. Therefore, investors and wage earners would also find it to their advantage to follow the plans, so that very little coercion would be needed. So far as the individual consumer is concerned, he would still be allowed to spend his money as he pleased, exercising his free choice among the commodities offered to him in the markets. It would not be necessary to regiment his consumption, but merely to forecast it intelligently.

The second requirement which a system of democratic planning would have to meet is that the organization through which the plans were drawn up and administrated would have to be genuinely representative. This means that every interested party would have to have some voice, through elected representatives, in making the decisions which would constitute the plans for industry. New machinery of government would have to be built up along these lines, thus carrying forward into a new sphere the traditions of representative democracy.

The development of a planning organization that would meet the above two requirements would have to be achieved by gradual experimentation. It is probably impossible to prescribe its detailed forms in advance. Some indication of the lines along which such machinery might be developed have, however, been suggested by other writers and may be briefly indicated here.

There might be set up in each industry an Industrial Planning Council, whose membership would be composed of people democratically chosen to represent investors, management, and labor in the industry concerned, and the consuming public at large. Existing trade and labor organizations in the several industries might be used as a starting point from which to develop suitable organizations for providing such representation. Some organization of investors might have to be worked out in order to provide for the selection of delegates from that group. Representatives of consumers might be appointed by the public authorities. Where remnants of the code authorities under the National Recovery Administration still exist, such organizations might form a nucleus for the planning councils.

The function of these bodies would be to gather data concerning plant capacities, available labor and materials, and possible outputs in their respective branches of production. They would make estimates of the probable growth of the industry and of its requirements for new capital and labor. On the basis of these data they would formulate tentative plans for the industry. The plans would specify the output to be scheduled for the ensuing year or years, with quotas for the individual businesses contributing thereto, the requirements of the industry for fuel and raw materials, the estimated costs of production, and the probable selling prices at which the products could be disposed of. These plans would not be final, but would be submitted to the central planning authorities for their guidance. The plans would constitute a sort of proposal from the industry as to what it was prepared to do for the economy.

At the head of the planning organization there would be needed a National Economic Planning Commission. This would be an arm of the Federal Government, probably headed by a Cabinet officer. Its membership should be of the highest caliber, and it would need to have at its command a large staff of technical experts, economists, statisticians, accountants, stenographers, clerks, and other office workers. In a country as large as the United States, subsidiary state or regional planning commissions, organized on similar lines, would be needed. The Commission would need to be clothed with sufficient authority to compel corporations and individuals to supply it with such information concerning their businesses as it needed for the formulation of its plans, and to prescribe the forms on which these data were to be reported.

The function of the National Planning Commission would be to receive and scrutinize the tentative plans submitted to it by the Industrial Councils. Forming its judgments on the basis of these plans and on information derived from a national survey of productive capacity and consumptive needs, it would draw up superplans for the economy as a whole for one-year, five-year, and perhaps longer periods. These superplans would indicate expected output, volume of employment, capital replacements and extensions, and the probable costs, wages, selling prices, and profits in each of the several industries. They would indicate where the market for the products would be found, and they would provide for the utilization of all the resources and labor power available. Some scheme of employment offices would presumably be developed for supplying labor where it would be needed in industry. Monetary policy would also have to be formulated by the Commission, or in close collaboration with it, so as to maintain a reasonably stable level of prices and to direct credit into the channels where it was expected to go.

The result of all this would be a kind of industrial budget or schedule for the Nation, so designed as to make the fullest possible use of existing resources, provide full employment for labor at the best wages industry could afford, and co-ordinate the various branches of industry—in short, to provide balanced abundance for the United States.

The comprehensive plans drawn up by the National Planning Commission should not have binding effect until acted upon by Congress. Otherwise, the danger of dictatorial regulation would be real; but if the plans were embodied in a bill to be fully debated and amended in Congress before it became the law of the land, they would have the democratic character which it is important to preserve.

When the plans were adopted by Congress and approved by the President, they should be put into effect through appropriate administrative machinery. The organization needed for this purpose should parallel that for drawing up the plans in the first place, but should not be identical with it. A certain amount of separation between those who made the plans and those who carried them out would probably be desirable, although they should cooperate closely. Those who formulated the plans would need to be guided by the experience of those who administered them, and the administrators should have some voice in the formulation of plans for the future. So it would be wise to set up a National Planning Administration as an arm of the executive branch of the Government, linked closely to the National Planning Commission, and similar state or regional planning administrations and industrial administrations paralleling the corresponding planning commissions and industrial councils.

The industrial administrative bodies would be charged with the function of carrying out in detail the plans that applied to their particular industries. It is here that the delicate matter of securing conformity with the plans without entire loss of individual liberty and initiative would arise most acutely. Execution of the plans would probably necessitate the setting of production quotas for the different enterprises in each industry and the enforcement of compliance with the adopted schedules on the part of individual business men and groups. However, it is to be remembered that these groups would have had some voice in formulating the plans in the first place, so that the restrictions forced upon them at the execution stage would not be arbitrary or onerous.

There might or might not have to be some regulation of prices and wages; this would depend on how successfully the plans succeeded in anticipating the demand, investment, and production which would maintain balance in the various industries. It does not appear that there would be any necessity for the rationing of consumption or for the drafting of capital or labor. Consumers would still be free to spend their incomes as they pleased, choosing such commodities as were offered by the market; investors would still be free to purchase such securities as were made available under the plans, just as they are now free to choose such stocks and bonds as are offered by the various corporations which issue them; and labor would still be free to enter such occupations and accept such employment as was open. But in all these matters, more information would be available for their guidance than under the present system of industry.

Enterprisers would still be free to direct the technical operation of their plants according to their best judgment, to buy such materials and employ such labor as was available at existing prices and wages, and to make profits by the economies of low costs made possible by efficient production. The amount of interference in the details of their businesses need not be any greater than that to which railroads and other public utilities are now subject under government regulation.

Such a program of planning as is here advocated promises two great advantages. In the first place, decisions reached through the machinery of planning would be based on much more accurate and complete information than the industrial decisions of an unplanned economy. The planning authorities, empowered with the authority of government and provided with machinery for collecting and correlating statistics from every branch of industry and from every part of the country, would have resources for gathering information far greater than those at the disposal of any individual business organization, no matter how large.

In the second place, through the machinery of planning, the thousands of decisions which have to be made in industry about such important matters as new investments and capital expansion, production schedules, and the flow of materials and semifinished goods through the various processes of industry, could be co-ordinated into a unified picture. As long as these decisions are made independently, many mistakes are bound to occur. The present competitive system depends for co-ordination largely on the rectifying of such mistakes *after they occur,* through the corrective reactions of prices. However, the system is so interdependent that mistakes made in one part of it lead to errors elsewhere, in a cumulative chain, until there is a general breakdown. Balance is not restored until after a severe depression, which sooner or later is repeated. Planning should succeed in *preventing* mistakes. This will not be done to perfection, of course, but it ought to be possible to keep errors at a minimum and to prevent them from becoming cumulative. As a result, the system of planned economy should enable industry to be maintained smoothly at a higher level of productivity than the world has ever known.

One of the most conspicuous tendencies of modern times is the increasing control of central governments over the affairs of men. General economic planning involves a still. further extension of such control. To many, this will be an argument against it, for they will see in it the final downfall of individual liberty and initiative. It is believed, however, that the democratic safeguards suggested in the foregoing paragraphs should suffice to protect the rights of the individual. If economic science has any practical significance for mankind, it must be found in the power which it gives to control and improve the functioning of economic life. The only agency which is qualified to exercise controls for society as a whole is the state itself. It is to be expected, therefore, that the state will continue to expand its regulation of industry. What is here advocated is that such control shall be planned instead of haphazard, and that the government which is to do the controlling shall retain its democratic character and be made as efficient as possible.

No. 120

TOWARD A PLANNED SOCIETY [1]

by George Soule

LIKE many other controversies over the conduct of human affairs, the debate about whether the United States should adopt economic planning has been carried on after the issue itself was decided. We already have planning. The argument has been like that in the seventeenth and eighteenth centuries as to whether the world should adopt capitalist industrialism. By the time the greatest single document in advocacy of the new

[1] George Soule, "Toward a Planned Society," *The New Republic* (November 3, 1939), Vol. 101, pp. 29-32. Reprinted by permission of *The New Republic.*

order was issued—"The Wealth of Nations," by Adam Smith—the change was already well established and nothing could have stopped it.

The terms in which the discussion has been cast have helped to create the false impression that planning is a patent new scheme to be accepted or rejected as a whole, that the nation is faced by a clear-cut alternative between voting to plan and retaining the familiar system. That has prevented many from seeing that planning is inherent in industrial civilization, and that what we have been advocating is really its extension and more skillful conscious use for socially desirable purposes.

Lest this be thought quibbling about terms, it is well to state briefly the theoretical issue as it is sometimes argued, and then show why it does not apply to the facts.

According to vulgar theory, what happens in economic life is the resultant merely of millions of choices of business men, investors, workers and consumers. They decide, as individuals, what to produce and how much of it, where to buy and where to sell, how much to save and where to invest it, whether they will pay the prices charged, how much to ask for their own products.

This system is supported as having two major virtues. In the first place, it is a "free one," since it rests on private enterprise and preserves the right of each individual to make his own economic decisions. In the second place, it is supposed to work better than any controlled system could. Competition ensures that those prdoucers offering the best values at the lowest price will survive and prosper. The return on capital in successful ventures stimulates saving and investment in productive facilities for those goods that the consumer most wants. The consumers' choices, in turn, determine the nature of production. The theory is elaborated further into endless refinements.

If one accepts this as the natural or existing state of affairs, then it is easy to argue against the introduction of planning. If you substitute decisions by groups or by government for those of individuals, you restrict freedom. Once economic freedom is gone, who knows where the tendency will stop? You are headed straight for dictatorship. And, in addition, you so upset the "natural" economic order by arbitrary intervention that it does not operate efficiently any more. Fix prices, limit profits or regulate production, and you throw into confusion that delicate system of dials and pointers that tells business men and investors when to produce more or less and where to invest and how much.

But this, of course, is a false way of stating the issue. The ideal world of the classical economists is not the one we have, or the one we have had for a long time, if ever. The intervention which prevented it from functioning satisfactorily came not from the advocates of social planning, but from the disposition of man himself. The elaborate classical theory rests on major assumptions which are not true. It assumes, first, that in every important economic field there will be an approximation to "perfect competition." It assumes that prices will move readily in response to forces of demand and supply, and that neither demand nor supply will be subject to "artificial" controls. It assumes that capital and labor will be "fluid." It assumes that men, in their economic activity, will be moved only by the purely economic motives of getting the best value for the least money, of buying low and selling high. And it assumes that in pursuit of these ends they will act rationally and with adequate knowledge of the facts. Individuals may make mistakes, but these will cancel out in the social result. Volumes would be required to show why and how these premises are false; many of the volumes have already been written. We may mention here two of the most important fallacies.

In the first place, the realm of private enterprise never consents to abide by the rules of free competition except where circumstances force it to do so, and it finds many ways to escape from them. Prices are determined by many factors, but only in a few instances simply by the forces of demand and supply. Habits, prestige, monopolies, quasi-monopolies, banking and currency control, patents, public regulation, tariffs, establishment of advertised brands, trade unions, farmers' cooperatives—these are only a few of the institutions which make prices less fluid.

In the second place, men are so far from being rational or well informed that the result of what they do as individuals even in "free markets" does not accord with the classical theories at all. A striking demonstration of this was recently published. One would think that if logical economic behavior and accurate foresight were to be found anywhere, they would be found in the capital market, where money is lent and borrowed by experts who have no other business, and by men of great wealth who are supposedly cold-blooded in their pursuit of gain. Mr. Frederick R. Macauley, expert statistician for the National Bureau of Economic Research, spent years in the study of interest rates, and published a scholarly book which traces their course in the United States since 1856. He calculated what the relation between long-term and short-term interest rates would have been if lenders and borrowers had had complete knowledge of the relevant facts and had made logical use of that knowledge. But statistical examination revealed that "the relations as they actually occur run *counter* to these theoretical rationalistic expectations." Not merely a deviation, mind you, to be accounted for by imperfections of logic and foresight, but an actual contradiction!

The correct assumptions for a valid economic theory have yet to be established; but we do know that the theory of the "free economy" is so far from the actual behavior of our world that it might as well be a metaphysical discussion of the flight of angels.

In saying that this nation is already practising planning, we do not mean that it has adopted planning of its total activities in the sense of a precise engineering technique, but merely that it is inexorably committed to the regulation of economic affairs in accordance with deliberate policies of one kind or another. This began before we were a nation at all. The colonies were conceived by England as a source of raw materials and a market for manufactured products. The regulations on currency, trade and manufacture imposed to prevent them from being anything else were irksome to the colonists and eventually resulted in the Revolution. No sooner had we gained our freedom than we adopted economic policies of our own. The Constitution was framed in large part to stabilize the currency and ensure the collection of taxes to recompense bondholders. The great controversies over the protective tariff and the National Bank arose from the plan to foster a native industry and to establish centralized control over the value of money, in the interest of capitalist accumulation. We even fought a Civil War about the issue as to whether the plantation-slave economy or the free-labor and industrial economy was to be dominant. After that war, the tariff and the currency policy were perennial subjects of politics.

The government subsidized railroad building by large bounties of land. The railroads in turn became subject to governmental regulation, first by states, then by the nation. Labor organized and, in many trades, established collective bargaining. The era of great industrial combinations, in the interest of price and production control, began. This, in turn, inaugurated the period of anti-trust legislation and trust-busting, in the interest of small competitors, consumers, and labor. Public utilities in traction, water, gas and electricity arose, were granted legal monopoly, were subjected to regulation. Before the first world war the country was engrossed in debate about national economic policy, and this, in Wilson's first term, resulted in new control devices such as the Federal Trade Commission and the Federal Reserve System for the banks. The federal income tax, with progressive rates for higher incomes, was established.

The war itself necessitated a hastily improvised but full-fledged planning system for purposes of war production. It involved administration of finance, foreign trade, shipping, railroads, fuel, food, war industries, labor and prices. Though most of these controls were quickly demobilized under the Republican reaction, important traces remained. We had a great elaboration of economic statistics, which are the first requisite for anything approaching scientific planning. And we had a wide array of trade associations in many industries, hitherto competitive, which quietly took over the techniques they had learned under government auspices. Some of their activities were beneficial to efficiency, like better accounting and engineering standardization, and some of them were devoted to control of output and prices in the interest of scarcity profits.

Both the war and the subsequent peace saw a tremendous development of scientific planning on an engineering basis in separate private industries. This era of industrial expansion is popularly thought of in terms merely of material factors, like automatic machinery, mass production with belt-line assembly and the like. But all this would have meant nothing without ability to administer enterprises of a size, extent and complexity hitherto believed to be beyond human executive capacity. What made possible the growth and success of huge organizations like the mail-order houses, General Motors and American Telephone and Telegraph was the maturity of scientific management, which is based upon a highly developed planning technique. This technique is not a theoretical dream of visionaries; it is a tested skill which is as definite and revolutionary an addition to our culture as the steam engine and the power loom. At the same time the planning of cities and of regions began to strike root.

The post-war era also saw the incubation of new social problems demanding attention to national economic policy. The farmers' surpluses gave rise to a long series of ingenious schemes pressed by the farm bloc. Finally, in Mr. Hoover's administration, this agitation broke through the stiffest sort of conservative opposition into the establishment of the Federal Farm Board and a new series of credit agencies. Once the ice was broken, the development of agricultural planning and control could not be stopped. Under the pressure of depression, it grew into the AAA, with its varied and changing devices. In spite of all the ridicule and opposition that it aroused, the Agricultural Adjustment Administration can never be demobilized; and the Department of Agriculture is to-day one of the most complete planning agencies existing in any government in the world. The fact that it has not solved its problem does not mean that we shall ever go back to the old helter-skelter order in agriculture.

It is unnecessary here to recapitulate the many new governmental agencies which came to life under the New Deal; their history is fresh in our memories. The important point to bear in mind, however, is that they were not random innovations imposed on an unsuspecting public by the President and a handful of brain-trusters, but the logical result of a long history of intervention into economic processes embarked upon by the government in response to pressures arising within the national community. A few of them, like the NRA of unhappy memory, have been abandoned, but most of them will continue in one form or another. We shall never demobilize the more highly integrated control that now exists over banking, credit and the securities markets, or the new measure of social security, or the regulation of minimum wages and maximum hours, or the TVA, or the Housing Administration, or the CCC. In discussing the future of planning, we do not have a clean slate to write on. The real question is not whether to intervene with the mythical "free economic system," but how to coordinate and supplement and plan the many interventions that have been necessary and that now exist.

The pertinent agitation for planning is now really a plea for the adaptation and introduction on a broader scale of the scientific planning technique that has already been developed and proved in single enterprises. We have been impelled to make policy decisions covering wider and wider fields, and to introduce more and more controls. Since these activities must go on and will probably be expanded, why not practise them as efficiently as we know how? Nothing is clearer than that without a high degree of intelligence and careful coordination these varied interventions may do as much harm as good. That was the trouble with the planning by separate industries in the Coolidge "new era." It was marvelous as far as it went, but the fact that it was confined to single enterprises, did not cover the no-man's land of coordination among them and did not cope with the larger problems of our economy, led to disaster. While planning of single units is necessary and desirable, it has gradually been borne in upon us that planning requires a more efficiently coordinated general economy as an environment for its decisions if it is to operate well.

The main principles of scientific planning are easily understood, even though its details are highly technical and varied. Yet, since they are so generally misapprehended, it may be well to state them again.

1. The planning agency is not executive but advisory. In military terms, it is not a "line" function, but a "staff" function. It is not the prerogative of the planners to decide upon major objectives or to execute decisions. These objectives are prescribed by some other policy-making body. In a private company, policy-making decisions are made by the officers or directors of the concern. In a democratic government, they are made by the elected legislature and executive or their agents. It is the duty of the planning agency, however, to study the conditions necessary to attainment of the chosen objectives, and to advise the policy-makers accordingly. Policy decisions will be affected by this advice, if planning is to work well.

From all this it follows that planning is not necessarily associated with any particular kind of objective or any special form of government. The major purpose may be good or bad; it may be efficiency in war or abundance in peace. The government served by planning may be a pure democracy or an absolute dictatorship, or anything between. A New England town meeting could be advised by a planning commission; some of them are.

2. The foundation of planning activity, given an objective, is research into the facts bearing upon the problem of achieving it. It is the essence of planning that its conclusions are formulated as little as possible on the basis of tradition, hunch or guess, and as largely as possible on the basis of objective research and experiment. The authority behind the planner is therefore not arbitrary authority, but the necessity inherent in the situation.

3. Given the objective and the information, the next step is the choice and mobilization of the means necessary to intelligent action. This involves coordination of all the relevant forces and factors, whether subject to control or not. An army staff, for instance, must take into consideration and make predictions concerning uncontrollable factors like enemy plans, the weather, the available resources. It must also devise ways and means for the coordination of its own controllable forces under these conditions.

Devices of planning in this stage may include, as in industry, specification, standardization, techniques of operation, schedules of production, criteria for the determination of price, accounting practices, budgeting, progress records, inventory control—all of those things that will enable a large and varied personnel to function in pursuit of the common objective.

This process of detailed formulation of plan is not a single effort, like the drafting of an architect's blue prints and specifications for a house. The plan is not drawn up and then left to work itself. The planning agency must engage in a continual process of checking and revision as the execution of the plan develops. It must be a going part of a continual and functioning organization, always foreseeing and ready to meet emergencies. Good planning makes the total organization not more rigid, but more flexible and adaptable.

4. Finally, the function of the planner is to assist the executive or policy-making body in obtaining the necessary cooperation of all concerned. It is faulty planning that relies upon arbitrary or dictatorial power in its executive to put the plan in effect. The kind of complex coordination required in a well planned enterprise will not operate without consent and a high degree of understanding on the part of those who have to do the work. Even if reluctance and sabotage are not encountered, mere rote work is inefficient. Thus, in the best planned industrial enterprises, standards of performance are set with the cooperation of organized labor. Agreed standards are a protection against speed-up and arbitrary discharge as well as an aid to

efficient production. This is merely an example to illustrate the general principle.

Furthermore, a good deal of decentralization is required for efficiency. Decisions that concern mainly subordinate units or individuals must be left with those units or individuals. The main function of the plan is to provide the proper environment for correct decisions, by reducing as much as possible the uncertainty regarding conditions that are beyond the control of the person deciding.

The tasks of our government are now large and responsible enough so that the introduction of planning technique of this scientific kind is indispensable. It already exists in various separate governmental agencies and for specific purposes. There are even approaches to it in the preparation of major decisions on governmental policy. What remains is only to expand the process, to make it explicit and understood.

If we shall be driven by circumstances to take part in war, we shall be forced into a general and explicit planning program almost overnight. We shall begin almost where we left off last time, and we shall do a much better job of it. It is significant that those who have been studying this problem have discovered that many fewer emergency bodies would have to be created than in 1917. The regular peacetime departments and special agencies of the government have been equipped with so much new information, so much better staffs and so many new powers that little would be necessary except to coordinate their activities about the objectives that war would demand.

If we successfully maintain our neutrality, an extension of planning activity will be necessary also. The least that could happen would be that the war would affect our economy so little that we should still be faced with the problems of mass unemployment and a deficiency in the flow of new capital investment. In that case the next job on the program of the New Deal, or of any following administration, would be to take concerted action to restore full production. A planned program for doing so, of which there already have been so many elementary hints, would be inevitable before too long.

The impact of the war may, however, produce other urgent problems, such as the necessity of controlling price increases and war profits, eliminating bottle-necks in our production and distribution, going to the aid of industries that are adversely affected by the shifting of demand. And any necessary war readjustment will have to be planned so as to make the shock of peace less disastrous than it was last time. We now have, for instance, means of preventing farmers from overextending their acreage on a basis that will produce an unhealthy inflation of land values and mortgage debt;

and we have means of restricting agricultural production the moment excessive demands for war exports cease.

If there is to be a decent and workable peace at the end of the war, it must arise from a degree of world economic cooperation that can be executed only on the basis of resourceful national economic planning. The belligerent nations may redraw boundaries as they please, but they cannot create a peaceful civilization without a recognition of economic necessities which transcend national lines. The tremendous task of demobilization and world reconstruction cannot be accomplished without the aid of the United States, and to give this aid we must have our own house in order.

National economic and social planning, then, is here and its further development is inevitable. But that does not mean utopia—far from it. We can use it for the wrong purposes just as easily as we have bungled the uses of natural science and invention. It constitutes added power, but also added responsibility. One thing is sure. We shall not use it well if we go on pretending that it does not exist and that we can operate merely according to the metaphysical principles of the mythical "free economy." That would renounce the potency of democratic planning in favor of those forces that would in the end deny the promise of democracy and an abundant life.

BIOGRAPHICAL NOTES

ADAMIC, LOUIS (b. 1899). Author. Born in Yugoslavia. Came to United States in 1913, naturalized 1918. Served with U. S. Army during World War I. Awarded Guggenheim Fellowship, 1932-33; awarded grant-in-aid by Rockefeller Foundation, 1937; now with the Immigration and Naturalization Service, Department of Justice. Author of *The Native's Return; My America; From Many Lands,* and numerous other books. Contributor to many leading periodicals.

ADVISORY COMMITTEE ON EDUCATION. This committee was appointed by President Franklin D. Roosevelt in 1936 to study the existing program of Federal aid for vocational education, the relation of such training to general education, and the extent of the need for an expanded program. In 1937 the work of the committee was enlarged to include consideration of the whole subject of Federal relationship to state and local conduct of education. The committee was headed by Professor Floyd W. Reeves of the University of Chicago.

BEARD, CHARLES A. (b. 1874). Professor of history and government. Columbia University, 1907-17; Johns Hopkins University, 1940—; President of the American Political Science Association, 1926, and of the American Historical Association, 1933. Director, Training School for Public Service, New York City, 1917-22. Adviser, Institute of Municipal Research, Tokyo, 1922. Adviser, Japanese Ministry of Home Affairs, 1923. Author of many books and articles on history and government.

BEARD, MARY R. (b. 1876). Author. Long experience in woman and labor movements; travel and study in Europe and Orient. Author of numerous books and articles.

BELLOWS, HENRY A. (1885-1939). Publicity director. Member of English Department, University of Minnesota, 1910-12; manager of radio station WCCO, 1925-27; member, Federal Radio Commission, 1927; Vice-President, Columbia Broadcasting System, 1930-34; Director and Chairman of Legislative Committee, National Association of Broadcasters, 1928-35; Director of Public Relations, General Mills, Inc., 1936-39.

BLAGDEN, RALPH M. (b. 1905). Journalist. Taught two years at Windsor High School, Vermont; spent nine years with *The Christian Science Monitor* as reporter, city editor, feature story writer, head of the radio production division, and assistant editor; taught journalism Boston University night school, for two years; chief editorial writer and associate editor, *Boston Evening Transcript,* one year; now one of the two staff editorial writers on the *St. Louis Star-Times.*

BOGART, ERNEST L. (b. 1870). Professor of economics. Indiana University, 1898-1900; Oberlin College, 1900-05; Princeton University, 1905-09; University of Illinois, 1909—. Regional Economist, Foreign Trade Adviser's Office, Department of State, 1919-20; adviser on currency and banking to government of Persia, 1922-23; member, Committee on Monetary Policy, U. S. Chamber of Commerce, 1933. Author of many books and articles.

BOYD, ERNEST (b. 1887). Author. British Consular Service, 1913-20—stationed at Baltimore, Barcelona, and Copenhagen. Editorial staff, *New York Evening Post,* 1920-22. Extensive literary work since 1922.

BUCK, A. E. (b. 1888). Governmental research specialist. On staff, Bureau of Municipal Research, 1917—; specialist on governmental organization and budgeting for Institute of Public Administration, 1921—; adviser to several states on governmental reorganization and budgeting; technical adviser to U. S. Bureau of the Budget, 1934-35; Consultant, President's Committee on Administrative Management, 1936-37. Author of *The Budget in Governments of To-day* and numerous other books and monographs.

BYE, RAYMOND T. (b. 1892). Professor of economics. University of Pennsylvania, 1916—. Author of *Principles of Economics, Getting and Earning: a Study of Inequality* (with R. H. Blodgett), and numerous other books and articles.

CALROW, CHARLES J. (1877-1938). Architect and public official. Architectural and engineering draftsman to 1898; construction superintendent and practicing architect to 1917; captain and major, U. S. Corps of Engineers, 1918-19; member of and consultant to the City Planning Commission of Norfolk, Virginia; chairman, Civic Improvement Committee, Norfolk Association of Commerce; District Administrator, Civil Works Administration, Southeast Virginia, 1933-34; Natural Resources Committee consultant and Director of the Virginia State Planning Board, 1934-38.

CANFIELD, DOROTHY (b. 1879). Author and novelist. Studied and traveled extensively in Europe; three years in France doing war work, first World War; member, State Board of Education, Vermont, 1921-23; member, National Institute of Arts and Letters. Extensive literary work.

CLOSE, UPTON—Josef Washington Hall (b. 1894). Author and lecturer. Investigating officer for U. S. Government in Shantung during Japanese invasion, 1916-19; newspaper correspondent in China, Japan, and Siberia, 1917-22; Chief of Foreign Affairs under Wu Pei Fu, 1922; lecturer on Oriental life and literature, University of Washington, 1922-26; speaker for National Industrial Conference Board. Frequent contributor to leading periodicals.

Coghlan, Ralph (b. 1896). Journalist. Editorial writer, *Louisville Courier-Journal*, 1920-22; special reporter and editorial writer, *St. Louis Post-Dispatch*, 1924-39; editor of editorial page, *St. Louis Post-Dispatch*, 1939—.

Commission of Inquiry on Public Service Personnel. This commission was appointed in 1933 by the Social Science Research Council with the approval of President Franklin D. Roosevelt to examine the broad problems of personnel within the United States and to outline a program for future action. The committee was headed by Lotus D. Coffman, then President of the University of Minnesota, and was composed of four other members: Louis Brownlow, Director, Public Administration Clearing House, Chicago; Ralph Budd, President, Chicago, Burlington and Quincy Railroad; Arthur L. Day, Vice-President, Corning Glass Works; and Charles E. Merriam, Department of Political Science, University of Chicago.

Cooper, Robert M. (b. 1907). Lawyer and public official. Special attorney, Department of Justice, 1934-37; Department of Justice representative as a member of the U. S. Codification Board, 1937-38; Department of Justice representative, advisory council of the Marketing Laws Survey, 1938-39; special assistant to the Attorney General of the United States, 1937—; assistant to the General Counsel of the Federal Communications Commission, 1939—.

Cornick, Philip H. (b. 1883). Governmental research specialist. Member, research staff, Institute of Public Administration; member, Land Committee, National Resources Planning Board; has made studies for a number of state and local agencies including the North Jersey Transit Commission, the New York Joint Legislative Committee on Taxation and Retrenchment, New York Commission for the Revision of the Tax Laws, New Jersey State Planning Board, the Westchester County (N. Y.) Commission on Government.

Coyle, David Cushman (b. 1887). Consulting engineer. Structural designer of New York Life Building, Washington State Capitol, Chamber of Commerce Building, etc. Member, Technical Board of Review, National PWA, 1933-35; Consultant to National Resources Committee. Author of *Brass Tacks, Age Without Fear, Why Pay Taxes?, Uncommon Sense,* and numerous other books and articles.

Cushman, Robert E. (b. 1889). Professor of government. University of Illinois, 1915-19; University of Minnesota, 1919-23; Cornell University, 1923—. Member, The President's Committee on Administrative Management, 1936. Author, *American National Government* (with S. P. Orth); editor, *Leading Constitutional Decisions;* frequent contributor to legal and other periodicals.

Daniels, Winthrop M. (b. 1867). Professor of transportation. Professor of political economy, Princeton, 1892-1911; member, Board of Public Utility Commissioners of New Jersey, 1911-14; member, Interstate Commerce Commission, 1914-23; professor of transportation, Yale University, 1923-40; trustee, N. Y., N. H. and H. R. R., 1935-37. Author of several books on transportation.

DAVENPORT, FREDERICK M. (b. 1866). Professor of law and politics. Hamilton College, 1904-29. Member, New York State Senate, 1909-10, 1919-25; Progressive nominee for Governor of New York, 1914; member of Congress from New York, 1925-33; President, National Institute of Public Affairs; Chairman, Council of Personnel Administration, United States Government.

DAVIS, WILLIAM H. (b. 1879). Patent lawyer and public official. Deputy administrator and National Compliance Director, N.R.A., 1933-34; member, Federal Commission of Industrial Analysis, 1936; member, Emergency Board under Railway Labor Act, 1937; member, President's Commission on Industrial Relations in Great Britain and Sweden, 1938; member, New York City Housing Authority, 1939; Vice-chairman, National Defense Mediation Board, 1941.

DAWSON, MITCHELL (b. 1890). Lawyer and writer. Director and secretary-treasurer, Chicago Civic Broadcast Bureau, 1934-35; chairman, Public Relations Committee, Chicago Bar Association, 1934-37; chairman, Public Relations Committee of Section on Bar Organization Activities, American Bar Association, 1936-38; editor, *Chicago Bar Record;* frequent contributor to leading periodicals.

DEMPSEY, DAVID (b. 1914). Journalist. Graduate of Antioch College; was successively: publicity worker for the Ohio Farm Bureau Cooperative Association, reporter on *Cleveland Plain Dealer,* and a research worker and writer for the American Civil Liberties Union. Now: staff member, Institute for Propaganda Analysis. Contributor to *The New Republic, Common Sense, The Christian Science Monitor* and other periodicals.

DERN, GEORGE H. (1872-1936). Business man, inventor, and public official. General manager, Consolidated Mercury Gold Mines, 1900-13; joint inventor of Holt-Dern ore roaster; member, Utah State Senate, 1915-23; Governor of Utah, 1925-32; chairman, Governor's Conference, 1929-30; Secretary of War of the United States, 1933-36.

DICKINSON, JOHN (b. 1894). Lawyer. Lecturer on government, Harvard University and Radcliffe College, 1924-27; professor of politics, Princeton University, 1927-29; professor of law, University of Pennsylvania, 1929—; Assistant Secretary of Commerce, 1933-35; Assistant United States Attorney General, 1935-37; General Solicitor, Pennsylvania Railroad, 1937—; author of numerous books and articles on legal and political subjects.

DIMOCK, MARSHALL E. (b. 1903). Professor of public administration. University of California, 1928-32; University of Chicago, 1932—. Second Assistant Secretary of Labor, 1939-40; Consultant, National Resources Committee, 1935—; Administrative Assistant, Immigration and Naturalization Service, Department of Justice, 1940—; author of several books and numerous articles in the field of political science.

EAGLETON, CLYDE (b. 1891). Professor of government. University of Louisville, 1918-19; Southern Methodist University, 1919-23; New York University, 1923—. Chairman, United States National Committee of International Student Service; International Law Editor, *New York University Law Quarterly;* member, Editorial Board, *American Journal of International Law.* Author of *International Government* and numerous articles on political subjects.

EDGERTON, HENRY W. (b. 1888). Judge. Private practice of law, 1914-21; professor of law, Cornell University, 1916-19, 1929-38, George Washington University, 1921-29; special assistant to United States Attorney General, 1934-35; Associate Justice, United States Court of Appeals for District of Columbia since 1938.

EDWARDS, WILLIAM H. (b. 1901). Professor of political science. He has held professorships at the University of North Dakota and Sweet Briar College, Virginia, and is now at New Mexico State College. He is one of the first among the critics of orthodox state reorganization plans to have presented a clear choice between two fundamentally different systems and to have made a strong case for independent boards. Author of numerous articles on state reorganization and related questions.

FLYNN, JOHN T. (b. 1882). Author and journalist. City editor, *New York Globe,* 1920; managing editor, 1920-23; adviser to United States Senate Committee on Banking and Currency, 1933-34; lecturer in contemporary economics, 1935-36; member, Board of Higher Education, City of New York.

FRANKLIN, JAY—John Franklin Carter (b. 1897). Commentator and author. Employed in American embassies in Rome and Constantinople, 1918-19; private secretary to American ambassador to Italy, 1920-21; Rome correspondent, *London Daily Chronicle,* 1922-23; *New York Times,* 1923-28; Economic specialist, Department of State, 1928-32; in office of Under Secretary of Agriculture, 1934-36; conducts a nationally syndicated column "We, the People."

FREY, ALEXANDER H. (b. 1898). Professor of law. Yale University, 1926-30; University of Pennsylvania, 1930-31, 1932—; Duke University, 1931-32. Fellowship from Carnegie Endowment for International Peace, 1921-23; Social Science Research Council Fellowship, 1928-29; Philadelphia Civil Liberties Committee since 1936. Author of *Frey's Cases and Statutes on Business Associations* and numerous articles.

GALLUP, GEORGE (b. 1901). Public opinion statistician. Head of Journalism Department, Drake University, 1929-31; professor of journalism, Northwestern University, 1931-32; Director of Research, Young and Rubicam Advertising Agency since 1932; professor, School of Journalism, Columbia University, since 1935; founder, American Institute of Public Opinion.

GARD, WAYNE (b. 1899). Journalist and professor of journalism. India correspondent for the Associated Press, 1921-24; Director of courses in journalism, Grinnell College, 1925; editorial writer for the *Dallas News;* contributor to a number of leading periodicals.

GLASS, CARTER (1858-1946). United States Senator. Member, Virginia Senate, 1899-1903; member, State Constitutional Convention, Virginia, 1901; member, United States House of Representatives, 1902-18; Secretary of the Treasury of the United States, 1918-20; member, United States Senate, 1920—.

GLOCKER, THEODORE W. (b. 1881). Professor of economics. Instructor in economics, Johns Hopkins University, 1907-08; assistant director of research, Boston School of Social Work, 1908-09, Director of Research, 1909-12; professor of economics and sociology, University of Tennessee, 1913-20; director, School of Business Administration, 1921—.

GOLDMAN, MAYER C. (1874-1939). Lawyer. Attorney in New York City, 1895-1939; leading proponent of the public defender plan for 25 years; member, Committee on Legal Aid Work, American Bar Association, 1937; Chairman, Committee on Public Defenders, New York State Bar Association; chairman, Committee on Public Defenders, New York City chapter, National Lawyers Guild. Author of *The Public Defender* and numerous articles on the same topic.

GROVES, HAROLD M. (b. 1897). Professor of economics, University of Wisconsin. Member of Wisconsin Assembly, 1930; member, Wisconsin State Senate, 1934-36; member, Wisconsin State Tax Commission, 1932. Author of *Financing Government* and other well-known books and articles in the field of public finance.

HAINES, CHARLES GROVE (b. 1879). Professor of political science. Ursinus College, 1906-10; Whitman College, 1910-14; University of Texas, 1914-25, University of California, 1925—. Executive Secretary, League of the Pacific Northwest Municipalities, 1912-14; President, American Political Science Association, 1939. Commissioner, Department of Water and Power, Los Angeles, 1939. Author of *The American Doctrine of Judicial Supremacy* and other books and articles on legal and political subjects.

HAMILTON, WALTON H. (b. 1881). Professor of law. Professor of economics, University of Michigan, 1900-14; University of Chicago, 1914-15; Amherst College, 1915-23; Brookings Institution, 1923-28. Professor of law, Yale University, 1928—. Member, NRA Board, 1934-35; delegate of United States Government to International Labor Organization Conference, Geneva, 1935; special assistant to United States Attorney General, 1938-40.

HARTMAN, ALAN (b. 1915). Journalist. Graduated from Harvard, 1937; assistant editor, *Survey Graphic;* now associate editor, *Decision* magazine.

HIBSCHMAN, HARRY (b. 1879). Lawyer, lecturer, and author. Member of the Illinois and Washington bars; practiced in Spokane, Washington,

1903-17; deeply interested in the law of the press and in modernizing and humanizing the law; frequent contributor to popular and legal periodicals.

HEER, CLARENCE (b. 1893). Professor of economics. Economist, Western Union Telegraph Co., 1921-24; governmental research, National Institute of Public Administration, 1925-27; professor of public finance, University of North Carolina, 1927—; consultant to several state tax departments and legislative committees; director of investigation of trends in taxation for President Hoover's Committee on Social Trends, 1932; research director, Interstate Commission on Conflicting Taxation, 1933.

HOWARD, DONALD S. (b. 1902). Research specialist and author. Formerly Director of Research and Statistics, Colorado Emergency Relief Administration; Director of the WPA Statistical Office, Denver. Now Research Assistant, Charity Organization Department, Russell Sage Foundation.

HYNEMAN, CHARLES S. (b. 1900). Professor of political science. Syracuse University, 1928-30; University of Illinois, 1930-37; Professor of Government and Director, Bureau of Government Research, Louisiana State University, 1937—; Director, School of Government and Public Affairs, Louisiana State University since 1938. Author of numerous articles in the fields of legislation and administration.

INSTITUTE FOR PROPAGANDA ANALYSIS, INC. This organization was established in October, 1937, to conduct objective, non-partisan studies in the field of propaganda and public opinion. The Institute publishes the results of its researches in monthly bulletins and special reports. The President is E. C. Lindeman, New York School of Social Work and its other officers and advisory board includes among others Charles A. Beard, Johns Hopkins University, Paul Douglas, University of Chicago, and Robert S. Lynd, Columbia University.

JACOBSON, J. MARK (?-1938). Lawyer and professor of political science. Instructor in political science, University of Wisconsin. Member of the New York bar; member, Legal Division, National Labor Relations Board. Author of *The Development of American Political Thought* and numerous articles on political and legal subjects.

JONES, HOWARD P. (b. 1899). Editor and public administrator. Editor of various papers and publications, 1919-29; public relations section, National Municipal League, 1929-32; Secretary, National Municipal League, 1933—; editor, *National Municipal Review*, 1933—; professor, School of Journalism, Columbia University, 1934-39; consultant, Governor's Committee on New York State Constitutional Convention; New York Civil Service Commission, 1939—.

KEY, V. O., JR. (b. 1908). Professor of political science. University of California at Los Angeles, 1934-36; Johns Hopkins University, 1938—; staff member, Committee on Public Administration, Social Science Research Council, 1936-37; research technician, National Resources Committee, 1937-38; member, Baltimore Commission on Governmental Efficiency and

Economy, 1940—. Author of *The Administration of Federal Grants to the States* and numerous articles.

KNEIER, CHARLES M. (b. 1898). Professor of political science. University of Texas, 1926-27; University of Nebraska, 1927-30; University of Illinois, 1930—; Director of Research, Illinois Legislative Council, 1938-39; consultant, TVA, 1939; author of *County Government and Administration* (with J. A. Fairlie), *City Government in the United States,* and numerous articles.

LAIDLER, HARRY W. (b. 1884). Author. Executive Director of the League for Industrial Democracy; director, National Bureau of Economic Research, 1920—; member, Social Service Commission, Federal Council of Churches, 1924—; chairman, National Advisory Council on Radio in Education, 1933-36; Chairman of Board, National Public Housing Conference, 1937—; member, New York City Council, 1939—.

LASKI, HAROLD J. (b. 1893). Professor of political science. Lecturer in history McGill University, 1914-16; at Harvard University, 1916-20; Harvard lecturer at Yale University, 1919-20; London School of Economics since 1920. Vice-chairman, British Institute of Adult Education, 1921-30; member of the Fabian Society Executive, 1922-36; member of the Industrial Court since 1926; member of the Lord Chancellor's Committee on Delegated Legislation, 1929; member of the Departmental Committee on Legal Education, 1932; member of the Council of Institute of Public Administration. Author of many books in the field of political science and many articles in the *Harvard Law Review, The Nation, The New Republic,* etc.

LERNER, MAX (b. 1902). Professor of political science. Assistant editor, *Encyclopaedia of the Social Sciences,* 1927,—later, managing editor. Member of faculty, Sarah Lawrence College, 1932-36. Director, Consumers' Division, National Emergency Council, 1934. Lecturer, Department of Government, Harvard University, 1935-36. Associate editor, *The Nation,* 1936-38. Professor, Williams College, 1938—. Author of *It Is Later Than You Think, Ideas Are Weapons* and numerous articles.

MacLEISH, ARCHIBALD (b. 1892). Author and poet. Appointed Librarian, Congressional Library, 1939. Recipient of Pulitzer Poetry Prize for *Conquistador.* Contributor to many periodicals.

McBAIN, HOWARD LEE (1880-1936). Professor of political science. George Washington University, 1907-10; University of Wisconsin, 1910-13; Columbia University, 1913-36. Dean of the Graduate Faculties, Columbia University, 1929-36. Special counsel for New York City before State Constitutional Convention, 1915; member, Board of Education, City of New York, 1916-18; member and secretary, New York City Charter Commission, 1921-23; associate editor of *The National Municipal Review* and *Political Science Quarterly.*

MERRIAM, CHARLES E. (b. 1874). Professor of political science. University of Chicago, 1900—. Alderman, Chicago, 1909-11, 1913-17; Republican candidate for mayor, 1911; President, Social Science Research Council, 1924-27; President, American Political Science Association, 1925; member, Hoover Commission on Recent Social Trends; member, National Resources Board, 1933-34; member, President's Committee on Administrative Management. Author of numerous books and articles in the field of government.

MILNER, LUCILLE B. New York School of Social Work, 1914-16; Secretary of the American Civil Liberties Union since 1920; worked with the National Civil Liberties Bureau during the first World War and prior to that served as executive secretary of the Missouri Children's Code Commission. In recent years she has been concerned with the plight of refugees and was sent to Europe in 1934 and 1936 to study the case of German refugees and the work of anti-Fascist organizations. She is a frequent contributor to a number of the leading popular periodicals.

MORRILL, FRED B. (b. 1858). Lawyer and author. Practiced law, Fargo, then territory of Dakota, 1883-1905; city alderman, city attorney and later prosecuting attorney in Fargo; Sergeant at Arms, National Republican Convention, 1892; practiced law, Spokane, Washington, 1905—; city attorney and criminal judge, Spokane; served in connection with the administration of the draft, first World War; author of several books and a contributor to popular periodicals.

MUNRO, WILLIAM BENNETT (b. 1875). Professor of political science. Williams College, 1901-04; Harvard University, 1904-29; California Institute of Technology, 1929—. Editorial writer, *Boston Herald*, 1907-21; member, Cambridge Charter Commission, 1913-14; member, city of Boston Budget Commission, 1915; chairman, Commission on Data and Information for Massachusetts Constitutional Convention, 1917-18; President, American Political Science Association, 1927; author of numerous books and frequent contributor to literary and political reviews.

OVERACKER, LOUISE (b. 1891). Professor of political science. Vassar College, 1920-22; Wilson College, 1924-25; Wellesley College, 1925—. Author of *The Presidential Primary; Money in Elections*. Frequent contributor to various political science journals.

PORTER, KIRK H. (b. 1891). Professor of political science. University of Iowa since 1918 and head of the Department of Political Science since 1940. Author of *A History of the Suffrage in the United States;* (ed.) *National Party Platforms; State Administration;* and numerous articles on politics and administration.

PRESIDENT'S COMMITTEE ON ADMINISTRATIVE MANAGEMENT. This committee was created by President Franklin D. Roosevelt, March 20, 1936, to make a study of administrative management in the federal government, and to submit recommendations to the President. The committee was composed of Louis Brownlow, Director, Public Administration Clearing House, Chicago; Charles E. Merriam, Department of Political Science, University of Chicago; Luther Gulick, Department of Political Science, Columbia University.

RADIN, MAX (b. 1880). Professor of law. Columbia University, 1918-19; College of City of New York, 1917-19; University of California, 1919—. Member of the bar of New York, California, and the United States Supreme Court. Author of several works on Roman law and legal history and numerous articles in philological and legal periodicals.

RANDALL, ROBERT H. (b. 1903). Engineer. Consultant to the National Resources Committee on state and regional planning; liaison between the National Resources Committee and the WPA; United States representative to the Public Works Committee of the International Labor Organization, 1938. Formerly president, R. H. Randall, Inc., civil engineers, and Randall Press, Inc., map publishers.

REDFIELD, WILLIAM C. (1858-1932). Business executive and public official. Treasurer, J. H. Williams and Company, 1887-1890, president, 1905; director, Equitable Life Assurance Society, 1905-13; Commissioner of Public Works, Brooklyn, 1902-03; member, United States House of Representatives, 1911-13; Secretary of Commerce, 1913-19; one time president, American Manufacturers' Export Association. Author of numerous articles dealing with public questions.

REEVES, FLOYD W. (b. 1890). Professor of educational administration. Rural school teacher until 1912; public school administrator, 1912-20; Transylvania College, 1923-25; University of Kentucky, 1925-29; University of Chicago, 1929—; director, American Youth Commission, 1939—; chairman, Permanent Commission on College Cost of the Association of American Colleges, 1926-28; Director of Personnel, TVA, 1933-36; member of staff, President's Committee on Administrative Management, 1936; chairman, Advisory Committee on Education, 1936; member, Advisory Committee on Administrators of the President's Committee on Civil Service Improvement, 1939—.

RIORDON, WILLIAM L. (1861-1909). Author and newspaper writer. Contributed numerous articles on the political views of George Washington Plunkitt, who was a New York State Senator and an important figure in the Tammany organization.

RODELL, FRED (b. 1907). Professor of law. Legal adviser to Governor Pinchot of Pennsylvania, 1931-33; Yale Law School, 1933—; member, Committee on Public Law, Association of American Law Schools, 1935-36. Author of *Fifty-Five Men, Woe unto You Lawyers* and a frequent contributor to legal journals.

ROGERS, LINDSAY (b. 1891). Professor of political science. Newspaper correspondent, 1909-15; teacher, Baltimore City College, 1910-15; admitted to Maryland Bar, 1915; professor, University of Virginia, 1915-20; lecturer, Harvard University, 1920-21; professor, Columbia University, 1921—; Research Assistant, United States Tariff Commission, 1918; Deputy Administrator, NRA, 1933; chairman, Board of Labor Review, PWA, 1934-36; Director, Social Science Research Council, 1936—; Trustee, Institute of Public Administration. Author of many books and articles in the field of political science.

ROOSEVELT, FRANKLIN D. (1882-1945). Thirty-second President of the United States. Admitted to New York Bar, 1907; member, New York Senate, 1910-13 (resigned); Assistant Secretary of the Navy, 1913-20; Democratic Nominee for Vice-President, 1920; Governor of New York, 1929-33; President of the United States, 1933-1945.

ROSEN, S. McKEE (b. 1902). Professor of political science. Fellow, Brookings Institution, 1926-27; instructor, University of Chicago, 1928-31; research associate, Hoover Commission on Social Trends, 1931-32; consultant, National Resources Committee and editor of its report *Technological Trends and National Policy*, 1937; staff of national workshop in the social sciences, University of Chicago, summer, 1940; head of the social science departments, Central Y.M.C.A. College, Chicago, 1931—. Author of *Political Process; Modern Individualism;* and co-author of *Technology and Society.*

ROSS, MARY. Journalist and public official. Graduate of Vassar College, 1915, and the Columbia University School of Journalism, 1916. Reporter, *New York World;* writer and editor for the American Red Cross, first World War; book reviewer, *New York Herald Tribune* since 1924; member, editorial staff, *Survey Graphic,* 1922-36; chief, Division of Publications and Review, Bureau of Research and Statistics, Social Security Board, 1936—. Frequent contributor to a number of the leading popular periodicals.

SABINE, GEORGE H. (b. 1880). Professor of philosophy. Stanford University, 1907-14; University of Missouri, 1914-23; Ohio State University, 1923-31; Cornell University, 1931—. Author of *A History of Political Theory* and numerous articles in the fields of philosophy and political theory.

SAYRE, FRANCIS BOWES (b. 1885). Professor of law and public official. Deputy Assistant District Attorney, New York County, New York, 1912-13; professor of law, Harvard Law School, 1919-34; jurisconsult to Ministry of Foreign Affairs, Siamese Government, 1925-30; Diplomatic Representative, Siamese Government, 1925-30; director, Harvard Institute of Criminal Law, 1929-34; member, Permanent Court of Arbitration at the Hague, representing Siam, 1925-34; Massachusetts State Commissioner of Correction, 1933; United States Assistant Secretary of State, 1933-39; United States High Commissioner to the Philippines, 1939—.

SCHAIN, JOSEPHINE (b. 1886). Author and civic leader. Settlement leader, 1916-24; Director of Department of International Cooperation, League of Women Voters, 1924-27; National Director of Girl Scouts, 1930-35; Executive Committee, National Peace Conference; chairman, National

Committee on the Cause and Cure of War; chairman of the Peace Committee and member of the Board of the International Alliance of Women.

SHOTWELL, JAMES T. (b. 1874). Professor of history. Columbia University, 1900—. Member, "The Inquiry" (preparatory committee for the Peace Conference, 1917-18); chief of Division of History, International Labor Legislation Commission at Peace Conference, 1918-19; member, Organizing Committee, International Labor Conference, 1919; Lecturer to the Nobel Institute, Norway, 1923; President, League of Nations Association, 1935—; Director, Division of Economics and History, Carnegie Endowment for International Peace, 1924—. Author of numerous books and articles in the field of international relations.

SIGERIST, H. E. (b. 1891). Professor of the history of medicine. University of Zurich, 1921-24; University of Leipsig, 1925-32; Professor and Director of the Institute of the History of Medicine, Johns Hopkins University, 1932—; author and editor of many books dealing with the history of medicine.

SMITH, ALFRED E. (1873-1944). Business executive, public official. Member, New York State Assembly, 1903-15; sheriff, New York County, 1915-17; President, Board of Aldermen, Greater New York, 1917-19; Governor of New York, 1919-20, 1923-28; Democratic Candidate for President of the United States, 1928; President, Empire State, Inc.; Director, New York Life Insurance Co.; Trustee, Catholic University of America; one of the founders of the American Liberty League.

SMITH, J. ALLEN (1860-1926). Lawyer and professor of political science. Practiced law, Kansas City, Missouri, 1887-92; Marietta College, 1895-97; University of Washington, 1897-1926; Dean of the Graduate School, University of Washington, 1909-20. Author of numerous books and articles on political and economic subjects.

SOULE, GEORGE H. (b. 1887). Journalist. Editorial staff, *New Republic,* 1914; Washington correspondent, *New Republic,* 1918; editorial staff, *New York Evening World,* 1919; director, Labor Bureau, Inc., 1920; editor, *New Republic,* 1924—; Special adviser to the Secretary of Interior, 1927; chairman, National Economic and Social Planning Association. Author of numerous books and articles.

SPROUT, HAROLD H. (b. 1901). Professor of political science. Miami University, 1926-27; Carnegie Fellow in International Law, 1928-29; Stanford University, 1929-31; Princeton, 1931—. Author of numerous articles for professional journals.

STERN, EDITH M. (b. 1901). Free lance journalist and novelist. Graduate of Barnard College. Author of several novels and contributor to most of America's leading magazines.

STUDENSKI, PAUL (b. 1887). Economist. Member of staff, Bureau of Municipal Research, 1914-17; director, Bureau of State Research, New Jersey State Chamber of Commerce, 1917-25; New York University, 1927—.

Consultant to New York State Old Age Security Commission, 1930; New York City Citizens' Budget Commission, 1932-33; New York State Commission on Revision of Tax Laws, 1934-38; President's Advisory Committee on Education, 1937; National Resources Committee, 1935-37. Author of many books and articles on public finance.

TREADWAY, WILLIAM E. (b. 1901). Lawyer and public official. Member, Indiana House of Representatives, 1934-38; member, Indiana State Tax Study Commission, 1935; member, Indiana Liquor Study Commission, 1936; Executive Secretary, Indiana Commission on Interstate Cooperation, 1938-41; Captain, Judge Advocate General's Department, United States Army, 1938-41; author of numerous articles in legal and academic journals.

WAGER, PAUL W. (b. 1893). Professor of political science. Department of Rural Social Economics, 1926-37, Department of Political Science, 1937—, University of North Carolina. Staff, Forest Taxation Inquiry, United States Forest Service, 1930-31; Regional Assistant, Land Policy Section, AAA, 1934-35; Regional Chief, Land Use Planning Section, United States Department of Agriculture, 1935-37; part-time economist, National Resources Planning Board, 1940—.

WALTER, DAVID O. (b. 1911). Professor of political science. Cornell University, 1934-37; University of Illinois, 1937-40; University of New Hampshire, 1940—. Author of a number of articles on political subjects.

WARNER, JOHN A. (b. 1886). Police officer. Entered the New York State Police at its organization in 1917 and served as Lieutenant of Troop "A," Batavia, New York, from June, 1917, to June, 1918; served as captain of Troop "K" at White Plains, New York, from June, 1918, to December, 1923; appointed Superintendent, New York State Troopers, December, 1923, and still holds that position.

WHITE, LEONARD D. (b. 1891). Professor of political science. Clark College, 1915-18; Dartmouth College, 1918-20; University of Chicago, 1920—. Guggenheim Fellow, 1927-28; investigator, Hoover Committee on Social Trends, 1930-31; member, Chicago Civil Service Commission, 1931-33; member, United States Civil Service Commission and Central Statistical Board, 1934-37; member, President's Committee on Civil Service Improvement, 1939-40; Editor in Chief, *Public Administration Quarterly*, 1940—. Author of many books and articles on public administration and the public service.

WHITE, WILLIAM ALLEN (1868-1944). Newspaper publisher, author. Proprietor and editor of the *Emporia Daily and Weekly Gazette*, 1895-1944. Sent to France as observer by American Red Cross, 1917; delegate, Russian Conference at Prinkipo; member, Republican National Convention, 1920, 1928, 1936; trustee, Rockefeller Foundation; president, American Society of Newspaper Editors; awarded gold medal for citizenship, Theodore Roosevelt Memorial Association.

WHITTINGTON, WILLIAM V. (b. 1904). Lawyer; Legal Assistant, Treaty Division, Department of State. Administrative assistant and clerk, Department of State, 1924-30; member of the District of Columbia and Illinois bars; general law practice, Washington, D. C., 1928-30; technical-legal assistant, Treaty Division, Department of State, 1930-35; delegate of the United States to an international radio conference, Lisbon, Portugal, 1934; special assistant to Commissioner, Federal Communications Commission, 1935-37; Editor of Treaty Index, Treaty Division, Department of State, 1937-38; Legal Assistant, Treaty Division, Department of State, 1939—.

WILLOUGHBY, W. F. (b. 1867). Economist. Expert, U. S. Department of Labor, 1890-1901; special agent, U. S. Commission to Paris Exposition, 1900; received Cross Legion d'Honneur from French government; lecturer in economics, Johns Hopkins and Harvard, 1901; treasurer of Porto Rico, 1901-07; secretary of Porto Rico and president of the executive council of the legislative assembly of Porto Rico, 1907-09; assistant director, U. S. census, 1909-11; member, President's Committee on Economy and Efficiency, 1911-12; professor of jurisprudence and politics, Princeton, 1912-17; constitutional adviser to the Chinese Republic, 1914-16; director, Institute for Government Research, 1916-32.

WITTE, EDWIN E. (b. 1887). Economist. Statistician, Industrial Commission of Wisconsin, 1912; secretary, Congressman John M. Nelson, 1912-14; special investigator, U. S. Commission on Industrial Relations, 1914-15; secretary, Industrial Commission of Wisconsin, 1917-22; chief, Wisconsin Legislative Reference Library, 1922-33; acting director, Unemployment Compensation Division, Industrial Commission of Wisconsin, 1934; member, Wisconsin State Planning Board, 1935-38; member, Wisconsin Labor Relations Board, 1937-39; member of staff, University of Wisconsin since 1920; chairman, Department of Economics since 1936.

WOOD, EDITH ELMER (b. 1871). Writer since 1890. Founder, 1906, president, 1906, 1907, 1909, Anti-tuberculosis League of Porto Rico. Chairman, National Committee on Housing, American Association of University Women, 1917-29; consultant, Housing Division, PWA, 1933-37; U. S. Housing Authority since 1938; member, New Jersey State Housing Authority, 1934-35; Vice-president, National Public Housing Conference, 1932-36; director, since 1936. Author of numerous books and articles on housing.

YOUNG, JOHN PARKE (b. 1895). Economist. Examiner for the Federal Trade Commission, 1917-18; economist, U. S. Senate Commission of Gold and Silver Inquiry (field study of 16 European nations), 1923-25; professor of economics and sociology and chairman of department, Occidental College since 1926; president, Young & Koenig, Inc., Los Angeles; member, Kemmerer Commission to government of China, 1929; member, Board of Economic Survey of Port of Los Angeles, 1933; member, Board of Governors, Investment Counsellors' Association of Southern California. Author of numerous books and articles.

Zeller, Belle (b. 1903). Professor of political science. Brooklyn College, New York. Conducted one of the first comprehensive investigations of lobbying activities ever made in a state capital. Author of *Pressure Politics in New York* and of numerous articles.